HEINEMANN
GNVQ

RESHMA
PATTNI

ADVANCED

BUSINESS

SECOND EDITION

DAVE NEEDHAM & ROB DRANSFIELD

Heinemann

Heinemann Educational,
a division of Heinemann Publishers (Oxford) Ltd
Halley Court, Jordan Hill, Oxford OX2 8EJ

OXFORD LONDON EDINBURGH
MADRID ATHENS BOLOGNA PARIS
MELBOURNE SYDNEY AUCKLAND SINGAPORE
TOKYO IBADAN NAIROBI HARARE
GABORONE PORTSMOUTH NH (USA)

© Dave Needham and Rob Dransfield 1995

First published 1995
99 98 97 96
10 9 8 7 6 5 4 3 2 1

A catalogue record for this book is available from the British Library on
request

ISBN 0 435 45255 X

Typeset by TechType, Abingdon
Printed in Great Britain by The Bath Press

Contents

Acknowledgements

The authors would especially like to thank Margaret Berriman, Jan Nikolic and Martin Coles for their invaluable contributions to this book. They would also like to thank:

Kay Kelly
John Merchant
Sue Friery
Alastair Clelland
Aubrey Nokes
Derek Smith
Alan Field

Laura Schuster
John Barnes
Bryan Oakes
Stephanie Howkins
Brian Yeomans
Mike Ellis
Derrick Scott

The authors and publishers are grateful to the following for permission to reproduce photographs and other material, and for providing advice and information:

Amalgamated Engineering Union, Automobile Association, British Gas plc, Business and Technician Education Council, BT Pictures, CMT (Computerised Marketing Technologies) Ltd, Cosworth Engineering, Department for Education, Department of Employment, The Economist, Greg Evans International, GST Software plc, HMSO, Honda (UK), ICI, Marks and Spencer, Microsoft Corporation, Mirror Syndication International, Nestle (UK), Nissan Motor Manufacturing (UK), the Northern Echo, Northern Electric plc, Pictor International, Procter & Gamble, Prontaprint, Rolls-Royce Motor Cars, Rover Group, the Royal Society for the Protection of Birds, Shell Education Service, Texaco, Unilever, Yorkshire Bank plc, Yorkshire Water plc, Virgin Group plc.

Finally, we would like to express our gratitude and appreciation to the teaching and library staff at Darlington College of Technology and at the Nottingham Trent University; to the editorial, production, marketing and sales teams at Heinemann Educational; to the officers of NCVQ; and of course to our families for their patience and understanding.

Rob Dransfield
Dave Needham
July 1995

Preface to the second edition

Welcome to our new edition of Business Advanced. We are pleased to have been able to change the structure and content of the book to meet the needs of students and tutors involved in GNVQ Advanced Business.

In particular, we welcome the revisions to the GNVQ Advanced scheme for 1995. We feel that the new scheme is based on sound progression and clear understanding of the needs of students who are engaged in developing knowledge, skills and attitudes in this field. The new scheme is set at an appropriate level and is designed to enable students to develop a broad range of important capabilities that will prepare them for the world of higher education, the world of work, and to be active and informed citizens in an increasingly complex and changing world.

In this new book we have set out to provide detailed background information and guidance to support students in developing an integrated understanding of the eight core units, combined with a wealth of opportunities to develop the core skills.

Performance criteria and range

In setting out the text we have worked through the performance criteria in a sequential order. The main headings in the book follow the performance criteria. For example, in Chapter 1 the first performance criterion for Element 1.1 is: 'Explain demand for goods and services'. The range for this performance criterion is:

Demand: satisfying consumer needs and wants, effective demand, spending and income, demand curves, price and income elasticity, causes of change in demand.

Our headings and sub-headings follow the performance criteria and range through the book, e.g:

The demand for goods and services

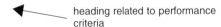

heading related to performance criteria

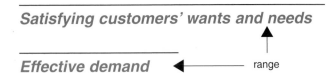

Satisfying customers' wants and needs

Effective demand ◄——— range

We have then provided a wealth of opportunities for students to provide evidence that they can meet the performance criteria.

Evidence collection points

Throughout the text we have provided evidence collection points. The evidence indicators are tasks designed to enable students to show that they have understood or have the skill to meet particular aspects of the range associated with performance criteria.

For example, when students are working to show that they can explain demand for goods and services, one of the evidence collection points we have provided dealing with the range 'spending and income' (in which students are expected to show they understand how spending varies with income) is as follows:

Evidence collection point

Set out a table which shows your income, spending and saving over the last three months. Of course, you may have spent more than you have earned. If this is the case we use the term dis-saving. For example, if in March my niece had earned £50 and spent £90 she might have had to dis-save by drawing £40 out of her previous savings. If you have dis-saved show this in your table and explain how the dis-saving was financed e.g. by borrowing, drawing on previous savings, etc.

If students work through the text using the evidence collection points, they will provide extensive evidence that they can meet the performance criteria. In addition, by working through the case studies, tasks, and evidence collection points they should be confident to take the end of unit tests knowing that they have met and understood the requirements of the scheme. Students will benefit from keeping the evidence they have collected in a neat and organised file.

Evidence indicators

In addition to the evidence collection points we have provided evidence indicators as specified by the scheme.

These evidence indicators should be regarded as assignments which enable students to provide clear evidence that they can meet the required performance criteria for Business and the core skills.

The evidence indicators appear at the end of each chapter and consist of a number of assignment activities. We have broken these down into separate sections which the student can tick off on the completion of each part.

For example, at the end of Chapter 2 we have set out the following evidence indicator which enables students to address the performance criteria for Element 1.2.

1 Explain types of markets
2 Compare competition within markets
3 Analyse behaviour of businesses in different markets
4 Evaluate the social costs of market operations
5 Evaluate the social benefits of market operations.

Evidence indicators

Produce a report setting out a comparative study of two different markets (e.g. the supply of tabloid newspapers/the supply of an exclusive magazine, the supply of computer software/household gas, the supply of contraceptives/hairdressing, the supply of petrol on a motorway/in a busy urban area.

The important thing is that you compare and contrast two markets, one which is competitive and the other which is relatively uncompetitive.

The following list should serve as a checklist. Please tick off each of the following when you have successfully covered them as part of your report. You need to be able to confirm that:

■ I have compared the numbers of suppliers in the markets. ☐
■ I have shown the size of the suppliers and the strength of demand in the markets. ☐
■ I have compared competition between two businesses in one market showing shifts in demand curves and explaining why these have occurred. ☐
■ I have described how competition can have an effect on consumers' choice and the quality of products. ☐
■ I have compared the behaviour of two businesses in two different types of market showing their use of both pricing and non-pricing strategies to improve market position. ☐
■ I have focused on activities undertaken by two businesses in order to show the social costs and benefits to the wider community (e.g. the siting of a new factory, the closing down of a plant, the creation of new jobs). ☐

The core skills

The core skills are a key part of any GNVQ course. The core skills of Communication, Application of Number, and Information Technology are essential for all students going on to higher education, into work and into the wider community.

We have therefore placed great emphasis on the development of core skills. In particular we have produced a Manual at the beginning of this publication which shows how to develop the core skills as a natural and ongoing part of business investigations. Business studies is a very broad field, and one in which we naturally use number, communication and IT in many ways. The Manual provides an invaluable guide as to how best to develop core skills.

In addition we have highlighted throughout the text the ways in which students can provide evidence of capability in the core skills as a natural part of evidence collection such as the following.

Evidence collection point

Research and then explain the methods used by a particular group of competing organisations to compete for customers. For example, you could look at local newsagents, taxi businesses, schools or colleges. Your work could provide evidence of core skills in Communication and, if you use a computer to present your findings, in Information Technology.

Use of core skills

The importance of action planning

Action planning is a crucial part of a GNVQ course. Planning is concerned with providing a structured and organised way of meeting objectives.

There are a number of important reasons why you should plan including:

1 to be clear about your objectives
2 to organise activities into a sequence
3 to organise the timing of events
4 to keep a check on progress
5 to make sure that the important things do not get left until last
6 to plan what resources and materials you need
7 to save time
8 to reduce stress
9 to look at present strengths and how they can be built upon.

We have found that a problem for many students is that while they have some idea about the goal or target they are working towards, they are not skilled at planning the steps required to achieve this target.

Action planning involves designing a series of sequential steps that will enable you to meet targets.

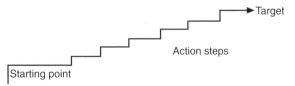

In a GNVQ course, a student's major targets will be to get assignments done on time and to make sure that work covers the appropriate performance criteria. The following guidelines will help to achieve this.

1 Be clear about your objective
E.g. to complete the Business in the Economy Assignment by Christmas, making sure that you cover the required performance criteria, and some aspects of the core skills performance criteria.

2 Organise activities into a sequence
E.g. set out a step-by-step plan of how you will complete this assignment, and how each step is related to the performance criteria.

3 Organise the timing of events
E.g. set out when each step in the assignment will be completed.

4 Keep a check on progress
E.g. how will you check that you are keeping to deadlines? Will you review your progress with another student, for example?

The importance of action plans is that they help you to get organised. You should be able to put your plan together quickly with the minimum of paper work. If an action plan involves a lot of paper and time, then throw it in the bin. Your action plan should be simple and easy to follow.

The headings in your action plan should be:

1 Area for development
What do you want to plan? Set out your targets.

2 Name of person responsible for the development
This will be you, or a small group of students. The responsibility lies with you, not with your tutor, take charge of your own learning.

3 Action steps
What steps will you need to take to see the plan through? Be specific about the steps that need to be taken. Set out the time when these steps will take place.

4 Review of progress
When and how will the progress of the action steps and the plan be checked? In writing out your plan you need to set dates for reviewing how successful you have been in carrying out the plan. For example, if you have eight weeks to complete an assignment, you could review your progress after two weeks, four weeks and six weeks. You will need to carry out this review with someone else. Two students can review each other's work, for example.

5 Evaluation
It is helpful to evaluate the success of your plan in order to help you to action plan in the future.

Please make sure that your action steps are clear and practical rather than 'airy fairy' and vague. For example, 'taking three books out of the library with chapters on supply and demand, and making detailed notes on each chapter' is a specific and practical step. 'Doing some reading' is vague. 'Going to computer services, taking out a manual on spreadsheets, setting out a spreadsheet of my research figures' is a detailed description of a practical step. 'Improving my IT' is not.

A useful layout for your action plan is shown on the next page.

You can see that the action plan we have outlined does not involve a lot of paperwork. However, it enables you to map out clear steps that you will need to take to meet your targets.

Too often in the past students have found themselves faced with three or four assignments to do at the same time and have left essential work to the last minute. Action planning helps you to spread out your work over a period of time.

Action planning is used widely in the workplace. If you learn to construct simple action plans now, you will have developed a useful life-skill. Finally, never write an action plan after completing an assignment. What a ridiculous waste of time that would be!

1 Area for development:

2 Name of person responsible for development:

3 Action steps:

Step (simple and practical)	Timing
a	
b	
c	
d	

(There may be quite a few of these to complete an assignment)

4 Review of progress (when reviews will occur and who will be involved)

5 Evaluation of plan (when and how it will take place)

Introduction: Wake up to Advanced GNVQ!

same type of job throughout their lives. Young people need to develop flexibility so that they can quickly adapt to changing demands in the workplace. New technologies and new products rapidly make previous technologies and products out-dated. All people, whatever their age or previous experience, need to be able to adapt to change. This involves developing a good understanding of business principles and ideas. It also involves developing skills such as the ability to communicate effectively, to use Information Technology, and to have a sound grasp of working with numbers to make calculations.

This guide has been written for students starting out on Advanced GNVQs in Business this year. It sets out to provide you with information about why GNVQs are important and how a GNVQ in Business is organised, and it gives some of the important terms which are used to describe features of the GNVQ.

Whatever type of work you want to do, you will need to develop a sound understanding of business principles, and a range of transferable skills

Why are GNVQs important?

A GNVQ is a General National Vocational Qualification.

General: The Advanced GNVQ Business course provides you with the knowledge, skills and attitudes that will be required in a variety of business occupations. Today, the world of work is changing rapidly. No longer can people expect to have the

National: The GNVQ qualification that you attain will be recognised nationally. A GNVQ course is a preparation for work and/or for further education and training. A GNVQ Advanced Business is nationally recognised as being the equivalent of two traditional A levels. Many employers and most universities recognise the GNVQ in Business to be an appropriate qualification for relevant university courses.

Vocational: A GNVQ course prepares students for the world of work. It provides real opportunities for students to develop understanding and skills that can be applied in many work situations – to produce real business documents, to communicate information in real business settings, to carry out market research, to prepare a business plan, to present ideas to a real audience, to prepare a set of accounts, etc. A GNVQ course in Business involves learning business theory that can then be applied in real situations. You use what you learn to make better decisions.

Qualification: A GNVQ is a nationally recognised qualification which enables you to walk tall. It tells employers and universities that you can work well with others, that you can express your ideas with confidence, that you have a good understanding of business and business issues, that you can use Information Technology to a good standard, that you will listen to others, can make informed decisions, and many other things.

Today GNVQs are more popular than ever. The National Employment and Training Targets agreed by employers, trade unions and the government involve raising the numbers of those with GNVQ Level 3 equivalents from about 30% of the working population in 1992 to 50% by the end of the century.

A GNVQ in Business helps you to walk tall

To complete a GNVQ course in Business you will need to cover successfully eight compulsory units, four optional units, and three core skills.

The eight compulsory units make up what is considered to be the heart of a Business course.

The four optional units give you some choice about the extra units you may cover to broaden your qualification.

How is Advanced GNVQ Business organised?

In this section we use as little jargon as possible so that you can get a clear picture of how the course operates.

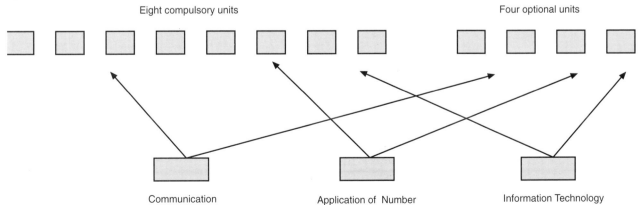

The core skills of Communication, Application of Number, and Information Technology are common to all GNVQs. The core skills are built into your work in Business rather than being taught separately. (However, students who feel that they are particularly weak in a core skill may be given extra tutorial support in special workshop sessions.)

The eight compulsory (often called mandatory) units in Business are:

Unit 1: Business in the Economy
Unit 2: Business Organisations and Systems
Unit 3: Marketing
Unit 4: Human Resources
Unit 5: Production and Employment in the Economy
Unit 6: Financial Transactions, Costing and Pricing
Unit 7: Financial Forecasting and Monitoring
Unit 8: Business Planning

Find out what optional units are available to you.

Learning and checking on outcomes

Each of the GNVQ Business units is divided up into smaller sections called elements.

When you work on a GNVQ course you will be aiming to show that you can successfully meet the performance criteria for each of these elements. For example, you will need to be able to show that you understand important aspects of business, or that you can do important business calculations, or that you can make an effective business presentation.

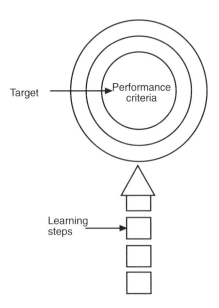

When you start a new unit your tutor will present you with a list of performance criteria that you are working towards.

Make sure that you understand fully what these performance criteria involve. Once you know where you are going you can plan the steps to get there.

How do I show that I can meet the performance criteria?

A GNVQ course involves working on your own or in groups to carry out work throughout the course to meet the performance criteria for each element.

The work that you carry out will take a variety of forms. For example:

- Carrying out library research
- Interviewing people
- Talking to people involved in business
- Group discussions
- Work experience
- Taking notes in formal lectures
- Making presentations
- Setting up and running a small business enterprise
- Using information technology to present and analyse data
- Making a promotional video.

All of these activities, and many more, should help to provide evidence that you can meet the relevant performance criteria for Business.

A portfolio of evidence

Every student following a GNVQ must build up a portfolio of evidence. This is a collection of material that you will submit for assessment. The portfolio may include all sorts of materials.

The bulk of the portfolio will probably be made up of assignments that you have presented using information technology tools such as word-processing, graphics plotting and spreadsheet packages. You may also include videos, disks and products that you have produced during the course.

You should take great pride in this portfolio of evidence. However, whilst presentation is important, a primary concern should be how the portfolio meets the performance criteria for each element.

End-of-unit testing

Your GNVQ is also assessed by an end-of-unit test. This test sets out to assess whether you have learnt the underpinning knowledge for each of the units that you study.

This year the end-of-unit test is composed of about 35 multiple choice questions. You will need to score over 70% in this test to pass the unit. In other words, out of 35 questions you will need to get 25 correct. You must therefore make sure that you have a firm grasp of the knowledge required in each unit. You can re-sit an end-of-unit test if you are not successful at the first sitting.

Starting out with your first unit

Now you are ready to start. Make sure that you clearly set out the title of the unit, and the titles of each of the elements to be covered.

Make sure that you have a copy of the performance criteria for each of the elements that you will be expected to cover. Find out how long you have to cover each element. Do you understand what the performance criteria mean?

Find out what kinds of evidence your tutors expect you to be putting into your portfolio of evidence for the first unit. When will the evidence for the first unit be assessed? Who will do the assessing?

When will the end-of-unit test take place?

Student checklist for Unit 1	✓✗
1 Do you know the title of the unit?	☐
2 What are the elements that are covered in the unit?	☐
3 What text can you refer to in order to give you the essential background reading for the unit?	☐
4 Do you have a list of the performance criteria?	☐
5 Do you understand each of the performance criteria?	☐
6 Who will help to explain the performance criteria?	☐
7 How much time should be spent on each element?	☐
8 How are core skills built into the unit?	☐
9 What will constitute evidence of performance?	☐
10 When will assignments need to be completed by?	☐
11 Who should receive completed assignments?	☐
12 When will the end-of-unit tests take place?	☐
13 What will the end-of-unit tests cover? Is it possible to see an example of a previous test?	☐

Getting ready for business

A GNVQ course contains two main component parts – a body of subject studies and a body of core skills. This is the great strength of the course.

As a result of following a GNVQ not only will you know much more about business. You will also know how to put this knowledge into practice. You will have developed some of the essential skills which make you an effective participant in business and social life.

Business knowledge in itself is of little value without the core skills. Employers today want people who can communicate, can apply number, and can use IT well. This book has been specially designed to combine the core skills with the development of business understanding in a seamless way.

We have therefore devoted the first section of this book to exploring ways in which you can develop an investigative approach to business studies. We outline how you develop the core skills. We have set out to show you how you can carry out research, present information, use IT, present data by applying number and many other things.

This first section of the book, therefore, should provide an invaluable insight for the student into investigating business activities – i.e. learning by doing.

Talk to most students who have followed a GNVQ course in Business and they will tell you that it has opened their eyes to learning – they have researched information for themselves, they have argued and discussed issues, they have worked in cooperation with others, and they have given presentations. The message is that core skills integrated with business understanding is a certain recipe for increased confidence in your own capability, for a broad-ranging grasp of real-world issues, and a capability to operate effectively in most organisations.

You will frequently want to dip into this introductory section as you work through your Business course.

Developing and showing evidence of the core skill of Communication

In today's competitive business world people with good communication skills are at a premium. A

GNVQ course therefore sets out to help you to develop effective communication skills so that you can become a confident and articulate member of an organisation.

Throughout this book you are encouraged to discuss issues, to write reports, to make presentations to audiences and many other aspects of communication. The main aspects of communication that you will be developing are:

1 taking part in discussions
2 producing written material
3 using images
4 reading and responding to written material.

Taking part in discussions

You will need to make contributions to discussions which are relevant to straightforward and also to more complex subjects. The purpose of your contributions should be to offer and obtain information and exchange ideas. The contributions that you make will need to be suited to the audience and situation.

These should be positive so that they take discussion forward rather than delay it. It is also highly important that you create opportunities for others to contribute.

Producing written material

In producing written material you should seek to include information which is accurate and relevant to the subject. Check that the text you produce is legible and the meaning is clear. Correct it if necessary.

You should make sure that you use accepted conventions for spelling, punctuation and grammar.

Use a writing format that suits the audience and purpose of the writing (e.g. report format, short notes, discursive writing, etc.). Make sure that the structure and style that you use emphasise the meaning you are trying to convey.

Using images

When you use images make sure that they clearly illustrate the points that you are trying to make and which are suited to the audience, situation and purpose of using the images. Use them at appropriate times and in appropriate places.

Reading and responding to written material

You will also need to select and read materials to obtain information. You should be able to extract relevant and appropriate information. Use appropriate sources of reference to clarify your understanding of particular subjects. You must also be able to summarise the information that you extract from these sources.

Carrying out research to collect evidence for your portfolio

One of the major attractions of a GNVQ course in Business is that it is based on you, the student, taking an active part in your own learning. You have moved beyond the days of simply sitting at a desk being taught information. You will now be asked to engage actively in investigation, to carry out research, to become involved in finding things out for yourself and presenting your findings to groups of other students and to outsiders such as business people. We have therefore compiled a set of notes to encourage you to engage in the research process. A key part of this work will involve the core skills of Communication. Information Technology and Application of Number. A starting point will be to carry out research to collect evidence for your portfolio, i.e. you should ask questions:

■ to find out information
■ to help you to make sense of information with which you are presented.

How much information do you need?

In business, decision makers will rarely have all the information they require. No matter how much detail is available, there is always more information which may be relevant in helping to tackle a problem. By asking questions you will become better informed and be able to use your information to show increased insights in a given area of study. Asking questions should also help you to make sense of information, views and ideas. You will also be clearer about the meaning of things by asking questions. Here are some typical questions to illustrate this:

■ What do I mean by....?
■ What does .... mean?
■ What does he or she mean by....?

You may want to ask questions about data you are given in class. Similarly, you may wish to ask questions about letters, leaflets and brochures you receive, and information in books and magazines. Sometimes, you may want to ask questions directly of people.

You will want to discuss these questions with friends, class-mates and your tutor. You will spend a lot of time thinking about the questions that you consider important. Asking questions is one way in which we make sense of the world around us.

What, why, when, who, how?

When preparing to do research make sure that you know *what* questions you will ask. You will also need to be sure *why* you are asking these questions. The reasons for asking questions should be that they help you to find out more information related to your main title question.

The acid test of a good question is that:

■ you understand why you are asking it
■ it helps you to answer your title question or problem.

When writing up your research explain why you asked particular questions.

When you ask a question is important. This should be done when the data are most likely to be available. A company may not be able to supply end-of-year sales figures if it has not had time to collect the relevant data. If you are going to interview people, do your interviewing at a time that is convenient to the interviewee.

Who you ask is also vitally important. Different people have different views. A company leaflet will give the company point of view whereas interviewing an employee will give that employee's point of view. Try to get a range of views (one person does not represent the strength of a particular view). Why do different people have different views? What evidence do people base their opinions on?

How should you ask? Make sure that you use a means that makes it possible for you to get an accurate record of the information you seek. A tape recorder may be helpful in recording spoken information.

However, if it is going to give inaudible results because of background noise then use some other means. Ask people to speak slowly if you are going to write down what they say. If you miss important points, then ask them to repeat these where necessary.

The data that you use for information purposes will be of two types:

- secondary data
- primary data

Secondary data

Secondary data is information (often contained in published materials), collected by somebody else. Collecting secondary data is often known as desk research, as you do not go out into the field to collect it.

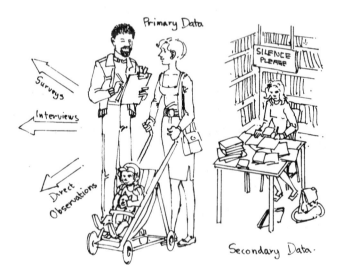

Golden rule – Always acknowledge any of the information you use either underneath its use or in a bibliography. The sources of quotations, tables, charts and so on should be clearly shown.

The type of data you collect depends upon your information needs. You should ask yourself:

- *What exactly am I trying to find out?* Make a list of what you need to know and the sort of information that would help you to achieve your aims.

- *What degree of accuracy do I require?* How are you going to measure the value of the information you obtain?
- *Where am I going to obtain this information?* Always make a list of possible sources of information. The more 'good and useful' sources that you use, and the longer the list, the more thorough and accurate your investigation will be.

Task

You are carrying out an investigation to find out why consumers buy one branded item rather than another.

- List six possible objectives of the research.
- How will you be able to test whether the information you collect is accurate enough to meet your research aims?
- List eight sources from which you could collect information.

Problems of using secondary data

Always be careful about how you use secondary data (Figure 1).

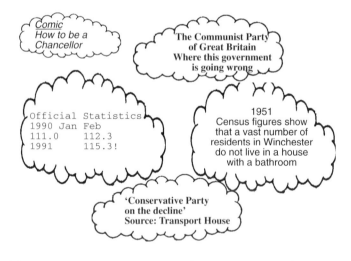

Figure 1 Would you use any of these sources of secondary information?

1 Make sure that you understand the information you collect. If you find it misleading or confusing, either ask for help or don't use it!
2 Remember that the secondary information you use was collected by other people for their own

purposes. In other words, the information they collected may not fit in closely with your own research aims.

3 The information could be out of date. Check when it was produced.

4 The information may be biased. Try to find out the motives of the person collecting the information. (For example, you might want to question information produced by a margarine producer showing that butter is bad for you!)

5 Information may not be reliable. For example, articles in many newspapers and other publications may only show one side of the picture, and may not be accurate.

> Do not copy out huge chunks of text.

Secondary data helps to support your course-work. Comment upon where you have obtained your secondary information. Show how the secondary information you have used has helped to support your research. (Figure 2).

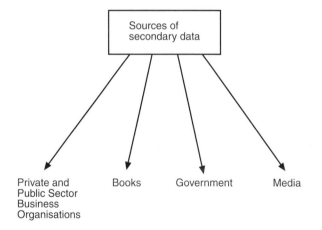

Figure 2 Secondary data sources

Private and public sector business organisations

Many different organisations receive requests from students for research information. Some of them have their own comprehensive educational services to deal with *your* requests for information. You may have difficulty in finding the right address. If you cannot find the address you require look in one of the following:

- *Yellow Pages*
- *Kelly's Directory* or
- the reference section of your school or college library.

If you cannot find what you need, consult your tutor or librarian.

The information you seek will often be close at hand. However, it may be difficult to find out who to ask, or where the information is kept. It is often necessary to ask first to find out what you want.

> Never give up at the first hurdle.

It is also important to remember that you should be specific about the information you require. If, for example, you want to find out how many people Shell UK employ in their marketing division, ask that specific question. If you simply request 'information about Shell' you stand only a limited chance of finding out the information you require.

 Task

Can you find some addresses? How did you find them?

You have seven days to find out the following addresses:

- The Consumers Association
- The Head Office of the National Westminster Bank PLC
- Your local Citizens Advice Bureau
- The Treasury
- Your local Livewire organiser
- An ICI factory
- Manchester United Football Club
- A Shell refinery
- The headquarters of your local police authority
- The local council offices.

Writing a letter to seek information

When writing a letter to seek information that will help you with your research make sure that you indicate the specific information that your require. A possible example is shown in Figure 3.

A few years ago an enthusiastic pupil of mine wrote to a company to ask for some information. After three weeks of waiting and no reply, he wrote again. He waited several more weeks in vain. I asked to see his third letter before he posted it and discovered the he had *not* put his address on! Most organisations will send you information free of charge. As a matter of courtesy always enclose a large stamped addressed envelope. You might receive a letter like the one in Figure 4.

Task

Study the letter from ICI in Figure 4 and answer the following questions.

1 Are ICI happy to deal with educational queries?
2 What do you think would be the wrong approach to use when contacting ICI?
3 What would be the best approach? Make a list of eight guidelines.

Making sense of the information you receive

Look carefully at all the information you have been sent. You will probably find that you have received more than you need. Mark the work that is useful and that which is not. Consider carefully how the information can be used to bring out the best in your coursework. You may find that you do not understand some of the information. Mark the parts that you are unsure about and, when you get the opportunity, ask your tutor what they mean.

Be careful about how you use resources which contain a lot of advertising materials emphasising the glossy nature of a business. These kinds of materials often just present one side of an argument or a particular point of view, so you need to be wary of them. Try to avoid advertising 'hype' or bias in your answer and paint a true picture of what you see.

Figure 3 A letter seeking information

Figure 4 ICI's letter of reply

- Only include relevant information
- Ask your tutor for help if you come across materials you do not understand.
- Try to avoid over-use of advertising materials
- Look out for bias
- Acknowledge your sources

Books

You may be able to find books that help with your investigation in:

- Your Business Studies department
- The school or college library

- Your local library
- The library of your local further educational establishment or college of technology.

Trying to find appropriate materials from books can sometimes be frustrating. Before you go into a library write out a list of topic headings and look in the index of every book in the section which covers your enquiry. If you are unsure about how to find specific information, the librarian is often more than willing to provide advice. If you decide to use your local college library, telephone the college beforehand to check that it is acceptable for you to do so.

A library will contain *textbooks* and *reference books* as well as many other types of books and publications. Textbooks will provide you with access to a wealth of information. Although it is unlikely that this information will refer specifically to the details of what you are studying, it may provide you with some helpful background information. For example, if you were studying the benefits of flow production to a particular company, you could look up information about the theoretical benefits of flow production and see how they relate to other companies and other systems.

Reference books are a good way of getting to know the topic you are studying. Some useful sources are:

- *Municipal Year Book* – information about local authorities in England and Wales.
- *Pear's Cyclopedia* – handbook with a section on events, office compendium, prominent people etc.
- *Whitaker's Almanac* – facts and figures about world affairs, business, names and addresses of associations, government offices and other organisations.

There are a number of *business dictionaries* which provide you with information about the meaning of various business terms. Useful sources are *The Top 20,000 British Companies* and *Kelly's Directory.* There are others which your librarian will be able to tell you about.

- *Who's Who* – lists people in the forefront of their professions.
- *Roget's Thesaurus of English Words and Phrases* – arranges words according to their meaning rather than alphabetical order.

The use of a good *dictionary* is essential to find out terms you do not understand as well as for checking spelling.

We feel that it is important to mention reference sources, not because we expect you to spend vast

amounts of time with a particular reference text but because an important business skill is being able to track down reference sources quickly. You also need to be able to express yourself in a clear and accurate manner.

Though working on your own in a quiet and often grandiose library is sometimes a little bit disconcerting, remember that the more research you do, the more ideas you should generate and the better the coursework you will produce.

Government statistics

Local and national government statistics are made up of facts and figures which are collected and assembled by local government officials and civil servants. These statistics are compiled for a variety of reasons. For example, they may be put together to help in estimating the number of schools to build, hospital beds to cater for, motorways to construct and so on. Statistical information enables planners to prepare for changes before those changes actually take place. Statistics may also be gathered to help the government understand and explain various trends such as changes in the population, the skills and qualifications of the people that make up the labour force and many other things.

Task

1 Make a list of ten types of information on which you feel it is important for a government to keep statistics.
2 Which of these are most important? Rank them from one to ten.
3 Prepare a short talk to justify the importance of those you have numbered one, two and three.

It is possible to gain access to most local and central government statistical publications at your local library, or by calling in and asking for information at your local council offices. If necessary, it is always possible to write to the appropriate government department.

Some publications you might find to be useful reference sources are:

- *The Monthly Digest of Statistics* published by the Central Statistical Office. This includes information on population, employment, law and order, various industries and many other useful areas of information.
- *Social Trends* contains a wide range of attractively displayed statistics with some analysis.
- *Annual Abstract of Statistics* contains wide range of statistical information. However, it is not an easy publication to use because of its complicated layout.
- *British Industry* published by the Department of Trade and Industry provides information about the volume of production in various industries.
- *Population Trends* is published by the Office of Population Censuses and Surveys. This gives detailed information about current and likely future changes in population.
- *Economic Progress Reports* is a monthly publication produced by the Treasury. It covers a wide number of statistics related to changes in the economy such as changes in the official unemployment figures, interest rates, money supply figures and many more.

There are also a number of local authority publications dealing with local statistics for unemployment, council expenditure and revenue, housing, and many other important areas of information.

There are several points to bear in mind when using statistics.

- Make sure that you understand the statistics that you use. It is often easy to draw the *wrong* conclusions.
- Try to explain what the statistics show, as well as why you are using them. Never just put them in without any explanation.
- Do *not* fill your coursework with statistics.
- State where you have obtained your statistics.
- Try to show the basis on which the statistics have been calculated. Who produced the statistics? Why did they produce them?

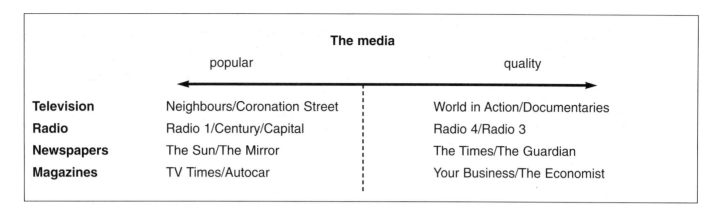

The media

	popular	quality
Television	Neighbours/Coronation Street	World in Action/Documentaries
Radio	Radio 1/Century/Capital	Radio 4/Radio 3
Newspapers	The Sun/The Mirror	The Times/The Guardian
Magazines	TV Times/Autocar	Your Business/The Economist

Figure 5 Defining the media

Media

'Media' refers to communication systems used to provide an audience with information. Often the word *mass* is added to media to emphasise that some forms of communication reach a very large audience. The media would include television, radio, newspapers and magazines. Though we take the media for granted in our everyday lives, many of you will be highly selective about what you read and watch. For example, when you watch television many of you will avoid the news, and if you read a newspaper, you may decide not to look at the business pages. But you are not alone – most people in this country spend little time watching and reading *hard news* items.

However, in order to find information which makes your work different and also keeps it up to date, it is useful to pay some attention to current events. Business activity takes place in a constantly changing world. Even the smallest business needs to be aware of changes in government rules about health and safety, changes in tax laws, how changes in credit laws will affect its business, and many other matters, knowledge of which can only be gained from an awareness of the environment in which a business operates. Watching topical television programmes and scanning current affairs and business pages in newspapers can be very helpful (Figure 5).

Here are some helpful hints to make studying for your coursework more effective.

■ *Television* Watch documentaries such as *World in Action* and other programmes such as *Watchdog* and *The Money Programme*. You will be amazed at how many ideas and themes they can supply for your studies.

■ *Radio* Listen to Radio 4. It is interesting to see how a presenter's sense of humour on the *Today* programme can make current affairs so pleasurable.
■ *Newspapers* Nearly all newspapers carry a business page and comment upon business activities. You will find many enlightening articles about small and large business organisations.
■ *Magazines* Local libraries keep a wide selection of magazines. Have a look at them. You might be surprised at how readable many magazines are.

Using a newspaper article as part of your evidence

Read the newspaper article (Figure 6) 'Tyneside flights are set to soar' (*The Northern Echo*).

Whenever you use an article, try to make notes on the points that you think are important in it. This particular article contains a host of information which could, for example, be used in a piece of coursework looking at the improving infrastructure or communications network in the north-east of England.

For example, when you read through it you may choose to note that:

■ air communications look set to improve in the north-east.
■ the improvement will mainly benefit business travellers
■ Manchester and then Birmingham are the most desired destinations for north-east business travellers
■ the fortunes of Newcastle Airport are improving.

Business
Trade and Finance

Tyneside flights are set to soar

BUSINESS travellers on Tyneside are expected to get a boost this spring with new flights set to be launched from Newcastle Airport to the Continent and the Midlands.

Glasgow-based Scottish European Airways has eight route applications to Europe which are expected to be reviewed by the Civil Aviation Authority next month.

"We feel pretty confident that we will soon be having more flights to Europe," an airport spokesman said.

The SEA has applied for direct daily flights from Newcastle to Frankfurt, Milan, Copenhagen, Geneva, Hamburg, Brussels, Gothenburg and Keflavik in Iceland.

If its application is approved, SEA plans to take delivery of four jets in late spring.

Belgium's national airline Sabena began twice-a-day flights to Brussels earlier this year.

Meanwhile, the CAA is also considering an application from Birmingham Executive Airways for a scheduled service between Newcastle and the Midlands.

Birmingham was second only to Manchester as a desired destination in a market survey completed late last year by the airport in co-operation with the Tyne & Wear Chamber of Commerce.

- Airport boss Jim Denyer, who is set to retire late this year after nearly 40 years in Newcastle, will be leaving on a high note.

The facility turned in record profits of £1.5m last year, a figure which equalled the record number of passengers.

And he has been awarded a silver medal by the Aerodrome Owner's Association for outstanding service.

Figure 6 A newspaper article on business travel

- Use a system which helps you to break information down into that which is more and less important.
- Beware of bias in the information you receive. Some magazines and newspapers deliberately represent a particular point of view.
- Try to use extracts from the information which will support your work. (Do not copy out large sections of text.)
- A limited use of pictures or charts from the media can help to support your work if the points they emphasise are sufficiently well explained.
- Make sure the information you use is up to date. Taking information from a magazine in my dentist's waiting room would be a mistake – unless I was writing a piece of history course-work!

Look everywhere for information. You will be surprised where it can be found.

Primary data

Primary data is information which you collect *first-hand* through your own research techniques. Primary research will often involve the use of questionnaires (see the next page) and other methods of recording data first-hand. The collection of primary data will be specific to a particular task. However, primary data may be difficult to collect because of the time involved, because of the difficulty of arranging appointments to meet the appropriate people, and for a number of other reasons.

When collecting primary information it is important that you use an effective method of *recording* this information.

- How will you record direct quotations?
- How will you record detailed statistical information?

Quotations can be very important because they are a record of 'authoritative statements' and points of view. However, they must be recorded accurately. Will you write down a person's words during speech, or will you use a portable tape recorder? Will you ask the person to repeat important phrases so that you can record those words accurately? You will need to give careful thought to these matters.

In collecting primary information you will often find that the speed at which you receive it is faster than you would like. You therefore need to devise some form of record sheet that will enable you quickly to record information in a way in which you can make sense of it later. This is particularly true when you are recording statistical information.

Figure 7 shows how a record sheet has been prepared to record goals, corners, off-sides and free kicks in a football match. The record keeper simply has to tick off these events as they occur.

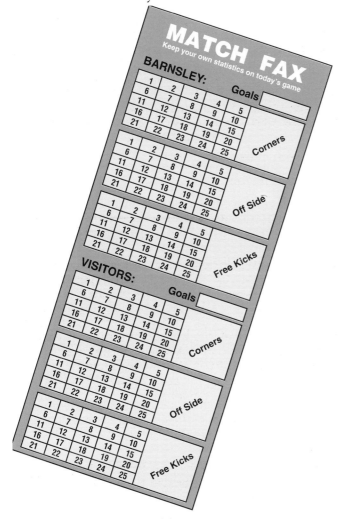

Figure 7 An example of a record sheet

Task

Prepare a record sheet that will enable you quickly to record the number of women passing you in the high street. You should allow for five different age groups, and women dressed in red, black, brown, blue or 'other colour' shoes. Try your record sheet for a 20-minute period. What problems did you encounter? How could you improve your record sheet?

Constructing a questionnaire

We have already seen that secondary data is information collected by someone else which you can then adapt to meet your own needs. Primary data, on the other hand, is information which you collect yourself, which is specifically designed to match your information requirements.

In business, companies constantly go out and gather information from customers. This is in order to find out what people think of their company's products or what sort of improvements they would like to see. This process is known as *market research*. Collecting primary information will often help you to improve the quality and accuracy of your finished work.

An important question that you need to consider is: 'What techniques should I use to obtain the information that I need?'

There are four basic methods that you can use.

1 *Direct observation* This simply involves watching and making a record of what you see or hear. Direct observation will reduce the problems of dubious data being recorded and is often considered to be the most accurate way of

collecting data because you are finding out exactly what happens, as and when it happens. For example, if you record the volume of traffic going past a junction, you are directly observing the traffic flow. However, a disadvantage of direct observation is that it can be time-consuming.

2   *Postal questionnaires* By writing to people you can try to obtain a range of responses to support your findings. Though this provides you with the opportunity to contact anyone you choose in order to get a response to your questions, usually few people bother to reply

3   *Telephone interviewing* This sounds quite imposing, but is really very simple. What it means is that you phone someone to try to persuade him or her to answer your questions. Cost is obviously dependent on what time of day the calls are made, how many calls you make and how long you stay on the telephone. This could be expensive and the responses may not always be encouraging if the person you telephone is busy.

4   *Personal interviews* Face-to-face interviewing often leads to more accurate and useful results being obtained. By working in a group, with several students conducting a series of interviews, you will find that you can pool a lot of information.

  Task

List two advantages and disadvantages of each of the following:

- direct observation
- postal questionnaires
- telephone interviewing
- personal interviewing.

Whatever technique you use, you will need to record the results. With direct observation you would keep a standard written record to note the number of occasions on which selected events happened. The other three methods, however, will require the design of a questionnaire.

What is a questionnaire?

A questionnaire is a systematic list of questions designed to obtain information from people about:

- specific events
- their attitudes
- their values or
- their beliefs.

Always make sure that the person answering the questions knows exactly what the purpose is of the exercise and is willing to cooperate.

There are two sorts of questionnaire. The first type involves handing or posting the questionnaire to a person who then fills it in and either gives it or sends it back to you. The second type involves carrying out structured interviews.

Telephone and face-to-face interviewing mean that the interviewer reads questions out and then writes down the answers. The main advantage of structured interviews is that if the questions lack clarity the interviewer can provide an explanation.

Task

Design three questions which will help you to find out about the hobbies and interests of another member of your group. These questions should need no further explanation and be suitable to form a questionnaire which may be handed to someone to fill in. If the questions are well worded, you should receive the information you are seeking.

Test the questions

- Has anybody attempted to answer a question which turns out to be vague or confusing and needs further explanation?
- Have the questions been successful? Have you found out the hobbies and interests of another member of the class?

- Has anyone found an example of (a) a bad question or (b) a good question?
- What important points have you learnt about questionnaire design?

> The questionnaire design is the most crucial part of the whole survey.

Though it is easy to design questions, it is very difficult to produce a good questionnaire. You must make your introduction simple, your layout clear and try to anticipate any misunderstandings. You want the questionnaire to provide you with the information you need. Do *not* include too many questions. A question should only be included if it relates to your needs.

Questions can be open or closed. Open questions are those which allow the person answering to give an opinion and which encourage him or her to talk at length. Closed questions usually require only a yes/no answer or one picked from a range of options. Questionnaires nearly always use closed questions. This tends to mean that the questions can be answered more quickly and more efficiently. It also means that, because the information is much more structured, the answers are easier to analyse. For example:

Do you find the layout of the new banking hall:

(a)

Very good	Good	Satisfactory	Poor	Very poor

   [Tick]

or

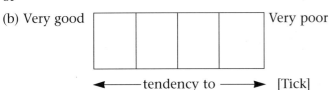

(b) Very good ⬚⬚⬚⬚ Very poor

◄——— tendency to ———► [Tick]

The purpose of this type of question should be to try to get people to commit themselves to a definite opinion – in this example, their feelings about the layout of a new banking hall, If instead you had used an *open question* the likelihood is that you would have got a variety of different answers. Closed questions tie respondents down so that they have to make a decision within a range of choices (in this case a range from very good to very poor).

Closed questions in which you suggest a range of answers can make it easy to sort your answers for analysis. For example:

Which of the following banks do you use most regularly? (Tick the relevant box.)

Barclays	⬚
National Westminster	⬚
Midland	⬚
Lloyds	⬚
Yorkshire	⬚
Others	⬚

To help you to operate the questionnaire, you may like to use a prompt card. This means that if several, or all of the questions in your questionnaire have the same range of set answers, you can number the possible answers, and then record the respondents' answers as numbers:

Example of a prompt card:

Barclays	01
National Westminster	02
Midland	03
Lloyds	04
Yorkshire	05
Others	06

Sometimes, you will need to ask open questions. For example, if you wanted to find out why people are unhappy or happy with the layout of a new banking hall, the range of answers you would have to provide might be too broad to be practical within a closed question. An open question will help you to discover people's real views on the new layout, and to communicate these views more effectively.

When designing your questionnaire you will need to give careful thought to how you can make sure that respondents concentrate on questions which are relevant to them, and skip over questions which do not relate to them. This will be important, for example, with questions which provide two possible answers. For example:

Question 1   Do you have a bank account?

                    Yes   ⬚
                    No   ⬚

If your answer is *no* skip to question 20.

(Questions 2-19 would then be filled in only by those respondents with bank accounts.)

Question 20	Why do you not have a bank account?

Receive wages in cash ☐
Use a building society ☐
Live too far from a bank ☐
Inconvenient ☐
Other reasons ☐

Make sure that your follow-up question relates to the objectives of the survey. For example, this questionnaire could have been designed to find out why people used different banks in a town. The follow-up question (20) could be used to find out why some people did not use the main banks.

Task

Set out a questionnaire (with ten questions) to find out whether members of your group have ever thought of setting up their own business, and what lines of business they would like to follow. Set out the questionnaire so that some of the questions can be skipped over by some respondents.

Task

Working on your own, list 12 problems which you might encounter in setting out a questionnaire. Now, discuss these problems with other members of the group.

- What are the most common problems mentioned?
- What solutions are there to help deal with these problems?
- What does your tutor think?

- Your questions should be simple and easy to understand.
- Make sure that whatever you ask relates to your *information needs*.
- Do not include too many questions.
- Make sure that your questions are logical and fit into an ordered sequence.
- Do not ask personal questions. You do not want to offend people.
- Try to make your questions unambiguous. Make the meaning of your questions clear.
- Before you start to construct a questionnaire, consider what you need to know. When you have finished it *test it*. Trial interviews are essential.
- Thank people for giving up their time to help you.

Survey on the use of the A1
This survey is designed to help assess whether the A1 satisfies the North East's business, industrial and leisure needs as an effective road link.
(Please tick the relevant boxes)

Question 1. Do you regularly use the A1?
Yes ☐   No ☐
If your answer is No, please skip to question 8.

Question 2. Do you use the A1?
Under 5 ☐   5–10 times ☐   more than ☐
times per   10 times
week

Question 3. Do you use it for?
Business ☐   Leisure ☐
Personal ☐   Others ☐

Question 4. How often do you find that you are delayed?
on every ⟨ table ⟩ never
occasion

◀— Tendency —▶

Question 5. Is the A1 adequate for your needs?

V. Good	Good	Satisfactory	Poor	V. Poor

Question 6. Would you suggest?
Leaving it as it is ☐
Providing a third lane ☐
Making it all motorway ☐
Making it into four lanes ☐
Making alternative routes ☐
Others

Question 7. Would an improved A1 help businesses in the North East?

Big improvement	Some change	No change

THANK YOU FOR ANSWERING THIS QUESTIONNAIRE

Question 8. You have stated that you do not use the A1. Is this because:
You do not drive ☐
It is too busy ☐
There are too many delays ☐
You have no need to use it ☐
It is too dangerous to use ☐
Others...

THANK YOU FOR ANSWERING THIS QUESTIONNAIRE

Figure 8 A short questionnaire that worked

A short questionnaire such as the one shown in Figure 8 can provide you with a wealth of information to help you with a coursework study of a particular issue, problem or area of interest such as the adequacy of the A1 as an integral part of the north east's transport system.

Task

A class of students set out to find if there was a demand for a second screen at their local cinema. They need to find the answers to questions such as how many people went to the cinema, how often they went, what sorts of people they were and the types of films they liked. This sort of information would show whether there was a large demand for a cinema, the people who would go most frequently, and what types of films should be shown in order to attract the biggest audience.

The class had already been given the information by the cinema owner that age was a very important factor influencing whether people went frequently or infrequently to the cinema and the sort of films they watched.

The class then set out to classify cinema-goers into different age groups, first by taking into account their own experiences and then by interviewing friends and relatives in different age groups.

How often do you go to the cinema?	5–15	16–25	26–35	36–50	51+
(a) More than once a week					
(b) Once a week					
(c) One a fortnight					
(d) Once a month					
(e) Hardly ever					
(f) Never					
What types of films do you mainly watch?					
(a) Horror					
(b) Adventure					
(c) Comedy					
(d) Romance					

Using this information they were able to classify the following age groups.

5-15 16-25 26-35 36-50 51 and over

Having chosen their main feature for classification they were able to set out a questionnaire containing all the other questions they wanted to ask. The questionnaire was simple to use in the field and easy to read off when completed.

A short section of the questionnaire is shown below.

Your task is to design a market research questionnaire to see if there is the demand for an additional screen at your local cinema. You should consider the following questions.

- What will you ask?
- Who will you ask?
- When will you ask?
- How will you ask?

Collect and record your information. Then, present a report of your findings and recommendations to your local cinema owner.

Alternatively you could research the demand for:

- a new supermarket
- a new leisure centre
- a new car park
- a new disco.

You will find it helpful to carry out a pilot survey to test your questions before you go for a full survey.

Carrying out an interview

- If you have arranged an interview, make sure you turn up on time.
- Ensure that your questionnaire is prepared and has been tested.
- If you are recording the interview, see that your cassette player works beforehand.
- Try not to stray from the topic.
- Make notes and think of follow-up questions.
- Try to be a good listener.
- Thank people for their help.

There is a good chance that you will choose to conduct personal interviews rather than telephone interviews or personal questionnaires. This is because the response rate to postal questionnaires is poor and it is expensive to send letters. The disadvantages of telephone interviews are that you disturb people, and unless you know them, or have arranged for such interviews, they may be too busy to talk to you.

Remember that when you carry out an interview, you are representing your school or college. Always tell people what you are trying to do and why you are doing it.

Task

Conduct an interview in a formal setting using the questionnaire you drew up for the previous task. Tape record your interview. Play back your interview.

- What went well?
- What went badly?
- What improvement should be made?

Recording and making sense of your information

The most common but probably the least effective way of writing down your information is on loose bits of paper. If you do it this way, you may soon find that your work lacks order and becomes confusing.

Many people use notebooks to record their information so that they don't lose important pieces of data. The problem with using this method is that things tend to get written down in the order they are collected, rather than in a logical pattern. Of course, it is possible to have several notebooks for different kinds of information, but this can be expensive and wasteful.

A loose-leaf notebook can be helpful, but you must take care to keep it in order. An advantage of using a loose-leaf book is that you can move sheets around to organise them in the way you see fit. A card index can be used in a similar way. You may like to use different coloured paper or cards for different subject headings.

You may like to store important information on a computer file. Databases and other computer applications can help you to store and sort information.

The computer is an excellent tool for storing information both in coursework and in business. The administration of any business depends on key files: records containing details of your customers, your employees, your suppliers and other important information. You can store your records on a computer disk which acts as your filing cabinet. The records that you might like to collect for your course-work may include answers to a questionnaire, details of local firms, and a range of statistics.

The records that you store can be saved and later retrieved under various headings known as fields. For example, if you are doing a survey of local businesses you might like to keep your records in the following fields:

- *name* of company
- *number* of employees
- *product* or service
- *location* of business.

Make sure that you know exactly what information you want to store in your database and that you can quickly retrieve the information you have stored.

Computer databases are particularly helpful in that they can sort out information for you. This can be a major advantage when you want to order the results of a questionnaire. For example, you may have made a number of entries on your database and then want to know which entries to your file contain specific information. You may want to find out how many people answering your market research questionnaire between the ages of 21 and 35 liked blue wrappers on chocolate biscuits. We can ask a computer to carry out a search for particular information by giving a simple instruction such as *Find* or *F* followed by whatever information we require.

It is very important that you record information accurately at the time it is available. When you are collecting coursework information you should always carry a notebook or portable tape-recorder. You should also keep a record of where, how and when you collected the information.

Sorting out your data

How you collect your data and the way in which you sort out your information are closely interwoven. You need to have some ideas about what you will do with your information before you start to collect. While you are sorting your information you may have fresh ideas about collecting new information.

Sorting data involves changing a loose collection of information into a form out of which sense can be made. To do this you will need to decide which elements of your data are important.

Two important skills in sorting information are:

1 Being able to classify data into different divisions. This helps you to put the data into manageable sections. For example, imagine that each of the boxes below represents a different piece of information.

You may feel that when carrying out your course-work you would like to collect and organise your work using the following classifications.

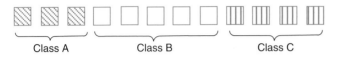

Class A   Class B   Class C

 Task

During the course of a piece of research a student found out the following information about the Better Biscuit company. The Manchester-based division of the company make ginger biscuits (1000 packets per day) and chocolate biscuits (3000 packets per day).

The ginger biscuits are sold in Britain and the chocolate biscuits are exported to the European Community. In Lincoln the company makes ginger biscuits (1000 packets per day), chocolate biscuits (1000 packets per day), cream biscuits (1000 packets per day). All these biscuits are sold in Britain. In Hull the company makes 10 000 packets of chocolate biscuits per day which are exported to the European Community.

List three different ways of classifying this information. Why is it important to think about the classification you will use before collecting information?

2 The second important skill in sorting information is being able to build up information by adding or joining items together. This would involve adding up categories of information.

For example, in investigating the activities of a company you may find that they operate three units. The sales figure for each unit is shown below:

Sales unit A =   300 000
Sales unit B =   150 000
Sales unit C =   50 000
Total sales are therefore 500 000

In a similar way, if you were investigating a new retail outlet or similar development you may want to group together all the individuals and organisations which are in favour of the development. You may do this in order to see if there is a common thread in their support for the development or to quantify the weight of the support.

Classifying under headings

It can be helpful to break down your investigation into a number of headings. These headings can be used for collecting information, sorting the information, and then for writing up your final coursework report. Alternatively, you may just use the headings for collecting information or for classifying it.

For example, an investigation of a new planning proposal could be carried out under the following headings:

- Background information
- The site
- The plans
- Arguments in favour of the proposal
- Arguments against the proposal
- Summary

When material is collected for a report it is often done in date order. However, you must be careful not to present your evidence in this way. For when a report is presented like this the conclusions often become lost in the main body of the report leaving the readers to sort out the information for themselves.

When you set out your coursework make a clear distinction between:

- the aims of the research
- the body of the findings
- the conclusions and recommendations

Conclusions and recommendations

Once the information has been organised and set out in a clear pattern, conclusions can be drawn. At this stage you must be very careful not to over-simplify. You should be aware that your data are often limited and biased by the value judgements of the people who have supplied you with information.

Usually there is more than one way of looking at evidence. This is one reason why different people have different viewpoints. When you look at evidence you should ask yourself:

- What does it mean to me?
- Why do I see it this way?

However, you should also consider:

- What it means to other people.
- Why they may use it that way.

In looking at data you should try to identify trends and sequences. For example, you may notice from the sales figures of a company that over the years sales have increased. You may then want to try to identify the causes of this increase. However, you must be cautious about the way you interpret evidence. There are usually several ways of looking at it.

Be careful not to draw false conclusions based on insufficient evidence. For example, the student who claimed that a company was better off because sales had increased by 10% failed to account for the fact that the company's costs had risen by 50%.

Sometimes the data that you collect will be very disappointing and you will have to abandon the task. However, it does not matter if you cannot get all the answers that you are looking for. You should try to be aware of the weakness of data that you collect and mistakes you made in collecting data. Data may be weak if lacking in quantity or quality. However, you will have learnt a lot if you are able to recognise what you did wrong and clarify the improvements you could make. Highlight your mistakes and explain how you would improve your research if you were to start again.

In writing a business report it is helpful to extract the main conclusions and/or recommendations and to restate them in a separate section at the end for emphasis. This makes it easier for the reader of the report to focus on your conclusions and helps you to draw your ideas together.

You have seen that the main pieces of advice in this section on conclusions and recommendations are the following.

- Be careful not to present your ideas in a simplistic manner.
- In looking through your data try to identify trends and sequences.
- Be careful not to draw false conclusions based on insufficient evidence.
- Make your conclusions clear, so that they have an impact on the reader.

Presenting your findings

The information that you gather should be presented in ways that are easy to understand both by yourself and by anyone else reading your report. There are many useful ways of presenting information.

> *Golden rule* – Do not use means of presentation other than plain text unless they help to make your report clearer to understand.

Many students get carried away with drawing charts and diagrams because they enjoy producing them and they look good. However, too many charts and diagrams can be confusing and can spoil the flow of a well-written report.

Task

- One member of the class should attempt to explain changes in the top 20 pop chart from the previous week without referring to any printed material.
- Another member of the class should attempt to explain the fortunes of the local football team without referring to a football league table.

Now each member of the group should look at a copy of these tables while the students that gave the original explanations give fresh explanations.

- Did the table improve the explanations? If so, how and why?
- What were the main advantages/disadvantages of using tables?

Tables of information

A table can be used to show a lot of information. It should be easy to read and clearly set out. The table

Top ten attractions		
visited by British and overseas tourists: number of visits in 1994		
1 Blackpool Pleasure Beach	6 750 000	(free)
2 British Museum	5 823 427	(free)
3 Strathclyde Country Park, Motherwell	4 000 000	(free)
4 National Gallery, London	3 822 371	(free)
5 Palace Pier, Brighton	3 500 000	(free)
6 Alton Towers, Staffordshire	2 618 365	
7 Westminster Abbey	2 500 000	(free)
8 Madame Tussaud's, London	2 449 627	
9 Pleasure Beach, Great Yarmouth	2 400 000	(free)
10 Tower of London	2 235 199	

Figure 9 A table showing visits to tourist attractions

in Figure 9 was used to show the top ten tourist attractions in the UK in 1994. For example, Blackpool Pleasure Beach was the most popular with 6.75 million visitors. Alton Towers was the most popular pay-for-admission attraction.

Tables are most frequently used to show information that can be presented in figures. However, this is not always the case, as is shown by the table in Figure 10. This table shows major companies that moved their offices away from London in the late 1980s.

A table can be used to present a wide selection of information in a way that can be quickly read and is simple to understand. The Stock Exchange page of a newspaper is a good example of a well-known table.

The table in Figure 11 was used to show some information about Grantham Town Football Club in

Company	Destination
Shell Chemicals	Chester
Lloyds Bank	Bristol
Mercury	Bracknell
Patent Office	Cardiff
Sealink UK	Ashford
Pearl Assurance	Peterborough
Sun Life	Basingstoke
BP Oil	Hemel Hempstead
Confederation Life	Stevenage
Securicor	Sutton
Mortgage Corporation	Woking
Lloyd's Register	Croydon

Figure 10 Major companies on the move

MATCHFAX – Grantham Town

		Team	COMP		SCORE	H	A	SCORERS
Aug	9	Gainsboro Tn	LC	H	3-3	403		Whitehurst (2) O.G.
	20	Halesowen Tn	BH	A	1–2		886	Burrell
	23	Ashtree Highfld	BH	A	1–2		90	Humphreys (pen)
	27	Dudley Town	BH	A	2–1		327	Whitehurst, Humphreys (pen)
	29	Tamworth	BH	A	3–1		1385	Humphreys (2 pens), Whitehurst
Sep	3	Boorwash Vic	FA	H	2–1	365		Humphreys (pen), Farrow
	10	Bilston Town	BH	H	2–1	356		Humphreys (pen), Whitehurst
	13	Mile Oak Rvrs	BH	H	2–1	328		Humphreys, Barber
	17	North Feriby	FA	A	2–1		150	Farrow (2)
	24	Shepherd Ch	FT	H	2–1	346		Farrow, Humphreys (pen)
Oct	1	Brignorth Tn	BH	H	2–0	401		Whitehurst, O.G., Anderson
	8	Nuneaton Bor	BH	H	3–0	422		Whitehurst. Ryder
	11	Corby Town	WF	H	2–2	329		Radford, Whitehurst, O.G.
	15	Stourbridge	BH	A	3–2			
	19	Corby Town	WF	A				
	22	Alvechurch	FT	H				
	29	Willenhall Tn	BH	H				
Nov	5	Atherstone U	BH	A				
	12	Gloucester C	BH	H				
	15	Rushden Town	BH	A				
	19	Bridgnorth Tn	BH	A				
	26	Forest Green	BH	H				
Dec	3	Banbury Utd	BH	A				
	6	Ashtree Highfd	BH	H				
	10	Hednesford Tn	BH	H				
	17	Wellingboro	BH	A				
	26	Spalding Utd	BH	H				
	31	Coventry Spt	BH	H				
Jan	2	Kings Lynn	BH	A				
	7	Sutton Coldfld	BH	A				
	14	Halesowen Tn	BH	H				
	21	Bilston Town	BH	A				
	28	Rushden Town	BH	H				
Feb	4	Stourbridge	BH	H				
	11	Mile Oak Rvrs	BH	H				
	14	Sutton Coldfld	BH	H				
	18	Atherstone U	BH	H				
	25	Tamworth	BH	H				
Mar	4	Willenhall Tn	BH	A				
	11	Wellingboro	BH	H				
	18	Coventry Spt	BH	A				
	25	King's Lynn	BH	H				
	27	Spalding Utd	BH	A				
Apr	1	Dudley Town	BH	H				
	22	Banbury Utd	BH	H				
	29	Hednedford Tn	BH	A				
May	1	Gloucester C	BH	A				
	8	Nuneaton Bor	BH	A				

KEY – BH: Beazer Homes Midland; FA: FA Cup; FT; FA Trophy, Wt: Westgate Insurance Cup; LC: Lincolnshire Senior County Cup.

Figure 11 Condensed information about Grantham Town Football Club

the early part of a recent football season. It shows the dates of the matches, teams played against, the type of competition involved, where the match was played, the score, numbers attending the match and who scored the Grantham goals.

Task

Reading a table

Read off the table the following pieces of information (up to and including 15 October)

1 How many games have Grantham won in the Beazer Homes Midland League?
2 How many goals have Granthan scored in the FA cup?
3 Who is Grantham's top goal scorer?
4 How many goals has Farrow scored?
5 What has been Grantham's (a) biggest home gate and (b) average home gate?

Task

Reading share price tables

Until they have had it explained to them people can be confused by the tables of share prices on the share page of a major newspaper. In fact, it is very easy to read the important details on a share page. Look at the table below.

Class of share	Price	±	High	Low
Breweries				
Allied	88	+2	94	80
Whitbread	74	−1	75	70
Oil				
BP	384		384	360
Shell	422	+1	422	416

The price column shows the previous day's closing price, the plus or minus shows the change from the closing price of the day before (the high shows the highest price the share has been this year, and the low shows the lowest).

You can see from the above information that Whitbread shares can be bought at 74p. They had fallen by 1p since the previous day. 75p is the highest price they have been this year and 70p the lowest.

Now try to read some information from the following table:

Class of share	Price	±	High	Low
Entertainment				
Tottenham Hotspur	88	−1	103	88
Ladbroke	233	+2	233	201·
Oil				
Atlantic	643	+85	643	420
BP	426	+5	441	418

- Which share has experienced the biggest rise in price since the previous day? (Can you give possible explanations for this rise?)
- What has been the cheapest price of BP shares for the year in which this table was constructed?
- When Tottenham Hotspur's shares were originally sold they were 100p each. How much were they selling for when the table was published?
- Collect information showing the price of ten shares on three consecutive days. Set out your own table, so that it is clear and simple. The table should show information about the change in these share prices over the three days.

Showing information on a bar chart

Bar charts are a particularly good way of making comparisons. In the same way that you can compare people's heights by asking them to stand back to back, you can quickly make comparisons by casting your eye over the columns of a bar chart.

A bar chart is a diagram in which lines, or bars, have lengths which represent the value of some feature. For example, if Major PLC employs 1.5 million people and Minor PLC employs 1 million this could be shown as in Figure 12.

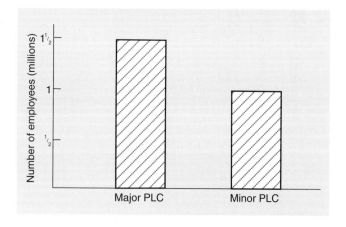

Figure 12 A bar chart

When setting up a bar chart it is particularly important to make it clear what measurements you are using on the axes of the chart. It is also important to use clear labelling and, if necessary, a key to indicate what the bars represent.

The bar chart shown in Figure 13 illustrates the way in which a well-constructed chart makes it possible to pick out information quickly and to make comparisons. The chart was used to show the results of a survey of 42 small businesses in the service sector. The sample included such businesses as accountants, solicitors, secretarial agencies and courier services, each of which employed fewer than 50 people. The sample of businesses was divided between two geographical areas – Sunderland and Cambridge. The survey set out to find out what types of new technology had been purchased by small companies in the two areas.

Just by glancing at the bar chart it immediately becomes obvious that most of the small firms surveyed in these two areas had invested in microcomputers, disk drives and printers. Obvious differences between the two areas can quickly be picked out, e.g. the use of Prestel by firms in the Cambridge area and facsimile machines by firms in Sunderland.

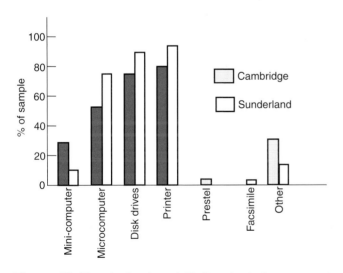

Figure 13 New technology initially adopted

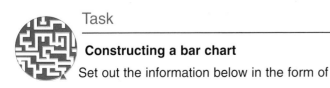

Task

Constructing a bar chart

Set out the information below in the form of a bar chart. The figures below show greetings card sales in the UK in 1994 in terms of (a) quantity sold and (b) value.

Types of card	Quantity sold	Value
Christmas/New Year	1.3 billion	£240.1 million
Valentine's day	20.4 million	£28.4 million
Mother's day	35.6 million	£37.4 million
Father's day	16.3 million	£15.4 million
Easter	23.0 million	£11.2 million

- What were the main problems you had in setting up your bar chart?
- How did you get round these problems?
- What were the main advantages of using a bar chart to show this information?
- What were the main disadvantages?
- What types of information do bar charts illustrate well?

Showing information on a pictogram

Many students enjoy working on pictograms to make coursework colourful and interesting. Pictograms involve the combination of tables, charts and other ways of showing information with an interesting illustration. Your illustration can be used to give a more dramatic impact to the information that is being presented.

Use pictograms when:

- they help you to understand your coursework better (and to enjoy your work)
- they make it easier for any outside reader to understand your work better (and enjoy reading it).

Pictograms can be used in a wide variety of imaginative ways. For example, the pictogram in Figure 14 illustrates how a bar chart can be combined with a map in order to show how business rents fall as one moves west from central London.

The pictogram in Figure 15 provides an attractive way of illustrating UK sales of Easter eggs and novelties in 1994.

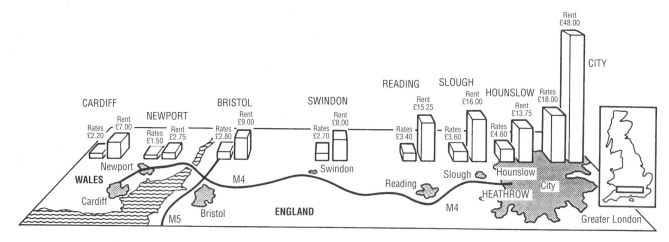

Figure 14 Moving west for rent and rates (£ per square foot)

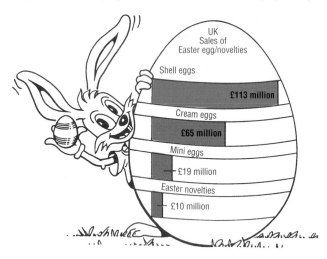

Figure 15 Illustrating UK sales of Easter eggs and novelties

![maze icon] **Task**

You have just carried out a piece of coursework which has involved comparing prices in the local corner shop with those in a large hypermarket. You have found out the information shown below.

How can you illustrate this information by means of a pictogram? Does your pictogram make the information more interesting and clearer to understand?

Line graphs

Line graphs are particularly useful for showing how things change over a period of time. On a line graph you will normally show how the value of specific items changes with time. Time should be shown along the horizontal axis and the variables (items whose values change) on the vertical axis. Line graphs can be a particularly useful way of presenting information in business reports.

The line chart in Figure 16, for example, illustrates changes in sales made by a business over a six-month period.

Line charts are particularly effective for comparing changes in a number of variables. For example, the chart shown in Figure 17 is a simple yet clear way of showing changes in the value of the pound against the dollar (USA), Deutschmark (Germany) and yen (Japan) in the first week of May 1995.

Item	Price of item	
	Corner-shop	Hypermarket
Washing powder (size E20)	6.20	6.00
Loaf of white bread (standard size)	0.75	0.70
Two litres of vanilla ice-cream	1.60	1.30

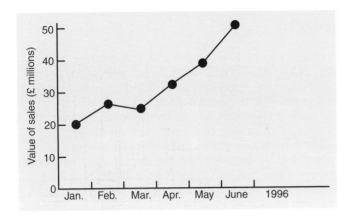

Figure 16 Changes in sales over a six-month period

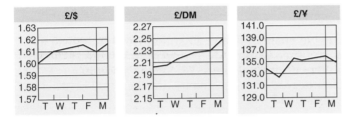

Figure 17 Currency movements

The vertical axis on a line graph will normally start at zero; but this need not necessarily be so.

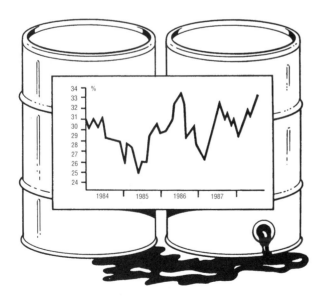

Figure 18 OPEC production (as a percentage of world output)

Line graphs can also be effectively built into pictograms. The pictogram shown in Figure 18 illustrates the percentage of oil produced by a group of countries known as the Oil Producing Exporting Countries (OPEC) between 1984 and 1988.

 Task

Study the pictogram in Figure 19 which illustrates the share price of Pennine Optical, an enterprise that makes spectacle frames.

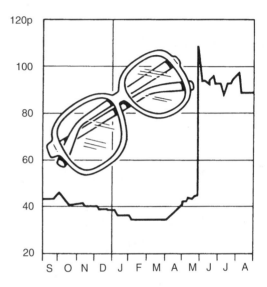

Figure 19 Pennine Optical share price

- What does this pictogram set out to show?
- Is it an effective means of presentation? Why?
- Is it eye-catching? Why?
- Is it easy to understand? Why?
- How else could the data be presented? Draw up your own alternative form of presentation.
- Look through a newspaper for a table of statistics that can be turned into a line graph. Then illustrate the information by means of a pictogram.

Line charts are particularly effective for illustrating inflows and outflows of money (or in any situation where one figure needs to be taken away from another). Using a line chart in this way makes it easy to draw comparisons quickly. Examples include the comparison of a company's sales figures with the cost of making those sales, and comparisons of a country's import and export figures.

The line graph in Figure 20 illustrates the profits and losses made by a firm over a six-year period based on the figures in the following table.

Year	Value of sales (£)	Cost of sales (£)
1	80 000	60 000
2	160 000	100 000
3	160 000	120 000
4	130 000	120 000
5	90 000	90 000
6	50 000	120 000

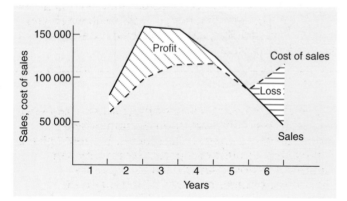

Figure 20 Line graph

Task

Illustrate the information below by means of a line graph. The figures are for Redland's inflation rate (%).

1986	1987	1988	1989	1990	1991	1992	1993	1994
3.5	4.0	6.5	7.5	10.0	4.0	2.6	2.7	2.0

- How would you set out the line graph?
- What are the main problems?
- How can you make it clear and easy to understand?
- Is a line graph a good way of presenting this information?
- How else could you go about presenting the information?

Pie charts

Pie charts can be used to present information in a clear and dramatic way. A circle is made up of 360 degrees and the total can be divided up into different sized segments, to present a very visual picture of how each proportion relates to the total. For example, if the value of a firm's sales is shared equally between two products then each could be represented by segments of 180 degrees in a pie chart (because there are 360 degrees in a circle) showing the total sales value of the company. So in this case the circle would be exactly divided in half.

Today, most business reports are presented by using a computer package. There is a wide range of software that makes it possible to set up pie charts quickly using a range of colours and different types of shading.

The pie chart in Figure 21 shows how the gross pay of an office worker Mr S. Singh can be broken down under various headings. Mr Singh's gross pay is £720. Each degree of the pie chart can therefore be used to represent £2.

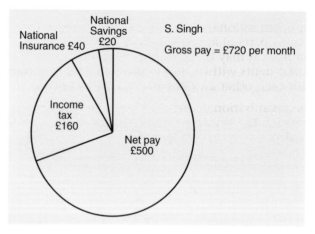

Figure 21 Pie chart showing the make-up of a pay packet

Singh's gross pay	= £720 (per month)	= 360°
Singh's income tax payment	= £160 (per month)	= 80°
Singh's NI contribution	= £40 (per month)	= 20°
Singh's national savings contribution	= £20 (per month)	= 10°
Singh's net pay	= £500 per month	= 250°

Task

Figure 22 shows The Body Shop's sales by region in 1994. Set this out in the form of a pie chart.

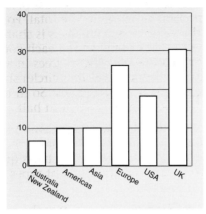

Figure 22　The Body Shop's retail sales by region (%)

Organisational charts

An organisational chart can be used to show how the various parts of an organisation fit together. For example, it may be used to show how various departments within an organisation communicate with each other and/or the chain of command.

The organisational chart in Figure 23 shows the way in which the three groups that make up a company are dependent on each other.

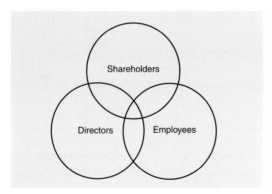

Figure 23　An organisational chart

The chart shown in Figure 24 is called an *organogram* and gives details of the structure of a small engineering company.

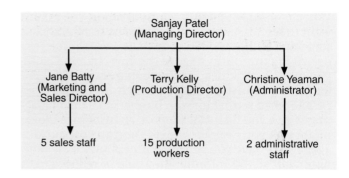

Figure 24　Organogram

Task

Draw an organisational chart to illustrate the structure of an organisation with which you are familiar, e.g. school, club, local petrol station, local bank or office.

Flow charts

A flow chart is a useful way of illustrating a sequence of events. The flow chart should summarise the various stages in a particular process. It should give a step-by-step account of a particular activity. For example, the flow chart shown in Figure 25 illustrates a number of stages which might be involved in turning a business idea into a growing business concern.

Figure 25　Flow chart

When you come to writing up your report you may want to spend quite a long time discussing a particular stage that is illustrated in your chart. For example, in describing the fourth stage in the flow chart in Figure 25 you may say that: negotiating support for a business idea could involve looking for help from a range of people when setting up your business. A bank manager might give you financial support, an insurance broker might give you insurance advice, and an Enterprise agency may give you general business advice. In your flow chart all this information would be reduced to the statement *Negotiate support*.

Task

Draw a flow chart to show the stages involved in buying groceries from a supermarket. The first stage should read:

Enter the supermarket

Task

The following report has been put together by a management trainee at Bonnie Charley PLC. It is a disaster!

- It is boring!
- It is difficult to make sense of!
- It is poorly presented!

What can you do with it to improve it?

Rewrite the report using charts and diagrams.

Who benefits from the activities of Bonnie Charley PLC – a report for shareholders and members of the company

Bonnie Charley has provided massive benefits for the community of Glenroy over the last five years. The profits of the company have increased year by year. In 1990 net profit after tax was 3.2 million, rising to 4.0 million in 1991, 5.1 million in 1992, 6.4 million in 1993, 6.6 million in 1994 and 8.4 million in 1995. The company operates in three main product areas. In 1994 65% of sales were of whisky, 25% of bread and 10% of barley. It is possible to compare the profits of Bonnie Charley with its main local rival Cambells PLC. Cambells' net profit after tax was 6.1 million in 1990, 6.4 million in 1991, 5.5 million in 1992, 4.2 million in 1993 and 3 million in 1994 and 1995.

Bonnie Charley PLC is a small company. The managing director is Elspeth McDonald and the three divisional managers are Harry O'Neill (whisky), Brian Mullen (bread), and Greg West (barley). The whisky and bread divisions each employ 30 production workers and there are 12 workers in the barley division.

Each year, divisional managers must establish their own targets for output, sales and profits. These figures will then be presented to Elspeth McDonald for approval. The managing director will either approve, or ask for changes to be made in the estimated figures.

The wages paid by Bonnie Charley are 10% higher than the average for the area. Bonnie Charley also contributes a quarter of a million pounds a year to local charities. Bonnie Charley products are widely consumed in the local economy and discounts are given to all local traders.

Bonnie Charley PLC is very much your company. A shining light in Glenroy.

Developing and showing evidence of the core skill of Application of Number

In presenting your findings you will depend heavily on the core skills of Information Technology, Application of Number and Communications.

In particular, in the previous section we have dwelt on a number of important skills involving the Application of Number. It is therefore helpful to set out the competencies which Advanced Business candidates are expected to develop.

Application of Number at Level 3

Being able to apply number is a very important business and life skill. There are some areas of Business in which accuracy and skill with the use of number is crucial, e.g. in finance and accounts. However, numeracy is also a general skill which is of great importance in many spheres of business activity, such as quantitative work in market and product research, business forecasting and economics, and in performance measurement in all aspects of business life.

In following a course in Business you will be given many opportunities to develop your number skills, particularly in the following areas:

1 Collecting and recording data
2 Tackling problems
3 Interpreting and presenting data

Collecting and recording data

You will need to be able to make decisions about what data to collect and then choose techniques which will suit a task involving numbers. Such techniques will include using percentages, ratios, fractions, estimates, measuring shape and space, and working with data collecting and handling processes.

You should be able to perform these techniques in the correct order, work in an accurate way and record data in the appropriate units, e.g. money, sales figures, and units of output.

You should always make sure that your records are accurate and complete and that you identify any sources of error and the effect that this might have on your calculations.

Tackling problems

You should be able to:

- Use number techniques which suit a problem that you are working on.
- Add, subtract, divide and multiply numbers of any size and make calculation using fractions, percentages and ratios, as well as formulae
- Make calculations involving measures such as National Income, the Retail Price Index, as well as shapes and spaces.
- Handle data using scales and tables, and work out and use the mean, median, mode and interquartile range.
- Perform techniques in the right order and choose and use appropriate units
- Work accurately and use mathematical terms correctly. Your calculations should be correct and you should check the procedures you have used.

Always make sure that the results you arrive at make sense when related to the problem you are tackling. Identify the effects of errors in your workings.

Interpreting and presenting data

You should identify the main features of the data you are working with, e.g. the main relationships and patterns, say, between sales revenues and profits. Choose and use appropriate techniques for presenting data. In particular, in Business you will frequently need to interpret and construct statistical diagrams (pictograms, bar charts, pie charts, histograms, scatter diagrams), interpret and construct graphs, interpret and compare modes, means, medians, the range and interquartile ranges. You should also be able to construct networks and two-dimensional drawings and present calculations using number.

You should follow conventions in presenting your work, e.g. using given axes and appropriate labelling of charts and diagrams.

Your interpretation and presentation of work should be accurate. Finally, you should be able to explain how the results make sense in the light of the problem being tackled.

Making an attractive final presentation

Presenting you final work well requires good communication skills. You want the reader or listener to understand the points that you make. You want him or her to interpret these points accurately. It is not unusual for a writer or speaker to make a point which is taken the wrong way.

The two examples given below of partners' letters to tutors may have sounded fine to their writer but, unfortunately, both are rather open to misinterpretation!

1 Dear Tutor
   Glynn was with me yesterday. I took him to the zoo to see my cousins...

2 Dear Tutor,
   I am writing to say that during the vacation I got married. Perhaps you would let me know what I am supposed to do...

Try to present your information clearly. Read your piece of work through to other people such as parents or friends and ask for their response. See if they understand what you have written.

Good communication also involves presenting information logically and fluently. Effective planning will help to ensure that your work follows a sequence of events which falls into place and which presents an overall picture of events, rather than a disorderly jumble of ideas.

Try to make sure that your work is neat so that it can be clearly understood by the reader. I am often criticised by my students for the way I mark their work. Students often knock on the door of my office to ask, 'What does this say?' Your examiner cannot ask 'What does this say?' Untidy work may be misinterpreted, will create a poor impression of what you can do, and may irritate the person who is marking. Make a special effort to present your work clearly.

Task

The list below represents the stages to be followed in an advertising campaign. It is not, however, in the most appropriate sequence. Put the stages into a more logical order.

- Developing the campaign
- Client approval
- Market research
- Testing the campaign
- Client commissions advertising campaign
- Test market
- Production of final advertisement
- The national launch

In presenting work for GNVQ assessment you can use a variety of appropriate media.

For example you may:

- Use a word processor/graphics package/multi-tasking computer package.
- Use video, tape-recordings, and other means.

Think carefully about the stationery you will need for assembling your portfolio of evidence. How will you keep your work together?

Task

Split up into groups of three or four. Discuss the sort of materials you will use for putting your portfolio of evidence together.

- Should your work be word processed or presented in some other way?
- What will be the best way of securing your materials together?
- Do you want to keep your work inside a folder and if so, what type of folder?

Presenting your work in an attractive and professional fashion should help you to take a pride in it. You will be presenting your work for assessment. This means that you will try to make sure that it is the best piece of work you have ever done.

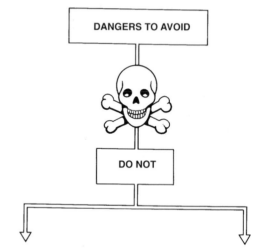

Use dictated notes or just copy extracts from books and other sources. Assessors want to see original work. They can tell!

Fill your work with pretty pictures from glossy brochures. Only use pictures where they enhance your explanations.

Look after your work. If you take it home don't lose it and don't let it get near the dog! Some of the most famous authors have lost manuscripts on trains and buses. An examiner recently put down a pile of students' scripts outside his house, while he popped back into the house to answer the phone. When he went back outside, the scripts had gone, and the refuse collection lorry was at the end of his street. Consider:

- Where are you going to keep the work?
- How will you keep it safe?
- Is there a chance of losing it?

Ask your tutor for help if you are likely to have problems with these points.

For example, if you were explaining the day-to-day activities of running a small jewellery business you might want to use the two photographs in Figure 26 to understand the following.

Figure 26 A small jewellery business

■ There are a number of important stages involved in jewellery making.
■ Personalised jewellery manufacture requires a lot of attention to detail.
■ Each stage in production is painstaking and slow.

■ Work requires a high level of concentration.
■ An investment is required in manufacturing equipment, paints, enamels, display cases and other materials.
■ The sole trader needs to be very versatile, but you can't do more than one thing at any one time. For example, what do you do if the phone rings and you are in the middle of an important manufacturing operation?

Your explanations would need to refer clearly to the pictures so that the reader could establish these points.

The form of presentation

You need to use a variety of different ways of presenting information, e.g. written work, displays and oral presentations (Figure 27). When you produce reports and/or use visual images make sure that they are relevant to the points being made and are appropriate for the audience. You may want to discuss presentation with your tutor. Look at published information from companies and other organisations that produce reports. Do they give you any hints?

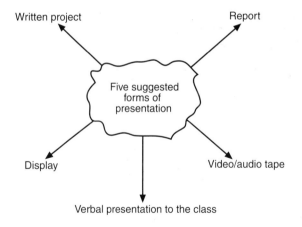

Figure 27 Forms of presentation

Task

You have collected the information below on the question:

'Do the owners of the St Damien's Hotel feel that they have chosen a good location?'

- How would you sort out the information?
- What titles and subtitles would you use?
- What order would you put the information in?

Rough notes:
The owners of the hotel are John and May Pulido.
They have owned hotels for the last twenty years. John says 'Hotels are in our blood'.
The most important reason they set up in Northampton is because there is a lot of business near the M1 motorway.
The hotel cost £500 000 to purchase.
There are good schools for children in Northampton.
They moved from Hounslow. They did not like Hounslow.
They paid £400 000 from savings and had a £100 000 loan.
There was plenty of land surrounding the St Damien's Hotel. It is in a pretty spot on the edge of Northampton.
There is room for expansion.
There are no other hotels on this side of town.
Business is good, £50 000 profits a year.
It is easy to get raw materials.
It is difficult to hire staff being on the edge of town.
They feel they have a 'prime location'.
Traffic is a bit noisy for guests
Taxes paid to the local council are low being out of the centre of town.
There is good access for cars, and delivery lorries.

Written project

For many writers the problem is where to start. You may have reams and reams of information but are not sure how to break it down. How can you structure it in a logical form? Making a plan is always useful. Work through your information, noting important areas under titles and subtitles. Then try to put these into a logical sequence.

You may find the following suggested outline for your written coursework helpful:

1 Title page to help display
2 List of contents
3 Main body of the work
4 Bibliography
5 Appendix
6 Index

The *title page* should be attractively presented and set out clearly what your assignment is about. Use some form of illustration to make it stand out.

Your *contents* page will list the subtitles or chapters into which you have divided your work. You should allocate a page number to each subtitle or chapter so that the reader can go directly to the sections referred to (Figure 28).

Contents		
SECTION A HOW ELECTRICITY IS MADE AND TRANSMITTED		8
Part 1:	Historical Perspectives	8
Part 2:	Workpacks, wordcards and resources for practical work	12
Part 3:	The priciples of electricity production	14
Part 4:	Radioactivity and the principles of nuclear power	15
Part 5:	The commercial production of electricirty	17
Part 6:	Nuclear power production	24
Part 7:	The distribution and transmission of electricity	28
SECTION B USING ELECTRICITY		32
Part 1:	General domestic applications	32
Part 2:	Cookery and catering	37
Part 3:	Industrial and domestic applications	39
SECTION C ENVIRONMENTAL STUDIES		43
Part 1:	Nature trail guides, workbooks and nature films	43
Part 2:	Industry and ecology	48
Part 3:	Nuclear waste and safety in the nuclear industry	50
SECTION D PLACES TO VISIT		52
Part 1:	Nature trails and field centres	52
Part 2:	Museums, exhibitions and power stations	54
Part 3:	The Molecule Theatre of Science	58
Part 4:	Other services	58
GENERAL INDEX OF TITLES		62

Figure 28 A contents page

The *main body* of the work can be divided into an introduction, the main contents and some form of conclusion.

In the *introduction,* outline the purpose of your study and indicate what you would like to achieve. Try to provide a broad view to your work and avoid adding personal opinion at this stage. Above all, try to make it interesting.

The *main contents* could consist of chapters or sections. It is perfectly acceptable to use a system of subsections or headings to run through your work. Sometimes it is best to decide upon a uniform system before you start. Any non-essential information which interrupts your flow should be contained in the appendix section.

Task

Working as a group, visit the library. Each of you should look at the organisation of a publication in which the author has carried out an investigation. A good example would be *Which?* magazine as it investigates, and compares different consumer goods.

- Look at the order in which information is presented.
- Make notes on the way in which the information has been organised. What have been the strengths and weaknesses of the pattern of organisation?

Members of the group should then report their findings to the whole class.

- What lessons have you learnt?

Think! Are all the charts, tables and diagrams you want to produce essential information? Some of your illustrations will help the reader to understand your work. However, too many will make the work confusing. Some of your tables and diagrams may need to go in the appendix section.

In the *conclusion* try to provide a summary of the results of your investigations. You might want to make recommendations or suggestions. Make sure that your conclusion clearly fits in with the aims and purposes which you outlined in your introduction to the study.

A *bibliography* is a list of references to information sources you have used to complete your work. Set your references out in a clear order. This is normally done alphabetically according to the surname of the author or by name of publication. Make sure that you include the correct title of the text, name of author and date of publication (you should be able to find this information on the first few pages), and the name of the publisher.

For example, if you wanted to put this book in a reference list, you would put:

Business Advanced, Dransfield and Needham Heinemann, 1995.

The *appendix* is a section at the end of a study which contains information which is useful to the study. It might include copies of letters you have written which illustrate the depth of your investigations, tables and figures which can be referred to and any other useful information. If you have anything else which you think would improve the study and which would indicate the extent of your investigations, put it in the appendix.

An *index* is not always essential but, when used, it will appear at the very end of a book or study. It should list topic areas in alphabetical order and indicate the corresponding page numbers. Some topics will appear on more than one page.

- Plan your work carefully. Make sure that it all fits into a logical sequence.
- Do not copy out large chunks of text.
- Only use photographs that support your text. Clearly show in the text why the photographs are important.
- Prepare a rough draft of your work. Then edit it, before producing the final work.
- Check your spelling. Use a dictionary or ask someone to help by reading through your first draft.
- Number the pages and secure them tightly together.
- Keep your work in a safe place and make sure that it is kept clean and does not get damaged.
- Acknowledge the sources you use.

Report writing

Many people, when they hear the word *report,* immediately think of a school report, others think of a news report.

A report is a written statement from someone who has made a study of something (such as an event,

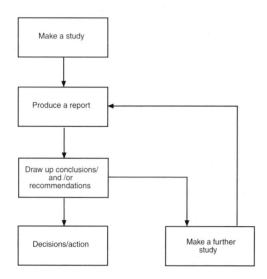

Figure 29 Turning research into action

the cause of some occurrence, or the performance of a person or organisation), which is then sent or passed on to someone else to be used for a particular purpose. Often the results of a business report will provide a basis for business decisions. The sequence of preparing for, writing up, and following up a report are shown in the flow chart in Figure 29. A written report is an important form of business communication and a perfectly acceptable and businesslike way of presenting your coursework.

A suggested form of presentation for a written report is:

1 Title page   5 Findings
2 List of contents   6 Conclusion
3 Terms of reference   7 Recommendations
4 Procedure   8 Signature

The *terms of reference* explain the reasons for the report by referring to the group or persons asking you to produce it. This section should explain why you are writing the report. For example:

'I am writing this report in response to a request from the local cinema owner, for our Business Studies group to carry out some market research to see if there is a demand for a second screen at the cinema.'

or

'I am writing this report to fulfil my unit assignment requirements for the GNVQ Advanced in Business by looking into the changes which have taken place in the pattern of retailing in the centre of Salford over the last 10 years.'

The *procedure* section will refer to the stages that have taken place in the build-up of your report. What letters have you sent? Which people have you interviewed? What else did you have to do?

Figure 30 Using a range of presentation aids

The *findings* will indicate what you have discovered as a result of your investigations.

Your *conclusion* will contain a summary of your findings. For example:

'Salford today has:

- more retailers
- more specialist shops
- fewer supermarkets
- more building societies
- ....'

Recommendations are only necessary where appropriate. For example, if you are trying to look at ways of resolving a problem through your coursework investigations, then the likelihood is that, as a result of your report, you will be suggesting some form of action.

Verbal presentations to the class

A verbal presentation is an excellent vehicle for allowing you to show what you can really do and fits in closely with real-world business (and everyday) practice. It also makes it possible for you to share your experiences by explaining your research to a group. Always be prepared to answer questions, but think beforehand about the types of questions you may be asked. Standing in front of an audience and trying to capture everyone's attention, while keeping them interested, can be extremely difficult. You can overcome any nervous feelings about this form of presentation by being well prepared (Figure 30).

Preparing a presentation

Making presentations is an important area of communication sills. Most students enjoy making presentations once they have overcome their early nerves. You will usually work together as a group to make a presentation. This will involve jointly planning work and then deciding on how your are going to structure your presentation,

A key rule is not to leave things to the last minute. You should run through your presentation in advance. The more you practise, the easier the words will come to you on the day. Remember that all the students in your class will also need to make presentations. They too will be nervous. Students should therefore seek to support each other. Indeed students will be judged partly on the way they support each other. Students should therefore not:

- seek the limelight, taking it upon themselves to do all the presentation
- refuse to be involved in making presentations.

In GNVQ Business the most able communicators and group members will be those who help others to make a success of presentations.

In preparing a presentation you will benefit from using the following checklist to prepare your presentation:

To plan and organise the presentation
Plan to:

- set out your objectives
- set out a main idea and a clear conclusion
- set out your introduction clearly
- think about your audience, their interests and their level
- brainstorm some main ideas
- plan handouts and overheads
- keep a clear thread linking main points.

To prepare for the presentation
Make sure you:

- practise
- check the equipment
- order your notes and handouts.

To develop the visual aids
Make sure you:

- make them clear and easy to look at
- choose the correct type of chart
- use computer graphics packages
- use 18-point or 24-point font sizes on overhead projectors
- have clear titles
- talk to the audience, not to the visual

- place yourself in the centre of the stage
- use a pointer, but not too often.

To stop being nervous
Plan to:

- take deep breaths
- move during the presentation
- establish eye contact.

Delivering your presentation
Plan to:

- be aware of what you say and how you say it
- speak with a strong clear voice, and don't speak too quickly
- be animated, clear and enthusiastic
- use your eye contact to make the presentation conversational and personal.

Questions and answers
Plan to:

- prepare for questions and practise the answers
- ask for questions by stepping forward with hand raised
- watch the questioner and listen carefully
- repeat the question to make sure everybody has heard it
- keep the same bearing as in your presentation
- use eye contact and look at the whole audience.

- Stand when you make your presentation.
- Do not just read from your work or from a prepared report. Make notes to guide you but talk freely, through your presentation (refer to notes using a series of headings or a system of small cards).
- Use slides, handouts, overhead projector transparencies, flipcharts, posters or any other form of visual aid to support your talk.
- Make sure that you keep to the point. Try to make your talk interesting, and sound cheerful.
- Do not gabble or talk too slowly.
- Start your talk by making it clear what your subject is and how you propose to present your ideas.
- Finish your talk with an appropriate ending which leaves an impression.

Display

In today's competitive business environment being able to display materials successfully is an important business skill. For example, look at the display of fresh vegetables shown in Figure 31. This photograph appeared in a promotional book for Geest, the international producer and distributor of a wide range

Figure 31 'Geest, first in the morning'

of fresh fruits, vegetables, flowers and a range of other products. The photograph appeared under the caption 'Geest, first in the morning'. The picture was used to illustrate the wide selection of fresh vegetables distributed by Geest. The largest proportion of fresh fruit and vegetables sold in this country still goes to the traditional greengrocer and market stall – hence the display of vegetables as if they were in a grocer's shop. Geest have displayed their products to make them interesting and appealing. Can you create attractive displays in your work?

Think carefully about whether the nature of your chosen coursework topic lends itself to a display of materials. Your tutor should be able to give you some helpful advice.

Work out a suitable pattern for displaying your materials and draw up a plan. Try to make your display look professional perhaps by using stencils for your headings. Make sure that all your charts, diagrams and pictures have adjoining notes and that your materials are kept in a place where they will not get damaged.

Video/audio tape

If you produce a video or audio tape you may want to introduce it with some short explanatory notes. (However, you may feel that you want to introduce the tape using that particular medium. Start the tape by explaining to the assessor – 'this is what the tape is about, this is how I set out my investigation'.)

You may want to present your ideas on a tape because you feel that you can express yourself better in this medium. Tape presentations are a particularly powerful means of communication. Most training activities used by major organisations today involve some form of video-recording.

Tapes also help you to capture events as they happen, and can be used to record reactions to events. They make it possible for you to record situations outside a classroom which you can then bring into the classroom for further analysis. You may want to use an audio tape for conducting an interview to make sure that you do not miss anything. Video-recordings enable you to capture details such as the complexity of a production process or the scale of a business park.

Make sure that before you start a piece of taped work you calculate how long it will take, and the steps and processes you will need to carry out.

Using a computer in presenting work

Most businesses today use computers and information technology applications. Using a computer to present your work should fit in well with your Business Studies course. It will help you to develop your information technology skills and to present your work in a business-like way.

The modern office is rarely complete without a computer. Computers are now in widespread use as word processors, for preparing databases and spreadsheets, as well as for playing games and producing artwork.

Word processing

A word-processing package can transform your computer into a machine which is different from a typewriter and a data processor. It makes it possible for you to type text, not onto paper but onto your display screen. Either before or after you've got it on the screen you will be able to perform automatically a wide number of 'star-typist' feats which once only a highly experienced secretary could perform without making a mistake or risking a mental breakdown.

A word processor is made up of:

- the keyboard for typing in material and instructions
- a visual display unit which displays the material on a screen
- a disk storage unit
- the printer for finished copy.

Some of the important things that you will be able to do with your word processor to help with your work will include:

- preparing your text, storing it on disk, changing it as and when required, printing up a final copy
- printing out as many copies of the final text as you require
- producing personalised letters to groups and individuals from whom you require information
- setting the line width, tabulation, page size and page numbering
- correct spelling errors in key words and correcting typing errors
- rearranging paragraphs into the most suitable order.

By using different software packages, a document can be produced on one machine which has both text and illustrations.

A simple word-processing package can present your data in a tabular form, which is the simplest method of presentation.

Figure 32 shows how a student has used a word processor to set up a table.

Granthanm Statistics 1993

	Total number Employer	School leaver recruitment 92	School leaver requirement 93
Bridalwear	295	32	29
Women's underwear/lingerie	175	19	14
Knitwear	160	10	25
Furniture covers	25	1	3
Women's outerwear	22	0	0
Others (approximate numbers)	30	?	?

Figure 32 A word-processed table

Such an illustration can easily be inserted without the need to input detailed command instructions to the computer.

To make use of more complex methods of presentation, a more specialised graphics package needs to be used. It is important to make sure that the word-processing and graphics packages are compatible with each other, otherwise it would be impossible to transcribe a picture into the text. You will benefit from using multi-tasking packages based on Windows.

Using a graphics program will produce a more varied collection of data presentation methods. These can include the use of bar charts, line graphs and pie charts.

In most cases these graphs will require some preparation to calculate values, although some of the more comprehensive programs only require to be told the actual data and will calculate their own values and assign a value to the scale.

Figures 33 and 34 were used by a student investigating the textile industry in the East Midlands as part of an assignment.

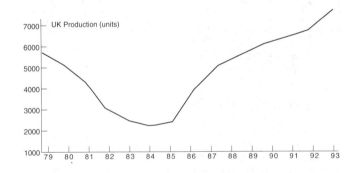

Figure 33 Illustrating UK textile production

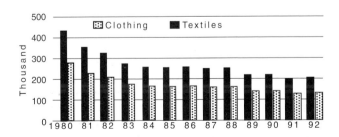

Figure 34 Employment in the textile industry

Layout and format

By using a computer, the layout of a document can be manipulated to produce almost any format that you want (Figure 35). Whole sections of text or pictures can be picked up and moved around. The pictures can also have their size altered to fit into any space desired.

In general you should prepare your text first and then decide on illustrations. You can then manipulate the text so that your pictures will fit into the text where needed. You can also alter the size of your pictures to fit into any space desired.

It is possible to use colour on screen, while to produce such results on paper would take a very long time and require you to be a good artist.

Five year record					
	1991	1992	1993	1994	1995
Turnover (£ million)	115.6	147.4	168.3	195.4	219.7
Pre-tax (£ millions)	20	25.2	21.5	29.7	33.5
Earnings per share (pence)	6.7	8.8	7.4	10.3	11.5
Dividend per share (pence)	1.22	1.60	1.70	2.00	2.40

Figure 35 Illustration of Body Shop's recent performance

Databases

A database is a store of facts that can be called upon to provide up-to-date information. Common business applications, for example, would include their use in banks or building societies to store information on the state of all the accounts. Data (information) is fed into the base in a well-defined form.

For example, if you were carrying out a piece of work looking at reasons for the location of light industry in a particular area you might want to look at the common locational requirements of a number of local firms. You would want to store the information in a number of fields, such as address, type of product, communication links used, availability of labour and so on.

When deciding on whether or not to use a computer database as part of your work you need to be sure that the advantages will clearly outweigh the disadvantages.

- Will the time taken be worth the effort?
- Will the database help you to sort out a lot of complicated data?
- Will the database be simple to set up and operate?

Spreadsheets

A spreadsheet is a table of numbers which can be organised and altered on a computer. A spreadsheet can be used to make forecast and calculations – the computer does the work for you. A common application for a spreadsheet is in making financial forecasts. For example, you may wish to forecast all the money that will come in and go out of a firm over a twelve-month period. You can then alter the inputs to calculate, for example, the effect or raising or lowering particular costs.

The overall benefit of using computer applications

Computer applications are widely used in modern business because they help the user to produce a better report. The computer is an ideal tool for recording information, storing information, helping to sort information, doing calculations, presenting information, changing the structure and layout of a report, checking spelling and helping to create a visual impact. There is a strong case for using a personal computer in doing a piece of Business Studies work.

We can now look at what is involved in IT capability, at Level 3 for GNVQs.

Developing and showing evidence of the core skill of Information Technology

Information Technology capability at Level 3

Throughout a GNVQ course in Business you will be provided with opportunities to practise and demonstrate your capability in Information Technology. At Advanced Level this covers a number of Elements:

1 preparing information
2 processing information
3 presenting information
4 evaluating the use of information technology.

Preparing information

To meet the performance criteria required you will need to select information in the form of text, graphics, and numbers which is appropriate to the task. You will then need to be able to enter this information into software in ways that will make it easy to edit.

You should keep the information that you need for a task and store it systematically, keeping back-up copies. In other words, you will need to be able to save your work in files so that you can make changes when required. You should be able to configure software to help you to input information. Of course, it will take you time to develop these skills.

Processing information

Processing information will involve finding the information that you require for a task, e.g. by locating and going into appropriate files. You will need to be able to use appropriate software to edit information, and process numerical information by using software to make calculations. For example, you should be able to add up totals and make calculations using spreadsheets and databases.

You should be able to reorganise information as required in a particular task that you are doing. It is very important that you regularly save your work.

You should be able to combine information from different sources and create automatic routines that help the efficient processing of information.

Presenting information

IT is a great aid in presenting work. You should be able to prepare work systematically for presentation, often presenting the information in different ways. You need to choose appropriate software carefully to display information, and then produce paper copies of your work that are attractive and interesting. You should be able to pull together information from several sources so that it looks consistent when you reorganise it for presentation. You should, of course, store information in files and make back-up copies.

Evaluating the use of information technology

You should know why and when it is appropriate to use information technology. You should be able to compare methods used by yourself and others to prepare, process and present information. You should evaluate different systems for managing information and describe software which can be used to carry out tasks.

In addition, you should be able to explain the effects on users of problems that occur when using IT such as faults in equipment or loss of information. Finally, you should be able to explain the importance of working safely and in line with good working practices.

Today IT capability is at a premium. All people starting work in modern organisations need this capability if they are to be effective members of these organisations. Throughout your Business course you will be given opportunities to build up this capability.

The use and abuse of statistics

Statistics are put together by people, and because we are all human, mistakes are made. Sometimes statisticians (the people who build up the statistics) use machines such as computers to help them. However, the programs that the computers run on are devised by human programmers and are therefore prone to error.

Statistics can be and often are inaccurate because of the following factors.

- People make mistakes. Simple errors of adding, subtracting, classifying, recording and drawing can happen.
- Some people deliberately choose to distort the figures to prove a point.

Using statistics can be compared to using a particular tool to overcome a problem. When a car breaks down a mechanic may need a socket set to take off a worn part. A doctor needs specialised tools to diagnose an illness. Tools to a statistician are the techniques used to draw conclusions. You looked at some of these techniques earlier when you studied questionnaires, sampling, tables, pictograms, charts and graphs. In order to produce an effective piece of Business Studies research you must be aware of these techniques and be ready to use them, but there are certain dangers. Therefore you must tread carefully.

Task

Benjamin Disraeli, a British Prime Minister in the nineteenth century, said: 'There are lies, damned lies and statistics.' What do you think he meant?

Stages in the preparation and use of statistics

There are four main stages in the preparation and use of statistics.

Design

The first step will be to design your research. How big a sample will you use? How will you decide on the necessary characteristics of your sample? How many questions will you ask? (Look back at the section on questionnaires.) What limitations are there in terms of time and money available? Will you conduct pilot research? Without effective design, the whole project may prove to be a waste of time.

Collecting the statistics

You may want to use existing secondary information or to collect new primary information.

Organising the data

Before you make sense of your data you will need to organise it into a structured form. You will then try to make sense of the data and to write up your findings.

Making the report available

The final stage involves making the report available to others so that they can look at it and interpret your statistics.

Why statistics are useful

Statistics provide a quick and easy method of making use of numbers. Most people are impressed in some way by numbers and figures.

What impression do you get when:

■ Someone tells you that his or her car has 130 brake horse-power and can do 120 miles per hour?
■ You hear that someone has been left £500 000 by a rich aunt?
■ You hear that Halifax Town have scored 20 goals in a match?

All the above measurements help you to quantify the events referred to. You can make some sort of judgement about the event that has taken place. This principle can apply to anything that can be measured.

Newspapers frequently use numbers in headlines to give a thumb-nail sketch of the enormity of an event. Examples of this are:

'Typhoon, 112 feared dead'

'57 killed in rail disaster'

However, it is important to remember that the evidence of numbers can be highly selective. For example, when the *Titanic* sank, the *Aberdeen Press and Journal's* headline was 'Aberdeen Man Lost at Sea'. You must be careful not just to choose those statistics that back up your own case. If you do, you will soon find that someone picks up another statistic that you have not used which 'discredits' your argument.

Task

Make a list of 10 pieces of information which indicate some form of statistics or numbers. For example, the number of persons in your household; how far you have to walk to school; the amount of money you spend each week on sweets and magazines; how much pocket money you get, and so on.

Read this list through to a partner and allow that person to read his or her information through to you. Has anyone discovered information that they find difficult to believe, or which they feel is rather dubious? Why is this information scarcely believable?

The wingspan of the Jumbo jet is longer than the first flight by the Wright brothers	More people today play bagpipes than ever before	A decapitated insect can live for as long as a year before it starves to death
A bee can haul more than 300 times its own weight	The top speed of a British grass snake is 4.2 mph	Australian earth worms can grow up to 10 feet in length

The information contained in each of these boxes is correct.

Perhaps the main benefit of statistics is that, by making sense of numbers, the resulting information can help someone to make a decision. In your case they can help you to analyse coursework data and to draw out some conclusions.

The conclusions that you make will only be as good as your statistical information and, as you are the person who is collecting this information, you must be careful about how it is collected. For example, your data may be inaccurate or *biased* because of the *type of questions* you have asked or because of the *sort of person* you have questioned.

Beware of biased data.

When you are constructing your questionnaire try to avoid asking people questions which they are unlikely to answer truthfully such as:

- How much do you earn?
- How old is your car? } Wealth

- How often do you bathe?
- Do you use a deodorant? } Cleanliness

- Do you vote Labour?
- Do you believe in private medicine? } Politics

- Are you successful?
- Would you describe yourself as an executive? } Aspirations

- Are you good at sport?
- How good is your eyesight? } Personal abilities

Personal questions involving areas such as wealth, cleanliness, politics, aspirations and personal abilities will lead the interviewee into opportunities to air strong views and even possibly to flaunt an ego (for example, questionnaires about sexual prowess are notoriously inaccurate). In this case your results will suffer. Of course, in some of your investigations it will be important to uncover strong points of view, and to try to make sense of different perspectives. However, it is important to keep a focus on the main issues and not to be sidetracked.

Task

Working as a pair, make a list of five questions that would lead to distorted

answers. Why are the questions poor? How could they be made to work?

Another common mistake when obtaining data for analysis is not getting a representative sample. Weak samples arise when you simply interview the first people who happen to come along; people who all come from a particular neighbourhood, members of one sex only, people from one particular age range or one socio-economic group. Any of these examples will produce results which reflect that group and which will not be representative of others.

Sampling

In collecting information it is essential that we use *accurate* samples. Sample surveys are the most common way to gather information by fieldwork.

A sample survey involves recording information about a small sector of the population which represents a particular group; e.g. married working women in Northampton aged 30-45 may represent all urban married working women in the UK.

Convenience sampling

This is taking information from any group which is handy – walking down a High Street, for example.

Judgement sampling

This is slightly more refined. The interviewer would select High Street respondents (people to question) on the basis of whether or not they appear to belong to a particular segment of the population – e.g. middle-class business people.

Quota sampling

This involves choosing to interview specific numbers of respondents with clearly defined characteristics, e.g. working-class Muslim teenagers aged 14-19.

Task

Make a list of the good and bad points of convenience, judgement, and quota sampling.

- What type of sampling will you use for your coursework?
- Give reasons for your choice.

If your sample is chosen by the correct method, every member of the relevant population will have an equal probability of being selected.

The larger the sample we use, the more likely it is to be representative. Let us suppose that we want to find out the proportion of all adults who are men. We know that it should be about half. If we chose a number of different samples, they would not give exactly the same estimate, but we would expect most of them to give roughly the right estimate; otherwise sampling would be of little value. The more samples we include in a total sample, the more accurate our estimate is likely to be. People are often surprised at the idea that one can estimate a quantity for a population of many millions from only 500 or 1000 people. But if it is a properly selected sample, the error will be only small.

Make sure that you show the whole picture

Although many statistics that we are presented with are reasonably accurate, there are many which are less accurate. We live in a competitive society and, for many manufacturers and politicians, there are clear advantages to be gained by using statistics to emphasise the good things rather than the bad. For example, a statement which boasts that 50% more is spent on nursery eduction today than five years ago sounds impressive. However, we need to find out how the figure was calculated. Does a 50% increase in money spending mean that there are 50% more nurseries as well? Does each nursery enjoy the services of 50% more staff and equipment? If only 2% more children nationally have the opportunity to attend nursery schools, we may start seriously to question the validity of the original statistic.

Similarly, a company might boast that it is exporting to more countries than ever before. However, it may fail to indicate that the value and volume of its sales overseas are falling.

Do your statistics support your argument?

When you draw conclusions or make judgements based on your statistics, make sure that the statistics fully support your view. For example, if you discovered that the number of employees in a company had fallen by over 40% in a 10-year period, you could not on the basis of this information assume that output had fallen. You would need to check the output figures to find the trends in production.

Similarly, if a company had just invested £10 million

in new technology, it would not necessarily mean that it was expanding its market share.

Think carefully abut the links you make between your statistics and the arguments, judgements and conclusions that you make.

Beware of advertising hype

Will advertising material always give a true record of the facts about a product? Will it present both sides of an argument fairly?

You may find that a lot of the literature you get from companies contains glossy sales material. Be careful how you use it. Much of it will have been designed to exaggerate in order to convince buyers that they are dealing with a market leader selling a number one product.

Task

Collect examples of advertisements which you think give fair and unfair representations of information. Explain your findings to the group. Do any of the advertisements below distort data?

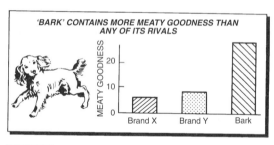

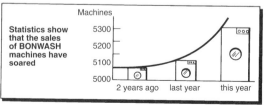

Accurate and fair information

Your information should be correctly presented and neatly labelled. If you quote figures in your work, quote them in units. Show exactly what the units represent and what they mean. Remember that statistics should be used to enhance your explanations and not be explanations in themselves.

If you are going to use a graph make sure that it gives an accurate representation of a trend. Because graphs are visual representations they are open to every trick in the field of optical illusion.

 Task

The Superior Bakery company had the following sales figures:

1991 £35 million
1992 £40 million
1993 £45 million
1994 £54 million
1995 £61 million

1 Set out the information above on a graph using a vertical scale of 0.5 cm = £10 million and a horizontal scale of 0.5 cm for each of the years.
2 Set out the information using a vertical scale of 2 cm = £10 million and a horizontal scale of 0.25 cm for each of the years.

Do the graphs give true and fair representations of the information?

Do you understand the statistics you use?

There is no point in using figures that you do not understand because the conclusions you draw from them will lack certainty and clarity. It is perfectly permissible to ask for help to interpret them. If you are still uncertain about their meaning do not use them.

Do statistics enhance your explanations?

Do not use statistics simply because everyone else in the group has done so or because you think it must be necessary to use them to produce an effective piece of coursework. There is no point in using them if they do not relate to your investigations. Remember, the purpose of statistics is to provide an effective device to enable you to draw conclusions.

Displaying statistics

A reader of your work should be able to understand quickly the results of your investigations by reading your coursework. Make sure your work flows and that all of your material falls into place. Check that all your tables, graphs, figures and diagrams have a title. Do not include complicated statistical calculations. Ask your friends and relatives to read your work and ask them questions to see if they can establish the points you are trying to make.

In an uncertain world statistics help you to make sense of data. Information from past events can be used to make estimates of future events such as numbers of employees, schools, factories, or cars on the road. Statistics are based on chance and probability. Today, statistical techniques are an important tool to be used by any business seeking to minimise risks. If you use your statistics well you will be taking an important step in business training. Statistics are very important. Treat them with care!

Work experience and research

- Make a preliminary visit to your work placement. Find out what you will be doing. Whom will you be able to ask for information at work? Whom will you be able to interview? What secondary information will you have access to?
- Next, write a letter to the company to check that they are happy to supply you with appropriate information and help. They may be able to provide you with extra help during your placement.
- Decide on the questions that you will ask and the method you will use to carry out your research. Make sure that you have your plan of action ready before you start your work placement.
- Make sure that you write up your notes at regular intervals during your placement. Your tutor may be able to arrange for your employer to set aside an hour each day for you to sit somewhere quiet to write up your notes. Do not wait until the last day of your placement to gather information.

You will often find that your employer is very interested in your research. He or she may want to spend an hour with you at the end of your work placement to talk over your work. Alternatively, a request may be made for you to send a copy of your research to your employer.

You may want to use your work experience to gather evidence for your portfolio. However, because a work experience placement is normally only for a short period of time you will need to have a good idea about what you want to find out before taking up the placement. (Of course, you can also use your part-time work to collect evidence.)

A few weeks before you start your work experience placement you should write to the person responsible for you at work to give details of your research requirements. The letter should include:

- the title of your research
- a brief outline of the information you are seeking
- an explanation of how the research fits into your school or college work.

Figure 36 is an example of the type of letter that would be helpful:

18 Summerfield Drive
Midtown
Midshire
MO6 5RD

Tel: (01432) 65713

7 February 1995

Mr P Patel
Personnel Manager
Manufacturers Ltd
Anystreet
Anytown
AN6 6BY

Dear Mr Patel

Work Experience place in Marketing Department

I have walked past your business every day for the past four years on my way to school, and have always wondered what it would be like to work there. I am particularly keen to work in your Marketing Department because my favourite subjects at school are Art and Business Studies and I am hoping to go into marketing when I leave school.

We have recently been studying marketing in our Business Advanced GNVQ class. I am hoping to do a piece of coursework of 3,000 words with the title "How did …… market their …… product?' I would appreciate it if I could carry out the research for this coursework by studying the marketing of one of your products whilst I am on work experience with you. Would it be possible for me to interview the people responsible for one of your marketing campaigns? I would like to evaluate the campaign and present my research findings to you. The coursework will count towards my GCSE grade.

Yours sincerely

Julie Head

Julie Head

Figure 36 A helpful letter

Writing a letter of thanks

It is very important to write a letter of thanks to the person responsible for organising your work experience. The letter should relate to the particular work you have been doing and show an appreciation of those who help you. Figure 37 is an example of the sort of letter you could write.

8 Rhos Bach
Bangor
BA1 8RE

8 March 1995

Mrs J Jury
Personnel Manager
Electronic Products Limited
Pecton
PT3 95J

Dear Mrs Jury

Thank you very much for inviting me to your factory for my work experience. I really enjoyed my time with you and feel I have learned a lot.

I didn't really believe that people could be so enthusiastic about their work. I was also impressed with their skill.

I enclose a copy of my GNVQ Business Advanced coursework: 'Could Electronic Products Limited survive without a Personnel Department?' I would be grateful if you and your colleagues could let me have your comments on it.

Would you please thank all the people who helped to make my work experience such an enjoyable one.

Yours sincerely

Ian Cottey

Ian Cottey

Figure 37 A letter of thanks

Some possible topics that you may like to explore on work experience include:

- What training does the company provide for the people that you meet at work? How effective is this training?
- How does your company use the profits it makes? In what other ways could it use these profits?
- Do employees enjoy their work? What factors in the working environment help employees to like/dislike their work? How important are the attitudes that employees take into work, in shaping impressions of work?

- What health and safety regulations operate in the workplace? How are these regulations met? Are health and safety standards adequate?
- What are the main inputs, outputs and processes involved in the production process?
- How is the company organised? What are the strengths and weaknesses of its pattern of organisation? (This would require some form of comparison with other organisations.)
- How are employees within a given organisation dependent on work carried out by other employees in their own and other organisations?

Of course, you should set out to use work experience and part-time work as an opportunity to gather evidence for your portfolio, both showing business knowledge and competence in the use of core skills.

This unit looks at the way in which the economy influences business activity. It is very important to understand how the economy works because it affects all our lives very directly. For example, if the economy is booming then we are more likely to have secure jobs. In this unit, therefore, we have tried to give you a clear picture of what the economy is, and how influential it is.

Business people make the decisions and take the actions that they think are right in the economic climate in which they are working. To make the right decisions it is important to understand the factors which affect the economic climate.

Chapter 1

The forces of demand and supply in business

This chapter looks at the ways in which businesses produce goods and services to meet the wants and needs of consumers. Business activity sets out to satisfy demand that comes from consumers. Businesses that successfully meet customers' needs can do so at a profit. However, not all organisations set out simply to make a profit – some, like charities, attempt to meet needs that profit-making organisations cannot serve.

The demand for goods and services

Satisfying customers' wants and needs

Everybody has wants and needs. At the moment I *would like* a new compact disc (CD) player and some CDs to go with it. When I have bought my new CD player I will probably make plans to acquire something else that I want. Before deciding to buy anything I will look around at the alternative models and brands. I will probably carry out some research to see what is the best offer on the market. However, I also *need* to have food, clothing and shelter to get me through the day.

Some of the things that I buy are regular purchases. For example, I read *The Independent* newspaper every day. I find it interesting and informative. However, if the standard of its stories and articles began to fall I might switch to another newspaper. If the quality of a different paper started to improve I might decide to switch to reading that one.

Every day, as well as making regular purchases, millions of consumers also make decisions to buy 'one-off' items, like a new car. Producers decide what products to make and in what quantities. In a market economy these producers will be guided by consumer demand.

Regular purchases	One-off items

Figure 1.1 Regular purchases and one-off items

Task

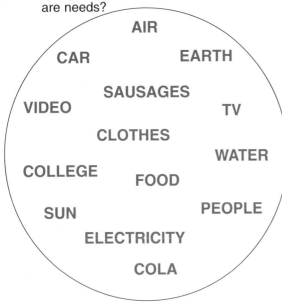

Look at the diagram below. Which of the things would you say are wants and which are needs?

AIR

CAR   EARTH

SAUSAGES

VIDEO   TV

CLOTHES

WATER

COLLEGE   FOOD

SUN   PEOPLE

ELECTRICITY

COLA

Now draw two circles, one with just 'wants' in it, the other with just 'needs'.

1   Which is the bigger circle?
2   Does everybody in the world have all their needs met?
3   What evidence can you draw upon to back up your argument?
4   If everybody does not have all their needs met, then why not?
5   Is it possible to change this?
6   Can you do something about this?
7   Who else needs to be involved to make the change?
8   How can changes be made?

As consumers, we like our wants and needs to be satisfied. These wants and needs will often be satisfied by consuming products. For example, when I am thirsty I will be satisfied by consuming a can of lemonade; when I want entertainment I will be satisfied (hopefully) by a visit to the cinema. Of course I will need to pay for these goods. If I cannot afford some of these goods then some of my needs and wants will go unsatisfied.

Effective demand

The demand for a product is a want backed up by money to make the purchase. If everyone starts demanding a particular item of fashion clothing then producers will rush to make that item.

Evidence collection point

1   Describe four products that you particularly want or need.
2   Explain how you could convert this want or need into a demand for the product.
3   What fashion items are currently in demand? Are there many producers making these items or just a few?

Spending and income

A person's ability to buy goods depends largely on his or her income. Income is the amount of money that you earn in a particular period of time. For example, in the first three months of this year my niece earnt £200 for delivering newspapers. Her income was:

January   £90
February £60
March   £50

However, she did not spend all of this income. She saved £30 each month. This can be shown in a table.

My niece's income and spending Jan–March, 1995

Month	Income	Spending	Saving
January	£90	£60	£30
February	£60	£30	£30
March	£50	£20	£30
3 month total	£200	£110	£90

Evidence collection point

Set out a table which shows your income, spending and saving over the last three months. Of course, you may have spent more than you have earned. If this is the case we use the 'term 'dis-saving'. For example, if in March my niece had earned £50 and spent £90 she might have had to dis-save by drawing £40 out of her previous savings. If you have dis-saved show this in your table and explain how the dis-saving was financed e.g. by borrowing, drawing on previous savings, etc. This work can contribute evidence for Core Skills in Application of Number.

Demand curves

Each year millions of students attend schools and colleges following a range of courses. One of the most popular is Business. All young people and many adult returners to education are entitled to follow courses which meet their needs. The government is keen to support GNVQ courses in Business because of the important part they play in preparing students both for the world of work and for life in modern society. Colleges receive funds from the government for each student place, up to a certain number. We can therefore say that there is a substantial demand for places on GNVQ courses. The students' wants are backed up by money.

Many goods are demanded for their own sake. This week you may purchase a new T-shirt or a pair of trainers. You are almost certain to buy something to eat, such as a sandwich or a packet of crisps. All of these items are demanded for their own sake. When goods are wanted for their own sake we say there is a primary demand for them.

Many other goods have a derived demand. Derived demand arises when a good is wanted not for itself but for what it goes into making. For example, a hairdresser does not buy scissors, curling tongs, shampoos, hairspray etc. because she likes having them in her salon but because she will use these items to cut and style people's hair.

 Task

Which of the following are examples of a prime demand and which of a derived demand?

- A farmer's demand for pesticides to spray on apples.
- A greengrocer's demand for apples to stock in a shop.
- A child's purchase of apples from the greengrocer.
- The purchase of a restaurant meal.
- A radio station's purchase of a popular compact disc.
- The Post Office's purchase of bicycles for its delivery people.
- A school child's purchase of a football strip.
- A Premier League football club's purchase of a football strip.

The demand for goods and services can be illustrated in a demand curve.

The amount of a good or service that is demanded is the quantity that a consumer will be prepared to buy at a given price. This can be shown by a simple example.

If the price of a colour printer for a computer is £500, John is prepared to buy one printer. If it is more than £500 he will not be able to afford one. If the price fell to £300 he might be prepared to buy two – one for his home and one for his office. We can set out John's demand for colour printers in a table:

Price	Quantity
More than £500	0
£500	1
£300	2

Quite clearly, as the price of printers falls they will become more affordable, and consumers will be prepared to purchase them instead of spending their money on alternatives. One printer will be very useful to John, as will two. However, if the price continues to fall there will come a point at which John has enough printers, and then further price falls will not encourage fresh purchases.

 Evidence collection point

Set out a table which shows how many chocolate bars you would buy in a week if the price of a bar were:

- 3p
- 25p
- 50p
- 15p
- 40p
- £1

For this exercise you should choose your favourite type of chocolate bar. Explain why you would choose different quantities at different prices.

So far, we have concentrated on individual demand for a product, i.e. how many a particular person would buy at different prices. Some goods are demanded by just a few customers; some will be demanded by a few hundred; whilst others will be bought by thousands or even millions of customers, e.g. Coca-Cola, Mars bars, Bic biros.

 Task

1 Identify four products for which total demand is limited to fewer than ten customers.

2   Identify four products that have a few hundred customers.
3   Identify four products that have a nationwide demand.
4   Identify four products that have a global demand.

Demand schedules can be set out by adding together the individual demand schedules of all consumers in a particular market. For example, the demand schedule below shows the likely national market for a particular type of printer in a six-month period – the figures have been collected from the market research carried out by the manufacturers:

Price of printer (£)	Quantity demanded
1 000	500
800	1 000
600	10 000
400	12 000
200	14 000

Evidence collection point

Study the demand schedule for printers.

1   What do you think would be the best price to charge for printers? Explain your answer.
2   Why would other prices be unsuitable?
3   What further information would you require to be able to select the most appropriate price to charge? (You may want to select a price which is not indicated in the table.) This task will help you to provide evidence for Core Skills in Application of Number.

The information in the demand schedule can be illustrated as a 'demand curve' (see Figure 1.2).

It is convenient for us to think of demand as fitting a nicely drawn demand curve, but of course in the real world demand patterns are not so simple. The demand for products varies considerably with fresh price changes. Some price rises will have little effect on quantities bought, whilst other quite small price rises may be critical.

Typically, we shall represent demand curves as neat curves or as straight lines (see Figures 1.3 and 1.4 below).

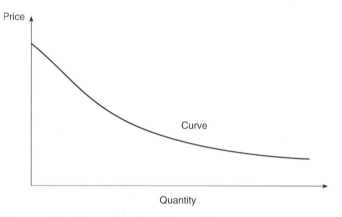

Figure 1.3 Curve showing demand

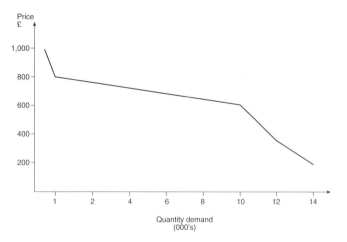

Figure 1.2 Demand for a company's printer at various prices

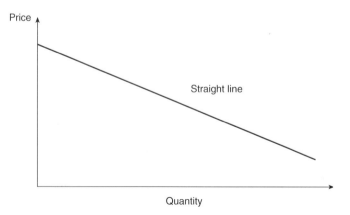

Figure 1.4 Straight line showing demand

Price and income elasticity

Some of you may find this next section on elasticity to be complex, particularly if you have not studied Business or Economics before. Don't worry if you have difficulty at this stage. Read through the section and try to understand as much as possible. See if you can work out some of the examples in the evidence collection points.

Here we try to present price and income elasticity in as simple a way as possible. A slightly more detailed explanation is given at the end of the chapter. You will need to familiarise yourself with the more detailed notes before you take your end-of-unit test.

Price elasticity

When you raise the price of most items, people will buy less of them. For example, when you raise the price of train fares, rail travellers may switch to car transport.

When you lower the price of most items, people will buy more of them. For example, when the price of computers fell, more households bought them.

Common sense therefore tells us that when prices change, so too will the quantities bought. However, businesses need to have more precise information than this – they need to have a clear

measure of how the quantity bought will change as a result of a price change.

A very useful measure of this relationship is called 'price elasticity of demand'. Price elasticity of demand is a measure of the percentage change in the quantity of a good demanded divided by the percentage change in its price.

We can show this in a simple formula:

$$\text{Price elasticity of demand} = \frac{\text{Percentage change in quantity demanded}}{\text{Percentage change in price of a good}}$$

For example, if a good fell in price by 50% (e.g. from £1 to 50p) and the quantity demanded increased by 100% (e.g. from 1000 to 2000), we could say that the elasticity of demand is 2:

$$\frac{100\%}{50\%} = 2$$

If a good fell in price by 50% (e.g. from £1 to 50p) and the quantity demanded increased by 25% (e.g. 1000 to 1250), we could say that the elasticity of demand is one-half.

$$\frac{25\%}{50\%} = \frac{1}{2}$$

From a producer's point of view it is important to understand what will happen to demand if you raise or lower price. There are clearly many advantages to be gained if people buy a lot more of our goods when (as a producer) we lower price.

In Business we use the term 'elastic demand' to describe a position where the quantity demanded changes by a bigger percentage than the price change.

We use the term 'inelastic demand' where the demand change is a smaller percentage than the price change.

We use the term 'unitary elasticity' where the demand change is of the same size as the percentage price change.

Evidence collection point

Study the table below.

Situation	% change in price	% change in quantity demanded
A	100	0
B	75	25
C	50	50
D	25	75
E	0	100

In which of the situations A, B, C, D and E do we have:

i   Elastic demand conditions?
ii Inelastic demand conditions?
iii Unitary elastic demand conditions?

To producers or sellers it is important to know how much demand will change as a result of price changes so that they can calculate the effect on sales and on the amount of money they receive from sales. Money received from sales is called 'revenue'.

- If a producer knows that demand for a product is elastic around the existing price:
  i   It may make sense to lower price – to increase sales and revenues
  ii It would be foolish to raise price – because sales and revenues will fall by a bigger percentage than the price rise
- If a producer knows that demand for a product is inelastic around the existing price:
  i   It may make sense to raise price – because revenues would increase
  ii it would be foolish to lower price – because even though you are selling a few more items you are losing revenues on all of the units that you sell

- If a producer knows that demand is unitary for a product around the existing price there is no justification for raising or lowering price.

Evidence collection point

Can you explain the following? A few years ago the railway companies in Sweden decided to almost halve the price of travelling by rail. This led to an increase in their revenues and profits.

People argue that such a policy in this country would not have the same effect. It would lead to a fall in the railways' revenues and profits.

We shall look in more detail at price elasticity of demand in the appendix at the end of this chapter.

Income elasticity

Another important measure of elasticity is income elasticity. The amount of income that people have is an important determinant of how much they can spend. As people become richer, their spending patterns change. When I didn't have so much money I generally bought white bread. Today I can afford to have a more varied diet, including garlic bread, pitta bread, wholemeal bread, and many more exotic varieties. What applies to me also applies to people in a country generally. As we become richer in this country our spending patterns change – for example, today we spend far more on restaurant meals than ever before. An important reason for this is that more people can afford to do so.

Producers need to look at income trends to see how these will affect spending patterns. For example,

some commentators argue that we are ten years behind the United States in spending habits because it will take ten years to catch up on average incomes. If we look at what the average American is spending his or her money on today this will give us some indication of what we will be spending our money on in ten years' time.

Income elasticity of demand measures how demand changes with income.

In most years the total income of a country rises (i.e. the National Income of a country increases). As incomes rise, so does the ability of consumers to buy new goods; people move into bigger houses, acquire bigger cars, buy a range of new gadgets, clothes and food. More expensive goods can replace inferior products.

Income elasticity can be measured by:

$$\text{Income elasticity} = \frac{\text{Percentage change in quantity demanded}}{\text{Percentage change in income}}$$

If incomes increased by 5% and demand for blueberry pie increased by 10%, we would say that the income elasticity for blueberry pie = 2. The higher the elasticity, i.e. 2, 3, 4, 5, 10, etc., the more responsive demand is to changes in income. It is helpful to producers to identify goods with a high income elasticity.

Normal goods are ones for which demand increases as income goes up, e.g. spending on leisure, restaurant meals, more expensive wine.

However, some goods are said to be 'inferior'. These are goods which people will buy less of as their income increases. For example, a person who buys a black and white or portable television set when they are less well-off may switch to a colour set as they get richer. Inferior goods will therefore have an income elasticity of demand which is negative. For example, as incomes rise by 4%, demand for black and white television sets might fall by 5%.

Evidence collection point

Divide the following items into two lists: which would you expect to have a positive and which a negative income elasticity of demand?

- The demand for Spam.
- The demand for Persian rugs.
- The demand for hard-back novels.
- The demand for Land Rovers.
- The demand for 'starter' homes.
- The demand for Mars ice-cream.

Group task

In this activity you will need to work together with two or three others. The object is to find out how a local firm makes a pricing decision for a particular product or small range of products. Obviously some product pricing decisions are sensitive areas for some companies. However, for many products this is not the case and local business owners will be pleased to discuss the matter with you.

The aim of the assignment is to find out:

a How the firm arrives at a pricing decision.
b The likely effect on sales of charging higher or lower prices.

Choose a group leader who will be responsible for coordinating the work. The duties of the group leader will be to ensure that the group works as a team, to manage the working environment, and to make sure that records are kept. A record sheet (see Figure 1.5) should be set out on a word processor and a suitable number of copies run off.

Local Pricing Assignment
Group record sheet

The group leader should hand this form to the supervisor or lecturer before the end of each session.

Group name ....

Date ....

Absentees ....

Checklist (tick when completed) ✔

All group members' record sheets completed and returned ☐

Textbooks returned/signed out ☐

Disks returned ☐

Computers switched off or left on main menu ☐

Area tidy ☐

Group task completed ☐

Memo for supervisor or lecturer ☐

Signed ....

Supervisor or Lecturer's reply

Figure 1.5 Group record sheet

1 At the beginning of each session the group leader should collect earlier record sheets and take note of any memos from the lecturer or supervisor. It is a good idea to keep a record of attendance.

2 The first few minutes of each session should be spent on group discussion, and checking progress on the assignment.

3 Ten minutes before the end of each session the group will need to discuss progress, update record sheets and prepare a memo for the lecturer or supervisor.

To start off the assignment the group will need to think about the sort of questions to ask a local business manager about pricing decisions. *Hints:*

■ Who at the company has this sort of information?
■ When and how are they most likely to be able to supply you with the information?
■ Will it be best to work through contacts that a group member has?
■ Is there someone at the place where you work part-time who may be prepared to talk to your group?
■ Will it be best to look at a range of contacts, bearing in mind that some companies will not be able to talk to you?
■ Will you need to do some background research so that you know a bit about the company and its products before you start the assignment?

You should then draw up a checklist of key questions about pricing. Set these out in a logical order.

In your group, draft a letter to make the necessary arrangements to visit the company or have someone come to talk to you. Discuss the draft with your lecturer or supervisor, who should countersign the letter before it is sent.

If you decide to make the initial contact by telephone, you will need to follow this up with a letter confirming the arrangements.

When you start to gather information, try to organise it in a way that is easy to understand. Put your ideas in the form of a report which you can present to other members of your group – and perhaps to members of the company that you have been working with. This work will provide evidence of Core Skills in Communication.

Causes of change in demand

We will now draw the demand curve as a straight line in order to simplify the text (see Figure 1.6).

■ If the price of a good rises we can refer to a 'move up the demand curve'. What happens to demand as the price rises to P_1 in Figure 1.6?

■ If the price of a good falls we can refer to 'a move down the demand curve'. What happens to demand as the price falls to P_2 in Figure 1.6?

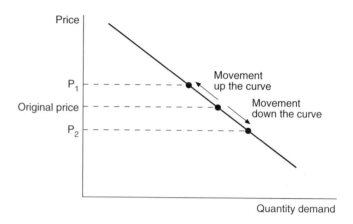

Figure 1.6 A simplified demand curve drawn as a straight line

Price is not the only factor that alters demand. Other factors include:

■ the price of complementary products
■ the price of substitute products
■ changes in tastes
■ changes in incomes
■ changes in population.

However, at the time we draw a demand curve we assume that these other influences do not come into play at that particular time. As time moves on, though, one or more of these other factors may exert an influence and cause the original demand curve to shift to the left or right. Indeed, in the real world these factors are constantly changing. Some may work in the same direction, or at other times against each other. It will be clearer if we first look at them in isolation before looking at a combination of their influences.

Complementary products

Complementary products are those you use together. For example, a computer keyboard complements a screen and printer; a business studies textbook is complemented by a workbook; and a car radio is complemented by a car! When the price of a desktop computer falls I may be more inclined to buy a printer as well. If the price of ham rises I may be inclined to buy fewer eggs.

Figure 1.7 Complementary products

Substitute products

Many goods compete with one another. When one brand of soap powder becomes more expensive I may switch to a cheaper rival. The same is true for canned drinks such as Coca-Cola and Pepsi-Cola, for brands of petrol such as Shell and BP, and for newspapers such as the *Sun* and the *Daily Mirror*. In Figure 1.8 we can see the effects of a rise in price of Coke on the demand for Pepsi, whose price remains unaltered.

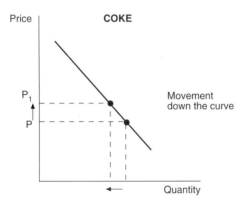

Figure 1.8 What happens to the demand for Pepsi when the price of Coke increases

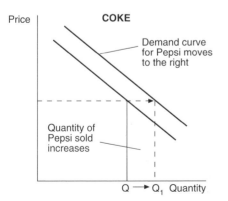

Tastes

Tastes obviously affect demand. Clothing fashions change not only with the seasons but from year to year. Many of this year's garments will end up as cast-offs. This year's car registration will drop in popularity once next year's appears. The life-cycle of a product depends very much on whether it is in a fashionable sector of the market or in a sector that lasts for a long period of time.

When tastes move in favour of a good its sales will boom, and when tastes move against a good its sales will fall. It may be quite difficult to think of products and brand names that are in decline; this is because many of them slip gradually from memory.

Income

Income is an important determinant of expenditure. In a period of recession, High Street sales will slump and expenditure on most goods will fall. This is particularly true of luxury items and incidental extras. In the boom years of the late 1980s, niche marketing developed. We saw the growth of firms such as Tie Rack, Knicker-Box and Sock Shop. Rather than selling a variety of goods, like Marks and Spencer, they chose a small area to focus on, and competed vigorously in this niche. In the early 1990s, with a period of recession, the profits of these concerns slumped as consumers had to hold back their expenditure for more essential items.

Population

When the population increases generally, so too will the demand for goods – in a particular country as well as on a global scale. However, population tends not to rise uniformly, and marketeers are more interested in the distribution of population. For example, they will be interested to note the current trend towards an ageing population – as we move towards the twenty-first century we have a far higher percentage of people past official retirement age than we have had before. Products can be developed for this group with promotion geared towards the channels that reach them.

Evidence collection point

Use diagrams to explain what movements are likely to occur in the demand for products in each of the following examples.

1 Reading becomes less popular in a time of recession. What will be the effect on the demand curve for fiction books?
2 The number of young children increases at a time when it is fashionable for children to have 'designer' clothes. What will be the effects on the demand curve for designer clothes for children?
3 The prices of cameras rise at a time when average incomes are increasing. What will be the effect on the demand for camera films?
4 The prices of newspapers rise at a time when people are reading fewer magazines, and people are using teletext as a common substitute for receiving news items. Show how this might affect the demand for newspapers.
5 The price of ice-cream falls owing to improvements in production methods during a long, hot summer. How might these changes affect the demand for ice-cream cornets?
6 Firework parties at home become more popular at a time when incomes are falling and people have fewer children. How might this affect the demand for fireworks?

We can see from the foregoing examples that there are many factors influencing the demand and that these frequently work against each other. Demand in the marketplace will be in a constant state of change. Market research is therefore essential to predict future changes and to raise awareness of current changes.

Case study – The changing demand for white bread

Answering the questions below will help you to provide evidence that you can explain the demand for goods and services.

In the 1980s, white bread acquired something of a social stigma. As a result, sales fell in volume by 7% while sales of other types of bread jumped by nearly 20%. Since about 1960, consumption of white bread has fallen from close to 40 oz per person per week to just 15 oz. Britain remains bottom of Europe's bread-eating league, consuming about 56 loaves per person per year against 100 in Italy and Germany.

But white bread looks to be back in favour. While wholemeal brands account for 22% of the market, brown bread 9% and wheatgerm and ethnic bread 1%,

white bread sales can still claim a massive 67% of a market worth £2 billion.

That share seems certain to grow, according to market research. The average white loaf today now costs about 12p less than the equivalent wholemeal loaf (because of cheaper flour, economies of scale and lower profit margins for distributors and retailers).

A recent survey by advertising agency Coley Porter Bell found that more than two in five consumers had not changed their shopping habits in the interests of health. Around 44% said that they had not stopped buying anything because they thought it was unhealthy, and 43% had not added anything to their weekly grocery basket on health grounds. Half of those asked were unable to name a manufacturer they associated with either healthy or unhealthy products.

The report concluded that nutritional value remains at the bottom of the list of reasons consumers give for buying food. Only 17% thought it was the most important factor, against 60% who cited taste and 23% who put cost first.

1 Identify different segments of the bread market highlighted above.
2 Explain how demand has altered in two of these segments in recent years. What factors might have affected these shifts in demand?
3 How would you go about finding out about possible future shifts in demand patterns? What sort of questions might you need to ask to elicit this information?
4 What is your opinion of the interpretation of these figures for changes in demand?
5 Carry out your own research into what factors influence the demand for different types of bread. What factors cause changes in demand? This work can contribute evidence for Core Skills in Communication.

Evidence collection point

Demand for most products changes fairly frequently. You can check this out by going to your local newsagent each day about 5 pm.

On some days the newspapers will be almost sold out, whilst on other days there will be a large stock left over. Demand varies with the weather, the news stories of the day, the day of the week and many other factors. Demand for newspapers falls off in the summer holidays and rises towards Christmas. Perhaps you could carry out an investigation to find out how demand fluctuates for newspapers at your local newsagent.

In the section on demand we have seen that the slope of the demand curve changes. Sometimes it is steep (relatively inelastic) while at other times it is flatter (relatively elastic). When the conditions of demand change, the demand curve will shift to the left or to the right.

In each of the situations below, explain what the likely effect on the demand curve will be for a particular newspaper, the *Daily News*.

1. A rival newspaper, the *Daily Planet*, goes out of business.
2. More people switch to newspaper reading and away from journals and magazines. This is because newspapers such as the *Daily News* begin to publish their own magazines and supplements.
3. In a period of recession people cut back on general household expenditures.
4. A newspaper with a similar format to the *Daily News* enters the market.
5. The price of all newspapers increases.
6. The average length of commuter journeys by train decreases.
7. The government bans the use of newspapers for wrapping up fish and chips.

The supply of goods and services

The profit motive

Organisations exist for a number of reasons. Etzioni (in *Modern Organizations*, published by Prentice Hall) defines organisations as 'social units that pursue specific goals which they are structured to serve under some social circumstances'. Goals can be defined as a future state of affairs which the organisation strives to achieve. Most organisations will set down guidelines for activity which serve as standards by which the success of the organisation can be judged.

In Chapter 4 we will look at the common features of organisations and the range of goals that they pursue. For the time being we will concentrate on a specific organisational goal, namely profit.

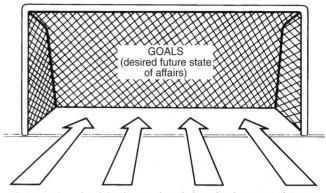

Organisations (social units, e.g. hospitals, schools, companies, one-person businesses).

Figure 1.9 Organisations directed towards goals

A firm's revenue is the amount that it earns by selling goods or services in a particular period such as a week, month or year.

For example, Joe has a hot dog stall outside the railway station on Saturday nights. On Saturday 15th December he sold 400 hot dogs at 50 pence each. His total sales revenue on 15th December was therefore:

$$400 \times 50p = £200$$

However, we also need to take into consideration Joe's costs. He has to pay business taxes to the local council for using the spot outside the station. The tax works out at £30 per week. In addition he has to buy bread rolls and sausages, amounting to £40 per week. Other costs such as petrol account for £30 per week. After all of these expenses Joe only takes home in profits £100 per week.

Revenues	Costs	
400 x 50p = £200	Tax	£30
	Materials	£40
	Other	£30

Therefore total profits on 15th December = £100

Figure 1.10 Joe's profits on 15th December

Figure 1.11 Higher profits attract new suppliers; profit acts as an incentive to production

Of course, calculations of profits are more complex than those outlined above, and we shall be looking at this in more detail in Chapter 24.

However, this simple illustration helps to emphasise the importance of profits. If Joe does not make a profit then he will not produce. The more profit that he stands to make, the more inclined he will be to produce hot dogs. The greater the profits from hot dog selling, the more likely is it that other hot dog sellers will enter the market, to provide Joe with competition.

Joe incurs costs from running his business operation. One way of looking at these costs is to divide them into two elements:

■ *Fixed costs* – which do not vary with the amount that Joe makes or sells.
■ *Variable costs* – which do vary with the amount that Joe makes or sells.

For example, one of Joe's fixed costs is the tax he has to pay to the council for his Saturday night pitch. If nobody bought any of his products he would still have to pay this fee. His variable costs will include the bread rolls and sausages that he buys in. The more he sells, the more bread and sausages he will need to purchase before each Saturday night. His total cost can be found by combining his fixed and variable costs.

The more output from a producer, the greater will be his or her costs.

Evidence collection point

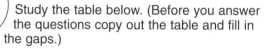 Study the table below. (Before you answer the questions copy out the table and fill in the gaps.)

Sales output (units)	Fixed costs (£)	Variable costs (£)	Total costs (£)
1	1000	50	
2			1100
3		150	
4			1200

1 What happens to fixed costs as output increases?
2 What happens to variable costs as output increases?
3 What happens to total costs as output increases?

A producer will want to know how costs or production will vary with the volume of production. Generally speaking, most producers will find that when they produce higher volumes they are able to do so at a lower cost per unit.

There are two main reasons for this:

1 By producing and selling larger outputs you are able to spread your fixed costs over a larger output.
2 As you increase output and sales you are able to use more efficient production and selling

techniques so that variable costs fall as a proportion of output.

There are many reasons for this increased efficiency. We refer to these as 'increasing returns'. Before exploring increasing returns, let us look at the factors that go into production.

Imagine that you are visiting a modern car plant. What would you see? The first and most obvious sight would be large areas of land and building. Inside you would find machinery and employees. In order for the machines to work they need to use energy, raw materials and semi-finished products – glass for the windows, tyres, electrical systems, etc.

A business enterprise is therefore a unit of production that sets out to bring together and to organise factors of production in order to produce goods and services.

The factors of production are the ingredients that make an enterprise work. They are: labour, capital, energy, materials and information:

- *Labour* is the energy provided by the employees. Work carried out takes a number of forms, such as handling information, sorting information, communication and control as well as more obvious manual tasks.
- *Capital* is represented by the machines and tools, without which there would be no production.
- *Energy* comes from the raw materials – the fossil fuels, electricity, gas and steam – that make machines work.
- *Materials* are needed to make any product, finished or semi- finished.
- *Information* is the know-how, all the accumulated experience of members of an organisation, that provides a driving force behind the enterprise.

Another way of looking at factors of production is to divide them into: land, labour, capital and enterprise.

Enterprise is then regarded as the factor that brings the other factors together to produce goods in order to make profits. Land is considered to be all the resources of nature (e.g. water, coal, farm land). Using this alternative classification, the rewards accruing to the factors of production are said to be:

Land	Rent
Labour	Wages
Capital	Interest
Enterprise	Profits

Increasing returns arise because as we produce more we are able to combine factors of production more effectively. Just imagine trying to operate a

supermarket with just one employee to stack the goods, price them, and serve the customers. The output and sales of that supermarket would be very limited. Employ two people and things would be a little better – the two could produce more than twice the output of the single employee. This pattern would continue as we increased the number of employees. We can therefore state that we are benefiting from increasing returns to labour. We can show the way in which costs fall as we increase output in the diagrams below. They show:

- Average fixed costs (Figure 1.12) i.e. the fixed cost per unit of producing more units as we expand production.
- Average variable costs (Figure 1.13) i.e. the variable cost per unit of producing more units as we expand production.
- Average total costs (Figure 1.14) i.e. the total cost per unit of producing more units as we expand production.

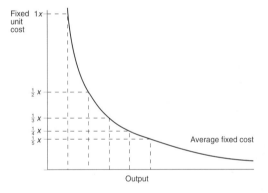

Figure 1.12 Fixed unit cost of production (where total fixed cost = £x)

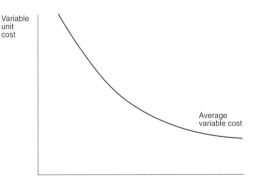

Figure 1.13 Variable unit cost of production (showing 'increasing returns' from employing more of a factor of production, e.g. labour in a supermarket)

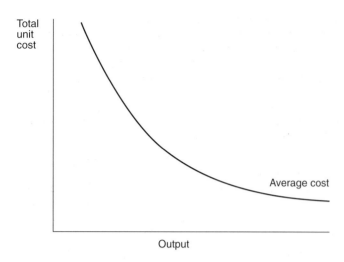

Figure 1.14 Total unit cost of production (i.e. combining the fixed and variable unit cost curves)

Of course, the picture outlined so far only indicates the efficient side of production. After a certain point, 'decreasing returns' begin to set in. For example, if we go back to our supermarket example, there will come a point at which you have the best possible number of staff working for you. Increase your staff and they start to get in each other's way, and to duplicate work. Beyond a certain 'best' point then unit costs will start to rise. We call this point the optimum point. We can now draw an average total cost curve which shows both increasing and decreasing returns as we increase the labour we employ (Figure 1.15).

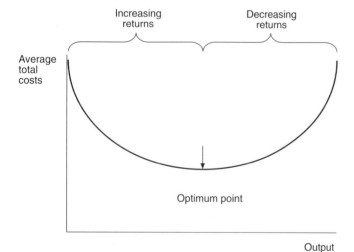

Figure 1.15 Increasing and decreasing returns

We are now in a position to illustrate the relationship between costs, revenues, output and profits.

Figure 1.16 illustrates the total cost of producing an increasing output of a particular type of good.

Profit maximisation occurs when there is the greatest possible difference between the total cost of production and the revenue gained from selling the goods. If we assume that all goods can be sold at a given market price, revenue can be shown on a diagram by a line which rises from left to right.

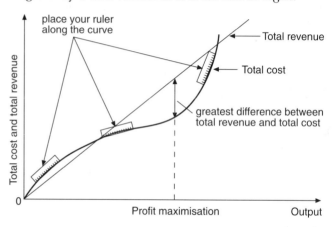

Figure 1.16 Profit maximisation

We shall see later that in fact most businesses have considerable freedom in setting prices so that in the real world the line would not be so simple.

Costs rise as a firm increases its output. Initially as this happens, the total cost of production rises, but the rate of increase falls. Place a ruler on the total cost curve in Figure 1.16 and you will see that as you move it up the curve the ruler begins to tilt downwards to the right. This is because as you increase output you are able to spread fixed costs (such as rent and rates) over a wider area. Then comes a point at which the curve begins to rise again more steeply (check this out with the ruler). Profit maximisation will occur at the point of greatest difference between total cost and total revenue.

The public service motive

The profit motive is not the only driving force behind supply. Another very important drive is that of public service. Many people in this country are involved in helping and serving others with no thought of their own gain, except from the pleasure of helping others. Obvious examples are St John's Ambulance volunteers who give their services freely at many public occasions when large numbers of people are gathered together, e.g. sporting events. Brownie, Cub, Scout and Ranger youth workers enjoy working with young people at considerable cost to their own purse and with no financial return. Charities and public welfare organisations are there to serve the less fortunate. We must be careful therefore not to assume that profit is the only motivation. A large number of people are far more committed to public service than to paid work organisations.

Evidence collection point

Research the work of one public service organisation. What does it set out to achieve? What motivates the people that work for this organisation?

Employing limited resources to get the best return

Suppliers of goods only have a limited amount of resources at their disposal.

For example, a bank may have a limited amount of finance which it can lend out to different types of borrowers. The bank will probably lend it out to those borrowers who are most likely to repay the loan, and at the highest possible return. For example, let us assume that a bank has been approached by 4 borrowers, each wanting to borrow £1000 for 6 months.

- Borrower A is prepared to pay a 25% rate of interest to start up a new, risky, business venture.
- Borrower B is prepared to pay 20% in interest to expand his highly successful business.
- Borrower C is prepared to pay 15% in interest to buy a new car. She is an existing bank customer who has never been in debt.
- Borrower D is prepared to pay 5% in interest. She earns an excellent salary and has never been in debt.

Task

The bank is in a position to lend only £2000. To which two of the above customers should they lend money?

Of course, the example above greatly simplifies the way in which banks operate. However, it illustrates the point that suppliers need to decide how to use their resources most effectively. If a factory machine is being used to make one type of food product, it cannot be making another food product at the same time. If an employee is engaged in maintenance work, he or she cannot be involved in production or selling at the same time.

Each of the above situations involves making a supply decision involving scarce resources. Production resources are relatively scarce: if we use a particular piece of wood to make a table, we cannot use the same piece to make a chair. Decision-making over a use of scarce resources involves:

- making a choice (either this or that cannot be done)
- making a sacrifice (if we choose to do this with a resource we cannot also do that).

Opportunity cost

The concept of opportunity cost is an important one in all decision-making, and particularly in the business world. Opportunity cost means the next best alternative that is sacrificed when we carry out a particular action. Individuals, groups, communities and nations are continually making decisions. When you make a decision to buy one thing you sacrifice options: for example, when you decide to buy a compact disc the real cost to you is the thing that you have to go without (e.g. a new item of clothing). When the government decides to build a new hospital, the real cost may be a new school that might otherwise have been built. When a business decides to invest in new computers the alternative sacrificed might be a wage increase to staff.

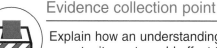

Evidence collection point

Explain how an understanding of opportunity cost would affect the business decision-making of each of the following groups of individuals:

1 Jill works for herself illustrating children's books. She works from home and frequently takes commissions over the phone from clients. Jill has been asked to give a talk at a school 100 miles from home. She will be paid a fee of £150 but no expenses. Jill has worked out that it will cost £15 for petrol and about £10 for wear and tear on the car.

She therefore anticipates making a profit of £125 for the day. She is not sure whether this will be worthwhile.

2   Southampton Boat Builders and Repair Yard is a business that normally does a lot of small repair jobs, and makes small fishing boats. They have recently received an order for three larger fishing boats from a big company. They have decided to refuse all other work to meet these orders. The job will take them six months and may lead to a larger order. They have calculated that they will make twice as much profit from concentrating on the large order.

3   John normally works a 30 hour week for £5 an hour. He has been offered a rate of £6 an hour if he will agree to work a 35 hour week. John has calculated that he will be better off by £60 a week.

Your work on these questions can provide evidence of Core Skills in Application of Number.

Choice of products

The choice of what products to supply will depend on all sorts of factors.

People choose to set up their own business for a variety of reasons. Most people at some time or another have said things like: 'If only someone sold *x* here they could make a fortune', or 'I have a good idea for a new product.'

■   At Christmas someone comes up with a new idea for hanging Christmas cards – a simple idea that would not require much capital. Perhaps it would present a business opportunity.

■   A group of teenagers notice that cars get stuck in a long queue at traffic lights in a busy area of the city. They decide to offer a car windscreen washing service. All they require are cloths, buckets, water, soap and a considerable amount of cheek!

■   A newspaper seller working outside a busy railway station finds that travellers arriving at the station frequently ask for the whereabouts of the nearest florist. He therefore has the idea of setting up his own flower stall located on the station forecourt.

There are many ways of coming up with a bright idea. Figure 1.17 shows a few suggestions. Try to add two examples of your own for each suggestion.

Most of the ideas that you come up with will already have been thought of and tried before, but sometimes a genuinely new idea arises. Examples are Rubik's cube and the Sony Walkman. However, most claims to 'new ideas' can rarely be attributed to just one person.

FOR EXAMPLE:	
Developing a hobby	Making wooden toys
Using your skills	Plastering/painting
A chance idea	A musical toothbrush
Spotting a gap in the market	A home hairdresser
Improving a product or service	A better restaurant
Combining two existing ideas	Coffee shop/bookshop
Solving problems for people	Financial adviser
Listening to people	Teenagers want a mobile disco

Figure 1.17   Some ways of thinking of business opportunities

Task

Your task is to examine the possible infringement of a patent. Imagine that the patent taken out on an invention has been challenged in a court of law by someone claiming to have invented (or patented) it first. In other words the idea may have been stolen.

Andreas Pavel filed a patent for an invention at the London Patent Office in 1977. The diagram shows what he invented.

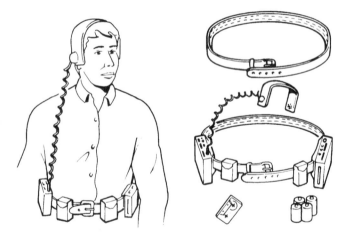

What do you think was the device that Andreas Pavel claimed to have invented?

In 1982, Pavel took a large international company to court. claiming infringement of his patent. The Sony Walkman became available in the shops in 1979.

There are two important requirements for a patent to be granted to an inventor of a new thing:

■   It must be a new idea.

■   It must have an inventive step (it should be more than just a development of an older idea).

Does the Sony Walkman infringe the patent taken out by Pavel in 1977? Set down your conclusions by using the following format.

Differences	Similarities
Conclusions	

Of course, the supply of a large number of goods today involves large business organisations. Sony, for example, make a wide variety of electrical and other goods.

One of the major influences determining what suppliers make will be the potential for profit. Suppliers will be looking to their return on capital employed. For example, if I have £100 and invest it in a building society for a year, I may find at the end of the year that my £100 is now worth £105 because of interest. My return on capital employed will therefore be 5%. Business organisations look to see where they are likely to make the most profits. Often this will involve diversifying into new products, although many firms may prefer to 'stick to their knitting', i.e. keep to those lines which they do best.

Case Study – Virgin

Virgin is one of the most famous business organisations in this country. Richard Branson started off Virgin as a record shop and soon developed a chain of record

shops. In 1986, Virgin became a public company with shares traded on the Stock Exchange. Branson then successfully moved into the airline business offering cheap flights across the Atlantic. In recent years Virgin has had a number of other major successes, often by moving into markets dominated by one or a few producers facing little competition. In the early 1990s Virgin moved into contraceptives – a market which at the time was dominated by one other major producer. Most recently Virgin has begun promoting Virgin Coke. Virgin identifies a business opportunity and then expands into this market. It then consolidates its position in that market. It does not try to do too much too quickly.

1 Why do you think that Virgin has chosen to supply the products that it has?
2 What risks has it taken by moving into new products?
3 Why is it important to expand and then consolidate?

Availability of finance for business

Businesses are decision-making units that supply goods and services. Some business units supply to the final consumer, whilst others supply to other producers. As you will find out during this course, it is not easy to supply the right goods, at the right time, in the right place and at the right price.

Suppliers need to be aware of the demand signals that come from buyers. They need to be able to anticipate likely changes in demand. Suppliers need to increase supply when demand is high and to reduce demand when supply is low. There are all sorts of business units concerned with making supply decisions, including:

- the ice cream van selling cones and choc-ices outside a park or school gate
- the large multinational clothes manufacturer selling its garments throughout the world
- the public service organisation, such as the meals-on-wheels service
- the charity organisation such as Oxfam working to supply famine relief.

People start their own business for a variety of reasons. Some have a bright idea that they think will make them rich; others find themselves unemployed and start their own business to survive. Some can only be themselves when they are their own bosses; others want to make a particular contribution to their community and can see no other way of doing it except by setting up on their own. Millions of businesses have been started up in the second half of the twentieth century. Some of them are today's household names such as Iceland, The Body Shop, and Virgin. Others are small business concerns serving a local market, such as the florist at the city railway station, the plumber or newsagent. Many other businesses have been set up, flourished briefly and then crashed.

None of these businesses, however, would have ever got beyond the ideas stage if they had not been able to get hold of a basic ingredient of business – FINANCE!

It is the availability of finance which will determine whether a business gets off the ground. We can see this for instance in the case of the Channel Tunnel – a huge project requiring massive investment.

Two of the principal sources of finance for Eurotunnel, the company mainly responsible for the tunnel link project, have been:

■ Selling shares to shareholders. Shareholders are members of the public who like an investment, as well as large financial institutions who are prepared to make a long-term investment.
■ Borrowing from the banks. Eurotunnel have borrowed vast sums of money from the banks. Each year the estimated cost of building the tunnel increased, requiring more and more money to be borrowed.

Much smaller organisations like a local plumbing or decorating business may not be able to borrow from the banks and they cannot sell shares. They therefore have to rely on the owner's own savings, and borrowings from family and friends. We shall look at sources of finance in more detail in Chapter 22. However, at this stage it should be very clear that the supply of goods is heavily dependent on business finance. Profit will only result if the firm manages its finances.

Weak financial management is one of the key reasons for business failures. Many businesses measure their trading success mainly in terms of their profits (the 'bottom line'). However, it is often the case that they should be more concerned about their cash flow.

Every business needs to have cash available at the bank to pay its bills. A manufacturing company, for instance, needs money to buy stock or raw materials to make the goods it intends to sell. But the company will not get its money back until it has sold the goods. If debtors (people and companies that owe money) are slow in paying the bills, then the manufacturing company could run into cash-flow problems.

Figure 1.18 The money cycle

A company should try to arrange its affairs so that if debtors are slow in paying, there is still enough cash in the company's account at the bank to pay important bills. Better still, the company should devise effective ways of preventing late payments.

Evidence collection point

A catering group rose like a soufflé. In little over ten years it grew to more than 60 trading outlets. The owner of the business, however, found it increasingly difficult to manage the organisation. First came complaints about hygiene, followed by a string of prosecutions. Then the main supplier insisted on putting in an accountant to probe the group's finances.

The group concluded a staff pay deal which raised wages by 50p an hour. This resulted in serious financial problems. Despite expert help and advice from the supplier, to whom the group owed £300 000, matters failed to improve.

Like a soufflé exposed to a blast of cold air, the company collapsed. Debts amounted to several million pounds.

1 What weaknesses can you identify in the company's growth as described above?
2 Why might some of the financial difficulties have arisen for the organisation?
3 Why is finance so important to the ongoing success of a business organisation?
4 To what extent does finance underpin an organisation's ability to supply?

Relationship between price and quantity supplied

The profit from selling a good or service is the difference between the price at which it is sold and the cost of producing it. The quantities of the good that the company offers will therefore depend on the price it receives for each unit sold relative to the cost of producing each unit.

As price rises (other things remaining the same), the company will at first make a larger profit on each item it sells. This will encourage it to make and sell more. However, the company may face rising costs as it expands (for example, the cost of paying employees at overtime rates will increase). For these reasons we should expect that companies will offer more for sale at higher prices, and as they increase their output they will ask for higher prices.

We can draw either a supply curve for an individual company, or a market supply curve from adding together all the individual supply curves. A typical supply curve will slope upwards from left to right (Figure 1.19).

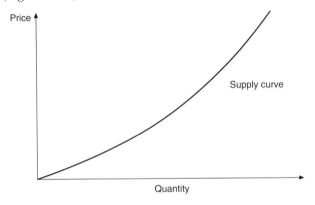

Figure 1.19 A simple supply curve

Evidence collection point

Study the supply curve shown in Figure 1.20. Draw the points shown on a piece of graph paper.

1 How much of the commodity would be supplied at:

   a 15p   b 14p   c 13p   d 12p
   e 11p   f 10p   g 9p   h 7p?

2 Draw in the supply curve and explain its shape.

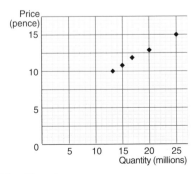

Figure 1.20 Supply curve

Supply curves

A supply curve shows the relationship between the price at which a good will be sold and the quantity that producers will be prepared to supply to the market at this price.

A steeply rising curve would indicate that producers would want to see relatively large increases in price before they expanded output.

In contrast, a shallow curve would indicate that producers would be prepared to increase their supply considerably in response to relatively small increases in price.

Elasticity of supply

An explanation of elasticity of supply helps us to understand the shape of the supply curve.

Elasticity of supply measures the responsiveness of supply to changes in price. It can be measured by:

$$\text{Elasticity of supply} = \frac{\text{Percentage change in quantity supplied}}{\text{Percentage change in price}}$$

Supply is said to be elastic when the quantity changes by a greater proportion than the price change.

Inelastic supply occurs when the quantity changes by a smaller proportion than the price change.

Time has a great influence on elasticity of supply. We can identify three time periods:

- *The momentary period.* At a moment in time it is impossible to alter supply. In a shoe shop at 3.30 pm on a Saturday afternoon there may only be three pairs of size 7 trainers. In business we define the momentary period as that in which it is impossible to alter both our fixed factors of production (such as the machinery or buildings in a processing plant) and our variable factors (such as labour and energy).
- *The short period.* Between 3.30 pm and 4.00 pm on a Saturday afternoon it may be possible to rush extra training shoes to the shop from a local warehouse. In business we define the short period as the period in which fixed factors remain fixed, but variable factors can vary.
- *The long period.* Because of a general increase in the demand for trainers, a factory producing trainers may expand its plant and equipment. In business we define the long period as the period in which all factors of production can become variable.

We can illustrate elasticity of supply in different time periods as in Figure 1.21. Momentary supply is represented by a vertical line, short-period supply by a relatively inelastic supply line, and long-period supply by a relatively elastic supply line.

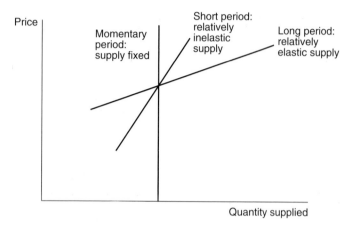

Figure 1.21 Influence of the time factor on elasticity of supply

What constitutes a short or long period varies from company to company and from industry to industry. For example, it takes a lot longer to increase fresh flower production than it does to expand artificial flower production. Some products have an extended long term (e.g. coffee and rubber), while others have a shorter long term. If you have ever grown cress on your window sill you will know that it can be grown within days.

Evidence collection point

Explain the following, using diagrams to make comparisons.

1 The elasticity of supply of Cup Final tickets on Cup Final day.
2 The relative elasticity of supply of meat in a butcher's shop:
   a at a particular instant in time
   b over a week.
3 The elasticity of supply of a particular popular newspaper early in the morning, at midday and in the evening.

Elasticity of supply also varies according to how close to capacity a company or industry is running. For example, if a factory is using only half its machines, it would be relatively easy to expand production.

However, if the factory is already working at full capacity, then the company would have to invest in new plant in order to expand its supply.

In order to expand production it is necessary to increase inputs. If inputs are readily available, then supply will be far more elastic than if inputs are scarce.

If the extra cost of producing additional units is rising sharply, then producers will be reluctant to expand output in response to higher prices.

Changes in supply – occurrence and causes

The cost of producing an item is made up of the price of the various inputs, including raw materials and the machinery used to make it. Rises in the prices of some of these factors will increase production costs, and this results in a reduction in supply at each and every price (Figure 1.22).

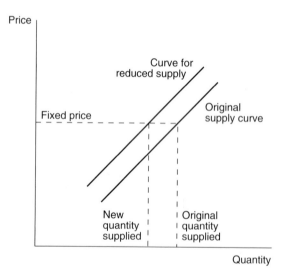

Figure 1.22 Shifts in the supply curve

The supply curve shifts to the left – at any given price less will be produced and offered for sale than before. For example, 1995 saw a rise in interest rates (i.e. the cost of borrowing money), and this increased the cost of production of many goods. Of course, a fall in production costs has the opposite effect.

Taxation imposed on output or sales has the same effect – producers and sellers are effectively taking less money at each price. On the other hand, improvements in technique, which make it possible for any given quantity of a product to be made or sold at a lower cost than before, will have the opposite effect.

The conditions of supply may be altered by such things as changes in the weather, fires, floods, dust-storms or earthquakes, although such changes are often only temporary. Weather conditions can lead to large or small harvests, and hence increases or shortages in the supply of wheat and other crops.

 Evidence collection point

Show how supply will alter in each of the following instances. Illustrate your answer with diagrams.

1 Improvements in technology in the car industry. (Show the effect on the supply of cars.)
2 Very high demand for tickets for a new musical show in London. (Show the effect on the supply of tickets for a particular performance.)
3 The development of more effective pesticides for use on cereal crops. (Show the effect on the supply of cereals.)
4 An increase in the cost of the raw materials required for housebuilding. (Show the effect on the supply of houses.)
5 An increase in demand for small-engined cars. (Show the effect on the supply of small-engined cars.)

Effects of customers on changes in supply

Customers play a major part in determining the quantity of products that will be supplied. There is no point in supplying a product unless there is sufficient demand for it. The size of the market and the intensity of demand will determine the number of producers that operate in the market and how much they are prepared to buy. For example, you will find that there is a fairly close relationship between the number of doctors (or fish and chip shops) in a town and the size of that town. When towns expand there will be an increasing demand for the services of doctors – eventually a critical mass will build up requiring the development of new doctors' surgeries in the town.

Effects of competitors on the supply of goods

Organisations today operate in an increasingly competitive market. In a competitive market,

organisations will need to out-compete rivals. Often this will mean supplying a larger volume of goods at a lower price. The existence of competition will act as a spur to businesses to increase supply in order to try to secure the largest share of the market.

Of course, when organisations are uncompetitive, their profits will fall and they may be forced out of a market. They may lead to a reduction in supply in the market.

Demand and supply interaction

The idea of a market price

Figure 1.23 shows the outline demand and supply curves for jars of strawberry jam in a particular week. We can combine these two curves on a single drawing to illustrate how prices are determined in the marketplace. The point at which the two curves cut is the point at which the wishes of both consumers and producers are met (see Figure 1.24).

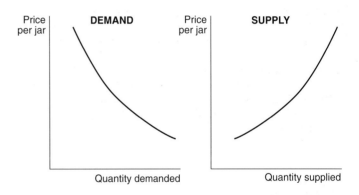

Figure 1.23 Demand and supply curves for strawberry jam

We can now see that, at a price of 60p for a 350g jar, 100 000 tonnes of jam would be bought in the marketplace each week. At this price consumers are happy to buy 100 000 tonnes and sellers are happy to supply this quantity.

This is called the equilibrium point because there is nothing forcing a change from it.

We can see why this point is an equilibrium one by considering non-equilibrium points. For example, at 80p a jar consumers would be prepared to purchase only 75 000 tonnes while suppliers would be prepared to make 125 000 tonnes available to the market. At

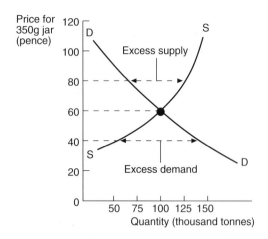

Figure 1.24 Market equilibrium for strawberry jam

this price sellers would be left with unsold stocks and would quickly contract supply to the equilibrium point.

If the price was below the equilibrium – at say 40p – demand would be for 150 000 tonnes with producers only willing to supply 50 000 tonnes; in this situation, strawberry jam would be snapped up as soon as it was put on the shelves, and stocks would run out. Prices would soon be raised towards the equilibrium point.

Evidence collection point

The following table sets out the demand and supply schedules for a particular make of sweet called 'Sweetsorts'.

Price per packet (pence)	Demand (million packets/ annum)	Supply (million packets/ annum)
0 pence	400	0
10 pence	320	0
20 pence	240	80
30 pence	160	160
40 pence	80	240
50 pence	0	320
60 pence	0	400
70 pence	0	480

1 Set the table out in the form of a graph.

2 What is the equilibrium price? Why is this the equilibrium price? What volume of goods will be supplied to the market at the equilibrium price?

3 Explain why 10 pence and 40 pence are not the equilibrium price.

The effects on business decisions of changes in demand and supply

The simple explanation of demand and supply of strawberry jam which we looked at earlier gives us an important insight into how markets operate. Producers and consumers respond to price signals, and in this way their wishes and plans are co-ordinated by the market mechanism. These wishes and plans change regularly since the factors influencing supply and demand are in a constant state of change.

For example, improvements in standards of living in a country will increase demand generally, but they will also affect costs – the money paid to an employee as wages for his or her work is income from the employee's point of view, but to the employer it is a cost. Furthermore, improvements in manufacturing techniques often increase the supply of particular goods without increasing costs. It is obvious that any change has knock-on effects throughout the marketplace. These changes are not isolated – they are happening all the time. Consider the case of up-market cook-chill meals sold by outlets such as Marks and Spencer and Sainsbury's.

If an increase in supply is coupled with a decrease in demand, the price of the good will fall. If a decrease in supply is coupled with an increase in demand, the price of the good will rise. However, if an increase in supply is coupled with an increase in demand, or a decrease in supply with a decrease in demand, we know that output is likely to increase in the first case and contract in the second – but we cannot be sure what will happen to price in these circumstances.

Changes in the marketplace lead to adjustments by consumers and producers. Demand and supply curves change shape and position, and very quickly a new equilibrium position is established. However, this will only be a temporary equilibrium point because markets are characterised by change. Indeed, one beauty of the marketplace is that it can quickly accommodate changes.

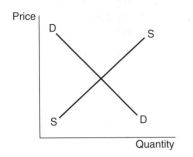
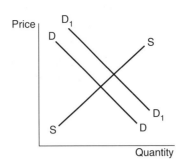
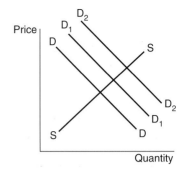

Figure 1.25 Demand shifts upwards

Shifts in demand curves

A shift in the curve for a product to the right indicates that consumers are becoming increasingly disposed to buy a particular product. We have already examined a number of important reasons for this shift, e.g. rising incomes, preference.

Initially, businesses will want to see whether the increase in demand will be sustained. If it is sustained, they will be more inclined to supply the goods in question to the market. For example, in Britain in the 1990s we see that housebuilding firms continue to supply new 'Executive' homes to the market, and that producers of GNVQ textbooks for Business continue to supply new texts.

Shifts in the supply curve

Shifts in the supply curve usually result because businesses have decided to produce more goods. When they do so, this can lead to a fall in price which in turn may discourage fresh increases in supply. However, if price falls, this may lead to an increase in demand, calling for further increases in supply (Figure 1.26).

Changes in market price and quantity sold

Changes in market price are the driving force which brings forward fresh supplies in a market economy. Businesses are constantly on the lookout for fresh opportunities. When prices rise in a particular sector, existing businesses and new businesses will have an incentive to move into this sector because it may offer higher returns on capital employed from the use of resources (Figure 1.27 on page 24).

Changes in quantities sold will also have an important impact on business decision-making. Businesses are highly sensitive to changes in sales. Nowhere is this more apparent than in the operation of a modern supermarket. When a consumer buys a product in a supermarket this

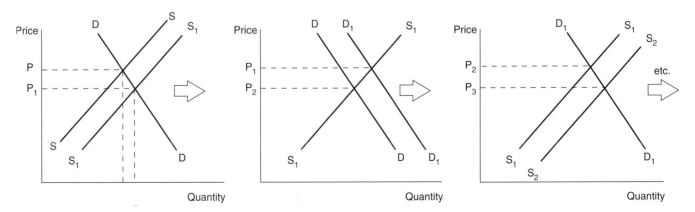

Figure 1.26 A shift in the supply curve and its repercussions

23

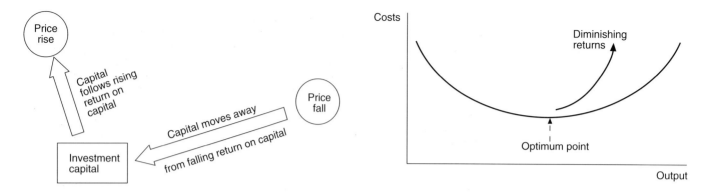

Figure 1.27 Maximising market opportunities

Figure 1.29 Costs rise when you go beyond the optimum point

information is immediately recorded, through the bar code, on the supermarket's computerised stock-control system. As soon as stocks run low, fresh supplies will be ordered from a central warehouse, which in turn orders supplies from manufacturers. Manufacturers will thus be able to respond quickly to changes in demand from the final consumer (Figure 1.28).

Increased costs for increased output in the short term

When a supplier increases the supply of a good, this will often lead to an increase in the supplier's costs. It will not lead to an increase in fixed costs of production (because these are being spread over a larger output). However, it will lead to an increase in variable costs.

This increase in variable costs is an important consideration in deciding whether to expand production or not. For example, a business may not be paid for the goods it sells until later (if it sells goods on credit). It may therefore be foolish to increase your sales. You may have borrowed a lot of money to finance your business. If you borrow any more in order to produce more goods you may run into financial difficulties.

Another consideration may be that the firm is already producing at the optimum point. Then if it expands output and sales, diminishing returns will set in, leading to rising costs (Figure 1.29).

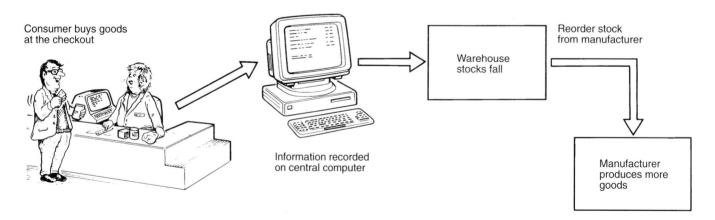

Figure 1.28 Business response to changing consumer demand/sales

Evidence collection point

The following table shows the average cost to a firm of producing different levels of output.

Draw the average cost curve on a piece of graph paper.

Output	Average cost
100	50 pence
200	40 pence
300	30 pence
400	20 pence
500	30 pence
600	40 pence
700	50 pence

1 What is the optimum output for the firm?
2 Why might the firm prefer to sell 400 units rather than 100 units?
3 Why might the firm prefer to sell 400 units rather than 600 units?
4 Why does the cost curve have the shape that it does?

Economics of scale in the long term

In the short term the firm's production is constrained by the fixed factors of production at its disposal. For example, a firm may only have a factory with a limited size, it may have a number of old-fashioned machines, its labour force may be poorly trained.

However, in the long term the firm can take action to improve the performance of its fixed factors. In the long term these fixed factors are no longer fixed in their potential. For example:

■ The firm can expand the size of its factory.
■ It can invest in new automated machines.
■ It can invest in the training of its employees.

We say the firm is able to benefit from economies of scale. This means that it is able to produce larger scale outputs at a lower average cost per unit.

The scale of operations is usually measured by the number of units produced over a period of time. Large organisations are able to produce their goods and services at more competitive prices because they can spread their fixed costs over a larger output. If the amount of production increases, average unit

costs over most production ranges are likely to fall because the organisation will benefit from economies of scale (the advantages it gains from being larger). All organisations aim for the scale of production which suits their type of activities best, and this is achieved when unit costs are at their lowest for the output produced. Beyond this point an organisation starts to find that inefficiencies or dis-economies of scale (the disadvantages of being too large) push unit costs up.

If output increases at a faster rate than the input, average unit costs will be falling and an organisation is said to be benefiting from increasing returns to scale. Beyond the point at which average unit costs are at their lowest, the increase in output will be less than the increase in input, so that average unit costs are pushed up and the organisation is suffering from decreasing returns to scale.

Internal economies of scale enable an organisation to manage its operations more efficiently. They result from an organisation being able to use better technology, management and business practices as it gets larger.

External economies of scale are factors outside the direct control of an organisation from which it benefits – such as an industry becoming larger or an area prospering.

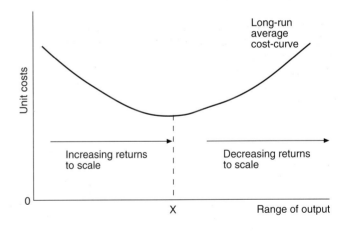

Figure 1.30 Returns to scale

Internal economies

■ *Technical economies*
Larger organisations have the ability to use techniques and equipment which cannot be adopted by small-scale producers of the same

good or service. For example, an organisation might have three machines, each producing 2000 units per week at a unit cost of £1. As the organisation becomes larger, it could replace these three machines with one machine producing 10 000 units per week at the lower cost of 75p per unit. If a small organisation tried to use such a machine, costs would be excessive in relation to its output and the machine would probably become obsolete before the end of its physical life.

- *Labour and managerial economies*
  In a very small business it is not unusual for one person to be 'jack of all trades', constantly adjusting skills and switching from one job to another. A large organisation, on the other hand, employs a number of specialised staff on its management team – accountants, marketing managers, personnel officers, etc. Specialist roles tend to improve the overall quality of work and decision-making processes, and reduce overall unit costs if the output is sufficiently large.
- *Commercial economies*
  In the commercial world, large organisations enjoy considerable benefits. For example:
  - they can afford to devote more resources to market research and product research
  - raw materials can be bought in bulk and larger discounts obtained
  - they can exercise buying power in their markets (e.g. demand extended credit periods)
  - they sometimes have a financial stake in suppliers or retail outlets
  - overheads may be spread over a larger output
  - centralisation may make the organisation more efficient
- *Financial economies*
  Large organisations are viewed in a different light by the financial world. As they are (usually) a more sound investment, they find it easier to raise finance, often at preferential interest rates. A further financial advantage is that they may be able to raise capital by issuing new shares on the Stock Exchange.
- *Risk-bearing economies*
  As well as having a financial stake in both suppliers and outlets, a larger organisation may have the ability to diversify across a range of products and operations to spread risks. By so doing an organisation covers itself against too much dependency on one area.

Evidence collection point

Explain why a small organisation may be at a disadvantage when attempting to serve the same market as a large organisation. Can you think of any advantages that the small organisation may enjoy?

External economies

Important external economies of scale are:

- *Concentration*
  If similar organisations develop in the same geographical area, a number of benefits arise – for example, a skilled labour pool, a reputation for the area for the quality of its work, local college courses tailored to meet the needs of that particular industry, and better social amenities.
- *Information*
  Larger industries have information services and employers' associations designed to benefit the members (e.g. the Motor Industry Research Association).
- *Dis-integration*
  In areas where certain industries develop, component industries or service industries develop to help with maintenance and support services.

Evidence collection point

Identify external economies which a specific firm has benefited from as a development of your local area, e.g. new road communications to other areas. Set out in detail the specific benefits from economies of scale.

Evidence indicators

You need to produce a report analysing the effect of supply and demand on business.

You will need to be able to:

- Report research findings about the demand and supply interaction and the price and sales for a particular product (Performance Criterion 5).
- Suggest future changes in demand and supply of particular products and suggest how these may affect business decisions about which products to supply and in what quantity (Performance Criterion 6).

The following list should serve as a checklist. Please tick off each of the following when you have successfully covered them as part of your report. You need to be able to confirm that:

- ■ I have analysed two products and explained causes of change in demand and supply of goods and services. ☐
- ■ I have analysed how the interaction of demand and supply influences decisions which businesses make about their products, and how much of them to supply. ☐
- ■ I have explained the importance to businesses of the relationship between price, demand and quantity supplied, and the relationship between price, profit and quantity supplied. ☐
- ■ I have explained the importance of customers and competitors in terms of their effect on demand, prices, supply and the consequences of shift in demand and supply in terms of output or sales. ☐
- ■ I have indicated that equilibrium between supply and demand will determine both the price and sales of a particular product, and indicated the effect on price and sales of changes in demand and supply. ☐
- ■ I have suggested possible future changes in demand and supply of particular products, and suggested how these could affect decisions made by businesses. ☐

Helping you to get started

Where to find information

Imagine that you have decided to investigate changes in the demand for and supply of fast food products in this country. You would need to look for newspaper and magazine articles relating to changes in the fast food industry. You will need to look at publications in the library such as the *Annual Abstract of Statistics* showing what is happening to people's earnings, what they are spending their money on, etc. You would also need to carry out your own primary research in your own locality, for example, by asking for information from fast food restaurants in your town. You might, for example, find that surveys have been carried out looking at local demand.

Presenting your evidence

In writing up your report, you will need to illustrate your work by using supply and demand curves

constructed from primary and secondary data from the local and/or national economy.

The report that you produce can use any medium, for example:

- ■ An oral report – a spoken presentation to other students. If you produce an oral report you will also need to produce written notes that prove that you understand the effects of demand and supply on business.
- ■ Audio-visual report – using tape recordings, videos, overhead transparencies, slides, etc.
- ■ Word-processed report.
- ■ Written report (as you progress through the course you should increasingly present your report by word processing rather than handwriting).

Starting evidence

You may be able to use some of the evidence provided below in assembling your report looking at demand and supply.

Evidence 1: UK National Income 1990–1994

The graph below is based on information produced by the research organisation Datastream. It shows production in the UK between 1990 and 1994. The starting point is 1990, which is given an index of 100 (if 1996 was 110 this would mean that the total output of all goods in the UK would have risen by 10% between 1990 and 1996).

The graph shows that 1991–1993 was a period of recession. Find out whether the upturn of 1994 has continued. Clearly if it has, this would have an impact on the demand for fast foods and other products.

Production index, 1990 = 100

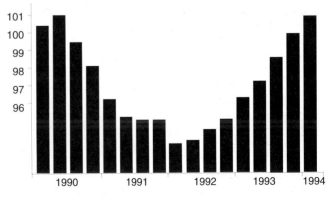

Source: Datastream

Evidence 2: Real disposable income (percentage change compared with a year ago)

The evidence shown in the chart below was produced by the Henley Forecasting Institute. Real disposal income is the amount that people have left in their pockets after taxes have been taken away. What does it show? Would it encourage suppliers of fast food to be optimistic about future demand patterns?

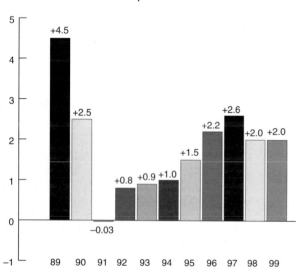
Real disposable income

Evidence 3: Adults purchasing a fast food meal as a percentage of the population

The graph below is compiled from a number of fast food surveys. What trends does it show? What would be the likely impact on the demand for fast food?

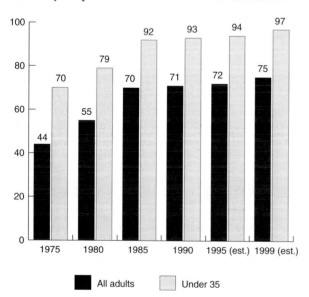

Evidence 4: Number of fast food take-aways and restaurants in 1989 and 1993

The graph shows the number of fast food outlets belonging to four major fast food chains in 1989 and 1993. What does it tell you about the supply of fast food in this country?

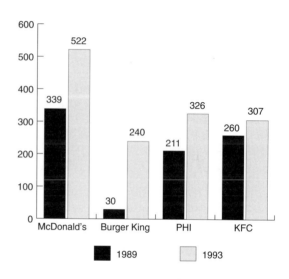
Fast food outlets

Evidence 5: McDonald's newspaper article

The newspaper article below is typical of that appearing in national newspapers in January 1995. What does the article tell you about the likely future supply of fast food in this country?

McDonald's plans to create 3000 jobs in Britain
The burger chain McDonald's is to open more than 50 new restaurants in 1995 and create more than 3000 full and part-time jobs throughout Britain.

The expansion, representing an investment of £65 million in construction and equipment, will take the number of McDonald's restaurants in Britain to more than 630. It is the first stage of a plan launched earlier this year which aims to double the number of their restaurants in Britain within 10 years.

The new restaurants will be in cities, motorway service areas, leisure centres and airports, and alongside A-roads. About one-third will be in London and the South, one-third in Wales, the Midlands and East Anglia and the rest in the North, Scotland and Northern Ireland.

The information provided above should give you some useful starting leads. You should now research your own information to build up a wealth of material to draw on so that you can set out clear evidence that you can meet all of the performance criteria for this unit.

Appendix: Elasticity of demand

Earlier in this chapter we stated that we would give a more detailed description of demand at the end of the chapter We hope you will feel confident enough to tackle this information now.

The downward slope of a demand curve shows that demand for a product rises as the price falls. However, frequently we need to know by how much demand will change as a result of a price change.

The slope of a demand curve is a fair indicator of the responsiveness of demand to price changes. A useful simplification is that the steeper the slope, the more inelastic the demand (Figure 1.31).

■ When demand is elastic the slope is relatively flat.
■ When demand is inelastic the slope is relatively steep.
■ When demand is unitary (the proportional change in demand and price are the same) then the curve will be a rectangular hyperbola.

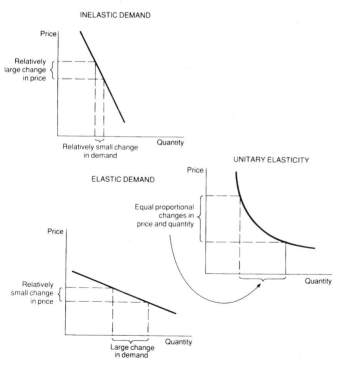

Figure 1.31 Simplified demand curves

It is important to stress that in setting out these general guides we are, in fact, simplifying mathematical reasoning.

Perhaps the easiest way of calculating the price elasticity of demand is to look at the change in total revenue as a result of altering price. If a producer wants to maximise revenue, then it makes sense to raise price if demand is inelastic and lower price if demand is elastic.

A useful way of thinking about elasticity is to remember that:

■ Demand is unitary when, if you raise or lower price, the total revenue earned remains constant.
■ Demand is elastic when, if you lower price the total revenue increases, and if you raise price the total revenue decreases.
■ Demand is inelastic when, if you lower price the total revenue decreases, and if you raise price the total revenue increases.

However, it is essential to remember that revenue is only one side of the profit equation. For example, if British Rail lowers ticket prices and gets a more than proportional increase in demand from passengers, its revenue will increase. However, it will probably lose out if it is too costly to use more carriages, or employ more ticket attendants etc.

Queens Park Rangers

If you are still struggling with elasticity of demand, it may be helpful to become a temporary supporter of Queens Park Rangers.

A simple formula for memorising elasticity of demand is:

$$\text{Elasticity of demand} = \frac{\text{Percentage change in quantity demanded}}{\text{Percentage change in price}}$$

That is, the Q goes on top and the P below – the first two letters of Queens Park Rangers.

The operation of markets and their effects on businesses and communities

This chapter looks at different types of markets and the level of competition that exists between organisations operating in the same or similar markets. It considers the various ways in which organisations compete, particularly emphasising the thinking which influences pricing decisions. It is also concerned with the way in which business activities in the marketplace can bring benefits and costs to society.

Different types of markets

The marketplace brings together consumers and producers. Consumers are able to signal their preferences and choices by 'voting' with their money for certain goods and services. This week Brussels sprouts may be highly popular, so they are quickly sold out. The sellers realise that there is a healthy demand, so tomorrow they may bring fresh stocks to the market and sell them at higher prices, and next year farmers may grow more sprouts to meet the expected demand. At the same time a particular type of apple may not be selling well, so shops are left with stocks which decay. Consequently the farmers will next year pick only a small quantity of these apples.

Every day millions of individual buying and selling decisions are made. When I go to buy a new shirt I am more concerned with my own buying decision than with the state of the market, but my decision to buy one shirt rather than another has a tremendous impact if there are thousands of other consumers

making decisions similar to my own. If we all want pink flowery shirts then it will pay manufacturers to switch resources (such as labour, machinery and raw materials) into making them. They may be able to make lots of them in a continuous production run at low cost and for a high profit. If I am the only person who wants a pink flowery shirt then I will struggle to find one, and I can expect it to be priced accordingly.

Competitive markets

A competitive market is one in which there are a number of producers supplying goods which are considered to be highly similar.

For example, if there were a number of small farmers producing apples which looked and tasted alike then their products would be very close substitutes.

In deciding whose apples to buy, a major consideration would be the price of the apples. The farmer who undercut the prices of rivals would be the one most likely to sell all of his or her stock.

The more competition there is in a particular market, the greater the similarity there will be between the offers being made by rival producers/sellers.

A good example of a competitive market is that of service stations. Service stations offer highly similar products and services:

■ A similar range of petrols, diesel, and other fuels.
■ A similar range of customer services, e.g. fast service, paper towels to wipe hands on after filling

Figure 2.1 The marketplace brings together consumers and producers

up, toilets, a range of extra products such as comics, newspapers.
- Light, flexible hoses.
- A place to check air pressure, vacuum the car, etc.

The higher the level of competition, the greater the pressure on individual service stations to rival the products and services offered by competitors.

Case study – Competition between the 'majors' in petrol retailing

Oil companies today compete in an increasingly competitive market. As a result of the increase in competition there has been a steady erosion of the big three's market share (Figure 2.2).

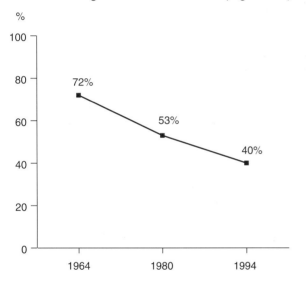

Figure 2.2 Market share of majors

The Monopolies Commission is a government body which is responsible for making sure that firms compete fairly in markets. In a report on the oil industry in the early 1990s the Commission stated that:

We were impressed by the diversity of approaches for attracting the customer. This reflects the vigour of competition for market share by majors, mini-majors and other wholesalers, and by independent retailers, particularly hypermarkets.

Hypermarkets have been particularly influential in creating cut-price competition between service stations. Hypermarkets do not set out to make more than a token profit from their petrol retailing operations.

The costs of entry into and exit from the petrol retailing market are quite low, so there are always people coming

in whenever there are big profits to be made and leaving when profit margins are squeezed. However, the majors have to be there through thick and thin; they have to price accordingly, which makes the market highly competitive.

The Monopolies Commission Report on the industry stated that for 90% of the country, in each 10 kilometre square there is on average a choice of 19 stations and eight different brands (Figure 2.3).

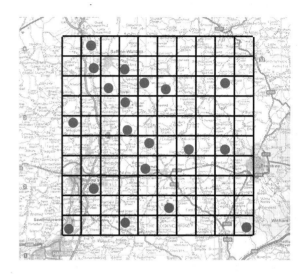

Figure 2.3 Average number of petrol stations per 10 kilometre square in 90% of the country

In urban areas the choice is even greater, with 75 stations in every 10 kilometre square and with 14 brands on offer.

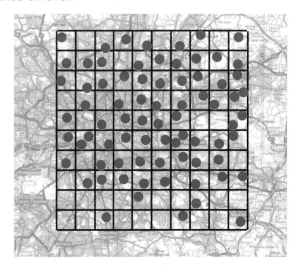

Figure 2.4 Average number of petrol stations per 10 kilometre square in urban areas

Research shows that about one-third of motorists will always go for the cheapest price even if it is a little out of the way. Another one-third balance price against other factors such as facilities and convenience. The remaining third tend to rely exclusively on convenience and prefer sites with a full range of modern facilities even if petrol there costs slightly more.

1 Who are the major competitors in the petrol retailing market?
2 Describe six ways in which they compete.
3 How can a particular company seek to gain a competitive edge? How is it possible to differentiate one product from another?
4 What factors are likely to (a) encourage, and (b) discourage competition in the petrol market?
5 In recent years hypermarkets have substantially increased their market share of petrol sales. Why are they able to do so?
6 How can rival petrol retailers respond to this challenge?
7 Is the petrol retailing market a competitive one? Explain your answer in detail.

Non-competitive markets

Competition occurs where two or more organisations act independently to supply their products to the same group of consumers. Some markets are characterised by an abundance of products and services so that customers have a considerable amount of choice.

In other markets there may be little (if any) competition and consumers may only be able to make a limited choice from the range of goods and services on offer.

Direct competition exists where organisations produce similar products which appeal to the same group of consumers. For example, this book is in direct competition with other books written for the GNVQ in Advanced Business.

Even when an organisation provides a unique end-product with no direct competition, it will still have to consider indirect competition. This occurs where potential customers examine slightly different ways of meeting the same needs. For example, instead of going on holiday to Bath or Bournemouth they might go to Majorca or Benidorm; instead of buying a tabloid newspaper they may buy a 'quality' broadsheet.

Evidence collection point

Copy the arrow in the figure below, and try to place the following products along the line depending on where you think the product lies in terms of a competitive–non-competitive continuum.

Competitive   Non-competitive

a types of Cheddar cheese
b makes of computer
c soap powders
d tabloid newspapers
e exclusive cars (e.g. Rolls-Royce)
f perfumes
g Advanced Business textbooks
h ways of crossing the Channel

The degree of competition in a market is likely to influence the level of sales and profits.

The firm that is first to the market with a new product may be able to make large sales and profits. However, in the course of time other firms will enter the market, so that sales will be shared between a larger number of producers. Each of these producers will be competing for market share, so that price wars may result, leading to falling profits.

Case study – Mexican food

UK sales of Mexican food have increased continuously in the 1990s. There has been a rush of UK companies into Mexican foods, which have become the fastest-growing sector in the UK 'ethnic' food market.

The sales mirror the American experience, where the popularity of Mexican food has soared. Salsa, the spicy Mexican tomato sauce, now outsells ketchup in the US. The fashion for tortilla chips has dented sales of crisps. United Biscuits and its rival Bensons, as well as a number of other producers, are stepping up their production of tortilla chips.

1 Why do you think that UK businesses are keen to start producing Mexican food?
2 What is likely to happen to profits and sales in this market sector over the next few years?

UK sales of Mexican food

£45.2 million

£28.9 million

£13.0 million

1989   1991   1993

3 How competitive do you think this market sector will become?
4 What will be the likely impact of increasing competition on profits and sales?

Monopoly

A highly competitive market exists when firms compete vigorously with each other.

Features of intense competition might include:

- producers supplying highly similar products (e.g. packets of salt and vinegar crisps)
- consumers having detailed knowledge of the offers being made by different suppliers (e.g. a shopper in a large supermarket who can check on the prices of different brands of products like soap powders)
- ease for producers and suppliers to enter a market (e.g. we saw that if prices and profits of petrol service stations increase, new small and large retailers can buy or hire a site and start trading).

A monopoly situation does not include these competitive conditions.

A pure monopoly exists if there is only one producer or seller. Because there is only one firm in the market it has considerable powers. For example, if you are not happy with the prices, quality or service, conditions of sale, etc. offered by the monopolist you cannot switch to a rival product because there aren't any.

A business that does not have direct competition is said to be a monopoly. It does not face outside pressure to be competitive. We must be careful, however, not to assume that monopolies are inefficient. Monopolies do not need to duplicate systems of administration, services and other processes. They can also put a lot of money into product development and research in order to keep up a long-term competitive edge.

In the real world there are unlikely to be many examples of pure monopolies because most manufactured goods can be copied. Some minerals are restricted to a few geographical areas; for example, a a large concentration of world gold reserves is found in the Commonwealth of Independent States and southern Africa. When a new product is invented, the firm that supplied it will initially have a monopoly. However, very soon other people will copy the product and provide close imitations. For example, it does not take long for an 'exclusive' perfume to be copied and to appear in a slightly modified form at a much lower price on market stalls and street corners throughout the land.

An understanding of monopoly, however, is very important in business. Monopoly powers help to explain how firms are able to make more than the normal amount of profit.

When a firm can restrict competition it is in a position to raise prices, and perhaps to exploit consumers. For example, if I desperately needed a loaf of bread when shops were closed, I might be forced to buy an over-priced loaf of not-too-fresh bread from a garage.

Oligopoly

Whereas monopoly means that there is one seller, oligopoly means that there are a few sellers. Oligopoly is typical of many markets in the United Kingdom where there are a few major sellers in national and local markets (although there may be additional smaller sellers).

Examples of oligopoly markets are:

- Quality newspapers, e.g. *The Times*, the *Independent*.
- Tabloid newspapers, e.g. the *Mirror*, the *Sun*.
- Contraceptive manufacturers, e.g. Mates (Virgin), Durex (London Rubber).
- Soap powders, e.g. Unilever, Procter and Gamble.
- Car manufacture, e.g. Peugeot, Honda.
- Confectionery, e.g. Cadbury, Rowntrees.
- Personal computers, e.g. IBM, Apple Macintosh.
- Petrol, e.g. Shell, BP, Esso.

Oligopoly markets have the potential for intense competition as well as the potential to restrict competition and act as monopolists.

Oligopolists could agree to share a market and to avoid potentially damaging competition, e.g. they could agree: 'Company A can dominate the North, Company B the South, Company C the West and Company D the East.' However, they would be unlikely to do this:

1 Because business organisations tend to have a natural desire to expand and dominate. For example, Company A may also want to be the major player in the South, East and West.
2 Because it is against the law to carry out uncompetitive practices. Companies that collude are using their powers to exploit less powerful groups and individuals. In this country this will lead to legal penalties.

Oligopoly markets are therefore often characterised by extensive competition. Competition acts as a spur, encouraging individual firms to improve their performance in order to increase their market share, sales, receipts and profits.

Case study – Competition between European airlines

Until the early 1990s, national airlines in Europe tended to have a monopoly over certain routes, particularly domestic routes within particular countries. This meant that Air France would have a monopoly in France, Lufthansa in Germany, etc. This is no longer the case. The European Union has now deregulated air transport in Europe – in other words, there is now open competition for routes in the European Union.

Europe has traditionally been one of the most expensive regions in the world in which to fly. This is no longer the case, and prices are tumbling. This is the message coming over loud and clear through the advertisements crowding hoarding and newspaper pages in the mid-1990s, offering cheap flights and special deals. Ticket prices are tumbling (Figure 2.5).

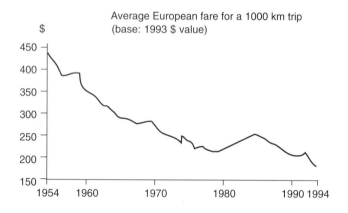

Figure 2.5 The changing price of air travel

For example, in the first quarter of 1995 Air France has halved its fares in special deals on two of its most lucrative routes, the Paris–Toulouse and Paris–Marseille runs.

The French government opened these routes from January 1st after pressure from the European Commission. Fares are on a downward path and will continue that way as new domestic and international competitors enter the market for existing routes.

Having led the way in the 1980s with its cost-cutting and efficiency improvements, British Airways is at the forefront of the skirmishes in Europe, British Airways is the major business organisation with the financial base to compete directly in France and Germany, Europe's two other main airline markets besides Britain.

1 Why did national airlines previously have a monopoly in domestic markets?

2 How has European Union deregulation changed this position?

3 What will be the likely impact on competition for European flights/

4 What is likely to be the impact on prices and services offered by airlines?

5 What is likely to be the impact on the profits of airlines?

6 To what extent is the European airline market going to be characterised by a competitive oligopoly situation?

Competition within markets

There are a number of important aspects of competition which we need to examine. Different organisations will focus on different aspects of competition at different times.

Competition for market share

Market share is often regarded by businesses as a key indicator of their current and future success. The argument is that if you gain market share then the profits will follow.

A firm will want to have a dominant market share in a particular market. For example in Figure 2.6(a) Patel's has 33% of the market, and its next nearest rival Robson's has 25%. Clearly it has the largest market share, but Robson's is still a threat. Patel's is more obviously a market leader in a situation where it has 33% of the market and its next two largest rivals have only 12½% each.

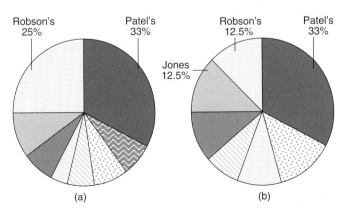

Figure 2.6 (a) Patel's just the market leader; (b) Patel's clearly the market leader

Research indicates that market share leads to market power. The advantages of having a large market share are striking. High market share companies are able to buy their ingredients and raw materials, or make them 'in-house', far more cheaply than smaller rivals. High market share companies are able to gain larger profits and plough this money back into research and development, which gives them a competitive edge. Companies with a high market share will continually be improving their products to keep them ahead of the market. For example, Heinemann Educational has been the leading book publisher in the GNVQ field. This has enabled them to spend more money on improving their books – making them more attractive and up-to-date than rival products which have dated quickly.

The Boston Consultancy Group has shown how market share leads to falling costs through an 'experience curve' (Figure 2.7).

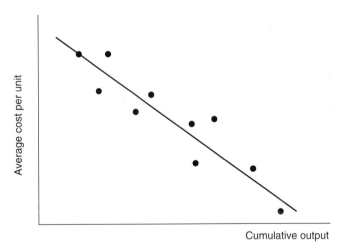

Figure 2.7 An experience curve

The cost of producing each unit will fall, as the total output that has been produced increases over time with experience.

Gains in efficiency stem from greater experience. The Boston Consultancy Group argues that this is a general principle and that, as a rough rule, average cost per unit fell by 20–30% with each doubling of experience. Greater experience stems from:

■ economies of scale
■ the elimination of less efficient factors of production

increased productivity stemming from technical changes and learning effects
improvements in product design.

The key lesson to be learnt is that the benefits of experience do not just arise – they need to be worked at. Companies must take steps to ensure that these benefits are reaped, through deliberate management policies.

Companies which have a high market share should be able to accumulate more experience. Therefore companies should strive for a high market share. The best indicator of market share is relative – that is, the ratio of a company's market share to that of its largest competitor:

$$\text{Relative market share of company A} = \frac{\text{Market share of company A}}{\text{Market share of nearest competitor}}$$

This indicator gives a clear measure of comparative strengths. The Boston Consultancy Group used statistical evidence to argue that a ratio of 2:1 would give a 20% cost advantage.

Competition for customers

Competition for customers is perhaps the most important aspect of competition. You are most likely to be successful in attracting customers if you have a clear picture of who they are and what they want. Market research is an important way of finding out about customers and their requirements. Once you have found out what customers want it will be important to give them:

what they want
at the right place
at the right price
promoted and offered in an appropriate way.

Case study – Attracting customers

'Loud, brash, American, successful, complacent, uncaring, unsensitive, disciplinarian, insincere, suspicious and arrogant.'

This was how Paul Preston, President of McDonald's in the UK, admitted that customers saw his company at the start of the 1990s.

McDonald's had been astonished to discover the sharpness of its customers' views in a survey carried out in 1991. 'What they told us was horrifying,' he told a meeting of personnel officers in Harrogate in 1995.

During the 1980s McDonald's had gone through a period of expansion, so that when it entered the 1990s it saw itself as being 'big and successful'. However, the reality was that it struggled through the first two years of the 1990s.

What customers wanted in the 1990s, the research showed was:

warmth
helpfulness
time to think
friendliness
advice.

They did not want brusque, brash American service. Nor did they think much of the latest McDonald's innovation of the period, the McPloughman's – a Big Mac version of the traditional cheese and pickle sandwich.

'Customers didn't want the product and McDonald's staff were embarrassed even to have to say McPlougman's.' McDonald's had failed to do market research to see if there was a demand for the product.

McDonald's now conducts regular customer opinion surveys.

1 What does this case study tell you about how to make sure that you are producing competitive products?
2 How important is customer research in enabling a business to remain competitive?
3 What weaknesses does the case identify in the McDonald's approach in the early 1990s?

Evidence collection point

Research and then explain the methods used by a particular group of competing organisations to compete for customers. For example, you could look at local newsagents, taxi businesses, schools or colleges. Your work could provide evidence of Core Skills in Communication and, if you use a computer to present your findings, in Information Technology.

Competition for product superiority

People buy those products which best meet their needs. Just listen to people who are buying a durable electrical good such as a freezer, television or a video. They are essentially concerned with making sure that they buy the product which is just right for them. They will discuss relative price, reliability, additional features and many other factors.

this was the jewellery chain Ratners. Gerald Ratner set up a highly successful chain of businesses selling low-price jewellery in the UK. However, in a speech to business people he was highly critical of the quality of his own products. These remarks led to the crash of the Ratner organisation as customers stopped buying the jewellery.

Price and image

For a discussion of competitive pricing strategies see pages 39–42. In some markets, however, a product's image is more important than its cost. This is apparent in some advertising of cars. Cars do not just offer you a way of getting from A to B, they also reflect your lifestyle. A particular type of car may give you the image of being a cautious, family person whilst another may present you as a risk-taking, exotic extrovert. Imagery is therefore very important in product competition.

Evidence collection point

Collect a series of 15 adverts which emphasise product superiority. Set out your adverts with a written commentary showing what aspects of product superiority are being emphasised in the advertisement, e.g. 'Lasts longer ...', 'Washes whiter than others', 'Provides all of those additional extras that ...'.

Evidence collection point

Contrast the images associated with and used to sell the following products:

1 Yorkie bars and After Eight Mints.
2 Peugeot 205 and Peugeot 405.
3 Chanel No 5 and Charlie perfumes.
4 Tetley Tea and Earl Grey Tea.

How important in imagery in competition between producers? Give examples. This work can provide evidence of Core Skills in Communication.

Competition for sales

Competition for sales is an important aspect of rivalry between organisations. The volume of sales is vital in many business areas.

The turnover of a business is measured by multiplying the average price of items sold by the number of items sold:

Turnover = average price of items × number of items sold

The more items that a business can sell, the more it can spread its costs over a larger output. The supermarket chains have benefited for a long time from policies of selling large volumes of goods. A popular business saying in America in recent times has been 'pile them high and see them fly'. The implication is that high sales at low prices will lead to low buying-in costs and hence to profitability. However, there may come a point at which goods are sold too cheaply and consumers lose confidence in the value of an item. A good example of

Competition between businesses to shift demand curves

Competitive edge gives a business an important advantage over rivals. Competitive edge will improve the position of an organisation's demand curve. This may mean for example that more of the product will be demanded at the same price as before, or that a higher price can be charged without losing a significant number of sales.

Figure 2.8 shows the effect on sales of two successful advertising campaigns for a product. At a market price of 80 pence it was originally possible to sell 1800 items; after the first advertising campaign demand rose to 3000, and after the second to 3700. Advertising is important in that it keeps products in the public eye. It also enables suppliers to describe the key benefits of their products.

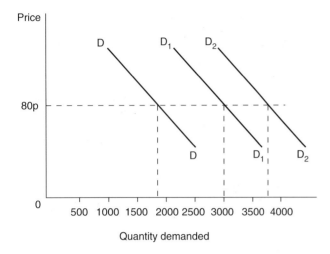

Figure 2.8 Shifts in the position of a demand curve resulting from advertising

Of course, advertising is not just concerned with shifting the demand curve in the way illustrated above. It is also concerned with making the demand curve more inelastic so that if price of the product goes up there is only a small drop in sales. Brand loyalty and commitment to a product will develop when consumers are able to appreciate the relative strength of a product when compared with their rivals' products.

In Figure 2.9 we can see that as we move up from the previous market price, demand becomes relatively more inelastic as a result of an advertising campaign.

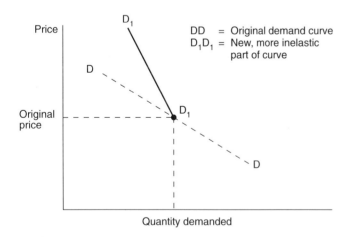

Figure 2.9 Demand becomes more inelastic above the market price

Merchandising is another way of making products more attractive. For example, merchandising might be concerned with creating an attractive and appealing display of goods in a shop to gain the attention and interest of consumers.

Because firms are able to compete to satisfy the wants and needs of consumers, they will produce a variety of similar but different products. Visit a sweet shop and count the hundreds of different types of chocolate bars and tubes of sweets on display – all meeting similar but subtly different tastes and requirements.

Competition also has the effect of acting as a spur to quality. If I am sold a poor quality good then I will switch to a better one. If a producer persists in supplying low-quality items, then they will quickly lose business as customers switch to rival producers. It only takes a small lapse in quality for people to choose not to buy a good. I used to buy my newspapers from a garage every day. Two days in a row the newspaper was dirty inside, where someone in the garage had spilled tea on it. I have never bought papers or petrol from that garage since.

Some people argue that today we have gone over the top in providing customer choice. They argue that there is so much to choose from that it is impossible to make a rational choice.

Evidence collection point

Make a study of consumer choice for a particular type of product which is sold in a supermarket. How many different types and brands of the product are on sale? How do the types and brands compete against each other? To what extent do consumers benefit from having this choice? Does variety lead to increased quality? What are the other benefits of variety? What are the drawbacks of having so much choice? Try to plan your product in such a way that it provides evidence of Core Skills in Application of Number and Information Technology.

The behaviour of businesses in different markets

In this section we will be looking at the actions and behaviour of business organisations in different markets. In particular, we will be looking at the pricing and non-pricing strategies which they employ in order to compete effectively.

Competitive pricing strategies

There are a number of pricing strategies which firms can employ in order to compete. These include:

■ skimming
■ expansion pricing
■ penetration pricing
■ destruction pricing
■ loss leaders
■ price wars.

Skimming

At the launch of a new product, there will frequently be little competition in the market, so that demand for the product may be relatively inelastic. Consumers will probably have little knowledge of the product. Skimming involves setting a reasonably high initial price in order to yield high initial returns from those consumers willing to buy the new product. Once the first group of customers has been satisfied, the seller can then lower prices in order to make sales to new groups of customers. This process can be continued until a larger section of the total market has been catered for. By operating in this way the business removes the risk of underpricing the product.

The name 'skimming' comes from the process of skimming the cream from the top of a milk product (Figure 2.10).

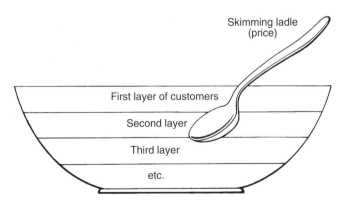

Figure 2.10 Skimming

Expansion pricing

Expansion pricing is used when a firm wants to expand its market share. The firm will first need to seek answers to questions such as, 'If we want to increase market share by 10%, what are the implications for pricing?' Clearly the benefit of increasing market share will be that you will be able to benefit from lower unit costs of production.

Expansion pricing occurs when economies of scale enable a firm to reduce its price. The process of expansion enables firms to produce higher volumes of goods at a lower cost per unit. For example, we can see this today in the mass production of motor vehicles. Large-scale producers are able to manufacture standardised cars in volume. As a result of this expansion it is possible to charge lower prices. The lower prices stimulate further demand, which encourages further economies of scale.

In deciding whether to follow a policy of expansion pricing you will need to have a clear idea of the sorts of actions that rivals may take. You will therefore need to anticipate their actions. Will they lower price too? What will the likely impact be?

Penetration pricing

Whilst skimming may be an appropriate policy when a seller is not sure of the elasticity of demand for the product, penetration pricing is appropriate when the seller knows that demand is likely to be elastic. A low price is therefore required to attract consumers to the product. Penetration pricing is normally associated with the launch of a new product for which the market needs to be penetrated (Figure 2.11).

● New product

● High fixed costs associated with set-up

● Need for large volume of sales

Penetration forces entry to: → **COMPETITIVE MARKET**

Figure 2.11 Environment appropriate for penetration pricing

Because price starts low, the product may initially make a loss until consumer awareness is increased.

A typical example would be that of a new breakfast cereal or a product being launched in a new overseas market. Initially it would be launched with a relatively low price, coupled with discounts and special offers. As the product penetrates the market, sales and profitability increase. Prices then creep upwards.

Penetration pricing is particularly appropriate for products where economies of scale can be employed to produce large volumes at low unit costs. Products which are produced on a large scale are initially burdened by high fixed costs for research, development and purchases of plant and equipment. It is important to spread these fixed costs quickly over a large volume of output. Penetration pricing is also common when there is a strong possibility of competition from rival pricing.

Destruction pricing

A policy of destruction pricing can be used to undermine the sales of rivals or to warn potential new rivals not to enter a particular market. Destruction pricing involves reducing the price of an existing product or selling a new product at an artificially low price in order to destroy competitors' sales (Figure 2.12). For example, when in late 1993 the new Costco stores entered the UK market, British supermarkets in the localities of the Costco stores slashed their prices to loss-making levels in an attempt to beat off the new American rivals.

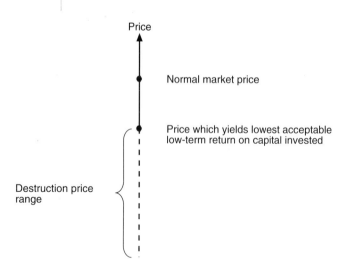

Figure 2.12 Destruction pricing

This type of policy is based on long-term considerations and is likely to lead to short-term losses. The policy is most likely to be successful when the company that initiates it has lower costs than its

competitors or potential rivals. However, it cannot be sustained in the long term because it will erode the profit base required to initiate research and development projects.

Loss leaders

Prices can be lowered from time to time to promote a product. Promotional pricing can be used to inject fresh new life into an existing product or to create interest in a new product.

Promotional pricing can be employed to increase the rate at which a product turns over. This can be used to reduce levels of stock or to increase the rate of activity of a business.

A form of promotional pricing is the use of loss-leaders. Supermarkets frequently use loss-leaders to boost sales. A loss-leader is a good which is sold at little or no profit or even at a loss. Only a small number of the items sold by supermarkets at one time are loss-leaders. The aim of selling in this way is to give the impression that all items in the shop are cheap – a shopper seeing that cornflakes are 10p cheaper in one supermarket may falsely expect all prices in the store to be cheaper. Another use of loss-leaders is to attract new customers, who will then spend on other, profitable items.

Price wars

A price war occurs when firms use price as an aggressive means of fighting competitors, usually for market share.

Businesses will engage in price wars usually when they can see a weakness in a rival. Perhaps a rival has a cash-flow problem or has been losing market share. Price wars can be short-term affairs or may be a regular feature of market activity. For example, newspapers have engaged in a price war since 1993, and it still continues in mid-1995. Oil companies frequently fight price wars to gain increased market share.

 Evidence collection point

Categorise the following examples into:

- skimming
- penetration pricing
- loss leaders
- expansion pricing
- destruction pricing
- price wars.

In each case explain why you have categorised the example in the way that you have:

1   A service station advertises and offers cut price oil.
2   A new book comes onto the market in hardback form at £25, two months later it comes out in paperback form at £15, the following year it comes out in a second edition at £10.
3   A new company enters the market, producing industrial chemicals in the North West of England. Existing large firms in the North West of England slash their prices to well below those of the new firm.
4   An existing business cuts its price in order to increase its market share.
5   A group of firms compete vigorously over price for an extended period of time. Some firms are forced out of the market.
6   A breakfast cereal manufacturer introduces a new type of cereal at a low price in order to attract customers to buy the product.

What type of pricing policy is being described in the following?

7   Reducing the price of an existing product or selling a new product at an artificially low price in order to wreck competitors' sales.
8   When there is little competition in the market, a relatively high initial price is set to gain high returns, then the price is subsequently lowered to strengthen market share.
9   Setting a low price to get into an existing market with a price increase when entry is secured.
10 Economies of scale leading to a lower price.

Price making

How much power do business organisations have in making pricing decisions? The answer to this question depends very much on the type of market in which the business is operating. Businesses will have most power to set prices when:

1   There is only one or a small number of producers. For example, the service station or café on a motorway which is fifty miles away from the next 'services' will have considerably more power to 'make' prices than the service station of café in a city centre which is surrounded by many competitors.

    We describe situations where there is a monopoly-like situation as being 'monopolistic'. Monopolistic firms will take a number of considerations into mind in setting prices. They

will want to cover costs and to make profits. Many businesses will 'make' a price which covers costs and gives a set minimum margin of profit which will enable expansion and growth.

2   There is a strong demand from consumers for the product because consumers need the product and cannot have their needs met by other suppliers. Again this is likely to be when there are few close substitutes.

Price taking

Price 'taking' means that the market sets the price and producers have to take this price from the market. This is likely to be the case in highly competitive markets. For example, a farmer with a small orchard would have to sell his apples at the existing market price. If he charged more than this price people would not buy his apples – competing apples are cheaper. If he lowered his price he would not make a profit. This is because the market is so competitive that any profits over and above those needed to keep people ticking over in business has been competed away (Figure 2.13).

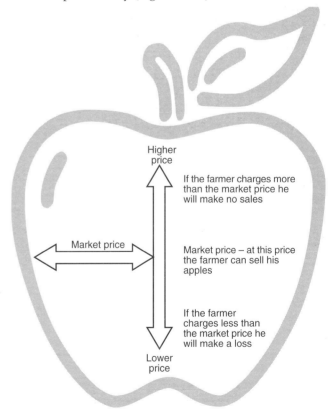

Figure 2.13   Price 'taking' in a competitive market

Price makers therefore have the power to set prices.

Price takers do not have the power to set prices. They 'take' the price set by the market.

Evidence collection point.

Explain why the following are likely to be price makers or price takers:

1 A village grocery shop.
2 One of a number of cinemas in a large city.
3 A bowling alley.
4 A fruit and veg stall in a market.
5 A garden centre.

Non-pricing strategies

Price is just one of many ways in which businesses compete. Businesses also compete by creating a business image. Our image is the way that others see us. Whether we like it or not it is our public face. People quickly form opinions about us from the images they get.

What sort of things do you notice about someone that you meet for the first time? Do you look at their clothes? Their hairstyle? What about the way they speak? Do you notice their facial expressions and gestures? First impressions are quickly formed on the basis of the images we receive.

Businesses also project images. A company's image gives a message about itself and helps people form a judgement about its quality, reliability and service. The image of the company will affect all the people it comes into contact with – customers, suppliers, employees, competitors, governments, communities and international bodies. A successful image will help convince people that it is worth dealing with that company and may give it an edge over the competition.

Logos are an obvious way in which companies use at-a-glance identifiers, signs or symbols which say 'this is Rolls-Royce' or 'this is a Shell service station'. In fact you will find that the logo generally appears on all of a company's products, advertisements, letters, brochures, etc.

Business image goes well beyond the logo. There is no point in having an image which does not meet the reality of how a company operates. 'Image' is a mixture of an individual's personal experience of a company or product, plus whatever he or she has read or heard from other sources. Advertising can help create or re-shape an image, but personal experience and the comments of other users are far more powerful.

Case study – Shell's brand image

Shell is a prominent brand name in the market, with an image built up over many years.

Maintaining a desired image is always hard work, and nowhere more so than at the customer interface. Shell service stations serve hundreds of thousands of customers every day. Each of those encounters can strengthen or weaken the image, depending on the personality and expertise of the people involved. Staff selection and training are both critical.

Shell hold special courses for everyone concerned at service stations – licensees, managers, cashiers, console operators, forecourt staff, cleaners – to make sure that the basic 'service' responsibilities like safety, cleanliness and product availability are properly understood, as well as such human touches as a friendly smile and a cheerful 'Hello'.

1 Why is a company or brand image an important part of the competitive mix?
2 What does this case study tell you about the way in which Shell works at its company and product image?
3 Why is it important to continually work to create an effective brand and product image?

Increasingly business organisations today are competing with each other by trying to create a one-to-one relationship with customers. A major way in which they are doing this is by providing a broad range of products to meet the individual needs of customers, e.g. customised cars in the motor industry (ones with a range of optional extras chosen by individuals).

Another way in which business organisations are competing is through customer service. Customer service is concerned with building a personal relationship between a customer and the company representatives.

Businesses are finding it more and more difficult to demonstrate product differentiation over competitors. Customer service on the other hand offers almost endless opportunities for superiority and differentiation. It covers the way a customer is treated by the sales staff, on the telephone, in the shop, at the check-out, the way queries and complaints are handled, the use of the latest communication technology to personalise even the most large-scale promotional campaign letters. All of these contribute to the ideal one-to-one relationship.

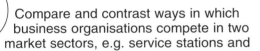

Evidence collection point

Compare and contrast ways in which business organisations compete in two market sectors, e.g. service stations and hotels.

The social costs of market operations

Market operations refer to competitive and non-competitive business activities which occur in a market economy (i.e. one in which most decisions about what to buy and what to produce and sell are influenced by price and competition).

Business activity creates benefits and costs for those both directly and indirectly involved with the business. Today it is recognised by many that industrial development will only be socially effective if it takes into account community losses as well as profits. Society as a whole has to decide what balance it wants to strike. How much pollution – even destruction of the environment – should we accept? Heavier lorries are most cost-effective in moving goods – but how heavy is too heavy? More factories and better roads can mean more jobs – but the price can be the loss of farmland. We therefore need to look at the social benefits and the social costs of market activity to get a clearer picture of net benefits.

- *Private benefits* are all the benefits accruing to an individual or group as a result of a particular activity, e.g. the profits from a business that are earned by the shareholders, the wages earned by the employees.

- *Private costs* are all the costs to an individual or group resulting from a particular activity, e.g. the cost to a sole trader of building and running a cinema.
- *Social benefits* are the private benefits plus all the beneficial effects for other members of the community resulting from a particular activity, e.g. the entertainment value received by cinema-goers, and the wages earned by the projectionist, cashier and ice-cream seller.
- *Social costs* are the private costs plus all the detrimental effects for other members of the community, e.g. the extra traffic congestion, parking problems and litter left on the street by cinema-goers.

The environmental impact of social costs

We need resources in order to be able to produce goods and services. However, there are not always enough resources to make the goods and services that consumers need and want.

Non-renewable resources are ones which are fixed in total supply and when used cannot be replaced. Their use will therefore diminish total supply. Fossil fuels and mineral deposits fall into this category.

Estimating the quantity of these resources is not always straightforward because the known reserves may only be a small fraction of the total actually in existence.

Resources fall into several categories. There are reserves:

- which could be economically extracted now (i.e. it would be profitable to extract them now, perhaps because they are easy to get at)
- which are marginally economic (i.e. only the very slimmest of profits could be made by extracting them)
- which are currently economic (i.e. they could only be extracted at a loss, for example because they may be deeply embedded in the earth's crust).

The degree of scarcity, in combination with the demand for the resource, determines its price. As resources become increasingly scarce, the price will rise and therefore demand will be reduced. Organisations operate today in a world which is increasingly being forced to take environmental concerns into account. Whether environmental consciousness has become a genuine concern in all organisations, or is being manipulated by some as a subtle marketing tool, remains to be seen. For example, it would appear that motor vehicle manufacturers are responding to environmental pressures, but the trend is still towards more and more car gadgets, which inevitably increase the car's weight and hence petrol consumption. The producers would argue that they are responding to consumer demand.

At the same time it is clear that the life-cycle of products (periods for which they are intended to last) is shortening in response to increased competition and change. Volkswagen, for instance, has recently reduced the life-cycle of its new products from 11 to 8 years.

With a shortening of the life expectancy of products it becomes easier to accommodate the 'green agenda' if consumers vote with their money for 'greener' cars. Some companies are currently designing vehicles with totally recyclable parts.

Many consumers are concerned by 'green' issues. Organisations therefore need to respond positively. This pressure clearly demands that organisations should make their employees more environmentally aware.

Case study – Poison in the water

On 6 July 1988, at 4.30 pm, the driver of a tanker from a chemical supply company arrived at the Lowermoor treatment plant in Cornwall with a delivery of aluminium sulphate. The gate was locked and the plant deserted. However,

the driver, who had never been to Lowermoor before, had been given a key by a colleague and so unlocked the gate and drove in. But where was he to put his delivery of aluminium sulphate?

He had been told that there was a tank 'on the left', but he found that there were several tanks on the left. He came to a hatch set in the ground and found that he could open it with the gate key. Concluding that this was the correct tank, he poured in the chemical.

The aluminium sulphate should in fact have gone into a separate storage tank from which it would have been dispensed at a maximum of 50 parts per million to help cleanse the water supply. Inadvertently the driver had poured it into a tank which allowed the undiluted chemical to join the water supply to be dispensed to consumers in the South West.

When the disastrous error was discovered, the water company blamed the chemical supply company. The water company said that the chemical should have been delivered on 4 July or 5 July, and that in any case it did not accept deliveries after 4 pm. It queried how the driver had obtained the key. The water workers union suggested that the key was one of a number handed out to contractors to help break the water workers' strike of 1983.

1 Comment on the seriousness of this incident.
2 What general lessons for organisational responsibility towards the environment can be learnt from the case?
3 What are the lessons for employers working for organisations?
4 What experiences have you had of working in situations in which your actions or inactions were a potential threat to the community? How well trained were you to prevent risks?
5 How high on an organisation's list of priorities should be a responsibility towards the external environment?
6 Do you think that environmental concerns provide too much pressure on the way organisations operate today?

Our environment is everything that surrounds us – where we live, the people we know, the living and non-living things around us:

Environment to each must be,
All that is, that isn't me.

All living things have four vital needs:

- Sun
- Air
- Earth
- Water

Plants and animals have been on this planet for millions of years. For 40 000 years they have shared it with humankind. In the last few decades, however, we have begun to destroy this world by damaging the balance of our four vital needs.

- We damage the balance of sunlight by making holes in the ozone layer.
- We fill the air with harmful gases.
- We put acid into the rain.
- We poison the earth with chemicals.

Everything we do to our environment affects us and every other thing which shares this world with us.

The surge of environmental awareness reinforced by pressure groups and political and media activity has resulted in an important cultural shift – environmental concern has joined other commonly held values. It is a shift that organisations cannot escape.

The environmental challenges to industry are now well established. First, there is regulation. The word regulation means setting down official rules, for example by government laws. Regulation can be seen as a relatively quick and visible way of changing industries' behaviour. In the UK, the Environmental Protection Act – and specifically 'integrated pollution control' – has changed the basis of pollution regulation. Membership of the European Community also forces the UK to adopt Community standards.

Perhaps most effective is consumer pressure. More consumers are looking for products that are 'ecologically friendly'. There is also investor pressure – those who provide finance for businesses are increasingly questioning the environmental soundness of their investments.

From inside there is employee pressure. People who are concerned citizens at home do not become environmentally irresponsible when they arrive at work. Management pressure is also very important. For example, the Advisory Committee on Business and the Environment, set up to help thrash out environmental issues with the government, is made up of senior managers from major companies.

The Environmental Protection Act of 1990 created two new systems for regulating industrial pollution. Integrated pollution control (IPC) applies to more than 5000 existing industrial processes with the largest pollution potential. It regulates all their releases to land, water and air. It is enforced by an Inspectorate of Pollution. The second system is enforced by local authorities and covers 27 000 complex processes, controlling only emissions to the air. Under both systems operators have to employ the 'best available techniques not entailing excessive cost', to minimise releases of the most polluting substances, and to 'render harmless' all releases from their processes.

IPC extends the sorts of control previously applied only to air pollutants to all the wastes – gases, solids and liquids – generated by companies. The Inspectorate ensures that 'the best practicable environmental option' (or Bpeo) is chosen to deal with these.

Task

Obtain some petroleum jelly, available from a chemist's shop if you do not have any at home. Take six stiff white cards and smear them with some of the jelly. Place the cards in a variety of places – some where you would expect the air to be clean (perhaps in a tree) and some where it is dirty (maybe near a busy street). Leave the cards in place for a few days and then collect them. Write down the signs of pollution you found and what they appeared to be from.

Develop a proposal for reducing some of these pollutants. Try to make your proposals fit in with the notion of being the best practicable environmental option (Bpeo).

There can be no doubt that we must all play a responsible part in preventing or reducing pollution. Individuals and organisations can work to control the pollution they cause.

An essential starting point is an awareness of pollution and its causes.

Water pollution

Much water pollution comes from factories, which take fresh water in from a river, use it in a manufacturing process, and then discharge it back into the river. The discharge often contains chemicals and oils which kill fish and other living things in their food chain. Other causes of water pollution are agricultural waste and chemicals which seep through the soil into rivers and lakes.

Oil is a potent pollutant. In March 1989, the ship the *Exxon Valdez* poured more than 10 million gallons of oil into Prince William Sound in Alaska, following which millions of fish and birds died. When seabirds dive through oily waters the oil sticks to their feathers, which then can no longer keep out the cold and wet. The birds die if the oil is not cleaned off.

Air pollution

As yet, we have not been able to harvest the forces of wind, sun or water to meet all our energy needs, and we will probably continue using coal, oil and gas for many more years. These are responsible for much air pollution. Power stations burning coal or oil pour dangerous sulphur dioxide into the air. Car and lorry exhausts add nitrogen oxide. To produce one unit of electricity, a power station sends into the air ten grams of sulphur, three grams of nitrogen oxide and a kilogram of carbon dioxide (one kilogram of carbon dioxide is enough to fill 20 balloons).

Task

Check your electricity bill at home and find out how many units of electricity your family uses in a day.

Multiply your units by the amounts of pollution given in the text to discover how much your family adds to air pollution from your use of electrical power alone. This work can help your provide evidence of Core Skills in Application of Number.

Noise pollution

Noise is experienced when the ear picks up unwanted vibrations, most of which come from machinery of some kind. At its most intense – for example, a jet plane taking off – noise can cause actual physical pain.

New roads can bring the nuisance of traffic noise into people's homes, often in areas which previously enjoyed peace and quiet. New road developments to carry freight to and from the Channel Tunnel are a case in point.

Noise is particularly annoying at night, when it can interrupt sleep. There is nothing new in this. In the times of the Roman Empire the capital's residents complained so vigorously about the disturbance caused by cart traffic that the Emperor Augustus put a ban on all carts leaving or entering Rome at night!

Case study – Public concern about the environment

The public's attitude towards the environment is a key influence on organisational activity. Opinion polls suggest that most people's concern for the environment is fickle and strongly influenced by media coverage.

When times are good and the economy is growing, people worry about the fate of the planet and that of future generations. When recession bites, these concerns tend to be pushed aside by more immediate concerns about personal security. However, polls do indicate that a substantial proportion of the population – about a fifth – have had their environmental consciousness raised permanently.

For example, once a month for a number of years MORI has been asking the public: 'What would you say is the most important issue facing Britain today' and 'What do you see as other important issues?' In the late 1980s the environment appeared high on the public's agenda of concerns.

MORI has also been asking people whether they have done any of the 12 'green activities' in the last year or two. These include walking in the countryside, buying 'green' products in supermarkets, joining an environmental group and writing letters on environmental issues to MPs and the newspapers. Those who answer 'yes' to five or more of these activities are counted as environmental activists. The percentage of those rose from 14 in 1988 to 31 in 1991 (Figure 2.14 opposite).

1 What conclusions would you draw from the bar-chart?
2 Do you feel that raised environmental awareness is likely to be a short-term or long-term trend?
3 What are the implications for organisational activities?

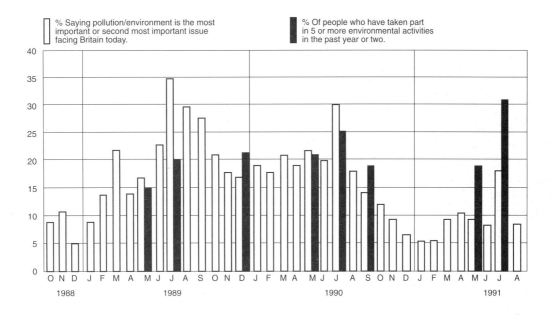

Figure 2.14 Concern for the environment – results of a MORI poll

4 Design an action plan for your organisation to improve its environmental consciousness.

5 Carry out a market research survey along the lines set out by the MORI survey. Do your findings coincide with the MORI findings? Explain your results and compare them with the MORI survey. This task could provide evidence of Core Skills in Communication.

Effects on health

The social costs of business activity can have a detrimental effect on health. An example of this which has received a lot of publicity has been the use of asbestos in the building industry. Today asbestos is rarely used but there are many buildings dating from the 1960s and beyond which have a lot of asbestos in them. Employees working in the building industry over the years have often been exposed to asbestos, resulting in cancers and other asbestos-related diseases. At the time when asbestos was used widely it was seen as being a cheap and efficient building material. It was only later that the full social cost implications were realised.

 Evidence collection point

The World Bank's World Development Report published in 1992 identified the environmental problems in the table as

Problem	Effect on health	Effect in my locality
Water pollution and water scarcity	More than 2 million deaths and billions of illnesses result from pollution; poor hygiene resulting from water scarcity	
Air pollution	Many acute and chronic health impacts; in urban areas particles in the air lead to 300 000–700 000 premature deaths a year, increased incidence of asthma and breathing difficulties	
Solid and hazardous wastes	Disease spread by rotting garbage and blocked drains	
Soil degradation	Reduces nutrition for poor farmers on poor soils; increased chance of drought	
Deforestation	Localised flooding	
Loss of bio-diversity	Potential loss of new drugs developed from natural resources	
Atmospheric changes	Diseases resulting from ozone depletion	

having an impact on health. Try to identify ways in which each of these problems has had an impact on health in your locality.

Effects of employment

Another consequence of market activity is the creation and destruction of employment. There are more people working in the United Kingdom today than ever before as a consequence of the rise in population. However, at the same time, the sorts of skills required are constantly changing.

Many jobs have been lost in agriculture and mining. The manufacturing base of the United Kingdom has been steadily declining for a long time. In the 1950s exports of manufactured goods were three times the quantity of imports. Today we import more manufactured goods than we export. Some of the factors that have been used to account for this deterioration include low quality and over-concentration on low-value products which many other countries now also produce.

Unemployment can be seen as a consequence of the failure of business to keep up-to-date. In a survey of products developed in the latter half of the twentieth century, Japan's Ministry of International Trade and Industry (MITI) found that Britons were responsible for 52% of what were termed 'revolutionary' ideas; the Americans produced 22% while the Japanese produced only 6%. But when it came to product development, this order was reversed. A number of UK commentators have pointed out that industry is not spending enough on the research and development required to bring new products and processes to market.

A contrasting view of modern unemployment is that it is a consequence of new technologies. A recent report by the West German Kommerzbank estimated that every robot employed in industry today replaces on average five workers, and that today 'intelligent robots' can replace at least ten workers in many assembly jobs.

What is evident is that the world of full employment is a thing of the past. In today's modern marketplace there is no scope for subsidised labour. International competition is very intense and even the most skilled and flexible employees are not guaranteed work any more. Employees need to be multiskilled, adaptable and prepared to work hard.

Evidence collection point

Examine two firms in your locality which have recently shed labour as a result of market forces, perhaps because there is no longer such a high demand for the products of those firms, or because other products are able to supply products more cheaply.

Uncertain unemployment conditions can lead to considerable levels of insecurity both for those in work and those who are unemployed. A survey published in *Personnel Today* in 1995 showed that in the 1990s many people are working longer hours. For example, white collar workers (office workers, junior managers, etc.) were working between 41 and 43 hours a week. Many managers work longer. Two out of five are putting in more than 50 hours and one in eight more than 60 hours. A survey by the National Association of Teachers in Further and Higher Education showed that heads of departments in colleges worked on average 55 hours. A catering company, Compass, published a survey in January 1995 showing that the lunch-hour is a thing of the past, the average time now taken being half an hour. Britain is recognised as having the longest working week in Europe.

Days lost from stress-related illness have increased from 37 million a year in the 1980s to 230 million a year in the mid-1990s. Heart attacks are on the increase, as are depression, anxiety, irritability and accidents in the workplace. People may overwork because there is more competition for fewer promotions, as a result of so many grades disappearing.

The social benefits of market operations

The marketplace generates wealth and income for people.

Wealth is the sum total of all the ingredients we have come to value as necessary for our material wellbeing. Comfortable houses, efficient transport, hospitals, health care and education to enable us to achieve our full potential – all these contribute to wellbeing. So everyone concerned in market processes is helping to create our wealth.

Income is the flow of new earnings which take place in a particular period of time. For example, if my salary was £20 000 this year, and I earned no other money, it would constitute my income.

Industry reacts to people's changing demands and produces the products that consumers are prepared to buy. Sometimes industry creates new demands by developing new products and then introducing them to the market. However, product development needs to go hand in hand with marketing activities.

Some new products are in advance of their time. Innovators develop these goods or services before introducing them to the wider public. For instance, the mass market did not know that it wanted a microwave oven. The product had first to be invented, then tested, test-marketed and researched. Finally, it was launched to a wide audience. Eventually it became a huge success.

Effects of employment

Millions of people are employed in industry and commerce. Some of them are doing enjoyable, creative work, while others are in boring, unimaginative environments where work is a burden rather than a pleasure. By creating employment the market also generates income:

■ shareholders receive profits
■ employees receive wages
■ lenders receive interest.

Market activity leads to rising living standards. Materially, most people are better off today than ever before. Figure 2.15 shows that real disposable income (i.e. the income that remains in your pockets after taxes and other deductions) has risen considerably between 1971 and 1991. The load of sliced white bread that could be paid for with 9 minutes' work in 1971 required only 5 minutes' work in 1991.

Investment

One of the most important factors of production is capital, i.e. the machinery and equipment that goes into making goods.

Buying capital is termed investment. Investment

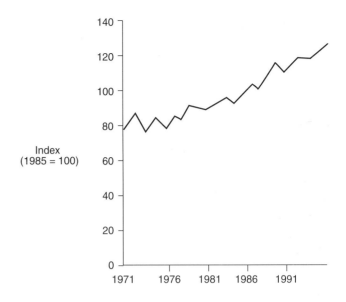

Figure 2.15 Real disposable household income for a married couple with only the husband working (1971–1995)

is thus a highly important activity. The more investment there is, the greater the number of goods that can be produced in the future.

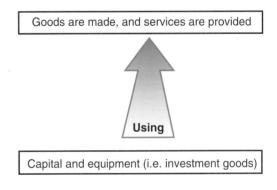

Figure 2.16 Use of capital for goods and services

In order to purchase capital and equipment, businesses will need investment funds. Some of these funds will come from the business owners' own savings or from ploughing back profits into a business. Other important sources of funds will include borrowing, e.g. from banks, and from the selling of shares to shareholders who become part owners in a company (Figure 2.17).

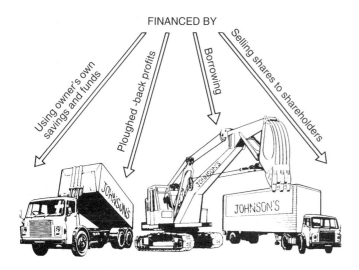

FINANCED BY

Using owner's own savings and funds

Ploughed-back profits

Borrowing

Selling shares to shareholders

Figure 2.17 Financing capital investment

Market operations create the investment process. Buyers express their wants and needs through demand. Suppliers are able to respond by making good with capital and equipment. Suppliers are able to get funds for investment by borrowing money from private individuals, banks and other financial institutions. These groups and individuals are prepared to lend money because they receive interest for lending money out, and receiving dividends (i.e. a share of the profits) if they have bought shares in companies.

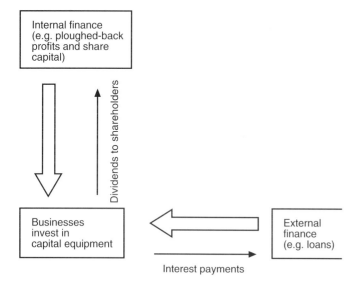

Figure 2.18 The investment process

Training

Another important benefit of market operations is that they lead to the training of employees. Just as organisations will invest in capital equipment, so too will they invest in the human resource. The more skilled, knowledgeable and capable the workforce, the better they will be able to contribute to production. The incentive to the employer is that having a high-class labour force will enable the company to produce high-class products at a competitive price. The market mechanisms can thus be seen as a driving force to ensure adequate training.

Individuals benefit from such a system in that it leads to them being more effective and employable members of the workforce.

Other benefits of the market system are that it creates the sorts of products that consumers want and that industrial activity and the resulting technological innovations can mean that people have more labour-saving machines and therefore more free time on their hands.

Hospitals, schools, museums and many welfare functions which we have come to take for granted are all supported by the wealth created by businesses in the public and private sectors of the economy.

The great benefit of a market economy is that it responds to the wishes and needs of consumers. Over the course of time consumers indicate by their purchases their preferences to suppliers, who are thus forced to change their practices.

Case study – Sweets disappearing from check-outs

In the mid-1990s we have seen a turnaround in the approach to selling sweets employed by the large supermarket chains in response to consumer pressure. Many customers did not like the supermarkets' practice of placing displays of sweets at check-outs.

The results of a survey by the 'Chuck Sweets off the Check-out' campaign, an alliance of health professionals founded in 1992, were published in January 1995. It covered 6200 check-outs in more than 600 stores.

The survey places Sainsbury's and Waitrose at the top, with 100% of check-outs sweet-free. Only those

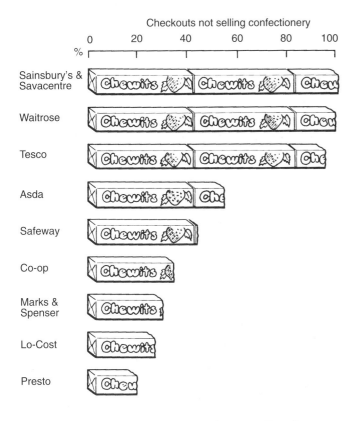

Checkouts not selling confectionery

| | 0 | 20 | 40 | 60 | 80 | 100 |

Sainsbury's & Savacentre

Waitrose

Tesco

Asda

Safeway

Co-op

Marks & Spencer

Lo-Cost

Presto

two and Tesco had such a check-out policy; but some Tesco counters still had sweets on them.

Of the other big stores Safeway has announced it will remove sweets from check-outs because of the 'hassle' the practice causes with young children. However, only 44% of its check-outs were found to be sweet-free.

Presto, owned by Safeway, has no policy and only 19% of its check-outs did not sell confectionery.

Marks and Spencer also comes near the bottom of the table.

The campaign, backed by organisations including the British Dental and Medical Association, argues that dental disease is the most widespread UK disease and that 'pester power' is a key factor in the purchase and consumption of sweets.

A survey commissioned by the campaign from Gallup found overwhelming support from parents. Eighty-seven per cent of mothers and 74% of fathers are against check-out sweet displays.

1 Why do you think that big stores originally stocked sweets near the check-outs?

2 Why do they appear to be reversing this policy?
3 What does this case study tell you about the social costs and benefits of business activity?
4 What does this case study tell you about the way in which market operations can be influenced by consumer pressure?

Evidence indicators

Produce a report setting out a comparative study of two different markets (e.g. the supply of tabloid newspapers/the supply of an exclusive magazine, the supply of computer software/ household gas, the supply of contraceptives/ hairdressing, the supply of petrol on a motorway/in a busy urban area.

The important thing is that you compare and contrast two markets, one which is competitive and the other which is relatively uncompetitive.

The following list should serve as a checklist. Please tick off each of the following when you have successfully covered them as part of your report. You need to be able to confirm that:

■ I have compared the numbers of suppliers in the markets.
■ I have shown the size of the suppliers and the strength of demand in the markets.
■ I have compared competition between two businesses in one market showing shifts in demand curves and explaining why these have occurred.
■ I have described how competition can have an effect on consumers' choice and the quality of products.
■ I have compared the behaviour of two businesses in two different types of market showing their use of both pricing and non-pricing strategies to improve market position.
■ I have focused on activities undertaken by two businesses in order to show the social costs and benefits to the wider community (e.g. the siting of a new factory, the closing down of a plant, the creation of new jobs).

Chapter 3

The effects of governments on markets

 This chapter considers the impact of government intervention on markets and how this affects businesses. It does not include the whole spectrum of government economic policy. However, students should build on their experiences and observations of government intervening in markets to understand the behaviour of markets and some of the consequences of government policies.

The chapter will look at:

- the reasons for government interventions in markets
- the means by which governments can influence markets
- the effects on markets of some UK government policies and European Union policies

The reasons for government intervention in markets

In the nineteenth century the UK government played only a small part in the control of the economy. Today, the proper role of the government is open to debate, but most people accept that it should at least try to influence economic activity. Why has this change in attitude taken place? We shall look at some of the more important reasons.

Widespread unemployment in the 1920s and 1930s

In some towns in the 1920s, over half of the potential labour force were unemployed. Many people felt in the light of the terrible suffering during this period that the government should play a central role in creating and sustaining employment.

Rapid inflation in the 1970s

The 1970s was a period of rapid increases in prices. People felt the effects of inflation in different ways,

depending amongst other things on how much power they had to raise their own incomes to cope with price rises.

The general effect of price rises is to distort the working of the price system. Trading ideally needs to take place in settled conditions. If you expected to be paid £100 in three months' time you would be very disappointed if you found that when you received payment you could only purchase half of the goods that you would have been able to obtain today.

If people become reluctant to trade, then fewer goods will be produced for sale. If fewer goods are made, fewer people are employed in production. Price disturbances can therefore cause the whole economy to stagnate.

The Citizen's Charter

Many industries previously owned by the government – such as telecommunications, fuel and power – have been privatised (sold to shareholders). Other industries, such as rail and coal, may be privatised in the future.

Services such as health and education operate in the 1990s far more on the basis of local management. This means that local managers (such as headteachers and school governing bodies) are responsible for setting and spending their own budgets. In this way they can use resources effectively in their own areas.

However, the government still continues to play the major role by providing funds from taxes and other sources – government spending still accounts for nearly half of all spending in the country.

The other side of this story is that there is far more emphasis on public accountability. Local managers need to be able to show how they are spending their funds. They need to manage their budgets wisely. Citizens are to be given far more right to complain. For example, under the government's Citizen's Charter, rail users will be entitled to refunds of their fares if trains fail to run on time, and motorway contractors can be fined for coning off sections of road when no work is taking place.

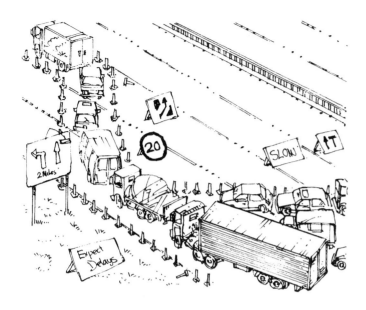

The way governments are chosen and operate

This section provides you with an introduction to the way governments are chosen and operate in the UK. It is important to have this sort of background before going on to look more closely at the reasons for government intervention in markets and the means by which governments can influence markets.

The electoral system

In the United Kingdom citizens are able to choose people to represent them at a number of levels.

At a national level they can choose Members of Parliament. MPs represent people who live in a particular area (a constituency). Who is your local MP? What is your local constituency? What political party does your local MP belong to?

At a European Union level, electors can choose Euro-MPs. The European Parliament is one of the three major Union institutions. It is the only directly elected institution, so it is particularly important that all European citizens exercise their right to vote. The Maastricht Treaty has given the European Parliament more powers, as we shall see later. Who is your Euro-MP? What party does he or she belong to? What is your Euro-constituency?

At a local level you can vote for local councillors. The local council is concerned with affairs in your

locality. What is your local council area? Who is your local councillor? What party does he or she belong to?

The electoral system for national government

In the British electoral system the country is divided into 651 single-member constituencies. Representatives are elected to Parliament by the first-past-the-post (simple majority) method, which awards seats in the House of Commons to candidates with the largest number of votes in each constituency. The boundaries of the constituencies are reviewed every 10-15 years to take account of population movements or other changes.

Under this system the strongest party in the House of Commons may have an absolute majority of seats despite having less than an absolute majority of votes. The system is generally considered to favour two-party competition, especially between parties whose support is concentrated geographically, and to discriminate against parties with support spread across constituencies. For example, the Liberal Democrats currently have a lot of support spread across the country, but only in parts of the West Country do they have the majority of voters behind them. The Labour Party is currently popular in inner London, the North East and North West. The Conservative Party has the bulk of the support in the South of England and in rural areas.

Forming a government

The party which wins most seats at a general election, or which has the support of a majority of members in the House of Commons, is usually invited by the Sovereign to form a government. The party with the next largest number of seats is officially recognised as 'Her Majesty's Opposition' and has its own leader (who is paid a salary from public funds) and its own 'shadow Cabinet'. Members of both parties, or any independent MPs who have been elected, support or oppose the government according to their party or their own view of the policy being debated at any given time. Because the official Opposition is a minority party, it seldom succeeds in introducing or changing legislation. However, its statements and policies are important, since it is considered to be a potential government – and would become so if successful at the next general election.

The law

Parliament is responsible for creating new laws. These can affect the ways in which markets operate in many ways, and so can also affect businesses. If the government raises income tax, for example, people have less money to spend, which affects sales. Government actions bring into play a wide range of changes to taxes – these changes then become law through a Finance Bill, which becomes an Act of Parliament (a new law).

Over the years a complex system of laws has developed. Some laws have not come from Parliament but have arisen through common practice. It is often impossible to find out when these laws first came into being (this is called 'common law'). An example is the right of people to walk on a particular village green. Other laws are new laws that are passed by Parliament (this is called 'statute law').

The law courts play an important role in protecting the rights of individuals and groups. When the law of the land has been broken cases are taken to the criminal courts, whereas when there is a disagreement between groups or individuals the case may be taken before a civil court.

Task

Which of the following would be taken to a criminal court and which to a civil court?

1 A firm catches one of its employees stealing the firm's property.
2 A firm is taken to court for making its employees work longer than the national legal limit.
3 A newspaper prints an inaccurate and defamatory story about the managing director of a major company.
4 A consumer buys a product which fails to meet the standard claimed in advertising.
5 A farmer claims that when a neighbour dams a river it is cutting off his water supply.
6 An employee who is sacked by his employer claims that he has not received sufficient compensation.
7 Two publishers produce books with the same title and with similar covers.

Government involvement in the marketplace

In this section we look at reasons why government involves itself in ensuring competitive conditions in the marketplace.

To increase competition

Competition is seen by many as a major driving force behind the market system. Competition between producers in the marketplace keeps prices down and ensures that goods are produced in line with consumer requirements. If a baker tried to charge more than competitors, trade would disappear; or if employees asked for more than the going wage, they would not be able to find work. If

landlords sought to exact a higher rent than others with property of the same quality they would get no tenants.

Government should ensure that competition can take place freely between competitors. The more competition the better, because this will lead to better quality products and lower prices, and acts as an incentive for producers to be better than their rivals.

To regulate competition

Whilst many people argue that competition is a good thing, they might also argue that there need to be guidelines and rules within which the competitive framework can operate. For example, whilst it may be beneficial to encourage competition between taxi firms, it is essential that they abide by health and safety regulations, e.g. concerning the number of people allowed in a cab at any one time, or the maximum length of time that a driver can drive without having a break.

National government and EU regulations provide a framework for competition in many markets. For example, while recent EU policies have encouraged competition between airlines on European routes, there are given standards which airlines must meet before they are allowed to carry passengers.

In recent years we have seen an increase in competition in industries such as gas, water and electricity. Regulators have been appointed to oversee the way in which new companies operate in these markets.

The large City of London markets like Lloyd's of London and the Stock Exchange need to be carefully regulated to ensure that fair trading practices are in operation.

To counteract anti-competitive activities

Anti-competitive activities come in a variety of forms. Examples include:

- Firms jointly agreeing to fix prices.
- Firms jointly agreeing who they will be prepared to supply goods and services to.
- Selling goods at one price to a particular group of customers, and at a higher price to another group.
- Limiting supply in order to raise price.
- Forcing rivals out of business by ensuring that their supplies are cut off.

All of these practices and many others involve the abuse of power in the marketplace and run counter to the principles of competition.

To ensure fair and honest trading

In business dealings it is important that all transactions are carried out in a fair and honest manner. Parties to bargains need to be clear about what they are committing themselves to and the consequences of making a deal or exchange. The government is responsible for establishing the legal framework within which trade takes place.

To protect consumers

Any product or services that it provided to the marketplace must meet certain standards. Some of these standards are established by law, some by voluntary codes of practice within an industry, and others by individual businesses.

Before the 1960s, consumers had very little protection under the law. They had to rely on their own common sense. The Latin expression *caveat emptor* – 'let the buyer beware' – applied. Businesses supply goods or services for consumers in return for payment. The legal system exists to provide a framework within which transactions can take place, and to provide a means of settling disputes. Large or well-developed organisations often deal with relatively small consumers, so there is a need for the law to make sure that this inequality in bargaining power is not abused.

 Evidence collection point

In which of the following instances might the government be expected to intervene to increase competition, to encourage fair trading, or to protect consumers? Explain why the government is likely to be involved.

1 A supplier agrees to provide a retailer with a given product for three months at a set price.
2 Suppliers agree to stop supplying a particular retailer who is cutting prices below those of other retailers.
3 Textile businesses engaged in cut-throat competition start employing child labour at very low wage rates.
4 Electrical suppliers sell cheaply produced, faulty goods to buyers.
5 Market traders use weighing scales they have designed themselves to measure out quantities of fruit and vegetables.

6 One firm is the sole supplier of goods in a considerable area of the country.

7 Two firms agree to split up a region so that one firm will sell goods in half of the towns and the other will sell in the other half.

To protect environmental and social interests

In recent times we have become increasingly conscious of our shared responsibilities for the environment. Gro Brundtland (*Our Common Future*, 1987) defined sustainability as 'development which meets the need of the present without compromising the ability of future generations to meet their own needs'. In *The Pearce Report*, David Pearce argued that 'sustainability ought to mean that a given stock of natural resources – trees, soil quality, water and so on – should not decline.' Many people believe that, left to its own drives and forces, the market might fail to take account of the need for sustainability. For example, businesses and individuals in pursuit of their own private ends may exploit resources too quickly. A famous quotation from Mahatma Gandhi (*Young India*) is relevant here:

> God forbid that India should ever take to industrialisation after the manner of the West. The economic imperialism of a single tiny island kingdom (Britain) is today keeping the world in chains. If an entire nation of 300 million took to similar economic exploitation, it would strip the world bare like locusts.

Government therefore has a key role to play in helping the market to create a sustainable future by taking measures to protect the environment as well as to look after social interests such as protecting the poor and needy from exploitation by the powerful.

Case study – Asthma: a growing epidemic

Scientists are now convinced that gas emitted from car exhaust exacerbates asthma, which has now hit one in every seven children in Britain. This neglected epidemic puts 100 000 people a year in hospital. It is now the greatest single cause of hospital admissions after heart disease and stroke, killing more than 2000 people a year. It is the only treatable chronic disease to be advancing in Western countries.

Britain has the worst record for monitoring nitrogen dioxide pollution in Europe. It has only seven official monitoring stations throughout the country. The EU directive controlling pollution lays down that the stations should be sited 'where nitrogen dioxide concentrations are likely to be among the highest, particularly "canyon" streets, carrying heavy traffic, and major intersections'.

1 To what extent is the market responsible for pollution?

2 Left to itself, is the market likely to provide solutions to this problem?

3 To what extent should the government intervene to limit or prevent pollution?

To stimulate consumer demand

Aggregate demand is the total level of demand in the whole economy. Aggregate demand is made up of:

■ demand by consumers for goods and services (call this C)

■ demand by producers for goods that go into further production (call this I, for investment demand)

■ government demand for goods and services (call this G)

Furthermore, we need to add the demand from foreigners for our goods and services (exports, X) and subtract the demand (M) by our citizens for foreign goods and services, because money leaves the country. A useful measure of aggregate money demand is therefore:

$$\text{Aggregate money demand} = C + I + G + X - M$$

Figure 3.1 (opposite) shows that aggregate demand is made up of demand from many sources.

We have said that the amount people spend in an economy will be received by the providers of goods and services. If we want to be absolutely accurate, however, we should also account for indirect taxes and subsidies.

If you buy a packet of sandwiches in a bakery the owner of the bakery will not be able to use all of this money in his or her business. Some of this revenue will be paid over to the government in VAT (value added tax) and other indirect taxes. When measuring aggregate money demand, therefore, we should subtract indirect taxes. Furthermore, some sellers will receive more than the sales price of their goods, probably as a result of government subsidies. A subsidy should therefore be seen as an addition to consumer demand, provided by the government. A more comprehensive definition of aggregate money demand (AMD) is therefore:

$$\text{AMD} = C + I + G + X - M - \text{indirect taxes} + \text{subsidies}$$

Aggregate monetary demand goes into purchasing all

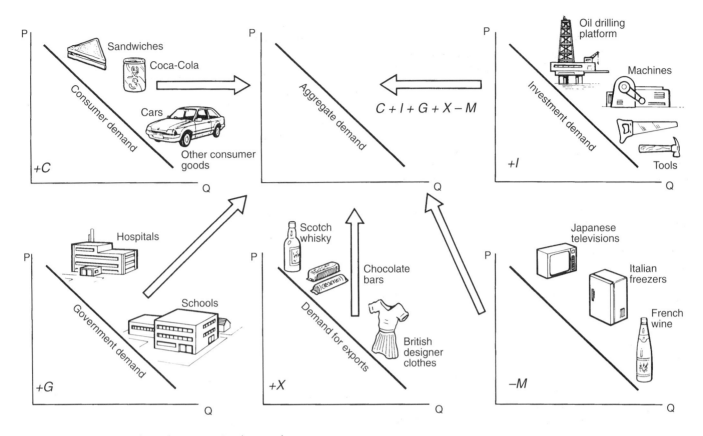

Figure 3.1 Examples of aggregate demand

the goods produced in a country, i.e. the national output. National output is another way of describing total supply (aggregate monetary supply).

When aggregate monetary demand (AMD) in the economy equals aggregate monetary supply (AMS), the economy is in temporary equilibrium (i.e. there is no reason why change in demand or supply

should take place). If this state of equilibrium remains then prices will remain steady, and so too will the level of production (Figure 3.2).

However, in the real world economic forces are continually changing. Conditions of aggregate demand and supply frequently alter, and economies tend to go through a trade cycle (Figure 3.3).

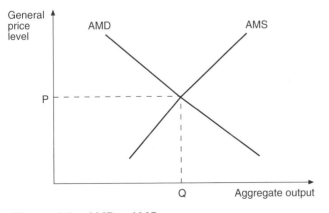

Figure 3.2 AMD = AMS

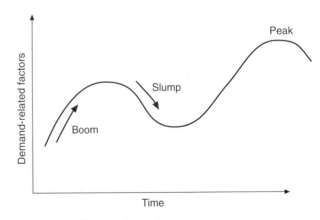

Figure 3.3 The trade cycle

For a few years demand increases, prices start to rise and unemployment falls. This is followed by a period of recession when prices fall and unemployment increases again.

During a boom, a number of economic indicators related to demand all tend to increase. The main indicators are:

- production
- employment
- sales
- interest rates
- investment

During a recession these indicators fall.

Evidence collection point

1 Explain how each of the following would add to or reduce aggregate monetary demand in this country:

- Consumers' demand
- Investment demand
- Imports
- Exports
- Government spending

2 Explain the difference between a recession and an upturn in economic activity.

Governments can play a major role in stimulating demand in the economy. The problem is that once a recession starts it tends to be self-perpetuating over two or three years (and sometimes longer).

Once demand falls from a peak, business people begin to get pessimistic about the future, and start to make cutbacks in production. Because they are making cutbacks in production they will invest less in capital equipment. This means that people earn less and spend less. The whole process is a vicious circle.

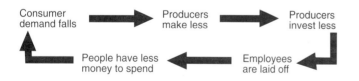

Figure 3.4 The vicious circle of recession

A small fall in consumer demand can therefore lead to a much bigger overall change in incomes and spending. We call this a 'multiplier effect', because the original fall in demand is multiplied. For example, if consumers reduce spending by £1m and this leads eventually to an overall fall in demand of £3m, we can see that the multiplier is 3.

$$\text{Multiplier} = \frac{\text{Overall change in demand}}{\text{Original change in demand}} = \frac{£3m}{£1m} = 3$$

We can illustrate the multiplier effect in a town of city with a large college or university. When students arrive in October with plenty of spending money, the economy begins to boom, Shops, cafés and bookshops take on more part-time staff, who receive wages for their work. These wages are then spent in the town or city and the multiplier effect continues. The original increase in spending by students is multiplied around the local economy. However, in the summer holidays, the reverse happens as students leave town and lots of part-time jobs disappear, leading to a localised recession.

The government operates in an environment in which the economy goes through a cycle of recession and recovery. It plays a major role in trying to ensure that a recession does not lead to a slump, i.e. falls in national output. The government therefore may want to take measures to stimulate demand when demand in the country is falling.

To improve levels of employment

For approximately 20 years prior to the Second World War, unemployment had averaged at least

10%. The war effort fully employed all our resources and in 1944 the government published a White Paper pledging the maintenance of full employment after the war.

The will to provide this was matched by the means as stated in the White Paper:

> The government accepts as one of their primary aims and responsibilities the maintenance of a high and stable level of employment after the war ... total expenditure must be prevented from falling to a level where general unemployment appears.

For the next 25 years, unemployment averaged only 1.8%. However, a major concern over the policy of maintaining full employment was that it was accompanied by inflation. When the Conservative government came to power in 1979 they placed a lot of emphasis on trying to cut back on price increases.

In recent years we have seen the resurgence of high unemployment, so that the 1990s have been characterised by unemployment at well over 2 million people in this country. Today unemployment is a problem confronting most industrialised countries.

When we look in detail at unemployment figures we are presented with some interesting findings. For example:

- Unskilled and semi-skilled manufacturing workers are twice as likely to be unemployed as skilled manual workers.
- Manual workers on the whole are twice as likely as non-manual workers to be unemployed For example, in 1991 unemployment for the latter stood as 3.1% compared with 16.3% for general labourers.
- For the 50+ age group in 1992, 39% of those unemployed had been out of work for over a year, compared with 24% for 18–25 year olds.

There is always considerable disagreement over the exact number of unemployed people in the UK at any time, because only those receiving state benefits and registered for work are counted in the official statistics. This misses out some married women who, if their husbands are working, cannot receive benefit. People on various training schemes are also not included, nor are men over 60 who have been unemployed for a long time. The unemployment figures therefore depend on the way they are collected.

There are many explanations of how unemployment is caused. One cause of unemployment may be downswings in the trade cycle, i.e. periods of recession. In a period of recession, with a downward multiplier, spending, income, outputs and thus employment will all fall. The term 'cyclical unemployment' is used to describe unemployment resulting from downturns in the trade cycle.

Another explanation of wide-scale unemployment refers to structural unemployment. Structural unemployment arises from longer-term changes in the economy, affecting specific industries, regions and occupations. For example, the coal industry in regions such as Central Scotland, South Yorkshire, the East Midlands, etc. has been in decline for a number of years because of the development of new substitute fuels such as gas, oil and electricity, and the importing of cheap coal from Australia, Nigeria, Russia and other places.

The result of these changes is demand for products like coal, steel, shipbuilding, textiles, shoes, etc. leads to structural unemployment as old industries decline. The effects of structural unemployment would be reduced if people moved away from declining industries and areas and into new, expanding areas. However, these changes do not occur smoothly so the economy suffers from 'structural problems' and hence 'structural unemployment' is a major cause of unemployment.

Other people argue that new technology is a cause of unemployment, i.e. technological unemployment. The argument is that the introduction of new technology is destroying jobs and trade while at the same time imports from low-wage developing countries are undercutting goods produced in this country.

However, a number of studies contradict this. For example, the *OECD Job Study* (June, 1994) argued that 'history has shown that when technological progress accelerates, so do growth, living standards and employment.'

New technology generates new products, new services and therefore new jobs. Fewer workers may be required in some production processes where specific tasks are taken over, but rising productivity boosts incomes and the demand for new jobs in the economy as a whole.

The above arguments indicate that there are considerable differences in opinion about the causes of unemployment. However, it is apparent that the government has a major role to play in ensuring that unemployment does not rise above 'acceptable' levels. But what those levels are is a subject for debate.

Evidence collection point

Look at the following views about unemployment. What arguments would you put forward to support or oppose the views shown?

To control inflation

Unemployment and inflation are economic problems which have repercussions for a large number of individuals and organisations. When unemployment is at a high level, the population as a whole has less money to spend, and this affects many firms and industries. In a period of inflation, rising prices are likely to affect everybody in one way or another.

Inflation is measured in several different ways. To the government, inflation means a general increase in the level of prices. Statistics use the retail price index (RPI), which is an average of price changes and shows the general change over a period of time. Some items in the index will rise, some will remain the same and others will fail.

The RPI is very useful in picking out general changes in inflation.

Evidence collection point

Figure 3.5 shows inflation trends since 1959. Briefly describe the trends that you can see. Which periods do you think would have caused the most concern to governments? What problems would inflation in these periods be likely to have caused in the economy?

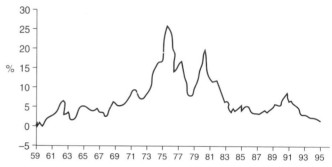

Underlying inflation in UK 1959–1995

Figure 3.5 Inflation 1959–1995

The Retail Price Index is calculated in the following way. About 7000 households throughout the UK keep a record of all their spending over a two-week period. This gives a picture of the 'typical items' bought by an 'average household'. The items are recorded in the index. Each month, government officers make a record of about 150 000 prices of some 350 different items up and down the country. The average price of each of these items is calculated.

Using these data the average inflation rate can be calculated. Each individual price change is given a 'weight' which depends on how important it is in the typical household's spending pattern. For example, food makes up about one-fifth of a typical household's spending, so that a 10% rise in the price of food would raise average prices by one-fifth of this – 2%.

Price changes are measured over a definite period of time so that it is possible to compare the changes from one period to another. The choice of a starting

(or 'base') date for an index is important, the aim being to choose a time which is 'normal' – that is, when nothing abnormal or unusual is happening.

The base date is given an index up to 100. We can then say, for example, that if in 1985 the RPI stood at 100 and today it is 350, prices on average have risen three and a half times over that time period.

Suppose in an imaginary country, Averageland, the family Average spend half their income on food, a quarter on clothing and the remaining quarter on entertainment. We can give these items 'weightings' out of 10: food 5, clothing 2.5, entertainment 2.5. In 1985 (the base year) food cost on average £1 per unit, clothing £5 per unit, and entertainment £2 per unit. In 1990, food in Averageland cost £5 per unit, clothing £7.50 per unit, and entertainment £3 per unit. We can analyse these changes in prices as follows:

	Original index	New index	Expenditure weighting	New index × weighting
Food	100	200	5	1000
Clothing	100	150	2.5	375
Entertainment	100	150	2.5	375

The total of the last column is 1750. In order to find out the new RPI in Averageland we must divide this total by the total number of weights (10), so:

$$\text{New RPI} = \frac{1750}{10} = 175$$

This shows that, on average, prices rose by 75%. Food doubled in price, while the other two items increased by one and a half times. Food was the most significant item in the index because the Average family spends as much on food as on clothing and entertainment combined.

Task

1 In Redland, the average consumer spends seven-tenths of his or her income on wine, two-tenths on bread and one-tenth on cheese. In 1993 (the base year) the price of all these items was £1 per unit. In 1996 wine has fallen to 50p per unit, bread has gone up to £2 per unit and cheese has risen to £4 per unit.
  a What is the new index for 1996?
  b Has it risen, fallen or remained the same?
  c Give at least three reasons why the weighting may need to be altered in 1996.
2 In Blueland, the public buy four items – eggs, cheese, bread and salt. Four-tenths of their income is spent on cheese, and two-tenths on each of the other three items. Between 1980 (the base year) and 1996, eggs doubled in price, cheese went up by 50%, bread remained the same and salt went down by 10%. Calculate the new index relative to the base year.

These tasks can help you provide evidence of Core Skills in Application of Number.

To stimulate growth

In the late eighteenth and early nineteenth centuries there developed in Western societies systems of thought which identified progress with advances in science, technology and industry.

Adam Smith, who produced the well-known book *Wealth of Nations* in 1776, argued that there was a propulsive force which put society on an upward growth path and a self-correcting mechanism that will keep it there.

The propulsive force was the 'desire for betterment' – or the profit motive. In Smith's words it 'impels every manufacturer to expand his business in order to increase his profits.' The main road to profit consists in equipping working people with machinery that will increase productivity. Thus the path to growth lies in what Smith called accumulation, or in modern terms investment. Because of increased productivity, society's output grows.

The rising demand for working people pushes up wages. As people become better off they became healthier and mortality rates fall. More people become available to swell the working population. As a result the demand for products increases and the rising working population prevents wages from rising and eating into profits. Because profits are sustained we have a self-correcting mechanism that enables growth to be maintained.

We can illustrate market-led growth in Figure 3.6 as an engine providing a propulsive force and a set of tracks that serve as a self-correcting mechanism enabling growth to take place.

Governments play a very important role in creating the conditions for sustainable growth. Growth will take place if there is sufficient demand in the economy to lead to increased supply. It will also take place if supply is becoming increasingly more efficient, e.g. better labour productivity resulting from training, or increased machine output resulting from the use of better machines.

Booms and slumps arise almost inevitably from changes in market demand and market supply on a grand scale. On the demand side, changes in demand are likely to come from:

- consumers
- investment decisions
- governments
- exports.

Consumer demand varies with incomes. When incomes are rising people are likely to spend more. When people have more disposable income, they will spend more – for example when taxes are lowered. People are also likely to spend more when it is easier to borrow money, and the cost of borrowing (i.e. the interest rate) is low.

Investment demand is likely to be high when the economy appears to be booming. At this time business people will be optimistic – they can expect good returns on their investments. Investment by businesses will also be higher when interest rates fall, because loans are less expensive.

Government demand is likely to be higher when the government is trying to encourage a boom. This may be to reduce unemployment or to make people feel better before an election. A government will also spend more if it believes this to be the right thing to do. For example, a government may feel that it has an important role in securing high standards of health care and education.

Export demand is likely to be high when a country's products are relatively cheap on world markets. The volume of world trade is likely to be highest when there is a general world boom.

Demand will be lower in situations which are the opposite of these outlined above.

On the supply side, output is likely to increase when goods can be produced more efficiently. This may be because factors of production become more effective, there are fewer problems in the production process, or when technology improves.

Propulsive forces i.e. profit motive

Self-correcting mechanism i.e. creation of demand

Figure 3.6 Market-led growth

Evidence collection point

1 Which of the following are (i) most likely, (ii) least likely to lead to growth in a national economy?

a An increase in demand for consumer goods after a period of recession.

b An increase in demand by home citizens for imports.

c An increase in the use of more efficient investment goods in the domestic economy.

d An increase in the demand for a country's exports.

e A fall in the productivity of labour in the home market.

f A rise in government spending on capital equipment during a recession.

2 Explain why the government may try to increase the rate of growth in the national economy.

Means of influence

Given that there are many reasons for government intervention in markets we will now go on to explore the means of influence by looking at:

- Legislation
- Regulation and deregulation
- The control of monopoly
- Monetary policy
- Fiscal policy
- Public ownership and privatisation.

Legislation

In Britain the government plays a very big part in all our lives. It encourages individuals and organisations to do some things and discourages other activities.

As a person grows from childhood to adulthood a multitude of regulations come and go. Here are a few:

5 You become of 'compulsory school age'. You can see a U film at a cinema unaccompanied. You have to pay child's fares on trains, and on buses and tubes in London. You can drink alcohol in private – for example at home.

7 You can open and draw money from a National Savings Bank account.

10 You can be convicted of a criminal offence if it is proved you know that what you were doing was wrong. If you are guilty of homicide you could be

detained 'during Her Majesty's pleasure' for a specific period – including a life sentence.

12 You can buy a pet. You can be trained to participate in dangerous public entertainment subject to obtaining a local authority licence.

13 You can get a part-time job, but there are restrictions – for example, you cannot work for more than two hours on a school day or a Sunday.

14 You can go into a pub but you cannot buy or drink alcohol there. You can possess a shotgun, airgun, air rifle, or ammunition. You may be employed on a weekday as a street trader by your parents.

15 If you are a boy you can be sent to prison to await trial. You can see a category 15 film. You can open a Girobank account.

16 You can leave school. You can marry with parental consent. A girl can consent to sexual intercourse. A boy can join the armed forces with parental consent. You can buy cigarettes and tobacco. You can have beer, cider or wine with a meal in a restaurant. You can enter or live in a brothel.

17 Criminal charges against you will be dealt with in the adult courts. You can hold a driving licence.

18 You are an adult in the eyes of the law. You can vote in elections. You can serve on a jury. You can buy alcohol in a bar.

21 A man may consent to a homosexual act in private with a partner over 21. You can become an MP. You can hold a driving licence for a heavy goods vehicle or larger passenger vehicle. You can apply for a licence to sell alcohol.

The above examples illustrate just a few of the ways in which the government limits or allows the activities of young people. In the same way there are literally thousands of laws and regulations that encourage or constrain the activities of organisations.

We will now discuss some of the legislation which is important to you as a consumer, citizen and member of an organisation.

Consumer protection

Any product or service that is provided to the marketplace must meet certain standards. Some of these standards are established by law, some by voluntary codes of practice within an industry, and others are set by individual businesses.

Businesses supply goods or services for consumers in return for payment. The legal system exists to provide a framework within which transactions can take place, and to provide a means of settling disputes.

Evidence collection point

Make notes on the following. When did you last make a complaint to a shop about something you had bought? How did you make the complaint? What rights were you aware of? What was the outcome of your complaint? You could provide evidence here of Core Skills in Communication.

How do disputes arise (see Figure 3.7)?

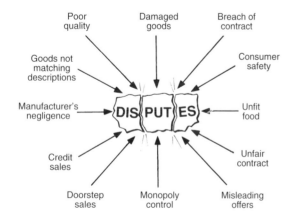

Figure 3.7 Some causes of disputes

- *Damaged or poor quality goods*. It quite often happens that purchased goods do not function properly. They may have been damaged in transit or they may be of poor quality and not suitable for the purpose for which they are intended.
- *Goods not matching descriptions*. Goods may not be as described on the packaging or in an advertisement.
- *Manufacturer's negligence*. Faulty manufacturing processes or bad design might lead to the personal injury of the consumer or damage to other goods. For example, a faulty electrical component might cause fire.
- *Breach of contract*. This could include the failure of the supplier to supply, a failure to meet the required quality, or a failure to supply by a given date. For example, a shop selling bridal gowns might fail to supply the dress by the agreed date.
- *Consumer safety*. Goods may not be safe and could cause injury to customers.
- *Unfit food*. Eating unfit food can have particularly unpleasant consequences and consumers need to be protected against this.
- *Misleading offers*. Consumers can easily be misled by offers, bargains and their rights concerning sales items.
- *Unfair contracts*. Contracts may contain exclusion clauses or disclaimers which might make the relationship between the buyer and the seller unreasonable. It would be unacceptable for a company to disclaim responsibility for an injury caused by its own negligence.
- *Doorstep sales*. There need to be guidelines to protect clients who might have been intimidated into buying goods from doorstep salespeople, particularly if these goods are expensive and have been bought on credit.
- *Credit sales*. Customers 'buying now and paying later' over an extended period leave themselves open to abuse. They could well be charged excessive interest rates, pay large administration costs or be tied to an expensive maintenance agreement.
- *Monopoly control*. We will look at monopoly control in greater detail below (see pages 69–74). Monopolies and mergers produce a situation where one or just a few companies control a market. Lack of competition can be to the disadvantage of customers in terms of quality and prices.

Evidence collection point

Interview a selection of 20 consumers to find out the sorts of disputes they have been in with sellers. Do most complaints fit into a small number of headings, or do their complaints go right across a wide range of areas? What actions did consumers take in each case? Is there scope for more consumer protection? If so, what form should it take? Your work could contribute evidence of Core Skills in Communication.

Legal processes of consumer protection

Consumers may need help to ensure that they get a fair deal when making a transaction with an organisation. Various Acts of Parliament set out to ensure that organisations honour their responsibilities.

The *criminal justice system* deals with cases where the laws of the country have been broken. These laws attempt to protect members of society and to punish offenders whose action have been harmful to the community. Cases might, for example, be brought to court for dishonesty or for selling unhygienic foodstuffs. Punishments could be fines, imprisonment or both.

The *civil law* is concerned with disputes between individuals and groups (Figure 3.8). Laws have been built up over the years dealing with buying and selling activities. Laws related to contracts set out the obligations that individuals have to each other every time they enter into an agreement, while the law of torts protects individuals and groups from others' actions, particularly if an individual or group suffers injury as a result of these actions. Individuals and groups enforce their rights by suing in the civil courts.

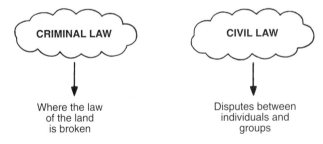

Figure 3.8 Criminal and civil law

Consumer laws

Numerous Acts of Parliament are concerned with consumer protection. Although it is not possible to know each Act in detail, it is necessary to understand the reasons for the more important Acts, and their

Figure 3.9 The three divisions of consumer laws

general effects. They all create legal responsibilities for organisations. We shall look at these Acts under three main headings (Figure 3.9).

Competition laws, which are concerned with creating a healthy climate of competition within the economy, are the subject of a separate section later in this chapter.

The *provision of credit laws* cover most forms of credit transactions. Under the Consumer Credit Act all businesses involved in some way with credit have to be licensed by the Office of Fair Trading. Advertisements offering credit have to state the annual percentage rate of interest (APR) so that consumers can compare the true cost of one credit offer with another.

It is illegal for traders to send you a credit card that you have not asked for. If you are refused credit, you can ask for the name and address of the credit reference agency that has reported you as a bad risk. You can then put the matter to rights if the refusal has been based on false information.

We now turn to Acts covering the *quality of goods or services.*

The Sale of Goods Act

Sellers must provide goods that are of 'merchantable quality' – that is, they must not be damaged or broken. Goods sold must also be fit for the purpose intended. If you bought a pair of shoes and they fell apart at the seams within a week, they would not have been fit for the purposes for which they were sold – serving as footwear.

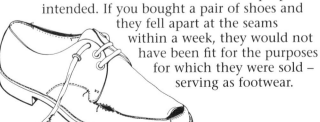

Figure 3.10 Unfit?

Figure 3.11 Won't fit?

Under this law you can ask for replacements if goods do not meet the requirements you specified to the seller. For example, if you bought spare parts for your car from a garage on the understanding that they were for a Mini, and found that they could only fit a larger car, you would be within your rights to ask for replacements or your money back.

The Trades Descriptions Act

The description given of the goods forms part of the contract that the buyer makes with the seller. This Act makes it a criminal offence for a trader to describe goods falsely. A type of case frequently prosecuted under this Act is the turning back of mileometers on used cars to make them appear as if they have covered fewer miles than they really have.

The main objective of the Trades Description Act is thus quite straightforward – descriptions of goods and services must be accurate. Articles described as 'waterproof' and 'shrinkproof' must be exactly that.

The Weights and Measures Act

The aim of this Act is to ensure that consumers receive the actual quantity of a product that they believe they are buying. For example, pre-packed items must have a declaration of the quantity contained within the pack. It is an offence to give 'short weight'.

The Food and Drugs Act

This Act is concerned with the contents of foodstuffs and medicines. The government needs to control this area of trading so that the public is not led into buying harmful substances. Some items have to carry warnings – tins of kidney beans, for example, must carry clear instructions that they need to be boiled for a fair length of time before they can be eaten.

The Act lays down minimum contents for various foodstuffs. For example, a sausage can only be called a sausage if it contains a certain amount of meat. Similar rules apply to items like Cornish pasties and beefburgers.

The contents of medicines are strictly controlled by this Act. Certain substances, e.g. mercury, are not allowed at all.

Case study – Food safety

Safety laws are passed both to protect employees at work, and to provide safety standards for the users of particular products.

Workers in a modern food processing plant follow strict procedures aimed at ensuring hygienic (i.e. germ-free) working conditions. For example, they must usually take off watches and rings, put on a hairnet and hat, a coat that is laundered daily and a pair of wellington boots. Any dressings on cuts or grazes must be replaced by metal-lined plasters that can be found by metal detectors should they fall off.

Despite these precautions, reported cases of food poisoning rose fourfold to about 75 000 between 1982 and 1992. Food manufacturers' sales and profits were hit by scare after scare, from salmonella to listeria, from botulism to bovine spongiform encephalopathy ('mad cow disease').

In January 1991 the government brought in a new Food Safety Act, giving environmental health officers the power to shut down offending premises immediately, and to seize suspect food before it reaches shops. Regulations on refrigeration temperatures, chemical residues in food and the use of certain technologies have been tightened, and from now on all food premises will be compulsorily registered, Staff training has to improve. Ministers have the power to oversee the introduction of new technologies such as irradiation. Perishable foods must carry 'eat by' rather than 'sell by' dates.

The European Union has agreed that member governments must achieve adequate standards of inspection at the point of production.

1 Why is food safety so important?
2 Could it be left to manufacturers and retailers of
  ' foodstuffs to regulate their own trades and
    industry?
3 Why is it necessary to update food laws constantly?
4 Comment on the likely effect of the new laws on:
   a the production of food
   b the sale of food
   c the quality of food
   d the price of food
   e consumers
   f the number of food producers in the industry
   g the use of new technology in food production.

There are numerous sources of help and advice for consumers, providing opportunities for people to follow up complaints and grievances. It is important to consider carefully the circumstances of each grievance before deciding on the most appropriate way forward.

The government protects consumers through a number of official bodies.

The Office of Fair Trading (OFT), a government body, was set up to look after the interests of consumers and traders. It publishes a wide variety of information and encourages businesses to issue codes of practice to raise the standards of their service. Traders who persist in breaking the law must give an assurance that they will mend their ways. As we shall see later in this chapter the OFT also keeps an eye on anti-competitive practices, monopolies and mergers and might suggest changes in the law.

Local authorities have trading standards departments that investigate complaints about misleading offers or prices, inaccurate weights and measures, and consumer credit. Environmental Health Departments enforce legislation covering health aspects of food – for example, unfit food, or hygienic storage, preparation or serving of food.

Nationalised industries are vast monopolies with the potential to put customers in a weak position.

Consumer and consultative councils represent consumers and aim to prevent the misuse of monopoly power.

Environmental regulations and planning controls

As we have seen earlier, the government is increasingly taking environmental considerations seriously, and is legislating to limit environmental pollution. For example, cars that create more than a set amount of pollution through exhaust fumes can be banned from the roads.

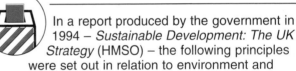

Evidence collection point

In a report produced by the government in 1994 – *Sustainable Development: The UK Strategy* (HMSO) – the following principles were set out in relation to environment and planning decisions:

■ Decisions should be based on the best possible scientific information and analysis of risks.
■ In cases where there is uncertainty, and potential serious risks exist, precautionary action may be necessary.
■ Ecological impacts must be considered, particularly where resources are non-renewable or effects may be irreversible.
■ Cost implications should be brought home directly to the people responsible – the 'polluter pays' principle.

Judgements have to be made about the weight to be put on these factors in particular cases. Some environmental costs have to be accepted as a price of economic development, but on other occasions a site, or an eco-system, or some other aspect of the environment, has to be regarded as so valuable that it should be protected from exploitation.

1 To what extent do you welcome the principles outlined above?
2 Illustrate how the principles might apply in an example involving planning and the environment with which you are familiar.
3 What do you think is meant by the 'polluter pays' principle?

In the late 1980s a new environmental law was passed in the United States. It did not require organisations to fix anything, install anything or clean up anything. All it obliged them to do was submit (to the Environmental Protection Agency) an annual list of the quantities of hazardous chemicals they had released into the environment. The Agency would publish the information in a Toxics Release Inventory. The aim of this law was to create a massive shift in power away from government and industrial regulation and towards the public.

Local communities in the USA are now able to knock on companies' doors armed with detailed information about what is being put into their air and water. Environmental groups have found the inventory a valuable campaigning resource. In industry, senior management and other employees have started asking pointed questions about why such large amounts of costly raw materials and valuable products are being thrown away. Many businesses have been able to set up new strategies for saving waste and cutting down on pollution.

In Britain there is growing pressure for environmental auditing. The Environmental Protection Act has paved the way for further registers on industrial pollution, waste disposal sites, contaminated land and so on.

Some of the 'green' investment funds have joined environmentalists in arguing for compulsory audits which provide information on companies' raw material and energy consumption as well as pollution. The Trades Union Congress (TUC) has urged its members to demand green audits in workplace negotiations.

In 1990 the European Commission proposed the idea of enforcing environmental audits on companies in a number of leading industrial sectors. However, the EU has produced a voluntary system rather than formal legislation.

Task

Carry out a rough environmental audit of the place where you work. Are there any obvious areas for environmental improvement? Are there policies which could be changed to improve the environment?

Regulation and deregulation

As well as imposing direct legislation to control market activities and the ways in which organisations operate, the government also regulates activities.

Regulation creates a framework in which organisations can operate and activities can take place.

For example, if the government was to regulate the local market for bus services, it might stipulate that:

- Only one bus company will be allowed to operate within that market.
- The buses must operate on specified routes, some of which might be loss-making (in order to provide a service to the community).
- Certain standards should be maintained. For example, buses should not be cancelled, staff working on the buses need to be trained to a certain standard, buses must be maintained to a certain standard, and should not be over a certain age.

Deregulation would occur when the government takes off some of the controls and restrictions in markets to encourage freer competition. For example, into the local bus market this might happen when:

- All bus companies that met minimum standards would be allowed to set up and compete in the market.
- Bus companies could select their own routes, timetables, etc.
- Companies could advertise and compete for customers, e.g. by reducing prices.

Case study – Battle on the buses

A bus war has broken out around Grantham, giving villagers a super-service of six buses an hour.

Lincoln RoadCar has moved into Reliance's patch in Barrowby (a village on the edge of Grantham), slashed fares and given residents in the village a service they can hardly believe.

The long-established Reliance operation gave Barrowby people four buses an hour into town. Now Lincolnshire RoadCar has introduced a Road Runner service, upping the numbers by two an hour between Barrowby and Grantham.

It has set the scene for a battle between the established operator and the newcomer. In the Reliance corner is owner Joe Simmons, with 20 buses, whilst in the RoadCar corner, the company, which is part of Yorkshire Traction, has more than 600 buses.

Joe Simmons has delivered 1000 leaflets to Barrowby homes stating that his service is reliable and well-known. RoadCar has chopped 5p off the 40p fare into town and Mr Simmons has matched the price cut. Mr Simmons is furious that the RoadCar schedule sees its Road Runner at bus stops just five minutes ahead of his service.

RoadCar is unrepentant and a spokesperson said, 'These changes are another step in the steady increase of our bus services. The introduction of the Barrowby route is just an extension of our success in other areas of the town.'

Figure 3.12 Battle on the buses (*Source:* Reproduced courtesy of the *Grantham Journal*)

1 Why did RoadCar move into Barrowby?
2 What were the company's short- and long-term objectives?
3 What about Reliance? Explain their reaction.
4 How did the changes that have have taken place affect the market?
5 How will this affect consumers?
6 What are the advantages and disadvantages of deregulating bus services?

The regulation of business activity has been of particular importance in industries which during the 1980s and early 1990s were transferred from being government-run to being in the private sector, i.e. owned by shareholders.

The four big industries that were privatised were:

■ water
■ gas
■ electricity
■ telecommunications.

When these industries were privatised, they became monopolies owned by private shareholders. The danger was that they would go all out to make large profits at the expense of consumers.

Therefore 'regulators' were appointed to safeguard competitive practices in these industries. The regulators (in 1995) are:

Water	Ian Byatt
Gas	Clare Spottiswoode
Electricity	Stephen Littlechild
Telecommunications	Don Cruikshank

The way regulation works in this country is that the regulator keeps an eye on the way in which concerns like British Gas and British Telecom operate and puts a 'cap' (limit) on the amount by which they can raise prices, so that a fair balance is kept between the interests of shareholders and consumers. The regulators can be and have been critical of the way in which new companies in these industries operate if their practices are anti-competitive. Fortunately some of these industries are becoming increasingly competitive; for example, the telecommunications industry has seen the growth of Mercury, Orange and a number of overseas competitors, creating a more competitive environment.

The government also regulates activities in markets by granting licences and franchises to companies to operate for a period of time. For example, the BBC has recently been granted a licence to operate into the beginning of the 21st century, However, such licences and franchises are granted only if organisations can show that they will meet minimum standards. If organisations do not meet these standards they can lose their licence or franchise.

The control of monopoly

United Kingdon competition law is made up of four principal Acts of Parliament, each dealing with separate aspects of competition policy. They are the

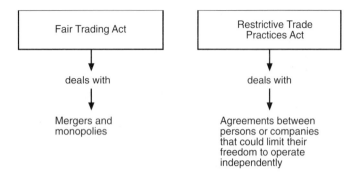

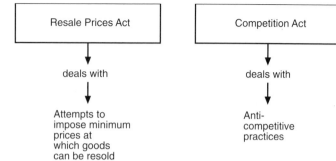

Figure 3.13 Four competition Acts

Fair Trading Act 1973, the Restrictive Trade Practices Act 1976, the Resale Prices Act 1976, and the Competition Act 1980.

Each Act gives the Director General of the OFT and the Commission of the Restrictive Practices Court different responsibilities.

These laws can be split into two categories:

- In the case of the Restrictive Trade Practices Act and the Resale Prices Act, action is taken in the courts.
- In the case of the Fair Trading Act and the Competition Act, practices are examined by the Director General, the Commission and the Secretary of State.

Evidence collection point

Keep a collection of newspaper cuttings dealing with cases involving the four laws relating to competition. What happens to companies that infringe these laws?

Monopolies

Where a company or group of companies has market power, there is the potential for the market to be harmed in a number of ways. Excessive prices, reductions in the level of services and unfair restrictions on entry into the market are typical examples of what can happen in the absence of effective competition.

Defining a monopoly

Although we normally think of a monopoly as the sole supplier to a particular market, United Kingdom law uses a wider definition.

Under the Fair Trading Act, a monopoly is defined first as a situation where a company supplies or buys 25% or more of all goods or services of a particular type in the whole country or in a particular area (e.g. the South East).

The Act also defines a complex monopoly as a situation where a group of companies that together have 25% of the market all behave in some way that affects competition.

Evidence collection point

Think of examples of national or local monopolies. In each case try to suggest why the monopoly position might help consumers, or be harmful to them. How would you go about testing this?

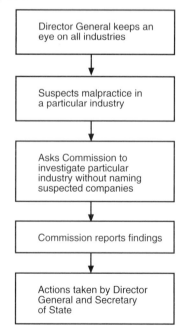

Figure 3.14 How monopoly malpractices are handled

The public interest

There is no assumption that monopolies are bad in themselves. The invention of a new device, for example, will inevitably make the inventor a monopolist to start with even if the device provides a benefit to the public. The 1973 Act simply defines situations where is is possible that market power could be misused, and recognises that this may be against the public interest. It is for the Commission to say what is and what it not in the public interest.

Dealing with monopolies

The Director General keeps a constant eye on British industry, looking at how major companies are operating and at allegations and complaints.

Once he or she feels that there may be evidence of monopoly malpractice in a particular industry, the case is referred to the Commission. However, at this stage no companies are named; it is simply suggested that the Commission should investigate a particular aspect of competition (e.g. prices) in that industry.

The Commission then investigates and makes a report to the Secretary of State, with suggestions for possible action. The Secretary and the Director General then decide what should be done. This might involve asking companies to make promises to change, or asking for promises backed up with measures to make sure that the promises are kept.

Evidence collection point

Newspaper distribution

In October 1991, the Office of Fair Trading decided not to refer the distribution of national newspapers to the Monopolies and Mergers Commission. The decision was described as a gross injustice by the National Federation of Retail Newsagents, which represents about 30 000 small newsagents and which campaigned for the enquiry.

Newspaper and magazine distribution in the UK is dominated by three wholesalers who together account for more than 80% of the market. W H Smith has a 45% share, followed by John Menzies at about 25% and Surridge Dawson at around 10%. The balance is accounted for by local wholesalers.

Newsagents are worried about changes in the distribution network which have led to major wholesalers obtaining exclusive distribution rights for titles in a particular area. The complaints were about a lack of alternative wholesalers for newspapers and magazines in their area. Increases in carriage charges, and being forced to stock publications they did not want. Although the OFT admitted there were restraints on competition in the way newspapers were distributed, 'it could see no reason for believing that there is any loss to the public sufficient to justify a reference.'

However, the OFT was concerned that there may be restrictive agreements between wholesalers. It was considering court action against one such local agreement in the Blackpool–Preston area. The OFT

Figure 3.15   Market power

found that one wholesaler had agreed not to supply certain newspapers and magazines in the Blackpool area.

1   Why is there considered to be a monopoly situation in newspaper and magazine distribution?
2   Why did retailers want this monopoly position to be investigated?
3   What does your local newsagent think? Perhaps you can also find out what the local wholesale manager thinks.
4   Does the case present any evidence of unfair monopoly practices?
5   Why do you think the OFT decided not to refer this case to the Commission?
6   Do you think the Director General was justified in failing to call for an investigation?

Anti-competitive practices

In a competitive market, companies can be expected to adopt policies intended to give them a competitive edge. This can lead to benefits in terms of efficiency, better quality goods and services, and so on. However, sometimes firms use practices which may be harmful to competition. Practices that may be acceptable in one market where competition is strong may be unacceptable in another where there is less competition.

Under the Competition Act, an anti-competitive practice is defined as any practice that has, or is intended to have, or is likely to have, the effect of restricting or preventing competition.

The ability of a firm to influence the market depends on its market power. Market power stems from having a large share of the market, having a leading brand name, or being able in some way to prevent new firms from entering the industry (perhaps as a result of patent rights). Companies are covered by the Act if they have more than 25% of a market or a turnover of more than £5 million.

If an alleged anti-competition practice is reported to the Director General, he or she can set up an investigative team to look at it. On the basis of the investigation the Director General must decide whether he or she thinks that it is anti-competitive. If it is felt to be so, the practice can be referred to the Commission. The Commission must decide whether it is against the public interest. A report is then produced within a period of four to eight weeks. The Secretary of State and the Director General may then insist that the business involved abandon the practice if it is felt to be unacceptable.

Resale price maintenance

Attempts by manufacturers or suppliers to enforce a minimum price at which their goods can be resold by dealers or retailers restricts competition and can keep prices higher than they would be otherwise. Resale price maintenance is unlawful under the Resale Prices Act except for goods granted an exemption. Goods exempted at present are books and pharmaceuticals. It is likely that very soon books will no longer be protected in this way.

Task

Why do you think that pharmaceuticals are exempted from the Resale Prices Act? Try to find out by interviewing someone in the pharmaceutical trade.

Under the 1976 Act it is unlawful to try to establish minimum prices. It is also unlawful to stop supplies or to offer less favourable terms to dealers whom the supplier believes to be responsible for price cutting. A supplier is, however, entitled to withhold goods from a dealer who is pricing them as 'loss leaders' (that is, goods sold at a loss in order to attract customers towards profitable items).

The Director General has the power to seek a court injunction to force the parties involved to scrap a retail price agreement.

Mergers

Under the Fair Trading Act, a merger is said to take place when two or more companies 'cease to be distinct'. The aim of competition policy is not to prejudge mergers but to examine the merits of individual mergers. The advantages in each case must be weighed up against the disadvantages.

The 1973 Act lays down two tests to decide whether a particular merger can be investigated:

■   *The assets test* – that the total gross assets of the company to be taken over exceed £30 million in value.
■   *The market-share test* – that as a result of the merger, 25% or more of the supply or purchase of goods or services of a particular description in the United Kingdom or a substantial part of it comes under the control of the merging enterprises.

The critical factor in deciding whether a merger should be allowed to take place is again the public

Figure 3.16 Examples of horizontal mergers

interest. Those most likely to cause concern are horizontal mergers, where two companies supplying the same sort of product or service combine.

Vertical mergers (where companies are at different stages of producing a product, e.g. a brewery merging with a chain of public houses) and conglomerate mergers (where companies that produce quite different products, e.g. baked beans and tooth paste) may also be investigated.

Companies are expected to notify the Director General if they hope to merge. The Director General will conduct a preliminary investigation before deciding whether to advise the Secretary of State to refer the merger to the Commission. Companies are not allowed to acquire each other's shares while the investigation is taking place. If they have already started to merge they will be ordered not to join the operations together.

The Commission reports to the Secretary of State who decides, in consultation with the Director General, whether or not the merger is in the public interest.

Case study – A merger in the public interest?

Two companies are hoping to merge. At present one company has 32% of the market and the other has 26%. The assets of each company are in excess of £50 million.

These companies both manufacture finished goods for retail sale. Because of the perceived high quality of their product they will only deal with selected retail outlets, and under the new (merged) company structure these outlets will be allowed to sell the

product only if they agree to a mark-up of exactly 35%. In addition there will be a number of regulations as to how the product can be displayed and offered to customers. The companies are confident that the new company will shortly capture all of this exciting and rapidly developing market.

Prices are expected to remain high in this industry, and product performance and quality are likely to improve rapidly with breakthroughs in research and development. The UK is a world leader in this product, and many new jobs will be created. UK prices compare favourably with those of the foreign competition.

1 List the facts making it likely that this proposed merger would be referred to the Commission.
2 What arguments can be put in favour of this merger?
3 What do you think the likely outcome will be?

Restrictive trade practices

All commerce is based on agreements of one form or another. The buying and selling of goods and services would be impossible without them. In such agreements, businesses agree to do certain things. However, some of these agreements may restrict competition.

The Restrictive Trade Practices Act covers agreements affecting goods and services. Companies must register certain types of agreement that they make with other companies. These may cover all sorts of areas including:

- restrictions on prices or charges
- conditions on which business is conducted
- geographical divisions of business
- people with whom business can take place

- the quantity of goods to be produced
- the manufacturing process to be used.

Agreements can be in any form, including the spoken word. All such agreements must be registered.

The Director General of Fair Trading refers suspect agreements to the Restrictive Practices Court, which will strike down any restrictions found to be against the public interest.

Parties to an agreement therefore need to be able to prove to the court that there are real benefits from their restrictive practices.

Evidence collection point

Describe the roles of the following in the United Kingdom's competition policy:

1 The Director General of Fair Trading
2 The Secretary of State for Trade and Industry
3 The Monopolies and Mergers Commission
4 The Restrictive Practices Court

Criticisms of the current system

The process is complex, slow and cumbersome, involving three separate bodies: the DTI, the Office of Fair Trading and the Monopolies and Mergers Commission. Each body has different responsibilities.

The OFT identifies a potential problem but cannot carry out a full investigation. Instead, it refers the problem to the MMC.

The MMC's investigations often start off by duplicating much of the research done by the OFT. It then makes recommendations to the DTI but has no power to put them into effect.

A frequent criticism is that neither the MMC nor the OFT has the powers to force companies to supply evidence for their investigations.

The final stage of the process is the DTI. Its head is the President of the Board of Trade, who has the final powers to put the MMC's recommendations into effect, or even to come up with new ideas (as happened over the review of newspaper wholesaling in 1995). The decisions of the President of the Board of Trade are likely to be influenced by political factors.

A criticism of monopoly and restrictive practices policy in recent years has been that the Secretary of State has been more concerned about UK businesses being competitive in world markets than with creating competition to benefit consumers at home. Restrictive practices have been allowed which give more powers to UK companies in fighting international competition. Consumers at home have suffered, in the short term at least.

The process of reviewing competition often takes months, or even years. For example, the review of the brewing industry lasted from 1986-89, resulting in the Beer Orders, which took three further years to be implemented.

European Community competition law

Since 1990 the European Commission has investigated matters relating to competition with a European dimension.

The European Union has its own competition regulations, which in a number of cases go above and beyond national laws.

Article 85 of the Treaty of Rome forbids agreements which may adversely affect trade between the 12 major states, and in particular which have as their object a limitation of competition within the European market. This includes price fixing, market sharing, restriction of production or technical development, and the imposition of discriminatory terms of supply. Such agreements are automatically not allowed unless given as exemption by the European Commission.

A European Merger Control Regulation allows the European Commission to control mergers which have a 'community dimension'. This is defined as those mergers where the parties have a total worldwide turnover exceeding 5 billion ECU and at least two of the parties have a Union-wide turnover exceeding 250 million ECU unless each of the undertakings achieves more than two-thirds of its

turnover in one and the same Member State. Special rules apply for banking, financial and insurance institutions.

The role of the European Commission

The European Commission is directly responsible for the application of European legislation in the United Kingdom. The Commission may act on the basis of agreements which have been made before them, on complaints or on their own initiative. They may seek information in writing or by inspectors making visits to firms. These inspectors would always be accompanied by staff from the Director General's Office. Commission inspectors have wide-ranging powers to ask questions and to obtain information.

Before deciding that a law has been broken, the Commission issues a statement of objection to the two parties concerned, who have then have the opportunity to reply to the Commission both in writing and orally, before representatives of Member States. The European Commission also hears the opinion of an advisory committee of competition experts from Member States, including a representative of the Director General.

Evidence collection point

The section above looks in detail at UK competition policy. You should concentrate on:

1 Understanding the four main areas covered by the legislation.
2 The main officials responsible for putting these laws into effect.
3 Actions which can be taken to create a more competitive environment.

A good way of studying this is to follow cases reported in the press. This should help you understand the varying interpretations of the 'public interest'.

Case study – Restrictive practices by Tetra Pak

In October 1991, the European Commission fined Tetra Pak, the Swedish/Swiss company that invented sterilised packaging for liquids, a record £52.5 million for abuse of its dominant market position. The Commission's investigation began as a result of a complaint in 1983 by an Italian competitor, Elopak.

Tetra Pak was accused primarily of adopting restrictive contract clauses. Sir Leon Brittan, the Commissioner responsible for competition policy, said: 'The infringements have involved almost all products manufactured by Tetra Pak and have had a damaging impact on competition in all EU member states.'

By insisting that customers use only Tetra Pak packaging machines and cartons, the company effectively stifled competition. Product guarantees were made dependent on this commitment.

The company also controlled delivery and fitting of spare parts for machinery owned or rented, and in many contracts imposed a monthly maintenance charge that was adjusted in line with customer loyalty rather than the actual maintenance required.

Rental agreements ran for a minimum of three years – nine in the case of Italy – and sometimes included punitive discretionary penalties for companies that allowed contracts to lapse. Carton labelling and, in some cases, monthly reports were required of clients, who risked finding themselves subject to surprise inspections.

The measures ensured that the company could safely adopt predatory pricing policies. The costs of machines and cartons in different Member States varied by factors of 300% and 50% respectively.

1 Why was the European Commission concerned with this case of abuse?
2 What seem to be the most telling allegations of abuse against Tetra Pak?
3 Give examples of the restrictive practices involved.
4 Which of these practices seems to be in the public interest and which against the public interest?
5 Why do you think Tetra Pak employed these restrictive practices?

Monetary policy

The government plays a key role in the economy in controlling the availability of money for spending.

Monetary policy is concerned with controlling:

■ the quantity of money in the economy
■ the price of money in the economy.

Monetary policy is felt to be important today. Most people now feel that there is a strong link between the amount of money in the economy and inflation. The view is that if people start spending money at a faster rate than new goods on the market, then prices will rise.

Monetarists believe that it is essential to eliminate general price rises because of the way they destabilise industry and the economy. Uncertainty about prices means that industry cannot concentrate on its main task – producing goods. People become dissatisfied and the whole economic order starts to crumble – people fail to pay up on time, businesses are reluctant to invest, there is more industrial unrest, and so on.

Definition of money

There is more than one way to express the quantity of money in the economy.

If all the people used only coins and currency notes to make their purchases, calculating the quantity of money would be easy. Instead people use a variety of forms of money, the most obvious being coins and notes, cheques, credit cards, and other forms of credit payments. Today it is also common practice for people to draw money out of building societies and other savings accounts to make purchases.

A wide range of new facilities for making payments is developing, so it is almost impossible for the government to know how much money is available to citizens to spend on goods at a particular moment in time.

In order to control the quantity of money, the government must decide on the definition of money which it thinks most accurately determines people's likely expenditure. It will then seek to control changes in the supply of money according to this chosen definition.

Case study – Little Mo

Different definitions of money are used by the government depending on what is being counted as money. These definitions are usually termed M0, M1, M2, M3, etc. The larger the number after the M, the wider the definition of money.

During the 1990s M0, or Little Mo, has been one of the most popular definitions of money. A close relationship can be seen between Little Mo and price rises (Figure 3.17). Generally when Little Mo falls, prices follow a few months after: when it rises, prices rise a few months later.

M0 is made up of two main elements:

■ The main part is notes and coins.
■ The other part is the banks' (NatWest, Barclays,

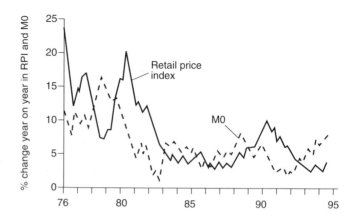

Figure 3.17 Little Mo and inflation

Lloyds, etc.) operational deposits at the Bank of England. These are the banks' own bank accounts.

Many economists think that M0 is a useful measure for giving advance warnings of changes in price levels.

1 What other measures are used apart from M0?
2 Build up a graph showing the relationship between M0 and the retail price index in the later part of the 1990s. Is there as close a relationship between them as there was between 1976 and 1995?

The role of banks

The Bank of England has an important part to play in controlling the lending of high street banks and other financial institutions. The measures available to the Bank for limiting increases in cash and lending include giving advice and instruction to other banks on how much to lend and who to lend to, and raising interest rates to discourage borrowing.

The lending institutions, such as banks, need to be carefully supervised by the government because of their tremendous powers of lending. They can grant overdrafts and loans and make a wide range of other lending arrangements with customers.

A bank's customers carry out a relatively small number of their transactions using cash. Financial institutions, by creating credit instruments such as cheques and credit cards, make it possible for individuals and organisations to borrow money and make payments by means other than cash. The more these credit instruments are expanded, the more purchasing power there is in the economy.

It is essential that the government does not let this spending get out of hand. It therefore sets targets and builds up a framework for controlling the financial system.

The Bank of England plays an important part in policing this system – it licenses financial institutions and keeps a watchful eye on their lending practices.

This policing is very important. If a bank collapses it creates a loss of confidence in an economy as well as leading to losses for depositors.

In 1995, for example, Barings Bank (one of the oldest merchant banks in this country) collapsed. The bank had not controlled the speculations of one of its dealers, Nick Leeson. He had been speculating with billions of pounds of bank assets. When his speculations were unsuccessful he gambled on the 'double or quits' principle. The bank collapsed and was sold for £1 to a Dutch bank. The Bank of England was criticised for not exercising enough control.

As well as controlling the quantity of money in the economy, the government can control the price of money. Minimum interest rates can be quickly altered by the Bank of England and the change will rapidly spread to all financial institutions such as banks and building societies. This is another way of controlling the quantity of money borrowed. If interest rates rise, people are more reluctant to borrow money.

Fiscal policy

Fiscal policy is the government's policy with regard to public spending, taxes and borrowing. The government can try to influence the level of demand in the economy through directly altering the amount of its own spending in relation to its total tax revenues.

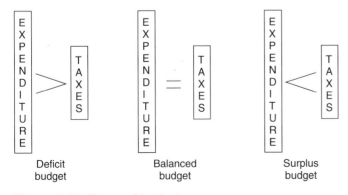

Deficit budget   Balanced budget   Surplus budget

Figure 3.18 Types of budgets

A deficit budget arises when the government spends more than it takes in taxes (Figure 3.18). The government can then borrow money from banks and other sources or sell stock in order to carry out its own expenditure policies.

The difference between government spending and tax revenue is known as the public sector borrowing requirement (PSBR).

The logic of the deficit budget is simple – if there is not enough spending in the economy to create enough demand for goods to give everyone a job who wants one, then the government can itself boost spending. However, as we have seen earlier, this may have inflationary effects. In a balanced budget the government matches its spending with taxes. The idea behind the balanced budget is that the government should not encourage price increases.There is also a belief that the government itself should spend as little as possible, because private individuals and groups are in a better position to make their own spending decisions.

A surplus budget arises when the government takes in more revenue than it spends. This is known as a deflationary policy because one outcome is a cut in inflation.

Balancing expenditure and revenue

Any form of government – whether it be at local, national or European level – needs to raise revenue in order to carry out its expenditure policies. Many economists feel that the smaller the role that the government plays in the economy the more efficient the system is likely to be. The larger the part that government plays in running things, the more employees it will need to carry out purely administrative tasks. For example, in 1993 the Scottish Office – which looks after the interests of 5 million people – employed over 6240 officials. On a wider front we are used to hearing criticisms of the bureaucracy of the European Community at Brussels.

Since 1994 the British government has announced its plans for both expenditure and revenue-raising at the same time (in the autumn). Figure 3.19 shows what the government planned to spend during the period 1993–94.

The sums shown in the table should be seen as representing the monies made available to different government departments for their spending. The departments then need to control their spending to keep in line with what is available to them. Each

77

Defence	22.0
Foreign Office	1.1
Overseas development	2.1
Agriculture, fisheries, food	2.6
Trade and industry	2.4
Employment	3.5
Transport	6.0
DOE – housing	7.4
DOE – environment	1.3
DOE – psa	0.1
DOE – local govt.	27.4
Home Office	5.7
Legal department	2.4
Education	8.9
National Heritage	0.9
Health	27.9
Social security	60.7
Scotland	12.6
Wales	5.9
N. Ireland	6.4
Chancellor's dept.	3.2
Cabinet Office	1.6
Local-authority self-financed spending	10.4
European Communities	1.3
Reserve	3.7
Control total	227.5

Figure 3.19 Planned expenditure for 1993–94 (£ billion) at 1992 prices in real terms

year government ministers argue the case for having more money available for their department (or at least to have as few cutbacks as possible). The figures are expressed in 'real terms' (in other words an allowance has been made against inflation).

Note that some of these figures are distorted because of transfers between departments. For example, the amount of money spent on education appears small. In fact much of the spending on education is carried out by local government. (Transfers take place between the following sectors: DOE, local government, education, health, social security, Scotland and Wales.)

Evidence collection point

Find out the most recent figures for government expenditure plans (these are published in national newspapers in the autumn) or look them up in a back number of *The Economist* magazine. How have expenditure plans changed since 1992–93? What have been the main

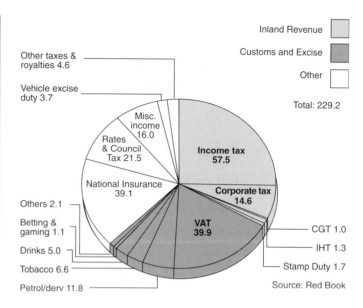

Figure 3.20 Budget revue estimates for 1993–94 (£ billion)

changes? What has caused some departments' expenditure totals to rise while others have fallen?

The pie chart in Figure 3.20 shows where the money to meet government expenditure was expected to come from in 1993–94. Taxes are collected by the Inland Revenue, the Customs and Excise Department and by other collecting agencies (e.g. the local council collects local taxes).

Public ownership and privatisation

The government influences the market in a major way through its policies of public ownership and privatisations.

For example, during the Second World War huge swathes of industry were taken over by the government in order to coordinate production to meet the war effort. Immediately after the war a number of industries were nationalised (taken over by the government by Act of Parliament), e.g. coal, steel and the railways. The Labour Party was in government at the time.

Later on the Conservative Party denationalised many of these industries so that once again they were owned by shareholders. During the 1960s and 1970 the Labour Party renationalised a number of industries.

In 1979 Margaret Thatcher's Conservative government came into power, and Conservatives are still in power in the mid-1990s. This government's policy has been one of privatisation, i.e. handing back industries to private owners and to the discipline of the market.

Case study – From protected monopoly to market competition

An interesting recent study (September, 1994) by Lawrence Gilson has looked at the process of deregulation of telecommunications, electricity and gas in the USA and Britain, water in Britain, and the railways and airlines in the USA.

It outlines five stages as these organisations move from government monopoly to competing in the marketplace.

■ *Stage 1 Equilibrium*
These organisations initially fit into a set of guidelines established for them by regulators. They set out to provide a universal (generally available) service. They subsidise consumers who cost more to serve, e.g. people in out-of the-way places. Customers are passive.

■ *Stage 2 Rumblings in the provinces*
The development of substitute products, and changes in technology and in public policy, mean that competitors begin to develop at the periphery of the industry.

This is particularly the case where profits are high, making it attractive for competitors to enter the market. Managers in the privatised concerns tend to think they will weather the storm because of their size.

■ *Stage 3 Identify crisis*
Stage 2 does not last long. Often the new competitors start to attract some of the most lucrative contracts, where the largest profits are made. Market dominance begins to crumble as more firms start to take away business. Existing concerns now become reluctant to subsidise consumers in the market.

The privatised concerns appeal for support from the regulator. When this fails they start to price cut and to use other competitive strategies.

■ *Stage 4 Refocus*
In Stage 3 a number of bankruptcies occur as competition steps up. In Stage 4 companies begin to focus on particular segments of the market where they are strongest. Mergers take place between organisations carrying out similar activities in the market.

■ *Stage 5 Dynamic competition*
This stage represent the full adjustment of the industry to competitive conditions. The success of organisations in the market depends on how smoothly they can adjust to changes in demand and supply conditions.

Evidence collection point

This case shows many of the complex steps that had to be carried out in privatising British Gas in 1986.

In 1948, the gas industry had been nationalised by the Labour Party in government. However, the Conservative Party from 1979 onwards was keen to privatise a number of industries.

Detailed plans for privatisation were set out by civil servants. On 7 May 1985, the plan was announced to the House of Commons.

A Bill has then to be presented to the House of Commons for discussion, as well as to similar committees of Members of Parliament who also raised questions and raised issues.

Bills need to be presented three times to the House of Commons, with amendments normally being made at each stage. The Bill then has to be presented to the House of Lords for approval. The Lords are able to suggest further amendments. The Bill is then presented back to the Commons.

Once the Bill has been approved it is presented to the Queen for her Royal Assent, when it becomes another Act of Parliament. At the end of this process, British Gas plc became a legally recognised body.

Now carry out some research of your own. Try to create your own illustrations or computer graphics which outline the steps involved in a major privatisation of the 1990s, starting from the date on which the Cabinet agreed that the industry or organisation should be privatised. This work can provide evidence of Core Skills in Information Technology and Communications.

The effects on markets of UK government policies and EU policies

When weighing up government policies there are a number of considerations which we need to bear in mind. You need to consider each of these when you examine government policies. They include:

British Gas

November 1986: Shares in British Gas launched on the stock market

24 August 1986: The State-owned British Gas Corporation ceases to exist, and British Gas plc established

18 August 1986: The Office of Gas Supply – the regulator of the industry – established

During first half of 1986: Government makes a series of announcements about the brokers who will handle the sale

25 July 1986: Bill receives Royal Assent

1948: Gas is nationalised

1973: The British Gas Corporation is established – a nationalised industry, responsible for finding, distributing and selling gas

---

21 July 1986: Commons consider, and agree, Lords' amendments to Bill

17 July 1986: Third reading of Bill in Lords

24 April – 9 July 1986: Bill considered in committee and then on report, over ten days

10 April 1986: Lords second reading

26 March 1986: Bill arrives in the Lords

25 March 1986: Third reading of Bill in Chamber

17 March 1986: Report stage of Bill

May 1979: Conservative government elected

1981: British Telecom successfully privatised

1982: Ministers begin to think of future privatisation plans

June 1983: Conservative government re-elected

---

17 December 1985–6 March 1986: Bill considered in standing committee, over 32 sittings

10 December 1985: Commons second reading

28 November 1985: Formal publication of Gas Bill – first reading in the Commons

May–November 1985: The Bill is drafted

7 May 1985: Plans announced publicly by a statement to the House of Commons

---

September 1983: Department of Energy civil servants begin work on plans to privatise gas industry

April 1985: Cabinet agrees that gas should be privatised in next parliamentary session

- business confidence
- changes in employment opportunities
- growth/lack of growth
- consumers' disposable income
- effects on demand
- trading conditions
- strategic decision-making
- business efficiency.

Business confidence

Business confidence varies a lot. Surveys of business confidence are carried out frequently. Business people are asked whether they are more optimistic or pessimistic about the next few months than the previous few months. Business confidence is very important in creating the conditions for investment and demand in the economy. When business people are pessimistic they will take fewer risks, borrow less money, take on fewer employees, etc. The government needs to create the conditions that encourage business confidence.

Changes in employment opportunities

Employment opportunities are very important. People look forward to having fulfilling jobs, security of employment, and opportunities for advancement. These opportunities will arise when the economy is growing and expanding. These opportunities will disappear in periods of prolonged recession.

Growth

Growth occurs when there is an ongoing increase in an economy's production of goods and services. Growth is conventionally measured in terms of expanding national output, although as we have seen we need to take account of the negative effects of pollution and environmental impacts. In evaluating economic policies an important consideration will be the impact on growth.

Consumers' disposable income

Disposable income is the amount of income remaining to income earners after deductions such as national insurance and income tax have been taken away. People frequently measure the effectiveness of government policies by their impact on the money in their pockets.

Effects on demand

Government policies will often be assessed in terms of their effects on demand. Business people welcome rises in demand because it means an increase in the money running through their tills. When the government pulls in spending, e.g. by running a budget surplus, then this will lead to a reduction in demand with a downward multiplier impact.

Trading conditions

Governments can have an important influence on trading conditions in the marketplace. Through its competition policies the government can create fair trading conditions and protect consumers. By encouraging free trade between countries the government can make it easier for our producers to sell overseas.

Strategic decision-making

Business decision-making needs to take into account long-term considerations: what products we should focus on over the next five years, which parts of the country we should focus our plant in, etc. Government policies should create a stable framework for long-term strategic decision-making. Businesses will look favourably on government policies that provide a suitable climate for long-term decision-making. They would not be happy with government policies that chopped and changed or penalised them for being efficient.

Business efficiency

Businesses will be efficient if they use resources in the most cost-effective way to meet and serve consumer needs. People generally welcome government policies that support and encourage efficiency. Many people would be quite critical of government interferences in the market if they supported less efficient firms, were based on favouritism or gave handouts to firms and allies who did not produce in an efficient way.

UK government policies

In this next section we will focus on a number of key policies used by governments to influence the marketplace, namely:

- interest rates
- personal income tax
- corporate tax
- value added tax
- public service wage levels
- public spending
- investment
- regional assistance.

However, before we go on to look at specific policies it is helpful to get an overall picture of broad views on managing the economy.

In an ideal situation there would be no price increases, no unemployment, a steady growth of national output, a healthy trading position with other countries and a steady and predictable exchange rate between our currency and that of other nations.

However, in the real world, prices increase, there are unacceptable levels of unemployment, national output increases in stops and starts, there are frequent balance-of-payment problems, and the exchange rate goes through highs and lows.

These five variables are the central focus for government economic controls. The way in which the government tries to influence these variables is very important. Government policies affect organisations in a direct way. The illustration in Figure 3.21 identifies the key variables that government controls and policies set out to manage.

In the next few pages we will therefore look at three different ways of dealing with the economy. Each way is supported by people with different views as to how the economy works. The three policies we look at are:

- laissez-faire
- demand-side economics
- supply-side economics.

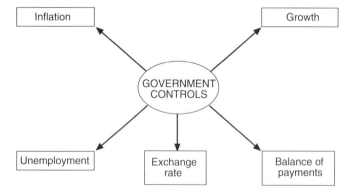

Figure 3.21 Government controls on economic variables

Laissez-faire policy

The French expression laissez-faire means 'leave it alone'. It therefore signifies government non-interference in the economy.

The theory behind laissez-faire is that free markets will lead to the best use of resources. If people want goods they will choose them by voting (with their money) for them to be produced. They will also make themselves available for work so that they can earn money to buy goods. Employers will employ labour so long as they can make a profit.

This theory was applied throughout the nineteenth century. The economy grew rapidly and many new products were invented and developed.

When some goods became old-fashioned they are replaced by new goods. Wages fall in some industries and rise in other industries. Some people will be temporarily unemployed, but they will be taken up in the newer industries. The natural state of affairs for the economy is thus one of full employment.

The mass unemployment of the 1920s could be explained by the fact that trade unions and other groups did not allow wages to fall in a period of recession. If wages and other prices had fallen then employers would have been prepared to employ labour in the new growing industries.

Demand-side economics

Demand-side economics was developed to provide an alternative explanation of the massive unemployment of the 1920s and 1930s.

Much of the early work in this field was carried out by the economist John Maynard Keynes. Keynes argued that full employment was just one possible state for the economy. Keynes maintained that the factors which create supply do not always lead to a demand for goods. Earners of money do not always spend it. This can lead to a fall in national expenditure, and to a reduction in output as suppliers are not able to sell stocks of goods.

We can illustrate this theory by using what is referred to as a circular flow diagram. In Figure 3.22 all income earned by a household is re-spent by them on goods and services.

In the real world, however, we do not re-spend all our income on domestically produced goods. Some of our money is saved, some goes in taxes, and some

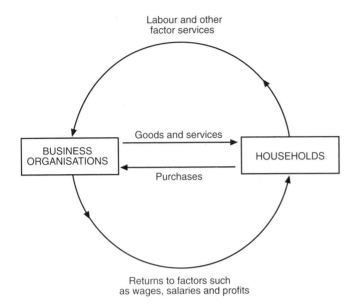

Figure 3.22 The simple circular flow diagram

goes on imports. In other words, some money is leaked from the circular flow.

At the same time, money demand is injected back into the system in the form of investment by businesses in new equipment and machinery. Some money demand is injected by government expenditure and some money demand is injected by export sales (Figure 3.23).

If we look at the demand side of the picture, we can see that aggregate monetary demand is made up of

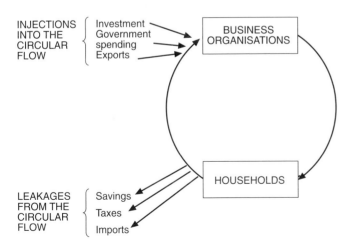

Figure 3.23 The amended circular flow diagram

consumers' expenditure, investment expenditure and exports. In the real world there is no guarantee that the total of this demand will be sufficient to create full employment. Indeed, demand fluctuates from one month to the next.

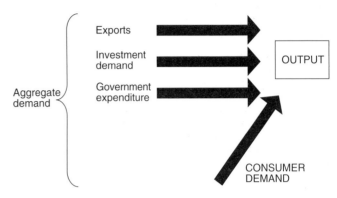

Figure 3.24 The demand for goods and services

In particular, investment demand is quite volatile. If business people are confident that the economy will boom for a period of time they will be keen to invest. However, when they are gloomy they will cut back heavily on investment projects. If you watch business news programmes you will frequently hear references to business confidence.

 Evidence collection point

What is the current state of business confidence in the economy? What are the likely effects for investment?

Changes in demand factors can have a dramatic impact. For example, when a building contractor loses a contract to build a new plant, he or she may have to pay off workers. These workers then do not earn wages. They buy less in local shops. The local shops then 'feel the pinch'. They buy in fewer stocks and reduce the overtime of staff. In turn these people have smaller incomes and they spend less. We have already seen that this is called the multiplier effect.

We can set out a simple rule which relates to the multiplier effect:

■ The greater the percentage of any fresh increase in demand that is leaked away, the smaller the multiplier effect will be.
■ The smaller the percentage of any fresh increase in demand that is leaked away, the larger the multiplier effect will be.

The accelerator

The accelerator is another simple but useful tool. It shows us that if consumers' demand falls slightly, this may have a much bigger consequential effect on the machinery and capital goods industries.

One way of classifying industry is into companies that produce capital goods and ones that produce consumer goods.

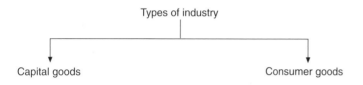

Figure 3.25 Classification of industry

Consumer-goods producers buy machinery from the capital-goods industries. Each year they will need to replace machinery that is wearing out. For example, they may replace 10% of their machinery. Now if the economy is in a slump they may not buy any new machinery at all. Just imagine the effect if all consumer-goods producers did the same thing. There would be little demand for capital goods. The capital-goods industry would have a massive downturn in orders. Many capital-goods companies would be crippled.

We can therefore say that a relatively small downturn in orders for consumer goods will have a vastly accelerated effect on capital-goods companies.

It is not surprising, therefore, that capital goods producers look carefully at the economic forecasts of booms and slumps. When they are gloomy they will start to make cutbacks, and these cutbacks may be multiplied into a slump in consumption which feeds back into an accelerated slump in investment. The accelerator and multiplier effects therefore work together.

The impact of demand

Our demand-side analysis so far has shown the tremendous power of demand to influence the fortunes of the economy, and hence of organisations. Falling demand leads to recession, unemployment and wasted resources.

For example, Figure 3.26 highlights some of the waste that occurred during the early 1990s in particular. During this time potential national output

THE GDP GAP

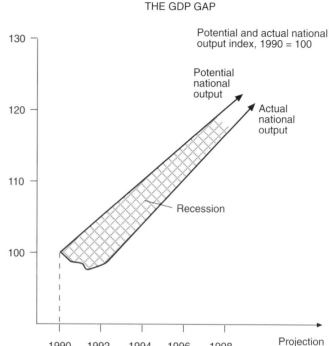

Figure 3.26 Recession creates waste

in this country was well above actual output because of recession and flagging demand and supply.

On the other hand, excess demand can lead to rising prices: inflation. Rising investment can have a multiplier effect on expenditure. The same is true of increases in exports, government spending or indeed an increase in consumer spending. If demand rises and supply is not able to expand at the same rate, then inflation will result.

The Phillips curve

Most economists recognise that there is a trade-off between unemployment and inflation. If the government is worried about inflation then it will need to dampen down demand. It can do this by, for example, raising interest rates to reduce borrowing and cutting back its own spending. This will lead to a slowdown in the economy and to unemployment.

If the government feels that the unemployment level is unacceptably high then it can increase demand, perhaps by lowering interest rates and increasing its own spending.

The Phillips curve is an attempt to show a statistical relationship between unemployment and inflation.

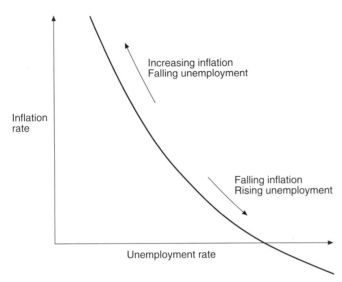

Figure 3.27 The Phillips curve

When inflation is rising, unemployment is falling, and when unemployment is rising inflation is falling. Today the notion of the Phillips curve is used to describe this trade-off. However, it is clear that the position of the Phillips curve moves from one period to the next.

Task

Upturns and downturns in the economy are frequently referred to in the media. When they occur they have a dramatic impact – closures, the opening of a new organisation to meet new demand, the spread of unemployment or inflation, etc. Every organisation will feel some of these effects.

Find out from your work placement or work experience how these external economic influences are affecting the organisation you are involved with. Try to develop a series of statistics which help to describe the trends that you outline. This work can contribute evidence of Core Skills in Application of Number.

Supply-side economics

During the 1980s there was a big switch in economic policy away from demand-side to supply-side theories. Whilst demand management had worked very well after 1945, the policy eventually ran into trouble.

After the war most governments used Keynesian policies (i.e. the ideas of Keynes). To counteract unemployment the government would use its own spending to pump up demand in the economy.

However, a major fault of this policy was that outdated industries were artificially supported. Instead of inefficient units being cut they continued to survive on government subsidies. This meant that the United Kingdom was losing its competitive edge in world markets.

The supply of goods in the economy rose very slowly in the 1960s and 1970s. Because supply was rising slowly, an increase in demand tended to lead to both rising prices and an increased reliance on foreign imports. Too many imports led to an increasing national debt, and the government was then forced to cut back in spending to reduce imports. Britain experienced 'stagflation' – a stagnant economy that was not growing, coupled with inflation. Demand management did not seem to be working.

The possible cure came with new policies that the Conservative government began to introduce in 1979. These policies concentrated on increasing supply rather than increasing demand. A whole host of measures was introduced to get supply going. These included:

■ reducing income tax to encourage people to work longer hours
■ reducing taxes on profits made by companies
■ reducing benefits to those out of work
■ reducing subsidies to loss-making industries
■ privatising rather than nationalising industries
■ reducing the size of the civil service
■ reducing government spending
■ passing laws to reduce trade union powers
■ measures against monopolies and restrictive practices
■ encouraging competition amongst groups such as solicitors, opticians, and even in the health service and schools.

The emphasis of the policy was to use supply as the means to drive the way forward.

Evidence collection point

How effective do you think supply-side measures have been? Select two or three of the examples of supply-side measures in the text and try to find out what the effects have been of implementing these policies. Why are different groups and individuals likely to have different views as to how effective these policies have been?

Let us now look as a range of government economic policies against the backcloth of these three major perspectives.

Interest rates

Interest rates represent the price of borrowing money. Generally speaking, the Bank of England will lower its base rate (the rate around which other interest rates are determined) when it wants to stimulate the economy. If you lower the price of borrowing, people will borrow more – and spend more (Figure 3.28).

The Bank of England will raise interest rates if spending is getting out of control. Higher interest rates discourage spending and dampen down business activity.

However, interest rates are not just used to influence spending in this country. Interest rates are also used to attract investment in this country from overseas. When foreigners invest in Britain they buy pounds sterling.

Sometimes the value of the pound falls because people are losing confidence in it. For example, if we were running huge trading losses then these losses would need to be paid for, often in pounds. If there are a lot of pounds on world markets the value of the

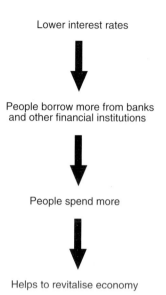

Figure 3.28 Lowering the price of borrowing

pound will start to fall. There comes a point at which this becomes undesirable. The government needs people to start demanding pounds again.

One way of doing this is to raise interest rates. So, if there is a run on the pound the government may be forced to raise interest rates. Higher interest rates will

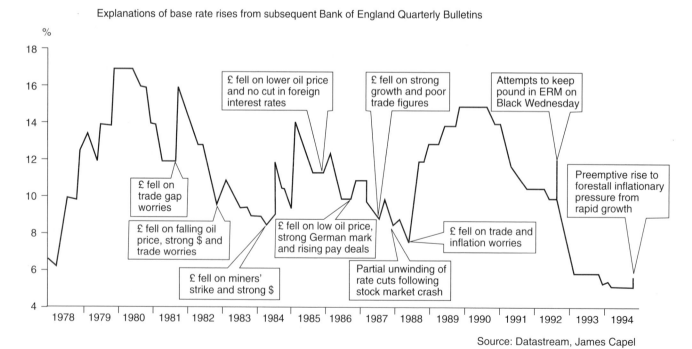

Source: Datastream, James Capel

Figure 3.29 Changes in interest rates since 1978 (major causes of rises)

attract foreign investors to invest in Britain because of the relatively high rewards to be gained.

Figure 3.29 sets out changes in interest rates in this country since 1978. You can see that interest rates have gone up following a decline in confidence in the pound or to discourage inflation in the home market.

Personal income tax

In 1992 the government raised £177.8 billion in taxes. The total was made up as follows:

Income tax	£59.6 billion
VAT	£40.0 billion
Local taxes	£22.1 billion
Corporation tax	£16.8 billion
Petrol duties	£11.8 billion
Spirits, beer, etc.	£ 5.3 billion
Tobacco duty	£ 6.6 billion
Vehicle excise duty	£ 3.2 billion
Taxes on capital	£ 2.4 billion
Customs duties	£ 1.9 billion
Other	£ 8.1 billion

Task

Set out the table of 1992 revenue in the form of a pie chart using a computer graphics package. Compare the figures with those for 1996. Use figures produced at budget time. This task will produce evidence of Core Skills in Application of Number and Information Technology.

Clearly, income tax continues to be the main source of taxation income for the government.

Personal income tax is the tax paid by individuals on their earnings in a given year. This will be earnings from a variety of sources: income from work, interest from savings, dividends from shares, rent from renting out property, etc.

The Conservative government since 1979 has continued to try to reduce the percentage of income that people pay in income tax. They believe that high income taxes discourage hard work and effort. They argue that if you reduce income tax then people have an incentive to work harder. In addition it enables the government to reduce its own spending. The argument is that individuals will spend their income to meet their own needs more effectively than if the government spends it on their behalf.

Evidence collection point

Find out by looking in back copies of *The Economist* or national newspapers (perhaps by using a CD-ROM), the amount of income tax that different taxpayers have to pay depending on their incomes.

Corporate taxes

Corporate taxes are those that are levied on business profits. Businesses that make over a certain level on profits must pay corporate taxes to the government. Of course, there are many items that can be offset against tax, such as money ploughed into investment projects. Businesses argue that corporate taxes should be kept to a minimum if business is to survive and to invest for future production.

Evidence collection point

Refer to this year's budget figures to find out the current rates of corporate taxes and what items can be offset against tax.

Value Added Tax

Indirect taxes are levied on expenditure as part of a payment for goods and services. They are called indirect because it is the retailer (or other middle person) who pays the tax charged to the government, rather than the consumer paying the tax directly.

Valued Added Tax (VAT) is levied on selling prices and is calculated at each stage of production. For example, if a retailer buys a box of goods for £500 and sells them for £800 then £300 has been added to the value of the goods. The retailer will only be responsible for the £300 worth of value that has been added to the goods when it comes to tax liability.

Direct taxes are more likely to be progressive, i.e. to take proportionally larger amounts away from the rich in order to reduce extreme inequalities in wealth or income. However, it is often argued that progressive taxes discourage effort and hard work (Figure 3.30 on page 88).

Many indirect taxes like VAT are said to be regressive in that they take a larger percentage of the income of the lower paid.

The Conservative government in recent years has switched the emphasis of the tax burden increasingly

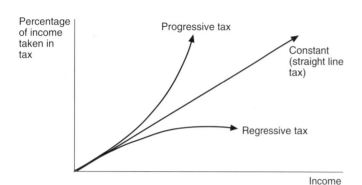

Figure 3.30 Types of taxes

from direct to indirect taxes as part of the theme of 'choice'. The argument is that people can choose whether to pay taxes. For example, you don't have to buy a bottle of wine, smoke cigarettes, and eat smoked salmon (all of which have considerable indirect tax components).

Evidence collection point

Research and outline some of the main components for and against (i) direct and (ii) indirect taxes.

Public services wage levels

There is one group of workers over whose wages the government has considerable control. These are people who work directly for the government, such as civil servants. Wage rises can and do often contribute to inflation. If the government wants to be seen to be taking a stand to reduce inflation it can limit the wage increases it gives to its own people. This then sets a standard for private industry.

In recent years we have increasingly seen the government take a 'hands-off' approach to employment. Increasingly, schools have become self-managing, we have seen the development of National Health Trusts, etc. The government therefore has become less of a direct employer. New bodies are self-managing and are responsible for pay bargaining with their employees.

However, these bodies get their funds directly from the government. The ability of National Health Trusts, Grant Maintained Schools, etc. to offer wages increases depends on how much they get from the government. For example, if the government in 1997

increases its funding for National Health Trusts by 2%, then the only way that these trusts will be able to give employees more than 2% extra will be by becoming more efficient, or by taking funds away away from other expenditure such as the treatment of patients.

The government is thus able to influence the economy semi-directly through the wages paid through public services.

Evidence collection point

Study a local example of pay bargaining by public service employees. To what extent is the money available limited by the government's policy on the economy at the time?

Public spending

Governments throughout the world are questioning the need for extensive government involvement in their economies. This is as true of Western countries as it is of countries emerging from communism in Eastern Europe. Tight control of public spending in the UK reduced the share of government spending as a percentage of all spending to 40% in 1990. However, it is unlikely that the government will be able to continue to reduce spending without causing serious weaknesses in existing services, such as education and health.

Figure 3.31 shows how government spending changed during the 1980s.

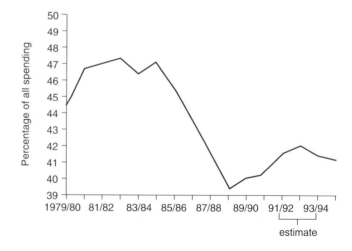

Figure 3.31 Government spending as a percentage of all spending

The Conservative government set out to cut government spending and to lower taxes. During the 1980s the government was able to cut back the growth in its spending by 12.6% over the decade. Because the economy was growing quickly this reduced the government's share of all spending.

In the early 1990s, government sending rose as a percentage of all spending. This was partly due to the recession. For example, as unemployment rose in the early 1990s the government had to spend more on social security. Also, with an ageing population (people are living longer), more will need to be spent on pensions and care for the elderly.

There has also been a change of emphasis. The 1980s philosophy was 'the less government the better', but now the government is more in favour of the 'social market'. This means that the government may intervene to make the markets work better. Public spending on training, roads, small businesses, etc. can help to improve the working of the market and to make firms more efficient. At the same time, education, health and other social services are vital if the quality of life is to be sustained and improved.

Evidence collection point

Explain how government spending can (i) help the working of the market, and (ii) hinder the working of the market.

Investment

The government is a major investor in the economy. It is responsible for huge investment projects such as the building of new motorways, bridges, and office complexes. Government investment makes a major contribution to investment expenditure and hence to demand.

Evidence collection point

Identify an example of a local investment project which is being carried out by the government. Outline the major spillover benefits for the local economy. Alternatively, identify an example of where the government is cutting back its investment in the local economy. What are the repercussions?

Regional assistance

In this country different regions and localities have had mixed economic fortunes. In the past, regions have been heavily subsidised by the government. There have been incentives for organisations to create jobs where industries are in decline. For example, government has provided grants to help in the purchase and hire of buildings and machinery, as well as subsidies for a set period of time for each employee employed.

In recent times there has been more of an emphasis on letting the market find its own solutions, for example by cutting back on subsidies to all but the most disadvantaged regions. The reasoning behind this is that if you subsidise inefficient regions you prolong the period of inefficiency.

However, some people argue that regional incentives still exist, e.g. in the form of government subsidies to Japanese car manufacturers to set up in this country.

Evidence collection point

Find out about regional subsidies to business organisations, particularly in your own region.

European Union policies

The UK is one of 15 European Union countries. These are:

France	Italy	Portugal
Germany	Ireland	Spain
Belgium	UK	Sweden
Holland	Denmark	Finland
Luxembourg	Greece	Austria

How the community is governed

The EU Commission is the controlling body of the European Union. Its headquarters is in Brussels, the capital of Belgium.

The Commissioners who sit on the Commission are chosen from the member nations of the EU. They serve for four-year renewable periods. On appointment they cease to act as Germans or Swedes or Britons and try to act only in the Community interest.

The Commission proposes new policies and laws based on the Treaties and other objectives agreed by Member States. It also has the job of ensuring that these laws, when passed, are properly enforced in the Member States.

The laws themselves are made by the Council of Ministers, but only after two other bodies have been consulted.

Consultation

First, an opinion on a proposed law has to be sought from the European Parliament. The European Parliament is made up of elected politicians from the many different European political parties and represents the views of the people. Besides its right to be consulted on all Commission proposals, the European Parliament has the final say on the Community's budget and has the power to censure the Commission. The Parliament is elected every five years (the next election is in 1999).

Second, the opinion of the Economic and Social Committee has to be sought. This is a committee of representatives from such bodies as trade unions, employers' associations and consumer groups throughout the Union.

Law making

Once opinions have been obtained from the representative bodies, the proposal passes to the Council of Ministers, which decides whether or not it should become Union policy or law.

The Council is composed of 15 Ministers, one from each Member State. Unlike the Commissioners, these Ministers act very much like representatives of their own country. Each one weighs up the proposal and, in the case of the more important matters, they all have to agree before it can become law.

In order to strengthen the Union's effectiveness, the number of cases where decisions can be taken on a majority vote has recently been increased. The European Parliament is more closely involved in majority decision-making.

The Commission mediates on Council debates, which are often animated as Ministers defend national viewpoints.

Once a proposal becomes law, it must be observed in all the Member States. Anyone breaking the law may be taken before either their own national courts or the Union's Court of Justice in Luxembourg.

A European Council, which is made up of the Heads of State of the 15 together with the European Commission President, meets at least twice a year in order to set broad guidelines for the Union.

We shall now go on to look at two EU policies which affect markets, namely regional assistance and the Common Agricultural Policy (CAP). We have already looked at Competition Policy (see page 69).

Regional policy

Jacques Delors, who was a major figure as European Union President until 1994, set out the Delors proposals covering the period 1987–97. The emphasis in these proposals was on moving the Union towards economic and social cohesion.

The Delors proposals recognised that the growth of free trade in the internal market of the Union would not lead to benefits for all regions. Therefore it was essential to provide assistance and support for economically backward and declining regions. Economic and social cohesion policies set out to make sure that the less favoured regions also benefit from the advantages of free trade among the 15 Member States. The Delors package therefore set out to double the money available for restructuring policies.

Between 1987 and 1992 the proportion of the EU budget allocated to structural funds increased from 17% to 27%. Funds were to be channelled to the four poorer nations among the 15 – Ireland, Portugal, Greece and Spain – particularly for developing infrastructure, e.g. transport and communications systems, and for training projects.

The Delors package set out that 33.5% of the entire EU budget should be made available for economic and social cohesion policies by 1997.

The EU is made up of an advantaged core and a disadvantaged periphery. The 'depressed south' is the most serious regional problem facing the EU at present. The European Commission identifies a number of types of 'disadvantaged' regions. These are:

1 *Lagging regions* – These are regions that have never really started to develop. There are a number of such regions in the Mediterranean zone with poor communications, low-output agriculture and very low incomes for many people.
2 *Declining industrial regions* – These are areas in which industry was once important but has now gone into decline, e.g. areas such as the north-west of England, and parts of South Wales.
3 *Peripheral regions* – These are regions that are far from the centre of large markets, e.g. the Highlands and Islands of Scotland, Ireland and Sicily.
4 *Border regions* – In the past a number of border regions were favoured because of the services they offered, e.g. warehousing for goods being traded between countries. With the lifting of border restrictions these areas now require assistance.
5 *Urban problem areas* – The big cities of Europe – e.g. Paris, Lyon, London – have particular social problems associated with crime, congestion, drugs, pollution, etc.
6 *Rural problem areas* – Some areas with poor climates for farming have particular problems. These areas have been adversely affected by reductions in subsidies to agriculture. The EU has a number of structural funds which provide help and support to these areas – for example, for projects in declining coal and steel communities, helping with assistance and training schemes to deal with long-term unemployed, the promotion of development schemes in rural and lagging areas, increased employment help for young people.

Evidence collection point

 Research and make notes about the types of regional assistance available from the EU to one locality in the United Kingdom.

The Common Agricultural Policy (CAP)

The Treaty of Rome (which originally set up what has become the EU) set out that the central aim of the Common Agricultural Policy (CAP) was to: 'Ensure a fair standard of living for the agricultural community'.

The main effect of this policy has been to guarantee incomes to farmers by setting minimum prices for agricultural products. These minimum prices set out

Figure 3.32 The CAP price

to ensure that farmers earn enough to keep farming. The price that the CAP guarantees will normally be higher than the free market price (Figure 3.32).

EU producers are also protected from cheaper imported foodstuffs from non-EU countries (e.g. American cereals). Imported non-EU foodstuffs can only be sold at a 'threshold price' (Figure 3.33).

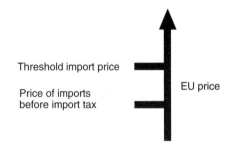

Figure 3.33 Some EU foodstuffs can be given a competitive edge

Import taxes are placed on these imports to bring them up to this threshold price. The effect of this important policy is to make EU foodstuffs more competitive within the internal market.

The result of guaranteeing farmers minimum prices is that more goods are provided than can be sold (because consumers cannot afford to pay the artificially high prices). The EU therefore has had to buy surplus produce and store it. This has given rise to the notorious wine lakes, butter mountains and beef mountains.

This is a very costly policy to run because not only does the EU have to buy up all the surplus stocks, it also has to build huge storage areas for products that often need to be refrigerated. Periodically, surplus stocks are sold off at the lowest possible prices to, for example, Russia and other East European economies.

Principles of the internal market	CAP
Removal of barriers to trade push down market prices	Prices administered by CAP
Open markets and competition lead to the survival of only the most efficient enterprises	Guaranteed prices allow inefficient farmers to survive
Removal of physical controls	Quotas used to restrict growth of output
Consumers will gain from price falls	Consumers will pay prices well above competitive world markets

In a widely acclaimed book *1992 – The Struggle for Power,* Tony Cutler and a team of writers argued that the CAP goes against the principles of a free market in Europe. Cutler contrasts the principles of the internal market and CAP.

The outline of the CAP above only gives a limited introduction. For a more detailed picture read *European Business Studies* by D. Needham and R. Dransfield (Stanley Thornes, 1994).

 Evidence collection point

The following letter appeared recently in a national newspaper. Read the letter and then carry out the tasks that follow:

Dear Editor

I am disgusted by the Common Agricultural Policy. Over 90 per cent of the European Union's Budget is spent on this policy. It is absolutely no use to hard-working British farmers. It simply serves to put money into the pockets of the French and German farmers who go on to produce butter mountain, and wine lakes. Under this scheme these farmers are paid according to how much they produce. They don't have to sell what they make. In fact they can leave their products to rot on the land. The UK never subsidised its own agriculture. British farms were simply the best in the world. Today our farmers are told not to grow produce on their own acres. They have to set it aside. This is so that French farmers can compete. The whole policy is a huge con. The sooner we scrap the CAP the better it will be for our farmers.

Yours angrily

A disgusted farmer

1 Make a list of points that are inaccurate in this letter.
2 Is there anything with which you agree in this letter?
3 Set out a letter in reply to 'A disgusted farmer'.

This work can supply evidence of Core Skills in Communication.

Evidence indicators

Using a video or tape recorder, organise a recorded discussion on 'why governments try to influence markets'. You will need to set out argument for and against government influence. You will also need to produce summary notes of a brainstorming session on the ways in which the UK government and EU policies influence markets.

In addition, produce a written summary of the effects of at least two of the means of government influence on a local or national market, e.g. the effects of privatisation or the impact of greater controls on out-of-town retailing developments. Tick the following boxes when you have completed the work.

- I can explain the reasons for government interventions in markets. (I have produced evidence of this in a tape recording/video of a recorded discussion.) ☐
- I have set our arguments for and against government intervention. ☐
- I have summarised the effects of at least two of the means of government influence on a local or national market. ☐

Business in the Economy: Unit Test 1

1   Effective demand occurs when:
   a   People have money in their pockets.
   b   The wish to buy a product is backed by the
       money to buy it.
   c   Producers are willing to produce more of a good.
   d   People's incomes are rising, enabling more
       saving.

2   Demand for a product is most likely to increase as
   a result of:
   a   Falling disposable incomes.
   b   A fall in the price of a complement.
   c   A fall in the size of the market
   d   A rise in the price of the product.

3   Which of the following demand curves represents
   demand at an instant in time?

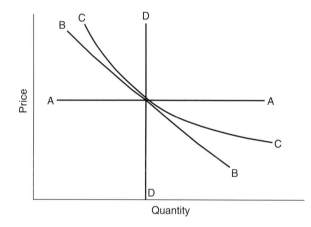

Quantity

4   Elasticity of supply measures:
   a   The responsiveness of the supply of goods to
       changes in price.
   b   The quantity of a good that will be bought at
       different prices.
   c   The responsiveness of supply to changes in
       demand.
   d   The responsiveness of supply to changes in
       income.

5   The government decides to build a new school
   instead of a new road. The opportunity cost of the
   school is:
   a   The cost of labour and materials.
   b   The new road
   c   The value to parents, children and teachers of
       the new school.
   d   Increased government spending on education.

6   In which of the following situations is elasticity of
   demand unitary?

Situation	% change in price	% change in quantity demanded
A	100	0
B	75	25
C	50	50
D	25	75
E	0	100

7   Which of the following best represents an
   organisation with a profit motive?
   a   The BBC.
   b   BP.
   c   The Boy Scout movement.
   d   Children in Need.

8   Which of the following has the greatest monopoly
   powers?
   a   A petrol station in a busy town.
   b   A petrol station at a motorway service area.
   c   A city newsagent.
   d   A High Street clothes shop.

9 The diagram below illustrates the market for CD players.

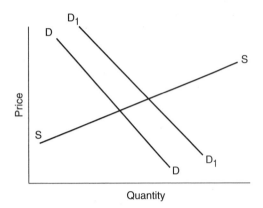

Quantity

Which of the following is likely to cause the demand to shift to D1–D1?
a An increase in the price of CD players.
b An increase in the price of compact discs.
c An increase in consumers' incomes.
d An increase in the popularity of mini-disc players.

10 Land, labour, capital and enterprise are:
a Factors of production.
b Chain of production.
c Divisions of production.
d Value of production.

11 The profit maximisation point for a firm occurs when:
a A firm obtains market leadership.
b There is the greatest difference between total revenues and total costs.
c Average costs are equal to prices charged for goods.
d The sales revenue from selling an extra unit of the good starts to fall.

12 Costs of production for business increase in the short term because:
a Fixed costs of production start to rise.
b Factors of production become increasingly more efficient.
c Variable costs start to rise once the optimum point has been reached.
d Costs can be spread over a large volume of production.

13 An example of an 'external' economy of scale would be when:
a Raw materials can be bought by a large firm

enjoying purchasing discounts.
b Larger organisations have the ability to diversify across a range of products.
c Similar larger organisations, developing in the same geographical area, benefit from shared research.
d Large organisations are able to borrow money from banks at preferential rates of interest.

14 An increase in the demand for jeans could result from:
a A fall in the price of cotton trousers.
b An increase in the supply of substitute products.
c A fall in disposable income.
d An advertising campaign for jeans.

15 If the price of chocolate biscuits falls, demand for them will:
a Increase.
b Decrease.
c Stay the same.
d Fall in proportion to the drop in price.

16 A market with a relatively small number of competing producers is best described as:
a Monopoly
b Perfectly competitive.
c Oligopoly.
d Monopsony.

17 A producer is faced with little competition in a particular market. The producer therefore sets a relatively high initial price in order to gain a high return with a view to lowering the price later on. This pricing strategy can be described as:
a Penetration pricing.
b Skimming pricing.
c Destroyer pricing.
d Expansion pricing.

18 Which of the following would be the best indicator of a non-competitive market?
a Easy entry for new firms into the market.
b Many firms operating in the market.
c Consumers have little knowledge about different products available.
d Businesses produce products which are identical in most respects.

19 Which of the following products is likely to have the most elastic supply?
a Seats at the Centre Court of Wimbledon on finals days.
b The supply of Brussels sprouts in summer.
c The supply of washing power in a supermarket.

d The supply of fresh cream buns in a corner shop.

20 Which of the following is the best example of a 'price taker'?
a The only producer of a particular product.
b A firm operating in a highly competitive industry.
c A business that tends to set prices which other firms follow.
d The Bank of England setting market interest rates.

21 Which of the following is the best description of destruction pricing?
a Setting a low price to gain entry into an existing market.
b Setting the market price which other firms are forced to follow.
c Setting a high initial price to gain a high return on sales.
d Setting the price of a product at an artificially low price.

22 Which of the following is an example of non-price competition?
a Selling goods with a free gift.
b Selling goods at a standard price.
c Selling goods as loss leaders.
d Buying goods at competitive prices.

23 Which of the following best exemplifies a competitive oligopoly situation?
a The supply and sale of gas.
b High Street banking.
c Fish and chip sales in a city.
d The sale of newspapers.

24 The demand for a new type of washing power would be elastic if:
a As a result of a reduction in its price revenue from selling the powder fell.
b A small increase in the price of the product led to a more than proportionate fall in the quantity sold.
c An increase in the price of the powder led to a proportionate fall in demand.
d As a result of a fall in the price of the powder revenue from selling the powder remains the same.

25 A construction firm is building a new motorway. Which of the following is an external cost to the firm of carrying out the project?
a The cost of employing labour for the project.
b The profit the firm will make from completing the project.
c Delays to motorists which occur while the road is being built.
d The cost to the firm of buying in the materials and equipment to build the road.

26 Which of the following is least likely to enable an organisation to reduce its unit cost of production?
a Increased specialisation of the labour force in producing larger outputs.
b Buying raw materials in bulk from suppliers.
c Borrowing money in larger quantities at a lower interest rate.
d Using more machinery to produce the same volume of output.

27 Expansion pricing occurs when:
a A business raises its price as a result of expanding its output.
b A business charges a relatively high price because it dominates a market.
c A business benefits from economies of scale enabling it to lower its price.
d A business lowers its price because the size of the market is contracting.

28 Increasing market share enables a business to lower its costs as a result of:
a Having to increase the quantity of its inputs relative to its outputs.
b The business benefiting from the 'experience curve' over time.
c Other firms lowering their costs in order to win back market share.
d Becoming a price taker with prices and costs being determined by the market.

29 Which of the following prices would a business that was engaged in destroyer pricing be most likely to charge?

30 Which of the following measures is the best indicator of 'relative market share'?

a $\dfrac{\text{Market share of Company A}}{\text{Market share of nearest competitor}}$

b $\dfrac{\text{Market share of nearest competitor}}{\text{Total market size}}$

c $\dfrac{\text{Market share of Company A}}{\text{Total market size}}$

d $\dfrac{\text{Total market size}}{\text{Growth in sales}}$

31 Which of the following is not an anti-competitive business practice?
a   Firms jointly agreeing to fix prices.
b   Firms jointly agreeing who they will supply to.
c   Firms trying to undercut each other's prices.
d   Selling goods at different prices to different people.

32 Which of the following is an example of a capital good?
a   Machinery.
b   Money.
c   Butter.
d   Insurance.

33 Which of the following reduces total demand for this country's products?
a   Investment.
b   Consumption.
c   Imports.
d   Exports.

34 Which of the following is the best example of monetary policy?
a   The government raising income tax.
b   The government lowering its own spending.
c   The government raising interest rates.
d   The government regulating business activity.

35 The opportunity cost to an individual of spending £10 on going to a pop concert is:
a   £10.
b   All the other things he/she could have spent £10 on.
c   The costs of getting to the concert.
d   The next best thing that could have been bought with £10.

36 The government would benefit most from an increase in taxes on tobacco when:
a   The demand for cigarettes is elastic.
b   Increases in the price of cigarettes lead to a proportional fall in demand for cigarettes.
c   The demand for cigarettes is relatively inelastic.
d   The demand for cigarettes is perfectly elastic.

37 Improvements in technology, such as computer-controlled manufactured systems, will:
a   Shift the demand curve for manufactured goods to the right.
b   Shift the demand curve for manufactured goods to the left.
c   Shift the supply curve for manufactured goods to the right.
d   Shift the supply curve for manufactured goods to the left.

38 Which of the following is an argument *for* nationalisation?
a   To give shareholders more control of the running of industries.
b   To expose businesses to the competition of the marketplace.
c   To ensure that essential services are organised by the state.
d   To increase the number of businesses operating in the market.

39 A surplus budget occurs when:
a   The government raises as much revenue from taxes as it spends.
b   The government increases the amount of money it raises from taxes.
c   The government spends less than it takes in revenue from taxes.
d   Government expenditures exceed revenues from taxation.

40 Which of the following has been privatised in recent years?
a   The Post Office.
b   British Telecom.
c   The BBC.
d   ICI.

41 Which of the following is most likely to lead to an increase in investment by businesses?
a   A rise in interest rates.
b   A general increase in consumer spending.
c   A downturn in the trade cycle.
d   An increase in pessimism in the business community.

42 Which of the following is a leakage from the circular flow of income?
a Consumer spending.
b Investment.
c Government spending.
d Savings.

43 Which of the following is an example of an *indirect tax?*
a Value added tax.
b National Insurance.
c Corporation tax.
d Income tax.

44 Which of the following is the best example of a horizontal merger between two businesses?
a An airline joining together with a soft drinks manufacturer.
b Two soft drinks manufacturers joining together.
c A bicycle manufacturer merging with a supplier of bicycle tyres.
d A toothpaste manufacturer merging with a manufacturer of shaving foam.

45 The major source of government taxation revenue in the 1990s has been:
a Income tax.
b VAT.
c Local taxes.
d Corporation tax.

46 Which of the following best represents a progressive tax?

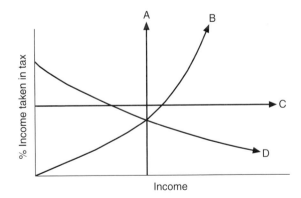

Income

47 Which of the following is a social cost of business activity?
a The creation of employment.
b The creation of pollution.
c The receipt of wages.
d The distribution of profits.

48 Government legislation concerned with the control of 'mergers and monopolies' is:
a Fair Trading Act.
b Restrictive Trade Practices Act.
c Resale Prices Act.
d Competition Act.

49 A 'complex monopoly' is deemed to exist when:
a A single firm dominates a number of complex markets.
b A group of companies which together have 25% of a market operate in an anti-competitive way.
c A number of businesses operating in a variety of different industries collude in pricing.
d A monopoly is complicated and difficult to understand.

50 A product will have a more inelastic demand:
a The larger the proportion of income spent on that good.
b The greater the number of substitute products available.
c The greater the strength of demand for that product.
d If it is bought only by people with higher incomes.

Business in the Economy: Unit Test 2

1 Which of the following is necessary for the existence of a market?
a A fixed location for trading to take place.
b A regulatory authority to govern trading in the market.
c Sellers of the goods or service to be in contact with buyers.
d Buyers and sellers are all in contact with each other at the same time.

2 In a recession businesses will expect to have:
a A fall in volume of sales.
b A rise in the volume of sales.
c No change in the volume of sales.
d A rise in profits.

3 Over recent years demand has increased for tea bags in preference to loose tea. One reason for this is that:
a There have been government health warnings about tea drinking.
b Tastes and preferences have changed among tea consumers.

c Falling incomes have led to the decline in tea drinking.

d Tea bags are seen by most people to be inferior product.

4 The wishes of producers and consumers are coordinated by the market mechanism. The point at which the demand and supply curves cut is known as the:

a Point of diminishing returns.

b Equilibrium point.

c Supply schedule.

d Demand curve.

5 Aggregate demand is the total level of demand in the economy. Which of the following is not part of aggregate demand?

a Investment.

b Government spending.

c Taxation.

d Consumer demand.

6 Aggregate demand and supply frequently alter as economies go through a trade cycle. The economic indicator which is least likely to fall in a slump is:

a Unemployment.

b Industrial production.

c Consumer spending.

d Investment.

7 When business activity creates pollution this can be described as a:

a Private benefit.

b Private cost.

c Social cost.

d Social benefit.

8 Which of the following would be a reason for privatising an industry?

a To control the production of harmful substances.

b To increase the power of the government in industry.

c To make the industry more answerable to shareholders and customers.

d To maintain the running of non-profit making services.

9 If the price of oranges falls, demand for them will:

a Increase.

b Decrease.

c Stay the same.

d Contract.

10 Which of the following is the best example of complementary goods?

a Salt and pepper.

b Tea and coffee.

c Fish and chips.

d CDs and cassette tapes.

11 The British Broadcasting Authority is:

a Owned by a group of shareholders.

b In the public sector of the economy.

c A government department.

d A public limited company.

12 Which of the following is an injection into the circular flow of income?

a Consumption.

b Exports.

c Savings.

d Taxes.

13 Jean Long sees a poster advertising men's underwear on a local billboard. She considers it to be indecent and wishes to make a complaint. To which of the following organisations would she be best advised to complain?

a The Advertising Standards Authority.

b The Office of Fair Trading.

c The Trading Standards Office.

d The police.

14 The diagram below illustrates the market for kiwi fruit. The shift to the left in the supply curve of kiwi fruit could have been caused by:

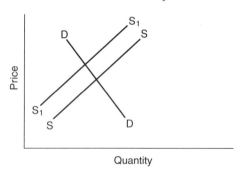

a An improvement in technical knowledge.

b A fall in production costs.

c Poor weather conditions.

d An increase in the number of suppliers.

15 Which of the following is most likely to lead to an increase in unit costs of production in a food-processing plant?

a Combining labour and capital more effectively.

b Reducing waste by more efficient production systems.

c Producing food dishes in greater bulk.
d Extending the delivery network to new destinations.

16 Which of the following best exemplifies a competitive market?
a Few sellers and many buyers.
b Almost identical products.
c Difficulty of entry for new firms into the market.
d Imperfect consumer knowledge of prices charged by sellers.

17 Which of the following is most likely to be a 'price maker'?
a A fruit and veg seller in a busy market.
b A city newsagent selling popular newspapers and magazines.
c The sole supplier of an exotic vegetable.
d A ticket tout trying to sell tickets at a greatly underbooked sports fixture on a rainy day.

18 The publisher of a new book initially sells the hardback edition at a high price, and several months later a paperback version at a lower price. This exemplifies:
a Penetration pricing.
b Expansion pricing.
c Destruction pricing.
d Skimming pricing.

19 Which of the following is an external economy of scale for a confectionery manufacturer?
a The development of new improved motorways and transport networks.
b The increased employment of specialist managers at a plant.
c The development and application of improved technology in the confectionery plant.
d The use of more specialist labour.

20 An example of horizontal integration would be:
a A brewery taking over a hop farm.
b A toothpaste manufacturer merging with a soap manufacturer.
c Two chains of chemists joining together into a single firm.
d A chemist's business being taken over by a brewery.

21 The most reliable indicator of a business organisation's market share is measured by:
a The sales turnover of the organisation.

b $\dfrac{\text{The market share of the company}}{\text{The market share of its nearest competitor}}$

c $\dfrac{\text{The market share of the company}}{\text{The market share of the company last year}}$

d The growth in the size of the total market from one year to the next.

22 The relationship between Gross National Product in 1994 and in 1995 could be used as a rough indicator of changes in:
a The rate of inflation.
b The level of unemployment.
c The rate of growth.
d The distribution of incomes.

23 Which of the following is the most likely result of an increase in demand for tickets for Centre Court at Wimbledon?
a An increase in the supply of seats.
b A reduction in the price of tickets for Centre Court games.
c A shortage of supply relative to demand.
d Excess capacity of Centre Court seats.

24 Which of the following are the best examples of substitute products?
a Different brands of washing powder.
b Salt and vinegar.
c Tapes and tape recorders.
d Butter and milk.

25 A function of a free market is to:
a Regulate the distribution of goods and services.
b Bring buyers and sellers together.
c Enable the government to restrict transactions.
d Impose minimum prices for important items.

26 A major form of aggregate demand for a domestic economy's products is:
a Savings.
b Public sector investment.
c Imports.
d Taxes.

27 Which of the supply curves shown below most closely represents perfectly elastic supply?

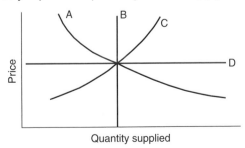

99

28 The government measure most appropriate for dealing with persistent inflation is:
a An increase in government expenditure.
b An increase in the money supply.
c An increase in interest rates.
d An increase in the public sector borrowing requirement.

29 If a 20% increase in price creates a 100% decrease in demand, the price elasticity would equal:
a 0.2.
b 1.
c 2.
d 5.

30 An example of an organisation in the public sector of the economy is:
a British Airways.
b Marks and Spencer.
c Mercury.
d The Post Office.

31 Which of the following represents the least competitive market situation?
a Oligopoly.
b Duopoly.
c Pure monopoly.
d Perfect competition.

32 Which of the following would be a social benefit of building a new hospital?
a The creation of jobs in the hospital.
b The expense of building the hospital.
c The traffic congestion caused around the hospital.
d The next best alternative that is sacrificed to build the hospital.

33 The government would gain most revenue from increasing taxes on wine and spirits when:
a The demand for wine and spirits is fairly elastic.
b The demand for wine and spirits is perfectly elastic.
c The demand for wine and spirits is unitary elasticity.
d The demand for wine and spirits is highly inelastic.

34 The radio that you bought last week fails to work. To whom should you first complain?
a The retailer.
b The manufacturer.
c Citizens Advice Bureau.
d *Which?* magazine.

35 The United Kingdom is called a mixed economy because it:
a Has public and private sectors.
b Imports and exports goods.
c Has industrial and commercial firms.
d Provides goods and services.

36 Which of the following is not a factor of production?
a Capital.
b Enterprise.
c Exchange.
d Labour.

37 Which of the following would be an example of non-price competition?
a Cutting production costs.
b Mounting an advertising campaign.
c Offering cheaper goods in a sale.
d Reducing business overheads.

38 Many state-owned industries such as British Telecom and British Steel have been privatised. What form of business organisation have they become on privatisation?
a Public Limited Company.
b Public Corporation.
c Private Limited Company
d Partnership.

39 A multinational company is a:
a Company with has branches in more than one country.
b Company owned by several different countries.
c Foreign company exporting goods to the United Kingdom.
d United Kingdom company trading with many other countries.

40 An increase in interest rates is likely to encourage:
a Spending.
b Withdrawal of savings.
c Savings.
d Hoarding.

41 When the ownership of public corporations is sold to the general public, this is called:
a Nationalisation.
b Privatisation.
c Communism.
d Public ownership.

42 Which of the following is not an example of fiscal actions by the government?
a Changing interest rates.
b Placing excise duty on tobacco.

c   Grants to businesses.
d   Changing rates of income tax.

43 The UK's international exchange rate describes:
    a   The total value of exports compared with imports.
    b   The amount of a foreign currency that can be bought with a pound.
    c   How much the UK is selling to other countries.
    d   The rate of inflation in the UK compared to other countries.

44 Consumers' disposable income is most likely to rise as a result of:
    a   An increase in income tax.
    b   A downturn in the level of economic activity.
    c   A reduction in National Insurance contributions.
    d   A fall in Gross National Product.

45 A business will have the greatest power to 'make' prices in a market:
    a   The greater the level of consumer power.
    b   The wider the variety of choice that consumers have.
    c   If it is able to use monopolistic practices.
    d   If it has several competitors.

46 Which of the following is an example of a financial economy of scale?
    a   The specialisation of labour.
    b   Spreading risks by producing several products.

c   Buying products in bulk.
d   Borrowing large sums of money at low interest rates.

47 Which of the following organisations best represents the 'public service' motive?
    a   Marks and Spencer.
    b   Shell UK.
    c   The Samaritans.
    d   BT.

48 For a want to become an effective demand the want must be:
    a   Extremely intense.
    b   Backed up by money.
    c   For consumer goods.
    d   For commonly available products.

49 A reason for an increase in the demand for compact discs would be:
    a   An increase in the price of compact discs.
    b   A fall in disposable incomes.
    c   A fall in the price of compact-disc players.
    d   An increase in Value Added Tax.

50 The central economic problem involves
    a   Costs.
    b   Choice.
    c   Money.
    d   Revenue.

All organisations exist for a purpose. They may provide goods or services designed to meet the requirements of consumers. Alternatively, they may simply exist to help others. For example, charities attempt to meet needs that profit-orientated institutions cannot serve. This unit looks at the many different types and structures of business organisation, both large and small, in both the private and public sectors. In doing so we look at many of the differences between types of organisational units, such as in their goals and objectives, as well as how these organisations are internally managed and administered in order to achieve their purpose.

Just like individuals, every organisation has a unique identity comprising a series of blended qualities which help to distinguish it from others. For example, by undertaking this course you are attending a college which may have communication and administrative systems as well as student facilities and internal management structures which are completely different from its nearest rival just a few miles away. This unit will help you to identify some of these differences and also understand why they exist. Your work placement may also provide you with a valuable source of information which will help you with the successful completion of this unit.

Business organisations

We live in a world of organisations. Organisations and their activities are central to our very existence and affect us daily in everything we do. They serve our needs and are an essential part of the fabric of our society. This chapter will help you to understand different types of business organisational activities ranging from those of multinational corporations to businesses such as your corner shop where you may buy your newspapers and confectionery. It will help you to understand how organisations work. When looking at this chapter you may find it useful to:

a contrast the ways in which organisations known to you work

b think about why many organisations differ so widely.

Objectives

The starting point for looking at organisations is to think about what an organisation is, and then what each type of organisation is trying to achieve. Organisations are a necessary part of the world in which we live. Though we probably do not think about it, we come across hundreds of organisations every day of our lives, for example your school or college, shops, radio and television stations, organisations which advertise through the media, as well as all of the other products and services we use daily which are provided by business organisations.

So, what is a business organisation? A business organisation is simply a unit that is set up by people to pursue certain *goals* in order to serve the needs of various groups of people. Etzioni (*Modern Organisations*, Prentice Hall) defines organisations as 'social units that pursue specific goals which they are structured to serve under some social circumstances'.

Goals can be defined as a future state of affairs which the organisation strives to achieve. Most organisations will set down guidelines for activity which serve as standards by which the success (i.e. the effectiveness and efficiency) of the organisation can be judged.

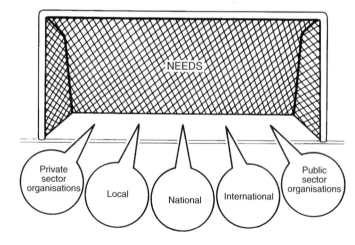

Figure 4.1 All organisations serve needs in pursuit of their goals

The prime responsibilities for all organisations is to serve their *stakeholders*. These are individuals and groups who have a stake in the running of the organisation and in the consequences of the organisational activities. For example, stakeholders may include shareholders, managers, employees, suppliers, customers, creditors and the public at large (Figure 4.2).

Figure 4.2 Examples of stakeholders

Stakeholders appear both within an organisation (managers and employees) and outside the organisation (customers and shareholders). The expectations of stakeholders will influence how an organisation seeks to achieve its objectives.

For example, owners and managers may set objectives which bring them rewards for the effort and risks they undertake. Customers will be concerned with value for money as well as a quality product. While most stakeholders will have common expectations, there may well be other areas over which disputes arise. For example, customers may want lower prices whereas shareholders want higher profits. Furthermore, the expectations of each group of stakeholders may change over time.

Goals and objectives provide a framework around which an organisation can satisfy stakeholder expectations and develop a strategy which involves making decisions and then measuring performance.

In doing so, this process provides a direction for an organisation to follow.

The objectives for each organisation will also be different. This is because they reflect the interests of different stakeholders, such as the power that each group of stakeholders may exert, as well as the size of the organisation, its business structure, the stage of development and the type of industry in which it operates – manufacturing, commercial services, public services, charity, etc.

When looking at statements of intent it is quite usual for different organisations to use various ways of describing what they are trying to achieve. One method of analysing these terms is to set them out into a hierarchy which shows the relative importance of each type of statement. We can then understand how they might influence the overall policy of the organisation at a range of different levels (Figure 4.3).

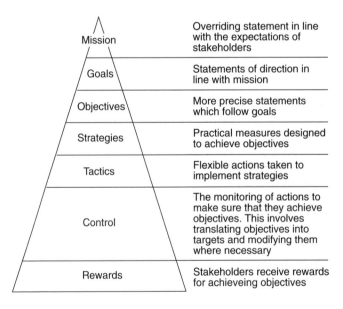

Figure 4.3 The hierarchy of objectives

National Power   We aim to be a world leader in power generation.

We will be the UK's top electricity generator and build profitable long-term business overseas.
Our purpose is to provide our shareholders with sustained growth in their development. We will stay ahead of current thinking in all we do:

■ with quality staff motivated to meet our customers' needs
■ by adopting best working practices
■ with a reputation for straight dealing
■ by good environment, safety and management practices wherever we work
■ with an open and friendly relationship with the communities where we work.

Glaxo   Glaxo is an integrated research-based group of companies whose corporate purpose is to create, discover, develop, manufacture and market throughout the world safe, effective medicines which will bring benefit to patients through improved longevity and quality of life, and to society in general through economic value.

1 In what ways are these statements
  a similar, and
  b different?
2 Which part of each statement would you describe as
  a their mission, and
  b their goals?

The *mission statement* shows stakeholders, both within and outside the organisation, what its core values are and provides a focus for action. Mission statements tend to be very general statements of intent and will usually focus upon how the organisation achieves its overall purpose, such as satisfying customer needs.

Goals expand upon the mission statement by providing a number of statements which indicate the direction the organisation will follow. They serve a number of functions. For example, goals may:

■ act as standards of performance
■ provide the basis for planning and management control
■ provide guidelines for decision-making
■ commit individuals to the activities of the organisation
■ show the true character of the organisation
■ serve as a basis for objectives and policies.

Etzioni distinguishes between three kinds or organisational goals. These are:

■ *Order goals* which restrict an organisation or prevent certain kinds of behaviour (for example, damaging the environment).
■ *Economic goals* concerned with the production of goods and services for customers.
■ *Cultural goals* which help to maintain the value systems of our society

The goals of an organisation are then translated into *objectives*. Objectives are more precise statements of what an organisation hopes to achieve and the desired end-results. In order to satisfy a range of goals an organisation must achieve its objectives in the future. Objectives may be *quantitative* or *qualitative* in nature. Quantitative goals may set specific targets, such as a sales volume of 100 000 units or a profit of £3 million. Qualitative goals will provide a series of statements or guidelines for the organisation, such as being good employers and providing good customer service.

One techniques which implements objectives is known as 'Management by Objectives' (MBO). This technique involves setting objectives for managers and employees and then upgrading or adjusting them according to changes and time limits (Figure 4.4).

Peter Drucker was particularly influential in stressing the importance of MBO. He set out to find out how best to manage a business to make sure that profits are made and that the enterprise is successful over a period of time.

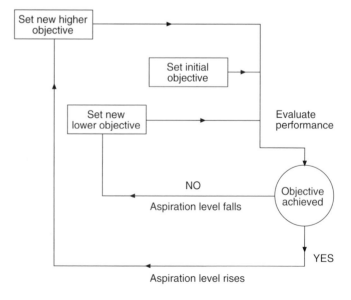

Figure 4.4 Management by objectives (MBO)

He felt that business objectives help management to explain, predict and control activities. The organisation should establish a number of objectives in a small number of general statements. These statements should then be tested in the light of business experience. It then becomes possible to predict business behaviour. The soundness of decisions can be examined while they are being made rather than by looking back on what has happened. Performance in the future can be improved in the light of previous and current experience.

In concrete terms, Drucker listed eight areas in which performance objectives need to be set out. These were:

- market standing
- innovation
- productivity
- physical and financial resources
- profitability
- manager performance and development
- worker performance and attitude
- public responsibility.

The major route to achieving objectives will depend upon *strategies*. Many businesses will use their *business plan* to outline their strategies. It is important to be clear what is meant by *strategy* and *tactics*. These terms originate from military use. Military strategy before and after a battle is the general policy overview of how to defeat the enemy.

Strategy involves developing the means to achieve objectives. Businesses sometimes use the term *policy* to describe strategies. A policy is a guideline for various kinds of action and implementation of objectives. A strategy/policy is distinct from an objective. For example, an objective might be to improve labour relations; the strategy would then be to set up schemes which help to do so. Having established its strategies an organisation can then work out its day-to-day tools and tactics to meet the strategic goals.

According to Professor Kotter (*A Force for Change*, Macmillan):

> The development of a good business direction is not an act of magic. It is mostly a tough, sometimes exhausting, information-gathering and analytical process. People who help develop such visions and strategies are not magicians. They tend to be broad-based strategic thinkers who are willing to take risks.

Strategy, therefore, involves looking at the larger picture and developing major decisions and directions for the organisation to move in. It is concerned with the 'generalship of business'.

Tactical decisions need flexibility. A tennis player might have a match strategy of playing with great power to force the opponents into errors. The player may practise his or her game to perfect the skills and power to implement this strategy (by, for example, practising forceful serving). During particular games that player may alter tactics (e.g. by serving long or short, to this side or that side of the court).

Task

Describe three situations in which you apply strategies to seek to attain particular goals. What sort of tactics do you apply to back up your strategy? How often do you alter your tactics? In what ways? How frequently do you have to modify your underlying strategy? How does this affect your actions?

In order to ensure that objectives are achieved, an organisation must translate them into workable practices and achievable targets which can be effectively monitored and controlled (Figure 4.5).

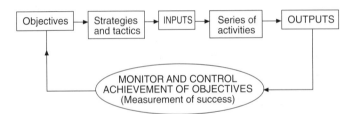

Figure 4.5 Monitoring and controlling objectives

By achieving objectives the organisation can then share the *rewards* among stakeholders. For example, shareholders may benefit from a good return upon their investment, employees from profit sharing and better employment security, consumers from better products and the community from reduced pollution or the use of bio-degradable materials.

Evidence collection point

Use yourself as a personal example to show how the various elements of the objective development process work. What is your mission? Outline your goals. Make a list of your objectives. What strategies and tactics are you going to use to achieve your objectives? How are you going to monitor your success and what rewards might you receive?

All organisations, no matter what sector they are in, turn inputs into outputs. However, their mission, goals and objectives may differ widely. There are millions of outputs in a modern economy based upon inputs.

It is, however, possible to classify the sort of objectives we would expect organisations to have on the basis of the type of industrial sector to which they belong. For example, business activity can be conveniently divided into:

■ extractive (primary)
■ manufacturing and construction (secondary)
■ services (tertiary).

Extractive industries – like farming and mining – take out things that are already provided by nature. Farmers grow and harvest crops, while miners take out fuel and minerals. Primary industries sometimes produce raw materials like iron ore (that go into making steel) and oil (that makes petrol, plastics, etc.), as well as producing final products like fish and oranges.

Manufacturing and construction industries make and assemble products. Manufacturers use raw materials and parts derived from other industries. A *semi-manufactured good* is one that is only partly made; most products involve several stages of production. Examples of manufactures are books, furniture, cars, chocolate and oil rigs.

Service/tertiary industries are particularly important in modern Britain. Services give something of value to people but are not physical goods. Examples of services are banks and public transport. Services are sometimes classified classified as *direct* (to people, e.g. the police, hairdressing) or *commercial* (to business, e.g. insurance, banking). However, this is not a very good classification because most commercial services like banking are used by individuals as well as by businesses.

Task

Set out column headings as below and then classify the following activities as primary, secondary or tertiary industries.

Primary   Secondary   Tertiary

Fishing, shoe making, shoe repair, coal mining, laundry, bottling spring water, market gardening, transport, key cutting, road sweeping, cloth making, mushroom growing, book illustration, road building, signwriting, theatre, window cleaning, oil refining, chocolate manufacture, building, advertising, insurance, retailing, civil service and oil drilling.

Manufacturing organisations

Industrial or manufacturing organisations are involved in changing natural resources or semi-manufactured goods into a tangible form of output, e.g. building a house, or manufacturing cars. Though some of the objectives for such organisations may be similar to the objectives of service organisations, others may vary considerably. For example, the following may be of greater concern for a manufacturing organisation.

■ *Health and safety* of employees and customers.
■ *Innovation* and use of technologies to provide continuous low-cost production runs.
■ Maintaining *output volume* levels.
■ *Environmental considerations*. For example, DuPont cite eight environmental goals:
  - the reduction of toxic air emissions
  - the reduction of carcinogenic air emissions
  - the reduction of emissions of 33/50 chemicals
  - the reduction of hazardous waste
  - to eliminate the land disposal of hazardous waste
  - to improve energy use
  - to cease production of chlorofluorocarbons
  - to equip ocean-going fleet with double-hulled tankers
■ *Worker performance* in a manufacturing or industrial environment, affecting employee relations, motivation and working practices.
■ *Minimum standards* of quality for various types of products and outputs.

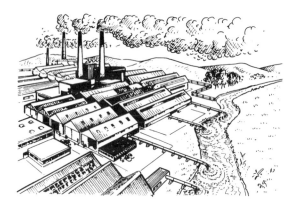

Evidence collection point

Talk to someone who works for a local business involved in industrial or manufacturing operations. From your discussion make a list of the objectives of his or her organisation. Underline/highlight the objectives which you think are unique to his or her *type* of organisation.

There has been a lot of talk about 'de-industrialisation' in Britain in recent years. The term suggests empty factories and shipyards. The general feeling is that de-industrialisation is a problem and not something to be welcomed.

The common-sense meaning of de-industrialisation is a decline in the importance of industry within the economy. But how do we measure this decline?

- Should we look at the number employed or the industrial output?
- Are we concerned with *absolute* decline or with *relative* decline compared with other sectors?

The concern with de-industrialisation has not been the result of falling industrial production in the advanced industrialised countries. Production has actually continued to increase. Today more products are produced, there is greater variety and new models have replaced older ones. For example, there is no comparison between a computer today and one of twenty years ago, a modern car uses fuel more efficiently, and living standards have risen.

However, as manufacturing has become better (not just in improving quality and efficiency but also in responding to environmental concerns and other challenges), it has also become smaller. In every advanced nation, industry employed a smaller proportion of the workforce in 1990 than it did in 1980; in virtually every nation, it also contributed a smaller proportion of the national output.

Everywhere, the 'slack' was taken up by services. It was in 1959 in the United States that, for the first time, the service sector of a nation became larger in terms of gross national product (GNP) than the industrial sector; in the 1990s the service sector in every country is much bigger, contributing 70% of the GNP in the United States, Britain and France, 64% in Italy, 60% in Germany and 56% in Japan.

Between the 1960s and 1993 the number of jobs in manufacturing in Britain fell from almost two-fifths (38.4% of the total) to less than a quarter (22%).

Case study – Texaco's strategic threads

Texaco aim to accelerate their process of continuous improvement by concentrating upon eight common strategic threads which are woven into the operations and plans of the whole company. These eight threads are:

- *Create value*   Being everything we do – from drilling for oil and gas to running a service station – the motivating force is the creation of value for our shareholders, customers and employees.
- *Become the company of choice*   We intend to become the recognised leader in our industry by strengthening the global value of the Texaco brand name, by performing as a strong, reliable and innovative business partner, and by working effectively with host governments to develop their countries' petroleum resources. And we certainly intend to be the company of choice for investors.
- *Be cost competitive*   We have been meeting this challenge by restructuring the organisation to enable people at all levels to act more quickly and decisively, not just to control expenses, but to apply advanced technology to re-engineer our operations and to guide us into new, profitable activities.
- *Leverage our technological leadership*   By creating, developing and exploiting new technologies, we can find and produce more oil and gas reserves, manufacture products more efficiently and remain a step ahead of the competition in bringing new products and processes to market.
- *Form strategic alliances* Few companies have been as successful in forming and maintaining alliances with governments, business partners and suppliers. Our successes range from the creation of the Caltex companies in the 1930s and the US joint venture Star Enterprises five years ago to our recent initiatives in China and in Russia.
- *Take a protective approach to the environment*   We are firmly committed to the highest environmental, health and safety standards in our operations, and we intend to use our proprietary technology to innovate solutions to the environmental challenges that face society. We will also maintain a leadership position in the public debate over the development of laws and regulations that protect the environment on a cost-effective basis.
- *Develop human resource excellence*   We are demanding more of ourselves – to join Texaco, to remain here and to advance with it. We are cultivating a workforce that is highly qualified, superbly trained, culturally and geographically diverse and empowered to assume responsibility and take action.
- *Build financial strength* Texaco is determined to remain a strong company, and our financial strategies to

control debt, build equity and be superbly credit-worthy are the cylinders powering our operating initiatives.

1 Make a list of types of stakeholders who may be interested in viewing these strategic threads.

2 What are they trying to do?

3 How different might Texaco's strategic threads be from those of a service organisation?

Services organisations

Some of the best-known names in the UK provide commercial services – Barclays Bank, General Accident, British Rail, Lloyds, to name but a few. Whereas many of the objectives of industrial organisation relate to the manufacture or construction of products and the effects of their manufacture for the community, service organisations may, similarly, have a range of objectives which relate to their operations in providing customer services. For example, their objectives may include:

- the need to develop or improve an *image* for the customer
- how they maintain or improve *customer satisfaction*
- the need to provide *reliable services* that are delivered 'first time'
- the ability to *differentiate* services from other service providers
- the need to be *caring* and customer orientated.

Evidence collection point

Imagine that you were setting up a taxi business in your local community. Make a list of objectives that you would have for your business.

There are three main reasons for the growth of the service sector of the economy.

First, as societies become richer, they choose to spend a higher proportion of their incomes on buying services rather than more tangible products.

Second, it has so far proved very much harder to wring additional *productivity* out of services than out of manufacturing. Greater productivity in a car plant means more robots on the production line: the product does not suffer, indeed probably the reverse. However, if greater productivity in a school is measured by fewer teachers in the classroom, quality of education suffers immediately.

Third, as countries become richer, they are able to 'export' their profits in the form of investment in other countries. It is evident that a number of countries have invested in manufacturing in developing countries. In turn the rewards are returned in profits, interest and dividends that can be spent on leisure services.

There is no sign at all that the shift in demand towards services will cease. Indeed, there is a powerful reason to expect it to accelerate – namely the ageing population in industrial societies. The proportion of people over 60 will continue to rise in every developed country for at least a generation. By the year 2020, more than 30% of the population of Germany and Italy will be over 60. Older people are more likely to spend their income on health care, holidays and domestic services. The countries that increase living standards most quickly in the future will be those that can improve the way they run service societies.

Services can be divided into four main groups: *financial services* and *distribution* tend to be in the private sector, whereas *health* and *education* tend to be in the public sector.

Technology can be used to transform each of these areas. In financial services we will see more than ever before the development of paperless money. Financial services are becoming increasingly tailored to the needs of individual customers. In distribution, the benefits of bulk retailing are likely seen much more widely, with resultant cost cutting. In health, technological advances have led to people living longer. The focus of health care will now shift to raising the quality of care and fitness throughout people's lives. Education, too, will become a continuous process, involving people of all ages. Workers can expect to be retrained to take on completely different skills several times during their careers.

Financial objectives

Though British Airways list seven corporate objectives they claim that their 'overriding objective' is 'to deliver a strong and consistent financial performance. As any business manager knows, you must make profits if you are to maintain and expand your business. The airline business is often regarded as cynical. We have to prove that we can produce good profits consistently.'

A business can work towards different types of financial objectives. For example, an organisation may strive for profit, and then to improve on that profit. Alternatively it may operate on a not-for-profit basis.

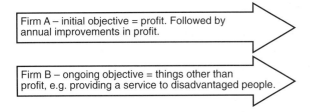

Figure 4.6 Objectives of profit and not-for-profit organisations

The large supermarkets are obvious examples of organisations which set out to make profits. The profits they make enable them to reward shareholders, and also to plough money back into the business in order to improve the quality of their services. Supermarkets operate in a highly competitive market. Firms that failed to make profits would not be able to improve their services and would rapidly lose trade. Most business and commercial organisations are profit motivated. They may not go all out to maximise profits, but they must make a profit or shareholders, and people who have lent them money, would lose confidence.

Not-for-profit organisations include building societies, friendly societies and charities. These organisations do not, strictly speaking, have a profit motive, but they still create a cash surplus which is distributed in a number of ways. Such organisations need to establish clear objectives so that their performance can be judged against appropriate standards. Without such standards there would be no way of checking how well an organisation is doing, and how its performance can be improved.

In recent years we have seen more and more organisations building the profit objective into their overall objectives. For example, charity shops today operate as commercial enterprises rather than casually run voluntary services. Increasingly, there is an appreciation of the importance of using scarce resources efficiently. For example, what would be the purpose of having an Oxfam shop on the High Street if it ran at a loss? It certainly wouldn't help famine relief. Organisations like building societies have increasingly switched to becoming public companies with shareholders, e.g. the TSB.

In the public sector it is unlikely that the overriding objective of any organisation will be pure profit maximisation. However, organisations such as schools, colleges and hospitals will have financial objectives based on:

- the need to meet financial performance targets
- offering value for money
- the provision of the best possible service for the lowest possible cost
- overall financial efficiency.

Evidence collection point

Find out the financial objectives for:
1   A small commercial business.
2   The school or college you attend.

In what ways are they (a) similar, and (b) different?

Market share objective

Many firms seek to be *market leaders*. Market share is regarded as very important in business today. If you are the market leader you stand a very good chance of being the most profitable organisation in the market or industry. If you can sell the most goods, then you will be able to spread the costs over a large output – e.g. advertising costs, production costs, distribution costs, etc.

Most businesses are all too aware of the importance of market share and will fight tooth and nail to gain supremacy. And when they succeed in gaining the lion's share they will broadcast their success far and wide. You can immediately identify major market leaders – once they have acquired an edge they are often able to hang on to it by ploughing money into investment, product improvement, and advertising and promotion. Coca-Cola is an obvious example of a market leader.

Evidence collection point

Find out who is the market leader in particular markets such as disposable nappies, washing powder and lawn mowers. What advantages do they have over competitors? How do they seek to protect their market leadership?

Another programme of research in the USA came up with another theory supporting this notion about market share. The study was called 'Profit Impact of

Marketing Strategies', more usually referred to as PIMS. This attempted to analyse the marketing factors which had the biggest influence on profits. Though a number of conclusions were drawn, the study highlighted the close relationship between market share and profitability as shown in the table.

Linking market share and profit (PIMS)

Market share	Profitability
Under 7%	9.6%
7–14%	12.0%
14–22%	13.5%
22–36%	17.9%
>36%	30.2%

The PIMS research showed clearly that organisations with a large market share were more likely to be profitable. This concept was taken further by the research to show that a high market share and increased performance were the results of moving along a 'learning curve', so that the more an organisation learnt about its market through market research, the better it would perform.

Rather than just try to increase market share, some organisations attempt to *sales maximise*. 'Turnover' is a term that means the value of sales in a given period of time. Clearly, if you are making sales then you may well be taking revenue away from competitors. The large the volume of sales the more your fixed costs can be spread. Business managers want the sales of their branch or department to be high, For one thing, this helps to boost the size of their department and hence their salary.

Task

Consider a firm that has fixed costs of £100 000 and additional costs of 50 pence for each unit produced. What would be the average cost per week to produce:

a 5000 units
b 20 000 units
c 500 000 units?

How does this example show the benefits of sales maximisation and the need for a large market share? What problems might be caused if the firm is not able to sell a lot of its output?

An organisation may also have the related objective of *growth*. A firm that grows quickly will find it easier to attract investors and will be able to produce on a larger scale. However, one of the biggest mistakes that business people make in the early days is that of over-trading. Running a large business is quite different from running a smaller one. All sorts of problems arise from over-trading: for example, there might not be enough cash to pay bills in the short term, managing more staff can be difficult, and so on.

Another related objective may be to operate in a wide variety of markets so that the organisation can spread risks. If one market fails, another may support the loss. However, opening into new markets also exposes a business to fresh risks. It may be better to operate in a small number of well-known markets rather than exposing yourself to new risks.

Public service objectives

There are many other types and groups of business objectives which organisations may pursue. As well as having objectives which directly address the areas of profitability and market share, these objectives may be concerned with public responsibilities which the organisation accepts that it has towards society and other stakeholder interests. For example, IBM publish a Stakeholder Report in which they summarise information under the following headings:

- *Employees* Population, earnings, graduates recruited, student unemployment, equal opportunities, etc.
- *Customers* Customer satisfaction, price/performance, customer training, customer visits, etc.
- *Suppliers* Amount of business, percentage of expenditure, investment in land and buildings, major construction projects, etc.

■ *The community* Secondments to community projects, support for enterprise agencies, contributions to charities, youth training, sponsorship, community projects, etc.

Though social objectives of this kind are considered to be of great importance, it can be argued that they may confuse managers over standards of performance so that they focus upon these areas instead of increasing profitability and market share.

Another area for corporate objectives is that of the environment and safety. Over recent years many organisations have set minimum acceptable environmental standards. For example, Cadbury Schweppes identify eight key commitments as part of their objectives:

■ To comply with applicable environmental laws and regulations and reflect industry best practice.
■ To undertake performance evaluation and compliance reviews.
■ To aim for efficient use of energy, raw materials and the minimisation of waste and pollution.
■ To promote efficiency in solid waste management.
■ To promote a healthy and safe environment, training and communication for employees.
■ To communicate environmental policies.
■ To institute procedures to implement policies successfully.
■ To have regular policy reviews and updates.

Public sector organisations have rather different objectives from those of commercial organisations. Their problem, however, is not primarily concerned with profitability or market share, but more *how* commercial they should become in order to carry out

their role for society. In doing so they have to meet the expectations of taxpayers, as opposed to shareholders, and provide them with value for money.

Evidence collection point

Write to or contact a local business organisation. Find out how it fulfils its role as a 'good corporate citizen'. Use examples to support your analysis. Organise your work so that you provide evidence of Core Skills in Communication.

Finally, in developing business objectives it is worth mentioning that many organisations adopt a policy of *satisficing*. A business may set itself the task of attaining clearly visible goals rather than maximising and stretching itself to the limit. This makes considerable sense when the firm does not want to take unnecessary risks. It may feel that it is better able to meet its orders with a margin to spare, to meet financial targets comfortably and to build up a reputation for delivering to its stated goals.

This does not indicate complacency. It may indeed be seen as sound business sense. Successful businesses trade and operate over many generations. (In the longer term a satisficer may make larger profits than a short-term high-flying maximiser).

Throughout the 1980s Polly Peck was heralded as the high-flying company of the decade, but in the early 1990s the company collapsed – it had over-traded and failed to keep proper account of its activities. In 1992, the ambitious Maxwell Corporation collapsed, with staggering debts. At the same time organisations with sound long-term strategies such as Marks and Spencer and Shell have gone from strength to strength.

Business organisations

Earlier in this chapter we looked at what an organisation is. We can also identify certain key features that are possessed by most organisations.

■ An organisation must have a *name* (e.g. Aston Villa Football Club, Edgbarrow School, St John's Ambulance Brigade, National Westminster Bank).
■ All organisations have *objectives*.
■ Organisations have *rules* and *regulations*. Some of these are written down formally on paper. Other informal codes of practice are not written down but people recognise and respond to them. Some

of the rules will be imposed externally by the government in the forms of laws.

- Organisations have *patterns* and *structures*. Usually there will be a chain of command. Some organisations are hierarchical, with decisions being passed from the top downwards. Other organisations will be more democratic, with many decision-makers with equal or similar powers.
- Within an organisation different members will have positions, ranging from the managing director to the caretaker. Positions are sometimes referred to as *posts* or *offices*. Each position will have set tasks associated with it.
- Organisations usually have a *chain of authority*. In a hierarchical organisation someone at a lower level may need to get permission from a superior to do something.
- Within an organisation different officers will have the *power* to carry out particular actions. Powers may be written down in a formal contract. Other powers may be informal. Individuals are recognised to have particular powers to carry out a course of action.
- *Records* are an important feature. Nowadays many records are kept in computer files – often in databases. Written records are also important. Most organisations will store records for several years.

Private sector

All organisations exist in either the *private sector* or the *public sector* of the economy (Figure 4.7). The private sector includes organisations which are owned and operated on behalf of private individuals. As we shall see, these organisations range from small one-owner businesses to vast multinational corporations. Private sector organisations include sole traders, partnerships, companies, franchises and cooperatives. Some private sector organisations are concerned with making goods – we call these *industrial organisations*. Some are concerned with buying and selling – we call these *commercial organisations*. Some are concerned with banking and insurance – these are *financial organisations*.

Evidence collection point

Using the template below, fill in the details of the different types of private sector organisations in your area. If you are unsure about the definition of each type of organisation turn to pages 117–124. For each category of organisation your list should include one example of a business engaged in industrial, commercial or financial activities.

	Sole trader	Partnership	Company	Franchise	Cooperative
Industrial					
Commercial					
Financial					

Public sector

Public sector organisations are all those which are in some way directly controlled by central or local government or are controlled indirectly through some form of government-created body. Government organisations are accountable to representatives elected by citizens and are concerned with the running, welfare and protection of the country and society in which we live.

An example of *central government* activities would include Departments of State such as Education, which is run by civil servants, and the armed forces, which provide protection for society as a whole.

Local government activities are the business activities provided by councils, such as car parks, swimming pools and leisure services.

Public corporations are owned by the government on behalf of the people. One example is the British Broadcasting Corporation. Such organisations seek to

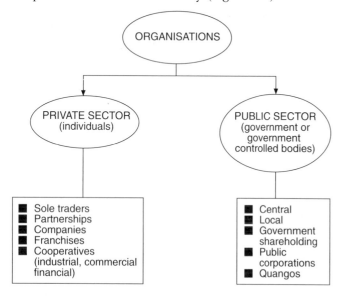

Figure 4.7 Private sector and public sector organisations

produce goods and services to serve all the people of the country.

Quangos, (quasi-autonomous non-government organisations) are elected public bodies. They are run by boards of directors to manage a particular initiative. For example, local TECs (Training and Enterprise Councils) are responsible for providing training opportunities and schemes on behalf on local employers.

Evidence collection point

Make a list of the ways in which organisations from the public sector affect your daily activities.

Charities

Charitable organisations have a special status in law. In the past charities were set up to provide for the helpless and needy (the poor, the homeless, etc.). Nowadays many organisations have adopted charitable status in order to gain tax and other advantages (e.g. public schools).

Evidence collection point

Make a list of organisations which have some form of charitable status. In what ways are they (a) similar, and (b) different?

Local organisations

All organisations have a different size or scale of operations. Often the size is determined by the nature of such operations as well as the type of market they serve. For example, there are many local electricians, plumbers and joiners within most communities who provide a range of services for householders. Such businesses, which may include local newsagents, Muslim butchers and local radio stations, are often better at tailoring services to the specific needs of members of each community.

National organisations

At a national level, organisations may cater for the needs of their customers across the country, Many are large and have become household names. They operate, however, largely within the UK and in general have not expanded their operations overseas.

This may be because there are few opportunities for that sort of business in other countries, often because other businesses are serving such needs or because the organisations were not designed to operate in other countries. Another reason may be that such organisations are either still in the public sector or have only recently been privatised.

Examples of organisations which operate at a national level include British Nuclear Fuels Ltd, Railtrack, political parties, legal organisations such as the courts or the Monopolies and Mergers Commission, and economic interest groups such as trade unions and the Confederation of British Industry (CBI).

International organisations

International organisations now have a membership in several nations whether at a government or at a private level. Examples are the European Union and the Red Cross/Crescent. Business organisations may also have tentacles in many countries (e.g. Marks and Spencer, Laura Ashley, BP, Unilever).

Evidence collection point

Make a list of organisations operating at local, national and international levels. In each case explain why such organisations operate at each level of activity.

Case study – Nestlé worldwide

The story of Nestlé and its activities within the UK is only a small part of the group's global approach to business.

Henry Nestlé was an enterprising man with vision. Born in 1814 in Frankfurt, Germany, he moved to the Swiss town of Vevey in 1843 where in 1866 he launched the world's first milk product suitable for new-born babies. It was soon so successful that physicians recommended its use in the fight against high infant mortality rates.

Nestlé came to Britain in 1868 and began manufacture at Aylesbury in Buckinghamshire in 1873. By 1905 the company had 18 factories, five of which were in Britain. Today, more than 125 years after its formation, the company employs 200 000 people worldwide in 440 factories in more than 60 countries and sells 15000 products across the world. Each year some 180 000 tons of Nestlé products are exported to 120 countries.

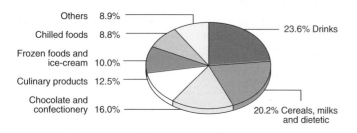

Worldwide sales of main product groups

Others 8.9%
Chilled foods 8.8%
Frozen foods and ice-cream 10.0%
Culinary products 12.5%
Chocolate and confectionery 16.0%
23.6% Drinks
20.2% Cereals, milks and dietetic

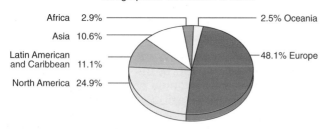

Geographical distribution of sales

Africa 2.9%
Asia 10.6%
Latin American and Caribbean 11.1%
North America 24.9%
2.5% Oceania
48.1% Europe

1 Make a list of Nestlé products which you either use or have come across.
2 What benefits do they gain from being a global business?
3 Contrast the activities of Nestlé with a much smaller organisation known to you.

Differences between types of organisations

The earliest forms of business organisation were sole traders and partnerships. Today many vastly different types of organisations exist, ranging from large public sector bodies to a small business in the private sector run by just one person. So, why are these organisations so different? There are many different reasons for this which go to the very depths of the history and development of the society in which we live.

In the early days, society evolved from feudalism towards a laissez-faire system in which there was little government intervention, and then forward again to capitalism with capital-owning employers and wage-earning workers. Under capitalism, the government takes some responsibility for the monitoring and control of activities through legislative law making.

Today, when we look at the private sector of the economy we often think of the industrial giants such as Unilever, Shell and Glaxo. But at the other end of the spectrum, we must not forget that big businesses started from small businesses, and these have an equally important role to play. For example, 3.2 million people in the UK are today classified as being self-employed.

There are a number of bases from which we can make comparisons of organisations. These include:

1 Types of liability
A share is a piece of paper showing that you are the part-owner of a business. Shareholders in companies and cooperatives have the legal protection of *limited liability*. Sole traders and ordinary partners cannot have limited liability.

Limited liability means that if the business goes bankrupt because it is unable to meet its debts, the shareholders/owners will not be liable (responsible by law) to lose their possessions to pay the money that is owed. The maximum amount that they could lose is the amount they have put into their shares.

Evidence collection point

Talk to some small business owners. Find out if they have limited liability. What views do they have either for or against having some form of limited liability?

2 Use of profit
The great benefit of being a sole trader is that all of the profits belong to the owner. However, so do the losses! A large number of sole traders go out of business each year.

In partnerships, an agreement between partners is set out in a *deed of partnership* which states how profits and losses will be shared. If a deed does not exist, then under the 1890 Partnership Act all partners are entitled to share equally in the profits of the business but must also contribute equally to the losses.

Owners of companies are known as *shareholders*. Shareholders may receive a benefit from owning shares in two ways. First, they may be paid a dividend upon the shareholding which is expressed as a return on the par value of the shares. Second, they may receive income by selling their shareholding at a value above that which they paid for it.

Traditionally *cooperatives* distributed profits as dividends which related to purchases by each member of the society. Thus profits were shared amongst customers. Some cooperatives still retain the dividend, others use trading stamps, while many have member benefit schemes which provide special discounts and offers.

Few businesses distributes all of their profits to their shareholders or owners. After tax has been paid and profits allocated, many organisations retain profit as a form of reinvestment for the business.

Public-sector organisations on the whole provide services which cannot be catered for by market forces. As a result, objectives vary from those for many private sector organisations. For example, though a health trust may run a few services for a profit, this would not be considered to be their most important function.

Public-sector expenditure has declined as a proportion of GDP since 1979. One declining sector has been nationalised industries, the sale of which through privatisation has been a feature of the last 15 years. Investment for such industries has either come from central government or through guarantees on loans from the private sector. Not all profits when made have been ploughed back into each business.

3 Sources of finance
A *sole trader will* have to provide capital from either their own sources or by taking out loans or an overdraft from a bank or other type of institution. A sole trader may also take out a mortgage.

Partnerships improve capital-raising opportunities by bringing in partners who may be able to contribute further capital for the business. However, limitations upon the number of partners may restrict capital-raising opportunities.

Companies provide opportunities for shareholders to invest their money without risking their personal assets. Whereas a private limited company can offer shares only to business associates, friends and family, a public limited company can offer its shares to the public through the Stock Exchange and this provides enormous capital-raising opportunities.

Public corporations, local authority enterprises and other forms of *public ownership* are largely funded by the state through various forms of taxation. However, since the Local Government Act 1988, many services have been put out to competitive tender to encourage competition with private sector organisations.

4 Control and legal obligations
As soon as one person starts to trade he or she becomes a *sole trader*. The sole trader business does not have a separate legal identity from that of the individual – in other words they are one and the same. They trade in their own name and assume all of the responsibilities of being in business and, therefore, if the sole trader breaches a contract, he or she has to meet the claim from personal resources.

Sole traders have the minimum of formality and have the advantage of maximum flexibility to do as they wish. Sole traders have the advantage of being self-employed which enables them, for tax reasons, to offset legitimate business expenses against income tax. Income tax liability is also assessed in arrears.

Partnerships can range from two people working together up to a maximum of 20, though certain professional partnerships may exceed this. The relationships between partners are generally determined by a Deed of Partnership between the partners; where no deed exists, the provisions of the Partnership Act of 1980 will specify the relationship between partners. Deeds normally cover areas such as capital, profit shares, responsibilities, salaries and procedures for dissolution.

Despite the Deed, partnerships in England and Wales do not have a legal personality and partners incur unlimited liability for the business. Partners are also responsible for the business debts of other partners. Partnerships may limit the flexibility of partners to sell or transfer their ownership as no partner may be able to transfer ownership without the consent of other partners.

As a result of *Salomon v Salomon & Co* (1897), a *company* exists as a separate legal identity from that of its owners. Assets such as property, as well as debts, belong to the company and not to individual members. To set up a limited company it is necessary to go through a number of legal procedures in order to gain recognition. This mainly involves the presentation of various documents and records to the Registrar of Companies. These documents are open to scrutiny.

All limited companies must present a Memorandum of Association and Articles of Association in order to receive a Certificate of Incorporation (Figure 4.8).

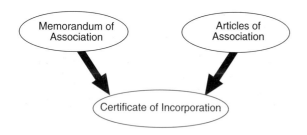

Figure 4.8 Documents required to set up a company

The Memorandum spells out the nature of the company when viewed from the outside. Someone reading the Memorandum would be able to obtain a general idea of what the company is and the business with which it is concerned. The Memorandum sets out:

■ the name of the company
■ the registered address of the company
■ the objectives of the company
■ the capital of the company.

Most companies will produce a fairly vague list of objectives in their Memorandum. This will give them the opportunity to alter their activities if market opportunities arise.

The Articles of Association set out the rules which governs the inside working of a company. They include:

■ the rights attached to the holding of the various types of shares offered by the company
■ the rules and procedures for issuing and transferring shares
■ the procedures and timings of company meetings
■ the details of how accounts will be kept and recorded
■ the powers and responsibilities of directors

■ the details of how company officers will be appointed.

Once these documents have been accepted the *private company* will be granted a Certificate of Incorporation and can start to trade. The Certificate of Incorporation sets up the company as a legal body in its own right. The company (not individual shareholders) enters into contracts and can sue or be sued in a court of law.

A *public company,* however, must take further steps before being granted a Certificate of Trading. The Memorandum of a public company must state that the company is to be a public company, and it must abide by a legal minimum figure for allotted share capital. Before a Trading Certificate is granted, shares allotted must be paid up to at least 25% of their nominal value plus the whole of any premium payable.

Public sector organisations may take a number of forms and are controlled by either central or local government and owned by the nation or ourselves as citizens of the nation. For example:

■ *Government departments* are run by ministers who are responsible to Parliament. Each department is staffed by civil servants.
■ *Nationalised industries* or *public corporations* are created either by Royal Charter or by a special Act of Parliament which sets out their legal rights and duties. They have wide powers which control their functions, legal status and methods of control. Each corporation has a semi-autonomous Board which is appointed by the government. Each industry is accountable to Parliament through its annual report. Parliament lays down a policy framework for the industry.
■ Nationalised industries which have been sold to the private sector or companies in which the government has some form of shareholding are usually subject to some form of government control. In some industries, the government retains a 'golden share' which enables them to veto certain decisions over some issues for a number of years.
■ *Local authorities* are corporations incorporated by Royal Charter or by a special Act of Parliament. As well as receiving money from local taxation and central government, they may finance their activities by issuing municipal stock or by raising loans. Ultimately their policies are controlled by government policy and local councillors, who are entrusted with responsibility for making decisions by local electors.
■ *Quangos* are created by Parliament, which

determines their powers and procedures. Quangos reflect a compromise between central government control and the needs of independence and flexibility of private sector organisations. Ministers have no direct control other than appointing the chairman.

Evidence collection point

Provide an example of each type of public sector organisation. In each instance find out more about the organisation and the people involved in running it. Comment in particular upon the control and legal organisation. If necessary write to the organisation to obtain more detailed information.

Types of ownership

The sole trader

The *sole trader* is the most common form of business ownership and is found in a wide range of activities (e.g. window cleaning, plumbing, electrical work, busking). The table shows a breakdown of sole proprietors into industrial groupings in 1991.

Evidence collection point

Provide examples of local businesses which could fit into each of the groupings in the

Percentage of the total for sole traders, broken down into industrial groupings (1991)

Grouping	Percentage
Construction	20.3
Production	5.7
Agriculture	6.9
Other services	8.7
Motor trades	6.0
Business services	5.0
Catering	7.9
Finance	10.2
Retailing	18.6
Wholesaling/dealing	5.2
Transport	5.5

table above. You could carry out a survey of local businesses, and store your information in a computer database. Present the information in the form of a pie chart using a graphics plotting package. This will help you provide evidence of Core Skills in Application of Number and Information Technology.

No complicated paperwork is required to set up a sole trader business. Decisions can be made quickly and close contact can be kept with customers and employees. All profits go to the sole trader, who also has the satisfaction of building up his or her own business.

But there are disadvantages. As a sole trader you have to make all the decisions yourself, and you may have to work long hours (what do you do if you are ill or want a holiday?). You do not have limited liability, and you have to provide all the finance yourself. As a sole trader you need to be a jack-of-all-trades, and just because you are a good hairdresser does not necessarily mean you have a head for business!

Task

Write a short case history of a sole trader in your neighbourhood. When did he or she set up? What is the business? What are the advantages and disadvantages to this person of being a sole trader?

The partnership

An ordinary partnership can have between two and twenty partners. Professional partnerships may have more. People in business partnerships can share skills

117

and the workload, and it may be easier to raise the capital needed.

For example, a group of vets is able to pool knowledge about different diseases and groups of animals, and two or three vets working together may be able to operate a 24 hour service. When one of the vets is ill or goes on holiday, the business can cope. The table shows a breakdown of partnerships into industrial groupings.

Percentage of the total for partnerships, broken down into industrial groupings

Grouping	Percentage
Construction	11.2
Production	6.5
Agriculture	16.0
Other services	6.0
Motor trades	5.2
Business services	3.4
Catering	12.5
Finance	7.3
Retailing	24.0
Wholesaling/dealing	4.8
Transport	3.1

Evidence collection point

Present the information from the table above in pie-chart format using a computer graphics plotting package. Compare the pie-chart for partnerships with that for sole traders. What are the key differences? Carry out a survey of partnerships. Try to find examples that would fit into each of the groupings outlined in the table. Plan this work so that it provides evidence of Core Skills in Communication, Application of Number and Information Technology.

Partnerships are usually set up by writing out a *deed of partnership* which is witnessed by a solicitor. This sets out important details such as how much each partner should put into the business, how the profits and losses will be shared, and the responsibilities of each partner.

Partnerships are particularly common in professional services (for example, doctors, solicitors, accountants). A small business such as a corner shop may take the form of a husband-and-wife partnership.

The main disadvantages of partnerships are that people can fall out (she doesn't work as hard as me!),

ordinary partnerships do not have limited liability, and partnerships can rarely borrow or raise large amounts of capital. Business decisions may be more difficult to make (and slower) because of the need to consult all the partners. There may be disagreements about how things should be done. A further disadvantage is that profits will be shared.

There is also a special form of partnership called a *limited partnership*. Limited partners (sometimes called 'sleeping partners') can put money into a partnership and have the protection of limited liability. However, they play no part in the running of the business. The business will be run by at least one non-limited partner.

Companies

A company is set up to run a business. It has to be registered before it can start to operate, but once all the paperwork is completed and approved the company becomes recognised as a legal body.

The owners of a company are its *shareholders*. However, other individuals and businesses do not deal with the shareholders – they deal with 'the company'.

Shareholders put funds into the company by buying *shares*. New shares are often sold in face values of £1 per share, but this is not always the case. Some shareholders will only have a few hundred pounds' worth of shares, whereas others may have thousands of pounds' worth (Figure 4.9).

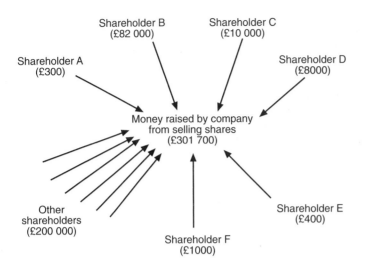

Figure 4.9 A company raises money from its shareholders

The capital of the company

The promoter or directors of the company can apply to the Registrar of Companies for permission to issue new shares. The amount that the Registrar agrees to is called the *authorised capital*.

The *issued capital* is the value of the shares that are actually sold to shareholders. A company may choose not to issue the full value of its authorised capital: it may hold back a certain amount for future issue.

Shares can be issued for payment in stages over a period of time. Each stage is then termed a 'call'. There may be three or four calls before the full price is finally paid. The *paid-up capital* is the money that has been received for these partly-paid shares.

Evidence collection point

Obtain the prospectus of a new company. This will show details of the offer of shares for sale. What is the value of the authorised capital? How much capital is actually being sought? What arrangements are being made for the payment of the shares?

Private companies

Private companies tend to be smaller than public ones (discussed below) and are often family businesses.

There must be at least two shareholders but there is no maximum number. Shares in private companies cannot be traded on the Stock Exchange, and often shares can only be bought with the permission of the *board of directors*.

The board of directors is a committee set up to protect the interests of shareholders. The members of the board choose the managing director, who is responsible for the day-to-day running of the business. The rules of the business set out when shareholders' meetings will take place and the rights of shareholders.

Private companies may find it possible to raise more cash (by selling shares) than unlimited-liability businesses. The shareholders can also have the protection of limited liability.

The main disadvantages compared with unlimited-liability businesses are that they have to share out profits among shareholders and they cannot make decisions so quickly. They cost more to set up.

Figure 4.10 Choosing the management in a private company

Evidence collection point

Study a local private company. Who owns it and who controls it? How much share capital does it have? What are the advantages and disadvantages of this organisational form for this particular company?

Public companies

A *public company* has its shares bought and sold on the Stock Exchange. Companies can go to the expense of having a 'full quotation' on the Stock Exchange so that their share prices appear on the dealers' visual display screens.

The main advantage of selling shares through the Stock Exchange is that large amounts of capital can be raised very quickly. One disadvantage is that control of a business can be lost by the original shareholders if large quantities of shares are purchased as part of a 'takeover bid'. It is also costly to have shares quoted on the Stock Exchange.

In order to create a public company the directors must apply to the Stock Exchange Council, which will carefully check the accounts. A business wanting to 'go public' will then arrange for one of the merchant banks to handle the paperwork. Selling new shares is quite a risky business. The Stock Exchange has 'good days' (when a lot of people want to buy shares) and 'bad days' (when a lot people want to sell). If the issue of new shares coincides with a bad day a company can find itself in difficulties. For example, if it hopes to sell a million new shares at £1 each and all goes well, it will raise £1 million; but on a bad day it might only be able to sell half its shares at this price.

One way around this problem is to arrange a 'placing' with a merchant bank. The merchant bank recommends the company's shares to some of the share-buying institutions with which it deals (pension funds and insurance companies, for example) who may then agree to buy, say, one-tenth of the new shares. In this way the merchant bank makes sure that the shares are placed with large investors before the actual date of issue comes round. Then, even if it is a bad day on the Stock Exchange when the shares are issued, the company's money is secure.

Another common method by which public companies raise share capital is to offer new shares for sale to the general public. Very often the shares will be 'underwritten' by a merchant bank. The company's shares are advertised in leading newspapers and the public are invited to apply.

When a company is up and running, a cheaper way of selling is to contact existing shareholders inviting them to buy new shares. This is a *rights issue*.

Case study – The growth of Floral Prints Ltd

In 1920, Mavis Stein set up her own dressmaking business in Norwich. She employed four seamstresses to work on the patterns she produced. The business flourished and was soon producing dresses for a number of wealthy private clients in Norwich.

Mavis then joined up with Jenny Jones, an up-and-coming fashion designer from the London School of Fashion.

The partnership they formed concentrated on high-quality 'up-market' garments. The garments were sold to

fashion houses in London and Norwich. The partnership deed set out that each would put £2000 into the business, share the work and the profits. They would be entitled to two weeks' holiday a year.

Mavis was to concentrate on the commercial side of the business (i.e. the buying and selling). She would purchase materials and equipment, and meet buyers. She would also handle the accounts. Jenny was to concentrate on the design and production and manage the workforce, which in the 1950s had risen to two tailor cutters and 16 seamstresses. They also employed a full-time secretary and bookkeeper.

In the 1960s, Mavis suffered a prolonged illness. The deed of partnership was altered. Mavis left her money in the business and became a sleeping partner, with the profits being divided 60:40 in Jenny's favour.

In 1970, Jenny retired and it was decided to form a private company known as Floral Prints Ltd. Initially shareholders were mainly friends and relatives. Mavis and Jenny between them held 55% of the shares. Shares were also sold to employees. A number of employees who had been with the business from the start were given additional shares. The board of directors, which was chaired by Mavis's daughter Rose, appointed Steven White as the managing director.

During the 1980s, Floral Prints established a national chain of boutiques. In order to finance this expansion the company went public. In 1985 the company was taken over by a large German company. It still trades under the original name.

1 Who originally owned and controlled the business?
2 What would be the benefits of becoming a partnership?
3 Would there be any drawbacks?
4 Why do you think the business became a private limited company?
5 What would be the advantages and disadvantages of becoming a private company?
6 Who owned and controlled the private company?
7 Why do you think the business became a public company?
8 What would be the advantages and disadvantages of becoming a public company?
9 Who owned and controlled the public company?

Franchising

In America over one-third of all retail sales are made through firms operating under the *franchise* system. It is a form of business organisation that is becoming increasingly popular in the United Kingdom.

Franchising is really the 'hiring out' or licensing of the use of 'good ideas' to other companies. A franchise grants permission to sell a product and trade under a certain name in a particular area. If I have a good idea, I can sell you a licence to trade and carry out a business using my idea in your area. The person taking out the franchise puts down a sum of money as capital and is issued with equipment by the franchising company. The firm selling the franchise is called the *franchisor* and a person paying for the franchise is called the *franchisee*. The franchisee usually has the sole right of operating in a particular area.

This type of trading is common in the fast-food industry, examples being Spud-U-Like and Pizza Hut. Further examples are Dyno-Rod (in the plumbing business), Tumbletots, Body Shop and Prontaprint.

Where materials are an important part of the business (e.g. hamburgers, confectionery, hair salons) the franchisee must buy an agreed percentage of supplies from the franchisor, who thus makes a profit on these supplies as well as ensuring the quality of the final product. The franchisor also takes a percentage of the profits of the business, without having to risk capital or become involved in the day-to-day management.

The franchisee benefits from trading under a well-known name and enjoys a local monopoly. Training is usually arranged by the franchisor. The franchisee is his or her own boss and takes most of the profits.

Task

Write down two lists to summarise the advantages of franchising to (a) the franchisor, and (b) the franchisee. Can you think of any more examples of firms operating under this system?

Cooperatives

Cooperatives are increasingly popular as a means of business organisation. At one time they were only to be found in agriculture and retailing, but in recent years the biggest growth areas have been in service occupations and in small-scale manufacturing.

The basic idea behind a cooperative is that people join together to make decisions, work and share profits. There are many different types of cooperative; we consider here the three most commonly found in business.

Retail cooperatives

The first successful cooperative in this country was set up in the northern town of Rochdale in the last century. Twenty-eight weavers clubbed together to start their own retail shop, selling a few basic grocery items. The profits were to be shared according to the amount spent, and everyone would have an equal say in how the shop was run.

The basic ideas started in Rochdale continue in today's Co-op. On buying a £1 share in the Co-op you are entitled to go along to the annual general meeting to discuss policy.

Consumer cooperatives are usually registered as limited-liability companies.

Evidence collection point

Find out how your local cooperative retail outlet is organised. How can you become a member? Where are meetings held? How can you have a say in policy? How are profits distributed? In researching this, you may be able to provide evidence of Core Skills in Communication.

Producer cooperatives

Producer cooperatives are usually registered as companies 'limited by guarantee', which means that

Annual Meetings of Members

GRANTHAM FRIDAY, 29th APRIL
THE LEISURE CENTRE, UNION STREET, at 7 p.m.

Members are warmly invited to join their Members' Council representatives
for refreshments from 6.30p.m. until 7p.m.

Admission on production of Members Share Book

CO OP Greater Nottingham Co-operative Society Ltd.

each member undertakes to fund any losses up to a certain amount. There are many types. A workers' cooperative, for example, is one that employs all or most of its members. In a workers' cooperative members:

- share responsibility for the success or failure of the business
- work together
- take decisions together
- share the profits.

Other examples of producer cooperatives are groups to grow tomatoes, to make furniture or to organise child-minding.

The main problems that such cooperatives face are finance and organisation. Cooperatives sometimes find it difficult to raise capital from banks and other bodies because they are not groups that seek primarily to make profits. A number of cooperatives in recent years have, however, been able to raise finance by selling shares. Some larger cooperatives have also found that it is necessary to set up a management structure in order to get decisions made.

Marketing cooperatives

Marketing cooperatives are most frequently found in farming areas. The farmers set up a marketing board to be responsible for, among other things, grading, packaging, distributing, advertising and selling their produce.

Businesses in the public sector

Most people expect *public-sector organisations* to seek to increase the welfare of all citizens. In recent years,

the shape and style of management in the national public sector has changed enormously. Today all three major political parties emphasise the role of *accountability* in the public sector. In other words, public-sector organisations are expected to show that they are using money wisely – that they are not wasting scarce resources. In 1993, for example, the new Head of the Prison Service and the new Chief Constable of the Metropolitan Police force were all chosen because of their business expertise.

From 1979 onwards, managers in government were repeatedly told that they were sluggish, inward-looking and even incompetent in comparison with their equivalents in the private sector. Public-sector managers were accused of being wasteful, unresponsive and resistant to new ideas. This is rarely the case today. In schools, hospitals, transport organisations and many other areas of the public sector, business planning takes place in a detailed way. Public-sector managers are explicitly defining tasks, pinning down who is responsible for doing them, measuring whether they have been done and how well, and establishing clearly what they cost, as well as controlling the cost.

The government has a shareholding in some businesses and direct ownership of a number of major enterprises. Local government also has a stake in some business activities.

Local government enterprises

Local councils often run business activities. For example, in municipal car parks attendants may be employed to collect parking charges and to check that no-one is using the car park without paying. Swimming pools, day nurseries, bus services, parks and leisure centres may all be run by the council, although services are increasingly being offered to tender by private firms.

Finance to run municipal enterprises usually comes from local taxes and from charges for using the services.

The local council may also sponsor *job creation schemes*. For example, it might set up *enterprise workshops* where people can start up a business in premises with a very low rental charge.

Central government enterprises

In the United Kingdom certain business activities are run by one of the following (see Figure 4.11):

- a government department
- a company in which the government has a shareholding
- a public corporation.

CENTRAL GOVERNMENT ENTERPRISES

Run by a government department

Example: Inland Revenue

Run by a company in which the government has a shareholding

Example: UK Nirex Ltd

Run by a public corporation

Example: British Rail

Figure 4.11   Central government's involvement in business

Activities run by a government department

When an activity is run by a government department, a Minister is in overall charge, and the department is staffed and run by civil servants. An example of this is the Department of Inland Revenue which deals with the collection of some taxes.

From a business point of view there are a number of criticisms of such an organisation:

- Decisions are made slowly because there are many links in the chain of command.
- The organisation is not forced to be efficient – there is no competitive spur.
- It is difficult to protect the public's interest by checking on how the department is run.

Companies in which the government has a shareholding

Over the years the British government has had shareholdings in a number of public companies, including BP and Rolls-Royce. The shareholding has often been a form of subsidy to the company to help it carry out research, compete with overseas companies, or avoid unemployment of the workforce.

In recent years the government has been selling off these shareholdings in the belief that companies should stand on their own two feet.

Activities controlled by public corporations

Public corporations, the main form of direct government involvement in business, are owned by the state on behalf of the people. They are felt to be a suitable form of *public ownership* because, although the state owns the corporations, their controllers are given a lot of freedom to make their own decisions.

Public corporations are set up by Act of Parliament, an example being the Coal Industry Nationalisation Act 1946. They are also called *nationalised industries*.

Although a public corporation provides a marketable good or service, it is different from a normal company in that the managers are not accountable to shareholders – instead they are accountable to the government. Also, although today public corporations are expected to be profitable, in the past they were given wider *social responsibilities*.

Contrasting public corporations with public companies

Public corporation	Public company
Set up by Act of Parliament	Set up by issuing prospectus and offer to buy shares
Owned by government	Owned by shareholders
Run by chairperson and managers appointed by government	Run by management team chosen by directors representing shareholders
Aims to provide a public service as well as having commercial goals	Commercial goals

Once a public corporation has been set up by Act of Parliament, a government Minister is made responsible for the industry concerned. However, the Minister chooses a chairperson (not a civil servant) to run the industry on a day-to-day basis.

The government sets yearly targets for the particular industry to meet, and the chairperson and managers must then decide on the best way to meet these. The government might, for example, set the British Broadcasting Corporation a target of making a 15% return on capital employed in 1997. The Corporation must then decide on how to meet this target in conjunction with its commitment to provide a high quality of programmes. In other words, it must decide how much to spend on programmes, how much to pay in wages and so on. The Corporation is supposed to have the freedom to make these day-to-day decisions and there is a lot of heated debate in the press and Parliament if the government tries to interfere.

Case study – Sweeping modernisation at the BBC

John Birt took over as Director General of the BBC in January 1993. He immediately promised an effective BBC which would clear away red tape, territorialism and confusion.

The BBC's television services had overspent by £38 million in 1992. Mr Birt therefore said that a priority was to appoint a new finance director. Key structural changes would include:

- streamlining the operation to focus on aims and objectives, policy and performance
- the separation of programme production from commissioning and scheduling in television and radio
- the creation of a separate resources, engineering and services department to run the production side of the BBC.

1 Is it important to be financially accountable?
2 What will be the effects of the restructuring on:
   a the number of people working for the BBC
   b the efficiency of its organisation
   c the quality of programmes?
3 Is it a good idea to buy in programmes rather than to make them?
4 The BBC will become more 'streamlined'. Is this a good thing?
5 Should the BBC have a business person as its Director General?

Up to 1979 many public corporations were given large financial subsidies by the government. There were two main reasons for this:

- to try to maintain jobs in declining industries (e.g. coal and steel) because they were major employers.
- to encourage the corporations to continue to run services which, although not profitable (and so of no interest to private firms), were of great social benefit to certain individuals, groups or communities.

Today public corporations are encouraged to concentrate more on meeting financial targets, and

to be more profit and client conscious. Members of the public do have some control over the running of public corporations. They can make a complaint to their local MP who can then raise the matter when the Corporation is being discussed in Parliament. In addition, a committee of MPs has the job of keeping an eye on each of the corporations, and each has a consumer council to which complaints can be made.

Privatisation

One of the major policies of the Conservative governments of the 1980s and early 1990s was *privatisation* – that is, putting public sector businesses into private hands. Examples of privatisations are British Airways, British Telecom and British Gas.

A number of reasons have been given for privatisation. First, it creates wider share ownership – the idea is that, by owning shares in public services like the telephones, electricity, water or gas, people will feel more involved. Second, privatisation is supposed to make these industries more competitive. It is felt that if some of these industries are encouraged to compete more they will produce a better service. In the past losses were made up by taxes; losses today could lead to bankruptcy. Third, money from the sale of the industries should enable the government to lower taxes. Fourth, the industries themselves can raise money more easily for investment. And finally, the Conservative government sees its role as deciding on policy and making laws, not running companies (Figure 4.12).

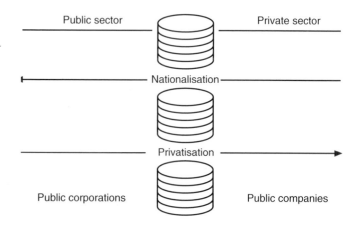

Figure 4.12 Privatisation and nationalisation

Evidence collection point

Carry out research to find details on two public corporations, two recently privatised concerns and four long-term public companies. Find out the date when each organisation was set up, nationalised or privatised. Who is the chairperson and/or chief executive of each organisation? What lines of business is it involved in? How many people are employed? What is the annual turnover? What is the latest profit figure? What other important data should you include in your database? Use Core Skills in Information Technology in presenting your data.

Organisational structures

If we look back in time we can see that there has always been a need to organise people. Probably the first large-scale organisations were Egyptian state monopolies used for building the pyramids. At the head of the organisation was the Pharaoh, whose authority was invested by divine right and who delegated authority to a vizier who acted as prime minister, chief justice and treasurer over an elaborate bureaucracy, at the bottom of which were the slaves.

During the medieval period serfs replaced slaves at the bottom of the economic and social order and, for a long time, businesses were viewed as a necessary evil. By about 1750 the ideological and cultural stage was set for the advent of the industrial revolution. Industrialisation resulted in the birth, growth and development of a massive number of organisations. At the same time there was a growing awareness of the need for coordinating and monitoring such organisations.

Simple structures

Nearly everyone at some time or other thinks about starting a business of their own. You often hear people say, 'Someone could make a fortune out of that' or 'I wish I had thought of that idea first'. So imagine that you decide, having left college and having worked for a large organisation for a few years, to 'go it alone' and set up your own business buying and selling jewellery by mail-order.

Consider your role in this new organisation. If you did not employ anyone else at the start, you would soon find that you needed to become a jack-of-all-trades, able to turn your hand to every aspect of the business.

For example, you would be involved in buying the jewellery, designing a catalogue and having it printed, finding out the sort of people who would like to buy the jewellery, putting together a mailing list and sending the catalogues out, taking orders by phone and mail, dealing with all correspondence, sending the orders out, keeping the accounts, getting the money in and banking it, as well as all the other issues needing daily attention.

We can show diagrammatically how this business is organised. Your role would be at the centre of a range of functions for which you would be personally responsible (Figure 4.13).

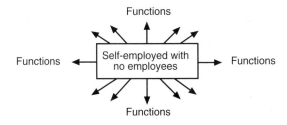

Figure 4.13 Organisation in a one-person business

Operating on your own is rarely easy. There are times when, as owner, you require the help or advice of others with special skills, such as an accountant, a bank manager or a solicitor.

As the business expanded you would find it necessary to employ some form of help, possibly part-time at first and then full-time. As you begin to employ other people you would relinquish some of the work you had been doing, and this would require a reappraisal of your role as well as the creation of roles for others within an organisational structure. For example, if you employed four other people you might give them roles of buyer, office junior, mail room clerk and accounts clerk (Figure 4.14).

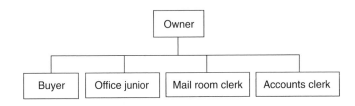

Figure 4.14 Organisation chart of small mail-order jewellery business

125

Notice that the business has been organised to reflect the *activities* of each of the members of staff. We can also see that each of these staff is responsible to one manager only, the owner. The chart therefore has a *pyramid* structure, in which the authority for management decisions starts from the top and extends downwards in a hierarchial pattern.

This simple example shows that, as an organisation develops, it has to consider the roles of everybody within it. It has to be organised in the best possible way to meet its objectives efficiently. This involves defining the relationships between departments, as well as between managers and other employees, so that all employees know what they should be doing, where they fit into the organisation, and to whom they are responsible.

Evidence collection point

Obtain an organisation chart either from your place of work or from the institution you attend.

What would need to happen if the jewellery business expanded? Perhaps a second warehouse is purchased, professional managers are taken on and more staff are employed. The business might also move into other product lines such as watches and clocks. As the organisation grew, the organisational structure would have to change to reflect such developments. At this stage the crucial decision would be *how to divide up the business* so that the various parts could be managed efficiently.

Dividing up the organisation

Dividing up an organisation is often referred to as *departmentation*. For example, because customers are all over the country it might be sensible to divide the business by regions. Or would it be easier to divide by functions, processes, etc.? The design of the new organisational structure would be crucial to the success of the business. It would have to:

- bring together every part of the organisation
- relate each part of the organisation to every other part
- show where the authority of individuals and departments lies
- enable those within the organisation to assess their roles and status.

Departmentation is the process by which certain activities or sections of an organisation are grouped

logically and then assigned to managers. The way in which this is done depends on the aims of the organisation. The five main methods of grouping employees are by:

- function
- product
- process
- geographical area
- type of customer.

As we shall see later, a *matrix structure* can be used to combine grouping methods.

Division by function

This is probably the most common way of grouping employees. *Functional organisation* means that the business is divided into broad sectors, each with its own specialism or function. Examples are 'Production' and 'Sales'. Though every organisation will have its own method of structuring its functions, we shall look at some typical division within a large organisation (Figure 4.15).

Figure 4.15 Division by function

- *The company secretary* The law requires that every company has a company secretary, who is responsible for all legal matters and often advises other departments. Duties include filling in the Memorandum and Articles of Association when the company is started. He or she also acts as a link between shareholders and directors and handles correspondence to and from shareholders, informing them of company meetings and important matters. Often a company secretary will have some other responsibilities, such as that of *office manager*.
- *The administration department* Many large organisations have a central administration office which is responsible for controlling paperwork

and supporting other departments with facilities such as filing, mail, word processing and data handling. Modern offices use computers and information technology extensively. It is common practice for an administration department to appoint an office manager with the responsibility for coordinating *office services* and offering expert advice to departmental managers. The work of an office manager might include organising clerical training, advising departments on layout, equipment and practices, coordinating the supply of equipment and stationery, standardising office practices and setting up an effective communications system within the organisation – such as mailing or phone systems.

Case study – Centralising office services

Many organisations prefer to centralise their office services within an administration department. This means that all paperwork is filed together centrally, that a typing pool deals with word processing requirements and that mail is dealt with by a mail room. It is thought that greater efficiency can be obtained if these and other services are carried out by a specialist department.

Viewpoint 1 Rob Butcher had been working at Smartco for 20 years in the accounts office. He enjoyed his job and felt that all the amenities and services he required were always at his fingertips. When office services were centralised the departmental secretary was moved to a typing pool, the photocopier was taken away so that all requirements were met by a print room, and all of the correspondence files were now filed centrally. If he required a service he found that he had to fill in a form to request it. He felt that this was a waste of time.

Viewpoint 2 Jan Smith was responsible for the reorganisation at Smartco. Despite resistance to the changes from some staff, it was her opinion that centralisation of office services led to easier covering for staff absences, a fairer distribution of work among clerical staff, and greater uniformity of procedures. She also felt that many of the savings could be spent upon better systems and equipment.

1 Examine the two viewpoints and explain whether your sympathies lie with Rob or with Jan.
2 Why might it be necessary to take into account the special requirements of some departments when centralising services?

■ *The accounts department* The *chief accountant* supervises the work of the accounts department. The managers of an organisation need to be constantly aware of relevant financial matters. Computers and calculators help to speed up accounting procedures.

The accounts department may be further subdivided into two sections. The *financial accounting section* will be responsible for keeping records of events as they occur. Records need to be kept of both cash and credit transactions. As well as keeping day-to-day records the section will be responsible for producing periodic records such as the annual accounts. The department will also have the responsibility of keeping accurate VAT records. The *management accounting section* will influence the direction of the organisation based upon its analysis of figures for the present and predictions for the future. Costings, budgets and targets for achievement are all vital. Wages, pensions, PAYE and National Insurance will all be handled by the accounts department.

■ *The marketing department* The marketing function is responsible for identifying, anticipating and satisfying consumer requirements profitably. Although sometimes marketing and sales departments are combined, there is an important distinction between the two. Marketing is concerned with ensuring that the organisation produces what the customer wants – sales is about selling what the organisation has.

The marketing department will therefore be primarily concerned with investigating consumers' needs and wants. This will involve *market research* to find out the nature of a chosen market, what products the market requires, where they want them, how much they will pay for them and the most effective way of promoting them. So that the wishes of consumers can be tied in with new product development, there will be close cooperation between the marketing department and the production planning/research and development departments.

■ *The sales department* The main responsibility of the sales department is to create orders for goods and services. The size of the department and the methods of operation vary considerably. For example, some organisations employ a large sales force working on a regional basis. Other organisations depend upon advertising to stimulate sales and employ only a small sales team.

■ *The information technology department* In a modern organisation, staff may work either directly with or have access to information technology. Information technology (IT) refers to the large and developing body of technologies and techniques which are used to obtain, process and disseminate information to employees.

The responsibilities of this department would include computing, telecommunications and office developments. Though these three areas used to be viewed as distinct, they are progressively merging together and playing a greater role in business activity.

The IT manager is there to exploit IT in the organisation and provide the guidance, support and expertise necessary to accomplish this.

■ *The production department* Production involves the activities necessary to produce a good or service that satisfies the customer. It is often argued that this part of the business is the most difficult to carry out. It involves getting the quality of the good or service just right, and it usually employs the largest amount of capital, assets and labour and other factors in the organisation.

■ *The personnel department* The personnel function has three principal areas of responsibility:
  – It is responsible for the recruitment and training of staff within the organisation.
  – It is responsible for ensuring that their terms and conditions of employment are appropriate, competitive and properly administered.
  – It is responsible for employee relations policy.

■ *The community projects department* Larger organisations in the UK are aware that they are more likely to thrive in a successful and receptive community. A community projects manager might be appointed with the responsibility of overseeing a range of projects – such as help to local small businesses, an educational service and environmental concerns units.

Evidence collection point

Prepare a series of relevant questions and then talk to a number of people from the world of work. Ask them what their job entails. Find out what sort of departmental structure exists within their workplace and where they fit into that structure. Plan this task so that it helps you provide evidence of Core Skills in Communication.

Division by product

As an organisation grows, so too may the range of products it offers. At the beginning it may be

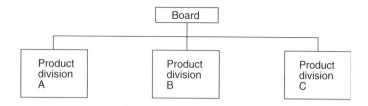

Figure 4.16 Division by product lines

straightforward to handle all the products with common facilities. As the range of products increases it may become more practicable to handle each type of product in a separate division of the company, so structuring the organisation upon *product lines* (Figure 4.16). For example, some publishers have a newspapers division, a magazine and periodicals division and a book publishing division.

Case study – Hanson PLC

As a multinational organisation with widely diversified business interests, Hanson PLC structures its activities in the UK by product. It has the following divisions:

■ The consumer group includes Imperial Tobacco with names such as Embassy, John Player Special, Lambert & Butler, St Bruno, Henri Wintermans and Castella; Every Ready with Silver Seal and Gold Seal; and Seven Seas, the world's largest supplier of vitamin and mineral supplements in capsule form.
■ Building products includes ARC, Greenways, London Brick, Butterley Brick, Crabtree and Marbourn.
■ Industrial products includes Robinson Willey, Smith Meters, Switchmaster, Berry Magicoal, SLD Pumps and Rollalong.

1 Comment briefly upon how Hanson PLC structures its activities within the UK.
2 Why might an organisation like Hanson PLC, which is a vast conglomerate, be more likely to structure by product?

The great advantage of dividing by product is that all divisions can concentrate on their own market areas. It also becomes possible to assess the profitability and effectiveness of each sector. For example, some organisations sell off or merge unprofitable divisions if the particular industry or area shows little promise; this allows the company to concentrate upon more profitable areas.

Division by product can also allow parts of organisations to engage in joint ventures with other companies. Coca-Cola and Nestlé both have interests in drinks and beverages, and they recently entered into a joint venture to manufacture a fresh range of ready-made beverages under the Nescafé and Nestea brand names. Deals like this are expected to become more common and are viewed as preferable to takeovers.

Evidence collection point

Look through a number of annual reports to find an organisation which divides either part or all of its activities by product. Extract figures from the report on the shares or turnover of each product division and chart these graphically. This work should help you provide evidence of Core Skills in Application of Number.

Division by process

Many manufacturing or services operations consist of sequences or processes. Each of these requires division of labour with separate skills, different types of machinery, and often in a different working environment (e.g. a paint shop, an upholstery workshop, a production line). Where this happens it could be appropriate to set up a department to monitor and manage each process. For example, a manufacturer of chicken nuggets could be divided by process (Figure 4.17).

Storage department	Manufacturing department	Freezing department	Packing department	Despatch department
Process 1	**Process 2**	**Process 3**	**Process 4**	**Process 5**

Figure 4.17   Division by process by a manufacturer of chicken nuggets

Division by process allows an organisation to set up teams of specialists involved with each stage. It allows point in the production process to be identified if things go either well or badly.

Division by process will, however, only work effectively if there is a steady flow from one process

to another. If one process department produces too much or too little, problems can occur as stocks build up or run out. This might occur if workers in one process department go on strike or if one department has particularly high absenteeism. Another problem might arise if departments fail to communicate with each other.

Division by geographical area

A large organisation may have branches and divisions not only throughout the country but also across the world. For example, BP boasts of its operations in more than 70 overseas countries. Such organisations, rather than attempting to control all their activities directly from a head office, may decide to divide up their operations according to regions or countries. A large retailer such as Marks and Spencer, which has shops on every major High Street in the UK as well as in cities across the world, will have groups of shops organised into regional and international divisions.

Figure 4.18 illustrates a company with five domestic divisions and three overseas divisions.

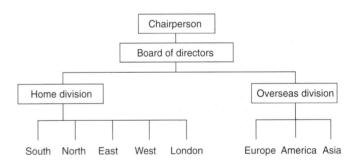

Figure 4.18   Grouping by geographical area

Case study – Yorkshire Water

Yorkshire Water is the guardian of a water environment which stretches from the industrial conurbation of south and west Yorkshire to the rural and recreational areas of the Yorkshire Dales, Moors and North Sea coast. Every day, around the clock, Yorkshire Water collects, treats and puts into the supply system on average some 302 million gallons of water serving around four and a half million customers and some 160 000 commercial premises. The scale and spread of

Figure 4.19 The region served by Yorkshire Water

activities across a large geographical area necessitate dividing the region into distinct areas (Figure 4.19).

1 Yorkshire Water is 'one of the ten water and sewage businesses of England and Wales'. Why do you think water companies are split according to regions and have further divided themselves geographically?
2 Make lists of the advantages and disadvantages of organisations being divided geographically.

Being organised geographically makes it easier for a large enterprise to respond quickly to local issues and problems and to tailor its strategies to local conditions (language, laws, customs, etc.). At the same time it might be possible to cut through a lot of 'red tape' if regional divisions are allowed to make their own decision. In addition, governments often look more kindly on divisions of foreign multinationals if there is a local head office and manufacturing facility.

However, having too many regional divisions can lead to duplication of facilities, lack of coordination and communication breakdowns. An extensive regional structure requires a series of management positions, and this might lead to a division taking on a life of its own, pulling against the parent organisation and ending up at loggerheads with the head office.

Division by type of customer

This type of division is particularly common where it is felt that different categories of customer require different treatment. For example, an organisation may treat its individual customers differently from its retail customers (Figure 4.20).

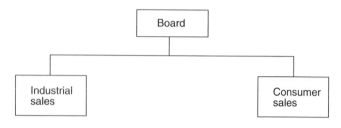

Figure 4.20 Division by type of customer

Banks, in particular, are divided in order to cater for various customer requirements. They have a foreign currency desk, a mortgage adviser, a separate desk for enquiries, and departments dealing with account services for private and for business account holders.

The main advantage of this approach is that each department can concentrate on the special needs of its customers. However, the departments may be costly to set up and run, particularly in terms of staffing, and may only be cost-effective when there is sufficient demand from all types of customers.

Task

Find an organisation that is divided by customer type. Comment on how this has been done and then indicate whether you feel the strategy has been successful.

The matrix structure

A matrix structure can be used to combine the grouping methods we have identified. In such a matrix it is probable that each member of the organisation belongs to two or more groups. A matrix is thus a combination of structures which enables employees to contribute to a mix of activities.

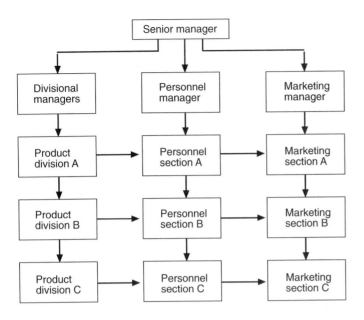

Figure 4.21 Part of a matrix structure

For example, in Figure 4.21 employees are organised both by function (personnel, marketing) and by product (product division). In this example some workers from each product division will be accountable to a personnel manager and a marketing manager, as well as to their divisional manager.

The matrix enables the organisation to focus upon a number of aims at the same time, and gives the flexibility to respond to new markets where there is an increase in demand for its goods and services – for example, servicing different types of customers with different products in different regions. Another great benefit is the cross-fertilisation of ideas between departments.

On the other hand, a matrix may be difficult to understand, so that employees lose sight of their operational aims. The system might also involve more than one chain of command, leading to power struggles, contradictory orders and general confusion.

Centralisation and decentralisation

However an organisation is divided up, there will always be some degree of centralisation or decentralisation. Centralisation or decentralisation represent two extremes within an organisation.

Centralisation occurs where authority, decisions and services are controlled by a central authority. For

example, office services may be controlled in part of a building instead of being spread throughout the organisation.

Decentralisation is similar to delegation but, whereas delegation is simply the passing down of authority from a superior to a subordinate, decentralisation goes much further – it is a philosophy of management which determines what lines of authority to pass down. It then develops policies to guide the staff who have this authority delegated to them, and implements controls for monitoring their performance.

There are many reasons for centralising activities. For example, centralisation:

- prevents parts of an organisation from becoming too independent and thus making decisions which might not fit in with an organisation's policies
- makes coordination and management control easier
- improves economies of scale and reduces overheads
- makes better use of equipment and facilities
- improves the speed of decision-making.

In direct contrast, decentralisation:

- enables decisions to be made at a level which is closer to the work
- improves the efficiency of support services which serve at a point which is closer to the workplace
- improves the morale and motivation of staff who have greater ability to make decisions affecting their activities
- provides staff with further authority.

Another great benefit of centralisation is that it reduces the chain of command. This may be better for improving staff flexibility when making day-to-day decisions.

Case study – Delegation and decentralisation

Phil works for a small company as a buyer. Though he normally works under close supervision, the Managing Director has asked him to cover while the Purchasing Manager is on holiday.

Sally works for a large company as a buyer. She is given an annual budget and a series of guidelines which determine what she can do and what she cannot do. The particular aspect of her job she likes is the freedom to make decisions. Her activities are constantly monitored in regular meetings with the supervisor, and each year she has an appraisal interview.

1 Explain how the two examples help to emphasise the principles of delegation and decentralisation. Which situation would you prefer to work in?
2 What are the dangers of too much delegation and decentralisation?

Flat and tall structures

The *scalar chain* refers to the number of levels within the structure or hierarchy of an organisation. It establishes the authority, responsibility and the framework which determines superior and subordinate relationships. It is important that any structure for an organisation provides a clear line of authority which enables managers to make effective decisions when managing the organisation.

Span of control refers to the number of employees who are directly supervised by one person. The manager who tries to supervise too many people may be so overworked that his or her staff are unable to perform their duties effectively. On the other hand, if a manager has too few people to supervise, his or her time may be wasted.

The scalar chain and the span of control help to create a pyramid shape of the organisation's structure and will also determine whether an organisation has a 'tall' or 'flat' structure. Where the spans of control are narrow and there are more levels of authority, an organisation will have a tall structure (Figure 4.22). In contrast, where there are broader spans of control and fewer layers of authority an organisation will create a flat structure (Figure 4.23).

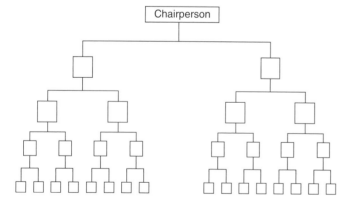

Figure 4.22 A tall organisational structure

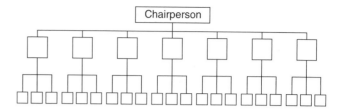

Figure 4.23 A flat organisational structure

Evidence collection point

Find out the organisational structure of the institution you either attend or work for. Determine the span of control and the number of layers of authority. Describe whether the organisation has a tall or flat organisational structure. Use diagrams and explanations to support your analysis.

There is no single ideal combination of span of control and scalar chain for any one organisation. It is, however, argued that fewer levels tend to improve decision-making, communications and morale. On the other hand, by 'delayering' and reducing the number of levels in the chain, this may reduce the opportunities for promotion and positions with higher status. This will limit the opportunities for the development of future managers.

Cooperative alliances

The structures of some organisations may be determined by the cooperative nature of their activities. These are sometimes called voluntary buying organisations. Examples are Spar, Wavyline or VG which organise themselves collectively for the purpose of buying, distributing and marketing. By doing this the benefits of bulk purchasing and marketing on a large scale enable them to sell at prices which compete with larger retailers. This also means that, within the organisational structure of the alliance, there may be many small independent units.

Comparing organisational structures

Organisational structures show the relationships between workers and the divisions of their work. Thus an organisation chart will show:

- how the organisation is divided
- the responsibility of different levels of employees and the person to whom each reports
- lines of communication
- possible lines of promotion.

There are many ways in which the structure of each individual organisation may be used in comparison with another in order to understand more fully the activities of each type of organisation. For example:

- The **size** of the organisation may be the major factor in determining the organisational structure. Within a very large organisation the chart provides a framework for the process of management. The structure will, therefore, help to make effective use of key activities and will provide supporting mechanisms for staff. It thus enables the activities of a very large organisation to be effectively planned, directed and controlled.

Similarly, within a small organisation an organisational structure is a useful guide to the division of work of members. This helps in coordination of their activities.

Case study – Yorkshire Bank PLC

Over the past 70 years Yorkshire Bank has undergone a process of growth in its activities. Today it is recognised as one of the foremost banking organisations in the UK, with branches across the county providing a comprehensive network of activities. Look at the bank's organisation chart (Figure 4.24).

1 How would you describe the scale of activities at Yorkshire Bank?
2 List the purposes of the organisation chart. That is, how might the chart be used?
3 Comment upon how the organisation is divided up.

- The **location** of an organisation's activities may also determine how an organisation is structured. Just imagine the problems a multi-product organisation has when having to organise activities across various regions of the world. (For example, to what extent did a lack of structure contribute to the problems to Barings Bank?) It is important in this situation that geographical

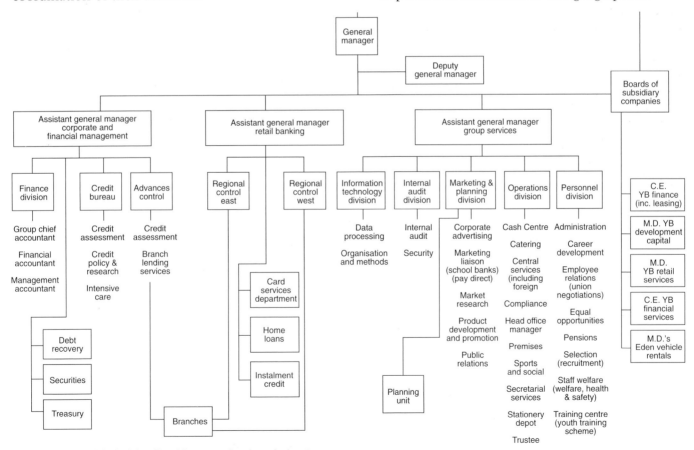

Figure 4.24 Yorkshire Bank's organisational chart

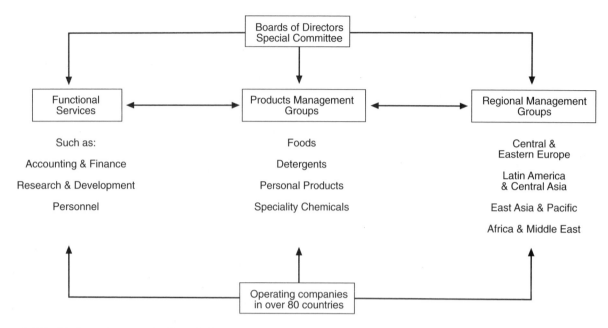

Figure 4.25 Unilever's organisational structure

groups are adequately accounted for within an organisation's structure, for example as with Unilever (Figure 4.25).

■ The **type of product** may also influence the choice of organisational structure. For example, some goods or services may require organising specialists into groups because of the nature of the product. For example, in a hospital, medical staff are arranged according to the type of service they provide – such as maternity or casualty. There is, however, always the danger that if an organisation is divided too rigidly by product, then this division may become too independent and present problems of control.

■ Dividing by **function** is probably the most common way of structuring an organisation. This type of structure shares the expertise of staff. For example, it may share the collective experience of scientists for the research and development function.

Many organisations use combinations of groupings to divide and structure their activities. For example, look again at the Unilever example. You can see that activities are structured not only *geographically* but also by *product* and *function*.

The aim for any organisation is, therefore, to provide a structure which helps the organisation to efficiently carry out its operations and meet its planned business **objectives.** The objectives of the organisation may often determine the type of

structure an organisation decides to adopt and provide a framework for its design. Objectives may also:

■ indicate the suitability of different levels for different activities
■ determine the relationships between them
■ facilitate systems of communication
■ assist in the measurement of performance in various parts of the organisation.

If the organisation is not meeting its objectives, it may well be necessary to improve efficiency by *restructuring* the organisation.

 Evidence collection point

Obtain an organisation chart from any type of organisation. Comment upon how the organisation is structured and then explain why the organisation is structured in that particular way.

Reasons for changing organisational structures

It is important for managers within an organisation to constantly assess how well the structure enables them to meet their overall business objectives. Poor design of an organisational structure can cause many problems for the organisation, for example:

- low morale resulting from inconsistent decisions based upon lack of clarity about job roles
- poor coordination of decisions
- poor response to new business opportunities and changes in the marketplace
- high costs from a tall hierarchy which contains a large number of managers in senior positions.

An organisational structure should, therefore, identify the responsibilities and relationships attached to every important position as well as the role that each person has to play within the decision-making framework of the organisation.

There may also be many deep-rooted reasons for changing an organisation's structure, based upon the need to improve the internal functioning of the organisation and pressures outside the organisation from the business environment (Figure 4.26).

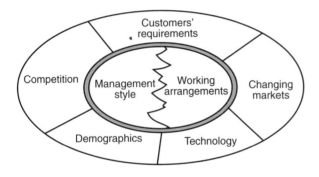

Figure 4.26   Reasons for change

The **effective working** of people within the organisation may be determined by the design of the organisation.

Management style may well be strongly influenced by the organisational structure. Many experts on human relations within the workplace advocate a structure in which there is increased participation for people at a range of levels within the decision-making process, and greater freedom for individuals to make decisions. They argue that formal structures with long chains of authority become bureaucratic and restrict the self-fulfilment of individuals, who instead feel failure and develop resentment.

The structure should therefore define the sort of leadership role that individuals should undertake and also define the power of its various members.

The operation of the structure will also influence the **working arrangements** of individual members within the organisation. For example, by changing a

structure individuals may have to rethink how they work, physically move to another working environment, develop new skills or perhaps adjust to new conditions. The structure must take into account the needs of individuals as well as how they work in order to improve the effective operation of the organisation as a whole.

Customer requirements within any market constantly change. As some products become less popular, other products become more popular. Greater emphasis may be placed upon providing better customer service or packaging. An organisation may frequently readjust its organisational structures so as to respond more closely to customer requirements in order to maintain its **competitive advantage.** Similarly, where competitors make product changes or start to compete in a different way, perhaps by emphasising a different aspect of their competitive advantage, a restructuring exercise may help an organisation to respond. These changes may take place not just because of the actions of a competitor but also because of wider changes taking place within the **market.**

The UK population is estimated to increase to 62.1 million by 2020. At the same time the population is ageing. Organisations need to view changes in **population** estimates and assess how they might affect their operations locally, nationally and internationally for years to come. This may means an organisation limiting its activities in some markets and trying to develop activities for others, e.g. manufacturers of trainers for young people may wish to restructure in order to revise their activities.

Another feature influencing organisational design is **information technology.** This plays an important role in changing the nature of business operations by giving people access to more information, thus enabling them to make more effective decisions. Computerised information and support systems may determine hierarchical structures, the organisation of support systems, the amount of decentralisation and the span of control. This has a significant effect upon the structure of the organisation as well as the way in which individuals work. It is frequently pointed out that IT tends to move an organisation towards a flatter structure with fewer levels of management.

Evidence indicators

Produce a report which compares and analyses three business organisations, one of which is in the public

135

sector and two from the private sector. You may wish to do this by writing to organisations, for example BP and the BBC, or you may wish to compare the functioning of your college as an organisation in the public sector with that of an organisation in the private sector.

The following list should serve as a checklist. Please tick off the following when you have successfully covered them as part of your report.

- I have managed to obtain information for three organisations, one of which is in the public sector and two in the private sector. ☐
- I have provided broad explanations of their profit and not-for-profit motives. ☐
- I have identified a number of circumstances in which one objective might conflict with another. ☐
- I have shown how a number of influences may affect the setting of objectives. ☐
- I have described the ownership of each organisation and contrasted each. ☐
- I have compared their organisational charts illustrating their different structures and shown how they help each organisation to meet its objectives. ☐
- I have also described how a number of changes both within and outside the organisation may influence their organisational structures and noted recent or planned changes to structures, location or functions. ☐

Administration systems

Administration plays an important role within all organisations. In administering an activity there is a need to organise, record, control, plan, communicate and make decisions. An administrator has to take responsibility not only for his or her own actions, but also for the activities of others. Most administrative tasks require a range of talents in addition to a knowledge of the work, experience and sound judgement.

In recent years the world of administration has been transformed by new technology which has brought about massive changes affecting people in their workplace. Administrators today have to balance the opportunities created by new technologies with the concern and understanding of their staff in order to build working practices which improve the administrative functions and procedures of the organisation.

In this chapter we look at the nature of administrative activities and examine how information technology can change and improve the workings of an organisation.

The administering and functioning of the organisation

Over many years, considerable efforts have been made by theorists to develop a clearer understanding of how managers and administrators can spend their time most efficiently. This work has contributed to the development of management theory as a science. For such theories it is possible to develop four broad functions that characterise all administrative activity. These are:

- *Planning* – deciding what provisions need to be made available in the future.
- *Organising* – making sure that all resources are available at the right moment.
- *Controlling* – making sure that things happen as they were planned.
- *Doing* – becoming actively involved in the task in hand.

It is possible to relate each of these four functions to a specific level of management responsibility (Figure

	Level of management or administration		
	Senior	Middle	Lower
Planning			
Organising			
Controlling			
Doing			

Figure 5.1 The activities of managers at different levels

5.1). Senior or top managers in an organisation tend to spend a lot of their time planning, some time organising, a lot of their time controlling but very little time actually involved in the tasks. Middle managers spend less time planning, more time organising, more time controlling and more time doing the work. First-line or lower managers contribute little to planning, are involved in some organisation and some control, but spend most of their time actively involved in the task at hand.

Evidence collection point

Conduct a series of interviews with people who work for a variety of organisations. How would you describe their day-to-day management responsibilities? Find out what time they spend planning, organising, controlling and doing. This task can contribute evidence of Core Skills in Communication.

Administration systems

When someone first starts to work for an organisation in a 'junior' position, his or her role is usually limited to a series of clearly defined tasks. As the employee begins to understand more about the functioning of the organisation, his or her duties can develop so as to include a range of simple administrative tasks. The employee's ability to be able to organise, control and make decisions will be crucial to many of these tasks.

Just as you have to organise and control your social activities, the success you have with your work role will depend on how well you can develop your organisational and administrative skills. Imagine you are arranging a party for a group of friends. You might have to:

- identify a mutually convenient date
- check that a suitable venue is available
- decide who to invite
- make sure that everyone knows when and where the party is taking place
- arrange for food and refreshments
- borrow some records, tapes and CDs.

Each of these tasks involves you in *organisational* activity. If you had the offer of help from a friend, you might ask that person to sort out the invitations, order some glasses from the off-licence and buy and prepare some food. At the same time you have to oversee all the activities to ensure that the preparations are going smoothly: you are involved in *administration.* You have to monitor the completion of the tasks, providing guidance and help where necessary. You have to make decisions. As the administrator of the event – the party – you set out the plan, work out what needs to be done, work on many of the arrangements yourself, delegate, monitor the preparations; and, finally, on the night you make sure that everything runs smoothly.

Administration is not just about people being well organised. It is also about the setting up of a *system* which ensures that events function as planned. The word 'system', therefore should include the tangible 'mechanics' of the operating environment which enables an organisation to carry out its functions

efficiently as well as the people themselves (Figure 5.2).

One definition of administration is provided by Brech, who defines administration as

> That part of the management process concerned with the institution and carrying out procedures by which the programme is laid down and communicated, and the progress of activities is regulated and checked against targets and plans.

In order to understand more fully what this definition means, we can look at each part of the definition.

- a 'management process' will involve the administrator taking responsibility and using organisational skills and judgement to make decisions
- 'concerned with the institution' means that administration forms part of the employee's work role
- 'carrying out procedures' are the activities as part of the work role
- 'by which the programme is laid down and communicated' are the guidelines which determine how a work role is undertaken
- 'the progress of activities is regulated and checked against targets and plans' shows that administrative activities have to fit in with the targets set by the objectives of the institution.

Another useful definition is provided by the Institution of Administrative Management which describes administration and office management as

> that branch of management which is concerned with the services of obtaining, recording and analysing information of planning, and of communicating, by means of which the

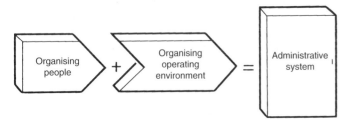

Figure 5.2 Combining people with the operating environment to produce the administrative system

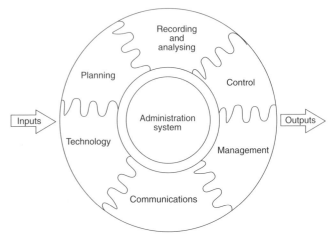

Figure 5.3 The administrative process

management of a business safeguards its assets, promotes its affairs and achieves its objectives.

Procedures

Administration is, therefore, an important part of every organisation. It is a 'backbone' which provides the systems necessary for other parts and functions of the organisation to operate efficiently (Figure 5.3 on page 138).

Case study – Administrative management at Marks and Spencer

These days, your local Marks and Spencer store has as much in common with the flight deck of Concorde as with the traditional corner shop. Take a close look, and you will discover a carefully coordinated team operation that uses state-of-the-art technology to deliver quality, value and service to customers and colleagues.

At the very heart of this operation is the Administration Manager – a pivotal figure within the management team. He or she makes sure that the many different systems which bring the store to life (including everything from the tills to the closed circuit television cameras) are operating as effectively as possible.

No other management category is harder to define, because no other category is developing as rapidly, or changing as radically, as Administration. The Administration Manager's remit is to protect store assets and ensure profitability. This involves monitoring store performance against budget, analysing sales figures and stock flow, and managing and motivating the Administration, Customer Service Desk and M & S Financial Services teams. On top of that, the Administration Manager also has to deal with a thousand and one other unforeseen challenges that arise every day.

So what makes a good Administration Manager? Obviously, in a role that is all about 'getting things done', leadership and team-working skills are vital, as is the ability to interpret and communicate numerical data. Commercial flair and creativity are important too, because Administration Management is not only about controlling costs, but also about taking the initiative and developing new ways of making the store more profitable. The fact of the matter is, the Administration Manager must be all things to all people: a financial advisor, a systems 'expert', a team leader, a commercially-driven retailer, and the store's resident problem solver.

1 Describe the sort of skills which are important for somebody involved with administration.
2 What does this case study tell you about the procedures and functions of an Administration Manager?
3 To ensure that a store functions effectively, an Administration Manager is responsible for the systems within the store. Describe the sort of systems which would help a store to operate efficiently.

Administrative systems and procedures and the role that administrators have in the management of the organisation may vary widely from one organisation to another. To understand this more closely you may like to refer to the role of the most senior administrator in your school or college. Think about the activities they control and the duties they carry out.

Administration procedures within an organisation may include:

- assisting functional department managers with clerical activities and the provision of suitable equipment
- setting up a series of clerical procedures and methods for all parts of the organisation
- providing services for other parts of the organisation such as purchasing, stationery, information technology
- setting up work procedures, schedules and output controls
- dealing with information – sorting, distributing, filing, etc.
- communications both within and outside the organisation
- control and protection of the organisation
- planning
- ongoing analysis of all the above.

The position of the administrator and his or her department may depend upon the type of organisation, its size and the way in which it is structured. If the volume of administrative work is very large, it may become a large departmental area under the control of an administration manager. A lot may depend upon the extent to which an organisation is either *centralised* or *decentralised* for administrative functions. In all situations, however, administration systems will provide some form of service for other functional departments (Figure 5.4).

Evidence collection point

Find out what sort of services are carried out by the administration system either from

Figure 5.4 Supporting functions with administrative systems

your school or college or any other organisation from which you can obtain information. Plan your work so that you provide evidence of Core Skills in Communication.

People in administration

There may be a range of employees with different levels of authority working in administration across the whole organisation. They may include:

■ administration managers controlling a large department
■ personal assistants to managers
■ supervisory staff heading key sections within the organisation
■ clerical staff providing day-to-day services for the rest of the organisation.

Though administrative staff are not themselves making goods or providing services for customers, they are still of great importance for the organisation as a *secondary* service which enables other departments to operate more efficiently.

Evidence collection point

Make a list of the type of work and possible job roles within the administration section of an organisation that may be associated with the following:

1 communication
2 storing
3 processing
4 analysing.

If possible present your conclusions using computer graphics, to provide evidence of Core Skills in Information Technology.

Administration equipment

A few years ago the 'electronic office' was regarded as a radically new idea. Today most organisations include some electronic office equipment. Indeed, in many organisations offices are extremely 'high tech'.

The range of office activities that can be automated is increasing all the time, as is the number of ways of automating them. On the computing side – as opposed to telephony, photocopy and other elements of the electronic office – word processing, electronic message handling, financial modelling and computerised personal organisers are commonplace (Figure 5.5).

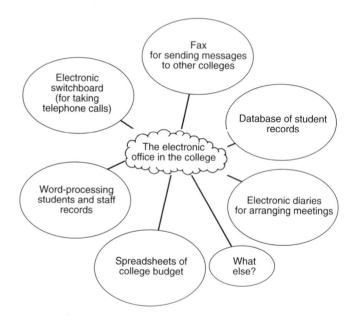

Figure 5.5 Some IT inputs

Evidence collection point

What elements of the electronic office are used in your college, or in another organisation with which you are familiar? Draw a diagram like the one in Figure 5.5 to show the range of applications. This task can provide evidence of Core Skills in Communication.

When looking at information technology across the range of administration activities it is useful to distinguish between:

- *general IT skills* needed across a range of jobs
- *specialist IT skills,* mainly at the professional level, needed for the development of sophisticated technology software and systems.

General IT skills

Very few jobs have been unaffected by information technology. Virtually all types of employees need some familiarity with the technology and its applications in their particular working environment (Figure 5.6):

- *Managers* need sufficient understanding of the latest developments to spot new business opportunities and to carry out changes.
- *Technicians, maintenance and craft workers* need to deal with IT components in plants and vehicles of all types.
- *Clerical workers* have to be familiar with a variety of word-processing, spreadsheet, database and similar applications.
- *Professionals* need to use specialist IT applications – including 'expert systems' – as an aid to their decision-making.

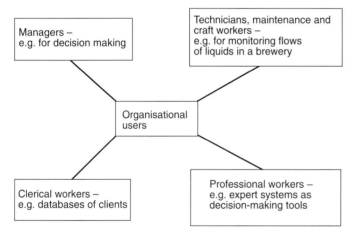

Figure 5.6 Users of IT in the workplace

Specialist IT skills

Many of the readers of this book will become (if you are not already) general users of IT. In particular, you will make use of the range of IT skills (as well as others) shown in Figure 5.7. Some readers of this book may also become specialist users of IT skills. About 1% of the working population

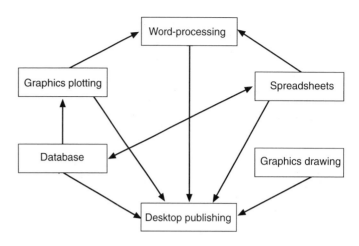

Figure 5.7 General IT skills

(approximately a quarter of a million people) are in one of the IT professions. The numbers have grown by about 20% since 1985. The number of recruits to this industry are expected to grow by 5% a year for the rest of the century. The growth of this job sector is therefore one of the fastest in the country.

Processing data

Information technology works within the administration system to process data in order to produce various kinds of information. Data is therefore the input and information is the output (Figure 5.8). (Note that data in computing is usually considered to be singular, so we say 'data is', not 'data are'.)

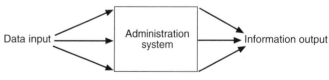

Figure 5.8 Processing data to produce information

The computer system comprises two main parts:

- *Hardware*
  This is the computer or other equipment or machinery providing IT services. It will consist of a physical electronic machine(s) which provides all the mechanical ingredients of the system. Items of hardware would include:

– the *personal computer* itself. The power of this is usually determined by the type of processor, for example, 486SX, 486DX or Pentium processor

– the *keyboard* for inputting data

– the *mouse* for selecting options and supporting the use of the keyboard

– the *monitor,* which may be a simple standard resolution monochrome monitor or a higher resolution colour monitor

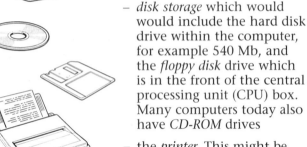

– *disk storage* which would would include the hard disk drive within the computer, for example 540 Mb, and the *floppy disk* drive which is in the front of the central processing unit (CPU) box. Many computers today also have *CD-ROM* drives

– the *printer.* This might be dot-matrix, bubble-jet or laser.

■ *Software*
Software is a term used to describe all of the programs and instructions which computing hardware requires in order to function. Software should be determined by the functions which the user wishes to carry out and be designed with the user in mind. It will comprise the *operating system*, which provides the environment in which the user works, and *applications software* used for different purposes.

In summary, we can say that administration systems provide the framework or internal infrastructure upon which the rest of the organisation depends.

Functions

There are many functions within the organisation which are largely determined by how the organisation has been structured and divided (see Chapter 4).

Research and development

This will depend upon the type of organisation as well as the industry in which it operates. *Research* is the system search for facts and information which will help to solve problems. Research may be:

■ *pure research,* concerned with researching new scientific principles to put an organisation at the 'leading edge' of developments in its field
■ *applied research,* involving the development of a practical business proposition from an idea.

Market research tries to anticipate the needs of potential and existing customers by means of a thorough understanding of behaviour patterns and the consumer environment. *Product research* then takes this further: it uses the knowledge of the customer to develop new products or make changes to existing ones.

Development involves the engineering work necessary to enable a product to reach the production stage. There are many stages in the development process; as new ideas and product developments go through successive stages, unsuccessful ones are eliminated (Figure 5.9).

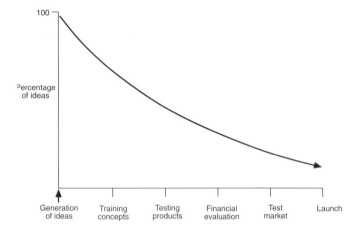

Figure 5.9 Stages in the development process

Case study – Reducing chlorofluorocarbons

DuPont have invested heavily in moving their production away from the harmful ozone-depleting chlorofluorocarbons towards a range of alternative products. The following extract was taken from a recent annual report:

Ice-cream is cold and we want to keep it that way. When CFCs were linked to ozone depletion. DuPont moved to find alternative products, and became the largest producer of a new line of coolants for refrigeration and air conditioning. At our plant, that meant replacing one manufacturing process and product line with another. Working in teams, that just what we did – under budget and ahead of schedule. We even recycled some of the manufacturing by-products for use in water treatment systems

1 What sort of research would DuPont have engaged in to find out whether alternative coolant products were available?
2 Describe the stages which would have followed this type of research.
3. How important is research and development for a company like DuPont?

Design

A new design is one for which the details are different are different from earlier products intended for the same use. Design is more than just appearance. It is about satisfying the customer with the performance, simplicity, operation and durability of the product.

For most products, a design team is established, led by a design manager. The team will remain with the project throughout its development. The process of design may determine the product's final shape, the materials it is made from, the dimensions and specifications. The product may be designed for economic production, function, ease of packaging and distribution and appearance.

Computer-aided design (CAD) refers to the applications of a computer to solve problems. A CAD system will consist of a computer, a workstation and a graphics board with a magnetic pen which enables the operator to touch symbols and select options so that a design can be made up. Such technology has transformed the role of the role of the designer. Developments in artificial intelligence, mathematical modelling and other areas of technology today represent fundamental changes in the ways in which the needs of consumers can be satisfied.

Evidence collection point

Track the changes in various aspects of product design for a product of your choice. Use a time chart to show *when* and *how* product design have changed. For example:

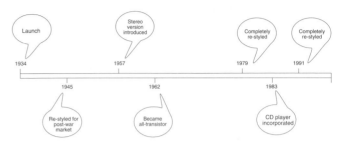

Marketing

Marketing involves everything that an organisation has to make happen if customers are to be satisfied with its products. For this to be done effectively and successfully, an organisation has to assess customer needs. The Chartered Institute of Marketing (CIM) define marketing as:

> The anticipation, identification and fulfilment of consumer need – at a profit.

Meeting consumer needs involves developing strategies which are then translated into a series of marketing plans. Marketing is, therefore, a strategic function which, by ensuring a business satisfies customers' needs and meets its business objectives, helps it to outperform its rivals.

Marketing planning should be viewed as a continuous cycle (Figure 5.10). Collecting and sorting information from the research process will help to develop plans and identify alternative sources of action. Plans can then be modified and controlled in the light of performance.

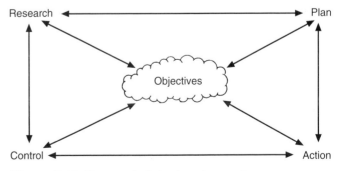

Figure 5.10 The marketing planning cycle

143

Communication

At the heart of all organisations is the need for effective communication. Communication refers to the ways in which people throughout an organisation communicate information both within and outside the enterprise. The contact may be between people, organisations or places and can be in a number of forms including speech, writing, data communication, actions and gestures. As communication probably takes up the largest proportion of managers' and administrators' time, the building and developing of communication skills must be viewed as a vital managerial requirement.

Evidence collection point

Find out more about communications activities in the workplace by referring to your own experiences of work, perhaps through your work experience. Make a list of all of the different communications techniques (paper-based, use of technology, meetings, etc). Plan your work so that you provide evidence of Core Skills in Communication and Information Technology.

Finance

In the previous chapter we saw that all organisations have a range of business objectives. Though many have a broad list of objectives, for businesses in the private sector the overriding objective may be the financial objective: its success in terms of profits – 'the bottom line'. In order to measure their profitability and performance, organisations set up and use an accounting system. This processes business data so that interested parties know how well or badly the organisation is performing (Figure 5.11).

There are a number of different approaches to accounting:

- *Financial accounting* This involves analysing an organisation's operations to ensure that they provide a 'true and fair' view of their activities. Financial accountants prepare financial accounts from which ratios can be extracted to show how the organisation is performing.
- *Management accounting* This information assists managers in the making of decisions, controlling various parts of the organisation's activities and planning for the future.
- *Social responsibility accounting* This method of accounting is becoming increasingly popular. It considers the wider effects of business activities upon society so that the organisation is aware of undesirable activities. Accounting statements can be used to show how an organisation has helped to reduce or overcome socially undesirable problems.

Producing goods

Producing goods involves transforming raw materials or components (inputs) into finished products (outputs) by adding value at every stage of manufacture. The management of these processes is often called operations management and involves planning and control of operations.

There are many decisions to be made when producing goods. One neat way of illustrating them is to break this function down into five broad areas called the five Ps, though in practice there is considerable overlap (Figure 5.12).

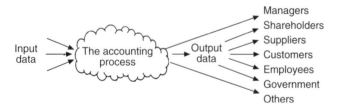

Figure 5.11 Generating accounting information

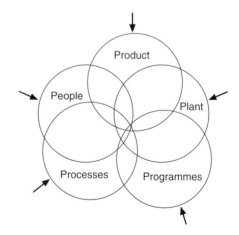

Figure 5.12 The five broad areas of production

- *Product* This is concerned with the research, design and development of the product, manufacturing it as economically as possible but also in a way which satisfies consumers, and then analysing the development of a portfolio of products.
- *Plant* In order to manufacture a product some form of plant is necessary. The location, size, capacity, design, layout, performance and safety of the plant are all of importance for the production manager.
- *Processes* To transform raw materials or part-finished goods into finished goods they have to go through one or more processes. They may, for example, go through as single items, in batches or in a continuous flow. They may be manufactured as single items or mass-produced products.
- *Programmes* These timetable the vast resources used by the production department.
- *People* The effective running of production processes depends upon people. Managers have to consider the background of the workforce as well as training required and then develop their 'organisation and methods' (O & M) in order to use labour most effectively.

Case study – Cosworth Engineering

Cosworth is one of the motor industry's best-known brand names and is involved with the design of high-performances engines for both road and racing vehicles. Their most celebrated customer is the Ford Motor Company, but products are also supplied for other manufacturers, including Aston Martin, Ferrari, General Motors, Harley-Davison, Jaguar, Kawasaki, Lamborghini/Chrysler, Maserati, Mazda, Mercedes-Benz, Nissan, Toyota and Yamaha.

The company was founded in 1958 and is based in Northampton with an additional manufacturing site at Wellingborough, Northants. In addition, it has two sites at Worcester for the Cosworth Casting foundry and process laboratories and an engine building factory in Los Angeles.

Cosworth Engineering designs and engineers advanced automotive engines for both road and racing vehicles. The company is well known for its work with the Ford Motor Company, especially the Sierra RS Cosworth Sapphire and the Escort RS Cosworth. As a result of successful progress on an additional development currently under way with Ford, further derivatives of the Cosworth V6 engine are being evaluated.

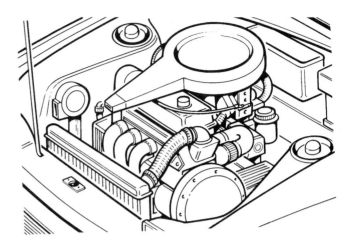

Cosworth builds a greater variety of racing engines than any other manufacturer and consistently achieves a high level in all major areas of motor sport. In 1993, Cosworth-designed engines were used by two of the top four teams in the Formula One Championship, both enjoying an excellent season with six Grand Prix victories.

Three prestigious awards were recently made to Cosworth. These were the British Design Award, presented by the Design Council, the Sir Henry Royce Award for the pursuit of superb craftsmanship and the Queen's Award for Export Achievement.

1 In not more than 50 words, describe the operations of Cosworth Engineering.
2 How would you describe their strengths?
3. In what fundamental ways will a manufacturing business like Cosworth (a) be similar to, and (b) different from, an organisation providing services?

Providing services

Modern society such as the United Kingdom are said to be in their 'third wave of development'. In the first wave most occupations were based upon agriculture; the second wave was dominated by manufacturing industry; while in the third wave the service sector has become increasingly important.

Tertiary or service production comprises commercial services such as banking and insurance and also direct services which are of benefit to individual members of the community such as policing, teaching and nursing.

Human resourcing

Human resource management is the management process which provides for human resource needs. It covers the complete employment spectrum of recruitment, selection, induction, training, appraisal, transfers, redundancy and retirement. It also includes welfare, health and safety, wage and salary negotiation, equal opportunities and all aspects of the management process which deals with people in their working environment.

Human resource management (HRM) today is concerned with using the workforce in a way which helps to achieve the goals of the organisation. Within the organisation, the HRM process will be concerned with motivating employees and making the most of the activities which they can provide through training and employee development. They may be concerned with a number of external pressures such as labour shortages, the industrial relations environment and legislation for the workplace (Figure 5.13).

Figure 5.13 Functions of human resource management

Evidence collection point

The following statement appeared in a recent report from the Fairey Group plc:

Fairey Group plc has a policy of encouraging its operating companies to provide information to their employees on a regular basis. This includes matters relating to their company's performance, its prospects in the markets it serves and the future outlook of its business.

The group publishes a house magazine *Fairey in Focus* which is made available to employees.

Financial participation in the group is encouraged through the Savings Related Share Option Scheme. The most recent opportunity to subscribe, in March 1993, was taken up by 375 employees, 29% of those eligible.

It is the policy of Fairey to recruit, train and promote disabled persons on the basis of their aptitudes and abilities. If employees become disabled, every effort is made to retain them and when necessary retrain them for appropriate posts.

Obtain a number of annual reports and look in each for a statement about employees. Describe how such statements help to provide a broad overview of the approach of each organisation to human resourcing.

Distribution

The main objectives of a firm's distribution policy is to make sure that products are where they are wanted at the time they are wanted. This will involve having a distribution network, often involving intermediaries linked by a communications system.

The process of distribution is not just concerned with physically moving goods from manufacturers to consumers. It is also concerned with choosing from available channels, deciding whether to use one channel or several and whether to sell direct to consumers or to go through intermediaries, and deciding how much spending to allocate to distribution and how much financial involvement to make in the existing channels.

The process of distribution must not be underestimated. For example, organisations such as Reader's Digest, Avon and Betterware have an approach to distribution which enables this area to provide their key competitive advantage.

Maintenance

Maintenance of plant and equipment is essential for the efficient provision of goods and services. A typical maintenance department in a large organisation will be able to call on the services of specialists such as electricians and joiners. The maintenance department will work to a plan to ensure that all equipment is checked and serviced in turn. The effectiveness of a maintenance department can be judged on the basis of freedom from emergencies.

Providing customer service

Over the last few years, given the increasingly competitive nature of the service environment, many organisations use the quality of their service as the key competitive factor in winning customers. Superior services help to differentiate their activities from those of other organisations. For example, financial institutions and airlines try to adopt a quality service approach which distinguishes them from their competitors.

Evidence collection point

Compare and contrast two competing services by identifying a number of key points which you would use to analyse customer service, for example waiting times, attitudes to staff, customer facilities, literature, after-sales service, service environment. Score each area out of 10. From your analysis, which service organisation is providing the best customer care? Present your work in a way that provides evidence of Core Skills in Application of Number.

Providing information technology service

Information is vital to decision-making in both commerce and industry. The quality of any decision depends on the reliance, accuracy and timeliness of the information available. The main task for the information manager will therefore be to identify the decision-makers' information needs, to decide how best they can be met, and to develop the systems for meeting them.

In a modern organisation a large proportion of the staff may work directly with, or have access to, computer terminals. Information technology (IT) refers to the large and developing body of technologies and techniques by which information is obtained, processed and disseminated and embraces computing, telecommunications and office developments. These areas are progressively merging together while, at the same time, expanding to play an ever greater role in business activity.

Information technology developments

A traditional business is often organised into functional specialisms. Each person in the organisation carries out one step before passing the job on to someone else. Often a job is passed from one department to another. Figure 5.14 shows this sort of flow. For example, market research is carried out by a few people in the marketing department,

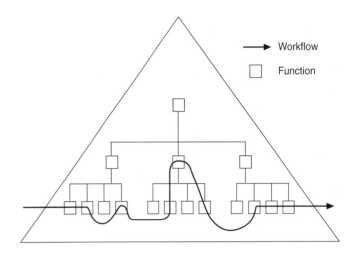

Figure 5.14 In a functional organisation the work flows step by step

who pass on the results to the technology department. The technology department comes up with some proposals which are passed on to production ... and so on.

The departments shown in the diagram have worked together in a flow on a particular 'business process', which is simply a set of work activities arranged logically to realise a business objective.

Task

Identify a business process in an organisation with which you are familiar. How are tasks passed on in a flow from one department to another?

Transformed businesses

Today many business writers use the term 'transformed business'. Such an organisation is run according to business processes rather than functional specialisms. The business processes are handled by teams of people from different functions, working together to achieve the aim of the process.

In a transformed business people involved in particular processes are given more freedom to make decisions and have more information at their fingertips by virtue of information technology. Instead of having to get permission from their line manager, they are allowed to make important decisions. Senior managers then become more

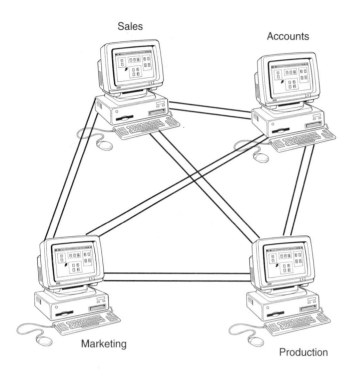

Figure 5.15 A network of information can be made available to the process team

concerned with external matters than with running the internal system.

Organisations based on business processes put a high premium on information and on sharing IT facilities. IT has a very important role to play. Groups working together in a team will need to share information, and computer terminals of different specialists are linked so that information is available to all (Figure 5.15).

One major benefit is a cost reduction as a result of simplifying the work flow. A job stays with one individual or team instead of passing in batches from specialist to specialist. The team is given authority to make decisions, as well as the information and tools needed.

Another benefit is the improved responsiveness to customers' needs. Front-line staff are given powers to act rather than pass problems up to line managers.

Improved job satisfaction can result. Staff can share customer satisfaction with a job well done. They are more challenged and fulfilled. The staff are part of a learning, adapting organisation focused on the customers' requirements.

Evidence collection point

Study an organisation which uses IT widely. To what extent is information shared in the organisation? What are the effects on decision-making? Can decisions be made more easily by individuals, or do they still need to be passed to supervisors or senior managers? Make lists of what you consider to be the major advantages and disadvantages of:

1 traditional functional organisations
2 process-based transformed organisations.

Hardware

Today people use phrases such as 'the information society' or 'the wired society' to refer to the way in which the revolution in information technology is transforming our lives. But what does this mean and what sort of machinery or hardware devices do today's managers and administrators have access to?

The *central processing unit* (CPU) carries out all of the operations of the computer and comprises the main box of the PC. It processes a large number of operations according to the instructions provided. When the computer is in use it uses the *random access memory* (RAM) which is made up of integrated electronic circuitry and chips. The RAM stores the software which is part of the operating system, the program in use and the data fed into the computer. When the PC is switched on it is the RAM that loads the system. The *processor* is the most important part of the CPU and determines the power of the system. Over recent years we have seen processors become faster and more powerful, moving from the 286 to the 386SX and then DX, to the 486SX and DX and finally to the Pentium processor, which, inevitably, will also be succeeded before long.

Floppy disks, either 5.25 inch or today's more popular 3.5 inch, contain a number of tracks which have sectors which provide storage. Most disks are double-sided and can be formatted with different densities of data. Recent developments are towards high-density disks which can be formatted with any density of data.

Hard disk drives are installed within the PC and are also used to store and retrieve data. Disk size will vary according to the PC but many today have more than 500 Mb. A program when installed on to the hard disk, particularly drawing and design programs such as Corel Draw, may take 30 Mb or more of hard disk space.

Larger storage spaces are available with *CD-ROM* (Compact Disc Read Only Memory) (Figure 5.16). Date on a CD-ROM is stored in the same way as on an audio compact disc and is safer as there is no danger that the head will make contact with the surface of the disk and destroy data. A single CD-ROM is able to hold the equivalent of 300 000 pages of A4 text. Over recent years CD-ROMs have been developed for multi-media uses which include sound, vision, photographs and video clips. CD-ROMs have become standard components of PCs but should be thought of as 'read only' devices. The great advantage is that data cannot be overwritten or changed.

Figure 5.16 CD-ROM

CD-I (Compact Disc Interactive) was launched in the UK in 1991 by Philips, Sony and Matsushia. The CD-I player is a standalone integrated system where materials are viewed via a monitor and interacted with via an infra-red joystick. Any combination of speech, sound or video may be decoded by a CDI player. CD-I has been marketed both as a consumer and commercial product with widespread applications for training.

The *monitor* is the vital part of the system for the displays it provides. Most monitors are in colour. The resolutions of the screen will determine how sharp the image is. For example, it may be possible to have a monitor with EGA, VGA and Super VGA. Higher resolution monitors will have more pixels and will provide a better picture.

Printers vary widely. Dot matrix printers have often been replaced by ink-jet and bubble-jet printers which make virtually no noise and provide a high quality of output. Laser printers have also been widely purchased and acclaimed by the business

world. The ultimate form of printer is the colour laser printer (Figure 5.17). Over recent years prices of all types of printers have steadily dropped.

Figure 5.17 The colour laser printer

There are a variety of ways in which systems can be upgraded. RAM is normally measured in megabytes; typical values are 2, 4, 8 or 16 Mb. Extra RAM will improve the performance of the computer. In order to improve storage capacity the hard disk can be changed, for example swopping a 170 Mb drive for a 540 Mb drive, and *graphics cards* can be inserted to improve the quality of the graphic screen display.

Networking involves linking together two or more computers to allow facilities and information to be shared. As we saw on page 148, this has the effect of decentralising information and communications so that managers have more information upon which to base their decisions. A computer network may be specifically developed for almost any type of organisation or application. Terminals may be just a few feet apart or they may exist in completely different parts of the world.

A *local area network* (LAN) may be used to connect computers within a single room, building or a group

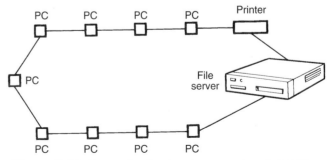

Figure 5.18 Example of a local area network (LAN)

of buildings on the same site, without the use of telecommunications links. LANs may be linked to a file server (Figure 5.18) which is a permanent data store which provides files and software on request for other PCs and also acts as a storage base.

A *wide area network* (WAN) may be used to connect computers on different sites by making use of telecommunications. The great benefit is that WAN networks extend the use of the computer beyond the office by using a *modem* (modulator/demodulator) which converts computer signals for transmission over the telephone lines before reconverting them back again.

Modems are used because telephone lines are for speech transmissions and not for use by computers. Waves travelling along lines are analogue waves where sound and images are converted into corresponding variations in electrical voltages or currents. Since 1990 BT has introduced a digitised network known as ISDN (Integrated Services Digital Network) which enabled transmission of video and voice signals in digitised format. As the ISDN is in itself digital there is no need to convert the computer's information into sound and therefore information transfer is faster and more reliable.

Uses for networks include:

- *Electronic mail (e-mail)* Here computers linked either through LAN or WAN send mail between terminals. Each user has his or her own mailbox which stores messages.
- *Teleconferencing* Discussions or meetings may take place with individuals widely dispersed, using a number of terminals.
- *Remote databases* These include Teletext or Prestel and provide users with vast amounts of information which may be constantly updated. Such databases may use 'fuzzy' logic search routines, which involves keying in clues to find the appropriate information required.
- *Electronic data interchange (EDI)* This allows users to exchange business documents and information such as orders and invoices by dealing directly through the telephone network.

Case study – 'Surfing the net!'

Though most of us have only recently heard of the Internet, it has been around for more than 25 years. It was born in 1969, the year of the Apollo moon landings and the Woodstock festival. Until recently it was used by computer buffs or 'Netties' who wallowed in their own brand of computer jargon, but today it has become widely accessible to a broader group of users.

The Internet began life as a defence network which linked computers of a few thousand researchers and military personnel. Today the Net might carry almost anything: the late-night ramblings of a Star Trek fan, the plight of a third-world refugee and computer games software. No matter how obscure the information, it will probably exist on the Internet.

The business world has spotted the potential of the Internet and in 1995 will attempt to turn its potential into profit. At the recent Internet World Conference there were more business people than buffs and enthusiasts in the audience. Some sessions at the conference analysed the potential to develop the net in a number of ways which included advertising, computerised local government, education, electronic shopping, banking and entertainment.

The biggest spur to the development of Internet, however, has been the realisation that it is a cheap way of communicating instantaneously with people on the other side of the world. For example, one recruitment agency in the UK has announced plans to place job-ads on the network; the main advantage being that the access offers employers the opportunity to select from a global pool of potential employees.

The latest development for the Internet is the World Wide Web, W3 or 'the Web'. This is a form of software which makes it easy for people with limited IT skills to use Internet. In fact it is a Windows equivalent which allows the user to manipulate information on a personal computer, and can be used to access sounds, graphics, text and video.

1 How far is Internet likely to transform global communications?

2 What are the arguments for and against using the Internet?

3 Identify any possible business uses for the Internet.

Evidence collection point

Draw a line diagram of a LAN network known to you. Show the location and type of all of the hardware attached to the network. Your work could provide evidence of Core Skills in Communication and Information Technology.

There are two key issues to mention about networks:

- *Security* It is important to prevent unauthorised access by hackers and others who may wish to make fraudulent changes to data. There may also be a problem if information contained on the network is of a personal nature. There are a number of methods of identifying a user, such as security cards and passwords.
- *Viruses* Networks are for multiple use and are therefore open to 'infection' by viruses. It may be necessary to set up a system of scanners and virus checks to make sure that virus attacks are speedily dealt with.

Software

It is not long since a high proportion of the population was frightened by computers. The machines appeared to be highly complex, came with daunting manuals and seemed to stop cooperating at the most inconvenient times. As a result of software developments modern computers have become more consumer-orientated, and a lot of thought has gone into making sure that they are user-friendly and that they meet organisational needs.

Computers rely on end-users telling them what to do, but the biggest problem many new computer owners face is discovering how to get the equipment to do what is asked.

A major improvement came with the development of Microsoft Windows, for which there have been a number of different versions. Windows 3.0 set a standard which was adopted for PCs across the globe. This was further improved by Windows 3.1/3.11 and Windows for Workgroups. The latest version is Windows 95 and the likelihood is that this will soon be superseded.

For the user, the chief advantage of operating the computer with windows is that of simplicity. On the

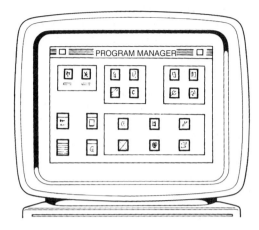

Figure 5.19 Using Windows

screen there are a number of windows which contain different tasks (Figure 5.19). Each task operates within a window. A window may fill the whole screen or just part of it, and it is possible to run more than one program at the same time. For example, it may be possible to be writing a document in the word-processing program while at the same time sorting an address list stored elsewhere in the system.

In Windows the user simply opens a window, points the mouse at the graphical user interface and opens a program. *Graphical user interfaces* (GUIs, or 'gooies') are making the technology easier to understand and

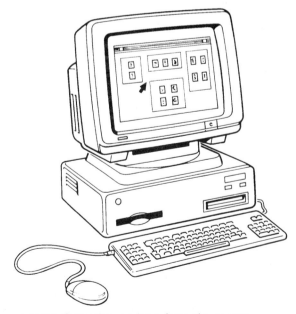

Figure 5.20 Selecting an icon from the menu

151

use – they are literally changing the nature of computers. A GUI presents the user with a series of small pictures, called icons, which represent the various options available. The mouse selects the icon for the desired course of action (Figure 5.20). If the user has selected a word-processing option, for example, the screen will provide the word-processing environment as well as the opportunity to use the mouse to select a further variety of options.

Microsoft Windows also provides many other benefits. For example:

■ Even if both windows are not on the screen at the same time it is possible to switch tasks easily without having to close down one program and open another.
■ Window sizes can be altered using buttons on the right-hand side of the window. The minimise buttons will reduce the window to an icon and double-clicking the mouse will bring it back to its original size.
■ Window sizes can be changed by moving the mouse to a corner of a window, holding the mouse button down and dragging the corner of the window in or out.
■ A window can be moved to another position on the screen to allow space for another application to be used.
■ Microsoft Windows also includes a number of other devices which may be of use for both the commercial and casual user. These include a:
 – **clock** which can be kept permanently displayed on screen
 – **paintbrush** program which is a useful package for constructing simple charts and drawings
 – **cardfile** for keeping useful addresses and other information
 – **calculator** which can be adapted for both scientific and standard use
 – **write/notepad**, both of which are simple word-processors, though Notepad can also be used as a text editor
 – **tutorial** which shows how the Windows package works
 – **calendar** which displays days as well as times of the day and also has an alarm
 – **file manager** which helps the user to keep their files in good order.

Evidence collection point

With the assistance of a Windows manual, use each of the devices within the Windows environment when completing an assignment.

Wherever possible, print from the devices. Plan your work to provide evidence of Core Skills in Information Technology.

Case study – Learning from the computer

Are PCs simple machines which do as we tell them, or is it soon going to become the other way around? When we use our PCs we undoubtedly develop habits which are not always efficient. Today there is a number of 'learning agents' on the market which, when installed on the computer, watch what you do, detect your pattern or work and then offer to take some of the repetitive tasks away from you.

One of the first packages around is called Open Sesame, which employs neural techniques that watch how you use the computer and then suggest ways in which it can work for you. This software is quite unlike any other application.

When using the computer you do not know it is there. It runs, however, in the background watching everything you do. When it has detected a regular pattern it will then make some suggestions. For example, it may by that time be handling the routine opening of documents and applications and be making suggestions about how you do regular 'housekeeping' jobs like back-ups.

The idea of smart or intelligent software is also beginning to catch on. WordPerfect, in order to differentiate itself from its rivals Microsoft and Lotus, recently released a Windows version which contains 'smart language agents'. WordPerfect uses intelligent editing to take out a space if one is left in front of a full stop. However, it now goes one stage further and deals with word and sentence construction.

So how far can these packages go? Future versions may well take a lot more of the brain strain away from the operator. They may also be able to communicate across different languages.

1 Describe how the packages mentioned in this study help the user.
2 What are the pros and cons of using each package? Might this sort of package interfere with what the user wants to do?

Word-processors involve using computer packages for the production of documents that contain text. The document is displayed on the screen and then recorded in the memory. A word-processor may be used for almost any textual application including letters, invoices, legal documents, books, articles, direct mail and so on. Features on the word-processor may include:

■ the ability to edit on screen, which means mistakes can be corrected after the document has been typed
■ saving the document to hard and floppy disk.
■ a spelling checker, a grammar checker and a thesaurus
■ many different types of font including Times New Roman, *Italics*, Garamond Book, `Courier New,` and **Bodoni Poster Italic.** The size of fonts may also be varied according to need.
■ different types of page layouts which include different margins, tabs, bullet points, etc.
■ template files for certain documents such as letters, mailshots and memos.
■ the ability to inset artwork, clipart, pictures and frames, often from other documents.

There are a number of leading software packages available, including Microsoft Word, WordPerfect for Windows (Figure 5.21), Lotus Ami Pro and Wordstar for Windows.

Information technology has revolutionised the ways in which accounting offices run. For example *accounting packages* assist in the capture and identification of information. Rapid capture enables, organisations to become more efficient; data can be processed more quickly and in a variety of ways. At the heart of the IT revolution has been improvements in software. Such developments have provided computer-based solutions to traditional financial problems.

Common applications of accounting packages include:

Figure 5.21 WordPerfect for Windows

■ *stock control* providing up-to-date information on stock levels as well as monitoring and checking the sales performance of each item
■ *sales ledger* keeping track of customers, what they buy, who they are, how much they owe and since when
■ *purchases ledger* keeping supplier records, who they are, what is purchased from them and how much you owe them
■ *VAT management* integrated into the package
■ *credit control* setting limits for customers and identifying late payers in order to improve cash flows
■ *invoicing/order processing* including the generation of documents
■ *management reports* providing a range of statements and other useful information
■ *small business accounting* packages for small business use providing a full records system
■ *payroll* an automated payroll system which includes employee details and statutory documents
■ *money management and financial decisions* some individual packages provide detailed packages which help individuals improve their management of money and help them to track their investments.

Much of the professional accounting software is produced by Sage – Sage Sterling is the leading brand of accounting software in the UK. Quickbooks is a useful package for non-accountants and Microsoft 3.0 for Windows provides a complete set of tools for money management.

Evidence collection point

Find out what accounting (or management) package is used within your school or college. Make a list of its functions and then comment upon the benefits of using such a package.

In the same way that word-processors are designed to manipulate text, *spreadsheets* are designed to manipulate numerical data. A spreadsheet presents the user with a grid comprising a large number of 'cells' which may each contain a number, a label or a formula which may refer to other cells. The spreadsheet can then use information for making forecasts, calculating information, drawing graphs and charts and presenting a wide range of information. Some of the more popular spreadsheets include Lotus 1-2-3, Microsoft Excel, Borland Quattro Pro and CA-SuperCalc (Figure 5.22).

CA-SuperCalc 1.0 *for Windows* is a complete analysis solution, offering the synergy of full-featured spreadsheeting and true multidimensional modelling, along with charting, analysis, auditing, security and automation. Also available, SuperCalc 5.5 for DOS.

Figure 5.22 CA-SuperCalc

One way of defining an electronic *database* is simply to describe it as a store of facts that provides information for users. However, it is really more than this. Databases are a powerful way of organising and manipulating information. Modern databases comprise a series of files which allow records to be created, collected, searched for, modified and printed. Most will provide file-searching facilities, calculations on fields for inclusion in reports, the ability to sort

records, index files and program files. Some of the more popular database programs include Microsoft Access and FoxPro, DataEase, Borland Paradox, Lotus Approach and Borland dBase for Windows.

Task

Compile a database of information about members of your teaching group. What information are you going to include in this database? Bear in mind that the database should be available for students to consult at any time. Is there any information you should definitely not put in? Your work can provide evidence of Core Skills in Communication and Information Technology.

Over recent years some of the most important developments of software for managers and administrators have been in the form of systems which have provided them with a range of information for decision-making purposes. These are called *management information systems* (MIS). One definition is provided by T. Lucey, who describes a MIS as:

> A system to convert data from internal and external sources into information and to communicate that information, in an appropriate form, to managers at all levels in all functions to enable them to make timely and effective decisions for planning, directing and controlling the activities for which they are responsible.

An MIS system, therefore, provides specific information for management needs and requirements at various functions and levels. The information may then be used for:

- problem solving
- decision-making
- improving the quality of decisions
- planning
- communicating information
- improving the efficiency of operations
- minimising the duplication of effort
- controlling activities.

MIS systems help managers in making decisions and are particularly important where information requirements can be anticipated in advance and where information is regularly required by a number of users.

Other commercial administration packages include:

- *desktop publishing packages* for the production of text and graphics in newsletters, magazines, posters and articles. These packages place emphasis upon the arrangement of information and appearance. Text can be imported from a word-processor, page layouts can be formatted into blocks, clipart can be used to enhance the text and drawings can be inserted. Some of the more popular commercial packages include Corel Ventura, Microsoft Publisher, Aldus PageMaker and GST Pressworks

■ *business presentation packages* which enable the user to develop high-quality presentations and slides and materials using a number of fonts and graphics and inserting these into a series of templates. These include Harvard Graphics, Lotus Freelance, and Microsoft Powerpoint.

■ *drawing, design* and *graphics* can be used for chart and graphic design and may also have advanced publishing capabilities. Examples are Corel Draw and Visio

■ *project management packages* enable the user to plan and monitor a project consisting of a number of interrelated activities. These include Microsoft Project, On-Target for Windows and CA-SuperProject.

■ *flowcharting tools*, *personal information managers*, *multimedia software*, *communications software* and *mapping and route planning tools*.

A number of packages have integrated a series of functions in order to provide a number of tasks within the same package. The advantage of using multi-tasking packages in that data can be easily transferred between applications, the user quickly develops familiarity with each of the functions and, given the range of applications, the packages represent value for money. For example, Microsoft Office includes Word, Excel, Powerpoint, Intellisense and Access. Lotus Smart Suite includes Lotus 1–2–3, Lotus AMI Pro, Lotus Approach, Lotus Freelance Graphics, Lotus Organiser and Lotus Notes Ready.

Evidence collection point

What sort of software have you at school, college or work? How is this software used? Find out about each type of software as well as the applications. Compile a report using graphics or a DTP to present your analysis. Your work can provide evidence of Core Skills in Communication and Information Technology.

Case study – Does software always have a use?

Berkley Systems began life as a small software company in California in 1987 developing software for sight-impared users. This serious purpose has involved the development of many important pieces of software for people who would not otherwise be able to use a PC. However, in developing software for such users an idea developed which instantly took off – screensavers.

The screensaver is a piece of software that waits until you have not used your computer for a while. The screen then blanks out and a graphic – such as a squadron of winged flying toasters – moves elegantly across the screen.

Screensavers are a rare example of humour on the PC which have also become big business. The packages rarely cost less than £30 and analysts IDC predict the worldwide market for moving-screen 'wallpaper' packages will more than double from £50 million in 1993 to £120 million in 1997.

1 It is argued that screensavers encourage users to take a break and have some fun! Are there any benefits of using screensavers in the workplace?

2 Are there any other examples of non-functional software on a PC?

Changing the way organisations work

In the 1960s, big and expensive computers were introduced by large organisations to handle major data-processing operations – such as payrolls, stock and inventory control. These machines were housed in large spotlessly clean (dust-free) rooms, and were managed by computer experts using systems that were difficult to operate. Keying in data was a monotonous task performed by semi-skilled staff, requiring accuracy and concentration but no knowledge of computers.

There have been great changes over the last 30 years. The development of integrated circuits led to the smaller, cheaper but equally powerful minicomputer. Hard on its heels came the tiny silicon-chip microprocessor carrying a vast number of electronic circuits. These chips make it possible to build sophisticated electronic control systems in very small spaces.

By 1990 personal computers (PCs) with equivalent power to the 1960s mainframes were to be found in offices large or small. These machines, costing sometimes less than a thousand pounds, can be used to run a range of software. Non-specialists can use PCs for many essential clerical and administrative tasks – word-processing, stock control, accounts, planning and so on. At the same time software is widely available and becoming increasingly easy to use.

Changes in the organisation of clerical and administrative work

When mainframe computers were introduced they led to centralisation of functions. As networking and PCs take over, decentralisation is following. Now different departments can use their own terminals to call up and update centrally held records. Typing is no longer carried out in the 'typing pool' – today word-processing can be carried out in any part of the building.

Low-cost microprocessors with user-friendly interfaces, e.g. keyboards, menus, mouses) mean that staff can routinely work on 'word and number crunching' (electronic textual and numerical processing), information storage and retrieval (database applications) and manipulating and analysing information (spreadsheets).

PCs are invaluable for many management functions including data analysis and forward planning. It is unfortunate that too many senior managers rely on 'chauffeured' use of this vital business tool, content that junior staff – often their secretaries – operate the computer terminal for them.

Trends in office automation in the next decade are likely to lead to a reduction in keyboard data entry, resulting in fewer clerical jobs. Senior clerks are also starting to take over some functions of managers. This could lead to an increase in senior clerical jobs and a reduction in the number of junior or middle managers.

Evidence collection point

Talk to a clerical worker about all of the changes that have taken place in their working environment over the past 10–15 years. Ask him or her what benefit these changes have provided and how they have affected the range of activities he or she is asked to undertake and how they have affected workloads.

For example, technology has enabled bank clerks to become 'personal bankers', using on-line computers to enable them to answer questions on financial services. Expert systems can permit insurance clerks to answer questions formerly the province of expert underwriters. Building society clerks have become adept at using spreadsheets to provide customers with instant details of financial options.

Throughout history, the office environment has reflected technological developments within society as a whole. Today's high-technology office equipment demands a clean working environment and the machines are accurate, efficient and fast. The traditional repetitive nature of office jobs can be minimised or eliminated and, as a result, offices are better places to work in and the type of work that employees undertake is more interesting.

Computers will usually help each user in a slightly different way. Imagine senior executives who have to spend a lot of time travelling on business. When they travel they may take a laptop or notebook PC which they can use on the train or plane. They may use word-processing, spreadsheet, database or graphics packages to analyse information and deal with correspondence. If they are giving a talk they may use a presentation package. Wherever they go, using a modem, they can call up their electronic mail. If they are unable, for some reason, to attend all meetings it may be possible to link up visually through a teleconferencing facility. Computers have, therefore, helped to increase the productivity of executives, putting information at their fingertips. At the same time the quality of their work has been enhanced and communication has been improved.

Improved customer service

Organisations spend a lot of money and time in developing systems which are designed to improve the ways in which the management and administrative function takes place with the ultimate objective of being able to satisfy customer needs more efficiently.

Perhaps the greatest benefit to all concerned is speed. Computers are fast and efficient. They help employees to carry out their functions speedily and efficiently. Organisations can use technology to respond much more flexibly by changing consumer patterns of demand and provide products which they want and where they want. For example, the use of bar scanners has reduced the time spent queuing in a supermarket. Rather than wait for an available till, bank customers can use teller machines. 'Quick Response' (QR) is a system used by many retailers to identify changes in consumer tastes from sales information – the system produces a closer relationship between demand and supply and enables retailers to respond quickly to any changes in fashion. For example, Marks & Spencer estimate that it has reduced lead times to under 10 days.

Using computers can also improve accuracy. When technology is used for administrative purposes, as long as the computer is programmed correctly, the accuracy of the output is virtually guaranteed. Many administrative systems will also introduce checking mechanisms which ensure that inaccuracies do not occur. In fact, almost always when or if mistakes do take place they are as a result of an error by a programmer and not as a result of computer error.

Computers help to reduce the costs of administration and these reductions can then be passed on to customers. For large and difficult jobs computers can provide considerable cost savings, particularly in terms of the number of staff who might otherwise have to be employed.

Technology and administrative systems may also enable organisations to provide improved types of services. Examples are home banking and shopping, messaging systems and answering services. Use of computers with access to data and stored information may also help employees to deal with specific problems as and when they arise if customers have any queries or complaints.

Computer-based administrative systems may also help to improve quality. Managers have more information upon which to base decisions and so, therefore, can make better decisions. These systems may also keep managers up-to-date with current developments, so making them better able to make informed decisions about the market.

Improving competitiveness

Technological changes in production, management and administrative procedures can exert a powerful influence upon all types of business organisations. In competitive markets organisations have to look at how the combined effects of computer, telecommunication and digital technologies can improve their efficiency, productivity and competitiveness in order to provide them with the best possible competitive advantage.

Evidence collection point

Using a computer program which is known to you, make a list of the potential benefits for users who might have to work with it on a day-to-day basis in the workplace.

Within this section we have used examples to show how technological advantages can increase workloads and further develop the role of the organisation. However, not everyone has the same reaction to technological and administrative change and when introducing new administrative systems it is important to be sensitive to their views.

One way of classifying people's reactions to change is to classify them as innovators, conservatives or inhibitors (Figure 5.23).

The *inhibitors* will resist change. They may see it as wrong or dangerous. They may only accept it when it has been adopted by the rest of the organisation.

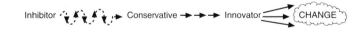

Figure 5.23 The different reactions to change

157

The *conservatives* will want to view the results of change before making a decision to accept any administrative changes. The *innovator* is a trialist and will applaud change and view it as a challenge. He or she may be excited by new ideas and concepts.

Case study – Using technology to improve competitiveness

The small company is often quoted as the loser in electronic technology. If a large customer tells it to gear itself up to receive orders electronically, it may then have to spend thousands of pounds to buy software and a computer system that may do little more than a fax machine. Keith Legg, information technology manager at the Ford Component Manufacturing plant in South Shields, has a positive view of electronic commerce. His company, which makes engineering parts, has a turnover of less than £5 million and employs 150 people. But, as early as 1988, when electronic trading was only three years old, he realised that many of their big customers, such as JCB and British Aerospace, would soon suggest that they should accept their orders electronically.

Before being pushed, Ford Component geared itself up for electronic trading. It wrote its own message-translation software and signed up with an electronic trading network. The expense of electronic trading was justified not on the lower cost of transaction, but on the marketing benefits.

For the first few years EDI (electronic data interchange) was used as an electronic fax and did not key into the in-house computing system. However, 18 months ago the systems were integrated. This is often considered the main problem with the spread of electronic commerce as it can be difficult to plug into accounting or production control software and, until recently, many accounting packages have ignored the potential of EDI.

Recently the Business Software Developers' Association have set up a working party to standardise links through EDI. The aim is to set up a system so that companies like Ford Components will go straight into it without having to experiment with expensive equipment. The future is now international electronic trade. The European Commission view electronic commerce as a 'glue' that could hold the single market together and has set up EDI awareness centres throughout Europe.

1 What does it mean when Mr Legg justifies 'the expense of electronic trading, not on the lower cost of transactions, but on the marketing benefits'?
2 What are the benefits of EDI for (a) Ford Components, and (b) customers?

3 Outline the sort of problems a business might encounter when introducing such a system.

Supporting the functions of an organisation

Administrative systems should be designed to successfully accomplish organisation goals. This can only happen if the system works efficiently and helps an organisation to operate smoothly. To do this the system has to be developed to solve specific problems and should, therefore, be fit for the purposes intended.

In developing an administration system, therefore, managers must realise that it must go though a systems life-cycle (Figure 5.24). This will include five distinct stages:

- defining the problem and setting objectives
- designing the system
- implementation
- operation and maintenance
- replacement.

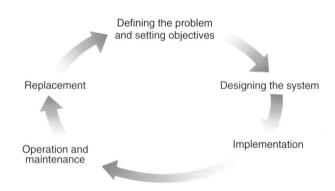

Figure 5.24 The life-cycle of an administration system

Defining the problem and setting objectives will be determined by the area which requires improvement. Analysts will need to collect information about the present system, look at current costs and performance capabilities and then determine what they would like from a new system. From this they should define the administrative problems to be solved and set a series of performance objectives. These may include customer service, cost efficiency, expansion, etc.

The system should then be *designed*. Design will involve determining the basic elements to the system and the setting of performance standards designed to match objectives. This may involve having to make trade-offs between the cost of a new system and efficiency required.

Implementation will involve purchase of hardware and selecting the software. It may also involve redesigning jobs, developing new documentation and procedures and training personnel.

As the system is used it will be important to *maintain* it and also monitor and evaluate its *operation*. This may involve periodic modifications. Finally, as business administrative objectives and goals change, and the system ages, administrators must decide when the system requires *replacement.*

A number of other criteria will determine whether a system is suitable for supporting an organisation's functions. These will include:

- ■ *System cost* One of the most important criteria for evaluation when introducing or developing a new system is cost. Such cost may have an important bearing upon the design of the system as well as how it operates. Administrators may have to perform a feasibility study to justify spending substantial amounts in order to ensure that they are receiving value for money.
- ■ *Security* If a system is accessible by a large number of users, then the need for proper security procedures becomes much more important. If a system introduces a Wide Area Network (WAN), then this gives the system greater exposure and may cause potential security problems. There are a number of security controls, including:
  - allowing only certain authorised personnel to use the system
  - physical controls such as keyboard locks, logs – or limited hour use
  - passwords which change periodically
  - making back-up copies of data and programs
  - network controls such as data encryption which codes data so that it cannot be understood unless it is first decoded
  - segmenting and rotating tasks of personnel so that each task requires several different people.
- ■ *Health and safety* As the use of computers has developed in the workplace a number of new issues have come to the fore, one of the most important being health and safety. It has been found that long periods at the keyboard can cause problems in the hands and arms known as *repetitive strain injury* (RSI). To help users, a number of organisations have used ergonomics – the science of matching machines in the work

environment to people – to develop products that reduce such problems.

The keyboard in Figure 5.25 provides a built-in palm rest for the palms between typing. The natural contour of the keys puts hands, forearms and shoulders in a more natural position and the wrist leveller provides for a straighter wrist posture.

Figure 5.25 The ergonomic keyboard from Microsoft

Another problem may be that of glare. Office lighting may create glare on the terminals and providing indirect lighting can eliminate this. Glare may also come from the screen. Screen filters provide protection against glare, as well as against static and radiation emissions.

Other health and safety issues within the office may include:

- noise pollution – the sound of computers and printers may be distracting and disturbing the type of workstation – poor workstation design may result in fatigue.

Improving administrative systems

In the society in which we live, we depend upon automation and technology to help with the generation of wealth. Computers, tele-communications and their effect upon administrative procedures today play an important role which influences how we work and learn, the work we undertake and the leisure we enjoy.

Organisations are units set up to pursue specific goals. To achieve these successfully within an increasingly competitive society, the organisations need to be able to operate efficiently and plan ahead.

Efficient administration systems which include extensive use of technology will help organisations to do this.

When new administration systems are introduced they may affect staff throughout the organisation. Jobs may be created, changed or lost. This creates a demand for staff training and retraining. Before any form of training starts, analysts have to develop a series of written standards and guidelines for using the system. These will help users to understand how the system works, deal with any emergencies or problems which arise and help them to adapt to its use.

Training on a new administration system should be considered as the development of a new learning opportunity. Use of the system will be improved by users developing:

- better *knowledge* of the system and its capability
- *skills* and *expertise* which help them to develop and improve the effective operation of the system
- *learning experiences* which help users to adapt to changing conditions and tasks so that they can improve the functioning of the system through their role.

If an administration system is not operating properly, this may be due to lack of training. Training will help to improve the efficiency of administration processes, help staff to cope with new or more complex techniques, raise operating standards and improve efficiency and morale.

Case study – Improving administrative procedures

Robin Hurst is a qualified accountant in his mid-20s. Most of his work has been with large accounting practices, but in search of partnership opportunities, he has recently been appointed by accountants – Dewhurst, Simkin and Taylor – in a rural Yorkshire town.

His first observations were that though the practice clearly needed developing, there were many businesses in the area and so plenty of opportunities for improving the client base. There are two qualified accountants currently within the business. Robin will be the third. The practice occupies an elevated position over the town market-place in an old building. The offices are in a state of disrepair and clearly need improvement. There are two clerical staff and two trainee accountants. The only computer within the practice is used by the clerical staff for word-processing only. There are few filing systems within the practice. Paperwork is stacked rather than dealt with in a more rational manner.

Most of the clients have been with the practice for many years. The senior partner is well-known locally and tries to emphasise the traditional virtues of the practice. However a number of small business have been moving to an accounting practice on an industrial estate in a larger town 15 miles away.

Robin intends to bring a fresh approach to the business. He is well aware of the challenges the practice faces but is willing to try to deal with them.

1 What overall objective might Robin have for influencing change?
2 Suggest a number of ways in which the administrative systems within Dewhurst, Simkin and Taylor could be improved or redeveloped. In your answer, refer to specific allocation of functions, types of technology, uses for technology, commercial packages and benefits that such changes might bring.
3 How will these changes provide clearer and safer procedures?
4 What problems might Robin face?

A modern office lies at the heart of any organisation. Like any system it needs to run well; in fact it needs to run in the best possible way. Inputs of raw data and semi-finished data need to be converted into finished information by using the most effective processes that are appropriate. It would be ridiculous for a small company to make a computer database out of sparse data relating to just three customers. It would be equally ridiculous nowadays for a company to rely purely on pen and paper records for dealing with thousands of orders. Organisations therefore need to use appropriate technology to meet their administrative needs.

Evidence indicators

In this activity you may refer to the organisation at which you undertook your work experience, may visit an organisation, or may use your school or college as a base for collecting evidence. Prepare a report which examines the functioning of the administration of one organisation.

The following list should serve as a checklist. Please tick off each of the following when you have successfully covered them as part of your report. You need to confirm that:

- I have examined the administration system used by a business organisation. ☐
- I have found out the purposes of the administrative system. ☐
- I understand how the functions of the organisation are supported by administrative procedures and processes. ☐
- I have explained how suitable the administrative system is for supporting the functions of the organisation (fitness for purpose). ☐
- I have described how information technology has supported the administrative process. ☐
- I have identified the positive and negative effects of information technology within the organisation. ☐
- I have, where possible, made suggestions for improvements to the administration system. ☐

Business organisations and systems

Chapter 6

Communication in business organisations

Central to all business systems is the need to be able to communicate both inside and outside the organisation. Communicating effectively with others can be very difficult. For example, how often have you failed to understand an instruction or have misinterpreted a statement? In all organisations the purpose of setting up an effective communication system is to create a mechanism that gets things done more efficiently. Such systems will ensure that messages are received, understood and accepted and then, as a result, action can take place.

This chapter looks at the nature and purpose of communication within the context of administrative systems. It looks at types of communications, their objectives and the effectiveness of communication to organisations within the context of business systems.

Communication in and between business organisations

At the heart of management at all levels of responsibility lies a fundamental requirement to be able to communicate. A manager must be able to communicate effectively with all people within his or her span of control. In fact, managers and administrators tend to spend by far the majority of their time communicating with others. If communication as a basic business skill takes up so much time, a knowledge of how to communicate well has to be viewed as a vital requirement for all managers and administrators.

Communication is the two-way process of passing on ideas and information. All organisations need good, clear paths of communication. In Chapter 4 we saw how systematic lines of communication help to create a structure which coordinates the activities between different parts of an organisation. Effective communication in an organisation, however, goes further than this. It enables an organisation to make everyone aware of what they can achieve. It also helps employees solve problems through the use of technical language referring to the more scientific aspects of their work. Finally, by providing a uniform way of giving people information and an opportunity

to put their ideas across, communication can be used to avoid misunderstandings, save time, resolve conflicts and provide all employees with a tool to express as clearly as possible what they really mean.

We all have to communicate. To communicate well requires the development of the basic skills of speaking, listening, reading and writing. In addition it involves an awareness and an understanding of the subject, the audience and the environment. Successful communication requires not only that information should be transmitted, but also that it should be fully received and understood. Listening and reading skills are therefore just as important as speaking and writing skills.

Task

Form small groups. Each member of the group should prepare a talk lasting for about one minute and then deliver it to the other members of the group. Analyse the problems encountered by both the speakers and the listeners. This will provide evidence of Core Skills in Communication.

The process of communication involves a *transmitter* (or sender) sending *messages* to *receivers*. A transmitter should put information into a form the receivers can understand, and this might involve oral, written or visual messages. This process is known as *encoding*. The transmitter chooses a particular medium to use to send messages to the receivers – letter, report, fax, phone call, etc. The receivers then interpret the messages through a process of *decoding* (Figure 6.1).

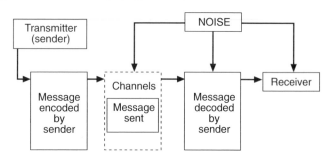

Figure 6.1 The communication process

Though a message flows from the sender to receivers, there is no guarantee that the receivers will either receive the full message or even understand it. This is because the process may be subject to some form of interference or barrier to communication which affects the smooth flow of information. Communication problems of this nature are known as *noise* and may lead to the downfall of the message. Noise can take the form of any barrier acting as an impediment to the smooth flow of information. Here are a few examples:

- *Language problems* The language used may not be fully understood, particularly if a receiver comes from a different background from the sender or has considerably less knowledge, technical or otherwise.
- *Jumping to conclusions* The receiver might read into the message what he or she expects to see, rather than what is really there.
- *Lack of interest* The receiver may not be prepared to listen to the message. The message has to be designed to appeal to the listener.
- *Competing environment* Background sounds (real noise) or interference from other activities in the work environment may influence the message, particularly if it is long or complicated and requires concentration by the receiver.
- *Channels of communication* Effective communication will be hampered if the means chosen to pass the message is poor.
- *Cultural differences* We all have different perceptions of the world according to our background and experiences, and this may result in our interpreting a message in different ways.
- *Steps in the message* If there are too many stages in the message (i.e. if it is too complicated), it may not be properly understood.

Task

Identify at least one situation in which a barrier to communication has affected your interpretation of a message.

Internal communication

Good communication plays an important role within an organisation. Communication may help to coordinate the activities of various departments, transfer information or initiate some form of action. The volume, type and nature of information may influence the type of communication methods used.

Internal communication may flow:

- downwards – from higher to lower levels
- upwards – from lower to higher levels
- horizontally – between people and departments at the same level
- multi-directionally – in all directions.

A *grapevine* will throw information out in all directions to all interested parties.

Evidence collection point

Make a list of all of the *internal* forms of communciation within the organisation you either work at or attend. Compare each type of communication under the following headings: speed, effectiveness, clarity, efficiency.

External communication

External communication is concerned with how an organisation is viewed by others. All of the actions of and communications from an organisation are encompassed. Every organisation has a public face or image, and this conveys a message which affects or influences everyone who has dealings with the organisation – customers, shareholders, suppliers, competitors, governments, communities, international agencies, environmental groups. Providing a positive image through external communication creates a better external environment for the organisation. Successful manipulation of public relations convinces others that the organisation is worth dealing with, and might provide it with considerable strategic and competitive advantage.

As with internal communications, external communications can be divided into verbal, written and visual communications.

Evidence collection point

Make a list of all of the *external* forms of communications from the organisation you either work at or attend. Compare each type of communication under the following headings: speed, effectiveness, clarity and efficiency.

Open or restricted channels

With any form of communication it is important to identify the purpose of the message as well as the people at whom the message is to be targeted. If the message is targeted at everybody within the organisation or groups outside and does not contain confidential materials, then the message is *open* for anybody to see or interpret; for example, notice boards, memos to all staff, staff magazines. On the other hand, if the message contains confidential materials, the likelihood is that it will be targeted at only a few groups of users either within a particular department or at certain levels of seniority, so that its use is *restricted*. It is important to build a communications network which provides a system whereby restricted messaged can be sent. For example, management information systems (MIS) (see page 154) ensure that certain information goes to specified people only and this can contribute to control, confidentiality and security of information (Figure 6.2).

The information needs to be received by several people in different places.
The information is highly complex, requiring extensive study.
The information needs to be referred to over a period of time.

The written word in some circumstances can be open to ambiguity if the receiver is not immediately able to question the sender. For this reason, even informal notes need to be accurate, clear in their meaning and easy to read. Documentation systems are widely used in industry to reduce elements of ambiguity and, very often, drawings and sketches are used to support the written text.

Some types of written communication are more easily read than others. For example, company accounts and other financial and quantitative information may be complex and require the reader to have specialist background knowledge. The target audience and the nature of the information are very important factors to take into consideration when deciding how to present data.

For many people, putting pen to paper implies creating something rather permanent, and there can be fear of being misunderstood, particularly if the document is directed 'upwards' or is to be viewed by a number of other colleagues. Confidence is important, as is the need to read through the message to make sure that you get the message right.

The word 'memorandum' (nearly always shortened to 'memo') derives from the Latin *memorare* which means 'thing to be remembered'. Today memos have a wider business use than just as memory aids, having become the most frequently used form of written communication within organisations. They are used to communicate instructions, information and enquiries. Though they are the internal equivalent of letters, there are one or two minor differences. An organisation's name does not normally appear on a memo for internal use, and it is not necessary to have a salutation or complimentary ending. Memos should be kept as short as possible and ideally should deal with only one item. Copies of the same memo are often distributed to a number of recipients (Figure 6.3).

The style of memoranda varies considerably. Instructions from senior management are likely to be written in relatively impersonal language, while a quickly scribbled message on a memo sheet to a close colleague may be in conversational English. It is often necessary to be more careful and diplomatic when writing memos up the seniority ladder, rather

RU   Restricted user

OU   Open user

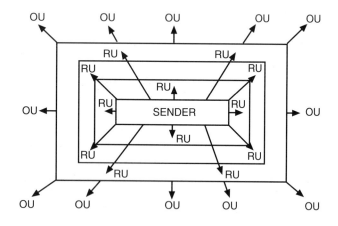

Figure 6.2 Open and restricted users

 Evidence collection point

What sort of information should be (a) open, and (b) restricted?

Written communications

Written messages vary from the very simple to the very complex. The following are examples where written communications are appropriate:

MEMORANDUM

To:	All staff	**Ref:**	BW/JK
From:	B Watson	**Date:**	12th April 199_
	(Personnel Manager)		

REVISED HEALTH AND SAFETY REGULATIONS

It has come to my attention that there have been a number of minor accidents in the last few weeks which have not been recorded in the Accident Book.

It is important that all accidents are logged. The company wishes to maintain a safe working environment for all its employees and can only do this if it is aware of defects.

Please make sure you are aware of your duties under the HASAW Act, now outlined in the revised Staff Handbook.

Figure 6.3 A specimen memorandum

than down. On all occasions it is important to take account of people's sensitivities and the position you hold.

Task

Imagine that you are a college administrator. Write a short memo to staff asking them to attend a meeting in the Main Hall on a date in the future. Ask them to contact you if they wish anything to be included as an agenda item.

Reports are another form of written communication. In simple terms, a report is a written communication from someone who has collected and studied some facts to a person who has asked for the facts (and possibly a recommendation) because he or she needs them for a particular purpose or to help with making a decision. It is therefore a basis for some form of action.

Reports may, for example, supply information for legal purposes (e.g. as a result of an incident or accident) or may be presented to shareholders. A report may attempt to assess the consequences of changes in company policy.

A well-written report is concise and does not contain anything the reader does not need to know. It should be clear and logically arranged but, at the same time, should not exclude anything that the reader needs.

Informal reports may be most suitably written or typed on a memo form. It is important to start with a title, and possibly a brief introduction, before going on to the body of the report. Recommendations for action should be clearly identified if these have been requested.

Formal reports will have many of the following features:

- Title page (subject matter, name and position of writer, date, etc.)
- Contents page
- Terms of reference (explaining the reason for the report)
- Procedure (how the task was completed)
- Findings
- Conclusions and/or recommendations.

When preparing a formal report, decisions have to be made on aspects such as language and style, circulation, and the presentation (including whether the report should have a cover and binding).

Evidence collection point

Imagine that you are asked by the National Union of Students to write a formal report on the facilities available for students at the college or other place of tuition you are attending.

Your report should be based on *research* covering areas such as library and IT facilities, recreational and social facilities, guidance and counselling, refectory, etc., and the strain (if any) put on these facilities by the numbers of students at the college.

Your conclusions and recommendations, clearly identified, should refer to the way in which the availability of facilities affects the working patterns of students at the college. Plan your work so that it provides evidence of Core Skills in Application of Number as well as Communication.

The *business letter* is still the most widely used form of external communication. It may be used, for example, to:

- make arrangements without the need for parties to meet

- provide both parties with a permanent record of such arrangements
- confirm verbal arrangements.

A well-written business letter conveys its message while maintaining goodwill. If a letter is sent promptly, is well set out and conveys its message accurately, the recipient will develop a favourable impression of that organisation, and is more likely to want to have further dealings than if the letter is delayed and inaccurate.

Writing an effective letter requires adequate preparation. It might be necessary to investigate the background to the letter by searching through previous correspondence, which may be stored in a file. As you research your letter, the contents will become apparent. For example, you might have to:

- seek information as the result of an enquiry
- confirm an order
- deal with a problem or fault
- obtain quotations
- seek payment for a debt
- place an order
- express an opinion
- seek references
- check credit-worthiness
- quote a price
- convey a personal message.

Evidence collection point

Collect examples of business letters you or your family have received from a variety of different organisations. What was each letter for? Comment upon the impression conveyed by each letter.

The layout, style and appearance of business letters – and even the envelope – varies from one organisation to another. Most will endeavour to create a good impression, particularly by giving attention to the heading and layout. Organisations often have a house style which they encourage all clerical staff to follow. Business letters are usually typed on A4 or A5 paper, and a fully blocked open-punctuated style is now the most common form of display.

A typical business letter will have the following features (Figure 6.4):

- a heading or **letterhead**
- a **reference** – enabling the letter to be filed and traced later
- a **date**
- the **inside address** – which is that of the recipient

- the **salutation** (Dear Mr Saunders)
- the **subject heading** (Manuscript of BTEC publication)
- the **body** of the letter
- the **complimentary close** (Yours sincerely ...).

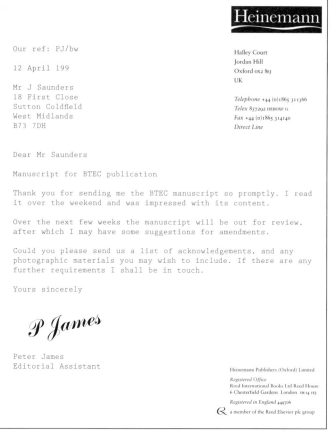

Figure 6.4 An open-punctuated fully blocked business letter

There is a convention about pairings of salutation and complimentary close. When the name of the recipient is not known, so that 'Dear Sir/Madam' is used, this should be paired with 'Yours faithfully'. When the name is known and 'Dear Mr/Mrs ...' is used, this should be paired with 'Yours sincerely'. If the recipient is addressed by his or her first name, this may be paired with 'Kind regards ... Yours sincerely'.

When a letter is sent with enclosures, this is denoted by 'Enc' or Encs' at the foot of the letter to alert the recipient to this fact.

When writing a business letter, always plan what you are going to say beforehand. Organise your information into a logical sequence and try to keep your language simple. Be courteous yet direct. After you have written the letter, check it for spelling mistakes and grammatical errors.

Evidence collection point

You have just received a batch of 50 reams of headed stationery from Monsons Press Ltd. Unfortunately the printer has used the wrong size paper and has used an out-of-date heading. It is generally unsuitable for office use. You have checked that the printer was given the correct information. Draft a letter of complaint and print a copy. Your work should provide evidence of Core Skills in Information Technology and Communication.

Minutes are a detailed record of a meeting and are often used as a form of internal communication. Such minutes displayed on noticeboards or sent to key staff inform people about decisions taken in various parts of the organisation. For example, in a school, copies of minutes of departmental meetings provide a useful guide to the headteacher on how staff might react to certain decisions. The same headteacher might put details of his or her meetings with deputies on a noticeboard so that other staff are kept up-to-date with developments. The minutes usually state who is responsible for specific actions arising from the meeting.

Before a meeting takes place, an *agenda* will list the items of business to be discussed and the order in which they will be taken. If an agenda is displayed on a noticeboard, a member of the organisation who is not invited to attend the meeting – and who might be concerned about a particular issue – will have the opportunity to have a prior word with someone who is invited.

Newsletters are a useful way of communicating changes and developments to staff, customers and other groups of people who may be interested in the functioning of the organisation. They may contain information about changes in staff, new product developments, charitable events and any other worthwhile activity (Figure 6.5).

Notices are another common form of written communication. They are placed in prominent positions and used to publicise any changes in policy, dates to be remembered, functions, events taking place, etc. Notices are usually short and related to a single subject. They might be supported by artwork to catch the attention of staff.

House magazines, *journals* and *newspapers* are a useful way of communicating policies, information, events and other activities. They are a particularly useful form of internal communication in large organisations where they can be used to help staff to develop a corporate identity and feel a sense of belonging.

Case study – St Michael News and M&S World

Marks and Spencer is a company that has always attached great importance to the care and training of its staff. According to Lord Rayner, Chairman of M&S from 1984 to 1991, 'the continued development of our business depends upon the calibre of our people'. The company provides training, personal development and motivational packages which recognise the contributions of all the employees.

The senior management believes that the commitment of staff is greatly enhanced when they feel involved and consulted. Communications groups have been operating in stores for some time. Training encourages staff to use their communication group as an effective vehicle for two-way communication. Another aspect of partnership is the suggestions scheme – called the 'Good Ideas Scheme' – which produces many contributions designed to improve efficiency and save money. Two further devices to keep employees informed is the staff newspaper called *St Michael News* and the magazine *M&S World* which is a company publication for Marks and Spencer management worldwide.

St Michael News is a bi-monthly glossy newspaper made available to all Marks and Spencer staff. It

NORTHERN ELECTRIC Review

Issue 1

CONNECTING WITH OUR CUSTOMERS

Welcome

Dear Customer,

Welcome to the first issue of *Review*, Northern Electric's new Customer newsletter.

Last year, in our Customer Service Guide, we told you that we would keep you informed of any changes to our services. This newsletter tells you a little about those changes, and about some of the activities of the Company and our staff.

In recent years, we have been able to:

▼ Reduce our prices - and your costs.

▼ Improve the standards of service we offer you.

▼ Raise investment in electricity network improvements to record levels.

▼ Offer support and sponsorship worth millions of pounds to the community.

Northern Electric has its roots in the North East, a region that pioneered so many developments in electricity in the past, and we are committed to delivering further developments in our service to customers in the future.

The Review is designed to help achieve that goal, so if you have any comments, complaints or suggestions about any aspect of our service, please write and tell me.

David Morris
Chairman, Northern Electric plc
Carliol House, Market Street, Newcastle upon Tyne, NE1 6NE

Service goes up, prices come down

Northern Electric's success rate in meeting the performance targets set in agreement with the industry Regulator are now running very close to 100%.

We have a far lower number of complaints referred to the Regulator than any other Regional Electricity Company in England and Wales.

In recognition of this and other aspects of customer service, Northern Electric was awarded the Charter Mark in 1993. But that doesn't in any way mean we are going to rest on our laurels.

Every year the company raises its performance targets still higher, with special emphasis on those aspects of our service we know will benefit our customers most.

We now offer improved appointments which includes morning or afternoon and two hour time slots when requested. We have extended our office hours to 8.00am - 6.00pm, and we are also currently testing an all-day Saturday service.

Tina Naylor, a Customer Service Representative, who helps answer over 1.5 million calls each year.

At the same time, we've actually cut our prices by 3% in 1993 and by a further 5% in 1994/95, on top of a further £10 rebate in 1993. In real terms, allowing for inflation, the ever higher quality of service we are now providing is costing our customers 15% less than in 1991, and over 20% less than in 1984.

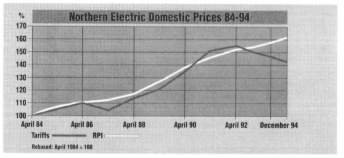

Northern Electric Domestic Prices 84-94

Tariffs ——— RPI ———
Rebased: April 1984 = 100

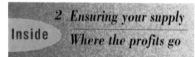

Inside

2 Ensuring your supply
Where the profits go

3 Breaking the barrier
Special service

4 £500 in prizes
Enterprise & Investment

Figure 6.5 Example of a customer newsletter

provides an opportunity for senior managers to communicate overall group strategy, successes and achievements and economic matters of interest to all employees – such as profits, store expansions, new systems and company policies. As well as this the newspaper acts as a forum for other events in the group – the introduction of new collections of clothes, new food ranges, homeware products, financial services, etc. Other articles cover information on the group's overseas activities, staff profit-sharing, community involvement, long-service awards, retirements, and competitions such as crosswords and 'Young Environmentalist of the Year'.

M&S World has been running for seven years and is published for M&S management. The magazine focuses upon the operations of the group around the world and examines developments in new products, technologies, stores and suppliers.

St Michael News and *M&S World* help to reflect the changing culture of the organisation from paternalism to partnership to ensure that values within the organisation are shared and not imposed. With more than 75 000 employees working for Marks and Spencer worldwide, it is generally felt that good communications will improve involvement and help to create a working environment in which everyone wants to contribute.

1 Comment upon why the Marks and Spencer management today places so much emphasis on partnership with the employees.
2 How important is a good internal communication system for creating such a partnership?
3 What methods, other than those indicated in the study, could be used to enhance communications within a large organisation?

Evidence collection point

Write to a number of organisations and talk to a number of people at work. Collect a series of different types of journals, newsletters and house magazines.

Oral communication

Oral communication involves the transmission of information effectively by word of mouth. Speaking is often a vastly underrated skill. It can be used to communicate ideas, reasons and conclusions. A good speaker is likely to have a far greater impact on the receiver of a message than a poor speaker and can provoke a far better response (Figure 6.6).

1 Express your ideas clearly, using language that is appropriate for your listeners
2 Say exactly what you mean – speak accurately using reliable information and never generalise with statements that go beyond the facts
3 Show empathy with the listeners, and convey enthusiasm
4 Try to be sincere and not put on an act – relax and talk naturally
5 Use tone, expressions and some body language (not too much)
6 Use appropriate pitch and volume
7 Articulate and enunciate well – a regional accent does not affect good diction if you speak clearly

Figure 6.6 How to be an effective speaker

Task

Think of anyone you know with good speaking ability. What makes him or her a good speaker? Make a complete list of the qualities of a good speaker. Discuss your conclusions with others in a group situation. This work should help you provide evidence of Core Skills in Communication.

For many people at work, verbal communications tend to be face-to-face exchanges for the purpose of relaying messages, personal discussion, giving advice, providing instructions and guidance, etc. Such exchanges are particularly appropriate for discussing personal matters and for conveying feelings or for confidential matters. Face-to-face contact can create a less formal relationship and allow communicators to get to know each other. Feedback can be instant, so that disagreements can be sorted out quickly. The main disadvantage of face-to-face contact, however, is that it is a time-consuming exercise which usually provides no permanent record of the message unless notes are written. Discussion may lack precision, and this can lead to misunderstandings.

Another area where verbal communications are important is in meetings. Nearly all employees at all levels in an organisation will spend some time attending meetings; administrative staff and managers will use a large proportion of their time in this way. Meetings are held to deal with issues, problems and areas of concern for an organisation. They provide an opportunity for a group of people to use their specialist backgrounds, experiences and knowledge to contribute to a range of matters.

Some meetings are called to generate ideas. Individuals have different backgrounds and the number of ideas being put forward tends to increase with group size. One popular problem-solving technique is *brainstorming*, which was originally used in the advertising industry to come up with new ideas. In a brainstorming session, the problem is stated and participants to the meeting are encouraged to produce as many ideas as they can, out of which the best is selected.

Meetings can be called to give people information or spread knowledge. These are particularly important if a lot of people need to be informed or if the information is confidential. Meetings allow parties from both sides of an issue to negotiate an agreement.

Often meetings are used to get collective decisions from members by democratic means. If an individual does not have the authority to make a decision, he or she might call a meeting so that others can agree to some proposals. Sometimes when a decision is made by a senior member of staff, it then needs ratification (confirmation) by others in a meeting.

Finally, meetings can be called to investigate something that has happened – for example, an accident or a series of thefts.

Meetings range from informal discussions or unstructured gatherings between a few people to formal, heavily structured meetings controlled by rigid rules and procedures.

Informal meetings involve the gathering together of individuals, often at short notice and without any set procedures. Informal meetings are flexible and can be called to respond to any issue, or can be used to share responsibility for a decision.

On the other hand, the rules and procedures for a formal meeting may be contained in a company's Memorandum and Articles of Association or in an organisation's standing orders or written constitution. The features of a formal meeting are:

- the meeting is called by a *notice* or *agenda*
- conduct in the meeting depends on the formal rules of the organisation
- decisions are reached by voting
- formal meeting terms are used
- the proceedings are recorded in *minutes*.

Formal meetings must be conducted according to legal requirements or a written constitution. It is usual to give *notice* of the meeting to every person entitled to attend according to the rules and regulations (Figure 6.7). The notice should be signed by the issuer and should specify the date, time and place of the meeting.

> NOTICE OF MEETING
> **CROWTHORNE FOOTBALL CLUB**
>
> The Annual Meeting of the Selection Committee will be held in the upstairs room of The Buckshot Inn on Monday 18th August 199_ at 7.45 pm. Any items for inclusion in the Agenda should reach me no later than 18th July 199_.
>
> Secretary:

Figure 6.7 A notice of meeting

A notice of a meeting will be accompanied or followed by an *agenda*, which is a list of topics to be discussed at the meeting. It will normally be sent to all those entitled to attend the meeting so that they can consider the topics in advance of the meeting (Figure 6.8)

> AGENDA
> **CROWTHORNE FOOTBALL CLUB**
> Annual Meeting of the Selection Committee
> to be held on Monday 18th August 199_ at 7.45 pm in The Buckshot Inn
>
> 1 Apologies for absence
> 2 Minutes of the last meeting
> 3 Matters arising from the minutes
> 4 Reports: Treasurer's report
> Team Secretary's report
> Chairperson's report
> 5 Proposal to redecorate clubhouse
> 6 Proposal to increase match fees
> 7 Any other business
> 8 Date of next meeting
>
> Secretary:

Figure 6.8 An agenda

Evidence collection point

In your role as Secretary to the Richmond Squash Club, prepare an agenda of a meeting to be held next Friday in the clubhouse at 8.00 pm. As well as the regular items, include the following: bar takings; redecoration of the clubhouse. Use a word-processor to display your agenda, to provide evidence of Core Skills in Information Technology.

A *chairperson* has certain duties and powers in a meeting. He or she makes sure that the meeting is properly constituted, preserves order, works through the agenda preventing irrelevant discussion, and ascertains the views of the meeting by putting *motions* and amendments to those attending.

Often a chairperson will have a special copy of the agenda known as the *chairperson's agenda*. On this, further information is provided for the chairperson's guidance, and space is provided on the right-hand side for notes to be made.

Shortly before the time a meeting is designated to start the chairperson makes sure that there is a *quorum* – this is the minimum number of people required for the meeting to go ahead according to the rules. He or she will also ensure that everybody has an agenda and that all new members are introduced.

The *secretary* then states whether any apologies have been received for absence, and reads through the official record – the minutes (Figure 6.9) – of the last meeting. If the minutes have already been circulated, it will be assumed that they have been read! Members are asked to approve them as a correct record of the last meeting and, if necessary, the secretary will amend them before they are signed by the chairperson.

At this stage any *matters arising* from the minutes will be discussed. For example, if the last meeting suggested that certain individuals undertake certain actions, these may be mentioned.

The chairperson then works through the business of the meeting according to the agenda. If reports are to be read (again, circulated reports are assumed to have been read) the writers may be asked to speak briefly about theirs. If a *motion* is proposed the chairperson will ask for a proposer and a seconder, allow for discussion of the motion making sure that all sides are heard, and then call for a vote. The chairperson usually has a casting vote if the voting is tied.

CROWTHORNE FOOTBALL CLUB

Minutes of the Annual Meeting of the Selection Committee held on Monday 18th August 199_ in The Buckshot Inn at 7.45 pm.

Present
Mr A James (Chairperson), Mr D Smith (Team Secretary), Mr R Pitt, Mrs H Johnson, Mr N Rees (Secretary), Miss E Walters (Treasurer)

1 Apologies	Apologies for absence were received from Mr R Cook and Mr S Turner.
2 Minutes	Minutes of the last meeting were taken as read, approved and signed.
3 Matters arising	Mrs Johnson reported that, since last season, she had taken on the task of writing the press releases and match reports that had regularly appeared in local newspapers.
4 Reports	Miss Walters presented the Treasurer's report. The club had a good season and finances were healthy. A copy of the audited accounts was distributed.
	Mr Smith presented the Team Secretary's report. The first team squad last season was strong and this was reflected in performances. The second eleven, however, struggled to attract players, and this was reflected in several dismal performances.
	Mr James thanked everybody for their hard work last season. Sponsorship had increased for the season ahead, and they had received a record number of enquiries from new players.
5 Clubhouse redecoration	Mr Rees said that this was long overdue and was conveying a poor image of the club to visiting teams and supporters. After further discussion it was agreed that this was a priority and the secretary was asked to obtain quotations and to bring these to the attention of the committee as soon as possible.
6 Match fees	Miss Walters pointed out that match fees had not increased over the last 3 years. Mr Smith expressed that if match fees increased too much this might deter new players from joining the club. It was agreed to increase match fees by just 50p per game.
7 Any other business	Mrs Johnson expressed that a small gift should be sent to Jim Robinson for running the line last season. Mr Pitt volunteered to visit local businesses to increase sponsorship.
8 Date of next meeting	It was decided to hold a short meeting of the committee on 5th September 199_ at 8.00 pm at the same location to discuss clubhouse redecoration.

Chairman
21st August 199_

Figure 6.9 Minutes of a meeting

Any other business is normally limited to non-controversial issues, because if it is felt that something deserves further attention it must be put on the agenda for the next meeting. At the end of the meeting a decision may be made about the date, time and place of the next meeting.

While a meeting is taking place, the secretary records the proceedings with a series of notes – the minutes. These should provide an accurate and clear record of what has taken place at the meeting. They are usually written up immediately after a meeting and are in the past tense:

- *Narrative minutes* include details of discussion and the decisions reached.
- *Resolution minutes* record only details of the decisions agreed.
- *Action minutes* have a column which indicates who is to follow up and take action upon any decision reached.

Whichever version is produced, the secretary only summarises the main points.

The secretary will usually have a folder containing agendas and minutes from previous meetings. It is important that such documents be kept as they provide a permanent record of issues that have been discussed and decisions that have been sanctioned.

Case study – The entertainments committee

Peter Jones, Dawn Williams, Tony Peters, Alison Sharpe, Donna Thomas, Alison Piper, Michael Sherbourne and Roger Hanson are all interested in setting up an entertainments committee at their local Community Centre. The centre's administrator has agreed to their request to set up a committee and has indicated that they can use the centre's hall on a trial basis on the last Friday of each month. He has, however, set certain conditions:

- Events should not make a loss.
- There will be no hire fee for the hall but half the profits from each event must be contributed to the Centre's funds.
- Events must not disturb local residents.
- Events should attempt to cater for as wide a range of residents as possible.
- The entertainments committee must have a chairperson, a secretary and a treasurer.
- All meetings of the entertainments committee must have a proper notice of meeting and an agenda, and minutes must be taken.

1 Consider whether you feel that the committee could be successful.
2 Have a preliminary meeting of the committee with seven colleagues. Make arrangements for a notice of meeting, agenda and items for inclusion to appear for the next meeting. Stage the meeting and take minutes.
3 Analyse your role in the meeting. What sort of contribution did you make? How could it be improved? This work should provide evidence of Core Skills in Communication.

At the majority of meetings you attend you will be a participant rather than the chairperson, secretary or treasurer. In such circumstances the sort of contribution you wish to make will be up to you. Raising a point at a meeting is something that many people do not feel comfortable about doing. The following might act as a useful guide.

- Scrutinise agenda items before you attend the meeting to see if there are any areas that may be of interest to you.
- Research such areas of interest and obtain any associated reading materials.
- Plan out, either in your mind or by making notes, what you might wish to say.
- Listen to what others have to say before speaking yourself.
- Timing is important – make sure the point you make fits into the discussion.
- Do not ramble on.
- Be tactful, and do not deliberately upset someone.
- Be assertive.
- Make your contribution coherent.
- Be ready for some sort of opposition by trying to anticipate the response you might receive to the points you are making.

Another form of oral communication may be in the form of a face-to-face exchange or discussion. In many administrative jobs employees are constantly

in situations where they are meeting customers, members of the public, representatives from suppliers, visitors, candidates for jobs, etc. Dealing with people on a daily basis requires a high degree of sensitivity. It is important to remain in control of the situation and resolve any dispute or problem using common sense.

Another form of verbal communication may be in the form of an interview. Within the organisation this may be for staff appraisal or perhaps a promoted post. Outside the organisation this may be from someone who is interested in something the organisation has done (e.g. press, television or radio). Part of a public relations strategy is to build up a positive perception of your organisation. Your response should therefore be designed to improve public understanding of your organisation's actions.

Evidence collection point

Imagine that you work for a government department as a civil servant. Make a list of rules for dealing verbally with the public on a daily basis.

Technological communications

Over recent years we have seen a revolution in electronic technology and its development for uses in data communication which, in one way or another, has influenced us all.

The only electronic communications technology we used to be dependent upon was the telephone, automatic switchboards and the teleprinter and telex systems. Today organisations have advanced capabilities for communicating written data and text, images and voice which all provide new ways in which they can improve their communication requirements and better meet customers' needs.

Electronic communications today are also capable of spanning long distances almost instantly. We have seen a globalisation of communications technologies providing many more opportunities for organisations to improve communication capabilities around the world.

With constant advances taking place in communications technologies and in expanding communication industries the costs and capabilities of communications are rapidly changing. At the same time organisations are spending more on communications technologies to try to increase their advantages over competitors.

Communications technologies are beginning to change our everyday lives, such as when we shop, keep in contact with friends, communicate with colleagues at work, enjoy our leisure time and receive information from the media.

So what are the components of data transmission? When communicating data, a communication channel is regarded as a highway which provides the mechanism for data to travel from one point to another. There are generally considered to be five different types of communication channel. These are:

1 *The telephone wire* This is the oldest form of communication channel, used mainly in the past for spoken conversations. Over recent years the telephone network has largely been transformed to an all-digital capacity which has developed an *Integrated Services Digital Network* (ISDN).

   The most significant element of this system is its ability to carry not only voice and data but also images and video pictures. ISDN has the capacity to do this because it has a large bandwidth. The potential for such a system is tremendous but it has been slow to take off. For example, it may be possible to access remote databases, communicate with clients from PC to PC on a daily basis at the same time, being able to demonstrate literature, teleshop using the computer, receive videos and films, carry out training to people in remote locations while still providing face-to-face contact. Think of all of the applications that this type of communications service could provide!

2 *Coaxial cable* This consists of a single wire supported by insulating material and surrounded by a metal sheath. This offers faster data communication than the traditional telephone wire and is frequently used for underground and underwater links.

3 *Fibre optics* With this type of system minute glass wires serve as the transmission medium. Lasers, which are a beam of light within a frequency range, are then used to carry the data. Fibres as thin as a human hair may carry 1300 voice conversations simultaneously and offer tremendous advantages in speed and capability.

4 *Microwave* Microwave signals are sent through relay stations or towers sending data through the air. Their great benefit is that they do without the need for wire or fibre-optic communication lines.

5 *Satellite* These links offer communication facilities spanning continents. The data is entered into a computer and then sent to a microwave station which then transmits the data to an earth station which beams the message to the orbiting satellite which in turn beams the message back again to

another ground station. The great benefit is that microwave transmission between earth and satellite offers almost error-free communication.

Evidence collection point

List at least one example of the use of each of the above types of communication channels.

There are many different types of communication using the above which cater for a wide range of applications.

One form of external communication which has experienced a massive expansion of recent years – and which is capable of sending both written and visual information – is *facsimile* ('fax'). Fax machines send documentary information electronically over telephone lines. It involves sliding a piece of information into a fax machine and having a duplicate appear almost anywhere in the world in 40 seconds or less. Instead of using a fax machine it is possible to send a *PC fax* (Personal Computer facsimile) where the computer combines document transmission with that of a fax machine so that files and documents can be sent over the phone using a fax board.

As an alternative to writing letters, many organisations today use *electronic mail*. The 'mail box' is a computer terminal linked to a telephone network; it can put messages into the system and store messages that have been sent through the system. Every user has a password to allow him or her to use the system. A message can be sent to several recipients at once. The message is stored in the terminal's memory until the mailbox is opened. There are now a number of subscriber-based systems, such as Telecom Gold. The main advantage over ordinary mail is the speed of transmission.

Another type of information service is that of *information retrieval*. It is possible to use the PC to access large amounts of information from remote databases. Examples of information that can be retrieved in this way include news, weather services, travel information, financial data and even travel reservations. The great benefit of this is that the database being accessed may hold a considerable volume of information, and this is constantly updated. Some communication services have become known as *electronic notice boards*.

Mobile phones have become an accepted part of everyday life. In fact many of the popular models of car today carry a mobile phone as a standard accessory. Mobile phones have been extremely influential in transforming the world of communications. Company employees may be able to access information or be able to keep in contact while travelling in other parts of the country or even in other parts of the world. This has helped to improve accountability, flexibility and decision-making.

Business television involves developing large audiences of selected employees and then broadcasting either a live or recorded link to them. It may be possible to gain feedback from the meetings using the telephone. This is particularly important for a franchising organisation, as this can help to provide better coordination, give up-to-date information and improve centralisation.

Case study – Business television

At 11.00 am all over Britain every Tuesday, BMW sales staff congregate in their showrooms to watch a message from their management. BMW are among the pioneers in the field of business television. This involves organisations transmitting words and pictures to their employees. BMW has been transmitting messages to nearly all of their dealerships in the UK. Staff typically view a 20–30-minute broadcast that is broken down into four or five segments. Items tend to involve a wide variety of areas and may include sales and marketing details, product information, details of competitors and so on. Though parts of the broadcast are recorded, other parts may have live sessions which enable employees to phone up, question the policy-makers and receive first-hand feedback.

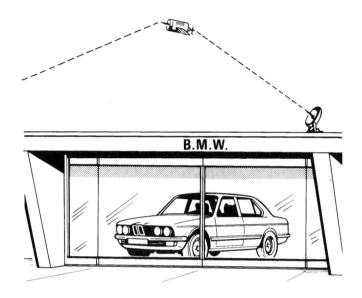

Peter Walker, BMW's marketing communications manager, says 'The primary advantage is immediacy.' He feels, 'TV has more impact than sending documents or video tapes. I wouldn't say we have saved a fortune yet, but we may end up reducing the number of conferences and meetings we hold. I think you end up communicating more.'

Business television first found favour among the large dispersed companies of North America and pioneers in the field included the electronics giant Hewlett-Packard and the brokerage house Merril Lynch. Research in the early 1990s revealed that US industry is spending about £200 million in private business networks. Gillian Greening, European marketing communications manager for Amdahl, the American computer manufacturer, recently decided to extend the company's broadcasts into Europe. Eight times each month employees in North America, and now Europe, gather to watch an hour-long programme, which concludes with a live question and answer session with senior staff. She feels, 'The spoken word is so much more effective than print. Business TV gives us the ability to communicate directly without the message becoming diluted down the management chain.'

Rockwell International also use business television. They feel that the main advantage of broadcasts is to spread information to sales staff. In a company with more than 10 000 products and sometimes several dozen new ones every month, they feel that business TV has become vital. They argue that it acts to bind together a large company, to create a culture or bond that makes staff feel closer to each other.

Assessing the real value of business TV is very difficult. The results of recent research showed that business TV would only help 40% of those watching the broadcasts to perform their jobs better.

1 What is business television?
2 How might business television improve communications for a large organisation?
3 What communication skills are required for those involved in the broadcasts?
4 Are there any dangers from using business television?
5 Why might business television help to improve the ways in which employees work?
6 How might business television help to cut down on paperwork?

A more selective alternative to business television is that of *video-conferencing*. This allows groups of people at two or more locations to hold meetings where everyone can see and hear what is going on. It may be used for product launches, press announcements or simply as a way of discussing and communicating information. The main benefit is that it is a convenient and economical alternative to business travel, thus saving not only travel costs but also hotel expenses.

Electronic funds transfer (EFT) is the electronic transfer into, out of and between bank accounts. For example, nearly all wages and salaries are today paid by electronic means. The increased efficiency of electronic communications has also moved towards *electronic funds transfer at the point of sale* (EFTPOS), where electronic funds transfer for a transaction would take place at the point of sale.

This type of arrangement has been further developed between customers and suppliers within industries through the process of *electronic data interchange* (EDI). This has the objective of simplifying and speeding business transactions between trading partners. It achieves this by allowing data, messages or documents to be transferred directly from one company's computer to another. The obvious benefits are savings on paperwork, time and the elimination of data rekeying. It follows that the more paperwork an organisation handles, the more apparent will be the potential benefits.

Although the early initiatives for EDI originated from the large manufacturers, retailers and distribution companies, increasingly the benefits of electronic trading are being experienced by mid-range and smaller companies (see page 158).

In the mid and late 1990s there is really no reason for trading with regular partners through the postal service. Now that communications software suppliers can deliver simple, automated systems for communicating EDI messages, electronic trading should rapidly become an accepted and preferred method of conducting business.

There are so many developments in the field of electronic communications that it is just not possible to name them all. However, the following are areas that we will hear a lot more about over the next few years.

- *Teleshopping* involves making purchases using a satellite TV channel. It is anticipated that the European market for shopping at home is about to explode with the launch of new shopping networks all over Europe.
- *Satellite technologies* have revolutionised voice, data, video and television transmissions. It is estimated that it will considerably reduce the need for business travel, massively increase video-conferencing facilities, further develop electronic mail systems and reduce the need for traditional paper-based communication systems.
- There are increasing numbers of *home workers* or *telecommuters*. The availability of data transmission facilities provided by personal computers enables individuals to work at home and yet still keep in close contact with their employers.
- *Voice messaging systems* allow users to send and receive messages which are then stored on computer media until accessed. This may be further developed by *voice input* so that computer users simply tell computers what to do and *voice output* where computer-generated voices use spoken words.
- There are increasing numbers of uses for, and development of, *expert systems* where computers help to provide the knowledge and experience of experts to help with certain areas.
- There will be further changes in the ways in which inputs into computers take place. For example, *light-sensitive pens*, the further development of *graphic input devices*, the *trackball* and *touch-panel screens*.

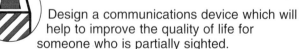

Evidence collection point

Over a two-week period look at and collect articles in the papers which refer to the many uses of newer technologies. Note that most of the broadsheets have a special page or a

number of pages dedicated to newer technologies on a particular day of the week – for example, *The Times* has an INFOTEC section on Fridays.

Meeting special needs

One of the greatest benefits from massive developments in technology and communication systems development is the help it provides for people with special communication needs across society.

Just imagine how frustrating it would be to have to spend all day every day in bed and for the majority of time to be left on your own. The 'Possum Link' enables people who have this kind of physical difficulty to turn lights on and off, to switch other electrical equipment on and off, to unlock doors and do many of the things that most of us take for granted.

For somebody with severe problems who is also without speech, communicating is extremely difficult. By using a display together with a light scanner, a communicator may help the user to develop computer-generated synthesised speech to ask for things they want or simply to carry out a conversation. Other communicating devices include:

- special keyboards or pads with foot, head, Braille or finger switches
- sign language which can be brought up on screen for certain TV channels
- automatic book-reading machines for the blind
- bionic limbs controlled by muscular signals
- medical alert transmitters which send a radio signal when help is required.

Evidence collection point

Design a communications device which will help to improve the quality of life for someone who is partially sighted.

Objectives of internal and external communication

In order to understand the importance of the communications process, it is useful to look closely at the ways in which communication systems may help to improve the efficient functioning of administrative systems.

Objectives of internal communications

Within the organisation efficient communications will help to provide facts and information for employees which will help them with their work. For example, informing employees may affect their daily responses to decisions or keep them aware of changes in procedures connected with health and safety, breaks, etc.

Whenever any activity takes place which involves two or more people, some form of communication is required. Communication helps to hold the organisation together. Communication systems can also be used for giving instructions, i.e. downwards from higher levels to lower levels. These may clearly influence how employees carry out their duties and provide managers with an efficient mechanism for control.

Internal communications may also provide a mechanism or basis for negotiation. Conflict exists in all organisations, but good internal communication mechanisms between the various parties to the dispute may help a dispute to be resolved easily and quickly.

Within the organisation communications may be used to present findings as the result of a piece of research. For example, a report may be circulated to many groups of employees to keep them informed of important issues and proposals.

Communication may help to motivate employees and improve teamwork. Informing employees about what is happening may improve their commitment to a process of change and help them to feel involved with this process. It also fosters teamwork because it brings employees together to focus upon one or more of a series of issues. In contrast, poor communication may not only affect the morale of employees, but this in turn may affect their performance and ultimately quality. Communication systems should also help employees to utilise their time more efficiently and this will also help to improve quality.

Communication systems help employees to carry out everyday functions more efficiently and ensure that they can do it better than they would be able to do without such systems. For example, communication systems may help employees to manage resources such as those in a warehouse, keep track of orders and know who to contact if there is a problem.

Evidence collection point

Make a list of all of the different forms of internal communication within the institution you either work for or attend. Explain the purpose of each type of communication.

Case study – E-mail – or junk mail!

Figure 6.10 Some personal communicators are able to transmit and receive electronic mail on the move

E-mail is cheap, almost instantaneous and transmittable across continents. With the developments in personal computers and personal organisers and communicators it is set to become more widely available over the next few years.

There is, however, a dark side to this development. Though it is easier to send an e-mail than walk down to the postbox, there is a danger that it could swamp employees with so much irrelevant digital 'bumph' that employees either fail to read it all properly or simply ignore it.

The more you look at e-mail the more you realise that past rules of written communication simply do not apply. People would normally carefully compose a reply to a letter, but with e-mail users simply compose spur-of-the-moment replies which may be brusque or thoughtless. Professor Staudenmaier, an e-mail expert, is in no doubt that it leads to sloppier letters. 'The speed and ease of it makes for carelessness.'

According to Professor Staudenmaier, e-mail is an excellent tool because it enables you to visit friends at very reasonable cost when you are far away and it lets you discuss complex problems at long distance.

177

However, when using it there is an unwritten rule that e-mail messages should be supported by voice-to-voice conversations or something begins to get lost in the communications process.

1 How useful is e-mail for communicating both within and outside an organisation?
2 What are the dangers of using e-mail?

Schools have changed a lot in recent years. Standards have improved, and there is wider choice.

Teachers, governors and parents have all played their part to bring this about. So have the Citizen's Charter and the Parent's Charter. They have brought:

on standards

- *new rights to information on how schools are performing;*
- *better arrangements for inspecting them;*
- *clear National Targets for Education and Training – for schools and colleges, employers and the Government;*

on choice

- *new types of school;*
- *more rights for parents; and*
- *improvements for parents of children with special needs.*

This updated Parent's Charter tells you all about these improvements. It is of particular importance to the parents of 5-16 year olds. But everyone, not just parents, should benefit from improved standards and choice. The Charter reforms are also the key to making the country more competitive. That is why we have sent this Charter to every home in the country.

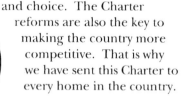

Figure 6.11 The Parent's Charter

Objectives of external communications

Organisations also have a number of external stakeholders such as shareholders, customers, government officials, suppliers and also the general public to whom they have to communicate. They could not exist without these stakeholder groups so it is important that external communications cater for the sensitivities of all of such groups.

Providing information is a useful service for these groups. For example, most organisations will produce an annual report for shareholders. Customers may wish to know of new services. Suppliers will want to know that the organisations they are dealing with are functioning efficiently and will be able to pay for their supplies. Within society as well people will want to know what an organisation is doing, how it is carrying out its activities and what the various outcomes are from such activities. Within the public sector many organisations have emphasised the need to inform others by creating a series of public service charters (Figure 6.11). For example, the Parent's Charter tells parents about their rights to know about their child's progress, reports from inspectors, performance tables, information about schools and annual reports from governors.

Another external objective may be to give instructions to individuals or employees working for other organisations. For example, it may be necessary to ask suppliers to deliver goods on a particular date or to ask customers to use products in a particular way.

One objective of external communications may be to confirm arrangements. This may include meetings and conferences or involve the confirmation of any transactions or details of transactions between two organisations.

External communications may also be used to improve customer service so that current customers are kept satisfied and new customers are won. Improved communication may help to reduce errors, provide customers with prompt and efficient feedback from their enquiries and be used to build a foundation for good customer service. In some circumstances good communications may be an integral part of the product provided for customers.

Another objective may be to provide access to customers through a series of marketing objectives., For example, they may be used for public relations purposes or to advertise to or reach targeted groups of customers. This may be used to improve competitive advantage, position the organisation in the market and differentiate products from those of competitors.

Evidence collection point

Make a list of all of the different forms of external communication from the institution you either work for or attend. Explain the purpose of each type of communication.

Analysing the effectiveness of communication

According to Chester Barnard, communication should occupy a central place in an organisation 'because the structure, extensiveness and scope of organisation are almost entirely determined by communication techniques'. Communication is, therefore, a foundation stone upon which other activities and functions of the organisation depend. To ensure that such activities and functions run efficiently an organisation has to develop effective communications.

If you were asked to analyse a communication system yourself, you may have your own impressions or views on how the system works based upon your own experiences. This would be a *subjective* way of analysing the effectiveness of a communications system. Not everybody will have experienced the system in the same way as yourself and so, in contrast, a more *objective* way of analysing an organisation's communication systems may be to encourage other groups of individuals, some of whom may be independent of the organisation, to analyse the system from different perspectives and perhaps to compare it with the functioning of other systems. This process of analysis is important because communication is a vital link between all parts of the organisation which depend upon the communication process in order to achieve their business objectives.

One way of analysing the effectiveness of a communications system is to carry out a communications audit. This would check the communication policies and practices of the organisation to ensure that they are achieving organisational goals. The audit may include an analysis of procedures, documentation and also user-attitude surveys. While undertaking the communications audit there will be a number of bases which can be used to analyse the effectiveness of communications:

- *Ease of use* Different users may have different views of the effectiveness of the system. Some may feel, particularly with paper-based systems, that the system is unnecessarily bureaucratic. They might have to obtain several signatures or fill in detailed forms in order to undertake a simple task! Technical jargon such as that which appears in many manuals may influence the use of various functions, as some staff may not fully understand how a communication activity either works or can be undertaken to its best advantage. Users may also suffer from information overload, which may mean that vital information is overlooked.
- *Access* It is important that all users of the system have access to the various communication mechanisms. For example, if some parts of the organisation do not have PCs, then the use of e-mail is restricted. Similarly fax machines, use of telephones and other equipment may be affected by the physical location of equipment. Speed of access is also important so that users, by responding to communications promptly and quickly, improve their operations and their flexibility through use of the system.
- *Effects upon the efficiency of the users* It is always important to take into account human factors when looking at the workings of communications systems within an organisation. When communications change this may demand job roles, work activities and job descriptions. Some individuals may find it difficult to adapt to changes in the ways in which they work, no matter how efficient they may seem to be. As a result they may resist changes in communication technologies and therefore such changes may be stressful. Some changes may not necessarily be better for some individuals. An interesting job role working with lots of people may be transformed into a job which may seem less worthwhile.
- *Improving interaction* There is an interaction between the communication system and how it is used by people both within organisations and between organisations (i.e. EDI). A formal structure sets up communication channels, helping individuals to understand their role in the use of interconnecting communications facilities or activities. Individuals, groups and work groups then set up an informal way of working with different communication systems and procedures.
- *Control* Communication systems should provide a range of information from various parts of the organisation, enabling managers to monitor, control and provide feedback from activities to ensure that they are meeting broader business objectives. Systems should also enable managers to

179

exert direct control over the nature, quality and type of communication activities.

- *Confidentiality* Much of the information stored in computer files – including addresses and telephone numbers – may be considered to be confidential. There is always the danger that this may fall into the hands of someone who may choose to misuse this type of information. Data privacy is, therefore, particularly important, and many issues are covered by the Data Protection Act (see page 196). A key element in developing a communication system must be the need to produce a system which safeguards data.
- *Security* Data kept with the communication system may be personal or could contain details about the business which may be of value for competitors. This type of data must only be accessed by people with the proper authorisation. Systems must also protect data from loss or corruption. For example, data may be lost due to equipment failure, variations in power, fire, human error or a virus. A number of measures are needed to support the system, such as back-up procedures, staff training, back-up power supplies and even dual computer systems.

Evidence collection point

What forms of communication do you use either at school, college or work? Using some of the above criteria, where relevant, comment upon how the effectiveness of these communications could be improved.

The effects of changes to communications

Communications systems should be designed to minimise errors which might damage an organisation's reputation or make work more difficult for employees. It is important, when planning a system, to involve the users. They will help in setting realistic and workable guidelines and also help decision-makers to understand the various factors which must be taken into consideration when developing a good system of communications.

Managers must set realistic goals. It is very easy to underestimate the time and effort required to develop a communication system suitable for all users. They may also have expectations beyond the capabilities of the system and not take into account delays or obstacles. Managers must, therefore, when making decisions about the changes to communication systems, balance both the positive and negative effects of changes to communications in organisations.

Case study – Videophone sales

Despite being available for nearly two years, videophones have not caught on. According to psychologists, the reason for this is that it is actually more difficult to get your message across on videophones than by using other means of communication.

According to Dr Claire O'Malley of Nottingham University, who has studied the subject with her colleague Steve Langton, and Professor Vikki Bruce of Stirling University, the difficulty is caused by the restriction of phone lines. A narrow bandwidth channel causes a delay of about half a second which disrupts conversation, leads to interruptions and people find it hard to time pauses. The problem disappears when ISDN links are used.

BT have recently introduced two videophones for ISDN lines, but they are not cheap. For example, the PC videophone, for connecting computers, costs £3300, plus the £400 connection cost for ISDN with £80 rental per quarter. Despite the cost, Adrian Butcher, general manager of videophones at BT, argues that people who need to meet regularly to discuss technical issues will find videophoning cheaper than travel. According to him, 'If you have a videophone call you get a much better impression of how people react, much more warmth – in most cases people wave goodbye.'

Psychologists, however, claim that videophones are not the same as a meeting. People find it difficult to manage conversations and miss the little cues that people give when they want to reply.

Professor Bruce has worries about technological rather than a more personal contact. 'What we do know is that face-to-face contact gives certain benefits. Video is not the same because it is restricted to face and shoulders,' she says. By using a videophone only peripheral vision is created. Subtle and manual gestures are lost. She feels that more research is necessary on how the design of videophones affect communication.

1 What forms of communication might videophones replace?
2 Make a list of both the (a) positive effects, and (b) negative effects of the use of videophones.

Positive effects of changes to communications

Managers spend a lot of time and money in developing communication systems, so it is essential to analyse their effects. The positive benefits of a change may be as follows:

- *Speed of communication* Improving communication techniques may massively increase the speed of communications. For example, a clerical worker may spend a lot of time 'holding' on the telephone while waiting to speak to people. Electronic mail virtually eliminates this problem. Video-conferencing may save considerable time which would otherwise be spent travelling and, in doing so, massively increase the flexibility and response of organisations to changes in trading conditions.
- *Improved access to communication* Not everybody within an organisation may have equal access to communication facilities. It should be possible to spread the use of networks to include further layers of staff and so further improve their ability to make well-informed decisions.
- *Better quality of decisions* Communications systems may provide accurate and reliable information on sales, marketing, accounts and personnel activities, thus making it possible for managers to make better-informed decisions.
- *Communications for wider audiences* Systems such as e-mail and business journals may help managers to communicate facts, figures and developments to wider audiences. For example, on an issue of safety it may be possible to reach all individuals who might be affected by a potential hazard.
- *Better quality of materials for presentation* Computers may be used at meetings or to present lectures or conferences. Programs such as Microsoft Powerpoint help in the preparation of overheads, handouts and presentation graphics.
- *Increase in personal productivity* Changes in communication techniques may help individuals to maximise the benefits arising from their use of time. Examples are the use of a mobile phone on the train or helping with routine tasks such as searching for information.

Negative effects of changes to communications

Changes in communications technology often arouses controversy. The prospects of machines which can think, make decisions and replace key workers easily stirs up fears. The negative effects of a change may be as follows:

- *Non-standardised equipment* The problem with buying new communications equipment is that it may not be compatible with existing equipment. For example, items of software may need a number of systems requirements which the office equipment does not have. The Novell Standard Perfect Office specifies 8 Mb RAM, a 386 MHz or higher microprocessor, Windows 3.1 or higher, and VGA display.
- *Cost* Keeping up with technological advances, particularly those made by competitors, may be extremely expensive.
- *Loss of jobs* Introducing a new telephone network, for example, may virtually eliminate the need for anybody operating a switchboard.
- *Exclusion from communication* Individuals within organisations may be excluded from using new technologies. Similarly, organisations which do not adapt their communication systems, for example to EDI, may find it more difficult to compete in the marketplace.
- *Training programmes* Wherever new technology is introduced it is important to train staff for the use of new communications equipment. This training may be costly and time-consuming.
- *Stress* Though changes in communications can improve working conditions, they may cause stress. Operators may fail to fully understand the functioning of a piece of software and feel that they are not getting the benefits from it.
- *Hazards* A number of influences may affect the operation of a computer system. These may include heat, smoke, steam and surges in electricity.
- *Security* It is important to ensure that information is neither lost or destroyed. Systems may be open to software piracy, industrial espionage, computer vandalism (virus infection) and other types of crime such as computer fraud.

Evidence collection point

Find one example where the process of communication has recently changed within an organisation. You may find a suitable example from the newspapers, by interviewing someone working for an organisation or even using your school, college or workplace as an example. Identify both the positive and negative effects of this change.

Suggesting changes to communications in a business organisation

In general, changes in communications both within and outside an organisation tend to happen slowly and in stages rather than overnight. The main problem is that change may cause considerable uncertainty for those involved in the change process.

Change may be influenced by a number of different factors. These may include economic conditions, changes in the marketplace, technological influences and customer perceptions and expectations. Usually change in communications will be necessary because of a combination of factors.

To achieve this performance criterion you are asked to analyse a business organisation and suggest changes to their communications system. To do this you need to think clearly of all the communications objectives and technologies which have been covered by this chapter as well as the positive and negative effects of such changes. Also, given the nature of communication technologies, many new products may be available today which might not have been covered by this chapter. To help you with your investigation the checklist opposite has been included.

Evidence indicators

For this activity, prepare a report which investigates the communications requirements of a business organisation. It is important when writing this report to think of as many reasons as you can to justify the changes to communication requirements you may suggest. Use the checklist to help you to complete this evidence indicator. Prepare a report which investigates at least four examples of internal and external communication in a business organisation. Please tick off each of the following when you have successfully covered them as part of your report. You need to confirm that:

CHECKLIST FOR CHANGES TO COMMUNICATIONS IN A BUSINESS ORGANISATION

1 Identify a business organisation which might require changes to its communications. (*Hint*: Think of an organisation which clearly requires a lot of changes to its communications systems.)

2 Find out about the communications systems within that organisation.

3 Distinguish between internal communications and external communications.

4 Comment upon current uses of technologies.

5 Find out about any communication problems which may currently exist within the organisation.

6 Make a list of their communication objectives.

7 How well are these objectives currently catered for?

8 Is it possible to improve communication systems to cater more precisely for these objectives?

9 Briefly analyse external changes which may affect the communication requirements of this business. These may include actions of competitors, new technologies becoming available, expectations of customers, etc.

10 Make a list of limitations which may affect your suggestions. Examples are cost, training requirements, security, expertise, size of organisation, exclusive or open access, restricted or open use.

11 Research your proposals. (Use catalogues, magazines and newspaper articles to support your analysis.)

12 Present your suggestions for change.

13 Explain how these suggestions meet the organisation's objectives.

14 Describe how they improve upon current communication techniques.

- I have identified a business organisation about which I am going to write this report. ☐
- I have investigated two examples of internal and two examples of external communication in this organisation. ☐

■ I have analysed at least one form of electronic internal and external communication. ☐
■ I have analysed the
 – effectiveness of use of each of the electronic forms of communication ☐
 – positive and negative effects of the use of each of the electronic forms of communication. ☐

■ I have proposed two changes to communications in the business organisation. ☐
■ I have justified these proposals in terms of their possible beneficial effects on the business organisation. ☐

Information processing

Broadly speaking, there have been three distinct generations of information development. The first era can probably best be thought about by referring to the Dickensian character of Bob Cratchit, working away for Ebenezer Scrooge, scribbling figures into leather-bound ledgers and copying correspondence for long hours in each day. The role of the clerk was that of a personal copier, secretary and accountant.

By 1900 the typewriter had appeared and mechanisation and productivity took over. Offices became large places for processing information with telephones, adding machines and typewriters outputting large volumes of information in a loud, automated environment.

The third generation began about 20 years ago – the information age. The computer has transformed information handling by providing systems which today lie at the very heart of modern management.

This chapter looks at information processing and the features and applications of modern technologies in the business environment. It looks at the purposes, functions and effectiveness of modern information systems.

The purposes of information processing

Information processing simply involves gathering data and then processing it to produce the information the user requires.

Today, information processing affects not only every organisation but also every part of each organisation. Modern systems enable employees to:

■ have information to which they would not have had access before
■ undertake a wider range of tasks
■ undertake such tasks more efficiently
■ have accurate data at their fingertips
■ use data in different ways
■ present data in many different forms.

We often hear people use phrases such as 'the information society' or 'the wired society' to refer to the way in which the revolution in information

technology is transforming our lives. This is nowhere more true than in the business environment.

A modern organisation can be seen as consisting of three sub-systems:

1 The *management* sub-system is concerned with all the people and activities involved in planning, controlling and decision-making.
2 The *operations* sub-system is concerned with all the activities, material flows and people directly involved with performing the primary function of the organisation, e.g. manufacturing operations or the provision of a service.
3 The *information* sub-system is made up of the people, machines, ideas and activities that are concerned with gathering and processing data in order to meet the formal requirements of an organisation for information. They may include the way in which information is collected, stored, handled, used, communicated and utilised for accounting purposes, monitoring stocks, or a wide range of other interrelated functions.

How important is the ability to process information efficiently for the modern business organisation? Although, as we shall see, there are arguments for and against different types of information processing systems, the ability to process information efficiently provides an organisation with a considerable number of advantages in the markets in which it competes. It is also important to note that information processing should affect everybody within an organisation at all levels. Information processing, however, should *not* reduce the importance of people. In the modern business organisation people are as important as ever.

Case study – The paperless office?

We used to talk about the prospect of a paperless office. It seemed the logical step in the revolution in information processing. However, it was recently reported that the use of paper in offices is increasing, despite the storage of vast quantities of information on computer.

There are a number of reasons cited for this. Many people do not like reading information from monitors. For example, information shown on monitors has little visual appeal. However, with much of the word-

In a modern office a number of operations make use of data. One way of looking at an organisation is as an 'information processing system'. As in any system there will be a means of transforming inputs into outputs by a number of processes. Today many of these processes are carried out with the support of information technology.

Here are a number of processes which take place in modern organisations, all involving data:

1	Capturing	6	Calculating
2	Verifying	7	Storing
3	Classifying	8	Retrieving
4	Sorting	9	Reproducing
5	Summarising	10	Communicating

1 *Capturing data* involves recording data generated by an event or occurrence, e.g. from invoices, sales slips, meters, counters.
2 *Verifying data* refers to checking that data has been correctly recorded/captured accurately, e.g. checking that an instrument is working correctly, or cross-checking recording procedures.
3 *Classifying data* entails putting different types of data into appropriate sections; for example, the sales of a company could be sorted into the different departments that made the sales.
4 *Sorting data* refers to the placing of data elements into a specified order; for example, an inventory file could be sorted into money value order, into code number order, etc.
5 *Summarising data* can be used to provide aggregate data. One way this can be done is to total up various figures, e.g. sales, or to draw up balancing figures for a balance sheet. Alternatively, it could be used to reduce data logically to a common form, e.g. by producing a list of all employees who were working on a night shift on a particular date.
6 *Calculating using data* involves computing various figures in a mathematical sense, e.g. by going through a series of processes such as adding and multiplying. For example, wages of employees can be calculated by multiplying hours by the wage rate and then subtracting the various deductions.
7 *Storing data* involves transferring data to the appropriate storage medium.
8 *Retrieving data* involves calling data up from the place of storage.
9 *Reproducing data* is the process of transferring the same data from one medium to another. At a simple level this could involve photocopying material, or calling up data from one screen to another as with Stock Exchange dealing.

processing and desktop publishing software today, it is possible to produce documents with a high visual appeal extremely easily. As the visual impact is important, information on paper then becomes the preferred alternative.

Though massive amounts of information can be stored easily on computer and accessed with tremendous speed and efficiency, the sheer volume of information as well as the need to find it, with the limitations of the scrolling nature of the computer, may mean that users prefer to rely on paper aids as information sources. Instead of these paper aids requiring storage, their role has become that of a temporary communication device. Once the information on paper has been read, it can then be discarded. The ease of printing and producing paper documents using faster and better printers and photocopiers helps this process.

So what about the coming of the paperless office? It would seem that the reverse has happened. Technological innovations, the availability of more information and the creation of new office structures have created a new role for paper within the office environment.

1 Why did so many people predict a paperless office and why has it not materialised?
2 What jobs can paper do better than computers and other forms of information processing?
3 Give specific examples of the new roles that paper may be playing within the office environment.
4 Conduct a survey within the institution you attend or work in. What role does paper play within the institution? Plan your survey so that you demonstrate Core Skills in Communication and Application of Number.

10 *Communicating data* refers to the transfer of data from one place to another. The ultimate aim of information processing is to provide information for the final user.

One way of demonstrating how information processing works is to use an example. An electricity company keeps records of customers and their outstanding accounts. It may keep a record of the amount owed by the Patel family who live at Greenlawns.

The company will keep a regular record of amounts owing for electricity used, the amounts paid by the family and the balance owed. Every now and then it will want to check on this information – for example, when the Patels have a query on their account.

The company may want to classify the information about the Patel's account under various sub-headings – for example, under the totals of electricity used at peak and off-peak times.

The information can be sorted in many ways – for example, into date order to show how much electricity the Patels used at different times of the year. The electricity company can sort out which customers have unpaid balances; and at the end of a quarter all the figures can be summarised to show the total amounts outstanding.

Calculations can be carried out with figures – for example, adding amounts owed and subtracting payments made.

All of the details relating to the Patels' account can be stored on files and retrieved from these files when required. This information can be reproduced, perhaps by making a copy of the Patels' records to send to them as a statement of account. This information can then be quickly communicated to them.

So, simply by looking at one account, we have been able to point to a wide range of information processing activities.

Evidence collection point

Describe how each of the data-processing activities outlined in the text can be related to (a) your own student records, and (b) your bank or building society account. Show how you use information processing to keep personal records – for example, in budgeting or keeping a diary.

Whenever information processing takes place, it happens within a system – for example, a telecommunications system or a computer network.

Within the system there is a group of devices called hardware, which are operated by a series of programs called software. Another way of looking at all of the information processing activities is to divide them into the various parts of the system where such activities take place. For example:

- *Input devices* – Receive information.
- *Storage devices* – Store programs so that they can be used again
- *The processor* – Uses information for processing.
- *Output devices* – Produce data in the required form for the user.

When these are put together they constitute the information processing system (Figure 7.1).

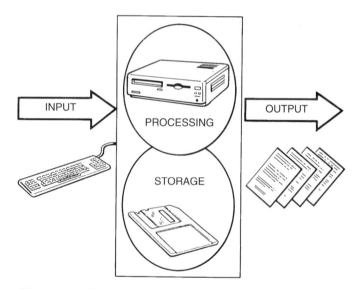

Figure 7.1 The information processing system

- *Receiving information* – There are many ways of receiving information, such as via keyboards, disk drives, telephones and optical readers. When information is received it will be converted into a form which is acceptable for storage and processing.
- *Storing information* – Storage technology has allowed storage capacity to grow and increase within both economic and size limits. Storage may include data, numbers, text, pictures and sound.
- *Using information* – The central processing unit (CPU) is the part of the system which controls computer operations. It receives data either from an input device or from storage; applications software then manipulates data to perform specific tasks such as accounting or secretarial functions.

■ *Communicating information* – Output devices communicate information to end users in the forms they require. Users will use the information from the output to help them with their professional job roles.

One way of looking at how an information processing system works is to look at an airline reservation system (Figure 7.2). A travel agent hundreds of miles away may be able to obtain flight information in seconds. The agent can enter the reservation for the customer, receive credit card verification and then print the ticket and boarding pass on the spot. They can even specify certain special requirements for customers such as food, wheelchairs and seat placings.

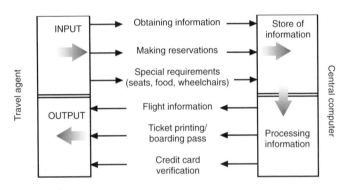

Figure 7.2 An airline reservation system

The system may be used not only by travel agents and their customers. It may also be used for:

■ *Crew information* The crew shifts, names and flight assignments may be set by the system.
■ *Aircraft information* The aircraft to be used for each flight can be identified, and its maintenance schedule and flight history can be coordinated.

Evidence collection point

Identify an example of either a manual or computer-based information processing system. Explain how the system receives information, stores information, uses information and communicates information. Use a diagram such as that shown in Figure 7.2 to present your analysis. Plan your work so that it provides evidence of Core Skills in Communication and Information Technology.

Information processing within a business organisation

Every organisation will have different information processing requirements, and these specifications will be customised to fit a wide range of tasks and activities. There are, broadly speaking, three different types of information processing systems (Figure 7.3).

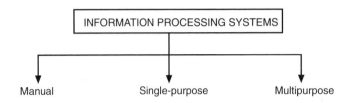

Figure 7.3 Information processing systems

A *manual system* may involve few technologies. The user may have set up a series of processes for receiving, storing, using and communicating information. This type of system may efficiently meet the requirements of the small business user or of a section of a larger organisation. That is, a large organisation may use advanced technologies which are not necessary for all sections within the organisation.

A *single-purpose system* runs a single program at a time, often with a single user. That program will access all of the computer's resources such as disk storage, keyboard, display and printer output. Once initiated the program will run until it is finished.

For most computer applications single-purpose is perfectly adequate. *Multipurpose systems* enable more than one program to be run at any one time; for example, the system could be printing while also enabling the user to work on a spreadsheet and a word-processor. A *multipurpose multi-user* system allows many users to run more than one program at any one time.

Evidence collection point

With reference to the above, describe the type of information processing system you use at school or college.

187

Word-processing

Word-processors are used to manipulate text. They display information on a screen and record in memory the text that a person enters on a keyboard. However, the word-processor can do far more than this. For example:

■ New text can be put on to the screen while existing text moves to create space for it.
■ Blocks of text can be moved around on the document that is being created.
■ The text can be spaced out to fill the whole line.
■ A word or phrase can be searched for, and can be removed or replaced by another word or phrase.
■ A header or footer (a piece of text that is printed at the top or bottom of each page) can be added.

You will know from your own use of word-processors that there are many other exciting features. For example:

■ Different printing styles (such as italics, underlined or bold text and so on) can be shown on the screen either as different colours or as they would appear when printed. This is referred to as WYSIWYG (pronounced 'wizzywig'), which stands for 'what you see is what you get'.
■ Text can be written in more than one column, as in newspapers.
■ Graphics can be put into the text.
■ A number of similar letters can be produced, with information specific to each letter added from a database. For example, if a business has a database of its suppliers and wishes to contact the local

ones, the database can be used to select all suppliers who are situated in the same county. The word-processor will then print a letter for each supplier, adding the individual information such as the name and address and salutation. This is called 'mailmerge'.
■ A spelling checker can be used. This checks all the text against a dictionary and points out any word that it does not recognise, perhaps because it is spelt incorrectly. However, if you have used a technical word of which the computer has no record, you can enter the new word into the computer's memory.

Evidence collection point

Using a word-processor, draft a letter to the person responsible for your work experience placement, thanking him or her for the help and support you have received. Print the first draft and discuss it with your tutor. Then do several redrafts of the letter until you are happy with the final format. Save and print the document at each stage so that you can discuss progress with your tutor. This work will provide evidence of Core Skills in Information Technology and Communication.

Desktop publishing

The improvements in word-processing systems, and their ability to produce graphics and to operate with great efficiency, have made desktop publishing (DTP) possible. Special computer programs make it possible

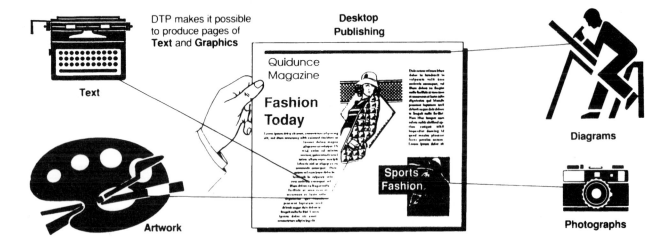

Figure 7.4 A layout produced by DTP

to produce pages of combined text and graphics to a very high quality.

Different typefaces can be used, diagrams can be placed on pages with text flowing around them, and so on. Pictures can be introduced into the document and stretched or shrunk to fit a space. DTP is used to produce items such as reports, company newsletters, training materials and advertisements (Figure 7.4).

Evidence collection point

If you have access to a desktop publishing system, use it to produce a cover sheet that can be adapted for each of your Business Studies assignments. The cover should be designed so that you can quickly amend it to word-process the new title of each assignment.

Number-processing

Computer software can also be used to process numbers. It is easy to forget that computers are best at dealing with numeric data! Computers can deal with all types of numeric information using a wide range of number-crunching techniques. Computer users may wish to use computers to analyse marketing information, to provide statistical summaries for staff throughout the organisation, for accounting purposes, or for advanced research.

Statistics is concerned with the collection, interpretation, analysis and presentation of numeric data, and can be an important tool for managers in an organisation. Packages such as Minitab and the Statistical Analysis System can perform almost any statistical operation.

Accounting packages (see page 153) have been developed especially for businesses and have a variety of applications. For example, they can record information, produce reports, improve cash flow and pay bills. Some number-based packages can also be used to help you to organise your personal finances.

Evidence collection point

What sort of number-processing activities might help you with your personal finances? Make a list and then find out more about the packages that are available.

Spreadsheets

A spreadsheet is a table of numbers which can be organised and altered on a computer. A spreadsheet is used when making forecasts and doing calculations – the computer does the work for you. Spreadsheets are used extensively in financial forecasting.

For instance, a firm will make a forecast of all the money that will come in and go out of the firm over a twelve-month period. The person using the spreadsheet can then alter the inputs to calculate the effect, for example, of lowering a heating bill by a certain amount each month. The computer will automatically recalculate the columns to change the heating figures, total cost figures and profits for each month. It will also recalculate total profit.

In this way a managing director, accountant or any other user of a spreadsheet can quickly carry out business calculations – such as working out the effects of minor changes.

Task

Imagine that you are responsible for the financial management of a service station, and you need to plan your budget for the coming year. A budget is a series of figures indicating the possible income of your business (i.e. the money that you expect to take) and the outgoings (the money you have to spend). You think that the possible sales income for the year of the service station may consist of the following:

	£
Petrol	1 440 000
Lubricants	15 600
Confectionery	48 000
Fast foods (sandwiches and drinks)	8 400
Groceries	10 800
Accessories (such as torches and batteries)	14 400
Newspapers/magazines	12 000
Toys/greeting cards	3 600
Books/tapes	4 800
Cigarettes/tobacco	78 000

You estimate outgoings for the year to consist of the following:

	£
Staff wages	36 000
Insurance	1 500
Heat/light/power	4 500
Security charges	1 200
Rent/rates	4 200

Maintenance/repairs	2 100
Office supplies	5 400
Petrol	1 080 000
Lubricants	12 000
Stock for the shop	150 000

Your first task is to prepare a computer spreadsheet to cover a twelve-month period, assuming that incomings and outgoings are spread evenly over all months of the year (Figure 7.5 can be used as a guide).

When your spreadsheet is completed you can experiment with some 'what if' situations:

1 What if petrol sales were twice your original estimate? How would this affect overall profit? You would obviously have to pay more for your stocks of petrol from the depot, but would you also have to spend more money on wages?

2 What if wages increased by 10% in June? How does this affect the end-of-year profit figure?

INCOME	JAN	FEB	MAR	APR	ETC.
Petrol					
Lubricants					
Confectionery					
Fast food					
Groceries					
Accessories					
Newspapers/magazines					
Toys/greeting cards					
Books/tapes					
Cigarettes/tobacco					
TOTAL INCOME					
OUTGOINGS					
Staff wages					
Insurance					
Heat/light/power					
Security charges					
Rent/rates					
Maintenance/repairs					
Office supplies					
Petrol					
Lubricants					
Stock for shop					
TOTAL OUTGOINGS					

Figure 7.5 The spreadsheet

3 What if rent and rates on the site were increased by 20% from 1 March?

4 What if the cost of petrol and lubricants rises by 10% in November with no corresponding increases in prices to motorists?

Evidence collection point

Use a spreadsheet to provide a forecast of your income and outgoings over the next two months on a week-by-week basis. Your work should provide evidence of Core Skills in Application of Number and Information Technology.

Databases

A database is a store of facts that can be called upon to provide information. A database may be used, for instance, in a bank or building society to store information on the state of all accounts. A database may be kept by a church to keep a record of all members of the congregation and their addresses. One may be used by a football club to keep a record of all tickets sold for various matches, and so on.

For example, a supplier might have a record of the account of Amin Stores. It would store the information in a number of fields – such as address, value of goods supplied, payments received, and balance of the account. If Mr Amin rings up asking for the state of his account, the supplier can simply order the computer to produce the appropriate information and display it on the screen.

Under the provisions of the Data Protection Act (see page 196) companies wishing to store any personal information on a computer system must register with the government-appointed Data Processing Officer. It is necessary to indicate the type of data being stored and the use made of it. Individuals have the right to request (on payment of a small fee) details of information held about them by any firm, and to require mistakes to be corrected.

Any work with a database needs careful planning. Once you have decided what you want to investigate you need to think:

■ What questions do I want to ask?
■ What information needs to be collected to answer the questions?

When using a database it is important to be consistent. For example, when entering figures you should not put 1.50 metres in one place and 150 cm in another place (they are of course the same thing).

If you use NAME, decide whether you mean first or second name. If you use GENDER, decide whether you will use male/female or man/woman; and so on.

Figure 7.6 shows a printout of information collected from one particular respondent to a market research questionnaire.

```
NAME     :  JONES
GENDER   :  MALE
BOVRIL   :  YES
CHEESE   :  NO
SALT/VIN :  YES
ONION    :  NO
PLAIN    :  YES
TOMATO   :  NO
FAV      :  SALT/VIN
```

Figure 7.6 A section of printout

When information is extracted from a database you can present it in a variety of different forms, including pie-charts and bar-charts. A database can be a very useful way of doing research, particularly if you are working in a group. You can work together to enter information into the base. However, make sure that you are aware of the purpose of the database and how to enter information consistently.

Evidence collection point

Undertake a piece of consumer research. Collate the information, enter it into a database and then display the information. Plan your work so that it provides evidence of Core Skills in Communication, Information Technology and Application of Number.

Graphics processing

Over recent years there have been a number of developments in the type and range of graphics processing packages available. Graphics packages enable data to be translated into a graphical form to help with the communication and meaning of data. For example, large volumes of information can be reduced to one or more pictures, designs or charts.

Programs include design, graph and charting packages. They vary considerably not only according to the type of graphics produced but also in how they are generated. *Presentation graphics* are frequently used for graphical presentations across a range of business uses, for example for direct transfer to screen, OHPs or

Timeworks Publisher and *Design*works are trademarks of GST Software Products.

Figure 7.7 Examples of clipart

high-resolution colour slides. *Illustration packages* enable illustrations to be created with the software and may include painting programs and drawing programs – such programs may be used in design. It is possible to allow images scanned into the computer to be added to original artwork. Clipart can also considerably enhance the quality of materials (Figure 7.7). *Computer-aided-design* (CAD) packages are mainly drawing programs which offer special features for engineers and architects.

Evidence collection point

Using the paintbrush program on a PC, attractively design a series of ticket/invitations for a party. Your work will demonstrate Core Skills in Information Technology.

Other information processing applications

Project planning

Computers and their databases can be used to assist in project planning. Packages are used to plan and monitor a project consisting of a number of interrelated stages called activities. First the activities are defined and the time taken by each is estimated. Then the way in which the activities depend on each other is defined. The computer calculates the total time for the project and shows the activities which must be completed on time for the project not to be delayed.

Here is a simplified example of the building of a new office. The activities and times may be:

1 Prepare land and build foundations   30 days
2 Build walls   30 days
3 Build roof   15 days
4 Install equipment   30 days
5 Equip office   20 days

Activity 1 must be done first, then activity 2, then activity 3. However, activities 4 and 5 – although they come after activity 3 has finished – can be done at the same time. Therefore the total time for the project is only 105 days (30 + 30 + 15 + 30), not 125 days. The computer output will also tell you that activity 5 is not critical; that is, it can start late or take longer than planned without delaying the project (Figure 7.8).

This IT tool therefore helps the project manager to determine the tasks that must be given top priority.

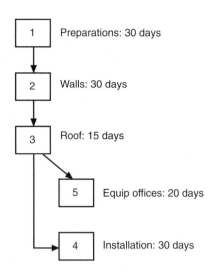

Figure 7.8 Planning the building of an office

Most versions of this computer program can also plan the use of resources or activities, record costs and produce a variety of reports. While this example would be too simple to require a program, we can see how useful such a facility could be in developing a project involving, say, 1000 or more activities.

Expert systems

Expert systems are becoming increasingly popular. They are computer programs consisting of a set of rules based upon the knowledge of experts. These rules can be used to form conclusions on information the program is given.

Imagine, for example, that you feed into the computer all the rules that experts know about a particular field – geology. Geologists could feed in all the information they know about the conditions in which particular minerals are likely to be found. The program can then be used to support researchers looking for new mineral fields. One oil exploration company's geological experts have formulated the rules they use in deciding whether a certain area is likely to contain oil deposits. Data on different areas can then be fed into the program and it will assess the chances of oil being discovered in a similar way to a human expert.

These programs are of particular use where a human expert is not available. One interesting use is in medicine where a program is being tested to aid diagnosis. It is used by the patient, not the doctor,

193

the idea being that for personal and intimate problems a patient may answer questions more easily from a machine than from a person. It also means that minor problems can be diagnosed without using the doctor's time.

One big problem with setting up expert systems is that it is often surprisingly difficult for experts to define exactly how they reach decisions.

Task

Describe three situations in which you think an expert system would assist decision-making.

The effectiveness of information processing

Information processing systems and their applications influence the ways in which business organisations operate and compete at all levels of decision-making. Given this vital role it is essential to constantly appraise the effectiveness of the systems to ensure that they provide the maximum possible benefits for the organisation.

One way of analysing the effectiveness of an information processing system is to look at a simple operating application. Imagine that a customer puts in an order. Now consider what happens. What if the organisation takes a long time to process the order? Having processed the order they then make mistakes with the transaction and deliver the wrong goods. From the customer's point of view they will be less than satisfied with the way the organisation has dealt with their order. The limitation of the information processing system has influenced a customer, who will not come back for repeat business. The system has, therefore, strategic and competitive implications.

An efficient system would, on the other hand, have meant that the customer was satisfied and would probably return for more business. Because information processing affects the ways in which an organisation competes, an effective information processing system therefore helps to provide competitive advantage.

There are a number of ways in which the effectiveness of an information processing system can be analysed:

■ *Fitness for purpose* Information processing systems must be developed to support the strategy of the organisation. This they do by focusing upon how best they can be used to provide the maximum help possible with operational activities. The aim must be to develop a system which helps with strategies for goods and services and performs a series of required activities.

By being fit for the purposes intended, information systems should help to provide solutions and not create problems. In doing so they should help organisations to achieve their goals and objectives. To ensure that a system does meet the required objectives, it is important to provide feedback on its activities and control over the output (Figure 7.9).

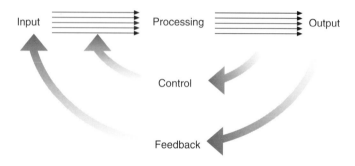

Figure 7.9 Feedback and control help to ensure that the processing system undertakes the required activities

■ *Cost* Cost has a clear influence upon the design of an information processing system. For example, a manager may have a budget constraint which determines how much can be spent upon its introduction. One danger of a tight budgetary constraint is that it can be too restrictive and can make it difficult to develop a system which undertakes activities as efficiently as originally required.

■ *Value for money* The most important element in any system design is that it should eventually result in the maximisation of benefit relative to cost. There are two ways of assessing whether or not a new system might provide value for money. *Quantitative* analysis identifies clear savings which have been made through the introduction of the new system – for example, fewer staff, less paperwork and reductions in other costs. *Qualitative* evaluation is more difficult as this identifies the ways in which a series of activities and services have improved as a result of spending on the new system. Though difficult to quantify, these are very important and may include higher morale, work which is less tedious and improved customer satisfaction.

Evidence collection point

Look at an information processing system. If possible find out (approximately) how much it costs. Undertake both a quantitative and qualitative evaluation of the benefits provided by the system (if necessary make up the figures).

■ *Effects upon the efficiency of the user* Information processing systems must be developed to meet the needs of a number of users. The overall aim should be to reduce the time taken to carry out activities, increase the speed with which output is generated, undertake a larger volume of work and make it easier for the user to access and operate the system. It is important, therefore, when developing a system to consider the needs of the users.

Evidence collection point

Make a direct comparison between the uses of an electronic typewriter for functions such as letter writing and typing invoices and a personal computer which does the same using a word-processor. In your analysis refer to reduction in time, volume of work, speed and ease of use.

■ *Capacity to retain and use information* The most important element in any system is its capacity to generate output. A good information system will have the right information available when required and in the form specified by the user.
■ *Meeting legal and other requirements* As we shall see, any system must take into account the requirements of the Data Protection Act and also meet other legal requirements such as those affecting health and safety.
■ *Improving security* If data or program security is important, a system must ensure that unauthorised people do not access it. Security features may include electronic controls such as passwords and data encryption to ensure that the system is kept secure.

Case study – Information and the AA

The mission statement of the Automobile Association (AA) puts priority on people and service. It aims to 'make AA membership truly irresistible' and 'to be the UK's leading and most successful motoring and personal assistance organisation'. The key to the AA's success is, therefore, the extent to which it manages to achieve its mission. In order to be able to do this, the AA has to manage a huge amount of information efficiently. It feels that effective information management is the vital component in providing a quality service.

If we consider the nature of the organisation, we can understand its needs for information management. For example, there are some 25m telephone calls to the AA each year, of which 8m calls are to its 0800 number. The AA also has to phone out and has some 8000 handsets. The AA's principal businesses are services to members and membership, which employs 7000 staff and runs 3600 patrols. Its services operations include insurance and financial services, which employ 4500 staff, as well as retail, travel services, the AA's own driving school and, of course, publishing – the AA is the UK's biggest publisher of maps and guides.

ICI has 16 mainframe computers installed with the AA, 8 of which are at the AA's corporate centre outside Basingstoke. The AA uses an IT system based on internationally recognised standards. They have chosen an open system approach that allows information systems to be developed in a coherent manner so that they can pursue new commercial opportunities. Their system also allows information to be accessed between systems so that opportunities for counselling services can be utilised. The implementation of the computer systems at the AA is so effective that it has become part of the DTI's open systems demonstrator programme.

The AA's annual expenditure on IT is over £40m. This high cost is partly due to the fact that the AA group is opening a new shop every 13 days and installing networked terminals in its shops and offices at the rate of 2 to 3 a day. Investment in computer technology is, therefore, running at £1m per month and computer usage is growing at an annual compound rate of 25 per cent. All of this is part of a tactical plan that covers aspects of hardware, software and communications.

The applications of the IT being installed at the AA are based on the fact that it is a service business. Key performance indicators are linked to response times for telephone answering, portfolio retention and break-down times. IT helps them to measure and improve these areas and, further, create an environment that attracts, develops and responds to customers.

1 What is the purpose of the AA's information processing system?
2 Describe the uses to which it might be put.
3 Make a list of the factors which might influence its effectiveness.

The effects of the Data Protection Act on information processing

One of the consequences of the increasing use of computers for information processing is the use of computers to store and process large quantities of information about individuals. For example, an electricity company may store account data about each of its customers, their addresses and telephone numbers, how they pay their bills and how long they take to pay. Some of the information kept in computer files may be perceived as being personal or private in nature. Even if the information is just a series of addresses or phone numbers, they may be considered to be private and there is a chance that someone who obtained this information may misuse it without their knowledge or consent. These are issues of data privacy and have concerned people for many years.

The Data Protection Act 1984 was passed to regulate the use of information for processing systems which relates to 'individuals and the provision of services in respect of such information'. The Act covers the holding of computer records and not manual records.

The Act requires those using personal data to register with the Data Protection Register and these registered data users must then follow the eight principles of the Act.

1 Data must be obtained and processed fairly and lawfully.
2 Data must be held only for specific lawful purposes which are described in the entry into the register.

3 Data should not be used in any other way than those related to such purposes.
4 Data should be adequate, relevant and not excessive for those purposes.
5 Personal data should be accurate and kept up-to-date.
6 Data should be held no longer than is required.
7 Individuals should be entitled to access their data and, if necessary, have it corrected or erased.
8 Data must be protected with appropriate security against unauthorised access or alteration.

There are a number of exemptions to the Act, including information kept by government departments for reasons of national security, information the law requires to be made public, mailing lists (as long as the data subjects are asked if they object to data being held for this purpose), payrolls and pensions information, clubs and personal data held by individuals in connection with recreational or family purposes.

To ensure that data is held only for legitimate purposes, many organisations appoint a Data Protection Officer.

Effects of the Act on individuals and organisations

Individuals

Information can be a powerful weapon, particularly if it is held by those who may misuse it. The Act provides a number of safeguards against those who may do this, particularly those who do so on the basis of racial, religious, political and sexual activities, beliefs or origins.

Because information from information processing systems may be passed on and sold to other organisations, one negative effect for individuals is that they may receive unsolicited communications from organisations who have obtained personal details through the purchase of mailing lists. Another danger is that of security, particularly if unauthorised employees access and try to use personal information for illegitimate purposes.

One positive aspect for individuals is their right to access, which enables them to obtain a copy of personal data held about them. When making such a request it should be made in writing and the data user may charge a small fee for dealing with it. If the individual is damaged by inaccurate data then they have a right to take action for compensation. They may also have inaccurate personal data erased or corrected.

If they believe that the provisions of the Act have been broken they have a right to complain to the Registrar.

Another important aspect of the Act is that employees have the right to access any information held about them and claim compensation for any distress caused by such information.

Organisations

The Data Protection Act made organisations acutely aware of the importance of the issue of data privacy. Before this procedures may have been lax and haphazard. This may have allowed information to get into the wrong hands and be open to misuse by unauthorised individuals. One of the negative effects has been the expense of setting up data protection procedures such as electronic or physical measures to protect rooms and access to software and the cost for many organisations of employing or allocating time for the activities of a Data Protection Officer. When requests for information are made, the organisation also has to allocate time for dealing with such requests and, where necessary, deleting or amending information.

On the positive side, now that organisations know what parameters determine how they may handle information, they may legitimately sell such information to others in the form of mailing lists.

Evidence collection point

All employees dealing with data processing should have a basic awareness of the Data Protection Act and its requirements. Imagine that you have been entrusted with the responsibility of producing a sign for the office which informs staff of the requirements of the Act. Use a word-processor to undertake this activity.

Carrying out this activity will provide you with the opportunity to show evidence of Information Technology Core Skills.

Evidence indicators

For this activity you are asked to write a report which explains the purposes of information processing in business organisations and also describes the systems used for processing numbers, graphics and text in one particular organisation. When looking for an organisation about which to write a report, try to choose an organisation that tends to rely heavily upon the support of information processing systems to help staff undertake their operational activities.

The following list should serve as a checklist. Please tick off each of the following when you have successfully covered them as part of your report. You need to be able to confirm that:

- ■ I have identified an organisation about which I am going to write a report. ☐
- ■ I have established the purposes of information processing in this organisation and described their information processing activities. ☐
- ■ I have analysed the effectiveness of these information processing systems, i.e. fitness for purpose, cost, value for money, efficiency, security etc. ☐
- ■ I have commented upon the influences of the Data Protection Act on the handling of information within this system with specific references to measures taken by the organisation. ☐
- ■ I have included an account of an individual's right to personal access to information, and the rights relating to security and accuracy of information. ☐

Business Organisations and Systems: Unit Test 1

1 Which of the following is unlikely to be an objective of a public sector organisation?
   a The provision of reliable services.
   b Client orientation.
   c Profit maximisation.
   d The efficient use of resources.

2 Quangos are:
   a Quasi-autocratic non-government organisations.
   b Quality-automated new organisations.
   c Quality-automatic new orders.
   d Quasi-autonomous non-government organisations.

3 If a deed of partnership does not exist, under the 1890 Partnership Act:
   a Partners are entitled to share the profits of the business equally.
   b Partners refer to their memorandum of association.
   c A decision is made at the annual general meeting.
   d Shareholders sell the shares of the business.

4 Partnerships generally contain:
   a 2–15 partners.
   b 2–20 partners.
   c 2–25 partners.
   d 2–30 partners.

5 Which of the following appears in the Articles of Association?
   a Name of the company.
   b Objectives of the business.
   c The capital of the company.
   d Timings of company meetings.

6 Which of the following is an example of a nationalised industry?
   a British Gas.
   b British Coal.
   c BBC.
   d Powergen.

7 The most common form of business ownership is the:
   a Partnership.
   b Private limited company.
   c Sole trader.
   d Public limited company.

8 In order to set up a company the relevant documents have to be sent to:
   a The Registrar of Companies.
   b The Ombudsman.
   c The Company Secretary.
   d Corporation House.

9 Putting public sector businesses into private hands is known as the policy of:
   a Nationalisation.
   b Privatisation.
   c Democratisation.
   d Business transfer.

10 A large multinational business with many overseas operations is likely to structure its operations:
   a By function.
   b By product.
   c By process.
   d Geographically.

11 Which of the following departments of an organisation is most likely to be responsible for administering statutory pension schemes?
   a Accounts
   b Marketing.
   c Production.
   d Sales.

12 A statutory requirement for a company set under the Companies' Act is:
   a To provide equal opportunities in the workplace.
   b To publish annual accounts.
   c To provide safe working conditions.
   d To ensure regular factory inspections.

13 A routine function of the wages department of a trading organisation is:
   a Recording purchases and sales.
   b Calculating employee pay totals at regular internals.
   c Preparing financial data for a stock market flotation.
   d Comparing actual expenditure with budgeted figures.

14 A major responsibility of a company secretary is:
  a Answering the telephone.
  b Handling correspondence to and from shareholders.
  c Taking minutes at staff meetings.
  d Welcoming important guests to an organisation.

15 The section of an organisation that would be responsible for keeping day-to-day records of moneys flowing into and out of a company is the:
  a Invoice section.
  b Management accounting section.
  c Financial accounting section.
  d Wages section.

16 Which of the following is least likely to be the responsibility of an office manager?
  a Organising clerical training.
  b Advising departments on office layout.
  c Advising departments on recruitment policy.
  d Coordinating the supply of equipment and stationery.

17 The most appropriate method for the relaying of verbal messages is:
  a Electronic mail.
  b Telephone.
  c Telex.
  d Fax.

18 An operational decision taken in the marketing function of an organisation is:
  a Selecting the best channels for distribution.
  b Deciding whether to launch a new product.
  c Collating information from survey results.
  d Developing a completely new corporate image.

19 Which of the following may threaten the security of a network?
  a Passwords.
  b Viewdata.
  c Internet.
  d Viruses.

20 A store of facts called upon to provide information is known as a:
  a Spreadsheet
  b Database
  c Word processor.
  d DTP.

21 The Health and Safety at Work Act:
  a Is only binding on registered premises.
  b Makes employers totally responsible for ensuring health and safety at work.

  c States that the Health and Safety Officer at a workplace need only be aware of general rather than specific laws.
  d Lays down training standards for employees in potentially hazardous occupations.

22 Which of the following is unlikely to result from the increased use of modern technology?
  a Rising wages.
  b De-skilling.
  c Repetitive strain injury.
  d Technological unemployment.

23 An example of an open channel of communication would be:
  a A letter.
  b A report.
  c Notice boards.
  d Memorandum.

24 Which of the following would not appear on a letter?
  a Letterhead.
  b Salutation.
  c Compliments slip.
  d Inside address.

25 A list of topics to be discussed at a meeting is called:
  a A notice.
  b An agenda.
  c The minutes.
  d An addendum.

26 EFT stands for:
  a Electronic Fees Transfer
  b Electronic Funds Transfer.
  c E-Funds Transfer.
  d Electronic Franchise Television.

27 Another name for a homeworker is:
  a Telecommuter.
  b Tele-employee.
  c Networked employee.
  d WAN.

28 A multi-purpose multi-user system:
  a Allows one program to be run at a time.
  b Allows two programs to be run after each other.
  c Enables more than one program to be run.
  d Allows many users to run more than one program.

29 A table of numbers which can be organised and altered on a computer is known as:
  a A word processor.

199

b Calculator.
c Spreadsheet.
d Database.

30 The Data Protection Act requires those using personal information to register with:
a The Data Protection Register.
b Their local council.
c TECs.
d The Data Protection Agency.

31 A disadvantage to the owners of a supermarket of the development of electronic technology is that:
a It is possible to keep a closer check on stock levels.
b Rivals may gain a competitive edge through using more advanced systems.
c Fewer employees are needed to operate checkouts because of the use of bar codes and scanners.
d Computerised recording of sales serves as a form of market research.

32 A major advantage of windowing systems is that they enable the user to:
a Carry out several tasks simultaneously.
b Save work automatically.
c Write memos and letters using a variety of fonts.
d Transfer information from one computer to another.

33 Robotics are of special benefit to jobs that are:
a Complex and require a variety of individual work tasks.
b Repetitive and do not require human manipulative skills.
c Unique and unlikely to be repeated again.
d Dependent on individual thinking operations.

34 Which of the following IT-based applications might best be used by an organisation seeking drilling sites for oil using established rules and knowledge about where oil is most likely to be located?
a Expert systems.
b Databases.
c Spreadsheets.
d Word processing.

35 To decide on the most comfortable and user-friendly form of IT system for employees, an organisation will use:
a Relative costs of different systems.
b Ergonomics.
c Economics.
d Different types of databases.

36 To help them to capture and store electronic data, many supermarkets use:
a More staff.
b Facsimile machines.
c Bar-code scanners.
d DTP.

37 The most appropriate accounting system for comparing actual with expected performance in the short period is:
a A balance sheet.
b A budget.
c A capital account.
d Cash-flow.

38 The most likely non-routine function for an administration system is:
a Making out sales invoices.
b Preparing a production schedule.
c Preparing a job specification.
d Introducing new health and safety checks.

39 In order to administer the VAT system effectively, an organisation must:
a Record the amount of VAT on all inputs and outputs.
b Add the value made by all its employees.
c Deduct value added tax from the sale price of each item it sells.
d Keep computerised records of all its employees is:

40 The most appropriate measure for a sales and marketing department to check on its effectiveness is:
a The size and number of outstanding debts.
b The increase in the number of new customers.
c The number of product defects detected by quality control.
d The length of time taken to research and develop a new product.

41 A weakness of a highly centralised administrative system is often:
a Administrative tasks can be carried out only by specialists.
b Functional areas within an organisation may be frustrated at the speed with which administrative tasks are handled.
c The central administrative team is able to carry out work on behalf of several departments.
d Centralisation allows economies of scale.

42 An objective of an internal communication system is to:
a Be a grape-vine for gossip.
b Take over the role of trade unions.

c Motivate employees.

d Communicate with other organisations.

43 For most organisations the most frequently used form of external verbal communication is:

a Telephoning.

b Faxing.

c Advertising.

d Meeting.

44 A specialist rather than a general IT skill is:

a Using word-processing packages.

b Working with a spreadsheet.

c Designing a computer program.

d Accessing a database.

45 A feature of the non-electronic office is:

a A fax for sending messages.

b A computer database of customer records.

c Word-processing of letters and other documents.

d A paper-based filing system.

46 The most likely users of an expert system are:

a Technicians.

b Professional workers.

c Craft workers.

d Clerical workers.

47 It would be most likely to be cost effective for an organisation to purchase and use a spreadsheet package when:

a The organisation keeps only a small number of records.

b The organisation is starting up and is faced with a severe cash-flow problem.

c The organisation is involved in making a large number of numerical projections.

d The organisation makes frequent use of word processing facilities.

48 A disadvantage of using electronic technology is:

a An organisation can communicate quickly with other organisations.

b An electronic system does not have to depend on paper-based records.

c The initial cost of installing the system may be high.

d Technical economies can be gained in the long term.

49 A specialist job using information technology is:

a Word processing.

b Stock control.

c Data storage.

d Writing computer programs.

50 Using the appropriate information technology in an organisation involves:

a Choosing the least-cost solution to problems.

b Using the most expensive applications that the organisation can afford.

c Using the applications that best meet the needs of the organisation.

d Using those applications which are most widely used by industry.

Business Organisations and Systems: Unit Test 2

1 Which of the following groups would not be stakeholders for a government department?

a Shareholders.

b Managers.

c Employees.

d Taxpayers.

2 A mission statement is:

a An operation undertaken by a group of employees.

b A report of an operation.

c A general statement of intent.

d A list of the objectives of an organisation.

3 An example of an extractive business would be:

a A chemical company.

b A mine.

c A car showroom.

d A manufacturing business.

4 Barclays Bank is an example of a business which provides:

a Commercial services.

b Services for the community.

c A social service.

d Distribution services.

5 One way of measuring relative market share is:

a Size of market share/number of competitors.

b Market share of company/market share of nearest competitor.

c Market/competitors.

d Competitors/size of market.

6 Which of the following is a public limited company?

a Department of Transport.

b Your school of college.

c BP.

d OFSTED.

7 After presenting a Memorandum and Articles of Association to the Registrar of Companies, the newly formed company will receive:
   a Shares.
   b A Certificate of Incorporation.
   c A trading lease.
   d A Royal Charter.

8 A one-person business is sometimes called:
   a The street trader.
   b A partnership.
   c A private company.
   d A sole trader.

9 The hiring of ideas out to other business organisations is sometimes called:
   a Franchising.
   b Leasing.
   c A cooperative.
   d Network marketing.

10 An example of a privatised business is:
   a BBC.
   b British Gas.
   c British Roadworks.
   d BPP.

11 The person within a company who deals with legal matters will be:
   a The company accountant.
   b The director's PA.
   c The company secretary.
   d The departmental administrator.

12 With a matrix structure a member of staff from an organisation may:
   a Belong to more than one project group.
   b Be directly responsible to one manager.
   c Work within a rigid hierarchy.
   d Only be employed on a temporary basis.

13 An advantage of manual information processing systems over electronic processing is:
   a Speed.
   b Accuracy
   c Less expense.
   d More personal.

14 The most appropriate IT system for internal communication within a branch of an organisation is:
   a A LAN
   b A WAN
   c Videoconferencing.
   d Teletex.

15 The division of labour has proceeded further in vehicle manufacturing than in vehicle repairing because:
   a Vehicle repairing requires larger units of capital than vehicle manufacturing.
   b It is possible be employ automatic machines and computer control in vehicle assembly.
   c Less quality control is required at vehicle assembly plants.
   d Assembly workers are more skilled than repairers.

16 The Data Protection Act:
   a Limits the quantity of data which an organisation is allowed to hold.
   b Makes it necessary for an organisation to indicate the type of data which it holds.
   c Protects organisations from having to disclose the data which they hold on individuals.
   d Makes it necessary for organisations to register all the information which they carry about other organisations.

17 A non-routine function for the personnel department of a manufacturing company would be:
   a Carrying out a job analysis.
   b Producing a job description.
   c De-layering the organisational structure.
   d Setting out an advertisement for a supervisor.

18 The term 'span of control' refers to:
   a The number of employees who are directly supervised by one person.
   b The functions that make up an organisation.
   c The hierarchical structure of an organisation.
   d The responsibility of each post within an organisation.

19 A flat organisational structure is one in which:
   a Decisions are passed down from managers to supervisors to line workers.
   b There are relatively few layers in the organisational chain of command.
   c There is a bureaucratic structure within the organisation.
   d Decisions within an organisation tend to be made at the centre.

20 Which of the following is not a common feature of a memorandum?
   a A number of copies are distributed.
   b They are sent externally.
   c They may have an organisation's name at the top.
   d They may have a subject heading.

21 Which of the following is an example of software?
   a Floppy disk drive.
   b Monitor.
   c Keyboard.
   d Word processing program.

22 Which of the following has made working with the visual display unit of a computer more user-friendly?
   a The mouse.
   b Graphical user interface.
   c The keyboard.
   d Bubble jet printers.

23 CD-ROM stands for:
   a Compact Disc Reading Off the Machine.
   b Compact Disc Raising Office Mechanisation.
   c Compact Disc Read Only Machinery.
   d Compact Disc Read Only Memory.

24 The main advantage of book computers when compared with other forms of computers is:
   a Size of memory.
   b Portability.
   c Applications that can be used.
   d Size of display unit.

25 An organisation is likely to gain the most benefit from the use of a computerised, rather than manual, database of customers when:
   a It deals with millions of undifferentiated consumers in a large mass market.
   b It deals with a handful of well-known customers who place single large orders.
   c It deals with a large number of known customers who need to be individually targeted.
   d It is just starting up and is unsure about the customer base.

26 A major disadvantage of using manual systems for storing data rather than using computerised systems is:
   a Records can be stored in paper form.
   b Records can be kept in a variety of ways to suit the needs of the user.
   c Large quantities of records can be stored using extensive storage space.
   d Records can be quickly retrieved and duplicated.

27 The most effective IT application for saving large quantities of important facts and figures in fields and records is:
   a A spreadsheet.
   b A graphics package.
   c A database.
   d A simulation.

28 The business function which lends itself most readily to computerisation is:
   a Wage negotiation.
   b Accounting procedures.
   c Advertising.
   d Dismissal procedures.

29 Which of the following items of office equipment is found in an unautomated office?
   a Answering machines.
   b Fax machines.
   c Photocopiers.
   d Filing cabinets.

30 ISDN stands for:
   a Integrated Services Digital Network.
   b In-service Systems Digitised and Networked.
   c Integrated Systems Digital Network.
   d Itemised Services Digital Network.

31 A non-routine function of sales administration is:
   a Making appointments to meet customers.
   b Researching media audience profiles.
   c Checking the success of a promotion.
   d Setting out a sales plan for a new concept.

32 A company needs suggestions to improve its administration systems. Which of the following is likely to produce the best results?
   a Article in in-house magazine.
   b Office memo to staff.
   c Quality circle.
   d A suggestion box.

33 The most effective measure of quality of service is:
   a The number of complaints.
   b The level of output.
   c The number of users of a service.
   d The level of customer satisfaction.

34 To connect users on different sites together an organisation would use:
   a A local area network (LAN)
   b A local networking area (LNA)
   c A wide area network (WAN).
   d The Internet.

35 An example of a remote database would be:
   a Windows.
   b Prestel.
   c Word.
   d dBase.

36 The computer application most commonly used for organising and manipulating numbers is a:

a Database.
b Spreadsheet.
c Desktop publisher.
d Word processor.

37 In a transformed business:
a IT makes most of the decisions.
b IT provides instant information which helps in decision making.
c IT shares business processes.
d IT increases the complexity of all operations.

38 User definable software means that:
a Software is easy to use.
b Software is based on well-defined graphics.
c Software can easily be adapted for the use of a particular business.
d Software can be obtained easily with appropriate hardware.

39 The most likely reason for a business organisation to use a computer-based accounting package is:
a The use of the computer will improve efficiency.
b There is very little spare time for training within the organisation.
c The use of the computer will improve presentation of results.
d Appropriate software applications are relatively cheap to purchase.

40 The aim of artificial intelligence is to:
a Create factory robots.
b Extend automation to a variety of administrative functions.
c Produce a machine which is able to analyse data and reason for itself.
d Implant intelligence from computers into human thinking processes.

41 A controller:
a Carries out a function automatically.
b Controls all outputs into a particular process.
c Controls all outputs from a particular process.
d Is a person who regulates inputs into a process.

42 Companies wishing to store personal information on a computer system must register with:
a The Office of Fair Trading.
b The Data Processing Officer.
c The Information Technology Ombudsman
d The Consumers' Association.

43 A person who makes an unauthorised entry into a computer system is known as:
a A programmer.

b A systems analyst.
c A virus.
d A hacker.

44 Which of the following is not an example of a spreadsheet program?
a Lotus-1-2-3.
b Word.
c Excel.
d CA-Super Calc.

45 A multitasking package is one which:
a Contains a single word processor.
b Involves use of a modem.
c Enables data to be transferred between applications.
d Contains software management drivers.

46 Which of the following is unlikely to be a security procedure?
a System used by authorised personnel.
b Back-up copies of data.
c Keyboard locks.
d Screen filters.

47 One example of a complimentary close would be:
a Dear Sir.
b Subject heading.
c Yours faithfully.
d Letter reference.

48 The system which can put and store messages onto a system is known as:
a Business post.
b Teleporting.
c Electronic mail.
d Business television.

49 Which of the following is unlikely to be used to appraise the effectiveness of a system?
a Efficiency
b Fitness for purpose.
c Value for money.
d Redundant skills.

50 One exemption from the Data Protection Act is information kept:
a By a personnel department.
b About illnesses.
c Relating to credit problems.
d For national security.

This unit introduces the major principles which underpin marketing:

- Anticipating what consumers in the marketplace will want and need, and identifying new opportunities.
- Satisfying consumer expectations by coming up with the goods and services that are required.
- Maximising the amount of income and profit generated by businesses, by successfully anticipating and satisfying consumer requirements.
- Maximising benefits to the organisaton.
- Successfully managing change (marketplaces change all the time) and being competitive.
- Coordinating activities in an organisation to achieve marketing aims.
- Making use of the latest technological developments.

- Improving the way in which customers see the organisation, as well as its products and services.

While you are working on this unit you will find that invaluable additional sources of information include:

- Business sections of national newspapers.
- Weekly magazines:
  - *Marketing*
  - *Marketing Weekly*
  - *Campaign*
- Sources of statistics and other information:
  - *HMSO Social Trends*
  - *HMSO Annual Abstract of Statistics*
  - *Key Note*
  - *Mintel*
  - *Market Research*

The principles and functions of marketing in organisations

This chapter looks at what marketing does (i.e. the principles of marketing) and how marketing operates (marketing functions). We will show that marketing is a central part of organisational activity which sets out to ensure that the organisation meets the needs of its customers.

Marketing principles

The marketplace is changing constantly. Organisations need to understand these changes or they will be left behind. Yesterday's successful organisation may find that if it fails to change then profits will drift away and be turned into losses.

Examples of this are all around us. Take, for example, the popularity of Economics as an A level subject. Fewer than 10 000 sixth formers took Business Studies A level in 1989, but that figure had risen to 27 000 by 1994. Business Studies has overtaken Economics in popularity (Figure 8.1) although the

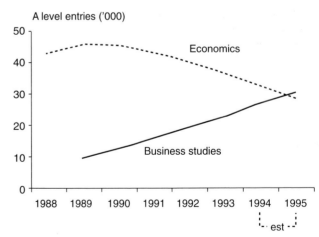

Source: Economics and Business Education Association

Figure 8.1 Numbers of students following A level courses in Business Studies and Economics

popular GNVQ Business is tempting students away from A levels.

There are a number of reasons for the change. One reason is that students perceive Economics as being boring compared with Business Studies. They often find role models such as Richard Branson and Anita Roddick to have more sparkle about them than economists they see on television. They also see that Business Studies degrees offer more chance of employment and higher salaries than Economics ones.

Business Studies is also seen as being more relevant to the real world than the dry theory of Economics. Economics used to be called the 'dismal science' because of its predictions of overpopulation and declining living standards. Today it is sometimes characterised as the 'dreary science' when contrasted with the 'sexier image' of Business Studies.

The response of Economics has been to revise syllabuses to cut out some of the more dry and theoretical elements of the course. New courses have also been developed which borrow heavily from Business Studies.

However, Business Studies teachers, too, are faced with the choice of either changing to meet the needs of their students or continuing to see numbers of students falling.

Another example of falling demand in recent times has been that of doorstep deliveries of milk (Figure 8.2).

Again there are a number of reasons for changing demand patterns. One has been that shoppers have increasingly turned to cheap supermarket supplies of milk in cartons. Families that consume large quantities of cereals with milk may be able to save £2 to £3 a week through supermarket purchases.

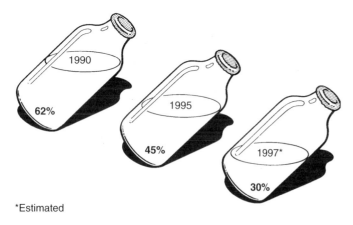

*Estimated

Figure 8.2 Delivered milk as a share of total milk sales

More people are doing a large weekly shop in supermarkets using the car to transport goods.

Another reason for the difficulties faced by doorstep deliveries has been the rising cost of milk from farms. In the past the Milk Marketing Board was responsible for milk supply in this country. In 1994 the government replaced the Milk Marketing Board (a regulated monopoly) with Milk Marque (an unregulated monopoly). The result has been that Milk Marque has been able to raise prices. Shoppers have opted for the relatively cheap supermarket cartons in a time of these rising milk prices.

The two examples highlighted above are typical of the millions of changes which are taking place in markets all the time. Successful marketing involves being able to anticipate these changes in order to make an appropriate response.

The economics teacher and the doorstep deliverer of milk who is unable to anticipate or cope with these changes may end up being left behind. The economist who responds by saying that teaching Economics is not the same as selling milk, Coca-Cola, beefburgers or whatever is missing the point.

The Chartered Institute of Marketing uses the following definition of marketing:

> Marketing is the management process responsible for identifying, anticipating, and satisfying consumer requirements profitably.

This definition places consumers at the centre of an organisation's activities – whether they be the pupils or parents of children at the local school, milk consumers, or people queuing to buy fish and chips.

Some organisations are physically very close to their consumers – for example, a newsagent in a small town. For other organisations consumers may be thousands of miles away – for example, Cadbury's selling sweets and chocolates around the world. The principle that the 'Consumer is King and Queen' is just as relevant to the organisation engaged in international marketing as to the local trader.

There are a number of key words in the definition given above (Figure 8.3):

■ *Identifying* This will involve answering questions such as: 'How do we find out what the consumer's requirements are?' and 'How do we keep in touch with their thoughts and feelings and perceptions about our goods or service?'
■ *Anticipating* Consumer requirements change all the time. For example, as people become richer

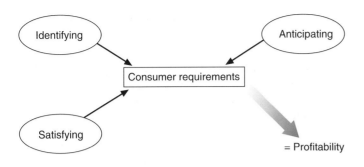

Figure 8.3 The ingredients of marketing

they may seek a greater variety of goods and services. Anticipation involves looking at the future as well as at the present. What will be the Next Best Thing that people will require tomorrow?

■ *Satisfying* Consumers want their requirements to be met. They seek particular benefits. They want the right goods, at the right price, at the right time and in the right place.

■ *Profitability* Marketing also involves making a margin of profit. An organisation that fails to make a profit will have nothing to plough back into the future. Without the resources to put into ongoing marketing activities, it will not be able to identify, anticipate or satisfy consumer requirements.

Figure 8.4 Marketing research antennae

One of the key components of marketing therefore is anticipating market needs and opportunities. A particular success of Virgin has been their ability to anticipate market needs: the development of cheap High Street record stores in the 1970s, cheap flights across the Atlantic during the 1980s, followed by contraceptives, and more recently Virgin Cola.

In order to anticipate change, organisations need to have an antenna which is highly sensitive to changes taking place in the buying population – what is happening to the age structure of the population, what is happening to tastes and preferences, what is happening to incomes, etc.

Market research is this antenna of an organisation (Figure 8.4). Market research is far more complicated than asking 100 people if they like a product and saying 'good' if 60 of them do. That, however, is really where it all starts. In the next chapter we shall look at market research in detail.

Evidence collection point

Explain how organisations can anticipate market needs and opportunities. Write an account showing how a particular organisation has successfully anticipated market needs and opportunities.

Satisfying customer expectations

Pedigree Petfoods, the leading producers of pet foods in this country, state:

> We work constantly towards identifying and satisfying consumer needs. It is the activity from which all else springs. We never forget that we cannot influence millions of consumer choices until we have convinced first one, then a second and a third consumer that our product is worthy of purchase. Our success is based on thorough research of the wide range of needs for pet animals and their owners. The knowledge which we gain is translated into our range of quality products which satisfy these needs better than any of our competitors.

It is the ability to satisfy customers that marks the difference between the successful and the unsuccessful organisation. This is why some schools have a huge demand for places, while others have falling roles. It is why some supermarkets have people crowding the aisles whereas others are practically empty.

Case Study – The growth of multiplex cinemas

In 1946 cinema attendance in Britain was 1.6 billion. By the 1980s it had fallen to an all-time low of 54 million – around one visit per head of population per year.

By 1994 cinema has revived – 114 million cinema tickets were sold. There are now nearly 2000 screens compared with 1271 in 1984.

CANNON
DARLINGTON

From Friday, June 16

BAD BOYS (18)
Weekdays & Saturday
2.05, 5.25, 8.15
Sunday 5.15, 8.00

SILENT FALL (15)
Weekdays 1.45, 4.05,
6.20, 8.30. Saturday 6.20,
8.30. Sunday 6.05, 8.20

RICHIE RICH (PG)
Weekdays & Saturday
1.40, 3.50
Sunday 3.55

BRADY BUNCH (12)
Weekdays & Saturday
1.55, 4.15, 6.20, 8.40
Sunday 4.15, 6.20, 8.35

BARGAIN PRICES
Adults 2.30. Children
£1.50. Senior Citizens
£1.5. Student £1.50.
All day, every day

24HR PROGRAMME
INFORMATION
(01325) 462745

The change in fortunes came with the arrival of the multiplex, which satisfied the needs of a new type of cinema audience. The first multiplex to open in the UK was the Point, a 10-screen cinema, in 1985. It was a large, bright and modern new building.

At the time critics felt that the multiplex had no future; they felt that the video had killed the cinema off. The UK had the largest expansion in both video machine purchase and the hiring of cassettes anywhere in the world.

However, multiplexes have gone from strength to strength so that by 1995 there are 75 in Britain, taking 40% of all cinema viewers.

The strength of the multiplex has been its ability to satisfy the needs of considerable numbers of cinema-goers. Before the multiplex, 60% of the cinema-going population was aged 16–24. Today it is people in their 30s and 40s, as well as families who typically attend multiplexes, in addition to the 16–24-year-olds.

The multiplex is attractive because it provides a relatively cheap and convenient night out. People can drive in, see the film and get back home quickly, so that, for example, baby-sitters do not have to stay up too long.

Multiplex tickets also vary in price from one part of the country to another, depending on what people in a particular area are able to afford. For example, a ticket in the West End of London may be as much as £8, whereas in Preston it is under £3.

The multiplex was not some sudden invention. It had previously been very successful in the United States and market research by the large American companies revealed that there was plenty of scope in this country.

1 How have multiplex cinemas been able to successfully satisfy customer expectations?
2 What sorts of customers do they appeal to?
3 What benefits do they offer to customers that are not available in more traditional cinemas?
4 Carry out a survey of multiplex users to find out why they are attracted to using the multiplex. What do they see as being the main benefits?

Generating income and/or profit

Milton Friedman, a well-known American economist, has stated that 'the business of business is business'. Businesses need to make money if they are to survive and grow. A business that failed to make a profit would not be able to give a share of profits to shareholders, pay its employees, or give contributions to charity.

Marketing therefore is responsible for identifying opportunities which enable goods to be sold in order to bring income into organisations and to enable them to make profits. Without profits an organisation cannot afford to modernise itself, install new technologies, or take commercial risks with, say, new product ranges. Nor can it justify the investment of its owners – private individuals or institutions such as pension funds and insurance companies – who must make the best possible use of their resources.

In a free competitive market, and in all but the shortest term, profit is the measure of how good a business is, how well-run, and how effectively it meets its responsibilities to the owners, customers, staff and the community.

Case study – Profitable lines in multiplexes

Multiplex cinemas only make a limited amount of profit from the films they show. Each film print costs at least £1000 and the costs of promoting and advertising the cinema and films are very high.

Multiplexes therefore rely heavily on a subsidiary form of income: food and drink. Over 25% of the revenue comes from selling items such as Coke, popcorn, sweets, chocolate and hot dogs. The profits that are made from these lines are much higher. Perhaps as much as 80% of all profits come from these subsidiary lines. Consumers at cinemas are far less likely to criticise a cinema for the high price of its food and drinks than for what they see to be its selling point – the film itself. Once cinema-goers are in the cinema they will often indulge themselves in sweets and drinks while they wait for the film to start.

1 What are the main sources of income for multiplex cinemas?
2 What are the main sources of profits for multiplex cinemas?
3 To what extent are the products sold in multiplexes complementary?

Maximising benefit to the organisation

Marketing sets out to enable an organisation to be successful. Success brings a host of benefits to the organisation. The organisation that is successful develops a good public image, people are keen to work for the organisation, the organisation can afford to give better rewards to employees, the organisation is able to plough money into research and development in order to secure a long-term future, the organisation is able to make a contribution to the wider community.

You have only to think of organisations which use marketing successfully to appreciate the benefits to the organisation which follow. For example, Mars produces a range of successful chocolate bars and ice-cream bars. This leads to high profits, and excellent working conditions in Mars plants. Shareholders benefit, as does the local community, e.g. in sponsorship for the London Marathon and other projects.

Evidence collection point

Identify an organisation in your locality which uses marketing successfully to anticipate and identify consumer requirements at a profit. What are the obvious benefits to the organisation?

Managing effects of change and competition

We have already looked at a number of markets which are experiencing changes. Indeed, you only have to walk down the aisle of a supermarket to appreciate the large number of competing brands of products. From time to time a new product will arrive which is subtly different from existing brands. If the new product is successful this will lead to a flurry of business activity as existing producers try to come up with rival versions. For example, in the early 1990s the German company Muller was highly successful in introducing 'twin pot' yogurts into this country (the fruit and yoghurt were stored in different compartments). This has led to the development of a variety of rival brands. Marketing in any organisation must constantly seek to enable the organisation to manage the effects of change and competition – by coming up with new products, advertising campaigns, price alterations, special offers, etc.

Case study – The spreading fats market

The spreading fats market provides us with a good example of a highly competitive market in which change occurs frequently, forcing organisations to adapt to cope with these changes. The table below illustrates some of the wide variety of products available in the spreading fats market.

209

Nobody worried about eating butter until 1980. Then, suddenly, it was bad for you. Then good for you. Then bad again. Current nutritional thinking (1995) is that foods containing high levels of saturated fats – such as butter – can contribute to heart disease. However, in the early 1990s some researchers announced that butter-eaters were less likely to have a coronary than margarine eaters.

The 'yellow fats' market including butter, margarine and low-fat spreads, is a £800 million market (1994). There have been big changes in demand in this market: in 1973, butter had 75% of the market, today it is nearer 20%.

The biggest producer of non-butter yellow fats is Unilever which has 40% of the yellow fats market. The butter producers are very sensitive to challenges from non-butter producers.

A good illustration of this occurred in November 1991. Unilever introduced a new brand called 'I Can't Believe It's Not Butter!' The Butter Council complained to the Independent Television Commission that regulates television advertising and had advertisements for the product banned. The main cause for complaint was that the product's name contained a double negative, inferring that if you cannot believe that it is not butter, then you must believe it is butter. In fact, I Can't Believe It's Not Butter! is a polyunsaturated fat-reduced margarine.

Market research suggests that the 22% of people who continue to eat butter do so because of the taste. If a product comes along that tastes like butter but is high in polyunsaturates – which reduces cholesterol levels in the blood – then the market could be blown wide open.

Clearly the yellow fats market is a dynamic one. Between 1983 and 1990, butter consumption halved, but margarine consumption also fell by 20% while sales of the new, reduced-fat products rose by 300%.

In the mid-1990s, with a strong interest in the environment and purer foods, some people have realised that butter is pure and natural. They see the antioxidants, E numbers, emulsifiers, colourings and stabilisers in margarine and decide on butter instead, so maybe there will be a swing to butter again!

1 How is the yellow fats market affected by competition?

Type of fats	Legal definition	Brand names	
Butter	Minimum 80 per cent fat (all milk fat), maximum 16 per cent moisture.	Anchor Country Life Wheelbarrow	Lurpak Kerrygold
Half-fat 'butter'	Fat 40 per cent (all milk fat), moisture 35 per cent.	Kerrygold Light	
Margarine	Made from fish or animal fats and vegetable oils; minimum 80 per cent fat (up to 10 per cent of which may be milk fat).	Stork Stork SB	Echo (hard) Blueband (soft)
Polyunsaturated margarine	Made from oils (e.g., sunflower oil) with high level of polyunsaturated fat: minimum 80 per cent fat, maximum 16 per cent moisture.	Flora Blueband	Vitalite
Fat-reduced margarine	Based on vegetable oil: fat 60 per cent, moisture 35 per cent.	Krona	Summer County
Mixed fat spread	Fat 70–80 per cent, moisture 15–25 per cent.	Clover Willow	Golder Crown Meadow Cup
Reduced-fat spread	75 per cent fat or margarine, based on vegetable oil.	Mello	Stork Light
Low-fat spread	Made from vegetable oils and 'dairy' ingredients, such as buttermilk: fat 40 per cent, moisture 55 per cent.	Outline Delight Flora Extra Light	Gold Clover Light Half-fat Anchor
Very low-fat spread	Vegetable oils and dairy ingredients: fat 40 per cent, moisture 60 per cent.	Gold Lowest	
Polyunsaturated low-fat	Made from oils high in polyunsaturated fat, sometimes with added milk products: fat 40 per cent, moisture 55 per cent.	Flora Light Sunflower	Shape

2 What are the main factors that are likely to affect consumer buying decisions? How do these factors alter over time?

3 What factors have caused changes in the demand for butter and margarine?

4 Why is it important for organisations to be able to manage the effects of change and competition in such a market?

5 What specific actions do you think that businesses are likely to take in order to manage the effects of change and competition? Use the example of a butter producer, and a margarine producer.

Coordinating activities to achieve marketing aims

Every organisation needs to have clear goals, and the major route to achieving organisational goals is strategy. It is important, therefore, to be clear about the difference between strategy and tactics.

These terms originate from military use (military strategy before and during a battle is the general policy overview of how to defeat the enemy). Developing a strategy involves establishing clear aims and objectives around which the framework for a policy is created. Having established its strategy, an organisation can then work out its day-to-day tactics to meet the objectives.

Marketing can thus be seen as the process of developing and implementing a strategy to plan and coordinate ways of identifying, anticipating and satisfying consumer demands, in such a way as to make profits. It is this strategic planning process that lies at the heart of marketing.

Putting marketing policy into practice and coordinating it can be viewed as an ongoing cycle of activities (Figure 8.5).

Reconnaissance involves checking out the market and product research to find out what customers want, how well the products are performing, and the strengths and weaknesses of competitors. This research should enable an organisation to make forecasts and predictions of likely future trends.

Strategy involves deciding on objectives and priorities for an organisation as well as laying down clear plans for marketing activities (e.g. what range of products will be made, their prices, and how they will be delivered to customers).

Operations involves putting the plans into practice –

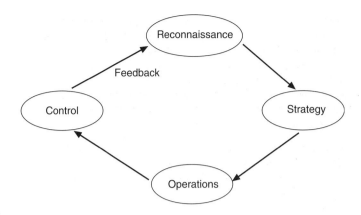

Figure 8.5 A cycle of marketing activities

organising advertising and selling campaigns, getting the goods to the right place at the right time, etc.

Control involves checking on the effectiveness of the marketing operation (e.g. checking on the volume of sales made, measuring the effectiveness of advertising, analysing the profitability of operations). Once again, this feeds back into reconnaissance. If sales are falling, why is this so? Why has an advert been so effective? The information that stems from control activities should feed back into fresh research.

Marketing planning is essential for an organisation. It enables the organisation to plan for the present and for the future and to learn from the past. The three main objectives of planning are:

1 To assess how well the organisation is doing in the various markets in which it operates.
2 To identify the strengths and weaknesses of the organisation in each of these markets.
3 To establish goals and objectives, so that resources can be used in an appropriate way.

Marketing must ensure that organisational activities are coordinated in such a way as to achieve marketing aims. For example, if market research indicates that people who visit multiplex cinemas are unwilling to stand in the rain queuing for an hour for the last seat to be sold just in front of them, then it is essential for the organisation to find solutions. In Manchester the UCI multiplex cinema has a bank of 90 telephone operators at the end of a Freephone number taking nationwide bookings. Consumers can say where they want to sit. The transaction takes on average 64 seconds. Marketing thus has a responsibility to ensure that all aspects of the way in which an organisation operates are geared to meeting consumer requirements.

Evidence collection point

Market research indicates that cinema-goers enjoy roomy, clean cinemas, where they can see a film at the stated time. What are the implications for the way in which a market-conscious cinema is organised?

Utilising technological developments

Technological advance means that yesterday's goods and services become dated. Organisations need to have their finger on the pulse of technological change. For example, Mars have been successful in recent years because they moved into Mars ice-cream in order to boost falling sales during the summer months. Rival chocolate manufacturers have copied Mars. Manufacturers of training shoes have used new technologies to create air-cushioned soles, giving trainers a light and springy feel. Computer manufacturers have devised new computers with much more memory and which can work much more quickly than in the past. Compact disc players have largely replaced record players.

All of these are examples of technology moving forward. Marketing has a responsibility to identify changes in technology, so that the organisation can make appropriate decisions to keep abreast of change. Too often organisations persist with outmoded technology while competitors leap ahead. It is essential to utilise new technological developments.

Evidence collection point

Identify examples where:

1 Organisations have utilised technological developments to give them a lead in the market.
2 Organisations have persisted in using outdated technologies so that they have been left behind in the market.

Enhancing customers' perceptions of the organisation, product or service

Customers' perceptions are vital. For example, some people will not use launderettes because they consider them to be dirty. Other people will not visit burger restaurants because they consider the food to be sub-standard and the packaging used to be environmentally unsound.

It is very important to gauge customer perception of an organisation. This can be carried out through market research.

Often organisations are quite surprised to find out what the view of the customer is (e.g. McDonald's survey, see page 36). Marketing plays an important role in making a comparison between customers' existing perceptions of a product, and the costs of things that customers would ideally seek in a product or service. Organisations that are armed with this information are best placed to make up the deficit.

For example, market research carried out on behalf of KFC in 1993 revealed that the rating of Kentucky Fried Chicken outlets at the time in terms of 'value for money' and being 'good for a complete meal' were behind those of some of its main rivals (Figure 8.6).

However, research also indicated that KFC was ahead of some of its rivals in other areas, e.g. its ratings on 'unique taste' (Figure 8.7).

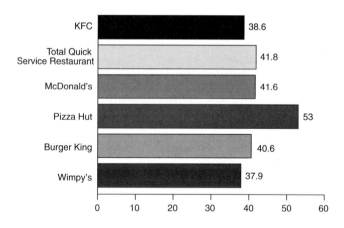

Figure 8.6 KFC rating on 'good for a complete meal' in 1993

Armed with this sort of information KFC were able to begin to change customers' perceptions. They started offering a wider variety of side dishes in their restaurants, and concentrated on providing value for money with competitively priced nourishing meals. Once they has transformed their products and services, they were able to advertise these changes on television to a national audience.

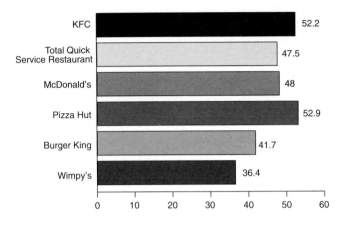

Figure 8.7 KFC ratings on 'unique taste'

This case outlines the importance of marketing in helping an organisation to be fully in tune with its market. Advertising will be of little use unless an organisation can genuinely provide the goods and services that customers require. You can only do this by using your antenna effectively.

Evidence collection point

Show by means of an actual example how marketing can be employed to enhance customers' perception of an organisation, its products and/or its services. Present your work so that you demonstrate Core Skills in Communication.

Marketing functions

Marketing performs a number of important functions in an organisation. These marketing functions are underpinned by marketing principles.

The implications is that we can only fully understand how marketing operates in the real world when we understand what marketing sets out to achieve. In the previous section we set out to identify the principles of marketing; we can now go on to look at how marketing operates in the real world based on these basic principles.

Managing change

In 1985, the Chartered Institute of Marketing adopted a new slogan:

MARKETING MEANS BUSINESS

The implication is that it is marketing that directs and drives successful business.

Marketing is now accepted in most well-run businesses as a strategic discipline or general management function. In this respect it must care for the future health of a business – especially enabling the organisation to deal with competition. This is because it is increasingly realised that although making a profit is important, an organisation should also develop its market share and search for brand leadership as well. So the marketer must monitor the profitability of the business and attempt to anticipate the likely trends. At the same time rival companies should be monitored and examined for vulnerable points.

Successful marketers must therefore be concerned with every aspect of their business, including future projects and other areas of their industry. Successful companies plan five or ten years or more in advance and often know as much about the competition as they know about themselves!

Marketing is not just a series of business-related functions, but is more far-reaching than this. It is a business philosophy designed to develop an attitude of mind which should be shared by everyone in an organisation, and is often enhanced by both frequent and open communication. Developing such an attitude of mind reduces the likelihood of crisis and contributes to the development of the overall future of an enterprise at both strategic and tactical levels.

At the heart of marketing lies the degree to which an organisation becomes marketing-orientated. The more committed a company is to its marketing activities, the more able it will be to pursue its corporate objective and develop and retain customers. Every business in existence relies on its customers for survival, and those who best meet customer needs will always survive a period of change.

With the accelerating increase in consumer power, the business which does not have the consumer at heart will become a dinosaur and will soon go the way of all the dinosaurs!

213

The marketing function is therefore an essential ingredient of corporate strategy, and this marketing focus should be communicated through marketing planning into all aspects of business activities (Figure 8.8).

```
┌─────────────────────────────┐
│     CORPORATE STRATEGY      │
│   underpinned by marketing  │
└─────────────────────────────┘
              │
              ▼
┌─────────────────────────────┐
│       communicated to       │
└─────────────────────────────┘
              │
              ▼
┌─────────────────────────────┐
│      all aspects of an      │
│   organisation's activities │
└─────────────────────────────┘
```

Figure 8.8 The marketing function is an essential ingredient of corporate strategy

So far in this chapter we have made constant reference to the changing marketplace. Marketing has a key part to play in keeping the organisation in tune with these changes.

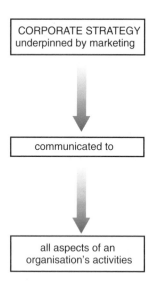

Case study – A changing environment for Philips

Over the past few decades the Philips laboratories have come up with the Video 2000 video-recorder system, the Laservision video-player, combining pictures with digital sound, and the compact disc. However, only the compact disc has turned into a clear success.

The biggest failure was the Video 2000. When the product was introduced in 1979, technicians acknowledged that it was far superior to the competing Betamax and VHS video systems, launched by the Japanese Sony and Matsushita companies respectively. But production failed to get off the ground, and one year after the official launch the product was still not on the shelves around Europe.

Later the Video 2000 was nicknamed the homing pigeon, since nearly half of the machines returned to Eindhoven for repairs.

The product failed partly because it was beaten to the market, and partly because of the mistaken belief that users would have little interest in hiring commercially produced videos from a video shop. The hardware was thus launched with no software backup! After four years Philips was forced to bring out its own VHS machines using Japanese technology.

The Japanese companies were thus able to make their products the standard ones and Philips lost over a billion guilders.

Another criticism of Philips at the time was that the national companies within the Philips group were too powerful. For example, the North American Philips Corporation would have nothing to do with Video 2000 and sold the Japanese systems instead. Many of the national companies ran their own campaigns and demanded specific designs.

Today things have changed at Philips. Managers of Philip divisions coordinate product launches and campaigns all around the world, while managers of business units are responsible for the entire life-span of a product, from development to sale.

1 Was Philips' failure with Video 2000 due to product inadequacy or to marketing failings?
2 What indications are given that Philips' corporate strategy at the time was not underpinned by a marketing philosophy?
3 How many of the problems that Philips encountered would you describe as:
   a external influences over which the organisation had little control
   b internal weaknesses?
4 How can an organisation plan for changes in its external environment?
5 How can an effective marketing organisation manage change within the organisation?

Coordinating marketing planning and control

Marketing planning is concerned with identifying clear objectives and setting out how those objectives can be achieved. The marketing objectives need to be built into all strategic and tactical thinking within an organisation, and govern the way in which an organisation operates.

The aim of any organisation is to satisfy the stakeholders who have most power and influence. Marketing, of course, is primarily concerned with serving the customer. The objectives of a market-driven organisation will therefore be chiefly concerned with satisfying the requirements of the consumer in the marketplace.

Marketing planning can therefore be said to be concerned with:

- establishing objectives and goals, allocating resources to meet these and setting out a clear plan of action
- setting out ways of evaluating performance against marketing targets
- assessing the position and performance of the organisation in the various markets in which it operates, and identifying its strengths and weaknesses.

A plan is set out with a clearly established time-line for developments. At the same time a review process is set in motion to check the performance of the marketing strategy. A key part of all planning stages is providing mechanisms that enable the company to evaluate marketing and product performance in the market as a whole and in individual markets in which the organisation carries out its activities (Figure 8.9).

A useful model for coordinating marketing planning and control is:

- *Diagnosis* Where are we and why? This usually involves some form of audit of company performance, which will then be analysed.
- *Prognosis* Where are we going? This involves looking at possible future scenarios in the light of present performance and trends.
- *Objectives* Where do we want to go? What is important?
- *Strategy* What is the best way of achieving our objectives?
- *Tactics* What specific actions will enable us to meet day-to-day targets?
- *Control* How far have we progressed? A company will need to establish performance indicators against which it can measure its success.

Evidence collection point

Briefly explain why it is important for an organisation to coordinate marketing planning and control.

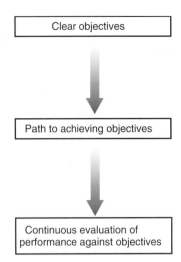

Figure 8.9 From objectives to performance evaluation

Customers have different needs, wants, likes and dislikes. Not every person likes the same make of motor car or has the same taste in clothes. If cost and production time were of no importance, manufacturers would make products to the exact specifications of each buyer. Unfortunately, this is not at all practicable. On the other hand, neither can it serve its customers successfully if it groups all of their needs and wants together.

Instead of trying to serve all customers equally, an organisation may focus its efforts on different parts of the total marketplace. Within the total marketplace it is possible to group customers with similar characteristics into market segments. Market segmentation is therefore a process of separating a total market into parts so that different strategies can be used for different sets of customers.

If you attempt to market a single product to the whole population, this is sometimes said to be like using a blunderbuss, firing shots to pepper the whole marketplace (Figure 8.10).

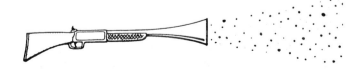

Figure 8.10 Marketing by blunderbuss

When it is not possible to satisfy all its customers' needs with a uniform product, an organisation will use market segmentation to divide consumers into smaller segments consisting of buyers with similar needs of characteristics, so that marketing becomes like firing a rifle instead of a blunderbuss. A rifle with an accurate sight will hit the target some efficiently, with wasting ammunition (Figure 8.11).

Figure 8.11 Marketing by rifle – hitting the target segment

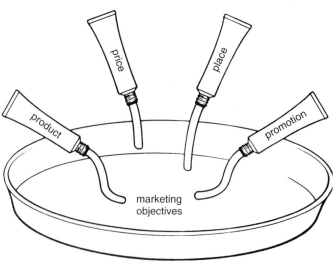

Figure 8.12 The marketing mix

Segmentation enables an organisation to follow market objectives. It also provides a means whereby an organisation can position its brands and products varieties in the marketplace. The marketing department can, by suitable promotion, establish a particular position in the market for each brand (e.g. up-market, mid-market, or down-market) and then tailor selling strategies for each position.

Implementing the marketing mix (product, place, promotion and price)

By splitting the marketplace and developing strategies to position products, any organisation can choose an appropriate marketing mix for each target segment. The marketing mix comprises a complex set of variables which an organisation combines in order to ensure that objectives are achieved. It includes strategic, tactical and operational elements and techniques.

The concept is usually analysed on the basis of the four Ps (Figure 8.12). To meet customer needs an organisation must develop products to satisfy them, charge them the right price, get the goods to the right place and make the existence of the product known through its promotion.

'Mix' is an appropriate word to describe the market process. A mix is a composition of ingredients blended together to fulfil a common purpose. Every ingredient is vitally important and each depends on

the contributions of the others. Just as with a cake, each ingredient is not sufficient on its own – but blended together it is possible to produce something very special. In the same way that there are a variety of cakes to suit various tastes, a marketing mix can be designed to suit the precise requirements of the market.

The marketing mix must have a time-scale. An organisation must have a plan that indicates when it expects to achieve its objectives. Some objectives will be set to be attained in the near future. Others might be medium-term (one to five years), and yet others might be visionary objectives for attainment in the longer term.

The mix must have strategic elements. These will involve the overall strategy of the organisation. They require considerable use of judgement and expertise and are only made by senior managers. Such decisions might involve the development of a new product or a new market strategy.

The mix must also have tactical or medium-term elements. The business environment has to be constantly monitored and decisions have to be taken according to whatever changes take place. External events might affect pricing strategies, product modifications or amendments to marketing plans.

There must also be short-term operational elements. These involve predictable everyday matters such as contacts with customers, analysis of advertising copy and minor decisions about packaging.

The commitment and support of a programme of planning with sufficient resources will underlie the manipulation of the marketing mix and will ultimately determine how capable an organisation is of achieving its objectives.

Evidence collection point

Choose a product you use regularly and comment briefly on:

1 the nature of the product
2 its price
3 its availability (place)
4 how it is promoted.

If you were given overall responsibility for this brand, how would you use the marketing mix to develop its core strengths?

We will now briefly look at the elements of the marketing mix in turn.

Product

The product is the central point on which all marketing energies must converge. Organisations have to analyse what their products mean to their customers. People and organisations buy goods and services for a variety of reasons, and a wide range of characteristics influence the decision to buy. For example, on the surface there are often clear and tangible benefits such as:

- shape
- colour
- size
- design
- packaging
- appearance.

The intangible features are not so obvious. They may include the reputation of the producer on certain issues, such as:

- after-sales service
- customer care policy
- availability of spare parts
- guarantees.

Task

Choose any product. List both its tangible and its intangible benefits.

At a basic level, people buy woolly jumpers to keep warm. They buy umbrellas to keep dry in the rain, and watches to tell them the time. However, human behaviour is a complex process. It is not uncommon to hear someone say 'I wouldn't be seen dead wearing one of those.' In other words, for many of us it cannot be any old jumper, umbrella or watch – it needs to be an item that fits in with a particular perception or self-image.

Products are not usually purchased to meet a single need; the ownership and use of a product involves a whole range of factors that make up the product concept.

For example, it may appear that a person chooses to holiday in the West Indies because he or she is attracted by the sand, sun and surf. However, it may come to light that the person is more concerned with 'image' – friends and associates will become aware that he or she is able to holiday in the West Indies. Holidaying in the West Indies is therefore associated with a particular lifestyle. In the public imagination it may represent being rich and able to afford exotic things.

Product benefits can be broken down into a number of important dimensions, of which we shall consider three:

- *Generic dimensions* are the key benefits of a particular item. Shoe polish cleans shoes. Freezers store frozen food. Deckchairs provide a comfortable seat on a sunny day. Hairdressers cut and style hair.
- *Sensual dimensions* of a product are those that provide sensual benefits. These include design, colour, taste, smell and texture. A ring doughnut has a shape, appearance, texture, taste and smell all of its own. The sensual benefits of products are frequently highlighted by advertisers.
- *Extended dimensions* of a product include a wide range of additional benefits. Examples are

217

servicing arrangements, credit facilities, guarantees, maintenance contracts and so on.

Research and development

Many people associate the research and development function of an organisation with the invention of new products. Whilst this is very important, the development of existing products is also significant. The task of product research and development is to combine with marketing activities to cater for the changing preferences of consumers and come up with the goods and services that will meet the needs of tomorrow's customers. Product research and development therefore goes hand in hand with market research, and considerable liaison is required between the two areas. For example, researchers will attempt to investigate all of the questions in Figure 8.13 before a final decision is made to go into production.

Product researchers use marketing information to help them develop well-designed products. Design involves developing goods and services in a form which both attracts customers and serves the intended purposes. The layout of a department store, for example, must be designed so that a customer is able to find the item he or she wants quickly, while the effective use of space is vital to ensure profitability. Product researchers must also consider production costs, ease of manufacture and selling price.

A company might be reluctant to change an existing design, particularly if it provides status (e.g. the radiator grille of a BMW car). Conversely, small changes may be made to products to give them a more up-to-date feel. A company logo may be updated to give it a 'modern look'.

Built-in obsolescence

Built-in (or planned) obsolescence can be, and frequently is, a feature of many products. Fashion clothes are designed to last for a season, and cars are built to last for only a few years. A manufacturer is able to sustain long-term market demand by limiting the lifespan of a product. Some commentators argue that this leads to a huge waste of resources, while others see it as boosting demand, employment and output in the economy.

Task

Draw up a list of arguments an environmentalist might put forward against built-in obsolescence. How might a major manufacturer respond to such arguments?

The product mix

Many organisations produce more than one product. One advantage of diversification is that it enables the company to spread its risks. The product mix is the complete range of items produced by an organisation. These products have to be managed and positioned in appropriately targeted market segments. The mix comprises all the brands, line extensions, sizes and types of packaging on offer.

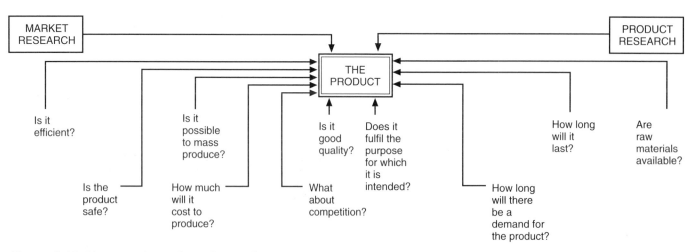

Figure 8.13 Key questions about the product

Task

Design three charts to show the product mixes of three well-known companies. Use a computer to present your work – this can provide evidence of Core Skills in Information Technology as well as Communication.

1 Explain why it is difficult for many American and European companies to compete in Japan.
2 What are the dangers of rushing out instant imitations too quickly?
3 Explains what is meant by:
   a product covering
   b product churning
   c parallel development.
4 How do the Japanese benefit by using off-the-shelf components?

The key to a good product mix is having an effective balance of products in line with the organisation's strategy. Effective management involves creating this balance. If a product is losing pulling power, it may need to be revamped, relaunched or replaced.

Case study – New product development in Japan

WESTERN companies are supposed to be the masters of innovation, marketing and incisive management. Japanese firms have a reputation for borrowing ideas from abroad, making painstaking improvements and then, when everything is ready, churning out better-quality products in huge volumes at low prices. This reputation may still be partly true for Japanese companies abroad. At home almost the opposite is the case, as many American and European companies trying to compete in Japan have been shocked to discover.

Foreign firms entering the Japanese market with a four-year technical lead have seen their products quickly matched – not copied, mind, matched – and then left behind. Once Japanese manufacturers relied on slick production techniques to make them into awesome competitors. Today their most effective weapon is rapid innovation.

Take Sony's best-selling CCD-TR55, a miniaturised video camera and recorder ('camcorder') that weighs a mere 790 grams (1.5lb). To make the product palm-sized, Sony had to shrink 2,200 components into a space one-quarter the size they occupy in a conventional camcorder. Yet only six months after introducing the CCD-TR55 in June 1989, Sony had competition. Matsushita, followed by its stablemate, JVC launched even lighter look-a-likes. Within a year, Sanyo, Canon, Ricoh and Hitachi were selling palm-sized camcorders as well.

The process of rushing out instant imitations is known in Japan as **product covering**. Rival manufacturers rush to produce their own versions just in case the pioneer's should prove to be a best-seller. With a target to aim at, the coverers know that the innovation is at least technically feasible. Reverse engineering – taking the product apart to see how it works – provides short-cuts. The top priority of companies is to prevent distributors and retailers from deserting their own camp.

Product covering is really just a part of an even more formidable Japanese process known as **product churning**. When developing a new product, western firms use a 'rifle' approach, testing the market constantly and revising the product each time until it exactly meets the customer's needs before launching it. Japanese manufacturers, by contrast, tend to use a 'shotgun' approach. For instance, around 1,000 new soft drinks appear annually in Japan, though 99% of them vanish within a year. New-product ideas are not tested through market research, but by selling the first production batch.

Kevin Jones, a consultant in McKinsey's Tokyo office, points out that nobody could imagine why people would want a hi-fi with not one, but two, compact-disc players. The doubters included Sharp, the firm that launched the machine. Nevertheless teenagers bought the machines to mix tracks from separate CDs onto tape. Within months both Sanyo and JVC followed with their own twin-CD machines.

Firms also engage in **parallel development** – developing second-and-third-generation products along with the initial version. As soon as the pack catches up, the original innovator has a replacement for its own hit product ready to go. Only weeks after Matsushita launched a rival to Sony's palm-sized camcorder. Sony hit back with two new models – one even lighter, the other with yet more technical features. Companies that fail to ride each successive wave of innovation risk being washed away.

This looks wasteful. But according to a study by McKinsey, Japanese companies develop new products in a third to half the time spent by their western counterparts, at a quarter to a tenth of the cost. Three factors help Japanese companies pull off this feat:

● **Japan's army of engineers**. Japanese companies are reaping the benefits of the country's enormous investment in education, especially in engineering schools. Technical literacy is now more widely diffused throughout Japanese business than anywhere else in the industrial world. Japan has 5000 technical workers for 1 million people. The comparable figure for America is 3500, for western Germany 2500; no other country comes close.

● **Catalogue design.** Instead of designing every component of a new product from scratch, Japanese engineers reach instinctively for the parts catalogue. By using off-the-shelf components wherever possible, they devote their most creative engineering skills to fashioning a product that is 90% as good as a product designed from scratch might be – but only half the price of a completely original version.

● **Free flow of information**. Unlike western firms, which tend to hand their suppliers the skimpiest of specifications when seeking a price quotation for a new component, Japanese manufacturers share their most secret plans, send their top staff to help out and hand over any proprietary know-how needed. They then leave the supplier to get on with the job of developing the part needed for the new product. With so much trust and exchange of staff, product-development information can flow

His master's CD

between a company and its suppliers while a new product is still only a gleam in an engineer's eye. The lack of job-hopping among Japanese engineers limits the leakage of information to competitors.

Even Japanese firms have not been able to transfer all these practices abroad. Flooding the market with new products, even imitations, is important in Japan because firms are determined not to lose access to scarce, and often rigid, dealer and distribution networks. Abroad, this matters less. Tarnishing their reputation with a poor product is also less of a concern because many new versions are aimed at a small core of sophisticated consumers who will try anything new. The extraordinary appetite of all Japanese consumers for new gizmos can also make an aging product-line fatal to a firm's prospects, as many failed camera manufacturers discovered in the 1980's.

Abroad, new products still have to be chosen and developed more carefully. A single dud can damage a carefully nurtured image. And falling a small step behind is not so threatening once brand loyalty has been established. Nevertheless, the new-product treadmill Japanese companies face at home has already given them an enviable prowess in foreign markets. Moreover, any western firm hoping to grab a chunk of the huge Japanese market will have little choice but to step on to the new-product treadmill too.

Source: The Economist Newspapers Ltd

5 Identify the areas of new product development in Japan which, in your opinion, use:
  a good marketing practices
  b poor marketing practices.
6 How is the Japanese consumer affected by such activities?

Price

We have already covered price in some detail on page 39. Of all the aspects of the marketing mix, price is the one which creates sales revenue – all the others are costs. For sellers, price is a key element in the marketing mix. It is an important selling point. 'Getting the price right' is an important tactical decision and as such it is a key factor influencing revenue and profit.

We all know of businesses that sold wonderful products which were just a little too expensive – they went out of business. We also know of businesses that sold their products too cheaply – not enough revenue was generated to cover costs adequately, and they also went out of business.

The importance of price within the marketing mix varies from one market to another and between different segments in the same market, In low-cost, non-fashion markets, price can be critical (for example in the sale of white emulsion and gloss paint for decorating). In fashion markets, such as fashion clothing, it can be one of the least relevant factors.

Certain products are designed to suit a particular price segment (e.g. economy family cars) whilst others perform a specific function regardless of cost. For consumers with limited budgets, price is a key purchasing criterion; whilst for others for whom 'money is no object', price is less important.

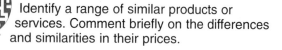

Task

Identify a range of similar products or services. Comment briefly on the differences and similarities in their prices.

There are many possible objectives in establishing prices. A key assumption of many business theories is that profit maximisation is the most important pricing target. Studies of actual business behaviour, however, reveal a wide range of objectives other than short-term profit maximisation.

A competitive price is one that gives a competitive edge in the marketplace. It is not necessarily lower than that of a rival, because other elements of the marketing mix add to the competitive edge. For example, it is possible to argue that Gillette razor blades are better quality than those of rivals, giving scope to charge a higher yet more competitive price.

A further aim of competitive pricing is to set a price that deters new entrants in a particular market, Large organisations with some degree of monopoly power may be inclined to keep prices relatively low in order to secure their long-term market dominance. From time to time you might hear the owner of a small organisation say: 'Of course we would like to diversify into producing X but we simply cannot compete with the prices being offered by the big boys.'

H. A. Simon put forward the view that a business may want to 'satisfice' – that is, achieve given targets for market share and profits from sales which may not maximise profits but which instead inflate boardroom egos. This situation can arise when the managers of an organisation are clearly different from the owners. If the managers can provide sufficient profits to keep the shareholders satisfied, then a proportion of the profits can be diverted to provide more perks for managers and large departments.

There are many other possible objectives in establishing prices. For example, a company might feel that it is important to maximise sales to create brand leadership, or it might want to establish a high price to create a reputation for quality.

Place

Though figures vary widely from product to product, roughly a fifth of the production cost of an item goes on getting it to the customer. The issue of place deals with various methods of transporting and storing goods, and then making them available to the customer.

Getting the right product to the right place at the right time involves the distribution system. Distribution is the process of moving goods and services to the places where they are wanted. It may involve a single step or any number of steps. The local baker might supply bread directly to customers. In contrast, the furniture store might supply chairs and tables produced in Scandinavia which have passed through a number of hands and have been stored two or three times before arriving at their final destination.

Transport can be a key cost component in many

products. Choosing the 'best' possible transport system involves weighing up and 'trading off' a number of key elements. What forms of transport should be used – road, rail, air, sea? Can these forms of transport be integrated? What are the best possible routes? Do you use your own fleet or outside carriers? How do you maximise safety? How do you minimise costs? How do you make sure that products arrive on time and in the best possible condition?

Task

Imagine you are the transport manager for an organisation that manufactures and delivers fresh cream cakes from Shildon, in County Durham, around the North East of England – particularly to Darlington, Sunderland, Durham, Newcastle and Consett. Work in groups to research and then discuss each of the transport issues mentioned in the text. Plan your work so that it provides evidence of Core Skills in Application of Number as well as Communication.

Different forms of transport have their own distinctive advantages and disadvantages.

Pipelines are expensive to construct, cheap to run and expensive to repair.

Roads give door-to-door delivery, are fast over short and some long distances, and make it possible to use your own fleet relatively cheaply. However, road transport is also subject to traffic delays and breakdowns, and lorry drivers may only drive their vehicles for a certain number of hours in a day.

Rail transport is relatively cheap and quick over long distances, particularly between major cities. However, it is not always appropriate for reaching out-of-the-way destinations and is costly for guaranteed speedy deliveries.

Air travel is very fast between countries, provided the ultimate destination is not off the beaten track. Air is generally used for carrying important, urgent, relatively light and expensive loads.

Sea transport is a cheap way of carrying high-volume bulky loads when speed is not of the essence.

Containerisation of loads has made possible the integration of these different forms of transport. Routes and services have been simplified to cut out wasteful duplication. Special types of vehicles have been developed to carry certain loads. Direct motorway connections between major cities have proved to be of major importance in determining

factory location decisions, as have fast inter-city rail services and air links.

Different methods of transport may prove to be more or less cost effective in different situations depending on the cost of transport relative to the type of good being transported, the price of the good, or the speed with which it is needed.

Promotion

People historically have always used hand signals, vocal patterns, symbolic drawings and facial expressions for the purpose of communicating (Figure 8.14).

Figure 8.14 Facial and hand signal communicating 'Hello, I like you!'

Today the exchange of information takes place through sophisticated media in order to accomplish the same goal. An efficient network of communications is essential for successful promotional activity.

The promotional mix comprises all the marketing and promotional objectives of the marketing mix. These methods can be broken down into two distinct areas: non-controllable and controllable.

Non-controllable methods are marketing messages which take place on the basis of word-of-mouth, personal recommendations and a consumer's overall perception of a particular product or service. For example, consumer opinions are influenced by a number of factors, such as whether their family has regularly used the product. A brand heritage, character, colour and image will also have helped to create brand loyalty and influenced regular purchasing patterns. On the other hand, public displeasure with a particular organisation, country or range of products might discourage purchase. For example, in recent years buyers have been hostile to CFCs in aerosols and 'dolphin unfriendly' tuna.

Controllable methods are marketing messages which are carefully directed to achieve the objectives of an organisation's promotional campaign. We will consider advertising and promotion in greater depth in Chapter 10.

Using the marketing mix

As we have seen, the marketing mix is a carefully constructed combination of techniques, resources and tactics which form the basis of a marketing plan.

Whenever objectives or external influences change, so the blend of ingredients in the marketing mix will need to be varied.

As a result, the marketing mix varies tremendously between one organisation and another and between different time periods. Each represents a different way of using resources.

Three broad approaches to the marketing mix are:

- undifferentiated marketing
- differentiated marketing
- concentrated marketing.

In *undifferentiated marketing,* a single marketing message is offered to the total marketplace. In other words all potential consumers are treated as if they had similar characteristics. This may be a relatively cheap way of tackling marketing, but its weakness is that it ignores individual differences (Figure 8.15).

Figure 8.15 Undifferentiated marketing

Differentiated marketing is the strategy of attacking the marketplace by tailoring separate product and market strategies to different sectors of the market (Figure 8.16). For example, the car market may be divided

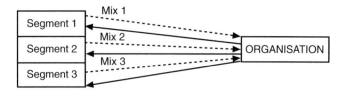

Figure 8.16 Differentiated marketing

into an economy segment, a luxury segment, a performance segment, etc.

This approach is very important because the reality of today's marketplace is that there are many discrete groups of consumers who need to be approached in different ways.

Task

The following diagram illustrates some of the main segments of the tea market, showing examples of teas sold in each segment.

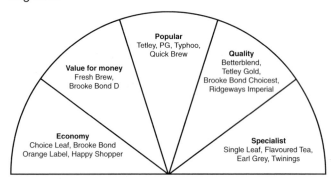

Figure 8.17 Segments of the tea market

Choose two of the segments and explain how you might use a slightly different marketing mix to appeal to consumers in these segments.

Concentrated marketing is often the best strategy for small organisations (Figure 8.18). This involves choosing to compete in one segment and developing the most effective mix for this sub-market. Jaguar, for example, concentrates on the luxury segment of the car market. Similarly, quality fashion retailers position themselves in this specific segment of the clothes market.

Although companies try to select and dominate certain market segments, they find that rivals are

Figure 8.18 Concentrated marketing

engaged in similar strategies. They therefore try to create a differential advantage. A positioning strategy will involve selecting a market segment and creating a differential advantage over rivals in that area.

Task

Look at two similar products. Comment on the similarities and the differences of their marketing mixes. To what extent are these due to positioning strategy? (Positioning relates to the market segments in which organisations choose to market their products.) What are the differential advantages each product has over its rivals?

The product life-cycle

An important aspect of the marketing mix is its use of the product life-cycle. The life of a product is the period over which it appeals to customers. We can all think of goods that everyone wanted at one time but have now gone out of fashion, obvious examples being hot-pants and beehive hairstyles.

The sales performance of any product rises from nought when the product is introduced to the market, reaches a peak and then goes into decline (Figure 8.19). Most products are faced by a limited

life-cycle. Initially the product may flourish and grow, eventually the market will mature and finally the product will move towards decline and petrification. At each stage in the product life-cycle there is a close relationship between sales and profits so that as organisations or brands go into decline, their profitability decreases.

The life-cycle can be broken down into distinct stages. In the *introductory* phase, growth is slow and volume is low because of limited awareness of the product's existence. Sales then rise rapidly during the period of *growth*. It is during this phase that the profit per unit sold usually reaches a maximum. Towards the end of this phase, competitors enter the market to promote their own products, which reduces the rate of growth of sales of the first product.

This period is then known as *maturity*. Competitive jockeying – such as product differentiation in the form of new flavours, colours, sizes, etc. – will sift out the weaker brands. During *saturation,* some brands will drop out of the market. The product market may eventually decline and reach a stage when it becomes unprofitable.

The life-cycle may last for a few months or for hundreds of years. To prolong the life-cycle of a brand or a product an organisation needs to readjust the ingredients of its marketing mix. Periodic injections of new ideas are needed – product improvements, line extensions or improved promotions. Figure 8.20 illustrates the process of injecting new life into a product.

A readjustment of the marketing mix might include:

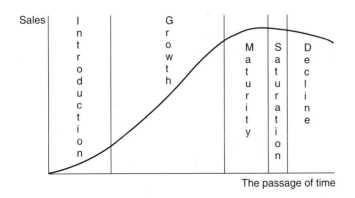

Figure 8.19 Stages in the product life-cycle

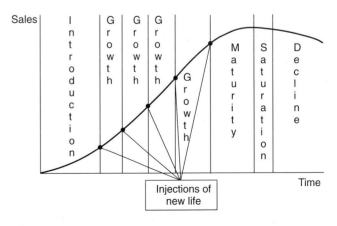

Figure 8.20 Periodic injections into the product life-cycle

223

- Changing or modifying the product, to keep up with or ahead of the competition.
- Altering distribution patterns, to provide a more suitable place for the consumer to make purchases.
- Changing prices to reflect competitive activities.
- Considering carefully the style of promotion.

 ## Case study – The relaunch of Madonna

In late October 1994, Madonna's new album 'Bedtime Stories' was launched. It remains to be seen whether this album will be as popular as her mid-1980s hits 'Like a Virgin' or 'True Blue' (see Figure 8.21). Pop stars, probably more than any other person or organisation, are faced by limited life-cycles. Madonna is all too aware of the finite nature of her product. In an interview with Norman Mailer in 1994 she said that 'as an unbelievably famous person you are only allowed to operate with everyone's approval for a limited amount of time.'

In the early 1990s some people argued that Madonna has moved her brand image too much in one direction. She played a leading role in the film 'Body of Evidence', for which press publicity emphasised the sexuality of her portrayal.

At the same time she produced a highly publicised book *Sex*, and on her album 'Erotica' the cover featured her as a dominatrix with a gold tooth in her mouth.

But perhaps this was just too much of the same thing! Public perceptions were becoming polarised. The new album 'Bedtime Stories' involved what can be seen as a subtle relaunch of a Madonna brand in the mature years of its life-cycle. The publicists argue that the new approach is 'bright, clean, clear and mellow'. Musically there is also a change in direction, with an increased emphasis on song-oriented rhythm and blues.

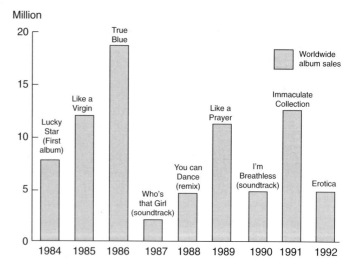

Figure 8.21 Madonna album sales

1 Does Madonna appear to have gone through a product life-cycle?
2 What stage does Madonna appear to be in the life-cycle?
3 What steps could be taken to inject life into the product life-cycle?
4 Use examples of other popular music artists who have sought to inject new life into their product life-cycles. How effective have they been?

The product portfolio

Most large organisations produce a range of products, each with its own life-cycle. By using life-cycles, companies can plan when to introduce new lines as old products go into decline. The collection of products that an organisation produces is known as its *product portfolio* (Figure 8.22).

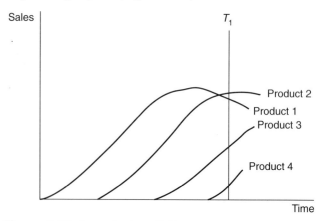

Figure 8.22 A product portfolio

In Figure 8.22, T1 represents a point in time. At that point product 1 is in decline, product 2 is in maturity, product 3 is in growth and product 4 has recently been introduced.

Task

The organisation you work for or attend will have a portfolio of products or services. Identify the elements of the portfolio and try to determine where these elements stand in their life-cycles.

If an organisation's products are launched at just the right time, it is likely to benefit from a continuous period of growth. Most organisations today are multi-product and provide a portfolio of products at different stages in their life-cycles. This helps to avoid serious fluctuations in profit levels and ensures that the most profitable products provide support for those that have not yet become so profitable.

Ensuring the survival of the business

No business can survive for any length of time without successful marketing. This is why marketing should be looked at as the *generalship* of business, that is, the function which has responsibility for directing and securing the long-term viability of an organisation.

Today, marketing assumes a significantly greater importance for many organisations than in the past. Many organisations have a 'total product' approach towards marketing, whereby all of the activities of the organisation are designed to fulfil the needs of the consumer. Such an approach relates quality to marketing and ultimately to success in the marketplace.

So what happens to organisations that ignore marketing? They will:

- be less responsive to consumer needs
- be less competitive
- lack overall direction
- rely on past achievements.

Evidence collection point

Identify two or three organisations in your locality that appear to:

1 place a great deal of emphasis on marketing
2 ignore marketing.

Identify which of these organisations are best placed to survive in the marketplace.

Branding

A *brand* is a particular product or characteristic that identifies a particular producer.

Many mass-produced products are almost identical. For example, most washing powders are very similar, as are different types of margarines. These goods tend to be produced by two or three large companies who encourage sales by creating a brand or marketing image which differentiates the products in the minds of the consumers.

The business of creating a brand is a particularly important function of marketing. Often people will buy the brand name as much as the product itself. You will see people in supermarkets pick up an item (which they have not seen before) and say, 'this must be a good one because it is made by so and so'.

Large organisations swear by the power of the brand. They will therefore fight tooth and nail to raise the status of their brands, and be determined that nothing should spoil the power of the brand.

The brand itself will often be recognisable by a logo or trade mark. For example, when you look at cereal packets you will be able to quickly pick out the Kellogg's logo which identifies the brand; when you are looking for toothpaste you will be able to quickly identify products from Colgate.

Organisations seek to create a portfolio of individual products which support the image of the brand. Well-known brand names will therefore emphasise quality throughout the organisation. They will be very careful about which products to add to the portfolio. For example, organisations with up-market images will be reluctant to merge with or acquire companies producing down-market products. When Virgin decided to move into cola it had to think long and hard about whether cola as a concept might spoil people's existing image of Virgin. Organisations need to consider whether new products and labels complement existing brands.

A brand which is held in high esteem is worth a lot of money to an organisation. There is a well-known saying in business that, 'an organisation can afford to get rid of all of its other assets, but not its brand image!'

Evidence collection point

Identify two or three brands of products in a particular market. To what extent could these brands be merged without spoiling the image of one of the brands?

Customer focus and an organisation's own needs

One of the main points we have been stressing in the text so far has been the importance in marketing of serving the needs of the customer. The effective organisation is one that anticipates, identifies and meets these needs. By meeting customer needs the organisation will best be able to meet its own objectives: profit-making, market share, public service or whatever. Unfortunately, however, in the real world of business some organisations forget about customers. They think they know best what customers require without carefully carrying out detailed research to find out what the market wants.

Market orientation versus product orientation

Few organisations operate in a static world. Today we live in a global marketplace for many goods and services in which technology, purchasing power, tastes and many other factors are all changing at the same time. In adapting to many of these changes, good marketing is a key factor.

Case study – Motorbikes

The classic example from the UK of failure to monitor customer requirements comes from the motorcycle industry.

In the 1960s foreign motorbikes were hardly ever seen on British roads. Great names such as BSA, Triumph, Ariel and Norton graced the highways with 'heavy, slow-revving, large-capacity machines'. The few imports available at the time were from Italy in the form of lightweight, high-revving machines and these were hardly given a second glance by British manufacturers. As British manufacturers did not make them, customers could not have them. At the time there was virtually no link between the marketing environment and the products which the manufacturers were producing.

For British bike manufacturers this did not matter. They were profitable and did not have to reinvest in costly research facilities. However, somebody else had identified that British manufacturers were failing to match the wishes of consumers in the marketing environment with the products they were making. Thousands of miles away research and development programmes were under way – Japan was about to enter the marketplace.

Today the transformation is complete. We only have to look on our roads to notice that motorbikes are nearly all Japanese and there are very few British manufacturers left.

If the British has looked outwards and identified customer requirements the position today might be very different.

1 Explain why the marketing process involves looking outwards and inwards.
2 What marketing activities should British motorcycle manufacturers have been carrying out in the 1960s?
3 Why did Japanese companies have a competitive edge?
4 Why do you think that it might be difficult to regain a competitive edge once it has been lost to a rival manufacturer?

Unfortunately, over the course of time, many organisations develop a product orientation rather than a market orientation.

Marketing orientation is based on the belief that if organisations do not satisfy the needs of customers, they will not survive. It is therefore essential to match the production and development of goods and services with the identification and anticipation of customers' desires and requirements.

This philosophy has been important for Japanese companies such as Sony and Honda for many years and today is becoming increasingly important for British companies. Customer needs and requirements are identified in every area of organisational activity, from the original idea and design right up until the final sale and then after-sale support.

The marketing orientation of a company can be contrasted with production and sales orientations. A production-orientated company holds the view that products will tend to find their own markets if they can be produced cheaply and be of good quality. Such companies spend relatively little time investigating consumers' wishes. As a result they often come to grief because, although their products are good in a technical sense, they do not provide the benefits that consumers require.

A sales-orientated company holds the view that success depends on effective advertising, selling and promotion rather than on achieving a real difference between the product it is selling and those offered by its competitors. This philosophy will be easily seen through if consumers shop around.

The real distinction between a marketing orientation and a sales orientation is that selling tries to get the customer to want what the company has; marketing on the other hand tries to get the company to produce what the customer wants.

Evidence collection point

Identify organisations and/or products which appear to be:

- product orientated
- market orientated
- sales orientated.

Which organisations and products are, or are likely to be, the most successful?

Cost of customer service versus productivity

Customer service requires attention to detail. Productivity is concerned with the output achieved from using an organisation's resources.

On the face of it there may be a contradiction between these two aims. We can illustrate this by an example.

A hairdresser can be highly productive if he or she cuts a lot of people's hair in a short period of time. It appears that the hairdresser is being productive. From the organisation's point of view this appears to be effective because resources such as capital and labour are being used to full capacity.

However, the reality is that productivity is not high when measured in terms of the revenue from the output. Hairdressing is a good example of a service which requires considerable personal service. We visit a hairdresser because we feel that they will help to make us look attractive and that attention will be paid to individual needs. Indeed, people are prepared to pay a lot of money to spend an hour at the hairdresser's.

The hairdresser who spends time on cutting two people's hair in an hour may receive £50 or more for their efforts. The hairdresser who rushes through six haircuts in a hour may be paid as little as £18 for their time. It is obvious where the productivity lies.

Creating a quality image is hard work, particular when dealing with customers. Effective encounters with customers strengthen an organisation's image. A good image enables an organisation to charge premium prices and ensures that customers come back. This is as true for a Premium League Football Club as it is for the producer of chocolates and the hairdresser. Effective customer service, then, should be seen as a desired goal for any organisation. Customer service should not be seen so much as a cost but as a benefit and as something that enhances productivity.

Evidence collection point

Identify three business activities in one or more organisations which are concerned with customer service. Show how these activities enhance productivity.

227

Cost of customer service versus profitability

Serving customers uses time and resources. Because there is a cost element to resource use, then costs need to be compared with revenues in order to assess profitability.

For example, a hotel may employ staff to make customers feel welcome and to serve the needs of consumers. Instead of having just one bartender, one porter, and one receptionist they may choose to employ several who are asked to make customers feel welcome and be proactive in seeking to help those who appear to have problems. The hotel thus gets a reputation for friendly and efficient service, so that it is always fully booked. The hotel makes a healthy profit because the revenues generated from having a full hotel by far outweigh the costs of having a few extra staff.

At the same time a rival hotel with a skeleton staff finds that most of its rooms are empty on a regular basis.

In the above example, the organisation's needs were to make profits for owners and shareholders. The hotel that was prepared to invest in the higher cost strategy was the more profitable one.

Organisations therefore need to strike a balance between customer service and profitability. For example, it would not be sensible for a hotel to increase its staff beyond a certain number.

The key is to find out what level of service customers want, and how much extra they are prepared to pay for such service. Anticipating, identifying and meeting customers' requirements for services is the recipe for success, and hence for profits.

Evidence collection point

Identify two organisations which need to exhibit high levels of customer service. Try to identify the levels of service which are most likely to yield maximum profits. For example, look at how the level of service in a local bank will determine the number of customers the bank will have. Does the bank need to emphasise customer service more? What will be the likely impact on costs and revenues? Your work could demonstrate Core Skills in Application of Number.

Cost of customer service versus accountability

Organisations are accountable to their stakeholders: shareholders, employees, consumers, neighbours, the government, the community, etc. There is a possible tension between serving customers and serving shareholders and other owners.

For example, if an organisation spends all its resources on pampering customers then shareholders may feel cheated. However, if an organisation fails to win customers then there will be no profits at the end of the day for shareholders.

A market-conscious company that serves customers by providing the right product, at the right price, in the right place, with the right promotion, stands a good chance of making profits for shareholders.

Nevertheless, tensions do occur. For example, in recent times there has been a tension in privatised industries between the consumer and the shareholder. Sometimes where regulators have insisted on capping prices charged to consumers shareholders have felt cheated out of profits. At other times when prices have risen customers have felt cheated by shareholders.

A 'good' business has several distinguishing features.

- It makes a profit by supplying products or services that people want to buy.
- It values and serves its customers.
- It makes a profit for its shareholders.
- It contributes to its own and the community's long-term prosperity by making the best possible use of resources.
- It minimises waste of every kind.
- It respects the environment, locally, nationally and globally.
- It sets performance standards for its suppliers – and helps in their achievement.
- If offers its employees worthwhile career prospects, professional training and job satisfaction.
- It expects the best from its employees and rewards them accordingly.

Evidence collection point

Which individuals and groups is a business organisation accountable to besides its customers? How can it balance the cost of customer service with accountability to its stakeholders?

Marketing activities in business organisations

So far we have been focusing on market principles and ways in which they underpin marketing functions. In particular, we have focused on ways in which marketing acts as a driving force behind business emphasis on the consumer.

Marketing activities are ways of putting principles into action. In particular, *marketing services* are the tools used by the marketing department. The marketing department will set out to identify the most appropriate marketing services to employ in order to make profits. These services may include public relations, trade and consumer promotions, point-of-sale materials, editorial publicity and sales literature.

Any communication with customers should ideally be the responsibility of the marketing function. The traditional areas of advertising, public relations and sales promotion are clearly marketing services. In addition, marketing services should also include the production of statements, invoices and even final demands, because the perception of the organisation by customers is too important to be neglected in any way.

Today many markets for goods and services have evolved to the point where the consumer has become of primary importance and has substantial control. In response to this changing balance of power, the successful business must produce the goods or services required to an appropriate standard at an acceptable price and distributed in a convenient manner.

Assessing market needs

As we have seen, an organisation must be aware of changes in its external environment as well as changes in the needs of its customers. It requires information. The gathering of such information helps it to plan its activities and reduce uncertainty.

The American Marketing Association uses a simple working definition of market research:

> Market research is the systematic gathering, recording and analysis of data about problems related to the marketing of goods and services.

We can break this definition down into its important ingredients:

- *systematic* – in other words, using an organised and clear method or system
- *gathering* – knowing what you are looking for, and collecting appropriate information
- *recording* – keeping clear and organised records of what you find
- *analysing* – ordering and making sense of your information in order to draw out relevant trends and conclusions
- *problems related to marketing* – finding out the answers to questions that will help you to understand your customers and other details about the marketplace.

It is the responsibility of the market research function within an organisation to find out as much as it possibly can about customers for all organisations if they are to meet the needs of their customers and remain competitive and profitable. It requires an organised way of finding answers to questions or solutions to problems and should be an on-going activity.

In order to sell to people what they want to buy, when they want to buy it, it is essential to build up a profile of customers – what they do, when and why they do it, and what would encourage them to use your products and services. In other words, you have to study their habits and motivations.

Market research also needs to find out what might make customers choose a rival product in preference to your own. For example, falling sales might be a result of changes in demand, the existence of an aggressive competitor or poor service on your part. We will look at market research methods in depth in Chapter 9.

Case study – Researching consumer needs

For Procter and Gamble (a major international manufacturer of detergent, personal care, cosmetic and food products), market research surveys are a way of life. In fact, they never stop. Over 200 000 customers respond to their questions each year, resulting in a research report nearly every day.

The changing patterns they reveal are fundamental to the firm's core business activities.

For example, in the immediate post-war years only 3% of households had any form of washing machine, and these were not automatic. Today over 80% have a washing machine, and automatic machines account for more than four out of every five machines bought. Sales of low-suds powders and liquids necessary for automatic washing machines grew for several years at a rate of around 20% each year.

Over the last 25 years the cotton content of the fabrics has halved, and today man-made fibres account for over half of fabrics sold. Around 80% of articles washed are coloured. In response, washing products have had to be developed which do not eventually bleach out colour and which wash as well or better at lower temperatures.

There has also been rapid change in the social patterns which affect the clothes-washing task. Today's variations across family sizes, occupations, leisure pursuits and so on are considerable. Sophisticated research techniques are required to build up an accurate picture of washing habits.

All of these different consumer needs have to be met by products which, though highly sophisticated and chemically complex, are easy and quick to use and relatively inexpensive. Only 20p of every £100 of household expenditure goes on washing products.

1 Describe briefly what has happened to the market for washing materials over the last 25 years.
2 Explain how market research helps Procter and Gamble to meet consumers' needs.
3 What might have happened to their core business activities if Procter and Gamble had not sufficiently researched the market?

Satisfying consumer requirements

The answer to the final question in the case study above is that failure to anticipate consumer requirements is likely to lead to falling sales, declining market share, loss of profits and loss of business. It is essential that businesses satisfy consumer requirements. At any given time consumers have a:

■ certain amount of income available for spending
■ given schedule of tastes and preferences.

However, both of these can and do change in the course of time. For example, a drastic change occurred in consumer spending with the arrival of the National Lottery at the end of 1994. By the start of 1995 the amount of money being spent on the National Lottery had made considerable inroads into average weekly household spending (Figure 8.23).

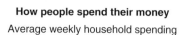

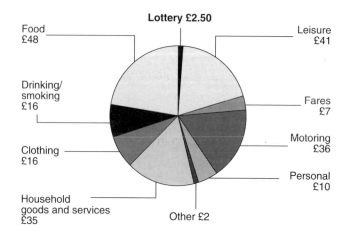

Source: Henley Centre

Figure 8.23 How people spent their money in 1995

Information like that shown in Figure 8.23 is of great importance to business organisations. For example, it can be seen that the average amount of money spent on leisure is £41. This figure has been rising in recent years, in contrast to money spent on cigarettes which has been falling.

The leisure market can be broken down into many different segments – such as health and fitness, sport and recreation, etc.

Marketing activities need to help an organisation to focus on the best ways of meeting the specific needs and requirements of particular groups of consumers. Marketing therefore needs to be a precise art. A precise understanding of the marketplace should translate into precise ways of meeting the needs of the market,which should underpin everything that an organisation does.

Case study – Mass customisation

Roy Westbrook and Peter Williamson have identified the latest stage in the process of sensitivity to customer requirements as being that of 'mass customisation'.

The authors identify the mid-1970s to the mid-1980s in Japan as being the period known as 'market in'. This involved cost savings through more efficient manufacturing coupled with adding features to standard products in order to increase demand.

However, by the late 1980s Japanese customers were again reaching saturation: 'They not only had most types of products, they now had a range of each. Worse still, the gadgets, bells and whistles were losing their novelty.' Product life-cycles were shortened.

A new strategy was therefore required for the 1990s – to personalise the product for each customer. This has involves responsive marketing to find out what customers need and coupling this with highly responsive production methods.

A good example is that of the Melbo company which makes customised suits, with a lead time of three days. You will not find the usual acres of racks, crammed with stock and occupying lots of expensive Toyko real estate. Instead the entire store carries fewer than a hundred suits, with a floor space requirement only a fraction of that needed by competitors. Melbo's customers do not come to fit themselves into a suit on the rack because the company's 'Ready Made Order System' will guarantee that a suit designed by houses like Givenchy, Daniel Hechter, or Nina Ricci, but individually cut and sewn to fit them, with a choice of over a hundred fabrics will arrive at their homes or offices within the week.

1 What do you understand by the term 'mass customisation'?
2 How is it likely to:
   a meet the requirements of consumers
   b benefit producers
   c lead to a more dynamic economy?
3 How is mass customisation likely to involve and influence the elements of the marketing mix?
4 Is mass customisation a way forward for all business organisations?

Managing the effects of change

All businesses operate within an environment of change. Some of these changes may be relatively slow, for example, a steady increase in population which may be predicted. Other changes may be rapid and dramatic, such as the sudden development of new technological processes, the entry of new competitors into a market or the fickleness of consumer demand.

The successful business needs to be able to anticipate and be ready for both types of change. Of course, it is the rapid shocks that are the most difficult to prepare for. The key is to build a flexible organisation which can quickly adjust to new changes.

Evidence collection point

Make a list of five rapid changes and five relatively slow changes which are taking place in the environment of a business with which you are familiar. What can a business do to anticipate and respond to these changes?

Evidence collection point

Here is a useful activity which will enable you to show evidence that you can analyse marketing activities in business organisations. It involves creating a SWOT analysis to analyse changes in the marketing environment in which a business operates, and then going on to devise marketing activities to take the organisation forward.

The task is best tackled by a group. It involves looking closely at a particular product, finding an appropriate market and deciding how to sell the product in that market. Your work on this project can provide evidence of Core Skills in Communications, Application of Number and Information Technology.

Introduction
At one time the privatised electricity companies had their own retail outlets selling electrical appliances. Today these have been sold off to independent concerns.

In this activity you are asked to help a manufacturer to promote one of its popular products – either cordless kettles or satellite dishes – which will be sold through independent retail outlets.

First you must do a SWOT analysis of one of the products. Then you must decide who you are going to sell the product to and how you will reach them. Lastly, you may like to produce a creative advertisement for the product.

What is a SWOT?
SWOT stands for

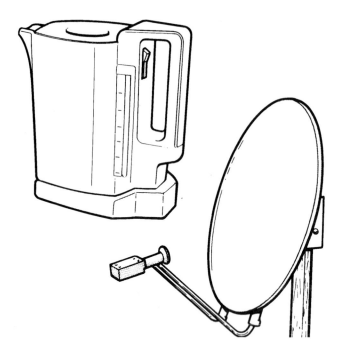

- Strengths
- Weaknesses
- Opportunities
- Threats

when you are marketing a product you should work out what are its strengths and weaknesses – then try to work out what are the opportunities that will help you to promote the product and the threats likely to be faced by your product in the near future.

For example, if Rowntree wanted to do a SWOT analysis of its product Smarties, it might say:

- Its *strengths* include the fact that everyone knows what a Smartie is: children love the different colours; they are not expensive; the packets look attractive in the shop; and so on.
- Its weaknesses might include that they are primarily a children's sweet, rather than for adults; they have been around a long time (perhaps people are getting bored with them).
- Its opportunities are that new European markets for Smarties are opening up, not just in the European Union but also in Poland, Hungary and so on; blue Smarties are new and exciting.
- Its threats might include the wide range of new sweets being sold; the arrival of M&Ms and the competition from European chocolate manufacturers; and so on.

What Rowntree needs to do then is to promote and improve strengths, play down and cut out weaknesses,

make the most of opportunities, and be aware of and respond to threats.

Do your SWOT analysis

Do your SWOT analysis for the manufacturer of cordless kettles or satellite dishes. Can you list three strengths, three weaknesses, three opportunities and three threats?

Decide how you will:

- maximise the strengths
- minimise the weaknesses
- make the most of the opportunities
- reduce the threats.

Use the SWOT analysis sheet to do this.

SWOT ANALYSIS	
PRODUCT _____	
STRENGTHS	WEAKNESSES
OPPORTUNITIES	THREATS

Who are you selling to?

You need to be able to identify your target market. This is the group of people you think will be interested in your product or service and who have the money to spend on it.

- Try to identify the target audience for your chosen product. You will probably target two or three groups to concentrate on. An example of a target group might be single women in the 18–24 year age-group on high income. Clearly you will be best placed to target an appropriate group if you do some original research of your own to find out which age group primarily makes the buying decision in households for these products.
- What type of media will be most suitable for reaching the target audience you have chosen?

Guidelines for promotions

To help you choose the most effective media for your

TARGET CUSTOMERS
PRODUCT ___

STATUS	AGE	INCOME H – HIGH L – LOW	TARGET AUDIENCE	SUITABLE MEDIA
MALE (MARRIED) NO CHILDREN	18–24	H / L		
	25–45	H / L		
	OVER 45	H / L		
FEMALE (MARRIED) NO CHILDREN	18–24	H / L		
	25–45	H / L		
	OVER 45	H / L		
MALE (MARRIED) + CHILDREN	18–24	H / L		
	25–45	H / L		
	OVER 45	H / L		
FEMALE (MARRIED) + CHILDREN	18–24	H / L		
	25–45	H / L		
	OVER 45	H / L		
MALE SINGLE	18–24	H / L		
	25–45	H / L		
	OVER 45	H / L		
FEMALE SINGLE	18–24	H / L		
	25–45	H / L		
	OVER 45	H / L		

MEDIA PLAN
PRODUCT ___

MEDIA			£COST	JAN	FEB	MAR	APR	MAY	JUN	JUL	AUG	SEP	OCT	NOV	DEC	SUB-TOTAL COSTS	COMMENTS
TELEVISION (CENTRAL AREA)	30 SECOND TV COMMERCIAL	OFF PEAK	600														
	OCT, NOV, DEC, MAR, APR, MAY	ON PEAK	4,000														
	30 SECOND TV COMMERCIAL	OFF PEAK	400														
	JAN, FEB, JUN JUL, AUG, SEP	ON PEAK	3,000														
LOCAL RADIO	30 SECOND SPOT		100														
NATIONAL PRESS	ONE INSERTION PER NEWSPAPER		5,000														
LOCAL PRESS	ONE INSERTION PER NEWSPAPER		500														
FREE TRADE PRESS	ONE INSERTION PER NEWSPAPER		200														
ELECTRICITY ACCOUNT INSERTS	ONE FOR EACH DOMESTIC CUSTOMER PER QUARTER		30,000														
DIRECT MAILING	1000 PACKAGES DELIVERED BY THE POST OFFICE (SELECTED AREAS)		450														
	1000 PACKAGES HAND-DELIVERED (SELECTED AREAS)		300														
TELEPHONE SALES	PER HUNDRED CALLS		10														
EXHIBITIONS	SMALL		250														
	MEDIUM		1,500														
	LARGE		4,000														
LEAFLETS	PER THOUSAND		250														
SHOP DISPLAYS	76 SHOPS		10,000														

233

promotions, consider the following guidelines. You will have detailed costs of these media outlets, and you should make a sensible selection to suit your chosen product.

This will be your media plan. (Use the 'Target Customers' sheet and 'Media Plan' sheet when making your decisions.)

Considerations when choosing appropriate media:

- *Television* In order to have a meaningful TV campaign you need at least ten on-peak and twenty off-peak spots in any one month. Some months are cheaper than others. Do you feel that spots during particular programmes are more desirable (e.g. *Neighbours, EastEnders*?)
- *Local radio* For maximum effectiveness you need 50 spots per month. This medium is particularly effective with the 16–25-year age-group and has high listening ratings during 'drive time'.
- *Press* Which newspapers and magazines would you use?
- *Electricity account inserts* Each quarter of the year millions of electricity company customers receive an electricity bill, nationwide. This provides an excellent opportunity to include promotional literature. Electricity companies would be keen to participate because the products are complementary.
- *Direct mailing* This is an excellent means of communicating with small customer groups (e.g. recent purchasers of cars, videos, microwave cookers) whose addresses can be readily obtained from existing sources. Direct mail can also be hand delivered. This will not be personally addressed, but posted through letter-boxes of everyone in a selected area. The method is therefore suitable for products that have a wider appeal.
- *Telephone sales* A member of staff is employed to phone direct to the customer.
- *Shop display* Adverts could be placed in shops selling these goods.
- *Exhibitions* The company may take part in local or national exhibitions, building its own stands, staffed by trained advisers who can promote the appliances.
- *Leaflets* These are a very useful promotional aid which a potential customer can take home, to help them to decide whether to buy after visiting a shop or an exhibition.

Producing a creative advertisement
Can you, as a group, produce an advertisement for a newspaper or magazine?

Preparing a media plan
Now that you have a clear idea about who your customers are you should prepare a media plan for the next 12 months. You can either do this on a copy of the 'Media Plan' sheet or set out your media plan on a spreadsheet.

Here are your media guidelines.

You have a budget of £750 000 to spend over 12 months.

If the campaign is going to be a success you will need to use several different types of promotion. You would almost certainly use the power of television as part of your campaign. Show on your chart or spreadsheet:

- during which months you will spend your money
- how much you will spend.

Remember to put in your sub-totals. Your total spending should not exceed £750 000.

Finally, you need to produce a creative advertisement. How will you present your ideas?

To finish off this activity you will do a presentation to the rest of your class. This presentation should be rounded off by a creative advertisement – a poster, a video, a talk, or some other creative advert.

The presentation will be divided up as follows:

2 minutes	To set up
2 minutes	To explain your SWOT analysis and to discuss your media plan, explaining how it will effectively communicate with your target customers
4 minutes	To present your creative execution in any way, shape or form, using chosen media
2 minutes	To pack away.

You should explain during your four-minute presentation how you would expect to maximise the product's strengths and overcome the weaknesses which you have identified in the SWOT analysis.

You should also indicate how your presentation relates to the target audience you have previously identified.

Points to consider:

- Do I need a personality? If so who?
- Do I need music? If so, what type?
- Do I need any promotional offers, e.g. interest-free credit, buy now pay later?
- How do I make it interesting, amusing, memorable, credible and original?

Managing the effects of competition

An organisation must at all times be aware of its competitors and the nature of what they are doing. There is competition when two or more organisations act independently to sell their products to the same group of consumers.

In some markets there may be a lot of competition, signified by an abundance of products and services so that consumers have a massive choice. These markets are characterised by promotional activities and price competition.

In other markets, competition is limited and consumers are able to choose from a limited range of products and services on offer – perhaps only one.

Direct competition exists where organisations produce similar products and appeal to the same group of consumers. The *Daily Star* directly competes with the *Sun;* and if you want to have a wall built, all the builders in your area looking for this type of work are in direct competition.

Even when an organisation provides a unique end-product with no direct competition, it still has to consider indirect competition. Potential customers might examine slightly different ways of meeting the same need. Instead of buying a car they might buy a moped; instead of buying a bag of sweets they could buy a box of chocolates from a different supplier.

It is frequently argued that competition is good for consumers and organisations alike. Organisations have to become more efficient and offer better products at prices acceptable to the market.

Marketing plays a key role in ensuring that organisations manage the effects of competition.

Case study – Getting rid of check-outs

It is possible that in the near future at least two-thirds of retailing jobs could go. Most of the main British supermarket chains, including Sainsbury's, the market leader, are considering replacing check-outs with do-it-yourself versions in which customers use hand-held laser scanners. This could cut costs and queues. It is believed that the first British trials will start in 1995. The system is currently being tried in the Netherlands.

Customers are given a magnetic identity card which is swiped through a rack to release a scanner the size of a mobile phone. The customer checks each item directly into a shopping bag and returns the scanner to a recharging bank, where the bill is printed, to be paid at an express check-out. There is no unloading or reloading of goods, less queuing and, if the customer pays by credit or store card, no need to go near the check-out.

Instead of having 40 people at tills ringing things up, there might just be five taking the cash.

1 What might be the effects of this new system on the cost of running a supermarket?
2 What are the implications for prices charged?
3 Why might supermarket chains need to adopt the new system?
4 What are the dangers of not adopting the new system?

The coordinating role of marketing

Creating a marketing plan for an organisation starts at a strategic level. In addition, it is also essential to plan carefully the tools and tactics of marketing. The various units involved in marketing will develop realistic plans setting out priorities and control mechanisms, as well as ways of evaluating the effectiveness of marketing.

The marketing plan will include plans for the following:

- Product mix
- Pricing
- Distribution
- Promotion.
- Market research
- Sales
- Advertising

The product mix plan

An internal audit of the current product mix involves listing the products and examining their performance over a period of years in order to identify trends.

The organisation will need to identify products that should be phased out, which should be modified, and which new products should enter the portfolio and at what time.

The pricing plan

A starting point will be to evaluate the quality of previous pricing decisions. It will then be necessary to assess the sensitivity of the market to price alterations in order to decide on the best price for different price segments. It will be important to assess what the competition is likely to do.

The physical distribution plan

Creating effective distribution channels will be critical in giving an organisation a competitive edge.

The promotional plan

In many large companies, promotions are tied to the life-cycle of the product. Promotional activity will be required at launch and periodically to inject new life into a product.

The market research plan

Market research planning is particularly important for products whose nature and market are constantly changing. The market research plan will cover three main areas:

- gathering of market data
- constant checking on performance in the marketplace and on the performance of competitors
- regularly testing products, markets, operations and ideas.

The sales plan

Many organisations will also have a discrete sales plan. This will set out targets and intended activities for the sales function in areas such as customer services and sales penetration.

The advertising plan

Large organisations may also have advertising plans which are separate from other promotional plans. However, the two will clearly need to complement each other. The advertising plan will contain details of which media to concentrate on, how to allocate the advertising budget, the type of audience to be reached, procedures for tracking the success of campaigns and other features.

Of course, planning will be ineffective without controls. For example, ratios will be used to assess performance on an ongoing basis. By monitoring performance against these ratios and other control measures an organisation will be able to adjust its performance in an appropriate way.

For example, if an organisation establishes a control ratio for distribution effectiveness and finds that the ratio is deteriorating then it will be able to take remedial actions.

Evidence collection point

Explain why planning and control is an important part of marketing activity.

Generating maximum income and/or profit

Income is generated by an organisation through selling goods and services to final consumers. It is all very well having the best product in the world but if nobody knows about it then you are unlikely to make a lot of income or profit.

Selling can be one of the most difficult of all business activities. Sometimes people in this country are not very good at selling themselves or their products. We are shy about saying 'I (or we) have come up with a great product which I think you will get a lot of benefit out of'.

Selling effectively involves finding and using the appropriate selling channels to get product messages and products to the end consumer. Selling involves finding out when and where people are most likely to buy products, how they like them to be presented and packaged, etc. Selling involves actually getting the product to the consumer, and taking in the sales revenue that makes up the income of the organisation.

Sometimes people tend to shun selling activities. They don't want to be seen to 'act like a salesman or saleswoman'. However, without this essential activity businesses would soon go under. If individuals have confidence and belief in products and services they should be prepared to 'sell' them.

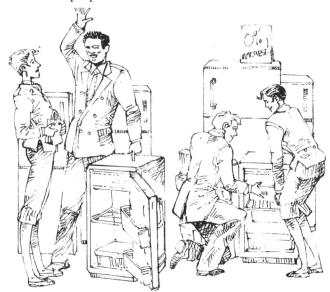

Selling should not be confused with dishonest activity. Selling is about communicating genuine benefits to people. Selling is looked at in much greater detail in Chapter 11.

 Evidence collection point

Choose a particular product which you feel provides genuine benefits to people. Highlight the main benefits of the product which you would be prepared to 'sell' to other people. What would be the best channels for selling the product? Would you feel comfortable in selling the product that you have chosen?

Optimising customer perception of organisations and/or products

We have already mentioned the importance of optimising customer perceptions (see page 37). What finally determines whether people buy a particular product or service depends on a variety of factors. First, obviously, is whether the product fits the needs of the prospective customer. If it does, other factors must come into play before the product is bought.

One factor is immediate need. For example, the immediate need of a motorist might be, 'the car's running out of petrol'. Another is common-sense and logic ('everyone's hungry so we must stop at the first service station that sells food'). If there is a choice between products that offer identical performance at identical prices, then 'image' ('I just feel happier dealing with that company and buying that product') becomes an important factor.

Today customer services is more important than ever before. Simply saying 'have a nice day' is not sufficient. Customers need to feel that they are being treated as individuals. The hairdresser who can remember personal details of a customer and how they feel about their hair is likely to be a success. The bartender who remembers the names of customers and what drinks they like is likely to attract business. Service is thus a key ingredient in giving competitive edge.

In addition, marketing communications (as we shall see in Chapter 10) are vital in communicating information to targeted groups of consumers through advertising, point-of-sale literature, etc.

Evidence collection point

Describe one example of how:
1 customer service
2 marketing communications

can help to optimise consumer perceptions of an organisation or product.

Perhaps using your own experience you will be able to recount positive experiences of organisations or products, e.g. a hotel you have visited, or a holiday company that you have used.

Growth of organisations

In this section we will briefly look at the growth of profit-making and not-for-profit organisations in terms of product development, and through markets.

Both profit and not-for-profit organisations need to have a marketing philosophy. There is no point in having a charitable organisation that is not there to serve its consumers. If they failed to serve consumers, who would they be seeking to serve? Doing good implies that you do good for someone who wants and needs help. It is therefore essential to find out the wants and needs of consumers of charitable and other not-for-profit products and services.

When we are looking at the growth of organisations, we are concerned therefore with the growth of all market-conscious organisations. You will need to carry out some research at the end of this chapter into ways in which profit and not-for-profit organisations carry out marketing activities.

Product development

The UK has always had a reputation for producing brilliant ideas but is generally regarded as failing to turn them into reality. Doing so usually implies that the good ideas are put into effect using innovative productive strategies, but that is not enough on its own. Someone – or some people – must have the vision to see that the product will be a success, be willing to take the risks involved, and be able to raise the necessary finance. Finally, the management team must have the organisational skills to make the whole process profitable.

There are a number of stages that can be identified in the preparation for launching a new product (Figure 8.24).

237

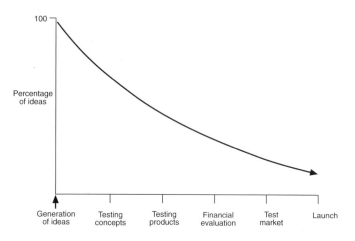

Figure 8.24 Stages in launching a new product

As new ideas and product development go through successive stages, unsuccessful ones are eliminated.

Testing a concept will involve trying to make sure that the product designs will succeed in the market-place. The following questions will need to be answered:

■ What benefits does this product offer?
■ How will it appeal to the consumer?
■ Does the product meet the needs of the market?
■ How could the idea be improved?
■ How long would demand last for such a product?

Testing the product will involve developing a model or prototype and then trying to see if it matches consumer needs. The objective at this stage is to understand areas such as:

■ quality, performance and safety
■ ensuring that the product works efficiently
■ ensuring that the product is aesthetically sound and that its appearance is pleasing to consumers
■ how to produce it economically
■ planned obsolescence (so that the product will need replacing after a given period of time)
■ the ingredients of the marketing mix.

In certain cases it may be worthwhile for a company to apply for a patent, which is a legal protection giving the firm the exclusive right to produce and sell a given item.

The financial evaluation of a new product's potential is essential for assessing whether or not it will ultimately generate profits. Techniques of investment appraisal, and cost–volume–profit predictions using costing techniques, are essential at this stage.

Predictions of sales, investments, costs and selling prices have to be made. A major difficulty at this stage is the reliability of data. Prediction always carries an element of risk.

A test market involves setting up a market situation that is as near to the real market as possible. Through this situation, the new product can be given a 'dry run' and the experience gained used to reduce the risks of the full launch. A test market also measures consumer behaviour in a real situation and provides valuable information which can be used to develop the marketing mix.

When a Japanese manufacturer wants to find out about changing consumer tastes and fashions, it will sometimes open a shop or restaurant where new product and service ideas can be tested and consumer responses monitored. Called 'antenna' shops because they are used both to 'broadcast' ideas from the manufacturer and to 'receive' ideas from consumers, they are concentrated in the fashionable districts of Tokyo and other major cities.

For Nissui, Japan's largest fishery company, the problem was that fish was becoming unfashionable among young Japanese, many of whom thought it smelly and unappealing. To counteract this trend, Nissui developed new fish products for modern tastes, such as frozen tempura and fresh frozen oysters. Spicy red chilli peppers were added to liven up canned fish, and ranges of fish hors d'oeuvre garnished with mustard relishes were launched. To taste-test its new ranges and to explore how the Japanese could be wooed back, the company opened up a number of 'antenna' restaurants, flying in fresh fish from around the world to try to start new food fashions.

The launch is the time when the product is presented to the market and is exposed to the ultimate critical test. Ideally, the launch will create an awareness of the product, followed by an interest in it and then a desire to purchase.

Product development therefore involves a number of important steps starting with the original research and innovation.

Some research is not expected to pay for itself within a foreseeable time-span. Large companies may allocate as much as one-tenth of their research budget to so-called blue-sky investigations whose most likely contribution is to the development of new products and a possible pay-off in the distant future.

In the course of development, products may need to be modified several times before they are finally regarded as suitable. Technological breakthrough involves making major strides forward which take products, or processes, to the stage at which they make new advances in product development.

Evidence collection point

Outline the major stages which were involved in the development of a new product which you are familiar with, or which you have researched.

Markets

In examining the life-cycle of a product we saw that products go through various stages from infancy to decline.

New markets arise from time to time, which gradually expand, sometimes to compete with or replace existing markets. For example, the traditional British holiday market lost a lot of ground in the 1970s and early 1980s as many people began to transfer their allegiance to Spanish resorts such as Benidorm. In more recent times people have looked further afield to West Africa, the Canaries, the West Indies and many other holiday destinations.

Changing market structures create new market opportunities. Business organisations thrive on spotting gaps in the market and opportunities for profits. In the 1980s 'niche marketing' became popular as companies like Tie Rack, The Body Shop, The Sock Shop and others spotted new market opportunities giving them scope for development in the marketplace.

Market share is important to business organisations. The Boston Consultancy Group have argued that the faster the growth of a particular market the greater the costs necessary to maintain position. In a rapidly growing market, considerable expenditure will be required on investment in product lines, and to combat the threat posed by new firms and brands.

The Boston Group developed 'The Boston Box', which relates closely to the product life-cycle. They identify four types of products in an organisation's portfolio (Figure 8.25). 'Problem children' are products that have just been launched. This is an appropriate name because many products fail to move beyond this phase. Such products are often referred to as *question marks*. Is it possible to develop these products and turn them into the 'stars' and 'cash cows' of the future? It might be, but first they will require a lot of financial support and will represent a heavy financial commitment.

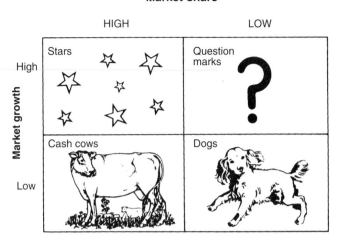

Figure 8.25 The Boston Box

Stars are products that have successfully reached the growth stage in the life-cycle. Although these products too will require a lot of financial support, they will also provide high cash returns. On balance, they will provide a neutral cash flow and are good 'prospects' for the future.

Cash cows have reached the maturity stage in their product life-cycle and are now 'yielders'. They have a high market share in markets that are no longer rapidly expanding. Because the market is relatively static, they require few fresh injections of capital; for example, advertising and promotion may be required to inject a little fresh life from time to time. However, the net effect is of a positive cash flow. Cash generated by the cash cows may be used to help the question marks.

Dogs are products in decline. These have a low market share in a low-growing or declining market. As they begin to generate a negative cash flow, they will usually be disposed of.

Evidence collection point

Using your own experience of a product portfolio provided by an organisation, identify its:

■ Question marks
■ Stars
■ Cash cows
■ Dogs

In each case explain what evidence you have for drawing the conclusions you make.

In order to maintain an effective portfolio development, it is important to have a balance of products at any one time. An organisation will require a number of cash cows to provide its 'bread and butter'. At the same time, it is important to develop the cash cows of the future by investing in the question marks. Fortunately, the stars should pay their own way. It is also important to identify the dogs and cut them out.

Products in the top half of the Boston Box are in the earlier stage of the product life-cycle and so are in high-growth markets. Those in the lower half of the box are in the later stages and so are in markets where growth will have slowed down or even stopped.

Ansoff has developed this theory further by outlining a product–market mix. This looks not just at the management of a product portfolio but also more widely at market developments and opportunities. Ansoff's matrix matches existing and new product strategies with existing and new markets (Figure 8.26).

Product / Market	Existing products		New products
Existing markets	Consolidation	Market penetration	Product development
New markets	Market development		Diversification

Figure 8.26 Ansoff's product–market matrix

In this way, his matrix suggests five alternative marketing strategies which hinge upon whether the product is new or existing and whether the market is new or existing.

- *Consolidation* implies a positive and active defence of existing products in existing markets.
- *Market penetration* suggests a further penetration of existing markets with existing products. This will involve a strategy of increasing market share within existing segments and markets.
- *Product development* involves developing new products for existing markets.
- *Market development* entails using existing products and finding new markets for them. These new markets will be identified by better targeting, market research and further segmentation.
- *Diversification* will lead to a movement away from core activities. This might involve some form of integration of production into related activities.

Evidence indicators

For this element you will need to record a discussion about marketing principles and marketing functions with supporting notes which explain how the principles identified underpin the marketing functions. The discussion and supporting notes should explain the ways in which business organisations manage to balance the interests of customers with the interests of their own organisation.

You also should produce a report which analyses marketing activities in two contrasting business organisations, one profit-making and the other not-for-profit. The introduction should explain how both organisations achieved growth using both product development and market development. The report should focus on how the businesses assess market needs by marketing research and how this information is used by marketing personnel. The report should conclude with an analysis of the marketing and selling activities used by both organisations to generate maximum income and where appropriate to maximise profit.

This work should enable you to produce evidence of using Core Skills in Information Technology, Application of Number and Communication.

You need to be able to confirm that:

- I have produced a record of a discussion about marketing principles and marketing functions. ☐
- This record is complemented by supporting notes which explain how marketing principles underpin marketing functions. ☐
- This evidence explains ways in which businesses balance the interests of the consumer and the organisation. ☐
- I have produced a report which analyses marketing activities in two contrasting business organisations (one profit-making and one not-for-profit). ☐
- I have explained how both organisations achieved growth using both product development and market development. ☐
- The report focuses on how the businesses assess market needs by marketing research and how this information is used by marketing personnel. ☐
- The report analyses ways in which marketing and selling activities generate maximum income and, where appropriate, maximise profit. ☐

The role of market research in identifying and monitoring markets and developing products

Business activities, by their very nature, are competitive. Within a dynamic business environment producers may be constantly entering and leaving the market. At the same time, changing customer preferences may provide signals for them to develop new strategies with different products and services. Whereas some organisations will succeed and achieve or surpass their marketing objectives, others will inevitably not perform as well.

So how does market research help? All organisational activities take place in an environment of risk. To reduce risk, market research provides an invaluable source of information to help organisations make decisions and develop strategies for products. For example, it will help them to:

- identify their competitors
- improve their knowledge of consumers and competitors so that changing trends can be identified
- use trends to forecast activities
- monitor their market position and develop plans and strategies
- improve their competitive advantages.

In this chapter we look at the importance of market research and its contribution to key marketing decisions about products in the marketplace.

Market research methods and their suitability for selected products

Case study – What do customers really want?

Corky Ra is an entrepreneur who likes a challenge and feels that he knows what his customers really require. In the 1970s he bet his father that he could open a vineyard in Utah, the American state where the mainly Mormon population consider drink and the devil to be cousins. He won his wager by building a 12-metre-high pyramid in Salt Lake City, making sacramental wine in it, and selling the produce to religious groups.

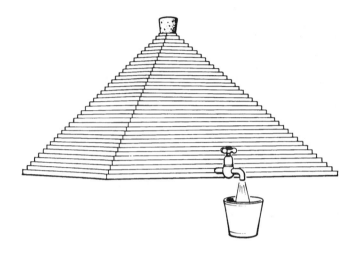

Seeking to diversify, Mr Ra moved into an industry ripe for some innovative marketing – the funeral business. Until his company arrived, burial and cremation were the two choices, but his research indicated that some potential 'clients' wanted something different – they wanted a way of preserving their remains so that they could be remembered.

Mr Ra's answer was a type of mummification. For around $700 clients can be pickled for eternity. Another $26 000 buys a bronze sarcophagus filled with an inert gas which does not allow body-eating bacteria to survive. One client has even specified a bejewelled interment costing $150 000. To help offset the expenses to customers, Mr Ra has managed to persuade the UK tax authorities that, unlike conventional funerals, mummification funerals should be tax-deductible.

There is, however, a snag – none of his clients has yet died. So far only his dog and cat have succumbed and sit mummified in his headquarters!

1 To what extent was it important for Corky Ra to find out what his customers really wanted?
2 What does 'Mr Ra moved into an industry ripe for some innovative marketing' mean?
3 Working in groups if possible, try to identify a good or service that does not appear to be offered by any organisation. Discuss your findings with other groups.

All organisations require answers to key questions. Answers will help decision-makers to understand the nature of the decisions they have to make about the products they provide and the markets in which they operate.

Questions may include:

- *How do we define the market?* What are its key features such as size and character, and what is the nature of competition?
- *What do customers require?* At the heart of marketing should be the ongoing activities of satisfying the needs and aspirations of customers.
- *Who are the target groups and how do we reach them?* The market may be made up of different groups and segments. Different distribution channels may be used to reach different groups of customers.
- *What strategies are used by our competitors?* It is important to know and understand how the actions of competitors might influence the market.
- *How do we measure our performance?* Market performance may be measured according to a number of key criteria, such as the value or volume of sales as well as brand or market share.
- *Where is our competitive position?* An important feature of marketing analysis is an ongoing review of where the organisation is within the market, its competitive advantage and how changes in its actions might influence market shape and market share.

In his statement to shareholders in the IBM Annual Report of 1993, Louis Gerstner wrote: 'no company is going to succeed without a clear set of tough-minded strategies grounded in a clear understanding of what's happening in the marketplace.' This simple statement helps to emphasise that, when planning ahead, although market research will not eliminate the risks associated with being in business, it will help to reduce them. The purpose of market research, therefore, is to provide information that cuts out unsubstantiated guesswork and hunches.

Marketing research methods

One of the most important things to remember is that what comes out of the market research is only as good as what goes in. Identifying the information required, successfully choosing the most suitable market research method and then the type and nature of the questioning should all be carefully considered before any project proceeds.

There are a number of different market research methods. The main ones are as follows.

Interview

Most interview techniques allow face-to-face contact between a researcher and a respondent. Interviews may allow an experienced researcher to glean more detailed and sensitive information. Interviews may also be flexible, and so gestures, facial expressions and other signs may be noted.

An interview with someone in a street is likely to be less friendly than a group interview in a home. A street interview is brief, impersonal and uses a broadly defined group of respondents, whereas a home discussion can be exactly the opposite – detailed, personal and with a tightly defined group of people.

One problem with face-to-face interviews is that, because of the nature of the interaction between the interviewer and the respondent, there is the risk that some of the answers become biased.

Evidence collection point

Find out the hobbies or leisure pursuits of people in your teaching group by briefly interviewing each of them. Present your results. Did you encounter any problems conducting your interview? Describe what these were. Look further at the other market research methods we cover; would any of these have been more suitable for obtaining the information you required? This work will provide evidence of Core Skills in Communication.

Observation

This involves looking at how consumers behave. For example, how do consumers behave when out shopping? Information like this can help to make decisions about packaging or influence the choice of point-of-sale materials designed to attract the attention of shoppers. It may also help to make decisions about where to place particular products in a shop – the process of putting products in a shop in the right place at the right time is known as *merchandising*. This is particularly important in the retail trade.

Today a number of sophisticated electronic devices can be used to monitor individual responses.

- A psycho-galvanometer measures perspiration and this may be used for a variety of forms of testing.

- An eye camera may record reactions such as visual stimulation.
- A tachistoscope exposes material for a short period and then measures responses.

Evidence collection point

Explain why the owners of small businesses are likely to know more about the behaviour of their customers than owners of large businesses. Briefly explain how they might use this information.

Questionnaire

Many of the other market research methods depend upon the use of a questionnaire as a form of data collection. A questionnaire is a systematic list of questions designed to obtain information from people about:

- specific events
- their attitudes
- their values
- their beliefs.

Questionnaire design is critical. Although it is easy to make up questions, it is very difficult to produce a good questionnaire – and a badly designed questionnaire may lead to biased results.

Another problem may arise if very few completed forms are returned, or if those returned are only partially completed. In addition, if the questionnaire is being administered by an interviewer's, there is always the danger that the interviewer may misinterpret the question and introduce his or her own personal bias in a way that prompts certain answers from respondents.

A good questionnaire will:

- ask questions which relate directly to information needs
- not ask too many questions
- not ask leading or intimate questions
- fit questions into a logical sequence
- use the language of the target group
- not use questions that are ambiguous
- avoid sexuality, politics and religion unless they are very relevant.

Sequencing the questions logically is very important. It may be useful to start with a few factual questions which are easy to respond to. These may be followed up by some form of multiple-choice questions before introducing questions that require the respondent to think about the issues being researched. The questionnaire may be closed with 'filter questions', which help to locate the respondent in the sampling frame.

The questions in a questionnaire may be 'open' or 'closed'. *Open questions* allow the person answering to give an opinion and may encourage him or her to talk at length. *Closed questions* usually require an answer picked from a range of options (which may be simply yes/no). Most questionnaires use closed questions, so that they can be answered quickly and efficiently, and the answers are easier to analyse (Figure 9.1).

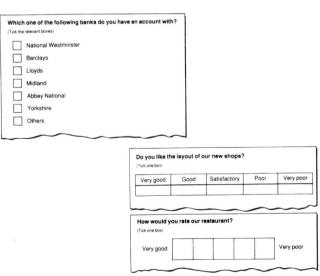

Figure 9.1 Three examples of closed questions

The purpose of a closed question is to get people to commit themselves to a concrete answer. The problem with open questions is that they are difficult to analyse. Closed questions tie respondents down so that they have to make a decision within a range of choices.

Task

Think back to any questionnaire or form which you have recently had to answer. (If necessary use your course enrolment form as an example.) What was the purpose of the questionnaire? Was it simple and easy to understand? Do you feel that this was well designed? If not, why not?

To help interviewers operate a questionnaire, sometimes a *prompt card* is used. This means that, if several or all of the questions in the questionnaire have the same range or set of answers, these can be numbered and then the respondents' answers can be recorded as numbers (Figure 9.2).

National Westminster	01
Barclays	02
Lloyds	03
Midland	04
Abbey National	05
Yorkshire	06
Others	07

Figure 9.2 An interviewer's prompt card

Some questionnaires are designed so that respondents can concentrate on the questions that are relevant, and then skip over questions which do not relate to them (Figure 9.3)

Question 1 **Do you have a bank account?**

☐ YES

☐ NO

If your answer is no proceed straight to question 20.

Figure 9.3 An example of a 'skip'

Evidence collection point

Collect questionnaires. Perhaps a good place to start is by obtaining a copy of your enrolment form. Collect any customer service or market research questionnaires that you or members of your family receive through the post. As you collect each questionnaire, comment briefly upon what you think each is trying to achieve, and describe the structure of each research activity.

Case study – The National Motoring Survey

In spring 1995, the National Motoring Survey was undertaken. The survey offered a series of prizes for respondents who filled in the questionnaire. A number of organisations sponsored questions within the questionnaire; for example, Imperial Tobacco Q57-63, First Direct Q44, Hidden Hearing Q40, Alliance & Leicester Personal Finance Ltd Q47, The Insurance Service plc Q25-30, 33 35, Vauxhall Motors Ltd Q13, 23 24. Read through the questionnaire and then answer the questions that follow.

1 Stating specific examples, explain how the answers provided to questions in the questionnaire will help organisations sponsoring questions to market their products.
2 Comment upon the nature of the questions (open/closed, easy to understand, etc.).
3 How easy (or difficult) would it be to analyse information from the questionnaire?
4 How would you suggest that this information be recorded?
5 Why is a prize draw used to encourage respondents to fill in and reply to the questionnaire? Discuss any alternative ways of encouraging a favourable response. Your work should demonstrate Core Skills in Communication.

Survey

Surveys are one of the most common ways used to collect market research information. They involve using one of the market research methods such as the various types of interviews to find out how respondents react to a range of issues often contained within a questionnaire.

There are two types of survey: a census and a sample. A *census* involves questioning a particular market. However, unless the market is very small this is unlikely to be practicable. Taking a *sample* involves

WIN OUR EXCLUSIVE PRIZE DRAW
BY PARTICIPATING IN THE NATIONAL MOTORING SURVEY

Dear Motorist,

Your opinions really CAN make a difference. Manufacturers and Motoring organisations need to understand who today's motorists are and what they want.

The information you provide will be held by CMT Ltd and safeguarded under the Data Protection Act. CMT uses your answers for market research and analysis purposes which will determine the offers you receive. CMT may make your responses available to other reputable companies who may wish to contact you with offers of goods and services. You can choose not to receive special offers by ticking the box on page 3.

As a thank you for completing and returning your survey you will be automatically entered into our motoring prize draw. If you don't want to answer that's OK - just skip to the next question!

Thank you for your valued help.

Ian McKenzie

Ian McKenzie, Research Director

EXAMPLE: Do you watch TV? 1 ☑ Yes 9 ☐ No

PLEASE REPLY WITHIN 14 DAYS

PLEASE PRINT

Your Surname: ____

First Name: ____   Partner's First Name: ____

Mr. 1 ☐   Mrs. 2 ☐   Miss 3 ☐   Ms. 4 ☐

Address: ____

Town: ____

County: ____   Post Code: ____

This questionnaire is divided into two main sections. The first section is specifically about Motoring and the second section relates to you and your lifestyle. All of this information will enable leading companies to produce a full picture of today's motorist.

1 Why do you drive?
1 ☐ To get to work   4 ☐ To get to shops
2 ☐ For leisure   5 ☐ Take children to school
3 ☐ For work   6 ☐ Other

2 Where do you do most of your driving? (Tick all that apply)
1 ☐ On Motorway   3 ☐ In the Country
2 ☐ In Town/Village   4 ☐ In Cities

3 Do you think the current motorway speed limit (70mph) is:
1 ☐ Too high   3 ☐ Acceptable
2 ☐ Too low

4 Do you agree that Motorway Tolls should be introduced in the UK?
1 ☐ Yes   9 ☐ No

5 When choosing a new car what are the most important factors you look for? (Tick all that apply)
01 ☐ Price   06 ☐ Style
02 ☐ Safety features 07 ☐ Environmentally friendly
03 ☐ Power   08 ☐ Extras
04 ☐ Economy (MPG) 09 ☐ Performance
05 ☐ Insurance Group 10 ☐ Others

6 If you could afford to buy and run any car what car would you choose?
Make ____   Model ____

7 Which petrol stations do you use most often?
01 ☐ BP   06 ☐ Jet   10 ☐ Shell
02 ☐ Esso   07 ☐ Mobil 11 ☐ Burmah
03 ☐ Fina   08 ☐ Q8   12 ☐ Texaco
04 ☐ Elf   09 ☐ Gulf 13 ☐ Other
05 ☐ Supermarket/Hypermarket

8 If you collect tokens/points please write the number of the company from Q.7 ____

9 What is the reason for choosing the petrol station you visit most often:-
1 ☐ It's on my regular route 5 ☐ Collect tokens
2 ☐ It's close to home   6 ☐ Friendly services
3 ☐ Price of petrol   7 ☐ Car wash
4 ☐ Shop facilities

10 When visiting your petrol station which of the following do you use:-
1 ☐ Car wash   4 ☐ Car Vac
2 ☐ Shop   5 ☐ Air
3 ☐ Water   6 ☐ Other

---

11 Besides cost what do you believe is the most important thing manufacturers need to do to improve their cars?
____

12 In your opinion what is the most important Act the government should pass to relieve congestion on the roads?
____

13 If you have a company car, can you:
Choose the make/model 1 ☐ Yes 3 ☐ No
Choose a Vauxhall   2 ☐ Yes 4 ☐ No

14 What in your opinion are the most key motoring safety issues the Government/manufacturers need to address? (Please tick a maximum of three)
1 ☐ A more rigorous test (including M-way driving)
2 ☐ Retests for banned drivers/dangerous driving convictions
3 ☐ Increase the legal driving age from 17 to 19
4 ☐ Mandatory safety devices on new cars eg ABS/airbags/side impact bars
5 ☐ Mandatory seat belts in all coaches, mini buses etc
6 ☐ Heavier fines for speeding in 30/40 mph areas
7 ☐ More use of speed cameras
8 ☐ More use of "sleeping policemen" in residential areas
9 ☐ Better road safety education for children

You & Your Car(s)

The following questions are all about your lifestyle. Both sections will be used together to enable leading companies to produce a full picture of today's motorist. If you don't want to answer some of the questions that's OK – just skip to the next question!

MAIN CAR

15 What cars do you have?

15 Make of Car? e.g. Ford ____

16 Model & Type e.g. Escort/XR3i ____

17 Registration Letter e.g. K ____ **CC:** ____

18 Who is the main driver? 1 ☐ You 2 ☐ Privately 1 ☐ By Company

19 Is the car owned? 1 ☐ Privately 2 ☐ By Company

20 Its yearly mileage? ____ ,000

21 Bought: 1 ☐ New 2 ☐ Used in 19 ____

22 Plan to change it: 1 ☐ 0-6mths 3 ☐ 1-2yrs
2 ☐ 7-12mths

23 Is the car: 1 ☐ Diesel 2 ☐ Automatic

24 Body type: 1 ☐ Saloon 4 ☐ Hatch
2 ☐ Coupe 5 ☐ Convertible
3 ☐ Off Road 6 ☐ Estate

25 Number of cars in your household:
1 ☐ 1 2 ☐ 2 3 ☐ 3 ☐ 3+ 9 ☐ None

26 When does your current car insurance expire? (If not sure of exact month, tick nearest)

Main Car:
01 ☐ Jan   05 ☐ May   09 ☐ Sep
02 ☐ Feb   06 ☐ June 10 ☐ Oct
03 ☐ Mar   07 ☐ July 11 ☐ Nov
04 ☐ April 08 ☐ Aug   12 ☐ Dec

SECOND CAR

MAKE ____

MODEL ____

Reg. Letter ____ **CC:** ____

1 ☐ You 2 ☐ Partner
1 ☐ Privately 2 ☐ By Company

Its yearly mileage? ____ ,000

Bought: 1 ☐ New 2 ☐ Used in 19 ____

Plan to change it: 1 ☐ 0-6mths 3 ☐ 1-2yrs
2 ☐ 7-12mths

Is the car: 1 ☐ Diesel 2 ☐ Automatic

Body type: 1 ☐ Saloon 4 ☐ Hatch
2 ☐ Coupe 5 ☐ Convertible
3 ☐ Off Road 6 ☐ Estate

27 How many years No Claims do you have?
You: 0 ☐ 0 2 ☐ 2 4 ☐ 4 ☐ 4+
         1 ☐ 1 3 ☐ 3 5 ☐ 5 ☐ Unsure
Partner: 0 ☐ 0 2 ☐ 2 4 ☐ 4 ☐ 4+
         1 ☐ 1 3 ☐ 3 5 ☐ 5 ☐ Unsure

28 Where do you keep your car(s)?
Main Car: 1 ☐ Garage 2 ☐ Driveway 3 ☐ Road
Second Car: 1 ☐ Garage 2 ☐ Driveway 3 ☐ Road

29 What do you use your car(s) for?
Main Car   Second Car
1 ☐ Social/Domestic/Pleasure 4 ☐ Social/Domestic/Pleasure
2 ☐ Travel to work   5 ☐ Travel to work
3 ☐ Business   6 ☐ Business

245

Your Interests

49 Please tick ALL the leisure interests and activities you and your partner enjoy regularly:

01 Coin/Stamp Collecting 12 Home Computing
02 Collectables 13 Active Sport/Exercise
03 Crossword/Puzzles 14 Pets
04 Do-It-Yourself/DIY 15 Playing Golf
05 Eating Out 16 Photography
06 Fine Art/Antiques 17 Record/Tape/CDs
07 Fishing 18 Snow Skiing
08 Foreign Travel 19 Theatre/Cultural/Art Events
09 Gourmet Foods/Wines 20 Wildlife/Environment
10 Grandchildren 21 Wines by Mail Order
11 Gardening

50 Please write the numbers of your three favourite activities from the list above:

You: Partner:

51 Do either of you bet on: (Tick all that apply)
1 Pools 3 Horseracing
2 Bingo 4 Other

52 Where have you been on holiday in the last 3 years? (Tick all that apply)
1 UK 3 USA
2 Europe 4 Rest of the world

53 How many times in the last year have you bought goods/services via the mail?
1 1 3 4-5 9 None
2 2-3 4 6 plus

54 Please tick all the newspapers that are REGULARLY read by your family:

	Daily	Sunday
Express	01	14
Independent	02	15
Mail	03	16
Mirror	04	17
Sport	05	18
Telegraph	06	19
Times	07	20
Other/Local	08	21
Guardian	09	
Star	10	
Sun	11	
Today	12	
Daily Record	13	
News of the World		22
Observer		23
People		24
Post		25
Sunday Mail (Scotland)		26
None 99		

55 What causes have you contributed to in the past year? (Tick all that apply) None 9
1 Wildlife 5 Helping the elderly
2 Environmental 6 Childrens' Welfare
3 Health Research 7 Disaster Relief
4 Third World Causes 8 Animal Welfare
0 Other

56 How do you contribute? (Tick all that apply)
1 By covenant 3 By post
2 In street/at door

IMPORTANT

If you or your partner smoke, each person must sign below so they can receive special tobacco offers.

Please sign that you are a smoker aged 18 or over:

YOUR SIGNATURE

PARTNERS SIGNATURE

Now please indicate for each tobacco product category which ONE brand you and/or your partner smoke most often.

57 CIGARETTES You Partner
B&H 01 51
B&H Superkings 02 52
Berkeley 03 53
Craven A 04 54
Dorchester 05 55
Dunhill 06 56
Regal 07 57
JP Special 08 58
Kensitas 09 59
Lambert & Butler 10 60
Marlboro 11 61

You Partner
Raffles 12 62
Red Band 13 63
Embassy 14 64
Rothmans 15 65
Rothmans Royals 16 66
Silk Cut 17 67
Stuyvesant 18 68
Superkings 19 69
Other: Under £2.20 20 70
Other: Over £2.20 21 71

58 Please tick if your brand is light/mild: 22 72

59 Please tick if your brand is menthol: 23 73

60 HANDROLLING You Partner
Golden Virginia 24 74
Old Holborn 25 75
Other Handroll 26 76

61 PIPE You Partner
Clan 27 77
Condor 28 78

PIPE You Partner
Dutch Blend 29 79
Gold Block 30 80
St. Bruno 31 81
Other Pipe 32 82

62 CIGARS You Partner
Café Crème 33 83
Classic 34 84
Castella Panatella 35 85
Hamlet 36 86
Hamlet Miniature 37 87
Hamlet Reserve 38 88
Henri Wintermans 39 89
King Edward Coronets 40 90
King Six 41 91
Panama 42 92
Other Cigars 43 93

63 How often do you/your partner smoke cigars? You Partner
Occasionally 44 94
1 pack per week 45 95
2-4 packs per wk 46 96
1 pack per day 47 97

---

30 Has anyone who drives your car had:
	Yes	No
An accident in the last three years?	1	3
A licence endorsement in the last 5 years? (not parking/speeding)	2	4

You & Your Home

31 Is your home a:
1 Flat 4 Semi-Detached
2 Maisonette 5 Detached
3 Terraced 6 Bungalow

32 When did you move to this address?
Year: 19
Month:

33 How many bedrooms do you have?
2 3 4 5 1 5+

34 Do you:
1 Own
2 Rent (Private) 2 Rent (Council)

35 When does your Home Contents insurance expire?
01 Jan 04 April 07 July 10 Oct
02 Feb 05 May 08 Aug 11 Nov
03 Mar 06 June 09 Sep 12 Dec

36 When does your Buildings insurance expire?
01 Jan 04 April 07 July 10 Oct
02 Feb 05 May 08 Aug 11 Nov
03 Mar 06 June 09 Sep 12 Dec

37 What are you and your partner's occupations?
	You	Partner
Craftsman/Tradesman	01	11
Education/Medical Services	02	12
Housewife	03	13
Manual/Factory Worker	04	14
Middle Management	05	15
Office/Clerical	06	16
Professional/Sen. Management	07	17
Retired	08	18
Shopworker	09	19
Student	10	20

38 Are you/your partner:
	You	Partner
Self-Employed/Business Owner	1	3
Running own in home business	2	4

39 Which cards do you or your partner have? (Please tick all that apply)
1 Access/Mastercard 3 Visa/Barclaycard
2 American Express/Diners Club 4 Store/Shop Cards 5 Other

40 Do you or your Partner have:
You: 1 Hearing Difficulties 3 A Hearing Aid
Partner: 2 Hearing Difficulties 4 A Hearing Aid

---

41 What are the dates of birth for:
You: Day Month 19 Year
Partner: Day Month 19 Year

42 Are you: 1 Married 3 Divorced/Separated
2 Single 4 Widowed

43 Please tell us the age of all your children living at home: 99 None at home
00 0-12 Mths 07 7 Yrs 14 14 Yrs
01 1 Yr 08 8 Yrs 15 15 Yrs
02 2 Yrs 09 9 Yrs 16 16 Yrs
03 3 Yrs 10 10 Yrs 17 17 Yrs
04 4 Yrs 11 11 Yrs 18 18 Yrs
05 5 Yrs 12 12 Yrs 19 19 Yrs
06 6 Yrs 13 13 Yrs 20 20 Yrs

44 Are you or your Partner considering changing your bank or building society current account?
You: 1 Yes 3 Possibly
Partner: 2 Yes 4 Possibly

45 Which group best describes your COMBINED annual household income?
1 Up to £5,000 5 £20,000-£24,999
2 £5,000-£9,999 6 £25,000-£29,999
3 £10,000-£14,999 7 £30,000-£34,999
4 £15,000-£19,999 8 £35,000 plus

46 How many prize draws, competitions or lotteries did you enter in the last year excluding the National Lottery? 9 None
1 1-3 3 7-10
2 4-6 4 11 plus

47 Do you forsee the need for a personal loan?
1 In the near future 3 In 12 months
2 In 6 months 9 No

48 Do you/your partner have any of the following? (Please tick all that apply)
1 Pension Plan - Private
2 Health Care (BUPA, etc)
3 Stocks and Shares
4 High Interest Investments & Unit Trusts
5 Savings Plan
6 Cheque Guarantee Card

PRIZE DRAW RULES: Open to everyone who completes a National Motoring Survey. Entry is free, no purchase necessary. The closing date for all entries is 5pm 31/10/95. The first prize is £1,000, plus 100 runners-up of £50 each. The winning numbers will be randomly selected on 30/11/95. No one professionally connected with the National Motoring Survey is allowed to enter. No correspondence can be entered into. No responsibility can be accepted for entries lost in the post. The prize draw is a CMT prize draw and may be offered across other CMT surveys. All winners will be notified by letter, by 31/12/95. For details of the prize winners, available from 31/12/95, send an S.A.E. to: Prize Winners List, National Motoring Survey, (B), PO Box 448 LIVERPOOL L70 1DW.
ADDITIONAL OFFERS: Thank you for completing this survey. CMT also provides you with the opportunity to receive offers for products and services from other reputable companies. Please tick here if you prefer NOT to receive these offers in future.

questioning a selection of respondents from the target market. In order to ensure that the results of a sample survey are accurate, the market research process must identify a representative group of consumers. If the selection is fair and accurate then information should be *statistically reliable*. If the sample is incomplete and does not accurately represent a group of consumers, misleading data is obtained – the sample is said to be *biased*.

There are a number of different ways of choosing a sample. These include:

- *Random sampling* With this method individuals and organisations are selected from a 'sampling frame', which is simply a list (usually numbered) of all the members of the market or population due to be surveyed. There are two main forms of random sampling:
  - *Simple random sampling* allows the researcher to choose the size of sample required and then to pick the sample on a purely random basis. The sample must be selected in such a way that every item in the sampling frame has an equal chance of being selected. On way of doing this is to use a computer to draw names and numbers from the list at random.

    Another way is to use *systematic sampling* which involves selecting items from the list at regular intervals after choosing a random starting point. For example, if it is decided to select a sample of 20 names from 1000, then every 50th name (1000 divided by 20) should be selected, after a random start in the first 50. If 18 is chosen as the starting point (possibly by using a table of random numbers), then the sample series would be: 18, 68, 118, 168, etc.
  - *Stratified random sampling* takes into account that some customers are more important than others. If therefore weights the sample on the basis of the importance of each group of customers in the market.

    For example, if an organisation has 5000 small users of products accounting for sales of £1 million, 4000 medium users accounting for £1 million, and 1000 big users accounting for £2 million, a random sample of 200 would not be representative of the whole market. To make the sample more representative would involve allocating the big users half of the sample because they make up half of the sales, with a quarter of the sample being allocated to medium users and a quarter to small users. The stratified random sample would then include 100 big users, 50 medium users and 50 small users, all randomly chosen from their respective categories.

- *Cluster sampling* With this method the population/customers are divided into small areas, but instead of sampling from a random selection of these areas, sampling is carried out in a few areas which are considered to be typical of the market in question. For example, you might divide the city of Newcastle into 200 segments and then, because of the nature of your survey, decide that you will only sample from a segment which contains at least one school, one church and one shopping centre, and any segments without these facilities are avoided.

- *Quota sampling* Although random sampling, if properly conducted, produces the best results, it can be expensive and time-consuming, and in some situations it is not possible to identify a random sample. *Quota sampling* is more commonly used.

  Interviewers are given instructions as to the number of people to interview with certain characteristics – such as sex, age, socio-economic group or other demographic detail. For example, if the interviewers are asked to investigate housewives aged 36–50, they will quiz every housewife 'fitting the bill' (possibly in interviews in the High Street) up to their maximum quota. The problem is that there is no assurance that the housewives interviewed are typical of housewives in that band, and the statistical accuracy of such sampling is questionable.

- *Convenience sampling* This involves gathering information from anybody available for the interviewer to survey, no matter what their background.

- *Judgement sampling* This involves selection of respondents by the interviewer based on his or her judgement that they seemed to be and looked representative of the group of customers in the market being researched.

Panels

Another market research method is to set up panels of consumers, which consist of groups of consumers who agree to provide information about attitudes or buying habits.

A consumer on a *home audit panel* will discuss consumer issues during a series of personal visits by a researcher. The great advantage is that this type of

panel will supply information over a long period of time from a willing participant who may agree to sample, test or use a range of products or who is simply asked to respond to questions on consumer issues.

Another type of panel is a *diary panel*. With this type of panel consumers record their purchases and/or media habits, usually in a diary. The purpose of the diary is not just to record purchases but also to provide research information which relates to demographic details and neighbourhood. For example, Audits of Great Britain (AGN) produces panel data across a variety of areas. Some panels, such as those set up by the Broadcasters' Audience Research Board (BARB), are designed simply to see how many people are watching the various television programmes at different times of the day.

The use of technology has transformed many consumer panels. For example, the use of hand-held barcode scanners has made it increasingly easy to improve the accuracy and speed of coding data.

Evidence collection point

Set up your own consumer discussion panel. Provide respondents with a suitable form and then ask five people to monitor their purchases over a fortnight. Think of some appropriate questions and then interview each person to discuss their purchases. Record your results. This work will provide evidence of Core Skills in Communication.

Telecommunications

Telephone interviewing is usually more appropriate for business surveys, as the respondents are often busy people and unavailable for long discussions. However, this method is often regarded as intrusive since it catches people unawares. This means that the respondent can start the interview with a negative viewpoint, which questioning will not necessarily overcome. However, it is a cost-effective way of reaching people, and the replies received are likely to be truthful.

Electronic interviewing is another market research method based on the telecommunications network and one which uses an interactive system. A respondent need only be a television and telephone subscriber and can respond instantly with a range of answers while a television campaign is actually being carried out.

Focus/discussion groups

Focus groups are an inexpensive method of obtaining useful qualitative information from consumers. For example, under the guidance of a chairperson, a group of users of the same product may be invited to provide opinions on its use. This method is frequently used in the motor industry. Car manufacturer Vauxhall states:

> Like other manufacturers, Vauxhall has to cope with a rapidly changing world and to keep pace it begins planning the next model even as the wraps are coming off a new launch.
>
> This begins with a series of 'clinics' where the reaction to a new shape is tested out on a number of preselected motorists. These motorists are recruited by an outside agency from owners of cars in the target group together with a small number positioned above the group (who may be persuaded to trade down) and below the group (who may be persuaded to trade up). They will be people who have no connection with the motor or advertising industries.
>
> Confidentiality is very important at this stage, so the cars are not badged and the respondents are not told which manufacturer is conducting the clinic. This also avoids any personal prejudices against a particular marque coming into play.

Field trials

Selected consumers may be asked to test a product prior to its launch. The purpose of this is to ensure that the product performs according to expectations in the home environment and provides an opportunity for any problems to be ironed out.

Evidence collection point

Make a list of the types of products that you would expect to have gone through extensive field trials before launch.

Experimentation

Experimentation involves setting up a research project to find out what might happen within the marketplace if certain things were to occur. For example, it may be possible to assess the reactions of a small group of consumers to a promotion.

Piloting

Prior to the national launch of a product, many organisations pilot the product within a part of the market. For example, many GNVQs were piloted in a few colleges. The purpose of the exercise is to obtain feedback from a partial launch so that any fine-tuning or adjustments can then be made to the product.

Quantitative/qualitative research methods

Having looked at a wide range of research methods it is important for us to realise that the research method used will largely determine the type of information obtained and this information may be either *quantitative* or *qualitative* in nature.

Quantitative information involves amounts or facts and figures, such as the average number of customers who may come into a shop at various times in a day. As this information is based upon hard facts it is considered to be *objective* (Figure 9.4).

In contrast, qualitative information involves descriptions, which may be made by respondents in surveys, such as attitudes, opinions, reactions and suggestions. This sort of information is more difficult

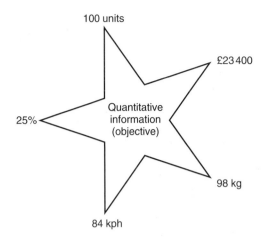

Figure 9.4 Quantitative information

to categorise and measure and because it is based on personal views it is said to be subjective (Figure 9.5).

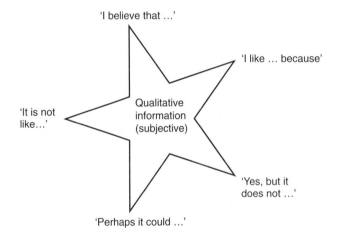

Figure 9.5 Qualitative information

Qualitative information often provides the context within which the quantitative facts operate. The 'What do you think about.....?' approach gives people the opportunity to offer a variety of opinions, reasons, motivations and influencing factors. A *group discussion* allows different opinions to be offered, which will frequently lead to a consensus, giving an idea of the popular view. People enjoy offering their opinions on subjects as diverse as the current political climate and the test of a particular margarine, and what this gives the researcher is an overall view of that particular audience's reaction to a proposition.

Quantitative data helps to produce an idea of the size and overall shape of markets and the effects of strategies on the demand for goods and services. Qualitative data helps to take this process further to show how goods and services have met the needs of current and potential customers (Figure 9.6).

Figure 9.6 Supporting quantitative data by qualitative information

It is usually necessary to use a number of market research techniques to obtain all of the information required. Whereas focus groups, interviews and home audit panels may obtain information which is more qualitative in nature, questionnaires, observations and diary panels will obtain hard facts.

Factors influencing market research methods

A number of different factors will determine the suitability of each type of market research method used for specific types of products:

■ *Accessibility* Different situations determine how good market research methods are at reaching targeted groups of respondents. For example, in organisational markets, telephones are particularly good for finding out information from people who may make decisions about products in their workplace. Diary panels enter the home to find out about purchases from consumers.

■ *Fitness for purpose* The market research technique chosen must be suitable for collecting information about different types of products. For example, car manufacturers use focus groups where the respondents can think about and discuss their requirements with others. This sort of information

could not be obtained through street interviews or questionnaires sent through the post.

■ *Validity* Market researchers must ensure that information obtained from various research techniques is valid. Precise quantitative data may be particularly important. With some research methods it may be useful to have a control group – a non-target group – to provide more depth to the research.

■ *Cost* Market research is an expensive process. Most methods will be analysed on a cost-per-response basis. For example, a questionnaire sent by post – depending upon the size of the sample – may be considerably cheaper than setting up a focus group or a telephone survey of the same number of respondents.

■ *Time* Some research methods may take longer than others. For example, a field trial or pilot may take more than a year to run and then the results have to be analysed. The danger is that this type of project provides signals for competitors who may then have time to develop their own products. In contrast, different forms of electronic interviewing may provide continuous market research information.

■ *Reliability* Many different factors may affect the reliability of a market research method. For example, interviewer bias may cause some respondents to reply to a questionnaire in a certain way. Sampling techniques may be incomplete. The questionnaire itself may be badly constructed and encourage respondents to reply in a certain way.

Evidence collection point

Using each of the factors above, undertake a comprehensive comparison of two market research methods.

Using sources to analyse market research information and make decisions

The real benefit of market research information is determined by how it improves the marketer's ability to make decisions. Good quality information will enable decisions to be made which satisfy the needs of the target market and also help the organisation to achieve its goals.

Cast study – Launching new Virgin products

In November 1994, Virgin Vodka was successfully launched within the M25 area as an initial test before a national launch. As a result of this a new division, The Virgin Spirit Company, was set up as a joint venture to coordinate the national launch in May 1995 and the launching of other brands in future.

The launch of the Virgin name into other areas is part of a programme of product developments and the launch of Virgin Cola, Virgin Vodka and Virgin Direct financial services is likely to be followed by Virgin spring water and a Virgin PC.

This move into spirits poses a serious threat to many established spirits brands. Spirits such as Scotch and Cognac are often associated by people under 35 with brands used by their parents. The name of Virgin, with its youthful and dynamic appeal, may seriously threaten existing products by capturing this market.

1 What sort of information might Virgin require before being involved in setting up a new brand?
2 How might Virgin use this information?

The use of market research represents a change from problem-solving by intuition to decision-making based on scientific gathering and analysis of information. The great advantage is that market research systematically provides information upon which managers may base product decisions.

Market analysis may, therefore, be used to identify:

■ *Changes in the market* The size and potential of any market must be constantly monitored for change. Analysis of sales trends as well as the size and potential of any market must be considered important. If the total size of the market is known, an organisation can thus work out what percentage of the market it has (*market share*) and then develop a strategy which helps it to increase its proportion of the market.

Market analysis may also be used to predict changes in the potential of the market both in the short and long term. Few markets are static and, as changes take place, it is important to understand about potential buyers as well as existing buyers.

For example, for the marketers of BSkyB it is as important to know how many households do *not* have satellite dishes as it is to know how many have them. If the market has potential new buyers, how long will it take to reach these buyers or to increase market share (Figure 9.7)?

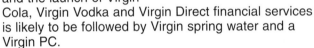

Figure 9.7 Market growth

In high-growth markets it is usually easier to meet growth objectives, and these markets are often considered to be more profitable. Low-growth markets, by their very nature, are more static and may even be declining. As the market size approaches the market potential, growth slows and competition usually intensifies.

Evidence collection point

Identify a product market which you feel has potential for growth. Explain briefly what sort of information would help you to analyse the changes taking place within that market. Present this in the form of a short report.

■ *Profit opportunities* As products go through their product life-cycle (see page 223) the profitability of different products changes. Marketing analysis helps to direct an organisation towards those activities where profitability and other business objectives can be best satisfied.

■ *The need to make changes to the product mix* The product mix comprises all of the products an organisation provides for its customers. Research will help managers to understand the sort of decisions they have to make about the product mix (Figure 9.8). For example it might:

– identify opportunities for the growth and development for new and existing products
– show how new products could replace existing products. This is known as *product substitution*
– show that some products are in decline – by modifying a product it may be possible to slow down its decline and sustain its profitability
– indicate that because a product is no longer satisfying a sufficient number of customers it ought to be deleted.

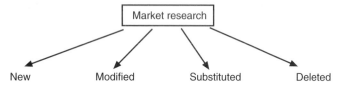

Figure 9.8 Analysis of research during the life of a product helping to make important product decisions

Evidence collection point

Analyse the behaviour of a product over a three-month period. What, if any, changes have been made to it and why do you think such changes have been made?

■ *Changes in consumer behaviour* The process of buying a good or service is not as simple as it might appear. A customer does not usually make a purchase without thinking carefully about his or her requirements. Wherever there is choice, decisions are made and these are influenced by complex motives.

Market research will help an organisation to understand *why* customers make particular decisions, particularly through the analysis of buying patterns, *who* buys, *what* they buy, *how* they develop preferences and how they buy. Analysing such changes will help an organisation to cater more closely for customers' needs.

■ *Changes in the activities of competitors* An organisation must at all times be aware of its competitors and the nature of what they are doing.

Competition exists when two or more organisations act independently to sell their products to the same group of consumers. In some markets there may be a lot of competition, signified by an abundance of products and services so that consumers have a massive choice. These markets are characterised by promotional activities and price competition.

In other markets, competition is limited and consumers are only able to choose from a limited range of products and services – perhaps only one. In these circumstances consumers may feel that prices are too high – they are not getting value for money.

Direct competition exists where organisations produce similar products and appeal to the same group of consumers. The *Daily Star* directly completes with The *Sun;* and if you want to have a wall built, all the builders in your area looking for this type of work are in direct competition.

Even when an organisation provides a unique end-product with no direct competition, it still has to consider *indirect competition*. Potential customers might examine slightly different ways of meeting the same need. Instead of buying a car they might buy a moped; instead of buying a box of chocolates on Mother's Day they could buy a bunch of flowers.

Task

Look at the market for one particular type of product (e.g. cars, electricity, insurance, beer, confectionery). Comment briefly on how the organisations supplying this market behave. In particular, is there a link between the numbers of competitors in this market and prices, promotional activities and choices?

■ *Changes in the effectiveness of other marketing mix ingredients* Market research will also provide valuable information about the use of other marketing mix ingredients. For example, what are customer perceptions of price, how effective is advertising, do distribution systems cater for customer requirements, what would be the effect on demand of changes in pricing policies?

Organising market research data

When an organisation has completed the important task of gathering information, it has to decide what to do with it. There are three stages involved:

- sorting and storing the information
- presenting the information
- making sense of the information.

Each of these stages has been transformed by the use of information technology.

Today, compilation, storage and analysis of market research may be undertaken by using specialist software, of which examples are the Statistical Package for Social Sciences (SPSS) and Minitab. Use can also be made of information received from bar-code analysis derived from electronic checkout and scanning systems located at the point of sale.

Electronic data processing (EDP) is frequently used for compiling and then categorising and summarising the results of market research. Questionnaire answers can be numerically coded for data entry. EDP makes it easy to deal efficiently and quickly with the results of lengthy questionnaires.

Presentation of data

Once statistical market research data has been obtained from all sources, it needs to be broken down and presented in such a way that its significance can be appreciated easily. Information can be displayed as text, tables, charts and graphs.

A table is just a matrix of rows and columns defining the relationships between variables; it summarises information into a form that is clear and easy to read. With suitable computer software, a table can be shown on a screen in the form of a *spreadsheet* – a grid of columns across the screen and rows going down the screen (Figure 9.9). It can also be manipulated though a series of calculations to show what would happen if alterations were made to any of the figures. As a result, one of the great benefits of spreadsheets is that they allow 'what if' questions to be asked and answered quickly.

OUTPUT	FIXED COSTS	VARIABLE COSTS	TOTAL COSTS	AVERAGE COSTS
10	300	20	320	32
20	300	120	420	21
30	300	200	500	16.6666667
40	300	260	560	14
50	300	300	600	12
60	300	320	620	10.3333333
70	300	390	690	9.85714286
80	300	460	760	9.5
90	300	620	920	10.2222222

Figure 9.9 A spreadsheet

Evidence collection point

Make up a spreadsheet containing the sort of data that might be useful for a marketing department. Show how the information could be manipulated and used. Plan your work so that it demonstrates Core Skills in Information Technology.

Pictograms are eye-catching and enable information to be presented in a form that can be readily understood. Items represented by a symbol may be supportes by a key (Figure 9.10).

Thompson's Boat Yard

Sale of boats

Figure 9.10 A pictogram

In a *pie-chart* each slice of the pie represents a component's contribution to the total amount. A circle is divided up in proportion to the figures obtained and, in order to draw the segments accurately, a protractor is necessary to mark off the pieces. The following formula can be used to find the angle (in degrees) for each segment:

$$\text{Angle for segment A} = \frac{\text{Amount of A}}{\text{Total}} \times 360°$$

Task

A company's sales are made up as follows:

Sales (£million)

Home	15
USA	4
Australia	3
EU	8
Middle East	10
Total	40

Draw an accurate pie-chart to present these sales figures. Label the chart. Your work should demonstrate Core Skills in Application of Number.

In *bar-charts* the areas for comparison are represented by bars – which can be drawn either vertically or horizontally. The lengths of the bars indicate the relative importance of the data.

Task

Look at the bar-chart in Figure 9.11, which shows the proportions of men and women in each job category in the marketing industry. Comment on:

1 the nature of the information
2 the form of presentation.

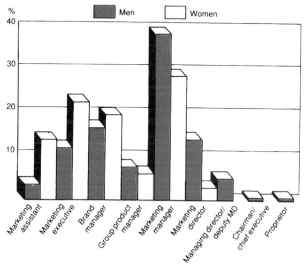

Figure 9.11 Proportion of men and women in each job category

Graphs are another visual way of displaying data. They show the relationship between two variables either in the form of a straight line or in the form of a curve. In particular, a graph shows how the value of one variable changes given a shift in the value of another. A graph may, for example, be constructed to show:

■ sales over a time period
■ the way the total cost of production varies according to the units of output produced.

Computers can be applied as a powerful tool to present information using *graphic packages* – drawings or pictures stored in a computer are known as graphics. A graphics package might be able to show a 'three-dimensional' shape as well as reduce and enlarge an image. Some programs allow bar-charts, pie-charts and graphs and other characters to be built up. Figure 9.12 shows a simple set of information displayed in three different ways, for comparison.

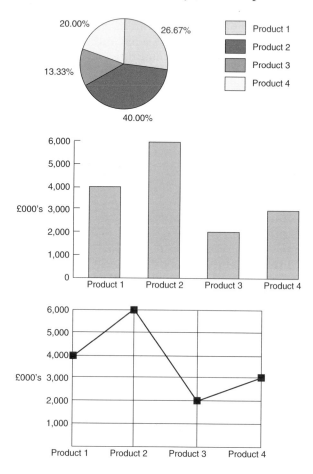

Figure 9.12 Sales figures for four products shown as a pie-chart, a bar-chart and a graph, using a computer package

Making sense of data

Statistical analysis of the hard-won information enables forecasting to take place. Decision-making techniques applied to the data allow decisions to be taken with greater precision and probability of success. Statistics are, therefore, a tool of management which tells managers what has happened in the past, what is happening now, and thus providing a more secure base for direction in the future.

One way of analysing market research information based upon a collection of values is through the use of *central tendency* – middle values. When we talk about middle values in everyday speech normally we think of an 'average'. This average is more correctly called the *arithmetic mean*. Two other measures of average or central tendency are the *median* and the *mode*.

The mean is quite simply the sum of a set of numbers divided by the number of items. For example, if sales figures (in pounds) over a six-day week were 165, 190, 185, 190, 180 and 170, the mean would be

$$\frac{165 + 190 + 185 + 190 + 180 + 170}{6} = \frac{1080}{6} = \pounds180$$

Therefore we can say that:

$$\text{Arithmetic mean} = \frac{\text{Sum of observations}}{\text{Number of observations}}$$

If data, such as daily sales figures is collected over a long period, adding up all the levels and dividing by the number of days may be time-consuming and prone to error. In these circumstances it could be useful to derive a *frequency distribution table*. For example, assume that a business's sales figures (in units) over 50 days are as follows:

5 6 2 6 5 2 6 4 6 5

5 6 4 5 3 5 6 5 6 5

6 5 3 3 2 4 3 2 3 5

4 3 5 2 1 4 2 5 1 4

5 4 4 4 5 3 5 2 4 5

These can be put into the frequency table shown below (Σ, which is the Greek letter sigma, stands for 'sum of').

Daily sales levels in units (x)	Frequency of occurrence (f)	Level × frequency (fx)
1	2	2
2	7	14
3	7	21
4	10	40
5	16	80
6	8	48
	Σf = 50	E(fx) = 205

On multiplying each value or daily sales figure (x) by the frequency with which it occurs (f), a total is achieved – Σ(fx). This can then be divided by the number of days to derive the arithmetic mean. The arithmetic mean is usually shown by $\bar{x}$ and the formula by which it is calculated is:

$$\bar{x} = \frac{\Sigma(fx)}{\Sigma f}$$

In our example the arithmetic mean is 205/50, or 4.1 units per day.

The *mode* is simply the value that occurs more frequently than any other value. If sales levels over four days were 15, 12, 15 and 17, the mode would be 15 because that number had occurred more than any other value in this period. If two or more frequencies occur the same number of times there is clearly more than one mode, and the distribution is *multimodal*. When there is only one mode the distribution is *unimodal*.

The *median* is the middle number in a distribution or array of figures. When figures are arranged into numerical order, the median is the one in the middle. For example, data ordered into the array 2, 7, 9, 12 and 15 would have the number 9 in the middle and so 9 would be the median value.

When calculating the median for a frequency distribution it is usual to say that the middle value is (n + 1)/2 if the total frequency (n) is an odd number.

In our earlier example of daily sales figures there was an even number of figures (50). If n is an even number, the median is taken to be halfway between the (n/2)th value and the (n/2+1)th value. In this example both the 25th and 26th values are 4, so the median reflects a daily sales figure of 4 units.

Evidence collection point

Conduct an interview of 50 consumers of breakfast cereals. Use the mean, median and mode to help with your analysis of the results. Explain how they helped with such analysis. Plan your work so that it demonstrates Core Skills in Communication and Application of Number.

Another way of analysing market research data using a measure of central tendency is by using *time series*. A time series is the name given to a set of figures recorded as they occur through time. The series may be plotted daily, weekly or monthly and it is usual for the horizontal axis to be used to denote the time dimension. If there is clear trend, these historical figures can be used to predict what will happen in the near future.

Figure 9.13 is an example of a graph showing a time series. Here the sales figures vary month by month, with troughs and peaks. The movement from trough to trough and peak to peak is called a cycle. However, what we need to know is whether the sales, while fluctuating, are steadily increasing in the longer term. Somehow, we need to decide how to distinguish the trend from the short-term fluctuations.

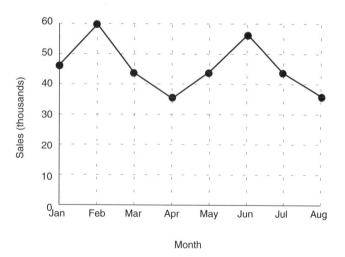

Figure 9.13 A time series showing monthly sales

To separate out a trend from a cycle we can use a statistical technique known as a *moving average*. Imagine that a business that sells financial services wants to keep a weekly moving average of sales in order to identify a trend. Its sales tend to peak every four weeks. The moving average smoothes out the peaks so that the underlying trend can be followed. The table shows how this is done, and Figure 9.14 shows the data plotted as a graph.

Week	Sales (thousands)	Four-week moving totals	Four-week moving averages
1	25		
2	28		
3	33		
4	38	124	31.00
5	34	133	33.25
6	37	142	35.50
7	42	151	37.75
8	43	156	39.00
9	39	161	40.25
10	42	166	41.50
11	45	169	42.25
12	48	174	43.50
13	43	178	44.50
14	47	183	45.75
15	50	188	47.00
16	52	192	48.00

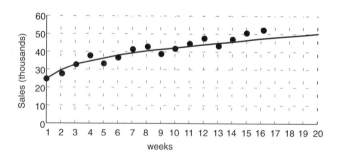

Figure 9.14 Weekly sales of financial services, showing a moving average with an extrapolated forecast

The moving average is calculated in three stages:

Stage 1 Calculate the four-week moving totals using the sales figures from the second column. For example:

$$25 + 28 + 33 + 38 = 124$$

The total then moves by deleting the first week and adding the following (fifth) week. The second total is

$$28 + 33 + 38 + 34 = 133$$

Stage 2   Calculate the four-week moving averages by dividing the four-week moving totals by 4. For example, 124 divided by 4 is 31, 133 divided by 4 is 33.25, etc.

Stage 3   The four-week moving averages show the trend. If the trend line in Figure 9.14 is extended to the right, this is known as a process of *extrapolation* will help to provide a forecast of sales activity in the coming weeks.

Sources of market research information

The first question any organisation has to ask is: 'What information is required'? To a certain extent this will depend upon the objectives of the organisation. Remember, the more accurate the information the more successful decision-making is likely to be. Decisions based upon little research or misleading information are likely to be poor.

There are three broad areas from which information may come (Figure 9.15). Existing organisations will have *internal information* kept within their own record systems. Secondly, a lot of information will already be published and available as *external* or *secondary information*. The third source of information will not already exist in any identifiable form and will have to be collected first-hand. This is *primary information*.

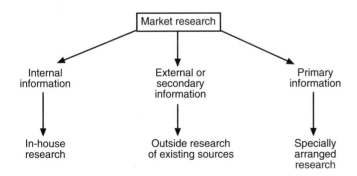

Figure 9.15 Sources of information

Internal information

Much of the information that an organisation requires about the marketplace is already held within its various departments. A lot of this internal information might be in filing cabinets, and at least some of it will be out-of-date. The secret is to know what you need, to discover where to find it, and then to retrieve it.

Nowadays, a lot of internal information is held on computer files. Computers have revolutionised the way information is stored, analysed and retrieved, and this has made the task of dealing with internal information much easier.

For example, in the past it was often difficult to get regular and reliable feedback from sales representatives, because their 'paperwork' was kept in their vehicles, was disorganised and bulky, and was rarely filed. This information was potentially valuable as it represented feedback from first-hand experiences – it is often said that the sales force is an organisation's 'eyes and ears'.

Computers have provided the means whereby information of this nature can be recorded in a simple manner, and contacts with each customer can be 'processed' so that information can be retrieved very quickly and then displayed in a way that is easy to understand, perhaps with the aid of a graphics software package. Techniques like this improve the quality of the market research process and enable organisations to direct their goods and services to those customers who are most likely to make a purchase.

In organisations using computerised records, files of information are stored on a *database*. This is a large amount of information stored in such a way that it can easily be found, processed and updated. The database may be central so that it can be accessed by users from all parts of the organisation.

Case study – The electricity distribution company

We can show how one type of database works as a source of market research information by looking at the activities of an electricity distribution company. Customers are given a *customer reference number* (CRN). To the CRN the electricity company can then attach a vast array of information that tells it about the consumer.

- *Tariff type* The price a customer pays for electricity can vary according to whether they are a home or business, a large or small customer.
- *Consumption* The company can then track the *amount* of electricity a customer uses, and *when*.
- *Method of payment* Some customers prefer prepayment rather than credit, others prefer to pay monthly rather than quarterly.
- *Change of tenancy* The company knows when customers move out of and into a property.
- *New buildings* The company knows when and where new buildings that use electricity are being erected, because an electricity supply is applied for.

From such information it is possible to obtain answers to an almost endless list of questions such as:

- What is the size of the market?
- What type of user uses the most/least electricity?
- How do customers prefer to pay?
- What is the average credit period?
- How many new users are coming on-stream?
- How many users is the company losing?
- What is the average consumption per user?
- What is the profitability for each type of customer?
- How does the use of electricity vary during the day?
- Where is the market expanding/contracting?

1 How will the answers to the sort of questions indicated here improve the way the electricity company manages it business?

2 What other questions might be answered from this type of database?

The internal information that has been collated needs to be put into context, since on its own it simply provides a snapshot of the organisation and its customers. In particular it tells the organisation nothing about how effective its performance is relative to that of its competitors, nor how the business could be threatened by those competitors.

External information

External information is more commonly called *secondary data* because it is often in the form of published materials, collected by somebody else. It can provide a broader dimension to data previously collected and can be used in two main ways.

Firstly, external information can enhance the company's existing knowledge. For example, postcodes help the computer to group customers geographically. By identifying and labelling certain characteristics of its customers, a company can make assumptions about their needs. Two examples of useful external sources are:

- *Domestic socio-economic data* Customers are classified by their house type, the assumption being that a certain lifestyle is associated with that type of house.
- *Industrial classification* Organisational customers can be classified according to the nature of the activities. Certain types of organisations can then be expected to have predictable demands for services.

Secondly, external sources can complement an organisation's own information by providing direct comparison with competitors, by putting performance within the context of the economy as a whole, and by identifying markets offering potential.

Task

Imagine that you are the owner or manager of a small shop selling sports equipment in your local neighbourhood. What sort of information might give you a better understanding of the decisions you have to make?

Government statistics

The government's statistical service is coordinated by the Central Statistical Office (CSO). Government departments prepare statistics and the CSO publishes both a monthly and an annual analysis. In addition, *Business Monitor* is published quarterly to provide a range of information about various markets. Information on particular groups of industries is identified by a code which relates to their Standard Industrial Classification (SIC) – for example, 'agriculture, forestry and fishing' and 'energy and water supply industries'. As the SIC is the government's official way of classifying organisations and markets, it is frequently used for market research.

Another useful source of information, particularly for industries selling in consumer markets, is census data published by the Office of Population, Censuses and Surveys. A full census is carried out every ten years, the last one being in 1991. This office also carries out two continuous surveys on Family Expenditure and General Households, which might also be useful for organisations to analyse for market research purposes.

Other secondary sources

Mintel is a commercial research organisation which, in return for a fee, provides a monthly journal containing reports on consumer markets – for example, bread, alcoholic drinks, insurance. The Mintel reports are up to about 20 pages long, with information such as market size, main competitors, projected growth, market share of main competitors, advertising spend of main brands, trends, etc. Mintel also produces in-depth reports in certain markets.

Task

Explain how and why information contained in Mintel reports might be useful.

Another research organisation which operates in a similar way to Mintel is Euromonitor. Its Key Note Reports cover a range of businesses and, at around 75 pages long, provide a good introduction to markets.

Some research establishments work exclusively in one particular sector. For the food industry, for example, there is the Leatherhead Food Research Association and the Food Policy Research Unit. *Business-to-business reports* are available for many sectors.

A. C. Nielsen and Retail Audits are research organisations that collect data of retail sales through supermarkets and large chains, and sell the figures to organisations wishing to buy them. These figures enable manufacturers to work out their share of the markets, the sales of different products, and the effects of any recent strategy such as price change or a promotional campaign. These audits, therefore, offer a window directly onto the marketplace.

There are many sources providing information about the media which might be of use to organisations wishing to look at how to get their promotional messages across to customers. *Benn's Media Directory* gives details of TV and radio companies, newspapers and magazines. *British Rate and Data* (BRAD) provides comprehensive coverage of virtually all the media selling and advertising space, together with rates. The *Advertisers Annual* makes detailed comparisons of advertising agencies.

Information about companies is available from several sources. Kompass publishes two volumes of products and services listed by the SIC codes mentioned earlier. Extel provides details extracted from the published accounts of all the public companies and from many of the larger private companies. The annual publication *Who Owns Whom* gives details of the ownership of subsidiary companies.

Evidence collection point

Visit the reference section and the periodicals section of either your school or college library or your local public library. Identify which sources of information may be useful for secondary market research purposes. Make a list of these reference sources.

Primary information

Internal and external data may not answer all of the questions an organisation may wish to ask. It may be out-of-date or it may not cover exactly the right market sector. Then, to meet an organisation's specific needs, *primary research* has to take place.

Primary data is first-hand knowledge, 'straight from the horse's mouth'. Information a company compiles from its own research efforts is called primary. The collection of primary data is a more lengthy, expensive and complicated process than the collection of secondary data and will involve using many of the techniques described on pages xxii–xxviii. Such techniques allow for data collection – it then has to be analysed and interpreted.

Using research for marketing decisions

Market researchers should constantly be feeding information through for planning and decision-making purposes. The type of information required will generally depend upon the objectives of the organisation.

There are five stages in the market research programme:

Stage 1	Research brief	Set objectives and define problem
Stage 2	Plan of work	Identify information requirements and plan the methods of collection
Stage 3	Collection of data	Collect data and check efficiency of collection
Stage 4	Evaluation of data	Store and analyse the data
Stage 5	Presentation of findings (report)	Make information available for managers, together with findings and conclusions

Having received this information, managers should be able to make clear and well-supported decisions about various part of the marketing mix. A market

259

research report is usually formally written and will summarise the findings from the market research.

It is important to realise that a market research report is not a 'tablet of stone'; managers still have a key role to play in using their experience and expertise to make decisions.

What type of decisions does market research evidence help managers to make?

■ *Product decisions* *Market research may:*
- analyse the market for existing products
- forecast demand for new and existing products
- identify market shares
- compare the features of competing products (types, brands, packaging)
- analyse consumer preferences
- test product concepts and features

■ *Pricing decisions* *Market research may:*
- analyse elasticity of demand to show the effect of changes in price on demand
- analyse the views of consumers about price levels
- identify customer perceptions of price
- evaluate the role of price in relation to other ingredients in the mix
- compare competing prices
- identify opportunities for the use of price as a strategic tool

■ *Distribution decisions* *Market research may:*
- provide information which helps with the evaluation of different channel alternatives
- emphasise the importance of different aspects of the distribution mix
- enable the organisation to cut distribution costs (inventory/ transport)
- identify a more efficient way of reaching customers
- compare channels used by competitors
- provide information about technologies which could improve the efficiency of distribution

■ *Promotional decisions* *Market research may:*
- analyse the effectiveness of advertising
- provide feedback on the effectiveness of sales techniques
- help with the development of a promotional policy
- analyse customer response to promotional techniques
- suggest ways of targeting groups of customers
- identify the most appropriate forms of media to use.

Evidence collection point

Choose a product which has recently been launched, e.g. a motor car. Explain how market research would help to provide information about each area of the marketing mix for this new product. Provide specific examples of the sort of problems it might help to solve.

When analysing research information it must be remembered that the marketing mix for every product comprises a unique blend of variables. Every ingredient is important and will depend upon others for their contribution to the successful marketing of a product. The research process provides vital information which can then be used to help the mix to be varied and as part of a marketing plan to suit the precise requirements of the market.

For example, think of two products which may seem similar but in reality have very different marketing mixes – such as an 'own brand' of cola and Pepsi. Both might be sold side-by-side in a supermarket. However, the own brand would not be promoted as a single product, would be sold only in that chain of supermarkets and would probably be cheaper. Pepsi, in contrast, will be sold in many supermarkets, and will have a higher price and a famous premium brand name which is widely promoted through advertising and other techniques.

Product developments

In any well-run organisation, market research has strictly commercial functions:

- to further the organisation's business objectives by creating better products
- to improve operational processes
- to provide information that serves as the basis for decisions by managers.

Some research processes will be expected to bring real returns in the near future, while others may not be expected to pay for themselves within a foreseeable time-span. These are known as 'blue-sky' investigations, which may lead to a pay-off in the distant future.

A new product may be one which:

- replaces an old product
- opens up a new market
- broadens an existing market.

It may involve an innovation, a technological breakthrough or simply be a line extension based upon a modification. It is often said that only about 10% of new products are really new. In fact, it is often possible to turn old products into new products simply by finding a new market for them.

Case study – Lolly technology

Many product advances are made possible by breakthroughs in production techniques. Twenty years ago, lollies were little more than tapered blocks of ice on a stick. The technology – pouring juice into a mould – restricted lolly-making to simple shapes. Then the lolly embraced rubber technology: by casting ice in a flexible rubber mould, the lollies could be shaped more intricately because the mould peeled off.

More recently, the Tangle Twister hit the High Street freezers. This was made possible by an ingenious invention from Wall's design engineers. They came up with a nozzle that could make a lolly by twisting together three separate flavours of ice. The innovation represented a quantum leap forward in lolly technology.

Such ideas are dependent on the combination of research and development, production engineering, investment funds, investment in people and the key edge of information technology.

1 What is meant by 'technology', and how does new technology provide for the development of new products?
2 Comment upon the impact of new technologies on the life-cycle of products.
3 To what extent does the case study emphasise the integrated elements required to bring technologies to the fore?

There are six distinct stages in the product development process. These are:

- Step 1 Ideas
- Step 2 Screening of ideas
- Step 3 Marketing analysis
- Step 4 Product development
- Step 5 Testing
- Step 6 Launch and commercialisation.

As new products go through each of these stages there is a mortality rate (Figure 9.16).

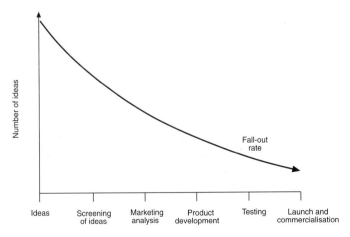

Figure 9.16 Fall-out from product development stages

Step 1 *Ideas* All new products start from ideas. These ideas may be completely new or simply be an update of an existing product. Ideas may come from:

261

- *Research and development* – product development and market research working together. Technological breakthroughs and innovations from research are very important.
- *Brainstorming* – involving a few people developing ideas from words and concepts.
- *Suggestions box* – cash incentives may encourage employees to contribute ideas.
- *Sales force* – working close to customers, the sales force understands needs and requirements and may contribute ideas.
- *Forced relationships* – sometimes one or more products can be joined together to form new products. For example, shampoo and conditioner.
- *Competitors* – monitoring the actions of competitors may provide a source of ideas.

Step 2 *Screening of ideas* Once ideas have been generated it is important to screen for the ideas likely to be successful and reject the rest. Considerations may include how well the product fits in with others, the unique elements of any idea that may make it competitive, the likely demand for the product, and whether or not it could be manufactured economically.

Step 3 *Marketing analysis* Once the ideas have been screened, further marketing analysis begins. This involves a thorough analysis of the product's market potential. This type of research helps to identify the market volume (units that could be sold) as well as the value of sales expected. It may also help to identify the market potential.

Step 4 *Product development* Having come through the test of marketing analysis it is now time to translate the idea or product concept into a product. Design, innovation and the uses of technology are very important for product development. An assessment of packaging and branding would also be involved.

Step 5 *Testing* Testing is a vital stage in the product development process. It may involve identifying valuable information through further market research which

helps to fine-tune the venture. Test marketing may comprise testing on part of a consumer market or trialling a product to ensure that it meets the required standards.

Step 6 *Launch and commercialisation* The launch is the most important day in the life of a product – it is finally revealed to customers. It may involve rolling from one TV region to another TV region. Today a common technique is to provide sneak glimpses of new products before they are launched.

Evidence indicators

For this activity you need to make a presentation of proposals for a new product to an audience. These may be visiting assessors, other students, lecturers or visitors to your school or college. Your proposals should show evidence of the collection of market research information from a number of sources and include both primary and secondary data. Proposals should describe the type of product, features of the product, packaging, sales outlets, promotion, selling price and timing of marketing communications.

The following list should serve as a checklist. Please tick each of the following when you have successfully covered them as part of your preparation. You need to be able to confirm that:

- I have worked either on my own or with a small group to identify a number of new product ideas. ☐
- I have developed a plan of the sort of information required to develop these ideas further. ☐
- I have identified market research methods to obtain this information. ☐
- I have collected the market research information. ☐
- The information has been presented and analysed using suitable IT packages. ☐
- From the research it is possible to draw certain conclusions and make recommendations. ☐
- I have prepared notes, OHPs, handouts and other materials for this talk. ☐

Marketing communications designed to influence a target audience

Within the context of marketing, communication activity refers to the processes used by an organisation to contact individuals and other organisations, more often than not for the purpose of persuading customers about the benefits of whatever is on offer.

This chapter explores the many areas of communication activity. It starts by helping you to understand the nature of the communication process, then looks at specific communication methods and at how these are targeted at specific groups of customers. Finally the chapter helps you to compare marketing communications and understand some of the controls over such communications.

The process of communication involves sending messages to consumers through various channels or media in order to create awareness and understanding of why they might wish to buy particular products or services.

Organisations are the *senders* in the communication process and consumers are the receivers. A sender will put information in a form that a receiver can understand. This might involve using oral, visual, verbal or written messages to transmit the ideas. This process is called *encoding*. The sender will also choose a particular medium to use to send the message to the receiver (e.g. television, radio, newspapers). If the consumer interprets the message as required, it should have the impact the seller wished for.

Though the message flows through to the receiver there is no guarantee that the receiver will either receive the full message or understand it. This is

because the process may be subject to some form of interference which affects the flow of information. This is known as *noise* and may lead to the downfall of the message. It will take the form of any barrier which acts as an impediment to the smooth flow of information and may include linguistic and cultural differences between the sender and the receiver.

Noise in the competing environment may affect communication so that the meaning of the message is lost. For example, nearly all promotional activities compete with activities from other organisations. One leaflet put through your door may be lost amongst a sea of direct mail from other organisations.

The communication process is illustrated in Figure 10.1.

To increase the chances of a message getting across, an organisation needs to think carefully about the target audience. For example, it is important to channel the message through the most appropriate media. It might also be necessary to repeat the message several times rather than rely on one transmission. It is important too, to understand noise in that media channel.

Feedback from the receiver to the sender enables an organisation to monitor its performance and satisfy itself that the messages are getting through and are having the desired effect.

An organisation needs to appraise the communication process carefully. It must have a clear idea of what a message should be, to whom it should be sent and the expected outcome of sending it. Promotional requirements will vary with geographic size, demographic dispersion and the nature of market segmentation. The more clearly an organisation can define its target audience, the more relevant the promotional mix.

To achieve its promotional objectives an organisation has to set its promotional strategy. A common mnemonic underlying a promotional strategy which is used to describe how to persuade a customer to make a purchase is 'AIDA'.

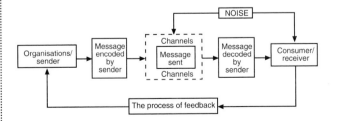

Figure 10.1 The communication process

A A customer's *attention* is captured and he or she is made *aware* of the product.
I The *impact* of the promotion stimulates the customer's interest.
D The customer is persuaded that he or she is *deprived* by not having the product, and this helps to stimulate a *desire* for it.
A *Action* involves the purchase of the product.

Using advertising and publicity

Advertising is a method of communicating with groups in the marketplace in order to achieve certain objectives. Advertisements are messages sent through the media which are intended to inform or influence the people who receive them (Figure 10.2).

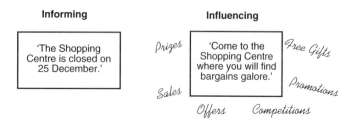

Figure 10.2 The difference between informative and persuasive advertising

According to the American Marketing Association advertising is: any paid form of non-personal presentation and promotion of ideas, goods or services by an identifiable sponsor

Advertisements may be used for two main purposes. These are:

■ to promote goods or services
■ to develop the image of the organisation.

With each of these purposes there may be a range of advertising objectives. For example:

■ Promoting goods and services
  – to assist with selling
  – to increase sales
  – to develop awareness of new products, or developments to existing products
  – to provide information that may assist with selling decisions
  – to encourage a desire to own a product
  – to generate enquiries.

■ *Developing the image of the organisation*
  – to provide information for a target audience
  – to soften attitudes
  – to assist with public relations activities
  – to change views
  – to provide a better external environment
  – to develop support from a community.

Evidence collection point

Compare and contrast two advertising campaigns, where one is clearly trying to promote goods or services and the other is trying to improve an image by developing public support for its activities. Comment upon how their approaches to advertising are (a) similar, and (b) different.

The starting point for an advertising campaign is to produce an advertising plan. This will involve allocating a budget to a range of activities designed to meet advertising objectives. There are seven steps in an advertising campaign. These are:

Step 1 Identify the target market
Step 2 Define advertising objectives
Step 3 Decide on and create the advertising message
Step 4 Allocate the budget
Step 5 Develop the media plan
Step 6 Execute the campaign
Step 7 Evaluate the effectiveness of the campaign.

Types of advertising media

Advertising messages may be sent through a variety of media forms, such as TV, radio and the press. Promotional materials supplied with a product, promotional events or company brochures are known as *publicity* and though they are not regarded as advertising, they do support the advertising process (see page 267).

At all stages in the advertising process it is important to assess how effectively advertisements have contributed to the communication process. In order to measure objectives, DAGMAR has become a fundamental part of good advertising practice. This stands for:

Defining Advertising Goals for Measured Advertising Results

In other words, before any advertising campaign is started, an organisation must define its communication objectives so that achievements can be measured both during and after the campaign.

Rank	Advertiser	Advertising expenditure			
		Total (£000)	TV (%)	Radio (%)	Press (%)
1	Procter & Gamble	94851	96.8	0.1	3.1
2	Lever Brothers (Unilever)	67425	94.2	–	5.8
3	Kellog Company of GB	60166	98.7	0.1	1.2
4	Ford Motor Company	56941	64.5	2.3	33.2
5	British Telecommunications	56419	61.7	1.8	36.4
6	Vauxhall (General Motors)	43035	40.5	2.2	57.2
7	Procter & Gamble (Health & Beauty)	39400	90.9	1.0	8.1
8	Rover Group (BMW)	39013	51.7	1.2	47.1
9	Dixons Stores	37749	8.3	3.5	88.2
10	Elida Gibbs (Unilever)	36851	91.3	–	8.7
11	Renault (UK)	36012	49.5	2.8	47.7
12	Birds Eye Wall's (Unilever)	35953	83.8	0.1	16.1
13	Peugeot Talbot	35643	33.5	0.5	66.0
14	Mars Confectionery	32322	95.9	0.8	3.3
15	VAG (UK)	30910	21.9	0.5	77.7
16	Citroën (UK)	29683	43.0	0.5	56.4
17	Nissan (GB)	29658	38.9	0.9	60.1
18	Gallaher Tobacco (American brands)	29264	–	0.2	99.8
19	Pedigree Petfoods (Mars)	28550	98.7	–	1.3
20	Brooke Bond Foods (Unilever)	27420	96.0	–	4.0

Figure 10.3 The top 20 advertisers 1993

Printed media

Printed materials make up by far the largest group of media in the UK. The group includes all newspapers and magazines, both local and national, as well as trade press, periodicals and professional journals. There are about 9000 regular publications in the UK which can be used by the advertiser. They allow the advertiser to send a message to several million people through the press or to target magazines of special interest from railways to snooker. They also allow the advertiser to communicate with people in a certain trade or profession and with those in a particular region.

The printed media also allows for accurate targeting and positioning. For example, look at Figure 10.4 which shows some of the women's magazines for sale. Think of all of the interests, hobbies, lifestyles and backgrounds of readers of such magazines. Types of customers can be identified by analysing readership profiles (see page 271).

The benefit of printed media are that long or complex messages can be sent and, as the message is durable, may be read repeatedly. If an advertisement appears in a prestige magazine it may take on the prestige of that particular publication. Colour quality is today offered in an increasing number of newspapers as well as nearly all magazines. Tear-off reply coupons which follow up advertisements are quite popular.

	Circulation (000s)	Women's readership (000s)	(%)		Circulation (000s)	Women's readership (000s)	(%)
Prima	665	2343	10	Mother & Baby	114	833	4
Good Housekeeping	457	2175	9	Country Living	182	791	3
Family Circle	346	1925	8	House Beautiful	308	724	3
Woman & Home	395	1889	8	'19'	197	707	3
Cosmopolitan	477	1837	8	Living	170	699	3
Vogue	179	1494	6	Looks	227	687	3
Ideal Home	250	1447	6	Practical Parenting	130	647	3
BBC Good Food	427	1362	6	New Woman	269	614	3
Homes & Gardens	175	1360	6	Woman's Journal	151	568	2
Essentials	410	1272	5	Company Magazine	250	549	2
Clothes Show Magazine	173	1220	5	Options	156	542	2
She	257	1079	5	Annabel	56	540	2
House & Garden	141	981	4	BBC Good Health	–	534	2
Elle	202	905	4	Hairflair	48	504	2
Marie Claire	314	902	4	Country Homes & Interiors	106	483	2
Needlecraft	90	882	4	Home & Country	85	438	2

Figure 10.4 Some of the women's magazines on sale

On the other hand, advertisements appearing in the printed media are sometimes criticised for having a poor impact. There are many competing messages which the reader is not forced to read, and some publications have a short time-span. Printed advertisements have static rather than dynamic qualities.

Evidence collection point

Pick two magazines and two newspapers. Describe how they differ. Using evidence to support the conclusions you make, build up a consumer profile of the sort of readers of each of the newspapers and magazines you have chosen. Your work should show evidence of Core Skills in Communication.

Broadcast media

Broadcast media includes commercial television and commercial radio. Television is the most powerful medium – it reaches 98% of households and viewing figures for some programmes can exceed 20 million. TV advertisements are usually of a highly creative quality, helped by both sound and colour. Messages are dynamic as they have voice, images, movement and colour, and can be repeated over and over again. The main disadvantage of such an expensive medium is that it is sometimes difficult to target a broadcast to a particular group of consumers.

Recent developments in television have seen franchise changes and the emergence of Carlton, GMTV and other companies. There have also been some mergers between television frachisees such as Yorkshire and Tyne-Tees. Direct broadcasting by satellite has been available since 1989 when Sky started using the Astra satellite, and this is today reaching an increasing number of households. Though cable TV penetration in the UK is low, it is steadily increasing.

There are more than 120 independent local radio (ILR) stations in the UK, including 12 in London. There are also several independent national radio

(INR) stations including Classic FM and Virgin. Radio is a good way of communicating a sense of urgency and action. Advertisements are low-cost in comparison with those of TV. One problem with radio, however, is that many regard it as only a background medium.

Posters

Posters include hoardings and screens and are particularly useful for providing frequency and supporting the images created through the broadcast media. If an outdoor medium is well sited, its impact may be considerable. Posters can be in colour and there is a wide choice of locations and sites with little competition from other advertising matter. In fact many posters become a sole attraction in places such as railway platforms, where people have little to do except look at an advert.

Posters do, however, suffer from the intrusions of noise and clutter from the immediate environment. Some may even go unnoticed. They may also be subject to vandalism such as graffiti, and many people feel today that hoardings intrude into the environment.

Evidence collection point

Look for a poster site located near to you. What sort of advertisements appear on the site? Is the site noticed? Conduct a short survey. How do local people feel about the poster site? Conclude by commenting upon whether you feel that the site is an effective form of advertising. Your work should provide evidence of Core Skills in Communication.

Cinema

Though cinema has declined in relative importance as an advertising medium, it tends to be popular with the young and is a good way of targeting a specific type of audience. A cinema has a captive audience, and the physical size and loud volume of advertisements makes them impossible to ignore. The quality of sound and vision helps the audience to recall cinema commercials better than those on television. The size of cinema audiences fluctuates widely and is dependent on the popularity of the film being shown. Commercials tend to be shown once during a programme and are not reinforced unless the recipient is a regular cinema attender.

Publicity

The term publicity refers to *non-personal communication* about an organisation and its products. In many cases, where publicity is provided free-of-charge by the press, publicity will not be paid for. However, this is not always true, as many organisations provide materials themselves as part of their own approach to developing publicity. As we will also see, there is a very fine dividing line between publicity and public relations and sales promotional activities. Whatever the case, it is very important that publicity is compatible with other areas of the promotional mix.

Activities involving publicity may include:

- *Sales literature* Organisations may produce a lot of literature which accompanies their products and activities. For example, they may send out catalogues, magazines, calendars, price lists, leaflets or brochures. These are particularly useful where goods have detailed specifications.
- *Signage* The names of some organisations may appear in a variety of places which are noticed by consumers. Logos may be particularly important. For example, just putting a logo on the product provides a form of publicity. Signs outside factories, as well as in any other place where they remind consumers of the organisation and its products, serve as a form of publicity.
- *Vehicle livery* This may help to provide a form of publicity, particularly if an organisation has a large fleet and the livery is distinctive.
- *Stationery* Distinctive headed paper, invoices or other stationery may provide reminders which act as a useful form of publicity.
- *Point-of-sale materials* These are designed to help consumers with product choices at the point of sale. They may include racks, displays, videos and interactive materials. An effective point-of-sale display attracts customers' attention and encourages them to approach and inspect the product before making the decision to buy.

Evidence collection point

Analyse the publicity generated by the activities of your school or college. Comment on how well areas such as signage and stationery help to enhance this publicity.

Case study – The interactive guide for Levi's

Levi's has turned on and tuned in to a new in-store touch-screen system which allows customers to go through the various styles of jeans without having to try them on.

The Interactive Fit Guide is on trial at the Levi's flagship store in Regent Street. It explains the difference between 517s, 569s and 818s with the aim of finding out the individual's perfect cut.

The guide has a series of options including men's and women's colour and slim-fit to super-loose. According to the system designers 'the system is intended to demystify the numbers'. It seems that most people know what 501s are like; few know what they are getting with 565s.

The Guide tries to capture the video culture by attracting customers with Acid Jazz music and clips from an up-to-date video catalogue. The company behind the scheme is presently negotiating to roll out the system nationwide on a cheaper CD-i system.

1 How does such a guide provide publicity for Levi's?
2 Explain how it helps customers.

Public relations activities

The forces in an organisation's external environment are capable of affecting it in a variety of ways. The forces may be social, economic, political, local or environmental and might be represented by a variety of groups such as customers, shareholders, employees and special interest groups. Reacting positively to such forces and influences is very important.

Public relations is the planned and sustained effort an organisation makes to establish, develop and build relationships with its many publics (Figure 10.5).

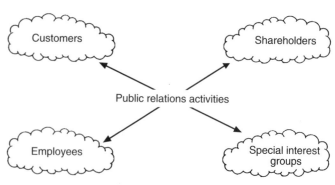

Figure 10.5 Public relations activities

The purpose of public relations (PR) is therefore to provide an external environment for an organisation in which it is popular and can prosper. Building goodwill in such a way requires behaviour by the organisation which takes into account the attitudes of the many people who may come across it and its products.

Whereas many of the other promotional methods are *short-term,* public relations is long-term, as it may take a long time for an organisation to improve the way people think more positively about its products and activities. For example, just think about the sort of public relations problems that chemical and oil companies have in a world where consumers have become increasingly environmentally conscious.

According to Frank Jefkins, PR involves a transfer process which helps to convert the negative feelings of an organisation's many publics into positive ones (see Figure 10.6).

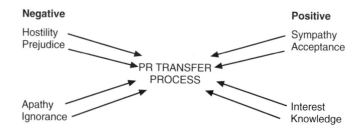

Figure 10.6 The PR transfer process

There are many different types of public relations activities:

- *Charitable donations and community relations* are good for an organisation's image, often provide lots of good publicity and also help to promote and provide for a good cause.
- *Hospitality* at top sporting events is a popular method used by organisations to develop their customer relations. For example, there are opportunities to entertain customers at events such as the FA Cup Final, Wimbledon and the Grand National.
- *Press releases* covering events affecting the organisation – such as news stories, export achievements, policy changes, technical developments and anything which enhances the organisation's image – are a useful form of public relations. Press conferences are used to cover newsworthy events which are of interest to a variety of media.
- *Visits* and *open days* are a popular method of inviting people to various events to improve their understanding of what the organisation stands for.
- *Sponsorship* of sporting and cultural events is viewed as a useful opportunity to associate an image with a particular type of function. For example, the NatWest Trophy, the FA Carling Premiership and the Embassy World Snooker Championship.
- *Lobbying* of ministers, officials and important people from outside interest groups, so that an accurate portrayal can be made of a problem or a case, may help to influence their views of the organisation.
- *Corporate videotapes* have become increasingly popular over recent years as a method of providing a variety of interested parties with information about a company's activities.
- *Minor product changes,* such as no testing on animals or environmentally friendly products, may provide considerable PR benefits.

Evidence collection point

Make a list of different public relations activities you either hear about, see or benefit from over a weekly period. Try to explain the purpose of each activity and evaluate their effectiveness.

Reaching a target audience with sales promotion methods

Sales promotion methods

Sales promotion describes a category of techniques which are used to encourage customers to make a purchase. These activities are effectively short-term and may be used:

- to increase sales
- to help with personal selling
- to respond to the actions of competitors
- as an effective alternative to advertising.

The Institute of Sales Promotion defines sales promotion as follows:

> Sales promotion is the function of marketing which seeks to achieve given objectives by the adding of intrinsic, tangible value to a product or service.

The essential feature of a sales promotion is that it is a short-term inducement to encourage customers to react quickly, whereas advertising is usually a process that develops the whole product or brand.

As you walk down a town High Street or through a shopping mall, you will see many different examples of sales promotions. Such promotions may serve many different purposes. For example, competitions, vouchers or coupons and trading stamps may be designed to build customer loyalty and perhaps increase the volume purchased by existing customers. Product sampling is a strategy that is often used to introduce new products into the marketplace. Clearance sales of overstocked goods will increase turnover during part of the year in which business might otherwise be slack. Many sales promotions are undertaken in response to the activities of competitors to ensure that an organisation remains competitive.

Sales promotions can be divided into two broad areas:

- promotions assisting with the sale of products to the trade
- promotions assisting the trade in selling products to the final consumer.

Selling into the pipeline is an expression used to describe promotions which move products from the manufacturer into the distribution system.

Selling out of the pipeline describes promotions which trigger the end-user to make a purchase (Figure 10.7).

Figure 10.7 Promotions into and out of the pipeline

There are many different types of sales promotion:

- *Dealer loaders* are among the inducements to attract orders from retailers and wholesalers. They may include a 'free case' with so many cases bought. For example, thirteen for the price of twelve is known as a 'baker's dozen'.
- *Competitions* may interest dealers and consumers. For dealers they may be linked to sales with attractive prizes for the most successful dealer. Scratch cards, free draws and bingo cards are popular promotional methods for consumers.
- *Promotional gifts* such as bottles of spirits, clocks, watches or diaries are considered useful bounty for dealers.
- *Price reductions* and *special offers* are usually popular with consumers. They can, however, prove expensive as many consumers would otherwise have been prepared to pay the full price.
- *Premium offers* may offer extra product for the same price. *Coupons* which offer money off or money back may also be attractive incentives for consumers. These may appear in magazines, be distributed door-to-door or appear on the side of a pack.
- *Charity promotions* can be popular with younger consumers, who collect box tops or coupons and send them to a manufacturer, which then makes a donation to charity.
- *Loyalty incentives* may be an important element in sales promotions. Dealers' loyalty might be rewarded with bigger discounts, competitions and prizes or even having their names published as stockists in advertisements. For consumers, loyalty incentives may be in the form of 'cash back', free gifts or a variety of other tangible benefits.

Targeting an audience

Not all customers are the same. Groups of consumers have different needs, wants and tastes. The process of dividing a market into parts at which different marketing inputs can be directed is known as segmentation. This is very important, because for communication activities to be effective as part of the marketing mix, they must be targeted at the most appropriate part of the market. Tom Cannon defines market segmentation as the 'sub-dividing of a market into distinct and homogeneous sub-groups of consumers where any group can conceivably be selected as a target market to be met with a distinct marketing mix'.

Market segmentation enables the organisation to maximise the efficiency of its communication activities by using a tailored marketing mix for each market segment in which there are consumers with different needs. To aim communication activities at the needs and requirements of part of a market, an organisation needs to understand the behaviour of consumers. There are many ways in which consumers can be divided or segmented because of their behaviour.

Socio-economic factors

One way of understanding how customers will respond to marketing activities is to divide them into socio-economic groupings based upon the types of

Socio-economic group	Social 'class'	Most likely types of occupation	Examples
A	'Upper' or 'upper-middle'	High managerial Administrative Professional	Surgeon Director of large company
B	'Middle'	Intermediate managerial Professional Administrative	Bank manager Headteacher Surveyor
C1	'Lower-middle'	Supervisory Junior managerial Junior administrative Clerical	Bank clerk Nurse Teacher
C2	'Skilled working'	Skilled manual workers	Joiner Welder Foreman
D	'Working'	Semi-skilled Unskilled	Driver Postman Porter
E	Lowest subsistence level	Low-paid Unemployed	Casual worker State pensioner

Figure 10.8 An example of a socio-economic classification

jobs they do. Dividing people into classes is called *social stratification*. The underlying assumption is that, as particular jobs tend to have certain life-styles attached, if the market can be divided by job classification then more appropriate products and services can be targeted towards particular groups.

One of the best-known classifications used to divide consumers in the UK is shown in Figure 10.8. According to this classification, an exclusive product would be advertised to groups A and B because they would be more likely to be able to afford it.

Socio-economic grouping provides a reliable picture of the relationship between occupation and income for the purposes of marketing. Members of each group have similar priorities, which influence their wants and needs. For example, we would expect those in groups A, B and C1 to spend some of their income on private education, private health care, new cars, antiques, etc. whereas those in groups C2, D and E would spend more of their income on necessities.

Age and gender

Segmenting a market by age is widely applied. People of different ages frequently have differing needs and wants. A good example is the way in which banks and building societies develop products for students, young children and elderly customers.

Many products are also segmented by gender. Clothing, alcohol, cosmetics and even cars are segmented in such a way. We can probably all think of magazines that are pitched at women or men of a certain age and lifestyle.

Case study – Newspaper readership profiles

Look at the readership profiles below and then answer the questions that follow:

1 Imagine you have been entrusted with the responsibility of increasing the circulation of one of the newspapers below. Working in groups, describe what audience your newspaper would be targeted at and what communication methods you might use to increase circulation.

2 Comment upon other areas of the marketing mix that you might change when developing your communication strategy.

	Tabloid/ Broadsheet	Circulation (1) '000	Adult readership (2) '000	%	Men %	Women %	Sex Age Class 15/34 %	35/54 %	55+ %	ABC1 %	C2DE %
Population profile					48	52	36	32	32	48	52
National Dailies											
The Sun	T	4071	9920	22	55	45	44	31	24	30	71
Daily Mirror	T	2493	7148	16	54	46	35	32	33	32	69
Daily Mail	T	1794	4456	10	50	50	28	34	37	65	35
Daily Express	T	1367	3482	8	52	48	27	32	41	60	41
The Daily Telegraph	B	1008	2617	6	55	45	23	34	44	84	16
Daily Star	T	747	2201	5	65	35	51	32	17	25	74
Daily Record (Scotland)	T	737	1925	4	53	47	40	35	25	32	68
Today	T	587	1777	4	55	45	40	38	22	44	56
The Times	B	485	1314	3	59	41	35	38	27	87	14
The Guardian	B	403	1344	3	55	45	39	39	21	84	17
Financial Times	B	297	739	2	72	28	37	45	19	89	11
The Independent	B	281	1055	3	62	38	45	38	16	85	15

Lifestyle

Over recent years many organisations have paid increasing attention to the lifestyle of consumers. A lifestyle is a pattern of behaviour adopted by a particular community or a sub-section of it. For example, someone upwardly mobile and ambitious would be seeking an affluent lifestyle and a higher material standard of living. The UK 'yuppy' is reputed to be young (24–35), well-educated, professional and upwardly mobile.

Evidence collection point

Make a list of the sort of products associated with a particular type of lifestyle, for example that of the 'yuppy'.

Psychographics is one way used to measure lifestyle. One example is the 'sagacity life-cycle' groupings which work on the principle that people have different behavioural patterns and aspirations as they go through life. Four main stages of the life-cycle are identified and then further sub-divided according to income and occupation groups (Figure 10.9).

The life-cycle stages are defined as follows:

- *Dependent* – mainly under 24s, living at home or full-time students.
- *Pre-family* – under 35s, who have established their household but have no children.
- *Family* – parents, under 65, with one or more children in the household.
- *Late* – includes all adults whose children have left home, or who are over 35 and childless.

The occupation groups are:

- *White* – head of household in the A, B, C1 occupation group.
- *Blue* – head of household in the C2, D, E occupation group.

Cultural factors

Culture encompasses standard patterns of behaviour and plays an important role in shaping our purchasing patterns. It stems from the traditions, beliefs and values of the community in which we live. For example, our religious beliefs, our attitudes towards alcohol, the food we eat and the importance of the family are all part of our culture.

Though a nation may be characterised by one dominant culture, there may be a series of sub-cultures within it. Sub-cultures are important for organisations that wish to target their output to those who share the values of that particular sub-culture – for example, youth markets, ethnic groups and senior citizens.

Self-image

Another attempt at explaining the behaviour of consumers is the self-image theory. The 'self-image' is an individual's thoughts about himself or herself as a person of a certain type. There are various ways to maintain and enhance this image, and in particular the individual makes choices of music, car, clothing and places to shop that fit his or her perception of 'self'.

By discovering how consumers wish themselves to be perceived, organisations can develop and promote products consistent with the image sought. For example, BMWs are carefully developed to match the self-image consumers would like.

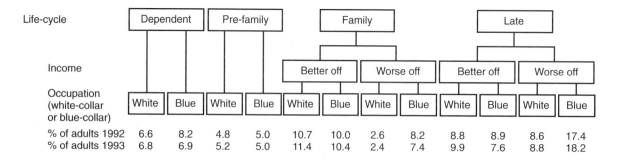

Figure 10.9 Sagacity life-cycle groupings

Personality

Closely related to the self-image theory is the personality of the consumer. By considering customers with similar personalities, it may be possible to promote products on the basis of such stereotypes. Fashion products, in particular, reflect the personality traits of customers.

Geographical location

Consumers in different regions may be affected by different factors such as climate, natural factors, cultures, population densities and levels of income. Certain regions also have different characteristics which affect buying patterns.

Evidence collection point

What types of products are local to the sort of people in your region? Make a list of these products and then compare them with products from another part of the country.

Economic factors

Another group of factors influencing consumer behaviour are the *economic determinants of consumer demand.* These include:

- *real disposable incomes* available to consumers to spend on goods and services. Any change in incomes will affect the types of goods and services they buy
- *the relative price of substitute products,* where the purchase may be viewed as better value for money
- *the size of population*
- *consumer tastes, fashions and habits*
- *government measures* influencing consumer behaviour.

Case study – Party, party, party

At a time when airlines are struggling to win passengers, an older rival is building up steam. Sea cruising, once the province of the leisured rich, is booming.

The typical passenger booking a cruise today is successful, in his or her mid-thirties and looking for a good time. In response to this trend, ships have been transformed into floating fun palaces. Discos with laser

lights and lavish floor shows have replaced a game of whist on the sun-deck. Gambling is an additional attraction. Customers also want shorter breaks – three to five days is the fastest-growing segment of this holiday market.

1 If you were a cruise operator, given the nature of the market indicated, how and where would you reach this particular type of customer?
2 Where else is there a market for cruises? Are there other groups of consumers for whom you could gear particular types of cruises? How would you promote such cruises?

Effects of marketing communication on product performance

Marketing communications require high levels of expenditure and therefore it is crucial to analyse the effectiveness of any investment. The effectiveness of any campaign will largely depend upon how effective a campaign is at influencing product performance or how well the campaign develops a brand image or customer perceptions.

There are a variety of different ways of evaluating the success of a campaign. It is important at the beginning of a campaign for marketers to have a good idea of what they wish to achieve. *Performance standards,* where actual performance can be compared with an expected level of performance, need to be set. For example, it may be possible to compare the number of products expected to be sold with the number actually sold. Given the influence of marketing activities on product performance, it is also useful to coordinate the activities of the marketing department with other areas of the business so that they can meet performance requirements set by the promotional campaign.

Evaluating the success of a campaign may involve testing the views of a *representative sample,* both before and after a campaign. Pre-testing will discover the sample's perception of a product before the campaign. Post-testing involves asking the same questions to discover how far knowledge and understanding of the product has improved (Figure 10.10).

For example, in the Creature Comforts campaign, customer perceptions were initially investigated. The campaign was 'tracked' with 10 000 interviews per month, and then the success of the campaign was evaluated by looking at the degree to which customer perceptions had changed in line with objectives. During the course of that campaign the proportion of consumers who viewed electric central heating as modern and up-to-date increased from 20% to 30%.

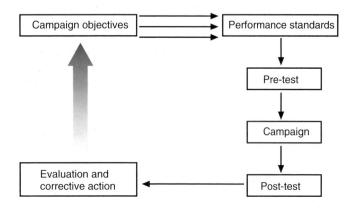

Figure 10.10 Evaluating the success of a campaign

Effective control of marketing activities will depend upon the quality and type of information received about the organisation's activities. There are a variety of different ways in which the influence of marketing communications upon product performance may be assessed:

■ *Sales levels* Using sales figures is probably the most tangible and effective way of evaluating performance. Sales may be measured in *volume* or units sold or *value* of sales achieved. However,

looking at sales figures alone is often not enough. For example, in a rapidly contracting market a small fall in sales might be considered to be a creditable achievement. Sales figures should be considered within the context of the market and should be compared with *market shares, growth, contraction* and *sales of competitors.*

■ *Customer loyalty, brand loyalty and repeat sales* Having the same customers come back again and again may be very important for the manufacturer or service provider. It helps to ensure that income levels are maintained and that extreme fluctuations do not take place in sales levels. The communication process can help to create:
  - *routine response behaviour* where buyers know of products, know they are acceptable and buy them without a great deal of thought and analysis.
  - reduce the consumers' *level of involvement* and time used for making the decision
  - improve their *familiarity* and *knowledge* of the product
  - create a *positive attitude* towards the product
  - reduce *cognitive dissonance* after the sale (doubt that they might have about the decision they have made to purchase the product).

Evidence collection point

Do you have any loyalties to certain products or brands? Explain why. List these products and show how often you purchase them. What features of the marketing mix of these products causes you remain loyal to them?

■ *Product life-cycle* In Chapter 8 we looked at the product life-cycle and the importance of matching changes in the marketing mix with the various stages in the cycle. In the early phases of the cycle communication activities should help to make buyers aware of its features and uses in the process of *building awareness.* During the latter part of the *growth phase* it is important to emphasise *brand loyalty* and *repeat purchase.* In the maturity phase, with a lot more competition in the market, competitors emphasise the differences between their products and others through product *differentiation.* During the decline phase the organisation may *reduce spending* on communication activities (Figure 10.11).

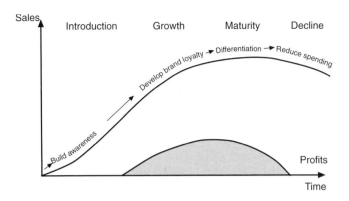

Figure 10.11 Communication activities during the product life-cycle

Evidence collection point

Look at a number of products and comment upon how communication activities reflect the particular phase they are at in their product life-cycle.

Direct marketing methods

Organisations are constantly looking for new ways to reach consumers. Over recent years, with changes and advances in new technologies, there has been an explosion of product-selling possibilities through the development of various direct marketing methods. Direct marketing is the process of using non-personal media, technology or telesales to introduce products to consumers.

Direct mail

Direct mail is personally addressed advertising sent through the post. Every month each British household receives an average six and a half direct mail items. By using direct mail an organisation may establish a direct relationship with its customers. The advertiser supplies promotional literature to encourage a sale and then tries to cater for the customers' perceived needs.

Mail-order is probably the most well-known form of direct marketing. Many firms use agents to help with sales. By cutting out the middle-men, mail-order firms have the opportunity to sell goods at competitive prices.

Dear Mr Lucky

First of all allow me, on behalf of my colleagues and myself, to offer you our warmest congratulations, because

You really are a winner in our 1995 super prize draw

Yes, you're off to a winning start, since one of our fabulous entry prizes is already yours, and may have even gone one better. If, as I hope, your personal lucky number 20676646 matches our 1st prize, you will also walk away with the prize of prizes, or the car, or £15 000 cash.

Figure 10.12 An inducement to respond to a direct-mail offer

The ability of direct mail to target precise market segments in a market makes it cost-effective, as it eliminates the supply of mailshots to those unlikely to buy. Geo-demographic and lifestyle systems such as PIN, ACORN and MOSAIC help the direct-mailer to identify types of consumer according to where they live and the lifestyle they follow. The majority of mailshots are read, and organisations often use sales promotions such as offers and competitions to encourage a response (Figure 10.12).

If a good impression is made with the consumer, direct mail can offer an organisation the opportunity to send a long message and some detailed copy. Organisations such as the Automobile Association, Reader's Digest, Consumers Association and the National Geographic are well established in using direct mail techniques. It is the easiest form of promotion to measure as it is possible to calculate the number of mailshots sent out, the cost of the campaign, the response rate and the number of sales made.

Royal Mail offers its 'Mailsort' service for volume mailings. By pre-sorting mail before handing the postage over, users can be provided with discounts on postage costs. Royal Mail points out that direct mail is the most selective form of promotional message reaching people in their own households, and it has a high impact in comparison with other advertising messages.

Telemarketing

The idea of *telesales* was born in the USA in the 1960s as a fast-action sales tool. When it came to the UK it failed to develop properly and established a poor reputation. This was the first generation of what is now known as *telemarketing*.

Telemarketing is the direct selling of products using the telephone. It may be based upon a *cold canvass* of the telephone directory or on a screened list of prospective clients.

During the 1970s, as more sophisticated telephone skills developed for research and account servicing, telemarketing began to be viewed as acceptable. Despite this it was rarely integrated with other direct marketing and selling activities.

The second generation of telemarketing involved spending large amounts of time and money on an exercise which was proving to be a poor investment – much of the information needed to make the system more efficient lay around the offices on pieces of paper, in card indexes or in the boots of sales representatives' cars. Potentially useful sales information was being wasted, opportunities were lost and more accurate targeting was made impossible.

From this muddle, telemarketing's third generation emerged with the aim of contributing to a database that could then be managed and integrated as part of the organisation's overall promotional mix. Such information was to provide the opportunity to

analyse the market and the position of competitors. It was to create a new and more powerful use of the phone to build, maintain and service accounts, whilst at the same time linking with other marketing activities.

A recent report from Datamonitor predicted that telemarketing will be the big growth area in direct marketing. The value of direct marketing will rise from £75 million to £108 million by 1998, an increase of almost 45%. This surge will require the setting up of 'carelines', which will be able to monitor customer reaction to sales.

Evidence collection point

From the consumers' point of view, make a list of the arguments for and against the process of telemarketing.

Other forms of direct marketing

Changes in technology today offer many more openings for telesales. The use of 'ISDN' lines may mean that more selling will be done downline with packages and presentation from PC to PC. Such savings may mean fewer reps and cars on the road, and more time spent selling. Recent research shows that telemarketing is particularly useful when combined with other communication techniques such as advertising and sales promotions.

Another area of growth is likely to be selling *off-screen* through satellite television shopping channels, where consumers can respond to direct marketing activities within their own homes.

Evidence collection point

Keep a log of how direct marketing activities affect both you and your household over a monthly period. How many of these activities have been effective? Comment on their success/failure rate. Your work should contribute evidence of Core Skills in Communication.

Case study – New Media Entertainment

New Media Entertainment was set up by Mercury to develop and evaluate demand for a variety of entertainment services. Their aim was to set up services using low-cost technologies which are available anywhere in the country via the telecommunications network.

One of their first steps has been to set up a national computer games network. Users with a PC and modem can play games with opponents from all over the country. Mercury has bought the rights to a number of games including Air Warrior, which lets players team-up into squadrons and fight each other. The service costs a couple of pounds per hour plus the cost of a local phone call.

Other services are also planned. These include:

■ chatlines
■ information services
■ theatre and concert information
■ booking services
■ home banking
■ home shopping.

1 What are the advantages for the consumer of using such a network?
2 What other forms of marketing activity may suffer as a result of the development of these forms of services?

Task

Lifestyle is a new brand of ice-cream comprising coconut-flavoured ice-cream and surrounded with plain orange flavoured chocolate. It is designed to compete in a highly competitive sector of the ice-cream market.

Imagine that you work for an advertising agency as an account executive. Work in groups to complete the following tasks:

1 Identify the target audience for this brand. Comment upon the various characteristics of this targeted group.
2 What types of media would you use to reach this targeted group? List the advantages and disadvantages of each type.
3 You have been asked to produce a media plan like the one shown below. If your campaign is to be successful it is advisable to use several forms of media. Your budget is £450 000.

Media plan			£ cost	Jan	Feb	Mar	Apr	May	Jun	Jul	Aug	Sep	Oct	Nov	Dec	Sub-total	Comments
Television (central area)	30 second TV commercial	Off peak	600														
	Oct, Nov, Dec Mar, Apr, May	On peak	4000														
	30 second TV commercial	Off peak	400														
	Jan, Feb, Jun Jul, Aug, Sep	On peak	3000														
Local radio	30 second spot		100														
National press	One insertion per newspaper		5000														
Local press	One insertion per newspaper		500														
Free trade press	One insertion per newspaper		200														
Direct mailing	1000 packages delivered by the Post Office (selected addresses)		450														
	1000 packages hand-delivered (selected areas)		300														
Bus sides	10 posters		1000														
Competitions	Each month		2000														
Coupons	Each month		1000														
POS materials	200 units		1000														

Control and guidelines for marketing communications

The *Office of Fair Trading,* a government body, was set up to look after the interests of consumers and traders. It publishes a wide variety of information, and encourages businesses to issue *codes of practice.* These codes refer to marketing activities considered to be acceptable, as well as those which are considered to be unacceptable. Their aim is simply to raise the standards of service. Traders who persists in breaking the law must give an assurance that they will mend their ways (see Chapter 3, pages 65–8).

The *National Consumer Council* represents the consumer to the government, nationalised industries, public services and businesses. It also carries out research and publishes recommendations.

Citizens' Advice Bureaux, of which there are some 900 in various parts of the country, cover many aspects of day-to-day life. A CAB will often agree to act as a 'go-between' in disputes between traders and consumers.

Local authorities have *trading standards departments* that investigate complaints about misleading offers or prices, inaccurate weights and measures and consumer credit.

Environmental health departments enforce legislation covering health aspects of food – for example, unfit food or unhygienic storage, preparation or serving of food.

Standard setters

The *British Standards Institution* is financed by voluntary subscriptions and government grants. Its primary concern is with setting up standards that are acceptable to both manufacturers and consumers. Goods of a certain standard are allowed to bear the BSI kitemark, showing consumers that the product has passed the appropriate tests.

Professional and trade associations promote the interests of their members we ell as the development of a particular product or service area. In order to protect consumers, their members often agree to abide by *voluntary codes of practice.* These codes aim to keep up standards and members will often set up funds to safeguard consumers' money. For example, the Association of British Travel Agents (ABTA) will refund money to holiday makers should a member company fail.

Independent consumer groups and the media

The *Consumers' Association* examines goods and services offered to the public and publishes the results of its research in *Which?* This magazine was founded in 1957 and has developed a circulation of over half a million. It has become an invaluable source of information for consumers.

The National Federation of Consumer Groups is a coordinating body for voluntary and local consumer groups. Local groups survey local goods and services, publish reports and campaign for changes.

There is no doubt that, when consumers' rights and obligations are abused or when dangerous goods are brought into the marketplace, feelings run high. The media – newspapers, television and radio – increasingly become involved in campaigns for changes.

Industry influences upon marketing activities

The Advertising Standards Authority (ASA) is an independent body that exercises control over all advertising except that on radio and television. The Authority draws up its own codes which it uses to ensure that advertisements are 'legal, decent, honest and truthful'. Advertisements should be prepared with a sense of responsibility to both consumers and society and conform to the principles of fair competition.

For example, a number of complaints were made to the ASA over a campaign by Rover to extol the virtues of wood panelling on the Rover 820 Se. Suspended by the main body of the text appeared a box with the words: 'A woman, a dog and a walnut tree, the more you beat them the better they'll be'. At Rover they insisted that the comment was only put there to inject some humour!

The ASA were also unconvinced of the cholesterol-reducing properties advertised in the showpiece launch of Common Sense Oat Bran Flakes. It brought in a team of top nutritional scientists after fears that the advertisement might create needless worry for consumers.

Evidence collection point

Over the period of a month look at the various types of advertisements by surveying magazines and periodicals. Make a list of advertisements (if any) that you feel are not altogether 'legal, decent, honest and truthful'. Explain why in each instance.

The *Chartered Institute of Marketing* has its own Code of Practice to which members are required to adhere. The code refers to professional standards of behaviour in securing and developing business, and demands honesty and integrity of conduct. The *British Code of Advertising Practice* is supported by advertisers, agencies and the media, whose representatives make up the *Code of Advertising Practice Committee*. The Code sets out the rules which those in the advertising industry agree to follow. It also indicates to those outside advertising that there are regulations designed to ensure that advertisements can be trusted.

Voluntary and statutory controls, and the formation of active pressure groups which often gain popular support from the media, have helped to develop a changing climate for marketing activity. Organisations today can no longer disregard groups of consumers, or wider issues in which they should be involved, and have to show increased sensitivity to their many publics.

Evidence indicators

For this activity you need to present a report which compares the advertising, publicity, public relations and sales promotion methods of two organisations. For at least *one* of these organisations you need to identify a business which has recently changed some of its marketing activities by moving towards an increased use of direct marketing with the accompanying use of new technologies. Track the marketing activities of these organisations over a period of time before presenting your report. The following list should serve as a checklist. Please tick off each of the following when you have successfully covered them as part of your report. You need to confirm that:

- I have identified two organisations upon which to base my report. ☐
- One of the organisations has recently used newer technologies and methods to communicate with its customers. ☐
- I have tracked the communication activities of two organisations over an acceptable time period. ☐
- I have identified the different types of marketing communications used by each organisation. ☐
- I have commented upon the use of these communications. ☐
- My report evaluates the use of promotional techniques in relation to product successes, sales, brand loyalty, consumer loyalty and consumer awareness. ☐
- I have commented upon how well activities keep within the various guidelines and controls over communication activities. ☐

Achieving customer satisfaction using sales methods and customer service

In this chapter we look at the changing way that goods and services are provided for almost all of our needs. In the 1970s and early 1980s would we ever have thought that banks and building societies would soon become financial supermarkets? It would have been impossible to imagine the vast shopping developments on the edges of towns, or that we would use our televisions as a form of shopping medium. Organisations today realise that they cannot compete on the basis of their products and prices alone. Satisfying customer needs has thus become the major weapon used by organisations to compete in the rapidly changing markets of the 1990s. Throughout this chapter we look at how such needs are satisfied by sales methods and customer service.

Meeting customer needs with direct and indirect sales methods

Customers are the most important people for any organisation. They are simply the natural resource upon which the success of that organisation depends. When thinking about the importance of customers it is useful to remember the following points.

■ Repeat business is at the backbone of selling. It helps to provide security and certainty.
■ Organisations are dependent upon their customers. If they do not develop customer loyalty and satisfaction they could lose their customers.
■ Without customers the organisation would simply not exist.
■ The purpose of the organisation is to fulfil the needs of customers.
■ The customer makes it possible to achieve everything the business aims for.

Many argue that all organisations have both *internal* and *external customers* (Figure 11.1). The belief is that the quality of customer service provided outside the organisation is dependent upon how well employees within the organisation treat each other. For example, if an employee makes an enquiry to personnel or writes out a requisition for some

stationery, he or she should expect to be treated with the same respect as a customer outside the organisation. This approach helps to encourage the teamwork and customer care which leads toward total quality management.

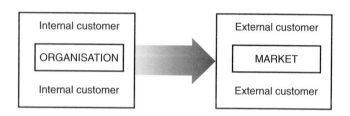

Figure 11.1 Internal and external customers

Many UK companies try to explain the concept of the internal and external customer by referring to the link which starts with the needs of external customers and then includes all of the people involved in bringing together resources to satisfy such needs. Everyone has a role in satisfying customers. This process helps to emphasise that all employees within an organisation are part of a quality chain which is improved with better teamwork, employee care and communication procedures.

Though the concept of the internal and external customer is widely used, it has been criticised for focusing an organisation's efforts internally upon itself instead of spending more time and attention upon using resources to satisfy the needs and expectations of external customers.

Customer satisfaction is at the heart of the selling process (Figure 11.2). One estimate is that it costs five times as much to attract new customers as it does to keep an existing one. The relationship between the customer and the organisation is, therefore, an important one.

According to Sarah Cook in her book *Customer Care*, customer relationships can be depicted in terms of a loyalty ladder (Figure 11.3). The willingness of individual customers to ascend the loyalty ladder will depend upon how they are treated when doing

Figure 11.2 Customer satisfaction is at the heart of the selling process

business with the organisation. Well-targeted sales methods and efficient personal service will help to convert one-off purchasers to occasional users, then to regular customers and advocates.

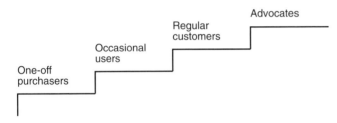

Figure 11.3 Loyalty ladder

In developing a relationship with its customers an organisation must concentrate on both the selling process and how the relationship between the buyer and seller is managed. This is part of what is widely known as *relationship marketing,* where an organisation has to develop all of its activities in ways which take into account how their activities may affect their relationships with customers. Examples are order times, reputation, the changing of goods or providing of refunds, dealing with faults, correctly addressed letters and the overall efficiency of operations.

Selling methods will depend upon how organisations or individuals wish to reach their customers. These methods will inevitably change where organisations feel that they serve their customers best with different methods. For example, Amstrad computers used to sell widely through computer shops. However, many people now do not buy computers in this way. As a result Amstrad decided to change the nature of their distribution from *indirect* selling to

direct selling through mail order. To do this they set up Amstrad Business Direct (Figure 11.4). Using carefully targeted customer information, customers benefit from lower 'factory prices' and direct technical support from the organisation as well as a number of other supporting benefits from a large mail order organisation.

Figure 11.4 Amstrad Business Direct

Direct selling methods

Direct selling involves contacting customers without the use of an intermediary (Figure 11.5). In the UK, direct marketing techniques have become increasingly popular, with an average annual rise of about 15%. Direct selling enables producers and providers of services to target specific groups of customers; this also provides them with a measurable response. In businesss-to-business industrial markets, direct marketing is particularly important. Major purchases such as installations, machinery and equipment are usually arranged between producer and user. Today direct sales methods have also spread to many consumer markets.

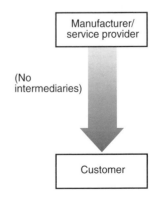

Figure 11.5 Direct selling

There are a number of direct selling methods, many of which have changed with the increasing use of different technologies. They may include:

- *Television selling* This is already big business, particularly in the USA and Australia, and has recently been introduced into the UK by satellite with a separate channel called QVC – a shopping channel open 24 hours a day, 364 days a year, with a special freephone number. In the USA the Homes Shopping Network became a huge success story in the late 1980s. The typical format is for each product to have a four-minute slot, during which viewers can phone in on one of 200 free lines, order an item and pay by quoting their credit card number. The products sold are mainly brand names, and they are presented in an entertaining and informative way.

Case study – Drawing money out of your personal computer

Soon the PC may be used to draw electronic money out of the bank, store it on a card and then use the cash to pay for goods and services over the Internet.

The idea for cash on a smart card is being developed by NatWest in conjunction with Midland Bank and BT. The card holds the money in encrypted digital form and is intended as an electronic substitute for cash. Trials have already begun. To fill your card with money you insert the card into a bank teller machine or into a slot in special phones. Paying for goods or services will simply involve putting the card into a slot in the till at a shop so that the till automatically debits the card.

The scheme also enables users to withdraw money from the bank and pay for goods and services over the Internet, by inserting the card into a reader installed on the PC and entering a few numbers on the screen. The potential for trade is considered to be enormous. Lots of people want to engage in transactions over the Internet. Waiting for a cheque is cumbersome and issuing credit card numbers over the network would be considered risky. The card would help many organisations to reach specialist users from large markets across the world.

1 How does this form of smart card differ from a credit card?
2 What are the benefits of this sort of card for a regular Internet user?
3 Is there any potential for this form of selling? If so, in what areas?

- *Radio sales* Commercial radio stations are constantly looking for new ways of reaching customers and securing advertising revenue. Businesses such as car showrooms, kitchen unit manufacturers and even colleges advertise on radio and provide follow-up details of their location or telephone numbers. Many radio stations also have programmes where listeners can ring up and either swap or sell goods.
- *Factory shops* As well as using intermediaries, many producers use factory shops to reach customers. This cuts out the retailer's percentage and allows goods to be sold at lower prices than those in the High Street. There are many examples, from Hornsea Pottery in East Yorkshire to the Moffat Woollen Mills and K Shoes at Kendal.
- *Telesales* This originated in the USA as a fast-action sales tool. When first developed in the UK it was regarded as intrusive and established a poor reputation. Since then telesales has become far more focused, with organisations carefully targeting customers and providing a number of supporting services to develop and maintain the telesales relationships. For example, many companies use 'carelines' to monitor the reactions of customers to new telesales promotions. The great advantage is massive reduction in sales expenses and more time which can be spent selling.
- *Door-to-door* Many organisations try to sell their goods directly into local communities either through door-to-door catalogue sales or by arranging other activities, parties and promotions. For example, Betterware, Tupperware and Avon are widely known for their different techniques for reaching customers. Parties and other events may be of help for a number of products such as clothes, saucy underwear (Ann Summers) and jewellery. Agents sell on behalf of the host organisation and usually receive a commission on their sales.
- *Pyramid selling* This involves setting up a network of salespeople to sell on your behalf. Each salesperson takes a commission from their sales and then also takes a commission from the sales of anybody they manage to get to join in the selling process. The more people they encourage to join, the larger the commission, as they stand at the top of the pyramid they have established. Some consumer goods, restaurants and many other areas rely on this form of selling.
- *Mail-order catalogues* Mail-order firms either sell goods through agents or by members of the public ordering a free catalogue. Some firms have

their own delivery service while others will use the Post Office or other carriers. As mail-order firms cut out the middleman, they have the opportunity to sell goods at competitive prices. They are also able to use computerised methods for handling orders and stocks and sell from large warehouses situated in locations where rates are cheap and communication links are efficient.

Indirect selling methods

Whereas direct selling methods are *zero-level channels* which do not use an intermediary, indirect selling methods use one of more channels of distribution through which goods are transferred from the producer to the end user. These channels consist of one or more individuals or organisations who help to make the products available for the end user (Figure 11.6).

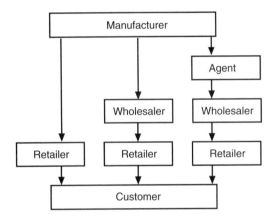

Figure 11.6 Indirect sales channels

International distribution channels

In international markets, distribution systems may be extremely complex. The international marketer has to deal with transporting products over larger distances, with many more choices of transport, often with significantly higher costs. It is also necessary to deal with distribution systems which reflect different economic, social and cultural developments, influencing the ways in which customers are reached through the market.

Such distribution systems may be completely different from those which marketers are used to in the home market. As a result, the international

marketer has to research the distribution systems relevant to a product before entering a market.

For example, when exporting to India one must choose between a local wholesaler or a manufacturers' agent. The local wholesaler sells on to a consumer wholesaler, who then sells on to a retailer. On the other hand, a manufacturers' agent either sells to a rural retailer or to another wholesaler (Figure 11.7).

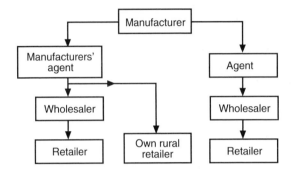

Figure 11.7 Typical distribution patterns in India

Wholesalers

These stock a range of goods from competing manufacturers to sell on to other organisations such as retailers. Most wholesalers take on the title to the goods and so assume many of the risks associated with ownership. They may provide a range of services which include:

■ *Breaking bulk* Manufacturers produce goods in bulk for sale but they might not want to store the goods themselves. They want to be paid as quickly as possible. A number of wholesalers buy the stock from them and generally payment is prompt. The wholesaler then stocks these goods, along with others bought from other manufacturers, on the premises, ready for purchase by retailers.

■ *Simplifying the distribution process* The chain of distribution without the wholesaler would look something like Figure 11.8. Manufacturer 1 has to carry out four journeys to supply retailers 1, 2, 3 and 4, and has to send out four sets of business documents, and handle four sets of accounts. The same situation applies to each of the manufacturers, so that in total 16 journeys are made and 16 sets of paperwork are required. (This is

283

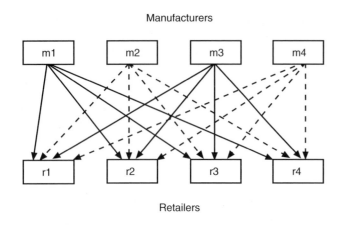

Manufacturers

Retailers

Figure 11.8 The distribution chain without the wholesaler

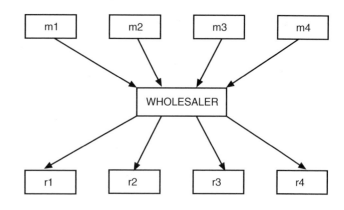

Figure 11.9 The distribution chain with the wholesaler

a simplification, because in the real world thousands of different transactions might be involved).

The wholesaler can simplify the costs and processes of distribution in the following ways:

- by cutting down on journeys, fuel and other costs
- by cutting down on paperwork – invoicing, administration, etc.

The chain of distribution with the wholesaler would look something like Figure 11.9. With the wholesaler everything is simplified.

■ *Storage* Most retailers have only a limited amount of storage space. The wholesaler can be looked upon as a huge cupboard for the retailer. Provided the retailer agrees to take supplies at regular intervals, the wholesaler will perform this important storage function. With the growth of

cash-and carry facilities, it has become easier for the retailer to stock up on supplies that are running down.

■ *Packaging and labelling* The wholesaler will sometimes finish off the packaging and labelling of goods, perhaps putting tags on goods or branded labels for supermarkets.

■ *Offering advice* Being in the middle of the process of distribution, wholesalers have a lot of market information at their fingertips. In particular, wholesalers know what goods are selling well. With this is mind they can advise retailers on what to buy and make.

There are a variety of different types of wholesalers. The largest single unit in the British wholesale trade is the Cooperative Wholesale Society (CWS). The CWS also manufactures own-brand lines, owns interests overseas, such as tea estates in India, and maintains a shipping and transport fleet.

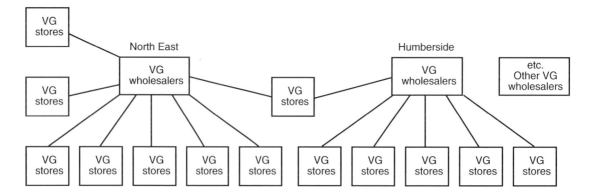

Figure 11.10 Voluntary groups

Most small retailers buy a large proportion of their stock from cash-and carry warehouses. Retailers are responsible for transporting the selected goods from the wholesale warehouse to their premises and are able to buy the goods at a trade discount.

Some wholesalers have set up voluntary groups. A voluntary group is made up largely of small retailers who agree to buy most of their stock from the group wholesaler (Figure 11.10). They include names such as VG stores, Late Shop, Happy Shopper, Mace, Spar and Wavyline. The group wholesaler buys goods in bulk from manufacturers at discount prices.

Agents and brokers

These differ from wholesalers in that they do not purchase the manufacturer's goods and take title, but, instead, earn a commission on the sales they make. In doing this, they assist in the transfer of goods between the producer and the end user.

An agent differs from a broker by working permanently on behalf of either a seller or a buyer. A broker only works temporarily on behalf of a business and normally transacts between a number of different sellers and buyers. Though agents and brokers perform few intermediary functions, they may have considerable specialist knowledge of a given type of market.

Distributors or dealers

Another way for a manufacturer to sell goods to the consumer is by using distributors or dealers. These enter into a contract to buy manufacturers' goods to sell to customers. Their function is similar to that of wholesalers and retailers, except that they will normally offer only a limited product range based upon the products of a single supplier. These products may be backed up by specialist services and facilities such as credit and after-sales servicing.

Retailers

The French word *retailer* means 'to cut again'. We have already seen that the wholesaler breaks down bulk supplies from the manufacturer. The retailer then cuts the bulk again to sell individual items to consumers. To categorise the many different types of retailer you need to consider the following:

1 *Ownership* Who owns the retail unit? Is it independently owned by a sole trader? Is it owned by a large multiple with shareholders? Is it a cooperative or a franchised outlet?

2 *Range of merchandise* Does the retail outlet specialise in a range of goods or does it have a spread of interests? Examples of specialised outlets include ice-cream parlours, furniture stores and fast-food outlets. Woolworths is an example of a more general outlet. Harrods at one time claimed to sell everthing from 'a pin to an elephant'.

3 *Pricing policy* Some retail outlets concentrate on the bottom of the price range. They offer discounts and low prices, buying in bulk and selling in large quantities. The early policy of Jack Cohen, founder of Tesco, was 'pile them high, sell them cheap'. In contrast, other retail outlets aim for an upmarket price image. This is true of exclusive fashion shops, clothing and jewellery stores. Here the mark-up may be several hundred per cent for many items.

4 *Location* Low-price stores frequently choose locations where business rates and other site costs are minimised. In contrast, large multiples and department stores need a town-centre location, or a site near a major road. Small 'corner' shops need a healthy volume of local custom for their livelihood – their strength is in offering local convenience.

5 *Size* Many variety stores are now over 50 000 sq. ft in area, but superstores and hypermarkets have areas from 25 000 to 100 000 sq. ft.

Draw a plan of your local shopping area. Make a list of all of the different types of retailers in the area. Your work should show evidence of Core Skills in Communication.

There are many different types of retail outlets, including:

■ *Independent traders* According to the Census of Distribution, an independent trader is a retail organisation with fewer than 10 branches. A typical number is one or two branches. The market share for these has been declining, particularly in food.

Many small shops in the UK are owned by one person whose business interests are confined to one shop. There are, of course, advantages and disadvantages of being a small operator (Figure 11.11).

Advantages	Disadvantages
Personal relationship with customers	Price competition from multiples who are aided by buying economies and scale of operations
They are convenient for shoppers, providing a local 'round the corner' service	
Can buy in stock to meet personal requirements of customers	The owner needs to be a 'jack of all trades', frequently lacking specialist retailing knowledge
Can work longer hours	Lack of capital to expand or improve business
Low overheads, low site costs	Located away from high-volume sales areas
Benefit from joining voluntary group	
Can offer personal credit facilities to shoppers	Growth of use of cars has led to one-stop shopping in large shopping centres
Can do home deliveries	

Figure 11.11 Advantages and disadvantages of small retail outlets

The number of independent retailers has fallen from 42.5% of commodity turnover in the early 1970s to 11.8% in the early 1990s. Joining a voluntary group, as described earlier, has been the best route for the survival of many small shops. Niche operating has also provided many opportunities, for example health food shops.

■ *Multiple chains* These are usually organised by joint stock companies, with a high degree of control being exercised by professional managers. The definition provided by the Census of Distribution is that a multiple store has more than ten branches. Some multiples are classified as specialist stores, concentrating on a narrow range of items, such as clothing (e.g. Dorothy Perkins, Top Man, Austin Reed). Others are variety chains like Marks and Spencer or Littlewoods.

Some key features of multiples are:

– centralised buying
– concentration on fast-moving lines
– merchandise is widely known
– located in busy shopping areas
– volume sales enable prices to be low
– shops project a strong corporate image
– many key functions of these shops are centralised.

Most multiples are members of the Multiple Shops Federation. This is a combined pressure group and sounding-board for ideas from some of the well-known multiples. Multiples continue to expand in importance despite many being hit by the recession of the early 1990s.

■ *Supermarkets* A supermarket is defined as a store with at least 2000 square feet (or about 200 square metres) of selling area, using mainly self-service methods and having at least three check-out points. The layout of a store is designed to speed customer flow and reduce time spent shopping.

Supermarkets are a key feature of shopping in the 1990s. New and large supermarkets continue to be developed in most areas of population growth.

Supermarkets have thrived with the development of brand names, the increasing number of working women with less time for shopping, and consumer preferences for easy shopping at low prices. They have high turnovers at a low mark-up – by maximising sales, they are able to spread their operating costs over a large output in order to minimise unit costs.

In recent years, supermarkets have been able to meet consumer demand for 'green' and organic products by using their considerable clout to influence producers. Because the supermarket business is highly competitive, it is also responsive to consumer preference changes.

The supermarket war has made the headlines for some time. The war has been marked by intense price competition, with the price of a can of baked beans falling to 7p and of a loaf of bread to less than 20p. While the margins of the retailing giants have suffered, consumers have reaped the benefits.

Somerfield, the former Gateway chain, is widely credited with starting the price war with its Price Check campaign. Its rivals could not ignore this competitive action. Tesco quickly followed with the introduction of its economy Value Lines range. Others were forced to respond. Sainsbury launched its Essential for Essentials campaign which cut the price on 300 own-label products, and Argyll pitched in with selective price cuts and multi-save promotions.

Probably the biggest factor influencing the ongoing development of the supermarket war has been the rapid expansion of *discount stores*. The aggressive pricing of many commodity items has appealed to recession-weary consumers and has lowered prices across the industry. Kwik-Save plans to open more than 160 new superstores over three years. Netto and Aldi are believed to be opening about 30 stores a year and, with the opening of the first warehouse club in Britain – Costco in Thurrock in December 1993 – retailers have a lot to be worried about. A recent survey by Verdict, the retail research firm, showed that the price of an average basket of shopping has dropped by 5.5% in a year, saving the average family £150.

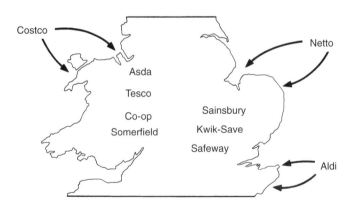

Figure 11.12 Some of the players in the supermarket war

The actions of the discount stores and continued new store development by the major chains have led to *overcapacity* in the market – supply growth has begun to exceed demand growth in many areas. At the same time the revivals of Asda and Somerfield mean that many large and capable players are competing for market share. Sir Ian MacLaurin, chairman of Tesco (Britain's second biggest supermarket chain) claimed that Tesco was emerging as one of the victors of the

supermarket war by reporting a 4% rise in like-for-like sales.

However, price competition has put operating margins and profits under pressure, and many belive that the next step in the war will see improved services as retailers try to differentiate their facilities in order to gain competitive advantage.

1 What were the probable objectives of the retail chains during the supermarket wars?
2 If a major retailer had ignored the actions of competitors, how might it have been affected?
3 Are there any winners and losers in such a war?

Evidence collection point

Look at the business information pages in a broadsheet newspaper over a two-week period and collect articles which appear about organisations involved in retailing activity. Accompany each article with a short statement which describes recent changes in retailing activity. Plan your work so that it demonstrates Core Skills in Communication.

■ *Hypermarkets* These are very large supermarkets. They have a massive selling area and offer a wide range of household goods at discount prices. As well as food and clothing, they stock lines as diverse as DIY equipment, motoring accessories, cosmetics, children's toys and hardware.

Their aim is to provide cheaply for all the basic shopping needs of an average household. They may also contain restaurant facilities and stock consumer durables like television sets at a discount.

■ *Department stores* The definition of a department store, as used by the Census of Distribution, is a store with a large number of departments and employing more than 25 people. They are to be found on 'prime sites' in the centre of most towns and cities.

A department store is divided into separate departments, each with a departmental manager and staff. It provides a very wide range of services and goods so that customers can do all their shopping under the one roof. The store generally provides a high standard of service and comfort with carpeted floors, a café, exhibitions and displays.

Department stores continue to be a force in the marketplace with their reputation for quality goods. However, whilst it is true that department stores have an up-market image, they can also offer discounts on many items. Department stores include many famous names such as Harrods,

Binns, Alders, John Lewis Partnership and Owen Owen.

In the last decade they have moved towards customer self-selection. They have also operated with a policy of 'leasing' shopping space to other retail names with a compatible image – this makes for better use of space and is an added attraction for many customers.

- *Discount stores* Today, specialist companies like Argos and Comet concentrate on selling large quantities of consumer durables at discount prices. The aim of these stores is to produce a high level of total profit by means of a very high turnover of stock. As the name implies, they attract custom by the discounts they offer. In recent years, these stores have moved away from the original warehouse-like service, and have increasingly begun to offer credit and other facilities.

Discount stores tend to be located at edge-of-town positions. They are well-stocked with a wide range of goods and brands. Recent examples are discount toy sellers and discount pet food sellers. They are located near to high densities of population.

- *Cooperative retail societies* Today there are fewer than thirty cooperative retail societies operating in various parts of the United Kingdom. There used to be several hundred, but over the years many of the smaller societies have joined together. The Co-ops have always tried to do more than just run a shopping business. They set out to serve the community in a variety of ways. For example, a Co-op might support a local education service for members, subsidise health care and other social activities, or finance cooperative theatre ventures and recreational facilities.

Evidence collection point

Compare and contrast two different types of retailing organisations. Look, for example, at their size, number of branches, location, range of goods, prices, and range of services for customers. Carry out a short shopping survey to find out which type of organisation customers prefer to use. Your work should provide evidence of Core Skills in Communication and Application of Number.

Needs of customers

In developing suitable sales methods, organisations have to balance their own objectives against the needs of customers (Figure 11.13). In order to be able to do this they need to understand how customers view their organisation as well as what their customers want from their organisatios.

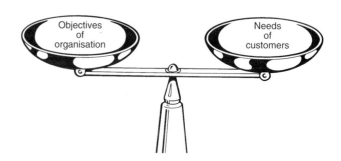

Figure 11.13 Balancing the objectives of an organisation against the needs of customers

The starting point is to identify potential customers and their expectations by listening to their views so that the organisation can then develop suitable service procedures which can satisfy such wants. They need to find out:

- what customers want
- how important this is for them
- why they need to have it
- how to provide it in the best possible way.

Roderick M. McNealy, in his book *Making Customer Satisfaction Happen*, refers to the 'Making Customer Satisfaction Happen' model (Figure 11.14). This, he

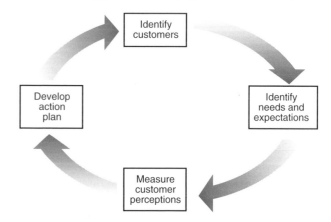

Figure 11.14 The Making Customer Satisfaction Happen model

claims, is a continuous circular process that provides an equation for satisfying customer needs which can then be used as part of the organisation's strategic approach to business.

Avis have a customer care balance sheet which takes into account business they may be losing both from customers who complain and from those who are dissatisfied but do not bother to complain (Figure 11.15). This emphasises the need to listen to customers and refers to the 'customer care balance sheet' which shows the annual sales lost from customers whose needs have not been met.

Figure 11.15 Customer care balance sheet

So, what do customers want and how can their expectations be satisfied by the different services and selling methods provided by an organisation? Customers may require:

- *Quick and easy purchasing procedures* For example, it is important that they understand purchasing procedures. At the same time they may wish to sample products, see how they function or ask for specialist help. Retail technology may help to reduce queue time and customer throughput.
- *Clear and accurate information* This may refer to products or purchasing procedures and may influence the final decision. In particular, consumers may wish for advice which helps them to weigh up a range of alternatives.
- *Clear refund procedure* Consumers are much happier to commit themselves to a purchase when they know that if the product does not match up to expectations, is damaged or does not perform its advertised functions, they can bring it back easily for a refund. Many supermarkets have a refund desk at the entrance and some large organisations have a good reputation for their dealings with returns.

- *Easy exchange of goods* Similarly, exchanging goods if they are not suitable helps to provide a service which closely meets the needs of customers.
- *Complaints procedure* There is nothing worse than customers having their complaints passed around from person to person and department to department. This creates a bad impression of the organisation, wastes time and may cause a lot of anguish. An efficient customer complaints procedure may help to retain business that might otherwise be lost if the complaint had been handled inefficiently.
- *Special services to meet special needs* Different groups of customers may have different needs. For example, how many stores can deal with wheelchair access or for mothers with young children in buggies? Similarly, will organisations provide specialist help or a wide range of services for their customers? Does free delivery extend outside the boundaries of a local town? What credit facilities will an organisation provide? Do the opening hours meet the needs of all customers? Does the product range stocked provide enough specialist products for all types of consumers? Is the organisation willing to order products on behalf of customers?

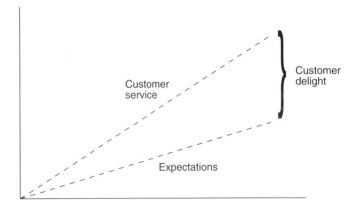

Figure 11.16 Exceeding customer expectations

Needs of organisations

Louis V. Gerstner, IBM's chairman and chief executive, in his 1993 Annual Report stated:

I want everyone in IBM to be obsessed with satisfying our customers ... The fact is, no company is going to succeed without a clear set of tough-minded strategies grounded in a clear understanding of what's happening in the marketplace. Some call it mission. Some call it vision. I call it strategy. And strategy is particularly important for IBM because our industry is going through a period of fundamental change at breakneck speed. So are our customers.

This statement emphasises the need to understand and satisfy customer requirements in order to achieve an organisation's range of objectives. It is, therefore, essential to match the production and development of goods and services with the identification and anticipation of consumer desires.

For example, providing services which help to achieve customer satisfaction may help to:

- improve *profitability* by providing a more flexible and secure customer base
- improve *market share* by retaining existing customers and also attracting new customers
- achieve *other business objectives*.

Evidence collection point

Obtain a copy of a recent annual report. Look at the statement from the Chairman and statements from other directors. Explain how that organisation uses customer service and customer satisfaction to meet some of its wider business objectives.

Sales campaign methods

At the heart of selling is the need to plan the activities of those involved in the selling process. Sales campaigns endeavour to match productivity goals relating to one or more products to the sales opportunities in the marketplace by providing a programme of activities enabling these opportunities to be grasped.

Sales objectives help to identify a focus for a sales campaign. They provide the sales force with direction and also enable performance standards to be set which provide a basis for evaluation. They may be stated in:

- value of units sold
- market share
- profitability generated by sales volumes.

It is usual for these objectives then to be translated into monetary values or sales volumes which relate to each salesperson.

Sales campaigns may take a variety of different forms and will largely depend upon the industry and the nature of the products. They may include:

- *Organising and allocating the sales force* The sales force has to be organised and allocated in a way which maximises effort and brings in optimum returns. If sales staff are in the field, the first factor is the *sales potential* of each territory. *Workload* is also important. It would be wrong to provide sales staff with a workload which went beyond their capabilities. The sales force may be allocated by area, by product, by customer, by type of market or even by type of customer service.
- *Setting realistic action plans* The objective of this is to match the realistic goals of those involved in the selling process to the orgainisation's goals for the market. In doing this it is important to consider how much time the seller should spend with each customer, the average order size, the frequency of order and the personal attention and degree of customer service required.
- *Training* The objective of training is to produce more effective sales staff, thereby increasing sales and improving customer satisfaction. If the sales campaign is for a new product, it is important to develop product knowledge.
- *Preparation of sales literature* Copies of this may be sent both to those involved in the selling process and to customers in order to generate interest. Literature must be attractive to ensure that it is not disposed of, contain an offer of service which will interest the recipient and also provide some form of follow-up, such as an opportunity to reply.
- *Sales meetings* At sales meetings there is an opportunity for dialogue between sales managers and sales staff. The meeting may be used to announce a new campaign, exchange ideas or further develop campaign details.
- *Sales conferences* In some circumstances it may be useful to set up a conference which large numbers of those involved in the sales campaign may attend. Sales conferences provide a useful opportunity for communicating large amounts of information about the new campaign and also provide the opportunity for sales staff to find out more from each other.

It is important to remember that many different groups of people may be involved in the selling process. For example, they may be shop counter staff in a retailing environment, specialist project engineers in an industrial environment or independent agents working on a commission-only basis. Sales campaigns have to take into account the different sorts or relationships in each of these circumstances.

Evidence collection point

Imagine that you are in the business of introducing:

a a new motor car
b a newspaper.

What sales campaign techniques would you use for each? How might they differ?

Responsibilities of salespersons

Most days in your life you are involved in some form of selling activity. It might be persuading a friend to come with you to the pictures, or asking a relative to buy something for you. What you are doing is using your relationship to sell your ideas to someone else.

Personal selling involves interaction between individuals or groups of individuals.

The objective of personal selling is to make a sale, and it is the culmination of all of the marketing activities that have taken place beforehand. It involves matching a customer's requirements with the goods or services on offer. The better the match, the more lasting the relationship between the seller and the buyer.

Evidence collection point

Make a list of situations in which you have recently been involved in some form of personal selling. Explain how the selling process took place in each instance. Did you have any responsibilities to the other person(s) involved in the exchange process?

The role of personal selling will vary from business to business. It is a two-way process which can be one of the most expensive areas of the promotional mix. This personal communication element can be very important as the final sale might come only as a result of protracted negotiations.

Personal selling is important in both consumer and organisational markets. However, in consumer goods markets, advertising often helps the process and is often the driving force which *pulls* a product through the distribution network. In organisational markets, on the other hand, personal selling may have to work harder to *push* the product through to the market (Figure 11.17).

Figure 11.17 The push–pull effect

The main benefit of personal selling is the ability to communicate with and focus on customers individually and with precision. For example, if you go into a travel agency and ask for details about a holiday, the sales assistant may explain and point out the features of various packages and any discounts or promotions they might offer. All the other areas of the promotional mix are targeted at *groups* of people.

Image

Though we may have mental stereotypes of the typical salesperson, selling involves special skills. Whereas there is a tendency to downgrade the role of the salesperson in the UK, in many countries (Germany, for example) sales staff require a high degree of technical competence and are generally accepted to be part of the corporate elite. Salespeople are key intermediaries who present information to customers and then provide feedback on customer needs.

Sales staff are representing an organisation and so need to reflect a positive image from that organisation. It is important that they do not offend customers by their appearance – the mode of dress should tend to match the nature of the products and the organisation. For example, a sales assistant in a fashion store should wear something up-to-date, whereas an insurance salesperson should wear more formal clothes. It is often said that the way we look determines the way others look at us!

Similarly, effective speaking will help to create the appropriate image and situation for the sale to take place. Good grammar, vocabulary, diction and voice tone may help to reflect the degree of professionalism required for the sale to take place. On the other hand, the use of poor grammar may create a bad impression of the organisation.

Many organisations spend more on personal selling than on any other area of the promotional mix, and within organisations large numbers of individuals may find that personal selling forms part of their role. Personal selling may involve individuals developing special skills and using them in many different operational situations. To do so, sales staff need to know their products and be well trained in selling techniques (Figure 11.18).

Figure 11.18 Stages in the selling process

Product knowledge

Selling in a highly competitive world means that preparation has never been so important. Though it has been said that salespeople are born and not made, nevertheless skills, knowledge and training can improve everybody's performance. Training is designed to build on people's selling skills and to use their personal abilities and understanding to follow the psychological stages of the sales process. Product knowledge is vital, as it allows for feedback from the prospective customer's questions about the product's technical specifications, benefits and functions.

Communicating effectively

Knowing their customers may help to determine how sales staff communicate with them. For example, some customers may prefer to be addressed with the more formal Mr or Mrs while others like to be called by their first name. It is important to remember:

■ Avoid phrases which might annoy customers, such as 'you know what I mean'.
■ Do not speak too rapidly.
■ Make sure that customers understand all of the points made during the presentation, particularly if they involve any detailed or technical understanding.
■ Vary the tone and use appropriate oral expression.

The presentation of selling is based on a strategy known as AIDA:

A   A customer's *attention* is captured and he or she is made aware of the product.
I   The *impact* made by the presentation stimulates the customer's interest.
D   The customer is persuaded that he or she is *deprived* by not having the product, and this helps to stimulate a *desire* for it.
A   *Action* involves the purchase of the product.

 Evidence collection point

Make a list of the skills somebody might require in order to become an effective salesperson.

Point-of-sale service

Probing is quite important in the early stage of the sales presentation, in order to find out the prospect's needs and where his or her priorities might lie. The salesperson can then try to match the product or service with the prospect's requirements. This may involve elaborating on the product's advantages, concentrating on aspects such as savings in costs, design ingredients, performance specifications, after-sales service, etc.

During the presentation, the salesperson must constantly evaluate whether the product is appropriate to the needs of the prospect. It is unethical to sell something that is not needed – although this may often happen! The larger and more complex the order, the more complex the negotiations over the conditions of supply. In many different situations it is important to provide a number of services to help with the process. For example, these might include:

- product demonstrations
- performance specifications
- sales literature
- samples
- a meeting to discuss details
- credit facilities
- sales promotions.

The prospective customer may have a variety of objections to the purchase. These objections may be genuine, or as a result of a misunderstanding. There might be a reluctance to make a commitment at this stage. Logical, well-presented arguments and incentives may overcome such objections.

Timing is crucial to closing the sale. A salesperson must look for *buying signals* which indicate that the prospect is close to a decision and almost ready to put a signature on an order form and discuss the contractual arrangements.

After-sales service

It is important to follow up the sale with post-sale support. Promises that might have been made during the negotiations will have to be fulfilled. If the salesperson guarantees delivery by a certain date, that date must be held. Servicing arrangements must be efficiently carried out, and any problems dealt with. Contacting customers to see if they are happy with the product will encourage repeat buying and improve the supplier's reputation for concern for its customers.

Evidence collection point

Using an example known to you, show how strong after-sales service may help to promote repeat purchasing patterns.

Sales administration

Sales staff may also have a number of other related functions. Communication, for example, is an important role. Sales staff act as an information link between suppliers and their customers. As a result, personal selling involves a boundary role – being at the boundary of a supplying organisation and also in direct and close contact with customers. The role is often not only one of selling but also one of

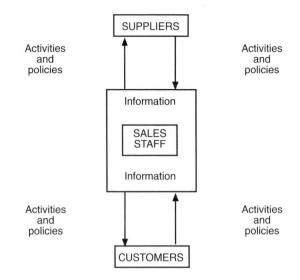

Figure 11.19 The information link between customers and their suppliers

interpreting the activities and policies of each organisation to the other (see Figure 11.19). A considerable amount of administration may also therefore accompany the selling role. For example, reports, schedules and computerised information such as inventory details are a part of daily life for a salesperson.

Comprehensive records on customers should be kept and updated after each visit. Keeping sales records enables the salesperson to respond exactly to each customer's individual needs. Knowledge of competitors and their products enables the seller to respond to queries about the relative merits and demerits of products.

Customer care

According to Drucker and Levitt, the purpose of every business is to create and keep a customer. The services provided by sales staff may:

- help to keep the business ahead of competitors
- ensure that customers remain loyal
- help with designing products to satisfy needs and requirements
- create a reputation for being a caring business
- generate goodwill
- reassure customers that their purchase decision was a good one.

Statutory responsibilities

In providing customers with products and services, sales staff also have a responsibility to keep within the law. In particular, under the Sale of Goods Act they must ensure that goods are of merchantable quality and fit for the purpose intended. Similarly, under the Trades Descriptions Act it is important that they do not falsely describe goods during the selling process. At the end of the day behaving unethically is simply counterproductive, as opportunities for repeat business will be lost.

Sales administration

As with all jobs, a certain amount of paperwork is necessary for the process of selling. Sales administration provides an important means of communicating with customers, keeping lines of communication open, maintaining information about accounts, pursuing new customer opportunities and dealing with other administrative functions efficiently.

Prospecting

Identifying customers is a traditional role fulfilled by a salesperson. 'Prospects' must be located before any selling can begin. Though sales staff will already have a list of customers or accounts, a salesperson will often have to carry out 'cold calling'. This involves visiting or telephoning a person or organisation with which the business has not previously had any dealings. Cold calling by sales representatives has unpredictable results and can be demoralising if there is a poor reception.

An alternative to cold calling might be the use of telephone canvassers, whose job it is to find potential customers and then pass on the details to sales representatives. Sometimes it is possible to use independent agents to find customers. Working on a commission-only basis, agents may reduce the numbers of sales representatives an organisation needs to employ, particularly if there are a number of low-value accounts. Insurance, for example, is sold by agents.

Many organisations today use direct-mail techniques to stimulate enquiries for sales staff to follow up. A good mailshot will make it clear what is on offer and help to initiate the selling procedure.

A growing selling approach is through the use of the telephone. Telemarketing (see page 282) is often regarded as a fairly cost-effective alternative to cold-calling in person.

Task

Imagine that you are Sales Director of a company that makes decorative plastic boxes. Most of the boxes are sold to supermarket chains who use the boxes for a range of own-brand products including chocolates, sweets, gifts and other items. The sales of the boxes are good but show little sign of increasing. Given that the cost of making boxes is increasing because of the rising price of raw materials and labour, you need to increase the efficiency of your production processes to produce 20% more boxes. Your role is, therefore, to sell 20% more boxes. You have to consider:

- whether you can sell more to existing customers
- how you can develop new markets
- whether you can identify different uses for the boxes
- how you can deploy and use the salesforce to sell more boxes.

Working in groups, produce a plan which shows how you might increase the sales of boxes by 20%.

Account management

Providing credit for customers is an important service, but is one which needs to be carefully managed within certain guidelines. On the one hand, the seller will wish to collect payment as soon as possible, but the terms of payment must also be acceptable to customers who may find better terms available elsewhere. There are a number of dangers in providing large amounts of credit. For example:

- When credit is provided, money is tied up in customer accounts. It may be difficult to collect this money quickly.
- Credit helps to provide finance for the business of the customer. If the customer's business encounters problems which mean that they cannot pay their bills, this will lead to a bad debt.
- A lot of time may be spent in account management, for example keeping and maintaining customer records and preparing statements and account reminders.
- At some stage the provision of credit may lead to a dispute with a customer over the amount of credit, credit periods, etc. and this may affect the selling process.

It is usual to place a credit limit on the account of each customer. These limits will normally depend upon some form of risk assessment. For new corporate customers it may be possible to go to Companies House and obtain statements. These can then be used to assess a company's financial position, but the process may take a lot of time. Another approach may be to contact a credit-rating agency for an assessment of the creditworthiness of a customer. These agencies may:

- provide a same-day analysis by computer
- analyse the ratios of the business concerned
- comment upon the credit position and financial position of the customer concerned.

In some situations it may be possible to ask for references on the creditworthiness of customers and to provide some form of credit clearance. After credit limits have been set for a customer, they may be subject to occasional rises as business contacts and relationships improve.

Credit control is an important part of the role of an organisation. In an ideal world customers would pay promptly, not demand long periods of credit and still be good customers for many years in the future. However, this is not always the case. Organisations may have 'marginal' customers whose reliability and ability to pay debts is not clear-cut. When sales orders are taken, the setting of credit clearance limits and the time allocated to the customer to pay should be judged carefully. Then, if customers exceed the time allocated to pay, they should be reminded about the need for prompt payment. Some systems allocate four categories of debtor – strong, average, marginal and weak. Different terms and conditions are then offered to each category. After the transaction has taken place the credit control section will keep up to date with credit accounts and identify where accounts become overdue.

There can be a danger of conflict between the sales force and the administrative staff. For example, salespeople in the field may want to concentrate simply upon the process of selling, but they have to take into account whether the customer base they create can provide payment for the purchases they make. This may often involve them in monitoring the accounts of their customers and advising them of due payments from time to time.

Processing orders

Sales staff are under an obligation to ensure that orders are processed quickly and efficiently. Precise details of order requirements and customer instructions such as those for packaging, terms of payment and dates of delivery should be provided. The original copy prepared by the sales staff may provide the basis for other documentation. For example, order details may include:

- name and address of customer
- date
- delivery date
- reference to salesperson
- quantity
- unit price
- value of order plus total
- special instructions
- terms
- relevant signatures.

Having received the order, the organisation must ensure that delivery dates are adhered to so that customer requirements are met on time. Follow-up from sales staff is important.

Evidence collection point

Make a list of reasons why sales administration is important for sales staff. Explain how computers and other forms of information technology may help with such administrative functions. (To help you to collect the appropriate evidence look at the information provided in Chapter 5.) Your work may provide evidence of Core Skills in Information Technology.

Using customer service to meet the needs of internal and external customers

It is often recognised that the service provided by internal customers (i.e. interaction between employees within an organisation) helps to determine how organisations treat external customers (see Figure 11.1).

Internal customers

Anita Roddick from the Body Shop recognises that 'my people are my first line of customers'. Service improvements between employees can help to empower them in a way which enables them to make decisions, develop teamwork and make use of suggestions and ideas within their workplace. There are many ways in which services between individuals in the workplace can be improved. For example:

- *Employee participation* Research suggests that most employees want to be involved in some form of participation in the decision-making process. Employees may have some useful ideas for improving efficiency and working practices. Where managers do not listen to staff, useful opportunities for improving service quality may be missed. *Quality circles* are a useful way of making service improvements through people. By involving people it may be possible to improve service quality and levels of productivity.
- *Understanding the roles of the different parts of the organisation* Some organisations try to break down the barriers between the different departments by encouraging staff to show other employees what their jobs involve. For example, British Airways encourage staff from each function to give presentations to show others what they do. When internal customers are then dealing with each other they can then show better understanding of their respective roles.
- *Employee care* Where employees exist in an environment of high employee care with good pay, equal opportunities, staff development, a range of employee benefits and good working conditions, they are likely to respond more professionally to their duties than they might do if they were treated badly.
- *Teamwork* As organisations move towards flatter structures, teamwork and cooperation between employees becomes a vital tool for providing customer service. A good team spirit will help to improve standards of service (Figure 11.20).

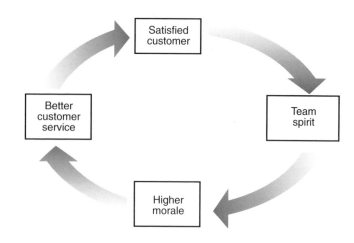

Figure 11.20 Improving customer service

- *Information* Where better information exists, employees are able to make more informed decisions. Use of technology may be able to provide more employees with information which can be used to improve customer service.
- *Relationships with suppliers* Suppliers also fall into the realms of customer service. It is important to provide the information which suppliers require, but also to maintain a close watch over the quality of products being delivered. They may also be opportunities to involve suppliers with new product developments.

Evidence collection point

Who are your internal customers at school or college? Explain who they are and then comment upon how improvements in relationships between each of these groups might affect the quality of the service provided in the classroom.

External customers

In providing high quality services for external customers, it is important to measure their perceptions of current performances. These performances may cover a range of areas such as:

- *Sales* It may be useful to measure how long it takes for customers to receive their order after they have placed it. For example, a promise of delivery within two days should *mean* delivery within two days. Similarly, are customers happy with the selling process? In a retail environment, do they have the opportunity to look at the goods and ask questions about technical specifications? In a business-to-business environment, how often will customers see sales representatives? Are customers satisfied with the sales service they receive?

■ *Complaints* How are customer complaints dealt with and then resolved? Are complaints dealt with individually and are the problems identified by such complaints properly addressed? If complaints are not dealt with adequately, customers may go and tell others what has happened to them. If they have had a bad experience it could have considerable effect upon an organisation, particularly if news of such problems reaches the media.

■ *Information* Customers will require information upon which to base their decisions and this information might need to be in a variety of forms. For example, many new car showrooms now complement their existing product information booklets with the use of CD-i so that customers can find out the answers to queries.

■ *Quality of product or service* How effectively does the product or service satisfy customer requirements? For example, does the finish, durability and performance of the product match the specifications? How long have customers been kept waiting either to be served or for the goods to be provided? When dealing with customers was all of the information accurate?

■ *Client/customer relationship* How are customers treated? Are relationships with customers good, and how does this help to generate repeat business?

Some organisations link customer satisfaction with the provision of awards for customer service. For example, the Woolwich Building Society ran a Tribute Scheme in which staff who achieved high standards of service were rewarded with gifts and activities. A scheme on BR's Southern Region invited customers to nominate a friendly BR worker.

Long-term customer satisfaction is about integrating quality customer service into the corporate culture. It should then become a way of life. By doing this an organisation creates a base upon which it can develop and build successful activities.

Evidence indicators

For this activity, prepare a report which compares the sales methods used by two different business organisations. It might be useful to contrast two organisations either known to you through work or which you might have come across in the High Street. The following list should serve as a checklist. Please tick off each of the following when you have successfully covered them as part of your report. You need to be able to confirm that:

■ I have identified two business organisations as the subject of my report. ☐

■ I have compared and contrasted their sales methods. ☐

■ I have explained how such sales methods meet the needs of customers and of the organisations themselves. ☐

■ I have identified a recent sales campaign from each organisation. Where I have been able to do so, I have found out details about each sales campaign. ☐

■ I have commented on how salespersons carry out their responsibilities. In doing so I have referred to the Sale of Goods Act and the Trades Descriptions Act. ☐

■ I have described how customer service helps to meet the needs of internal and external customers. ☐

Marketing: Unit Test 1

1 The professional body which represents the activities of professional marketers is known as the:
   a Chartered Institute of Management Accountants.
   b Advertising Association.
   c Chartered Institute of Marketing
   d Marketing Association.

2 The process of dividing the marketplace into discrete sections so that goods or services can be targeted at particular types of customers is known as:
   a Planning.
   b Market research.
   c Undifferentiation.
   d Segmentation.

3 Which of the following is not included in the marketing mix?
   a Product.
   b Personnel.
   c Price.
   d Place.

4 A product's extended dimensions will not include:
   a Colour.
   b Servicing arrangements.
   c Credit facilities.
   d Maintenance contracts.

5 Concentrated marketing involves marketing to just one segment. For the motor industry an example would include:
   a Ford.
   b Rover.
   c Vauxhall.
   d Aston Martin.

6 An example of a product in the mature phase of its product life-cycle would be:
   a Ford Galaxy.
   b Sky television.

   c Heinz tomato sauce.
   d Pentium processors.

7 Which of the following would not be considered to be a brand?
   a Smarties.
   b Snickers.
   c Nestle.
   d M&M's.

8 SWOT stands for:
   a Strengths/weaknesses/opportunities/threats.
   b Strengths/weaknesses/opportunities/targets.
   c Strengths/weaknesses/outlets/targets.
   d Strengths/weaknesses/outlets/threats.

9 Which of the following would not fall into the promotional mix plan?
   a Public relations.
   b Advertising.
   c Promotional pricing.
   d Sales promotions.

10 A test market involves:
   a Finding out what the market wants.
   b Testing products in a laboratory.
   c Testing a new product in part of the market.
   d Testing the product for a relaunch.

11 Products which generate high positive cash flows are known as:
   a Cash dogs.
   b Cash goats.
   c Stars.
   d Cash cows.

12 BRAD stands for:
   a British Rate and Data.
   b Broadcasting Rates and Descriptions.
   c British Rates and Diagnosis.
   d Broadcast Rates and Data.

13 Wentworth Electrics has nearly 2500 customers. They are in the process of undertaking some primary research. To do this they have constructed a survey which, though it is intended to be randomly sampled, is weighted on the basis of the importance of each group of customers in the market. This is an example of:
a Simple random sampling.
b Cluster sampling.
c Quota sampling.
d Stratified random sampling.

14 If a sample is incomplete and does not accurately represent a group of consumers, it is said to contain:
a Too much information.
b A distorted census.
c Bias.
d Too much objective analysis.

15 A good example of an opinion poll is:
a Panels.
b Gallup.
c Discussion groups.
d Bar code analysis.

16 Dividing people into classes which reflect purchasing habits and lifestyles is called:
a Social division.
b Social stratification.
c Socialising.
d Class divisions.

17 Which of the following might happen in a vertical market?
a Supplier would have to keep many customers happy.
b Supplier would be dependent upon the customer.
c Customer behaviour changes frequently.
d Because there are many customers, there will be a lot of competition.

18 For a manufacturer, franchising is a good example of a system of:
a Transport.
b Distribution.
c Advertising.
d Promotion.

19 A question that allows a respondent to express an opinion is a:
a Free question.
b Closed question.
c Open question.
d Variable question.

20 If all questions have the same range of answers an interviewer may use:
a A prompt card.
b An add lister.
c A census.
d A reminder card.

21 The organisation which attempts to maintain standards in the travel industry is:
a BSI.
b Travel Agents Bureau.
c CBI
d ABTA.

22 Gathering information from anybody available for an interviewer to survey is known as:
a Cluster sampling.
b Quota sampling.
c Judgement sampling.
d Convenience sampling.

23 Focus groups are useful for collecting:
a Qualitative information.
b Quantitative information.
c Census information.
d Large samples.

24 Using new products to replace existing products is known as:
a Product modification.
b Line extensions.
c Product substitution.
d Product extension.

25 An example of direct competition would be:
a Jaguar and Ford.
b BP and ICI.
c *The Sun* and *The Telegraph*.
d *The Mirror* and *The Sun*.

26 One useful form of market research is using:
a Computer files.
b Feedback from sales representatives.

c Spreadsheets.

d The legal influences upon the organisation.

27 The Standard Industrial Classification is an example of:

a Primary data.

b A retail audit.

c Use of a questionnaire.

d Secondary information.

28 An important reason for primary research may be that other information is:

a Too expensive.

b Out-of-date.

c Difficult to understand.

d Decentralised.

29 Which of the following ways of collecting primary information would have the lowest response?

a Face-to-face interviews.

b Telephone questionnaires.

c Postal questionnaires.

d Observation.

30 Census data is published by:

a DTI.

b Central Statistical Office.

c Census Information Service.

d Office of Population, Censuses and Surveys.

31 If a questionnaire is badly designed this may lead to:

a An incomplete sample.

b Biased results.

c Too many open questions.

d Incomplete sampling.

32 Questioning a selection of respondents is known as:

a Census.

b Primary survey.

c Sample.

d Marketing database.

33 The strategy of using the same marketing mix for all segments in the marketplace is known as:

a Niche marketing.

b Undifferentiated marketing.

c Differentiated marketing.

d International marketing.

34 The main purpose of the Advertising Standards Authority is to:

a Keep up advertising standards.

b Control advertising expenditure.

c Ensure that advertisements are legal, decent, honest and truthful.

d Supervise the advertising industry.

35 A government body which looks after the interests of consumers and traders is the:

a Office of Fair Trading.

b Department of Employment.

c Department for Consumer and Commercial Affairs.

d Treasury.

36 To distinguish a trend from a cycle we can use:

a The median

b The mode.

c The arithmetic mean.

d A moving average.

37 An example of an organisation which collects details of retail sales through supermarkets and large chains is:

a Retail Audits.

b BARB.

c BRAD.

d AA.

38 The technique used where a few people develop ideas in a group from concepts and key words is known as:

a Meeting.

b Television conferencing.

c Brainstorming.

d Suggestions box.

39 One example of a public relations activity would be:

a Discount tokens.

b Charitable donations.

c Dealer loaders.

d Personal selling.

40 A person in the C1 socio-economic group would have an occupation such as:

a Brain surgeon.

b Postman.

c Porter.

d Teacher.

41 Which one of the following is involved in direct marketing?
a Vauxhall.
b *Reader's Digest.*
c Mars.
d Heinz.

42 Direct selling by using the telephone is known as:
a Mailsort.
b Television marketing.
c Telemarketing.
d Telematics.

43 Hornsea Pottery is an example of:
a Factory sales.
b Pyramid selling.
c Door-to-door.
d Chip marketing.

44 A sampling frame is a list of:
a Interviewers.
b Sampling techniques to be used.
c Members of the market.
d Methods of collecting data.

45 The butter market in the UK is worth £350 million per annum. As female shoppers account for 70.6% of food sales per year, how much butter do males purchase each year?
a £247.1m.
b £102.9m.
c £105m.
d £103.2m.

46 One factor affecting demand for consumer goods can be:
a The cost of raw materials.
b Changes in the prices of substitute goods.
c Improved technology.
d Social factors.

47 Which of the following is part of the marketing mix?
a Pressure.
b Price.
c Personnel.
d Performance.

48 An example of a product reaching maturity is:
a Home control systems.
b Satellite televisions.
c 4-wheel-drive cars.
d Microwaves.

49 If you wished to complain about unhygienic preparation of food you would go to:
a The National Consumer Council.
b The Office of Fair Trading.
c Environmental Health Department.
d Citizens' Advice Bureau.

50 Setting up a network of people to sell on your behalf, from whom you may take a commission, is known as:
a Personal selling.
b Linked selling.
c Pyramid selling.
d Telesales.

Marketing: Unit Test 2

1 One important function of the wholesaler is:
a Breaking of bulk.
b Direct selling to customers.
c Credit to consumers.
d Product manufacture.

2 Which of the following would not be classified as a multiple?
a Harrods.
b W H Smith.
c Top Man.
d Austin Reed.

3 The marketing strategy of an organisation will be reflected through its:
a Sales promotions.
b Advertising campaign.
c Marketing mix.
d Marketing budget.

4 The process of building a product only to last a few years is known as:
a Product liability.
b Built-in obsolescence.
c Product depreciation.
d Sales maintenance.

301

5 The integration of different forms of transport has been made possible through the use of:
  a The Channel Tunnel.
  b Containerisation.
  c Motorway services.
  d Transport terminals.

6 An example of an injection of new life into a product may include:
  a Reducing advertising expenditure.
  b Increasing the price.
  c Better product differentiation.
  d Research into other areas.

7 Market research is the systematic gathering, recording and analysis of data about problems related to:
  a Producing goods and services.
  b Sustaining operations.
  c The marketing of goods and services.
  d Advertising.

8 Quantitative data is concerned with:
  a Product descriptions.
  b Hard facts.
  c Sampling methods.
  d Primary research.

9 An example of gathering primary information is:
  a Researching government statistics.
  b Telephone interviewing.
  c Use of industry research establishments.
  d Reading the *Financial Times*.

10 In a report from A C Nielsen you would expect to find:
  a Media information.
  b Corporate reports.
  c Detailed information about the market.
  d Profit forecasts.

11 The electoral register is a good example of:
  a A list of census data.
  b A sampling frame.
  c A market segment.
  d Differentiated marketing.

12 If a relationship exists between two variables, such as promotional expenditure and the sales of a commodity, then by changing parts of the relationship, it will be possible to forecast what the outcomes of such changes will be. If the relationship is close then there is said to be a positive:
  a Reaction.
  b Correlation.
  c Relationship.
  d Deviation.

13 Which of the following is least likely to affect consumer demand?
  a Disposable incomes.
  b Price of substitutes.
  c Technology.
  d Fashions.

14 A tangible product benefit would include:
  a Colour.
  b Servicing.
  c Performance.
  d Reputation.

15 Cliff Richard would be in what stage of the product life-cycle?
  a Introduction.
  b Growth.
  c Research and development.
  d Maturity.

16 The Act which ensures that goods are of merchantable quality is:
  a The Trades Descriptions Act.
  b Fair Trading Act.
  c Consumer Credit Act.
  d Sale of Goods Act.

17 Visiting an organisation with which you have not previously done any business is called:
  a Credit selling.
  b Door-to-door selling.
  c Hard selling.
  d Cold selling.

18 A postman would fall into socio-economic group:
  a B.
  b C1.
  c C2.
  d D.

19 Which of the following is least likely to be a marketing objective?
   a To increase market share.
   b To develop a brand.
   c To be a good neighbour.
   d To develop a global strategy.

20 How might a business extend the life-cycle of a brand?
   a Launch competing products.
   b Readjust the ingredients of the marketing mix.
   c Undertake more secondary research.
   d Analyse the economic determinants of consumer demand.

21 If a change in the quantity demanded of a good is of a greater proportion than the change in price that initiated it, then demand for that product is said to be:
   a Declining.
   b Inelastic.
   c Elastic.
   d Increasing proportionately.

22 CAB stands for:
   a City Advisory Banks.
   b Citizens' Advice Bureaux.
   c Council for Advice and Backing.
   d Consumer Advice Bureaux.

23 Which of the following is least likely to be a reason for undertaking market research?
   a To remain competitive and profitable.
   b To build up a profile of customers.
   c To find out why customers might buy a rival product.
   d To improve production techniques.

24 Demographic data based upon a survey published every 10 years is published by:
   a Central Statistical Office.
   b DTI.
   c Treasury.
   d Office of Population, Censuses and Surveys.

25 Which of the following is a primary source of data?
   a Observation.
   b Mintel Reports.
   c Excel.
   d Desk research.

26 Which of the following is a form of random sampling?
   a Quota sampling.
   b Systematic sampling.
   c Cluster sampling.
   d Judgement sampling.

27 By looking for an area which is considered to be typical of a market, you are engaging in:
   a Stratified random sampling.
   b Convenience sampling.
   c Judgement sampling.
   d Cluster sampling.

28 The total value of the market for beer in 1992 was £13 300 million. Given a population of 58 million, this means that average spending per head on beer per week is roughly:
   a £0.44.
   b £4.40.
   c £44.00.
   d None of the above.

29 One method of presenting data is by using:
   a Questionnaire.
   b Median.
   c Moving average.
   d Scattergraph.

30 In 1992, 54.9% of all new car registrations were imported. As the number of new registrations was 1 594 000, the number of new cars manufactured in the UK was:
   a 875 106.
   b 718 894.
   c 717 867.
   d 723 876.

31 If a good is a basic necessity it is likely to have:
   a Unitary elasticity of demand.
   b Elastic demand.
   c Inelastic demand.
   d Derived demand.

32 An example of a good which appeals to a person's self-actualisation needs might be:
   a A Mercedes motor car.
   b A large house.
   c A meal in a restaurant.
   d An opportunity to go on an Arctic expedition.

33 Which of the following is not part of the marketing mix?
  a Place.
  b Position.
  c Price.
  d Promotion.

34 The pricing technique where you add a margin to unit cost is known as:
  a Cost-plus pricing.
  b Contribution pricing.
  c Demand-orientated pricing.
  d Competition-orientated pricing.

35 If consumers do not receive the actual quantity of a product that they believe they are buying, then they may take action under the:
  a Trades Description Act.
  b Fair Trading Act.
  c Foods and Drugs Act.
  d Weights and Measures Act.

36 In order to market effectively an organisation must:
  a Advertise extensively.
  b Employ a large sales force.
  c Produce low cost, cheap and desirable products.
  d Satisfy customer needs.

37 Secondary research is sometimes called:
  a Primary research.
  b Internal research.
  c Desk research.
  d Field research.

38 Selecting respondents on the basis of how they look is called:
  a Cluster sampling.
  b Systematic sampling.
  c Random sampling.
  d Judgement sampling.

39 If it is decided to sample systematically 40 names from a sampling frame containing 1000, and 16 is chosen as the random staring point, the next number to be sampled will be:
  a 51.
  b 41.
  c 56.
  d 66.

40 One reason a person might wear designer clothes may be because he/she is concerned about:
  a The price of substitute products.
  b Self-image.
  c Cultural factors.
  d Product value.

41 Which of the following regions has the highest population?
  a North.
  b South West.
  c Scotland.
  d South East.

42 Grouping customers together with similar characteristics so that an organisation can focus its efforts upon different parts of the marketplace is known as:
  a Positioning.
  b Market segmentation.
  c Cultural targeting.
  d Market division.

43 Competing in just one segment in the market is known as:
  a Concentrated marketing.
  b Differentiated marketing.
  c Undifferentiated marketing.
  d Marketing management.

44 During which period of the product life-cycle does the rate of growth begin to slow down?
  a Decline.
  b Growth.
  c Saturation.
  d Maturity.

45 To plan an advertising campaign an advertiser will usually consult:
  a A newspaper.
  b An advertising agency.
  c A TV station.
  d A local PR agency.

46 A good example of a franchised outlet would be:
  a BHS.
  b Woolworths.
  c W H Smith.
  d Spud U Like.

47 The organisation that publishes *Which?* is the:
   a Consumers' Association.
   b Office of Fair Trading.
   c The *Which?* Consumer Organisation.
   d The National Consumer Council.

48 When selling to a new customer an organisation may set a:
   a Sales budget.
   b Credit clearance limit.
   c Profit target.
   d Standard cost budget.

49 One way of measuring quality of customer service is by looking at the number of:
   a Sales.
   b Complaints.
   c Late payments.
   d Service calls.

50 A very large supermarket with a massive selling area is known as:
   a A discount store.
   b A department store.
   c A hypermarket.
   d A multiple store.

This unit aims to give an overview of the main features of human resourcing. It analyses the rights and responsibilities of employers and employees and examines the legal and ethical constraints which influence the behaviour of public and private sector organisations. You will examine ways of upholding the rights of employers and employees, including the role of trade unions in negotiating conditions of service and resolving conflicts.

Human resources should not be seen purely as the concern of the personnel departments but as an integral part of many job roles. You will investigate the changing nature of roles and the challenges of introducing and implementing changes at work.

You will have opportunities to acquire skills both as an interviewer and an interviewee in recruitment, selection and appraisal situations. Through this you should develop skills in appraising interviewers and interviewees by observing, preparing questions and completing interview appraisal documents.

Chapter 12

Human resourcing

This chapter looks at the rights of employers and employees in the workplace. It explains employer and employee responsibilities in human resourcing and identifies procedures available to employers and employees when rights are upheld. It also explains the roles of trade unions and staff associations, and explains employers' methods for gaining employee cooperation.

The rights of employers and employees

When you go to work you will find that you have a number of rights in the workplace. These rights are very important because they provide you with levels of protection against unscrupulous employers. At the same time employers have rights which mean that they can expect certain things of employees.

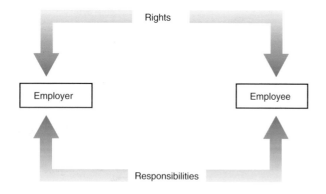

Figure 12.1 Rights and responsibilities – a two-way process

It is very important for you to be aware of both your rights and responsibilities in the workplace (Figure 12.1). Nearly every day we read cases in the national press of employers and employees who have been taken to court for not keeping their side of the bargain.

When a new employee is taken on, he or she must be given a written contract of employment within 13 weeks of starting the job. Under the Contract of Employment Act 1972, the written contract must include the following:

- title of the job
- date the job starts
- hours of work
- rate and method of pay
- holiday arrangements
- period of notice that must be given
- pension scheme arrangements
- rights concerning trade unions
- the organisation's discipline rules.

The employer will agree on a date with the employee for work to start, and the contract of employment becomes binding from this date. The period of notice that an employee must be given when being dismissed is stated in the contract, which is a legal document.

Case study

A contract of employment may be laid out in the following way – see Figure 12.2, which shows only the first part of a contract of employment.

1 How clear do you find the contract of employment to be? Which features of a contract of employment are

SUPERIOR CHOCOLATES PLC

PARTICULARS OF TERMS OF EMPLOYMENT

HOURLY PAID EMPLOYEES

This document defines the terms and conditions for hourly paid employees of SUPERIOR CHOCOLATES and is compiled in accordance with the requirements of the Contracts of Employment Act 1972 and the Amendments thereto under the Employment Protection Act 1975.

To: (Name)......Daniel Sykes...............................

Of: (Address). ....24...Nottingham..Lane..............

Grantham,.Lincs,.NG31.9HL.......................

Job title: .....Production..Line..Operative.........

This Contract to take effect as at .....9...a..m............

Your employment with Superior Chocolates commences on ......30th..September,..1995.......

1. Remuneration

Your rate of pay and overtime rate is as established by the Domestic Agreement between the Trade Union and the Company. A copy of this Agreement is available for reference in the Personnel Department.

Your current rate of pay is £3.50 per hour for a 35 hour working week, and is paid in arrears, normally on the Thursday.

Each payment will be accompanied by an itemised pay statement. The pay week commences on Monday morning and ends on Sunday midnight.

In addition to the above rate of pay, the Company operates an Incentive Bonus Scheme for direct operatives. A copy is available in the Personnel Department for reference.

Figure 12.2 Part of a contract of employment

    set out in the contract above?
2 Can you provide a contract of employment from your own place of work? Show how the features of a contract are set out in your contract. Perhaps this could be done in a short presentation to other students.
3 Alternatively you might like to design a contract of employment for a fictitious job, where you are already familiar with typical features of the line of work concerned.

Health and safety at work

Employees are expected to comply with rules and regulations covering health and safety in the workplace. At the same time employers must ensure safe and healthy working conditions.

Figure 12.3 Hazards at work

Task

Look at the pictures in Figure 12.3. Can you spot the dangers illustrated?

List them, and suggest possible action to be taken in order to ensure a safer working environment in each case.

Official regulations covering health and safety occupy thousands of pages of text. The details are very important. We shall examine some of the main laws that apply.

The Factories Act covers most businesses that use machinery. It therefore applies to a wide range of premises, including garages, printing works, engineering works and building sites. Note that it does not apply just to 'factories'. Some of the important details of this Act are:

- Adequate toilet and washing facilities must be provided.
- The inside of buildings must be properly heated and ventilated.
- Floors, stairs and passageways must be free from obstructions such as boxes and furniture.
- Floors must not have slippery surfaces.
- Machinery such as presses must have fenced screens to prevent injury.
- Fire escapes must be provided and kept in good order.
- Fire exit doors should not be locked or obstructed.

The Offices, Shops and Railways Premises Act

This Act is particularly important in relation to office and shop conditions:

- Temperatures must not fall below 16 degrees Celsius in places where people work for any length of time.
- There must be adequate supplies of fresh or purified air.
- Toilet and washing facilities must be adequate for the number of employees and kept in a clean state. There must be running hot and cold water with soap and clean towels.
- Suitable lighting must be provided wherever people walk or work.
- The minimum amount of space for each person is 12 square metres of floor area.

The Health and Safety at Work Act

This Act establishes a responsibility for both employers and employees to provide safe conditions at work. The employer's duty is to ensure, so far as is reasonably practicable, the 'health, safety and welfare at work of all employees'. The employee's duty is to take reasonable care to ensure both his or her own safety and the safety of others who may be affected by what he or she does or does not do. Employers or employees who do not abide by these rules can be punished in a court of law.

An example of an area covered by the Act is protective guards for cutting machines, such as food-slicing machines, and industrial presses. Accidents occur if the guards are faulty or if they are removed. Generally the workplace should be designed in such a way as to minimise the risk of accidents.

The Act also lays down training standards for employees in potentially hazardous occupations.

This Act is backed up by a Health and Safety Executive which includes representatives of employers, employees and local authorities. Inspectors make sure that the law is being observed.

Reporting of Injuries, Diseases and Dangerous Occurrences Regulations 1985 (RIDDOR)

Injuries that result from accidents at work where an employee is incapacitated for three or more days must be reported to the authorities within seven days. Injuries involving fatalities must be notified immediately by the most practical means, e.g. by phone. Listed diseases must also be reported.

Control of Substances Hazardous to Health Regulations 1988 (COSHH)

Employers must carry out an assessment of work tasks that are likely to create risks for the health and safety of employees. Following on from the assessment, decisions need to be made on how to prevent or limit risks of exposure to such substances.

Workers dealing with dangerous substances should be given appropriate information and training. Measures taken under COSHH need to be continually monitored.

Substances covered by the Act cover all substances potentially harmful to health, whether in solid or liquid form or in the form of gas or vapour.

Noise at Work Regulation 1989

Employers have an obligation to reduce the risk of hearing damage to employees to the lowest level practical. The employer has an obligation to make sure that, when the sound reaches or exceeds a set level, ear protectors are worn.

Other regulations

Other regulations cover the use of electricity in the workplace, the provision of first aid facilities and training, fire precautions and other important areas. Enforcement of the laws is principally by the Health and Safety Executive backed up by local authority inspections. Inspectors have substantial powers, including the right to enter premises, to obtain information and to take possession of articles and substances. Offending organisations can be taken to court and given substantial fines and the persons responsible can receive prison sentences.

Negligence at common law

An employee can claim for damages resulting from an employer's negligence if the employer fails 'to abide by the duty of care to the employee so that the employee suffers injury or damage to health'.

The employer has a duty of reasonable care for the safety of employees, and this responsibility extends to when he or she sends employees to the premises of third parties.

Negligence occurs when there is a breach in the duty of care. The applies to:

- Safe premises
- A safe system of work
- Safe plant, equipment and tools
- Safe fellow workers.

The European dimension of Health and Safety

Health and safety is an important part of the Single European Act which lays emphasis on providing safe working conditions in all Member States. The emphasis is on harmonising working conditions. In addition, new Directives have been established about the technical requirements and safety standards for specific products.

A manufacturer needs to show that products are produced to European standards. This should involve:

1 A manufacturer's declaration backed up by test results.
2 A certificate of standard from an independent body.
3 The provision of test results by the independent body.

The Directives include such areas as:

- Personal protective equipment
- Machinery safety, including mobile machinery and lifting equipment.

Evidence collection point

Investigate the health and safety features that apply either to you in your place of work, or to a parent or friends at their place of work. Set your findings out in a written report.

If you have the facilities, work in a group to produce a video to highlight the health and safety lapses that affect the members of your college. This video could be a short 'commercial' lasting no more than 45 seconds. You should construct a storyboard to clarify your ideas before you shoot the video. This work will provide evidence of Core Skills in Communications.

The safety officer of an organisation must be aware not only of general laws, but also of specific laws and codes relating to particular industries. For example, there are special laws relating to workers in mines, the explosives industry and textiles. On top of this, many industries establish their own safety regulations, often in conjunction with trade unions. A firm's safety officer will normally attend conferences and refresher courses on safety as a regular feature of his or her work.

Compliance with non-discriminatory legislation

Equal opportunities are very important in the modern workplace. Providing equal opportunities involves providing the same opportunities to all employees and prospective employees regardless of their sex, age, disabilities, ethnic origin, sexual orientation, etc.

Discrimination against anyone on the grounds of their sex, race, colour or national origin is illegal, whether it be in recruitment, conditions of work, promotion, training or dismissal. Job advertisements must clearly not discriminate. It is then necessary to make sure that interviews are fair, pay is equal for similar work and that there is no sexual or racial harassment.

Task

These advertisements appeared in a local newspaper. Do you think that they discriminate in any way?

RESPONSIBLE PERSON

required to deliver newspapers
in Middleton Village

Phone Middleton 5557

SALES REPRESENTATIVE REQUIRED

Get in the fast lane with one of the
fastest growing frozen food firms

Excelsior Foods

Excelsior need a Sales Representative in the Midlands

You should be presentable and articulate, able to assimilate the latest sales strategies and be able to develop new food outlets. Experience of the food trade would be helpful.

In return we offer an attractive remuneration package and a company car.

Send your CV together with a hand-written letter explaining why you should fill this demanding post to:

Jane Jones
Excelsior Food
Middleton
M13 8TU

WE WANT YOU TO WORK FOR US

Are you young and dynamic with the right sort of personality to work as an office administrator with us? We are looking for someone who has good interpersonal skills and is prepared to work with others. You may be expected to work extra hours with the managing director of this go-ahead company.

Write to: John Proudfoot
Middlewich Disposal Products
Middlewich
MI35 9BQ

There must be no discrimination of any sort. Alleged cases of discrimination can be taken to an industrial tribunal or a body such as the Race Relations Board.

The Sex Discrimination Act set out rights for both men and women. Unlawful discrimination means giving less favourable treatment to someone because of their sex or because they are married or single, and can be either direct or indirect. The Act also covers victimisation. Direct sex discrimination means being treated less favourably than a person of the opposite sex would be treated in similar circumstances. For example, a policy to appoint only men to management positions is clearly illegal.

Direct marriage discrimination means being treated less favourably than an unmarried person of the same sex. A policy not to recruit married people for a job that involved being away from home would not be allowed.

Indirect sex discrimination is less easy to identify. It means being unable to comply with a requirement which on the face of it applies equally to both men and women, but which in practice can be met by a much smaller proportion of one sex. For example, organisations may be indirectly discriminating against women if access to certain jobs is restricted to particular grades which in practice are held only by men.

Victimisation means being treated less favourably than other people because you have in good faith made allegations about discrimination in relation to the Sex Discrimination Act or any other regulation.

A person who thinks he or she has been treated unfairly with regard to sex discrimination can lodge a complaint with the Central Office of Industrial Tribunals within three months of the alleged wrongdoing.

An industrial tribunal is a relatively informal 'court' which will usually meet locally. It consists of a legally qualified chairperson and two ordinary members of the public with experience of industry and commerce (Figure 12.4).

Figure 12.4 An industrial tribunal panel

As complainant, you can either present your own case to the tribunal or seek help from the Equal Opportunities Commission. If the tribunal finds in your favour it can do any or all of the following things.

■ Make an order declaring your rights.
■ Order that you be paid compensation, which could include lost earnings, expenses, damages for injury to your feelings or damages for future loss of earnings.
■ Recommend that the person or organisation you complain against should take a particular course of action within a specified period – for example to consider you for promotion within the next year.

Case study – Discrimination in the workplace

In March 1995 the case of Wendy Underwood was presented to an industrial tribunal. Mrs Underwood claimed that she was forced out of her £17000-a-year job after seven years upon becoming pregnant, and told it would not be a 'good idea' to go back.

The tribunal was told the former flight lieutenant – who is claiming unfair dismissal on the grounds of sexual discrimination – was not told she could return to her post as an air traffic controller at RAF Cottesmore following the birth of her first daughter in June 1990.

In December 1989 Mrs Underwood discovered she was 12 weeks pregnant and immediately told her bosses. After talks with her commanding officer it was agreed she could remain at her post until the 20th week of her pregnancy.

Mrs Underwood said that all attempts to try to sort out her future in the RAF were met with a dismissive attitude which made her feel 'like a persona non grata'.

'Nobody wanted to tell me anything about what I should do or what I was entitled to. Nobody made it clear what my position was in the RAF.'

At the time she had no idea she was entitled to re-enlist after the baby was born and was unaware of the RAF's policy to actively recruit women with children into the service. When she asked about coming back after having the baby she was told by the station officer that it would not be a good idea.

Mrs Underwood contrasted her treatment with that of her husband who has been given unlimited time off to pursue his rugby career. Mr Underwood plays rugby for England.

1 What do you consider to be the main issues of concern in this case?
2 Do you think that the case outlined involves discrimination? Explain your answer.
3 What do you think the judgement of the Industrial Tribunal would/should have been?

Evidence collection point

Study the three cases below and then explain why each case could be said to involve discrimination in the workplace.

Case 1: Jane Delaney vs Northshire County Council

The following advert recently appeared in a national publication advertising a job in the primary school where Jane works.

Jane had been working at the school for ten years. She

> ### DEPUTY HEADSHIP
>
> Committed primary teacher wanted to take on this post of responsibility. We are looking for someone with a broad range of interests and experience. The successful applicant should be able to take charge of music, drama and boys' PE.

already ran the school music department and had a keen interest in drama. She felt that she would not be given a fair opportunity at interviews for the job.

Case 2: Winston Roberts vs Household Insurance

Winston Roberts has been working for Household Insurance for three years. Mr Roberts had brought up their child for two years before deciding to return to work. Winston's firm has a crèche for employees who have worked for the firm for two years and over. When he applied to put the child in the crèche he was told that he could not do so because the crèche was only for the children of female employees.

Case 3: Milo Kovaks vs International Sales

Milo Kovaks has been working in the marketing department of International Sales for several years. Recently the company advertised for an international sales officer who would be in charge of departments in Brussels, Rome and Paris. The job entails a lot of travel.

Milo applied for the job but was not selected for the interview, though a number of those who were had far less experience. However, Milo did notice that they were all single people – he is married.

The Race Relations Act makes it unlawful to discriminate against a person, directly or indirectly, in the field of employment on the basis of race, colour or national origin. Direct discrimination means treating a person, on racial grounds, less favourably than others are or would be treated in the same or similar circumstances. Segregating a person from others on racial grounds constitutes less favourable treatment.

Indirect discrimination consists of applying a requirement or condition which, although applied equally to persons of all racial groups, is such that a considerably smaller proportion of a particular racial group can comply with it. Examples are:

■ a rule about clothing or uniforms which disproportionately disadvantages a racial group and cannot be justified
■ an employer who requires higher language standards than are needed for safe and effective performance of the job.

The Commission for Racial Equality has produced a code of practice for the elimination of racial discrimination and the promotion of equality of opportunity in employment. This code aims to give practical guidance which will help employers, trade unions, employment agencies and employees to understand not only the provisions of the Race Relations Act and their implications, but also how best they can implement policies to eliminate racial discrimination and to enhance equality of employment. This code covers a variety of areas including recruitment, training and appraisal.

Evidence collection point

You are the personnel officer for a large, well-established building society. You have been set the task of reducing the turnover of female staff in the building society, the Artt, Davies and Deaves Building Society.

The Society has branches all over the country. The society was founded in 1938 by Messrs. N. Artt, D. Davies and L. Deaves, all of whom are still active in the management of the organisation.

Concern has recently been aroused within the Society following the completion of a five-year study by the personnel department. The study has highlighted an increasing turnover of female staff. In addition to the study, a recent survey within the organisation has shown that there is a feeling that women are discriminated against.

Staff level	Male	Female
Executive Officer	74	6
Principal Officer	220	100
Administrative Officer	50	910

(from a sample of 80 branches across the UK)

As personnel officer you have been given the brief to produce a report for discussion within the personnel department. Plan your work so that it provides evidence

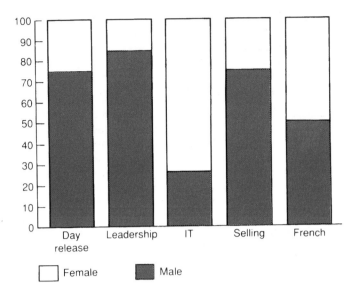

Figure 12.5 Male/female breakdown of staff sent on training courses

of Core Skills in Communication, Application of Number and Information Technology. Your report should cover the following areas:

1 What does 'equal opportunities for all' mean?

  a Set out a series of objectives in the form of a diagram such as in Figure 12.6.

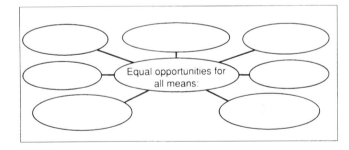

Figure 12.6 Equal opportunities for all

  b How can Artt, Davies and Deaves communicate these objectives to all members of the organisation?
  c How can Artt, Davies and Deaves keep a check that these objectives are being applied?
2 From the evidence provided in the text, suggest possible reasons why there has been an increasing turnover of staff.
3 Suggest possible ways of reducing this turnover.

4 Highlight the laws which Artt, Davies and Deaves need to comply with in providing equal opportunities.
5 In your conclusion, put forward some hard-hitting suggestion for future policy. Set out a programme of suggestions for future changes in a series of clear action steps.

Employer responsibilities in human resourcing

There is an increasing emphasis in organisations on Human Resource Management (HRM). What this means is that people are seen as being a vital resource in the workplace. There are two main schools of thought about Human Resource Management.

The hard approach

The hard approach is concerned with treating people as a vital resource, but in a calculating sort of way as you might do with other resources. For example, HRM would be concerned with trying to maximise outputs from given inputs by considering the most cost-effective ways of doing things.

Employees are encouraged to see their interests as being tied up with those of the organisation. Recruitment is concerned with taking on those employees who best fit in with styles and practices in the organisation, and are thus likely to be most productive. People are vital but they must fit in with the organisation's needs.

The soft approach

The soft approach is also people-centred but it recognises that people are different from other resources. People need to be nurtured, motivated and made to feel important. It recognises that people have feelings and that these need to be the focus for HRM.

A soft approach therefore emphasises involving employees in the management of work – for example, by creating self-managing teams – and is concerned to build commitment to the organisation by informing employees about the organisation's purposes and values.

Some people argue that Human Resource Management approaches are more often talked about than practised. Often organisations just treat people

Human resource management	
Hard approach	**Soft approach**
People most important resource	People most important resource
People need to be used in a cost-effective way	People's feelings should be considered
People should be used in a productive way	Ways of motivating people and involving them in decision-making and shaping work need to be found
People help the organisation to meet its goals	People need to be involved in helping the organisation to shape its goals.

as they do any other sort of resource. We have witnessed this recently in the way in which organisations hire and fire large numbers of people at very short notice.

However, there are other organisations which feel strongly that when people feel that they are an important part of an organisation and help to make decisions – a process called empowerment – they will be highly motivated and highly productive, resulting in effective and profitable organisations.

Clarifying business objectives

If a business is to be successful then it needs to have clear aims that people can work towards. Today these general aims are often set out in a mission statement. The mission is an agreed purpose for an organisation, e.g. 'to be leaders in providing high quality medicines to our many customers.....', 'To give the highest possible standards of public service in....'.

Many organisations will display their mission statements in prominent places so that all employees and customers can see what the organisation stands for. The organisation will then break down this general mission into specific objectives, e.g. to increase sales in 1996 by 10%, to answer all letters to the organisation with seven days.

Organisations have a responsibility to ensure that employees are aware of business objectives. An understanding of these objectives helps individual employees to pull in the right direction.

Individuals who work in a department of an organisation should know what the department's

objectives are for a particular period of time. Nowadays, also, individuals will often be involved in setting their own objectives through the process of appraisal (see next chapter).

Evidence collection point

If you currently have a part-time job, try to establish the objectives which your section/department is working towards. What specific objectives have been set for you in the workplace? What are the benefits of knowing the objectives you are working towards? (An obvious parallel is the performance criteria that you are working towards in a GNVQ Business course.)

Offering and facilitating training and professional development

Training and development are absolutely essential to organisational success. One of the quickest routes to making an organisation more productive is by increasing the potential of employees.

The purpose of training is to ensure that, as quickly as possible, people can reach an acceptable level of performance in their jobs.

Training sets out to fill the gap between what a person can do and what they should be able to do (Figure 12.7) It is concerned with building up skills and knowledge to increase the competence of people in the workplace.

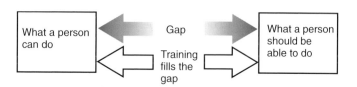

Figure 12.7 Training fills the gap between what a person can do and what they should be able to do

Development can be defined as 'the modification of behaviour through experience'. Development operates at all levels in an organisation, from the new apprentice to the managing director. Development sets out to enable individuals to do better in their existing jobs.

Employers and individuals will only invest more of their own time and money in training if they are convinced that, for them, 'training pays'.

Examples of benefits to employers of training are:

- savings in materials costs due to reduced wastage in production and better stock control
- improved delivery performance and the amount of 'down-time' of equipment
- lower staff turnover and hence lower recruitment and induction training costs
- improved quality, reliability and range of products or services to customers
- faster adaptation to new production technologies and materials
- more efficient scheduling of work and improved responsiveness to specific customer requirements
- improved employee commitment and a more flexible and adaptable workforce.

Individuals also recognise the benefits of training. Research shows that training and education are associated with high earnings. There is some evidence that the earnings gains from education and training, particularly higher level qualifications, may have increased during the 1990s.

As well as financial gains, many people report other benefits from training and development in terms of increased satisfaction from work, more interesting work and improved access to jobs with more scope for the exercise of responsibility and creativity.

Evidence collection point

You have been asked to present the case for the development of a training programme for all staff at a hotel. You will need to sell the benefits of training to both managers and employees.

Recently you developed a training programme for a similar hotel. The results were an increase in business from repeat and recommended guests – from 58% to 70% of bed nights over two years. The conference and banking side of the business grew as a result of customer satisfaction. There was fall in staff turnover and negligible absenteeism.

Produce a five-minute presentation using visuals such as overhead transparencies to outline the benefits of a training programme for staff. This work will provide evidence of Core Skills in Communication.

Training should be seen as a responsible investment in the workforce. It is not only to meet short-term

organisational objectives but also to develop employees personally and create a long-term future for them. This can help them to achieve their ambitions, undertake responsibilities and, at the same time, increase their sense of belonging to the organisation.

In on-the-job training, an individual is placed into a job and trained to perform the task under close supervision. This is training for a specific function, but an increasing amount of training today is directed towards improving employees' understanding of how the organisation operates. Induction training also fulfils this aim.

Staff development provides skills and qualifications for promotion. This will often include off-the-job training acquired by attending courses.

A soft approach to Human Resource Management would stress the importance of developing employees personally so that they can fulfil their personal needs. Of course this will benefit the organisation in the long run but the emphasis is on individual rather than organisational needs.

Case study – Management discover training

The tendency of management in the UK to regard training simply as a cost rather than as an investment is well-known. When a recession occurs it tends to be one of the first areas to suffer cutbacks (Figure 12.8).

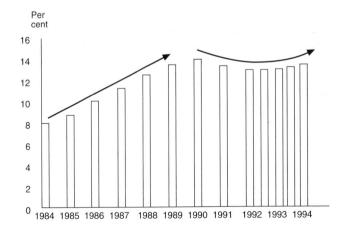

Figure 12.8 Employees receiving job-related training (men aged 16–64 and women aged 16–59): 1984–1994

315

This weakens the ability of organisations to hold and recruit staff and undermines their ability to cope with problems. For example, a recent study by the Small Business Research Trust suggested that lack of management training was a significant factor in the reluctance of small firms to pursue a growth policy.

Professor David Ashton from Lancaster University believes there has been a significant change in attitude in recent years by larger companies, though the old weaknesses persist amongst smaller companies. Among larger businesses he has seen increasing interest in management qualifications rather than training alone. This has led to a provision by business schools of a range of programmes tailored to the requirements of business, such as the Master of Business Administration.

Projects on which managers work in such programmes are often viewed as key to future business success. Companies themselves have also responded to the demands of managers and seem to view management development as a valuable strategy for retaining personnel.

Professor Ashton's findings are supported by a survey carried out by Harbridge Consulting Group. This indicated that today a more thoughtful approach is taking place in management development. More organisations feel that training should take place entirely on individual needs, and management development is also being discussed more frequently at board level than ever before.

Management development is, however, usually planned on a one-year basis in most companies. The Harbridge report indicates a need to bring an understanding of long-term issues into the process of planning for management development. This will enable organisations to cope with demographic changes in the structure of the workforce.

1 Why is training sometimes regarded simply as a cost rather than as a benefit?
2 How might training help to retain personnel?
3 Express your views as to whether or not training should be based upon organisational needs or individual needs.

Managing change

The human resource management environment today is one of change. These changes can and often do lead to large-scale changes within organisations. These changes need to be managed in a constructive and careful way.

For example, one of the major changes that has been taking place has been that of downsizing. Instead of organisations employing thousands of people for life, in tall organisations with many layers of management, these organisations have become flatter with layers of management being stripped out (see page 132).

Increasingly organisations have been getting rid of hundreds, and even thousands, of routine administrative workers and middle managers. Information technology has had a lot to do with this. Information technology makes it possible for large organisations to handle vast quantities of information and routine procedures with fewer administrators. At the same time increasing competition has meant that slow-moving, top-heavy organisations are less responsive to market changes.

Employers therefore have a major responsibility in managing change. Managing change involves:

- Identifying necessary changes (e.g. the need to downsize).
- Involving people in the process of preparing for change.
- Communicating and explaining clearly the reasons for change.
- Convincing people that change is necessary.
- Creating a vision of necessary changes.
- Creating commitment to change.
- Making the required changes.

Of course, change is not an easy process. People who have done the same job in the same way for many years will be reluctant and even resistant to change. People who are faced with the prospect of redundancy may be shattered by the implications. Managing change is thus not an easy business.

Evidence collection point

Choose an example from a local or national newspaper of a case where management is having to manage change over a human resource issue, e.g. the relocation of a business, the downsizing of a company, the closure of a plant. What are the main issues concerned? How has management prepared the workforce for change? How have the employees reacted? To what extent has the management of change been successful or unsuccessful?

Recruitment

Recruitment is an important responsibility of an organisation because it is often seen as the starting point in what is termed 'the employment procession' (Figure 12.9).

Employees have needs from the time of their selection for employment until they cease working for the organisation. The employment procession starts with the recruitment process – finding potential new recruits and choosing whom to take on. New staff then need to be helped to 'fit in', so they go through a period of induction. During their employment they will need to be trained to upgrade their skills and knowledge and be involved in the process of development. When the need arises they may need to be transferred to other jobs or areas.

When they finish working for the organisation they need to have their jobs terminated in a satisfactory way – this includes making sure that pension and other matters are dealt with according to law.

From the employer's point of view, the purpose of recruitment is to buy in and retain the best available human resource to meet the organisation's needs, although as we have seen a softer approach would be one which also recognises individual needs. In recruiting employees, organisations must abide by the principle of equal opportunities. We will look at the process of recruitment in greater depth in Chapter 14.

Negotiation of pay and conditions

Employers have a responsibility to negotiate pay and conditions with employees and/or their representatives. Traditionally pay and conditions have been set by collective bargaining between trade unions and employers' groups. In recent years bargaining arrangements have been fragmented as local pay bargaining has developed. For example, instead of wages for nurses being established at a national level we are now seeing a situation in which individual hospitals are creating local bargaining structures with their own group of employees.

Until recently there were mechanisms to protect low-paid workers from exploitation by unscrupulous employers. For example, Wages Councils established minimum wages for poorly paid workers in a number of industries.

In the early 1990s the government abolished Wages Councils. The argument they put forward was that if the UK was to be competitive then employers and employees should have the freedom to set their own wage levels.

However, it is not all doom and gloom. A counter-trend in the 1990s has been for large UK companies to set up Works Councils for the negotiation of pay and conditions.

This stems from our being part of the European Union. An EU directive covering companies with more than 1000 workers or with over 150 employees in a second European Union country must set up a consultative process for negotiations. Under the system, companies have a duty to inform and consult employees on the commercial performance of the organisation and on employment policies.

Any organisation that has not arranged a voluntary deal by 1996 will be forced to set up a Works Council which meets the detailed provisions of the directive.

Many UK companies have been setting up Works Councils, including Coats Viyella and Courtaulds in the textile industry, GKN the engineering company, Guinness, Bowater and United Biscuits. Because the UK has opted out of the EU Social Chapter, British

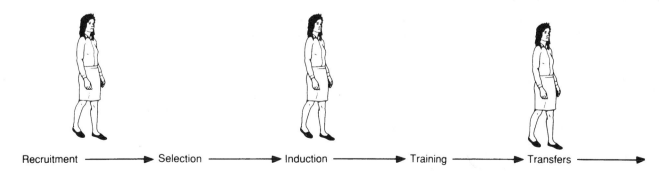

Recruitment ⟶ Selection ⟶ Induction ⟶ Training ⟶ Transfers ⟶

Figure 12.9 The employment procession

companies cannot be forced to set up Works Councils. However, at least half of the top 100 UK companies have already done so.

Some large companies recognise the importance of setting up such arrangements, others fear that soon they will be forced to by EU directives, while yet others feel that if the Labour Party comes into power in the late 1990s they will be forced to step into line.

Evidence collection point

Explain why employers have an important responsibility to establish procedures for the negotiation of pay and conditions.

Handling disciplinary procedures

Employers need to establish a clear framework of disciplinary procedures in the workplace. This is important because employees will need to be seen to be dealt with in a fair way.

Disciplinary matters should wherever possible be dealt with within the organisation rather than having to be taken to an outside tribunal.

Employers should therefore:

- Be made aware of the consequences of breaking rules
- Be given a clear indication of the type of conduct that may warrant summary dismissal.

Key features of disciplinary procedures are that they will:

1 Be set out in writing.
2 Specify to whom they apply.
3 Make it possible to deal with matters quickly.
4 Set out the disciplinary actions that might be taken.
5 Set out the levels of management who will be involved in particular disciplinary actions.
6 Make provision for individuals to be informed of complaints against them.
7 Give individuals the opportunity to present their side of a case before decisions are taken.
8 Make provision for individuals to be represented by a trade union official or representative of their choice.
9 Set out that except for gross misconduct an employee cannot be dismissed for a first break of discipline.
10 Ensure that disciplinary action is not taken until the case has been investigated thoroughly.

11 Make sure that individuals are given a reasonable explanation of any penalties imposed.
12 Provide the right of appeal.

The usual chain of events in imposing discipline in the workplace is:

1 A formal warning, followed by
2 Written warning, followed by
3 Final written warning, followed by
4 Disciplinary transfer, suspension or dismissal.

Dismissal without notice is only legal if employees do something which effectively cancels or breaks their contract of employment.

Examples of conduct which could lead to summary dismissal would include:

- dishonesty
- disclosing trade secrets to competitors
- assault on the employer
- refusal to obey a reasonable order
- damaging the employer's property.

More frequently, employees will be dismissed 'with notice'. The employee cannot be forced to accept less notice than is legally set out in the contract of employment. However, payment of wages instead of notice is allowed.

Possible fair reasons for dismissal would include:

- The employee not having the capability or qualifications to perform the work which they were employed to do.
- The conduct of the employee.
- Redundancy of the employee (i.e. the employee's job being no longer required).

Complaints of unfair dismissal will be presented to an industrial tribunal. Appeals against an industrial tribunal decision will go to the Employment Appeal Tribunal. From there, appeals go on to the Court of Appeal and finally to the House of Lords. Today, appeal cases can be presented to the European Court of Justice.

Evidence collection point

The action which management takes to deal with the misconduct of an employee should depend on the type of misconduct. You are the personnel manager in a small High Street retail shoe shop. What actions would you take (a) in the first instance in dealing with the following examples of misconduct at work; (b) if the misconduct continues?

1 Minor misconduct – this includes trivial acts such as persistent lateness by members of staff.
2 Major misconduct – this includes serious acts such as fighting and swearing which affects customers and/or clients, and breach of safety regulations.
3 Gross misconduct – this includes extremely serious cases of misconduct such as theft and dishonesty.

Handling grievance procedures

From time to time grievances will occur in the workplace. A grievance is a real or imaginary wrong causing resentment which can be regarded as grounds for complaint. Grievances will come in all shapes and sizes and will include allegations of:

■ sexual harassment in the workplace
■ lack of equal opportunities for career progression
■ unfair treatment of individuals and groups

The employer will need to create channels so that informal complaints can be dealt with speedily and with the minimum amount of fuss and disruption. If this does not resolve a grievance then evidence will need to be taken in written form, involving interviewing parties to the grievance. The next step may be to present the grievance to an industrial tribunal and then to the courts.

It is essential that all grievances are taken seriously because they can rapidly escalate.

Evidence collection point

What do you understand by the term grievance? Why do employers have an important responsibility for dealing with grievance procedures?

Implementing non-discriminatory legislation

It is not enough to have equal opportunities legislation. In addition, organisations need to develop policies and codes of practice and procedures for putting them into action.

Case study – Equal opportunities at Melton College

The following is extracted from the Policy Statement and Code of Practice on Equal Opportunities for Melton College in 1995.

Policy statement
The Governors, all staff and all students of Melton College are firmly committed to the implementation of the following Equal Opportunities policy.

Statement
1 The atmosphere and physical environment of the College will ensure that equal value is given to all members of the institution regardless of gender, race or ability.
2 Every effort will be made to ensure that equal access to the College is available to prospective staff or students and racial or gender stereotyping is avoided.
3 The College categorically condemns the expression of attitudes and dissemination of materials which are discriminatory in nature. Incidents of discriminatory behaviour will be dealt with under the appropriate section of the Code of Practice.
4 All staff and students should accept their individual and collective responsibility for challenging racist and sexist attitudes. Development programmes for staff and students should recognise Equal Opportunities as a high priority area.
5 The content and delivery of the curriculum will be reviewed with the aim of countering discrimination and promoting positive attitudes.

The above statement is in accordance with national guidelines and the legal requirements of the Sex Discrimination Act (1975, amended 1986) and the Race Relations Act (1976) which make unlawful discrimination in employment, training and related matters on the grounds of sex, marital status, colour, race, nationality, ethnic or national origins.

Code of Practice
The Code of Practice aims to provide a set of recommendations and guidance on how discriminatory behaviour in relation to race, sex and special needs can be identified at Melton College.

Identification of racist behaviour
Racist behaviour will be identified as being behaviour which is motivated by a lack of respect for or hatred of another racial group.

Examples of racist behaviour are listed below (the list is not exhaustive):

1   Jokes and name-calling stressing racial characteristics.
2   Racist graffiti.
3   Possession and distribution of racist literature and insignia.
4   Refusal to work with other students on the grounds of race.
5   Physical assault.
6   Dissemination of racist myths and misinformation.
7   Use of racist comments for disciplinary purposes, e.g. 'We don't do that in this country'.

Identification of sexist behaviour

Sexist behaviour is behaviour which discriminates between people on the grounds of gender. Sexual harassment will be deemed to fall into this category.

Whilst blatant harassment (e.g. physical assault) will be obvious to both victim and perpetrator, the following examples may help victims to identify more subtle instances. In all cases, the emphasis is on unwanted and unwelcome attention which is sexual in nature and which can apply to either sex (the list is not exhaustive):

1   Jokes, innuendo and name-calling stressing sexual characteristics.
2   The use of derogatory and/or condescending names intended as a put-down.
3   Attention being drawn to body and clothing by verbal or non-verbal means.
4   Following and touching which is unnecessary in the course of college activity and in professional relationships.
5   Leering, gesturing, catcalls and whistling.
6   The display of pin-ups and posters of an offensive nature.
7   The use of sexist comments for disciplinary purposes.

Action on discriminatory behaviour

1   Students and staff should challenge the behaviour directly if they feel they can.
2   Any graffiti or offensive materials should be reported immediately to the Administration Manager.
3   If students wish to complain about such behaviour, they should tell their course tutor or student counsellor or other member of staff. They should ensure the incident is recorded, without detail at this stage.

    If students wish to take their complaint further, they should write down the details and take them to the Director of Client Services.

4   If staff wish to complain of discriminatory behaviour, they can, in the first instance, go to their Sector Manager, or the Director of Client Services. They should ensure the incident is recorded, without detail at this stage.

    If staff wish to take their complaint further, they should write down the details and taken them to the Director of Client Services.

5   In cases reported by both students and staff, the Director of Client Services may refer the matter to the principal.

6   All recordings of incidents and the action taken should be made on the form available from the General Office and these should be lodged with the Director of Client Services.

7   All recordings of the detailed complaints and action taken must be lodged with the Director of Client Services. Access to those records will be restricted.

Disciplinary action

The Disciplinary Code of the College for staff and students is available to be invoked when dealing with incidents of a disciplinary nature.

1   What do you consider to be the major strengths of the policy and procedures outlined above?

2   To what extent do the policy and procedures provide the basis for actual practical steps to ensure that equal opportunities are a reality in the college?

Implementing health and safety regulations

We looked in detail at the beginning of this chapter at the health and safety responsibilities of organisations. As with equal opportunities legislation it is essential for organisations to provide practical steps for putting policy into action. Every organisation should have officials with a responsibility for health and safety. Usually in larger organisations there will be health and safety committees who have the responsibility for checking and monitoring health and safety procedures. The committee will be made up of representatives from various departments in an organisation and will be accountable to the Health and Safety Executive.

The responsibilities of health and safety committees will be to canvass the views of members of the organisation, and to ensure that training is provided in health and safety procedures. Health and safety notices will need to be placed in prominent positions. A number of such notices, e.g. relating to fire escapes and fire doors, must be placed in prominent positions by law. It is essential that health and safety regulations are not broken or premises can be closed down.

Evidence collection point

Carry out some research to find out what the major health and safety regulations are in an organisation in which you work and/or study. What procedures does the organisation follow to ensure that health and safety regulations are implemented?

Meeting quality standards

When we use the term 'quality' in business we refer to products or services that 'do what they claim to do, and what their customers expect of them'. In other words they must be 'fit for their purpose', as the British Standards Institution defines quality.

There are two aspects of this definition. The first is measuring up to specification. The second is meeting customer requirements (Figure 12.10).

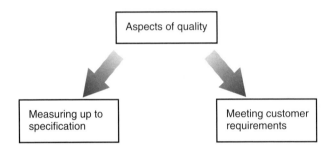

Figure 12.10 Two aspects of quality

The first aspect is often summed up as 'fitness for purpose or use'. This is sometimes called the producer definition of quality. Quality for the producer is achieved by its products or services meeting a predefined specification in a consistent fashion. Quality is demonstrated by a producer having a system, known as a quality assurance system, which enables the consistent production of the goods or service to a particular standard.

The second aspect is concerned with meeting customer requirements. Consumer satisfaction will be the best measure of this aspect of quality.

In terms of human resourcing, employers have a responsibility to ensure:

■ The employment opportunities that they provide meet set standards and specifications.

For example, if employers set down that jobs will need to be carried out in a particular way then they will need to provide the opportunities for employees to carry out the job in that way if they are to be done to quality standards.

If an employer sets out that particular post-holders will require certain types of training if they are to meet given standards, then appropriate training will need to be provided.

It is only by setting quality standards for human resourcing that people at work will be able to produce quality products.

■ Human resource opportunities at work should meet consumer requirements. For example, employees will be important consumers in the workplace. If they are satisfied with their jobs then they will be highly motivated. Dissatisfaction would be indicated by high levels of labour turnover, poor productivity, etc. The end result would be poor performance and sub-standard products.

Employers therefore have a responsibility for providing quality conditions for human resourcing, by setting standards and by ensuring that employees are satisfied with jobs and working conditions.

 Evidence collection point

What do you see as being the main responsibilities of employees in providing quality working conditions?

Employee responsibilities in human resourcing

There are many rewards from employment, but these come with a number of responsibilities. Employees have important responsibilities to their employers, fellow employees, customers and to other groups.

Compliance with terms of contract

The contract of employment sets out the terms and conditions under which an employee will work. The contract will make it fairly clear what an organisation expects of an employee.

For example, employees would be expected to work to the times set out in the contract and to have the required levels of qualifications. An employee who arrived late to work on a regular basis or who had lied about previous experience and qualifications could be dismissed.

It is up to an industrial tribunal to decide on the 'fairness' of a dismissal. A worker can be 'fairly' dismissed without notice. This would involve proving a case against the employee on grounds such as:

■ wilful destruction of company property
■ sexual or racial harassment
■ continuous bad timekeeping
■ a negligent attitude at work
■ inability to do the job which the employee was appointed to do
■ sleeping on the job.

It is very important for an employee to study his or her contract and to be sure of keeping within its terms. Contracts vary according to the nature of the work. They become very important when cases are brought to the courts. For example, in 1995 a nurse was censured for carrying out a small part of an operation which went beyond her contractual duties. Keeping to the terms of a contract is important because it gives you protection as well as responsibilities.

Evidence collection point

Study a contract of employment. Make a list of the main contractual responsibilities that are set out in the contract. Perhaps you could contrast two different contracts for different types of work.

Compliance with health and safety at work regulations

When we looked at health and safety at work regulations we saw that employees have an important part to play in ensuring safe working practices in the workplace.

To take a simple example: an employee working in a supermarket is informed that a customer has spilt yoghurt onto the floor. The supermarket employee must then immediately put up a sign by the spilled yoghurt showing that there is a slippery floor. He or she will then inform their supervisor and steps will be followed to ensure that the floor is cleaned. The sign will remain in place until the floor has dried. The employee must be given prior training in following these procedures, or all sorts of things may go wrong. For example the employee may start to mop up the yoghurt without putting up a warning sign. Customers may then slip and injure themselves.

An employee who knows health and safety regulations and does not abide by them is guilty of negligence and will be liable to dismissal.

Health and safety requirements are an essential part of the training of employees and important health and safety requirements will be prominently displayed at the place of work. Health and safety laws place a requirement on an employee to 'take reasonable care to ensure both his or her own safety and the safety of others who may be affected by what he or she does not do'.

The emphasis is on the word 'reasonable', because accidents will always happen. However, we frequently read about employees who have been negligent. For example:

■ The underground guard or train driver who was under the influence of alcohol.
■ The ferry door operator who did not check that doors were fully closed.
■ The production line operative who slept at work.

Evidence collection point

Produce a five-minute presentation including overhead transparencies outlining the health and safety requirements for employees at a place of work that you are familiar with. This work will provide evidence of Core Skills in Communication.

Non-discriminatory behaviour

Employees have a responsibility to ensure that they are not party to discriminatory behaviour. This will involve complying with the requirements of the Sex Discrimination Act and the Race Relations Act.

Individuals can and are frequently found guilty of discrimination at work. The newspapers regularly inform us of men and women who have harassed others in the workplace.

This may take the form of innuendo. For example, in March 1995 the newspapers reported the case of a female employee who had not been considered for promotion because she had shunned the sexual advances of her male work superior. In the same month we read of a male employee who had been continually pestered by his female superior.

Harassment may take the form of bottom pinching, lewd jokes and physical intimidation. For example, we have all read reports of some of the brutal initiation ceremonies to some sectors of the armed forces. We have read about racial name-calling and taunting in many occupations. More and more cases of harassment at work are coming to light, perhaps because more people are prepared to report cases.

From the employee's point of view it is important to note that discrimination of any sort is a serious offence and will be dealt with as such in the courts. Anyone who engages in any form of open or secret discrimination has no place in a modern workplace.

Evidence collection point

Collect a press cutting which identifies discrimination in the workplace by an employee. What sort of punishment does the discriminator receive?

Working towards organisational objectives

Organisations work towards specific objectives. Objectives tend to be set at an organisational level, at a departmental or divisional level, and at individual levels. Modern organisations should communicate to their employees what these objectives are so that employees can work towards them.

Employees have a responsibility to find out what specific objectives they should be working towards so that they can work towards set standards. If you know what you are expected to achieve then you are best placed to measure your performance.

For example, in a production plant a particular operating unit may be set the objective of producing 100 units of output a day. Your objective may be to produce 10 of these units. A restaurant may have the objective of increasing the number of customers by 10% in the coming month through attention to customer detail, quality food, neat presentation of staff and friendly attitudes. If you are a waiter in the hotel your personal objectives might be to make each individual customer feel special, to be neat, and to be alert in your work.

Evidence collection point

What are the objectives of an organisation that you work for? How are you expected to contribute to meeting these objectives?

Meeting customer needs

Market-orientated organisations (most businesses today) set out to satisfy consumers. Attention to detail and to customer service are essential ingredients. This is as true for a beautician as it is for someone working in a fast-food restaurant. There is a saying that 'the customer is always right', the implication being that employees consider the customers' needs and requirements first.

Responsibilities to other employees

Employees rarely work alone today. Even the lighthouse keeper of days gone by is being replaced by automatic lighthouses. Increasingly the emphasis is on teamworking, in which groups of people share work and expertise. In teams you need to be with people who are supportive and helpful rather than just in it for themselves. Individuals have a responsibility to others for shared work targets, health and safety, shared quality standards, etc.

Meeting quality standards

Employers have a responsibility to employees in providing an appropriate working environment that enables them to produce quality work.

Employees have a responsibility for making sure that the products they make meet set specifications, and also meet the needs of customers.

Procedures available to employers when rights are not upheld

So far we have been studying a number of major rights and responsibilities for employers and employees in the workplace. However, from time to time some of these rights are not upheld or responsibilities are not carried out.

In this section we explore the procedures available to employers in these situations. We shall look at the procedures available to employees in the next section.

Negotiations with individuals

The obvious starting point is to talk things through with the individuals concerned. For example, an employee may have a poor attendance record, or may feel that employers are preventing them from doing the training which they feel they need.

The first type of negotiation might be an informal 'off-the-record' chat. If this is unsuccessful the next step may be a formal chat, with a written record being made of points at issue. Wherever possible, issues should be thrashed out in a friendly way. It is important to be frank and honest.

Negotiations with trades unions

Here we are referring to interactions between employers and trade union representatives concerning disciplinary and grievance procedures. These may be a result of either breaches of an organisation's (or the state's) regulations and codes of practice or an individual employee's perception of having being wronged or ill-treated.

Employers and employees need to have a system for communicating their views and requirements to each other. The aims of a business organisation may be to win more orders and to make sales and profits; employees working for that business, on the other hand, may be more concerned with having a longer holiday break, job security and improving their wages and conditions of service. A forum of some description needs to be set up to make these different viewpoints known (Figure 12.11).

Employers and employees need to come together to discuss their needs and problems. Arrangements for such industrial bargaining vary considerably.

The media's reporting of trade union activities can easily give the wrong impression of the full role of unions in modern industries. Unions are, in fact, involved in all aspects of industrial relations.

A trade union is an organisation of employees, which aims to protect and promote the interests of its members. A trade union is therefore a promotional pressure group and a protective pressure group. It exerts pressure by means of collective bargaining with employers.

We will look in greater detail at the role of trade unions below (see page 327). However, at this stage it is important to note that unions play an important role in supporting individuals and groups of

Figure 12.11 Viewpoints require a forum

employees in negotiations over their rights in the workplace. Representatives of the union will represent their members' rights in particular instances.

It is in the interests of managers and employees to establish a clear set of workable negotiating procedures. A negotiating procedure sets out a framework in which parties can establish terms and conditions of employment.

This framework will cover four main elements:

1 The area (which may be geographical, occupational grouping, etc.) in which the union's representative role is acknowledged. Where several unions are involved this may clarify the 'territory' of each; for example, 'This agreement covers industrial relations between Sunny Bakeries plc and the Bakery Union.....'.
2 Those issues that will be subject to negotiation, such as wages and salaries, conditions at work and union recognition.
3 The steps by which agreement will be sought; for example, 'In the first instance a meeting will be

organised between the personnel managers of individual plants and the divisional officer of the trade union.'
4 The steps to be taken when there is a failure to agree; for example, the matter may be put before an outside negotiating body such as ACAS (see below).

Evidence collection point

Identify a case from a national newspaper where a particular union has been asked to represent employees in order to protect their rights. What specific actions has the union taken?

Negotiations through the Advisory, Conciliation and Arbitration Service (ACAS)

The Advisory, Conciliation and Arbitration Service (ACAS) was set up in the 1970s to act as a 'third party' in industrial disputes. It can do this in a number of ways.

Conciliation is a process through which an independent outsider, such as an ACAS official, tries to act as a channel of communication between an employer and a union. The conciliator will usually meet the parties separately before trying to bring them together.

Mediation is a stronger process whereby an independent outsider proposes the basis for a settlement. However, the parties involved do not have to accept it.

Arbitration involves both parties agreeing to accept the recommendations of an independent body like ACAS (Figure 12.12).

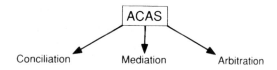

Figure 12.12 The functions of ACAS

The greater part of the work of ACAS involves individual grievances. Each year in the 1990s ACAS has had to deal with over 50 000 cases of individual arbitration. Individual disputes involve a variety of cases including unfair dismissal and sex discrimination applications.

ACAS has a legal obligation to try and resolve individual grievances before they reach industrial tribunals. Most individual cases will be resolved either through conciliation or because the complaint is dropped. Nine out of ten disputes involving ACAS are settled before industrial action is taken.

The rest of ACAS's resources are dedicated to advisory work involving both unions and employers, including surveys, projects, training activities and advisory visits.

Evidence collection point

The national and local press frequently refer to industrial relations issues in which ACAS has been involved. Keep a diary of such events over a three-month period. What actions did ACAS take? How was it involved in different disputes?

Industrial tribunals

We have already outlined the nature of industrial tribunals (see page 311). Industrial tribunals play a very important part in the bargaining process in that they are seen to take a neutral stance. Both employers and employees feel that they have been given an impartial hearing by an industrial tribunal and the outcomes are widely credited as being 'fair' judgements.

Court action

Court action is of course the next step up in disciplinary and grievance procedures. Court action is inevitably a far more formal process, and is one which takes longer and is more costly.

A civil court will be responsible for adjudicating between two parties when a criminal offence has not been committed, e.g. a dispute over contractual terms. Criminal courts will involve criminal offences such as harassment in the workplace.

When satisfaction is not given in a lower court then cases can be taken to appeal eventually to the High Court or to the European Court of Justice. The higher the level of the court the greater the length of time and expense involved.

Plaintiffs wishing to make appeals to higher courts will often need some form of backing, e.g. by a trade union, if costs are not to be prohibitive.

Evidence collection point

Identify an industrial grievance that has recently been to a court of appeal. Explain the issues involved in the case.

Procedures available to employees when rights are not upheld

Negotiation with employer

Negotiation with an employer is the obvious starting point for making a complaint or for airing a grievance. Often such issues can be dealt with in an informal way. The employer may not have realised that a particular action or procedure was inappropriate. However, if no action is taken by an employer or a complaint is not taken seriously, then it will be necessary to make a written complaint, perhaps by writing a letter. Copies of documentary evidence should be kept by the employee. In making a complaint against another employee or supervisor, it is important to write to the person responsible for the person you are making a complaint against.

Negotiations through trade unions

Employees who are members of trade unions have the security of knowing that they can call on the services of skilled negotiators. Unions are used to handling grievance procedures, and will have considerable expertise in this matter. Unions will generally negotiate on your behalf after first taking as much evidence as possible to support a claim or assertion.

Negotiations through ACAS

We have already seen that ACAS is an important channel for grievance procedures and other disputes. Individuals or trade unions can present cases to ACAS.

Industrial tribunals

Industrial tribunals will look into cases presented to them by individuals or their representatives.

Court action

Court action is the next step up for individuals and groups wishing to follow civil and criminal actions.

Industrial action

As we shall see below, industrial action is a way of exerting pressure to redress a grievance or resolve a work-based dispute.

The role of trade unions and staff associations

Trade unions are organisations formed, financed and run by their members in their own interests, and several have existed for over 100 years. There are many trade unions, covering a wide range of employment areas.

In British law, a union must be 'independent' – that is, it must not rely on an employer for funds, facilities or organisation. It must show that it can provide adequate services to its members and that it is able (if necessary) to sustain itself during disputes.

In the United Kingdom there are over 200 certified independent trade unions, although the vast majority of members belong to the largest few unions. They can be divided into three main categories:

- manual worker unions
- white-collar unions
- managerial/professional unions.

Task

Using newspapers, library sources and your memory of news programmes, write out the full names of the unions listed in Figure 12.13.

	Initials	Full name of union
Manual	NUM	
	GMB	
White collar	NUT	
	CPSA	
Managerial and professional	NATFHE	
	BALPA	

Figure 12.13 Some familiar unions

Try to find out the names of other major unions. For example, look in *A Handbook of Industrial Relations* by B. Towers (Kogan Page)

A staff association is slightly different from a trade union. It is a group of employees who share a common purpose, i.e. to further their interests in the workplace. Generally speaking, a staff association will be made up of white-collar employees. The staff association will not usually be a member of the TUC (Trades Union Congress) though there are exceptions to this.

A staff association will usually be made up of people working for a particular organisation rather than being made up of people working for many different organisations.

Today there is not a great deal of difference between staff associations and trade unions.

Perhaps the biggest difference is that the term staff association sounds slightly more up-market than trade union.

During the 1980s and 1990s there has been a decline in union membership. However, the fall in numbers has not been fastest in the UK under a Conservative government – it fell faster in France with a Socialist government. Indeed, union membership as a proportion of the workforce fell in every major industrial country.

In the UK the proportion in 1988 was 41% and in France 12%. By 1993 it was down to 33% in the UK.

The central causes of union decline are the changes in the industrial structure and the nature of the workforce that have been taking place across the industrial world. These changes include the decline of numbers employed in 'heavy' industries such as coal and steel, the shift of manufacturing employment from production to design and marketing, the increase of women in the workforce, the shift to part-time work, the growth of small companies and self-employment.

Lower inflation in the 1980s may also have contributed because people did not have to fight so hard to keep their pay up with price levels.

Another cause of union decline has been the human resource management practised by employers which is designed to build a web of individual relationships, with flexible employees; this is coupled with the needs of the business, buying employees' commitment in return for investment in the development in their skills. Human resource managers are committed to people as an investment. There is thus less scope for the trade unions to combat the 'unfeeling' employer.

Internationally, the main area where unions have kept their memberships – though not necessarily their influence – has been the public sector. Where unionisation is lowest, as in France or the United States, the public/private sector balance of union membership is even more heavily skewed towards the public sector.

It is likely that union membership will continue to decline as the factors which created the unions become less significant. It is possible that trade unions will, by the beginning of the twenty-first century, be seen as having had a natural life of a little more than 100 years, for the conditions that led to their growth will no longer apply.

The appalling abuse of workers by industrial management that made the unions necessary rarely occurs today in the developed world, and the ineffective management that operated in the public sector will no longer be tolerated.

As industry in the developed world increasingly shifts production (though not design, finance and marketing) to less developed countries, where labour costs are lower, union membership will be further eroded. This shift is already widespread in the USA and Japan.

Trade unions and staff associations play a number of roles including:

- negotiating pay and conditions
- giving advice and information
- defending employees' rights
- resolving conflict.

Negotiating pay and conditions

Trade unions and staff associations set out to look after their members by:

- protecting their levels of wages and other payments
- negotiating their hours of work and other working conditions
- keeping an eye on health and safety at work

The first stage of union communication with management prior to industrial action should be through the negotiation process. Ram Singh exemplifies the process of negotiation in diagrammatic form (Figure 12.14).

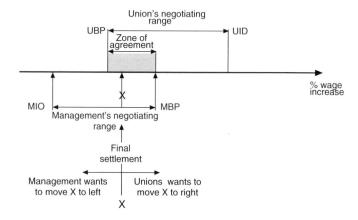

Figure 12.14   A zone of agreement in bargaining (after Ram Singh)

He points out that in negotiations, management and unions tend to choose positions that favour their own interest. The starting-point in a wage dispute would be the union's initial demand (UID) and the management's initial offer (MIO). One party is unlikely to be able to persuade the other to accept its starting position; therefore there has to be a movement towards a central, compromise position.

There is, however, a limit to this process, which can be called the break-point or fall-back point. Neither party is prepared to go beyond its own break-point. In Figure 12.14 the management's break-point (MBP) overlaps with the union's breakpoint (UBP). There is therefore a zone of agreement in which a settlement can be made. The point at which the final settlement is made (point X) depends on the bargaining strength and skill of the two parties.

Giving advice and information

In medium-sized and large organisations it is not really possible for each employee to negotiate individually with management on every issue or grievance that arises. Instead, trade unionists elect or appoint representatives who negotiate on behalf of all the members. These representatives can be divided into two groups.

Shop stewards are elected by union members at their workplace, their task being to represent the views of trade unionists on day-to-day issues. They are not paid a wage by the union since they work at their own job when not involved with union business. However, they are trained by the union to carry out their union duties.

Full-time officials of a union are either elected by the members or appointed by the union's executive team. They are paid out of the union's funds.

To do their job well, trade union representatives need skill in talking to their members and in gaining a clear view of their problems. They must be able to organise and speak at meetings and present arguments to management, and have an understanding of accounts, production levels, the market and basic economics. They must also have a good knowledge of present laws concerning health and safety, dismissal, redundancy and employment in general. The job of a trade union official is therefore an extremely demanding one.

With all this expertise, union officials are a great source of advice and support for individuals at work. They are able to advise you about your rights, and your obligations. They are the first people to turn to in the case of grievances and disputes.

Evidence collection point

Identify your local representative of the National Union of Students. Try and find out what sorts of advice this official is asked for in a typical week.

Defending employees' rights

Full-time officers in most unions are in three or four grades.

At the top is the general secretary, who is an elected official. Next come the national officers, who are usually recruited internally and operate from their union's headquarters. A third band of officers run the union in the regions or districts, and they are responsible for the first-line officers who not only organise the union at local level, but also are closely involved with the union membership at the place of work and the local branch. The first-line officers make up the vast majority of all full-time officers (Figure 12.15).

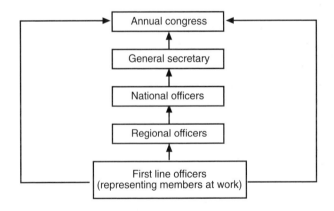

Figure 12.15 A typical union structure

Case study – Changes in the labour force

Over the next few years there will be dramatic changes in the structure of the labour force. These will stem from shifts in population structure, advances in technology, changing attitudes at work and other factors.

329

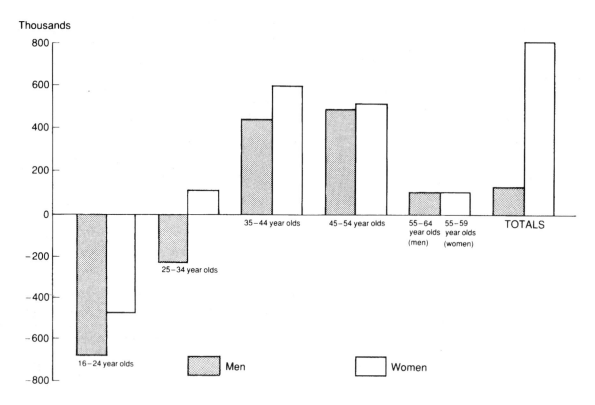

Figure 12.16 Projected changes in the UK civilian labour force of working age, 1989-2001

Figure 12.16 shows the projected changes up to the year 2001.

What impact are these changes likely to have on the size, structure and influence of trade unions in the UK?

Trade union representatives help to ensure the smooth running of industry. Wherever people work or meet together, disputes and grievances will occur, and in industry the problems of new technology, complicated payment systems and work that lacks stimulation are bound to create occasional dissatisfaction. Many of these everyday problems are easily dealt with by meetings, discussion and bargaining.

It is the trade union representative who expresses the views of employees and defends their rights. Shop stewards often complain that, while most of their activity is concerned with preventing disputes or strikes, such information is not printed in the papers.

Types of industrial action

■ *Non-cooperation* This can take the form of working without enthusiasm, a go-slow or a work-to-rule. Working to rule means sticking firmly to the rule book, elements of which might normally be set aside to speed up procedures.

Figure 12.17 A P&O picket line

■ *Overtime ban* This is a weapon that needs to be used carefully because employees lose earnings while employers pay out less in wage and production costs. It can be most effective when management has important orders to meet.

- *Strike* A strike is the ultimate weapon of a trade union and occurs when employees withdraw their labour. A strike will normally involve some form of picketing action. A picket is a union representative who stands outside the place of work to explain to people why the strike is taking place and why they should not go into the workplace (Figure 12.17).
- *Sit-in/work-in* In response to being made redundant, employees may continue working and 'lock-out' the management until negotiations take place.

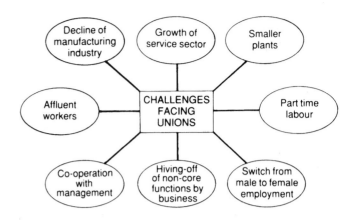

Figure 12.18 Challenges facing trade unions

Types of employer action

Employers and management can themselves take industrial action to put pressure on employees. Actions can include the withdrawal of overtime, mass suspensions, changes in working standards and payment rates, locking employees out, the closing down of enterprises and the removal of plant and machinery at the workplace. The withdrawing of overtime or mass suspensions, for example, are sometimes used by the management to put over the point to union negotiators that it proposes to stand firm on a particular point.

Resolving conflict

Disputes usually occur when all the available channels of discussion and negotiation have been tried. Reasons for disputes are usually very complicated, and one needs to be cautious about saying that one party is 'wrong' or 'right'. If the causes of disputes were that simple, then they would rarely occur.

A major function of trade unions and staff associations is to resolve conflict in the workplace. Employees' representatives are there principally to smooth working relationships rather than to ruffle feathers. The whole structure of industrial relations in this country is there to manage and resolve conflict.

Earlier in this chapter we saw that the number of people in trade unions has declined. There are many challenges and changes which trade unions must face in their environment today (Figure 12.18), not least of which is the increased affluence of the general labour force.

Another change has been the decline of manufacturing industry – the traditional base for large unions – and its replacement by the supremacy of the service sector of the economy. Large factories and plants have increasingly been replaced by smaller units of employees, but where large concentrations of employees still work together they tend these days to be part-time or unskilled workers with limited bargaining powers.

The separating-off of non-core service functions by large businesses means that individual employees have closer contact with their immediate managers.

There has been a move towards increased cooperation between managements and employees. A new style of management increasingly stresses the importance of including employees in decision-making processes, and in return employees are expected to take on wider responsibility for their own actions. For example, multi-skilling involves employees being prepared to do many different jobs rather than concentrating on a single job skill. At the same time many employers have introduced single-union deals – rather than bargaining with many individual trade unions they recognise and bargain with a single union.

Alan Cave has recently argued in his acclaimed book *Managing Change in the Workplace* that what we need today are what he calls 'reinvented unions' which should be there to support the human resource management initiatives of employers.

He argues that unions would be more popular if they focused on their role of representation and problem-solving, principally through the following.

- An employment advice service giving easy access to the best possible advice to those struggling in deregulated labour markets.
- A support service for 'mobile career workers', taking the hassle out of all the pensions, taxation, contract and training tangles they face.
- Partnership in change – offering firms, in effect, advice drawn systematically on the practical experience of union members with new techniques and technologies.
- Flexible friendship helping firms to face the headache of resourcing the more complex, flexible patterns of employment, and to raise the quality of the labour they employ.

Case study – A single-union deal

In November 1991, engineering union leaders and Toyota signed a single-union agreement that was heralded at the time as likely to give the company the lowest labour costs in the motor industry. Five unions competed for the prize of recognition for up to 3300 workers to be employed at Toyota's new plants at Burnaston in Derbyshire and on Deeside. The deal offered workers 'stable employment' in exchange for total flexibility between skills and a commitment to maintain production goals.

Wage levels offered were at a high level for the time. Employees were expected under the agreement to work a 39 hour week despite the Amalgamated Engineering Union's successful campaign for the introduction of a 37-hour week throughout the engineering industry.

The Japanese owners wanted to establish productivity levels comparable to those of Japanese plants. The agreement also sorted out arrangements for industrial action. If the two sides could not be brought together in their thinking by an independent third party, then a ballot of members would need to be called before any industrial action could take place.

The expected output from the plant is 200 000 cars a

year from a tiny labour force compared with that of domestic competitors. Workers will have representatives on the company board and they have also been given the strongest commitment to job security in the car industry.

1 What have the management at Toyota contributed to make this deal a success?
2 What contribution has the Amalgamated Engineering Union made?
3 How will each side benefit from the deal? Who else might benefit?
4 What weaknesses can you see in this deal?
5 What ingredients of this arrangement do you see as 'forward looking'?

The Trades Union Congress

The trade unions as a group have their own organisation, known as the Trades Union Congress (TUC). Every year delegates from the separate unions meet together at a conference to discuss and vote on general union policy. The TUC itself has a permanent body of national officials under the leadership of a president. The TUC puts forward the unions' collective point of view to the government and others. It has a major interest in employment laws, training and conditions at work.

Professional associations

A professional association offers exclusive membership for suitably qualified people in order to enhance the status of their work. There are many types, reflecting the wide range of professions, and many were established under the Companies Acts or by the granting of a Royal Charter. Their functions include:

- Acting as examiners of standards and providing study facilities and guides (for example, prospective bankers take exams organised by the Chartered Institute of Bankers).
- Controlling entry into the professions.
- Preserving high standards of professional conduct in order to protect the public.
- Providing members with technical information and keeping them in step with new knowledge.

With more specialisation in the professions, and more people working in the service sector, professional associations have increased in number in recent years.

Employers' associations

Just as employees have formed and joined trade unions in order to protect their common interests, so employers have formed and joined their own groups. Examples are the Confederation of British Industry (CBI) and the National Farmers Union. These associations have two main functions:

■ to represent employers in dealing with trade unions
■ to give help and advice to employers on a wide range of issues, such as training and calculating tax.

In some industries an employers' association will bargain with trade unions to establish a minimum wage for a given period of time. Individual employers then negotiate additional payments at a company, plant or workplace level with shop stewards.

Most employers' associations today operate principally at a regional rather than a national level.

The Confederation of British Industry

This body was set up to provide a national organisation giving the views of employers. The CBI acts as a mouthpiece for the employers to present their opinions and feelings to trade unions, government, the media and other interested parties.

The CBI collects and makes known information on a wide range of matters. Its Industrial Trends survey, published quarterly, gives up-to-date information on the state of business. It also produces a magazine, *CBI News*, giving employers up-to-the-minute information on a wide range of business issues.

The CBI has a permanent staff involved in collecting statistics, processing information, publishing articles and dealing with queries from industrialists. It is led by a Director General.

The government and industrial relations

The government plays a major role in establishing the industrial relations climate and in organising talks between itself, employers' representatives and employees' representatives.

Throughout the 1980s and 1990s the government has established a comprehensive set of laws limiting the actions of trade unions.

Important pieces of legislation have been the banning of secondary picketing (i.e. the picketing of premises not directly involved in a dispute), establishment of the right of individuals and groups to sue unions for damages (including lost business) caused by illegal industrial action, and provisions for balloting members on strike action.

New aspects of industrial relations in the 1990s include the following.

■ Seven days' notice to be given of industrial action.
■ The right of an individual to join the union of his or her choice.
■ The right of workers not to have union deductions made from their pay without their individual consent.
■ The right of members to information about their union's affairs, including the salaries of principal officers.
■ New rights to combat fraud and vote-rigging in union elections, including the right to inspect voting registers.
■ The right to an independently scrutinised postal ballot before strikes.
■ Postal ballots on union mergers.
■ Collective agreements to be legally binding unless they include provision making them unenforceable.
■ New powers for the government-financed Certification Officer to investigate mismanagement of union finances.
■ Higher penalties for union leaders who fail to keep proper accounts.

Employers' methods for gaining employee cooperation

Today the emphasis in many organisations is on human resource management. Instead of responsibility for people at work being just in the hands of the personnel department, it is today recognised as being a strategic organisation function that works across all members of the organisation. In order for people to feel valued and motivated they therefore need to be involved more deeply in organisational processes.

Representation

Representation involves enabling employees to be a part of decision-making processes within an organisation. Employees may, for example, have representatives present at management meetings in an organisation. The benefits of employee representation are that it enables employees to have a clearer picture of organisational objectives, it reduces the 'them and us' divide in the workplace, and it enables employees to make a contribution to decision-making. Employee representatives may be able to bring invaluable inside information to the decision-making process.

Case study – Employee representation in Germany

The German union structure has been shaped by the country's history. In the 1920s the German economy was racked by huge inflation and strikes. In reaction, a new concept known as *Mitbestimmung* (co-determination) grew up. This was based on the radical idea that workers and managers should have equal power in a company.

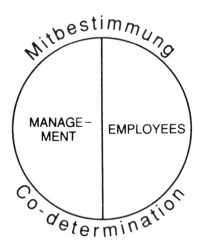

Under Hitler, unions were suppressed, but came back after the Second World War. Ironically it was the British who were largely responsible for the shape of the post-war unions in Germany. As the occupying power they saw the need for stable industrial relations, and brought in experts to create the structure that still survives.

A small number of unions were created (there are now sixteen, headed by the engineers' IG Metall, the biggest union in the world) and a one-plant-one-union rule was established. With everyone from cook to toolmaker in the same union, there was never any possibility of demarcation (who does what) job disputes.

Mitbestimmung took on a definite legal form. It was introduced first in the steel industries and later spread to all large companies. Its basis was a two-level board

system, with the workforce and employers equally represented on the supervisory board. If it came to the crunch, employers could always get their way, but the set-up did have a calming effect. Management was able to find out the wishes of labour early on in negotiations.

In addition, a works council – a non-union body that represents the workers' interests except on pay – has been in place since 1972. Conflict is illegal. The principle of co-determination sets the scene for the whole industrial relations atmosphere, which is remarkably free from confrontation.

But the other leg of the system – the legal framework – ensures that even if the unions do want to push wages up, their actions are strictly limited.

Wage talks are carried out between unions and employers' organisations. Some are countrywide, while IG Metall negotiates state by state. One state will be chosen by the union; the battle will be fought there, and other states will fall into line.

The idea is to thrash out collective deals which set basic pay levels for different grades of employee. These are binding and, as individual companies are not involved in the negotiations, there is no scope for one company to offer bigger wage increases than another.

The basic wage level is, however, rarely paid, because virtually every company adds a top-up that can boost basic pay by perhaps 25%. These top-ups reflect local skill shortages, and tend to be more generous in large companies. So the idea of the centralised coordinated pay settlement in Germany is really a myth.

1 What are the main differences between the union structures in Germany and in the UK?
2 How and why did the differences develop?
3 Which do you think is the better system?
4 How does the German system incorporate the representation of employees in decision-making processes?
5 What are the advantages of employee representation?

Consultation

Consultation is the process of discussing with and seeking the advice of others.

Increasingly, business organisations see the benefit of spreading the decision-making process as wide as possible. By consulting groups of employees you are inviting them to take joint ownership of decisions. This can be tremendously motivating. Employees respond well to being asked for advice. When decisions are finally made they are then able to see that they have had a joint input. People are likely to work harder to achieve targets and objectives that they have helped to construct.

Setting up a joint consultative committee is a way of bringing employees and managers together in the workplace to share decision-making. Such a committee meets formally and sometimes (but not always) involves union representatives. It is essential to disseminate the information coming out of joint consultative committees around the organisation. Minutes should be posted on notice boards.

Evidence collection point

Suggest ways of increasing participation in one organisation that you are familiar with.

Teamworking

Teamwork and the development of a team spirit can go a long way towards increasing the sense of satisfaction that people obtain from their working environment, and providing them with a sense of purpose.

For example, imagine what it would be like if you played in a team where other members did not like passing the ball, or if you were in a play in which the actors were competing with each other to impress the audience. In both situations confusion would arise. The group or team would not perform well because individuals would be working against each other – teamwork would be lacking.

Task

Choose one example of a team or group situation in which you operate. How important is it that you cooperate with other members of the group to perform an activity? What would happen if you did not?

At work, lack of teamwork might lead to a job not being completed, or if it is completed, it might be finished badly. Working relationships might be fractious. People might not listen to each other or respect others' views. They would be working as individuals and not heeding advice or providing suggestions. Group values, pride and purpose would not exist.

A team can be defined as 'a collection of people with a common purpose who communicate with each other over a period of time'. In a team the contributions of individuals are complementary. At the very centre of team operations is collaboration.

Whenever a team undertakes a task, there are three elements involved in making decisions about its completion (Figure 12.19):

Figure 12.19 Working together for a common purpose

- The *task* is the content of the work. For example, the team may be involved in a project or in the provision of a goods or service.
- The *process* is all of the interaction which takes place between the different members of the group. It involves people working together, the relationships they establish and the feelings they generate within the group. One test of a good team is how well its members can contribute to a sequence of activities when they work apart.
- The *action schedule* is how the team is organised to undertake a particular task. It will set out who does what and all the procedures necessary for completing the task.

Task

In *Making It Happen*, Sir John Harvey-Jones says 'When I took over as chair of ICI one of my first actions was to arrange for the executive directors and myself to spend a week away together in order to discuss how the board should lead the company, and how we should organise our work'.

How does this statement by Sir John relate to the task, process and action schedule discussed above?

Forming teams

The ability to work in a team is an important element in the learning process. When employers look for new staff, they do not just concentrate upon those with the right qualifications, important though these are. They look for people with the right

335

personality for the job, who can cope with the work involved and also work with others.

SmithKline Beecham Pharamaceuticals recently advertised a management post in a daily newspaper. As the following extract from the advertisement shows, the company was looking for someone with both technical and business skills who could work well with others:

> You will lead a small team which is involved in all stages from negotiation with key suppliers to the provision of first-class user support services. The implementation of new technology in the scientific environment presents special challenges, and you will need to combine a confident and persistent approach with tact, diplomacy and excellent communication skills. We are looking for someone whose high level of technical expertise is matched by business and management skills.

The success of any project usually depends upon all the members of the team. For example, imagine a group of workers building a house. The completion of the project and the quality of the final product depends upon when each specialist turns up and how well they carry out their task. If anyone fails to pull their weight the success of the project is affected. Or imagine a group of people putting up a marquee: if they do not work together and pull on the ropes at the same time, it is not possible to erect the tent.

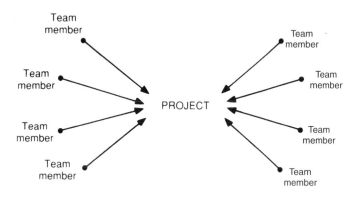

Figure 12.20 Working together as a team

In an organisation, groups or teams may be formed by people who share workstations, who have a similar specialism or who work on the same project.

This sometimes involves working with others from different departments or other areas.

Before any team can be put together a number of issues have to be addressed. These include:

- the size of the team
- the nature of the project
- the requirements of the group
- the roles of members of the team
- the abilities of the group members
- the norms of the group.

Case study – Ignore teamworking at your peril

Heslegrave Gill, a Yorkshire-based consultancy, recently claimed that UK companies are ignoring one of their greatest assets by failing to harness the talents of the people working for them. They feel that giving more attention to teamworking would enable UK firms to emulate the success of the Japanese and point to several examples to prove the case.

Teams of shift workers at the Scunthorpe Rod Mill in South Humberside were looking at ways of achieving greater levels of productivity. Team leaders were instructed in skills such as time management, identification of training needs and problem-solving. The teams were given scope to manage their own work and introduced initiatives to improve both product quality and customer service.

At Penine SCS, a small Halifax firm supplying pneumatic equipment to British Steel and British Coal, the teamworking approach was used to involve employees in the running of the business. Mel Westwood, the company's Managing Director, commented:

> 'We have now installed what we call profit centre managers. These are people from the workforce who are in charge of each department. They are provided each month with a profit and loss report and have set up their own budgets. We have introduced a profit-sharing scheme and they know exactly what the financial position of the company is. We don't hide anything.'

The employees at Penine SCS became so committed to the best interests of their company that they insisted on postponing the profit-sharing scheme for a year so that a reinvestment programme could lay a solid foundation for the future. They showed that they wanted rewards in the future and not in the short term.

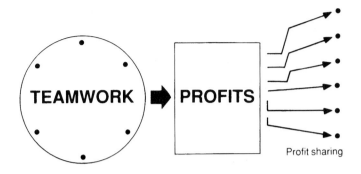

Figure 12.21 Benefiting from teamwork

1 Why do you think that many UK companies have ignored the talents of their workforce?
2 What are the benefits of teamworking?
3 Comment briefly on how teamworking has helped:
   a Scunthorpe Rod Mill
   b Penine SCS.

A strong team is one having a sense of purpose, with clear objectives and goals. Within the group there will be norms of attitude, behaviour and discipline. Individual team members will be open about their views, be prepared to confront where necessary, but will be prepared to cooperate with decisions made by the group. Support and trust are important in a team, as are good relationships across the whole group.

Task

Work in teams of four to design and build a spaghetti bridge to span a gap of half a metre and be capable of supporting the weight of a boot. The bridge should be supported at each end by a tower constructed from a sheet of cardboard. Glue and sticky tape may be used.

Summarise the following:

a How you planned your bridge
b How the team worked together
c The role undertaken by each member of the team.

Your work should provide evidence of Core Skills in Communication.

Team roles

Within every team, various roles can be identified. In general there are four types of functions.

- Leaders
- Doers
- Thinkers
- Supporters.

A *leader* is someone who influences others with his or her actions or words in order to pursue the goals of the organisation. Many leaders have great strength of personality or charismatic qualities, while others are quietly forceful or persuasive.

A *doer* is a more practical person who gets things done and wants to get on with the job once decisions have been taken. A doer will quite often side-step problems rather than spend time trying to find the best solution.

A *thinker* inspires others by providing solutions to problems. A thinker is capable of deep thought, is inventive and can be a constant source of ideas.

A *supporter* is somebody who creates harmony in the team by looking for ways to overcome any problems or destructive undercurrents. A supporter can be particularly useful in a crisis.

Evidence collection point

Imagine that you have been asked to form a small team consisting of yourself and a few of your friends. The team must contain a leader, a doer, a thinker and a supporter. What role would you give yourself, and which friends would you ask to fill the roles? What leads you to believe that they fall into the categories you have assigned to them?

Employee share ownership

A popular form of motivation of employees is to give them shares in the organisation as a bonus for good work. By giving shares to employees they are able to share in the profits of the organisation. Their own efforts are then directly related to the rewards of the organisation. Of course, this policy can be on shaky ground in times of poor profitability.

Quality circles

Making the most of what employees have to offer and valuing their contributions is becoming increasingly important for businesses wishing to remain competitive.

The old-fashioned idea that employee involvement was just about collective bargaining through trade unions is steadily disappearing. Today's ideal form of consultation tends to be by means of groups or teams of employees in quality circles.

The concept of quality circles originally came from Japan in the early 1960s. They were developed in order to improve quality and productivity in manufacturing. It was not, however, until the early 1980s that they started to appear in Western industry. Originally they captured the attention of management specialists as they brought together workers in a consultative process which involved group dynamics.

As a result, over recent years quality circles have attracted a lot of attention and thousands of companies have set them up. To coordinate the diverse activities of quality circles, the International Association of Quality Circles has been formed.

Quality circles are made up of small groups of employees engaged on any sort of problem affecting their working environment – for example safety, quality assurance, efficiency. They are a means for employees to improve their working life by putting forward their points of view on day-to-day issues. They are therefore a form of indirect consultation designed to meet both employee and management needs. They also allow employees to identify their

actions more closely with the success of the organisation and this increases their degree of job satisfaction.

Like many management theories the quality circle is easy to understand. A typical circle consists of between eight and twelve people from similar working backgrounds. They meet perhaps once a week, usually during working hours. Each circle has a leader. Figure 12.22 indicates what a quality circle does.

Evidence collection point

Form a quality circle of between eight and ten people. You have been asked by management to suggest practical ways of improving the quality of your course. Discuss your ideas and make recommendations.

A great benefit of quality circles is that an organisation can use line specialists, who know their jobs and understand how they work, to resolve problems without having to call in management consultants. Furthermore, the management's support of quality circles implies that the employees are trusted to solve problems and their contributions are valued. This helps to develop stronger links between managers and employees and improves morale, as well as the quality of performance.

Job security

A final way of gaining employee cooperation is to create job security. Individuals will work harder for an organisation that they feel will look after them today, tomorrow, and for a long time into the future. When an organisation is committed to individuals, individuals will be committed to the organisation. However, increasingly people are being employed on short contracts. The days of job security for life have disappeared.

Evidence collection point

Interview two or three close friends and relatives. To what extent have their jobs become less secure in recent times? How has this influenced their commitment to organisations?

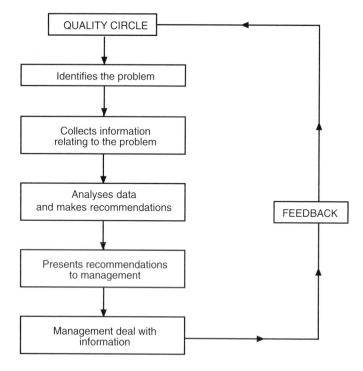

Figure 12.22 How a quality circle works

Evidence indicators

Produce a report which analyses the features of contracts of employment, especially pay and disciplinary procedures.

Compare two working environments with regard to health and safety regulations and non-discriminatory legislation.

The following list should serve as a checklist. Please tick off each of the following when you have successfully covered them. You need to be able to confirm that:

■ I have outlined information about:

– contracts of employment ☐

– working conditions ☐

– health and safety at work regulations ☐

– discrimination at work ☐

■ My report compares:

– contracts of employment for remuneration including ☐

– holiday and sick pay ☐

– procedures for disciplinary action ☐

– conditions for termination of the contract. ☐

■ My report compares two working environments for:

– compliance with or contravention of health and safety regulations ☐

– compliance with or contravention of non-discriminatory legislation. ☐

■ My report outlines the procedures which are available to employers and employees to uphold their rights when these are contravened. ☐

■ A section of my report explains the role trade unions and staff associations can play in negotiating pay and conditions, providing advice, information and legal representation for aggrieved parties. ☐

■ A section of my report explains employer responsibility for negotiating pay and conditions and handling grievance procedures, and discusses how employee cooperation can be gained. ☐

Job roles and changing working conditions

This chapter identifies job roles in business organisations before going on to describe the responsibilities for human resources that are involved in job roles. It then proceeds to explain the reasons for changes in working conditions in recent times. Finally, it looks at ways a business might plan to implement changes to working conditions.

Job roles in business organisations

Directors, managers and supervisors all have responsibilities relating to human resource management. Individuals' job roles extend and expand as they progress upwards in an organisation, moving from the handling of daily routine tasks to making strategic decisions.

On the whole, the larger an organisation the more complicated its organisational structure. Large organisations often require several 'layers' of command. Some people spend a lot of time making important decisions while other are mainly involved in carrying out routine tasks and following set procedures.

Directors

Directors are individuals with legal responsibility to the business's customers, employees, suppliers and shareholders.

It is the directors who generally make the strategic decisions in a business or organisation.

The Board of Directors is thus the top level of a company. Directors sit on the board because they have specialist expertise in a particular line of business, or because they have generalist business experience or, sometimes more importantly, good contacts.

People are 'approached' by a company to become directors, though their appointment must be approved by shareholders. The Board of Directors will usually include a financial expert, an expert with detailed knowledge of the product or service concerned, an expert in getting things done ('a

mover and shaker'), a marketing expert, someone with a lot of contacts, and other key directors depending on the business or industry.

The Managing Director is the head of the organisation. He or she needs to be a person of considerable influence, intelligence, and with the ability to get the board to work together and in the right direction.

When choosing directors it may be wise to appoint someone who is also a director of a variety of other companies in order to draw on their general experience. Politicians are also often invited to be directors because of their political influence (Figure 13.1).

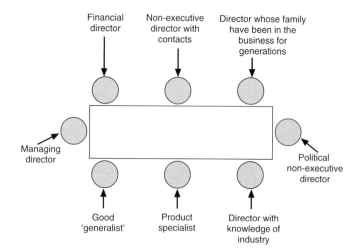

Figure 13.1 A Board of Directors for a public company

A distinction is often made between 'executive directors' and 'non-executive directors'. Executive directors are those who are directly involved in the day-to-day running of the organisation, taking a responsibility for 'executing' decisions. Non-executive directors are influential directors who will simply attend board meetings. The non-executive directors bring to the business extra experience and influence. As a company moves on into new fields and product lines, some directors will no longer be required while new directors with different skills will be taken on.

Evidence collection point

Obtain the prospectus of a large public company. Look at the pages showing the directors of the company. Try to explain why particular directors have been chosen to sit on the board of that company. Which directors are also involved in other activities?

Managers

Managers have the job of deploying an organisation's resources and making policy decisions. Managers use and develop systems for 'organising the organisation'. In the past students used to learn the functions of management by learning the mnemonic:

POSDCORB

This stood for:

Planning
Organising
Staffing (i.e. getting the right people for the right posts)
Directing
Coordinating
Budgeting

It was often described as 'getting things done with or through other people'. This involves deciding on objectives, making decisions to ensure that the objectives are met, and then planning, organising and coordinating activities. The manager's function is particularly concerned with bringing together sets of activities and tasks which contribute towards the completion of whole projects. It also involves controlling, i.e. making sure that things are going to plan. Of course, budgeting is a key aspect of management. That is, the manager must be able to forecast incomings and outgoings from the organisation in order to better control finance and other resources.

The above description makes management sound rather like a highly calculated process. Indeed, a number of people would like us to believe that this is the reality of management. However, research into what managers actually do presents us with a slightly different picture. Most managers in the real world spend a lot of time chasing after things, and reacting to events after they have happened. This is often

because the work environment is so fast moving and unpredictable that it is difficult to predict future events.

Managers therefore needs to be highly alert and able to make quick and appropriate decisions. This requires considerable intelligence, experience, and an understanding of the environment in which they are operating. Indeed, some researchers indicate that effective managers often appear to be quite 'scatty'. The great quality of an effective manager is the ability to get on with people and to be able to influence people to work in a positive direction. Managers also need to be healthy and have the ability to absorb pressure.

Strategic (senior) managers

Strategic managers make top-level decisions concerning the scope of an organisation's activities. These decisions set out what the managers want an organisation to be like and to be about. Strategic decisions are therefore vital for the development and welfare of an organisation. They require detailed analysis and considerable use of skilled judgement.

Examples of strategic decisions include deciding to develop a new product, to open up new markets, or to carry out major investment projects. Of course many of these strategic decisions will need to be approved at Board of Directors level. Some top managers will have a dual role as Directors.

In a college the principal and vice-principals would be examples of senior managers.

Middle managers

Middle managers organise and control the resources of an organisation within established guidelines. Middle managers do, however, usually have considerable scope for using their own judgement and for bringing in new ideas after consultation with senior management.

Examples of middle management decisions include setting out and controlling a departmental budget, organising a sales force, and changing prices of products in response to changes in the market.

In a college, a head of school or department would be an example of a middle manager.

Junior/supervisory management

Junior managers are usually concerned with short-term operational decisions, as well as longer-term ones. Operational decisions are routine and frequently recurring tasks that can be carried out following straightforward rules. Examples include managing stock, arranging schedules for the delivery of goods, and organising hours worked by staff.

Management implies a level of responsibility in an organisation. In a college, lecturers can in some ways be looked at as junior managers – looking after day-to-day lectures, organisation of stock, management of the temperature in the classroom, etc.

However, they also will be involved in some middle management decisions – planning of courses, and course development in conjunction with team leaders.

Unfortunately, the title 'junior manager' or 'trainee manager' is sometimes used by organisations to encourage people to work hard for relatively low pay, because the title 'manager' seems to give a certain status. Anyone taking on a job described as a junior manager should check on the opportunities for promotion.

Evidence collection point

Explain what you understand by the term 'manager'. Study one organisation with which you are familiar. What is the management structure within the organisation? Are there distinct layers of senior, middle and junior management? Determine the nature of the decisions made at each level, and give examples.

Supervisors

Supervisors are quite often the backbone of an organisation. They are people who know how things should be done at 'ground level'. They work with middle and junior managers to put plans into practice at an operational level (Figure 13.2).

Supervisors know the capabilities of all the resources (machines, people and materials) because they work in among them every day.

Supervision is a skilled and demanding job. The supervisor is like a sergeant major in the army giving orders to the ground troops. He or she will be first in line to deal with day-to-day problems as and when they occur.

Organisations therefore look for people with good qualifications to fill supervisory roles. They are likely to have mathematical and communications skills as

Figure 13.2 A supervisor's operational duties

well as a good knowledge of the technology of their industry (today this will almost certainly involve information technology).

Supervisors may have risen 'through the ranks' of their organisation by hard work and the ability to cope with responsibility, so they need to have their skills periodically upgraded through training courses.

Evidence collection point

Figure 13.3 shows the specification for a supervisor in a large office.

1 What does the specification tell you about the qualities that a prospective employee would need to have to fill the post?
2 What does the specification tell you about the role of the supervisor?

Operatives

Whilst operational activities may be routine, they need to be done with great care and precision. There are many different types of operatives. In a supermarket there are shelf fillers and check-out staff; in a textile company there are cutters, stitchers and packers; etc.

Operators need to feel that they are valued, and there should be opportunities for them to learn new skills, so that they can move on to higher grade work.

Attributes	Essential	Desirable
Physical		
Health	General good health	
Grooming	Well dressed and good presentation	
Voice		Well spoken, friendly
Attainments		
Job experience	Experience with administration work, reports, memos, and documentation	
General education		4 GCSEs including Maths and English
Job training	Willing to be trained to required level	
Special aptitudes		
Skill with words		To a good standard of written and spoken English
Skill with figures		Good level of numeracy
Interests		
Social	Able to socialise with staff and customers	
Intellect	Common sense and a good level of intelligence	
Disposition		
Leadership	To be responsible for staff and to be responsible to management	
Self-reliance	To be punctual and to act in mature and reliable way	
Other points	To follow and abide by company rules and to help other staff	

Figure 13.3 Specification for a supervisor

The word operative is sometimes used to describe someone who works a machine, or someone who has a particular skill.

Assistants

The term assistant is also frequently used in business to describe someone who helps others to carry out their work effectively. For example, the terms clerical assistant, dental assistant, and kitchen assistant are used commonly.

The assistant will carry out very routine operations but during this process will be learning 'on the job'. The work of an assistant is very important. Without assistants, work could not be carried out to a high standard.

Evidence collection point

Identify five people in a particular organisation who hold different job roles, e.g. director, manager, supervisor, operative, assistant. Briefly describe what each of the jobs entail.

Task

A National Vocational Qualification (NVQ) is a statement of competence relevant to work, which is intended to help entry to, or advancement in, work, training or further education.

Currently there are five levels of NVQs (these are on a par with GNVQ levels). For example, NVQ level 3 Advanced is at the same Level as the GNVQ Level 3 that you are studying.

Look at the five levels below. Identify which levels would be appropriate to:

- managers
- supervisors
- operatives.

- *Level 1 (Foundation)* Competence in the performance of work activities which are, in the main, routine and predictable, or provide a broad foundation for progression to a higher level.
- *Level 2 (Intermediate)* Competence in a broader and more demanding range of work activities, involving greater individual responsibility and autonomy than at level 1.
- *Level 3 (Advanced)* Competence in skill areas that involve performance of a broad range of work activities, including many that are complex and non-routine. In some areas, supervisory competence may be a requirement at this level.
- *Level 4 (Higher)* Competence in the performance of complex, technical, specialised and professional work activities, including those involving design, planning and problem-solving, with a significant degree of personal accountability. In many areas supervision or management will be a requirement at this level.
- *Level 5* Competence which involves the application of a significant range of fundamental principles and complex techniques across a wide and often unpredictable variety of contexts. Personal accountability and autonomy feature strongly, as does often significant responsibility for the work of others and for the allocation of substantial resources.

Responsibilities for human resources in job roles

The world of work has changed dramatically. In the past many large organisations worked on the top-down approach. Orders and decisions were passed downwards and there was little room for personal autonomy at lower levels. In the past, responsibility for people at work was largely the responsibility of the personnel department.

Today, attitudes are changing. Increasingly it is recognised that a responsibility for 'human resources' rests with all decision-makers in an organisation. If people at work are going to be motivated and concerned to work well for the organisation, they will do so best when they are supported by a network of positive interpersonal relationships.

In this section we will therefore concentrate on these human resource management aspects of the modern workplace.

Identifying business objectives

Business objectives are usually established at the top of an organisation. The Board of Directors will be responsible for deciding on a mission statement which identifies the core values of an organisation. This will then be translated into organisation-wide objectives and policy statements.

Managers then have the responsibility of translating these objectives and policies into divisions and/or departmental objectives.

Managers will need to work closely with supervisors to plan ways of meeting objectives and policies. This will involve translating these objectives into programmes, and schedules for activities.

Operatives will then need to carry out scheduled activities in such a way as to meet targets and objectives that have been set for them (Figure 13.4).

Of course there needs to be continuous monitoring of these activities for control purposes. For example, over-ambitious objectives may need to be scaled down.

Working with others

If an organisation's activities seem to run smoothly it is easy to take the employees for granted. If something goes wrong, it is equally easy to blame

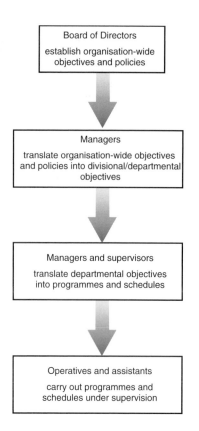

Figure 13.4 Business objectives throughout the organisation

them. Such an approach ignores the needs of employees and fails to take into account the reasons *why* something is or is not taking place.

All organisations must plan for and manage effectively the people they employ to achieve the most from the skills and experiences they possess. An organisation's most valuable asset is its people and the work they do; each is indispensable to the other.

Think what might happen if a manager failed to manage his or her employees and organisation effectively. Initially this might cause bottlenecks, inefficient procedures, possibly poor communication. Staff would be put in difficult and uncomfortable situations. They might lose time, not know what to do, be put under pressure unnecessarily, have to apologise to customers, and so on.

How would employees react to these events? In the early stages many would put up with the inefficiencies of management in the hope that things would improve. If the weak management remained, morale would start to wane, some employees might become resistant to events taking place, and become more time-conscious about the hours they worked. After a period many might leave, and some of those leaving might be key members of staff with important functional responsibilities – for which they have never been properly recognised and rewarded. Replacing them with staff of an equal calibre could be impossible without extensive delay and training costs.

Over recent years the concept of human resource management has become increasingly recognised. HRM places more emphasis upon people in the working environment and how their activities and needs should be understood, provided for, maintained and satisfied.

Case study – Using the workforce properly

Using the workforce properly is a key to Australian industry becoming truly competitive, according to Dr Michael Deeley, the chief executive of ICI Australia.

Dr Deeley believes that improved competitiveness requires a fundamental shift in direction in relationships with employees: 'We need to move from seeing employees as an undesirable and variable cost, to seeing them as an important investment; as the key to improving performance through fully utilising their talents.'

Dr Deeley thinks that this can be achieved by moving away from a workplace where employees are controlled to a workplace designed to make them more committed: 'This is where employees are trusted and empowered, where management provides support and motivation by focusing on performance and outcome.'

This idea would create a workplace based upon commitment. An individual would have a job that was flexibly defined within a career structure and with opportunities for further advancement and training. Dr Deeley feels that 'where people have control over their jobs, where they have freedom to act and an ability to influence their working environment, they have job satisfaction and an outlet for their creativity. This in turn leads to more committed employees with secure and satisfying jobs.'

In support of these views is the Institute of Personnel Management of Australia (IPMA), which launched its annual Human Resources Week with the theme 'Our Workforce – Use It or Lose It', designed to raise public

awareness of the importance of people to Australia's future. During the week the role of human resource management in Australia was discussed and debated.

1 How will using the workforce more effectively help Australian industry?
2 What fundamental shift in attitudes did Dr Deeley suggest?
3 Why did Dr Deeley suggest more participation by the workforce?
4 How might a Human Resources Week improve the ways in which organisations manage people?

Increasingly, job advertisements today stress the importance of being able to work with others. For example:

'To work as part of a well established and highly successful team'.

– Teaching advertisement

'Ability to work with others is essential.'

– Nursing advertisement

'Effective interpersonal skills are the most important requirement for this job.'

– Personnel advertisement

'The ability to work with others and to manage a high performance team.'

– Advertisement for a general manager

Teamworking becomes more significant when operating processes and/or technology require considerable interaction between people who may be

carrying out different functions but who share a common purpose. This sort of situation is common to most jobs today. As organisations become flatter by stripping out layers of management and supervision, it becomes increasingly important to have successful teamwork.

Teamwork is also particularly important in periods of crisis or change. Teamwork is an essential part of modern GNVQ courses, in which the core skills of communication and interpersonal relationships are vital.

Working with others is essential at all levels of an organisation, from the managing director down to the assistant. Managers and supervisors need to be able to motivate others, and to smooth out interpersonal difficulties between people. Operatives and assistants need to work effectively as part of high-performance cooperative teams.

Evidence collection point

Identify five job roles in an organisation. Describe ways in which people in these job roles are involved in working with others.

Meeting targets

Targets and deadlines are an important feature of business activity. If targets are not met, an organisation will not reach its objectives. If deadlines are not met, orders may be lost, contracts cancelled, wastage increased, etc.

If targets are to be met they need to be set out clearly. Tasks and activities will need to be delegated. Effective delegation involves setting out:

- what needs to be done (i.e. the details of the task and activities)
- who needs to do it (i.e. the organisation members responsible)
- why a particular member of staff should do it (objectives and motivation)
- how activities and tasks should be carried out (details)
- when it should be completed by and to what standard (deadline and performance standards).

Strategic targets will be identified by the Board of Directors. Operational targets will be set by managers and supervisors. At each level of an organisation employees will need to know what their targets and their responsibilities are. In this way they are made accountable for meeting targets.

Current thinking is that at each level in an organisation people should be involved in helping to establish their own targets and objectives. In this way realistic targets can be set, and motivation is increased through the process of participation.

Evidence collection point

Identify ways in which five job holders in an organisation are given targets to aim for and how they go about achieving these targets.

Monitoring performance

Performance is the act or process of carrying out a particular activity. Some performances are a lot easier to measure than others. For example, we could quite easily measure the number of tea cakes produced on a production line within an hour, but it would be a lot more difficult to measure the performance of a lecturer or concert pianist within an hour. Some performances can be quantified, others we measure in a more qualitative way – e.g. 'that was a wonderful performance' (a comment that you will frequently make to your lecturers!).

In the workplace it is important to keep a check on performance, particularly if standards of performance have been set. A standard can be defined as an accepted or approved example of something against which others are judged. Managers and supervisors in organisations will take most responsibility for establishing standards and for monitoring performance of people as well as other resources. However, increasingly, people at work are being encouraged through the appraisal process to become involved in setting appropriate performance standards for themselves on an ongoing basis.

Evidence collection point

Identify standards of performance that have been set for five job holders. Explain how actual performance is monitored.

Implementing changes in working conditions

Working conditions are being transformed in today's businesses. We will look at some of the more important changes in working conditions in the following pages. Obvious examples of changes include the increase in part-time work to replace full-time work, the increased requirement for people to work with new forms of technology – particularly information technology – the changing nature of work contracts, and the development of flexible working practices.

Many of these changes in working conditions have been forced on businesses by the external environment in which they operate and as a result of competition.

Boards of Directors have been responsible for taking decisions to downsize companies and to introduce new patterns of working conditions. Managers are then responsible for implementing these changes. However, the changes we have seen in recent times are not without repercussions for managers. The de-layering of organisations has led to the stripping out of layers of middle managers, administrators and operatives.

Introducing new working patterns involves the skilful management of change. Managing change involves making people aware of the need for changes in practices, involving them in the change process, and hopefully making them active participants in introducing change in a constructive way.

Supervisory staff are engaged in the process of making change work as well as suggesting ways in which change can be managed. Supervisors are the front-line staff in terms of making sure that changes in procedure and practice are implemented. At an

operational level employees will need to adjust to change and to adopt new working conditions.

In a very important book published in March 1995, *Jobshift: How to Prosper in a Workplace without Jobs* by William Bridges, the author points out how jobs are changing today. No longer are employees dependent on an organisation for a job for life. Instead:

- Employees are contingent workers, i.e. everyone's job depends on the results that organisations can achieve. Poor results mean that jobs disappear.
- Employees need to see themselves as people whose value to the organisation must be demonstrated in each successive situation. They cannot rely on previous results. It is their value now that is important.
- Employees need to develop an approach to their work and a way of managing their own careers that is more like that of an external supplier than that of a traditional employee.
- The wise company will build positive relationships with these new types of employees. The nature of this relationship will be different from the past. The emphasis today needs to be more on the nature of the work rather than benefits such as sick leave, pensions, etc.
- Employees need to act more like people in business for themselves, setting out their own plans for career development, taking personal responsibility for health care, insurance and pensions.
- Increasingly, work in organisations will be carried out by project teams who are brought together for a particular purpose. This is exactly the same process as you working in a group or team to carry out a GNVQ group assignment. Employees will need to have the skills to move rapidly from one task to another and to build up working relationships in their project teams.
- Increasingly, employees will need to accept that they will need to transfer from organisation to organisation during their working lives rather than working for a single company.

All of these changes involve important challenges to organisation members, requiring an increasing ability to implement changes in working conditions.

In a document entitled *Planning for the 21st Century* (Spring, 1995), the Skills and Enterprise Network set out the challenges of preparing employees for changes in working conditions:

As we enter the second half of the 1990s, talk of planning for the skills we will need in the year

2000 and beyond is no longer crystal ball gazing. It is hard reality. Many individuals who take up the training and education which is currently being planned will not have completed it before the year 2000. And the skills gained from most training completed before this time will need to last into the 21st century.

There is wide agreement that improved skills and qualifications are central to securing our future competitiveness.

Those planning vocational education, training and enterprise provision need to aim to produce skills that will be wanted by employers immediately, as well as giving a good basis for developing the new skills that will be needed in the future.

Employees will not only need to develop the abilities to work in new working environments, they will also need to develop the skills that enable them to function effectively in future labour markets.

Case study – Flexibility and flexible skills

The following quote is taken from *Planning for the 21st Century*:

It is no longer enough to think simply of the specific skills needed by specific jobs. New work organisations are leading to jobs which cut across old boundaries and demand a broad range of skills.

People need vocational skills which are relevant to a broader range of related jobs, and which can form a foundation for more specific skills. GNVQs are an example of more stress being placed on broader skills which are needed in groups of occupations. Job-specific skills remain important. But with increased job-changing, and more frequent changes in the demands specific jobs make, they may have to be provided in shorter bursts throughout an individual's working life.

There is an increased requirement to develop core skills which individuals need in a wide range of jobs. Use of new technology, and increased emphasis on customer services and quality, are becoming a standard part of a wide range of jobs.

Other core skills include literacy, numeracy, and the ability to communicate and work well with others.

More and more individuals also need the ability to motivate themselves and others, and to respond flexibly to deal with new problems. The organisations they work for are increasingly likely to have to respond to new challenges to remain competitive. And they themselves may have to be flexible in changing the basis of their employment, for example by working on a flexible contract basis or becoming self-employed.

1 Why are general vocational skills and abilities, as opposed to specific vocational skills, becoming more important?
2 What are the implications for the development of individuals?
3 What are the implications for ways in which organisations help people to make these changes? What should organisations be doing to develop their people?

Providing training

Training is the process of systematically guiding or teaching employees to do something by subjecting them to various exercises or experiences, so that they improve job-related skills and knowledge.

Lack of training may lead to a reduction in the possible production level, to errors and to waste.

Employees who have good potential may decide to leave in frustration.

It would be quite foolish to expect a teacher to instruct a class of pupils without an extensive period of preparation, so that skills and abilities can then be

applied to the job. The problem is made worse by the fact that the teachers do not realise that they are making mistakes, because they have no standard for comparison. One of the tragedies of the early 1990s was a government scheme that involved placing untrained teachers straight into a school environment. A number of these teachers simply floundered, leading to wide-scale inefficiencies and resource waste.

Poor preparation costs an organisation time and money. It can also lead to injury in hazardous environments.

Training is a key part of working life. It adds to the skills and abilities of the labour force and thus increases its supply; it is also a great motivator. Training helps to give employees a sense of purpose. Training for future needs is a long-term investment. Unfortunately it is an area of expenditure that is easy to cut back in difficult times without immediately affecting productivity. Expenditure in the UK on training is quite low by European standards.

Data from the Labour Force survey for 1995 indicates that training for employees is usually focused on their current job: 80% of employees receiving training said the training was intended to improve their skills to do the type of work they were currently doing or had done before.

The remaining 20% said the purpose of the training was to give them skills for a completely different type of work.

Much of the training received by employees is of short duration: 43% did training lasting less than a week. However, 24% of employees were doing training courses lasting for more than a year.

Off-the-job training was the most common method used. About a third took place on the employer's premises; 38% at a university, college of further education or other educational institution; 8% at a private training centre; and 7% in the employee's home (e.g. distance learning packages such as Open University courses).

One of the main reasons for training was the introduction of new technology – particularly information technology.

Training takes place predominantly in establishments with over 25 employees rather than smaller workplaces. Training is most common for employees in public administration, education and health, financial services, and energy and water. Employees in professional and technical occupations are most likely to train.

Training is most common amongst those with management responsibilities. In 1995 roughly 20% of managers and 16% of supervisors had received training. Figures are much lower for other employees: 15% for secretarial workers, 7% for plant and machine operatives.

New employees are most likely to receive training. The amount of training tends to decrease the longer a person has been at work. Young employees are the group most likely to receive training.

In a large organisation there will be a training manager responsible for identifying training needs. Some training managers will focus on the needs of the organisation, whereas others will focus on the needs of individual employees.

Management within an organisation should be responsible for encouraging training. This might involve developing training policies and programmes with training officers. For example, many large supermarket chains encourage employees to take NVQs. This has the dual effect of increasing competence in the workplace and in increasing the motivation of employees.

Today organisations can qualify as 'Investors in People' if they meet certain quality standards related to human resource management. Being an Investor in People may encourage people to apply for jobs with you because they see that you are a caring employer concerned with the ongoing development of staff.

Employees have a responsibility to themselves and their organisations to acquire training in order to improve their performance at work and their ongoing career.

Evidence collection point

Either:

1 Identify a firm which encourages its employees to train. What does the firm see as being the main benefits of training both for the organisation and for the employee?

Or:

2 Identify individuals who have recently received training. What do they regard as the main benefits to their employing organisation, and to themselves?

Giving advice

Providing expert advice is an important element of some job roles. For example, Directors will give advice to the Board of Directors, particularly relating to their specialist field. Directors will also give advice to managers on the best ways of handling particular business policies.

Managers, because of their inside experience of running a business, are able to give advice to the Board. They will also give advice to other managers on particular issues. For example, a personnel manager in an organisation may give advice and support to divisional, departmental and functional managers on ways of handling human resource issues. Managers will also give advice to supervisors on how to implement particular programmes and activities. In addition, some managers will give advice to, and seek advice from, other employees by 'walking about' the organisation. Peters and Waterman in their book *In Search of Excellence* talk about the importance of 'management by walking about' whereby a manager continually monitors the way an organisation operates by going around talking to people in their work situations.

Supervisors play a key advisory role in giving advice to management on tactical and operational activities, which helps to inform programmes and policies. In addition, supervisors will advise operatives on the best ways of carrying out operations. They may also play a mentoring role in showing employees how to carry out tasks and advising them on performance.

"AND WHAT HAPPENS IF I PRESS THIS THEN?...."

Operatives play an important role in feeding information to supervisors, and giving advice to fellow workers. In the past new employees were inducted into practices through a process known as 'sitting by Nelly', i.e. sitting alongside a more experienced employee who acted as an adviser and guide.

Evidence collection point

Interview five different job holders in an organisation. Identify the ways in which they give and receive advice about work activities in a typical day. Your work should demonstrate Core Skills in Communication.

Discipline

Disciplinary procedures within an organisation take a top-down route. An employee is accountable to a line manager or team leader. In the first instance it is this person who will be responsible for discipline. Of course, if matters are serious they may need to be dealt with at a more senior level.

For example, in March 1995 a cleaner at Boots in Nottingham was fired for eating an After Eight mint that she had been clearing away after an official function. She was seen by her supervisor who reported the matter to her line manager. The cleaner was initially sacked. However, the employee, who had over ten years of commendable service for the company, was later reinstated by a full management meeting. It was felt that although the offence was serious the punishment was disproportionate.

Within an organisation there will be set disciplinary procedures. You will find that in the first instance you are immediately accountable to a superior who is responsible for giving informal, followed by formal, warnings. Should the matter proceed further the employee will receive a formal written warning, which may come from the personnel manager.

Handling grievances

Grievance procedures within an organisation will be handled in a similar way to disciplinary ones, i.e. in an upward direction. Often grievance procedures will involve some form of representation, frequently by a trade union. In the first instance grievances should be taken up in an informal way with those concerned. In an open organisation grievances should be allowed to come to the surface.

It would be a poor organisation in which employees could not trust their immediate superiors. However, if the superior is part of the grievance, e.g. through sexual or racial harassment, then it may be necessary to leapfrog that part of the grievance procedure.

Management within an organisation has the responsibility for creating the frameworks and policies that enable grievances to be dealt with. There should be named officials who set procedures and to whom employees can take their grievances. In the first instance grievances should be kept within an organisation, except where the law has been broken.

Evidence collection point

Identify the grievance procedures within your school or college. What are the formal channels for handling grievances?

Reasons for changes in working conditions

The working world today is dramatically different from the way it used to be.

We will first look at some of the changes to working conditions and then go on to identify some of the more important reasons for these changes.

In 1984, Charles Handy wrote that the old patterns (of work) were breaking down – gone are the 1960s and 1970s with the wide availability of work and security: 'The new patterns are on their way whether we welcome them or not.'

Handy said that the signs are, to put it bluntly, that there are not going to be enough jobs to go round – not full-time, lifetime jobs – and this will be true whatever government is in power over the next twenty years.

So it is argued that we must learn to live with a different notion of work, which will affect not only those seeking employment, but also those currently employed.

If there will not be enough full-time jobs to go round, it may be preferable to give everyone a job for part of their lives, or a part-job for most of their lives.

The principle of work-sharing is increasingly put forward as a possible solution to the problem. The

extent to which this is feasible depends not only on the nature of the job (not all jobs might be suitable for job-sharing) but also on the willingness of those involved to accept lower incomes.

A shorter working week and a reduction in overtime work might be seen as a way of reducing the supply of labour – but it is unlikely to increase the number of full-time jobs.

Early retirement has become increasingly common in recent years, but employers are likely to use the opportunity of early retirement to slim down their labour force, or reorganise without any direct replacements being employed in order to cut costs and increase productivity.

Case study – Downsizing at Shell

At the beginning of April 1995, Royal Dutch Shell announced that it was to cut 1200 jobs at its headquarters in London and The Hague as part of a dramatic reshaping of the group. Instead of having over 100 regional organisations – Shell UK, Shell Ireland, Shell Denmark, etc. – it will now have five large business units answering to a small corporate centre. The key to this process is to cut back on the large administrative core and to create self-managing businesses.

Cor Herkstroter, the group's Chairman, argued that Shell's structure must become simpler, less costly and more responsive to customers. The business environment in the late 1990s is characterised by low oil prices with flat profit margins. The market is highly competitive with major firms striving for higher productivity, innovation, quality and effectiveness.

The redundancies were programmed for the second half of 1995, taking out 1200 of the 4000 headquarters jobs.

At one time Shell employees would have expected a job for life. Today this is a thing of the past. In 1990 Shell employed 135 000 people worldwide; In 1995 they employ 106 000 and the number is falling.

The operational parts of Shell are concerned with:

- exploration and production
- oil products
- chemicals
- gas
- coal.

These operational components have been supported by the 100+ service companies, i.e. the regional organisations. However, the operational companies feel that they have been supporting inefficient regional organisations which have been duplicating roles. The services and support operations are thought to cost Shell about $1bn (£625m) a year.

What is happening at Shell is mirrored in many other large organisations today. Jobs are being shaken out, in a relentless drive for efficiency in a very competitive climate.

Flexible working

One of the major changes in working conditions in recent times has been the ongoing development of flexible working.

Labour market flexibility has been recognised by governments for some time. For example, a 1985 White Paper (*Employment: The Challenge for the Nation*) included references to flexible hours, job-sharing, home-working and self-employment.

There are a number of definitions of flexibility. Numerical flexibility refers to the ability of firms to adjust the number of workers or the number of hours worked in line with changes in the level of demand for their goods and services. Typically this refers to the use of part-time, temporary and sub-contracted workers.

Large supermarket chains commonly vary the number of hours they allocate to employees in the following week depending on the profit figures in the previous week.

Temporal, or working time, flexibility can be seen as a particular form of numerical flexibility, relating to changes in the number and timing of hours worked from day to day or week to week, for example through flexitime or annual hours contracts.

The use of more temporary and contract workers and other methods of flexible working will permanently change Britain's employment patterns. These changes are due to the need for increased productivity, flexibility and cost control.

In the first half of the 1990s the vast majority of the UK's largest organisations were restructured, leading to job losses at all levels.

The flexible firm

A business concept that has been growing in importance has been that of the 'flexible firm'.

In the past many large organisations had a large core of full-time workers who expected a job for life. Throughout the country, employees would start working with an employer like Boots or Raleigh after leaving school. Brothers, sisters, parents, grandparents, uncles and aunts might all work for the same employer.

Today, the pool of core workers in an organisation has been severely slimmed down. Instead, organisations rely more and more on peripheral and external workers to carry out work tasks (Figure 13.5).

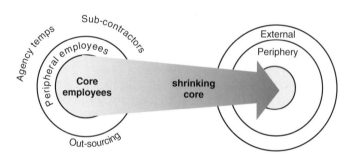

Figure 13.5 The shrinking core

Today, core workers tend to be:

■ multi-skilled, full-time, enjoying good pay conditions and benefits.

Peripheral workers are:

■ short-term, temporary, part-time and receiving less favourable pay, conditions and benefits.

External workers are:

■ those who are not employees of the firm (agency temps, workers in contracted-out services and the self-employed).

The flexible firm sets out to cut its labour costs to a minimum by limiting core workers, relative to peripheral and external workers.

Evidence collection point

Identify the core, peripheral and external workers in an organisation that you are familiar with.

The table below sets out in a fairly dramatic way the impact of the flexible workforce in today's labour market. The figures show that, of the 25 million plus workers in employment today, 38.2% are not in full-time employment. What is even more obvious is that 52.1% of women are not in full-time employment. Both men and women contribute significantly to the flexible workforce.

UK employment 1993/94 (000s and %)			
	Total	Men	Women
Total in employment	25 381	13 934	11 446
Full-time permanent employees	15 685	10 204	5 480
As percentage of total in employment	61.8	73.2	47.9
All other workers	9 693	3 729	5 964
As percentage of total in employment	38.2	26.8	52.1

Clearly, firms find it increasingly convenient to take on flexible workers.

Task

The following comments have been made about flexible working practices. Explain how a business organisation's view of each of these comments may vary from those of employees.

Flexible conditions mean that in a boom it is easy to take on extra labour. In a recession cutbacks can be made quickly.

It is possible today to give employees a 'no hours' contract. The staff have a contract to work for us, but it does not specify the number of hours to be worked!

We can now look at some of the reasons why changes in working conditions are being progressively introduced.

Labour mobility

Labour is far more mobile in modern Britain than it was in the past. There are two main types of labour mobility: geographical mobility and occupational mobility.

Geographical mobility

Geographical mobility occurs when employees are prepared to move around the country or within a region to where the jobs are. If people are not prepared to move, this accentuates the depressed conditions that exist in a particular area.

Norman Tebbit (a government Minister in the Thatcher era) was noted for suggesting that people should 'get on their bikes' to move to where jobs are available. However, this is not as easy as it sounds. Many people have strong social bonds with a particular area – they may have an aged grandparent living in an old people's home there, their children may be in school, they may simply love a particular area and its people.

The Conservatives have throughout the 1980s and 1990s reduced the state benefits that enabled unemployed people to stay put. However, the collapse in jobs in recent years means that people are reluctant to uproot themselves to move to jobs which are at best surrounded by uncertainty.

Occupational mobility

Occupational mobility involves changing from one job to another. Increasingly, individuals are needing to become more flexible in their skills, in order to be able to adjust to new job requirements. Individuals may retrain to take on new jobs and responsibilities with an existing employer or with a new employer.

Flexible labour markets in the UK seem to be delivering a number of benefits.

- There was less productivity decline in the recession in the early 1990s.
- There was a quicker decline in unemployment after the recession.

353

■ Flexibility allowed workers to combine employment with other responsibilities.

Evidence collection point

List what you consider to be the five main benefits to:

a employers
b employees

of increases in labour mobility.

A past feature of the British industrial scene was demarcation disputes. These were arguments over who should do what. The trade union movement insisted that only members of a relevant trade union could be asked to do particular tasks (e.g. mend a broken machine). This led to a great waste of time and other resources.

Multiskilling involves training employees to do a range of tasks in the workplace. A machine operative can be trained in the art of performing routine maintenance work and in doing straightforward repairs. This can be a great motivator because it gives a job variety and opportunities for higher pay. It means that a plant can be continuously productive, more competitive, and therefore possibly better able to provide good wages and conditions (because the demand for labour is derived from the demand for the final product).

Task

In the new Japanese Toyota and Nissan car plants in the UK, the managements have agreed single-union deals. Only one union operates in each plant, and operators are flexible and able to do a number of different tasks. When Nissan started its car plant in Sunderland there were only three job classifications, whereas in the past some British car plants have had as many as 500 different job classifications!

1 Why might managers prefer to have multiskilled workers in a narrow range of job classifications?
2 Why might employees prefer such a scheme?
3 Why might some employees and trade unions oppose such a scheme?
4 What are the benefits and drawbacks to the economy of allowing these schemes to operate?

Improving productivity

The drive to improve productivity is essential to businesses operating in competitive conditions. We have already looked at examples of how Shell and other companies are downsizing, how businesses are introducing flexible working practices, and the development of multiskilling in Japanese- and UK-based companies.

There is a saying that productivity leads to performance which leads to profits:

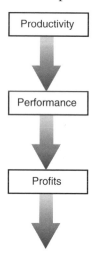

The reverse is inevitably true. Organisations that do not increase productivity quickly lose competitive advantage when everyone else is producing better-value quality products. Productivity relates to all of the factors of production employed by businesses, and, particularly today, also to people.

Evidence collection point

Many thousands of people today in the slimmed-down, super-efficient, highly productive world of work in the late 1990s are being asked to do the work of two or three members of staff for much the same money with no extra support and no special thanks (a process known as the intensification of work).

This has been described elsewhere as the 2:3:2 formula – half the people are now doing thee times the work for twice the pay, compared to the early 1980s.

Interview five individuals in business organisations to find out whether this pattern is reflected in their working conditions.

What do they see as being the advantages and disadvantages of the 2:3:2 formula? What are your personal views?

Improving employee motivation

One of the main reasons for changing working conditions is to improve employee motivation.

There has been extensive research into motivation and the behaviour of people at work. One of the leading early theories was that put forward by Maslow, which provided an insight into people's needs. Maslow's study of human behaviour led him to devise a hierarchy of needs with basic needs at the bottom and higher needs at the top (Figure 13.6).

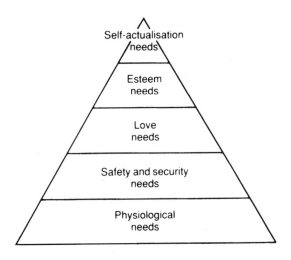

Figure 13.6 Maslow's hierarchy of human needs

Maslow claimed that people want to satisfy a lower level of need before moving on to a higher need:

■ *Physiological needs* are basic. Food, shelter and clothing are required to meet the needs of the body and for physical survival. This basic level of need will be typically met at work by the exchange of labour for a wage packet or salary and by the physical conditions of the working environment.
■ *Safety and security needs* involve protection from danger and the provision of a predictable and orderly workspace. Security of employment, and pension and sick-pay schemes, are also relevant here.
■ *Love needs* are concerned with the individual's needs for love and affection. This involves

relationships and a feeling of 'belonging'. At the place of work these needs can be satisfied by the companionship of fellow workers, working in a group or team, and company social activities.
■ *Esteem needs* are based on an individual's desire for self-respect and the respect of others. Employees have a need to be recognised as individuals, to have a job title or some form of status or prestige, and to have their efforts noticed.
■ *Self-actualisation needs* are concerned with personal development and individual creativity to achieve one's full potential. In order to meet these needs at work, individuals need to be provided with the opportunity to use their creative talents and abilities fully.

Maslow felt that as an employee moves up the hierarchy he or she becomes more 'complete', someone who enjoys work and feels a direct involvement in it. However, the theory has its critics, who question the realism of a hierarchy where needs are structured in such an ordered way. Maslow has also been criticised for producing a theory which only reflects middle-class values in American society.

Task

Can you recognise the needs in Maslow's theory in your own behaviour? If so, on what point in the hierarchy are you currently concentrating? How does society influence the way you satisfy these needs?

Another famous theory of motivation is that of Herzberg, and this in many ways complements Maslow's findings.

Herzberg investigated how satisfied people were at work. Following a series of interviews he came to the conclusion that certain factors tended to lead to job satisfaction while others frequently led to job dissatisfaction.

Factors which give rise to satisfaction Herzberg called motivators or satisfiers; those tending to give rise to dissatisfaction he called hygiene factors or dissatisfiers.

The most important motivators or satisfiers are:

■ a sense of achievement
■ recognition of effort and performance
■ the nature of the work itself
■ responsibility
■ the opportunity for promotion and advancement.

355

Hygiene factors or dissatisfiers included:

- company policy and administration
- supervision and relationship with supervisor
- working conditions
- salary
- relationships at the same level in the hierarchy
- personal life
- relationships with subordinates
- status
- security.

The main difference between motivators and hygiene factors is that motivators bring satisfaction whereas hygiene factors can at best only serve to prevent dissatisfaction. The theory thus makes a distinction between factors causing positive satisfaction and those causing dissatisfaction.

Task

Look at Herzberg's motivators and hygiene factors. If you were a manager or employer, how useful would a knowledge of these be if you wanted to improve the morale and commitment of your employees?

The work of Maslow, Herzberg and others has led to considerable research into ways of increasing employee motivation.

Job enrichment involves loading a job vertically to maximise responsibility, achievement and recognition. This may mean increasing the variety of individual tasks an employee undertakes at different levels of responsibility. It could also mean increasing his or her area of supervision so that the person's contribution is perceived as more highly valued. Other possibilities are to upgrade the job, give more control over the job, provide more challenging tasks, provide feedback, etc.

Herzberg did, however, recognise that not every job can be enriched with other levels of responsibility, and that some employees feel happier in conditions of predictability.

Job enlargement, on the other hand, involves loading a job horizontally with more tasks of a similar nature. The idea behind this is to increase the challenge and variety of the work and provide employees with a broader range of skills to cover work at that level. Increasing the variety of an individual's tasks can satisfy more work needs and allow the employee to see his or her contribution to the whole.

Task

Interview five individuals in different job roles. To what extent are their jobs loaded horizontally or vertically? How could their jobs be enriched or enlarged? Your work should contribute evidence of Core Skills in Communication.

An organisation can attempt to motivate employees by developing special groups or teams. For example, quality circles have been a particularly important motivator in recent years.

Quality circles are typically small groups of seven or eight people who voluntarily meet on a regular basis to identify, investigate, analyse and resolve quality-related matters or other work-related arrangements using problem-solving techniques. Members tend to be from the same work area or do similar work.

Quality circles are about participation, teamwork, job satisfaction, self-esteem and organisational commitment. They have been particularly effective in Japanese industry where they have been responsible, it is claimed, for loyalty coupled with high productivity.

Case study – Nissan

On 1 February 1984, Nissan and the UK government signed an agreement to build a car plant near Sunderland in the North East of England. Within months the company had appointed its first British employee, the personnel director. Since then their ten-year British tenure has been a success.

Nissan's aim is to build profitably the highest-quality car sold in Europe. The company also wants to achieve the maximum possible customer satisfaction and ensure the prosperity of the enterprise and its staff. To assist in this, Nissan aims to achieve mutual trust and cooperation between all people in the company and to make Nissan a place where long-term job satisfaction can be achieved.

Nowadays, 'kaizen' is a word much used in Sunderland. It is Japanese, the literal translation being simply 'continuous improvement'. The improvement is gained by slow and steady change, and once achieved it is maintained at that level until such time as the next improvement step takes place.

During the 1950s, Japanese industry made great efforts to improve the image of its product quality. These efforts were assisted by two prominent American specialists who visited Japan. Their influence caused Japanese industry to take a fresh look at its strategy, and in 1962 the first quality circles were formed and registered. By the mid-1960s most of the larger Japanese companies were supporting a great many quality circles, and currently Nissan in Japan has over 4000 active circles.

In the whole of Japan there are over 10 million members of some 1.2 million quality circles covering manufacturing industries, service industries and commerce. Such circles have been viewed as a powerful force for promoting a company-wide quality awareness and for encouraging contributions from an organisation's greatest resource – the workforce.

Figure 13.7 Final assembly area – Nissan Sunderland

At Nissan's UK plant the 'kaizen' programme has been developed as a replacement for periodic quality circle activity. It encourages constant quality awareness and is better suited to the needs and aspirations of the British workforce. 'Kaizen' assumes the total involvement of all employees but recognises that participation depends on individuals genuinely feeling part of the Nissan team. The company policy is that:

■ All staff have a valuable contribution to make as individuals, and this contribution can be most effective within a team environment.
■ 'Kaizen' team activity helps develop leadership and presentation skills as well as enabling people to understand, acknowledge and learn from others.

'Kaizen' is one way in which employees may participate in issues that affect their workforce.

The 'kaizen' philosophy may be applied anywhere at any time. Everyone is encouraged to participate in the activity, and, as members of a team, learn how to analyse situations logically and factually and discuss issues meaningfully and efficiently. People who contribute to the activity include:

■ *leaders* who receive special training in the 'kaizen' process and then apply these skills to team activities

■ *members* who participate in the activities, often from the same work unit or area
■ *specialists* who assist a team with a particular project.

A steering committee develops the policies and guidelines under which the activity operates.

The 'kaizen' process is designed to enable a team to move on from the stage of dealing with current problems or areas in need of improvement to a stage where sources of concern are dealt with in advance of their actual occurrence.

1 Explain how and why 'kaizen' activity or the process of participation through quality circles might motivate employees.
2 Refer to a group or team activity with which you have been involved (e.g. sports, hobbies, clubs). Explain how membership of the group or team affected your approach to the activity.

Adapting to technological changes

The skill needs of existing employees are rising. In a survey in 1994, 63% of employers reported that the skills needed by their 'average' employee were increasing. Larger establishments, and particularly service sector ones, were most likely to report a rising need for skills.

Increases in skill needs were particularly strongly associated with the use of computerised or automated equipment. Three-quarters of the users of such equipment had seen skill levels in their jobs increasing.

An increasingly wide range of general work skills are demanded in many jobs. Job enlargement and job enrichment have brought about an increasing need for multiple skills. Much of this change is the result of new technology and restructuring of the workforce.

The transforming effects of technology have meant that today groups of employees can be networked together in project teams. Information technology has reduced the need for many administrative workers. For example, in banking thousands of workers are being stripped out of organisations as new electronic technology takes over.

Organisations have had to adapt to these and other technological changes, which has meant that work is organised in different patterns, new skills are required by new team workers, and that a premium is placed on training in the new technologies.

Identify ways in which the work of five job holders has been altered in recent years by developments in technology. What personal changes have these individuals had to make to prepare themselves and cope with these changes?

Employing new skills

The introduction of new technologies, increasing international competition and industrial change continue to be powerful forces placing skill demands on the labour force (Figure 13.8).

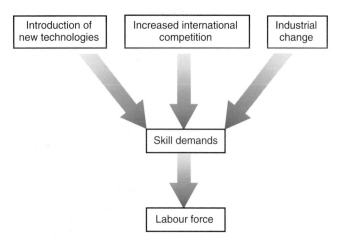

Figure 13.8 Forces demanding new skills

There are three main types of increased skill demand.

■ *Occupation trends* – higher level occupations are expanding at the expense of lower ones. For example, professional and managerial jobs are expanding at the expense of routine administrative jobs.
■ *Higher skill needs* – there are increasing skill requirements within specific jobs. As work becomes more complex, it becomes more skilful.
■ *Broadening work demands* – general trends in the labour market are leading to a wider range of skill requirements and greater flexibility in many jobs.

As work changes, people at work need to be able to use new skills. Increasingly these skills are ones that require general capabilities and core skills such as communication, interpersonal relationships and the use of information technology.

Evidence collection point

Identify the types of new skills that five job holders are having to use in their place of work.

Evaluating changes to working conditions

We can now move on to look at some of the different types of working conditions that are developing in response to changes in organisations.

Fixed short-term contracts

The number of people working on short-term contracts is increasing in most occupations. For example, instead of teachers receiving contracts of employment that provide them with long-term job security, they may be given a one-, two- or three-year contract. This gives the employer the flexibility to terminate the contract quickly, thus enabling the employer to control costs. An employee in this position cannot consider himself or herself to be a core worker. Employers may work exceptionally hard in order to try and secure a permanent contract. Alternatively, they may simply tread water because they do not feel a part of the organisation.

Evidence collection point

Interview someone who has, or who has had, a fixed short-term contract. What does he or she see as being the strengths and weaknesses of such contracts?

Long-term contracts

Many people still work to long-term contracts. The advantage of a long-term contract is that it gives a sense of security and personal value to the employee. Long-term contracts usually set out a number of important contractual rights – to a pension, benefits, etc. Core workers will be permanent employees working with long-term contracts.

However, the nature of such contracts is changing to accommodate increasing flexibility. For example, annual hours contracts are becoming increasingly popular, whereby employees are contracted to work so many hours a year, rather than working a nine-to-five pattern. About 10% of employees currently work to annual hours contracts.

Long-term contracts do not guarantee lifetime employment. Nevertheless, they do mean that individuals cannot be dismissed at the whim of an employer. There needs to be a valid reason for fair dismissal to take place. However, in today's fast-moving labour markets, jobs can and frequently do disappear through redundancy.

Flexible hours

Flexitime is a system that permits flexibility of working hours at the beginning or end of the day, provided an agreed period (core time) is spent at work.

There are many different arrangements for flexitime, so the following should simply be looked on as examples.

A firm's working day might be divided into three sections:

1 *Band time* This is the total period for which the business is open, e.g. 8 am to 8 pm.
2 *Core time* This is the period in which all the members of the firm are expected to be working, e.g. 10 am to 12.30 pm and 2 pm to 4 pm.
3 *Flexible time* This is the period of time in which employees can select the hours they work e.g. 8 am to 10 am and 4 pm to 8 pm.

If, for example, employees are expected to work 36 hours in a five-day working week and they work 20 hours of core time, then they choose the other 16 hours in which to work. Some employees may prefer to work more in the morning, others in the afternoons. Other employees may vary their hours.

The advantages of flexitime are as follows:

- It gives workers more control of when they work. Workers may enjoy this type of freedom. Flexibility also enables them to fit in private engagements such as hair and dental appointments.
- At least for the basic core time, all the workforce is operating together.

Staff may be responsible for keeping their own record of the hours they have worked, or they may 'clock in' and 'clock out', perhaps by using an electronic swipe card.

Holiday pay

Most contracts of employment will build in a period of annual leave which employees can take at an

appropriate time. In many organisations employees will need to 'book in' their holidays. This is to ensure that there are enough staff working at any one time to deal with customers, answer phones, handle queries, deal with essential problems, etc. Holiday pay is given to the employee during paid leave. Employees will under some circumstances be allowed to take non-paid leave, for example if a child is sick, for a wedding, or if they wish to take an extended holiday.

Sick pay

The contract of employment will set down short periods of time which employees are allowed to take off through sickness. Normally employees will continue to be paid during this time. The government has made businesses largely responsible for paying sick pay to employees: this is called statutory sick pay (SSP). These payments are made if an employee is sick during normal working days.

Effects of changes to working conditions

In this section we briefly evaluate some of the changes to working conditions in terms of:

- costs to business
- benefits for business
- costs to individuals
- benefits for individuals.

Costs to business

In this chapter we have focused on two main themes which characterise the management of changing job roles and working conditions today.

One theme has been the dramatic impacts of changes in technology and the growth of dynamic competition in the marketplace. These changes have resulted in increasing uncertainty in the marketplace. People cannot be certain that they will be able to sell their products tomorrow and in the future, and hence it is impossible to guarantee employment.

The other theme that we have explored is that of the development of human resource management as a way of ensuring that the human resource is used to maximum effect in business organisations.

These two themes are intertwined, although there are some obvious tensions.

People who feel that they are valued in the workplace are most likely to be productive. People who are allowed to make their own contribution in the workplace are most likely to be innovative.

However, the increasing trend is towards new forms of contracts – part-time contracts, flexible-hours contracts, no-hours contracts, and other forms of loose contracts. The question is whether employees will maintain their loyalty and motivation under such arrangements.

One aspect of the shrinking-core concept is that today firms increasingly contract out their non-core activities.

For example, Shell UK, instead of employing a pool of photographers at Shell Mex House working from their own office with Shell equipment, now have only one full-time photographer, and buy-in (contract out) photography work from private contractors (often former Shell employees).

One impact of such a change is that Shell benefits from cutting down its employment costs. However, the question is whether Shell loses out through losing employee loyalty. This may be a hidden cost of new working conditions.

There was a steady increase in sub-contracting during the 1980s. Seventy per cent of large firms now sub-contract non-core functions, and 72% of all establishments sub-contract at least one service.

On the face of it, businesses seem to be able to reduce their costs by adopting these new working conditions. They are able to employ part-time labour at a fraction of the cost of full-time employees.

However, there may be a real danger that things will start to fall apart when you only have part-timers who do not take an overarching responsibility for the success or failure of a business.

The problems of coordination also increase. For example, if two employees job-share, there may be important linking activities which are missed out through lack of communication.

Benefits for business

As employers continue to experience the same competitive pressures, they are likely to continue to seek more flexibility from their workforce. Survey after survey in the mid-to-late 1990s has shown that employers expect to contract out more, and expect increases in part-time work and work-sharing amongst their core staff.

Government policy also seeks to encourage further flexibility, so the need for increased flexibility is likely to be of profound importance for both employers and individuals as they consider their current and future skill needs.

Benefits for business of new working conditions include:

- the ability to motivate employees through human resource management practices
- lower overheads through slimming down and restructuring processes
- opportunities to make use of a pool of employees in ways that may not have been possible in the past
- opportunities to build individual contracts with individual employees, rather than mass, collectively bargained contracts
- opportunities to use resources to their full potential, e.g. continuous production using a shift system.

All of the above factors, and others outlined earlier in the text, provide opportunities for organisations to produce larger outputs at lower costs. The cumulative effect of benefits is to create competitive advantage in a competition-intense environment.

Evidence collection point

Use a desktop publishing package to produce a newspaper editorial highlighting the costs and benefits to businesses of adopting new working conditions and practices. Plan your work so that it provides evidence of Core Skills in Information Technology, Application of Number and Communication.

Costs to individuals

New working conditions have brought with them considerable costs for individuals.

For example, we now have much higher figures for male unemployment, and although more women are working they tend to be in lower paid, part-time work.

The mid-1990s has seen the departure of tens of thousands of middle-class employees from well-paid jobs and brought the fear of unemployment for many others.

In some areas of industry the middle manager is a fast-vanishing species. The British Institute of Management says that just as the 1980s witnessed the shedding of manual workers, the 1990s has seen the removal of whole layers of management. People might at one time have thought that if they had a job with a bank or a big company, they were there for life. But many of these people have been made redundant and many others are miserable because they think they could be next. Reports from sectors such as banking, telecommunications and the civil service all make reference to a climate of fear, increased stress and plummeting morale, with insecurity the norm.

Case study – Changing opportunities in Grimethorpe

Structural changes have made themselves felt in whole communities almost wholly dependent on one activity.

This is well evidenced by the village of Grimethorpe, which in the 1980s had 2500 people employed in its colliery. When the mine closed down in 1993, the place was emasculated, cut off from productive society.

A recent survey showed that less than 5% of the population in the village works, with the rest struggling by on benefits, topped up for many by what they can

pick up around the place. There exists a scavenging economy – a vulture culture.

But there are those who believe that the village does have a future, despite having lost its self-confidence, becoming benefit-dependent and having its choices taken away.

Initiatives are centred around education, building up a workforce which could attract a hi-tech investor, similar to one on another abandoned colliery site nearby.

But the challenge is whether anyone can do anything for the hard-core, the unsocialised, the marooned. According to the local parish priest, it may be necessary to face up to the fact that, for whatever reason, a lost generation has been bred, one that has never worked and will never work, having lost all the social structures that go with work. Ultimately it is suggested that only a major economic revolution will save them.

1 What does the above case tell you about changing economic fortunes and new patterns of work?
2 To what extent are some individuals relatively powerless in a changing economic climate?
3 How can individuals best adjust to changing work patterns like those outlined above?

Costs to individuals from changing working conditions include:

■ loss of job security
■ loss of permanent core jobs, to be replaced by peripheral and external work
■ loss of bonding between employee and traditional employers
■ wide-scale destruction of jobs
■ loss of contractual rights
■ loss of group powers, as collective bargaining is replaced by individual bargaining
■ loss of benefits such as holiday pay, sick pay, and redundancy pay by those working on temporary contracts.

Evidence collection point

What other costs to individuals can you list which result from changes in working conditions.

Benefits for individuals

There are many benefits for individuals, however, resulting from new working conditions. Flexible working is a boon to many people who want to fit work around their other commitments.

Flexible hours might mean that an individual is able to take children to school, do the week's shopping, etc. The existence of part-time work means that people can work without a full-time commitment. Job-sharing and other arrangements mean that employees can just commit themselves to part of a job.

Compared with other EU countries, women in the UK can be seen as being in some ways well placed relative to men in the current labour market. The UK is the only country in the EU where the overall unemployment rate for women is lower than for men. The main factor in this is the low unemployment rate for married women, which has fallen very steeply from about 10% in 1984 to nearer 5.5% in late 1994. This may be due to the increased availability of part-time and flexible working arrangements.

Teleworking is another benefit to employees of changing working conditions. Teleworking involves working from home with the tools of information technology – mainly a network of personal computers and databases, backed up by fax or other transmission systems.

The availability of information technology is changing the nature of office work. More and more tasks are skill- and knowledge-based 'think work' which, although it is at present carried out in centralised offices, does not need to be. Groups of specialists will still be able to work as a team, even if they are separated by large distances. Employers will be able to tap into the workforce in any part of the country. This may create more employment for skilled men and women with young families, and for others for whom commuting is an inconvenience.

Today there are nearly three-quarters of a million home-workers. Approximately half of these are in clerical or secretarial jobs. In 1992 it was estimated that about 1 employer in 10 uses some form of home-based workers, and about 1 in 20 uses

teleworkers. Amongst the largest employers about 1 in 5 may use telework/home-working.

Evidence collection point

Explain in about 300 words some of the prime benefits to individuals of new working conditions.

Planning ways for a business organisation to implement changes in working conditions

Changes in working conditions within an organisation need to be planned if they are going to be managed successfully.

Planning

Planning for change must start with deciding on your aims and objectives.

In military terms, your aim is your main focus for concern – for example, to win a war. Your objectives are the main means you establish to pursue your aim – to fight a number of battles, to ensure that you have available the best possible weaponry, to strike when you have the maximum advantage.

The plan could include the following details:

- Area for development – the main changes which are planned.
- Name of the main person responsible for implementing the change.
- The task group. Who will support the main initiator in bringing about the change? How will they be involved in preparing and carrying the plant?
- Statement. This should be a clear statement of what the plan sets out to achieve. It must be clearly understood by all those involved in making the changes.
- Roles. Who will be responsible for what in actually preparing and carrying out the changes?
- Analysis of needs. This should be an analysis of the strengths, weaknesses, opportunities and threats in relation to making the proposed changes. This is a SWOT analysis (see Chapter 8) and should be carried out by the task group. It could be done on a large sheet of flip-chart paper set out like Figure 13.9.

STRENGTHS	WEAKNESSES
OPPORTUNITIES	THREATS

Figure 13.9 Template for SWOT analysis

- Action steps. List the main steps that will need to be carried out in the planned change. List them both in order of importance and in the order in which they will need to be carried out. The action steps will help to make it clear what needs to be done, and what resources are needed to help make the changes.
- Targets. These are a key ingredient of the planning process, and they make it possible to measure performance and to check on progress. Targets should relate to specific dates and to specific measures of performance, e.g. by November next year 10% of employees will have been up-dated on new health and safety requirements.
- Evaluation. Criteria will need to be established to assess the success of the action steps. It is very important that these criteria are set out at the start of the planning process. Only by setting them out at the onset will it be possible to measure the success of the plan.

Training

In planning changes in working conditions, one of the key aspects will be training of people involved. New working conditions cannot simply be imposed – they need to be understood. It will therefore be necessary to identify who needs training, what forms of training they need and how long the training will take. A key part of the management of change is the training process.

Monitoring progress

It is essential to check on the progress that is being made with the plan. This is why it is so important to set targets and standards. Checks must then be made on the extent to which these targets and standards are being met.

Measurements will need to be made to monitor performance against standards. For example, if a target of training 10% of the workforce within a three-month period has been set, the monitoring process might reveal that after two months only 5% of the workforce has received training. The review process will then be concerned to identify why training seems to be falling behind target and what can be done to bring it up to the 10% standard in the final month.

Evidence collection point

Produce a plan which is designed to implement changes to working conditions in a particular workplace. The plan should identify those job roles which would have a responsibility for implementing the change, and should be concerned with procedures for planning, setting targets, training, and monitoring progress.

Evidence indicators

As part of this element you should produce a report that identifies five individuals in business organisations who hold the range of job roles: director, manager, supervisor, operative, and assistant.

For each individual, the report should describe their responsibilities in identifying and meeting targets, working with others, training, discipline and implementing change in working conditions.

The report should explain why working conditions are subject to change, and explain in depth one reason for changes to working conditions.

You should also produce a plan to implement change to working conditions. The plan should also identify those job roles which would have a responsibility for implementing the change.

Carrying out this assignment will enable you to show evidence of meeting Core Skills requirements in Communication and Information Technology.

The following list should serve as a checklist. Please tick off each of the following when you have successfully covered them as part of your report. You need to be able to confirm:

■ I have identified and explained the part played in organisations by five individuals with different job roles ☐

■ For each individual I have described their responsibilities in:

– identifying and meeting targets ☐

– working with others ☐

– training ☐

– discipline ☐

– implementing change in working conditions. ☐

■ I have explained why working conditions are subject to change. ☐

■ I have explained in depth one reason for changes to working conditions. ☐

■ I have produced a plan to implement changes to working conditions. ☐

■ In the plan I have identified those job roles which would have a responsibility for implementing the change. ☐

Chapter 14

Recruitment procedures, job applications and interviews

This chapter is designed to help you to develop an understanding of current good practice in the recruitment of employees, including an informed overview of how employers and job applicants communicate. You will need to be able to produce and evaluate letters of application and curricula vitae which meet conventional business formats. You will also need to take part in interviews for jobs, appraisals and reviews.

Procedures for attracting and recruiting applicants

An organisation's most valuable resource is its workforce – the people who work for it. Managers therefore need to give careful thought to the needs of employees. An organisation can have all the latest technology, and the best physical resources, but unless it looks after its people it will never thrive and achieve optimum results.

Recruiting individuals to fill particular posts within a business can be done:

- internally, by recruiting within the firm
- externally, by recruiting people from outside

The advantages of recruiting from within are that:

- Considerable savings can be made. Individuals with inside knowledge of how the business operates will need shorter periods of training and time for 'fitting in'.
- The organisation is unlikely to be disrupted by someone who is used to working with others in the firm.
- Internal promotion acts as an incentive to all staff to work harder within the organisation.
- From the firm's point of view, the personnel staff should already have been able to assess the strengths and weaknesses of an insider. There is always a risk attached to employing an outsider who may prove to be desirable only 'on paper'.

The disadvantages of recruiting from within are that:

- You will have to replace the person who has been promoted.

- An insider may be less likely to make the essential criticisms required to get the company working more effectively.
- Promotion of one person in a company may upset another.

AREA MANAGER

Southern England

£24–28k + car + benefits

The concept of Mothercare is unique in the world of retailing. With over 250 stores nationwide and a clear market leadership in its chosen field, it is an essential part of life for nearly all of Britain's parents-to-be and new parents.

We are seeking an Area Manager to operate in the South with responsibility for around 20 stores. Your role will be to maximise sales, working closely with your Store Managers and appreciating the individual needs within your area . . .

Imagination, flair, an entrepreneurial attitude and problem-solving skills are just some of the qualities you will need, as well as the ability to lead and motivate your team. Our culture is changing and our Area Managers are at the forefront of this. Substantial retail experience is obviously essential . . .

Figure 14.1 Advantages and disadvantages of internal recruitment

We will now go on to look at some of the important procedures that need to be carried out in recruitment.

Advertising vacancies

Job advertisements form an important part of the recruitment process. An organisation is able to communicate job vacancies to a selected audience by this means. Most job advertisements are written (or at least checked) by the personnel department, a task involving the same skill as marketing a product. Advertisements must reach those people who have the qualities to fill the vacancy.

The nature of the advert will depend on:

- who the target audience is – potential managing director, supervisors, operatives, etc.
- where the advert will be placed – on a notice board in a factory, in the *Financial Times,* at the local job centre, etc.

Job advertisements therefore take many forms, according to the current requirements. Good advertisements contain at least the following information (check the list against Figure 14.2).

New Globe Theatre Company

DIRECTOR

London

Basic £20k + car + bonuses

The New Globe Theatre Company is a new group which will be staging productions in major London theatres. The Director will receive an initial salary of £20 000 but can expect to progress steadily to higher rates as the size of the company increases and the scale of operations expands.

We are looking for someone with extensive experience of theatre production and management who will probably have worked in a similar capacity for at least five years in regional theatre productions.

If you wish to take the opportunity of pioneering this new and exciting venture, please forward a letter of application to:

Director of Personnel,
The New Globe Theatre Company,
1001 The Strand,
London WC2 0NG
Telephone 0171 900 1234

Figure 14.2 Advertising a job nationally

- *Job title* This should form the main heading, possibly in bold print.
- *Job description* This should highlight the major requirements of the job in a concise format.
- *Organisational activities and marketplace* There should be a brief description of the environment in which the organisation operates.
- *Location* Applicants need to know the location of the organisation and the location of the job (which may be different).
- *Salary expectation* Figures are not always necessary, but an indication of the salary level (or a recognised grade) should always be given.
- *Address and contact* This should appear, with a telephone number if appropriate.
- *Qualifications* Certain jobs require a minimum entrance qualification, which should be clearly stated.
- *Experience* This should be quantified as it will have a bearing on the expected salary level for the job.
- *Fringe benefits* The advertiser may wish to mention a company car, a health insurance scheme and so on.
- *Organisation identity* This may be in the form of a logo (or simply the name of the organisation).

A good job advertisement, while providing prospective candidates with helpful information, also helps to discourage applications from people who do not have the required qualifications for the job.

Presentation of the advertisement is very important, as it gives prospective employees a first impression of the organisation.

Evidence collection point

1 Cut out three newspaper job advertisements. Mount each separately on a piece of paper or card. Identify each of the points made above on the advert. You could draw arrows indicating job title, job description, location, etc.

Summarise the strengths and weaknesses of each of the advertisements.

2 Think about the features of what you would consider to be an ideal job for you. Try to make out a realistic job advertisement to describe this job. You may need to carry out some research to find out such features as a realistic wage and the experience required.

Your work should provide evidence of Core Skills in Communication.

Job vacancies will need to be advertised in the appropriate media well in advance of the closing date for applications. For example, if a business organisation wants to interview in March it may place an advert in a national newspaper in early January, stating that the closing date for applications is 8 February.

Shortlisting

Imagine that a college has advertised for a new Human Resource Management Lecturer. They have advertised this post in:

- the local newspaper
- the educational section of two national newspapers
- a specialist magazine for teachers and lecturers.

The college wants to secure the best lecturer for the post and is pleased when there are over 50 applicants for the job.

The Head of Business Studies and a lecturer in Human Resources together with a member of the college senior management team and an outside governor then sift through the applications.

They will discard any applications that do not meet certain criteria they are looking for. In this case they want someone who:

1 Has experience of working in industry in human resource management.
2 Has a teaching qualification, plus a minimum of three years' lecturing experience.
3 Has an established record of research and published articles.

When they have carried out this process they are left with only 12 candidates.

They then decide to reduce this number to a short list of eight by looking at the relative strengths of the candidates. Next, they take a more detailed look to reduce the number to five, whom they will call for interviews. The five candidates who make it to the final cut will be notified well in advance so that they have plenty of time to prepare themselves for an interview.

Evidence collection point

Find out how shortlisting is carried out in a place of work with which you are familiar.

Dealing with references

In business, references for employees will usually be taken up by an employer before a contract of employment is agreed. For some posts prospective employers will send for references as soon as an employee is being considered for a job. This is often the case with fairly routine work. Employers will not even consider the job applicant before they have seen a reference from a school/college or previous employer. This is also often the case in first appointments and for part-time work.

However, a more common practice for many jobs in industry is for the employer to send for references after an interview has taken place. The main reasons for this are that:

1 This reduces the paperwork involved in the recruitment process. You only process the papers of the prospective employees you are really interested in.
2 Many prospective employees do not want their existing employers to know that they are looking for work elsewhere. For every job offer made there will be many candidates who are disappointed. If these people are already employed, sending for references might sour their relationships with existing employers.

When sending for a reference from an employer it is helpful to set out the key points on which you want to receive comments. References should be relatively brief because they must not be too time-consuming for the writer.

Assessing candidates

Candidates should be assessed against set criteria for a job. For example, in choosing a lecturer in Human Resource Management, you should be looking for the most knowledgeable candidate, with the best teaching record, the ability to work with others in a team, and the ability to inspire and enthuse students. There will of course be other criteria, too. Today it is common practice when selecting lecturers to assess them by asking them to do a presentation which should illustrate their current knowledge of a subject and their ability to teach in a simulated classroom situation.

Recruitment and selection are closely tied together. Selection is the process of choosing people to work in an organisation.

The selection system should attempt:

- to get the best people within existing budgets – that is, those with the most appropriate skills, experience and attitudes
- to select people who will stay with the organisation for a reasonable time
- to minimise the cost of recruitment and selection relative to returns.

Selection interviews should be well organised. They should be arranged at convenient times and at convenient locations, and should present to candidates a realistic picture of what the job entails and what working for the organisation would be like.

Before selecting candidates for interview, the organisation should have a clear picture of the 'ideal' candidate. As we have seen, it is then a matter of sifting through all the applications to find candidates who best meet the organisation's requirements and drawing up a shortlist.

As part of their interviews, candidates may be given tasks to complete to test their aptitude. Also, to check whether applicants are likely to stay with the organisation, it is important to ask them about their future intentions, and to show them the working environment. While the organisation needs to select suitable employees, it is also important that employees select the right organisation.

Evidence collection point

At the B&Q do-it-yourself store in Macclesfield, the average age of the sales staff is 57. The store works very efficiently and consistently achieves profits that are 30% ahead of the targets.

B&Q now has a policy of aiming job advertisements at older people. A national advertisement prompted 7000 replies, and more than 600 over-50s applied for 57 job vacancies at Macclesfield.

The scheme was started because of B&Q's difficulties with the youngsters it employed – in some areas the staff was turning over faster than the stock, so senior

management decided to see whether older people would stay longer. Research has indicated that they do, and they take fewer days off for sickness. Employee turnover at Macclesfield is nearly one-sixth that at similar stores, and absenteeism is 40% less. Shoplifting is also low.

As a result of this experiment, B&Q's target is to have 10% of its national workforce aged over 50. The company feels that older staff are prepared to work harder. In addition, many have had a lot of experience of using the materials that the company sells, so that they can give useful advice to customers.

1 What qualities do you think B&Q looks for in its sales staff?
2 Set out these qualities in the form of a job specification for a sales person.
3 Would older people fill this job specification better than younger workers?
4 What disadvantages will there be to B&Q from employing older sales staff?

Confirming employment

Once the selection procedure has been carried out it will be necessary to confirm employment with successful candidates. This will usually involve writing to say that the business will offer to employ them subject to the receipt of suitable references. It will then be necessary to finalise the terms of any offer that has been made and to agree a suitable date for work to start. The contract of employment will then place employment on a formal and legal basis.

Evidence collection point

Interview three employees to find out what arrangements were involved in formally confirming their employment.

Dealing with unsuccessful candidates

For every successful job applicant there will be many more unsuccessful ones. Unsuccessful candidates need to be dealt with in an honest and sympathetic way, both for the purpose of helping the development of these candidates and in order to prevent resentment building up against the business.

When people fail to secure a job they may feel quite hurt, because they have been rejected. They may feel that they have been treated badly. It is therefore very important to make sure that unsuccessful applicants are informed of the reasons why they have been rejected. In particular it is important to point to the selection criteria – e.g. we are looking for candidates with at least three years' experience of working in industry. It is important to make it clear that the decision has not been made on personal grounds but through following fair procedures.

Most of us have experienced rejection in job interviews. We would like to know why we have not been selected. An important procedure therefore is to brief applicants to explain why they have not been taken on for a particular post: 'I will not be able to take you on for this post because..... You may benefit from doing x, y or z in order to improve your chances of taking on a similar post.' Candidates may still feel resentful that they have been rejected. But at least they have been given an explanation, and something to work at!

Evidence collection point

Interview three people who have been unsuccessful in job applications. Find out how they were dealt with in these situations. What are their views about how decisions were or were not explained to them?

Job descriptions

A job description will set out how a particular employee is to fit into the organisation. It will therefore need to set out:

- the title of the job
- to whom the employee is responsible
- for whom the employee is responsible
- a simple description of the role and duties of the employee within the organisation.

A job description could be used as a job indicator for applicants. Alternatively, it could be used as a guideline for an employee and/or line manager as to his or her role and responsibility within the organisation. (It is not, however, a contract of employment.)

Job descriptions can be used by organisations to provide information for use in drafting a situations vacant advertisement and for briefing interviewers.

Job title

One of the most important parts of a job description is the job title. The job title should give a good indication of what the job entails. For example, you may hear people in organisations make statements such as: 'She's supposed to be the Managing Director, let her make the decision,' or 'Leave the word-processing of letters to the secretary, that's not your job'. I heard a conversation between a lecturer and a porter concerning the carrying of boxes which ended up with the remark: 'You're supposed to be a porter – get porting!'

When looking through job advertisements the first thing that job applicants will look for (apart from the salary) will be the job title.

From time to time job titles will change, often to give a slightly different feel to some jobs or to confer new status – the Principal of a College may become Chief Executive, a dustbin man may become a 'disposal services officer', etc.

Position within organisational structure

A job description will often establish where an individual stands in a particular organisational structure. This will mean that it can be clearly set out who the post-holder is accountable to, and who is accountable to him or her.

The position within an organisation will also give a clear idea of responsibilities. Job applicants will be interested to locate their position in order to ascertain whether their previous experience will be extensive enough and to assess the kind of commitment they will be expected to make to the organisation.

Duties and responsibilities

A further important aspect of the job description will be that which sets out the duties and responsibilities of job-holders.

Prior to setting out a job description an organisation may carry out an analysis of the tasks which needs to be performed by a job-holder, and of the skills and qualities required.

If this is done carefully, then organisational planners will have a clear picture of how particular jobs fit in with all the other jobs carried on in an organisation. It also helps job applicants to get a clear picture of what is expected of them, and it helps job-holders to understand the priorities of their work.

Job analysis is very important in creating a clear job description. For example, the job of a trainee manager in a supermarket could be described under the following key headings:

■ Title of post
■ Prime objectives of the position
■ Supervisory/managerial responsibilities
■ Source(s) of supervision and guidance
■ Range of decision-making
■ Responsibilities for assets, materials, etc.

Evidence collection point

Imagine that you are a personnel officer with a large High Street retailer. Currently you do not have enough shop assistants to meet the demands of customers, particularly at weekends. There are long queues at the tills, and it has become impossible to stack shelves neatly or to price all items accurately.

Set out a job analysis for a shop assistant, by answering the following questions:

a What tasks need to be performed?
b What skills and qualities are required?
c How can these skills be acquired?

Alternatively, examine two job descriptions produced by an organisation (perhaps the organisation you work for). Explain how successful these job descriptions seem to have been in matching applicants with vacancies.

Person specifications

A job specification often goes beyond a simple description of the job, by highlighting the mental and physical attributes required of the job holder. For example, a recent Prison Service advertisement specified the following: 'At every level your task will call for a lot more than simple efficiency. It takes humanity, flexibility, enthusiasm, total commitment and, of course, a sense of humour.'

The personnel department may therefore set out, for its own use, a 'person specification', using a layout similar to the one shown in Figure 14.3.

Summary of job			
Attributes	**Essential**	**Desirable**	**How identified**
Physical			
Qualifications			
Experience			
Training			
Special knowledge			
Personal circumstances			
Attitudes			
Practical and intellectual skills			

Figure 14.3 Layout for a person specification

The person specification can be used to:

■ make sure that a job advertisement conveys the qualities that prospective candidates should have
■ check that candidates for the job have the right qualities.

Personal attributes and achievements

A person specification is concerned with identifying those people who have the right qualities to fit the jobs you are offering.

For example, personal attributes for a member of the Paratroop Regiment might include physical toughness and alertness. The personal attributes of a teacher may include the ability to work well with others and to find out about the learning needs of pupils. The personal attributes of a shop assistant might include punctuality and smartness of appearance.

Personal achievements give a good indication of the existing abilities of given individuals. For example, someone who has achieved the Duke of Edinburgh Award shows qualities of enterprise and initiative. Personal achievements can be good indicators of qualities such as the ability to work in a team, to help others, to persevere, etc.

Qualifications

Qualifications are another important ingredient in person specifications. For example, when recruiting a new Human Resources lecturer it would be essential to appoint someone with formal teaching qualifications and some form of academic qualification such as a degree in Business Studies.

Qualifications are a good measure of prior learning. This has been simplified in recent years by the development of NVQs and GNVQs which are nationally recognised qualifications.

For example, in appointing someone at a a managerial level you would be looking for at least NVQ Levels 4 and 5.

The idea of a qualification is that it prepares you to do a particular job or activity. In creating a job specification, organisations will therefore need to consider the level of qualification required by a job holder.

Experience

There is a well-known saying that there is no substitute for experience. Someone with experience in carrying out a particular post or who has had particular responsibilities should be able to draw on that experience in new situations.

For example, an experienced lecturer has already taught, assessed, administered, and carried out a variety of other duties in a college. A new lecturer has not had the same advantages.

We talk about the learning curve which results from experience. The implication is that the good learner will learn at a progressively faster rate as they draw on their experience. A person specification should therefore set out the required experience for a job-holder.

Competence

Competence is a word that is widely used today. Competence implies that a person has sufficient knowledge or skill to carry out particular tasks or activities. Most people would rather visit a competent than an incompetent doctor, or be taught by a competent rather than an incompetent teacher.

Person specifications should set out levels of competence required by a particular job-holder. Modern qualifications like GNVQs and NVQs are based on a competence model. Hairdressers, for example, need to show competence in a range of performance criteria that make up the elements of hairdressing work. A hairdresser would be foolish to take on a new stylist for dyeing purposes who had not first exhibited competence in mixing and applying hair dye.

Evidence collection point

Examine two person specifications for particular jobs. Write a commentary that explains how successful these have been in matching applicants with vacancies. Show how the person specifications set out the personal attributes and achievements, qualifications, experience and competence required for specific jobs. Plan your work so that it provides evidence of Core Skills in Information Technology and Communication.

Letters of application

We are now in a position to look at job applications and interviewing from the applicant's point of view.

However, before you do this look through the two flow-charts in Figures 14.4 and 14.5 which indicate the selection process for a job (a) from the employer's point of view, and (b) from the applicant's point of view. They present you with a clear picture of this process and one which you should be familiar with before you start applying for jobs in earnest.

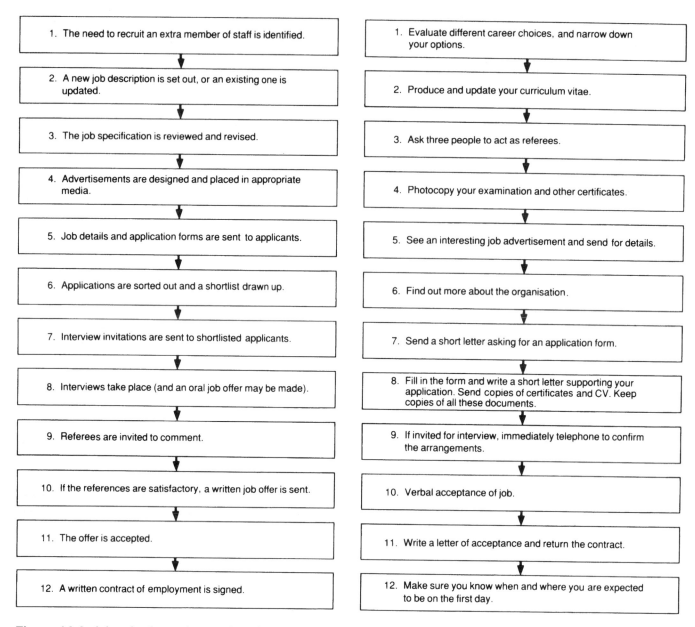

Figure 14.4 Job selection – the employer's schedule

1. The need to recruit an extra member of staff is identified.
2. A new job description is set out, or an existing one is updated.
3. The job specification is reviewed and revised.
4. Advertisements are designed and placed in appropriate media.
5. Job details and application forms are sent to applicants.
6. Applications are sorted out and a shortlist drawn up.
7. Interview invitations are sent to shortlisted applicants.
8. Interviews take place (and an oral job offer may be made).
9. Referees are invited to comment.
10. If the references are satisfactory, a written job offer is sent.
11. The offer is accepted.
12. A written contract of employment is signed.

Figure 14.5 Job selection – the applicant's view

1. Evaluate different career choices, and narrow down your options.
2. Produce and update your curriculum vitae.
3. Ask three people to act as referees.
4. Photocopy your examination and other certificates.
5. See an interesting job advertisement and send for details.
6. Find out more about the organisation.
7. Send a short letter asking for an application form.
8. Fill in the form and write a short letter supporting your application. Send copies of certificates and CV. Keep copies of all these documents.
9. If invited for interview, immediately telephone to confirm the arrangements.
10. Verbal acceptance of job.
11. Write a letter of acceptance and return the contract.
12. Make sure you know when and where you are expected to be on the first day.

All students who are following this course will need at some stage to produce letters of application for jobs. It is important that you get this process right. Over the years we have seen many students applying for jobs. It is surprising how often there are two students who are almost identical in terms of qualifications, appearance and ability, but one is offered many interviews while the other receives only a few. Usually the difference is in the quality of their letters of application.

A letter should have a clear structure, with a beginning, a middle and an ending. It should state:

- your reason for applying for the job
- the contribution you can make to the organisation
- how you have developed your capabilities through training and education
- the skills and knowledge you have acquired that would help you to do the job well.

The letter needs to be interesting – you are writing about (i.e. selling) yourself. It should contain just enough information to support your application form and CV (see below), highlighting the most relevant evidence. You will know that you are writing effective letters if they lead to interviews.

Here are some important rules to remember.

- ■ Use good English with accurate spelling. Always check in a dictionary if you are unsure of the spelling of a word.
- ■ Use your own words rather than simply copying those in the advertisement.
- ■ Do not try to be too clever by using long words.
- ■ Keep the paragraphs short.
- ■ Try not to use 'I' too much.
- ■ Word-process letters if possible. Failing this, draft a handwritten copy before producing the final typed copy.
- ■ Follow the correct convention of addressing people. A letter beginning 'Dear Sir/Madam' should be ended with 'Yours faithfully', whereas one that begins 'Dear Mr Ramprakash' should be ended with 'Yours sincerely'.
- ■ Keep a copy of what you have written.

Evidence collection point

The letter opposite was sent by an applicant for the post of trainee accountant with British Rail. What weaknesses can you spot?

Evidence collection point

Write a letter of application for the post described below.

The position: Trainee Manager at Marks and Spencer

The company: One of the top ten companies in the UK by turnover and a leading retailer. The company employs over 50 000 people and continues to grow.

A manager: Managers at all levels are expected to show responsibility. The company is looking for people who are tough and talented. They should have a flair for business, know how to sell and be able to work in a team.

The training: The first year's training will introduce the new manager to the stores and to working in a management team. In the second year trainees can specialise in personnel, selling or administration.

Salaries: £8500–£11 500 p.a.

```
                                    21 Wade Park Avenue
                                       Market Deeping
                                         Peterborough
                                            PE6 8JL

20th September 1995

BR Finance Manager, Anglia Region
Room 109
East Side Offices
Kings Cross Station
London
N1 9AP

Dear Sir,

I noticed in my local paper that you have a job
avalable for a junior accountant. I am very
interested in the post because I see it as
presenting a good opportunity. I have always
been very interested in accounts. I am also
studing accounts at collage. I understand that
on your accountancy training scheme there will
be good oppertunities for promotion. I am also
studying GNVQ course in Business. This is a very
interesting course and I have had good reports
from all my tutors on the course. As part of the
course I am studying accounts. I have found the
accounts to be the most exciting and interesting
parts. I am also interested in train spotting.
   I am working at the Anglia Co-operative
Society. This is a part time post but it involves
a lot of responsibility. I have to check the
stock and make sure that shelves are well
organised. I also have had my EPOS training.
   I am currently working on my cv and will send
it to you next week. Many thanks for your
interest in my application.

Yours Sincerely,

Norman Major
```

Curriculum vitae

A curriculum vitae (usually called simply a CV) is a summary of your career to date. There are three stages you should follow when setting out your CV.

- ■ assemble all the facts about yourself
- ■ draft the CV
- ■ edit the document several times.

Try to create a favourable impression (but always be truthful). Omit negative statements about yourself. Do not be vague.

Always use a word-processing package with an impressive, yet conservative, font.

Assembling the facts

At this initial stage you are trying to get together as many relevant facts as possible about your career to date. It does not matter if you put down too many to start with – make a list of *all* your educational, work-based and leisure achievements, as well as training activities and courses you have been on. Make brief notes about each of these as well as about projects and assignments you have been involved in.

Drafting the CV

A CV should be divided into suitable headings and sub-headings, for example:

1 Name
2 Date of birth
3 Address
4 Telephone
5 Education and training
6 Qualifications
7 Other relevant achievements
8 Interests
9 References

Remember that the key part of the CV is the career history, so the sections that go before should not be too long. For example, when dealing with training, list only the most important and relevant training course, and then if necessary include some of the others under 'other information'.

When you set out your responsibilities and achievements, decide whether it is necessary to put some of them under sub-headings. It is normal practice to start your career history with your most recent job and work backwards in time, because employers are usually more interested in your recent experience.

If some of your experience is of a technical nature, try to present it in a way that can be read easily by the general reader (rather than only by a specialist).

Try to use dynamic words in your CV. Here are some good examples:

accomplished	achieved	conducted
completed	created	decided
delivered	developed	designed
directed	established	expanded
finished	generated	implemented
improved	increased	introduced
launched	performed	pioneered
planned	promoted	redesigned
reorganised	set up	solved
succeeded	trained	widened
won	work	wrote

CURRICULUM VITAE

Name:	Prakesh Patel
Date of birth:	1.3.78
Address:	50 Palmerston Road Reading RG31 9HL
Telephone:	01604 76321
Education and training:	Waingels' Copse School, Reading Sept 1990-July 1995
Qualifications:	Mathematics (B) English (C) Business Studies (A) French (C) German (A) Technology (C) History (C) All July 1995
Interests and activities:	Captain of school rugby team, house captain and prefect (1994–95). Venture Scout. Bronze Award for Duke of Edinburgh. Member of Woodley Chess Club.
Work experience:	Assistant in Heelas (Department Store) in Reading on Saturdays
Referees:	Mr I. Marks Waingels' Copse School Denmark Ave Woodley Reading RG3 8SL	Rev. R. Babbage St Jude's Church Street Reading RG4 7QZ

Figure 14.6 A skeleton CV

Editing the CV

You may need to alter your CV slightly for each job application so that it concentrates as closely as possible on the requirements of a particular job. Look at the details of the job and ask yourself whether your CV suggests that you have the requirements for the post. Imagine yourself in the employer's shoes; what qualities do you think the organisation is looking for?

 Evidence collection point

Produce your own up-to-date CV. Ask someone else to evaluate your CV against the following checklist:

1 Have you given a good impression of your skills, knowledge, experience and personality?

2 Are these set out in a concise and readable fashion?
3 Do significant achievements stand out?
4 Have you eliminated confusing terms, jargon and obscure abbreviations?
5 Are all words spelt accurately, have you used correct grammar, and is the layout clear and organised?
6 Does the CV have a good 'feel'?
7 Would the person reading it understand it easily?

Interviewer techniques

As part of your GNVQ course it is very helpful to arrange simulated job interviews in the classroom. There are a number of benefits to be gained from this.

One benefit is that it provides excellent opportunities to rehearse the Core Skills of Communications, particularly when working with adults in a realistic situation (for example, you might invite personnel officers from local organisations to take part in the interviewing process).

Another benefit is that it helps you to rehearse and practise for the real interviews that you will be having shortly when you apply for jobs. The structure and format of a simulated interview will be very similar to the real thing. If you have practised in front of a student audience you should be better prepared and less nervous in future.

Another very important benefit is that it gives you an insight into the interviewing process. You will gain an idea of what it is like to be in the interviewer's chair, and this will help you to identify the kinds of things that the interviewers are looking for. Perhaps groups of students can act as interviewers. What are they looking for? What are the main criteria that they are using to judge candidate performance?

It is very helpful to make a video of the job interviews so that you can critically evaluate performance. Useful things to look out for are:

■ the effective use of body language, and eye contact
■ the completeness of answers given to questions (rather than answering 'Yes or No')
■ whether interviewees listened to questions and gave appropriate responses.

Let us first look at some interviewer techniques. By studying these carefully we can get a useful insight into what the interviewer is thinking about and looking for.

Opening the interview

Generally speaking, interviews should try to make the interviewee feel relaxed. For example, they might ask the interviewee about his or her journey to the interview on that day: 'Where have you come from?' 'Did you find it easy to get here today?', etc.

Of course, there are exceptional times when interviewers deliberately set out to make the interviewees feel uncomfortable to see how they react, for example by putting them on a wobbly chair or placing them at a lower height than the interviewer's chair.

However, the important thing to remember is that modern business organisations are not run like the Gestapo. Generally they should find some means of making the interviewee feel comfortable, so that the interviewee can show his or her best side.

When there are several interviewers a starting point might be to introduce the interviewee to each of the panel in turn.

Asking questions

The next stage is to ask the interviewee a set of pre-determined questions. The questions asked should relate to the person specification and job description. Remember that you are looking for the candidate who is best able to meet the organisation's requirements. The interviewer will have a copy of the candidates application form and curriculum vitae. Interviewers will normally want to make notes to check how each interviewee meets the job requirements.

For example, they may have a sheet like that shown in Figure 14.7 in front of them. By setting out a score-sheet like it is possible to compare candidates'

Post: Shop supervisor		
Candidate name: Melissa Graham		
Requirements	Score (1–5)	Notes
Tidy appearance	3	Untidy hair.
Intelligence	5	Answered questions quickly, and with good attention to detail.
Punctuality	1	Turned up 2 minutes late for interview.
etc.	etc.	etc.

Figure 14.7 Interviewer's score-sheet

responses to questions, and behaviour in the interview situation.

The questions chosen by the interviewer should be carefully thought out in order to ensure that they make it possible to draw accurate comparisons. For example, in interviewing lecturers to teach on a GNVQ Advanced course in Business, the interview panel might ask all candidates questions such as:

■ What can you tell us about the best way to organise the teaching of core units on an Advanced Business course?
■ What do you see as being the strengths of group work?
■ Can you tell us about your experience of teaching GNVQ students?

Interviewing also requires a considerable amount of intelligence and inventiveness. When candidates answer your questions you may feel that you need to ask them a little bit more in order to get a more complete answer. Follow-on questions are very important here. Some follow-on questions may be planned in advance, while others may need to be developed on the spur of the moment.

For example, when an interviewer talks to someone applying for a job as a shelf stacker in a supermarket, he or she may get the following responses:

Interviewer: Have you had experience of shelf stacking in a supermarket before?

Interviewee: Yes, I worked at Marks and Spencer doing it for three months.

Interviewer: (Follow-on question) Can you tell me exactly what you were responsible for doing in your shelf stacking job? (And why you left it!)

Without follow-on questions an interview can pass very quickly with little being found out about the true strengths (and weaknesses) of job applicants.

Using body language

People do not just talk to each other through words. They also talk through their body language. An interviewer who wants to draw the best out of candidates for a job will use appropriate body language. The interviewer should be seated at the same height as the interviewee with a good frontal or open posture. The interviewer should not cross his or her arms or make threatening gestures such as pointing a finger or banging a fist down on the table. He or she should smile and use clear eye contact.

Closing the interview

The usual way of closing an interview is that, when the interviewer or interviewing panel have finished their list of questions, they will ask the interviewee if there is anything he or she would like to ask. When this is completed the interviewer will say something like: 'Thank you very much for coming to the interview, I hope you have a safe journey back. You will be hearing from us by...' The interviewer will clarify the arrangements through which the interviewee will be informed of arrangements, and explain how any administrative task such as claiming for expenses should be done.

Giving feedback

Often candidates for a post will be given feedback on how they performed in the interview situation. They should be told about their strengths and weaknesses and the reasons why they were or were not chosen for the post. This feedback should be seen as a positive process concerned with the ongoing development of the interviewee.

Interviewee techniques

Interviews can be nerve-racking. In a short space of time the candidate must convince the interviewer that he or she is the person the organisation needs.

Preparing

Both the interviewer and the candidate need to be prepared. The candidate can prepare by practising answers to the questions likely to be asked, possibly with the help of a friend who takes the role of the interviewer.

It must be remembered that interviews are a two-way activity. The candidate has a chance to ask questions and find out if the organisation and the job are suitable. Questions can, for example, be asked about training, promotion prospects and social facilities.

There are all sort of things that you can prepare before an interview. For example, you may want to try out the clothes that you will wear to the interview beforehand, perhaps by wearing them to some sort of public occasion. There is nothing worse than feeling uncomfortable in the clothes you have chosen for an interview. Many people like to plan the route they will take to get to the interview, even doing a dummy run beforehand.

You may like to prepare yourself by thinking about the kinds of things that interviewers will be looking for in you. The interview assessment form shown in Figure 14.8 gives you some useful indications of the qualities that are looked for in many job holders.

Factors	INTERVIEW ASSESSMENT					
	Rating					Remarks
	A	B	C	D	E	
Appearance Personality Manner Health						
Intelligence Understanding of questions						
Skills Special skills Work experience						
Interests Hobbies Sports						
Academic						
Motivation						
Circumstances Mobility Hours Limitations						
OVERALL						

A = Exceptional   B = Above average   C = Satisfactory
D = Below average   E = Unsuitable

Figure 14.8 An interview assessment form

The checklist shown in Figure 14.9 should also be helpful in giving you some useful preparatory advice for interviews:

Showing confidence

It is important for interviewees to appear confident but not over-confident. You should be confident in your own abilities. One of the most important attributes to have in the interview situation is enthusiasm. An enthusiastic person will tend to radiate confidence. Candidates who appear hangdog

DO ✔	DON'T ✘
Find out about the firm before the interview	Be late
Dress smartly but comfortably	Smoke unless invited to
Speak clearly and with confidence	Chew gum or eat sweets
Look at the interviewer when speaking	Answer all questions 'yes', 'no', or 'I don't know'
Be positive about yourself	Be afraid to ask for clarification if anything is unclear
Be ready to ask questions	Say things which are obviously untrue or insincere

Figure 14.9 A candidate's interview checklist

and timid will be viewed in a poor light, particularly for posts that require some degree of responsibility and initiative.

Body language

At an interview it is important for you to adopt the right body language. Look alert and eager. Look the questioner in the eye. Avoid nervous movements, and try not to cross your arms in a defensive position. Try not to threaten the interviewer by pointing your finger or making sudden violent movements. Sit up straight and try to look confident and at ease – not apathetic and too laid back.

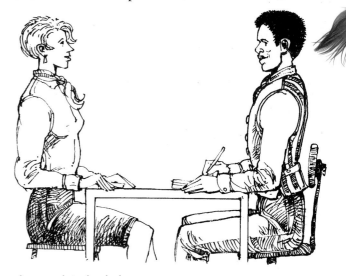

Appropriate body language

Do not give brief one-line answers, but try to expand on your answers so that the interviewer can

Inappropriate body language

Inappropriate body language

see you at your best. Smile, and at all times try to appear interested and enthusiastic about what is being discussed. You do not have to let yourself be pushed around by an aggressive interviewer – be assertive by standing up for yourself, without taking it to the extreme by becoming heated and argumentative.

Listening to questions

When you are being interviewed, listen carefully to the questions that you are asked. If you do not understand a question or have not heard it clearly, it may be helpful to say, 'Please could you repeat that question?' If you give an inappropriate answer to a question that you have misheard then the interviewers may doubt your intelligence. The golden rule is to concentrate on the questions being asked.

Responding to questions

When answering questions you will need to expand on points rather than giving a simple yes/no or a short answer. Try to give detailed and clear responses. Remember that the interviewers are judging you against certain criteria. Try to think about what those criteria might be and prepare full answers which enable them to give you high scores for your answers.

Try to be clear, enthusiastic, and interested in the questions. However, don't speak for too long, or ramble. This may give the impression that you are disorganised. Don't oversell yourself. The person who goes on and on about having wonderful skills is likely to appear both boring and pompous. The interviewing panel will often have to work with you. They won't want to work with an inflated egotist, or someone with verbal diarrhoea.

Asking questions

At the end of the interview you will be given opportunities to ask questions. Try to ask a small number of relevant questions. Don't ask questions that simply involve the repetition of material that you have already been told.

If you are not sure whether you want the job or not, then ask questions that will enable you to make a more informed choice.

Be clear and concise

Good verbal communication involves asking and answering questions in a clear and concise way. The person who is straightforward, interesting and direct will often sway an interview in a positive way.

Remember that the initial impressions you gave are very important. It is often in the first few minutes of an interview that the panel make up their minds about which candidate to appoint.

Any job interview involves a certain amount of luck and the outcome depends on how you do on the day.

A recent study reported that the person who is first on the interviewer's list is three times less likely to be hired than the last name on the list.

Monday is the worst interview day because managers are under pressure on the first day of the week, while Friday offers the distraction of a coming weekend. Early morning interviews are not recommended because managers are too preoccupied, while those after 4 pm are unhelpful because interviewers are anxious to get home!

Evidence collection point

In groups, carry out mock interviews for an imaginary post. Before the interviews take place the interviewing panel will need to establish the qualities they are looking for in the successful applicant. The interviewing panel will also need to establish a set of questions. The same questions need to be asked of each applicant if the interviews are to be fair.

The 'applicants' will each need to produce a CV and a written application. They will also need to research the nature of the organisation and the post.

After the interviews, all interviewers and interviewees should fill in an evaluation sheet containing the following questions:

1   How did you feel about the interview?
2   How did you consider that the interview went?
3   What impression do you think you gave?
4   What did you think of the interviewers'/interviewees':
    a   planning and organisation
    b   preparation for the interview
    c   performance at the interview?

Appraising interviewers and interviewees

As part of your GNVQ course you will benefit from carrying out mock interviews for a fictitious job (as in the evidence collection activity above) or for a real job but in a simulated interview situation.

Carrying out successful mock interviews will involve considerable planning and preparation. An effective approach will be for one group of students to prepare to interview candidates for a particular post. This group of students will prepare a job advertisement and person specification, and organise the interview schedule. The interviewing team will need to decide what questions to ask, in which order and by whom, and think of follow-on questions. Students will need to make sure that the questions they ask are appropriate to the qualities they want to find out about in the job applicant.

The second group of students will play the part of the interviewees. They will need to study the job description and person specification. They will need to prepare for the interview as if it were the real thing. They will need to consider issues such as body language, preparation and answering and asking questions.

It will be helpful if the whole process can be videotaped to enable effective feedback on performance.

Appraising own performance

Individual students should prepare an appraisal form for analysing their own strengths and weaknesses in the interview situation.

This should be a very helpful process because it encourages you to be objective in your self-criticism. You can then use the form to reflect on your performance. Prepare the form before the interview takes place either by watching a video showing you interviewing or being interviewed, or simply by recalling your thoughts and feelings.

Appraisal of my performance as interviewer/interviewee:

Aspect of performance	Rating				
	Very good	Good	Fair	Weak	Very weak
Eye contact					
Body language					
Appearing confident					
Answering questions					
etc.					

The types of things you need to put on the form might include those shown in the table.

You can then use another section of the form to identify opportunities for improvement. For example:

Eye contact

I noticed when I watched the video that I did not look the interviewers in the face, and I didn't keep my head still. This is an aspect of my performance that I need to concentrate on more in group work.

Body language

I started off the interview sitting up straight but I soon became flustered and crossed my arms in a defensive position. I then became quite aggressive because I was anxious and started pointing in a menacing way.

The purpose of the self-assessment is to enable students to improve their own performance by being honest about their strengths and weaknesses.

Interaction between participants

For interviews to be successful there will need to be an effective interaction between participants both in simulations and in the real thing. Interviewees are most likely to be successful if they can generate positive interactions. It is important therefore to appraise these interactions.

Once again all participants in the role play should construct an appraisal form looking at aspects of interactions, as shown in the table.

More detailed comments will also need to be recorded about each of these aspects.

Success of the interview

It will be important to appraise the overall success of the interview. One of the key considerations will be whether the interview was an appropriate way of selecting the best candidate for the job, i.e. the one who most closely fitted the person specification and was able to fulfil the job description.

The job interview will need to be carried out in a professional way. This means that students should not select candidates on a friendship basis but purely on fitness for the job.

Students will also need to appraise the interview in terms of the way it meets legal and ethical

Appraisal of interactions during interview:

Aspect of interaction	Rating				
	Very good	Good	Fair	Weak	Very weak
Individuals' support for each other					
Interview conducted in a positive atmosphere					
Clear communication between participants					
etc.					

obligations. Recruiters have legal obligations relating to areas such as race relations, sex discrimination, opportunities for disabled people and equal pay. At the same time staff engaged in the recruitment process need to work to a professional code of ethics embracing concepts of objectivity, confidentiality and honesty.

Legal and ethical obligations in recruitment procedures

Equal opportunities

In Chapter 12 we looked at the importance of equal opportunities in the workplace. This concept is particularly important in the interview and selection process. Consider the following interview questions from the equal opportunities viewpoint. Commentary is provided in italics.

Mrs _____, I see you are married. Do you intend to start a family soon?

The question is not relevant to whether the interviewee is capable of going the job. It also shows direct sex discrimination, because a man is not likely to be asked the question. This question must not be asked.

What will happen when your children are ill or on school holidays? Who will look after them?

The question has no relevance as to whether the interviewee is capable of doing the job.

Your hair is very long, Mr _____ If offered the job are you prepared to have it cut?

This question is only relevant if a safety aspect of the job is involved (e.g. use of machinery). Otherwise the standard of dress expected by the company could be discussed (e.g. the correct image for dealing with customers).

Mr _____ , as you are 55 do you think it's worth us employing you?

This question may not be relevant because, at this age, it should not stop the person from doing the job. However, if the interviewee is 60 years of age, the company might feel that any necessary training would not be worthwhile.

Miss _____ , as a woman do you think you are capable of doing the job?

This question cannot be asked as it discriminates on the grounds of sex.

Do you think your disability will affect your performance in the job?

This question can be asked but might be better phrased: 'Do you have any health problems that may affect you in this job?'

How do you feel about working with people from a different ethnic background from yourself?

This question should not be asked because it suggests race discrimination.

As a woman returner, Mrs _____ , do you feel you will be able to cope with the new technology in the office?

This question cannot be asked, as it reveals sex discrimination. Also, it should be accepted that as a woman returner Mrs _____ will probably need some retraining.

As a man, Mr _____ , you will be working in a department consisting mainly of women. Are you easily distracted?

This question is not relevant as it will not affect the way the applicant performs the job.

Miss _____ , don't you think your skirt is rather short?

This question should not be asked because it shows sex discrimination.

Case study – Employee Recruitment Policy Statement for Melton College

Study the following policy statement and outline what you consider to be its major strengths.

1 Recruitment, Promotion and Training Decisions

All decisions in relation to the above will be taken, having regard only to the requirements of the job (or of the training proposed). Promotion and training opportunities will be available to all employees, irrespective of race, ethnic origin, religion, sex, marital status or possible family commitments, sexual orientation or disability.

2 Shortlisting, Interview and Appointment Procedures

Interview and appointment procedures shall be adopted so as to minimise any disadvantage suffered by the handicapped, members of ethnic minority groups or either sex. Accordingly, except in so far as it is necessary for particular appointments, questions will not be asked at interview regarding the following: prospects of marriage, future family plans, religion or sexual orientation.

Application for all posts will be by standard job application forms. A copy of this statement shall accompany every application form issued. All members of interviewing panel should receive appropriate training, be familiar with this policy and be aware of the guidelines to be followed.

3 Induction

Induction procedures will include arrangements to ensure that such procedures are clearly understood by everyone. (This particularly applies to instruction and notices in respect of the Health and Safety at Work Policy.) For disabled people with mobility difficulties, special attention will be paid to emergency evacuation procedures.

4 Other decisions

It is implicit in this policy that employees should not be treated more favourably or less favourably in all matters of employment (except where an exception is necessary and is allowed under the law) because of race, ethnic origin, religion, sex, marital status or possible family commitments, sexual orientation or disability. It is possible that discrimination can be implicit in unnecessary job requirements of experience and qualifications, the arrangements and timing of training courses and any other unnecessary aspects of the structure and conditions of the work which are, or may be, difficult for members of certain groups to comply with.

5 Monitoring

Monitoring of this policy in relation to employee recruitment will be by the Senior Management Team together with the Curriculum and Employment Committee of Governors.

Contract of employment

We have already seen that new employees must be given a contract of employment within thirteen weeks of starting a job. However, the contract of employment becomes legally binding once the employee agrees to work for the employer, and the employer agrees to pay the employee a wage or salary. Where this is discussed in an interview it is important to consider the contractual implications.

Evidence collection point

Produce a set of written notes explaining the issues underlying examples of discrimination in recruitment procedures.

Honesty

When you fill in an application form you must sign it to certify that the details you have provided are accurate. Failure to disclose certain information, or including information you know to be false, is an offence in law and will mean that any contract you sign is not legally binding.

In a similar way, the job description and details provided by the organisation have to be described accurately and honestly.

For example, a job advertised as involving a 30-hour week which actually involves working 40 hours can be said to be unfairly described.

When you are at an interview you must speak honestly about yourself and your qualifications. The interviewer should also provide an honest description of working conditions and the nature of the job.

Objectivity

Objectivity is an important part of the recruitment process. In particular, from the employer's point of view this involves looking at all candidates on their merits in a dispassionate way. This might involve asking each candidate in an interview the same set of

questions and judging these against an objective set of criteria (rather than changing the questions and the criteria).

Fairness

Fairness is particularly important. It involves avoiding discriminatory practices such as choosing someone who is a member of your rugby club, or because he knows your brother-in-law.

Confidentiality

Confidentiality is important. Information disclosed in an application form or an interview should not be passed on. In the same way as the doctor does not go around telling the world at large about a patient's ailments, the interviewer must protect the disclosures of interviewees.

Evidence collection point

Produce a short series of notes explaining the ethical issues involved in recruitment, outlining examples of unethical behaviour.

Evidence indicators

As part of the element you should produce a report based on the recruitment procedures used by either a business or a recruitment agency.

The following list should serve as a checklist. Please tick off each of the following when you have successfully covered them as part of your report. You need to be able to confirm that:

■ I have produced two job descriptions and two person descriptions with a commentary which identifies the most appropriate applicant for the vacancy. ☐
■ I have produced two application letters and two curricula vitae (one of which is my own, and the other is for a person with several years' work experience). I have evaluated the curricula vitae for:

  – Clarity of language ☐

  – Quality of presentation ☐

  – Relevance to the job applied for. ☐

■ I have produced and filled in two interview appraisal forms (which record a self-appraisal and an appraisal by others) of my performance in the roles of interviewee and interviewer through two mock or real interviews. ☐

■ My interview appraisals are supported by notes which explain the issues underlying examples of the discrimination and unethical behaviour in recruitment. ☐

Human Resources: Unit Test 1

1 Which of the following measures is most likely to lead to employee cooperation in the workplace?
   a Demarcation of job task.
   b Production line working.
   c Team working.
   d Top-down instruction.

2 An example of on-the-job training is:
   a An employee learning from a more skilled colleague.
   b An employee attending a college course on day release.
   c A manager following an Open University degree course.
   d A manager taking a break from work to study at home.

3 A director in an organisation is usually responsible for what level of decision-making?
   a Operational decisions.
   b Strategic decisions.
   c Routine decisions.
   d Day-to-date decisions.

4 Appraisal of people at work involves:
   a Selecting candidates for an interview.
   b Carrying out an interview for a job.
   c Helping employees to monitor their progress and prospects.
   d Dealing with individual disputes involving people at work.

5 A function of human resource management is:
   a Ensuring the company's products are well received in the marketplace.
   b Providing rewards and motivations for employees.
   c Ensuring all aspects of quality control in an organisation.
   d Supervising day-to-day production activities.

6 The job of a shop steward is best described as:
   a Representing union members at a national level.
   b Participating in the recruitment of new employees to a firm.
   c Representing all employees in a business organisation.
   d Representing union members' interests at plant level.

7 The term kaizen means:
   a Quality control.
   b Continuous improvement.
   c Hierarchical management.
   d Trade union recognition.

8 The National Union of Teachers is an example of a:
   a Craft union.
   b Industrial union.
   c White collar union.
   d General union.

9 All employees have certain legal rights when they start a new job. Which of the following would a new employee need to be provided with during the first three months?
   a A job analysis.
   b Contract of employment.
   c Job specification.
   d Union membership certificate.

10 It is illegal for unions:
   a To operate an overtime ban.
   b To strike.
   c To carry out secondary picketing.
   d Not to cooperate with management.

11 The heading least likely to be included in the job description of a trainee manager in a supermarket is:
   a Range of decision-making.
   b Responsibility for materials.
   c Prime objectives of the post.
   d Responsibility to shareholders.

12 The best definition of a 'real team' is:
   a A collection of individuals who work together.
   b A collection of individuals with a clear performance need.
   c A collection of individuals who work together on particular tasks and activities with a shared performance goal.
   d A collection of people with common skills who are committed to a common purpose, and with shared goals for which they feel jointly accountable.

13 A firm advertising the post of production-line operative would be most likely to use:
 a Cinema advertising.
 b National newspapers.
 c Local newspapers.
 d Specialist trade journals.

14 An employee is held back from promotion because of her use of English (which is her second language) even though the job she has applied for does not involve speaking. Which of the following laws has been contravened?
 a The Sex Discrimination Act.
 b The Factories Act.
 c The Health and Safety at Work Act.
 d The Race Relations Act.

15 A major advantage of external recruitment is:
 a The firm knows what it is getting.
 b It saves on recruitment costs.
 c New ideas are brought into the organisation.
 d There is a saving on induction costs.

16 A candidate at a job interview should:
 a Bring a friend into the interview room.
 b Before the interview, decline an invitation to look round the organisation.
 c Be assertive when handling difficult questions.
 d Interrupt the interviewer when questions are being asked.

17 An example of indirect sex discrimination is:
 a Being treated less favourably than other employees after making allegations about sex discrimination.
 b A decision to appoint only single women to positions in a company.
 c A decision to apppoint only men to senior management positions.
 d Where access to particular jobs is restricted in particular grades which in practice are held only by men.

18 Which of the following employee organisations would most likely represent lawyers and solicitors?
 a Professional associations.
 b General unions.
 c White collar unions.
 d Craft unions.

19 Encouraging employees to attain skills and competences for a particular job is a description of:
 a Appraisal.
 b Training.

 c Development.
 d Education.

20 The Health and Safety at Work Act places the responsibility for safe working conditions on:
 a The employee only.
 b The employer only.
 c Employers and employees.
 d Employers and the government.

21 An employer and an employee are deemed to have formed a contract of employment:
 a After the employee has been working for 13 weeks.
 b When the employer is satisfied with the employee's work performance.
 c When the employee agrees to work for the employer, and the employer agrees to employ the employee.
 d After the employer has received a satisfactory reference about the employee.

22 Which of the following would be included in a job description for a trainee manager in a supermarket?
 a Holiday entitlement.
 b Prime objectives of the position.
 c The age of the post holder.
 d Hours of work.

23 Which one of the following would most likely be responsible for doing routine tasks in an organisation?
 a Senior managers.
 b Middle managers.
 c Supervisors.
 d Operatives.

24 An organisation's selection process should always set out to:
 a Increase the number of employees working for an organisation.
 b Ensure that there is a high turnover of labour within an organisation.
 c Minimise the cost of selection relative to returns.
 d Ensure that the budget allocated for selection increases from year to year.

25 A candidate at a job interview should:
 a Avoid looking at the interviewer when speaking.
 b Tell the interviewer how much he/she wants to earn and how much holiday is expected.
 c Find out about the firm before the interview.
 d Avoid asking for clarification of difficult points.

26 Modern 'human resource management' stresses that:
   a HRM is specifically the province of personnel and no one else.
   b Human resources are motivated solely by financial rewards.
   c The best way of motivating people is through their pockets.
   d All managers have a responsibility for the human resource.

27 When someone is treated less favourably than other people, because he or she has in good faith made allegations about discrimination in the workplace, this is an example of:
   a Direct marriage discrimination.
   b Direct sex discrimination.
   c Indirect sex discrimination.
   d Victimisation.

28 Which of the following would not normally be included in a contract of employment?
   a The date the job starts.
   b Hours of work.
   c The period of notice that must be given.
   d Opportunities for promotion.

29 The form of leadership style likely to encourage the highest level of participation in group decision-making is:
   a Autocratic.
   b Bureaucratic.
   c Democratic.
   d Centralised.

30 The role of a supervisor in an organisation is to:
   a Arrange business meetings.
   b Make strategic decisions.
   c Make sure management instructions are carried out.
   d Take responsibility for Health and Safety at work.

31 A curriculum vitae should include:
   a Positive and negative statements about the job applicant.
   b Achievements of the job applicant.
   c A reference from a previous employer.
   d Examination certificates belonging to the job applicant.

32 When an organisation tries to recruit individuals who have not applied for a particular post, this is called:
   a Job-seeking.

b Professional recruitment.
c Head-hunting.
d The employment profession.

33 Job enrichment involves:
   a Ensuring that employees work longer hours.
   b Increasing bonuses available to individuals.
   c Increasing the variety of tasks carried out by an individual.
   d Training an employee before he or she starts work.

34 A male engineer finds that female contemporaries earn more money for doing the same work. He may seek redress under:
   a The Health and Safety at Work Act.
   b The Equal Pay Act.
   c The Data Protection Act.
   d The Factories Act.

35 Conciliation in an industrial dispute is a process whereby:
   a An independent outsider proposes the basis for settlement.
   b Both parties agree to accept an outside decision.
   c Both parties find it impossible to agree on principles.
   d An independent body tries to act as a channel of communication between the two sides.

36 Which of the following is not a feature of multi-skilling?
   a Flexibility of employees.
   b Demarcation in the workplace.
   c An emphasis on training of employees.
   d Responsibility of employees in work areas.

37 A reason for the decline in trade union membership in recent years has been:
   a The growth of the working population.
   b The reduction in the number of trade unions through amalgamation.
   c The decline of employment in the 'heavy industries'.
   d The increasing exploitation of employees in the workplace.

38 Which of the following roles could be described as a middle manager?
   a Company director.
   b Shareholder.
   c Computer operator.
   d Departmental head.

39 Which of the following appears in a job description?
a Title of post.
b Name of superior.
c Name of holder.
d Holiday entitlement.

40 Which of the following would appear in a job advertisement?
a Required sex of the applicant.
b Job analysis.
c Experience required.
d Job specification.

41 Which of the following would best exemplify an Equal Opportunities interview for a job?
a Unstructured schedule of questions.
b Each candidate being asked the same questions.
c All candidates being of the same age and sex.
d All candidates being able to ask questions.

42 An outline of a job applicant's career history should be given in an:
a Application form.
b Curriculum vitae.
c Testimonial.
d Reference.

43 Introducing new employees to an organisation and giving them an outline of what is expected of them, as well as telling them about their rights and entitlements, is best described as:
a Education.
b Training.
c Appraisal.
d Induction.

44 A Quality Circle may be introduced to an organisation to:
a Involve employees in the decision-making process.
b Strengthen a 'top-down' approach to human resource management.
c Identify inefficient members of an organisation.
d Increase the need for final inspection of products.

45 Which one of the following questions is an interviewer allowed to ask at a job interview?
a Your future intentions for child care.
b Your sexual orientation.
c Your reasons for applying for the job.
d Your political views.

46 The most suitable place to advertise for temporary staff to work in a local supermarket will be:
a Postcards in shop windows.
b National newspapers.
c Local newspapers.
d Professional journals.

47 Which of the following will provide an employer with specific information that they have asked for?
a Job description.
b Application form.
c Letter of application.
d Curriculum vitae.

48 Which of the following job roles would most likely to involve responsibility for monitoring the work performance of others?
a Operative.
b Assistant.
c Supervisor.
d Shop steward.

49 An ingredient of an effective letter of application for a job would be:
a The use of long sentences.
b Passages copied from the job advertisement.
c Good English with accurate spelling.
d A rambling and wide-ranging writing style.

50 A requirement which on the face of it applies equally to both men and women, but which in practice can be met by a much smaller proportion of one sex, illustrates:
a Direct marriage discrimination.
b Direct sex discrimination.
c Indirect sex discrimination.
d Victimisation.

Human Resources: Unit Test 2

1 An employee may be dismissed 'fairly' for:
a Belonging to a trade union.
b Being late on the first day at work.
c Having a negligent attitude at work.
d Asking for a pay rise.

2 An employee who removed a protective guard from a machine would have contravened:
a The Factories Act.
b The Equal Opportunities Act.
c The Office, Shops and Railway Premises Act.
d The Health and Safety at Work Act.

3 The human resource activity of buying in and retaining the best available human resources for an organisation is best described as:
  a Recruitment.
  b Training.
  c Termination.
  d Appraisal.

4 Which of the following would most likely be included in a job description?
  a The prime objectives of the position.
  b An outline of job promotion prospects.
  c An analysis of the human resource procedures of the organisation.
  d Details of skill requirements of the post holder.

5 An applicant for a job should present details of his or her personal history, education and experience in a professionally produced:
  a Letter of application.
  b Application form.
  c Job description.
  d Curriculum vitae.

6 Which of the following would not normally be part of the role of trade unions and staff associations?
  a Negotiating pay and conditions.
  b Defending employee's rights.
  c Supervising employees at work.
  d Resolving conflicts at work.

7 A person who thinks he or she has been treated unfairly with regard to sex discrimination can lodge a complaint with:
  a The Central Office of Industrial Tribunals.
  b The Trades Union Congress.
  c The Confederation of British Industry.
  d The House of Lords.

8 An advantage of internal recruitment at work is that:
  a New ideas are brought into the organisation.
  b It saves money on recruitment costs.
  c There is no 'buzz' of efficiency from new ideas.
  d The turnover of labour in an organisation is increased.

9 Systematically comparing the requirements of a job with similar posts in order to set a suitable salary can be described as:
  a Job description.
  b Job evaluation.
  c Job advertisement.
  d Appraisal.

10 A structured interview:
  a Takes the form of an informal conversation between the interviewer and the interviewee.
  b Outlines the pay structure and conditions of work within an organisation.
  c Involves asking each interviewee a number of pre-set questions to a clearly set-out pattern.
  d Involves asking an interviewee personal questions relating to his or her curriculum vitae.

11 According to Maslow's hierarchy of needs, the highest level of needs is that of:
  a Self-actualisation.
  b Love.
  c Esteem.
  d Safety and security.

12 Which of the following payment systems does not link pay to results?
  a Performance-related pay.
  b Profit-related pay.
  c Piece rates.
  d Time-related pay.

13 Which of the following would best indicate dissatisfaction of employees with their work?
  a A high level of overtime worked.
  b A high level of labour turnover.
  c A willingness of employees to participate in decision-making.
  d A high level of union membership.

14 Which of the following would be least likely to appear in a person specification?
  a Pay scales.
  b Personal attributes and achievements.
  c Experience.
  d Competence.

15 An individual with legal responsibility to a business's customers, employees, suppliers and shareholders, and who generally makes strategic decisions, is a:
  a Supervisor.
  b Manager.
  c Operative.
  d Director.

16 The ventilation has broken down in an office. The staff claim that this is making them feel ill and they demand it is mended. Which law gives them protection in the case?
  a Health and Safety at Work Act.
  b The Factories Act.
  c The Office, Shops and Railway Premises Act.

d Equal Opportunities Act.

17 An organisation advertising the post of financial director would be most likely to use:
  a An employment agency.
  b A local newspaper.
  c A professional journal.
  d Television advertising.

18 Which of the following provides the best example of good interviewing technique?
  a Making the interviewees feel uncomfortable.
  b Asking the candidates if they have any questions they want to ask.
  c Explaining the weaknesses of the previous holder of the post.
  d Finding out about the candidate's family and personal commitments.

19 In which of the following situations is a trade union likely to have the greatest bargaining powers?
  a The union represents part-time employees.
  b The demand for the product is relatively inelastic.
  c A small percentage of the labour force is unionised.
  d The business operates in a competitive market.

20 A job description for a job role includes the following: overseeing work being carried out, setting daily schedules; introducing new staff to work tasks; keeping checks on the level of production. The activities described are most likely to be the responsibility of:
  a An operative.
  b A senior manager.
  c A middle manager.
  d A supervisor.

21 Which of the following words would be most appropriate for you to include in your achievements in a curriculum vitae?
  a Average.
  b Uninteresting.
  c Performed.
  d Satisfactory.

22 A firm advertising the post of maintenance operative would be most likely to use:
  a Cinema advertising.
  b National newspapers.
  c Local newspapers.
  d Specialist trade journals.

23 Outlining the title of a post, prime objectives of the position, range of decision-making, responsibility for assets, materials etc. in a way that can be clearly understood by applicants is best described as:
  a Job analysis.
  b Preparation of a job description.
  c Preparing a person specification.
  d Producing a job advertisement.

24 The most appropriate pathway for staff development is:
  a De-skilling of existing work operations.
  b Limiting entry to a profession by strict entry requirements.
  c Making sure that only a few really keen employees are encouraged to improve their work skills.
  d On-the-job training for new employees in the workplace.

25 The European Union's Social Charter can best be described as:
  a An attempt to create flexible working practices in European industry.
  b A package of measures designed to harmonise working conditions throughout the EU.
  c A package of measures designed to make EU industrial relations similar to those in the Pacific Rim.
  d An agreement to create a socialist labour market in European Union countries.

26 The term 'downsizing' refers to:
  a Organisations hiving off non-core functions and shedding jobs.
  b The relatively small size of some organisations.
  c The process of selling off public sector businesses to the private sector.
  d The diseconomies of scale which result from expanding too quickly.

27 The representatives of shareholders in an organisation are the:
  a Employees.
  b Managers.
  c Directors.
  d Operatives.

28 An operative in a car plant is able to carry out a variety of production operations, as well as maintaining his or her own equipment. The term applied to this is:
  a Deskilling.
  b Demarcation.

389

   c Multiskilling.
   d Redundancy.

29 Trade unions whose members are civil servants are best described as a:
   a Craft union.
   b White-collar union.
   c Blue-collar union.
   d Industrial union.

30 Enabling employees to improve and develop their existing job skills can be described as:
   a Training.
   b Recruitment.
   c Selection.
   d Transfer.

31 Which of the following does not form part of the 'employment procession'?
   a Induction.
   b Negotiation.
   c Selection.
   d Recruitment.

32 Modern 'human resource management' is concerned with:
   a Making sure that all managers share a responsibility for development of the human resource.
   b Making sure that human resource management is concentrated in the personnel function.
   c Developing scientific management principles for managing people.
   d Maximising the productivity of labour through time and motion study.

33 A benefit to business of increasing flexibility in the workplace is that:
   a Employees are able to concentrate on rigidly demarcated lines of work.
   b Employees are able to do a variety of work tasks in the process of production.
   c Organisations need to employ more people to ensure that tasks are performed accurately.
   d Labour is able to replace work which was previously carried out by machinery.

34 Studying the movements made by operatives in the workplace and how long they take to perform each task is called:
   a Appraisal.
   b Time and motion study.
   c Ranking.
   d Productivity of labour.

35 Periodically reviewing progress and achievement in job roles is called:
   a Education.
   b Training.
   c Appraisal.
   d Induction.

36 Which of the following is not an objective of trade unions?
   a Representing members in disputes at work.
   b Protecting promotion opportunities and seeing that employees get fair treatment.
   c Setting the wage rate for different occupational gradings.
   d Negotiating hours of work and other working conditions.

37 Which of the following would not be classified as a case of 'fair' dismissal?
   a Wilful destruction of business property.
   b Sexual harassment of other employees.
   c Inability to do a particular job.
   d Taking time off work for certified illness.

38 Redundancy is the term applied to a situation in which:
   a Employees are given 'the sack'.
   b Employees are no longer required because a job disappears.
   c Employees retire from work.
   d A business replaces older employees with younger ones.

39 Which of the following is a type of employer action in industrial disputes?
   a Working to rule.
   b Mass suspension.
   c Strike.
   d Overtime ban.

40 The national body which represents the interests of employers is:
   a The TUC.
   b ACAS.
   c The CBI.
   d The Employer's Federation.

41 An example of 'off-the-job' training is:
   a An employee learning from a more skilled colleague.
   b An employee learning from experience in the workplace.
   c An employee attending a training course at the local college.

d A new employee being inducted into company working practices.

42 Which one of the following measures is most likely to increase employee motivation?
   a Standardisation of jobs.
   b Job enlargement.
   c Top-down decision-making.
   d Reduction in employee responsibility.

43 The heading least likely to be included in the job description of a shop assistant would be:
   a Title of the post.
   b Responsibility for materials.
   c Objectives of the post.
   d Qualifications required.

44 A candidate at a job interview should do all of the following except:
   a Set out their answers in a positive way.
   b Avoid eye contact with the interviewer.
   c Arrive well on time for the interview.
   d Think before answering questions.

45 The number of people in trade unions in recent years has fallen because:
   a Increasingly men are replacing women in the workforce.
   b Trade unions are breaking up into smaller units.
   c More and more people are working part-time and with flexible working practices.
   d The government has encouraged trades unions.

46 An advantage of external recruitment is that:
   a The organisation benefits from an influx of new ideas.

b It is cheaper than recruiting internally.
c It encourages the development of internal employees.
d The recruitment process is quicker than internal recruitment.

47 Being treated less favourably than other people because you have, in good faith, made allegations about discrimination against you in the workplace is known as:
   a Direct marriage discrimination.
   b Direct sex discrimination.
   c Indirect sex discrimination.
   d Victimisation.

48 An employer-led body that provides training in given localities in known as a:
   a Training Agency.
   b TEC.
   c CBI.
   d TUC.

49 The job of a manager is best described as involving:
   a Doing routine tasks.
   b Planning, organising, and coordinating work.
   c Assisting others to carry out their work.
   d Processing materials in an orderly way.

50 The mental and physical attributes required by a job holder are described in:
   a Job description.
   b Job analysis.
   c Job advertisement.
   d Job performance.

Production and employment in the economy

The aim of this unit is to explore the 'production' of goods and services by businesses. Production should not only be thought of in terms of manufactured goods but also in terms of primary production of goods such as oil, coal and agricultural products, and services such as banking, insurance, travel and catering. You will need to develop an understanding of the terms 'productivity' and 'value added'.

Chapter 16 focuses on employment – in order to deal with general production issues, you need to identify changes taking place in the labour market and understand their implications. Chapter 17 looks at ways of improving industry's

competitiveness, focusing in particular on UK businesses operating in the world market.

Your work should span large companies, middle market companies (usually employing between 20 and 300 people and accounting for around 30% of total UK employment), local authorities and other public-sector organisations (e.g. Benefits Agency, National Health Service). It is suggested that you use sources of information such as work visits, case histories, work experience placements and school-based enterprise activities as a starting point for investigations.

Chapter 15

Production in business

This chapter is concerned with identifying the ways in which value added is achieved in production and why business aim to add value. It identifies and gives examples of changes in production, analyses the effects of changes in production on business and identifies way of improving production.

Ways to achieve value added

Production is a broad term which is used to cover all the processes of adding value by the private and public sectors in the provision of goods and services to consumers and customers.

The notion of value added lies at the heart of business practice. We can illustrate the process of adding value by means of an example.

Here is a list of some of the ingredients that go into making a typical car:

- *Raw materials:* steel, iron work, aluminium, other non-ferrous metals, paint and solvents, textiles and leather, plastics.
- *Finished products:* windows, tyres, engines.
- *Fuels:* gas, electricity, oils.

If the car producer purchases during a year £70 million worth of raw materials and finished products, and makes 30 000 cars which are sold for £10 000 each, the firm receives £300 million for its cars. The value added in the process of production is therefore £230 million:

Revenue from selling cars	£300m
Cost of buying components and materials	£70m
Value added	£230m

The business will seek to operate in the most effective way to add value to its inputs. It will then sell its finished products in the marketplace.

Success in business is concerned with adding the most value. Figure 15.1 indicates what a firm can do with the value it adds. The left-hand side shows the value of sales to customers. We must deduct from this the value of goods and services bought from other firms. This gives us a figure for the gross value added by the

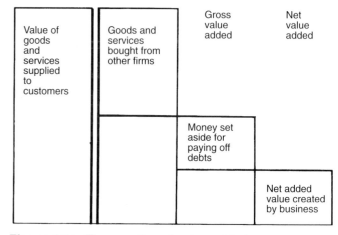

Figure 15.1 The creation of value added

392

business organisation. We can then deduct money which needs to be set aside for paying back debts from the past, finally arriving at a figure for net added value created by the business in a particular time period (we have followed European conventions here).

We can then look at how this added value is distributed. Some will go to the government in taxes, some in dividends to shareholders, some in interest to investors. Usually the largest chunk (often as much as 70%) will go in wages and salaries. The remainder can be retained as profits by the business. This profit which is kept in the business is very important because it can go into expanding or consolidating the business in the next year.

One of the key things you should learn from a business course is the importance of adding value. The more value you can add in the process of production the better your competitive advantage will be and thus your ability to survive, expand and flourish.

Businesses constantly seek ways of adding value to products. Value can be added to products by making them more desirable so that more people are prepared to buy them and at higher prices. For example, value is added to motor cars by creating desirable additional features such as mobile phones, automatic route finders, increased safety features and economy fuel consumption.

One of the most important ways of adding value to products in today's competitive market conditions is through service – personal attention to customers' requirements, friendly relationships with customers, etc.

The value added by a business to its input materials is thus more than simply physical improvement – it also involves non-tangible considerations such as service and 'image'. There is an essential human dimension. A business has to benefit not only the people who buy the products and services, but also its own employees, its suppliers and the community at large.

Benefits, whether tangible, in the form of scientifically measurable product differences, or intangible, in the form of 'image' or service, are comparatively easy to add. However, the key is to add benefits which go above and beyond those being offered by competitors.

Evidence collection point

Identify the added benefits which persuade you to purchase one organisation's products rather than alternatives. For example, what extra added value does your hairdresser provide compared with rivals?

Marketing as a source of added value

Marketing is the key to adding value to products. It is concerned with identifying those benefits which consumers are looking for in products, i.e. in identifying the kinds of added values that consumers want and need. In today's competitive marketplace producers need to build special relationships with customers by directly serving their needs.

For example, if we look at the market for car tyres we can see that there has been a switch in emphasis in consumer requirements. In the past, tyre adverts emphasised the importance of speed, for the motorists who fancied themselves as debonair racing drivers. Today, consumers of cars and tyres are more concerned about the safety aspects. Reasons for this include the fact that women today have a major say in car purchases, and families and individuals are increasingly concerned about the risks of motoring.

Other aspects of this awareness and concern are also being addressed by motor manufacturers in the design and production of cars, for example by the use of side impact bars and airbags.

The market-conscious car manufacturer and tyre manufacturer will today add most value to products by concentrating on meeting consumers' requirements for safe products.

Evidence collection point

Produce a short written report identifying ways in which two 'new' products have concentrated on adding value through marketing consciousness.

Producing this report will help you to provide evidence of using the Core Skill of Communication.

Adding value through quality assurance

In his widely acclaimed book *Thriving on Chaos,* Tom Peters argued that consumers' perception of the quality of a product or service is the most important factor in determining its success.

Quality as defined by the consumer, he argued, is more important than price in determining demand for most goods and services. Consumers will be prepared to pay for the best quality. Value is thus added by creating those quality standards required by consumers.

Figure 15.2 Consumer quality standards

Figure 15.3 Moving to total quality management

Figure 15.2 highlights what is meant by quality standards from the consumer's point of view.

Peters emphasises the importance of Total Quality Management, which involves taking quality to new heights. Peters identifies three stages in the development of quality:

1 quality control
2 quality assurance
3 total quality management.

1 Quality control is an old idea. It is concerned with detecting and cutting out components or final products which fall below set standards. This process takes place after these products have been produced. It may involve considerable waste as defect products are scrapped. Quality control is carried out by Quality Control Inspectors. Inspection and testing are the most common methods of carrying out quality control.

2 Quality assurance occurs both during and after the event, and is concerned with trying to stop faults from happening in the first place. Quality assurance is concerned to make sure that products are produced to predetermined standards. The aim is to produce with 'zero defects'.

Quality assurance is the responsibility of the workforce, working in cells or teams, rather than an inspector (although inspection will take place). Quality standards should be maintained by following steps set out in a QA system.

3 Total Quality Management goes beyond quality assurance. It is concerned with creating a quality culture, so that every employee will seek to delight customers. The customer is at the centre of the production process.

Companies like Marks and Spencer and Sainsbury's have been following this policy for a long time. It

involves providing customers with what they want, when they want it and how they want it. It involves moving with changing customer requirements and fashions to design products and services which meet and exceed their requirements. Delighted customers will pass the message on to their friends.

Customer preferences will constantly change – the organisation therefore has to provide new ways of responding to changing tastes, needs and wants. For example, the second edition of this book has been produced even though the first was highly successful. It is recognised that in the second half of the 1990s students want a book which closely follows the performance criteria and range for GNVQ Advanced, and provides even newer case studies.

Evidence collection point

Use a desktop publishing package to illustrate ways in which a particular organisation or product creates value added through total quality management.

You can use the work you produce in this activity to provide evidence of Core Skills of Information Technology and Communication.

Ensuring the best relationship between costs of inputs and value of final product (productivity)

Productivity can be looked at as the relationship between costs or inputs (e.g. people marketing, materials, finance, distribution) and the revenue from outputs (e.g. income from sales, repeat sales, continuity of sales).

A productive system can be thought of as a whole economy or simply a group of people working together. The productivity of the system is the amount of output that can be produced from a given set of inputs:

$$\text{Productivity} = \frac{\text{Output}}{\text{Input}}$$

The productivity ratio therefore measures how efficient a system is in converting inputs of resources into useful outputs.

Increases in productivity can be gained by:

- output increasing while input remains the same
- output increasing while input increases at a slower rate
- output staying the same while input decreases
- output falling while input falls at a faster rate.

Measuring the productivity of labour

If we wanted to find out how productive the employees in a food processing plant were, we could do so by studying the following ratio:

$$\text{Productivity} = \frac{\text{Number of units of goods produced per month}}{\text{Average number of people employed per month}}$$

Multifactor productivity ratios

Outputs are not produced by labour alone. We also need to take account of machinery and raw materials. A multifactor productivity ratio like the one shown below takes into account other inputs:

$$\text{Productivity} = \frac{\text{Output}}{\text{Labour} + \text{materials} + \text{fixed assets}}$$

In the real world the most common calculation made is for labour productivity. This is because labour is the most commonly used factor of production. Industries that use a great deal of labour are said to be labour-intensive.

Today, however, with the introduction of new technology, capital is becoming more and more intensive. Many new industries are employing more and more capital – that is, they are becoming increasingly capital-intensive. Value can be added to products by switching to high-tech capital equipment which is far more productive than traditional methods. High outputs can be produced at much lower unit costs.

Evidence collection point

What do the pie-charts in Figure 15.4 tell us about the changing importance of labour in manufacturing? What do these charts suggest about the way in which value is currently being added through production processes?

Measuring productivity over time

It is important to be able to monitor productivity trends over a time period to see whether an organisation is becoming more efficient or less efficient. Clearly, if a company increases the training of its workforce, increases the automation of its plant, or successfully reorganises the production process, it will expect to see an increasing productivity ratio. This can be tracked over time. Value is thus added through increasing productivity because revenues can be added to at a quicker rate than costs rise.

Task

Productivity figures for different industries appear from time to time in national newspapers, and are available on request from the Department of Employment. Study the productivity figures for a particular firm or industry and observe how these vary over time. Try to give reasons for the changes. Show which industries are making the biggest value added contributions to the national economy.

Calculations which you do for this task can be used to provide evidence of Core Skills in Application of Number.

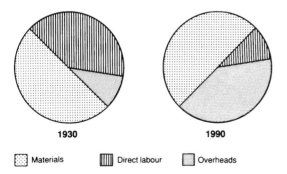

1930   1990

Materials   Direct labour   Overheads

Figure 15.4 The breakdown of manufacturing costs

Changes over time can also be measured by means of an index (see Chapter 3):

$$\text{Productivity index} = \frac{\text{Productivity ratio in time period}}{\text{Productivity ratio in base year}} \times 100$$

Useful comparisons can then be made between firms in the same industry, and between the economic systems in different countries.

Measuring productivity of inputs by value

As we have already seen, it is possible to measure productivity by value. For example, we can use a multifactor measure of productivity:

$$\text{Productivity} = \frac{\text{Sales revenue}}{\text{Labour + materials + overheads}}$$

This can be broken down further to measure the productivity of particular inputs:

$$\text{Labour productivity} = \frac{\text{Sales revenue}}{\text{Wages}}$$

$$\text{Capital productivity} = \frac{\text{Sales revenue}}{\text{Value of capital items}}$$

$$\text{Materials productivity} = \frac{\text{Sales revenue}}{\text{Value of materials used}}$$

Productivity of the national economy

We could try to measure the productivity of the national economic system in a similar way, by using the formula:

$$\text{Productivity} = \frac{\text{Total national output}}{\text{Land + labour + capital}}$$

However, this would be almost impossible to measure because it would be very difficult to add together the factors of land, labour and capital. Economists therefore use a quantity known as the gross national product (GNP). This involves measuring the outputs of each of the industrial sectors that make up the economy – manufacturing, energy and water, agriculture, forestry and fishing, service, construction, etc.

The most productive system (i.e. the one in which most value is added) will be the one which best combines factors of production. High productivity involves the skilled combination of resources, through efficient planning systems, through using effective resources, by developing resources (e.g. through training), etc.

Just-in-time production

Just-in-time (JIT) manufacturing is one of the strengths of the Japanese production system and is one which has enabled Japan to have a highly productive economy.

Just-in-time production is a very simple idea:

1 Finished goods are produced just in time for them to be sold, rather than weeks or months ahead.
2 The parts that go into a finished product arrive just in time to be put together to make the final product, rather than being stored (at some cost) in a warehouse.

The idea is to run a company with the smallest possible levels of stock and work-in-progress. Clearly this needs careful planning.

■ All sources of uncertainty must be removed from the manufacturing process. There must be absolute reliability of production targets, supplies, and levels of output achieved.
■ The time to set up machines must be reduced to a minimum so that components and finished products can be produced in small batches as and when required.
■ Bottlenecks must be eliminated.

Using a JIT system requires a complete reorganisation of the traditional factory. Factories have traditionally been organised into 'shops', each working at a particular stage in producing a final product. With a JIT system the factory is reorganised so that people are grouped together around the products they produce. The may need to have access to a family of machines (e.g. a lathe, a milling machine, a drill and a grinder), as in Figure 15.5.

A recent survey has shown that two-thirds of Western manufacturing companies are trying to use JIT. However, the ability to make JIT successful may depend on the organisation and environment in which the idea is applied.

Evidence collection point

In Japan, just-in-time production is widely used by business organisations. However, in that country the business environment has the following characteristics:

■ There is lifetime employment in many large corporations, so that labour mobility between companies is limited.

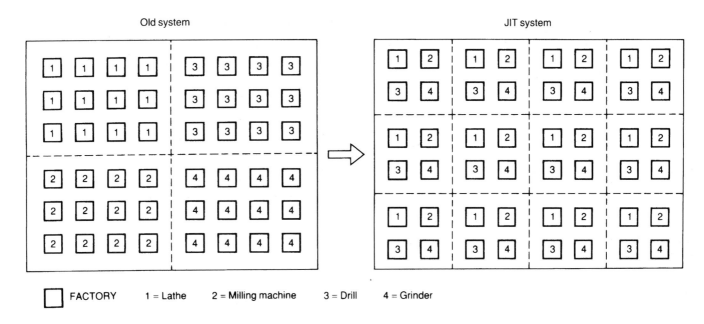

Old system   JIT system

☐ FACTORY   1 = Lathe   2 = Milling machine   3 = Drill   4 = Grinder

Figure 15.5 Adopting the JIT system

- Unions are based around companies and not on trades or occupations.
- JIT relationships between firms and their suppliers have built up over a long period.

1 How many of the above apply in British companies?
2 Which would be easy for British companies to adopt and which would be more difficult?
3 What factors are likely to influence the success of British companies in adopting JIT practices?
4 List six main recommendations that you would make to a company developing JIT practices in this country.

Using human resources effectively

Human resource management has been at a premium in recent years. Most organisations have realised that the best way of creating value added is through people. By involving people in decision-making processes and encouraging them to take the initiative, organisations have been able to reap tremendous productivity advances.

Why business aims to add value

To meet international competition

World trade is dominated by huge trading blocs of countries. In the mid-1990s there are three huge exporting blocs accounting for a large proportion of world trade. These blocs are East Asia and the Pacific, NAFTA (the North American Free Trade Area) and the European Union.

In 1994 the total of world exports was worth $3376bn. The major exporters were:

USA	$398bn
European Union	$375bn
Japan	$314bn
Other East Asian and Pacific States	$251bn

If we look at the growth of exports in recent years we can immediately see the importance of the East Asian and Pacific countries in contributing to this growth. For example, at the start of the 1990s the increase in the volume of exports was:

East Asia and Pacific	10.2%
USA	4.0%
Japan	4.0%
European Union	4.4%
World	4.1%

In the 1990s there has been a flood of capital and investment to China, South-East Asia and parts of Latin America, fuelled by the possibilities of growth in these regions. Many Asian countries enjoy annual growth rates in excess of 10 per cent. It is understandable that companies increasingly want to locate production facilities in or near these countries.

The development of Asian economies presents both a threat and a challenge. Clearly, there are many areas

397

of manufacture – e.g. computers, electronics, televisions and cars – where Asian economies can produce in large quantities and at low costs using automated technology.

However, there are also considerable benefits to be gained from the expansion of these markets for British exporters. In recent times British exporters have been doing much better in competitive markets than in the past, often by employing total quality and just-in-time systems.

In addition, the Single Market process developing in Europe since 1992 has made it easier for British companies to sell on the European continent by forcing them to change the technical standards to which they worked. The German DIN standard became the norm after 1992. UK companies cursed as they adjusted to it – but now they are reaping the rewards by selling into our biggest market in Europe.

Adding value effectively is an essential ingredient of international competitiveness. If we fail to increase the value we add to products at the same rate as our rivals, then our products will become less desirable. There will always be new rivals who want to muscle in on market opportunities.

To meet customer requirements

Business people frequently refer to the 3Cs as forming the basic 'facts of life' of business success. These three Cs are costs, competitiveness and customers (see Figure 15.6).

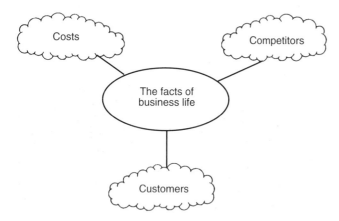

Figure 15.6 The facts of business life

Only by keeping costs down are you able to offer goods and services at acceptable prices. Only by matching or beating the competition will you be able to make your offers better than those of rivals. And only by making sure that your offer is the one that customers are looking for will you be able to sell a winning product.

Once again we return to the basic requirement of business to be in tune with the customer. Today the emphasis needs to be on creating those added values for which the customer signals a preference.

'Value' is a blend of price and benefits. Both are critical. Unless the price is right, the best combination of desirable benefits will not be considered good value by the customer. Nor, in the long term, will the customer think it good value if the benefits are added irresponsibly – at the cost of the environment, for instance. And the customer's decision is final.

The difficulty is determining which benefits people want and then producing them at an acceptable price and in an environmentally acceptable way.

Benefits offered by a product or service include:

- availability
- ease of use
- technical assistance and advice
- performance consistent with specification (i.e. does it do what it says it will do?)
- superiority over competitors
- accountability – if things go wrong, the manufacturer will put them right
- courtesy and helpfulness of staff
- attractive, appropriate and efficient design and packaging
- image – a category that covers a great many benefits, including 'peace of mind' (you can trust the company), 'empathy' (this company understands my needs) and 'lifestyle' (this product fits my idea of myself or my company).

The overall value of a product is a trade-off between one or more of these benefits and the price. An efficient supplier will be continually testing various combinations of benefits and price to make sure that the customer is satisfied with the value offered.

The concept of added value is a part of a larger concept – 'conformity with requirements' or 'fitness for purpose'.

Edward de Bono in his significant book *Surpetition* argues that modern businesses need to go beyond competition. It is no good just checking out the competition to be ahead of them – instead, you need to give yourself an uncatchable advantage through 'surpetition' i.e. continuously improving your own position in order to provide the range of benefits that best meets the needs of consumers.

Consumers do not simply seek a single benefit from a product, they seek a whole cluster of benefits. A car is not simply something that you drive around in. In addition it is something that needs to be parked, to represent the consumer's lifestyle, to provide safety, to be compatible with a clean environment, to be able to carry the shopping. The producer therefore needs to be constantly seeking ways of adding value to products to ensure that the product provides the complete set of benefits that are required at any one time.

For example, in producing this book we have set out to produce a product that goes beyond simply being competitive – we are looking for surpetition. This edition of the book has added value to the first edition, by covering the Range set out for GNVQ in Business, by setting out appropriate Evidence Collection Points to enable you to build up an effective portfolio, by providing a student-friendly introduction to help you to familiarise yourself with the terminology of GNVQs, by being written in student-friendly language, by the use of clear diagrams, by the use of colour and clear icons, by the use of the most recent case studies, by identifying opportunities for developing Core Skills, etc. Surpetition involves transforming products that are better than the competition to products that anticipate the full set of benefits required by consumers.

Evidence collection point

Identify a product that provides a number of important benefits which are required by consumers. To what extent do those benefits match or exceed those offered by the competition? If the organisation was seeking surpetition, how else could it add value to the product to ensure that it provides the full set of benefits required by consumers?

To improve profit

We have emphasised the importance of profit in business many times in this text. Without profit an organisation is unable to grow, or to develop new ways of adding value to products in order to meet ongoing consumer requirements.

Organisations need to be profitable if they are to make use of new technologies, modernise themselves, and to take the sorts of commercial risks which are necessary for ongoing development of the organisation and the wider community.

In business there is a common saying that profits will follow market share. Market share will be created by providing attractive offers to consumers, i.e. by adding value to products over and above those offered by alternatives. In a dynamic business environment it is therefore essential to add value to goods and services in order to improve profit margins.

Evidence collection point

Follow the financial reports in a quality newspaper in order to identify organisations which have made increases in profits in recent times. To what extent can these profit improvements be attributed to ways in which these organisations have recently added value to their products?

To survive and grow

Organisations operate in many and varied circumstances. Some operate in expanding markets with plentiful opportunities. Others exist in contracting markets. However, whatever market environment an organisation operates in, its best chance of success will rest in its ability to create benefits and to add value to products.

In shrinking markets you will see the 'survival of the fittest'. Often this will be because the organisation has identified new benefits which will continue to attract customers, whereas rival producers have stuck to making 'old-fashioned' offers. Visit any farming area and you will notice that while many farms

which tried to maintain traditional patterns of agriculture have disappeared, there will be farmers who have adopted more innovative practices who have survived and prospered. This does not mean that the organisation abandons all of its previous practices; instead, it develops an effective combination of the old and the new.

Visit your local High Street and you will still find amongst all the new modern multiples some family businesses that have been in trade for generations. However, these businesses will have changed with the times. They will have sought ways of adding value which enable them to survive and in some cases to grow.

Evidence collection point

Identify two or three business organisations in your area which have survived and perhaps grown by providing new benefits in order to add value to the goods or services that they offer. To what extent have they retained old ways of creating benefits, and to what extent have they blended in new ways of adding value?

Examples of factors which can contribute to changes in production

Production needs to be a dynamic ingredient in the creation of value. With each passing year we are experiencing quicker and more widespread advances in production techniques. Some of these changes are quite breathtaking, making it difficult to anticipate the shape of future production. Those people involved in making decisions about the purchase of new automated production technologies must build into their calculations shorter and shorter time-spans. Today's new supercomputer or automatic machine may quickly become tomorrow's dinosaur.

In this section we will therefore identify some important factors contributing to changes in production.

Price

All around us we see new technologies coming into wider use to replace older ones. Very quickly we see previous technologies become old-fashioned.

Case study – The development of optical fibres

In the past, copper cables were the main medium for communication transmission, e.g. for telephones. Nowadays we have optical fibres, which are made of thin threads of glass through which light can be beamed from one end of the fibre to the other. Not only can text and speech be sent, we can now also transmit pictures and images. Instead of the voice-only telephone we will soon all be buying picture and image phones.

Optical fibres have a number of important advantages:

- They take up less space than copper cables.
- They can carry far more. For example, 16 fibres can carry all trans-Atlantic communications.
- They are relatively cheap to maintain and install.

1 How will the development of optical fibre communication alter the ways in which people are able to communicate?
2 What will be the likely impact on the cost of communications?

In the marketplace the price of products can and frequently does change. It is not just end-product prices that change, but also intermediate product prices such as raw materials and energy sources. The cost of producing products falls and rises with new developments.

Price acts as a signal to channel resources into different lines of production.

When new products are developed and consumers signal their preferences for these products, then producers will set out to make them.

When the first ballpoint pen was developed it was very expensive. However, as it became increasingly popular it became possible to mass-produce. Originally there was a single firm producing ballpoint pens – soon there were several. Prices continued to tumble. Today there are many manufacturers of ballpoint pens and their prices are very low (although there are many varieties of ballpoint pens offering different benefits, and at different prices). The basic functional ballpoint pen is very cheap.

In the late 1980s and early 1990s CD players came onto the market. Originally they were quite expensive. Today, most families have CD players and their prices have continued to fall. As the price of products fall, producers need to seek ways of producing these products at an increasingly low cost, e.g. by using the most up-to-date technology for mass production.

Evidence collection point

Identify a product which has needed to be produced in different ways as a result of a fall in the price of that product on the market. Explain how and why the price of the product has fallen. Explain how and why the techniques for producing that product have altered.

Technology

Here we will look at ways in which technology has contributed to changes in production in particular through the development of:

- Management information systems
- Automation
- Robotics
- Computer-aided design
- Computer-aided manufacturing

Technology is concerned with applying practical and mechanical knowledge and understanding to the world of business and industry. This knowledge is continually being developed through research and development. It is therefore essential to create the conditions which enable these developments to be put to use.

At any one time there are some products that are growing and some that are in decline. Some new products are being researched and others are in a period of infancy or growth.

There are various ways of maintaining the sales of products (Figure 15.7). One way is to introduce a new product as the existing one becomes obsolete, so that there are overlapping cycles. This is a common practice with motor vehicles. A second alternative is to modify the existing product in order to extend its life-cycle. This is the case with many modern desktop computers – improved models with more memory, a wider range of applications and greater speed continually update old models. A third option is to change the production technology itself to make the product more competitive – for example, by employing better production technology in the textile industry.

In fact most business organisations today employ a mixture of these three ways of extending product life-cycles.

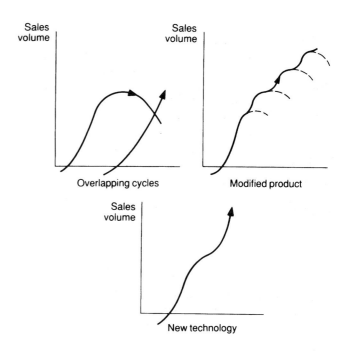

Figure 15.7 Three ways of extending product life-cycles

In modern competitive markets it is essential for businesses to be able to innovate. Freeman, in *The Economics of Industrial Innovation,* argued that for a large business organisation, 'not to innovate is to die'. Indeed, such organisations are trapped on an 'innovation treadmill'. Inevitably, therefore, employees who work for these organisations need to be prepared to adjust to new styles of operation and management.

As industries become more mature the emphasis on change is placed on the processes of production as opposed to the products themselves. In their early days, new products can set their markets alight with their flair and product originality. As time passes, other businesses will copy them, so that if companies want to remain as market leaders they will need to rethink their methods (Figure 15.8).

Two major trends have become noticeable in the production process in recent years. The first is increasing specialisation, so that the processes can be split into many separate operations. The second is increasing standardisation of these separate operations so that they can be done by semi-skilled and unskilled labour. This is particularly so during the mature phase of a product's life-cycle.

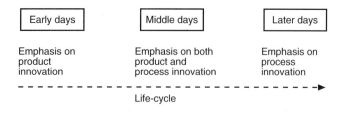

Figure 15.8 Moving the emphasis of innovation

Many of the declining industries are therefore characterised by more old-fashioned working practices, lower-paid employees and resistance to change.

Hirsch produced an interesting picture to show the relative importance of different factors of production during the life-cycles of products. This is presented as Figure 15.9.

Life-cycle phase			Factors of production
NEW	GROWTH	MATURITY	
2	3	1	Management
3	2	1	Scientific and engineering know how
1	2	3	Semi-skilled and unskilled labour
3	2	1	External economies
1	2=	2=	Capital

Figure 15.9 Relative importance of factors of production at different stages of the product life-cycle

It is important to remember that different products have different production methods. Also, although many modern products are made in automated plant, this does not necessarily mean that they have to be produced on a large scale. Traditional automation is geared to high-volume standardised production, but newer flexible manufacturing systems are quite different.

With flexible manufacturing, different products can be produced on the same line. Flexible manufacturing means that economies can be achieved for both large-scale and small-scale production. A flexible automation system can turn out a small batch or even a single copy of a product as efficiently as a line which is geared to producing a million identical items.

Management information systems (MIS)

A management information system (MIS) is a large, usually computerised, databank to which managers have access. It is made up of number of files consisting of key data which are regularly updated.

Armed with such information, managers are able to keep up-to-date and on top of all current developments in the business environment and in business activities. Managers are able to have a much clearer understanding of how businesses are developing on an ongoing basis and to have a clearer appreciation of the implications of decisions that they might make.

A criticism of such systems in the past was that, while the data was extensive, it was not necessarily constructed in the way that best suited the user. The organisation would put a lot of information into the system without thinking clearly about how it would be extracted. A newer approach involves manager-operated computers which are 'user-friendly' and with data that is 'needs-driven'. Managers can use the system to create their own models which are then built into the management system. This helps managers to think about the decisions that they are making.

For example, a management information system for a school or college might include information about current student numbers, and the money received from various sources for each student. Managers should then be able to manipulate the 'models' built into the system to project the likely impact of increasing recruitment of student numbers in the coming year on future budgets for the next few years. Managers will also be able to check on the implications for staffing and courses in the college.

Evidence collection point

You have been given the task of designing a management information system for your school or college. What sort of data would be most useful for inclusion in this MIS? What sorts of operations would managers most like to be able to perform with this data?

Automation

Mechanisation involves the use of machinery. The machine is, however, controlled directly by the operator.

Automation, on the other hand, involves the creation of a control unit to control the machine. Instructions are fed into the control unit, which then controls operations.

Machines are at work in our homes. Examples of machines controlled directly by the operator include food mixers, hair dryers and vacuum cleaners. Automatic machines, however, are under automatic control. These machines are able to control themselves once they have been fed instructions. Examples include washing machines, central heating systems and video recorders (Figure 15.10).

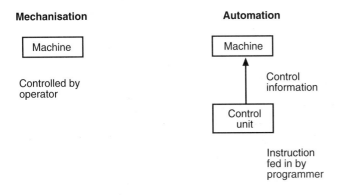

Figure 15.10 The difference between mechanisation and automation

An automatic machine needs to have some method of controlling itself. It must be able to sense and measure when and when not to take action. An example of the way this operates is the central-heating system of a house. Generally this system will be triggered by one of two mechanisms – the timer, or the thermostat. The system can be programmed to switch on and off at set times, or to come on whenever the temperature in a building falls below a certain level.

Today many industrial and commercial processes are automated, and clearly this facilitates high levels of production at low unit costs. Organisations that fail to automate their processes will be at substantial cost disadvantages.

Case study – Automation in a modern brewery

In the UK today the beer and lager market is dominated by a few large breweries. These firms are able to produce high outputs at a low average cost per unit. The brewing process is controlled by a central computer which checks that the mixing of ingredients has taken place correctly and takes regular readings on temperatures and fermentation.

Bottles returned from public houses and other outlets are on pallets containing several crates of bottles. Each crate is lifted off the pallet automatically and a machine picks up the bottles to pass them down a line into a washing machine. The bottles are then checked for faults by an electronic device that examines the structure of the bottle.

The bottles are automatically filled and an electronic eye checks that the contents reach a certain level in the bottle. The machine line will then label and cap the bottles.

They are placed in crates and the crates are automatically placed on a pallet, which is stacked on an out-going lorry.

The whole process is predesigned to eliminate the need for labour in the main line of production. Labour is only required to supervise the computer, maintain the machinery and keep an eye on it in case it breaks down.

1 Why is the beer and lager market suitable for mass production?
2 What other production lines can you think of that are suitable for automated production?
3 What types of production might be unsuitable for automation?
4 Who benefits from automation?
5 Who loses out as a result of automation?

The word 'control' means the ability to direct or restrain. A controller carries out a function automatically. For example, in a washing machine, once a programme has been set the controller takes over, switching the heater on and off, regulating the water supply and outlet, and switching the motor that rotates the drum (Figure 15.11).

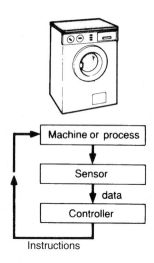

Figure 15.11 Basic features of control

Evidence collection point

Identify a recently automated process either at home or in a workplace that you are familiar with. Explain how this process has enabled production to take place more effectively.

Robotics

Robots are really an application of automatic control. They are of special benefit for jobs that are repetitive and where human manipulative skills are not required. Another application is in dangerous or unpleasant work areas.

Robots vary in the method of programming. Some are programmed by keying in instructions, but this is laborious and liable to error. In other cases the robot can learn to copy movements carried out by a human operator. (It is ironic that the operator teaching the robot may be the person to be replaced by it!) As robots become more 'intelligent' they increasingly also have some system for checking progress (e.g. an electronic eye or camera).

The benefits of using robots are therefore:

■ people can be replaced by robots in mundane jobs where human intelligence is not required (e.g. routine assembly work)
■ robots can be used where working conditions are difficult or dangerous (materials may be heavy,

hot or radioactive, or deep underground or under water).

The disadvantages of using robots are:

■ further erosion of craft skills may result
■ greater levels of capital investment increase the pressure for shift working
■ a new physical danger is introduced into the workplace – fatalities have already occurred as a result of using robots at work.

Computer-aided design (CAD)

Thirty years ago designers spent a lot of time at drawing boards. The skills brought to the job included:

■ creativity (thinking up ideas, styling, etc.)
■ analysis (calculating strengths, quantities, etc.)
■ mechanical drawing (putting the ideas on paper).

Although the central role of the designer was to carry out creative and analytical work, much of the time was spent on drawing and redrawing. Today, with the development of sophisticated computers, it is possible to use a computer screen instead of a drawing board. This saves considerable time and effort.

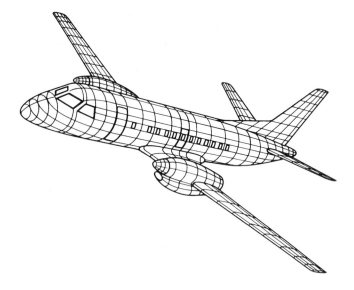

A designer employing a CAD program uses a keyboard (or mouse), a screen and a graphics pad. The designer is able to program the computer to perform many quick calculations of angles, volumes, dimensions, etc.

Having drafted the design, the designer can view the item on the screen as if from different positions, and view it as a solid object instead of just a series of lines. The computer can then be asked to calculate all the important features of the design, and to show how these change when, for example, one dimension is altered.

CAD in industry has revolutionised almost every area of industrial design, from wedding dresses to supertankers.

Evidence collection point

If possible make use of a CAD package available in your school or college to draw some simple examples of robot arms that could be used to lift items on and off a production line. The robot arms should not be complex mechanical drawings. They should show simple structures that can be used for grabbing an item, moving it up and down, left and right.

The evidence you collect while doing this activity could be included in your portfolio of evidence to show your capability in the Core Skill of Information Technology.

Computer-aided manufacturing (CAM)

Over recent years many developments have taken place in production industries. As well as computer-aided design (CAD), developments have taken place in machine tools. Many are now controlled numerically by a computer (computer numerical control – CNC).

Other developments have taken place in robotics. With CADCAM (computer-aided design/computer-aided manufacturing), data from the CAD system is used to drive machines, making the CAD system part of the manufacturing process. With CAM, computers play a key role in organising and supervising the manufacturing process, ensuring that production is carried out according to specified standards.

Computers may be able to check standards, alter production runs and processes and carry out other operations far quicker and with a much greater degree of accuracy than human operators. Computer-aided manufacturing has been one of the driving forces behind 'just-in-time' manufacturing because of its high level of quality control.

There are three major reasons which businesses usually cite when investing in information technology. These are:

- to achieve improvements in productivity
- to achieve a competitive advantage

- to improve the flexibility of the organisation so that it can respond more readily to changes in the marketplace.

For example, when British Telecom first introduced digital telephone exchanges (a long time ago), a frequently quoted joke was that the new exchanges only needed a man and a dog to run them: the man was needed to feed the dog and the dog to keep the man away from the equipment.

Today we are seeing many large organisations increase their investments in information technology in order to speed up operations, to cut out waste, and to improve accuracy and quality control while reducing costs. Particular examples are banking and insurance operations.

Of course, the ability of an organisation to raise productivity depends on the careful application of IT to create effective solutions.

Information technology can be used by organisations to give it a competitive advantage, by using improved systems to carry out existing operations. For example, airlines can adopt an electronic booking system which is accessible to all travel agents. Of course the reality is that all its rivals will purchase and operate similar systems. However, the point is that the business that stays still while all its rivals are moving forward will quickly encounter problems.

Finally, organisations can become more responsive to customers by adopting IT systems. For example, the financial services industry has been revolutionised by IT, allowing personalised banking whereby consumers can be provided with on-line information about the current state of their accounts, the availability and cost of new financial services, etc.

Evidence collection point

Identify an organisation in your locality which uses computer-aided manufacturing. Investigate and explain how computer-aided manufacturing has benefited this organisation.

Case study – Artificial intelligence

In the 1970s and 1980s great things were expected of the development of artificial intelligence (AI) through computers. It was hoped that their tremendous ability to calculate would enable them to 'think' at a higher level than mere mortals. The aim was to produce a machine able to analyse data and reason for itself. It was hoped that the knowledge of an expert could be recreated within a machine using a system of rules and facts.

Why has AI failed to live up to expectations? One of the reasons is that researchers underestimated how difficult it was to encode expert knowledge and ordinary wisdom into rules. They also failed to recognise how time-intensive and expensive it would be to keep such devices up-to-date, and how people are reluctant to rely solely on a machine for important answers. Although such expert systems are successful in specialised fields of engineering and finance, forecasts that we would all be using them in everyday life have never come true.

Now, in the mid-1990s, rather than trying to out-perform human beings in problem-solving skills, there are signs that AI applications are earning their keep by processing routine tasks, enabling people to concentrate on more demanding work.

Typical of the new approach is work at the Veterans Medical Centre in Dallas on producing a cost-effective assistant for doctors in specialist clinics. The aim is not to increase expertise but to cut costs and time. A recent device developed by the hospital is called Epileptologist Assistant, and is used by nurses in a follow-up clinic to question epileptic patients before their examination by a doctor.

A doctor can spend 60–80% of his or her time on relatively trivial matters. About 20% of the time is spent on interesting and exciting cases, and just 1% on treatment that needs special research or consultation with a colleague. Rather than developing an expert system to concentrate on that 1% (the original idea of developing an expert system), it is possible to provide the best assistance to manage the 60–80% of routine work.

The 'Assistant' prompts the nurse to ask between 30 and 50 set questions from a choice of 300. Each line of questioning is dictated by more than 200 rules, and at the end the program delivers a full report of patient responses as well as suggesting changes in treatment which the doctor can adopt or alter during consultation.

1 What was the original view of the value of expert systems?
2 What is the new view of the value of artificial intelligence highlighted above?
3 What other areas of organisational life could benefit from the use of AI?
4 Think of familiar situations in which AI could be used routinely. What would be the chief benefits resulting from its implementation in these cases?

Contracting-out

A major change in production that has taken place during the 1980s and 1990s has been in the growth of contracting-out.

Before this time there was a tendency for organisation to integrate and to expand. The aim of integration was for an organisation to take control of all stages of the production of a product. For example, the jeans manufacturer would want to control both the retail outlets that sold jeans and the cloth manufacturers that produced the denim and other cloths used in production (Figure 15.12).

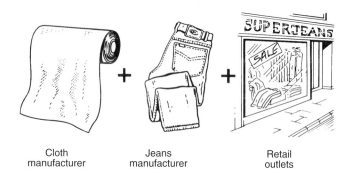

Cloth manufacturer · Jeans manufacturer · Retail outlets

Figure 15.12 An example of backward and forward integration

There were obvious advantages to this integration in that the organisation took total control over standards. It was in charge of all operations, and all activities were focused around the needs of the organisation. It was not just the manufacturing side that would be controlled by the organisation, it was all the services involved in running the business as well – office administration, public relations, advertising, selling, etc.

Today the emphasis is far more on the leaner and fitter organisation. Manufacturing and service activities are frequently contracted-out to independent suppliers. Organisations concentrate on their core strengths and use contractors to do the rest.

For example, oil companies in the early 1980s typically employed their own people on oil rigs. Today they award contracts to independent firms to staff the rigs. Today car manufacturers may buy in their raw materials and components from many different suppliers, setting out tight contractual schedules for quality and performance.

The emphasis is on an organisation focusing on its core strengths and contracting-out non-core production and services to independent organisations. Smaller core organisations are much easier to manage and control. They can also impose very tight standards on suppliers (Figure 15.13).

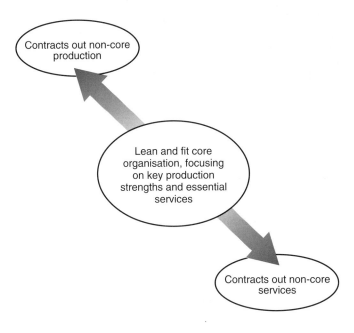

Figure 15.13 Contracting out non-core production and services

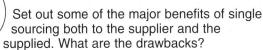

Evidence collection point

Identify an organisation which contracts out a lot of its production activities and services. Explain how and why the organisation contracts out these activities and services.

Single sourcing

A common feature of modern production is that of single sourcing, i.e. obtaining supplies from a single supplier. Whilst this trend is associated with modern business practice it is by no means new.

Marks and Spencer, for example, typically contracts work out to single sources: recipe dishes in an M&S store may all come from a single supplier, e.g. Fenland Foods in Grantham; all of a particular range of underwear might come from a particular supplier in Leicestershire, etc. These suppliers are responsible

for developing new products for the Marks and Spencer range, which will be purchased by M&S buyers. M&S is thus able to insist on the very highest quality standards.

M&S knows that products will be produced to a consistent standard to meet their requirements. However, it will be the supplying organisation that is responsible for all the logistics of getting the goods to where M&S wants them.

Fenland Foods will want the M&S order because it will provide them with a steady livelihood, and it makes more sense to supply one contract rather than several. M&S will insist that Fenland work for them only. There will be an understanding that if supplies fall in standard then the contract will be terminated.

Single sourcing is an important ingredient of just-in-time manufacture. Companies like M&S will not need to hold extensive stocks because they have a guarantee from their suppliers to provide new stocks 'just in time'. Modern Japanese car manufacturing is based on a very similar system.

Evidence collection point

Set out some of the major benefits of single sourcing both to the supplier and the supplied. What are the drawbacks?

Labour flexiblity

This term is used to describe a number of aspects of employment, including:

- flexible contracts of employment
- wage or earning flexibility
- subcontracting and outworking
- ability of employees to move from one job to another
- functional flexibility and the breakdown of job demarcations
- flexibility in the place of work
- numerical flexibility
- working-time flexibility.

Flexible contracts

One way in which firms achieve greater flexibility is by increasing the use of temporary and part-time contracts, thus reducing job security and reducing the number of employees employed permanently and full-time.

Subcontracting and out-working

Some organisations have chosen not to take responsibility for certain activities which were previously carried out internally, e.g. cleaning services and advertising. In the public sector many of the services traditionally provided by Local Authority employees have been contracted out, e.g. street cleaning.

Ability of employees to move from one job to another

Organisations can gain flexibility within their labour force by having the option of moving employees to different jobs and geographical areas according to changing economic conditions.

Functional flexibility

This relates to the reduction of job demarcations between occupations in order to allow the more flexible use of labour. Peter Wickens, in a widely read book *The Road to Nissan,* quotes from a company agreement with the trade union the AEU:

> To ensure the fullest use of facilities and manpower, there will be complete flexibility and mobility of employees. To ensure such flexibility and change, employees will undertake training for all work as required by the Company.

In the Japanese motor industry many assembly workers, for example, handle routine preventative maintenance and minor breakdowns and will assist the maintenance staff when they arrive. Instead of having a specialist skill, then, the implication is that people will need to acquire a whole range of skills to allow them to work productively across many tasks.

Flexibility in the workplace

Increasingly, large numbers of people are working away from the traditional workplace, e.g. home-workers working from their own homes.

Numerical flexibility

The ability of firms to adjust the number of workers or the number of hours worked in line with changes in the level of demand for their goods and services is referred to as numerical flexibility. Typically firms achieve numerical flexiblity through the use of part-time, temporary and self-employed (subcontract) workers.

Working-time flexibility

This relates to changes in the number and timing of hours worked from week to week or day to day, through overtime, short-time working, annual hours contracts and flexitime (start and finish times vary within a broad band).

 Evidence collection point

Using evidence from a workplace with which you are familiar, show how increased labour flexibility has affected production.

Legislation

There are many thousands of laws in force. Many of these have implications for production. You are not expected to have a detailed knowledge of them but you should be able to show how laws, and changes in laws, can affect production.

An obvious example is Sunday trading. Now that retail outlets are allowed to operate on Sundays this means that large retailers have to adapt their systems to operating seven days a week. There are clear implications for the delivery of goods and the timing of stock changes on the shelves. There are also implications for the recruitment of labour.

Laws such as the Deposit of Poisonous Wastes Act, the Clean Air Act and the Pollution of Rivers Act set standards for emissions into the air, sea, rivers and other natural depositories. Organisations need to comply with these laws or face heavy fines and other penalties. The emphasis is on forcing polluters to clean up their processes.

Standards have been set for the emissions of poisonous and harmful substances from car and lorry exhausts. Recent checks have shown that the worst polluters are usually business users. In 1995 vehicles with the worst exhaust emissions were taxis; 38% of those stopped had illegal levels. Light vans were next, with 15% of those stopped having illegal exhaust emissions.

Legislation has the impact of forcing businesses to change their activities to comply with the law. The taxi firm that creates unacceptable pollution will be faced with the prospect of its vehicles being banned from the road, and perhaps a heavy fine.

Evidence collection point

Identify ways in which a particular piece of legislation, e.g. the Clean Air Act or the Pollution of Rivers Act, affects the way a business organisation carries out its production.

Competition

Competition is one of the most important factors contributing to changes in production. For example, in the competition between rival supermarket chains in the past, supermarkets were able to gain a competitive advantage by using automatic scanning devices known as Electronic Point of Sale (EPOS).

Increasingly, all supermarket chains changed the way they operated to take advantage of the resulting cost advantages.

They then sought to secure other competitive advantages, e.g. by offering a range of environmentally friendly products.

In recent times we have seen Tesco's seek further competitive advantage by ensuring that customers never have to wait for more than a very short time at check-outs. And of course the latest development has been the move towards the abolition of the check-out counter. Assuming that over the next few years some supermarkets replace staffed check-outs with do-it-yourself versions, we can expect all competing chains to come into line with this innovation.

Case study – Technological advance at Rover

The Rover Group is at the forefront of the technology of rapid prototyping in this country. Rapid prototyping allows designers to turn 3D computer drawings swiftly into solid models.

The company is typically cutting development time by 60–90% and costs by 40–70%.

For example, designing a heater case by the traditional route costs £200 000; using rapid prototyping this has been cut to £50 000 and can be completed in one-third of the time.

Rapid prototyping systems work using a layering technique. Special software cuts a computer-aided design of a component into slices and feeds the data for each layer into the rapid prototyping machine.

The most common technique used is called stereolithography. The data describing each slice controls a laser which 'draws' the slice on a layer of photosensitive resin that is immediately solidified by the laser. The slice is then lowered into a bath of resin and the next layer is built on top; and so on until the model is completed.

1 What are the main benefits of such technological advances:
   a to producers
   b to consumers
   c to the wider economy?
2 How are competitors likely to react to the use of such advances by Rover?
3 Why are Rover unlikely to rest on their laurels in using this new advance?

Quality standards

Total quality management is the name given to a process of structured good management practices which result in measurable continuous quality improvement. It is this ongoing process of quality improvement which contributes to changes in production.

The process, as we have seen, requires clear identification of customers and their needs, and development of products and services that conform with the customers' requirements and are 'fit for the purpose'.

'Fit for the purpose' is the key: a Rolls-Royce is a quality vehicle for use at a wedding; a Land-Rover is a quality vehicle for rough terrain. They are very different, but both meet their respective customers' needs.

TQM is a management discipline that focuses on requirements and responds with products which are defect-free for a particular use.

This involves three stages:

■ *Stage 1 Quality planning*
  This is the process of identifying customers, defining their needs or requirements and designing products and services to meet them.
■ *Stage 2 Quality control*
  This is the process of measuring, comparing and correcting to make sure that products and services are designed and made to meet requirements.
■ *Stage 3 Quality improvement*
  This is a continuous effort to cut out wasteful practices and improve quality.

Failure to conform with requirements costs money, because customers do not want products and services to contain faults. There are plenty of rival products for customers to turn to if they are not satisfied.

Evidence collection point

Explain how quality improvement will lead to changes in production.

Analysing improvements in production

In this section we will analyse improvements of production in terms of:

■ causes of change
■ impact on production
■ research and development needed
■ human resourcing changes
■ changing customer and supplier relations.

We will look at these improvements in production in terms of:

■ better productivity
■ quality assurance
■ investing in research and development, training and technology
■ reducing pollution
■ changing working methods.

The causes of change

The profit motive, supported by competition, acts as a propulsive force to drive forward changes. This is a process with a long history – we have long since seen the disappearance of the hand-held plough in commercial farming in this country, and the cooper or barrel-maker has been replaced by automated beer-barrel production. Advances in technology enable new methods and processes of production to be employed. Consumers frequently want new products and they will quickly abandon outmoded ones. Most households, for example, use an electric kettle rather than boiling water on the stove, they watch the television more frequently than they listen to the radio, and they use central heating rather than coal-burning stoves.

Today the wider economic environment is particularly significant in determining the pace of change and the level of competition in international markets. Particularly important changes in this wider environment in recent times have been:

- the reduction in trade barriers and frontiers
- the development of mass global markets
- the growth of new economic powerhouses
- the unpredictability of demand
- the growing importance of environmentalism
- the ever-present impact of new technologies.

The reduction in trade barriers and frontiers

In the late 1990s the world contains many huge trading areas. Goods can flow freely between countries in these trading areas. The Single European Market is one example of this.

In recent times we have seen the opening up to trade of huge mass markets such as those of Russia, China and India. These countries have populations of hundreds of millions of people who are increasingly able to generate disposable income to purchase consumer goods.

At the same time, in 1994 a fresh General Agreement on Tariffs and Trade was signed, effectively reducing import taxes and tariffs on many products sold in world markets.

This opening up of trade has both enabled and forced manufacturers to employ more competitive production techniques. Mass markets make large-scale production possible. However, they also enable competitors to produce on a large scale.

The development of mass global markets

Today we are seeing the development on a global scale of mass markets which can be reached quickly by large-scale producers. The quantities of products like Coca-Cola and Marlborough cigarettes that can be sold throughout the world are vast.

It is interesting to note that when the Rolling Stones brought out a new disc in 1994 it quickly reached a much higher global sales figure than any of their 1960s and early 1970s records had done at the height of their popularity in the UK and America.

The modern music business can quickly reach a global audience through modern communications and distribution systems. The earnings of stars like Michael Jackson and Madonna have been phenomenal.

The growth of new economic powerhouses

The success story of the Japanese economy since the Second World War has been well charted, and has been followed by many East Asian economies in recent times.

We talk of the Pacific Rim countries as being the new economic giants. They are strategically placed to benefit from the enormous increase in earning power in Asia and the Pacific. The export growth of countries like South Korea, Malaysia and Thailand has left Western economies lagging well behind.

These countries are able to benefit from a massive internal market so that they are able to produce on a large scale at low unit costs, operating with highly efficient labour forces which are not restricted by the tight employment regulations that exist in the West.

The unpredictability of demand

We cannot predict the direction in which change will take place, or what kinds of demands the marketplace will make in the future. Today we live in a highly uncertain environment, and chaos theory has become an increasingly influential school of thought. Chaos theory relates to all sorts of disciplines, but basically it states that there are so many variables causing changes in the world today that it is impossible to predict what the impact of all these changes will be when they operate together. The extreme example often cited is that of a butterfly flapping its wings in Sydney, Australia, setting in motion air currents that lead to a hurricane in the United States the following week.

Today we have millions of organisations developing new products and new ideas in competition with each other. The impact of these changes often

411

revolutionises the ways in which other products are made. Overnight, processes and methods may become outdated. Organisations need continually to update production methods and techniques in order to keep abreast of the wave of change.

The growing importance of environmentalism

In recent years there has been an increasing emphasis on the environment. Citizens and governments have become more concerned about the quality of life. This has led to greater control on the creation of environmental wastes and the way in which resources are used. Countries like Germany are at the forefront of environmental protection. Compulsory and voluntary regulation and legislation covering the environment have forced through changes in production methods. Increasingly, 'green consumers' are demanding new ways of producing goods.

The impact of new technologies

The modern age is characterised by technological changes. New technologies continually replace old ones, and have revolutionised most products. For example, food technologies have created Mars ice cream bars and microwave meals. New technologies will continue to revolutionise production.

Evidence collection point

Prepare an oral presentation highlighting ways in which a particular change in production has forced through change in your local area. For example, the use of new technology by an overseas producer might have forced local

companies to adopt new production methods.

Evidence that you collect from this activity can be used as evidence of the Core Skill of Communication.

Impact on production

Production methods today are subject to frequent changes. You will not have to travel very far to find organisations which employ management information systems, robotics, automation, computer-aided design and manufacture, that contract out work, that take advantage of a flexible labour force, etc.

Some of these changes will have been forced on the firm, i.e. the firm will be striving to catch up with production techniques employed in America, Japan, Korea, etc. Some of the changes will have stemmed from the fact that the organisation seeks to stay ahead in its field.

Whether the stimulus for the change is internal or external, it will have an impact on production.

New technology can transform the way in which goods and services are made. Technologies also tend to interact so that research and development in one field can have spin-off effects in many other areas. For example, the non-stick frying pan was a spin-off of materials development for the space programme.

In another example, very recently the firm Charles Glassware, which puts the logos and badges on finished glass for British breweries (including Carlsberg-Tetley, Whitbread and Guinness), developed a way of controlling 'nucleation'. This is the process in which dissolved carbon dioxide is released as bubbles, giving lager its fizz and creating the head. The new process helps lager to keep its head and bubbles for up to an hour after being poured.

Improvements in production mean that the way in which goods are produced changes – instead of ten employees being required for a particular process you may only require two (or in some cases you may require none at all as they are replaced by robots or computer-aided manufacture).

Evidence collection point

Follow newspaper or magazine reports of changes in production. Identify ways in which production processes have been altered in a particular instance.

Research and development

Most changes in production are the result or research and development.

In any well-run organisation, research and development will seek to further the organisation's aims by creating better products, improving operational processes and providing expert advice to the rest of the company and to customers.

There are two essential ingredients of research and development – to make the best possible use of resources, and to take maximum care of the environment. The continued success of the organisation depends on these two ingredients. The cost of research and development needs to be measured against the value of output.

The cost of ongoing research can be considerable. In some sectors, such as aerospace or some chemical and pharmaceutical sectors, research costs alone will account for by far the largest percentage of costs, rising for some types of aircraft to as high as 50–60%.

What is certain is that without a flow of new improved products and processes, no organisation can expect to remain successful.

Some research cannot be expected to pay for itself in any foreseeable time span. Many companies allocate a proportion of their research budgets, as much as 5–10% in some cases, to so-called 'blue-sky' investigations that just may produce spectacular commercial results in the short term, but whose more likely contribution is to the long-term understanding of products and processes – with a possible pay-off in the far distant future.

Research workers may spend many years of painstaking research before they come up with a discovery of tremendous import, such as a cure for AIDS. To take another example, for many years electricity has been highly efficient to produce but highly inefficient to distribute. Suddenly, at the end of 1993, some French scientists made a breakthrough which may mean that electricity can be carried at almost room temperature with hardly any wastage at all – i.e. the creation of a highly efficient supply of energy. The impact of such a discovery on the way in which goods are produced in future could be tremendous.

Evidence collection point

Identify two changes in the way that goods are produced which have required considerable input of research and development.

Human resourcing changes

When you change the way in which goods are produced you will almost inevitably change the way in which you employ people at work. For example, when you move from manual operations to automated production you will replace human muscle power with 'machine muscle power'. This may mean that fewer operatives are required and that they are different types of operatives – i.e. they may become checkers and controllers.

The term 'Fordism' is often used to describe the situation in which goods were processed on an assembly line which itself determined the rate at which workers worked, e.g. in the production of motor cars. Each worker performed a relatively simple operation, lasting a few seconds.

Some commentators saw this process as being de-humanising in that the operative is simply an extension of the machinery. Of course today, most if not all standardised operations have been automated in car manufacture and other industrial processes. As we shall see in the next chapter, this has meant that work has been radically transformed.

Changing customer and supplier relations

Making changes in the quality standards required by producers has implications for their relationships with suppliers. For example, a failure to meet the producer's quality standards could jeopardise the production process and subsequently damage customer supplier relations.

We have already seen that the emphasis on production today is very much on managing quality in order to ensure the highest possible standards. Sub-standard work is simply not acceptable, and in societies in which consumers are alert to their rights and to the choices that are available, the sub-standard producer will quickly go out of business. Just imagine going into a bakery and finding that the bread was slightly stale, or buying a pair of trousers on which the buttons had not been stitched properly. Quality is paramount in modern business practice.

413

Figure 15.14 Quality in modern business practice

Evidence collection point

Explain why total quality is an essential ingredient of the successful production process.

Improvements in production

We will now go on to look at some of the major aspects of improvements in production.

Better productivity

We have already seen that improving productivity involves using inputs more effectively to produce outputs. The factors we identified earlier in this chapter such as improved technology, the use of robotics, automation, improved quality standards, etc. can all lead to improvements in productivity.

Of course, there is always the danger that inappropriate changes in production may lead to limited improvements or even to falls in productivity.

One of the key criteria that a business uses when introducing changes in production methods and techniques will be that of improved productivity. In analysing changes in production, therefore, you should try to estimate the likely changes on productivity.

Evidence collection point

Identify a change in production methods that is being introduced by a business

organisation with which you are familiar. Show how this change is expected to lead to improvements in productivity. What are the major pitfalls associated with the change?

Quality assurance

Resources spent on quality assurance, including training, improvement to equipment and systematic revision of processes, are almost always far less than the cost of poor quality. The typical cost of poor quality, in US and European businesses can amount to around 20–30% of a company's annual expenditure.

The benefits of quality assurance are tremendous. Organisations develop a reputation for quality and reliability. They are associated with appropriate standards. It is highly important therefore to develop quality as a way of life in organisational activity.

We have already mentioned the importance of total quality management (TQM) in an organisation. TQM is achieved by a series of small-scale incremental projects. The Japanese word for this approach to continuous improvement is 'kaizen' (step-by-step improvements).

Kaizen involves small projects that seek to build success and confidence, and develop a base for further ventures in improvement. By way of

Figure 15.15 'Kaizen' – breaking down elephant-sized projects into bite-sized assignments

illustration, Joseph Juran (one of the great pioneers of TQM) talks of 'elephant-sized' and 'bite-sized' projects. He argued that the best way to tackle the 'elephant-sized' projects is to divide them up into manageable 'bite-sized' assignments. He recommends assigning one team the task of 'cutting up the elephant' (Figure 15.15).

Case study – BS 5750

The increasing demands for quality from customers and suppliers alike in the late 1990s have meant that more and more organisations today are creating quality standards that match BS 5750. BS 5750, states that:

> The supplier's management shall define and document its policy and objectives for, and commitment to, quality.

Once the system is set up:

> The supplier shall carry out internal audits to verify whether quality activities comply with planned arrangements and to determine the effectiveness of the quality system.

BS 5750 was introduced in 1979 and has been updated recently to bring it into line with European and international standards. It is made up of a series of national standards that can be used by any organisation, whether it employs 10 or 10 000 people.

Such standards identify basic procedures and criteria that help to ensure that organisations provide goods or services that meet customer requirements.

Achieving BS 5750 standards may take an organisation between one and two years, and the costs will vary. Many organisations employ an adviser to help them reach the standards.

The great benefit of BS 5750 is the economies it helps to create. For example, systems are improved, customer needs are identified and then satisfied and overall product requirements provide genuine market and competitive benefits.

1 Using a desktop publishing package, produce a leaflet highlighting the benefits to an organisation of achieving BS 5750. You could use this leaflet as evidence of your capabilities in the Core Skills of Information Technology and Communication.
2 Would implementing BS 5750 be useful to the organisation you work for or the college you attend? Explain why.

Quality assurance could include implementing the sorts of quality standards outlined above, changing management styles or altering design to eliminate errors.

Investing in research and development, training and technology

Improvements in production can stem from investing in a number of important areas including research and development, training and technology.

We have already seen that research is a premium function of an organisation. Research involves investment for the future. Research that bears fruit, whether it be tomorrow or in ten years' time, can help to create a competitive edge. Many of Britain's most successful companies such as Shell, BP and Marks and Spencer, spend considerable sums of money on research and development.

Investment in training is also vital. Increasingly employees need to be able to work with new production systems. Systems that are used effectively will be highly productive ones.

Research carried out by Professor Sig Prais of the National Institute of Economic and Social Research indicates that UK manufacturing is working with its hands tied behind its back. He argues that our lack of vocational training explains much of Britain's poor productivity compared with industrial rivals.

Britain's biggest skills shortfall is among intermediate-level crafts, of the sort that are commonplace on Continental and Japanese production lines, where a high level of skills encourages employees to maintain their machinery well and to put simple faults right.

A low level of skills means that there are more breakdowns and longer delays in putting things right. The workers on the production line have to wait for the maintenance specialist, rather than doing it themselves. Managers therefore have to design production schedules to allow for periodic hold-ups. Highly skilled workers also often have to do jobs themselves which, in competing countries, might be done by more flexible lower-skilled employees. Low skills also mean that British manufacturers are less able to produce short and specialised production runs because of the time taken to change the production line.

Investments in new technology are an important ingredient of competitive advantage. However, it is not just a matter of investing in technology for the sake of it. The key is investment in 'appropriate technology'.

Evidence collection point

Interview a representative of a local business organisation to find out how investment in:

- research and development
- training
- technology

have helped to give the organisation a competitive edge. Write up a report of your findings.

Reducing pollution

A statistical analysis carried out by the New Economics Foundation and the *Independent* newspaper in 1994 revealed that, far from being the 'Dirty nation of Europe', Britain has one of the better environmental records (Figure 15.16).

Eleven issues were considered, covering air and water pollution, nature conservation, car use, energy efficiency and household waste.

Each country was awarded a score of between 0 and 100 for each issue – with the best scoring 100 and the worst 0 – and the scores were then averaged out.

The green league table

Nations' environmental scores out of 100

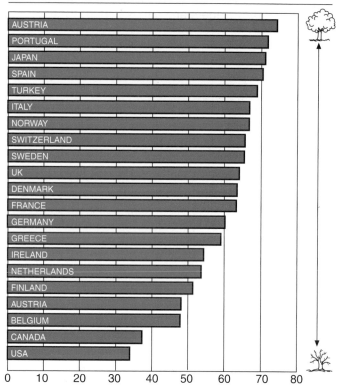

Figure 15.16 Table of environmental pollution

Austria came first with 76% followed by Portugal (73%) and Japan (72%). Britain with just under 64% came 10th of the 21 OECD countries.

Less developed countries such as Turkey, Spain and Portugal tended to score highly for their low air pollution, car use and refuse production, but poorly for low levels of sewage treatment and lack of nature reserves and national parks.

Attempts are being made to develop more sophisticated ways of monitoring environmental damage and pollution. For example, Her Majesty's Inspectorate of Pollution are developing ways of auditing and reporting on such areas as chemical release into the environment by companies, and in specific regions of the UK.

Increasingly, business organisations are being judged by the level of pollution they cause. For example, shareholders are asking questions about the pollution created by their companies.

Evidence collection point

Collect a series of eight articles from newspapers and magazines concerning the way in which pollution is created by production processes. In each case produce a commentary identifying ways of reducing this pollution.

Evidence collected from this activity could be placed in your portfolio to provide evidence of Core Skills in Communication.

Changing working methods

There are a variety of ways in which changes in production can lead to changes in working methods. These include distance working using computer networks, working in problem-solving teams such as those which bring together design, production and marketing personnel and greater flexibility including multiskilling. We shall look at these in greater detail in the next chapter.

Evidence indicators

Produce a report which describes ways in which businesses add value and explains why they add value through production. One section of the report should identify and give examples of factors which

can contribute to change in production. It should analyse at least two possible improvements in production explaining the causes of change and its consequences for the business, its employees, its customers and suppliers.

Producing this report should enable you to provide useful evidence for your portfolio of the Core Skills of Communication and, hopefully, Information Technology.

The following list should serve as a checklist. Please tick off each of the following when you have successfully covered them as part of your report. You need to be able to confirm that:

- I have set out in a report format an assignment which describes ways in which businesses add value and explains why they add value through production. ☐
- One section of the report identifies and gives examples of factors which can contribute to changes in production. ☐
- I have analysed at least two improvements in production. ☐
- I have explained the causes of change. ☐
- I have explained the consequences of change for:
  - the business ☐
  - its employees ☐
  - its customers ☐
  - its suppliers. ☐

417

Production and employment in the economy

Chapter 16

Investigating and evaluating employment

This chapter explores the nature of employment in business. This is an important aspect of business to understand as, for most people, employment takes up a large proportion of their lives.

We have therefore set out to present a picture of the main features of employment and how employment trends are changing in the United Kingdom and the European Union, and the implications of these trends.

This chapter therefore sets out to:

- identify and explain types of employment
- evaluate the effects of changes in types of employment
- identify implications of employment trends in the local economy
- evaluate the implications of employment trends in the local and national economy.

Types of employment

Until recently, most jobs were permanent full-time jobs. Today this picture has changed and there are very many different types of employment. Larger organisations in particular will operate a variety of different employment arrangements. The most common ones are shown in Figure 16.1.

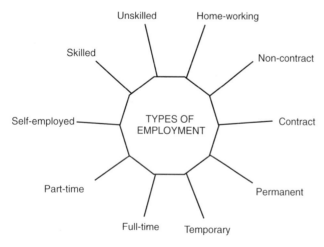

Figure 16.1 Different types of employment

Self-employment

Self-employment grew significantly in the 1980s and an upward trend has now reappeared following a fall during the recession in the early 1990s. At the end of 1994, 13% of those in employment were self-employed compared with 11% in 1983.

The term self-employment simply indicates that an individual works for himself or herself rather than for a larger organisation. The classic example of the self-employed person is the window cleaner, plumber, or corner shop owner. Nowadays there are many self-employed people in dynamic sectors of the economy, such as IT specialists (e.g. with a desktop publishing service), business consultants and designers.

Full-time

In 1850 the normal working week in the UK was 60 hours, spread over 6 days at 10 hours each. By the early 1960s this had been reduced to 40 hours spread over 5 days. The average full-time working week now lies between 35 and 40 hours, still spread over 5 days.

In reality it is difficult to come up with a hard and fast definition of full-time work. A dictionary definition provides us with 'for the entire time appropriate to an activity'. For example, a full-time teacher would work to the full contractual time established by the school – perhaps from 8.30 am until 4.00 pm each day for 180 days a year. A full-time lecturer in a college may work a set number of contractual hours a year, e.g. 800 hours of contact and preparation time a year.

In its statistical work the Labour Force Quarterly Survey accepts respondents' definitions of whether they are full-time or part-time.

It is interesting to note that, according to respondents' own assessments, the average number of hours worked by full-time employees was 39.2 hours in the Autumn of 1993 and 39.7 hours in the Autumn of 1994.

Part-time employment

Part-time employees are, as the name implies, people who do not 'work for the entire time appropriate to an activity'.

Traditionally, jobs which did not require more than a few hours a day to complete, such as school cleaners or dinner supervisors, have been employed on part-time contracts. The number of part-time employees has increased dramatically in recent years and is directly linked to a greater proportion of women in the labour force.

Recently European Union regulations have set out that part-time employees have entitlements to pensions, redundancy pay and other employment rights.

The Labour Force Survey in the autumn of 1994 revealed that, on average, part-time employees are working 15.4 hours a week. In 1994, 24% of those employed had part-time jobs compared with 20% in 1983.

Evidence collection point

The following figures relate to changes in the numbers of part-time and full-time employees between 1981 and 2001. The figure for 2001 is based on a projection. (A projection is not a precise prediction of what the future will be. Instead it shows what tomorrow will look like based on

certain simple assumptions about patterns of behaviour. Most projections are based on the assumption that past trends and patterns of behaviour will continue.)

Year	Numbers working part-time (millions)	Numbers working full-time (millions)
1981	4.5	18.0
1991	6.0	16.5
2001	7.0	15.0

Use a graphics plotting package on a computer to set out these results in the form of a bar chart. Work out the percentage of employees working part-time and full-time in each of these years. Set this information out in a pie-chart.

You can use the work that you produce for this task to show evidence of capability in the Core Skills of Application of Number and Information Technology.

The reasons why employees may choose to work part-time are:

- they have greater flexibility in working hours
- they can use part-time employment as a supplement to other income, e.g. their student grant
- it enables them to enjoy more leisure time
- they can use it as a 'hobby' job, rather than doing nothing during the day
- full-time work is not available.

The reasons why employers may want part-time employees are as follows:

- it provides them with a more flexible arrangement. It is easier to recruit part-time staff to work evenings and weekends, for example. This is particularly useful in retailing.
- part-time employees are generally lower paid.
- part-time employees do not have the same legal rights as full-time employees, although EU legislation has somewhat reduced this imbalance.

Permanent employment

Permanent employees are those who have a contractual commitment from their employers to continue employment, irrespective of whether they work full-time or part-time.

A simpler definition is that the employees have an open-ended rather than a fixed-term contract.

This open-ended contract can be ended only when either party gives 'notice of termination'. The length of the notice period will depend on the length of time the employee has worked there and the period of notice specified in the contract of employment.

Temporary employment

A temporary employee will have a work contract for a limited time period only. They can be employed on a full-time or part-time basis. Many factories, for example, take on temporary packers before Christmas to cope with increased orders.

When employees have worked for an organisation for a given period of time, often three years, they may legally come to be regarded as full-time employees. Organisations often get round this by employing someone for less than three years, and then replacing him or her with another employee.

Reasons why organisations may employ temporary employees would include:

- to cover staff sickness or holidays
- to assist with exceptionally large orders
- to cope with seasonal changes in demand, e.g. in the hotel and tourism industry
- to work on special projects with a limited time span
- to clear backlogs of work.

Contracted and non-contracted employees

Today short-term contracts are becoming more and more common. In times of economic uncertainty, employers are finding greater flexibility in giving short-term contracts for one or two years to new employees, e.g. in teaching/lecturing. This gives them the option to renew or not to renew at the end of the period. Computer programming is another example of an area where short-term contracts are commonplace.

The term contracted worker refers either to a fixed-term contract worker, employed for a specific period of time, or to a subcontractor. A subcontractor is hired to do work that someone else has been contracted to do. Subcontractors are very common in the construction industry where builders will contract other companies or individuals to do electrical, plumbing and other work.

A fixed-term contract could be one-off or renewed on a periodic basis. Many of the catering staff in schools are on fixed-term contracts, which are reviewed annually. Professional footballers usually work to fixed-term contracts.

Skilled/unskilled employment

A skilled job is one which requires skill (i.e. special ability) or special training. It is no longer enough to think simply of the specific skills needed by specific jobs. Change within jobs, and demands for greater flexibility between jobs, mean that we need to think in terms of giving people broad vocational skills which can form a foundation for more specific skills.

The development of GNVQs is an obvious example of the stress being placed on the broader skills needed in groups of occupations. Job-specific skills remain important, but as changing jobs becomes more the norm, they are increasingly likely to have to be provided in shorter bursts throughout an individual's working life.

Evidence collection point

What sorts of (a) job-specific, and (b) general skills would be required by:

1 a hairdresser
2 a professional footballer
3 a teacher or lecturer.

Skills can be acquired through practice, experience and by detailed study and training. Employees who are properly prepared for skilled jobs are likely to be most effective.

Some people have more natural aptitude for particular skilled occupations than others. However, it would be unlikely that someone could become skilled without training or practice. Darren Gough is a world-class cricketer and Steffi Graf is a world-class tennis player – however, they both got where they are today through many hours of practice as well as natural aptitude.

Home-working

Home-working is simply work that is done one at home for pay. This type of work was common in the days of cottage industry prior to the industrial revolution, and in recent times has again become popular. For example, many sales representatives and professionals (accountants, consultants) are based at home. This is possible because of improved communications and technology – faxes, computers, etc. Some business organisations encourage home-working to reduce overheads and there is the additional benefit to many people of reducing the stress associated with commuting.

 Evidence collection point

1 Obtain a daily newspaper and study the job advertisements.

You will find these in the appointments section.

2 Select four job advertisements. Each of these four should fulfil a different criterion based on the features of employment:

full-time, part-time, permanent, temporary, contract, non-contract, skilled, unskilled, home-working.

Of course, a number of them will cover several criteria.

3 Explain how the jobs advertised match these criteria.
4 Perhaps you could repeat this activity by visiting a job centre and examining jobs advertised.
5 Which of the above features of employment seems to be the most common in your sample? Try to explain this trend.

The effects of changes in types of employment

Changes in types of employment can be viewed from two main perspectives.

1 From the point of view of the employee. We can look at employee needs in terms of:
■ pay
■ benefits
■ career progression opportunities
■ job security
■ working conditions.

2 From the point of view of the business. We can look at business needs in terms of needing to:
■ control costs
■ maintain profits
■ maintain levels of productivity
■ maintain customer satisfaction.

Before we go on to look more closely at the above factors, it is important to build up a picture of the trend towards flexible working practices which is characterised by the move to increased part-time working and self-employment in the economy. Businesses and individuals are increasingly using alternatives to full-time permanent employment on standard contract terms. The flexible firm has become very important in business thinking (Figure 16.2).

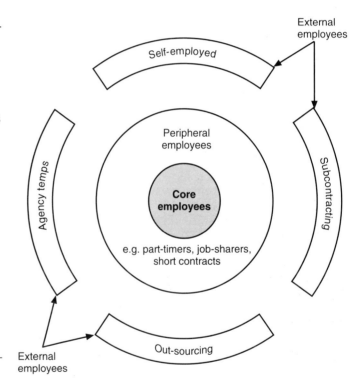

Figure 16.2 The flexible firm

As discussed in Chapter 13, the flexible firm distinguishes between:

■ *Core workers* These are employees who are multi-skilled (i.e. educated and trained to do a variety of job tasks), work full-time and who receive good pay, conditions and benefits.

- *Peripheral workers* These are short-term, temporary and part-time workers, who receive less favourable pay, conditions and benefits.
- *External workers* These are not employees of the firm, but are, for example, agency temps, workers in contracted-out services and the self-employed.

The flexible firm, as we have seen, cuts its labour costs by limiting core workers relative to peripheral and external workers. For example, in the Central Office of Rank Xerox, direct wage payments in recent times have accounted for less than one-third of total labour costs. Many former Rank Xerox employees work from their own homes using computer equipment linked to the Xerox network. These independent employees are free to work for other clients apart from Rank Xerox.

There is no need for a large business organisation to take responsibility for transporting goods, for advertising and for many other activities which can be contracted out. In the public sector, contracting-out has been the order of the day. For example, in the BBC many programmes are now produced and made by outside contractors who sell their products to the BBC (which is thus able to reduce its operating costs and the size of the organisation to a manageable core).

The days of the massive, large-scale employing organisations in both the private and the public sector are over. The secret is to employ the minimum number of core employees required for maximum efficiency. In an obituary for the musician Frank Zappa I read that Zappa abandoned his policy of employing a large number of musicians in his band one day when he saw a celebrated American jazz band leader having to dip deep into his own pocket to scrape together enough cash to pay his large group of full-time musicians at the end of an engagement.

In the Civil Service, contracting-out is becoming increasingly common. Today many Civil Service jobs are under threat as private firms are invited to run government services. 'Efficiency scrutinies' have been used to find areas where cutbacks can be made. When Margaret Thatcher became Prime Minister in 1979 there were nearly three-quarters of a million Civil Servants. By the mid-1990s the figure is closer to half a million. The government now intends to reduce the size of the Civil Service further by 50 000 before 1998.

The old distinctions between full-time and part-time, contracted and non-contracted, permanent and non-

permanent employees are being eroded as business organisations and individuals develop broad ranges of new working agreements and relationships. We need to bear in mind this broad diversity when evaluating different types of employment.

Evaluating the effects of changes in employment in terms of employee needs

Pay

A full-time contract is most likely to secure better pay over the medium to long term. Employers are most likely to take workers on full-time if there is a clear need to retain that person within the organisation. For example, a full-time lecturer is not just expected to contribute to class teaching, but also to the development of long-term working relationships and course development in a college. Full-time employees are core workers who are closely associated with the organisation and are expected to take on greater responsibilities than part-time workers. One would expect the pay of such employees to be correspondingly higher than other workers'.

This is not to say that part-time workers will always be low paid in the short term. Many part-time workers are in the lowest paid jobs. However, in some cases they may receive very high pay packets – perhaps because they are helping to fill a short-term gap. For example, a supply teacher will receive a higher daily rate of pay than a full-time teacher on the same scale. However, the supply teachers will not be paid during the holidays or when they are not working.

As a general rule, part-time pay is low-paid work. A labour force survey in early 1994 revealed that while there was a fall in 1994 of 19 000 in full-time jobs there was a rise of 57 000 in part-time jobs. Almost all of the new positions were in the service sector, and over 60% of these were taken by women.

An important statistic is that women fill 85% of part-time jobs and 77% of part-time work is paid below the Council of Europe's decency threshold – which in 1995 was £5.75 an hour. Much part-time work pays less than £3 an hour.

Skilled employees receive considerably more pay than unskilled ones. There is a clear relationship between the amount of experience and training that people have received and their pay levels. Training can therefore be seen as an important investment by an individual. Particularly important today is the acquisition of core skills and competencies which will be required in a broad range of occupations. Levels of pay for most jobs rise on an incremental basis which may be tied in with performance appraisal.

The pay of self-employed workers varies widely. Some people are prepared to accept very low pay because they would rather work for themselves than for someone else. Some business people are forced to work for years with very little return because they are unable to make profits. Other self-employed people make vast fortunes because they produce something which is in great demand.

The pay of home-workers also varies considerably. For example, a leading journalist may be able to do much of his or her work from home and receive very high sums for each article written. In contrast, some home-workers are among the most exploited in the land. For example, people who fill up children's 'gift bags' at home may be paid in pence rather than pounds for each hour worked.

Permanent workers will often be paid more than temporary ones. Temporary employees may be prepared to accept low wages simply to gain employment. Of course some temporary employees may be highly paid, e.g. a film star with a temporary contract for a few months to complete a film with a particular studio.

Evidence collection point

Study advertisements for different types of employment. Compare and contrast the different rates of pay offered for these types of work. Are there any general rules that emerge from your study? You may use the evidence which you present to show capability in the Core Skills of Application of Number and Communication.

Benefits

Generally speaking most of the work benefits will be received by core rather than peripheral workers. Core workers will be entitled to such benefits as company pensions, use of company cars, part or complete payment of phone bills, subsidised meals or luncheon vouchers, holiday and sickness pay, etc. The benefits received by part-time workers will be far fewer. You have only to study job advertisements to appreciate the difference in benefits being offered to full-time and part-time employees.

Evidence collection point

Produce a short written report comparing the benefits offered by a number of jobs advertised in the local newspaper so that you cover: full-time, part-time, permanent, temporary, contract, non-contract, skilled, unskilled jobs and, if possible, homeworking.

This report will help you to provide evidence of the Core Skills of Communication and, possibly, Information Technology.

In choosing a job an important consideration will be the benefits offered. For example, it is very important to plan for the future by making sure that you receive more than just your state pension when you retire. An important advantage of full-time and permanent work is that it usually offers some form of occupational pension scheme whereby employees put money aside for their future retirement. Employees who receive benefits such as company cars and subsidised phone bills are effectively reducing their day-to-day living costs.

Part-time, temporary employees, and the self-employed have none of these advantages. It is essential that when you choose a job you think about the long-term as well as short-term considerations.

Career progression opportunities

Career progression involves moving up an incremental ladder so that you move to new posts of responsibility, higher pay and more rewarding work. Clearly these opportunities will most likely exist if you are a full-time employee doing permanent work with a permanent contract of employment.

In the past, individuals would expect to work for an organisation and be rewarded over time by career progression within their jobs. Today the suggestion is that individuals are more likely to follow portfolio careers. It is quite possible now to begin working life as a credit analyst in a bank, move into financial management in a larger company, start and grow a small business, and then work as a management consultant. Or perhaps begin as an environmental engineer, do a spell in teaching and then move into marketing. The movable career path has been christened 'the portfolio career'.

People following a GNVQ course in Business need to be aware that in their working lives they will have to cope with over- and under-employment (i.e. having too much or too little work to do), constant activity, redundancy, parenthood, living with others or alone, staying in one place, or, probably, frequently moving homes or even countries. The move to increased flexibility means that career progression opportunities are less likely to be there within a single organisation.

Full-time work may offer career progression within an organisation, or it may not. It may be necessary to move to another organisation if you want promotion. Full-time workers will constantly need to consider the sorts of training and personal development that they will need if they are going to achieve career progression. This will involve developing a portfolio of skills such as information technology, effective presentation skills, the ability to use business calculations, etc.

Part-time, temporary, non-contract and unskilled work are least likely to offer career progression.

Career progression may be an important need for employees who increasingly take on greater responsibilities as they grow older. The single person will have fewer commitments than the married person with children to support, a mortgage to pay, and loan repayments on the car and other household durables.

Evidence collection point

Interview five individuals of roughly the same age who have been working for a number of years in different employment situations, e.g. part-time, full-time, permanent, temporary, contract, non-contract, skilled and unskilled. Find out about how career progression opportunities vary between the individuals that you have identified.

Job security

We live in times of increasing uncertainty in which job security has largely disappeared. Groups such as bank employees, teachers and lecturers are increasingly finding that full-time, permanent work is less certain. For many, this uncertainty has always been a feature of working life, e.g. the construction worker building a road on a short-term contract or the hotel porter working the summer season.

The demand for labour is derived from the demand for the product that the labour produces. In today's competitive climate jobs can disappear overnight.

The *Times Educational Supplement* (8 July 1994) reported that 51 000 teachers in England and Wales

were on fixed-term contracts. Many of these contracts were limited to one year, while others were for less than a term's work. This figure accounted for 8.6% of the teaching force compared with 4.6% in 1983.

The principal cause of this huge growth in uncertainty about jobs is the growth of local management of schools, whereby schools have the responsibility for managing their own budgets, coupled with less money being made available for education. Head teachers and governors, worried by the prospect of not being able to balance their books if pupil numbers fall (leading to a drop in income), are hedging their bets and creating what they consider to be an easily disposable category of teacher.

Job security is more likely to be associated with full-time, permanent, skilled and contracted labour than with part-time, temporary, unskilled and uncontracted labour.

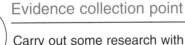

Evidence collection point

Carry out some research with people you know in order to compare the job security of different types of employment.

Working conditions

Working conditions vary from industry to industry, and from employer to employer. However, generally speaking, working conditions are most likely to favour full-time, permanent, contracted and skilled labour who provide the core of the workforce. Employees seeking the best working conditions should therefore try to find this sort of work.

Part-timers are frequently treated as a disposable asset who may have only limited commitment to the organisation. However, this is a very short-sighted way of handling human resources, particularly as organisations today are coming to rely more heavily on part-time, temporary employees.

Case study – Poor treatment of the human resource

The following extract is based on an account by a supply teacher of her work in the mid-1990s.

'Where does one get a cup of coffee?' I asked a teacher passing through the staff room. 'No idea', she replied. Not an unusual experience in an agency supply teacher's day!

I managed to get posts as a supply teacher by answering an advertisement offering £75 a day working with a team of supply teachers.

Once started, supply teachers phone in for work for the following day until a job becomes available. The first school I was sent into as supply cover said they hadn't booked me, and were only prepared to pay me for half a day's work. The second school was for emotionally and behaviourally disturbed children, for which I had had no training. I endured a day of youths literally hanging from the rafters of the classroom.

In any school, the children look up and see you coming and have the attitude: 'We don't need to take him seriously – he's only the supply cover.' You know little of the codes of conduct of the school, who to turn to, what the procedures are. Very often little work has been set for the pupils, and often you are expected to cover the most disruptive classes.

With no direct contractual obligations between the supply agency and the school, neither party invests in making the arrangement work. Arriving at the office door of one school, I was instructed to take a box of stationery and go to room 12. There were not even courtesies, directions or any information given to me. Briefing of supply teachers is virtually non-existent.

1 What does the above case tell you about:
   ■ the pay
   ■ job security
   ■ working conditions
   of supply teachers?

2 Cite other examples you are familiar with which show that part-time, temporary workers are subject to unfavourable conditions in their workplace.

Evaluating the effects of changes in employment in terms of business needs

To control costs

In a survey of top Japanese executives carried out by the Kyodo news agency in early 1994, 86% said the lifetime employment system (under which Japanese employees were guaranteed a job for life with a particular company) was set to disappear. An even larger 95% said that companies would increasingly adopt pay scales based on merit, rather than the current system under which employees are rewarded according to seniority. In today's competitive climate, businesses throughout the world are increasingly adopting more flexible approaches to working patterns.

The second annual Survey of Long-term Employment Strategies, published in late 1993, reported that the use of more temporary and contract workers and other methods of flexible working will permanently change Britain's employment patterns.

The prime reasons for these changes are the need for increased productivity, flexibility and cost control. Between 1988 and 1994 more than 90% of the UK's largest organisations have restructured, and this has led to job losses at all levels. Sixty-six per cent expect to be involved in further restructuring by 1997.

One of the prime imperatives of business is cost control. Rising costs force an organisation to raise prices or to jeopardise other competitive advantages such as delivery times, quality, etc.

Organisations therefore need to create the most effective balance between the various types of employees that it uses. In recent years we have seen the stripping out of layers of full-time, permanent

contracted employees from organisations. One of the major purposes has been to raise productivity and increase cost competitiveness with rivals.

A large permanent staff creates an ongoing burden for an organisation. Each year employees grow a year older, so that they are entitled to pay increases, salary upgrades, larger pension contributions, etc. From the organisation's point of view it may make sense to shrink the core of the organisation, particularly when people can be replaced by technology.

Evidence collection point

The table below shows average earnings in Britain by gender, 1990.

1 What does the table tell you about the relative cost to employers of using male rather than female labour?
2 Why might this sort of evidence encourage employers to substitute part-time for full-time employment?

To maintain profits

In order to secure maximum profits, organisations will seek to employ the best possible combination of employees. This, for example, helps to explain the growth in the number of home-workers in recent times. Home-workers provide a potential pool of highly skilled employees who may be relatively cheap to employ. For example, teleworkers with IT skills may be prepared to accept wages which are lower than those which they would want if they had to work in an office.

At the same time, organisations need to retain a committed group of core workers who work full-time and are the lifeblood of the organisation, giving it its distinctive culture and image. Core workers need to be highly proficient and skilled, involving an

	Male Manual £	Non-manual £	All £	Female Manual £	(% of male)	Non-manual £	(% of male)	All £	(% of male)
Weekly earnings (incl. overtime)	237.20	354.90	295.60	148.00	(62.4)	215.50	(60.7)	201.50	(68.2)
Hourly earnings (excl. overtime)	5.08	9.02	6.89	3.66	(72.0)	5.73	(63.5)	5.28	(76.6)

Average earnings in Britain by gender, 1990

investment in training. However, this should be more than repaid in the form of higher productivity.

The employment of part-timers gives an organisation flexibility, enabling it to maintain profits.

To maintain levels of productivity

An important consideration from the employing organisation's point of view is that of maximising productivity. Organisations will maximise productivity by creating an employment structure which rewards and motivates its employees.

The policy of rewards should:

- ensure that the organisation can recruit both the quality and the quantity of staff it requires
- foster staff loyalty
- provide rewards for good performance as well as incentives
- create differentials between jobs
- reflect market rates for different skills
- be easy to understand
- be cost-effective.

The organisation will also secure productivity by making sure that employees are committed to the organisation, for example by providing them with the right sorts of career opportunities and working conditions.

An important concept in motivating employees is that of empowerment, i.e. giving power or authority to individual employees to make decisions or to contribute to decision-making rather than having it handed down to them. Empowerment requires willing acceptance as well as willing (if probably nervous) distribution. Empowerment is meaningful only if it is a contract based on trust.

Empowerment is most likely to work when employees feel that they are valued by an organisation. The growing move to flexible workforces may work against productivity through empowerment. When people feel insecure, or that they do not really belong to an organisation, e.g. part-timers and non-contract workers, they may be reluctant to make decisions.

In recent years there have been considerable criticisms of the delayering of organisations. Some people feel that the traditional permanent full-time worker was committed to an organisation. Stripping out middle-management layers and supervisors has created uncertainty and lack of direction. The employment of too many part-timers can lead to disorganisation and falling levels of productivity.

Another way in which organisations can change the way in which they operate is to enhance the skill levels of employees, i.e. to employ a more skilled workforce.

Qualification levels in the workforce as a whole have improved. In 1995, 39% of the workforce was qualified to NVQ level 3 or equivalent. Some industries, however, currently have low levels of qualification (e.g. agriculture, 24%), others higher (e.g. energy and water, 50%).

To maintain customer satisfaction

It is essential that an organisation's employees give a desirable impression of the organisation. Therefore it is important to have the right people in the right places. For example, it may be cheaper for an organisation to employ a temporary secretary to answer phones. However, if he or she is clueless about how the organisation works the organisation may lose a lot of business. The better trained and more highly skilled an organisation's employees are, the better their chance of giving satisfaction to customers. Organisations therefore need to secure just the right balance between the types of employment they use.

Case study – Evaluating performance of counter staff at a fast-food restaurant

The following checklist is used by managers to evaluate counter staff performance:

Greeting the customer	Yes	No
1 There is a smile		
2 It is a sincere greeting		
3 There is eye contact		

Taking the order	Yes	No
1 The counter person is thoroughly familiar with the menu		
2 The customer has to give the order only once		
3 Small orders (four items or less) are memorised rather than written down		
4 There is suggestive selling		

Assembling the order	Yes	No
1 The order is assembled in the proper sequence		
2 Grill slips are handed in first		
3 Drinks are poured in the proper sequence		

4 Proper amount of ice
5 Cups slanted and finger used to activate
6 Drinks are filled to the proper level
7 Drinks are capped
8 Clean cups
9 Holding times are observed on coffee
10 Cups are filled to the proper level on coffee

Presenting the order	Yes	No
1 It is properly packaged		
2 The bag is double folded		
3 Plastic trays are used if eating outside		
4 A tray liner is used		
5 The food is handled in the proper manner		

Asking for and receiving payment	Yes	No
1 The amount of the order is stated clearly and loud enough to hear		
2 The denomination received is clearly stated		
3 Change is counted out loud		
4 Change is counted efficiently		
5 Large bills are laid on the till until change is given		

Thanking the customer and asking for repeat business	Yes	No
1 There is always a thank you		
2 The thank you is sincere		
3 There is eye contact		
4 Return business is asked for		

1 To what extent would you say that the competencies listed above make the job skilled rather than unskilled?
2 Would training be required to create the competencies listed?
3 What sorts of employees would be best able to perform the job as outlined above? (Part-time, full-time, permanent, temporary, contract, non-contract?)
4 What factors would the employer need to consider in deciding what types of employees to use?
5 How will the employer's choice of types of employees to carry out the job affect:
   a costs
   b profits
   c levels of productivity
   d customer satisfaction?

The implications of employment trends in the local economy

You may find it helpful while studying the next sections to use a variety of additional information sources so that you can compare the appropriateness of information from different sources. The changing national and regional patterns of employment could be explored using UK and EU information available such as computer-based data (e.g. SECOS). Local councils and Training and Enterprise Councils (TECs) are valuable sources of local data. The *Employment Gazette* includes an extensive breakdown of employment statistics.

Employment and unemployment

Many students who follow GNVQ courses in Business will go on to obtain jobs in the local economy. It is essential therefore to have an understanding of changes in employment and unemployment at an international and national level and of how these affect the local economy.

Recently I had a conversation with a young school leaver who told me that she didn't need to go to college because she was guaranteed a job in the local textile factory. She left school in May, worked for three months and then the factory closed down. The student, and many others like her, did not have a clear picture of the wider economic environment in which her own local industries were operating. It is precisely this sort of underpinning knowledge that should inform a course in Business.

Full employment seems to be a thing of the past. This is not only true in the UK but in nearly every other country: France, Germany, the United States, etc. Unskilled and semi-skilled manufacturing workers are twice as likely to be unemployed as skilled manual workers. Manual workers as a whole are twice as likely as non-manual workers to be unemployed. It seems likely that economies are currently unwilling or unable to take up the slack in employment. We have a situation in which those in work are having to work longer and longer hours, while we have an increasing residue of people who are out of work.

Deskilling

Deskilling can be defined as mechanising or computerising a job so that little skill is required to do it, or depriving employees of the opportunity for skilled work. In many industries jobs have been deskilled as automated processes take over, leaving operatives little to do but press buttons and watch machinery do the work. Examples are automatic key cutting and photographic development processes. Of course, at the same time we have seen the growth of the process of multiskilling, whereby operatives are expected to do a variety of work tasks in a particular work environment. For example, Peter Wickens in his book *The Road to Nissan* cites the example of the Ford motor company which offered their workforce financial awards, conditional upon them agreeing to changing working practices. For example, mechanical and electrical craft workers were required to be flexible and versatile across the full range of their respective skills.

Similar arrangements related to production operatives who were expected under an agreement to:

> perform all tasks and undertake any necessary training programmes in order to create flexibility and mobility within and between departments.

Retraining

An important change in the world of work has been the considerable demand for retraining as existing skills and jobs become outmoded.

The increasing and changing demand for skills means that most of the workforce should already be regularly updating and upgrading their skills. The emphasis now needs to be on lifelong learning.

In the past, a typical pattern was for people to go through a period of schooling, which was a broad educational process preparing them for work. They would then experience a period of training in the early part of their working lives, followed by working on the job.

The emphasis today has changed, so that education should be more vocationally orientated, and training and development should then become a lifelong process in a flexible world.

Male employment and female employment

Patterns of male and female employment have been and continue to be dramatically different in this country. In 1985 the number of men in employment (full-time and part-time) exceeded the number of

women by more than 45% – 13.1 million against 9.4 million. In May 1993 the figure was 10.7 million against 10.1 million (Figure 16.3).

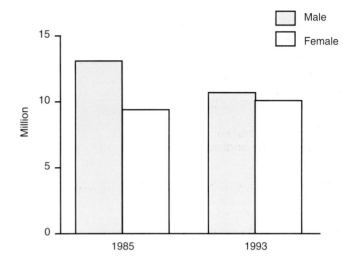

Figure 16.3 Male and female employment

However, evidence shows that women are less likely to be core workers, more of them being part-time peripheral workers. Almost half the women are in part-time jobs. Large numbers of these, and a large percentage of their colleagues in full-time work, are, by any standards, low paid.

In the early 1990s, women accounted for only 27% of managers and only 1% of top managers.

Case study – 'Scandalous' treatment!

The Equal Opportunities Commission in 1995 attacked as 'scandalous' the under-representation of women at boardroom level and challenged business to eliminate discrimination at all levels.

The Commission pointed out that women made up almost half of the workforce and more than 50% of graduates but accounted for only 3% of directors and were paid only 79% of male earnings.

The Chair of the Commission, Kamlesh Bahl, warned companies of the escalating costs of awards in discrimination cases. Compensation awards had risen seven-fold since the £11 000 ceiling was lifted in 1994.

1 What factors do you think account for the under-representation of women at board level?

Life phase	Group	Working time issues
Young, independent phase	Men and women	Longer holidays More time for education and training Longer hours for more money and promotion
Parental phase: Partners with pre-school children	Women	Maternity, paternity and parental leave More flexible hours Career breaks
	Men	Paternity and parental leave More flexible hours Option to work shorter hours
Partners with school-age children	Women	Term-time working/longer holidays Time for education and training/retraining Working hours that fit with partner's. Option to move into full-time work
	Men	Four-day week/longer weekends. Opportunity to work longer hours
Older independent phase	Women and men	Time for education and training/retraining; sabbatical leave Four-day week/longer weekends Longer holidays
Older, caring phase	Women	Option to reduce working hours
Pre-retirement phase	Men and women	Option to work shorter week/part-time Longer holidays
Retirement phase	Women and men	Flexible retirement (individual choice of retirement date; option of part-time retirement) Earlier retirement by choice not compulsion

2 Can you produce evidence to show that this trend is being, or may in the future be, reversed?

A recent survey has indicated that males and females currently have different views about working time at different periods of their lives. Of course, this picture is a generalisation. How accurately do the results of the survey reflect your attitudes and those of your family and friends?

The chart shown here is split into three columns. The first column indicates the life phase that a person is currently in. The second column shows the group concerned, i.e. male or female or both. The third column shows the issues which most concern them about the use of their working time.

Employment trends

National levels of employment

The Institute of Employment Research at Warwick University has forecast that employment will continue to grow until at least the year 2001.

Between 1993 and 1997, employment is projected to grow by 640 000 (0.6% per year on average). However, a faster rate of growth of 0.9% per year is shown for the latter four years resulting in an extra 950 000 jobs between 1997 and 2001. By 2001 employment is expected to rise to 26.2 million.

The decade as a whole will see an extra 1.6 million jobs, an increase of 6.4% on the 24.6 million 1993 level.

Evidence collection point

Find more recent evidence in magazines and newspapers to indicate recent changes in employment. How do these changes compare with the Warwick forecasts? Show your information by using a graphics package.

The work you produce can provide evidence of your capability in the Core Skills of Information Technology, Application of Number and Communication.

The shift from manufacturing to service industries

There has been a lot of talk about 'de-industrialisation' in Britain in recent years. The term suggests empty factories and shipyards. The general feeling is that de-industrialisation is a problem and not something to be welcomed.

Figure 16.4 De-industrialisation – a good or bad thing?

The common-sense meaning of de-industrialisation is a decline in the importance of industry within the economy. But how do we measure this decline?

■ Should we look at the numbers employed or the industrial output?
■ Are we concerned with absolute decline or with relative decline compared with other sectors?

The concern with de-industrialisation has not been the result of falling industrial production in the advanced industrialised countries. Production has actually continued to increase. Today more products are produced, there is greater variety and new models have replaced older ones. For example, there is no comparison between a computer today and one of twenty years ago; a modern car uses fuel more efficiently; and living standards have risen.

However, as manufacturing has become better (not just in improving quality and efficiency but also in responding to environmental concerns and other challenges), it has also become smaller. In every advanced nation, industry employed a smaller proportion of the workforce in 1995 than it did in 1985; in virtually every nation, it also contributed a smaller proportion of the national output.

Everywhere, the 'slack' has been taken up by services. It was in 1959 in the United States that, for the first time, the service sector of a nation became larger in terms of gross national product (GNP) than the industrial sector; in the 1990s the service sector in every country is much bigger, contributing 70% of the GNP in the United States, Britain and France, 64% in Italy, 60% in Germany and 56% in Japan.

Between the 1960s and 1993 the number of jobs in manufacturing in Britain fell from almost two-fifths (38.4%) of the total to less than a quarter (22%).

Factors causing the decline in manufacturing

The decline of manufacturing is not a uniquely British phenomenon. The same pattern is typical of all major industrial countries. However, the British case stands out as being an early and extreme case of de-industrialisation. The number of people employed in manufacturing has fallen since the early 1960s at an accelerating rate. Whether or not this is seen as a problem depends on why such a change has taken place.

There is considerable evidence that, as economies develop over time, gradual shifts take place between the primary, secondary and tertiary sectors. At early stages of development there is a shift away from agriculture towards industrial and service activities, as the relative importance of agricultural products (food in particular) declines, and manufactured goods and services become more important. As incomes continue to rise, the share of manufacturing in output and employment tends to decline, and that of services tends to increase.

Important causes of de-industrialisation

There are many explanations of de-industrialisation. Here are two important ones. (You can read more about the process in *Industrialisation and Development* by Hewitt, Johnson and Wield, Oxford University Press.)

1 De-industrialisation can result from a change in the pattern of industrial specialisation. A country that discovers a natural resource is likely to experience some de-industrialisation. Production of this new sector will increase rapidly and the share of other sectors, including manufacturing, is reduced. Can you think of an example?

   The obvious one was the discovery of North Sea oil. This changed Britain from being a net importer to being a net exporter of oil and led to a reduction in the share of manufacturing industry in output and employment. This type of de-industrialisation is not necessarily bad. With the development of oil as an export Britain did not need such a large manufacturing base.

2 Lack of competitiveness in manufacturing can lead to de-industrialisation. It is this case which is really the major cause of concern. A country that is becoming less competitive in manufacturing will see its share of world exports of manufactures decline and its imports increase. Declining employment in the manufacturing sector will not be sufficiently offset by increased employment of labour in other sectors.

   The slow growth of domestic manufacturing will lead the country to fall further behind its competitors as productivity increases lag, and a vicious circle of decline is set in motion, with rising unemployment and a deteriorating balance of payments.

The growth of the service sector

There are three main reasons for the growth of the service sector of the economy.

First, as societies become richer, they choose to spend a higher proportion of their incomes on buying services rather than products.

Second, it has so far proved very much harder to wring additional productivity out of services than out of manufacturing. Greater productivity in a car plant means more robots on the production line; the product does not suffer, indeed probably the reverse.

However, if greater productivity in a school is measured by fewer teachers in the classroom, quality of education suffers immediately.

Third, as countries become richer, they are able to 'export' their profits in the form of investments in other countries. It is evident that a number of countries have invested in manufacturing in developing countries. In turn, the rewards are returned in profits, interest and dividends that can be spent on leisure services.

There is no sign at all that the shift of demand towards services will cease. Indeed, there is a powerful reason to expect it to accelerate – namely the ageing population in industrial societies. The proportion of people over 60 will continue to rise in every developed country for at least a generation. By the year 2020 more than 30% of the population of Germany and Italy will be over 60. Older people are more likely to spend their income on health care, holidays and domestic services. The countries that increase living standards most quickly in the future will be those that can improve the way they run service societies.

Services can be divided into four main groups: financial services and distribution, which tend to be in the private sector; and health and education, which tend to be in the public sector.

Technology can be used to transform each of these areas. In financial services we will see more than ever before the development of paperless money. Financial services are becoming increasingly tailored to the needs of individual customers.

In distribution, the benefits of bulk retailing are likely to be grafted on to much wider swathes of the industry, with resultant cost-cutting.

In health, technological advances have led to people living longer. The focus of health care will now shift to raising the quality of care and fitness throughout people's lives.

Education, too, will become a continuous process, involving people of all ages. Workers can expect to be retrained to take on completely different skills several times during their careers.

Evidence collection point

Identify different firms in your local region which are growing or contracting. What types of new jobs are being created or destroyed? Are these jobs in manufacturing or in service industries?

Case study – The ageing of the working population

One of the most important trends in employment in recent years which has implications for all of us has been the ageing of the population.

Welfare expenditure on the increasing numbers of the elderly places a heavy burden on industrialised economies unless steps are taken to encourage longer and more flexible working lives.

Public pension expenditure and health care for the elderly will become the largest budget items for most industrialised countries at the start of the next century. With employees either choosing or being forced to retire earlier and living longer, fewer economically active people are paying the taxes or earning the wealth to support the rising numbers of the elderly.

By 2025 in Europe, there are likely to be only 1.5 people working for each ageing dependent. In Germany there may be more pensioners than workers.

We are arriving at a situation where baby-boomers will shortly be retiring. They will be out of the labour force for 20 years or more after they retire.

Extending retirement age alone – as Italy, Portugal, the United States, Germany and Greece have done – is not enough. Companies and governments need radically to alter their perception of older workers and the incentives for them to keep working.

The numbers retiring earlier, either from choice or from redundancy, are rocketing. Barely a half of 60–64-year-old males now work in the UK as compared with 90% in the early 1960s.

1 What are the main trends identified in the case above?
2 What do you see as being the major implications for:
 a governments
 b business organisations
 c individuals?
3 What solutions would you put forward for solving some of the problems which are likely to be caused by the ageing population?

Full-time and part-time employment

We have already identified the important changes that are taking place as many full-time jobs disappear to be replaced by part-time work and contracting-out.

Statistics produced by the Labour Force Survey in late 1993 show the increasing importance of new types of working arrangements. The Survey distinguishes between the traditional workforce and the flexible workforce (Figure 16.5).

	All employees (000s)
All in employment	25 381
Traditional workforce, i.e. full-time permanent employees	15 685
Flexible workforce consisting of:	
Full-time temporary employees	659
Part-time permanent employees	4 718
Part-time temporary employees	624
Full-time self-employed	2 590
Part-time self-employed	589
Government training schemes	359
Unpaid family workers	154

Figure 16.5 The traditional and flexible workforce in 1993

There are all sorts of new working arrangements which give greater flexibility. These include:

- Flexitime arrangements
- People working short working weeks
- An hour off each day, where some workers work for an hour shorter than the normal contract. A similar arrangement is the nine-hour fortnight.
- Shift-working – a long-established form of flexible working.
- Job-sharing – two or more people sharing a

particular job, e.g. a morning and afternoon secretary

■ Longer working days complemented by longer periods off work
■ Term-time jobs so that men and women can be with their children during the school holidays
■ Weekend working
■ Individual working hours where the work schedule is negotiated on an individual basis.

Evidence collection point

Identify three employees who are not members of the traditional workforce, i.e. they work some form of flexible arrangements. Set out the details of the arrangements which are worked.

Permanent and temporary employment

With the development of the flexible workforce we have seen the expansion of temporary at the expense of permanent employment in a wide range of industries and business organisations.

Evidence collection point

Identify organisations in the local economy which have expanded temporary at the expense of permanent employment. What are the major reasons behind these changes?

Skilled and unskilled employment

Recent years have seen very encouraging progress in the growth of educational and vocational qualifications in the labour force. In Spring 1994, 40% of the employed workforce of working age were qualified to NVQ level 3 or its academic equivalent (2 A levels or a GNVQ Advanced).

The increasing and changing demand for skills means that most of the workforce should be updating and upgrading their skills regularly.

In the late 1980s there was a major increase in job-related training. This trend has again increased in the mid-1990s after falling off during the recession.

Many commentators in the United Kingdom feel that if we can improve our education and training then the output of goods and services will be increased because employees will become more productive.

People are often surprised that we are not further behind in our productivity. Our national output per head in 1990 was 87% of that in the former West Germany and 92% of that in France. One explanation of the relatively small gap is that workers in this country work longer hours. There is evidence that because Britain is increasingly employing flexible approaches to work and because of an increased emphasis on training, our productivity increases are greater than those of rival economies.

Training in crafts and technology in this country still lags behind that in France and Germany. Britain awarded 30 000 mechanical and engineering qualifications in 1990 compared with 98 000 in France and 134 000 in Germany.

The shortfall in intermediate skills training leads to the familiar problems suffered by British businesses near the peak of any boom. They cannot find enough skilled people, and therefore enter into a wage-bidding war that aggravates inflation. British managers have to make production systems foolproof because they cannot dispense with unsatisfactory workers. Downtime (time when production lines are not working) is greater than on the continent because workforces are unable to repair faults and have to await specialised skilled maintenance and repair teams. Stocks have to be higher to avoid bottlenecks.

Case study – The German system of vocational education

The German education system is based on dividing schools into three groups: grammar, technical and vocational. The vocational group is put through a methodical system of apprenticeship training – 70% of Germany's labour force has passed through this system. It is firmly based in the private sector. Teenagers leaving school between the ages of 15 and 19 sign with an employer, who trains them for two or three years in one of 380 occupations. They become craftworkers, machinists, secretaries, sales assistants, etc.

The system is administered by chambers of commerce, which register the apprentices, certify the trainers, regulate the programmes, and organise the exams. The qualifications are recognised throughout Germany and increasingly throughout Europe.

The trainees receive not more than a quarter of the wage paid to qualified employees. Since the training is based in the workplace, the apprentices are among adult workers and so have models to emulate. And their reward for completing the course is clear – their wages are quadrupled.

However, major weaknesses of the German technical schools are that they lack good libraries and study space. They are overcrowded and there is little assignment or project work.

1 What aspects of technical education in Germany, outlined above, might we benefit from in the UK?
2 What are the major weaknesses outlined?
3 Try to find out more about German technical education, perhaps by interviewing German visitors to this country, or people with experience of working in Germany.

It is important that employers train their existing workforces in order to improve their productivity and remain competitive. The major responsibility for training rests with employers, not with the government. Unfortunately, in periods of recession employers are likely to cut back substantially on their training budget. It becomes cheaper to recruit skilled labour from the pool of the unemployed.

Employers can benefit from:

■ supporting the development of employer-led Training and Enterprise Councils (TECs) and the initiatives created by TECs to deliver training schemes
■ offering placements on employment training schemes.

The availability of job-related training varies according to employment status and age. Part-time employees are less likely than full-time employees to be offered training, and the self-employed are significantly less likely to get training (Figure 16.6). The older an employee, the less likely it is that he or she will be offered job-related training.

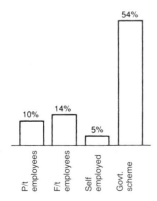

Figure 16.6 Job-related training according to employment status in recent years

Male and female employment

In recent years the number of women in employment has risen both numerically and in percentage terms compared with men, so that women now make up nearly half of the workforce in the United Kingdom.

Demographic changes have meant that there are fewer young people in the labour force and frequently these have been replaced by mature women, often doing part-time work.

In recent times the average hourly earnings of women have been nearly a quarter less than those of men. A major cause of women's lower earnings has been lack of access to overtime. However, as well as earning less than men, recent studies show that women also tend to be concentrated in low-paid occupations such as distribution, hotel, catering and other services, accounting for a quarter of all female employment.

Public administration, education, health, leisure and personal services account for just over 40% of female employment. Surveys show that in none of these occupational groups do women earn more than men.

A large proportion of the growth in female employment is due to an increase in the number of women working part-time. Some official definitions define part-time work as that which involves less than 30 hours per week of work. The vast majority of part-time employees are married women (almost 75%).

There are two main reasons why a large number of women work part-time.

1 They tend to have greater responsibility for childcare and domestic work.
2 The poor provision for childcare in the UK.

Evidence collection point

Investigate employment in a particular business which is a large-scale employer. Make a comparison of the types of jobs which are carried out by men and women in the organisation.

The growth of the underground economy

The 'underground economy' is the term currently used to describe economic activity which is undeclared for tax purposes. Most countries have substantial underground economies where people are paid for work by cash in hand rather than through formalised paperwork. The underground economy has always been with us, but in recent years people have been developing increasingly sophisticated methods of tax evasion.

Regional levels of employment

It is helpful to contrast regional levels of employment in particular sectors of the economy with the national picture, and to examine ways in which this picture is changing over time. The best source of this information is to study the Regional Annex of *The Labour Market and Skill Trends* produced by the Skills and Enterprise Network.

This publication can be obtained from:

Skills and Enterprise Network
PO BOX 12
West PDO
Leen Gate
Lenton
Nottingham NG7 2GB

This data will enable you to get a good picture of changes in employment structure in your particular region.

Evidence collection point

Identify the major changes in employment in your region which will be taking place up to the year 2001.

Differences in pay

The ability of an organisation to pay high wages depends on the value of the output of employees and the price at which the organisation can sell its products. The same is true of the whole economy.

A high-wage economy is one that produces products that command premium prices. A low-wage economy is one that produces basic items at prices that have been forced down to a low level by competition.

Figure 16.7 shows that there is a substantial difference between the pay received by some categories of employees (e.g. doctors) and others (e.g. hairdressers). The chart relates to the spread of pay in 1993. We can also see that within an occupational group there is a considerable spread in pay – some doctors were earning about £20 000 while others were getting nearly £50 000. In 1993 the average salary of doctors was £32 000 but 10% of all doctors earned less than £19 292 and 10% earned more than £48 229.

The figures shown in the chart were produced by the New Earnings Survey. The survey broke occupations down into the following ten categories according to earning power (the lowest are shown first).

1 Hairdressers, beauticians, kitchen porters
2 Dry-cleaning staff, waiters, cleaners
3 Assistant nurses, receptionists, packers
4 Caretakers, stores clerks, secretaries
5 Debt collectors, factory workers
6 Laboratory technicians, car workers
7 Librarians, sales reps

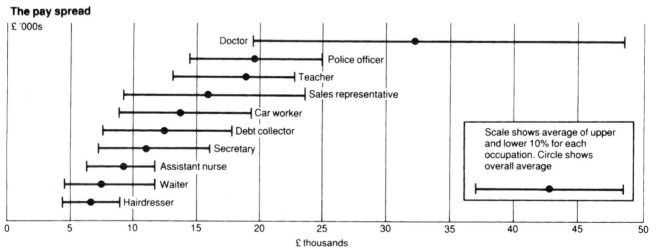

The pay spread

Source: Department of Employment, New Earnings Survey 1991 parts (A&D)

Figure 16.7 The pay spread

8   Teachers, electricians, scientists
9   Accountants, production managers
10 Bank managers, doctors.

Evidence collection point

The following illustration indicates estimated earnings in 1995 of a number of top earners in this country. How would you account for the earnings of these people when compared with the earnings of people in other occupations such as yours and mine?

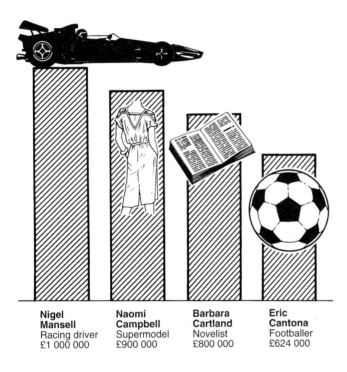

Nigel Mansell
Racing driver
£1 000 000

Naomi Campbell
Supermodel
£900 000

Barbara Cartland
Novelist
£800 000

Eric Cantona
Footballer
£624 000

Evaluating the implications of employment trends in the local and national economy

In examining the changes in types of employment and in employment trends that we have outlined so far it is important to evaluate the implications of these trends in terms of their effects on:

■ individuals in employment
■ the unemployed
■ communities
■ government revenue and expenditure.

Effects on individuals in employment

The effects of the changes we have outlined should be considered in terms of individuals' personal relationships, attitudes, health, and income and spending power.

More and more people are building a living wage out of a portfolio of low-hours employment. In other words they are doing several part-time, perhaps temporary, jobs with a variety of different contractual arrangements.

Jobs for life in most cases are history. The days are gone when a school leaver could expect to work for a single firm until retirement.

The days of the 'permanent temporary' have emerged. The broadening appeal of the permanent temp is directly related to changes that took place during the 1980s which created a demand for interim management. Such demand was created because companies cut staff numbers and then found they could not cope when the workload increased. It is estimated that at least 15% of major companies now use interim managers.

Whilst the formula of 'half as many people, paid twice as well, producing three times as much, equals productivity and profit' seems to be very much in existence, this can have a dramatic impact on workers' lives.

Case study

A newspaper article recently printed the story of a senior manager in his mid-40s who works an average 63 hour week, travels 180 000 miles a year and has taken only four days' holiday in the last year. When not abroad on business he is at his desk by 8.15 am and never leaves before 7 pm. He was recently told that he would have to work longer hours if he valued his job.

Ten years ago someone who worked fewer than eight hours per week was a rarity unless they were looking after children. But changes in 1988 to National Insurance Contributions offered cost savings to firms that sub-divided work into part-time units, thus promoting the supply of jobs offering low weekly hours, as opposed to permanent full-time jobs with increased fixed costs.

In the wake of a lengthy recession, workforce flexibility becomes even more attractive for employers, at a time when low-hours jobs have become feasible for the growing ranks of single-parent families and for students in full-time education whose incomes have been adversely affected by the reduced level of state support.

Case study – The development of the symmetrical family

In the 1970s the sociologists Wilmott and Young looked forward to the development of the new symmetrical family. The belief was that instead of men going out to work and women being responsible for the housework, we would move to a situation in which both men and women would go out to work and housework would be shared.

However, this situation does not seem to have materialised. Instead, today many women with children have a 'double burden'. Half of women who have a baby are back to work in nine months (in the 1950s the figure was 8 years). Survey after survey reveals that women continue to do most of the work in the home. Men are increasingly helping with the shopping and clearing away after meals. However:

- one-fifth never prepare a meal
- two-thirds never wash or iron clothes.

Women on average are in sole charge of the children for 25 hours a week, compared with 6 hours for men.

1 What is meant by 'double burden' of women?
2 How accurately do the figures outlined above tally with families that you are familiar with?

3 Why do you think that women continue to carry a 'double burden'?

The dramatic changes which are taking place in the world of work have a profound impact on relationships. For example, people who work very long or irregular hours may be able to spend little time with their families.

As working conditions change, this will have a profound effect on people's attitudes. For example, those who suddenly find that their job security is being eroded may begin to feel disenchanted and less motivated to work for a particular organisation. Alternatively, fear of losing a job may encourage people to work much harder.

People who enjoy more leisure time may be able to benefit from a healthier lifestyle. There are obvious benefits to health from the decline of hard and unpleasant jobs such as underground mining. However, there will be obvious costs if there is no suitable alternative work.

For those in work, stress is an increasingly common problem. The classic stress situation occurs in jobs with high demands but low support. Perhaps the route to reducing stress is not to reduce demand on people but to increase support. People want demanding jobs that provide interest and variety. The biggest predictor of ill-health is boredom and monotony. Employees need high support both from their boss and colleagues, and in feedback from the work itself.

What can be done to reduce overwork? Under the Health and Safety at Work Act, companies have an obligation to provide a safe environment for staff at work. Some provide what are called Employee Assistance Programmes (EAPs) which are stress management schemes for their staff, while others carry out stress audits or employee satisfaction surveys.

Changes in the world of work will also have a dramatic impact on the spending and earning power of individuals. Those that work long hours and are part of the core workforce stand to make large sums of money. In addition there are others, such as certain self-employed people and those with a high market value, who are able to negotiate contracts which give them very high salaries. However, there are many part-time, non-contracted, temporary staff whose rewards from work are negligible.

For example., in recent times social commentators have identified what they refer to as an 'underclass'. These people can be found in pockets all over the country. They lack any power and receive the worst of everything. The group includes some youngsters with poor qualifications, pensioners, some single-parent families, and some members of particular ethnic groups. For example, a report in 1993 by the charities Barnardos and Youthaid reported that there were 100 000 16- and 17-year-olds with no job and no training place. Hardship payments of £33.60 per week were available for youngsters awaiting training places, and the number of payments made had risen dramatically in the early 1990s.

At the other end of the scale, since the 1950s there has been a steady decline in the numbers of low-skilled jobs and a great increase in the numbers of professional and lower and middle management positions. There are now more high-status jobs around. Commentators refer to the 'new working class' which is particularly concentrated in the South of England. These workers have more spending power and access to goods and services.

Evidence collection point

Interview two individuals to find out what the major effects of the changing world of work have been on them in terms of the factors outlined above.

Effects on the unemployed

People can become unemployed for all sorts of reasons. Particular groups may be more prone to unemployment. For example, in 1994 the rate of unemployment for those between the ages of 45 and retirement age was 8% compared with 16% for 16–24-year-olds. However, if older workers (over 50 years of age) do become unemployed, they are likely to spend a longer period out of work than other age groups. In 1994, 58% of unemployed people aged 50 to retirement age had been unemployed for more than a year. This compared with 45% for the population as a whole.

Prolonged unemployment amongst older workers tends to lead to the 'discouraged worker' effect. Discouraged workers are those who would like a job, but believe there are no jobs available, and so have not looked for work. Many older workers are likely to leave the workforce when they become discouraged.

A host of factors can affect an individual's chances of finding work. Where they live can play an important role. Unemployment rates vary by region – for

example, in 1994 Greater London had an unemployment rate of 13% compared with 7.4% in East Anglia.

Changes in the world of work have meant that employment favours the best qualified, the most experienced, and the most skilled. Those without these advantages are most likely to be employed in part-time, temporary, unskilled and non-contractual work.

Effects on communities

The effects of employment changes will have an overall impact on communities in terms of a general feeling of wellbeing, prosperity or poverty, health and security.

The nature of work is such that as traditional patterns change, then work changes its locations. Former mining communities may be characterised by heavy levels of male unemployment – this will lead to a downward spiral in people's health, wellbeing, security, income, etc.

Evidence collection point

Contrast two localities which have had different experiences resulting from the changing location of work – compare an area which is prosperous with one which is declining. Compare the two localities in terms of wellbeing, prosperity/poverty, health and security.

Effects on government revenue and expenditure

As employment in the national economy increases, the amount of tax collected increases and the cost of social security benefits falls.

As employment in the national economy falls, the amount of tax falls and the cost of social security rises.

For example, when Freda Jones lost her job working as a printing press operative she no longer received a weekly wage of £110. From this income she had typically paid income tax and national insurance of £23. The government had also received taxes from the money she spent on goods through Value Added Tax, the money she had spent on her car through Vehicle Licence Tax and Fuel Tax, as well as a number of other taxes that she had paid. Instead it had to pay her a state benefit of £56 a week.

Evidence indicators

In order to meet the performance criteria for this unit you will need to produce a report which identifies and explains types of employment, and evaluates how at least four types of employment have changed. It should evaluate the effects of changes in terms of employee and business needs.

The report should illustrate national and regional trends in:

- employment in one manufacturing and one service industry
- full-time and part-time employment
- male and female employment
- differences in pay

and explain the implications for:

- employed or unemployed people
- communities
- government revenue and expenditure.

Evidence that you produce during this assignment should help you to meet the standards for the Core Skills of Information Technology, Application of Number and Communication.

The following list should serve as a checklist. Please tick off each of the following when you have successfully covered them as part of your report. You should be able to confirm that:

- I have produced a report in the correct format. ☐
- I have identified and explained types of employment. ☐
- I have evaluated how at least four types of employment have changed. ☐
- I have evaluated the effects of changes in terms of employee and business needs. ☐
- I have illustrated national and regional trends in:
  - employment in one manufacturing and one service industry ☐
  - full-time and part-time employment ☐
  - male and female employment ☐
  - differences in pay. ☐
- I have also explained the implications for:
  - employed or unemployed people ☐
  - communities ☐
  - government revenue and expenditure. ☐

The competitiveness of UK industry

In this chapter we look at some of the most useful ways of comparing the economic performance of the UK economy with that of its competitors, and identify who these competitors are. We then go on to describe some business strategies intended to improve competitiveness, including government strategies. Finally we look at ways of evaluating some of these strategies.

Competitiveness is not constant – it changes all the time, as individuals, organisations and economies strive to improve on their previous best performance. Inevitably some economies, industries and business organisations will grow in strength over time while others decline.

When you study this unit you should seek information from current magazines, journals, and newspapers which analyse the competitiveness of different economies, and different sectors and organisations within an economy. You will benefit from using the contemporary media covering business and government economic strategies.

It is useful to build up a file of newspaper stories on the performance of UK industry; this should introduce you to competing and sometimes conflicting strategies. It is helpful if this sort of study takes place during a time of public debate (e.g. when the Chancellor of the Exchequer presents a Budget or at election time).

Comparing the performance of the UK economy with major competitors

When comparing economic performance we need to use a range of economic indicators. For example, if we simply measured economic performance by looking at whether inflation was under control, we might fail to notice that unemployment is soaring and export sales are low. We therefore need to get a picture of a variety of interconnected variables. In this chapter we identify the following as being valuable performance indicators (Figure 17.1).

- Economic growth
- Investment
- Inflation
- Exchange rate
- Share of world trade
- Research and development
- Technological development
- Productivity.

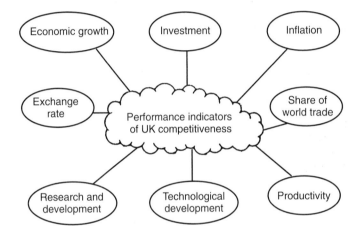

Figure 17.1 Performance indicators

Note that some of the information contained in this chapter looking at economic statistics has been obtained from Barclays Bank Economic Department.

Calculations of changes in national income, inflation, unemployment, etc. are updated regularly as trends and forecasts alter. For the most up-to-date information for your research into UK competitiveness you can obtain country reports (free to Barclays Bank customers) from:

The Librarian
Economics Department
Barclays Bank
PO Box 12
1 Wimborne Road
Poole
Dorset
BH15 2BB

Economic growth

Measuring growth is not an easy business, as we will see below.

One simplistic way of measuring growth is by comparing the gross national product of one year with that of the next, or comparing the GNP of one country with that of another. Measuring GNP is a statistical exercise carried out by the government and recorded in so-called 'Blue Books' of National Income Statistics.

If you look at the circular flow diagram (Figure 17.2) you can quickly get an idea of how GNP can be measured. The illustration shows that households provide factor services to businesses, while buying goods from firms.

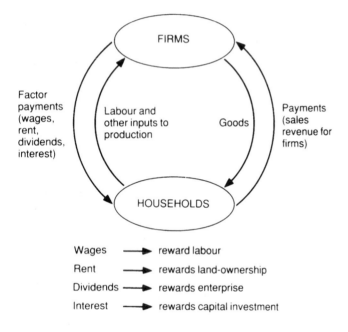

Figure 17.2 The simple circular flow system

You can see that the National Income (GNP) is the total of all incomes earned in a particular period of time by households in wages, rent, dividends and interest. Adding up the GNP would therefore involve counting up these factor incomes, for example in a year. This could be done mainly from tax returns.

Another way of measuring GNP in a time period would be to total up all the final spending by households on goods produced by firms.

Using this simple model we can see that the economy would grow if firms produce more goods,

so that they pay out more in wages, rent, dividends or interest. The economy would also grow if households were able and willing to spend more on buying goods produced by firms.

Business organisations make a contribution to GNP through the value that they add. A business buys in inputs and converts them through its business system into finished outputs. The more efficient the business is, the better the use it will make of its inputs. The business also contributes to national income by paying out factor incomes.

The clear message is that an economy can grow when:

- business increases the value it adds to production
- factors of production increase the value they add to production.

Growth should lead to increasing standards of living so that consumers have bigger baskets of goods to consume (Figure 17.3).

Figure 17.3 Economic growth enables consumers to enjoy more goods

However, we need to be very careful about how we measure and compare growth. GNP only includes the value of things that are bought and sold, missing out huge swathes of the non-money economy. The value of you cleaning your own home is missed out, while the value of industrial cleaning is counted. Caring for Granny at home is out, but nursing-home care is in.

The more self-sufficient people are, the lower their GNP will appear to be.

Since GNP only measures things which are bought and sold for cash, it ignores clear air, pure water, silence and natural beauty, self-respect and the value of relationships between people – all of which are central to the quality of life. Increasingly, more sophisticated ways are being used to measure GNP, but this continues to be a problem.

An additional problem of using GNP as a measure of growth is that it fails to take account of the way we use up scarce resources, which are then not available for future growth or future generations. *The Economist* magazine has recently highlighted this weakness by reporting that 'a country that cut down all its trees, sold them as wood chips and gambled the money away playing tiddly winks would appear from its national accounts to have got richer in terms of GNP per person'.

It is important to appreciate that measuring GNP can be useful in giving a helpful indicator to show how productive an economy is in a particular period of time, i.e. in adding value in the process of production. People have a cause for concern if GNP is not increasing very fast or is falling.

When our competitor's GNP is rising at a faster rate than ours over a sustained period of time this gives a helpful indicator of our falling competitiveness.

Evidence collection point

Study the following information, which sets out details of changes in real national income for some of the UK's main competitors in Europe.

Produce some brief notes covering the following points. The work that you produce would help you to show evidence of the Core Skills of Application of Number and Communication.

Changes	Average 1984–1991	1993	1994	1995	1996	1997
Belgium	+2.6	−0.8	+0.3	+1.0	+1.4	+2.0
France	+2.5	−1.0	+1.5	+2.5	+2.5	+3.5
Germany	+3.1	−1.5	+1.0	+2.0	+2.5	+3.0
Netherlands	+2.7	+1.0	+2.0	+3.5	+3.0	+2.5

What is the main picture that these statistics show about changes in National Income in these countries over the time period shown? How would you explain the difference in growth rates in the periods shown?

Look up comparable data for the UK during the same period, e.g. by using the National Income Blue Books, or researching information from *The Economist* magazine. How does the UK's growth pattern compare with that of these European competitors?

The following information may be of use in helping you to start researching the UK's recent growth performance:

1990	1991	1992	1993	1994
1.0	−2.0	−1.0	+2.0	+4.0

Today, most people recognise that there is far more to a person's quality of life than simply being able to purchase a bigger basket of goods.

In measuring the quality of life the following list of factors is perhaps more comprehensive and useful:

1 The quantity of goods and services produced and consumed
2 The quality of the environment, including space, energy, natural resources and plant and animal species
3 The fraction of people's time available for leisure
4 How fairly – or unfairly – the available income is distributed
5 How good or bad working conditions are
6 How easy it is to get a job – supporting oneself by one's own work is one of the essentials of life and a reduced possibility of doing so means a considerable loss of welfare.
7 The safety of our future
8 How healthy we are
9 The level of cultural activity, the standard of education and the ease of access to it
10 The quality of the housing available
11 The chance to develop a satisfactory religious or spiritual life
12 The strength of one's family, home and community life.

Task

Look at each of the factors outlined above which purport to measure aspects of quality of life. How do you fare at a personal level in terms of each of these factors?

How easy would it be to develop an index which measured these factors in order to replace a simple GNP index?

Are there any factors which have not been listed above which could be included in a measure of quality of life?

Investment

A report produced by the Department of Trade and Industry in July 1993 showed that British industry is lagging behind its international rivals with a productivity gap of about a quarter compared with France, Japan and Germany.

The report showed that expenditure on research and development has slipped behind in the previous ten years, with British industry spending less as a proportion of GDP than Japan, Germany, France and the United States.

Investment is essential to ongoing competitiveness because it is an investment in the future.

Investment means the purchase of goods which go into further production. Examples of investment goods are factory buildings, machines, tools, company vehicles, oil rigs, computers used by businesses, hospitals and schools.

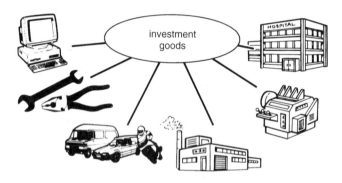

Case study – Investment in the future

Davinder Kaur set up her own business in the late 1980s producing women's clothes. She purchased some old cutting and pressing machines to make the clothes. At the time the economy was booming and there was a healthy demand for her fashion garments.

Davinder's business was highly productive, adding a lot of value to the materials that she purchased. She was soon making healthy profits. At the time a lot of her friends had set up successful businesses and this seemed to be a national picture. It was the days of

'spend, spend, spend' – people were buying new houses, new cars, new luxury goods and holidays abroad.

There seemed little point in replacing the machines because they were so profitable.

However, in the early 1990s a lot of businesses like Davinder's began to suffer. In a period of recession orders began to contract, and because her machines stated to break down her costs of production began to increase. She was in a weak position to face the new climate of competition and quickly her business collapsed.

1 How and why did Davinder fail to invest in the future?
2 What should she have been doing in her profitable period?
3 How would investment have enabled her to weather the storms of the 1990s recession?
4 How can this lack of investment lead to national economic problems?

Business people are most likely to invest when they are optimistic about the prospects for the economy. If they think the economy is booming then they will be confident that they will be able to sell their goods and that investment in the future will be worthwhile.

If business people are pessimistic they will be frightened about investing in case they are unable to sell their goods, and so are unable to make interest payments and repayments of sums borrowed to finance the investment. A high investment economy is one which is most likely to benefit from long-term growth.

Evidence collection point

Study newspaper and magazine reports setting out the UK's recent investment performance when compared with that of Japan, the United States, France and Germany. What is the likely impact of such investment for UK international competitive performance?

Set out your findings in the form of a newspaper editorial to include in your portfolio of evidence. This will enable you to provide evidence of capability in Core Skills of Communication and Information Technology.

Inflation

Inflation occurs when there is a general rise in price levels. Inflation is a highly destabilising force. A

"I SEE THE JONES'S HAVE HAD ANOTHER PAY RISE. IT'S TIME THAT YOUR UNION GOT YOU ONE!"

Evidence collection point

The following table compares price changes in some of the UK's major competitors (% price changes):

Changes	Average 1984–1991	1993	1994	1995	1996
Belgium	3.1	3.0	2.5	3.0	3.5
France	4.1	2.3	2.5	2.5	2.5
Germany	1.9	4.0	2.8	2.5	3.0

Find recent statistics showing the UK's recent inflation performance.

The figures below should help to start you off on your research:

1990	1991	1992	1993	1994
10.0	4.0	2.6	2.7	2.0

Contrast UK performance with that of Belgium, France, Germany and the Netherlands. What are the implications for UK competitive performance and the performance of individual businesses?

small increase in prices can rapidly escalate as people whose wages and other incomes have fallen behind try to catch up, leading to further increases in costs and prices.

Inflation is harmful to trade. Manufacturers generally sell goods on credit. When they seek repayment they find that the money they receive is less than they expected. They therefore become reluctant to trade.

Inflation can also lead to unemployment. Businesses faced by rising costs may be forced to cut back on production and on the number of employees.

Comparative inflation rates are frequently used as an indicator of international competitiveness. If prices are rising faster in the UK than in Germany, France, the United States, Japan, Pacific Rim countries and other competing countries, then we will find it increasingly difficult to sell our goods abroad.

For example, suppose that a German bicycle and a British bicycle are the same price on international markets in 1995 but British domestic prices are rising faster than German ones. This may mean that in 1996 the German bicycle becomes cheaper than the UK one. Over a period of time this loss of competitiveness can be catastrophic.

During the 1970s in particular, the UK lost a competitive edge because of poor productivity and rising prices in the UK. Large swathes of industry were destroyed, never to revive again.

You need to have a clear picture of some of the descriptions of inflation which you will hear being used on the television and see in the newspapers.

- *The headline rate of inflation* – is the increase in the Retail Price Index over a 12–month period.
- *The underlying rate of inflation* – is the Retail Price Index not including mortgage interest payments.
- *The government's target range for inflation* – sets out the target which the government would like to see achieved over a 12–month period and is usually represented by a band covering a lower and an upper figure, e.g. 1–2%.
- *Manufacturing prices* – is inflation as represented by the prices that manufacturers are charging.
- *Core inflation* – some prices are very volatile and may give an unrepresentative view of real price changes. Core inflation is calculated by removing volatile prices such as petrol prices from the index.

Exchange rates

The exchange rate is the rate at which one currency will exchange against other currencies. When your currency rises in value against other currencies this makes your goods more expensive when you export them.

It is important that your currency exchanges at a high enough rate to bring in proper revenues from selling goods overseas. However, if the value rises too much, foreigners will become reluctant to buy your products.

If the value of your currency falls too much it will be easy to sell products abroad – but it may not be worth doing so if each product does not yield much revenue.

International competitiveness is measured by comparing the relative prices of the goods from different countries when these are measured in a common currency.

For example, at a constant exchange rate of dollars/sole (US and Peruvian currencies), Peruvian goods would have become 14 times as expensive in dollars in 1980 as they had been in 1970. Since American goods in dollars were only twice as expensive in 1980 as 1970, Peruvian competitiveness would have been reduced seven times.

The importance of exchange rates in the competitiveness equation cannot be overestimated. Business people often suffer from an ongoing fall in competitiveness caused by exchange rate changes either because the pound sterling is too strong or because it is too weak. The key is to secure just the right balance which makes our goods competitive without being too cheap.

It is important that exchange rates remain stable over a period of time so that traders know what to expect when they exchange goods. In recent years there has been a lot of emphasis on creating stable exchange rates within the EU. The ideal is that at some stage in the future there will be a single currency.

In recent years, sterling has proved to be a volatile currency and this makes life difficult for our exports. Factors which cause the exchange rate to fluctuate include:

- domestic interest rates (raising interest rates helps to raise the value of the currency)
- the UK balance of trade and balance of payments (when we sell more exports then foreigners demand more pounds to buy them, so pushing up the price of the pound)
- the performance of the UK economy (good performance leads to confidence in the UK and its currency, pushing the currency price up as more people want it).

In October 1990 the UK joined the Exchange Rate Mechanism (ERM), which established fairly fixed exchange rates between European Union currencies. However, it was not able to keep within the system for long, as it found it was being forced to carry out policies which went against the interests of the UK economy. The UK therefore left in September 1992, so that once again we have a volatile currency.

The following table shows the sterling exchange rate against the French franc.

	1984–91	1993	1994	1995
Sterling exchange rate	10.51	8.65	8.0	7.6

The figures shown above are quite revealing. For example, if you had gone on holiday to France in the late 1980s with £1000 you would have been able to exchange it for about 10 500 francs. However, if you took £1000 in 1995 you would only have received 7600 francs – you would have been able to buy a lot fewer goods. Expressed in these terms you can see how important the exchange rate is in determining international competitiveness.

Evidence collection point

Set out a spreadsheet showing the exchange rate between the pound and the US dollar, the pound and the Japanese yen, the pound and the French franc, and the pound and the German mark over a six-month period.

Illustrate these changes on a graph, and explain:

a the major factors causing any major or underlying changes
b the likely impact of these changes on exporters and holidaymakers in these countries.

You can use the evidence you collect to provide evidence of capability in the Core Skills of Application of Number, Communication, and Information Technology.

Share of world trade

Today there can be no doubt that UK trade is closely tied to the EU; for example, over half of our exports by value go to EU countries.

We can see the importance of the EU to the UK in the table in Figure 17.4.

A country's share in world trade is a useful performance indicator. During the nineteenth and

	1982	1986	1990	1992
Total trade	55 558	72 988	103 692	108 506
European Union total	24 424	34 996	55 025	60 702
France	4 492	6 211	10 895	11 485
Belgium and Luxembourg	2 310	3 833	5 649	5 715
Netherlands	4 643	5 442	7 561	8 503
Germany	5 413	8 549	13 169	15 213
Italy	2 024	3 463	5 553	6 147
Ireland	2 889	3 554	5 313	5 739
Denmark	1 098	1 212	1 419	1 561
Greece	255	356	683	771
Spain	872	1 906	3 621	4 405
Portugal	429	472	1 032	1 164
Sweden	1 936	2 308	2 712	2 439
Finland	513	664	1 041	997
Austria	251	403	706	795

Figure 17.4 The value of UK exports to selected European countries (£m)

early twentieth centuries, the UK was a major force in world trade. Because we were one of the first countries to industrialise and to develop global trading relations we were world leaders.

However, as time moved on our competitive advantage deteriorated. This was not surprising because the UK is a relatively small island economy with limited supplies of natural resources.

Today we have tied ourselves to the European Union and the performance of our economy in world trading needs to be looked at in terms of the performance of the EU in world markets.

In the early 1990s the EU had 20% of the world market in goods and services both for imports and exports. The United States' import figure was slightly below this and its exports amounted to 15% of the world total. Japan's share was just under 10%. Three-quarters of the EU's trade was in goods and a quarter in services, as shown in Figure 17.5.

The bulk of the EU's trade with other countries is with the Western industrialised countries (about 60%), being made up mainly of manufactured products (64% of imports and 83% of exports). Machinery and transport equipment made up the

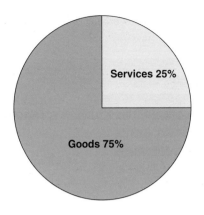

Figure 17.5 Relative market share of goods and services

biggest proportion of trade in manufactured product (40% of exports) followed by miscellaneous manufactures and chemicals.

Case study – The performance of UK exports in 1994

1994 and 1995 were very good years for British exports. Figure 17.6 highlights some of the major increases in British export sales in 1993/94.

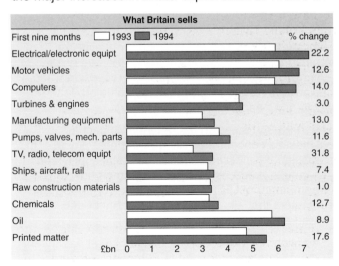

Figure 17.6 Major increases in British export sales 1993/94

Figure 17.7 highlights where some of these major increases in sales were going.

447

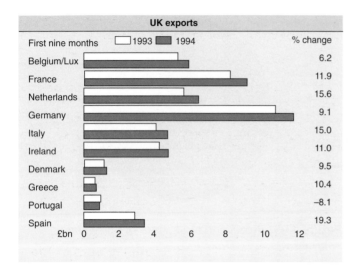

Figure 17.7 Destination of increases in UK exports 1993/94

Because of EU requirements it is now necessary to examine two separate sets of figures for exports – one for exports outside the EU and one for 'dispatches' within it.

In 1994 and 1995 conditions for UK exports were highly favourable. A combination of weak domestic demand, a competitive currency, and strong growth in other countries was a sure-fire formula for success.

Increasingly, UK businesses have been gaining a competitive edge and a reputation for quality. An improvement in management standards and quality assurance took off after the 1980-81 recession when businesses realised that if they did not improve they would go under.

The 1990-91 recession had a further impact as businesses concentrated on applying best practice. In particular, businesses began to use total quality and just-in-time practices. It is not uncommon now to find a large number of UK plant and factories equipped with computers that allow employees to monitor and measure product quality.

In addition, the advent of the Single Market has meant that products are produced to European standards.

In recent times we have seen a fall in the value of the pound against other currencies and we can see a surge in demand for UK exports. A widely quoted recent example of UK success was that when Mercedes-Benz looked at British component suppliers they found that the British suppliers could produce the same quality for 60% of the cost in Germany.

The influx of Japanese companies to the UK has been of tremendous benefit in introducing new working practices and in creating exports. Much of the volume of sales came from the build-up of Japanese-owned plants selling to Europe.

But the most spectacular successes came outside Europe, where car sales rose by 28% in 1994. The Americans were the biggest non-EU customers. Rover took the American market by storm with its Range Rover and Discovery models.

Asia has also proved an excellent market for motor vehicles, with Rover selling 8000 Minis in Japan. Car sales have also been soaring in Malaysia, Thailand and Singapore.

In 1995 it is estimated that Germany, with its 'supermark', will be easier to sell to. There will also be tremendous opportunities in fast-expanding markets in Asia and in new markets in Eastern Europe.

1 Why did the performance of UK exporters improve in 1994–95?
2 Why is export performance an important indicator of overall economic performance?
3 Try to find out more recent evidence of UK performance in world trade.
4 What factors help to explain more recent changes?

Research and development

Research and development should be seen as a considerable investment in future profitability. In a survey of products developed in the latter half of the twentieth century, Japan's Ministry of International Trade and Industry (MITI) found that Britain was responsible for 52% of revolutionary ideas; America came up with 22%, while Japan produced only 6%. But when it came to product development, this order was reversed.

A number of UK commentators have pointed out that industry is not spending enough on research and development to bring new products and processes to market. Research and development in the UK accounts for about 2.5% of national income.

 Evidence collection point

Set out some brief notes gleaned from newspaper articles pointing to the UK's recent performance or lack of performance in research and development in business. Explain why R&D is so important to international competitiveness.

Technological development

Technological development is the process of using new techniques to improve and enhance industrial performance. In an increasingly hi-tech world it is necessary to be at the leading edge of development. Competitors will certainly make use of this edge.

At any one time society has a given stock of knowledge about ways in which goods can be made. Technical advance can come through:

- *invention* – the discovery of new knowledge
- *innovation* – building new knowledge into production techniques.

Invention can lead to spectacular increases in technical knowledge, and successful inventors are always at a premium in society because they help us to leap forward – for example, the creation of crisps, followed by putting flavourings into crisps, followed by being able to produce crisps in a variety of shapes.

Innovation will usually require investment in new machinery and other capital items. This is an area where Britain is sometimes criticised as being slow. The Japanese MITI, in comparison, is very good at making sure that government money is available to convert new inventions and ideas into developed products.

Major new inventions can lead to periods of investment and innovation as these ideas are put into practice. Today we are seeing a wave of new products replacing old ones as new technologies

sweep away old ideas. If we allow innovations to take place we can benefit from an ongoing process of growth.

Case study – Hi-tech gives the edge

Price Waterhouse, in conjunction with the *Business Independent on Sunday*, has during 1994 and 1995 run a competition for 'Middle Market' companies.

Results of their research in late 1995 showed that modern technology was highly important in creating a leading edge.

In 1994 Elonex, the computer company, was top. In 1995 Morse Group, another computer company, led the field. Second-placed Inter-capital Group insisted that their success was based on the use of computers, while third-placed Astec group is involved in mobile telephones.

Ten companies in the table (of 50) are in the computer field, and many others made use of the technology. The leading firms in the competition attributed a large part of their success to concentrating on what they did best, i.e. finding a niche in the market and sticking with it rather than spreading their interests.

Morse used computer technology extensively to achieve its leading position. The company concentrates on financial services of a specialist kind.

Dart, the computer software system in which the company invested a great deal of money, was seen as a way of gaining an edge over the competition. It has become so successful that it is now a profit centre within the organisation and is sold to clients – about 20 banks throughout the world.

1   Why is technology so important in giving an organisation a competitive edge?
2   How can the use of computer systems enhance the performance of organisations?
3   Why is it important to the competitive edge of the UK economy to have new firms being successful in new growing sectors?

Productivity

Modern production depends on the combination of research and development, production engineering, investment funds, investment in people and the effective use of information technology.

When businesses succeed in raising productivity, they are increasing output using fewer real resources.

449

They are breaking down resource constraints and creating opportunities for growth. Just-in-time stock control, CAD/CAM, quality control and teamwork are just some of the strategies with potential in this respect.

A report produced by the Department of Trade and Industry in July 1993 indicated that in terms of value added per hour worked, in manufacturing, the gap between Britain and three other nations – Japan, Germany and France – stood at 20–25%, while it was nearer 70% compared with the United States.

The Confederation of British Industry's national manufacturing council called in Autumn 1992 for a 5% increase in productivity each year for the next ten years. The government is cautious about endorsing specific timescales for improvements, saying that the onus should be on individual industries and companies to compare their productivity month by month with the benchmark standards set by the world's best performance.

Evidence collection point

Use newspapers and magazines to find information about the UK's recent productivity performance. Compare this performance with that of three of the UK's major rivals. What explanations are put forward for the UK's level of performance? Is increased productivity enabling the UK to improve its competitive edge?

Major competitors

European

Who, then, are the UK's major competitors? Clearly UK firms operate in a wide variety of markets, in which they will be faced by different groups of competitors.

For example, in the oil market companies like BP and Shell (which is a Dutch/British company) are faced by major competition from US multinationals like Texaco, and Middle Eastern multinationals like Q8. Clearly these firms are competing on a global scale in a variety of markets.

In markets such as textiles, UK manufacturers will be faced by competition from producers in the Far East and Eastern Europe.

Generally speaking, UK industry has increasingly positioned itself in the markets for high-value-added goods and services as opposed to high-volume, low-cost manufactured goods. Increasingly the UK's markets are for the kinds of goods and services that will be purchased by consumers with higher disposable incomes, e.g. financial services, insurance, whisky and confectionery.

The UK is the fourth largest economy in the EU behind Germany, France and Italy. The emphasis in the UK economy is very much on services, and the work of the City of London makes a substantial contribution to invisible earnings. The City of London continues to be the world's major financial centre and this gives us a considerable competitive advantage.

However, while the invisible trade balance has shown a consistent surplus over the past ten years, this surplus has been declining (see Figure 17.8)

1988	1989	1990	1991	1992	1993	1994
+6	+4	+5	+4	+5	+3	+5

Figure 17.8 UK invisible trade 1988–94 (£bn)

Particularly worrying has been the series of crises which have faced Lloyd's of London, which until recent times had been a model for Britain's efficiency in providing financial services.

The UK still has some important manufacturing industries including chemicals, whisky manufacture, pharmaceuticals and machine tools. You have only to visit a large supermarket abroad to appreciate the real impact that whisky sales make on our balance of payments. Major British companies such as BP, Unilever and ICI have a major international presence.

Over the years there has been a recognition that competitive advantage has been lost in industries such as coal, iron and steel, engineering and textiles. The car industry declined seriously in the 1970s and early 1980s. However, Japanese car manufacturers have had a major impact in turning this around with their plant in this country.

The 1970s and 1980s saw a considerable restructuring of manufacturing companies. This was also a period of extensive privatisation as telecommunications, gas, water, steel, electricity and other concerns were sold off to the private sector and substantially reduced in size. The emphasis is still on privatisation but it has become increasingly difficult to place industries such as railways and coal with private investors.

The agricultural sector of the economy accounts for a very small percentage of the labour force, but it is highly productive.

During the 1970s and 1980s the British economy benefited considerably from North Sea oil and gas. In the mid-1990s BP and Shell have again come up with intensive finds off the Shetlands, but it is not clear how valuable these reserves will be with the current depressed price of oil.

Case study – France

France is the largest country in Europe by geographical area. Nearly 65% of its exports are within the EU. Manufacturing industry is responsible for nearly 25% of national output.

In recent years the French government has managed to hold back inflation and this has enabled it to achieve some slow growth, although unemployment levels are relatively high and are likely to remain so.

In 1992 it looked as if the French franc might not be able to keep within the bands expected by the Exchange Rate Mechanism. However, the storm was weathered and the French economy now appears to be in a relatively strong position, enabling it to play an important role in Europe. Labour costs have been falling and, importantly, the level of inflation is lower than that in neighbouring Germany.

However, France is plagued by high levels of unemployment and this has led to serious social hardship. There are many political activists in France who feel that the level of unemployment is unacceptable, and this has led to industrial action and civil disturbance.

In the 1980s French businesses tended to concentrate on selling to a protected home market and to less-developed countries. In recent years there has been more emphasis on selling to industrialised markets. The French have been successful in this area, and that has been a major feature of improving external trade.

The general economic policy of France is a balance between free enterprise and government intervention. In the past, levels of protection were quite high; however, with the development of the EU more and more large French companies have looked outwards to international markets. Many companies have become international in stature, e.g. Chanel in cosmetics and Renault and Peugeot in car manufacture.

	1994	1995	1996*
Change in national income	1.5	2.5	2.5
Unemployment rate	12.5	12.5	12.5
Prices (%) change	2.5	2.5	2.5
Current a/c (Fr bn)	0.7	0.8	−0.5
Interest rates (%)	4.0	4.0	5.0
Sterling exchange rate	8.0	7.6	?

*Forecast

Figure 17.9 French economic statistics (1994–96)

Evidence collection point

Identify the major changes which have been taking place in the French economy in the last year. How do these changes fit with the economic statistics provided for the French economy?

Case study – Germany

East and West Germany were reunited as a Federal Republic of Germany on 3 October 1990. Since the Second World War, West Germany has been one of the powerhouses of the world economy and a major force in the EU.

During the late 1980s the German economy was starting to slow down, and in the early 1990s the Germans were faced with the tremendous costs of reunification as much of former East German industry became redundant overnight.

The former West Germany was a free enterprise, Western economy merging with a state socialist, Eastern bloc country in which pollution had been a major external cost of industrial activity.

The process of unification led to a temporary boom as consumers in the East were able to purchase new consumer durables for the first time. The boom ended in the second half of 1992, leading the economy into a recession as sharp as any since 1945. Manufacturing took the brunt of the downturn.

Some commentators feel that German manufacture should have been reduced at an earlier stage. Today Germany typifies the high-cost Western economy with highly paid labour trying to compete with low-cost labour in the new Pacific Rim economies. It seems likely that manufacturing in Germany will need to be trimmed

451

considerably, with smaller workforces, shorter working weeks and fewer producers. German growth is likely to be slow because of loss of competitiveness within the EU.

A recent study by a German research institute has shown that, in 1992, West Germany had the highest hourly wage rates among developed economics. Major problems were caused by the strength of the German currency in international markets and by social security and welfare payments which amounted to almost 50% of labour costs. Also, Germany's excellent environmental standards added to the cost of production.

Evidence collection point

Carry out some research into a local manufacturing company which operates in an important industrial sector, e.g. chemicals, food or confectionery. Identify the organisation's major European competitors. Show how competition has changed over the last ten years, and how the business has fared competitively. Set out your findings in a written report which could be used to provide evidence of the Core Skill of Communication.

Non-European

You have only to look at the major sources of UK imports in 1958 and 1991 to appreciate who some of our major non-European competitors are both in home and foreign markets (Figure 17.10).

Imports from (% of total)	1958	1991
Germany	19.5	23.5
Belgium	17.8	13.0
USA	11.3	8.1
France	2.8	7.0
Japan	0.8	5.4
Italy	1.8	3.4
Spain	0.4	1.4

Figure 17.10 UK imports in 1958 and 1991

The USA and Japan have been and continue to be major competitors for UK businesses.

Businesses in these countries have been able to benefit from large production runs of products and very high quality standards. In particular we talk about the Japanese 'economic miracle' after the Second World War and how the Japanese have created a new style of quality products, particularly in the field of manufacturing.

Case study – Japan

The growth of the Japanese economy is usually heralded as the major 'economic miracle' of the twentieth century. However, the seeds of this growth really occurred in 1868 when the Japanese first decided to build a modern economy and from that time grew at a faster rate than other economies. From 1960 to 1974 real income per head grew at an average annual rate of nearly 10% and this growth has continued until the present date.

During the late 1970s and early 1990s the Japanese have built up a reputation for high quality and high performance at reasonable prices. The emphasis in Japan has been very much on providing goods which meet the 'fitness for purpose' requirement of quality.

Important ingredients of Japanese success have been the high-quality management of organisations, who plan the introduction of new products over many years. Another aspect has been the responsibility given to workforces who are expected to contribute to decision-making through quality circles.

Japanese employees have been very loyal to their companies and in large organisations there has until recently been a guarantee of jobs for life. In Japan there has also been a strong emphasis on bonus payments which provide an incentive for individual workers to care about the profits made by corporations.

In addition the government works closely with firms, particularly through MITI, in helping to finance the research and development of new products and in providing a secure economic environment.

Recently Corporate Identification (CI) has been very important in Japan and is the process whereby a 'clear and good corporate image [is projected] to the public by advertising the unique character and culture of the corporation using various kinds of slogans and signs.' Corporations work long and hard to develop CI so as to provide a strong relationship with customers.

At the same time the emphasis in Japan is on providing the right products at the right price. This is achieved by strong marketing programmes in which products are designed to meet consumer requirements. There is also a continuing emphasis on lowering costs while maintaining the quality of products. Factory automation has been a major weapon in making this possible, e.g. by using robots and computer numerical control machine tools coupled with automated warehouses and unmanned vehicles.

The emphasis in Japan is on reducing waste to a minimum through high quality standards. The watchword is 'fool-proofing', whereby systems are organised in such a way as to minimise the likelihood of mistakes.

We have already seen that 'just-in-time' is central to the Japanese system. All ingredients in the production process are carefully planned so that they arrive just in time and in just the right sequence to enable smooth production.

Quality control circles are organised so that small groups of grass-root level employees meet together regularly to discover and analyse daily problems in order to come up with the most effective solutions.

The aim of Japanese industry is total quality management. TQM is seen as the prime way of achieving competitive advantage.

In recent times we have come to talk about the 'Japanisation' of British industry. Not only have British companies been able to benefit by learning from the increasing number of Japanese companies operating in this country, but also they have been able to benefit from taking on board the overall approach used by industry in Japan.

The process of 'benchmarking' involves adopting the very best standards which are used by other firms and industries, particularly in your own industrial sector. UK companies have increasingly worked towards the benchmarks established in Japan. This has enabled many UK companies to make advances and to win exports in the mid-1990s. One of the main advantages that the Japanese economy has had over the years has been the very high savings ratio in Japan, which at times has been over 100% higher than that in the UK. This money has then been available for investment in both the Japanese economy and in other countries.

The money that has been channelled into investment has then made possible the great increases in productivity (Figure 17.11).

In the mid-1990s we have seen an increase in savings in this country coupled with increased investment in modern production techniques. Correspondingly we have been more competitive in export markets.

At the same time we have seen more instability in the Japanese economy. The 'high yen' has meant that

Figure 17.11 The path to a 'miracle"

Japanese exports are less competitive than in the past. Many people in Japan are less inclined to save than previously. Many Japanese organisations are no longer prepared to offer 'jobs for life'. However, the Japanese economy continues to be very strong and Japanese organisations still have a powerful name for quality.

1 What are the major factors which have contributed to the strength of the Japanese economy?
2 What lessons can British business learn from Japan?

Case study – The United States

The United States has been a major competitor of the UK from the late nineteenth century onwards. In particular, the USA has been able to benefit from its large size (a large home market) and a relative abundance of raw materials and land. The opening up of the USA through railways and, later, roads helped to create a massively powerful international economy with rich deposits of natural resources such as oil and fertile agricultural land.

In particular, the USA has been able to be highly competitive in products that it can produce in bulk – wheat, iron and steel, coal, automobiles, agricultural equipment, computers, telecommunications, etc.

During the early part of this century the term 'Fordism' was coined to describe the large hierarchical American companies which thrived on mass production of standardised products such as the Model T Ford.

The American economy provided both an opportunity and a threat to UK producers – an opportunity as a large market and a threat as a producer of relatively cheap, high-quality products such as the Massey-Ferguson tractor, Coca-Cola and IBM computers.

During the 1970s and 1980 US manufacturers increasingly lost ground to the Japanese and other growing economies such as South Korea. However, most large US corporations have now adopted Japanese style manufacturing techniques and quality controls.

In the late 1980s the US economy was characterised by increasing moves to labour flexibility. Many US corporations restructured by delayering, and reducing their workforces by thousands. Old-style contracts based on full-time, permanent work were replaced by new flexible arrangements. This meant that after an initial period of growing unemployment, people were then able to find work with a number of part-time, temporary contracts, and many other flexible arrangements.

Today US business is leaner and fitter, and US corporations tend to focus on their best lines rather than producing a variety of unrelated products.

1   What advantages have US producers had which have enabled them to develop a competitive edge in particular markets?
2   How can UK producers learn from the UK experience?

Case study – The Pacific Rim

In 1989 Australia was instrumental in encouraging the development of a new trading organisation and alliance, Asian-Pacific Economic Cooperation. This organisation is made up of Asian and Pacific Rim countries. It includes the world's two largest economies, the USA and Japan, and the fastest-growing, China. Also among APEC's 15 members are East Asia's up-and-coming economic powers: South Korea, Taiwan, Malaysia, Thailand and Singapore. APEC accounts for more than half the world's economic output and two-fifths of its trade, but it is only a relatively loose organisation of trading nations when compared with the EU.

However, its significance is that it presents new alliances in trade. Today, for example, United States' trade across the Pacific is already 60% higher than that across the Atlantic.

APEC has set itself the target of becoming a well-organised free trade area by 2010. There is little doubt that, historically speaking, Europe's economic fortunes are in decline and those of Asia-Pacific are in the ascendant. A Harris poll of European business leaders in mid-1995 revealed that 45% thought China and South-East Asia would become the most powerful economic region over the next 10–15 years.

We are left with the question as to what Europe should do about these changes. The rise of Asia-Pacific marks a shift in the global economic centre of gravity. The UK has to learn, assimilate and cooperate. Just as we have learnt to adopt through 'benchmarking' the best principles of our rivals and competitors, so we need to learn from the best principles that emerge from Asia-Pacific. The UK should be looking to development in Asia-Pacific as an opportunity as well as a challenge.

1   Why has Asia-Pacific developed as an economic powerhouse?
2   What are the major implications for UK organisations?

Evidence collection point

Set out a brief report outlining the strengths of five of the UK's major competitors. One side of A4 for each country should be adequate.

Business strategies intended to improve competitiveness

There are many different strategies that can be employed by UK businesses to improve their competitiveness.

We will look at these strategies under a number of headings:

- Organisational structure
- Human resourcing
- Marketing
- Scale of production
- Finance
- New technology.

Organisational structure

An organisation needs to operate in such a way as to give it a competitive edge. In today's competitive markets organisations must respond quickly to dynamic change, so they will need to have loose and flexible arrangements which empower people to make appropriate decisions in diverse markets.

Today a lot of emphasis is given to creating the architecture for business success. Professor John Kay of the London Business School defines the 'architecture' as 'the network of relational contracts within, or around, the firm'. He cites Marks and Spencer as an example of a company with a strong architecture that depends very little on any individual or group of individuals.

All too often, however, businesses are limited because an effective organisational architecture is not put in place. Members of an organisation should feel proud to belong to it. Frequently they do not and this is a severe limitation to competitiveness.

Maintaining morale implies both motivating people effectively and creating an organisational structure which is tailored to the needs of the business concerned. The quest for efficiency often leads businesses to change the nature of their management structure. This can improve morale but it can also be destructive of individuals' security and sense of well-being.

Evidence collection point

Interview a manager at a local organisation that trades internationally. Find out how the organisation has recently changed its 'organisational architecture' in order to gain or maintain a competitive edge.

Human resourcing

People are the most important resource of organisations. It is necessary to ensure the commitment of individuals to the success of an organisation. Human resource management involves seeking to develop individuals to the best of their potential.

Individual development is best for the organisation and for the individual because it encourages commitment. Individuals also need to be encouraged to become decision-makers in their own right. This helps to create a thinking organisation rather than one in which decisions are simply passed downwards.

Jon Katzenbach and Doug Smith in their book, *The Wisdom of Teams; Creating the High-Performance Organisation* (Harvard Business School Press, 1993),

argue that there is a threshold that a group must come through before it becomes a team. They define a team as:

> A small number of people with complementary skills who are committed to common purposes, performance goals, and an approach for which they hold themselves mutually accountable.

They argue that human resource managers should seek to create a 'high-performance team'. As well as meeting the definition for a real team, this group will also be deeply committed – even beyond the team set-up – to the personal growth and success of its members. It will significantly out-perform other teams. They identify a performance curve as teams move towards team effectiveness (Figure 17.12).

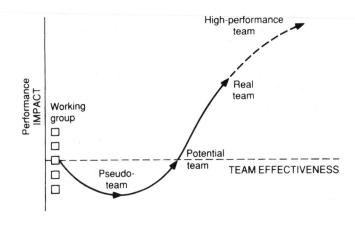

Figure 17.12 The performance curve

Evidence collection point

Identify ways in which a human resource management approach in a local organisation enables it to gain a competitive edge.

Marketing

Market saturation is a problem that can face a firm all too quickly. The market may be saturated because limited demand has been quickly satisfied. Alternatively, weak marketing may mean that potential demand has not been effectively identified.

Effective marketing involves identifying consumers' requirements and meeting them in order to make a profit. Ineffective marketing involves failing to identify and meet consumer requirements at a profit.

The ability to extend a product life-cycle is often essential if firms are to continue to grow.

The 'spotlight' technique is a useful way of analysing the strengths and weaknesses of a business.

The spotlight technique employs four spotlights:

1 *Market penetration* This spotlight help you to test how well you are selling in your chosen market. Improvement could be made by increasing sales to current customers or attracting new ones in the same sector.
2 *Market development* This spotlight lights up new markets for your product or service.
3 *Product development* This spotlight illuminates products that you can develop, or change, to make the most of your current markets.
4 *Diversification* This spotlight sheds new light on possibilities for developing new products and/or services in order to open up completely new markets.

Evidence collection point

Interview a local business manager whose organisation is involved in exporting. Find out how they use marketing to take advantage of new opportunities. Can you relate their marketing to the spotlight approach?

Of course, in looking at marketing we should emphasise the importance of research and development as a key part of this activity. Market research should focus on finding out exactly what consumers require and then this information should feed into product development.

Scale of production

The scale of production is a major factor in giving a competitive edge for nearly all products for which there is a high demand. Coca-Cola and Mars are prime examples of organisations being able to spread their fixed costs over very large outputs. The fixed cost contribution that goes into a Mars bar is almost zero.

The way to achieve large-scale production is to sell successfully into a large market. Exporting can therefore be very important in reducing costs.

The UK has only a relatively small domestic market. However, if we consider the market to be the European Union we are faced with a sizeable market. If producers then think about making global sales they are in a position to produce very large outputs at extremely low unit cost.

Evidence collection point

Make brief notes showing how a particular UK producer is able to benefit from producing low-priced products as a result of large-scale production.

Increasing the scale of production can lead to greater productivity. However, there are examples of new technology allowing small-scale production to be competitive. For example, breweries that start up by using the latest automated equipment, which is relatively cheap to install, are able to produce specialist beers at a comparatively low cost.

Finance

Finance is one of the biggest stumbling blocks to business expansion. It is not just a case of having enough finance, it must also be of the right type. In particular there must be sufficient cash flow to meet day-to-day trading needs.

The Association of British Factors and Discounters calculated that in 1993 £50 billion was owed in unpaid bills, with the average business having to wait 81 days for payment.

Businesses also need to be careful not to borrow so much that they cannot make their repayments. Rising interest rates in the late 1980s and early 1990s forced many businesses into liquidation. Any organisation needs to structure its financing carefully so as to meet its key objectives – whether they be to maintain a liquid position, or to provide funds for investment projects.

Finance is essential to organisations wishing to secure a competitive edge. The key is to have the right type of finance, in the right place, at the right time. In this respect the government can play a key role in making sure that organisations that develop new ideas are supported in their ventures.

Financial control is also an important element of business activity. It is essential that businesses carefully control the costs of labour, production and marketing in order to obtain a competitive edge.

Evidence collection point

Interview a local business manager to find out how his or her organisation carefully controls the cost of labour, production and marketing in order to gain a competitive position.

New technology

The record that a country has in employing new technology will be a key determinant of the competitive edge that the country is able to obtain.

For example, many of the former Communist countries in Eastern Europe operated their industry during the 1980s using outmoded technologies. This was not a major problem at the time because they were operating in highly protected markets. The products that were made managed to sell, although it is clear that consumers were often frustrated by what they were 'forced' to buy.

However, when Eastern bloc countries were opened up to the storm of international competition many of the old businesses collapsed overnight (although many continued to be subsidised). The reconstruction of the former East Germany has been an expensive business because it has involved the replacement of old with new technology. Nevertheless, it seems clear that in the longer term

this will pay off as the employment of new technologies will create competitive advantage.

Evidence collection point

Show how the employment of new technology by a local business (e.g. a college or school) has enabled it to gain competitive advantage.

Government strategies intended to improve the competitive position of UK industry

The government has a major role to play in helping business within a country to secure competitive advantage.

Case study – Government intervention in industry

In 1987 Michael Heseltine, before he became the government minister responsible for industry, published a book called *Where There's a Will*. In it he argued the following case:

> The capitalist economies with which we have to compete do not operate on the theory held in Britain that government is an onlooker in the industrial game or at best a referee. In most of these countries, there are partnerships between the government and the industrial world.

457

France and Germany share with Japan the sense of national purpose which so many observers note in our competitors but do not find in Britain. This purpose is based on partnership.

In many of the high technology fields, the role of the government is the manifestation of French will..... We would not have a major civil airframe manufacturing capability in Europe today if it were not for France. We would not have a launcher capability in the space field but for France....

It is not intervention that is wrong: in the modern world, it is unavoidable. What was wrong before was the subsidising of losses and the cosiness and lack of professionalism associated with that. Intervention and featherbedding are not the same thing. The trick is to distinguish between them.

The evidence is that there will be continuing development and growth in, for instance, aerospace, robotics, telecommunications and biotechnology. These are all areas which Britain's competitor governments are supporting. Government and industry in Britain must talk together about what markets exist, could be created, or are under threat.

In his 1989 book, *The Challenge of Europe: Can Britain Win?*, Heseltine argued:

Government will have to fund much of the seed-corn exploration which alone can lead to breakthroughs but which is too costly or too risky for the private sector to pay for without assistance. Above all, there is one cardinal rule for intelligent, responsible politicians: they should stop pretending that this sort of industrial support is a doctrinal intrusion into the working of the market place.

1 What is Michael Heseltine saying about the role of the government in supporting industry to develop a competitive edge in international markets?
2 What is he saying about the extent to which government should (a) get involved, and (b) not get involved in providing such support?

The government can and does get involved in many interrelated strategies to improve the competitiveness of UK industry.

We will look briefly at:

■ exchange rate policy
■ control of inflation
■ privatisation
■ deregulation
■ reducing the role of the government

■ investment in new technology
■ improving training and education
■ taxation affecting aggregate demand
■ government expenditure
■ European market integration
■ participating in the World Trade Organisation (WTO).

Before reading on you may benefit from referring back to notes we made under many of these sub-headings in Chapter 3.

Exchange rate policy

Money is demanded in order for it to be used to buy and sell goods and services. The price of the pound therefore depends on its demand and supply.

Let us assume that one pound exchanges for ten French francs (as was the case at the end of the 1980s). Demand for pounds may come from two sources. Firstly, when British producers sell goods in France they will want payment in pounds, but will often be paid in francs. Secondly, French citizens who want to purchase shares in British assets, e.g. shares in Laura Ashley plc or Marks and Spencer, must change their francs into pounds to buy them.

On the other side of the equation, a supply of pounds may arise in the foreign exchange market because UK firms and households want to purchase French goods, and because UK citizens want to purchase French assets.

Figure 17.13 illustrates the demand and supply for pounds in our simplified foreign exchange market.

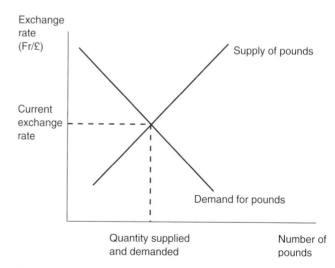

Figure 17.13 Determining the market exchange rate

If Marks and Spencer sells ties at £5 each, with an exchange rate of 10 Fr/£, a tie will cost a French consumer 50 francs. However, at 8 Fr/£ (the exchange rate which prevailed in late 1994) it will cost only 40 francs. We would therefore expect M&S to sell more ties (and other goods) at the lower exchange rate. We can therefore make a generalisation that a larger quantity of pounds will be demanded at lower franc–sterling exchange rates. Hence, the demand curve for the pound slopes down from left to right.

Today, as we have seen, we are experiencing massive shifts in global trading relations and in competitive advantage. Many Western European economies have lost their competitive edge in many fields of manufacture to Pacific Rim countries. These countries are able to match and beat Europe in high technology production, and to undercut Europe in terms of wages and other costs (e.g. through lower environmental standards).

This means that many manufactured products are sold into highly competitive markets in which consumers have a keen awareness of alternatives on offer and are interested in quality. There may be little advantage to be gained by many British manufacturers from depreciation in the exchange rate since competition does not focus on price.

At the same time, increases in the value of the pound can erode a very thin competitive edge for many UK firms.

The key to business success through exchange rate fluctuations is to ensure that you have a competitive advantage. This involves giving your product that little bit extra to make it into a 'unique selling proposition' (USP), whether it be through after-sales service, delivery or additional features of the product. UK firms need to ensure that they are ahead of the field so that, like Marks and Spencer, they give that little bit extra when compared with the competition.

The UK government has a very important role to play in managing exchange rates to ensure that they are appropriate to creating competitive advantage.

The exchange rate will depend on the demand and supply for the pound in international markets. Foreigners will demand British goods if they are attractive. Hence the government has a role to play in helping UK industry to produce quality goods. Foreigners will demand pounds for investment purposes if they feel that the UK is a secure place to put their money. The government therefore has a role to play in creating a secure environment with effective economic policies.

The level of UK interest rates will also play a part in attracting overseas investment in this country.

The government can also manage the exchange rate by instructing the Bank of England to buy and sell pounds on international markets. If the pound is falling (perhaps because of loss of confidence in the government) then the government can instruct the Bank to buy pounds using gold and foreign currency reserves. If the pound is becoming too strong the government can instruct the Bank to sell in order to lower the value of the pound by making it more plentiful.

However, it must be remembered that the Bank of England does not have a bottomless pit of gold and foreign currency reserves to trade.

Generally speaking, as an economy becomes less competitive over time the value of its currency will fall. A major reason for this lack of competitiveness may be that government economic policies are inappropriate.

Managing the exchange rate is crucial. If the pound is valued too low then exporters will increase the volume of their sales, but the value may fall. If the pound is too high the volume of sales will fall, and so too may the value.

Evidence collection point

Study changes in the value of the pound over a three-month period. Identify the major causes of changes in its value. How has the government been involved? How have changes in the value of the pound affected local businesses that export?

Evidence that you produce from this activity may be used to show evidence of capability in the Core Skills of Application of Number, Communication and Information Technology.

Control of inflation

The control of inflation is very important in creating competitive advantage. For example, the German economy has been very successful in the second half of the twentieth century because among other policies it has set out to limit inflation.

Rising prices feed quickly into rising costs, including rising wages. It does not take long to lose a competitive advantage. Perhaps this year your prices are rising by half a per cent more than those of rivals

– next year this may be one-and-a-half per cent, and so on.

Inflation is always a problem because it sets up a vicious cycle of further wage and price rises.

In a period of inflation, savings are discouraged. Savers are reluctant to save because the real value of their savings falls. With less being saved there are less funds available for investment, pushing up interest rates and other business costs.

In a period of inflation, not only will exports become dearer and less competitive, but also imports will become relatively cheap. People in this country will start to buy more (cheaper) imports and fewer (more expensive) home products.

Once inflation takes off it can deteriorate into a spiral in which people lose confidence in the currency. This state is called hyperinflation and can lead to massive price rises with money becoming worthless.

Governments can employ a range of policies to control inflation.

The government exerts a big influence on how much is spent in the economy. It can deliberately manipulate the amount of spending in the economy through fiscal policy. As we have seen, fiscal policy is the relationship between government spending and taxes.

To increase spending in the economy, the government can increase its own spending, lower taxes or impose a combination of lower taxes and increased spending.

To reduce spending in the economy, the government can reduce its own spending, raise taxes, or impose a combination of reduced spending and raised taxes.

The government can also influence demand in the economy through its monetary policy. In the UK the government is responsible for printing money and controlling the banking system through the Bank of England. If it increases the amount of money in the economy then there will be more available for spending in shops, pubs, clubs, cinemas, etc. The government can print more money to finance its own spending.

As well as controlling the quantity of money in circulation, the government also sets the price of obtaining money. The price of borrowing money is the interest rate. Raising interest rates discourages borrowing and spending. You will find that one of the first actions that the government will take if spending starts to increase too quickly (leading to

rising prices) is to raise interest rates. Of course, it will look long and hard before doing this because raising interest rates can have a dampening effect on economic activity.

For example, in May 1995 it was suggested that the Chancellor of the Exchequer should raise interest rates because the pound was falling in value and inflation was starting to rise. However, the Chancellor resisted raising interest rates (at least for a while) because he wanted the economy to pick up and demand to become more lively.

 Evidence collection point

Set out a league table comparing the current rate of inflation in the UK with that of three major competitors.

How do differences in inflation rates help to give each country a competitive advantage or disadvantage? Describe two policy measures that would enable the UK to reduce its inflation rate.

Privatisation

Privatisation is seen by some people as a way of increasing competitive edge. The argument is that the freedom of the market and the existence of competition 'forces' organisations to be more competitive and efficient.

Privatisations have reduced the role of the UK government to one of the lowest in Europe, although it remains higher than in the United States (Figure 17.14).

Country	Percentage of national income produced by nationalised industries
France	17
Italy	14
UK	11
United States	1

Figure 17.14 The role of the state in production in selected countries

Nationalised industries before privatisation were characterised by what is referred to as 'X-inefficiency', i.e. waste caused by bureaucratic inefficiency and clumsiness. There were simply too many employees doing too little, and not enough incentive for managers to cut out waste. When industries such as gas, airlines, water and electricity distribution were placed in the private sector the emphasis was on more competitive structures and accountability to shareholders.

Public corporations, too in recent years have been increasingly expected to operate as if they were in the private sector.

In a number of cases it is clear that industries have benefited from the process of privatisation in that they have been able to become more competitive, particularly in facing European and worldwide competition. In other cases the evidence has been less clear.

What is clear is that the Labour Party under Tony Blair will not renationalise industries which the Conservatives have privatised during the 1980s and early 1990s. However, the impetus to fresh privatisation has lessened as some state concerns prove to be unsuitable for privatisation while privatisation of others, e.g. the Post Office, is opposed by MPs and the public.

Case study – Productivity growth of privatised industries, 1972–80 and 1980–88

The illustrations below are derived from information collected by the London Business School covering the performance of privatised industries. (Remember that the privatisation process followed the election of the Conservative government in 1979.)

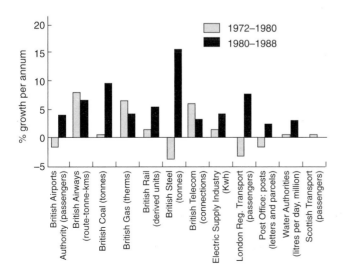

What do the illustrations above tell us about the change in productivity in privatised industries? Why do you think that some changes have been greater than others?

Can you gather more recent evidence relating to the performance of privatised concerns, particularly those that operate in international markets?

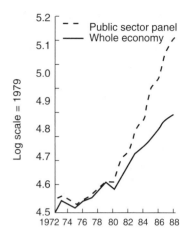

Deregulation

Deregulation involves the freeing up of controls on business activity. The problem with regulation is that it can lead to a mass of controls and administrative procedures that need to be carried out, leading to inefficiency. A good example was the way in which before the development of the Single Market in the European Union exporters had to fill in many documents when exporting and importing. With the creation of the EU this was reduced to a single simplified document covering goods in transit between countries.

When you deregulate business activity it becomes possible for businesses to concentrate on making goods, rather than hiring people to check their paperwork and the way in which they operate, continually having to be careful not to fall foul of administrative procedures. Deregulation means that industry can concentrate on satisfying the consumer and producing quality goods rather than quality paperwork.

Evidence collection point

Interview a local business manager to find out one good example of ways in which deregulation of business or industry has enabled them to become more competitive.

Reducing the role of the government

Those in favour of the free market use the slogan, 'Best government is least government'. The view is that the smaller the part the government plays in directing economic activity the freer businesses will be to satisfy the real needs and wants of consumers.

461

A free market exists when the government plays no part in controlling markets. Decisions are made freely by buyers and sellers. Buyers continue to buy items provided they feel that they are getting value for money.

If consumers consider that they would get better value for money by buying one brand of petrol rather than another, they will buy it. Producers will increase their output in response to consumer demand.

The advantages of a free market without government control and regulation stifling economic activity are:

- Consumers are able to 'vote with their money' for the goods they want to be produced. Popular items are likely to be produced in larger quantities and at relatively low prices.
- Because demand represents consumer needs and wants, resources are channelled into these lines. Resources will not be channelled wastefully into unpopular lines.
- Because the government does not interfere in the economy, consumers can spend their own money in the ways that they see fit. The argument is that you know what purchases will give you most satisfaction. A government official spending money on your behalf is less in tune with your needs and wants.
- A free market system can respond quickly to changes. In other words it is dynamic. In the 1960s and 1970s teenagers tended to buy records, but today they are far more likely to buy tapes and compact discs. The music industry helped to bring about the changes and today music shops supply what the consumer wants.
- Scarce resources do not have to be wasted on administering the system.

The Conservative government from 1979 into the 1990s focused on reducing the part played by the state in directly running the economic system. Increasingly the emphasis was on reducing government spending and government control of industrial activity. The argument was that the unfettered market would lead to increased efficiency. Indeed, during this period many UK industries began to gain competitive advantage. However, there was an increasing feeling during the 1990s that the government had lost touch with popular opinions about social justice.

Case study – Crisis for democracy

In November 1992, Anthony Sampson's *The Essential Anatomy of Britain* was published by Hodder and Stoughton. Anthony Sampson is a widely respected analyst of political power in Britain.

Sampson argued that thirty years ago the landscape of British power was much more varied than it is today. In the 1960s there were far more people who could influence decisions, including trade unionists, outspoken professors, indignant scientists and eccentric church leaders. Now all the spotlights are trained centre-stage, where a single party had been in power for 13 years (up to 1992), led by politicians whose experience is largely limited to politics and finance, and who are removed from grass-roots public opinion. He sets out three major factors that have led to the crisis for democracy.

First, during the 1980s the traditional powers that counterbalanced government power were cut down by Margaret Thatcher. These were, for example, local government, the unions and the universities.

Second, the continuation of a single party in office greatly limits the choice available to voters, and makes civil servants far more dependent on the patronage of one set of people for their jobs. The ideas of civil servants are likely, therefore, to reflect those of their political masters.

Third, and most importantly, far more decisions are being made in Europe, by the Commission and the Council of Ministers and by national politicians making decisions in secret with their key advisers.

 Evidence collection point

What evidence can you provide to indicate that:

a the government in the UK has played an increasing role in the economy in recent times?
b the government in the UK has played a decreasing role in the economy in recent times?

What factors have led to this increasing or decreasing role?

Investment in new technology

If business organisations are to invest in new technology then they need to have a positive lead from government. Governments can provide this lead by:

- investing in new technology themselves, e.g. government departments and public corporations
- providing subsidies and other means of support to private sector organisations particularly for new initiatives, e.g. the government is currently looking at ways of supporting educational institutions wishing to use networked IT systems

■ publicising and promoting the use of new technologies in industry, e.g. by organising conferences and other ways of disseminating good practice in the use of new technologies.

Evidence collection point

Study newspaper and magazine articles to document ways in which the government has recently been involved in encouraging the investment in new technologies. Show how this enhances the competitive performance of the UK economy.

Improving training and education

We looked in considerable depth at ways of improving training and education in Chapter 12 Investing in training and education is an investment in the future skills base of this country and hence in productivity and performance (Figure 17.15).

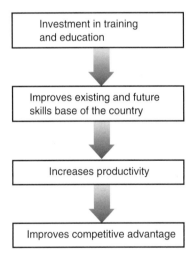

Figure 17.15 Achieving competitive advantage through education and training

GNVQ courses like the Advanced Business course are designed to provide students with the broad-based capability to engage in a wide variety of business-related occupations or further study. In particular, core skills are an essential preparation for employees of the future who will need to be more numerate, have good communication skills, and to have effective IT capabilities as well as be able to work with others, solve problems, and have a persevering and innovative attitude.

Evidence collection point

Identify a recent education or training initiative which has been designed to improve the competitive advantage of UK industry.

Taxation affecting aggregate demand

The government uses its taxation policy to influence the total level of demand in the economy. Raising taxes has the effect of taking money out of the economy so that people have less to spend.

Lowering taxes puts more money in people's pockets. The government's budget strategy in recent years has been concerned with reducing future government spending and cutting the government's borrowing requirement. This has been part of a policy of reducing government's role in the economy.

The intention has been to make sure that industry can get on with producing the goods that people need without the government taking too large a share of the national cake and adding to industry's costs.

The 1995 Budget set out its intentions for public finance as shown in Figure 17.16.

Receipts (bn)	1994/95	1995/96
Income tax	64.2	70.1
Corporation tax	20.1	26.4
Value added tax	43.4	49.0
Excise duties	26.3	28.0
Other taxes	39.7	43.0
Social security receipts	42.5	44.5
Other receipts	16.3	17.8
Total receipts	252.5	278.9
Expenditure (bn)		
Total	295.2	305.0
Privatisation proceeds (bn)	6.3	3.0
Public sector borrowing requirement	34.4	21.5

Figure 17.16 1995 Budget

The effect of successfully carrying through these intentions would have meant that instead of the PSBR being 5% of GNP it would have fallen to 3%. The government would thus need to borrow less money, which would have enabled it to keep inflation down. The fact that the government taxed less would mean that people had more money to spend, and industry had more money to invest in the private sector.

The intention therefore was to increase the UK's competitive edge by having a more dynamic private sector.

Evidence collection point

Explain how reductions in taxes can enable the private sector of the economy to become more competitive.

The most important taxes in terms of total revenue for the government are income tax and value added tax. Income tax is a direct tax which is taken from people's incomes. The higher the standard rate of tax the greater the government's revenue from it is likely to be, although taxes that are too high will discourage effort and hard work.

The Conservative government reduced the standard rate of tax so that in 1995 taxpayers paid 20% on the first £3200 that they earned after allowances. The tax rate then rose to 25%, which was the maximum that most taxpayers paid. Higher income earners paid 40% on some of their income.

Value added tax is an indirect tax. The Conservatives felt that it was important to change the burden more from direct to indirect taxes. This was because it was felt that there is a greater element of choice in paying indirect taxes.

Government expenditure

In terms of creating competitive advantage, it is important for government spending to be carried out in a productive way rather than be used to featherbed inefficient industries.

In 1995 the Conservative government's intention was that planned government spending should fall from 44.2% of national income in 1993/94, to 43.5% in 1994/95, to 42.5% in 1995/96 and then on to 39% by the year 2000.

Of course this is only one perspective on how a government should operate to create competitive advantage. An alternative view would be that the government can stimulate the economy through wise spending on social welfare provision.

Evidence collection point

Identify recent changes in government expenditure plans and explain why these have come about.

European market integration

The development of an economic community within the EU can be seen as involving a number of steps with each step leading to closer cooperation (Figure 17.17).

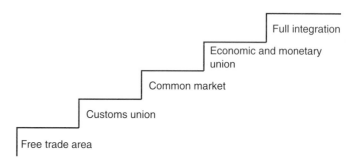

Figure 17.17 The development of a trading community

Free trade area

Developing a free trade area involved getting rid of some of the barriers to free trade. In particular, it involved the removal of quotas and tariffs between members of the trading community.

Customs union

In 1986 the EC created a customs union with moves towards positive integration of economies. In addition to the free trade area Member States operated a common external tariff. This meant that an import from a non-EC country, e.g. from Canada, would pay the same tariff whether it entered France, Germany, Belgium or any other Member State. Within the customs union the Member States developed common trading policies and moved towards equal conditions for individuals, firms and groupings operating within the customs union.

Common market

The creation of a common market took the integration process a step further. A common market involves the free movement of factors of production (land, labour, capital and enterprise) and the free movement of goods. Over the years, we have seen a harmonisation of policies designed to create freedom of movement. The Single European Act of 1986 highlighted what are known as the four freedoms (Figure 17.18).

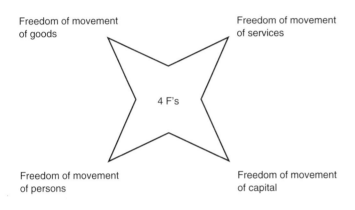

Figure 17.18 The four freedoms

Economic and monetary union

It would appear that complete economic and monetary union (EMU) is still a long way off. The aim of EMU is to provide a fixed exchange rate or single currency at some stage in the future.

A fixed exchange rate would exist if a given amount of pounds sterling could be changed into a set number of French francs today, next week, next year, and into the foreseeable future.

A single currency would exist if an ECU could be used in Luxembourg, Athens, Helsinki, Dublin or Copenhagen to pay for goods and services.

However, attempts to create exchange rate stability have not as yet been successful, although an important new step was the creation of a European Central Bank in Frankfurt in 1993. Germany, France, the Netherlands, Belgium and other countries have enjoyed some exchange rate stability and are working towards greater monetary union.

Full integration

Full integration of economies remains a future ideal. Integration would involve common economic policies decided upon by union institutions in conjunction with state governments through the creation of some sort of United States of Europe.

It has not been easy to create economic integration. However, in a world that is increasingly dominated by huge trading blocs it has been essential.

Since 1957 the EC has expanded internally from 6 to 9 in 1973, 9 to 10 in 1981, 10 to 12 in 1986 and 12 to 15 in 1995. Each step involved the need to integrate new markets.

Before the European Union created a single market, competitive edge was reduced by:

- the high administration costs in dealing with different national standards and requirements
- higher transport costs because of border regulations
- the higher cost of smaller production runs to meet different national standards
- duplication of costs as a result of having separate research and development projects
- the high cost of non-competitive government activities, e.g. buying only from producers in your own country (rather than cheaper, higher quality goods and services from other EU countries)
- higher prices and reduced choice for national consumers.

If the EU is to be competitive on a global scale it will need to create an internal market which is at least as competitive as those of other huge global trading areas, e.g. the North American Free Trade Area (NAFTA), the Pacific Rim countries, and the Commonwealth of Independent States.

Benefits of the Single Market which add to competitive advantage include:

- a wider choice of goods and services as barriers to trade are removed, and greater assurance about the quality and safety of imported products as clear guidelines become legally binding on business
- easier travel, for example cheaper air fares, as competition increases
- more jobs as business opportunities grow (although unemployment is a major problem facing all EU Member States as we move towards the next century)
- wider recognition of qualifications, making it easier for people to live and work where they

choose in the Union
- an end to routine customs controls at ports and airports and the freedom to bring back any goods bought, duty and VAT paid in other EU countries, for personal use.

Evidence collection point

Study recent press reports to build up a portfolio of cuttings identifying benefits of European market integration. Produce a short commentary to accompany each report.

Participating in the World Trade Organisation (WTO)

The General Agreement on Tariffs and Trade (GATT) was created in 1947 and operates on three levels as:

- a set of trading rules ('the rules of the road for trade')
- an international agency for helping to resolve trade disputes between countries and groups of countries
- a mean by which countries get together to create freer trade and cut down existing barriers.

The period of growth during the 1980s was supported by a period of the freeing of trading conditions in the world.

At the end of 1993 there were 112 members of GATT, accounting for 90% of world trade. With China and Russia joining the World Trade Organisation (Figure 17.19), this was extended to nearly all of world trade.

Figure 17.19 The WTO – an umbrella organisation

With the completion of the Uruguay Round (a round of talks which started in 1986, the eighth such round of reductions in barriers in trade since 1947), the World Trade Organisation (WTO) was created to replace GATT. The WTO is a powerful umbrella organisation. Underneath is an agreement on trade in goods and services and intellectual property.

If there is a consensus among most Member States, the WTO is able to force terms on members that do not want to make changes. The WTO is in effect an international trade organisation with full-time officers.

Clearly such an organisation acts as a spur to competition and international specialisation. It is essential for modern trading nations to be members of such an organisation.

Evaluation of business and government strategies intended to improve competitiveness

In this chapter we have described business and government strategies to improve competitiveness. You should try to evaluate the effectiveness of these policies by examining such indicators as:

For business
- Market share
- Sales
- Revenue
- Efficiency
- Productivity
- Product quality
- Service

For government policy
- Trading conditions
- Standard of living
- Levels of employment

Market share

Market share is always a useful indicator of business performance. Time and time again in this book we have stressed that profits frequently follow market share. When you examine the success of a UK business, you should try to find out figures for market share in specific markets and if possible in international markets generally.

The drive for market share is particularly important to the success of business. For example, in recent times Sainsbury's, the supermarket group, has been involved in gaining market share both in supermarkets and in DIY:

In 1983 it took a minority interest in Shaw's, the US food retailer.

In 1988 it took full control of Shaw's assets.

In 1994 it bought a 16.7% stake in Giant Food, a US food retailer.

In 1995 It took over the Texas Homecare chain of DIY stores so that it became the second largest player in the UK's £9 million DIY market. At a stroke Sainsbury's, with its existing Homebase stores, doubled its percentage share of the DIY market to 10% (only 4% behind market leader B&Q).

Sales

Volume of sales is an important indicator of business performance. You need to examine very carefully the volume of sales of businesses competing both at home and in international markets in evaluating their competitive edge. In particular, you should look at the way in which sales are expanding over a period of time.

Revenue

Revenue is the money received from making sales. We have already stressed the importance of increasing sales revenue over time because it is a company's revenues that pay its way.

Efficiency

Efficiency is a measure of how well available resources are used. Efficient organisations do not waste resources. In this chapter we have seen that one of the great achievements of Japanese business has been in minimising waste through a process known as 'fool-proofing'.

In evaluating the achievement of competitive edge you should look at how efficient organisations are in the way they use people, capital, raw materials, land and other resources.

Productivity

Productivity is measured by the output that is produced by a given quantity of inputs. Increased productivity is a clear indicator of competitive advantage.

Product quality

In Chapter 15 we looked at product quality in terms of 'fitness for purpose' and in meeting consumer requirements. Product quality is a key ingredient of business success.

Service

Today the service side of business is at a premium. Businesses can often gain competitive advantage by offering better service than rivals offering similar goods at similar prices.

Evidence collection point

Carry out some detailed research into a business concern in your locality which faces international competition. Produce a report showing how this organisation is able to gain a competitive edge by concentrating specifically on its: market share, sales, revenue, efficiency, productivity, product quality and service.

Trading conditions

Governments have an important part to play in providing effective trading conditions which enable businesses within the economy to flourish. In this chapter we have looked at the development of trading within the European Union and how the UK has benefited from the freeing of trade, and have looked at its participation in the World Trading Organisation.

The government has a key role to play in creating favourable trading conditions through its ability to influence exchange rates and inflation, and also through its demand- and supply-side policies, e.g. taxation and spending.

Standard of living

The government also has an important part to play in creating the economic conditions that enable its citizens to enjoy increases in their standards of living. The government can introduce measures which encourage people to save or spend, to invest, to export or import, etc.

The government needs to balance its policies in order to ensure an increasing standard of living and quality of life for existing and future generations.

Levels of employment

Involuntary unemployment exists when people who want to work cannot find jobs. Unemployment occurs for a number of reasons:

- A lack of demand for products on a wide scale. This occurs in a period of recession when there is a reduced demand for all goods, from building blocks to industrial machinery, from confectionery to cars.
- A change in the structure of demand. As times move on, the whole structure of demand for products changes – new products come in to replace outmoded products. For example, CD players replace record players, synthetic fibres replace natural fibres.
- Technology means that some products and processes can be carried out with a much smaller labour input, for example the use of machinery in farming and the use of automated production lines in car factories and breweries.

Unemployment leads to a great waste of resources in an economy. It is also socially demoralising. Combating unemployment therefore requires the generation of fresh demand in an economic system, the training and retraining of employees to take on new jobs, and other policies.

The level of employment or unemployment in an economy can be used as one indicator of the success or failure of government economic policy. After all, how competitive is an economy if many of its people (human resources) are out of work?

Evidence indicators

To provide evidence that you have met the performance criteria for this unit you should produce:

- A set of league tables comparing the UK economy with at least three major competitors.
- A short report describing how one business faces competition.

The following list should serve as a checklist. Please tick off each of the following when you have successfully covered them in your evidence. You need to confirm that you have produced:

- A set of league tables supported by a summary comparing the UK economy with at least three major competitors. ☐
  The tables compare:

  Economic growth ☐

  Investment ☐

  Inflation ☐

  Exchange rate ☐

  Share of world trade ☐

  Productivity ☐

- A supporting summary which explains and justifies the choice of performance indicators. ☐

You also need to confirm that you have produced a report in which you have:

- Described how one business faces competition. ☐
- Described the strategy used by the business to improve its performance in a competitive world market. ☐
- Evaluated the strategy in terms of its effects on employees and on the business. ☐
- Evaluated government strategies which affect the business and shown how these may help or hinder the competitiveness of the business. ☐

Production and Employment in the Economy: Unit Test 1

1 About three-fifths of all employees in the UK are engaged in:
 a Manufacturing.
 b Self-employment.
 c Services.
 d Work-related government training.

2 A business firm uses £20 000 worth of inputs in a month. The total value of its output in that month is £50 000. The value added by that firm in the month is:
 a £20 000.
 b £30 000.
 c £50 000.
 d £70 000.

3 Short-term, temporary and part-time workers who receive less favourable pay, conditions and benefits are usually described as:
 a Core workers.
 b Peripheral workers.
 c External workers.
 d Teleworkers.

4 A feature of just-in-time manufacturing is:
 a Finished goods produced well in advance of being sold.
 b Time to set up machinery is increased in order to iron out technical weaknesses.
 c An organisation operates with the smallest possible level of stocks.
 d Stockpiling occurs to prepare for fluctuations in orders.

5 Building in some means of inspection at every stage of the production process is often described as:
 a Scientific management.
 b Multiskilling.
 c Total quality control.
 d Time and motion study.

6 A disadvantage of specialisation is:
 a Workers become less dependent on each other.
 b Output levels increase only slowly.
 c Traditional skills are passed on from one generation to the next.
 d Employees may not be able to do a range of tasks.

7 The money value of the output of labour is best measured by:
 a Physical output.
 b Revenue product.
 c Employment.
 d Wages.

8 A useful way of measuring economic growth is to calculate:
 a Gross national product in different years.
 b The retail price index.
 c The balance of payments.
 d Regional employment patterns.

9 Which of the following countries is a member of the European Union?
 a Switzerland.
 b Norway.
 c Finland.
 d Turkey.

10 Which of the following major UK industries has benefited most from Japanese companies setting up in this country?
 a Coal mining.
 b Textiles.
 c Engineering.
 d Motor vehicle manufacture.

11 The region of the UK with the most people in employment is:
 a South East.
 b East Anglia
 c Yorkshire and Humberside.
 d Scotland.

12 The 'underground' economy is:
 a Economic activity which is undeclared.
 b The mining sector of the economy.
 c Income which is saved rather than spent.
 d The self-employment sector of the economy.

13 The most likely condition to prevail in the labour market during a period of boom is:
 a Wages will rise and unemployment will increase.
 b Shortages of labour will start to occur and wages will rise.

c Wages will fall and unemployment will fall.
d Wages will rise and the demand for labour will fall.

14 The best example of a labour intensive industry is:
a Car assembly.
b Hairdressing.
c Brewing and bottling.
d Production of heavy chemicals.

15 An organisation is least likely to recruit additional employees when:
a Faced by a temporary surge in consumer spending on a national scale.
b Faced by a structural increase in demand for the product which is makes.
c It wins an important contract which involves increasing output to complete the contract by a fixed date.
d Faced by an increase in the productivity of its existing labour force coupled with an increase in orders.

16 The largest chunk of value added by organisations will normally go as:
a Rent.
b Wages.
c Profits.
d Interest.

17 Which of the following is not true about quality assurance?
a Quality assurance is concerned with trying to stop faults happening in the first place.
b Quality assurance is concerned to make sure that products are produced to pre-determined standards.
c The aim of quality assurance is to produce with 'zero defects'.
d Quality assurance is only concerned with the inspection of finished products.

18 Total Quality Management is principally concerned with:
a Inspection of products.
b Detection of faults.
c Prevention of faults.
d Continuous improvement.

19 Productivity can be measured by:

a $\dfrac{\text{Inputs}}{\text{Outputs}}$

b $\dfrac{\text{Revenue}}{\text{Outputs}}$

c $\dfrac{\text{Outputs}}{\text{Inputs}}$

d $\dfrac{\text{Inputs}}{\text{Revenue}}$

20 The factor least likely to lead to an increase in wage levels in the textile industry is:
a An increase in productivity in the textile industry.
b The imposition of a national minimum wage.
c The increased demand for UK textiles.
d An increase in training and skills among textile workers.

21 A feature of 'teleworking' today is that:
a Teleworkers are most commonly found in the secondary sector of the economy.
b Teleworkers work most or part of their time at a distance from the office.
c Over one in three employees in the UK is currently engaged in 'teleworking'.
d There are more 'teleworkers' in the UK than in any other country.

22 The aggregate demand for labour in an economy will:
a Increase during a slump.
b Contract during a boom.
c Depend on the productivity of labour.
d Not depend on the level of economic activity.

23 If the demand for labour increases while the supply of labour falls this is likely to lead to:
a An increase in unemployment.
b An increase in wages.
c An increase in the rate of emigration.
d No change in the labour market.

24 Loading a job horizontally to increase the challenge and variety of work is described as:
a Job enrichment.
b Job enlargement.
c Quality circles.
d Kaizen.

25 Which EU economy is being described? This economy experiences considerable disparities between a high wage north and a low wage south of the country. Official statistics show that it is the third most productive EU state.

a The UK.
b Greece.
c Italy.
d Germany.

26 Self-employed people who may work on a contract for a 'flexible firm' are termed:
a Core workers.
b Peripheral workers.
c Managers.
d External workers.

27 The most likely reason for redundancies in an organisation in the short term is:
a Government regulations requiring that all organisations publish a Health and Safety policy.
b An increase in employers' National Insurance contributions.
c The arrival of a new competitor in an existing market segment.
d An increase in the productivity of labour.

28 A feature of a quality circle is:
a Concerned with checking on the quality only at the end of the production line.
b They are made up entirely of production workers.
c Employees can bring forward their points of view on day-to-day issues.
d Emphasis on making sure that products are produced and stored.

29 The largest numbers in employment today are in:
a Coal mining.
b Agriculture.
c Financial services.
d Shipbuilding.

30 Which one of the following is not part of the Pacific Rim trading area?
a Japan.
b Malaysia.
c Australia.
d Ireland.

31 Which of the following is an example of a tertiary industry?
a Newspaper production.
b Pottery making.
c Retailing.
d Coal mining.

32 Which of the following measures would be most likely to reduce the level of unemployment? An increase in:

a Income tax rates.
b The quantity of exports.
c The rate of interest.
d Indirect tax rates (e.g. VAT).

33 The General Agreement on Tariffs and Trade is an attempt to:
a Regulate trade by imposing tariffs.
b Discourage countries from reducing tariff barriers.
c Reduce import taxes and quotas through international agreement.
d Establish ways in which debtor countries can pay for imports.

34 The best example of supply-side government economic policy is:
a Increasing government expenditure to raise aggregate expenditure.
b Reducing income tax to encourage people to work longer hours.
c Increasing the size of the government's budget deficit.
d Making it easier for people to buy goods using credit facilities.

35 In an economy citizens: save one-fifth of their marginal income; are taxed one-tenth of their marginal income; spend one-tenth of their marginal income on imports. If there is an increase in government spending of £200 million in this economy, what will be the overall effect on expenditure in the economy?
a An increase in expenditure of £200 million.
b No change in expenditure.
c An increase in expenditure of £500 million.
d An increase in expenditure of £1000 million.

36 One reason for the decline of the manufacturing sector is:
a The industry has reinvested too heavily.
b The goods were of a poor standard.
c There is cheaper overseas competition.
d Only poor quality of labour is available.

37 If the rate of pay for computer programmers goes up in the South East, then this will:
a Cause other rates of pay to fall.
b Encourage programmers to move to the South East.
c Spread wage increases to other parts of the country.
d Increase the demand for labour in the South East.

38 In the 1990s working practices have been increasingly been characterised by:
a Labour market flexibility.
b Organisational culture.
c Job enlargement.
d Piece work.

39 Wage differentials refer to:
a Similarities in pay.
b Annual rates of pay.
c Differences in wage rates.
d Productivity levels.

40 Division of labour involves:
a Introducing specialist tasks into the production process.
b Making the factory less flexible.
c Decreasing labour productivity.
d Increasing the number of service sector jobs.

41 Redundancy occurs when particular types of jobs are no longer required. One reason for having to make redundancies is:
a The business is expanding.
b Part of an organisation closes.
c New employees are required.
d Employees are members of trade unions.

42 The new umbrella organisation supervising international trading relationships and encouraging freer trade is:
a The International Monetary Fund.
b GATT.
c The World Trade Organisation.
d The World Bank.

43 At the start of 1993 an important change for the countries of the European Union was that:
a They started to use the same unit of currency.
b Barriers to trade between members were removed.
c Member countries adopted the same tax system.
d Member countries adopted minimum wage legislation.

44 In 1995/96 how many countries were there in the European Union?
a 7.
b 10.
c 12.
d 15.

45 In order to combat regional decline in Britain, a government might:
a Give incentives to industry to move to areas of high unemployment.
b Give financial assistance to firms wishing to set up in areas of low unemployment.
c Increase unemployment benefits.
d Subsidise unemployment in all areas of the country.

46 The group most likely to have the widest pay spread is:
a Waiters.
b Hairdressers.
c Debt collectors.
d Doctors.

47 When calculating national output it is necessary to count only the value added by each industrial sector so as to avoid:
a Measuring the value of production.
b Double counting.
c Tax evasion.
d Counting the contribution of primary industries.

48 A business sells its goods for a total sales value of £100 000 in a year and buys inputs of £90 000 in that year. The value it has added through the process of production is:
a £190 000.
b £100 000.
c £30 000.
d £10 000.

49 Which of the following would lead to a decrease in productivity?
a Output falling while input falls at a lower rate.
b Output staying the same while input decreases.
c Output increasing while input increases at a smaller rate.
d Output falling while input remains the same.

50 Which of the following is most likely to lead to cyclical unemployment?
a The voluntary redundancy of employees.
b The fall in demand for a particular type of labour.
c A general slump.
d Temporary unemployment while employees change jobs.

Production and Employment in the Economy: Unit Test 2

1   Multi-skilled workers who work full-time and who receive good pay and conditions are termed:
    a   Core workers.
    b   Peripheral workers.
    c   External workers.
    d   Teleworkers.

2   The quantity of goods produced by labour is best measured by:
    a   Physical output.
    b   Revenue product.
    c   Employment.
    d   Wages.

3   A business purchases £20 000 of inputs in a month and converts this into £30 000 of outputs. The value added by this business is:
    a   £50 000.
    b   £30 000.
    c   £20 000.
    d   £10 000.

4   In 1995 the European Union was enlarged by the entry of:
    a   Austria, Norway and Greece.
    b   Norway, Switzerland, and Sweden.
    c   Sweden, Finland, and Austria.
    d   Norway, Sweden and Finland.

5   The area which has been expanding its trade most rapidly in recent times has been:
    a   The North American Free Trade Area.
    b   The European Union.
    c   East Asian and Pacific states.
    d   Japan.

6   The industry that was the first major industry in the UK today only employs less than half a million people as it strives to compete with cheap imports. This industry is:
    a   Electricity.
    b   Car manufacture.
    c   Railways.
    d   Textiles.

7   The demand for labour is derived from the demand for:
    a   Capital as a factor of production.
    b   The marginal productivity of labour.
    c   The products that labour produces.
    d   Enterprise.

8   An organisation is least likely to recruit additional employees when:
    a   Faced by a temporary surge in consumer spending on a national scale.
    b   Faced by a structural increase in demand for the product which it makes.
    c   It wins an important contract which involves increasing output to complete the contract by a fixed date.
    d   Faced by an increase in the productivity of its existing labour force coupled with an increase in orders.

9   Which of the following is an accurate statement about unemployment rates in the European Union?
    a   Spain and Ireland have rates of unemployment which are below the EU average.
    b   Luxembourg and Portugal have rates of unemployment which are above the EU average.
    c   The rate of unemployment in Luxembourg is below that in Ireland.
    d   The rate of unemployment in Spain is below that in Portugal.

10   In a 'third wave' society:
    a   The emphasis in employment will be on the growth of the secondary sector.
    b   The primary sector becomes more important than the secondary sector.
    c   Automated plant and equipment become obsolete.
    d   There is a major switch in employment to the service occupations.

11   Automation involves:
    a   The use of machinery controlled directly by employees.
    b   The creation of control units to control the operation of machines.
    c   The replacement of capital by more labour-intensive processes.
    d   The division of labour to carry out more complicated work tasks.

12   Which of the following is *not* an advantage of using robots in industrial production?
    a   Robots can be used where working conditions are difficult or dangerous.
    b   Greater levels of capital investment increase the pressure for shift working.
    c   Robots can speed the rate of routine assembly work.
    d   Robots are more efficient at standard checking procedures.

13 Which of the following payment systems is linked to results?
   a Holiday pay.
   b Christmas bonus.
   c Time-related pay.
   d Piece rates.

14 If the labour force in the confectionery industry becomes more effective, the initial effect will be to:
   a Shift the demand curve for confectionery to the right.
   b Lead to a movement up the supply curve for confectionery.
   c Lead to a shift in the supply and demand curves for confectionery to the right.
   d Lead to a shift in the supply curve of confectionery to the right.

15 A feature of a GNVQ is that:
   a The qualification is based on national standards.
   b The course prepares students for specific jobs.
   c The qualification is of equivalent value to three traditional A levels.
   d Courses must be completed within a two-year period.

16 Of the following industries the most labour intensive in the UK is:
   a Motor vehicle manufacture.
   b Motor vehicle repair.
   c Computer manufacture.
   d Agriculture.

17 An effect of imposing minimum wages would be:
   a An increase in employment.
   b Some job losses for low-paid workers.
   c An increase in the competitiveness of UK businesses.
   d A rise in everyone's standard of living.

18 Employees of an organisation who may have fewer rights than other more established employees are known as:
   a Core workers.
   b Directors.
   c External workers.
   d Peripheral workers.

19 Which of the following is least likely to lead to an increase in wage levels in the UK computer industry?
   a An increase in training and skills among UK computer workers.
   b An upturn in the world economy leading to higher spending.

   c An increased demand for computers.
   d An increase in the supply of people with computing skills in the UK.

20 Primary industries include:
   a Construction.
   b Insurance.
   c Engineering.
   d Farming.

21 Which of the following is *not* a fringe benefit?
   a Discount on company products.
   b Travel allowance.
   c Luncheon vouchers
   d Pay.

22 Which of the following can be deducted from a worker's pay at source?
   a Value Added Tax.
   b Vehicle Excise License.
   c National Insurance contributions.
   d Corporation Tax.

23 Monetary policy is concerned with controlling the quantity and price of money in circulation. An example of monetary policy is:
   a Creating a budget surplus.
   b Reducing interest rates.
   c Increasing government spending.
   d Curbing public sector wage increases.

24 The elasticity of demand for labour shows how the demand for labour:
   a Fluctuates at different times of the year.
   b Falls to meet supply.
   c Is determined.
   d Changes as a result of a change in wages.

25 Value added created by a business would be distributed among:
   a Wages, taxes, interest, dividends and profits.
   b Wages, interest, government spending, and profits.
   c Wages, government spending, taxes and imports.
   d Dividends, profits, taxes and government spending.

26 Making sure that a business has sufficient resources to meet production requirements with the minimum possible stocks is termed:
   a Quality control.
   b Just-in-time production.
   c Capital intensive production.
   d Computer-aided design.

27 A car producer purchases during a year £70 million worth of raw materials and finished products and makes 30 000 cars which it sells at £10 000 each. The value added in this process of production is:
  a £300m.
  b £230m.
  c £70m.
  d £30m.

28 Which of the following statements is true?
  a There are more men than women working in part-time employment.
  b Men are predominantly employed in part-time work.
  c Women are predominantly employed in part-time work.
  d The average earnings of women are greater than those of men.

29 Most of the growth of the labour force since 1981 has come from increased participation by:
  a Full-time employees.
  b Female employees.
  c 16–21-year-olds.
  d Male employees.

30 A reduction in the level of unemployment in a country might come from:
  a A reduction in labour productivity.
  b A rise in wage rates of employees in the country's industries.
  c An increased use of labour-saving devices in new automated factories.
  d An improvement in comparative advantage of the country's products on world markets.

31 The most capital-intensive industrial activity is:
  a Strawberry picking.
  b Personal insurance.
  c Steel manufacture.
  d Fashion design.

32 A likely effect in the fall of the pound sterling against the French franc would be that:
  a The French would buy more United Kingdom goods because they would be cheaper.
  b The French would buy less United Kingdom goods because they would be more expensive.
  c The United Kingdom would import more French goods because they would be cheaper.
  d Trade between France and the United Kingdom would remain the same.

33 The United Kingdom's more important imports by value are:

  a Agricultural goods.
  b Raw materials.
  c Manufactured goods.
  d Chemicals.

34 A seller's market exists in the labour market when:
  a The number of school leavers increases considerably.
  b The supply of labour is scarce relative to the demand for labour.
  c It is easy for employers to recruit skilled labour.
  d There is a considerable net migration of people from a country.

35 Between 15 and 16 million people were employed in which sector of the labour market during the 1990s?
  a Manufacturing.
  b Services.
  c Self-employment.
  d HM forces.

36 If the demand for labour increases while the supply of labour falls this is likely to lead to:
  a An increase in unemployment.
  b An increase in wages.
  c An increase in the rate of emigration.
  d No change in the labour market.

37 Production of goods is complete only when they have:
  a Left the factory for a wholesaler.
  b Left the wholesaler for the retailer.
  c Been offered for sale by the retailer.
  d Been sold by the retailer to the consumer.

38 Which of the following measures is most likely to reduce inequality of income?
  a Value added tax at 20% on all consumer goods.
  b Progressive income taxes.
  c Council tax.
  d Regressive expenditure taxes.

39 The largest share of value added in production goes as a reward to:
  a Capital.
  b Enterprise.
  c Labour.
  d Land.

40 Where the government uses its spending and taxation policies as the major means to regulate the economy this is best described as:
  a Laissez-faire policies.
  b Monetarism.

c Demand-side policies.
d Supply-side policies.

41 An example of a direct tax is:
   a VAT.
   b Excise duties.
   c Income tax.
   d Customs duties.

42 Which of the following exemplifies both secondary and tertiary industry?
   a Fishing and the processing of fish into fish pies.
   b The growing of organic vegetables and their sale to the public.
   c The mining of coal in a private colliery for sale to local households.
   d The sale to the public of hand-made jewellery.

43 The most likely event to encourage demand-pull inflation is:
   a An increase in income tax.
   b An increase in government spending.
   c A fall in investment.
   d An increase in savings.

44 A feature of what is sometimes referred to as 'the new working class' is:
   a Lack of any real power.
   b Concentration in non-manual occupations.
   c Increased spending power and access to goods and services particularly in the south of England.
   d Tendency to be contracted in service sector occupations.

45 An organisation agrees to pay extra sums of money to a selected number of employers, depending on their achievements for the organisation in a given period of time. This is best described as:
   a Performance-related pay.
   b Profit-related pay.
   c Scientific management.
   d Appraisal.

46 Preparation for a broad range of educational training and employment opportunities based on building up transferable knowledge and skills is appropriately carried out through:
   a GCE A levels.
   b GNVQs.
   c NVQs.
   d Youth training.

47 A perk of a particular job may be:
   a Basic salary.
   b Private health care.
   c Employer National Insurance contributions.
   d Tax allowances.

48 Which of the following states has opted out of the European Union's Social Chapter because it favoured more flexible working practices?
   a The UK.
   b Greece.
   c Germany.
   d Italy.

49 When the productivity of labour in Industry X is rising and in Industry Y is falling, this leads to:
   a Increased employment in Industry Y and decreased employment in Industry X.
   b The relative decline of Industry X.
   c Increased wages in Industry X and falling wages in Industry Y.
   d The substitution of capital for labour in Industry X and the substitution of labour for capital in Industry Y.

50 A feature of 'just-in-time' manufacturing is:
   a Large stockpiles of raw materials and components.
   b The unplanned production of goods.
   c Components arrive shortly before being assembled.
   d Stockpiles being left not in use for a long time.

The aim of this unit is to introduce the concepts underlying a profit-motivated business. You will need to explore 'added value' from the financial point of view – its distribution, its associated 'money cycle', the financial transactions involved in that cycle and the documents supporting those transactions. You should understand that the cost of providing goods and services is linked through the concept of break-even point to pricing concepts.

Added value, the distribution of added value and the money cycle

On completing this chapter you should be able to:

1 Explain the trading cycle of goods or services in a business and their added value.
2 Explain the distribution of added value.
3 Explain the money cycle.
4 Explain factors for consideration when selling.
5 Explain factors for consideration when buying.

The trading cycle of goods or services in a business

Order, supply and payment

The trading cycle gives us a useful starting point for beginning to look at financial transactions in an organisation, and at the way in which value is added through production.

In a manufacturing company the trading cycle starts with the purchase of raw materials, and then goes through production and the warehousing of finished goods ready for sale, finishing with the eventual sale of those goods. Let us take a real-life example to illustrate this process.

Fenland Foods is a manufacturer of recipe dishes which are sold in Marks and Spencer stores. In order to make their recipe dishes they need to buy in lots of raw materials including:

■ meat
■ carrots
■ pasta
■ spices
■ potatoes
■ packaging materials.

In their factory at Grantham all of these ingredients are blended together to make highly popular recipe dishes which are stored briefly in the Grantham

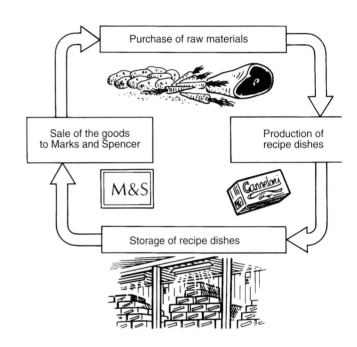

Figure 18.1 The trading cycle for Fenland Foods

storehouse ready for distribution to Marks and Spencer stores (Figure 18.1). The advantage of selling direct to M&S is that payment is prompt and goods are guaranteed a sale.

Evidence collection point

Illustrate the trading cycle for a manufactured product. The best way of gathering this evidence will be to visit a local manufacturing organisation in order to see the stages in the production cycle for yourself.

Evidence you collect from this activity could be used to show competence in Communication.

477

Processing raw materials or components for a service

Not all organisations manufacture products. Many are engaged in providing services. However, the trading cycle process for services is very similar to that for products in that it is concerned with processing inputs into finished outputs. For example, in a retailing company the trading cycle starts with the purchase of stock for resale and ends with the sale of that stock.

We can illustrate this by taking another real example. Marks and Spencer purchase recipe food dishes from Fenland Foods. They then stock these in their shop ready for resale. Customers buy these dishes from Marks and Spencer (Figure 18.2).

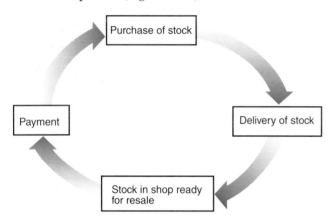

Figure 18.2 Marks and Spencer trading cycle for recipe food dishes

The cycle provides a useful and easy way of thinking about how businesses operate and trade.

Evidence collection point

Research the activities of a local retailing organisation. Show how they engage in the trading cycle. Draw a diagram to illustrate this – perhaps you can include fictional figures to represent their purchases of stock and sales.

Meeting customer requirements

The ultimate purpose of the trading cycle is to meet customer requirements. We live in a society in which the production of most goods is market driven.

Organisations that fail to meet customer requirements can quickly go out of business. If the goods that manufacturers make, or retailers stock, do not meet the requirements of customers they will not be sold. Unsold stock leads to poor profits, and reduces the ability of an organisation to carry on trading. If Marks and Spencer buy a recipe dish from Fenland Foods that is not popular they will ask Fenland to produce an alternative product.

Making a return on investment

Organisations need to make a return on the money that is invested in them. We have seen in Chapter 4 that sole traders are owned by one person, partnerships by 2–20 partners (in most cases) and companies by shareholders. Each of these people will need to make a return on the capital they invest in a business. For example, if I invested £1000 in Shell UK this year, I would be very pleased to receive a dividend of £100 in the first year – this would represent a 10% return on the capital that I had invested with them. If they paid me only £10 I would be very disappointed – this would only represent a return of 1%. I would have been better off putting my money in a Post Office account. The trading activity of business organisations therefore needs to be carried out to make a return on investment which is at least as good as other investments with similar risks.

Making a trading profit or loss

When you carry out trading activities you want to make sure that you make a profit from doing so. Without profit you will quickly go out of business. We can illustrate the business of making a profit by looking at a retailing organisation.

A retailing organisation needs to set up its operation in order to make sales. For example, it will need to employ people to make the sales for it and pay them salaries. It will also need to set up a branch network (i.e a chain of shops) to make the sales.

It can then go about selling its goods. It will (hopefully) make a surplus from making more in sales than it costs to pay salaries, run the branch network, and buy in goods for resale. Out of its surplus it can pay taxes, and dividends to shareholders. It will also carry forward a residual balance of retained profits within the organisation (see Figure 18.3).

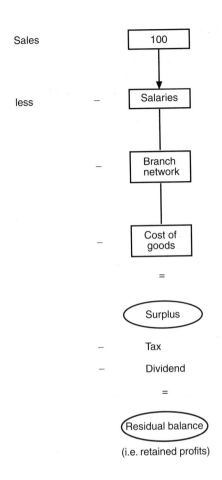

Sales   100

less   –   Salaries

            –   Branch
                 network

            –   Cost of
                 goods

            =

                 Surplus

            –   Tax

            –   Dividend

            =

                 Residual balance

                 (i.e. retained profits)

Figure 18.3 What is involved in making a profit

Adding value

Adding value lies at the heart of business activity. In the trading cycle we have seen that businesses buy in inputs and sell outputs in most cases for a higher price.

Industry, commerce and direct services create products. Value is added at each stage of production. A simple example of adding value is the carpenter converting relatively inexpensive material into furniture. The difference between the cost of the wood and the price of the finished article is the value added (Figure 18.4).

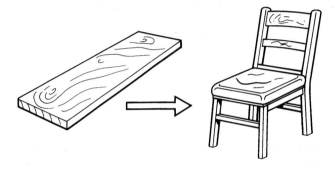

Figure 18.4 The carpenter adds value in creating a chair

Case study

The following figures are taken from the accounts of Marks and Spencer plc for the year ended 31 March 1994. Set the figures out in the format shown in Figure 18.3. Did Marks and Spencer make a profit from their trading activities?

	1994 £million
Cost of purchasing merchandise sold	4247.0
Branch network and associated support services	704.9
Wages and salaries	737.8
Tax paid to the government	272.2
Dividends paid to shareholders	256.6
Receivable from customers	6541.2

Value of goods or services supplied

At the end of the trade cycle producers supply goods which are bought in the marketplace, i.e. at their market value. For example, in 1996 our carpenter may sell £20 000 worth of chairs to customers.

Cost of goods or services bought from others

In trading activity, nearly all organisations will buy in raw materials, components and finished goods from other trading organisations. The cost of buying in goods or services from others is clearly not included in the value added by a particular organisation.

Calculation of added value

The added value created by an organisation is therefore the difference between the value of goods or services bought from others and the value of goods or services supplied.

479

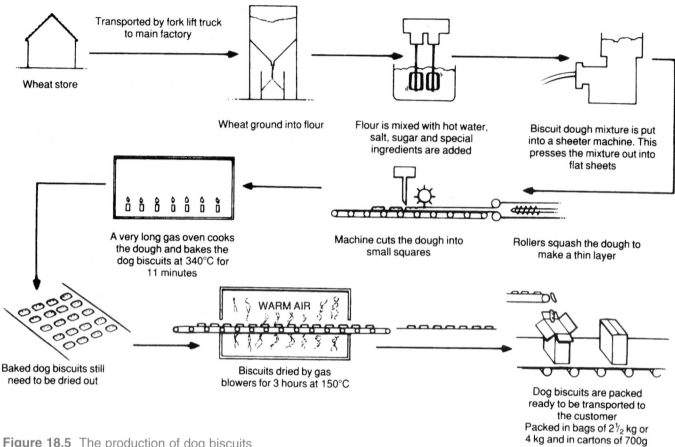

Figure 18.5 The production of dog biscuits

Value of goods or services supplied – value of goods or services bought in = Value added

For example, if the carpenter had bought in £10 000 of goods and services to produce his chairs which he sold for £20 000, we would have:

£20 000 – £10 000 = £10 000 value added

In the world of industry and commerce there are many stages involved in adding value to products. For example, Figure 18.5 shows the various stages involved in adding value in dog biscuit production.

Of course, there will also be many different types of inputs required to make outputs (Figure 18.6).

Evidence collection point

The following figures are taken from the accounts of Marks and Spencer plc for the year ended 31 March 1994.

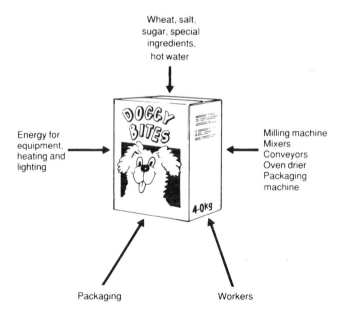

Figure 18.6 Inputs needed to make dog biscuits

	1993 £ million	1994 £ million
Cost of purchasing merchandise sold	3879.6	4247.0
Branch network and associated support services	648.4	704.9
Wages and salaries	686.3	737.8
Tax paid to the government	239.5	272.2
Dividends paid to shareholders	225.1	256.6
Receivable from customers	5950.8	6541.2

1 Prepare a diagram that illustrates the trading cycle of Marks and Spencer plc. Use the figures for 1994 to show the cost and accumulated cost up to each stage. Complete the trading cycle by showing the amounts received from customers. Highlight the profit earned by the company.
2 Prepare 'value added' statements for 1993 and 1994 in the format shown in the table below.
3 Describe and comment on the distribution of added value for each year.
4 For what purposes might some of the added value be retained in the business?

You can use some of the evidence that you gather from carrying out this activity to provide evidence of the Core Skill of Application of Number.

In a particular trading period, organisations will not necessarily be able to complete all the products that they set out to make. This means that there will be some 'work in progress' (WIP), i.e. materials which are partly processed. Of course, some value has been added to these materials, but there is still more to be added. Some products will be completely finished and others will be in a semi-finished state.

We should mention here the importance of the purchasing (procurement) function of an organisation in adding value to products. It is essential to make sure that what you buy in is of the right quality and arrives in time. If it does not meet these criteria you may not be able to add as much value to your products as you would like. You may be late in getting goods to your customers, and they may be less than happy with the finished quality – all of which limit your ability to add value.

The distribution of added value

There are many claims on the value which is added by an organisation:

- Employees need to be paid wages and salaries.
- Taxes need to be paid to the government.
- Interest needs to be paid to lenders
- Money is required to pay off debts.
- Dividends must be paid to shareholders.
- Profit is retained in the business.

Figure 18.7 illustrates these.

Wages and salaries

Wages and salaries tend to take the largest share of value added in many organisations in the private and public sectors. Wages may account for over 70% of the value added by an organisation – for example, in schools, where much of the budget will be spent on teachers and other employees' salaries.

	1993 £ million	Percentage of added value	1994 £ million	Percentage of added value
Charged to customers				
Less cost of bought in goods and services				
Added value				
Distribution of added value				
To employees				
To government				
To shareholders				
Retained in the business				

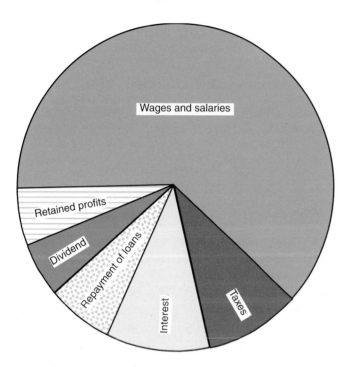

Figure 18.7 The share-out of value added by the organisation

Taxes

Taxes have another claim on value added by an organisation. One such tax is corporation tax, which is a tax on an organisation's profits over a certain amount.

Of course, businesses will pay value added tax (VAT). However, it is important to remember that value added tax can be claimed back by organisations on the inputs they buy from other organisations (see Chapter 28 for information on the payment of VAT).

Interest

Interest is paid to people who have lent the organisation money, e.g. in the form of loans or debentures. This is money which is lent to the organisation by people who are outside the organisation (i.e. it does not include shares).

Money required to pay off debts

Some business organisations have debts outstanding in the form of loans which they have received in

previous trading periods. Part of the value you add in a particular trading period may therefore be needed to pay off these outstanding debts. Indeed, many organisations will make provision to pay off debts in a systematic way.

Dividends paid to shareholders

An important 'call' on the value added by an organisation will be that from shareholders. Shareholders invest in an organisation because they expect to make a healthy return. Organisations therefore need to make sure that they reward shareholders in an appropriate way through dividends.

Profit retained in the business

Businesses should also retain profit within the business, in order to expand and grow, and to provide a safety net of funds to secure ongoing trading.

The money cycle

Every business needs to have cash available at the bank to pay its bills. A manufacturing company, for instance, needs money to buy stock or raw materials to make the goods it intends to sell. But the company will not get its money back until it has sold the goods. If debtors (people and companies that owe money) are slow in paying their bills, then the manufacturing company could run into cash-flow problems.

A company should try to arrange its affairs so that if debtors are slow in paying, there is still enough cash in the company's current account at the bank to pay important bills. Better still, the company should devise effective ways of preventing late payments.

The money cycle therefore consists of:

- *Initial cash*
  The business has cash available with which to purchase stock or raw materials.

- *Purchase materials*
  Cash is then converted into stock or materials in order to enable the organisation to add value to them.

- *Produce goods*
  Value is added by organisations producing goods

in a variety of ways – the hairdresser cutting and styling hair, the building firm building new houses, the confectionery company manufacturing chocolate, etc. All of these operations are dependent on the smooth running of the cash cycle.

- *Sell goods on credit*
  Generally speaking, most goods are sold on a credit basis. The standard period may be one month to payment, three months to payment, or even longer. When manufacturers sell goods they need to give wholesalers and retailers time to resell goods before they can pay for them.

- *Goods are paid for*
  Goods need to be paid for within the terms set down for the credit period, e.g. 28 days. When the goods are paid for, this will bring cash back into the business.

Figure 18.8 shows the money cycle in the form of a simple illustration.

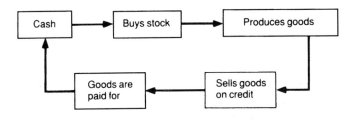

Figure 18.8 The money cycle

Residual cash

As a result of going through the money cycle, the business will be left with cash. Of course, most of this cash will be returned into the money cycle in order to buy new stock, etc. If the residual cash is greater than the initial cash the business will have made a profit out of its operations which is available for sharing out as value added. Indeed, the aim of business is to make cash work for you in order to generate value added, which can be shared amongst all members of the organisation.

However, there may be situations in which residual cash is less than initial cash, and in this case a loss is made. This restricts the trading capacity of the organisation in the ensuing trading period. We can set out a simple table to illustrate this situation:

	£
Initial cash	10 000
Buy goods	3 000
Add value	7 000
Finished goods	10 000
Sell at loss	−1 000
Residual cash	9 000

The obvious consequence is a depletion in resources.

Evidence collection point

Set out a spreadsheet which shows how the money cycle for some goods or services mirrors the trading cycle and starts and ends with cash.

Evidence that you provide can be used to contribute to your portfolio in respect of the Core Skill of Information Technology.

We can conclude by saying that in a manufacturing company the cash cycle starts with payments for raw materials and ends with the receipt of payment from customers.

In a retailing organisation the cash cycle starts with payments for stock and ends with the receipt of cash from customer sales.

It is interesting to note that today many supermarkets have a rather unusual money cycle. Goods are delivered to them quickly by manufacturers on a credit basis. The supermarket then quickly gets the goods out onto the shop shelves. The supermarket will sell the goods to customers and receive payment before they have paid for them themselves!

Factors for consideration when selling

When selling goods it is important to give careful consideration to how and when you will be paid for your goods and services. There are obvious disadvantages in having to wait for payment and indeed in recent times this has led to many businesses ceasing to trade.

Cash

Cash is a secure way of being paid. You produce goods, offer them for sale, and receive immediate payment in notes and coins, or by cheque. Immediately you can use that cash to support the ongoing trading cycle.

Credit

Goods sold by one business to another are often sold on credit as opposed to cash.

A typical credit transaction is illustrated in Figure 18.9.

Date	What happens	Payment
1 Jan	Forester delivers wood to carpenter	
8–31 Jan	Carpenter works on chair manufacture	
1 Feb		Carpenter pays wages
3 Feb	Carpenter delivers chairs to furniture shop	
3 March		Carpenter pays forester for wood
31 March		Furniture shop pays for chairs

Figure 18.9 Trading on credit

Credit worthiness

When dealing with customers you will need to make an assessment of their credit worthiness. Many a business has been brought down because the organisation it sells to ceases to trade before payments have been made.

This was particularly true in the unpredictable times of recent recessions, when some of the best-known names went under.

You should therefore take great care to assess the credit worthiness of the organisations or individuals you are dealing with. You may ask someone to whom you are selling to provide trade references from other people he or she deals with, or you may require some sort of testimony, e.g. from a bank. Credit reference agencies will carry out a check for you to find out the credit status of people you do business with.

In dealing with new customers for the first time you may be extremely cautious and ask for money 'up front', or for some form of payment guarantee, in the early days of trading with them. Of course, you may also want to examine their accounts, in order to see what their current position is.

Payment terms

Payment terms are an important consideration. Businesses generally offer a discount for prompt payment, e.g. quoting 'less 5%, 28 days'. This means that customers will have 5% taken off the amount they have to pay if they pay within 28 days.

Businesses may also impose penalty clauses as part of the payment terms, e.g. adding an interest charge for each day that payment is overdue. It is important to use terms for trading in order to speed up the money cycle.

Credit control

There are certain dangers in credit transactions. Many customers may take too long to pay their bills and some may not pay the bills at all. This leads to bad debts. Cash discounts are used to encourage customers to pay promptly, but they do not always work.

Large firms employ credit controllers whose job it is to ensure that a regular review is made of all customers, that credit limits are not exceeded and that payments are prompt. Letters and phone calls are used to remind customers about payment and, in some cases, legal action has to be taken.

Bad debts

Businesses can also sell their debts to a factoring company. This simply involves selling off bad debts to a third party for less than they are worth. Many small businesses need cash to keep the business ticking over. It makes sense to sell off debts for less than their face value in order to make more money by producing new goods. Banks in Britain offer a wide range of factoring services for good-quality debts.

During the 1990s many companies have been slow in paying debts. This makes life difficult for other firms that have supplied goods on credit. The government is considering passing a law to limit the amount of time a firm can hold back payment.

Firms can take out bad-debts insurance with an insurance company to cover themselves against non-payment. The disadvantage, of course, is the cost of the insurance premium.

Before granting credit, a firm will usually ask for a trade or bank reference. A trade reference is given by a supplier who has previously given credit to a business, vouching for reliability.

Before giving credit, the firm could also make enquiries with a credit reference agency, which is a firm specialising in keeping lists of people who have defaulted on payments. The agency will verify, for a fee, whether a particular firm has ever had problems or whether it has a clean record of reliability.

Evidence collection point

Produce a set of notes explaining why the finance department in a business would have to consider the credit worthiness and payment terms which they offer to customers.

Factors for consideration when buying

When buying raw materials, or goods as part of the trade cycle, there are a number of important considerations to bear in mind. One of the most important considerations is that the quality of your inputs to the trading cycle will have a key influence on the quality of your outputs from the trading cycle.

Assessing suppliers

Assessing suppliers involves deciding from whom you are going to buy your raw materials and products. Clearly you will be looking for the best value for money and for quality products (expressed in terms of fitness for purpose).

Key considerations will be the price the suppliers will supply at, the terms they offer, how quickly they can deliver the goods, what payment terms they expect, etc. You will need to compare the offers made by competing suppliers to decide on the best terms.

An effective organisation like Marks and Spencer will have a well-organised buying department which works carefully to ensure the best possible supply of inputs to its trading cycle, as the following case study shows

Case study – The organisation of a buying group at Marks and Spencer plc

Marks and Spencer is perhaps the world's best known High Street retailer. Some of the products they sell include recipe dishes. To provide these dishes in the way that the customer requires involves getting together a team of specialists (Figure 18.10).

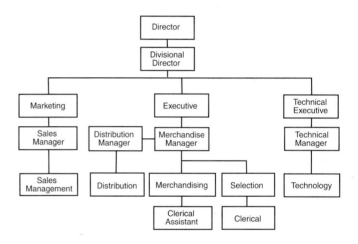

Figure 18.10 The organisation of an M&S buying group

The selectors must choose the recipe dishes that they want to be prepared for sale. They work with top chefs and restaurants to come up with state-of-the-art dishes. Creating a dish includes finding 'a source of excellence'. For instance, if it is an Italian dish the selectors consult with the best Italian chefs and cookery schools in search of the best idea. When the recipe has been selected, the selectors will choose a food manufacturer to make the product.

The merchandisers are responsible for negotiating prices, estimating the quantities of ingredients and fixing up production schedules with manufacturers.

The technologists work out how the dish can be made in bulk. They look at any difficulties that might arise in production. They are concerned with quality and such things as 'sell by' dates.

The distribution manager will be concerned with working out schedules for getting the goods to the stores.

The marketing and sales managers will look at how goods are selling in the shops, which lines to expand and which lines to cut.

1 Explain why each of the departments described above is important to the total buying operations of Marks and Spencer.
2 How are Marks and Spencer able to maintain the quality of their supplies?
3 Why are different specialists required to maintain the quality of the purchasing operation?
4 What sorts of factors would you expect buyers to take into account in deciding which suppliers to work with?

Specification

It is essential when buying to come up with a precise specification of what it is you want. This includes a precise identification of the goods/service required, the quality of goods and in many cases precise delivery arrangements (e.g. using a Just-In-Time approach).

Just-in-time is a very simple idea:

1 Finished goods are produced just in time for them to be sold, rather than weeks or months ahead.
2 The parts that go into a finished product arrive just in time to be put together to make the final product, rather than being stored at some cost in a warehouse.

The idea is to run a company with the smallest possible levels of stock and work-in-progress. This needs careful planning.

It is therefore very important to produce precise specifications when buying in goods and to make sure that your suppliers meet these specifications. You need to get a guarantee of quality from your suppliers. Marks and Spencer and other organisations will give out contracts to sole suppliers on the understanding that they meet specifications for quality, delivery time etc. If a supplier fails to meet the specification you stop trading with them. They would be foolish to fail to meet specifications because your order goes towards providing them with a livelihood.

Quantity

Quantity is an important consideration when deciding who to purchase from. You need to make sure that

they have the capabilities to produce the quantities you require. It is all very well producing quality tennis racquets, but if you need to sell many thousands of racquets a year, you need to make sure that the firm to which you give the contract has enough productive capacity to make up the required order.

Price

Price is always a major consideration. With modern automated production, many suppliers are capable of producing highly similar products. You may therefore want to place an order with the business that offers you the lowest price. Of course, at other times you will prefer to pay a little bit extra for a much better product. Consideration of price will also take into account discounts for quantity, cash payment and prompt payment.

Delivery date

Delivery time is another critical factor in buying decisions. If your customers want products now, there is little point in dealing with a supplier who will deliver next week. In the meantime your customers may have gone to another seller whose supplier can supply immediately.

 Evidence collection point

Produce a set of notes which explain why the quantity ordered, price paid and delivery date are significant in terms of both the trading and money cycles.

In this chapter we have set out to demonstrate the important link between the trading cycle of a business and its money cycle. You need to understand that money is the lifeblood of any business. High sales and a healthy profit are not enough for a business to survive. Insufficient money to pay creditors may lead to delays in receiving new supplies. This in turn gives rise to problems in production and distribution, leading to restricted sales and an even lower supply of money.

Evidence indicators

The following evidence indicators should serve as a checklist to show that you can meet the performance criteria required for this unit. Tick off each of the following when you have successfully covered them. You need to be able to confirm that:

- I have produced a diagram which illustrates the trading cycle of the goods or services produced by one business. ☐
- The diagram is supported by approximate annual figures for the business. ☐
- The figures show the accumulated costs of goods or services bought from other businesses, the final value of the goods or services when sold to the customer and the resulting added value. ☐
- The figures are supported by a commentary which suggests how the added value could be distributed, and explains why profit might be retained in the business, used to pay off debts or paid to shareholders. ☐

- I have produced a spreadsheet which shows how the money cycle for these goods or services mirrors the trading cycle and starts and ends with cash. ☐
- I have produced notes explaining why the finance department in the same business would have to consider the credit worthiness and payment terms which they offer to customers, and why the quantity ordered, price paid and delivery date are significant in terms of both the trading and money cycles. ☐

Chapter 19

Financial transactions and supporting documents

All organisations are required to keep records of their activities. By keeping records accurate and up-to-date, organisations can measure their performance, improve their overall financial control and take action when problems arise.

In this chapter we look at the purpose and use of business documentation for generating accounting data which can be used to create accounting information. In doing this we look at a range of business documents which originate from business transactions.

Despite the advent of information technology, paper documents and recording procedures are still an essential part of business life. Although most records today are stored on computer databases, we need to identify the types of documents that records relate to.

The purposes of using documentation for financial transactions

When we buy goods from a shop, there is rarely a need for much documentation. We might pay directly by cash or, if we pay by cheque, credit card or debit card, we will have to sign some form of business document. Organisations, however, require a lot more documentation to cover the requirements of a transaction. There are a number of reasons for this.

- Most organisations buy goods or services on credit. For example, the good or service is first supplied and then payment is made at a month-end or later. At each stage in the processes involved, documents help to record what is happening.
- Documentation provides the source data for the recording of purchases and sales. They help to ensure that this process is carried out efficiently and is free from error so that appropriate payments are sent out on time and that mistakes are not made when sending documents to customers.

- Accounts are generated from the documents. These can be used to provide feedback on various transactions. They can also be totalled and summarised to provide an overview of different aspects of the organisation's performance.
- Documents help to create records which then meet the legal requirements of the organisation for the Department of Inland Revenue and the Department of Customs and Excise. For example, they may wish to know sales figures for the purpose of VAT calculations.
- It is important that parties to a transaction know precisely what they have agreed to, for example in terms of discounts, amounts and prices. Documentation serves to confirm arrangements, thus helping to create a mutual understanding between the buyer and seller.
- Specific requirements may be met by the use of certain documents, for example petty cash vouchers and stores requisitions.
- Documents also help to monitor business performance so that information is created for the purpose of internal planning and control.

Case study – Monitoring and controlling your business

The following key points appear in a Barclays Bank business advice booklet *Monitoring and Controlling your Business*:

- Keep all your records and write them up promptly and regularly. Do not allow invoices and receipts to accumulate in a drawer.
- Have a look at various ready-made record systems that are on the market. They could simplify matters for you. Larger and more complicated businesses may find a computer package helpful, but first discuss this with your accountant.
- As always, get good professional advice if you are in any doubt about your records.
- Remember that the Inland Revenue and Customs and Excise are interested in your records. Do not try to mislead them or yourself.
- Accurate and up-to-date records can help your business to avert a crisis as well as saving money with your accountant.

1 Give at least two reasons why a small business should not allow documents to accumulate.
2 Identify two benefits of keeping accurate and up-to-date records.
3 Who will be interested in such records?

Source documents are documents that relate first-hand to transactions between customers and organisations. Their importance should never be underestimated. Imagine the sort of confusion that might arise if a source document is mislaid. For example:

■ Goods might be sent to the wrong customer.
■ The wrong goods might be despatched.
■ Payment could be delayed.
■ General confusion might arise, leading to complaints and loss of further business.

There are many types of business documents and electronic processing systems, several of which we look at in this chapter. Business documents required for transactions capture the details of accounting events, are necessary as proof of business dealings, and are a way of checking goods ordered and received.

Financial information is the end-result of a process which may involve the following stages (Figure 19.1).

1 The preparation of source documents.
2 The entry of data from source documents into source records.
3 The posting of data from source records into a more permanent record of data called the *ledger*.
4 The presentation of accounting reports from ledger information.

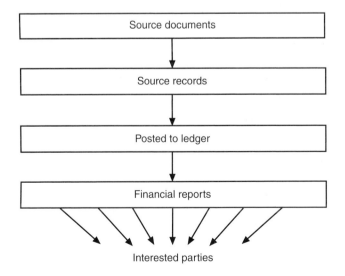

Figure 19.1 Generating financial reports

Data-flows from source documents are today, more often than not, channelled through a management information system or accounting system. These are used to meet the needs of managers for planning and control. Source documents provide the raw data for such purposes.

Evidence collection point

Over the period of one month collect all of the business documents you come across. Examine the uses for and purposes of each type of document.

Purchase documents

The first stage in the purchasing process will be to make decisions about the goods or services required. A letter of enquiry may be sent to several suppliers to find out what they can offer, and so that various details and specifications can be compared. A buyer will wish to find out many things before placing an order – for example prices, details about the goods, delivery dates and times, and discounts.

In response to the enquiry the potential seller may supply a quotation or a catalogue with a price list. The buyer will then compare quotations or analyse details from the catalogues. A quotation provides details of availability and of terms being offered. For example, '5%-30 days' indicates that if the bill is paid within 30 days, the buyer can deduct a cash discount of 5%.

Orders placed

Once a buyer has decided upon the best quotation or has scrutinised a series of catalogues, the next step may be the issuing of a purchase order. In the example, a firm called Customised Caravans of Carlisle is ordering raw materials from J.P.P. Evans & Co. of Dudley (see Figure 19.2).

Information appearing on a purchase order may include the following.

■ Order number so that it can be traced easily, and matched against invoices and statements.
■ The price which will have been obtained from a price list, quotation or catalogue.
■ The purchaser's name and address. Source documents are usually headed with the name and address of the organisation. It is possible for the delivery address to be different to the above.

489

PURCHASE ORDER
CUSTOMISED CARAVANS
Scotland Road
Stanwix
CARLISLE CA3 8JB
Tel 01748–8397421   Fax 01748–8397428

J. P. P. Evans & Co.   Order No.: KL 2322
Birmingham Road
DUDLEY
West Midlands   Date: 8th May 1995
B34 7BB
                              Delivery: Above address

QUANTITY	CATALOGUE NO.	DESCRIPTION	PRICE
10	B345	Tins Henna Red Paint	£5.00 per tin

Authorisation: *R Robertson*

Figure 19.2 A purchase order

- The name and address of the supplier.
- A description of the goods required.
- The catalogue number/reference number of the goods or service required.
- Authorisation such as the signature and date.

Task

Look at the specimen purchase order in Figure 19.2. Explain what might happen if:

1 the date was omitted from the order
2 the reference/catalogue number was missed from the order.

Advice note/despatch note

Before despatching the goods the seller may send an advice note to say that the goods are being sent and that they will arrive shortly. If the goods do not arrive, the buyer can then contact the seller to find out why the delay has arisen.

Delivery note

A delivery note is usually sent with the goods. This simply lists the items that have been sent. The buyer can use it to check that the goods have arrived.

Purchase invoice

From the buyer's point of view the invoice is known as their 'purchase invoice'. It is an official request for payment and is therefore an important document in any transaction. It shows the details of the transaction, the amount charged and the terms (Figure 19.3).

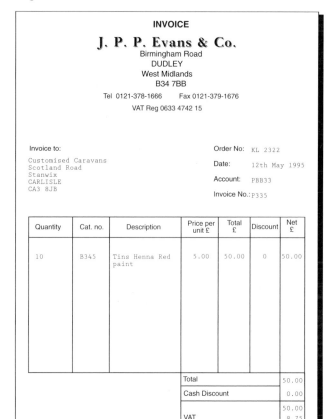

INVOICE

J. P. P. Evans & Co.
Birmingham Road
DUDLEY
West Midlands
B34 7BB
Tel 0121-378-1666   Fax 0121-379-1676
VAT Reg 0633 4742 15

Invoice to: Order No: KL 2322
Customised Caravans
Scotland Road   Date: 12th May 1995
Stanwix
CARLISLE   Account: PBB33
CA3 8JB
                                     Invoice No.: P335

Quantity	Cat. no.	Description	Price per unit £	Total £	Discount	Net £
10	B345	Tins Henna Red paint	5.00	50.00	0	50.00

Total	50.00
Cash Discount	0.00
	50.00
VAT	8.75
Total	58.75

Terms:
Net monthly
E & OE

Figure 19.3 An invoice

Information appearing on a purchase invoice may include:

- *Order number* This can be used to check the goods delivered against those ordered.
- *Terms* This shows how much time the buyer has to pay for the goods, and the cash discount which may be given for quick payment.
- *Carriage* If this appears it will show how transport costs should be paid for. 'Carriage paid' means that the seller will pay for the transport and 'Carriage forward' means that the buyer is expected to pay.
- *E & O E* This stands for 'errors and omissions excepted', which means that the seller can correct any mistake on the invoice at a later date.
- *Trade discount* This may be given for a variety of reasons. It will be deducted from the invoice price.
- *VAT* If a good or service is subject to value added tax, this will be added to the amount appearing on the invoice.
- *Invoice number* This makes it easy for the accounts department of both the buyer and the seller to identify the invoice quickly.
- *VAT registration number* Most organisations print their VAT number on their invoices for convenience.

If the seller has not transacted any previous business with the buyer, or perhaps if the buyer has been late with payments in the past, the seller might send the buyer a *pro forma invoice*. This document is sent to the buyer before the goods are delivered and sets out the charges which then have to be paid in advance. The goods are then delivered after the payments are made.

Credit note to the buyer

A credit note to the buyer may be sent by the seller to adjust the amount which appeared on an invoice (Figure 19.4). A credit note reduces the invoice price. The invoice price might be reduced because a mistake has been made, or because goods have been found to be faulty or damaged, or simply because the wrong goods have been delivered.

Information appearing on the credit note may include:

- the original invoice number
- the date
- addresses
- the reasons for the credit being given.

A credit note is sometimes printed in red.

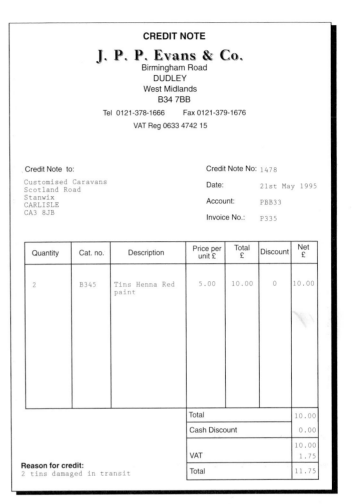

Figure 19.4 A credit note

Goods received note

A goods received note is used internally to inform various departments about the arrival of orders. For example, copies may be sent to the department that ordered the goods, purchasing and also the accounts department where it will be checked against the invoice before the supplier is paid (Figure 19.5).

Evidence collection point

Draw a chart to show how purchase documents relate both to the seller and to departments within the organisation. You work should provide evidence of Core Skills in Communication.

491

GOODS RECEIVED NOTE

CUSTOMISED CARAVANS

Goods from:

J. P. P. Evans & Co.
Birmingham Road
DUDLEY
West Midlands
B34 7BB

GRN No: 842

Date: 14th May 1995

Quantity	Catalogue No.	Description	Order Number
10	B345	Tins Henna Red Paint	KL 2322

Received by _P Williams_

Condition of goods		Copies to:	
shortages		Production	✓
damaged	✓ 2 tins damaged	Purchasing	✓
good condition		Accounts	✓
		Stores	

Figure 19.5 A goods received note

Sales documents

The major responsibility of the sales department is to generate orders for products. The size of the sales department and the overall nature of its operations will depend largely on the type of industry in which the organisation operates. For example, selling to industrial markets will normally require a lot of personal selling, whereas in retail markets promotional activities stimulate sales and organisations will generally operate the smaller sales teams.

Orders received

A sale is concluded when a customer completes an order form. When an order form is received for a credit sale a copy is usually sent to the credit control department for approval. This is because there are many dangers with credit transactions. Some customers may take too long to pay their bills or may even not pay their bills at all.

The credit control department reviews all accounts, sets credit limits, ensures that limits are not exceeded, and tries to ensure that payments are

made promptly. These actions constantly influence the cash flow and liquidity of the organisation.

Before granting credit for the first time, a supplier may ask for a trade or bank reference. A trade reference is provided by a supplier who has previously given credit to a business and may vouch for the reliability of their custom.

Sales invoice

From the seller's point of view the invoice is known as their 'sales invoice'.

When goods have been despatched to the customer by the stock control department, a copy of the sales order stating the date of despatch is sent to the sales invoice section of the accounts department, who then prepare the invoice.

The invoice contains the relevant details of the transaction – such as the quantity and price of the goods ordered and the amount due from the customer. When the invoice is prepared, prices should be checked, discounts should be calculated, VAT should be added where necessary, and all other details should be checked carefully.

Task

The blank Heinemann sales invoice shown as Figure 19.6 is extracted from a pack of continuous stationery.

1   Name two advantages of handling invoices by computer.
2   On the sales invoice identify the VAT number, the invoice number, the address where the invoice is to be sent, payment details, and the column which refers to trade discount.
3   Explain why the invoice address might be different from the delivery address.
4   What details mentioned in the text do not appear on the invoice?

Delivery note

The delivery note is usually sent with the goods, often in the care of the driver of the company delivering the goods. The person receiving the goods will be expected to sign it, after having checked the quantity of goods delivered. If the goods are posted, the delivery note will tend to be packed with the goods (Figure 19.7).

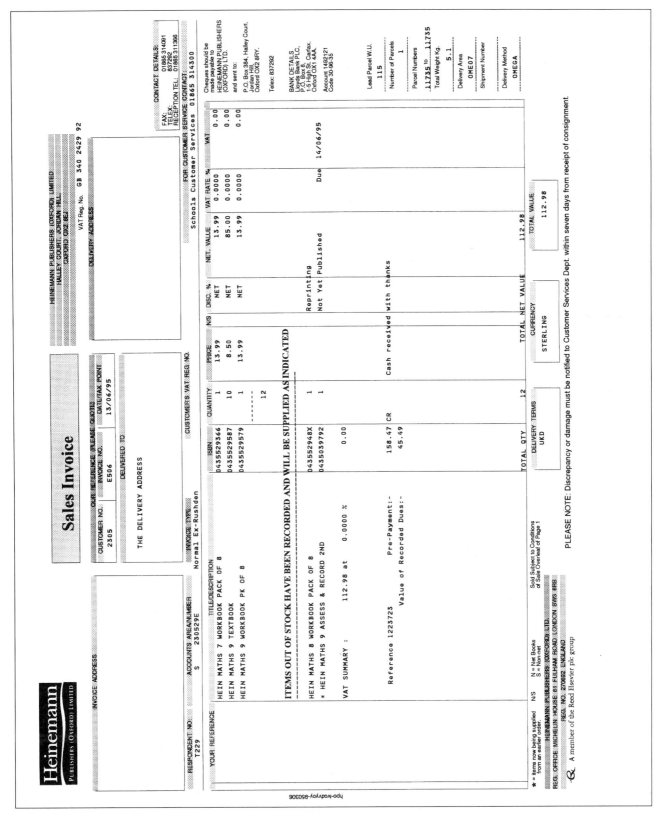

Figure 19.6 A specimen sales invoice

Information appearing on the delivery note may include:

■ the purchase order number
■ the method of delivery
■ the catalogue reference number and quantity supplied
■ the signature and printed name of the person receiving the goods.

Statement of account and remittance advice

The seller will send all regular customers a statement at the end of every month. This is simply a copy of the customer's account in the sales ledger and usually contains a record of all transactions with the customer during the month. The statements will contain details of all invoices which have been issued to each customer, any payments which have been made and any credit notes which have been issued.

Information appearing on the statement may include:

■ the addresses and customer account number
■ the date

DELIVERY NOTE

J. P. P. Evans & Co.
Birmingham Road
DUDLEY
West Midlands
B34 7BB

Tel 0121-378-1666   Fax 0121-379-1676

Date:	12th May 1995
Order No.:	KL 2322
Delivery:	Van
Delivery Note No.:	476

Customised Caravans
Scotland Road
Stanwix
CARLISLE
CA3 8JB

Quantity	Catalogue No.	Description
10	B345	Tins Henna Red Paint

Signature	*P Williams*	Name	*P WILLIAMS*

Figure 19.7 A delivery note

■ details of invoices issued
■ any credit notes issued
■ details of payments made
■ the amount outstanding.

STATEMENT

J. P. P. Evans & Co.
Birmingham Road
DUDLEY
West Midlands
B34 7BB

Tel 0121-378-1666   Fax 0121-379-1676

VAT Reg 0633 4742 15

Date: 30th May 1995

Account: PBB33
Customised Caravans
Scotland Road
Stanwix
CARLISLE
CA3 8JB

REMITTANCE ADVICE

J. P. P. Evans & Co.
Birmingham Road
DUDLEY
West Midlands
B34 7BB

Account: PBB33

Date	Reference	Value £	Outstanding £	Outstanding £
12/5/95	INV P335	58.75	58.75	58.75
	CN 1478	11.75		
	TOTAL		58.75	58.75

Figure 19.8 A statement and remittance advice

In the statement in Figure 19.8, a tear-off slip known as a remittance advice is attached. The buyer can detach this from the statement and then send it with the amount due to their supplier. If a statement does not have remittance advice attached, buyers may prepare their own remittance advice to send with the cheque.

Case study – Working as an auto-electrician

Peter Birch recently set up in business as an auto-electrician in York. Peter's business is located in an area that has a large number of garages, many of which have expressed an interest in using Peter's specialist services. Peter also hopes to attract a lot of work from personal customers. He has paid for an advert in *Yellow Pages* and has advertised in local newspapers.

Peter has been surprised by the extent of the documentation he has to handle in the day-to-day running of his business. He has opened accounts with several local suppliers of parts and has already received an assortment of documentation, including advice notes, delivery notes invoices and statements. Peter is also concerned about the type of documents he should provide.

1. Explain briefly the purpose of each of the types of documents mentioned above.
2. Advise Peter on the sort of documentation he should be providing for his customers. Though all of his personal customers will be paying by cash, garages will expect to be allowed to pay by credit.
3. Advise Peter on the benefits of using a computer or some form of information technology to help with the documentation process.

Payment documents

Most business transactions involve at some stage a transfer of money from one person or organisation to another. Whereas in the past transactions involved payment by notes and coins, today most involve the use of automated systems which transfer money directly from one place to another without any direct movement of cash.

Cheque

The most significant document used for payment and transferring funds is clearly the cheque (Figure 19.9), which is issued through the mechanism of the banking system. Though cheques are not legal tender, their use and acceptability today is widespread. The definition of a cheque is as follows:

> A cheque is an unconditional order in writing drawn on a bank, signed by a drawer, which requires a bank to pay on demand a sum of money to the order of a named person or to the bearer.

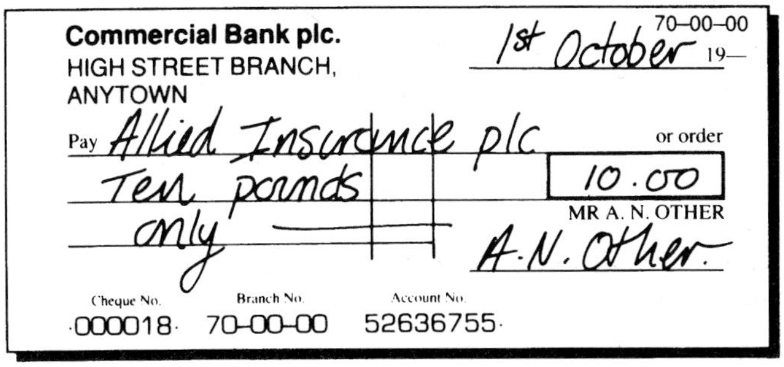
Commercial Bank plc.
HIGH STREET BRANCH,
ANYTOWN
70–00–00
1st October 19–
Pay Allied Insurance plc or order
Ten pounds only
10.00
MR A. N. OTHER
A.N. Other
Cheque No. 000018 Branch No. 70–00–00 Account No. 52636755

Figure 19.9 A specimen cheque

Evidence collection point

Write a short booklet entitled *How to write out a cheque.* Use a series of dummy cheques to illustrate the various features of cheques and the points you would like to make. Plan your work so that it provides evidence of Core Skills in Communication and, if possible, Information Technology.

The meanings of the various parts of the above definition of a cheque are:

- *Unconditional* Payment cannot be dependent upon certain conditions being met.
- *Writing* A cheque must be in ink or print.
- *Signed* A cheque must be signed by the drawer who is the person paying the money.
- *On demand* The cheque will be paid when presented to the bank.
- *A sum of money* This must be written on the cheque in words and figures.
- *Named person or to the bearer* The cheque must be payable to someone by name or to the bearer (the person in possession of the cheque).

Bank giro credit

Another document associated with receiving or transferring payment is a bank giro credit (Figure 19.10). This allows for the credit transfer of money into a bank account and may be used for putting takings into an account, for the payment/receipt of bills and payment of salaries. Credit clearing works in a similar way to cheque clearing – it involves the transfer of money between accounts.

Banking documents are source documents of entry for an organisation's cash book. It is from these books that company accounts are drawn up – both management accounts which project and analyse business performance and financial accounts which record past performance – many of which are required by law.

Remittance advice

Another payment document, as we saw earlier, is a remittance advice which accompanies a payment document such as a cheque. With some systems a computer will print out a remittance advice as well as a cheque to be sent on to a supplier.

Petty cash voucher

Another regular form of payment which most organisations will have to make is that of petty cash. A petty cash book is usually set up to record low-value payments made by members of staff for relatively small purchases such as travelling expenses, items of stationery, etc. Such small items are not

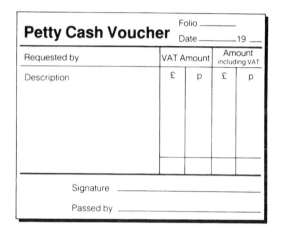

Figure 19.11 A petty cash voucher

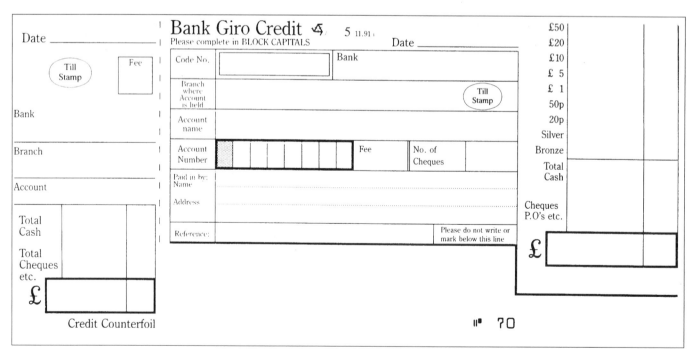

Figure 19.10 A bank giro credit

entered in the main accounting system; instead, a petty cashier will control the money and make the necessary payments. Payments of petty cash are usually made against a petty cash voucher (Figure 19.11) – the voucher is then authorised and payment is made in cash.

Other methods of transfer through the banking system

It is estimated that more than eight million cheques are processed through the banking system each working day. Dealing with such large volumes of documentation has become a very expensive process. Banks have therefore increasingly sought to use information technology to reduce costs and increase the efficiency of the system. In doing this, bankers and the banking system have opened up and developed other methods of payment transfer. Examples are:

- *Standing orders* Customers can advise their banks to make regular payments on certain dates for fixed amounts. If the amounts or the dates are to be changed, the customer simply advises the bank of such changes.
- *Direct debits* With this system the customer tells the bank what to pay and when. The receiver provides the documentation requiring payment. This system can deal with variable payments.
- *BACS (Bankers' Automated Clearing System)* This system was set up to deal with bulk electronic clearing for payments purposes. It removes the need to send vast amounts of paper around the system and is used for standing orders, direct debits and salary credits. The user of the system provides the bank with data in the form of magnetic tape, diskette or disk and this is then sent to the BACS computer centre for processing. If the information is sent down the telephone line, it is known as BACSTEL. The input is processed and debits and credits are made to relevant accounts.
- *Credit cards* Customers are provided with a card and a credit limit and can buy goods up to that limit. Every month a statement is sent to the credit card holder who may either pay the amount on the statement or pay it at some stage in the future.
- *Debit cards* These allow customers to buy goods and services using the card. They can have their account debited immediately with the cost of the item.

Electronic Data Interchange (EDI)

As we saw earlier in the book, Electronic Data Interchange (EDI) has the objective of speeding up business transactions between suppliers and their customers. It achieves this by allowing data, messages or documents to be transferred directly from the computer of one organisation to the computer of another. The great benefit is that it cuts paperwork and the chances of errors by sending pre-formatted data between trading partners. Once in place EDI dramatically cuts paperwork and reorders automatically with the ability to review and edit orders.

Evidence collection point

Make a list of the advantages of using cheques and other methods of banking transfer in preference to cash.

Receipt documents

Receipt

As well as documents associated with making payments, documents are also used to record receipts. The most basic and common document used to show a receipt of payment is simply a sales receipt. This is evidence that money has been received and may show the various elements comprising the transaction. For example, Figure 19.12 shows a sales receipt for petrol. Note the VAT number, the date and the total value of the receipt.

Figure 19.12 A sales receipt

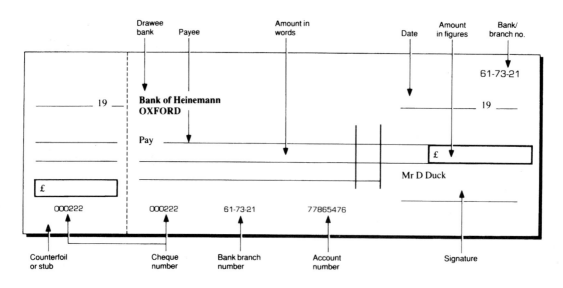

Figure 19.13 The parts of a typical cheque

Cheque

One of the most important jobs in a cashier's department is to record incoming cheques. Cheques are today the most widely accepted form of payment. The various parts of a cheque are illustrated in Figure 19.13.

When recording cheques it is important to make sure of the following:

- Cheques contain current dates.
- The amounts in words and figures are the same.
- The payee's name is correct.
- The cheque is signed.
- Any alterations are clear and have been signed.

Paying-in slip

A paying-in slip is used when paying cheques and cash into an organisation's bank account. A paying-

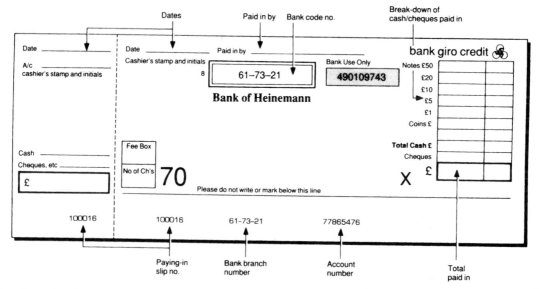

Figure 19.14 A paying-in slip

in slip is illustrated in Figure 19.14. Where a number of cheques are paid in on one slip, they are listed on the reverse of the slip.

Task

Imagine that you work in a cashier's department. In the morning post there are a number of remittances. These include:

- a cheque for £8.76
- a cheque for £7.89.

In addition, the following cash payments are received during the day:

- 8 x £10 notes
- 9 x £5 notes
- 8 x £1 coins.

Prepare a paying-in slip for all of the above to be paid into the bank. Make up suitable account and code numbers.

Bank statement

Banks send statements to their customers at regular intervals. The bank statement simply provides a detailed record of all the transactions which have taken place (Figure 19.15).

Information appearing on a bank statement may include:

- a balance which is brought forward from the previous statement
- account details
- a list of deposits paid into the account
- a list of withdrawals from the account
- a balance after each transaction.

Bank of Heinemann
Oxford Branch

Confidential

Sheet Number

784

Telephone 01865-322222   30th May 1995

Account Number   75283122

Date	Details	Withdrawals	Deposits	Balance (£)
1995				
May 2	Balance from sheet 783			183.45
May 4	Cheque 476124	15.00		168.45
May 5	Cheque 476125	18.50		149.95
May 6	Oxford Council DD	73.85		76.10
May 7	Oxford Telecom credit		956.32	1032.42
May 8	Cheque 476126	149.30		883.12
May 18	Cheque 476129	350.00		533.12
May 25	Cheque 476127	200.00		333.12

Figure 19.15 A bank statement

- reduce the effects of any form of error by detecting an error shortly after it takes place
- provide a system which makes fraud virtually impossible.

One way of doing this is to set up an audit trail. This uses a series of analysis documents which check that all of the steps in the accounting process are error-free and also serves to identify errors when they are made.

There are a number of consequences of incorrect completion of source documents, as illustrated in Figure 19.16.

Consequences of incorrect completion

With every organisation it is important to ensure that business documents are correctly completed. Internal checks to ensure that day-to-day transactions are correctly recorded will help to detect errors and fraud. They will also help to:

- limit the responsibility for particular actions to one or more individuals
- ensure that the records confirm the facts

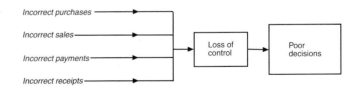

Figure 19.16 Incorrect completion of documents affects the quality of decision-making

For example, just think about some of the possibilities of the incorrect completion of source documents:

- The organisation fails to send out a large sales invoice or puts a figure on the invoice which is too small (i.e. £1000 instead of £10 000). This means that profits will then be understated.
- The organisation sends out invoices upon which amounts are too large. This will annoy a number of customers who consequently might consider taking their business elsewhere. Profits will be overstated.
- An incorrect payment is made to a supplier. It may be difficult to recover this payment.
- A cheque is lost and not recorded. This may not even be noticed, and will cause considerable problems as a consequence.

All of this leads to poor and inaccurate information filtering through to managers, who may have based their decisions upon this poor quality information. There are other dangers as well. For example:

- Not keeping accounting statements which provide a true and fair record of business activity may lead to a breach under the Companies Acts for false accounting.
- A lot of time which could otherwise be better spent may have to be allocated to finding mistakes and dealing with minor inaccuracies. This costs money.
- Managers may be optimistic about business performance and base their decisions upon the wrong information. In the accounting context they may feel that the business has a strong cash-flow position. If as a result of errors this is not so, this could lead to a liquidity crisis.
- If mistakes have been made, information may be permanently lost which may make it virtually impossible to recover debts.

Evidence collection point

Think about your personal financial situation. What would be the worst possible consequence of the incorrect completion of a source document for your bank or other personal account?

Security checks for business documents

There are a number of security checks which are necessary for many of the different types of business documents:

- *Orders* These should be authorised. Copies of the orders should be sent to the receiving department, the stock control department and the accounts department for the checking of prices and discounts. It may be necessary to check that order levels fall within prescribed spending limits, i.e. that members of staff are not exceeding their authority by ordering something of too high a value.
- *Invoices* These should be checked against the original order to ensure that the correct goods have arrived, that prices are correct, that discounts have been correctly calculated and that VAT has been applied correctly. Invoices should also be checked against the goods received note to ensure that the details correspond to the goods which have been delivered. Invoices which are incorrect need to be sorted out with the seller. After invoices are checked they can then be authorised for payment.
- *Credit notes* These should be kept safely and amounts deducted from the prices which appear on invoices.
- *Cheques* Once invoices have been authorised, eligible cheque signatories may then sanction payment. All organisations will have signed a bank mandate which will set out the names of those employees empowered to sign cheques.

Evidence collection point

Explain why every organisation requires a range of security procedures which check documentation. Find out the security checks carried out in either the organisation you work for or the organisation you attend.

One list of security checks was provided by the Auditing Practices Committee. These recommend:

- *Segregation of duties* This means that job tasks would segregate or break-up the roles of those who both record and process a financial transaction. For example, it would not be a good idea for the same person to receive the cash and also be responsible for recording it and taking it to the bank.
- *Physical controls* These ensure that access to valuable assets within the organisation is restricted through a variety of security measures involving use of documentation.
- *Authorisation and approval* All transactions within

the organisation should require authorisation and approval by the person responsible.

- *Management* Outside the internal controls of the system, managers should be able to use supervisory controls over various procedures.
- *Supervision* Supervisors should be able to review and oversee the day-to-day recording procedures.
- *Organisation* Organisations should have a plan which defines the roles of individuals and comprises a series of controls which include the delegation of authority and responsibility.
- *Arithmetical and accounting* There should be controls within the organisation which ensure that information is accurately recorded and processed.
- *Personnel* It is important to ensure that staff have the appropriate personal and professional characteristics to carry out their roles.

Tasks

1 Look closely at the purchase order in Figure 19.17, and then answer the following questions:
  - a Why might failure to quote the order number lead to delayed payment?
  - b Why does the 'date work required by' appear on this order?

2 Look at the invoice in Figure 19.18. Check the details on the invoice and suggest where amendments should take place.

3 Imagine that you work for Jevons General Maintenance Co. Ltd and that you have been asked to design a suitable goods received note to be used within the company. Use a word-processor to help you with your design. Aim to make the design simple and effective.

4 Look carefully at the order in Figure 19.19 and then answer the following questions:
  - a How is the number on the order to be used?
  - b Why does the order require confirmation of delivery date?
  - c Why does the order contain instructions regarding:
    - i delivery
    - ii packing
    - iii invoicing?

5 Imagine that you work in the office of Reading and District Joinery Supplies, 3 Everside Way, Earley, Reading, Berkshire RG3 7BB. Your accounting records highlight the following details about your transactions with B Roos:

ORDER NUMBER
2693 / /0-43 /

HEINEMANN EDUCATIONAL
Hailey Court, Jordan Hill
Oxford OX2 8EJ
Telephone Oxford (0865) 311366
Telex 837292 HEBOXF G
Facsimile (0865) 310043

FROM:

TO:

ADDRESS:

DATE:

TITLE:

When invoicing please quote title and ORDER NUMBER. Failure to quote this will delay payment. Please send your invoice addressed to

INSTRUCTIONS:

DATE WORK REQUIRED BY:

SIGNATURE: DATE:

Please sign both copies (before commencing work), and return the duplicate copy to

Figure 19.17 Purchase order

WORKWISE LTD
4 Cottingham Street
HULL
HU8 7YT

Invoice No. 7643
Order No. 93/876
Account No. 89/78

VAT No. 765 6543
9th July 199–

To:
Watchet Works Ltd
4 Sonnet Corner
PICKERING
YO13 5FK

Code	Description	Quantity	Unit Price	Total
F300	Overalls	16	£12.50	187.50
G567	Shirts	25	£9.50	237.50
		Goods total		425.00
		Less 10% discount		42.50
				380.00
		Add VAT 17.5%		66.93
		Grand Total		313.07

Figure 19.18 Invoice

Print Order

Heinemann

Order Number

3269 / / 0-43 /

Ref your Estimate/Scales _____

Heinemann Educational Publishers
Halley Court
Jordan Hill
Oxford OX2 8EJ

TO: _____
Title: _____

Telephone 0865 311366
Telex 837292 HEBOXF G
Fax 0865 314239

Date: _____

MATERIAL ENCLOSED/TO FOLLOW: _____
(Please show proofs/imposed ozalids)

PRINT QUANTITY: _____ x _____ pp Trimmed page size _____ x _____ mm No. of colours _____

PAPER: _____
Quantity: _____
Size: _____ gm²
In stock with you/we to supply/print up to paper supplied
Delivery due _____

COVER: Print _____ copies
Supplied by: _____
No. of colours _____ UV Varnish/Laminate
Material: _____
In stock/we supply by: _____

BINDING/PACKING: _____

ADVANCE COPIES TO   AT OXFORD
SEE ADVANCE COPY FORM ATTACHED

DELIVERY DATE REQUIRED _____
Confirm by return

INVOICING – Invoices must include our Order Number (as above), together with details of our paper/cover material usage. Please send invoices to Finance Dept. at above address.

ARTWORK/CRC – PLEASE RETURN TO THE UNDERSIGNED

SIGNATURE: _____

DELIVERY INSTRUCTIONS – Bulk stock with advice note to Reed Book Services Ltd., Warehouse No. 2, Sanders Lodge Industrial Estate, Rushden, Northants NN10 9RZ

PACKING INSTRUCTIONS
All books must be packed in binders parcels/cartons (in 30s), each with a maximum weight of 15 kilos per parcel/carton.
Each parcel to have label showing: TITLE, ISBN, EDITION, QUANTITY, BAR CODE, PUBLISHER, PRICE (if known). (Pack in multiples of 10 where possible.)

PALLETS
Use
1000 x 1110 mm
2 way entry
non-reversible
pallets as illustration
on the left.
Do not mix titles
on one pallet.

No overhang on pallets. Maximum height including pallet 1250 mm. To avoid movement in transit, strap and shrink wrap each pallet.

Figure 19.19 Order

1st Jan   Balance due £345.00
2nd Jan   Goods sold £567.88, invoice no. P335 (including VAT)
3rd Jan   Goods sold £243.77, invoice no. P339 (including VAT)
7th Jan   Received cheque for £345.00
9th Jan   Goods sold £44.55, invoice no. P366 (including VAT)
11th Jan   Goods sold £39.00, invoice no. P366 (including VAT)
20th Jan   Goods returned, £14.00, credit note CN66 issued

Prepare a statement of account to be sent to B Roos at her address: 44 Cornice Grove, Finchampstead, Berkshire RG12 5GG.

6 Fill in and sign the cheque and counterfoil below, making it payable to RS Stores Ltd for £177.89. Date for today.

7 Form a group of four. Two of you should then act for a buying organisation and two of you for a selling organisation. For each organisation make up either a set of documents associated with purchasing or with sales. Use the documents across a number of transactions to illustrate how they work.

8 You have been appointed office manager for a small factory. You are concerned about security procedures in the office. Design a notice for staff which lists the security procedures for documentation. (Use the guidelines from the APC on pages 500–501 to help you to draft these.)

9 Find out more about the operation of Electronic Data Interchange. Write to a number of large companies to ask about whether or not they use it and how it is used. Research the technical pages of magazines,

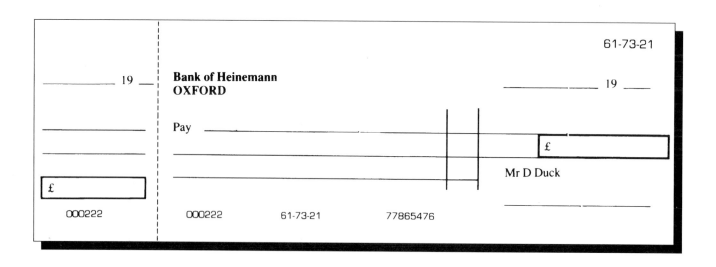

newspapers and periodicals to find articles about EDI.

10 Obtain a copy of a bank statement. Explain the meaning and purpose of each entry. In what ways is a bank statement (a) similar to and (b) different from a statement of account sent by a company?

Evidence indicators

For this activity you need to complete a set of purchases documents, sales documents, receipts documents and payments documents. Use a word-processor and/or other supporting packages to help you to complete your documents.

The following list should serve as a checklist. Tick off each of the following when you have successfully covered them as part of your operation. You need to confirm that:

■ I have accurately completed a set of purchase documents. These include a purchase order, goods received note, and purchase invoice. ☐

■ I have accurately completed a set of sales documents. These include a sales order received note, a delivery note, invoice, credit note, and statement of account. ☐

■ I have accurately completed a set of payments documents. These include a cheque, a bank giro credit form, a remittance advice and a petty cash voucher. ☐

■ I have accurately completed a set of receipts documents. These include a receipt, a bank paying-in slip, a cheque and a bank statement. ☐

The cost of goods and services

Have you ever made and sold anything or provided a service for somebody else? What have you charged for the good or service you supplied? Did your calculations include costs?

Nearly all business managers have to deal with products and their costs, sometimes on a day-to-day basis. A knowledge of costing techniques is therefore an essential part of the process of planning business activities. In this chapter we look at how to calculate the cost of a good or service using costing techniques.

Direct and indirect costs of businesses

The word 'cost' has several meanings, even in everyday language. The cost of items we purchase is something we come across daily – it is a money sacrifice we have to make for the things we want.

Organisations frequently refer to calculating the cost of business activities to determine the cost of providing the customer with their final good or service. In this context they are using a knowledge of costs together with a knowledge of revenues to determine whether or not something they are planning will ultimately reap the rewards they desire. Today cost accounting and the use of costing techniques provides a useful source of data for management accountants.

Nearly all of an organisation's activities involve some sort of cost. A sound knowledge of these costs and their influence is fundamental for assessing profitability, as profits are only a reflection of income over and above such costs. Costs from the past – which therefore have already been incurred – often provide a guide to likely costs in the future.

There are two broad approaches to the classification of business costs:

1 One method categorises costs by their type and identifies whether they can be directly related to the final product or service of the business.
2 The other approach is to analyse costs according to whether they remain fixed with changes in

output levels. This forms the foundation for decision-making, which is further developed in the next chapter.

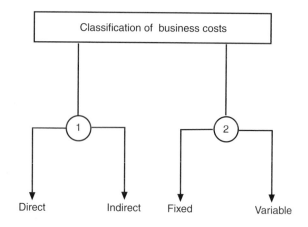

Figure 20.1 Classification of business costs

Direct costs

Direct costs are those costs that can be clearly identified with the product or service being provided. Typical examples include:

- *Direct labour* – payments made to workers who make products or provide services. An engineering firm may incur direct wages paid to machine operators and an office-cleaning firm will pay direct wages to cleaners.
- *Direct materials* – the cost incurred for materials used to make specific products or provide specific services. An engineering firm may require materials in the form of base metals and ready-made components, the cleaning firm will require chemicals and materials for specific cleaning contracts.
- *Direct expenses* – other costs may be incurred specifically for the final product or service. These may include payments to the product's designer (royalties), payments made to other businesses for work they have done as sub-contractors to help provide the finished product or service for the

consumer and sometimes power and depreciation, *but only if there is a direct link between the cost unit, the use of power or the depreciation taking place.*

Evidence collection point

Make a list of the direct costs of the school or college you attend.

Indirect costs

Indirect costs are those that cannot be classified as direct costs. Wherever possible, costs incurred by businesses are identified with specific products or services, as this provides the most accurate costing of a firm's output.

However, many costs incurred by businesses cannot be easily related to specific units of production or service. For example, it is usually very difficult and time-consuming to relate precise amounts of electricity used and property rents incurred to specific units of output.

Indirect costs can be classified as follows:

- *Indirect labour* This would include the cost of management, administration and marketing personnel. Even the cost of many 'blue-collar' workers may need to be classified as indirect labour if they are not doing work that results directly in a product or service. Examples are maintenance workers and stores personnel.
- *Indirect materials* These include small items which are difficult to relate directly to items of output. In fact, the costs of relating them to specific items of output would outweigh the benefits of slightly more accurate product costs. Examples of indirect materials include lubricating materials, rags for cleaning and small nuts and bolts.
- *Indirect expenses* These include a wide range of costs such as property rents, power, stationery, rates, telephone and other running expenses as well as depreciation of fixed assets (see the paragraph below about depreciation of fixed assets). Total indirect costs are often called overheads.

Evidence collection point

Make a list of the indirect costs of the school or college you attend.

Fixed assets and depreciation

Fixed assets describe those items that can be used in the business for a fairly long time period (generally over one year). Examples include land and buildings, machinery, office equipment and motor vehicles.

Although fixed assets can last for many years, they do not last for ever. They wear out and have to be replaced. When the firm purchases a fixed asset it will have an expectation that it will have a certain lifetime over which it will provide benefits for the business. It is therefore normal practice to spread the cost of the fixed asset over its expected life and this results in a 'depreciation' charge to be included with all the other business costs.

As we saw earlier, depreciation is classified as an indirect expense:

$$\text{Depreciation per annum} = \frac{\text{Cost of asset}}{\text{Useful life of asset in years}}$$

For example, a motor vehicle is purchased for £9600 and is expected to be in use in the business for four years:

$$\text{Depreciation for one year} = \frac{£9600}{4}$$

$$\text{Depreciation for one month} = \frac{£9600}{48}$$

Task

Calculate the amount of depreciation to be charged for each of the following assets for one month, one quarter and one year:

a A building purchased for £99 000 to be used for 30 years
b A computer purchased for £540 to be used for 3 years
c A factory machine purchased for £27 000 to be used for 10 years.

Unit of production or service

In order to calculate the cost of a good or service it is important to identify the unit cost of the good or service being produced. For example, for a manufacturing business a unit of production may be one car or one football. Output here is easily quantifiable into a product, and may also be represented as the number of products produced and sold over a period. The period may be one week, one month or one quarter. The period must be consistent with the period used for determining total costs.

For example, the number of units of production for a manufacturing business produced over a range of time periods may be:

Month	Quarter	Half-year	Year	Total cost period
243 cars	730 cars	1460 cars	2920 cars	

The units of output used by service businesses will depend upon the nature of the service.

- *Garage workshop* services may be charged out on a *labour-hour basis*. (The cost of repair or servicing each car will then depend upon the period of time spent on each job.)
- *Bus company* units of output may be determined by *the cost per passenger mile*. (The cost of running each bus will then be determined by the mileage.)
- For a *computer help-line* it may depend upon the *cost per call*. (The cost or providing help will then depend upon average cost per call.)
- A *hotel* may determine the *cost per room*. (Costs will then depend upon the cost for letting each room.)

The units of production or service to which costs are charged are known as *cost units*. From the examples we have seen, we know that a cost unit may be either a unit of goods or a unit of service.

 ## Task

Consider the following service businesses:

a Solicitor
b Dry cleaner
c Grass cutting for parks and sports grounds
d Maintenance engineers for heating systems
e Painters and decorators
f Hotel
g School

1 Identify the unit of output for each
2 Identify as many costs for each business as you can and then analyse them into direct and indirect costs.

Allocating direct and indirect costs to a time period

It is important to translate all costs, direct or indirect, to a *common time period*. For example, when provided with cost information it may not all cover the same time period. Electricity and telephone bills may be paid quarterly or monthly, rent may be paid half-yearly, business rates may be paid monthly, workers paid weekly, etc. Costs now have to be *converted into the common time period* which is going to be used for each unit of goods, or service.

For example, if it is decided to use one year as a base for a unit of goods, or service:

- Bills paid quarterly will have to be multiplied by 4.
- Bills paid half-yearly will have to be multiplied by 2.
- Bills paid weekly (e.g. wages) will have to be multiplied by the *weeks worked*. (Note: the business will not be working 52 weeks a year due to holidays.)
- Bills paid monthly will have to be multiplied by 12.

Example

Claire runs a small manufacturing business. Her costs are as follows:

- *Direct materials* each week cost £150.
- *Direct labour* per year costs £10 000.
- *Direct expenses* are £6000 payable every 6 months.
- *Indirect materials* cost £100 each half-year.
- *Indirect labour* costs £5 per week.
- *Indirect expenses* are £900 per half-year.

Claire's business is going to be costed according to unit of production, which is going to be measured on a per-week basis over a 50-week working year. The total cost per week will therefore be:

Direct materials	£150
Direct labour (10 000/50)	£200
Direct expenses (6000/25)	£240
Indirect materials (100/25)	£4
Indirect labour	£5
Indirect expenses (900/25)	£36
Total costs per week	£635

Task

1 Peter runs a small advertising agency for which his costs are as follows:

- *Direct materials* £300 per week
- *Direct labour* £15 000 per year
- *Direct expenses* £150 per week
- *Indirect materials* £1000 each half-year
- *Indirect labour* £10 per week
- *Indirect expenses* £1000 per year.

Peter has decided to cost his business according to the unit of service provided to customers over a 50-week year. Translate the above costs into yearly values to find the total costs for the year.

2 Rachel runs a playgroup for which the costs are as follows:

- *Direct materials* £150 per week
- *Direct labour* £12 000 per year
- *Direct expenses* £80 per week
- *Indirect materials* £300 per half-year
- *Indirect labour* £80 per month (assume a 4-week month)
- *Indirect expenses* £500 per year.

Rachel is going to cost her business according to the number of hourly units of service provided each week, assuming a 50-week year. Translate the above costs into weekly values to find the total cost for each week.

Total (absorption) cost of a unit of production or service

Having identified the unit of output and whether it is to be calculated according to the number of products made or a unit of service such as labour-hour rate, the next stage is to translate the total of direct and indirect costs into the cost of a unit of production or service. This process is known as *absorption,* where total costs are then absorbed into each cost unit (see Figure 20.2).

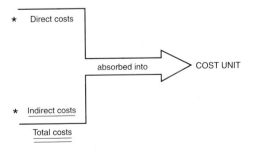

Figure 20.2 Absorbing total costs into each cost unit

$$\text{Cost per unit of production or service} = \frac{\text{Total costs (direct + indirect)}}{\text{Number of units of output}}$$

Example: Costing a good

Robin Williams is about to set up his own business making pottery miniatures and wants to know how to cost the goods he is going to make.

Stage 1 The first thing Robin must do is to identify the unit of production. In this instance, his production is a good, so his cost unit will be a unit of output – in other words, *one* pottery miniature. Robin has decided to relate the unit of production to a weekly period.

Robin anticipates that he will work 30 hours per week making the miniatures, and then spend 10 hours on the administration. He can make two miniatures per hour, so his production for each week will be 60 miniatures. He anticipates working a 50-week year.

Stage 2 Robin anticipates his direct and indirect costs to be as follows:

- *Direct materials* The clay and boxes required for each miniature will cost £3.00. As he is making 60 miniatures each week, his weekly cost of direct materials will be £180.
- *Direct labour* Robin works a 40-hour week, 30 hours on making the miniatures and 10 hours on administration. He hopes to draw £150 per week for his wages. The cost of direct labour spent on making the models will therefore be £150 × 30/40 = £112.50.
- *Direct expenses* Robin calculates that, with each firing, his kiln will depreciate by £2 and with eight firings per week, this will be £16 per week.

Total direct costs (per week):

£180 + £112.50 + £16 = £308.50

- *Indirect materials* Robin anticipates that he will spend £1000 per annum on stationery and leaflets.
- *Indirect labour* Robin will be spending 10 hours per week on administration. As he earns £150 per week this cost is likely to be £150 × 10/40 = £37.50 per week.
- *Indirect expenses* The cost of electricity and the use of telephone is likely to be £1200 per year.

Total indirect costs per week:

Indirect materials (1000/50)	=	£20.00
Indirect labour	=	£37.50
Indirect expenses (1200/50)	=	£24.00
		£81.50

Total costs for the week will therefore be:

Total direct costs per week	=	£308.50
Total indirect costs per week	=	£81.50
Total costs per week		£390.00

The cost per unit will be:

£390	(Total costs)
60 miniatures	(Units of output per week)

The cost of one miniature is therefore £6.50

Example: Costing a service

Helen aims to set up a home design business. Her intention is to provide first-hand consulting upon decorating and interior design for homes.

Stage 1 As Helen is providing a service she has decided to cost her service on a per-hour basis, so that each hour of consulting will be the cost unit. She has decided to relate these hours to a weekly period.

Helen anticipates working 40 hours per week. Of these 40 hours, she anticipates spending 35 hours directly providing services for customers and 5 hours on administration. There are therefore 35 hours to spend on consulting each week.

Stage 2 Helen anticipates her direct and indirect costs to be as follows:

- *Direct materials* Helen uses a computer to help with her design work. Each week she expects to spend £30 on stationery and disks.
- *Direct labour* Helen works a 40-hour week, 35 hours on providing services and 5 hours on administration. She hopes to draw £300 per week for her wages. Her direct labour will therefore be £300 × 35/40 = £262.50
- *Direct expenses* Helen's only other direct expense is software, which she estimates to be £10 per week.

Total direct costs per week:

£30 + £262.50 + £10 = £302.50

- *Indirect materials* Helen anticipates spending £1500 per year on computer accessories, leaflets and other indirect materials.

- *Indirect labour* Helen spends 5 hours per week on administration. As she hopes to draw £300 per week for her wages, her indirect labour will therefore be £300 × 5/40 = £37.50.
- *Indirect expenses* The cost of electricity and telephone is likely to be £1800 per year.

Total indirect costs per week:

Indirect materials (1500/50)	=	£30.00
Indirect labour	=	£37.50
Indirect expenses (1800/50)	=	£36.00
		£103.50

Total costs for the week will therefore be:

Total direct costs per week	=	£302.50
Total indirect costs per week	=	£103.50
Total costs per week	=	£406.00

The cost per hour will therefore be:

£406.00	(Total costs)
35 hours	(Units of output per week)

The cost of Helen's service on a per-hour basis is therefore £11.60.

Task

1 List two direct materials which are likely to be used for the production of each of the following:

- a bookcase
- a motor vehicle
- clothes
- tins of spaghetti.

2 Jane Soames has set up in business on her own, making pine cupboards. She wants to find out how much it costs to make each cupboard. The following information is available.

- It takes 5 hours to produce one cupboard.
- The pinewood for each cupboard costs £7.00.
- Other direct materials for each cupboard such as handles and screws cost £1.50.
- There are no other direct expenses.
- Jane expects to work 40 hours per week over a 50-week year. 30 hours per week will be spent on making cupboards and 10 hours per week on administration.
- Jane wants to draw £150 per week for her wages.
- She expects to spend £1500 per year on indirect materials such as leaflets, stationery and other items.

- The cost of other running expenses such as telephone, rent and electricity is £2000 per year.

a Classify costs under the headings of direct and indirect costs.
b Identify an appropriate unit of production.
c Work out the number of units produced in a week.
d Calculate the direct and indirect costs per week.
e Calculate the cost per unit of production.

Evidence collection point

Select a business organisation of your choice. For the organisation you choose, identify the unit of production or unit of service. Calculate the direct costs and indirect costs for a time period. Work out the unit cost of the good or service. Your work should provide evidence of Core Skills in Application of Number.

Variable and fixed costs

Another method of classifying costs, as mentioned at the beginning of the chapter, according to their relationship with changes in output levels. This identifies costs as either *fixed* or *variable*.

Fixed costs are those costs that do not increase as total output increases. For example, if an organisation has the capacity needed it might increase its production from 25 000 units to 30 000 units. Its rent, rates and heating bills will be the same, since they also had to be paid when the organisation was producing 25 000 units.

Variable costs are those that increase as the total output increases, because more of these factors need to be employed as inputs in order to increase outputs. For example, if you produce more items you will need more raw materials.

You have been introduced to two different classifications of cost. One describes the nature of costs incurred (direct and indirect costs) and the other how these vary with the level of production (variable and fixed costs). You may find it useful to relate these two different classifications as follows:

- Direct costs can be generally considered as variable costs.
- Indirect costs can be generally considered as fixed costs.

Although this is in some ways a simplification, these statements should help your basic understanding of business costs. We can now identify total business costs using the two classification methods:

Total costs = Direct costs + indirect costs

Total costs = Variable costs + fixed costs.

Calculating the variable costs of a unit of production from given data

As output increases, total variable costs will increase but the variable cost per unit will stay the same (unless the levels of output are moving towards maximum capacity – see the first Task below). For example, if the only variable costs are direct materials and direct labour and these are 50p for every unit of output produced we can see that:

	100 units	500 units	1000 units
Total variable costs	£50	£250	£500
Variable costs per unit	50p	50p	50p

Task

Stake Out Ltd is a private company, manufacturing small, high-quality canvas tents for hillwalkers and campers. Business has been healthy over the past two years as the recession has encouraged people to invest in lower-budget holidays and because of increasing growth in the leisure market for camping equipment.

The company is managed and owned by Rachel Hunter, who is the Managing Director, and Kuldip Gill, who supervises operations. They have a small factory unit on a trading estate and they employ 15 full-time employees – a foreman, 12 machine operators who cut out canvas for part-time workers and two despatchers. The part-time workers are employed as contractors, using their own sewing machines at home to make up the tents from the cut-out pieces that have been sent to them.

The foreman is paid £250 per week, the machine operators £200 per week and the despatchers £180 per week. The part-timers are paid £50 for each tent they produce.

Other business costs include:

- electricity at £120 per week
- rent and rates at £560 per week
- loan repayments, including interest, at £220 per week
- other fixed costs at £100 per week
- directors' salaries for Rachel and Kuldip at £400 each per week

■ material costs for each tent at £15.

The existing capacity for Stake Out is 160 tents per calendar week. If it needs to produce more than this, it has to pay higher rates to cover overtime put in by part-time workers, which results in an increase in part-time costs from £50 for each tent to £65 for each tent, up to and including a capacity of 180 tents, and from £65 to £95 for each tent up to a maximum capacity of 200 tents.

1 Calculate the variable cost per unit.
2 Construct a table to show the fixed, variable and total weekly costs at each rate of production up to the maximum capacity of 200 units.
3 Explain why the variable cost per unit increases as output moves towards maximum capacity.

Task

Timberworld manufactures quality tables and chairs using traditional hand-made processes. Production output is measured in terms of dining-room suites of which 30 were made during the month of May. The following costs were incurred during May:

Wood	£150 per suite
Rent and rates	£1000
Power and telephone	£650
Administration and selling costs	£3250
Motor expenses	£600
Direct labour	£240 per suite

The business also uses equipment in its workshops that costs £9600 and is estimated to last eight years.

1 Analyse the costs into fixed and variable costs.
2 Calculate the total costs for May.
3 Calculate the total cost of one dining-room suite.

The marginal cost of a unit of production or service

Marginal cost is the cost of producing one extra unit of production or service – i.e. because it is the cost of producing one extra unit of production or service it comprises the variable cost per unit.

We have identified that as output varies, some costs also vary but others remain fixed. It is because of this fact that average unit cost will change as production varies. The cost of producing more output or the saving in producing less output is the marginal cost per unit (variable cost), and this is not the same as total cost per unit.

Example

Roadrunners & Co. operate a courier service for documents and parcels using small motor vans. The business charges its customers on the basis of the number of miles to be travelled. Fixed costs are £2000 per month and variable costs 20 pence per mile. During March the business's vehicles travelled 5000 miles and in April they travelled 7000 miles. Calculate the total costs and cost per mile for both months.

	March £	April £	Marginal cost £
Fixed costs	2000	2000	0
Variable costs at 20p/mile	1000	1400	400
Total costs	3000	3400	400
Number of miles	5000	7000	2000
Cost per mile £	0.60	0.49	0.20

The marginal cost comprises just the variable cost of travelling the additional 2000 miles.

Case study – Britain's twilight homes

At Tony Acton's elegant mews house there is nothing to betray his role as chairman of a conglomerate with products ranging from kitty-litter to nursing homes. Acton is one of a growing band of corporate executives who are keen to profit from demographic changes which will see Britain's over-85 population increase by 40% by the year 2000. Welfare subsidies and the Community Care Act have recently encouraged more development of nursing homes in the private sector.

However, according to the industry's trade associations, nursing and residential homes are closing at the rate of four a week, due to high interest rates, rising staff costs and falling occupancy rates. The nursing home sector, previously dominated by husband-and-wife teams, had become ripe for rationalisation and for large organisations to move in. One such organisation is Takare. Takare's blueprint is to build nursing homes to its own specifications. All except one are in single-storey 30-bed units built round a central management facility. The company believes it can benefit from greater economies of scale. The chairman feels that the company's proven formula enables it to 'give twice the care for half the cost'. Where others seem to be failing, Takare seems destined for success.

1 Explain how larger organisations are able to run nursing homes more efficiently than smaller organisations.
2 If you were running a small nursing home, in the sort of market indicated here, how would you attempt to manage the finances of your business? What decisions might you have to make?

Task

You are a trainee accountant working for the regional office of a large petrol company. You have been presented with this memo (above) from your senior accountant.

Working in groups prepare the presentation requested in the memo. The notes (below) provided by the senior accountant give some useful background information.

Volume

The quantity of product that you sell is a critical factor in the success of every kind of business. The reason for this is that every business has to pay two different types of cost: fixed costs and variable costs.

Fixed costs

So called because they remain the same no matter how many units of product you sell. For instance, a shop still has to pay the same rent, rates, heating and lighting, staff wages, insurance and much else no matter how large or small its sales are in a particular month. The same applies to a factory, or any other kind of business.

MEMORANDUM

TO: *Trainee Accountant*   REF: RD/BC
From: Rita Daines   DATE: 10 APRIL 199–
      (Senior Accountant)

PRESENTATION TO LOCAL SERVICE STATION MANAGERS

I want you to prepare a presentation for six service station managers which will take place in the Boardroom on 15 May. You will need to show the managers the importance of selling high volumes of petrol in order to keep down unit costs. Please prepare four overhead transparencies to support your presentation.

You must also work with Jane Johnson the Sales Manager to come up with at least six clear suggestions as to ways in which more motorists can be encouraged to buy petrol.

You will need to calculate how much the margin is at each of the three retail outlets shown in the pie charts (see my notes below) using the figures given for sales. Also explain why retail outlet No 3 will be in the best position to improve its premises and equipment.

You may use my notes to develop some ideas for the first part of the presentation.

                                    RD

(Of course, if sales remain low over a long period, say a year, then the owners of the business will have to think of reducing its fixed costs, by taking smaller premises, for instance, or employing fewer people.)

Variable costs

These are costs that vary with the number of units you sell. For instance, if your shop sells confectionery, the more units of confectionery you sell to customers, the more you have to buy from the wholesaler; if your factory makes furniture, the more units of furniture you make, the more wood and other materials you have to buy from your supplier. In other words, your costs vary directly with the number of units you sell.

What is the margin?

The difference between the variable costs of each unit of product and the price paid by the customer is called the 'margin'.

The proportion of fixed costs to the margin changes with the number of units you sell. For instance, if your fixed

511

costs are £1000 a year and you sell 100 units, then each unit has to carry £10 of fixed costs. If the margin is £20 then the fixed costs represent 50% of the margin.

If you sell 500 units, then each unit has to carry only £2 of fixed costs – which is 10% of the margin.

Fixed and variable costs

Fixed costs at a service station include: staffing, insurance, heat/light, security, business rate and office costs.

Variable costs are the costs paid by the service station to the refinery for bulk supplies of petrol, diesel and lubricants, plus items such as stationery and sales promotion.

The left-hand side of Figure 20.3 below shows a typical value for the total fixed costs of a typical service station. The right-hand side shows a typical value for the variable costs. The table has been simplified for the sake of clarity, and of course the figures given are examples only.

Fixed costs		Variable costs expressed in pence per litre (ppl)	
Staff	£35 000	Fuel	30.00ppl
Insurance	£2 000	Bank charges	0.30ppl
Heat/light/		Sales promotion	
power	£5 500	& advertising	0.15ppl
Security	£1 500	Postage &	
Business rate	£6 000	stationery	0.03ppl
Maintenance			
& repair	£2 000		
Office	£6 500		
Depreciation	£3 500		
Total	£62 000	Total	30.48ppl

Figure 20.3 Typical fixed and variable costs of a service station

Note: To cover fixed costs of £62 000, a service station selling 500 000 litres a year must add 12.4 per litre (£62 000 divided by 500 000) to the variable costs.

A similar sized but more successful service station selling 3 million litres a year would only have to add 2.06p per litre (£62 000 divided by 3 000 000). In other words, the minimum price per litre (before profit) that the lower volume station must charge its customers is 42.88p (30.48p + 12.4p). The higher volume station can cover all its costs, fixed and variable, by charging only 32.54p (30.48 + 2.06p).

The higher volume station can afford to charge less per litre, and still make a bigger margin – to be used for further investment and distribution to shareholders.

These figures are examples only. There is a further fact to remember: the variable cost of fuel (the price the service station has to pay) can go up or go down (because of currency fluctuations or bulk deals) over a period.

Figure 20.4 shows how the per-unit ratio between fixed costs and variable costs changes with the number of units sold.

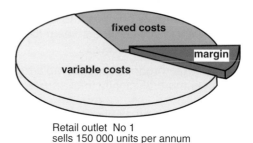

Retail outlet No 1
sells 150 000 units per annum

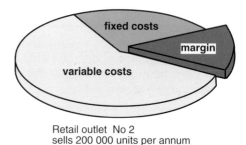

Retail outlet No 2
sells 200 000 units per annum

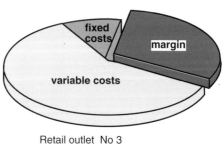

Retail outlet No 3
sells 500 000 units per annum

Figure 20.4 Cost and margin per unit sold

The more units sold, the lower the proportion of the unit price taken by fixed costs.

Assume:

- Each unit has a retail price of £1.
- Variable costs per unit are 60p.
- Fixed costs are £50 000 per annum.
- Each of the three retail outlets (1, 2 and 3) have the same fixed costs (rents, rates, staff, depreciation, etc).

Task

The Rilton Hotel measures its output in terms of number of guest nights. It provides food and drinks only to overnight customers. It has incurred the following costs over the last two trading quarters:

	To June £	To September £
Food	4500	6000
Rent	5000	5000
Casual staff	3600	4800
Permanent staff	6000	6000
Drinks	900	1200
Laundry	1350	1800
Power	2650	2650
Depreciation	3000	3000

The number of guest nights in the June to September quarters were 900 and 1200 respectively.

1 Analyse costs into fixed and variable costs.
2 Calculate total costs for each quarter.
3 Calculate total cost per guest night.
4 Calculate the marginal cost for one guest to stay one night at the hotel.

Task

Clone-it Ltd assemble personal computers from components purchased from other firms. The following bill of materials lists the components required to make one PC.

Description	Number
Casing	1
Motherboard	1
Hard disk	1
Floppy disk drive	2
Processing chips	1
Wiring	2 m
Cable	2
Keyboard	1
Monitor	1
Output ports	3

The components are ordered from suppliers in the following batch sizes:

Description	Number	Total order value (£)
Casing	100	1000
Motherboard	200	8000
Hard disk	50	7500
Floppy disk drive	200	6000
Processing chips	300	6000
Wiring	200 m	50
Cable	250	200
Keyboard	50	1500
Monitor	50	3500
Output ports	150	3000

Employees working in the assembly department earn £8 an hour and take 6 hours to assemble and test one computer. Employees working in the packaging department take one hour to pack one computer and earn £5 an hour. Management and clerical staff cost £8000 per month.

Other costs include power at £2400 per quarter, telephone at £500 per month and distribution costs of £50 per PC. The business uses premises that cost £192 000 depreciated over 40 years and equipment that cost £30 000 depreciated over 5 years. The production and sales volume for June was 500 computers. Required for the month of June:

1 Identify, with explanations, which costs are direct costs and which are indirect.
2 Calculate total costs for Clone-it Ltd for the month of June analysed between direct and indirect costs.
3 Calculate the total cost of one PC for June.
4 The business has capacity to produce 600 computers per month. If the business could secure orders for a further 100 computers during July what would the total extra cost be? How much is the marginal costs for each additional PC? Explain why the marginal cost is different from the total cost of one PC calculated in 3 above.

Evidence indicators

For this activity you need to produce a set of calculations which shows the breakdown of total cost and marginal cost of a unit of production or service for an organisation. Your evidence may be either in the form of a spreadsheet or manually generated, but must include explanations which relate to the figures.

The following list should serve as a checklist. Tick each of the following boxes when you have successfully covered them as part of your preparation. You need to confirm that:

- I have identified the direct and indirect costs of an organisation. ☐

- I have related these costs to a time period. ☐
- I have used these costs to calculate the absorption cost of a unit or production of a good or service. ☐
- I have identified the marginal cost. ☐
- I have shown how the marginal cost relates to the production of an extra unit or service. ☐
- Where necessary, I have used appropriate diagrams, figures and illustrations. ☐

Chapter 21

Pricing decisions and break-even

Earlier in the book we looked at a range of pricing strategies (Chapter 2) as well as the important role that pricing has within the marketing mix (Chapter 8). This chapter takes the concept of pricing further to help you to think more widely about all the factors and practical issues involved in setting prices. It is important to emphasise at this stage that although marketing personnel make decisions about pricing, finance personnel help them to understand the consequences of the strategies which they may choose.

The *Oxford English Dictionary* defines price as the 'sum of consideration or sacrifice for which a thing may be bought or attained'. A major problem in setting a price is that 'price' has different meanings for different groups of people. For example:

- for *buyers* price is an unwelcome cost
- for *sellers* price is a key element in the marketing mix
- for the *government* prices have an influence upon the general price level – and hence votes.

Factors determining price and related pricing strategies

A number of situations can be identified in which pricing decisions have to be made. The most important of these are:

- *When a price needs to be set for the first time* This can happen when a new product is launched on the market, when new outlets are used or when new contracts are made.
- *When it becomes necessary to make a change in the pricing structure* This may be because of the development of competition, the movement along the product life-cycle or a change in demand or cost conditions.

The only time a business has complete freedom to set prices is before it has committed itself to developing and marketing a new product. Once the product has left the drawing board, many factors will affect the pricing decision. Some of these will be internal and others external to the organisation.

For example, internal influences on price include:

- the objectives of the organisation (e.g. profit maximisation, satisficing)
- the pattern of direct and indirect costs
- existing prices of similar and other products produced internally by the organisation
- existing ideas on price-setting in the organisation
- the organisation's knowledge of the market
- pressures from feedback from salespeople and other members of the organisation
- levels of research and development and the pace of new product development.

External influences upon price may include:

- the strength and behaviour of competitors
- the attitudes and influences of other groups involved in the chain of production and distribution
- pressure from suppliers of raw materials and components used in the product
- elasticity of demand for the product
- existing and anticipated government policies
- general conditions in different markets.

Because there are so many variables involved in pricing decisions, and because information available to organisations at any one time will be imperfect, it will be necessary to select certain 'basic' factors to help make pricing decisions.

Basic factors

A number of different factors determine how prices are set. These include the following.

1 *The need to make a profit* The ability to make and maximise profits is a key target for many business organisations. In reality, however, studies reveal that most organisations tend to aim for realistic or satisfactory profits rather than very large ones.
2 *Prices of competing products* The nature of competition has a very important effect upon price. Where competitors in the marketplace compete on price, particularly for similar goods or services, consumers are likely to be influenced by this and will opt to buy from the cheapest seller.
3 *Under-used capacity* Imagine a theatre which is only half-full. The theatre may be profitable but

the empty seats could have been sold at slightly lower prices to encourage more ticket sales. The income from these extra ticket sales would have helped to pay fixed costs. The action would have had a dual function, i.e. (a) increasing the use of the theatre and (b) improving profitability. One very important factor may therefore be to use pricing in a way which helps to make use of capacity and the influence that this has on profits.

Related pricing strategies

Cost-plus pricing

This is the related pricing strategy for the *need to make a profit*. This type of pricing strategy recognises that in anything but the short term, a business needs to make a profit. As a strategy it adopts the following approach for each unit:

Cost price + profit = selling price

The cost price is described in Chapter 20 as the total costs, direct and indirect, absorbed into one cost unit. Many owners of small businesses will tell you that they 'cost out' each hour worked and then add a margin for profit.

The process of cost-plus pricing can best be illustrated in relation to large firms where *economies of scale* can be spread over a considerable range of output.

For a large firm, unit costs will fall rapidly at first as the overheads are spread over a larger output. Unit cost then becomes relatively stable over a considerable quantity of output. It is therefore a relatively simple calculation to add a fixed profit margin (e.g. 20%) to the unit cost. The firm is able to select an output to produce and to set a price that will be 20% higher than the unit cost of production (Figure 21.1).

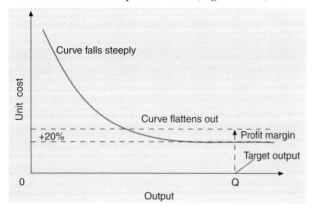

Figure 21.1 Select a target output OQ and then add a 20% profit margin to the unit cost to get price

While cost-plus pricing is very popular, there are many dangers associated with it. If the price is set too high, sales may fall short of expectations; if the price is set too low, then potential revenue is sacrificed. However, the greatest danger of cost-based pricing is that it indicates a *production-orientated approach to the market*. Emphasis on costs leads to tunnel vision that looks inwards at the company's product rather than outwards to the customers' perception of the product.

Evidence collection point

Make a list of the arguments for and against adding a profit margin to cost price in order to arrive at a selling price.

Market lead pricing

This is the related pricing strategy which takes into account *prices of competing products*. If a product is faced by direct competition, then it will compete against other very similar products in the marketplace. This will constrain pricing decisions so that price setting will need to be kept closely in line with rivals' actions.

In contrast, when a product is faced with indirect competition (i.e. competition with products in different segments of the market), there will be more scope to vary price. This opens up the possibility for a number of strategies. For example, a firm might choose a high-price strategy to give a product a 'quality' feel. In contrast, it might charge a low price so that consumers see the product as a 'bargain'.

The level of competition is a key determinant of price. Where there are many close competitiors, there is little or no scope to charge a price which is above the market price. In a situation where there is no competition, the seller can often charge a relatively high price. However, the seller cannot charge more than the consumer is prepared to pay. At the end of the day consumers can spend their income on alternative products. Between these two extremes, we find hundreds of different markets. In some the consumer has most power, in others it is the seller.

Case study– Aldi supermarkets

Aldi supermarkets are a good example of an organisation exporting its low-price strategy to more and more markets. Initially the company operated in its home base of Germany using a formula of concentrating on a small range of high-turnover non-perishable items in very basic shops with no frills attached. This formula gave Aldi a dominant position in the German discount market.

The company concentrated on roughly 500 fast-selling lines such as tinned and packaged groceries, dairy products and fruits and vegetables. Most of these products were Aldi exclusive lines developed for them by manufacturers and based on high-quality standards. Because there were so few lines the items were not price-marked – checkout staff were expected to remember the prices of all items or consult a list. Each supermarket had a very small staff.

Market research showed that three-quarters of all German householders shopped for some items at Aldi, and the company had a market share of over 20% for tinned vegetables, tinned meat, tinned milk, margarine, sherry, tea and spirits.

From the power base of its existing home market, Aldi has been able to spread out progressively into new international markets. In the early 1990s it had a strong presence in several neighbouring European states, with 102 stores in Denmark, 220 in Belgium, 270 in the Netherlands, 104 in Austria, 16 in north-east France as well as 225 in mid-western United States. In the 1990s it has also moved increasingly into the UK market, and its presence has had a considerable impact here. It now seriously threatens the big retail groups including Sainsbury, Tesco, Dee Corporation/Gateway, Argyll/Safeway, Asda and the Co-ops.

In the mid-1990s the UK is seeing the increasing spread of new forms of low-cost stores, such as Kwik Save, Safeway's Lo Cost stores, the Co-op's Pioneer shops and more recently Costco from the United States. These are all essentially straightforward discount stores along the Aldi lines.

1 What influence is the Aldi approach to pricing having upon other supermarkets?
2 How effective have low-cost discount stores been in the UK in recent years?
3 What is likely to be the long-term effect of low-price competition in the UK supermarket sector?

Marginal cost/contribution pricing

This is the related pricing strategy which takes *under-used capacity* into account. Contribution or marginal cost pricing involves separating out the different products that make up a company's portfolio in order to charge individual prices appropriate to a product's share in total costs.

When a firm produces a range of individual items or products, or sells products in a variety of markets, it is easy to determine direct costs, but not indirect costs. For example, in a food-processing plant producing 100 different recipe dishes it is easy to work out how much goes on each line in terms of raw materials, labout input, and other direct costs. However, the same process cannot be applied to indirect costs – the salary of the managing director, the business rates applied on the factory building, and so on.

When the *contributions* of all the individual products that a firm produces have been added together they should more than cover the firm's indirect costs.

> **Contribution** is the sum remaining after the direct costs of producing individual products have been subtracted from revenues.

There are strong arguments in favour of contribution pricing because of the way it separates out the individual products and analyses them *in terms of their ability to cover the direct costs which can be attributed to them*. A new product may be brought 'on-stream' because it can be shown that it will cover its direct costs and make a contribution to covering the company's total indirect costs.

In contrast, if we were to analyse individual products in terms of the relationship between their total revenue and total costs, calculations might show a loss. For example, if two products used the same distribution facilities, it would not make sense to expect both products to cover their own distribution costs individually. Contribution pricing enables a more rational analysis of individual products. Prices can be set in relation to each product's own direct costs (Figure 21.2).

Contribution is an excellent way of pricing for firms selling to a range of international markets which share a common fixed cost base. However, while contribution pricing is possible in many situations, it is not so easy in others.

Evidence collection point

Make a list of types of organisations which would clearly benefit from having a pricing policy designed to maximise use of capacity. Investigate at least two of these types of organisation locally and then explain in your own words whether you think that they adopt such a policy.

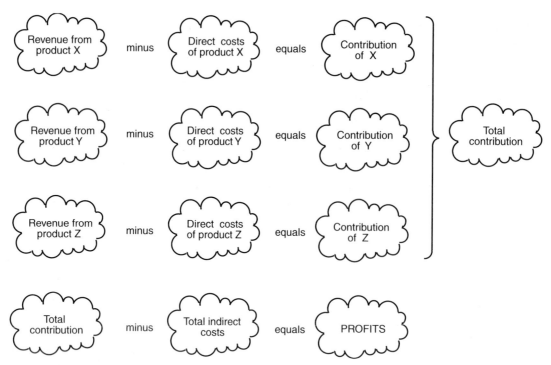

Figure 21.2 Calculating profits using contributions

Break-even point

> The **break-even point** is the point at which sales levels are high enough not to make a loss, but not high enough to make a profit.

The concept of break-even is a development from the principles of *marginal costing*. Marginal costing is a commonly used technique which uses costs to forecast profits from the production and sales levels expected in future periods. The great benefit of marginal costing over other costing methods is that it overcomes the problem of allocating fixed costs – only variable costs are allocated, as we shall see.

The difference between an item's selling price and the variable costs needed to produce that item is known as the *contribution* (that is, its contribution to the whole profit).

> **Contribution** = selling price per unit *less* variable costs per unit

By producing and selling enough units to produce a total contribution that is in excess of the *fixed* costs, an organisation will make a profit.

For example, Penzance Toys Ltd manufactures plastic train sets for young children. It anticipates that next year it will sell 8000 units at £12 per unit. Its variable costs are £5 per unit and its fixed costs are £9000. From the above formula we can deduce that the contribution is £12 minus £5, which is £7 per unit. Therefore – for each unit made – £7 will go towards paying fixed costs. We can also show this using totals to show how much profit will be made if the company sells 8000 units (see Figure 21.3).

	(£)
Sales revenue (8000 × £5)	96 000
Less marginal costs (8000 × £5)	40 000
Total contribution	56 000
Less fixed costs	9 000
Net profit	47 000

Figure 21.3 Profit statement for Penzance Toys Ltd

The problem can also be looked at by constructing a table as in Figure 21.4.

Units of production	Fixed costs (£)	Variable costs (£)	Total costs (£)	Revenue (£)	Profit (loss) (£)
1 000	9 000	5 000	14 000	12 000	(2 000)
2 000	9 000	10 000	19 000	24 000	5 000
3 000	9 000	15 000	24 000	36 000	12 000
4 000	9 000	20 000	29 000	48 000	19 000
5 000	9 000	25 000	34 000	60 000	26 000
6 000	9 000	30 000	39 000	72 000	33 000
7 000	9 000	35 000	44 000	84 000	40 000
8 000	9 000	40 000	49 000	96 000	47 000
9 000	9 000	45 000	54 000	108 000	54 000
10 000	9 000	50 000	59 000	120 000	61 000

Figure 21.4 Profit table for Penzance Toys Ltd

Task

Rovers Medallions Ltd produces a standard size trophy for sports shops and clubs. It hopes to sell 2000 trophies next year at £9 per unit. Its variable costs are £5 per unit and its fixed costs are £4000. Draw up a profit statement to show how much profit it will make in the year. Also construct a table to show how much profit it will make at each 500 units of production up to 3000 units.

Marginal costing is particularly useful for making short-term decisions – for example, helping to set the selling price of a product, or deciding whether or not to accept an order. It might also help an organisation to decide whether to buy in a component or whether to produce it themselves.

Break-even analysis is a concept which is central to the process of marginal costing. Breaking-even is the unique point at which an organisation makes neither profit nor loss. If sales go beyond the break-even point, profits are made, and if they are below the break-even point, losses are made. In marginal costing *it is the point at which the contribution equals the fixed costs.*

To calculate the break-even point there are two stages:

■ Calculate the unit contribution (selling price less variable costs).
■ Divide the fixed costs by the unit contribution:

$$\text{Break-even point} = \frac{\text{Fixed costs}}{\text{Unit contribution}}$$

For example, in Penzance Toys Ltd (see above) the contribution per unit is £7 and the fixed costs are £9000. The break-even point would therefore be:

$$\frac{9000}{7} = 1286 \text{ units (to nearest unit)}$$

The *sales value* at the break-even point can be calculated by multiplying the number of units by the selling price per unit. For Penzance Toys this would be:

$$1286 \times £12 = £15\,432$$

Penzance Toys has covered its costs (fixed + variable) and broken even with a sales value of £15 432. Anything sold in excess of this will provide it with profits.

If an organisation has a *profit target* or selected operating point to aim at, break-even analysis can be used to calculate the number of units that need to be sold and the value of sales required to achieve that target.

For example, we can imagine that Penzance Toys wishes to achieve a target of £15 000 profit. By adding this £15 000 to the fixed costs and dividing by the contribution, the number of units can be found which need to be sold to meet this target. Thus:

$$\frac{£9000 + £15\,000}{£7} = 3429 \text{ units (to nearest unit)}$$

The difference between the break-even point and the selected level of activity designed to achieve the profit target is known as the *margin of safety.*

Task

B Hive Beehives Ltd is a small business selling hives to local keepers. Each hive is sold for £25. Fixed costs are £18 000 and variable costs are £13 per unit. The company wishes to achieve a profit of £18 000.

1 Calculate the break-even point in both units and sales value.
2 Calculate both the units and sales value necessary to achieve the selected operating point.

Drawing a break-even chart

A break-even chart can be used to show changes in the relationship between costs, production volumes and various levels of sales activity. The following is the procedure to construct a break-even chart (you may find it helpful to look forward to Figure 21.5.)

- Label the horizontal axis for units of production and sales.
- Label the vertical axis to represent the values of sales and costs.
- Plot fixed costs. Fixed costs will remain the same over all levels of production, so plot this as a straight line parallel to the horizontal axis.
- Plot the total costs (variable costs + fixed cost). This will be a line rising from where the fixed-cost line touches the vertical axis. It is plotted by calculating total costs at two or three random levels of production.

- Sales are plotted by taking two or three random levels of turnover. The line will rise from the intersection of the two axes.

The break-even point will be where the total-cost line and sales line intersect. The area to the *left* of the break-even point between the sales and total-cost lines will represent *losses,* and the area to the *right* of the break-even point between these lines will represent *profit*.

As always, an example will make this clearer. Eddie Bowen plans to set up a small restaurant. In doing so he knows that he will immediately incur annual fixed costs of £10 000. He is concerned about how many meals he will have to sell to break-even. Extensive market research indicates that a typical customer will pay £8 for a meal, and Eddie knows that variable costs – such as cooking ingredients and the costs of serving customers – will amount to about £3. Eddie has set himself a profit target of £14 000 for the first year of operation. Our task is to advise Eddie on the number of meals he has to sell and to indicate to him his margin of safety.

Eddie's unit *contribution* is:
£8 – £3 (selling price – variable costs) = £5 per meal

His *break-even point* in units will be:
£10 000 (fixed costs) ÷ £5 (unit contribution) = 2000 meals

The *sales value* of the meals will be:
2000 meals × £8 (selling price) = £16 000
His *profit target* will be achieved by:

$$\frac{£10\ 000\ (\text{fixed costs}) + £14\ 000\ (\text{profit target})}{£5\ (\text{unit contribution})} = 4800\ \text{meals}$$

The *margin of safety* will be the difference between the selected level of activity and the break-even point. It will be between 4800 meals with a turnover of £38 400 and 2000 meals with a turnover of £16 000.

The three random levels of variable costs and sales chosen for the purpose of plotting the break-even chart are at 1000 meals, 3000 meals and 5000 meals:

	1000 meals (£)	3000 meals (£)	5000 meals (£)
Variable costs (£3/meal)	3 000	9 000	15 000
Fixed cost	10 000	10 000	10 000
Total cost	13 000	19 000	25 000
Sales	8 000	24 000	40 000

We can now plot the break-even chart (Figure 21.5) which shows graphically the break-even point of 2000 meals with a sales revenue of £16 000. The margin of safety can be seen on the chart if we identify the selected level of profit (at 4800 meals) and the targeted turnover (of £38 400), and compare this point with the break-even point.

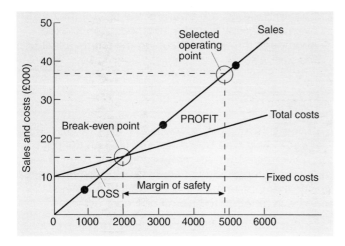

Figure 21.5 Eddie Bowen's break-even chart

The break-even chart is a simple *visual tool* enabling managers to anticipate the effects of changes in production and sales upon the profitability of an organisation's activities. It emphasises the importance of earning revenue and is particularly helpful for those who are unused to interpreting accounting information.

Evidence collection point

Make up an example of a business selling a product of your choice. Construct a break-even chart and then comment upon how the chart could be used for the purpose of making key decisions within the organisation. Your work should provide evidence of Core Skills in Application of Number and Communication.

Analysing the break-even chart

The break-even chart can be used to explore changes in a number of key variables. These may include:

- *Sales volume and value* By looking at the chart it is possible to predict the effects of any changes in

sales trends. For example, a sudden fall in sales may lead to a loss and a sudden increase may improve profitability.
- *Profits or losses at given level of production* The break-even chart enables a business to monitor levels of production. By doing this important decisions can be made if changes take place.
- *Prices* It is possible to use the break-even chart to analyse different business scenarios. For example, given market research information, what would happen if we reduced price by £2?
- *Costs* The effects of any sudden changes in costs can be plotted on the break-even chart.

Any of the above may affect an organisation's ability to achieve its selected operating point and margin of safety. The break-even chart is a useful management technique upon which to base action which enables an organisation to achieve its plans.

Task

John Smith had a visit from an aged relative who wanted advice. For many years she had run a small hotel in a market town in the Thames valley. After careful consideration she had decided to 'call it a day' and retire, but she was keen to see the business continue and wished to retain her ownership in it.

John is interested in a proposition she has put forward, which involves running the hotel on her behalf. The hotel has been allowed to deteriorate over the years and, in John's opinion, it is obvious that extensive refurbishment is necessary before he could realistically consider her proposal. The hotel is, however, in a prime spot, was extensively used little more than ten years ago, and John feels that with hard work it has the potential to become successful again.

He arranged for a number of quotations to be made for building works. The most favourable quotation received was for £180 000, which involved extensive interior redecoration and refurbishment as well as completely reorganising the reception and kitchen areas.

John's intention is that the finance for the building work should come from a five-year bank loan with a fixed annual interest rate of 10%, payable each calendar month, and based upon the original sum. The loan principal would be paid back in five equal annual instalments.

He has estimated the following fixed and variable costs:

Fixed
Annual loan repayment £36 000
Annual interest on loan £18 000
Business rate and water rates £7000 p.a.
Insurance £4500 p.a.
Electricity £1300 per quarter year
Staff salaries £37 000 p.a.

Variable
These include direct labour such as cleaners and bar staff, as well as the cost of food, bar stocks etc. After careful research John has estimated these to be £2000 for each 100 customers who visit the hotel.

John has had a local agency conduct an extensive market research survey and feels confident that the hotel will attract about 100 customers per week, who will each spend on average (including accommodation, food and drinks) about £70 in the hotel.

1 Work out the break-even point for the hotel in both numbers of customers and value.
2 Work out the number of customers required to make a gross profit of £35 000.
3 Draw a break-even chart showing the break-even point, the profit target and the margin of safety.
4 What other information might John Smith require before deciding whether to go ahead with the project?

Task

Theme Holidays Ltd is a private company that specialises in providing holidays for adults and children alike who require a unique form of entertainment. All their holidays involve overseas packages based on a theme. With the opening of Disneyland Paris they are finding that half of the packages they now provide are based on this one resort, while the other half are to theme destinations in the United States.

Theme Holidays is currently reviewing its profitability for 1995. They anticipate that their fixed overheads will be £450 000 for the year. With the Disneyland Paris packages, a quarter of the variable costs go in travel costs, at an average of £30 per package. They anticipate selling packages at an average of £160 per holiday in 1995.

The American holidays are sold at an average price of £650 per holiday. Travel costs of £200 for the American holidays comprise half of the variable costs of the holiday.

Market research has revealed that, during 1995, Theme Holidays expect to sell 400 holidays.

1 Work out the contribution for both the European and American holidays.
2 Calculate the company's profit for the year before tax and interest.
3 Market research also revealed that if Theme Holidays reduced their prices by 10% they could sell 300 more holidays per year. Calculate how this would affect profitability and advise accordingly.
4 Theme Holidays are aware of the size of their fixed overheads. How would a 10% reduction in fixed overheads through cost-cutting measures affect both the above?

Task

Insolvency specialists, it seems, are not the only type of business to flourish during a recession. As many companies drive to improve efficiency and cut costs without compromising quality, many have turned to contracted business services in an effort to hive off non-core activities.

CleanEasy has benefited enormously from this process. They claim that conditions are booming as many companies wake up to the benefits of utilising professionally managed external support services. CleanEasy have noted the rapid growth of the contracted services sector with pleasure and feel confident that this area will continue to grow. They have responded rapidly to this growth by undertaking an expansion programme that has resulted in an increase in their fixed costs so that they are now as follows:

	£
■ Loan repayments and interest	230 000
■ Rent and rates	95 000
■ Insurance	980
■ Staff salaries	325 000
■ Other fixed overheads	100 000
■ Promotion	5 000

The average contract size for CleanEasy is £24 000 per annum and they currently expect to increase their number of contracts for the forthcoming year to 130. Each contract will cost them at least £12 000 in direct labour and at least £4000 in direct materials. Other variable overheads will be about £1000.

1 Work out the break-even point for CleanEasy in terms of value and volume (to the nearest contract).
2 Draw a break-even chart to illustrate the above.
3 How much profit will they make with 130 contracts?
4 Given the nature of their investment, CleanEasy wish to make £300 000 profit for the year. How many contracts would they require to achieve this?

5 One strategy CleanEasy are proposing to adopt is to increase their promotional budget. If they increase this budget to £50 000, research has indicated that they will achieve at least 35 more contracts. How will this affect profitability?

6 Another strategy they are considering is to decrease price. Further research has revealed that if the average contract price fell to £22 000, they could expect to gain at least 45 new contracts. How will this affect profitability?

Limitations of break-even analysis

Break-even analysis is often considered to over-simplify organisational behaviour by reducing it to an equation: how to generate sufficient contribution to cover fixed costs and provide a surplus (profits). Its limitations are several:

■ It can be argued that, in real situations, fixed costs actually vary with different activity levels, and so a stepped fixed-cost line would provide a more accurate guide.

■ Many organisations fail to break-even because of a limiting factor restricting their ability to do so (e.g. shortage of space, labour or orders).

■ The variable-cost and sales lines are unlikely to be linear (i.e. straight). Discounts, special contracts and overtime payments mean that the cost line is more likely to be a curve.

■ Break-even charts depict short-term relationships, and forecasts are therefore unrealistic when the proposals cover a number of years.

■ Break-even analysis is (like all other methods) dependent upon the accuracy of forecasts made about costs and revenues. Changes in the market and in the cost of raw materials could affect the success of the technique.

Reasons for using a break-even chart

The principal use of a break-even chart is to be able to *find a break-even point* given certain important information about sales and costs. Decisions may then be taken to select levels of operating activity which will provide required profits and also create a margin of safety.

As a tool, one of the great benefits of using a break-even chart is the ability to change and manipulate information so that predictions can be made about a range of different situations. This is known as *'what if?' analysis.* For example, if we could reduce variable costs by 10%, how would this affect profitability? What would happen if we reduced prices by £3 in order to achieve a predicted 15% increase in sales? All these situations can be plotted on a break-even chart. As a result, the chart is a useful device for quickly manipulating information so that outcomes can be anticipated.

The break-even chart is also a useful way of *anticipating and measuring profits and losses.* This is particularly important because, even though it reduces business to a diagrammatic equation, it is an important tool for predicting various levels of activity and then following actual levels of activity to see if plans are met.

Break-even analysis can be used to work out how easily fixed costs can be covered from contributions made from sales. In a range of circumstances break-even analysis can provide help with increasing profitability by providing information which enables a business to provide *different services at different prices* in order to make the most of a business's ability to use all its capacity or as much as possible. For example, a hotel might be profitable with a 40% occupancy rate, and bookings may always be at around 50%. The owner, however, knows that by providing cheaper beds after six o'clock at night, the occupancy rate is increasing, and although he or she is not getting as much to contribute to fixed costs and profitability as early bookings, the hotel is receiving something towards those costs and, of course, increasing its profitability.

In the previous chapter we looked at the cost of providing a good or a service. In this chapter we have considered the price of selling such a good or service, together with the concept of profitability. This type of approach to costing is particularly useful for small businesses who need to work out their costs and sales in order to forecast their profits accurately. A break-even-chart or some form of break-even analysis is frequently included in a business plan.

Evidence collection point

Obtain a copy of a business plan from a bank. What sort of information do they require about costs and sales levels? Show how this information could be presented for a small business idea of your own. Plan you work so that it provides evidence of Core Skills in Communication.

Task

Competition in the air-travel business is fierce – witness the price competition between carriers on transatlantic flights.

One such airline is Richard Branson's Virgin Atlantic. This operates on only the busiest international routes, where it can fill most of its planes' seats. It is the only way a small airline can compete with the likes of British Airways.

Although Virgin is competitive on price, Branson knows his firm cannot compete on this alone. Bigger airlines benefit from economies of scale. So Virgin attempts to provide a better service for a lower fare than its rivals.

Virgin launched a new service in 1992 called Mid Class for the full price of an economy ticket. By reducing the number of Economy Class cabins, there are fewer seats on a plane, but Branson thinks Virgin gains in two ways:

- by filling a greater proportion of seats as flights rarely operate at full capacity
- by encouraging more early bookings and less need for last-minute price discounting.

The rationale behind the move was that customers who are prepared to pay the full price of an economy ticket would prefer to travel with Virgin if they got better service for their money.

The following are some illustrative costs and revenues for a full-capacity return flight operation to North America:

	£
Depreciation of plane	25 000
Fuel	27 000
Flight crew costs	3 000
Cabin crew costs	6 000
Food	4 000
Selling costs and administration	10 000
Landing fees	15 000
Maintenance	10 000
	100 000

Total cost for identical Mid Class and Economy Class.

A plane with large Economy Class can carry 375 passengers with an average revenue per passenger of £350. A plane with Mid Class can carry 325 passengers with an average revenue per passenger of £425.

1 Analyse and then comment on the fixed costs and variable costs in this operation.
2 Identify the break-even point for a standard economy class plane and a plane with the new Mid Class (draw a break-even chart for each level of service and identify the break-even point for each).
3 If 80% of seats were filled, how much profit would each type of service make?
4 Some airlines sell tickets at £100 each. How can last-minute price discounting make sense?
5 Evaluate Richard Branson's decision to introduce Mid Class.

Evidence indicators

For this activity you need a report which explains the basic factors influencing pricing decisions and uses a break-even chart. Your report may be based upon a real business, a fictitious business or upon the efforts of a group-work exercise which considers the setting up of a business organisation. Make sure that you provide explanations and supporting analysis to accompany the figures you use.

The following list should serve as a checklist. Tick each of the following boxes when you have successfully covered them as part of your preparation. You need to confirm that:

- I have explained the basic factors influencing pricing for a real or fictitious business. ☐
- I have described a related pricing strategy for one good or service. ☐
- I have explained the significance of the concept of break-even. ☐
- I have drawn a break-even chart using appropriate labels. ☐
- I have supported my chart with notes and explanations which help to explain the significance of the information which can be drawn from the chart. ☐
- I have explained how and why the chart might be useful in a business situation. ☐

Financial Transactions, Costing and Pricing: Unit Test 1

1 Value added occurs at:
   a The first stage of production.
   b The last stage of production.
   c Every stage of production.
   d When the product is sold.

2 Value added is defined as:
   a The difference between the value of goods/services bought and goods/services supplied.
   b The sum of goods/services bought and goods/services supplied.
   c Goods/services bought x goods/services supplied.
   d Total profits.

3 Most of the cash from the money cycle will usually be used to buy:
   a Debtors.
   b Machinery.
   c New stock.
   d Capital.

4 Most goods sold from one business to another are usually sold:
   a By cash.
   b By cheque.
   c Using credit cards.
   d On credit.

5 To encourage customers to pay their bills promptly a business may use:
   a Cash discounts.
   b Trade discounts.
   c Courtesy discounts.
   d Credit cards.

6 If debtors fail to pay the amount owing from their account this may lead to:
   a Industrial action.
   b A bad debt.
   c Reduced sales.
   d Stock problems.

7 A document which records credit transactions between customers and organisations is known as:
   a Financial recording document.
   b Source document.

   c Debiting document.
   d Recording receipt.

8 A person to whom you owe money is known as:
   a A debtor
   b A creditor
   c A customer.
   d A credited supplier.

9 The document usually sent with the goods is the:
   a Order.
   b Statement.
   c Delivery note.
   d Credit note.

10 Which of the following is not sent from the seller to the buyer?
   a Credit note.
   b Invoice.
   c Statement.
   d Purchase order.

11 To improve the efficiency of purchasing an organisation may wish to identify values which they consider desirable in their suppliers. This they can do through:
   a Customer rating.
   b Supplier rating.
   c Contract tendering.
   d Cost contracting.

12 Accounting information is largely:
   a Qualitative in nature.
   b Determined by feedback.
   c Quantitative in nature.
   d Used for controlling cash.

13 Which of the following is not considered to be an accounting body?
   a Chartered Institute of Management Accountants.
   b Chartered Association of Certified Accountants.
   c Chartered Institute of Public Finance and Accountancy.
   d Chartered Association of Certified and Management Accountants.

14 At the end of a period, financial accountants prepare statements called:
   a Performance indicators.
   b Ledgers.
   c Journals.
   d Final accounts.

15 MIS stands for:
   a Management Induction System.
   b Management Information Systems.
   c Managers Introduction to Systemisation.
   d Measuring Information Scientifically.

16 A copy of the purchase order is unlikely to be sent to:
   a Receiving department.
   b Sales department.
   c Stock control department.
   d Accounts department.

17 Absorption costs:
   a Do not include overheads as part of total costs.
   b Include overheads as part of total costs.
   c Are sometimes called fixed costs.
   d Are useful for marginal costing.

18 The cost of wages paid to assembly-line workers who are involved in the process of product manufacture could be described as:
   a Direct costs.
   b Indirect costs.
   c Fixed costs.
   d Product overheads.

19 The total cost divided by the number of units produced is called the:
   a Marginal cost.
   b Fixed cost.
   c Unit marginal cost.
   d Absorption cost.

20 One example of direct costs might be:
   a Lighting and heating.
   b Rent.
   c Telephone.
   d Raw materials.

21 Peter Robinson intends to sell sledges at £50 per unit. Variable costs are £10 per unit. With total fixed costs at £2000, the break-even point in units will be:
   a 33.
   b 50.
   c 25.
   d 40.

22 If output doubles a fixed cost will:
   a Double.
   b Halve.
   c Remain the same.
   d None of the above.

23 A part of a business such as a department for which costs are collected is known as a:
   a Costing unit base.
   b Cost centre.
   c Cost analysis centre unit.
   d Costing unit.

24 The document which informs departments about the arrival of an order is:
   a The advice note.
   b The goods received note.
   c The delivery note.
   d The invoice.

25 E & E O stands for:
   a Errors and omissions excepted.
   b Entries and omissions excepted.
   c Errors and omissions excesses.
   d Entries and omissions excesses.

26 Which of the following may be printed in red?
   a Invoice.
   b Order.
   c Statement.
   d Credit note.

27 When recording incoming cheques it is important to make sure that if an alteration has been made it is clear and has been:
   a Dated.
   b Completed in duplicate.
   c Initialled.
   d Written in capitals.

28 The department which reviews accounts and sets credit limits for customers is known as:
   a Credit reference department.
   b Customer audit department.
   c Credit control department.
   d Creditor supervision office.

29 Royalties paid to a designer and which are based upon the number of goods manufactured would be:
   a A direct expense.
   b An indirect expense.
   c Indirect labour.
   d Direct labour.

30 Nuts and bolts would be considered to be:
  a Direct materials.
  b Indirect materials.
  c Direct expenses.
  d Indirect expenses.

31 If we divide the cost of an asset by its useful life in years, this would then tell us:
  a The margin for the asset.
  b Its value.
  c Depreciation per annum.
  d How long it will last.

32 If a motor vehicle is purchased for £10 000 and is expected to last 5 years, depreciation over each six months will be:
  a £5000.
  b £2000.
  c £1000.
  d £500.

33 The unit of output for a hotel is likely to be:
  a Cost per hour.
  b Cost per room.
  c Cost per customer.
  d None of the above.

34 Costs that do not increase as total output increases are known as:
  a Variable costs.
  b Director costs.
  c Allocated costs.
  d Fixed costs.

35 The related strategy for cost-plus pricing is the need to:
  a Break even.
  b Overcome excess capacity.
  c Make a profit.
  d Satisfice.

36 The sum remaining after the direct costs of producing products has been deducted from revenues is known as:
  a Value added.
  b Contribution.
  c Profit.
  d Total fixed costs.

37 The break-even point is found by dividing:
  a Fixed costs by unit contribution.
  b Unit contribution by fixed costs.
  c Variable costs by profit per unit.
  d Contribution by variable costs.

38 Whenever a business transaction takes place it creates:
  a A shareholder and a debtor.
  b A creditor and a debtor.
  c A borrower and a creditor.
  d A lender and a supplier.

39 An unconditional order in writing drawn on a bank, signed by the drawer, which requires a bank to pay on demand a sum of money to the bearer is usually called:
  a A standing order.
  b A direct debit.
  c A bank statement.
  d A cheque.

40 If a mistake has been made on an invoice and a customer has been undercharged, it may be necessary to send a:
  a Statement.
  b Debit note.
  c Credit note.
  d Further invoice.

41 What part of a bank giro acts as a receipt for a deposit?
  a Account number.
  b The counterfoil.
  c The signature.
  d The paying-in slip number.

42 To ensure that a cheque cannot be cashed over a counter and that it is only paid into a specified account, a cheque may be:
  a Crossed 'drawer only'.
  b Crossed 'account payee only'.
  c Left open.
  d Crossed 'drawers branch only'.

43 Costs which are proportional to the amount of product being manufactured are called:
  a Fixed costs.
  b Indirect costs.
  c Standard costs.
  d Direct costs.

44 The cash cycle starts with payments for raw materials and ends with:
  a Payments for expenses.
  b Payments to creditors.
  c Receipts from customers.
  d Receipts of tax.

45 The Department of Customs and Excise will require details of:
a Income tax paid.
b Exports and imports.
c Sales and purchases.
d National Insurance contributions.

46 The document usually sent before the goods which indicates that they are on the way is known as the:
a Delivery invoice.
b Delivery note.
c Statement.
d Advice note.

47 If the sellers have not transacted with the buyers before, they may decide to send a:
a Cheque.
b Pro forma invoice.
c Credit note.
d Advice note.

48 A remittance advice is usually attached to:
a An invoice.
b An advice note.
c A credit note.
d A statement.

49 Payments from petty cash are usually made against a:
a Petty cash receipt.
b Petty cash voucher.
c Petty cash number.
d Credit card.

50 EDI stands for:
a Electronic Data Interchange.
b Electronic Dating Initialisation.
c Electronic Data Inquiry.
d Electronic Data Issue.

Financial Transactions, Costing and Pricing: Unit Test 2

1 Which of the following is least likely to be included in the money cycle?
a Cash.
b Stock.
c Fixed assets.
d Debtors.

2 Before granting credit for the first time to a customer a business will normally ask for:
a A cash discount.
b A trade reference.
c A payment period.
d Credit discount.

3 To find out what suppliers may be able to offer, a potential buyer may send out:
a An order.
b An advice note.
c An invoice.
d A letter of enquiry.

4 Which of the following is unlikely to be used to transfer money?
a BACS.
b Statement.
c Cheque.
d Standing order.

5 If faulty goods are delivered you may be sent a:
a Statement.
b New invoice.
c Credit note.
d Debit note.

6 Before a junior member of staff sends out an order, as a security precaution, it may be necessary for it to be:
a Stamped.
b Dated.
c Rewritten.
d Countersigned.

7 The document which is normally sent with the goods is known as:
a The invoice.
b The statement.
c The delivery note.
d The credit note.

8 When paying cheques and cash into a bank account, a cashier may use:
a A standing order.
b A direct debit.
c A bank draft.
d A bank giro credit.

9 One electronic method of transferring funds is known as:
a BACS.
b INTERSTEL.
c STABS.
d ICC.

10 If payments are not made promptly this could affect an organisation's:
  a Accounting procedures.
  b Audit methods.
  c Liquidity.
  d Audit.

11 To record receipts and payments of cash an organisation will use:
  a The bank account.
  b A cash book.
  c The petty cash book.
  d None of the above.

12 The total of direct costs is sometimes called:
  a Total cost.
  b Semi-variable cost.
  c Fixed cost.
  d Prime cost.

13 All costs are items of:
  a Revenue expenditure.
  b Capital expenditure.
  c Fixed expenditure.
  d Variable expenditure.

14 An example of capital expenditure would be:
  a Workers' wages.
  b Rent and rates.
  c New machinery.
  d Depreciation.

15 Selling price less variable costs per unit equals:
  a The break-even point.
  b The contribution.
  c Total fixed costs.
  d Direct costs.

16 If a cost is described as direct, then if sales double the cost will:
  a Halve.
  b Double.
  c Remain constant.
  d Probably none of the above.

17 The point at which the contribution equals the fixed costs is:
  a The margin of safety.
  b Unit cost.
  c The profit target point.
  d The break-even point.

18 Which of the following is not a purchase document?
  a Order.
  b Goods received note.

  c Credit note to the buyer.
  d Receipt.

19 In response to an enquiry a seller will usually send:
  a A statement.
  b An order form.
  c A price list.
  d A credit note.

20 Which of the following will not appear on an invoice?
  a E & O E.
  b Date.
  c Seller's signature.
  d Trade discount.

21 The goods received note is usually checked against the:
  a Price list.
  b Invoice.
  c Statement.
  d Credit note.

22 The document normally sent with the cheque is the:
  a Paying-in-slip.
  b Remittance advice.
  c Bank-giro credit.
  d Counterfoil.

23 When customers advise their banks to make regular payments on their behalf on fixed dates for fixed amounts, this is known as:
  a Direct debits.
  b Statementing.
  c Standing orders.
  d Debit cards.

24 One great benefit from EDI is that it:
  a Increases staff.
  b Reduces paperwork.
  c Reduces dependence upon technology.
  d None of the above.

25 To set up a series of internal checks upon an accounting system, it may be possible to create an:
  a Error-free zone.
  b Audit trail.
  c Accounting break.
  d External audit.

26 VAT will not appear on:
  a Invoice.
  b Statement.
  c Delivery note.
  d Credit note.

27 Which of the following would be unlikely to improve the security procedures for an accounting system?
  a Segregation of duties.
  b Transaction authorisation.
  c Employ more staff.
  d None of the above.

28 Which of the following is not a cost?
  a Telephone bill.
  b Fixed asset.
  c Stock.
  d Cash sale.

29 Administration wages would be considered to be:
  a Direct labour.
  b Indirect labour.
  c Direct expense.
  d Indirect expense.

30 If a machine costs £24 000 and is expected to last four years, the monthly depreciation charge would be:
  a £6000.
  b £3000.
  c £1500.
  d £500.

31 The unit of service for a computer help-line is likely to be:
  a Labour hour basis.
  b Cost per computer.
  c Cost per call.
  d None of the above.

32 Cost per unit of production or service equals:
  a Total cost/units of output.
  b Units of output/total cost.
  c Marginal cost/units of output.
  d Contribution/fixed costs.

33 Costs which increase as total output increases are known as:
  a Variable costs.
  b Indirect costs.
  c Spillover costs.
  d Fixed costs.

34 The pricing strategy which takes into account the prices of competing products is:
  a Skimming.
  b Cost-plus pricing.
  c Contribution pricing.
  d Market lead pricing.

35 At the break-even point an organisation will:
  a Make a profit.
  b Make a loss.
  c Have to cut jobs.
  d Make neither profit not loss.

36 The difference between the break-even point and the selected operating point is known as:
  a The margin of safety.
  b Elasticity of demand.
  c Total costs.
  d Safe operating profit.

37 R Times sells books for £10 each. Variable costs are £8 per unit. Fixed costs are £100 000. Calculate the break-even point in sales.
  a £5 000.
  b £50 000.
  c £500 000.
  d £5 000 000.

38 Using the example in question 37, if prices were increased by £2 to £12, the unit break-even point would fall by:
  a 2500 units.
  b 25 000 units.
  c 250 000 units.
  d None of the above.

39 VAT stands for:
  a Value Added Tax.
  b Volume Aided Transaction.
  c Value Added Transaction.
  d Volume Added Tax.

40 The discount offered for prompt payment is called:
  a Debtors discount.
  b Trade discount.
  c Cash discount.
  d Settlement discount.

41 A credit note:
  a Increases the invoice price.
  b Reduces the invoice price.
  c Means that goods have to be paid for in advance.
  d None of the above.

42 Sending bulk electronic payments down the telephone line for clearing through the banking system is known as:
  a EDI.
  b BACS.
  c DD.
  d BACSTEL.

43 The card which enables payment to be made immediately when purchasing goods or services is:
  a A cheque guarantee card.
  b A credit card.
  c A debit card.
  d A banking card.

44 Office stationery would be a good example of:
  a Direct materials.
  b Indirect materials.
  c Direct expenses.
  d Indirect expenses.

45 Which of the following is a variable cost:
  a Office equipment.
  b Raw materials.
  c Motor vehicles.
  d Debtors.

46 Cost-plus pricing indicates the following approach to pricing:
  a Customer-focused.
  b Production-orientation.
  c Sales-orientation.
  d Technological-orientation.

47 The pricing strategy which helps to utilise under-used capacity is:
  a Cost-plus pricing.
  b Market-lead pricing.
  c Skimming.
  d Contribution pricing.

48 The point between the total sales and total cost lines to the left of the break-even point will represent:
  a Marginal cost.
  b Profits.
  c Fixed cost.
  d Losses.

49 When transferring money to pay a large number of salaries it may be possible to use:
  a A bank giro credit.
  b A paying-in slip.
  c Standing order.
  d Director debit.

50 EDI allows data to be transferred:
  a From computer to computer.
  b From paper to computer.
  c Without any form of records being kept.
  d None of the above.

In Chapter 4 we saw that all organisations have a range of aims and objectives. Although some of these may be broad, the successful achievement of such objectives frequently depends upon one overriding financial objective – financial success in terms of profits (the bottom line). Achieving this objective depends upon efficient financial planning and control throughout the organisation.

The use of business data which we looked at in Chapter 18–21 helps to provide control for the organisation's activities and provides information that can be used to draw up financial statements which comply with legislative requirements. In this section we look at the financial requirements of business organisations, at how such finance is controlled, at supporting financial statements and at how to use and understand such statements.

Sources of finance and financial requirements of business organisations

In all organisations money comes in and then flows out. From time to time managers might pose questions such as:

- Can we afford X or Y?
- Are we going to be able to pay our workforce this month?
- We seem to be profitable and have plenty of work but why do we never have any money?
- If we borrow money to buy a new machine, can we meet the repayments?

Every organisation has financial requirements and there are many issues involved in financing any proposition. To answer such questions and to make the right critical decisions, an organisation has to engage in some form of financial planning.

This chapter looks at the financial requirements of different types of business organisations and shows how such requirements may be met by various sources of finance.

Financing requirements

Financial planning involves defining objectives and then developing ways of achieving them. To be able to do this, a financial manager must have a realistic understanding of what is happening and what is likely to happen within the organisation; for example, when is money going to come in, what is it need for, and would it be possible to use some of it for expansion and development? In the 'money-go-round' (Figure 22.1), capital and sales revenue come into a business, but is there enough left over, after paying all of the costs, for expansion and development?

We can appreciate the importance of financial planning by considering a report prepared by the

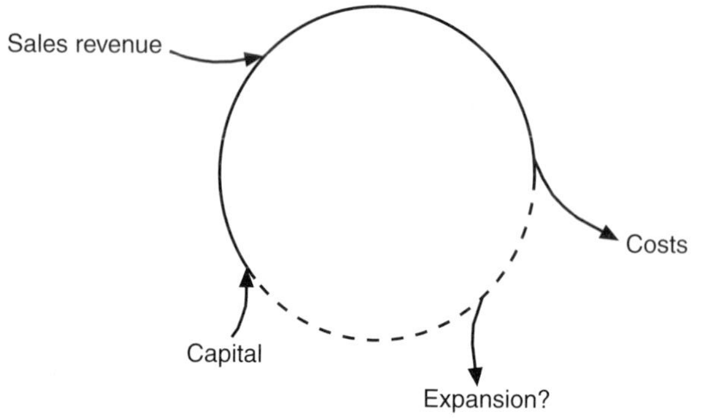

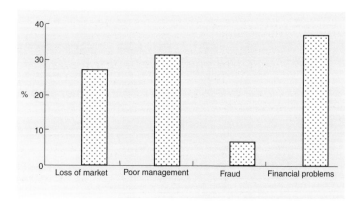

Figure 22.1 The money-go-round

Society of Practitioners of Insolvency during the recession of the late 1980s–early 1990s, which produced statistics to show why business failed. As you can see from Figure 22.2, the biggest single cause of business failure was financial problems, which accounted for 36% of business failures: 20% because

Figure 22.2 Causes of business failure

of cash-flow problems, 5% because of loss of finance when lenders in the market became cautious about who they lent to, and 11% because of bad debts when businesses failed to pay their bills.

For organisations to operate successfully they need to pay for the use of resources. These may include:

■ *Fixed assets* These are relatively permanent items which the business owns and operates, such as premises, equipment, plant and machinery, motor vehicles, furniture and other tangible items.

Capital expenditure is the form of expenditure which relates mainly to fixed assets. This is because expenditure upon some assets lasts longer than one year. As we will see later, when deciding to use fixed assets such as cars and machinery, purchasing them using capital expenditure is not the only option. It may be possible to lease them. As the organisation does not own them the item will not then appear in the balance sheet as a fixed asset.

■ *Working capital* Working capital is more usually defined as current assets minus current liabilities.

Working capital provides the short-term funds which enable the organisation to operate – for example, paying for stocks of raw materials and paying the running costs of the business. *Revenue expenditure* relates mainly to the shorter-term running costs of the organisation because it is on items which last less than one year.

Evidence collection point

Within the educational establishment you attend, think of five examples of relatively long-term assets which are fixed and five examples of items which are short-term and will have been sourced by working capital.

■ *Asset finance* Fixed assets are relatively long-term items which are owned by the organisation. There are many sources of finance available to owners who might wish to purchase such assets. For example, in a very small business, the owner may decide to buy the assets on his or her own by putting in his or her capital:

Assets = Capital

The business will then owe the capital to the owner. Alternatively, he or she may decide to put some capital in and borrow the rest by raising a loan, perhaps from a bank. As the loan would then be a liability, the equation would then be:

Assets = Capital + liabilities

As we shall see when we look in more detail at the different sources of finance, some sources are more suitable than others for acquiring items which last over a longer period. For example, mortgages are a long-term source of finance for premises.

■ *Working capital finance* Current assets are sometimes called 'circulating assets' because the form they take is constantly changing. A business will require finance to hold stocks of finished goods in readiness to satisfy the demands of the market. They may also require finance to make products and create work in progress. When a credit transaction takes place stocks will be reduced and the company will incur debts. Debtors will have bought goods on credit and therefore owe the company money. After a reasonable credit period, payment will be expected. Out of this inflow, profits will have been created which can be used to restart the trading cycle (Figure 22.3).

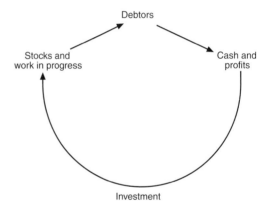

Figure 22.3 The trading cycle

Current liabilities are the debts of the business which need to be paid in a fairly short period of time (normally within one year). Creditors are normally suppliers of goods on trade credit for which the business has been invoiced but has not yet provided payment. Current liabilities may also include a bank overdraft, any short-term loans and any taxes owed to the Department of Inland Revenue.

Assets and working capital

Assets

Assets are items that are *owned by* an organisation and money and other items that are *owed to* the

533

organisation. The asset side of a balance sheet will normally be set out in what is called an inverse order of liquidity. The means that items that are difficult to convert to cash quickly (i.e. are *liquid*) appear at the top of the list. By examining the order in which they are listed, you can gauge the ease with which successive assets can be converted to cash until you come to the most liquid asset of all, cash.

Assets are classified into two types:

1 *Fixed assets* The simple distinction is that all fixed assets have a lifespan of more than one year. Fixed assets may include:
    Land
    Buildings
    Production machinery
    Transport (vehicles)
    Office machinery
    Fixture and fittings
2 *Current assets* These are short term and regularly change when trading takes place. Current assets may include:
    Stocks: raw materials
            work in progress
            finished goods
    Debtors
    Cash
Note that for manufacturing businesses, stocks will start off as raw materials. As they go through value added processes they will become work in progress. When they are complete, they are then finished goods.

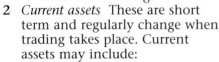

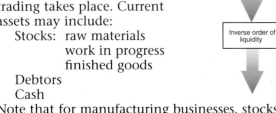

Working capital

As we saw earlier, working capital is simply current assets minus current liabilities. It is simply all of the assets which can be converted into cash fairly quickly less the debts which are owed in the near future. A prudent ratio of current assets to current liabilities is considered to be 2:1 (Figure 22.4), although most businesses operate with a slightly lower ratio than this. It is now more commonly thought that a satisfactory working capital ratio will depend upon the company concerned, the type of business operation, stock levels and other factors.

Task

Put the following current assets and current liabilities into an order which is similar to the one above:

Creditors	£24 000
Debtors	£19 000
Stocks	£23 000
Cash	£4 000
Bank overdraft	£22 000

What is the ratio in this situation? Would this ratio be prudent?

Working capital is often considered to be the portion of capital that 'oils the wheels' of business. Funds employed in fixed assets are concerned with producing goods and services. Working capital provides stocks from which the fixed assets may produce. It allows the sales force to offer trade credit and create debtors. Firms with insufficient working capital are in a financial straitjacket. They lack the funds to buy stocks, and to produce and create debtors. In these circumstances providers of finance may well call a meeting of creditors and appoint a liquidator. Clearly, a business must always have adequate short-term funds to ensure the continuation of its activities.

The operating cycle expresses the connection between working capital and movements of cash. It can measure the period of time between:

- the purchase of raw materials and the receipt of cash from debtors
- the time when cash is paid out for raw materials and the time when cash is received from sales (Figure 22.5).

	£	£
Current assets		
Stocks (raw materials/work in progress/finished goods)	20 000	
Debtors	15 000	
Cash	5 000	
		40 000
Less current liabilities		
Creditors	15 000	
Bank overdraft	5 000	
		20 000
Working capital		20 000

Figure 22.4 A ratio of 2:1

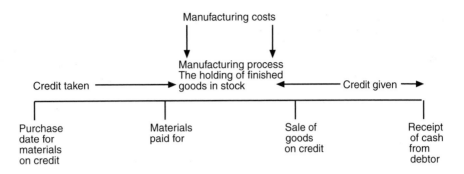

Figure 22.5 Managing the credit cycle

Example

A firm buys raw materials on two months' credit and holds them in stock for half a month before issuing them to the production department from which they emerge as finished goods. These are held on average for one and a half months before sale. Debtors take three months to pay. The cash cycle would be:

	Months
Raw materials credit from suppliers	(2)
Turnover of stock of raw materials	0.5
Turnover of stock of finished goods	1.5
Debtors' payment period	3.0
Cash cycle	3.0 months

Not only does this cycle show the time ingredient; it also shows that income from debtors should be more than enough to cover any manufacturing costs and overheads encountered. The dangers of insufficient working capital are clear to see:

1 A company with limited working capital will not be able to buy in bulk and could miss out on opportunities to gain trade discounts.
2 Cash discounts will be lost as the business will avoid paying creditors until the last possible opportunity.
3 It will become more difficult to offer extensive credit facilities to customers. By shortening the credit period, customers may well go to alternative suppliers.
4 The business will be unable to innovate. Limited finances will hinder its ability to develop new products or improve production techniques.
5 The business's financial reputation as a good payer may be lost.
6 Creditors may well take action. As capital becomes squeezed, a business will be forced to finance its activities by overdrafts and trade credit. A point could well be reached where its future is dependent upon the actions of creditors.
7 Overtrading can take place. This would involve financing a large volume of production with inadequate working capital, often from short-term loans. This can lead to a complete imbalance of the working capital ratio.

Accountants will constantly review an organisation's asset structure to ensure that resources are utilised efficiently. Depending on their review, it might be necessary to increase working capital. This might take place in a number of ways:

1 Reducing the period between the time cash is paid out for raw materials and the time cash is received from sales will provide funds for regeneration. Although the improved efficiency of the cash cycle will help working capital, it might be unpopular with creditors.
2 Fixed assets such as land and buildings might not be fully utilised, or space might be used for unprofitable purposes. Space could be rented, sold or allowed to house a more profitable operation so that cash flow could be improved. A business's cash flow might be improved by selling assets and leasing them back, although this can commit the firm to heavy leasing fees.
3 A company could review its stock levels to see if these could be the subject of economy measures. If the stock of raw materials is divided by the average weekly issue, the number of weeks' raw materials held in stock can be calculated. Some companies attempt to maximise liquidity by using a 'just-in-time' approach so as to hold the minimum stocks possible. Although this might save on expenses associated with running a large store and looking after stocks, the company might lose out on trade discounts and be susceptible to inconsistent supplies.
4 Many businesses employ a credit controller to economise on debtors. A credit controller will vet

new customers and set them a credit limit, ensure that credit limits are not exceeded and encourage debtors to pay on time. Credit controllers are often caught in a conflict with the sales department, whose staff wish them to extend credit limits, and the accounts department, who want debtors to pay quickly and so increase their working capital.

5   As we have seen, cash budgeting can be used as an important control mechanism to predict the effects of future transactions on the cash balance of a company. Cash budgeting can help a company to take actions to ensure that cash is available when required.

6   A number of short-term solutions are available to increase working capital. Companies might extend their overdraft or bring in a factoring company. It might be possible to delay the payment of bills, although this obviously displeases creditors.

Evidence collection point

Divide the list of assets from the last evidence collection point into fixed assets and current assets using an inverse order of liquidity.

Common methods of finance

The first important decision about any finance is for how long a period you require it. Though short-term funds tend to be the most expensive, they are also more flexible – and this benefit can offset the lower cost of long-term funds, which might not be fully employed if fluctuations take place in business activity.

Many organisations expand by using short-term finance and then replace this type with long-term finance through a funding operation. Funding in this situation therefore raises long-term finance to pay off short-term finance, so that further short-term finance is then made available for the organisation to expand again (Figure 22.6).

Trade credit

A useful form of finance for all organisations is that of trade credit allowed by suppliers. The credit period is the time between receiving the good or service and being obliged to make payment for it. Credit

Figure 22.6 Short-term and long-term finance

periods are usually governed by the type of business and the relationship between the purchaser and the supplier. Although no rate of interest is attached to trade credit, cash discounts may be forfeited if payments are not made within the agreed time.

Organisations trying to extend trade credit in order to improve their short-term cash situation endanger their reputation with suppliers.

Overdraft

An overdraft is the most frequently used form of short-term bank finance and is used to ease cash-flow problems. Arrangements are made between the customer and the bank to include an agreed limit on an account beyond which the customer will not draw. Interest is calculated on the level of the overdraft on a daily basis. Often a bank will make a special charge for arranging an overdraft and committing the bank's money, whether the withdrawal facilities are used or not. After an agreed period, the bank will examine the account and make a decision about whether to revise or reinstate the limit.

Whereas the account of a personal customer will show a regular input of income per month and a regular pattern of expenditure (Figure 22.7 (a)), this does not happen with a business customer who is

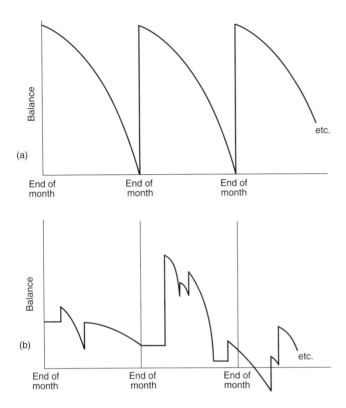

Figure 22.7 (a) Personal account, (b) Business account

dependent upon debtors paying their bills. As a result, it is easy to understand why business customers often slip into an overdraft situation (Figure 22.7 (b)), and need this flexible form of short-term finance.

Task

Make a list of the advantages and disadvantages of arranging for an overdraft facility.

Factoring

In order to overcome a short-term financial problem, and instead of arranging an overdraft, a bank or other financial institution may provide the use of a *factoring service*. Trade debts can be tied up for periods extending beyond three months. A factoring company offers immediate payment against these debtors (normally 80%) and the rest when the debt is paid. In this way, the firm improves its liquidity with immediate funds and ensures that its assets are not

tied up in debtors. The factoring company can take away the burden of running the sales ledger and the problem of collecting payments. It charges interest on the sum and also administration charges.

Case study – Late payments damage health

The recent UK recession claimed a record number of victims. Many of them blamed their demise on more than just high interest rates and overall economic downturn. They claim that, having supplied goods and/or services, particularly to large companies, late payment by those customers frequently dealt the final blow.

It is difficult to establish the number of cases where late payment has contributed to business collapse, but one indication is a near doubling of county court judgements in the early 1990s used to demand payments.

Many organisations today deliberately delay payments to creditors in order to improve their cash flow position but, in so doing, they often cause serious problems with their suppliers. Suppliers find it very difficult to fight back and always risk losing vital business if they do so. A recent survey by accounts Pannel Kerr Foster finds that 70% of small and medium-sized companies believe that late payments made the recession worse and that an overwhelming 96% believe that it adds to business problems. For example:

- 76% of firms have to wait three months or more for their bills to be paid
- only 14% receive their money within the contractual limit of 30 days
- manufacturers fare worst as eight out of ten of them have to wait up to three months for payment
- 96% say it adds to their business problems and 30% say it seriously affects their business.

Many feel that small businesses face a 'Catch 22' position. Businesses need to sell goods and/or services but do not want to take their largest customers to court. Some of the largest British companies are subjected to the greatest criticism. Many of these companies generate up to a third of their profits from their large cash reserves, instead of using such reserves to pay suppliers on time.

Delaying payment seems to have become part of the British business culture. Many organisations have become aware of the benefits of holding on to money as long as they can and feel that it is only common sense to do so. Large companies not only have the resources for monitoring credit, but also have easier access to funds. Whereas a small business requiring cash might go to a bank and be charged interest at base plus from day one, a plc will be able to go to the Stock Market, float a rights issue and then not have to pay shareholders until the first dividend some six months later.

There is general agreement that imposing interest on overdue debts might improve the situation. Of companies that already charge interest on delayed payments, nine out of ten feel that they have not lost customers as a result and that the system has encouraged prompt payment.

Another solution seems to lie in the Courts and Legal Services Act 1990. This provides for most debt cases to be handled by county courts rather than the High Court. It also provides for the client to be represented by a debt-collecting agent rather than a barrister and for the debt-collector's fee or commission to be recoverable by the court.

Packages of measures designed to improve prompt payment have appeared in recent budgets. These measures today mean that large companies will have to reveal in their accounts the length of time they take to pay bills. Companies awarded government contracts will also have to commit themselves to paying their sub-contractors promptly – normally within 30 days. The Department of Employment has agreed to provide up to £90 000 to small business associations to set up support services for their members in areas where the problem of late payments is severe and will also provide them with advice on how to pursue offenders.

Whether the above measures work remains to be seen. Late payments are hardly likely to disappear overnight. However, as long as large businesses continue to borrow, in effect, from their suppliers' banks instead of their own banks, they will continue to place their suppliers at a severe competitive disadvantage.

1 Explain why organisations deliberately delay the payment of their bills.
2 How might delayed payment affect the working capital of each business organisation in the transaction?
3 What would you consider to be a reasonable credit period? Explain why.
4 How might delayed payments have contributed to the recent recession?
5 High might factoring help organisations suffering from delayed payments?
6 Why might large organisations be less likely to suffer from delayed payments than small organisations?

Leasing and hire purchase

Major banks have links with finance houses which provide a variety of schemes enabling customers to receive goods and make payments over time. Goods on *hire purchase* remain the property of the finance company until the customer has made all of the payments, whereas other *credit purchasing* schemes enable the goods to belong to the customer from the first payment.

Another way in which a company can gain the use of an asset without having to pay for it is through *leasing*. The lessee uses the asset and makes regular payments to the lessor, who owns it. An operating lease is for a small amount, and a capital or finance lease is for a large item over an extended period. As the asset does not belong to the lessee, it will not appear in the balance sheet.

The procedure for leasing is for a company to choose the equipment it requires, which is then purchased by the leasing company. A contract determines the rent payable and the conditions, e.g. options to purchase, maintenance agreements, etc. The benefits of leasing are that:

1 It enables a business to have complete use of an asset without having to use risk or loan capital to finance it.
2 Leasing payments are an expense and are charged to the profit and loss account before tax is assessed.
3 Leasing enables businesses to change their equipment more often and thereby to keep up to date with modern technology.
4 Tax allowances can be claimed by the lessor and be filtered through to the lessee in lower lease payments.

Although leasing enables the lessee to manage expenditure more easily, the lessee does not own the equipment. If income falters, lease payments may impose a considerable burden on a business; furthermore, loans cannot be secured on assets that are leased.

Loans

Borrowing is considered an acceptable feature of commercial activity. The charge for borrowing is interest, and a crucial element in calculating the interest charge is the amount of risk involved with the loan. For example, longer-term loans tend to carry higher rates, as will loans made to small businesses with unproven track records. In order to obtain a loan, an organisation needs to use its business plan to convince its financial backers of the viability of its proposition. Many financial institutions involved with lending activities will try to provide a package of lending facilities to match the specific requirements of each borrower.

Although loans can come from a variety of sources, the main source is the bank. Banks offer a range of types of loans for businesses, including the following:

1 *Business starter loans* These are designed to help new businesses or businesses that have been operating for less than 12 months. The loans range from £1000 to £15 000 and carry a fixed rate of interest. They are usually repayable over a term between one and ten years. (*Note:* Secured loans tend to be at a lower rate of interest.)

2 *Business development loans* These loans are for business development and expansion. They can be for virtually any purpose and usually come with fixed interest rates and fixed monthly payments. Loans can range from £2000 to £250 000 and be repayable from anything between one and 20 years.

3 *Franchise finance* Banks can specifically tailor business loans to aid with the purchase and running of franchises.

4 *Small firms loans guarantee scheme* This is a service offered by banks and supported by a guarantee by the DTI for businesses that do not have a proven track record. The government guarantees a proportion of the loan up to £100 000 over two to seven years.

Banks usually offer a range of loan protection schemes to cover situations such as accident or sickness which might affect the ability of a business person to make regular repayments.

Large, publicly quoted organisations may borrow money by issuing *debentures*. A debenture is an acknowledgement of a debt made to a company for a fixed rate of interest which specifies the terms of repayment at the end of a period. It is therefore a long-term loan which is transferable on the Stock Exchange. A debenture holder is not a shareholder but a creditor. This means that interest payments are an expense to the company and are allowable against profits.

Although holding debentures is much less risky than holding shares, their value in the marketplace will very according to interest rates. For example, a debenture that pays a 10% rate of interest will be worth 10/8 or 1.25% of its face value when interest

rates are 8%; if interest rates rise to 15% it would only be worth 10/15 or 0.66% of its face value. Thus, if interest rates rise the value of the loan falls and vice versa.

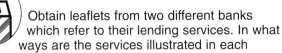

Evidence collection point

Obtain leaflets from two different banks which refer to their lending services. In what ways are the services illustrated in each leaflet (a) similar, and (b) different? Your work could provide evidence of Core Skills in Communication.

Mortgages

A mortgage is a loan secured upon a property. The size of the mortgage will depend upon factors such as the age of the property, the length of repayment period (often 25 years) and the income of the borrowers. The lender of the mortgage has certain legal rights over the property, including the right of sale, if the borrower is unable to meet the repayments. There are many different types of mortgage. For example, with a straight repayment mortgage the customer is paying off interest and capital throughout the loan so, as the amount of the mortgage reduces, so does the interest. With an endowment mortgage the customer takes out an insurance policy. When the policy matures the sum insured pays off the outstanding mortgage.

Banks may provide *bridging loans* with mortgages. If a customer wishes to purchase a new property before the sale of the old one, the bank may advance the sum to do so and the bridging loan is replaced by the proceeds of the sale when it takes place. Organisations may also wish to raise money by *re-mortgaging*. A re-mortgage simply replaces one mortgage agreement with another.

Profit retention

One of the most important sources of finance for businesses is profits that have been ploughed back. Initially, profits are subject to corporation tax, payable to the Department of Inland Revenue. Then a proportion of what is left is allocated to shareholders as dividends. The directors will recommend how much profit should be distributed in this way. The board needs to satisfy shareholders while at the same time ensuring that sufficient funds are available for reinvestment (Figure 22.8). Directors do not want shareholders to express dissatisfaction at

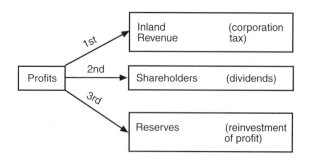

Figure 22.8 Order of profit allocation

the annual general meeting or to sell their shares and thus cause share prices to fall so that under-valuation leave the business vulnerable to takeover. The profits retained in the business will be shown in the balance sheet as reserves, and the funds represented by these reserves will be spread among the assets.

Government grants

An important source of finance for many businesses is the availability of government grants, 'soft loans' and subsidies. Government help may come from the EU as well as from central and local government and can be provided by a variety of different agencies. For example:

1 *The Enterprise Allowance Scheme* (EAS) provides an allowance for people starting a new enterprise for up to 40 weeks.
2 *Development agency loans* for 'desirable' businesses are available in a location where there is high unemployment.
3 *The British Technology Group* (BTG) may offer finance to companies wanting to develop new products and processes.
4 *Regional selective assistance* may provide grants for capital investment projects within development and intermediate areas. It also provides access to loans from the *European Investment Bank* (EIB) and from the *European Coal and Steel Community* (ECSC) for projects that create jobs in areas suffering from job losses in the coal and steel industries.

Venture capital

Another valuable form of finance for businesses is venture capital. Venture capital companies provide

finance in return for an equity shareholding in the organisation and an element of control. 3i is the largest venture capital company of this type in this field. In recent years the law has changed to allow companies to buy back their capital if certain safeguards have been met.

Case study – Investment capital from 3i

The British motor trade has been subject to vast structural changes over the last few years. Though many big groups have been divesting themselves of individual businesses, some small companies have become larger, even during the recession. One reason for this has been that long-term capital has been available for the well-managed business. For example, 3i invested £14m in the motor trade during 1990–91. Much of this involved helping small businesses to grow.

As a large investment institution, 3i has access to massive resources but, as well as engaging in multimillion-pound transactions, it is also willing to provide capital to smaller investors. Roughly half of its investments are for less than £200 000. The purposes of the funding vary quite widely – it may be to enter a new market, launch a new product, expand or install a new plant. 3i state that they are not always concerned about the size of any venture, but are often more interested in the quality of management and the prospects for growth.

3i considers itself to be a 'hands off' investor that takes a long-term view rather than a short-term investor that might wish to see quick returns. Their investment usually involves the provision of equity or venture capital rather than loan capital. Thus, 3i becomes a part-owner of a business, usually as a minority shareholder. The great benefit of this is that share capital strengthens the balance sheet by reducing the level of gearing. An organisation can thus raise loans in the future if they are required. Many of the businesses hit badly by the recession were too highly geared.

Packages from 3i for the motor trade have enabled businesses to take a more strategic view towards financing. Long-term capital has been provided for long-term growth, allowing businesses to then raise short-term capital for short-term needs.

1 Distinguish between venture capital and a loan.
2 What are the benefits of having an institutional investor such as 3i as a minority shareholder?
3 Explain what is meant by the following terms:
   a structural changes

b hands-off investor
c quick returns
d equity.

Equity

This type of capital will depend upon the type of organisation.

A *sole trader* business is easy to set up and is the most common form of business ownership. Though a sole trader has considerable flexibility, this type of business carries a lot of risk. Thus a sole trader often relies on finance from personal sources and additional sums can be difficult to raise.

Sole traders frequently expand by taking in *partners*. Partners can bring in further capital together with greater expertise. They are particularly suitable for the professions, but limitations on numbers can restrict capital-raising opportunities.

In order to achieve the benefits of limited liability and extend their capital-raising opportunities, many partnerships transform themselves by a legal process into a registered company, and issue shares.

As we have seen already, companies can be either *private* or *public*. A *private limited company* has certain restrictions on the rights of members to transfer shares, and there are limits on the ability of the public to subscribe for share ownership. A fully listed public limited company has almost endless opportunities to raise fresh capital from the financial markets.

For example, a public limited company can create a *public issue by prospectus*. An issuing house (probably a merchant bank) organises the issue of shares by compiling a prospectus (a brochure), accompanied by an advertisement and an invitation to buy shares. This can be expensive – something like 7% of the money raised by the issue can go to meet the costs.

Another method for a public company to raise finance is to make an *offer for sale*. The public company issues shares directly to an issuing house, which then offers them for sale at a fixed price. This too is an expensive method and is best used when the size of the issue is too small to need a public issue by prospectus.

A *rights issue* is a cheaper method of obtaining finance – existing shareholders are offered shares directly at an advantageous price. Another method which avoids the expense of 'going to the market' is a placing, whereby shares are placed with a number of investors through an intermediary (a share dealer).

In a public limited company most capital is held usually in the form of *ordinary shares*. An ordinary share is a fixed unit of ownership and gives the holder the opportunity to share in the profits or losses. Most ordinary shares carry voting rights at shareholders' meetings. Shareholders elect the Board and sanction the level of dividends proposed. *Authorised capital* is the maximum amount of share capital a company is empowered by its shareholders to issue, whereas *issued capital* is the nominal amount of share capital issued to shareholders.

Another class of shares is *deferred shares* (or *founders shares*). These are issued to members of the family which built the business, and they sometimes carry enhanced voting rights so that a small group of people can maintain control of a family business.

Preference shares are a less flexible class of share. Owners of these shares are not, strictly speaking, part owners of the company and their exact rights will be found in the company's Articles of Association. However, they do have preferential rights to receive dividends if profits exist and, in the event of a company winding up, will receive the face value of their shares before the ordinary shareholders are repaid. On the other hand, dividends on preference shares are limited.

Some companies issue *cumulative preference shares* and this avoids the difficulty of having to pay preference shareholders if profits are too small. The holder of the cumulative preference share will receive arrears of dividends accumulated from the past in later years. *Redeemable preference shares* enable the company to buy back the shares from the shareholders. Redemption can be made from profits or reserves or it may be financed by a fresh issue of more shares. *Participating preference shareholders* receive dividends above the fixed rate when ordinary shareholders have been paid and if the company has done well in a particular year.

It should be noted that organisations in the public sector are publically owned and – unless they are going through the process of privatisation – cannot go to the Stock Exchange for capital. They can, however, use the financial markets for loans.

Evidence collection point

Obtain an annual report from a publicly owned company by writing to its Head Office. Though parts of the report may seem rather complex, look carefully through the report. Identify at least two sources of finance for this company.

Gifts

Sometimes relatives or very close friends may provide gifts or possibly an inheritance which helps individuals to develop their business opportunities. Such gifts may then be put into the business as capital.

Sources of finance

There are many different individuals and organisations who today provide sources of finance. Ten years ago the distinctions between the various suppliers of finance were much easier to identify. For example, loans were from banks and mortgages from building societies. Today, since the Financial Services Act there has been increasing competition from different organisations to provide a range of sources of finance.

Suppliers of finance include:

- *Sellers* When buying goods from sellers they are providing trade credit as a source of finance. This may be particularly useful for organisations who then need to sell the goods so that they can pay their creditors.
- *Banks* Banks today provide a wide range of services for their customers. Advances or lending to personal and business customers is by far the most profitable of their activities.
- *Factoring companies* Factoring companies and the services they provide have become an increasingly popular source of finance as they free money

which the business already has but has not managed to collect.

- *Leasing and hire purchase companies* Although businesses never become the owners of the equipment they lease, this has today become a very popular way of obtaining items. With leasing and hire purchase, organisations eliminate the worries of ownership and manage to spread costs evenly over a longer period.
- *Building societies* Many of these have become key competitors in the provision of finance. Since the Building Society Act of 1986 they can now offer loans to personal customers. The merger of some building societies and the formation of public companies e.g. Abbey National plc, have put them into direct competition with banks.
- *The business* Reinvestment of capital is an extremely important source of finance for the business. Funds from profit retention can then be spread out amongst assets and represented by reserves.
- *Venture capital companies* These are non-banking commercial organisations which attract money from investors to reinvest in limited companies. The problem with these companies is that they require control over their investment.
- *Savings* All businesses, no matter how small, generally involve some form of cost. Owners must show that they have confidence in their own ideas and abilities by contributing some form of investment into the capital of the business, some of which is likely to come from savings.
- *Share issues* As we saw earlier, though there are restrictions upon share issue in private limited companies, public limited companies may issue a range of different types of share through the Stock Exchange.
- *Government grants* The government will provide different types of grant to both new and established organisations. This may be through regional aid from the Department of Trade and Industry's 'Enterprise Initiative', Loan Guarantee Schemes from the Department of Employment or finance from Training and Enterprise Councils (TECs).
- *Non-profit organisations* Clubs and societies may receive membership fees to provide their sources of finance. Charities may receive donations and trade unions may receive subscriptions from their members.

 Task

Name two common sources of finance for each of the following:

a small corner shop
b a large multinational business
c a professional partnership
d a large charity.

Evidence collection point

Carry out a detailed study of one organisation providing sources of finance. Find out what types of organisation most frequently use finance from this source. Plan your work so that it provides evidence of Core Skills in Communication and Application of Number.

Characteristics of sources of finance

Lenders always try to minimise the risks of loan finance. When providing finance for a limited company, it is possible for the lender to demand a *personal guarantee* of repayment from the main shareholder, and this effectively removes that shareholder's limited liability and puts him or her in a similar position to a partner or sole trade. Lenders also frequently ask for *security* or *collateral* against a loan. In this way certain assets are 'secured' and, if the business has to be wound up, the lender has priority over other creditors in claiming any money raised from the sale of these secured assets (office furniture and equipment, vehicles, machinery, etc.)

Case study – Applying for a loan

When a potential borrower is applying for a loan, a bank manager will wish to view a *business plan* as this will show what the business is, the resources and expertise at its disposal and its proposed developments.

At the first meeting the bank manager will ask: 'What is the money required for?' It might be needed for working capital or to purchase fixed assets. The bank will expect the borrower to provide evidence that the money really is needed for a specific purpose and that it will be spent as indicated.

The bank manager will also wish to know *how much* is needed, *for how long* it is required, and *how it is to be paid back.* How much could depend upon the amount put into the business by the owner. Assessing the cost of fixed assets is usually fairly straightforward; however, anticipating working capital requirements will require a detailed estimate of cash flows. Projecting how long

finance is needed for will require detailed projections of costs and sales taking into account all eventualities. Paying money back should take into account the cost of borrowing the money and the use of realistic cash-flow projections.

In deciding whether or not to grant the loan, the bank manager will use certain principles of lending which can best be remembered by using the mnemonic IPARTS. This stands for:

- Integrity
- Purpose
- Amount
- Repayment
- Term
- Security.

Customer *integrity* is an important consideration in determining whether or not a customer is going to honour a debt. The bank will not wish to resort to legal action to recover the loan. The past history of the customer will therefore be very important.

The bank will wish to know the *purpose* of the loan and how it is to be used. It will also wish to know whether the *amount* requested is the right amount; for example, will the customer require more, or has he or she asked for too much?

Repayments are an important consideration in lending. Given customer projections of cash flow, is the firm going to be able to meet the repayments? The period over which the loan is required will be an important consideration of risk. The longer the *term*, the larger the interest repayments; however, 'long term' means higher risks and a greater likelihood of something going wrong.

Finally, *security* will provide some form of insurance against default by the customer. The bank will then have an asset that it can sell in order to recover the loan.

Whatever the business proposition, there is always a level of uncertainty. Those wishing to borrow money have to show a level of personal financial commitment to the business process and to use their business plans to predict carefully the chances of a business succeeding.

1 Explain why a bank manager will wish to examine a business plan. In your answer, identify at least four areas that should be included in the plan.
2 Risk is always an important feature of lending money. Name two factors that would indicate some degree of risk.
3 What measures might a bank take to reduce the risks of lending?
4 Obtain a copy of a bank loan application form and comment briefly on the information it requires.

543

There are a number of different characteristics and features of the process which identify the most appropriate sources of finance. These include:

- The *time* over which the source of finance is required. For example, an overdraft would be short term, business loans would tend to be short and medium term and a mortgage would be long term.
- The *arrangement fee*. In some cases, as with overdrafts, it is usual to charge an arrangement fee.
- The *annual percentage rate* (APR). Interest rates are a charge upon the use of funds. With personal borrowing, banks usually charge in relation to APR. With business borrowing, banks generally charge at a rate above *base rate* according to risk and other factors.
- The *type of institution/person* to approach for finance may very widely.
- The *relative benefits of each source*. For example, look at the comparisons between the uses of loan capital and risk capital shown in Figure 22.9.

Evidence collection point

A business wishes (a) to acquire more heavy machinery, and (b) to reduce the time it takes to pay its creditors. Advise on the best source of finance for each purpose. Compare and contrast the characteristics of each source.

Usual sources of finance for different organisations

	Sole trader	Partnership	Private limited company	Public limited company	Non-profit making
Trade credit	*	*	*	*	
Overdraft	*	*	*	*	
Factoring	*	*	*		
Leasing and hire purchase			*	*	*
Loan	*	*	*	*	*
Mortgage	*	*			*
Profit retention			*	*	
Venture capital			*		
Equity	*	*	*	*	
Grants	*	*	*		
Gifts	*				*
Fees					*

Advantages of using risk capital
1. If the business has had a bad year, the company is under no legal obligation to shareholders.
2. Unlike loans, whereby the principal has to be returned at the end of a period on a contracted date, the company does not have to pay the share capital back.
3. Interest on loan capital is an overhead which reduces profits, whereas share capital does not create overheads.

Disadvantages of using risk capital
1. It can be expensive to issue shares.
2. Companies have to undergo the rigorous financial requirements of the Stock Exchange to be listed, and then demands for shares are subject to the uncertainties of the marketplace.
3. The creation of more shareholders may dilute the influence of the founders of the company and affect their ability to make decisions.

Advantages of using loan capital
1. In relation to raising funds through share issue, it is cheap.
2. Inflation will benefit the borrower because the value of the interest payments will diminish; the loan and the interest will be worth less in real terms.
3. Interest payments are a company expense and appear in the profit and loss account before corporation tax is assessed.

Disadvantages of using loan capital
1. Any loan charge must be paid irrespective of business performance.
2. A highly geared company would reduce its ability to allocate profits to shareholders.
3. Excessive loan capital may affect a business's flexibility. Repayments will have to be met at certain times and these dates might not match incomes from sales. Covenants, guarantees, etc. could affect decision-making.

Figure 22.9 Comparing the use of risk and loan capital

Evidence indicators

For this activity you need to describe the financial requirements of two different business organisations. In doing so you must emphasise the difference between asset finance and working capital finance. Base your analysis upon a general overview (without using figures) of the financial requirements of two businesses known to you. Remember to respect the confidentiality of those concerned.

The following list should serve as a checklist. Tick off each of the following when you have successfully covered them as part of your preparation. You need to confirm that:

- I have identified two business organisations about which I have provided a general overview of their financing arrangements. ☐
- I have described how they have financed their activities. In doing so I have shown the differences between asset finance and working capital finance. ☐
- I have compared the characteristics of each different source of finance. ☐
- I have evaluated the appropriateness of each different source for the purposes used. ☐

Forecasts and cash flow for a small business

Looking into their future helps all organisations to plan their activities so that what they anticipate and want to happen can actually happen. This process of financial forward planning is known as budgeting. It is considered to be a system of responsibility accounting because it puts an onus on budgeted areas to perform in a way that has been outlined for them and its success will depend upon the quality of information provided. Businesses that do not budget may not be pleased when they view their final accounts. Budgeting helps the financial manager to develop an understanding of how the business is likely to perform in the future.

In this chapter we describe the use of forecasts in the planning process for a small business. In doing so we look at three components of forecasts; the capital budget, the trading forecast and the cash flow forecast.

Purposes and components of forecasts

We all budget to a greater or lesser extent. Our short-term budget may relate to how we are going to get through the coming week and do all the things we want to do. Our slightly longer-term budget may involve being able to afford Christmas presents in two months' time. Our longest-term budget could involve the planning necessary to afford the car tax, MOT and motor insurance which all fall due in ten months from now. Also, when can we afford to replace the car?

In exactly the same way, businesses try to see far into the future. The problem is that, the further one looks into the future, the most difficult it is to see accurately.

A budget is a financial plan which is developed for the future. Many businesses appoint a budget controller whose sole task is to coordinate budgetary activities. A short-term budget would be for up to one year, a medium-term budget would be for anything from one year to five years and a budget for a period longer than this would be a long-term budget (Figure 23.1).

Figure 23.1 The budgetary period

Budgeting is an important function for almost every type of organisation. In this chapter we look more specifically at the process of budgeting within a small business where the budgeting process is probably likely to affect everyone.

Wherever budgeting takes place it is important to draw upon the collective experience of people throughout the business. A budgeting team might consist of representatives from various areas of activity. The team will consider the objectives of the budgeting process, obtain and provide relevant information, make decisions, prepare budgets and then use these budgets to help to control the business (Figure 23.2).

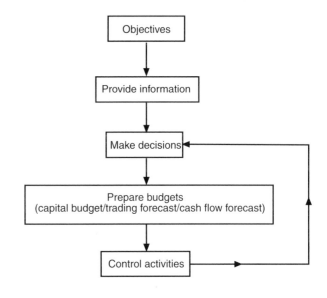

Figure 23.2 The budgetary process

So what are the purposes of budgeting?

- Budgeting helps to predict what the organisation *thinks will happen*. Given the experience within the organisation, they help to show what is likely to take place in the future.
- Budgets create opportunities to *appraise alternative courses of action*. Information created for budgeting purposes forms the basis of decisions which have to be taken. The research necessary for budgeting will look at alternative ways of achieving the organisation's objectives.
- Budgets set *targets*. If communicated to people throughout the organisation, the budgets will help them to work towards the targets which have been set.
- Budgets help to *monitor and control performance*. This can be done by studying actual results, comparing this to budgeting results and then finding out why differences may have taken place.
- Budgets are fundamental to the *process of business planning*. They provide a series of quantitative guidelines which can be used for coordination and then followed in order to achieve the organisation's business objectives.

Budgeting may also have some useful spin-offs. Every year the business is reviewed and this gives members of the various departments a better understanding of the working of the organisation as a whole. In fact, by participating in the budgetary process they feel that their experience is contributing to policy decisions. The process may also highlight areas of concern.

Budgeting also increases cooperation between departments and lowers departmental barriers. In this way members of one department can become aware of the difficulties facing another department. By being involved in the budgetary process, non-accountants also appreciate the importance of costs.

Evidence collection point

Identify a range of activities in which you participate that you think could be helped by some form of budgeting (for example, personal finances, club responsibility, etc.). Explain how in each instance.

In reality, budgeting may take place in almost all parts of an organisation. Budgeting should also be viewed as something which is going on all the time and as a source of useful information and guidance for managers. In this chapter, however, we will describe only three components of budgetary forecasts. These include:

- *The capital budget* The word 'capital' refers to the buying of fixed assets. Do we plan now for the money we will need in the future to buy another car? The capital budget is a simple statement of intent or forecast which specifies the planned purchase of assets, the date of intended purchase and the expected cost of purchase.
- *The trading forecast* The trading forecast is a simple statement of intent which takes into account sales, the costs of the planned production as well as overheads. The surplus left over once costs and overheads have been deducted from sales is the profit.
- *The cash flow forecast* This forecast looks at the cash coming into an organisation as well as the cash going out. It is a prediction by a business of how much money it thinks it will receive and how much it thinks it will pay out over a specified period of time.

Evidence collection point

Explain how each of the above might be used by a business organisation.

Capital budgets

Capital expenditure refers to the aquisition of fixed assets. Capital budgets are prepared to plan for the purchase of fixed assets.

The capital budget is prepared after reviewing fixed asset needs for the budget period. This will be done in the light of business objectives and planned strategy for the budget period. The next step is to consider the condition and capacity of existing fixed assets. For example, a planned expansion into new markets will require a review of existing assets to ensure sufficient business capacity is available. Capital expenditure may also be required to renew existing assets, such as worn-out equipment. In recognising that more fixed assets are required, it is necessary to plan their purchase including the time and cost of aquisition.

It follows from the nature of this type of expenditure that some years will require more capital expenditure than others. Together with the fact that for many businesses the value of fixed assets used is significant, it is important that capital budgets are prepared to ensure that adequate finance is planned.

Classifications of capital expenditure will follow those you are already familiar with from constructing

Jason Robards Ltd: capital budget for the year ended 31 December

	Jan. £	Feb. £	March £	April £	May £	June £	July £	Aug. £	Sept. £	Oct. £	Nov. £	Dec. £	Total £
Replacement													
CNC machine						50 000							50 000
2 motor vans								20 000					20 000
Computer			5 500										5 500
Expansion													
Building extension									50 000				50 000
Production line										40 000			40 000
Health & Safety													
Air conditioning		9 500											9 500
Total	**0**	**9 500**	**5 500**	**0**	**0**	**50 000**	**0**	**20 000**	**50 000**	**40 000**	**0**	**0**	**175 000**

the fixed asset section of the balance sheet. Typically they include:

- land and buildings
- factory plant and machinery
- office fixtures and fittings
- computer equipment
- motor vehicles.

Expenditure may be further analysed into assets required for:

- expansion of existing product ranges
- expansion into new products
- replacement of existing assets and
- satisfying health and safety regulations.

In this way information is provided as to whether the business is expanding or just maintaining its productive capacity. It may also indicate whether items of capital expenditure are essential or merely desirable.

When evaluating expenditure on capital items the business managers will consider the likely returns of making the investment and the associated risk of not reaping the hoped-for benefits. Wherever possible, the cost of purchasing assets will be evaluated against the financial benefits that should result (for example, increased sales or reduced costs). In many cases numerical information to support an investment decision is not readily available. In these cases it is necessary to perform a cost–benefit analysis to recognise the more qualitative aspects of the proposal. For example, expenditure on welfare facilities such as employee social clubs and catering facilities will be evaluated for the goodwill and lower staff turnover that such facilities may encourage.

Once prepared, the details from the capital budget are incorporated into the cash budget.

Task

Whitehills Leisure Centre provides customers with a gym, swimming pool and team sports hall. The centre's management is reviewing capital expenditure needs for 1996. They intend to expand facilities during the year with four squash courts and more equipment for the gym. The squash courts will be built in May at a cost of £75 000. The additional gym equipment will comprise three exercise bikes costing £1000 in March, a rowing machine costing £1200 in July and weight-lifting equipment costing £2000 in November. The receptionist has been complaining about the number of repair visits required recently for the computerised cash till and so it has been decided this will be replaced in January at a cost of £1600. The floor surface round the swimming pool is too slippery when wet and so management has decided this should be replaced in January to minimise the risk of accidents. It has also been decided to refurbish the dressing rooms. New lockers and benches will cost £5000 in June.

Prepare a capital budget for Whitehills Leisure Centre for the year ended 31 December 1996 with separate sections for expansion, replacement and health and safety.

Trading forecast

As we explained earlier, the trading forecast is a simple budget forecast of sales as well as planned production costs and overheads on a month-by-month basis over a period of time. In this forecast sales is the only area generating income, and everything else is either a cost or an expense. If these are then deducted from the sales figure and there is a surplus left over, this surplus is the *net profit* (see Chapter 24). On the other hand, if there is a deficit from trading activity this is a net loss.

It is important to emphasise that the profit of a business may be significantly different from the cash flow and this budget helps to highlight such differences. This is because the trading forecast identifies sales and purchases *when they are made* and not when they are paid for. (Note: many business transactions take place on credit, where the goods are paid for at a later period in time.) The cash flow forecast, on the other hand, only recognises amounts when receipts or payments have been made.

- *Sales* This is the number of goods sold at the selling price over each month. It is not the money received each month from sales.
- *Purchases of raw materials* These are the amounts of raw materials bought which are to be turned into finished goods and sold. So that we can call our surplus a profit or deficit a loss, we are assuming that no stocks of raw materials or finished goods appear either before or after our forecast.
- *Expenses* Organisations soon incur a wide variety of expenses during the course of their trading activities. These may include advertising, electricity, business rates, interest charges and salaries. When we looked at the cost of a unit of production or service in Chapter 20 we encountered the concept of depreciation. Depreciation may be included in trading forecast but would not appear in a cash flow forecast as it does not represent a movement of funds.

- *Net profit/loss* This is the final profit or loss a business makes after the deduction of all expenses. Where a profit is made this may then be used by the owner(s) of the business.

Task

Peter Atkin makes window frames. Prepare the monthly trading budget for Peter Atkin from the following information:

1 Peter sells each frame for £550 each unit. He anticipates selling the following units in 1996:

Jan.	Feb.	Mar.	Apr.	May	Jun.	Jul.	Aug.	Sept.	Oct.	Nov.	Dec.
10	12	10	8	5	7	6	6	8	10	11	11

2 Peter buys the raw materials for production in the same month that he uses them to complete a sale. (He carries no stocks of raw materials.) Raw materials for each frame cost £180. However, he has heard that this is to increase to £200 from 1 July.
3 Other monthly expenses are as follows:
wages £1100
depreciation of machinery £500
telephone £150
loan interest £180.

Evidence collection point

Imagine that you are running a small business making a product of your choice. Make up a simple trading forecast. Your work will show evidence of Core Skills in Application of Number.

Rachel Williams Ltd: trading budget for the year ended 31 December

	Jan. £	Feb. £	March £	April £	May £	June £	July £	Aug. £	Sept. £	Oct. £	Nov. £	Dec. £	Total £
Sales	400	450	500	540	640	500	550	500	500	450	400	370	5800
Raw materials	120	140	120	130	150	150	130	150	150	130	120	110	1600
Wages	50	50	50	50	50	50	50	50	50	50	50	50	600
Telephone	40	45	45	45	45	45	45	45	45	45	45	40	530
Expenses	200	200	200	200	200	200	200	200	200	200	200	200	2400
Total	410	435	415	425	445	445	425	445	445	425	415	400	5130
Net profit/loss	(10)	15	85	115	195	55	125	55	55	25	(15)	(30)	670

Note: net losses appear in parentheses

Purpose of cash flow

Whereas profit is a *surplus* from trading activities, cash is a liquid asset which enables an organisation to buy the goods and services it requires in order to add value to them, trade and make profits. It is therefore possible for an organisation to be profitable while, at the same time. creditors have not been paid and liquid resources have not been properly accounted for.

On the other hand, an organisation must look carefully to see that its use of cash is to its best advantage. For example, if it holds too much cash in the bank it might be sacrificing income it could otherwise earn.

An organisation must therefore ensure that it has sufficient cash to carry out its plans, and ensure that the cash coming in is sufficient to cover the cash going out. At the same time it must take into account any cash surpluses it might have in the bank. The organisation is said to have a certain *cash-flow* position.

Looking carefully at the availability of liquid funds is essential to the smooth running of any organisation. With cash planning or budgeting it is possible to forecast the flows into and out of an organisation's bank account so that any surpluses or deficits can be highlighted and any necessary action can be taken promptly. For example, overdraft facilities may be arranged in good time so that funds are available when required.

Case study – When the numbers fail to add up

Every year thousands of businesses fail as a result of cash-flow problems. The root cause of these problems seems to be weak financial management, which is frequently identified when the businesses are wound up. Today it has become one of the key reasons for business failure.

The importance of effective cash management is stressed again and again in booklets, guides and starter packs. For example:

'Finance … is where your numbers stand up and be counted.' (Price Waterhouse)

'The banker is far more concerned by the cash flow that trading generates.' (Ernst & Young)

'Many businesses fail to make profits or to have enough cash at the right time, because the management has not planned ahead.' (National Westminster Bank)

'The big question in cash flow is: what would happen if … …?' (Barclays Bank)

Despite these points being made in every booklet and guide, the message concerning weak financial management seems slow to penetrate.

Lee Manning, a senior manager at Buchler Phillips, says that 'weakness in company management and the information available to it' is a common theme running through reports of business reviews carried out for lenders. He identifies five principal components within that theme:

- Most companies which suffer long-term financial difficulties are victims of inadequate and insufficient management information, with particular emphasis on up-to-date cash-flow information.
- Cash-flow forecasts are generally prepared at the start of the business period and not reviewed again until the period has elapsed, thus defeating the object of cash-flow analysis.
- Cash-flow forecasts are generally highly optimistic.
- Management tends to ignore the quality of debtors and tends to look at the face value of invoices rather than how easy it is to get the money in.
- Companies are often brought down by large speculative projects which represent a move away from their core business.

According to one firm of accountants, businesses often reach crisis conditions before thinking about their cash flow. The major lesson to be learnt from accounting is that 'cash is king'.

1 Explain why an organisation's cash flow is considered important by its bank.
2 What does Barclays Bank mean when its representative says 'The big question in cash flow is: what would happen if … …?'
3 Why, in your opinion, do so many businesses ignore cash flow?

The cash-flow forecast is an extremely important tool within an organisation and has a number of clear purposes. For example:

- The forecast can be used to *highlight the timing consequences* of the capital budget and the trading forecast. For example, the capital budget may point to when machinery needs to be replaced, and this can then be included in the cash-flow forecast. Similarly, the trading forecast may have within it expenses such as water rates which may be paid quarterly or half-yearly – these again can be included within the cash-flow forecast.

- The cash-flow forecast is an essential document for the compilation of *the business plan*. It will help to show whether the organisation is capable of achieving the objectives that it sets. This is very important if the business is apply for finance, where the lender will almost certainly want to know about the ability of the applicant to keep on top of their cash flow and meet the proposed payment schedules.
- The cash-flow forecast will help to boost the *lender's confidence* and the *owner's confidence*. By looking into the future it will provide them with the reassurance they require that their plans are going according to schedule.
- It will also help with the *monitoring of performance*. The cash-flow forecast sets benchmarks against which the business is expected to perform. If the organisation actually performs differently from these benchmarks, then the cash-flow forecast may have highlighted an area of investigation. Investigating differences between forecast figures and actual figures is known as variance analysis.

Significance of timing

Credit periods

In order to prepare a cash-flow forecast you need to know what receipts and payments are likely to take place in the future and exactly when they will occur. It is important know the length of the lead time between incurring an expense and paying for it as well as the time lag between making a sale and collecting the money from debtors. The art of successful forecasting is being able to calculate receipts and expenditures accurately.

Most business transactions take place on credit and, as we have discussed earlier in this book, most payments are made either weeks or months after documentation has been sent. For example, suppose a business sells the following goods at £10 each on credit:

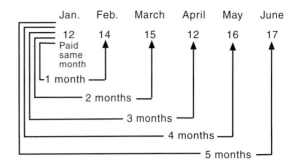

Assume that the cash for these sales is received three months after the sale. This means that in April the cash will be received for January, in May the cash will be received from February and son on. From the other viewpoint, if you have been given 3 months' credit you would pay for goods bought in January during April and so on.

> When working through a cash flow forecast it is important to look carefully at the timing **of every entry.**

Illustration

A cash-flow forecast for the six months ended 31 December 1995 can be drafted from the following information:

1   Cash balance 1 July 1995: £4500.

2   Sales are £15 per unit and cash is received three months after the sale. For the period in question, the sale of units is:

1995										*1996*	
Mar.	Apr.	May	Jun.	Jul.	Aug.	Sep.	Oct.	Nov.	Dec.	Jan.	Feb.
60	60	75	90	55	140	130	150	150	160	170	150

3   Production in units:

1995										*1996*	
Mar.	Apr.	May	Jun.	Jul.	Aug.	Sep.	Oct.	Nov.	Dec.	Jan.	Feb.
40	50	80	70	80	130	130	150	145	160	170	160

4   Raw materials cost £4 per unit and these are paid for two months *before* being used in production.

5   Wages are £5 per unit and this is paid for the same month as the unit produced.

6   Running costs are £4 per unit, 50% of the cost is paid in the same month of production while the other 50% is paid for in the month after production.

7   Sundry expenses of £50 are paid monthly.

551

Receipts from sales

							£
July	60	(April)	×	15	=		900
August	75	(May)	×	15	=		1125
September	90	(June)	×	15	=		1350
October	55	(July)	×	15	=		825
November	140	(August)	×	15	=		2100
December	130	(September)	×	15	=		1950

Payments

July

						£
Raw materials	130	(September)	×	4	=	520
Wages	80	(July)	×	5	=	400
Running costs	80	(July)	×	2	=	160
	70	(June)	×	2	=	140
Sundry expenses					=	50
						1270

August

						£
Raw materials	150	(October)	×	4	=	600
Wages	130	(August)	×	5	=	650
Running costs	130	(August)	×	2	=	260
	80	(July)	×	2	=	160
Sundry expenses					=	50
						1720

September

						£
Raw materials	145	(November)	×	4	=	580
Wages	130	(September)	×	5	=	650
Running costs	130	(September)	×	2	=	260
	130	(August)	×	2	=	260
Sundry expenses					=	50
						1800

October

						£
Raw materials	160	(December)	×	4	=	640
Wages	150	(October)	×	5	=	750
Running costs	150	(October)	×	2	=	300
	130	(September)	×	2	=	260
Sundry expenses					=	50
						2000

November

						£
Raw materials	170	(January)	×	4	=	680
Wages	145	(November)	×	5	=	725
Running costs	145	(November)	×	2	=	290
	150	(October)	×	2	=	300
Sundry expenses					=	50
						2045

December

						£
Raw materials	160	(February)	×	4	=	640
Wages	160	(December)	×	5	=	800
Running costs	160	(December)	×	2	=	320
	145	(November)	×	2	=	290
Sundry expenses					=	50
						2100

	July	Aug.	Sept.	Oct.	Nov.	Dec.
Receipts						
Sales	900	1125	1350	825	2100	1950
Total receipts	900	1125	1350	825	2100	1950
Payments						
Raw materials	520	600	580	640	680	640
Direct labour	400	650	650	750	725	800
Variable expenses	300	420	520	560	590	610
Fixed expenses	50	50	50	50	50	50
Total payments	1270	1720	1800	2000	2045	2100
Receipts – payments	(370)	(595)	(450)	(1175)	55	(150)
Balance B/F	4500	4130	3535	3085	1910	1965
Balance C/F	4130	3535	3085	1910	1965	1815

VAT

VAT is charged by many businesses on the goods and services they provide. HM Customs and Excise administer the VAT system and ensure that businesses comply with the regulations.

To forecast the cash flows of business accurately it is important that you have some knowledge of VAT regulations.

- VAT is charged as an addition to the selling price of a business's goods or services.
- Businesses have to pay the VAT they receive from customers to Customs and Excise.
- The standard rate of VAT is set by Parliament (17.5% in 1995/6).
- Like private individuals, businesses that are registered also pay VAT on goods and services provided by other VAT-registered businesses. However, businesses that are registered for VAT can claim back the VAT they have paid by deducting it from the amount they have to pay to HM Customs and Excise.
- Businesses have to register for VAT and charge it on their sales if annual turnover is over £46 000 (in 1995/6).
- VAT is usually accounted for in three-monthly periods – tax quarters. Businesses will be informed of the quarter dates they have account for VAT when they register for VAT.

VAT quarter dates

A	31 January	30 April	31 July	31 October
B	28 February	31 May	31 August	31 November
C	31 March	30 June	30 September	31 December

VAT has to be charged if three conditions are satisfied:

- the goods or services are classified as a taxable supply
- the supply of goods or services is in the UK
- the supply is made by a VAT-registered business, whether it is a sole trader, partnership, or company.

Many things that a business buys and sells are classified as a taxable supply, but some items are specifically excluded.

When preparing a cash flow statement we must include the VAT that is added to taxable sales and purchases. In addition, we must also remember to plan for the VAT payment to Customs and Excise.

VAT payable = VAT on sales – VAT on purchases

Classification of financial transactions for VAT purposes

Taxable at standard rate – 17.5%	VAT is charged on
Most items not specified as being non-taxable, e.g. Petrol	Food
	Water and sewerage
	Books and periodicals
Maintenance and repairs	Certain supplies to charities
Materials	Public transport
Factory and office equipment	Transactions in land and
Stationery	buildings including rent
	Financial services
	Insurance
	Postal services by Post Office
	Betting and gaming
	Wages paid to employees
	Drawings
	Dividends

Timing of cash flows

The difference between the VAT charged to customers and the VAT paid on supplies has to be paid to Customs and Excise by the end of the month following the VAT quarter. Let us look at a business that has a VAT quarter at the end of February:

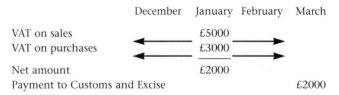

	December	January	February	March
VAT on sales			£5000	
VAT on purchases			£3000	
Net amount			£2000	
Payment to Customs and Excise				£2000

The net VAT payable of £2000 must be paid to Customs and Excise by 31 March.

Illustration of a cash-flow forecast with VAT

Jane Covey is preparing a cash forecast for her first six months of trading to August. She will start March with a cash balance of £1000 and will purchase equipment for £1000 during that month. There will be no credit transactions and forecast figures each month are: sales £5000, wages £2000, rent £500, materials £2000. The equipment, sales and materials are subject to VAT at 17.5%. Jane's VAT quarters end on May and August.

Answer

Care should be taken to ensure that VAT is calculated only on those items that are subject to tax.

1 The VAT on sales will be £5000 × 17.5% = £875 per month.
2 The VAT on purchases will be based on payments for equipment and materials. Rent and wages do not attract VAT.

The VAT to be paid to Customs and Excise is payable in the month following the VAT quarter, in this case June. (VAT is charged and paid only on equipment and materials in this instance.) It is made up as follows:

- VAT on sales for the quarter
  (£875 + £875 + £875)   =   £2625
- VAT on purchases for the quarter
  (£525 + £350 + £350)   =   £1225
- VAT payable to Customs and Excise =   £1400

The VAT due for the next three months will not be paid until September, so will not appear in the cash-flow statement.

If the business pays more VAT in a quarter than the VAT it charges customers, the difference can be reclaimed from Customs and Excise in the form of a refund. If this situation arises an additional 'VAT refund' line should be inserted in the receipts section of the cash-flow statement.

Task – Cash-flow forecast with VAT

Dallington Roofing Ltd requires you to prepare a cash-flow statement for the six months to June. All transactions are on a cash-only bases. The following figures are forecast for each month: sales £7000, materials £1600, wages £3500 and rent £1000. The difference between VAT charged to customers and claimed on purchases for the quarter to December of the previous year amounted to £1500. This will have to be paid in January. It is also forecast that the business will buy additional equipment in March for £2000 plus VAT. The company will have £3000 in its bank account at 31 December.

Note: For small businesses and for the purposes of this element it is permissible to account for VAT when cash is paid or received on a cash-flow basis rather than on an invoice basis.

Cash-flow headings

Cash-flow headings may vary according to the nature of the business and the complexity of the exercise as well as the range of possible in-flows and out-flows which it is possible for a business organisation to have. Some of the more likely cash in-flow headings are as follows:

Jane Covey: Cash-flow statement for the six months to August

	March	April	May	June	July	August	Total
Receipts							
Sales	5 000	5 000	5 000	5 000	5 000	5 000	30 000
VAT on sales	875	875	875	875	875	875	5 250
Total	5 875	5 875	5 875	5 875	5 875	5 875	35 250
Payments							
Equipment	1 000						1 000
Rent	500	500	500	500	500	500	3 000
Wages	2 000	2 000	2 000	2 000	2 000	2 000	12 000
Materials	2 000	2 000	2 000	2 000	2 000	2 000	12 000
VAT on payments	525	350	350	350	350	350	2 275
VAT paid to C&E				1 400			1 400
Total	6 025	4 850	4 850	6 250	4 850	4 850	31 675
Receipts – payments	(150)	1 025	1 025	(375)	1 025	1 025	3 575
Balance B/F	1 000	850	1 875	2 900	2 525	3 550	1 000
Balance C/F	850	1 875	2 900	2 525	3 550	4 575	4 575

- *Start-up capital* This would be the capital put into the business when trading activities begin.
- *Loan receipts* If a business receives monies from a loan it would appear as a receipt.
- *Miscellaneous receipts* A business organisation may have a number of miscellaneous receipts which could inject finance into the cash-flow forecast (for example, rent received and income from the sale of an asset).
- *Sales receipts* Clearly the most common form of receipt, this is simply income from sales.
- *VAT recoveries* If more VAT is paid on purchases than is received on sales, then the VAT recovered from Customs and Excise would be an inflow. (Note: this is unlikely to happen very often.)

Cash out-flow headings include:

- *Payments for assets* Asset purchase will be predictable through the capital budget and the amounts used for each purchase will be deducted from the cash-flow forecast.
- *Raw materials* This is likely to be a regular outflow which may relate to a production schedule or the volume of sales.
- *Expenses* These might include water rates, telephone bills as well as many other running costs. They will *not* include depreciation as this is not a movement of funds.

- *Interest payments/loan repayments* Where these appear they are regular payments for the use of capital.
- *VAT payments* As we have seen, VAT is usually charged for three-monthly periods.

Producing cash-flow forecasts

At this stage it is necessary for you to show that you can produce a cash-flow forecast from a range of information. Use the approach shown in Figure 23.3 for setting out your cash-flow forecast.

The tasks detailed below vary widely both in structure of difficulty, use of source information and number of types of out-flows and in-flows.

Task

C. Moon Ltd has £500 in the bank on 1 January. The owner, Christine Moon, anticipates that her *receipts* over the next six months are likely to be as shown on the next page:

		Jan. £	Feb. £	March £	April £	May £	June £
Cash in-flows	**Receipts**						
	Start-up capital						
	Loan receipts						
	Miscellaneous receipts						
	Sales receipts						
	VAT recoveries						
	Total						
Cash out-flows	**Payments**						
	Assets						
	Raw materials						
	Expenses						
	Interest payments						
	Loan repayments						
	VAT payments						
Receipts less payments for each column	Total						
	Receipts – payments						
Running cash balance	Balance B/F						
	Balance C/F						

Figure 23.3 Outline for a cash-flow forecast

Jan.	Feb.	March	April	May	June
£2300	£1400	£5300	£6100	£4700	£1400

She has also worked out what her payments are likely to be over the next six months:

Jan.	Feb.	March	April	May	June
£1400	£4100	£5600	£5000	£3100	£900

Christine Moon is concerned about whether she needs an overdraft facility and, if so, when she is likely to need it. Construct a cash-flow forecast and advise her on her financial requirements.

Task

Prepare the cash-flow forecast of S. Todd Ltd. The business has £250 in the bank and the owner anticipates that his *receipts* over the next six months are likely to be as follows:

Jan.	Feb.	March	April	May	June
£1400	£1600	£1500	£1000	£900	£700

He has also worked out his payments and expects these to be:

Jan.	Feb.	March	April	May	June
£1100	£700	£900	£1400	£1000	£900

The cash-flow forecasts we have considered so far have shown monthly totals. In real life, however, the information is likely to be broken down into specific components. It is useful to ascertain when each of these components needs to be applied and what the effect of each is. It is therefore possible to modify the cash-flow forecast by making it more detailed.

Task

Andrew Nut sets up in business as a manufacturer of string vests by putting £28 500 into a business bank account on 1 January. For the first six months of the year he anticipates or *budgets* for the following situations.

- His forecasts for the purchase of raw materials and sales receipts for finished goods, based upon extensive market research, are as follows:

Purchases (£)		Sales(£)
January	6 500	5 500
February	7 000	7 100
March	7 300	8 000
April	7 500	14 000
May	6 100	17 000
June	6 500	14 300

- Andrew Nut has arranged one month's credit from suppliers, so raw materials purchased in January will have to be paid for in February.
- He expects one-half of sales to be for cash and the other half on credit. He anticipates two months on average to be taken by credit customers; i.e. sales made in January on credit will not be settled until March.
- Wages are expected to be £1000 per month, paid in the same month.
- Machinery must be purchased for £15 500 on 1 January and must be paid for in the same month.
- Rent for his factory is £6000 per annum, payable in equal instalments at the start of each month.
- Other costs (*overheads*) are £1500 per month, and these are assumed to be paid in the month following that in which they are incurred.
- In April, Andrew Nut expects to receive an inheritance from his Aunt Kitty of £8000, which he will put straight into the business bank account.

Prepare Andrew Nut's cash-flow forecast for the first six months.

Task

Albert Spanner sets up as a manufacturer of machine tools by putting £17 400 into the business bank account on 1 January. For the first six months of the year he anticipates or budgets for the following:

- His forecasts for the purchase of raw materials and sales receipts for finished goods, based upon market research, are as follows:

Purchases (£)		Sales(£)
January	3 200	2 000
February	3 350	4 000
March	4 185	6 200
April	5 500	7 000
May	5 700	8 200
June	5 900	8 400

- Albert Spanner has arranged two months' credit from suppliers.
- He expects one-quarter of sales to be for cash and the other three-quarters to be on credit. He anticipates two months' credit on average to be taken by credit customers.
- Wages are expected to be £800 per month, paid in the same month.
- Machinery is to be purchased in January for £2500 and in April for £3500. On both occasions the owner anticipates making payments in the month following purchase.
- Rent for his factory is £3000 per annum, payable in equal instalments at the start of each month.
- Other overheads are £1000 per month, to be paid in the month following that in which they are incurred.
- In May, Albert Spanner will take out a loan for £4000, which he intends to put straight into the business bank account.

Prepare A. Spanner's cash-flow forecast for the first six months of the year.

Task

Claire Roberts sets up a business on 1 January by putting £1000 capital into the business bank account. (Assume a nil bank balance on 1 January.) Her projected income and expenditures are as follows:

Receipts:

- from clients January £3000, February £3400, March £3300, April £3500, May £3300, June £3800
- loan in February for £8000.

Payments:

- purchase of motor car March £7000
- salary £1000 per month
- raw materials £1200 per month paid in the month following
- loan repayment from February £250 per month
- loan interest £15 per month
- electricity £50 payable in March and June
- telephone £80 payable in May
- water rates £300 payable in June
- vehicle expenses £50 per month payable from month in which the car is purchased

- post £90 per month
- rent £1000 per annum payable quarterly.

Draw up the cash-flow forecast for the first six months.

Task

Robin Chilton sets up in business as a joiner on 1 January. His transactions are on a cash-only basis. He forecasts that the amount his business charges for work completed will be £8000 per month. VAT is to be charged on sales and is paid for raw materials and equipment only. He expects to pay £10 000 for equipment in January and £3500 for raw materials each month. Expenses include rent £100 each month, water rates £50 every 3 months, wages £2500 per month. VAT should be paid in April. Robin had £1350 in his bank account on 1 January. Prepare his cash-flow forecast.

Consequences of incorrect forecasting

It must be remembered that cash-flow forecasts are only forecasts and that the best-laid plans may go wrong. It may be useful for an organisation to be prudent about its forecasts so that it ensures that it will have sufficient liquidity to meet problems as and when they arise. These problems might be:

- *A shortage of working capital* As we saw in the previous chapter, working capital is important in order to keep the trade cycle operating. A business which does not have sufficient working capital will not be able to pay debts as and when they arise. This could lead to insolvency.
- *The inability to make plans work* If an organisation has used its forecasting for the planning process and the forecasts are inaccurate it may not be able to buy the machinery or other assets it requires.
- *The refusal by the business's bank to pay cheques to suppliers when bills are due for payment.* A loss of goodwill may result from suppliers and this could cause damage to the business's reputation.

Evidence indicators

For this activity you need to complete the capital budget, trading forecast and cash-flow forecast for a small business over a twelve month period. These need to be completed using a computer-generated spreadsheet. (Note: The great benefit of using a spreadsheet is that is is possible to consider 'what if' questions and then understand how various options relate to the forecast. For example, what if debtors pay a month later than expected? The computer will rewrite the calculations based upon such a change.) Please tick each of the following boxes when you have successfully completed them as part of your activity. You need to confirm that for this activity:

- I have produced a capital budget, trading forecast and cash-flow forecast for a small business.

- I have used a spreadsheet to compile these forecasts.
- I have supported each budget with an explanation which explains the rationale and significance of the figures.
- I have described the benefits an organisation may receive from using these forecasts, particularly in terms of raising finance.
- I have referred to the consequences of an inaccurate forecast in my analysis.

Profit and loss statements and balance sheets

In this chapter we will describe the outlines of a basic accounting system which would be suitable for a small business. We will then identify and explain accounting periods before showing how to extract a trial balance from a given set of accounting records. We will indicate how you can identify each account on the trial balance correctly in relation to profit and loss or balance sheet items. We will show how you can produce profit and loss and balance sheets in vertical form from the trial balance figures. Finally, we will explain the purposes of balance sheets and profit and loss statements.

A basic accounting system

A useful definition of accounting is: 'The art of preparing accounting reports from book-keeping records in accordance with acknowledged methods and conventions.' Let us look at the components of this definition:

1 *Book-keeping records* Traditionally records of accounts have been kept in books or ledgers. These records have been kept in a systematic way. (Today, of course, most book-keeping and accountancy procedures are carried out using computers – i.e. computerised accounting.)
2 *Preparing accounting reports* It is necessary to summarise the entries which appear in book-keeping records in such a way that they can be presented for analysis and examination. Accounting reports summarise the entries which have been made in the books.
3 *Acknowledged methods and conventions* There are set ways of recording accounts which have been acknowledged over a period of time. Records need to be set out to meet these methods and conventions. This is so that other people can look at these records, and comparisons can be made between one set of figures and another.

The accounting process therefore can be seen as consisting of two parts:

■ Developing and keeping an accurate, full and useful record of the business's financial activities (this part is normally referred to as book-keeping).

■ The interpretation of these records, i.e. the preparation of accounting reports.

There are a number of stages involved in putting together and keeping a basic accounting system:

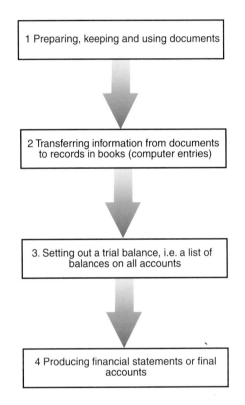

1 Preparing, keeping and using documents

2 Transferring information from documents to records in books (computer entries)

3. Setting out a trial balance, i.e. a list of balances on all accounts

4 Producing financial statements or final accounts

Documents

In Chapter 19 we examined a variety of documents which are used for the trading of goods, e.g. purchase documents, sales documents, payments and receipts documents.

These documents provide the basis for a book-keeping system. Book-keepers will transfer information from individual documents into accounting records.

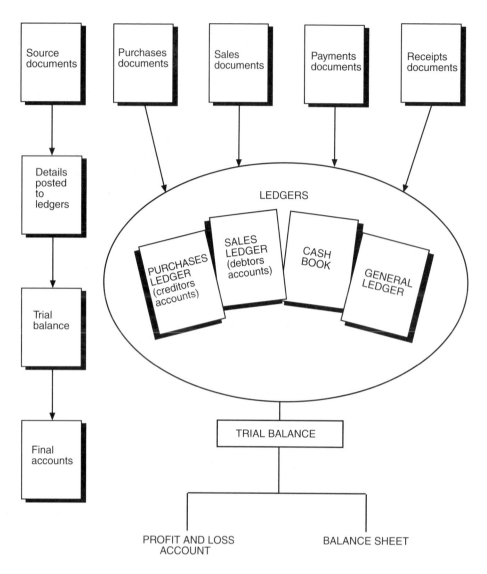

Accounting records

In this country accounting records have traditionally been kept in ledgers. We associate ledgers with clerks toiling long hours in dark and gloomy office conditions writing entries with quill pens into big musty books. Today this picture has long since disappeared and many accounts clerks work in bright and airy offices, with modern computers!

The ledgers are often referred to as the *books of prime entry* because this is the first place book-keeping records will be kept. Ledgers are subdivisions of the complete records kept by a company.

The *sales ledger* is used for making records of all the sale transactions carried out by a business. It contains

the accounts of debtors – customers to whom goods/services have been supplied on credit.

The *purchases ledger* is used for making records of all the purchase transactions carried out by a business. It contains the accounts of creditors – suppliers to whom the organisation owes money.

The *cash book* is a very useful record of all the cash and bank transactions of a business.

You can immediately see the value and simplicity of the cash book if you study the example shown below. The book is divided into two major columns, the left-hand side for receipts and the right for payments. You can then divide these columns into as many sections as you want. The entries below show some receipts in the first week in October 1996.

You can see cash entries being made for cash sales and money coming in from customers settling all or part of their accounts by cheque.

The entries below show some payments in the first week in October 1996.

You can see that the business bought £26.50 of stock from Sax Ltd by cheque on 1 October. On 2 October it paid its rents by cash. On 4 October it bought £10.00 worth of stationery by cheque.

At the end of each week, month, etc. we can quickly rule off the book and produce total figures for receipts and payments.

The *general* or *nominal ledger* is used for recording all the other records of a business, e.g.:

- An asset account records the business's assets such as machinery, fixtures and fittings, etc.
- An expenses account shows all the day-to-day expenses of running the business.
- An owner's capital account shows what the owner has put into the business.
- A drawings account shows moneys drawn out of the business by the owner or owners.

In ledgers, transactions are recorded using the *double-entry* system whereby, with each transaction, one account is debited and another is credited. This means that for every debit entry into one account there is always a corresponding credit entry into another account. Such a system assumes that all entries into an accounting system reflect a process of exchange. In other words, every transaction involves two parts which need to be recorded in the books of account. For example, if we buy equipment for cash we lose cash but gain equipment.

We would therefore record the loss in cash in a *cash account* and the gain of equipment in an *equipment account*. This dual element is carried through to the trial balance and then on to the final accounts (Figure 24.1).

The use of information technology has meant that today integrated software packages contain the books

Receipts

Date	Details	Bank	Cash	Cash	Credit	Other
Oct.	Bal b/f	100.00	160.00			
1	Till		50.00	50.00		
3	J. Brown	40.00			40.00	
5	Till		65.00	65.00		
	Total	140.00	275.00	115.00	40.00	0.00

Payments

Date	Details	Chq	Bank	Cash	Stock	Misc.	Overheads
Oct.							
1	Sax Ltd	36	26.50		26.50		
2	Rent			60.00			60.00
4	Stationery	37	10.00			10.00	
	Total		36.50	60.00	26.50	10.00	60.00

561

Sylvia buys a hairdryer for her hairdressing salon for £250

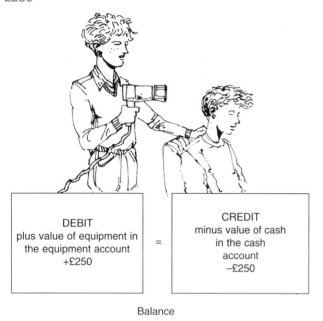

| DEBIT
plus value of equipment in the equipment account
+£250 | = | CREDIT
minus value of cash in the cash account
–£250 |

Balance

of first entry and these are linked to a system which updates all records whenever a transaction takes place.

Trial balance

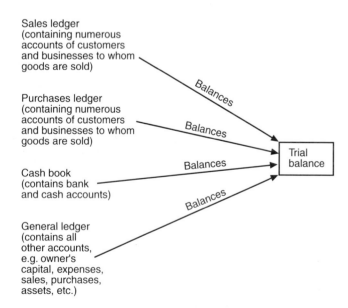

Sales ledger (containing numerous accounts of customers and businesses to whom goods are sold)

Purchases ledger (containing numerous accounts of customers and businesses to whom goods are sold)

Cash book (contains bank and cash accounts)

General ledger (contains all other accounts, e.g. owner's capital, expenses, sales, purchases, assets, etc.)

Balances

Balances

Balances

Balances

Trial balance

Figure 24.1 All balances transferred to trial balance

The trial balance is a list of all the accounts from all the ledgers. It should balance because for every debit entry into one account there should have been a corresponding credit entry into another. This list of balances provides the raw material for accountants to draw up the final accounts.

Financial statements or final accounts

Accountants provide valuable information to answer critical questions such as:

- How is the business doing?
- What sort of returns on investments will the owners receive?
- Can the business meet its short- and long-term debts?
- Is the business in a position to expand?
- How much taxation is the business liable to pay?
- What are the financial prospects of the business?

Much of the information that accountants provide appears in the form of final accounts. These are drawn up regularly by each organisation's auditors and are used to assess performance.

Final accounts are made up of the following three elements:

1. A trading account
2. A profit and loss account
3. A balance sheet.

We shall look at these elements later in this chapter.

First, however, you may find it useful to know more about different types of accountants.

Accountancy falls into two broad areas. *Financial accounting* involves fulfilling the legal requirements to keep books of account and prepare annual accounts for shareholders and the Inland Revenue. Limited companies must have their books audited by a qualified chartered or certified accountant to vouch that the accounts are a 'true and fair' view of the company's financial affairs. *Management accounting* provides detailed information about many aspects of a business and helps managers with decisions they have to make.

Accountants work in three main fields:

- In private practice accountants work for firms which provide a range of services to fee-paying clients. Such firms range from large international organisations to small practices with just one accountant.
- In industry and commerce accountants work in almost every organisation.

■ In public service, such as central and local government and the National Health Service, the work of accountants is fundamental to allocating resources efficiently.

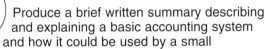

Evidence collection point

Produce a brief written summary describing and explaining a basic accounting system and how it could be used by a small business. You may find it helpful to interview a small business owner to find out how he or she records information from documents in the company's books and then into accounting records.

The summary may help you to provide evidence of the Core Skills of Application of Number and Communication.

Accounting periods

In setting out accounting records you need to be specific about the time period covered.

Monthly

Monthly records are very important for keeping an ongoing check on financial performance. Of course, today it is far easier to provide financial information on a monthly basis because of the use of computer spreadsheets which enable data to be rapidly stored and sorted. For example, records of purchases and sales can be inputted instantly and accounts updated. Thus trial balances can be generated straight away. It is relatively easy to produce a cash-flow chart and profit and loss account on a monthly basis. It is very important to keep monthly records in order to have a view of such things as how solvent a business is, i.e. whether at a given moment in time it is able to meet outstanding short-term debts.

Quarterly

It is also common practice to produce quarterly records of financial information, i.e. every three months. Records will be presented for the first quarter, second quarter, third quarter and fourth quarter of the year. It is then possible to check one quarter against the next. One can also check the position, say, in the first quarter of the year (January–March) against the first quarters in previous years.

Annual

Annual records give a good view of business performance over the longer term. For example, the annual balance sheet is regarded as a highly important accounting record summarising the balances from a company's liabilities and assets accounts. Businesses will produce forecast balance sheets predicting what their balance sheets will look like over the next one, two or three years. Forecast annual information can then be compared with the actual results.

Every year a company will produce an annual report containing the balance sheet and profit and loss account for that year's trading. These final accounts can then be compared with previous years in order to have a clear view of how the business is progressing.

Evidence collection point

Study accounting information that is available to you, e.g. trial balances, profit and loss accounts, balance sheets, etc. Identify the time period covered by each set. Explain why this information has been produced for the given time period (month, quarter, year, etc.).

Producing a trial balance

At the end of an accounting period, either annually, quarterly or monthly, accounts are balanced. These balances are then listed in a trial balance. The trial balance lists all the balances from all the accounts in all the ledgers.

The trial balance is *not* part of the system of double-entry. It does, however, provide a useful mechanism for checking the accuracy of accounting entries and also provides a list of balances which can then be used to prepare the final accounts.

As we have seen, ledger accounts have either debit balances or credit balances. The trial balance must be constructed in a way which takes these two types of balances into account. Given that each transaction involves part of a transaction being recorded as a debit and the other parts as a credit, it will follow that when all the accounts are listed together, the total of the debits must equal the total of the credits.

563

Example

Trial balance of Rebecca Snowden as at 31 December 1995

	Dr £	Cr £
Purchases	15 000	
Sales		45 000
Stock 1 January 1995	8 500	
Wages	4 500	
Interest paid	3 200	
Travel expenses	4 000	
Light and heating	3 500	
Advertising	2 500	
Premises	50 000	
Motor vehicles	15 000	
Plant and machinery	25 000	
Debtors	14 000	
Bank	8 000	
Cash	2 000	
Creditors		17 000
Drawings	10 000	
Bank loan		30 000
Capital		73 200
	165 200	165 200

The total of the debit and credit columns is the same. (Note: the trial balance will help to detect only certain types of error – for example, where the debit entry has been made into one ledger account and the credit entry has not been made into another.) It must not always be assumed the because the trial balance balances, it is always correct. For example, one error which would not be detected would be if an invoice was misread so that £5000 was transferred to two accounts instead of £50 000.

We have not numbered each of the accounts. It would be normal practice to have a folio reference number for each account so that entries can be traced.

Another way of presenting a trial balance is to list entries in a *single column*. When this is done, debit entries are added and credit entries – which are shown in brackets – are deducted. The balance at the bottom of the trial balance should then be zero.

Example of a single-column trial balance

Trial balance of Rebecca Snowden as at 31 December 1995

	£
Purchases	15 000
Sales	(45 000)
Stock 1 January 1995	8 500
Wages	4 500
Interest paid	3 200
Travel expenses	4 000
Light and heating	3 500
Advertising	2 500
Premises	50 000
Motor vehicles	15 000
Plant and machinery	25 000
Debtors	14 000
Bank	8 000
Cash	2 000
Creditors	(17 000)
Drawings	10 000
Bank loan	(30 000)
Capital	(73 200)
	zero

Task

1 The following balances have been extracted from the books of R. James as at 31 December 1995. Use them to construct both a single-column and double-column trial balance.

	£
Purchases	12 400
Sales	65 700
Stock 1 January 1995	7 100
Salaries	14 400
Wages	2 500
Interest paid	3 200
Rent paid	4 000
Light and heating	3 500
Land and buildings	45 000
Machinery	14 000
Motor vehicles	8 000
Debtors	18 000
Bank	7 500
Cash	2 000
Creditors	18 400
Drawings	8 000
Bank loan	15 000
Capital	50 500

2 The following balances have been extracted from the books of A. Jenkinson as at 31 December 1995. Use them to construct both a single-column and double-column trial balance. (Note: use 'Capital' to balance both trial balances.)

	£
Bank	4 100
Premises	8 400
Fixtures	4 000
Bank loan	6 000
Wages	5 000
Advertising	6 000
Rent paid	5 000
Cash	3 000
Debtors	14 000
Creditors	4 000
Purchases	6 000
Sales	18 000
Stock 1 January 1995	4 000
Drawings	5 000
Capital	X XXX

Relating accounts in the trial balance to profit and loss or balance sheets items

All entries into the trial balance form the basis upon which entries can be made into the final accounts – for example, the profit and loss account and the balance sheet. Each entry into the trial balance will then appear once in one of the final accounts.

One way of relating accounts in the trial balance to final accounts is to use a simple extended trial balance. To do this we will refer again to the trial balance of Rebecca Snowden.

1 The trial balance includes a stock valuation for the beginning of the year. At the end of the year the stock is again valued and this figure appears in the trading account as a credit entry and the balance sheet as an asset.
2 Gross profit is the difference between debit and credit entries in the trading account. It also appears as a credit entry in the profit and loss account.
3 Gross profit less overheads equals the net profit. This is a debit entry in the profit and loss account. Net profit also appears under liabilities and capital in the balance sheet.

Task

Look at the previous tasks concerning R. James and A. Jenkinson. Prepare an extended trial balance for each, taking into account a closing stock figure on 31 December 1995 of £6500 for R. James and £5400 for A. Jenkinson.

The profit and loss account

The basic financial statements of a sole trader include:

- a trading account
- a profit and loss account
- a balance sheet.

Sales, cost of sales, gross profit

The trading account can be likened to a video giving ongoing pictures of an organisation's trading activities. For many businesses trading involves

Extended trial balance of Rebecca Snowden

Entry	Trial balance as at 31/12/95		Trading account for period ended 31/12/95		Profit and loss account for period ended 31/12/95		Balance sheet as at 31/12/95	
	Dr	Cr	Dr	Cr	Dr	Cr	Assets	Liabilities and capital
	£	£	£	£	£	£	£	£
Purchases	15 000		15 000					
Sales		45 000		45 000				
Stock 1 January 1995	8 500		8 500					
Wages	4 500				4 500			
Interest paid	3 200				3 200			
Travel expenses	4 000				4 000			
Light and heating	3 500				3 500			
Advertising	2 500				2 500			
Premises	50 000						50 000	
Motor vehicles	15 000						15 000	
Plant & machinery	25 000						25 000	
Debtors	14 000						14 000	
Bank	8 000						8 000	
Cash	2 000						2 000	
Creditors		17 000						17 000
Drawings	10 000						10 000	
Bank loan		30 000						30 000
Capital		73 200						73 200
	165 200	165 200						
Stock 31 December 1995			5 000				5 000	
Gross profit			26 500			26 500		
Net profit					8 800			8 800
			50 000	50 000	26 500	26 500	129 000	129 000

buying and selling stock. The difference between the value of the stock sold (sales) and the cost of producing those sales – which is the production costs of manufactured goods for a manufacturing company, or the cost of purchasing the supplies for a trading company – is known as the gross profit. The trading account simply shows how gross profit is arrived at:

> Sales minus cost of sales = gross profit

'Cost of sales' has to take into account the value of stocks.

'Opening stocks' is effectively a purchase as these will be sold in the current trading period. On the other hand, 'closing stocks' must be deducted from purchases as these will be sold next year. The true cost of sales is therefore found by applying the formula:

Cost of sales = opening stocks *plus* purchases *less* closing stocks

Overheads, net profits

The profit and loss account may be drawn up beneath the trading account and covers the same period of trading. The gross profit figure from the trading account becomes the starting point for the profit and loss account.

Some organisations receive income from sources other than sales. There may be rents received, profits on the sale of assets, etc. As these are extra income they are added to the gross profit.

In addition, every organisation incurs expenses and a range of overheads, and these are deducted to show the true net profit of the business. The expenses might include:

- rent of premises
- gas
- electricity
- stationery
- cleaning costs
- insurances
- business rates

- depreciation
- bad debts
- interest on loans
- advertising costs
- sundry expenses
- motor expenses
- accountancy and legal fees.

Figure 24.2 shows how the final account might look. The part of the account up to and including the gross profit is the trading account, while the remainder is the profit and loss account. Net profit is the final profit in the business and will belong to the owner.

Net profit = gross profit *plus* income from other sources *less* expenses

	(£)	(£)
Sales		27 500
Less cost of sales:		
Opening stock	9 000	
Add purchases	15 000	
	24 000	
Less closing stock	3 750	
		20 250
Gross profit		7 250
Add other income:		
Profit on sale of plant		2 000
		9 250
Less expenses:		
Electricity	510	
Stationery	125	
Business rate	756	
Interest on loans	159	
Advertising	745	
Depreciation of motor vehicles	1000	
Insurances	545	
Sundry expenses	124	
		3 964
Net profit		5 286

Figure 24.2 Trading and profit and loss account of E. Blyton for year ended 31 May 19X1

Most sole traders employ an accountant to draw up their accounts. Nevertheless, whoever prepares them, it is the sole trader who remains responsible for their accuracy and for correctly declaring the amount of the profits. The tax authorities will need to be satisfied that the accounts supplied to them represent the true results of the business.

It is essential to keep full and accurate records from the start of the business. Well-kept books make the preparation of the annual accounts easier, and save the accountant's time (so keeping down the fee charged).

Evidence collection point

A sole trader has come to you for help. During 1995 she has kept her ledgers accurately and has been able to extract the following figures for the year. However, she is not sure how to present them in the form of a profit and loss account.

Set out the details in a clear trading and profit and loss account.

	£
Closing stock	64 000
Opening stock	45 000
Purchases	20 000
Sales	92 000
Rent	2 000
Insurance	500
Wages	32 000

Task

A business sells £100 000 worth of goods during 1996. Its stock at the beginning of the year is worth £10 000. During the year it makes a purchases worth £50 000 and its stock at the end of the year is worth £20 000. It has three main expenses: rent of £5000, rates of £5000 and advertising costing £10 000. Show a trading/profit and loss account for the year ended 31 December 1996. Your work should show evidence of Core Skills in Application of Number.

Balance sheets

Whereas the trading account gives an ongoing picture, a balance sheet is a snapshot of what an organisation owns and owes on a particular date. It is a clear statement of the assets, liabilities and capital of a business at a particular moment in time (normally the end of an accounting period, e.g. quarter, year, etc.).

Looking at the balance sheet can thus provide valuable information because it summarises a business's financial position at that instant in time.

The balance sheet does balance simply because the accounts record every transaction twice. For example, if you give me £100 we can say that:

■ I owe you £100 (a liability or debt)
■ I now have £100 (an asset, something I own).

Look at Figure 24.3. Does it seem odd to you that 'capital' is owed by the organisation? This will become clear as you read on.

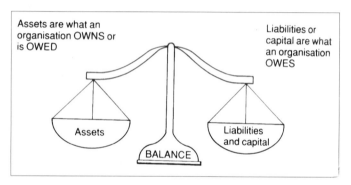

Figure 24.3 Assets equals capital plus liabilities

At the end of a trading period a business will have a number of assets and liabilities. Some of these will be for short periods of time while others will be for longer periods. Whatever the nature of the individual assets and liabilities, the balance sheet will balance.

Task

Make lists of six probable assets and six probable liabilities of a small corner-shop. Do the same for a public house.

Every balance sheet has a heading which contains the name of the organisation and the date at which the snapshot is taken. You will find it helpful to refer to Figure 24.4 as you read this section.

	(£)	(£)
Fixed assets		
Land and buildings		80 000
Machinery		13 200
Motor vehicles		8 700
		101 900
Current assets		
Stocks	9 700	
Debtors	3 750	
Bank	2 100	
Cash	970	
	16 520	
Less **Current liabilities**		
Creditors	9 000	
WORKING CAPITAL		7 520
		109 420
Less **Long-term liabilities**		
Bank loan	9 000	
Mortgage	30 000	
		39 000
		70 420
Financed by:		
Capital		70 000
Add net profit		5 286
		75 286
Less drawings		4 866
		70 420

18052

Figure 24.4 Balance sheet of E. Blyton at 31 May 19X1

Assets

The assets side of the balance sheet is normally set out in what is called an *inverse order of liquidity*. This means that items which may be difficult to convert into cash quickly and are therefore liquid appear at the top of the list of assets. By looking down the order it is possible to gauge the ease with which successive assets can be converted to cash, until we come to the most liquid asset of all, cash itself.

Evidence collection point

Explain what the term 'asset' means.

A small bakery has the following assets. Try to put them into an inverse order of liquidity with the most liquid at the top and the most liquid at the bottom:

- cash in the tills
- bread in the shops
- a bakery van
- the baker's oven
- supplies of flour
- money in the bakery's bank account
- money owed to the bakery by firms
- the baker's premises.

Assets can be divided into *fixed* and *current*. Fixed assets tend to have a life-span of more than one year. They comprise items that are purchased and generally kept for a long period of time. Examples of fixed assets are premises, machinery and motor vehicles. When a business buys fixed assets it does so by incurring capital expenditure.

Current assets

Current assets are sometimes called 'circulating assets' because the form they take is constantly changing. Examples of current assets are stocks, debtors, money in the bank, and cash in hand.

A manufacturing business holds stocks of finished goods in readiness to satisfy the demands of the market. When a credit transaction takes place, stocks are reduced and the business gains debtors. These debtors have bought goods on credit and therefore owe the business money; after a reasonable credit period payment will be expected. Payments will have to be made on further stocks, so that the business has a cash cycle. 'Cash' or 'bank' changes to 'stock', then to 'debtors', back to 'cash' or 'bank' and then to 'stock' again (Figure 24.5.)

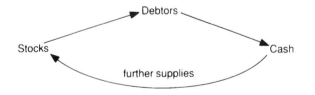

Figure 24.5 The cash cycle

Evidence collection point

Identify (with reasons) which of the following items should be considered as a current asset of a newsagent:

- the fixtures and fittings of the shop
- cash in the tills

- money in the bank
- money owed by the newsagent to the suppliers
- money owed by customers for newspaper bills
- the delivery bicycle
- stocks of newspapers in the shops.

Current liabilities

Current liabilities are debts which a business needs to repay within a short period of time (normally a year). These liabilities include creditors, who are suppliers of goods on credit for which the business has been invoiced but has not yet paid. They may also include a bank overdraft which is arranged up to a limit over a time period and is, technically, repayable on demand. Other current liabilities may include any short-term loans and any taxes owed.

The balance sheet is set out so as to show working capital because this is always an important calculation for an organisation. The working capital is the current assets less the current liabilities.

The working capital ratio is the ratio of current assets to current liabilities:

> Working capital ratio = current assets:current liabilities

It is important for an organisation to maintain a sensible ratio. The level of ratio depends on the type of business, and the likelihood that funds will be required quickly to meet liabilities (e.g. creditors demanding repayment quickly). For most businesses a ratio of 2:1 is regarded as a sign of careful management, but some businesses have lower ratios.

Working capital is important because it provides a buffer to 'keep the wolf from the door'. Many businesses have suffered the consequences of having too many of their assets tied up in liquid assets.

Long-term liabilities and owner's capital

A long-term liability is sometimes called a *deferred liability* as it is not due for payment until some time in the future. By convention, in a set of accounts this means longer than one year. Examples for a sole trader could include a bank loan or a mortgage.

Capital is provided by the owner of the business and is therefore deemed to be owed to the owner by the business. The balance sheet keeps an updated record of the amount owed by the business to the owner.

569

During a year's trading the owner's capital may be increased by the inflows of profits (profits for the period) and decreased by outflows of drawings (money or other assets taken out of the business for personal use). Having taken these into consideration, a new capital figure is calculated at the end of the year. So the balance sheet shows how the capital has increased (or decreased) since the last balance sheet was prepared.

Producing profit and loss and balance sheets from the trial balance figures

The trial balance is a list of balances extracted from the ledger. Entries to the ledger are supported by source documentation (i.e. documents such as purchase and sales documents).

Accountants make use of the trial balance to prepare the final accounts. The trial balance contains a list of all the business's accounts. Accounts will have either a debit balance or a credit balance. Debit balances will generally comprise the assets of the business, expenses and the totals of purchases and costs. Credit balances will comprise any liabilities such as capital and creditors as well as the income from sales.

Each item in the trial balance will appear once in the final accounts. It is useful to tick each item in pencil as it is entered, so that none is missed. The closing stocks figure taken at the year end is not listed in the trial balance but is shown as a note underneath the balance. The closing stocks will appear twice, once in the trading account and then again in the current assets in the balance sheet.

Evidence collection point

From the following trial balance of J.O. Nory draw up her trading/profit and loss account for the year ended 31 December 1997, together with her balance sheet at that date. The closing stocks at 31 December 1997 were valued at £10 300.

	(£)	(£)
Stock @ 1 Jan 1997	12 700	
Sales		81 250
Purchases	18 325	
Electricity	1 451	
Stationery	1 526	
Business rate	1 845	
Loan interest	3 955	
Advertising	2 150	
Sundry expenses	1 205	
Land and buildings	161 000	
Machinery	4 900	
Motor vehicles	18 300	
Debtors	12 100	
Bank	4 250	
Cash	325	
Bank loan		10 000
Mortgage		20 000
Creditors		4 300
Drawings	9 350	
Capital @ 1 Jan 1997		137 832
	253 382	253 382

In this element we have considered the account of only a sole trader. If you wish to look further at the accounts of other types of organisations you may wish to work through the following section.

Final accounts of a limited company

It will help our understanding of the accounts of a limited company if we first go over some of the essential features of this type of organisation. As we have already seen in earlier chapters, in limited companies:

- the company has a legal identity separate from that of its owners
- the owners are known as shareholders
- shareholders have limited liability
- management is delegated to a board of directors, who may or may not be shareholders
- corporation tax must be paid on profits made.

Companies must comply with the Companies Acts, and the Companies Registration Office controls their formation. There are two types of limited companies:

- public, which have their shares traded on the Stock Exchange, and
- private, for which there are restrictions on the trading in their shares.

To set up a limited company it is necessary to go through a number of legal procedures. This mainly involves the presentation of various documents to the Registrar of Companies. All limited companies must produce a Memorandum of Association and Articles of Association to receive a Certification of Incorporation.

The Memorandum spells out the nature of the company when viewed from the outside. Someone reading the Memorandum should be able to gain a general idea of what the company is and the business with which it is concerned. The Memorandum sets out:

- the name of the company
- its address
- its objectives (i.e. what types of activities it will engage in)
- its capital.

The Articles spell out the rules which govern the inside working of the company. In particular they set out the details of how accounts will be kept and recorded.

Once a private company has lodged these documents with the Registrar and had them accepted it can start to trade. The Certificate of Incorporation sets up the company as a legal body *in its own right*. The company (not the individual shareholders) enters into contracts and can sue or be sued in a court of law.

A public company, however, must take further steps before being granted a Certificate. A Prospectus has to be issued and shares have to be allotted.

One clause of the Memorandum of Association states the share capital of the company and indicates how it is to be divided into separate shares. Authorised share capital is the amount the shareholders have authorised the directors to issue. Issued share capital is the amount that has actually been issued by the directors.

There are a number of types of shares. For example, there are ordinary shares, for which dividends are normally expressed as a percentage of the nominal value of the shares or as a monetary value per share. There may be preference shares, which carry a preferential right to receive a dividend. Companies can also issue debentures, which are split into units in the same way as shares; they are in effect loans made to the company and secured by specific assets of the company.

The trading/profit and loss accounts

The **trading account** of a limited company is similar to the trading account of any other type of organisation. However, in the profit and loss account:

- directors' fees or salaries may be included, because these people are employed by the company and their fees and salaries are an expense

- debenture payments, being the same as loan interest, also appear as an expense.

The appropriation account

Beneath the profit and loss account of a company will appear the **appropriation account**. This is designed to show what happens to any profit and how it is divided.

Corporation tax is the first charge on profits and has to be paid to the Inland Revenue. For example, the tax rate was 33 per cent for the tax year 1991/92 for company profits over £1 250 000. Shareholder dividends are the portion of the profits paid to shareholders.

Reserves are the portion of the profit which the directors and the shareholders prefer not to distribute as dividends. This money is set aside for another purpose.

Any profit left over at the end of the year, after taxes and shareholders of all kinds have been paid, is added to the balance of profit from the previous year, to give the new retained profit.

> Balance of profit at end of year = net profit from this year *plus* retained profits from previous years *less* corporation tax *less* dividends *less* transfer to reserves

An example of an appropriation account for a company with a net profit of £250 000 is shown in Figure 24.6.

	(£)	(£)
Net profit		250 000
Less Corporation Tax		100 000
Profit after taxation		150 000
Less proposed dividends:		
Ordinary shares	70 000	
Preference shares	20 000	90 000
		60 000
Less transfer to General Reserve		40 000
		20 000
Add retained profit from previous year		30 000
Balance of retained profit		50 000

Figure 24.6 An appropriation account

Task

Workhard Ltd has just announced a net profit of £300 000. Prepare the appropriation account from the following details:

a The taxation rate is at 25%.
b There are 500 000 ordinary shares of £1 each, fully paid. A dividend of 10 per cent is proposed.
c There are 300 000 10% preference shares of £1 each, fully paid. The 10% dividend is to be paid.
d £50 000 is to be transferred to General Reserve.
e Retained profit from the previous year was £125 000.

The balance sheet

In the **balance sheet** of a company the fixed and current assets are presented in the same way as in any other balance sheet.

The current liabilities are the liabilities due to be paid within 12 months of the date of the balance sheet. In addition to those which normally appear in this section, limited companies also have to show the Corporation Tax which is due to be paid during the next twelve months, as well as the ordinary and preference share dividends due to be paid. Long-term liabilities may include debenture payments.

At the beginning of the 'Financed by:' section of the balance sheet, details will appear of the authorised capital, specifying the type, value and number of shares that the company is authorised to issue. These are in the balance sheet for interest only and their value is excluded from the totals. The item on issued share capital contains details of the classes and numbers of shares that *have* been issued (obviously the issued share capital cannot exceed the authorised).

Reserves are shown beneath the capital. Reserves and retained profits are the amounts the directors and shareholders decide to keep within the company.

Example

From the trial balance of Wargrave Ltd and the notes below, we can prepare the trading account, the profit and loss account, the appropriation account and the balance sheet for the year ended 31 December 19X2:

Notes:

- The closing stock is £12 250.
- Corporation Tax is charged at 25% of profits.
- There will be a 6% dividend on ordinary shares.
- The 10% preference share dividend is to be paid.
- £2000 is to be allocated to the General Reserve.
- Authorised share capital is 400 000 ordinary shares of £1 each and 100 000 10% preference shares of £1 each.

	(£)	(£)
Stock @ 1 Jan 19X3	21 300	
Sales		118 100
Purchases	35 000	
Electricity	8 000	
Stationery	5 000	
Business rate	1 300	
Loan interest paid	1 000	
Debenture interest paid	800	
Advertising	3 200	
Sundry expenses	1 350	
Directors' salaries	12 000	
Land and buildings	320 000	
Machinery	24 000	
Motor vehicles	12 000	
Debtors	7 100	
Bank	23 200	
Cash	500	
Bank loan		10 000
10% debentures		8 000
Creditors		500
General Reserve		4 000
Retained profit @ 31 Dec 19X2		35 150
Issued share capital:		
200 000 ordinary £1 shares		200 000
100 000 10% £1 preference shares		100 000
	475 750	475 750

The accounts and balance sheet based on this data are shown in Figures 24.7 and 24.8. Relate each item to its corresponding entry.

	(£)	(£)	(£)
Fixed assets			
Land and buildings			320 000
Machinery			24 000
Motor vehicles			12 000
			356 000
Current assets			
Stocks		12 250	
Debtors		7 100	
Bank		23 200	
Cash		500	
		43 050	
Less **Current liabilities**			
Creditors	500		
Proposed dividends:			
Ordinary shares	12 000		
Preference shares	10 000		
Corporation Tax	10 350	32 850	
Working capital			10 200
			366 200
Less **Long-term liabilities**			
Bank loan		10 000	
10% debentures		8 000	
			18 000
			348 200
FINANCED BY:			
Authorised share capital			
400 000 ordinary shares of £1			400 000
100 000 10% preference shares of £1			100 000
			500 000
Issued share capital			
200 000 ordinary shares of £1 fully paid			200 000
100 000 10% preference shares of £1 fully paid			100 000
			300 000
Reserves			
General Reserve		6 000	
Balance of retained profit		42 200	
			48 200
			348 200

Figure 24.7 Balance sheet of Wargrave Ltd for the year ended 31 December 19X2

	(£)	(£)
Sales		118 100
Less cost of sales:		
Opening stock	21 300	
Add purchases	35 000	
	56 300	
Less closing stock	12 250	
		44 050
		74 050
Gross profit		
Less expenses:		
Electricity	8 000	
Stationery	5 000	
Business rate	1 300	
Loan interest paid	1 000	
Debenture interest paid	800	
Advertising	3 200	
Sundry expenses	1 350	
Directors' salaries	12 000	
		32 650
Net profit		41 400
Less Corporation Tax		10 350
Profit after tax		31 050
Less proposed dividends:		
Ordinary shares	12 000	
Preference shares	10 000	22 000
		9 050
Less transfer to General Reserve		2 000
		7 050
Add retained profit from previous year		35 150
Balance of retained profit		42 200

Figure 24.8 Trading, profit and loss and appropriation account of Wargrave Ltd for the year ended 31 December 19X2

Task

From the following trial balance of Twyford Ltd and the attached notes, prepare the trading account, profit and loss account, appropriation account and balance sheet for the year ended 31 December 19X2.

	(£)	(£)
Stock @ 1 Jan 19X2	7 300	
Sales		123 400
Purchases	12 500	
Electricity	4 100	
Advertising	3 200	
Business rate	800	
Salaries	16 000	
Directors' salaries	18 000	
Loan interest paid	4 400	
Debenture interest paid	1 000	
Land and buildings	124 000	
Motor vehicles	16 000	
Debtors	7 000	
Bank	15 000	
Cash	1 000	
Bank loan		25 000
10% debentures		10 000
Creditors		4 000
General Reserve		3 000
Retained profit @ 31 Dec 19X1		4 900
Issued share capital:		
50 000 ordinary shares (£1)		50 000
10 000 pref. shares (£1)		10 000
	230 300	230 300

You have been informed that:

- The closing stock has been valued at £3400.
- Corporation Tax will be charged at 25% of profits.
- The 10% share dividends are to be paid.
- £3000 is to be allocated to the General Reserve.
- Authorised share capital is the same as issued share capital.

Statements of cash flow

The profit and loss account provides information which matches sales and costs, and a balance sheet is a static statement showing a business's financial position. Neither of these shows how a business has *used* its funds and cash.

In 1975 the tenth Statement of Standard Accounting Practice (SSAP) was issued which required a business with an annual turnover of £25 000 or more to provide a statement to fill this gap, as part of its final accounts. This was called a **funds flow statement**.

Funds flow statements were prepared through a process of comparison. If a company's balance sheets for two successive years were listed alongside each other, then clearly the changes during the year could be seen. Differences between the two years were then listed and grouped together either as sources or as applications of funds.

Sources of funds included profits, new loans, share issues and profits on the sale of assets. Applications of funds included purchase of fixed assets, tax paid, dividends paid, and loans repaid.

	(£)	(£)	(£)
	31 Dec 19X0	31 Dec 19X1	Comparison
Premises	3 000	3 000	0
Stocks	8 000	10 000	+2 000
Bank	3 000	3 000	0
	14 000	16 000	
Capital	14 000	14 000	0
Creditors	–	2 000	+2 000
	14 000	16 000	

Figure 24.9 Two balance sheets for B. Regis

The example in Figure 24.10 shows how an increase in stocks could have been financed. Clearly this increase in stocks has been financed through the credit provided by suppliers, and this fact is shown in the form of a statement (Figure 24.10).

Sources of funds – creditors	£2000
Application of funds – increasing stocks	£2000

Figure 24.10 Funds flow statement for B. Regis

Another way of presenting this sort of statement was to have a section which analysed *working capital changes*. The reason for this was to enable managers to exert a firmer grip upon these changes. The change in working capital between the two balance sheets would then equal the difference between the sources and applications of funds. This is illustrated in Figure 24.11.

```
Balance sheets
                          (£)        (£)        (£)
                        31 Dec     31 Dec    Comparison
                         19X0       19X1

Fixed assets             450        550        +100
Long-term investments    500        450         -50
Current assets less
  current liabilities    150        200         +50
                        ─────      ─────
                        1 100      1 200

Capital                  360        400         +40
Profits                  300        500        +200
Loans                    440        300        -140
                        ─────      ─────
                        1 100      1 200


Funds flow statement
                                    (£)        (£)

Sources of funds:
 Capital                             40
 Profits                            200
 Sale of investments                 50        290
Application of funds:
 Fixed assets                       100
 Loan repayments                    140        240

Increase in working capital                     50
```

Figure 24.11 Balance sheets and funds flow statement for H. O. Gate

```
                                           (£m)      (£m)
Net cash inflow from operating
activities                                            6

Returns on investment and servicing
of finance
  Interest received                          2
  Interest paid                             (4)
  Dividends paid                            (4)
Net cash outflow from returns on
investment and servicing of finance                  (6)

Taxation
  UK corporation tax paid                            (4)

Investing activities
  Purchases of tangible fixed assets       (4)
  Purchase of subsidiary undertakings
    (net of cash and cash equivalents
     acquired)                            (18)
  Sale of plant and machinery               4
Net cash outflow from investing activities          (18)
Net cash outflow before financing                   (22)

Financing
  New secured loan repayable in 1995       17
  Repayment of amounts borrowed            (2)
Net cash inflow from financing                       15
Decrease in cash and cash equivalents                 7
```

Figure 24.12 A cash flow statement for the year ended 31 March 19X2

The new way: cash flow statements

As we saw in Chapter 11, in 1990 the Accounting Standards Board took over from the Accounting Standards Committee and this heralded a new era in accounting standard-setting. All accounting standards (SSAPs) now come under the authority of the ASB and are to be subject to scrutiny and change.

In September 1991 the ASB set out the first Financial Reporting Standard (FRS1) on cash flow statements. The standard supersedes SSAP10 on sources and applications of funds, discussed above. The new standard FRS1 will change the nature of the third statement in a company's accounts. The aim is for the cash flow statement to be viewed as just as important as the balance sheet and the profit and loss account.

The problems with funds flow statements were that:

- companies drew up their statements in different ways
- they were difficult to use to compare one business with another
- they looked at funds or profit rather than at cash
- the meaning of funds was not very clear.

The new cash flow statements focus on something which all business managers can identify with – the need for a steady cash flow. Figure 24.12 shows an example. The bottom line is the change in what is called 'cash and equivalents'. The cash flow statement explains the movement by placing all cash flows into five categories. Note that in this example we have adopted the more usual convention of putting outflows of cash in parentheses, rather than using a minus sign as we have been doing. Further information is given in notes, in particular a reconciliation of operating profit to operating cash flow.

The idea is that a user can see at a glance the extent to which, for example, cash flow from operations has or has not paid for dividends, tax and new investments, or the extent to which those items had to be financed by the raising of new capital. The statement should expose more quickly than before those companies that are not generating cash – even though they may be reporting profits.

The statement in Figure 24.12 shows that:

- the operations provided cash inflow of only £6 million
- £6 million was used up in dividends and interest
- £4 million was used up in paying tax
- £18 million was used up in new investment
- the cash balance *decreased* by £7 million
- to make all of this possible, £15 million had to be obtained by way of new finance.

It is clear immediately from the example that the operations were not even supporting the dividends and the tax payment. The company is using up cash without even considering further investment. This is exactly the kind of thing a cash flow statement is intended to bring out. This sort of information should help to provide readers of accounts with clearer warnings of business failures.

Task

If you were an investor in a company, what sort of information would you require about your investment? Make a list.

Case study – King cash

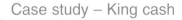

SSAP10 on sources and applications of funds has formed an integral part of final accounts for all but the very smallest of businesses for many years. However, today it is replaced by a cash flow statement. The change has been:

- to improve the *quality* of information provided in published accounts
- to bring the UK accounting procedures into line with international practices.

The monitoring of cash flow is probably the most significant aspect of the successful operation of any organisation. It is one thing to have a 'theoretical' profit reported in the profit and loss account, but another matter – and probably more important – to have the

physical resources available to meet payments to short-term creditors.

This need for businesses to have short-term liquidity and long-term profitability is illustrated by today's emphasis upon cash flow. Particularly in times of recession many firms strive to report a book profit figure but ignore the need to meet short-term creditors.

Many criticisms have been levelled at funds flow statements over recent years. These concentrated upon funds as movements in working capital at the expense of examining in more detail general changes in funds. Also, their format and content varied considerably between companies and this caused difficulty with interpretation and comparison. Cash flow statements will provide more information on the connection between liquidity and profitability. They will also actually record the cash flow generated by an organisation over its financial year. Cash flow statements will therefore assist in emphasising to investors the risks they are undertaking.

FRS1 should now be adopted by all organisations as their standard in respect of financial statements relating to reporting periods on or after 23 March 1992. SSAP10 was withdrawn as of that date.

1 Why is it important to improve the quality of information in published accounts?
2 Why is it necessary to bring UK accounting practices into line with international practices?
3 Explain the difference between profit and cash.
4 What might happen if a business fails to pay creditors?
5 Write a short report explaining why cash flow statements will improve the quality of final accounts.

The final accounts of other types of organisations

So far in this chapter we have looked at the final accounts of two types of business organisation, the sole trader and the limited company. These are not the only types of business organisation and each of the other different types will also be required to produce a series of financial statements.

Partnership statements

In seeking to develop their businesses further, many sole traders take in partners. An ordinary partnership can have between two and 20 partners.

Normally a **partnership agreement** will be established which will contain the following guidelines:

- details of profit sharing (for example, 75% to one partner and 25% to the other)
- whether interest is to be paid on the capital each partner has invested in the partnership and the rate at which it is to be paid (for example, the partnership might pay partners 10% upon the amount of capital which each partner has invested)
- whether interest is to be charged on the drawings and the rate at which it is to be charged (for example, partners might be charged at 5% on the amount of drawings they make during the year).

Alternatively the members of the partnership may wish to cement their agreement in accordance with the Partnership Act of 1980.

This defines a partnership as:

'the relation which subsists between persons carrying on in business in common with a view of profit.'

The Partnership Act has the following rules:

- profits and losses should be shared equally between partners
- no partner should receive a salary
- partners are not entitled to receive interest on their capital
- interest is not to be charged on partners' drawings
- if a partner contributes more capital than agreed, he or she can receive interest at 5% per annum on the excess.

There are **two** main differences between the financial statements of a partnership and those of sole trader. These are:

1 After the profit and loss account an appropriation section appears which divides the profit between partners.
2 In the balance sheet, the capital section shows each of the partners' capital and current account balances.

Example

In the business of Smith and Jones, interest on drawings is charged at 10%. At the start of the year Smith draws £10 000 and Jones draws £20 000. Smith has a salary of £4000 per annum and 10% interest is paid on partners' capitals.

Smith has a capital of £30 000 invested with the business and Jones has a capital of £20 000 invested with the business. When they come to divide profits

	(£)	(£)
Net profit		18 000
Add interest on partners' drawings:		
Smith	1000	
Jones	2000	3000
		21 000
Appropriation of profits		
Salary: Smith		4000
Interest on partners' capitals:		
Smith	3000	
Jones	2000	5000
Share of residue:		
Smith (60%)	7200	
Jones (40%)	4800	12 000
		21 000

Figure 24.13 Appropriation account of Smith and Jones

their partnership agreement determines that 60% are to go to Smith and 40% to Jones. Their net profit for the current year is £18 000. Their appropriation account will therefore appear as shown Figure 24.13.

Task

During the current year Black and White have made a net profit of £27 000. Interest on drawings is charged at 5% and over the year Black has made drawings of £8500 and White has drawn £7000 from the business.

White has a salary of £9000 and 10% interest is to be paid on partners' capitals. Black has a capital of £35 000 invested in the business and White has a capital of £30 000 invested in the business. Profits are divided equally. Draw up their appropriation account.

In the balance sheet, the capital account of each partner is fixed and only changes if partners increase or decrease their contributions. The current account balances fluctuate and to each:

- share of profit is added
- salary is added (if applicable)
- interest on capital is added

- drawings are deducted
- interest charged on drawings is deducted.

Example

A balance sheet extract from a partnership may appear as in Figure 24.14.

FINANCED BY:			
Capital accounts	(£)	(£)	(£)
Tate		30 000	
Lyle		20 000	
			50 000
Current accounts	**Tate**	**Lyle**	
Opening balances	2 300	3 100	
Add: salary	5 000	–	
interest on			
capital	3 000	2 000	
share of profit	7 500	2 500	
	17 800	7 600	
Less: drawings	4 000	3 000	
interest on drawings	200	150	
	13 600	4 450	18 050
			68 050

Figure 24.14 Extract from the balance sheet of Tate and Lyle as at 31 December 19X3

	(£)	(£)
Current accounts: Adam		580
Eve		140
Capital accounts: Adam		25 000
Eve		20 000
Drawings: Adam 8 000		
Eve 2 000		
Freehold premises (cost) 40 000		
Stock 1/1/–3	5 600	
Purchases and sales	15 000	52 480
Wages and salaries	6 850	
Business rate	2 400	
Advertising	3 750	
General expenses	8 200	
Fixtures and fittings		
(cost)	2 400	
Motor vehicles	3 500	
Debtors and creditors	4 500	7 100
Bank	3 100	
	105 300	105 300

Notes as 31/12/–3
* Stock is valued at £7500
* Interest on drawings is to be charged at 5%
* Interest on capitals of 10% is to be paid.

Figure 24.15 Trial balance of Adam and Eve 31 December 19X3

Task

Adam and Eve run a small lighting wholesaling business in which they share profits equally. The trial balance in Figure 24.15 was taken from their books as at 31 December 19X3. Prepare final accounts as at the date of the trial balance.

The purposes of balance sheets and profit and loss statements

A balance sheet is a financial statement summarising the balances from a company's liability and asset accounts. It tells us where a company's money is invested and where it came from, and this enables us to assess what we consider the risk to be. It is a 'snapshot' of the company's financial position at a moment in time.

A profit and loss statement compares a company's incomings and outgoings over an accounting period. If a balance sheet is a snapshot, this account is like a video which has recorded how the business has performed over a period of time.

Informing owners

The owners of a business such as the sole owner, partners or shareholders will want to have a clear picture of the assets and liabilities of the organisation, and the profits and losses made in a particular accounting period.

Informing managers

Managers will want information about the relationship between assets and liabilities, and how well the business is performing in order to make financial decisions such as whether to reduce the length of credit allowed in order to increase the liquidity of assets, or to change prices if profits seem to be falling.

Securing finance

In securing finance from outside backers it is essential that you can show a 'sound' balance sheet, i.e. one in which different types of assets are 'matched' to liabilities and 'healthy' profits are being made.

Maintaining finance

Finance of various types is required to 'oil the wheels' of business activity. It is essential for a business to be able to attract and retain finance of the right type. For example, retained profits can be ploughed back into investment, cash can be used to service the cash cycle, loans need to be attracted for capital expenditures, etc. It is therefore important to maintain the right type of finance within the organisation.

Monitoring performance

Balance sheets provide an excellent way of monitoring financial performance (as well as the real trading performance) of an organisation. The snapshot provided by the balance sheet gives a good indicator of the financial 'soundness' of the business and of the extent of its assets and liabilities.

Profit and loss statements summarise the revenues and expenses of a business for a past accounting period or forecast for a future accounting period. They show the overall profit or loss for the period and the extent to which profits are paid out as dividends or retained in the business.

Fulfilling statutory obligations

Companies are obliged to file accounts each year at Companies House. These accounts are open to public inspection and need to be set out in a required format. Organisations will need to present a clear balance sheet and profit and loss account. Other organisations are expected to file accounts with the appropriate body. For example, registered charities have to file annual accounts with the Charities Commission.

Assessing taxation liability

Accounts also need to be produced and filed with the tax authorities. For example, the accounts of a sole trader with a turnover of more than a certain amount need to be filed with the Inland Revenue. Self-employed people are subject to income tax. Companies will need to pay corporation tax.

 Evidence collection point

Explain how profit and loss statements and balance sheets are used to secure and maintain finance from lenders.

Evidence indicators

The following evidence indicators will help you to show that you can meet the performance criteria for this unit as well as capacity in the Core Skills of Application of Number, Communication and Information Technology.

Please tick each of the following boxes when you have successfully covered them as part of your preparation. You need to confirm that for this activity:

- I have produced a brief summary which explains a basic accounting system and how it could be used by a small business. ☐
- I have produced a trial balance, profit and loss statement and balance sheet for a small single-product business such as a sole trader running an ice-cream kiosk or a self-employed decorator. ☐
- The trial balance, profit and loss statement and balance sheet which I have produced are supported by a commentary which explains how profit and loss statements and balance sheets are used to secure and maintain finance from lenders. ☐

Chapter 25

Data employed to monitor a business

In this chapter we describe the key components of the data employed to monitor a business. We explain who would want to use such information and why they should want to use it. We also set out how comparisons can be used to monitor the performance of business, and explore the ratios that can be used to analyse the profitability, solvency and performance of businesses.

Financial information

Business data are the inputs for an accounting system. The output is financial information.

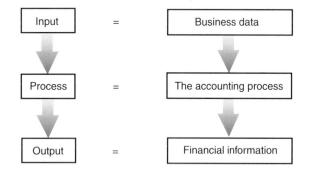

The financial information that is the output of the accounting process is very useful to a number of end users, in particular:

- the owners of an organisation
- managers
- providers of finance
- tax authorities
- the general public
- employees of an organisation.

Owners

The owners of a business will be keenly concerned to know how well it is performing. Owners may be a sole trader, or partner, or shareholders in a company.

They will want to know how much profit they are making, the total value of their outstanding debts, the value of their assets and many other things.

Managers

Managers need the information in order to be 'on top' of their handling of the business. For example, they will need to keep a regular update on the cash flow position, and how successful they have been in creating profits. They will want immediate information on improvement or deterioration in performance.

Providers of finance

A provider of finance such as a bank or debenture holder will want to know how secure are their loans to the business, when they are likely to be repaid, and at what rate of interest. For example, a bank that had lent money to an organisation may not be too pleased to find that the organisation was increasing its borrowing to such an extent that it may not be able to pay back its loans.

Tax authorities

Tax authorities such as the Department of Inland Revenue and Customs and Excise will want financial information to find out how much they are due in tax. For example, Customs and Excise will want to know how much value added is being produced by an organisation, the Inland Revenue will want to know the size of the profits made by sole traders, etc.

The general public

The general public will also have an interest in accounting information. For example, people may be thinking about becoming shareholders. They may want to know how much profit companies are making.

Employees

Employees have a right to know how well a company is performing. For example, if your company makes massive profits you may feel that you deserve an increase in pay. If it has large outstanding debts, you may feel that it is time to move to another job.

Case study – The Vaux Group

The tables and charts in Figure 25.1 give a picture of the financial performance of the Vaux Group in recent years.

Study the information in Figure 25.1 and the notes below before answering the questions. As this stage do not attempt a detailed financial analysis. Just give simple commonsense answers.

The Vaux Group was associated with breweries for many years, particularly in North-East England. Vaux is concerned with brewing, inns and beer wholesaling. It also owns hotels and nursing homes. The fortunes of its beer operations have been declining due to industrial decline in the North-East, and also because of changing tastes as people drank more wine and lager.

At the same time Vaux is making more profit from old people's homes (there are now many more old people in the UK) and from its hotel businesses. The result in the six months to 18 March 1995 was a decline in the share of total trading profits from beer and pubs from 57.7% to 53.6% and an increase from Swallow Hotels and nursing homes from 42.3% to 46.4%.

Collectively, the four businesses produced a 13% increase in taxable profits to £11.7 million, a solid

Trading record	1992	1993	1994	1994	1995
	Year to 30 Sept.			Half-year to 18 March	
Turnover (£ billion)	247.3	234.9	243.5	109.1	115.1
Pre-tax profits (£million)	20.4	26.6	29.3	10.3	11.7
Earnings per share (pence)	11.38	16.57	17.88	5.87	6.45
Dividends per share (pence)	9.35	9.50	9.85	3.35	3.45

Market value: £331.3 million, share price 236p

Operational analysis Half-year, £million

Share price Pence

Source: Datastream

Figure 25.1 The Vaux Group

performance given that during this period that there was £500,000 of reorganisation costs and £220,000 of property losses. The interim (half-year) dividend rose 3% to 3.45p.

Importantly, occupancy rates of Swallow Hotels (i.e. the percentage of rooms that were occupied) rose from 58.3% to 62.9%. This was partly due to the fact that as we came out of recession there was a bigger demand for the use of conference rooms and overnight stays by business clients.

Hotel profits increased and are likely to grow. The profit from St Andrew's (old people's) Homes increased slightly.

Beer sales fell in Vaux Inns but there was an increase in revenue from food, although only about 50% of Vaux Inns currently sell food.

Group profits overall (i.e. profits for all the Vaux businesses combined) will rise. However, a rising tax charge will erode much of that gain so there will be only a very small increase in earnings per share.

581

1 Why might shareholders be interested in reading this information? What can it tell them about the future prospects for their shareholdings?
2 List two specific actions that management at Vaux could take on the basis of their financial analysis of this information. (For example, would they try to increase beer production?)
3 Why might employees of Swallow Hotels and St Andrew's Homes be interested in reading this information?
4 Why might banks that had lent money to the Vaux Group have an interest in this information?
5 Who else might be interested in this information?

Your analysis of this case study should help you to provide evidence that you can identify users of accounting information and why this is helpful to them.

Reasons for monitoring a business

There are a number of important reasons for monitoring the financial performance of a business. These include:

- checking its solvency
- checking and assessing profitability
- calculating taxation liabilities and payments
- maintaining the finance of the organisation
- comparing performance with targets
- improving performance.

Solvency

The word 'solvency' means 'to be able to meet financial obligations'. A company becomes 'technically insolvent' when it has sufficient assets to meet all its financial obligations but insufficient time to convert these assets into cash. It is 'legally insolvent' if it is in a situation of permanent cash shortage.

A number of users of accounting information will want to check regularly on the solvency of business organisations. For example, owners and shareholders will want to know that their money is 'safe'. In this respect they will want to look at the distribution of assets and liabilities that a company has. The company may have money coming in at 'some time in the future'. However, unless it has money coming in now, tomorrow, and the next day it may face cash flow problems so that it becomes 'technically insolvent'.

Lenders of money to organisations want to know that their loans will be repaid and that interest will be paid at regular intervals. Employees and other stakeholders in organisations will want the security of knowing that the organisation is solvent.

Managers will want to know the extent of solvency so that they can restructure assets and liabilities into an appropriate form. Solvency is a base line for ongoing business operations.

When auditors carry out a periodic audit of an organisation's accounts one of the key areas they would need to emphasise would be how solvent the organisation is.

Profitability

In this text we have continually stressed the importance of profitability. Indeed, if you follow the financial reports in any paper, one of the key aspects they will headline will be profits.

'First-quarter results yesterday confirmed that BP is firmly on track to meet projected full-year profits of £2bn by 1996!'

'Life is getting tougher in the insurance business – but no one seems to have told General Accident. Its pre-tax profits beat City expectations by jumping 79% to £110.2m in the March quarter of 1995!'

Profits are a key indicator when judging business performance. It is the first point of reference for many organisational stakeholders.

It is all very well saying that sales have risen, productivity is soaring, and the organisation is growing. However, shareholders and providers of capital will always ask the question:

As we saw in the previous chapter, profits can be calculated through the profit and loss account, and this information is a key financial indicator.

But have you been making a profit?

Taxation

It is very important that all organisations, as well as self-employed people, keep detailed records of their financial transactions and accounts for taxation purposes.

Taxation rules change from time to time and business organisations need to employ professional accountants to set out their accounts so that tax due is paid in an appropriate way. Value Added Tax (VAT) will be calculated according to the rules set out by the Customs and Excise at a particular time. The Inland Revenue calculates the profit on which tax should be paid. Corporation Tax is the tax charged on the profit of a company after it has been adjusted for income and expenses or allowances recognised or ignored for tax purposes but not for accounts purposes. Corporation Tax will be paid several months after profits have been made.

It is important that fair and accurate accounts are kept and that these are set out in a consistent way from one year to the next.

Any inaccuracies would mean that incorrect taxes are calculated. Organisations that deliberately falsify accounts are guilty of 'fraud'.

Maintaining finance

The accounts of an organisation are monitored to make sure that finance is maintained within it. Managers must make sure that the organisation has an adequate supply of finance to meet its trading and investment requirements, its cash flow and other areas. Financial managers will seek answers to such questions as:

■ 'When is finance going to come in?'
■ 'What is it needed for?'
■ 'Do we have enough finance to meet current requirements?'
■ 'Do we have enough finance to meet future requirements?'

For example, a manufacturing company may need to replace machinery at regular intervals. Therefore it needs to make sure that it puts finance aside or acquires fresh finance to meet this requirement.

A trading organisation must generate enough cash to purchase fresh stocks. It needs to be sure that it can generate sufficient cash or be able to buy new stocks on credit.

Studying accounting information enables managers to get a picture of how well placed they are to maintain finance.

Outside providers of an organisation will be pleased to supply an organisation with fresh finance if they can see that the organisation is in a position to maintain its finances.

Comparison with targets

Financial planners will set targets for financial performance. For example, targets may include a given return on capital invested in the company, a target for sales, a target for profits, etc. Monitoring of actual performance then makes it possible to identify what areas are performing well or badly. For example, we have seen that in 1995 BP was well placed to meet projected full-year profits of £2 billion in 1996. By continually monitoring profits (each month) between now and the target date, BP is able to note whether things are going well or badly and then to take remedial action if necessary.

Improving performance

Monitoring financial performance provides invaluable indicators to how an organisation can improve its performance. For example, a company may have three divisions with two of these divisions showing increasing profitability and the third, declining profitability. Then the organisation may decide to restructure the failing division or to sell it off. If an organisation notices that debtors are taking longer to pay then it may decide to create incentives for early payment and penalties for late payment. It is only by closely monitoring your financial performance that you can make these changes. We will be looking later in this chapter at a number of ways of judging the financial performance of organisations.

Evidence collection point

Interview a business owner to find out how and why they monitor financial information to check on the solvency and profitability of their business for taxation purposes, to maintain finance, to make comparisons with targets and to improve performance. Set out your finding in brief notes. The evidence that you collect from this activity will enable you to provide evidence of the Core Skills of Application of Number and Communication.

The use of comparisons and variance in monitoring a business

In assessing business performance it is very useful to be able to compare the performance of the business with desired standards with that of previous years as well as with the performance of similar firms.

For example, let us assume that a business had set itself a budgeted target of making £100 million in profits before tax in 1996. This is intended to improve on its 1995 performance of £90 million.

In the event, it makes a profit of only £90 million but this can be explained by a downturn in the economy leading to lack of demand.

In fact the performance is regarded to be quite good because the firm's nearest rival (which is exactly the same size and similar in almost every respect) performed less well. Its profit before tax was £90 million in 1995, but had fallen to £82 million in 1996. We can set out these comparisons in a table.

Comparison of profits with previous year	Comparison of budgeted profit with actual profit	Comparison with nearest rival's profit
1996 = £90 million	Budgeted = £100 million	Rival 1996 = £82 million
1995 = £90 million	Actual = £90 million	Rival 1995 = £90 million

Clearly, comparisons will need to be made using a range of important financial factors such as gross and net profit, turnover, sales, market share.

Comparing actual with forecast

In planning activities you need to plan financial forecasts so that you have a target or standard to achieve. You should then compare your actual performance against this standard to see if any variances occur.

'Variance' is the difference between what you intend and what actually happens. For example if you intend profits to be £100 million and they are only £65 million, you may have a 'negative variance' of £35 million.

In planning and monitoring financial performance, assessing variances can be used as a way of checking and then (if possible) making corrections or amendments to business activities in order to put the

business back on track to achieve standards. Of course, the remedial action required may be to create a more accurate forecast (Figure 25.2).

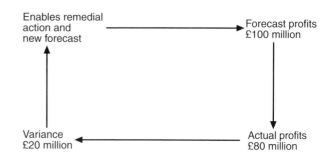

Figure 25.2 Planning and monitoring financial performance

Variance analysis can thus be used to measure the difference between budgeted (intended) and actual outcomes. Feedback from such analysis can be used to inform decision-making in the next accounting period.

Variance analysis makes it possible to detect problems and it enables managers to take speedy action to improve performance and profitability. It gives managers greater control over performance.

In the trading cycle, businesses will plan to spend a given sum on purchasing stock. If there is an increase in the amount the business has to spend over time then it will be necessary to explain the variance, e.g. because of:

- increased wastage
- materials damaged in transit
- inefficiency by operators
- inefficient buying

By identifying a variance it becomes possible to identify weaknesses and to correct them immediately.

For example, a business found that, of its three divisions, two were easily keeping up with forecast profits while the other increasingly lagged behind. When a team of auditors looked into the operation of the weak division it found that it was purchasing raw materials at vastly inflated prices. By shopping around it could have reduced its cost of materials by a third.

Comparison of actual performance with that of previous years

It is always a good indicator to compare a business's performance with its achievement in previous years. Of course, the business will change and so too will its external environment. Over a period of time we are able to build up a picture of how the business is doing. We can illustrate this by means of an important case study.

Case study – ICI in 1995

In 1995 ICI was engaged in the following activities: paints (Dulux, Gidden, ICI Autocolor); materials (acrylics, plastic films, polyurethanes); explosives; industrial chemicals (PET resins, surfactants, catalysts, titanium dioxide pigments, CFC replacements).

Important financial figures were:

	1993	1994	1995
Turnover	£8.4 billion	£9.2 billion	£10 billion
Pre-tax profit	£374 million	£408 million	£713 million
Net profit	£257 million	£188 million	£367 million
Earnings per share	35.7p	26p	54p
Dividend per share	27.5p	27.5p	29p

ICI used to be regarded as the benchmark of British industry, i.e. its performance was an important indicator of how business in the UK fared in general.

In 1993 ICI was broken up by a process of demerger. Zeneca, its pharmaceuticals operations, was hived off to become a separate company. There was a feeling that pharmaceuticals were carrying the rest of ICI and that the other divisions should be forced to stand on their own two feet. The public could then see how strong the remainder of ICI was.

The chemical industry always goes through a cycle of expansion and decline. In mid-1995 it began to reach what was regarded to be the peak of its cycle. Many critics wonder how strong the various parts of the revamped ICI will be to weather the downturn in the chemical industry cycle.

The new chair of ICI is Sir Ronald Hampel, who took over in April 1995. He has set out new tough performance standards for ICI, claiming that in the 1980s the good businesses in ICI had not been driven hard enough (i.e. they had not been set sufficiently high performance standards).

One of his first actions was to pull ICI out of the loss-making petrochemicals and chlor-alkali industries. The remaining parts of the ICI group, i.e. paints, explosives and industrial chemicals, were told that they had to earn an average rate of return on capital employed of at least 20% over 5 years. This was to be subject to a minimum of 10% at the bottom of the cycle, implying that they really had to make money in the good times, or else the 'For Sale' sign would go up pretty quickly. (This would mean that, for example, in a five-year period if an ICI business made 10% at the bottom of its profit cycle it would need to make at least 30% at the top.)

In the first quarter of 1995 pre-tax profits of ICI more than doubled from £103 million to £244 million. However, it is important to remember that this is near the top of a cycle. Some experts are very pessimistic about future profits. Industries with strong up- and down-cycles are difficult to manage. In a down-cycle investors start to worry about falling profits. In an up-cycle investors are concerned about how long it will last, and how soon the cycle will start to go down again.

In recent times, as well as half-sizing by splitting off from Zeneca, ICI has concentrated on three main themes:

1 Focusing strongly on business in which it can have a strong competitive edge, e.g. by technology and position in the market.
2 Seeking to concentrate on providing value through building stronger businesses.
3 Responding to changes in the world market. For example, ICI is currently growing rapidly in Asia.

It is very important for ICI to set tough financial performance standards because most people recognise that in 1996 and 1997 the chemicals cycle may be in a downturn.

1 Describe the tough cyclical market in which ICI operates.
2 Why did ICI split from Zeneca?
3 Why have ICI set high performance standards for its businesses?
4 Why does ICI need to make high returns on capital employed in the upturn in the chemicals cycle?
5 Why do ICI businesses need to compare one year's financial figures with those of the next?
6 Why might ICI investors compare financial performance in one year with that of the next?
7 Try to obtain figures for ICI performance in terms of turnover, pre-tax profits, net profit, earnings per share, and dividend per share in 1996 and 1997. Try to explain any changes in these figures from previous years.

585

Evidence collection point

Compare the performance of a business over a three-year period and try to explain variations that have occurred. You will find that the Business News section of *The Independent* newspaper provides superb analysis of business results in a readable and easy-to-understand format.

Inter-firm comparisons

The purpose of comparing two businesses or two sets of data is to identify differences between them (variances) and then to interpret these variances in order to improve business performance. Inter-firm comparison enables you to compare two businesses in the same industry.

In particular, business people will want to compare their own performance with that of rival firms. Businesses will want to know how their market share has changed and compare this with that of rivals, e.g. pre-tax profits, return on capital employed, sales, etc. Visit any board meeting which is looking at financial performance and you will see that much discussion is on how their business is doing compared with that of their nearest rivals.

Of course, if you want a representative indicator of how well a business is doing it is often best to compare it with a business of a similar size operating in similar market segments and using similar technologies.

For example, the case study below gives a good idea of how a firm might compare its performance with that of a rival!

Case study – We've beaten Tesco! says Sainsbury's

The information below is typical of that produced in a number of newspapers in May 1995.

It has taken Sainsbury's a month to challenge Tesco's claim that it now has the biggest share of the grocery market. But the reply seems fairly convincing.

Sainsbury's Chair David Sainsbury revealed that Sainsbury's sales rose $7\frac{1}{2}$% to £12 billion in the year to 11 March, compared with Tesco's £10 billion. Its pre-tax profits rose $10\frac{1}{2}$% to £808 million against Tesco's £595 million and its market share edged up by nearly 0.5% to 11.7% compared with Tesco's 11.4% as calculated by Central Statistical Office Data.

Indicator	Sainsbury's performance 1994/95	Tesco's performance 1994/95
Sales	£12 billion	£10 billion
Pre-tax profits	£808 million	£595 million
Market share	11.7%	11.4%

In his annual statement David Sainsbury said: 'The discount stores are not the threat they seemed years ago and Tesco's Clubcard is having little effect on our stores. Since the year end our supermarket sales have grown by 8%. Tesco's food sales may be growing faster in the short term, but Sainsbury has a big edge on sales and profits, thanks to its big stake in the DIY market through its Homebase chain and in America through the Shaw's supermarket chain.'

1 Why is it important for businesses like Sainsbury's to compare its results with those of its rivals?
2 What types of actions might Sainsbury's take as a result of analysing their financial performance during 1994/95?
3 Which figures do you think are most important in analysing financial performance? What other figures would you like to see which are not mentioned in the case?

Later in this chapter we shall look at a range of measures used for judging aspects of business performance.

Key components of information

The key components of information required to monitor a business are:

1 forecasts
2 actual performance
3 previous year's performance.

We shall look at each of these in turn.

Forecasts

In planning for the future it is important to make a forecast of what the balance sheet and the profit and loss account will look like after a particular period and of cash flow.

In forecasting it is essential to focus your plans on likely events and transactions in the current accounting period, which will normally be for the

	Forecast for month 1		Forecast for month 12	Annual forecast
Income:				
Sales				
Other income				
Total income				
Expenditures:				
Materials				
etc.				
etc,				
Total expenditure				
Net/profit or loss				
Cumulative profit or loss				

next year. By setting out your intentions and expectation you can produce a detailed set of figures showing what your targets are. For example, you will want to set out your anticipated incomes and expenditures in your profit and loss account. You will normally do this on a monthly basis, and then add up all these figures to arrive at a forecast annual profit and loss account. A simplified form of this is set out above.

Similarly, you will set out a cash-flow forecast. A highly simplified form of this is shown below:

	Month 1	Month 12
Receipts		
Payments		
Net cash flow		

Also you can draw up a forecast balance sheet based on your expected activities during the year, including the purchase, sale, and depreciation of fixed assets.

Actual information

Actual information is the results of business activity. This would need to be set out in the following way so that a comparison can be made between the forecast and actual results.

	January Forecast	Actual	Total Forecast	Actual
Income				
Expenditures				
Net profit/ or loss				
Cumulative profit or loss				

We could set out the actual cash flow in a similar way:

	January Forecast	Actual	December Forecast	Actual
Receipts				
Payments				
Net cash flow				

Also we can put together an accurate balance sheet which shows the true state of affairs at the end of the year.

It now becomes possible to compare forecast with actual information to find out what went right and what went wrong, and to try to explain any variances.

Evidence collection point

Invite an accountant to explain to you how forecast cash flows profit and loss accounts and balance sheets were assembled for a particular business, and how the major differences between the forecast and the actual can be explained.

Previous years' information

As well as looking at forecast and actual financial information it is also helpful to study past information to get a better picture of change within the organisation. This also shows how the organisation is performing. For example, in looking at the balance sheet of the business you can see changes in:

- the size of the fixed capital base of the organisation
- the asset structure
- the relationship between assets and liabilities
- the dependence of the organisation on outside finance
- the extent of debtors and creditors to the organisation.

By looking at the profit and loss account you are able to see changes in:

- the sales made by the organisation
- the expenditures of the organisation
- the net profit or loss of the organisation.

You can also study previous years' figures to gain information on changes in the speed at which the organisation is having debts repaid or at which it is paying creditors, etc. In the previous chapter we looked at how you set up balance sheets and profit and loss accounts. While studying this chapter you should obtain actual published accounting information to make comparisons of forecast, actual, and previous years' information. Below we will consider ways of judging the performance of businesses by using such published information to examine solvency, profitability, and performance ratios.

Task

Write to major public companies to acquire copies of their annual reports, including copies of their published accounts. Interpret this information by working out ratios.

The performance of a business

Financial information can be used to establish the performance of a business. In looking at this information you will need to look for a number of aspects of performance.

Solvency

To what extent is the business solvent? In other words, does it have enough money flowing in to pay out money that must meet its debts?

Profitability

To what extent is the business profitable? You will need to extract information about profits from profit and loss accounts and compare this with other information. For example, in assessing the efficiency of management of a business you should look at the amount of profit generated in relation to the total value of assets for which managers are responsible.

Achievement of targets

A key business activity is to set targets for itself. Without targets it will have nothing to aim at and will not be able to assess how successful it has been. You should look at the financial targets set by a company and assess whether it is meeting its targets, and why it is succeeding or not.

Better or worse than targets?

You should use financial information to judge whether an organisation is performing better or worse than targets. For example, you can do this by comparing forecast (budgeted) figures with actual figures.

Establishing tax liability

You should look at how financial information can be used to assess the tax liability of a company. In particular, when looking at company reports you should compare the profits made before tax with the tax liability. Of course, the tax authorities will use financial information to establish the extent of tax liabilities.

Minimising tax liability

Businesses will try to minimise their tax liabilities by offsetting various items against tax. Try to find out how an organisation can present its information in such a way as to minimise tax liabilities.

Maintaining funding

Most businesses need outside sources of funding to carry out their operations. Investors will examine accounts in order to check that their money is safe. Look at the way in which accounts are presented to try to ensure that their funding is maintained. We present below a number of ratios that suppliers of funds to organisations will use in deciding whether to keep their money in that organisation.

Comparison with others

Financial information is widely used to make comparisons with organisations, particularly those in the same industry and of a similar size and nature. When studying financial information try to make such comparisons.

Evidence collection point

Produce some brief notes explaining why it is important to examine the financial performance of a business by analysing available information.

Use of solvency, profitability and performance ratios

When assessing business performance it is important to have some way of measuring:

- solvency
- profitability
- performance.

You will find it helpful to use a number of important ratios which enable you to see how a business is performing. These ratios are therefore performance indicators.

Solvency ratios

Two useful ratios to measure solvency are:

- the current ratio
- the acid test ratio.

In assessing the solvency of a business we need to compare the current outgoings and debts of the company with the amount which the company can turn into cash in a short period to pay off these demands.

We can illustrate this point by using a simple example involving personal finance. Suppose that I owe the electricity company £100 and have already received my final reminder from them. They have threatened to take me to court if I have not paid up by next Wednesday. Currently, I have only £50 in my bank account and £20 in cash in my pocket. I am due to receive £500 in three weeks' time as my student grant. Fortunately, my father has said that he will give me £150 tomorrow.

In this case I am solvent because my current assets are greater than my current liabilities, i.e.

Current liabilities

£100 owing to electricity company

Current assets

£20 cash

£50 money in bank account

£150 advance from father

Therefore current assets are £220 and current liabilities are £100.

The term 'liquidity' refers to the ease with which a firm can convert its short-term or current assets into cash to cover payments as and when they arise. Stocks are the least liquid of the current assets because they must first be sold (probably on credit) and the customer will be provided with a credit period. As a result, there is a time lapse before stocks

589

are converted into cash. It is the responsibility of the company to ensure that it can meet debts likely to arise in the near future. Current liabilities are items that have to be paid for the short period.

Current ratio

The current ratio is an important way of measuring an organisation's ability to settle current liabilities (immediate debts). It is measured by the simple formula:

$$\text{Current ratio} = \frac{\text{Current assets}}{\text{Current liabilities}}$$

Clearly, some current assets are more liquid than others, and the time factor involved in transferring them to cash is something an experienced manager should be able to estimate. A prudent ratio is sometimes 2:1. This may not be the case if stocks form the bulk of the value of current assets. Companies have to be aware that bank overdrafts are repayable on demand and that figures extracted from a balance sheet, while reflecting the position of current assets and liabilities at a moment in time, do not reflect the current assets:current liabilities ratio at other times. In practice, most businesses operate with a ratio slightly lower than 2:1.

Case study – Current ratio

The following extracted figures show the current assets and liabilities of a small business:

Total stocks:
Raw materials	500
Work-in-progress	300
Finished goods	800
Total stocks	1600
Trade debtors	1000
Cash/bank	400
Current assets	3000
Trade creditors	500
Tax due	300
Loan interest due	200
Current liabilities	1000

Your can see from the above figures that the business has a current ratio of 3:1, i.e.

$$\frac{3000}{1000}$$

Acid test ratio

A major problem is that you may not be able to convert your stocks rapidly into cash. For example, in our illustration we have £500 of raw materials and £300 of partly finished goods.

Businesses therefore often use a more severe ratio to test whether they have the ability to meet current liabilities. This is called the 'acid test ratio' and does not include stock in the liquid assets of the business. The acid test ratio is measured by:

$$\text{Acid test ratio} = \frac{\text{Liquid assets}}{\text{Current liabilities}}$$

In the example we have used, the acid test ratio is 1.4:1, i.e.

$$\frac{1400}{1000}$$

The acid test ratio is measured by current assets minus stock:current liabilities. This is sometimes called the 'quick ratio'.

It is a very important ratio. It is sometimes referred to as the Plimsoll line of a business. The Plimsoll line is a line drawn on a ship's hull. If the ship slips below this line in the water then it is in danger of sinking.

Evidence collection point

Study the current assets and current liabilities of a business by extracting this information from a balance sheet.

Illustrate the current ratio and acid test ratio of the organisation by setting out a diagram similar to that in Figure 25.3.

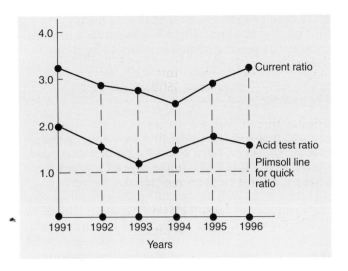

Figure 25.3 Solvency ratios

Profitability ratios

The profitability of a business should be measured by looking at the general profitability of the investment made in a company or at the profits that the company makes on its sales.

Return on net assets

The return on net assets of a company is a useful measure of profitability because it shows the profit earned on the net assets used in the business.

Just as a person who puts money into a building society will ask 'What am I getting from my investment?', the owners of a business will want to know 'What return am I getting from my investment in the business?'

Return on net assets can be measured by:

$$\text{Return on net assets (\%)} = \frac{\text{Net profit}}{\text{Net assets}} \times 100$$

The net profit of a business is extracted from the profit and loss account and shows the net profit before tax. Net assets are calculated by adding together the total assets of the business and then subtracting the current liabilities.

Return on net assets thus provides a good idea of the efficiency of a business as a profit-making concern for its owners.

There are three other ways of measuring profitability of investment in which you may be interested.

The return on capital employed (ROCE) (%)

This measures the amount of profit earned from every pound invested in the business. ROCE is widely used as a profitability indicator and is measured by:

$$\frac{\text{Profit before interest and tax}}{\text{Capital employed}} \times 100$$

(Note: capital employed = net assets before deduction of long-term debt.)

The figure for capital employed is usually taken as that at the start of the year, as this is the capital that generated the profit in the following year. The best way to think about the percentage return is to compare it with other investments. For example, if you invest £100 in a building society and receive £10 a year in interest (before tax), then you can see that you are getting a return on your capital of 10%. This is a good measure of how effective your investment is. ROCE is therefore a quick and useful way of calculating the effectiveness of an investment in the business; it relates profitability to alternative investments.

Return on shareholders' funds (%)

This measures the returns that shareholders make on the capital they invest in the business and is measured by:

$$\frac{\text{Profit after interest and tax}}{\text{Shareholders' funds}} \times 100$$

Profitability (%)

This is a useful way of measuring the performance of management by comparing the profit generated against the total value of assets used by management and is measured by:

$$\frac{\text{Profit before interest and tax}}{\text{Total assets}} \times 100$$

Evidence collection point

Show that you can work out return on net assets (%) from the following figures.

- The profit and loss account of a business indicates that its net profit before tax is £20 000.
- Its balance sheet shows the following (fill in the missing figure for net assets employed).

Balance sheet as at 1 October 1997

	£	£	£
Fixed assets:			
Premises			70 000
Current assets:			
Stock	50 000		
Cash-in-hand	80 000		
		130 000	
Current liabilities:			
Creditors		30 000	
Net working capital (current assets – current liabilities)			100 000
Net assets employed			170 000

Your work should show evidence of Core Skills in Application of Number.

Gross profit (%)

The gross profit (%) is a ratio that is extracted from the trading account. It relates gross profit to sales revenue:

$$\text{Gross profit \%} = \frac{\text{Gross profit}}{\text{Sales revenue}} \times 100$$

For example, if sales of £100 000 produced a gross profit of £25 000 then the gross profit percentage is 25%. In terms of buying stock and selling it, this means that every £1 of sales gives a 25p gross profit. The gross profit percentage should be calculated at regular intervals, and if it rises or falls the reason should be investigated. If the percentage falls this may indicate that stock is being stolen or damaged. Alternatively, it could mean that the cost of stock is rising and the increase has not been passed on to the consumer.

Profit margin (%)

This is a very important profitability ratio because it shows the profits that the business is making on its sales. It indicates the profit that results from every pound of sales revenue. Clearly, a business will want to increase its profit margins in order to be more efficient.

$$\text{Profit margin} = \frac{\text{Profit before interest and tax}}{\text{Sales revenue}} \times 100$$

If you can increase the profit that you squeeze out of the same volume of sales you are clearly being more efficient. If you can increase your profit margin out of a larger volume of sales you are also becoming more efficient as well as spreading the efficiency over a larger number of sales. The profit margin should be similar from year to year, and should be comparable with the ratios for other enterprises in the same field of business. It takes business expenses into account.

If the gross profit percentage is consistent from year to year, any changes in the net profit percentage could indicate an increase in overheads (fixed costs) as a proportion of sales revenue and a need to make economies or to adjust prices.

Evidence collection point

The following figures show the profit and loss statement of a business over a period of time. Look at the figures and then set out a graph to show how the gross profit (%) and the profit margin altered over the time period shown. What factors might account for these changes? Doing these calculations will enable you to show that you understand how to calculate profitability ratios and give evidence of the Core Skills of Information Technology and Application of Number.

£000	Year 1	Year 2	Year 3
Sales	900	1200	1610
Less: Cost of goods sold	450	600	930
Gross trading profit	450	600	680
Total fixed costs	270	290	430
Net profit before tax	?	?	?

Performance ratios

There are a number of other ratios which we need to consider briefly. These also give us useful information on the current performance of an organisation. The ratios help us to measure how successfully the business is being run and/or how well management is handling different aspects of the business.

We have chosen four areas:

- sales performance
- asset turnover performance
- stock turnover performance
- debtor collection period.

Sales performance

One of the main purposes of an organisation is to sell goods efficiently. We need to have some way of measuring what it costs to make sales. If these costs can be reduced in proportion to the sales that are made then the organisation can be said to be becoming more efficient. We can set up a ratio to compare the expenses of running an organisation with the sales made, or a ratio which compares the overheads of running the organisation with the sales made, i.e.:

$$\frac{\text{Administration costs}}{\text{Sales}} \times 100$$

or

$$\frac{\text{Overheads}}{\text{Sales}} \times 100$$

Asset turnover performance

Turnover ratios are a group of ratios that are used to measure the number of times a specific type of a company's assets have been 'turned over' (i.e. sold) in a particular trading period (this is normally one year). They are calculated by dividing sales revenue for the year by the average value of the assets at the start and end of the period.

The general asset turnover ratio can be calculated by:

$$\text{Asset turnover} = \frac{\text{Sales}}{\text{Net assets}}$$

This ratio indicates how effectively fixed assets are being used to generate sales. It is really an efficiency ratio designed to show how well managers are using fixed assets in the running of the business. The ratio will depend on the type of business concerned.

Stock turnover performance

Stock turnover is a very important measure of the liquidity of a business's stocks. The value of the stocks is related to sales revenues in order to find the number of times that they have been 'turned over' during the period. It can be measured by:

$$\text{Stock turnover} = \frac{\text{Sales revenue}}{\text{Stocks}}$$

Stock turnover is the average length of time an item of stock is held in stores before it is used or sold. The adequacy of this ratio depends upon the type of industry. For example, a greengrocer would expect a much higher stock turnover than a furniture business. Many firms hold smaller stock levels today than in the past. They may operate a 'just-in-time' system (i.e. being supplied with just enough stock to meet current demand) and consequently have a higher stock turnover.

 Evidence collection point

Work out the stock turnover for a business from the following figures.

(£000)	1994	1995	1996
Average stocks	260	380	500
Sales revenue	1200	1600	1900

Explain the implications of the changes in stock turnover over this period.

Debtor collection period

This is calculated by using the formula:

$$\frac{\text{Debtors}}{\text{Average daily sales}}$$

where average daily sales are calculated by dividing sales by 365.

The normally accepted debt-collection period is about 60 days. It may be possible to improve liquidity by reducing this period. Customers who are late in paying their debts are receiving free finance for their business. This ratio indicates the average number of days of credit received by customers before they provide a payment.

Evidence collection point

Interview a business manager with some responsibility for accounts to find out the debt-collection period in his or her organisation and how they seek to reduce it.

Of course, it is helpful to remember the basics of good debtor control, namely:

- *Invoice quickly* As soon as the goods have been delivered and accepted, invoice!
- *Invoice correctly* If your customers want you to attach a copy of the purchase order, or quote the order number, make sure that you do. Ensure that your invoice is clear and well laid out.
- *Check creditworthiness* Find out whether your customers are able to pay and their reliability. If you agree a level of credit, keep to it.

Evidence indicators

These are useful for showing that you can meet the performance criteria for this unit as well as providing evidence of the Core Skills in Application of Number, Communication, and Information Technology. Tick each of the following boxes when you have successfully covered them as part of your preparations. You need to confirm that for this activity:

- I have produced a description of the key components of the information used to monitor a business. ☐

This includes:

- An explanation of who would want to use such information. ☐
- Why they should want to use it. ☐
- Why comparisons and variances can be useful when monitoring the performance of a business. ☐

In addition, I have produced:

- A summary of two given sets of accounting information for two comparative businesses which explains and uses ratios to illustrate:

1 profitability (gross and net) ☐

2 solvency ☐

3 performance ☐

for the two businesses.

Testing your understanding

Study the profit and loss account and balance sheet of Jolly Trading in Figures 25.4 and 25.5. Use the figures to calculate:

- profit margin (%)
- gross profit (%)
- return on net assets (%)
- current ratio (%)
- acid test ratio (%)
- asset turnover
- stock turnover

This should help you to provide evidence of Core Skills in the Application of Number.

	£	£
Sales		120 000
Cost of sales:		
Purchases	80 000	
Closing stock	10 000	
Cost of sales		70 000
Gross profit		50 000
Overheads	20 000	
Depreciation	2 000	
		22 000
Net profit before taxes		28 000
Drawings		24 000
Retained profits		4 000

Figure 25.4 Jolly Trading Profit and Loss Account for the period ending 31 December 1996

	£
Fixed assets:	
Premises	20 000
Fixtures and fittings	8 000
Current assets:	
Stock	10 000
Debtors	2 000
Cash-in-hand	2 000
	14 000
Current liabilities:	
Creditors	6 000
Net working capital	8 000
Net assets employed	36 000
Financed by:	
Owner's capital introduced	32 000
Retained profits	4 000
	36 000

Figure 25.5 Balance sheet of Jolly Trading as at 31 December 1996

Financial Forecasting and Monitoring: Unit Test 1

1 Which of the following is a fixed asset?
  a Debtors.
  b Stock.
  c Fixtures and fittings.
  d Mortgage.

2 P Strong Ltd pay the £2 000 they owe to A Weak Ltd on the 10 March. In A Weak's balance sheet this will:
  a Increase working capital by £2000.
  b Decrease working capital by £2000.
  c Increase working capital by £4000.
  d Have no direct effect upon the size of working capital.

3 Current liabilities are sometimes described as:
  a Long-term liabilities.
  b Short-term liabilities.
  c Debtors.
  d Equities.

4 Which of these shares may be bought back from shareholders?
  a Participating preference shares.
  b Ordinary shares.
  c Deferred shares.
  d Redeemable preference shares.

5 With cash balance of £2450 at the beginning of a period, receipts of £6840 and payment of £7150 during a period, the trial balance at the end of a period will be:
  a £2760.
  b £5520.
  c £2140.
  d £4280.

6 An example of a cash inflow may include:
  a Receipts from creditors.
  b Introduction of new capital.
  c Interest charges.
  d Loan repayments.

7 Poor cash flow forecasting may result in:
  a Receipt of interest.
  b Loss of confidence by debtors.
  c Having to arrange finance at short notice.
  d The need to employ more staff.

8 Which of the following will not appear in a cash-flow forecast?
  a Rates.
  b Income from sales.
  c Payments for assets.
  d Depreciation.

9 To help to produce a cash-flow forecast it may be possible to use:
  a Word-processor.
  b Database.
  c Graphics package.
  d Spreadsheet.

10 Katy Jackson expects to sell £15 000 of goods in March. One-third of sales are always for credit and two-thirds are for cash. Two months' credit on average is taken by customers. If sales in May are £21 000, how much will Katy expect to receive in May?
  a £10 000.
  b £14 000.
  c £19 000.
  d £21 000.

11 Which of the following is not a final account?
  a Balance sheet.
  b Trial balance.
  c Trading account.
  d Profit and loss account.

12 Stock turnover is which sort of ratio?
  a Solvency ratio.
  b Profitability ratio.
  c Performance ratio.
  d None of the above.

13 Under which of the following headings would you place a van which you have purchased?
  a Current assets.
  b Long-term liabilities.
  c Current liabilities.
  d Fixed assets.

14 If the gross profit is £9350 and the cost of sales is £16 720, then sales will be:
  a £7370.
  b £14 740.

c £26 070.

d None of the above.

15 Which of the methods below would be used to calculate the debtor collection period?
   a Gross profit/sales.
   b Net profit/sales.
   c Current assets/current liabilities.
   d Debtors/average daily sales.

16 In order to obtain a bank loan an organisation will have to draw up:
   a Trial balance.
   b Business plan.
   c Profit and loss account.
   d Appropriation account.

17 If creditors increase this would:
   a Decrease the size of the working capital.
   b Have no effect upon the working capital.
   c Increase the size of working capital.
   d Increase long-term liabilities.

18 A source of finance which would not be available for a sole trader would be:
   a A bank loan.
   b Issue of shares.
   c Mortgage.
   d Use of savings.

19 The working capital ratio is the ratio of:
   a Current assets to fixed assets.
   b Current assets to long-term liabilities.
   c Current assets to capital.
   d Current assets to current liabilities.

20 The major cause of business failure is often identified as:
   a Weak financial management.
   b Too much stock.
   c Poor communication.
   d Bad time-keeping.

21 Rachel Thomas has £500 in the bank. Over the next six months she expects to earn £1450 per month and have to pay out £900 per month. At the end of six months her cash balance is likely to be:
   a £3300.
   b £3800.
   c £15 100.
   d £4300.

22 Rob Tall has arranged two months' credit from his suppliers. This means that if he buy goods for £3500 in June, he will have to make payments in:
   a April.
   b July.
   c August.
   d September.

23 One solution to a cash flow deficit may be to:
   a Buy more goods.
   b Create more creditors.
   c Incur other overheads.
   d Sell fixed assets.

24 Figures which can be used to make estimates of cash flow are likely to come from:
   a The balance sheet.
   b Previous cash flow forecasts.
   c The trading account.
   d The trial balance.

25 Negative cash-flow figures are recorded by:
   a Putting a minus sign in front of the figures.
   b Placing brackets around the figures.
   c Highlighting the figures in a box.
   d Underlining the figures.

26 The difference between budgeted cash-flow figures and the actual cash-flow figures could be called a:
   a Deficit.
   b Surplus.
   c Cash fund.
   d Variance.

27 Final accounts are drawn up from information supplied by the:
   a Journal.
   b Cash-flow forecast.
   c Cash book.
   d Trial balance.

28 Which of the items below would be deducted from capital?
   a Drawings.
   b Net profit.
   c Assets.
   d Shares.

29 The financial position of a business at one moment in time is shown in the:
   a Profit and loss account.
   b Balance sheet.
   c Trading account.
   d Cash book.

30 Which of the following is not considered to be a fixed asset?
   a Freehold premises.
   b Fixtures and fittings.
   c Stocks.
   d Motor vehicles.

31 The figures for which of the following appear in the credit column of the trial balance?
   a Capital.
   b Purchases.
   c Current assets.
   d Fixed assets.

32 Current assets are sometimes called:
   a Circulating assets.
   b Cash-flow.
   c Acid test ratio.
   d Working capital.

33 Which of the following assets would be considered to be the most liquid?
   a Land and buildings.
   b Debtors.
   c Stocks.
   d Motor vehicles.

34 A form of short-term bank finance used to overcome cashflow problems would be:
   a Bank loan.
   b Bank draft.
   c Direct credit.
   d Overdraft.

35 A service which offers immediate payment against debtors is called:
   a Standing order.
   b Bank finance.
   c Factoring.
   d Loan finance.

36 One way in which a business can use an asset without having to save to pay for it is through:
   a Credit control.
   b Bank loan.
   c Share finance.
   d Leasing.

37 The method of raising finance which involves some loss of control is known as:
   a Executive shareholding.
   b Venture capital.
   c Debentures.
   d Loan capital.

38 The maximum amount of share capital a business is allowed to issue is called:
   a Issued capital.
   b Preference shares.
   c Rights Issue.
   d Authorised capital.

39 APPR stands for:
   a Annual Performance Ratio.
   b Annual Percentage Rate.
   c Allowable Performance Rate.
   d Allowable Percentage Rate.

40 Capital budgets are prepared to plan for the purchase of:
   a Current assets.
   b Stocks.
   c Fixed assets.
   d None of the above.

41 The final profit a business makes after payment of all expenses is known as the:
   a Gross profit.
   b Surplus.
   c Accumulated profit.
   d Net profit.

42 The standard rate of VAT set by Parliament is:
   a 20%.
   b $17\frac{1}{2}$%.
   c 15%.
   d 10%.

43 If more VAT is paid on purchases than received on sales, then some VAT could be:
   a Lost.
   b Recovered.
   c Paid twice.
   d Paid at a lower rate.

44 If a person buys £8000 of goods and sells 75% of them for £10 000, then the gross profit is:
   a £2000.
   b £4000.
   c £6000.
   d £8000.

45 Net profit plus expenses less other income would equal:
   a Cost of sales.
   b Gross profit.
   c Sales.
   d Purchases.

46 If sales are £4000, gross profit is 20% of sales and net profit is 10% of sales, expenses are:
a £1200.
b £800.
c £400.
d £1600.

47 Asset turnover is shown by the ratio:
a Assets/sales.
b Sales/net assets.
c Net assets/profit.
d Sales/net profit.

48 Which of the following would not appear in a balance sheet?
a Fixtures.
b Creditors.
c Bank overdraft.
d Sales.

49 Which of the following would not be a consequence of incorrect forecasting?
a Cash flow problems.
b Bad debts.
c Incorrect working capital.
d Insolvency.

50 'Going public' as a way of raising funds is more likely to be an option for a:
a Sole trader.
b Partnership.
c Private limited company.
d Public limited company.

Financial Forecasting and Monitoring: Unit Test 2

1 A loan secured on a property is called a:
a Debenture.
b Mortgage.
c Bank loan.
d Building society indemnity.

2 Selling a product which cost £400 for £500 on credit will:
a Increase working capital by £500.
b Decrease working capital by £100.
c Have no effect upon working capital.
d Increase working capital and capital by £100.

3 One way of raising capital for a sole trader may be to:
a Introduce partners.
b Issue debentures.
c Factor debts.
d Create a rights issue.

4 The maximum amount of capital a company is empowered to issue to shareholders is called:
a Equity capital.
b Issued capital.
c Authorised capital.
d Share capital.

5 The surplus from trading activities is usually called:
a Cash.
b Current liability.
c Profit.
d Debtors.

6 Patricia Jones has £800 in the bank. Her income from 1 January is only £600 per month but her anticipated monthly expenditure is £900 per month. In which of the following months is she first likely to require an overdraft?
a January.
b February.
c March.
d April.

7 Peter Jones buys 100 units in January at £3.75 per unit. He has arranged 3 months' credit from his suppliers. This means that he will have to pay:
a £350 in March.
b £375 in April.
c £370 in May.
d £375 in March.

8 One advantage of using a spreadsheet for producing a cash-flow forecast is that it makes it possible to examine:
a The benefits of IT.
b Where to obtain an overdraft.
c Alternatives.
d Various sources of finance.

9 Which of the following appears on the debit side of the trial balance.
a Sales.
b Capital.
c Creditors.
d Motor vehicles.

10 In which of the following statements is net profit calculated?
a Balance sheet.
b Trading account.
c Trial balance.
d Profit and loss account.

11 The percentage of gross profit to the cost of sales is 25%. If sales are £18 000, then gross profit is:
   a £13 500.
   b £9000.
   c £4500.
   d £2250.

12 Which of the following is included in working capital?
   a Bank loan.
   b Fixtures.
   c Drawings.
   d Bank overdraft.

13 Accounting transactions are recorded in ledgers using the process known as:
   a Financial bookkeeping.
   b Ledger control.
   c Double-entry accounts.
   d Double-entry bookkeeping.

14 If gross profit is £1000 and the net profit is 25% of the gross profit, expenses will be:
   a £250.
   b £750.
   c £375.
   d £500.

15 To find out if stock has been stolen or damaged it would be necessary to calculate the:
   a Gross profit percentage.
   b Current ratio.
   c Net profit percentage.
   d Stock turnover.

16 Which of the following is likely to have the highest rate of stock turnover?
   a A clothes shop.
   b A sandwich bar.
   c A jeweller's.
   d A furniture store.

17 The current ratio measures:
   a Liquidity.
   b Profitability.
   c Asset usage.
   d Capital structure.

18 To draw up an accurate cash-flow forecast it is important to know the:
   a Number of debtors an organisation has.
   b Timings of receipts and payments.
   c Level of working capital.
   d Profit margin.

19 The difference between forecast cash flow and actual cash flow is known as:
   a The closing cash balance.
   b A variance.
   c The profit.
   d The opening cash balance.

20 On 1 April Sarah Fletcher has £300 in the bank. Her monthly income is £450 and her expenditure for the next few months is likely to be £600 per month. In which of the months below will she first require an overdraft?
   a April.
   b May.
   c June.
   d July.

21 Raw materials are paid for two months before being used. Raw materials paid for in August will relate to raw materials used in:
   a June.
   b May.
   c September.
   d October.

22 Pauline Thompson expects to sell £18 000 of goods in April. One third of goods are sold for cash and two thirds on credit. One month's credit on average is taken by credit customers. If sales in May are £21 000, how much will she expect to receive in May?
   a £19 000.
   b £13 000.
   c £16 000
   d £14 000.

23 An example of an inflow or receipt into a forecast could be:
   a Production expenses.
   b Fixed costs.
   c Interest received.
   d The bank balance.

24 Cash flow simply involves matching:
   a Profits with losses.
   b Credit sales with cash sales.
   c Income with expenditure.
   d Purchases with sales.

25 Which of the following appears in a trading account?
   a Discounts.
   b Net profit.
   c Expenses.
   d Purchases.

599

26 Which of the following is likely to change in value because of depreciation?
  a Current assets.
  b Current liabilities.
  c Fixed assets.
  d Capital.

27 If opening stock is £2315, closing stock is £3710 and purchases are £8245, then the cost of sales figure will be:
  a £9640.
  b £6850.
  c £2215.
  d £1470.

28 Which of the following would not appear in a profit and loss account?
  a Rent received.
  b Light and heat.
  c Motor vehicles.
  d Advertising.

29 A trial balance is:
  a A balance sheet.
  b A list of balances extracted from the ledger.
  c The balance extracted from the bank statement.
  d The final balance of the cash book.

30 If the gross profit is £27 500, sales are £44 900, the closing stock is £4000 and the opening stock is £6500, purchases must be:
  a £19 900.
  b £14 900.
  c £27 900.
  d £6900.

31 Stock turnover over a period is usually described as a:
  a Number.
  b Ratio.
  c Percentage.
  d Proportion.

32 If an organisation is not liquid it will not be able to pay:
  a Short-term debtors.
  b Short-term creditors.
  c Customers.
  d Capital back to shareholders.

33 An example of a cash outflow could be:
  a Payments by debtors.
  b Cash sales.
  c Rent and rates.
  d Receipt of an inheritance.

34 Debra Walker has £450 in the bank in January. She expects to earn £500 per month in each of the next six months. However, in order to pay for her holiday her outgoings are likely to be £800 in the first two months and £400 thereafter. In which month is Debra first likely to require an overdraft facility?
  a January.
  b February.
  c March.
  d April.

35 Given the information provided in question 34, what is Debra's cash balance at the end of six months likely to be?
  a £(50).
  b £150.
  c £250.
  d £350.

36 If a business anticipates a cash deficit it may improve its position by:
  a Making payments more promptly to customers.
  b Taking money out of the bank.
  c Delaying the payment of expenses.
  d Overtrading.

37 When trading on credit, the money owed by credit customers should appear in the cash-flow forecast when:
  a The sale is made.
  b The goods are delivered.
  c The payment is made.
  d None of the above.

38 Which of the following is not an asset?
  a Investments.
  b Fixtures.
  c Debtors.
  d Capital.

39 The percentage of gross profit to sales is 40%. If sales are £16 000, the cost of sales is likely to be:
  a £6400.
  b £12 800.
  c £4000.
  d £9600.

40 In the trial balance the sales would be shown:
  a In the credit column.
  b In the debit column.
  c In the credit column when payments have been made.
  d As an adjustment beneath the trial balance.

41 Which of the following is a current asset of a newsagent?
 a Money owed by customers for newspaper bills.
 b Money owed by the newsagents to suppliers.
 c Fixture and fittings.
 d Bank loan.

42 Which of the following appears in the profit and loss account?
 a Stocks.
 b Sales.
 c Purchases.
 d Net profit.

43 Which of the following will increase the owner's capital?
 a Drawings.
 b Profits.
 c Losses.
 d None of the above.

44 Which of the following is not a current liability?
 a Bank loan.
 b Creditors.
 c Bank overdraft.
 d Taxation owed to the Inland Revenue.

45 If a customer wishes to purchase a new property before the sale of an old one, the bank may arrange:
 a An overdraft facility.
 b A bank loan.
 c A bridging facility.
 d A second mortgage.

46 An example of a company which provides venture capital by paying for equity in small businesses is:
 a ICI.
 b IMI.
 c 3i.
 d IBM.

47 The most common source of finance for a club or society is likely to be:
 a Bank loans.
 b Shares.
 c Subscriptions.
 d Retained profits.

48 Which of the following is not an advantage of using loan capital?
 a It is cheap.
 b Inflation benefits the borrower.
 c Interest does not always have to be paid.
 d Interest appears before tax.

49 VAT is collected by:
 a Department of Inland Revenue.
 b DTI.
 c Department of Employment.
 d HM Customs and Excise.

50 Which of the following is not a fixed asset for a joiner?
 a Workshop.
 b Wood.
 c Motor van.
 d Machinery.

The aim of this unit is to help you to understand the depth of planning which must be carried out before a finance provider may be willing to risk investing in a business idea. The unit brings together much of the knowledge and understanding developed through the other units.

You will need to consider a business idea; supply a rationale and information to support a loan application; and show how you will monitor and carry out your business plan. You should be able to organise and produce your business plan to a standard such that you can communicate it with confidence to possible providers of finance.

As a result of studying this unit you should develop the ability to think through business scenarios from the human, marketing, production, timing and financial points of view. You should present this information in a way which would persuade a finance provider to support the business.

You will also be required to analyse your own strengths and weaknesses with regard to employment and self-employment.

If in your college or school you are involved in an enterprise which takes place over a period of time, then you will be able to present evidence from this activity to show that you can meet the required performance criteria.

In producing your business plan you should show that you fully understand the use of balance sheets, cash-flow forecasts and break-even point, and that you can justify the projections in the plan.

You are not expected to produce a detailed production plan, although you should understand the timing and resource implications of production.

Chapter 26

Preparing work and collecting data for a business plan

This chapter focuses on how planning needs to be carefully carried out and data collected for a business plan. The chapter identifies a number of preparatory stages in developing a business plan. You can best put these ideas into practice by setting up either a fictional or real business for part of the final year of your course.

The stages identified are as follows:

1 Explain the purposes of a business plan.
2 Identify the business objectives and collect supporting information for the business activity for which a plan is to be prepared.
3 Identify the legal and insurance implications of the business objectives.
4 Discuss the feasibility of proposals with others.
5 Estimate resource requirements to design, produce, promote and sell the goods or service.
6 Produce a flow-chart illustrating estimated time-scales.
7 Identify potential support for the plan.
8 Prepare an action plan identifying actions to be taken to finalise the business plan for presentation.

Purposes of a business plan

A business needs a plan so that it has a direction to follow.

The business needs to know:

■ Where it is going
■ How it will get there
■ What resources it will need.

A business plan can be defined as:

A plan presented to a bank or other source of finance describing what the business intends to do, and explaining what its costs will be, what it expects to earn, how it will repay money borrowed and how soon it will make a profit.

The plan enables the owner(s) to check and monitor progress. Planning therefore gives structure and direction. The business plan is also needed to show other people the direction the organisation is following. Support from people outside the organisation will almost certainly be needed – these are people who will supply the business with resources (including financial ones). If we are looking for a loan or overdraft for the business, we need to show a bank manager how much we will need, for how long, and when we will be able to repay the loan. Lenders of money will also be interested to see cash-flow projections, estimates of profits, etc. Would you lend money to a business that had no clear plans?

 Evidence collection point

As you work through this chapter you should begin to prepare work and collect data for the first draft of a business plan.

We can therefore review the purposes of a business plan as follows.

To seek sources of finance

When you set out in business you will normally need to secure outside sources of finance to help you start off. Some of your start-up capital will come from your own savings. However, in addition you may need to borrow money from friends and relatives, or other outside bodies such as banks.

Outsiders will not be keen to invest their money in a venture which has not been carefully thought out. Your business plan should therefore set out where and how you hope to seek additional sources of finance in addition to your own capital.

To gain finance

The people who will lend money to your business or invest in it will be concerned with two major factors:

- Whether in a given period of time the business will earn more money than it costs to run.
- Whether cash will flow into the business at a rate which enables it to meet ongoing demands for payment – i.e. cash flow.

Investors and lenders will want to know that their money is secure. For example, they will need to know that if your business runs into difficulties then the sale of assets will be sufficient to pay off debts. They will want to know that you are competent to run a business and that you are making fair and reasonable assumptions about things such as the sales you will make, the costs you will incur, etc.

To monitor progress

Planning should be seen as an ongoing process. In setting out targets and activities you should also be setting out ways of checking that targets are being met, and that activities are being carried out in an appropriate way.

For example, a business may anticipate that sales will follow the pattern:

	January	February	March	April
Sales	300	450	600	750

This business will need to devise ways of checking sales in each of these months so that actual performance can be checked against expected performance. That is:

	January	February	March	April
Expected sales	300	450	600	750
Actual sales	30	100	200	150
Monthly variance	−270	−350	−400	−600
Cumulative variance	−270	−620	−1020	−1620

In the above example, we can see a stark picture of a business that seems to be heading for disaster. Clearly, the business has overestimated the number of sales that it is likely to make. The accumulated variation between what the business expects to sell and what it is actually selling is a cause for considerable concern.

The illustration, however, does show the importance of using planning as a means to monitor progress. In setting out a plan you will need to set out time-scales and objectives. Then it will be important to review the plan in the light of actual performance. For example, you may plan to rent premises within a certain budgeted rental figure – what will be the implications of failure to find these premises or to keep within the budget? You may plan to purchase insurance with a given premium – what will be the implications of premiums going up?

In setting out a business plan you will need to be clear about what will be the main indicators of performance, and then you will need to monitor these indicators closely. Important indicators will include sales figures, revenues, costs and profits.

It is important for managers to be involved in business planning because this will give them a clear overview of how the business operates. Objectives can be set for different elements of business activity.

Evidence collection point

Produce a short leaflet for people thinking about setting up in business explaining why they should create a business plan, and what the main purposes of business planning are.

Business objectives

It is essential to have business objectives because this gives you a direction to follow.

Businesses have a range of objectives. Some organisations are primarily concerned with making a profit, whilst others may have charitable purposes. They may be concerned with sales volume, so that an objective is to sell x products per month; or they may be interested in sales value (e.g. to make £x of sales per month). Some businesses may have the objective of being the market leader, whilst others may set profit targets. Some may seek just to break even. Business objectives may also vary between the short-term and the long-term. This year your objective may be to hold on to your market share and break even, but in the longer term you may seek to make 20% return on capital invested and become the market leader.

To make a profit

Making a profit is a sensible business objective, particularly for businesses that need to raise finance from outside sources. Profits provide a business with

SALES FORECAST: number of units (Q) = _____

price per unit (P) = _____

GROSS TURNOVER ($Q \times P$) = _____

Minus: variable costs (of making forecast sales) = _____

Gives GROSS PROFIT = _____

Less overheads = _____

Gives NET PROFIT/LOSS = _____

Figure 26.1 Profit and loss forecast for 1998

a 'surplus' or 'cushion' which supports their activities in future trading periods. For example, it may be sensible in future periods to use profits to finance business expansion rather than having to rely on loan capital.

In simple terms, 'gross profit' can be calculated by subtracting the variable costs involved in making sales from the income from these sales.

In calculating expected gross profit you will therefore need to do the following calculation:

Expected sales (units) $\times$ price charged = Expected sales revenue

Expected sales (units) $\times$ variable cost per unit = Expected sales costs

Expected sales revenue – expected sales costs = Gross profit

In order to arrive at the figure for net profit you will then need to take away your overheads (i.e. fixed costs).

A chart setting out expected profits can be set out as shown in Figure 26.1.

To break even

A number of businesses may simply seek to break even, particularly in the early days. The volume of sales called the 'break-even point' occurs where the gross profit is equal to the costs, i.e. the business has made neither a profit nor a loss. It is important to remember that when you set out your business plan you will want to set out a wage for yourself or for all the members of your business. These wages need to be paid out of overheads. In other words the owners' wages are quite distinct from the profits of running the business.

Bank charges and interest payments on money borrowed would also need to be included in your overhead costs.

Breaking even therefore is a considerable achievement because it means that you have paid your way in any given year. You have not only covered the variable costs of production but also the complete set of overheads for a business, which include:

- wages
- National Insurance
- local council taxes including water charges
- rent
- fuel (e.g. electricity, oil and gas)
- telephone
- postage
- printing
- advertising and promotions
- repairs and maintenance
- insurance
- professional fees (e.g. to a solicitor or accountant)
- interest payments and bank charges
- vehicle and travel costs
- depreciation of vehicles
- depreciation of other assets (e.g. machinery, computers)
- other overheads.

Breaking even is therefore a considerable objective to achieve. The business-person who can pay himself or herself a 'decent living wage' as well as paying interest payments and bank charges is likely to be viewed as presenting a viable business proposition to outside providers of finance.

Of course, the provider might look on the proposition even more favourably if the business was likely to generate profits and to be able to pay back some of the loan capital.

To be subsidised

Not all businesses set out to make profits or to break even. Some businesses recognise that they will need to be subsidised. For example, some government services

such as ferries between the remoter islands of the United Kingdom can operate only on a subsidised basis.

Arguments for subsidising the ferry service would be that the ferry provides the only regular links between islands, e.g. for medical supplies, mail, food, tourism and other contacts, and that there are considerable benefits resulting from the operation of the ferries through the supplies and people going to the islands.

Many charities will also operate on the basis of subsidies. For example, a charity may carry out some of its trading activities at a loss, but this loss will be covered by subsidies from members' donation. Although, on paper, activities may appear as a financial loss, this does not take account of the extent of the benefits arising from such activities, e.g. providing employment for blind people.

The important thing, however, in business planning is that you identify the expected subsidy that you will require from particular business activities and justify why this subsidy will be required. People who are involved in supporting business activities are often prepared to provide a subsidy which has been justified. What irritates providers of capital is when the actual subsidy required turns out to be very much larger than that expected or budgeted for.

To make goods and to provide services

Many organisations set out to produce goods, while others set out to provide services.

For example, in your town or locality you will find young people who have set up their own enterprises producing goods such as a sandwich-making and delivery service, making pizzas, or making clothes or

Income from ferry passengers = £100 000
Cost of running ferries = £200 000
Subsidy = £100 000

1 To produce and sell gingerbread.
2 To trade under the name Simply Super Gingerbread.
3 To purchase ingredients in bulk at trade prices (wherever possible).
4 To produce gingerbread on the morning it is sold.
5 To sell gingerbread from a market stall on Saturday mornings.
6 To sell gingerbread at prices 10 per cent below those charged by other sellers of gingerbread.
7 To set production and sales targets, and to monitor these targets at regular intervals.
8 To review trading objectives at regular intervals.

Figure 26.2 A clear set of objectives

engineering parts, as well as ones who have concentrated on services such as hairdressing, financial services and running their own shops.

The wider public has most confidence in enterprises which clearly set out objectives and produce a clearly definable good or service. 'Shady' businesses tend to be ones about which you will hear it said: 'I don't know exactly what they do – they are a bit of an unknown quantity.' When you set out your own business plan it may be helpful to set out some clearly defined objectives. Figure 26.2 shows some of the objectives established by a group of young people with a mini-enterprise making gingerbread.

Evidence collection point

Set out some brief notes which clarify what major objectives enterprises might have when they first set up. Also try to discover the objectives of a local business.

Find out from the owners:

a How and why the objectives were established.
b How successful the organisation is in meeting its objectives.
c How and when the business reviews its objectives.

Then, identify the business objectives for a business activity for which you are going to prepare a business plan.

One of the most important parts of your Business Advanced course will be involved with setting out your own business plan. Hopefully, you will do this in conjunction with setting up your own enterprise activity in school or college.

When you set up your enterprise you will need to carry out detailed research in order to get a business plan off the ground. In this chapter we are focusing on the preparatory work that is required. The next chapter focuses on the production and presentation of your business plan.

When you start to set up your enterprise:

- Choose an enterprise activity which will sustain your interest.
- Choose an activity which can be carried out on a small scale.
- Choose an activity which will involve all members of your group.
- Make sure that you keep accurate records of business activities. All members of the group should be aware of everything that is going on.
- Choose an activity involving a product with a definite demand. Market research will be essential;

it is also essential that you produce a quality product.

Supporting information

In preparing work and collecting data for a business plan it is very important to prepare supporting information including information about:

- competing products
- demand for the product
- estimated number of customers
- likelihood of repeat business
- likely volume of sales
- possible value of turnover
- possible profits.

Competing products

There is a saying in business that an 'enterprise is only as successful as the competition allows it to be'. There is no point in producing a product which is more expensive and less reliable than an existing product.

Case study – Sell N Serve

The leaflet in Figure 26.3 was produced by a group of college students who set up their own business enterprise, Sell N Serv.

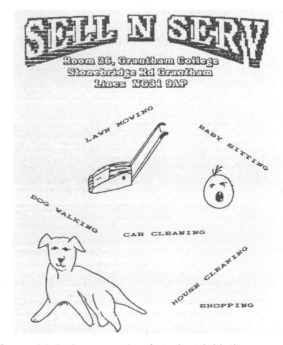

Figure 26.3 An example of student initiative

1 Which of the activities do you think would be successful?
2 Which of the activities do you think would have involved the students in the greatest competition?
3 What do you think the students would need to find out about the competition in each case in preparing work for their business plans?

It is always helpful to study the competition in order to gain additional ideas for your own product. The competition will give you a starting standard from which you can start to plan your own operation. Look at the size of their operation, the type and quality of their products or the characteristics of the service they offer.

What sort of image do your potential competitors put over? How can you outcompete the competition?

By studying the competition, you will be able to see how you can be different, and what additional benefits you will be able to offer.

Demand for the product

It is important to get a strong feel for the likely demand for your product or service. The quantity you sell will determine your likely sales revenue. Fall short of expectations and your budgeted figures will fall sadly apart.

In particular, you will need to have a good understanding of what sorts of people are likely to buy your product and why they want to buy the product. Demand is a want or need for a product backed up by money purchasing power. The demand for a product is the number of items that will be sold at different prices. You will want to know what the main factors will be which influence demand.

For example, price may be an important influence on demand. If this is the case you will need to make sure that your prices are no higher than those of direct competitors.

Income may be another important factor influencing demand. If this is the case you will need to be cautious about setting up during a recession when incomes may not be rising or may even be falling.

Case study – Flower selling

John and Julie have just left school and they would like to set up in business selling flowers from a market stall. They will be able to hire a small stall for £20 a day and a larger stall for £40 a day. The market is open each day from Monday to Saturday from 9 am to 5 pm except for Thursday when there is half-day closing.

John and Julie will be able to purchase stocks of flowers and plants from a local grower. Prices vary according to the season. However, John and Julie have found out that as a 'rule of thumb' they can mark up flowers by 300% in winter and 200% in summer.

They have decided to carry out some market research before finally deciding to set up in business.

1 How can John and Julie research their market?
2 What questions should they ask in their market research?
3 Whom should they ask?
4 How can they obtain accurate predictions of what the future demand for their product is likely to be?

Evidence collection point

How would you go about developing a detailed picture of the likely demand for a product or service that you propose to develop?

Carry out some research to find out what the demand is likely to be for your goods or service.

Estimated number of customers

Setting out an estimate of the likely number of customers for your goods or service is not a matter of plucking numbers out of the air. You will need to carry out some detailed and precise research.

You will need to specify your likely customers as accurately as possible. You therefore need to narrow down your list of potential customers. For example, you could do this by geographical area. Are you selling your product countrywide, in the East Midlands, in Lincolnshire, in South Kesteven, in Grantham or just in your college? The process of narrowing down your group of customers is called 'segmentation'.

Therefore, you need to identify:

- the segment, or segments, that make up your market
- the total size of this segment
- your likely share of this segment.

There are all sorts of ways of segmenting markets – by area, by age, by interest, by income and status, etc. You will need to identify the most important characteristics that will define the segment that you are aiming for. Once you have defined your segment you will need to draw out in detail the characteristics of the customers to whom you are aiming to sell. The most important questions that you need to answer are:

- How many customers are there in your chosen segment?
- Where are they, and how can they be reached?
- Exactly what will they be most likely to demand (e.g. size, colour and quality of product, terms of payment, packaging)?
- How much will they buy? That is, what quantities will they buy and how often?

To obtain this information you will need to collect data by asking questions of potential customers. You will need to know the prices they currently pay for similar goods and services, and how much they would like to pay. Find out what they look for in the current goods and services that they buy, and what weaknesses they see in these goods and services. What suggestions do they have for improvement?

You need to take advantage of the information given by potential customers about the market segment to which you want to sell your products.

Evidence collection point

Carry out some research and collect data to find out in which market segment you should be selling your goods, and the characteristics of customers in this market segment. Find out the best ways of capturing a large share of this segment.

Based on this research, estimate the likely number of customers that you will be able to gain.

The likelihood of repeat business

Selling goods and services should not be seen as a one-off business. For example, on pages 605–6 we gave the sample of a group of students who made gingerbread. If they had sold that gingerbread and then found that people had not liked it, they might not have had any repeat orders. In nearly all business lines it is important to obtain repeat orders. For example, in producing this textbook we would hope that the quality will be such that teachers and lecturers who have used the book will recommend it to future students.

A great deal of effort needs to be put into making sure that products are based on quality standards, i.e. 'fitness for purpose'. If products meet these standards then this will lead to repeat orders. In making calculations of demand you will need to build in calculations for repeat orders.

For example, if you found that in selling gingerbread there was a demand for 500 biscuits at a price of 25p each, you would need to find whether this was a regular demand. That is, would a student who was prepared to buy three a week continue to buy three a week for every week that you ran your business? If a shop was prepared to buy 20 biscuits for resale, would it want 20 biscuits every week or just every now and then?

Evidence collection point

Produce a short set of notes explaining why repeat orders are important to business.

Find out the extent of repeat orders for a product or service you intend to produce.

Likely volume of sales

Volume of sales is a measure of the total quantity of goods which you would expect to sell within a given time period.

For example, if you expect to sell 500 Christmas candles in December, this would represent your volume of sales. If you produce more than one product, then you should calculate the volume of sales for each product line.

Evidence collection point

Prepare work and present data to show the likely volume of sales for products or services that you intend to offer in a given period of time.

Possible value of turnover

Figures for value of turnover will be of more use to a business in making financial calculations than figures that simply show volume.

Volume is helpful in showing quantities of raw materials that will be required, the amount of storage space needed, etc. However, figures represented in values are more helpful because they involve the common denominator of money.

For example, suppose that a business sells:

15 books at £5 each
100 magazines at £2 each
300 newspapers at 50p each.

In volume terms we can say that the business has sold 415 items.

However, it may be far more useful to know the value of its sales, i.e. the value of turnover, which in this case will be £425.

As we have seen earlier, we need to know the value of sales in order to be able to calculate break-even, gross profit, net profit, etc.

Evidence collection point

Prepare work and collect data to show the possible value of turnover for a business idea that you are working on. Explain how the figures for the value of turnover were arrived at.

Possible profit

In preparing estimates for a business plan we can only talk about possible profit. Actual profit will be arrived at by calculating actual sales revenues and costs after a period of trading.

We saw earlier that the estimated profit figure will be arrived at by calculating:

Gross turnover – variable costs = Gross profit

Gross profit – overheads = Profit/loss (before tax)

Evidence collection point

Set out a rough estimate for profit/loss for a particular business idea that you are working towards as a result of making a detailed calculation of gross turnover and costs. Bear in mind that it is very difficult to accurately forecast sales and costs at this stage. Try to set out some alternatives, for example:

- a high sales forecast
- realistic sales forecast
- pessimistic sales forecast
- optimistic costs forecast
- realistic costs forecast
- pessimistic costs forecast.

The legal and insurance implications of the business objectives

Rules and regulations introduced by both central and local authorities will influence the actions of businesses and therefore need to be taken into account in business planning. Frequently, small business owners will need to consult either their local enterprise centre or accountants, solicitors and tax consultants for advice.

Some of the main areas that need to be considered include:

- *Inland Revenue* A statement of income and expenditure must be submitted to the designated Inspector of Taxes.
- *Value Added Tax* When total turnover rises above a certain level, the owner must notify the local Customs and Excise Officer and register for VAT.
- *Business names* Although sole traders and partnerships can trade under their own names, if a business name is used it must follow the procedures laid out by the Business Names Act, 1985.
- *Planning control* Where the use of premises is to be changed, the planning authority must be consulted.
- *National Insurance* Contributions to the Department of Social Security have to be made both for owners of the business and for their employees.

- *Licences* These may be required for selling alcoholic products, operating as a driving instructor, providing credit services (Consumer Credit Act) and importing certain goods.
- *Insurance* It is a legal requirement to have vehicle insurance and employer's liability insurance.
- *Data Protection Act* A business will have to register if it keeps information about people on computer.
- *Health and Safety Act* This places a duty on employers to ensure the health and safety of the workforce.
- *Employment law* A business should be aware of the law relating to areas such as redundancy, unfair dismissal, sex discrimination and union membership.
- *Consumer protection* Businesses should be aware of various consumer-related acts which are designed to protect consumers from faulty products, unfit food, misleading descriptions, etc.

We will now look at some of those areas which you may need to research in identifying the legal implications of your business objectives.

Employment law

In Chapter 12 we looked at the responsibilities of employers for abiding by employment laws. If you are setting up a business which employs people, you will need to look carefully at requirements concerned with contracts of employment, with the appointment and dismissal procedures and at the requirements of Equal Opportunities, Race and Sex Discrimination Acts. These laws are very important because not only do they provide the basis for sound business policy, but also failure to comply with them can lead to severe penalties.

Evidence collection point

Produce a four-sided desktop-published leaflet outlining to employers the main features of employment law with which businesses need to comply.

Work done in producing this leaflet will help you to provide evidence of the use of Core Skills in Information Technology and Communication.

Health and safety regulations

In Chapter 12 we looked in depth at the most important ingredients of health and safety regulations affecting businesses today. They showed

that it is the responsibility of both employers and employees in this country to comply with safe working practices.

Health and safety is always one of the most important considerations for any organisation. It only takes a few seconds for an accident to occur. Most injuries are caused by pure accident. However, there are other cases where negligence is involved.

For negligence to be proven it is necessary to meet three conditions:

1 A business must owe a duty of care to a plaintiff, e.g. an employer to his or her workforce or customers.
2 The duty of care must be shown to have not been carried out.
3 Damage must have occurred.

It is essential for people carrying out business activities to ensure that they are not negligent.

For example, if you set up a baby-sitting group, and for a few minutes you left a group of very small children unattended with the door leading to a road unlocked, the consequences could be terrible.

If, during the course of manufacturing a food product, you dropped a jar and a sliver of glass found its way into the ingredients, imagine the consequences!

Evidence collection point

Prepare work and collect data exploring the health and safety regulations which particularly relate to a product or service you intend to provide for an enterprise activity.

Environmental regulations

In setting up and running a business there are a number of important environmental regulations that need to be considered. Examples of these are planning permission requirements, noise controls, waste controls, and fire regulations.

Planning permission requirements relate to using buildings for particular purposes, changing the use of buildings, putting up new premises, etc. For example, if you wanted to convert an ordinary house into a restaurant or take-way facility you would need to apply to the local council for planning permission. There are a number of factors to be considered, including the road transport facilities in the area, the existence of other business premises or residential

accommodation in the locality and the strength of local feeling. Other residents have the right to object to planning proposals and change of land use in a particular area.

Noise controls are being given increasing priority since 1995. Before this time it was very difficult to bring prosecutions against noise disturbance. Now the controls have been 'beefed up'. Promises which make more than a certain amount of noise, e.g. through the use of electric saws, are not allowed within a certain distance of residential property.

In addition, there are tight environmental controls covering the discharge of wastes into sinks, rivers, the sea, etc. Harmful substances cannot simply be poured down the sink or taken to the local council dump. There are very tight controls covering the disposal of such substances, and substantial fines for non-compliance with regulations.

Another important area is fire regulations, which cover the amount of space needed between buildings, the placing of fire doors, the practice of fire drills, etc.

Evidence collection point

Identify the environmental regulations which need to be considered for a business idea that you are planning for. Look at each of these regulations in detail in terms of how it relates to

your business proposal. What do you need to do to ensure that you comply with regulations? Set out a checklist identifying important requirements.

Trades Descriptions Act

The Trades Descriptions Act sets out that goods must comply with descriptions that are given of them in any form, verbal as well as written. It is very important that any claims that you make about a product can be proved.

For example, if you claim that your product only contains natural ingredients, then you will get into trouble if you include artificial substances. If you produce shrinkproof cloths, then they should not shrink when washed at the correct washing temperature.

Evidence collection point

Examine the details of the Trades Descriptions Act, with particular reference to a product or service for which you are producing a business plan. Set out in writing how your product is complying with the requirements of this Act.

Insurance implications

All types of businesses require a similar set of policies. The purpose of insurance is to provide cover against losses which might be incurred through business activity.

For example, a group of students carrying out an enterprise activity decided to produce a presentation to outline their business proposal to prospective providers of finance. In preparing an overhead for their presentation they used the wrong type of transparency, which melted in the photocopier. The students tried to repair the roller in the photocopier, causing £400 worth of damage. This incident illustrates why it is essential to insure business and trading activities.

Asset insurance

In carrying out business activity you may need to purchase expensive assets such as machinery and equipment, or you may hire such assets. It is essential to make sure that any such assets are insured.

The size of the premium will depend on the value of the asset, and on the insurance company's estimation of the risk involved.

Public liability insurance

A firm can cover itself for the compensation it is liable to pay out if it is sued by someone who is hurt on its premises. Businesses must pay a premium to receive this cover. However, it is very important that a business and its employees are trained in safety procedures. In the case of negligent behaviour, insurance policies may be invalidated and the business may be responsible for liabilities incurred in the case of accidents.

In addition to public liability insurance, a business must also take out employers' liability insurance. This is a compulsory insurance to cover the money it may need to pay out if it is sued by an employee who is hurt while working on the company's premises.

Product liability insurance

A firm can insure itself against being sued by a consumer who suffers injury or loss caused by the firm's products. For example, food products must be produced to very high quality standards – from time

to time you will read about pieces of glass and even staples being found in food. You read of cases where hairdressers have mixed hair dye in the wrong way so that people's hair falls out or turns green.

In America, product liability cases can result in compensation claims for millions of dollars – sometimes for seemingly outrageous cases, like the woman who successfully sued the supplier of a microwave oven. She had attempted to dry her cat in the oven after bathing it, and it died. She claimed that the manufacturer should have warned her against such an event taking place!

Evidence collection point

Produce a short report (about 500 words) setting out the types of insurance cover that you would need to take out for your business idea. Visit a local insurance broker to find out what levels of premium you would be expected to pay, and what cover this would give you.

Discuss the feasibility of proposals with others

When you have a good business idea, who do you turn to for advice about feasibility? Of course, you turn to someone with business experience. For example, your local Enterprise Agency has business consultants available to give such advice. A High Street bank will not only be able to give financial advice, but will provide more general guidance on other aspects of setting up a business. Most High Street banks provide starter packs giving guidelines on how to construct a business plan, and bookshops offer a range of slim volumes on the subject.

You may also seek advice from someone who has already experienced the problems. For example, if you were thinking of setting up as a mobile hairdresser you would want to consult someone who already operates in this field. So the first step is to consult a knowledgeable person about your overall business idea, or several 'experts' on different aspects of it.

Evidence collection point

At this stage it will be helpful to review the work you have been doing to date and to consolidate it in a useful form. Prepare a presentation which will outline the following:

- Demand for the product.
- Likely customers.
- Likely start-up requirements and year one expenses to be financed – in other words how much money you will need to start up your enterprise, the expected expenses over the first year (try to set these out month by month in the form of a budget forecast), and how you would expect to finance these start-up requirements and ongoing expenses.
- The level of sales and profitability needed to ensure survival. (Perhaps you should present this in the form of a cash-flow forecast.)
- The number of people needed in the enterprise and the degree of expertise each would need to have if the business is to be a success.
- The levels of stocks and extent of associated equipment or fixtures and fittings needed.

When you have made your presentation you will need to discuss the feasibility of your proposals with others. These could be teaching staff or external experts and advisers from other organisations (e.g. a local bank). Discussing the feasibility of the draft plan at this stage should avoid doing too much work on ideas that are unrealistic, and will enable you to become more skilful at discussing your ideas.

You should record your evidence from this activity in written notes, illustrations, tape recordings and/or video recordings to enable you to show evidence of capability at the Core Skills of Communication, Application of Number and Information Technology.

Estimating the resource requirements to design, produce, promote and sell the goods or service

The next step that you will need to carry out is to estimate the resources that will be needed to carry through the plan.

A new product should be *designed* to meet the needs of customers. A 'new design' is a product with details that are different from earlier products intended for much the same use.

Customers should be able to identify features of the new product that are different from and better than those of competing products. Good product design is generally agreed to relate directly to commercial success.

For most major projects a design team is established, led by a design manager. The team then remains with the project throughout its development.

An organisation's *product* (and hence production) is the good or service it offers to consumers. All organisations have to analyse what their product means to their customers. Too often, in the past, organisations have ignored marketing information and developed products simply because production costs appeared to be low, or because efficient use could be made of materials; they did this instead of looking at how they could develop products to meet customer needs.

Promotion involves using a variety of means to ensure that consumers are aware of the product that the organisation is offering in the marketplace. There is no point in having a good product unless you are going to take the time and trouble to promote it.

Selling is concerned with putting over the benefits of your product in such a way that people buy it. The sales arm of an organisation is a vital ingredient because without selling, the organisation will not make any revenue.

The organisation will therefore need to work out what resources it will require to carry out these essential activities, i.e. for:

- design
- production
- promotion
- selling.

The resources needed to produce goods and services are described below.

Human resources

People are perhaps the most important resource of any organisation. You will need to work out what skills you have which can be applied to the business, and the skills that will need to be contributed by others. Mental and physical labour will be required to carry out work tasks; management experience will be needed to control and coordinate the use of other resources.

Task

Set out a list of work responsibilities for the business organisation you hope to set up. Show how these work responsibilities will help to achieve the objectives that you have discussed and agreed. Carry out an audit of the skills of members of your group who are involved in setting up an enterprise. Identify any gaps between existing skills and those required to make the business a success. How might this gap be filled? Check that you have sufficient human resources to design, produce, promote and sell your product.

Physical resources

Physical resources will include the materials and equipment required, such as raw materials and stock. Because the business is producing products it will need ingredients (i.e. raw materials). It will also usually need to have some goods available to supply to consumers immediately (unless all goods are made to special order).

Evidence collection point

Outline the physical resources that will be required to ensure that your business idea is carried through successfully. What physical resources will be required to ensure the successful design, production, promotion and sale of your chosen product or service?

Financial requirements

The financial requirements should set out the capital and cash requirements of the organisation:

- *Capital, equipment and premises* The business will need to have somewhere to operate and machinery to produce outputs.
- *Cash resources* Cash is the lifeblood of a business. It needs to have money available to buy stock and to pay off debts. Without cash, other vital resources that the business requires will quickly dry up.
- *Financial resources* In addition to cash, the business may need to have other financial resources to set up, buy materials, and to pay off debts. For example, it may have an overdraft, loan or mortgage. Many businesses also require land.

Evidence collection point

Set out the major financial requirements for your business plan to cover the design, production, promotion and sale of the good or service.

In addition, a business will need information and communication resources. An organisation today will require means of communication with its internal and external customers. It will benefit from the use

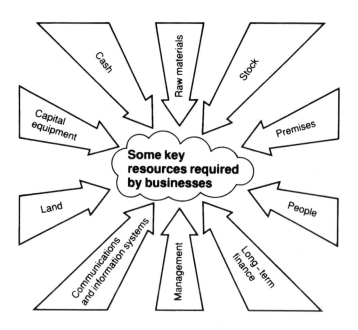

Figure 26.4 Resource requirements for a business

of IT systems, and other key ways of processing and communicating information.

The key resources required by a business are summarised in Figure 26.4.

Producing a flow-chart illustrating estimated time-scales

In preparing work and collecting data for a business plan it is essential to produce a flow-chart estimating the time-scale from the conception of a business idea to the opening of the business.

The flow-chart can be a simple diagram prepared either by hand or using information technology. The purpose of setting out the flow-chart is not to develop technical skills, but to encourage you to consider the diverse activities undertaken in creating a workable business plan, and how one activity may depend on the outcome of another.

You could set out the flow-chart in either a horizontal or vertical format. The best way of tackling this activity is to use an A3 piece of paper or a sheet of flip-chart paper. Students should then work together as an enterprise group. You should brainstorm ideas of the steps that will be required from conceiving the business idea to the opening of the business.

Obviously many of the steps can take place at the same time, but some of the steps can only take place after previous ones have been completed. For example, you could only estimate the size of your market after you have decided what your product is, and who your likely customers will be.

A useful way of looking at the sequence of activities involved in the production of new products is set out in the analysis of stages of product development shown in Figure 26.5.

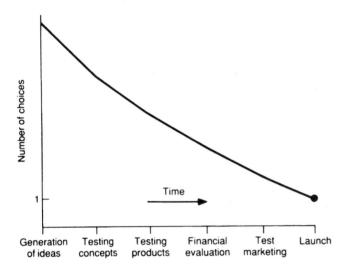

Figure 26.5 Time-scale to the launch of a new product

A number of steps can be clearly identified in the production of a new product. As ideas and products go through successive steps of research and testing, those considered less likely to succeed are eliminated (Figure 26.5).

Testing concepts involves assessing whether or not product designs might succeed in the marketplace. This means asking questions such as:

- What appeals to the customer?
- What benefits would this product offer?
- Does the product meet the needs of the market?
- Could the idea be improved?

Testing products of the manufactured kind involves developing models or prototypes. At this stage the designer will be looking at such areas as quality, performance, safety, ergonomics and appearance. The economics of production must be taken into

account, and it may be decided to build in planned obsolescence so that the product will need to be replaced after a certain period of time.

Financial evaluation of a new product's potential is essential. Will it ultimately generate profits? Techniques of investment appraisal, and cost–volume–profit predictions using break-even analysis, are essential at this stage.

Test marketing involves setting up a market situation that is as near to the real thing as possible. This is a 'dry-run' and brings back information to reduce some of the risks of a full launch. Test marketing often takes place in a chosen small market rather than in the total market.

The launch is the time when the product is presented to the market and is exposed to the ultimate critical test. Ideally, the launch will create an awareness of the product, followed by an interest and then a desire to purchase.

The above example is meant to illustrate the sequential steps which are involved in moving from an idea to the actual realisation of a product. In your flow-chart you will need to carry out a similar exercise in which you identify the time sequence involved in getting your business off the ground. You will need to identify all the activities involved and then organise them into a logical sequence. Some of these activities will involve finance, others marketing, etc.

Time-scales will need to be calculated under a number of headings:

- Planning
- Production
- Marketing
- Selling
- Distribution
- Lead time to break-even.

Planning

You will need to identify the planning activities that will need to take place, and when they will take place – when and how will you decide what to produce, when and how will you create a projected cash flow and plans for raising finance, when and how will you create a marketing plan, etc.

Production

Identify the various stages that will take place in producing the product. The steps in the time

615

sequence may be very similar to those identified in Figure 26.5 which showed steps from the generation of ideas for a new product to its launch.

Marketing

Identify the various stages in marketing – market research, identifying the target market, test marketing the product, etc.

Selling

Identify the activities that will be involved in selling the product, and the sequence of tasks involved.

Distribution

Identify the different stages involved in getting the product to customers, and when and how each of these will take place.

Lead time to break-even

Identify, by a series of calculations of anticipated revenues and costs, the lead time until the business reaches the break-even point.

Evidence collection point

Set out a flow-chart which shows the time-scales involved from the conception of the business idea to the opening of the business. The flow-chart should include planning, production, marketing, selling, distribution, and the lead time to break-even.

Identifying potential support for the plan

You should identify people and/or institutions who could be called on to provide moral, specialist, financial or legal advice or resources for the business plan. People providing support would include people within your own institution, such as business studies lecturers, specialists such as people responsible for planning the financial budget of the school or college, or anyone within the organisation responsible for some form of project planning.

In addition, you should be able to call on expert help from people outside the institution, e.g. people who work full-time in finance, the law, marketing, or production. You should make appointments to discuss parts of your business plan with specialist advisers. Alternatively, specialists should be invited into the school or college.

It should be stressed, however, that you will need to present your ideas in a professional form to specialists. You will be wasting their time if you present 'half-baked' ideas on a scrappy piece of paper.

Evidence collection point

Set out in about 300 words details of the types of people who might be able to give you specialist help with your business plan. What sorts of specialist help would you expect to derive from each of these 'experts'?

Finalising the business plan for presentation

The next chapter includes consideration of how you will be able to prepare a presentation of your business plan to an invited audience. You should now set about creating an action plan which is concerned with preparing your presentation.

The action plan should set out:

1 The area for development, i.e. what do you want to plan or change? In this case you are planning to make a presentation of your business plan.
2 The action steps required, i.e. what steps will you need to take to see the plan through? In this case you will need to set out step by step what you will need to do in order to be ready for the presentation. A very important element of this will be to set out a time-scale for each of these steps.
3 Review of progress. In setting out the plan you will need to set out clearly from the start the dates at which you will review progress towards meeting your targets, i.e. ensuring that your action steps are performed on time. Ideally you should review this progress with somebody else. The most sensible suggestion would be for you to work with another student who can be relied upon to pressurise you to achieve your deadlines. The review of progress should look at how successful you have been in carrying out action steps on time and at what else needs to be done.

4 Evaluation. Evaluation of your action plan should be concerned with answering the question: 'When and how will I measure the success of the plan and the steps that I have taken?'

All of the above are essential ingredients of your action plan. If you fail to take the action plan seriously you will fall behind and will be unlikely to make an effective presentation.

Evidence collection point

Prepare an action plan identifying actions to be taken to finalise the business plan for presentation.

Evidence indicators

Produce the first draft of a business plan, outlining the goods or services to be provided and relevant supporting information on marketing and finance.

The following list should serve as a checklist. Please tick off each of the following when you have successfully covered them as part of your report. You need to be able to confirm that:

- I have:
  - planned time-scales ☐
  - considered legal and insurance implications ☐
  - worked out first estimates for resource requirements ☐
  - obtained possible support for the plan from financial, legal, marketing or production specialists ☐
  - listed action points identifying next steps to complete the business plan. ☐
- I have produced a supporting statement explaining the purpose of producing a business plan. ☐

617

Producing and presenting a business plan

This chapter has been designed to enable you to go through the various stages in producing a finalised business plan. The chapter has been set out in sequence to enable you to:

1 Describe and explain business objectives for a business enterprise
2 Outline a marketing plan for a business enterprise
3 Outline a production plan for a business enterprise
4 Outline the resource requirements for marketing and production
5 Produce financial data and forecasts to support the business plan
6 Identify monthly profit and loss and balance sheet monitoring and review procedures of the business plan
7 Present and explain the business plan to an audience.

You will need to understand the details of planning – especially the financial details – which prospective lenders demand of a business plan. In addition, you should be aware of the needs and expectations of other parties interested in the plan, such as co-directors, partners, shareholders, investors and employees.

Although you may wish to present your plans on paper, in an appropriate presentational style and format, this has cost implications (it may be more cost-effective with the development of electronic mail to include a disk or a network reference in the portfolio). The portfolio should contain the visual aids prepared to support the oral presentation; these are likely to duplicate the content of the business plan. If a potential provider of finance is not available, that role may be simulated, for example by the Business lecturer.

Describing and explaining business objectives for a business enterprise

When you set out in business you need to have a clear idea of what you are trying to achieve. So, first of all, set out what you are in business for. For example, if you are in business to become rich, then how rich, and how soon do you want to be rich? If you are in business to be independent, what level of income will you need to achieve from the business to maintain that independence? If you are in business to pass on a healthy growing concern to your heirs, then what level of annual growth will you want to achieve?

There are thus three essential ingredients to setting out your objectives:

■ a definition of the objectives
■ a value or target figure that you are aiming for
■ a time-scale in which to achieve these targets.

For example, the following are examples of these three ingredients:

■ to increase personal income by £60 000 in three years
■ to increase profits by 20% per year over the next 3 years
■ to successfully build up the enterprise so that it can be floated on the Stock Market in five years.

 Evidence collection point

Start off your detailed business plan by setting out the following:

■ Introduction
■ Details of the business
■ Business objectives

Introduction

This should give a brief summary of the business idea. It will explain the objectives of the business and how it is intended they should be achieved. Perhaps you can include some personal details – brief relevant work experience, skills and education. The name of the business is very important – it will need to give the impression of 'quality' (fitness for purpose). Points to consider include:

■ Does your business name give you a competitive edge? (Look at names used by the competition.)

- Is your business name linked to quality?
- Are you benefiting from association with a competitor?

Details of the business

This should include the business name and address, and a detailed explanation of the product or service being offered. Try to show what makes your product or service different from that of competitors, and why your product will sell.

Business organisation

This should state whether the organisation will take the form of a partnership, a private limited company, etc. Also spell out the management structure of the organisation – be brief and concise, showing key personnel and what their functions are.

Business objectives

In this section of your work you will need to show potential lenders that you know exactly what you are doing, i.e. that you have clear objectives. Your objectives will need to cover the following:

- *Supply of goods or service* What exactly is it that you are supplying to the market? Is it a product or service? What exactly is this product or service? This is not always clear, particularly if you are launching a new idea. You will need to show how your good or service is distinctive and how it differs from other products or services.

  Remember that 80% of all new products that were launched in the mid-1990s were unsuccessful. The implication is that if people are going to be convinced by your idea then they need to feel that it is a really good one.

- *Achieving sales volume* One of your objectives will be to achieve a given sales volume, i.e. how many items you expect to sell in each sales period. You will need to set out this expected sales volume in your introductory objectives. In the marketing section of the plan you will then need to justify this figure and show how it is likely to be achieved.
- *Achieving sales value* We have already seen that the value of sales is perhaps more important than the volume of sales. The sales value shows the total revenue that will actually come into the business, and which will be a major determinant

of profit. Briefly, in your objectives section set out the sales value which you hope and expect to achieve; later on you can justify this.

- *Making a profit* Calculating profits will involve detailed estimates of sales value, sales costs and overheads. In your initial objectives it is helpful to set out the sorts of profits that you are hoping to make. People who lend you money will be convinced if they can see the real potential for profits.
- *Break-even point* It is also helpful to show the break-even point, i.e. when a business makes no profit and no loss. Lenders of money will feel most secure if it does not take long for the business to achieve the break-even point.
- *Meeting time-scales* The other important element of objectives is the time-scale concerned. What will be the sales value and volume in particular time periods? When will the break-even point be achieved? When will profits be made?

 Evidence collection point

While studying this chapter you should start to assemble a five-part business plan for a small business enterprise, presented on paper or electronically.

You should now be able to produce Part One of your plan:

- Part One: Introduction and objectives – explaining the key objectives of the plan.

This should enable you to provide evidence of your capability in the Core Skills of Communication, Application of Number and Information Technology.

Outlining a marketing plan for a business enterprise

You will not be able to sell anything unless there is someone out there willing to buy what you are offering. Market research will therefore need to provide the basis on which you produce your marketing plan.

In carrying out market research you will be seeking to find out: 'Is there anyone out there wanting to buy our good or service?' As a first task, therefore, look at your proposed market and see whether it is large enough to generate the business you need.

The marketing plan you produce will need to cover a number of important ingredients:

- *The demand for the good or service* How strong or weak is the demand? Who will want to purchase the product, i.e. what is your target market? What are the features of people in this target market? What factors will influence people demanding your product?
- *Naming* What will you call your product or service? How did you choose this name? What are the benefits/drawbacks of using this name?
- *Pricing* What price will you charge? How and why have you chosen the price structure?
- *Packaging* What packaging will you use for presenting your good or service?
- *Promoting* How will you promote your product? Why have you chosen to promote your product in this way?
- *Distributing* How will you distribute your product? Why have you chosen particular distribution channels?
- *Merchandising* Why have you decided to merchandise your product in the way you have selected?
- *Selling (targets, volumes)* What sales targets and volumes do you expect to be able to achieve? Provide details of why you have chosen these targets and volumes. What evidence do you have to show that they are feasible?
- *Timing* How will the plan be phased in terms of what will be achieved by when?
- *Marketing communications* Which communications methods and means such as advertising, public relations, sales promotion, direct marketing, etc. will most effectively communicate to, and influence the decision-making of the target audience?
- *After-sales support* How will you provide after-sales support to consumers of your products or services? Why are you providing after-sales support?

You will need to read through the following section before starting on your marketing plan. It should provide you with a wealth of ideas about what to include in this plan.

Anyone with business experience who looks at a business plan will focus on a key question: does the person who made the plan understand his or her market? In simple terms this involves looking to see whether the plan shows an understanding of why people will buy the good or service, and whether the competition has been researched.

The plan needs to show that you understand the marketing mix from the consumer's point of view.

What product does the customer want? What price does the customer want to pay? Where does the customer want the product? What promotion does the customer want?

If you are going to be able to convince someone that your marketing plan is well thought out, you will need to show that a sufficient quantity of customers will purchase your product. Set out to give answers to the following questions:

1 What benefits will your product or service offer to customers?
2 At what price will your goods or service be offered?
3 Will price be an important influence in the buying decision?
4 How and where are you going to sell the product or service?
5 How are you going to launch your business or service to gain maximum possible interest and take-up? What promotional and publicity methods will you employ?

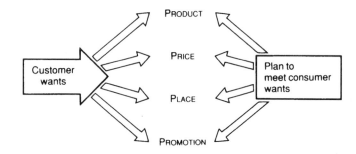

Figure 27.1 Planning to satisfy your market

In your marketing plan you should also give an indication of how you will **sell** your product. Selling can be a weak point in a business. In order to sell a product you will need to think about how you are going to communicate with customers, including what you are going to tell them. Selling is concerned with presenting solutions to a buyer's needs or problems. How are you going to meet your customers, explain your solutions to their problems or needs, counter any worries that they may have, and then complete the deal (as well as offering after-sales service)? An outline of these details must be built into your plan.

You should also mention the **timing** of your marketing and sales activities. Perhaps you could construct a flow-chart showing when market research will occur, when promotion will occur, when prospective customers will be contacted, etc.

Case study – Washing machine repairs

Jane Brown is seeking financial support from her bank to finance a washing machine repair service. She has supplied her bank with the following information:

> I have decided to move into washing machine repairs because I have always been interested in mending things. I have been able to repair some washing machines for households in this area, where I have friends. People always seem to be satisfied with my work. I have decided to charge £12 an hour for my labour, and will charge for parts and petrol as well. I expect to be able to take the market by storm and within a year should have over one-third of the market in this town. I expect the market to grow as more and more people struggle with old models of washing machines.

It would appear that Jane does not know a lot about marketing. Look through the information she has supplied and identify the strengths and weaknesses of her presentation. What parts of her research and planning do you feel need improvement? What questions should she be seeking the answers to and spelling out in her marketing plan?

As well as providing information for outsiders, the marketing plan sets the targets for a business. Performance can then be monitored against these targets. Progress should always be checked against initial plans.

Jane Brown's marketing plan failed to answer a number of questions:

- *Why will people buy her product?* Some market research would have answered this crucial question. She might have found, for example, that older washing machine users and those lacking mechanical skills prefer not to carry out the complex and dirty task of mending, servicing and repairing their own washing machines. This might be particularly true for people whose washing machines are becoming dated. Market research would have indicated the benefits that different groups of consumers were looking for. She would then be in a better position to provide these benefits.
- *Who will buy her product?* Market research would have indicated the main groups wanting her product. She might then have been able to target benefits at specific groups.
- *How much will her customers buy?* Will they have repeat orders? Finding out how often customers would need washing machine repairs would give her a clear idea of the quantity of sales she could expect to make. This information would be vital in planning targets and in seeking financial support for her business.
- *Who are her competitors?* Research into the competition would enable Jane to find out what benefits they were offering and whether she would be able to compete with them. She would need to find out the strengths and weaknesses of her competitors. She could then concentrate on

those benefits that her customers required but which the competition was weak at supplying, and make sure that she was also effective in supplying the benefits in which competitors were strong.

■ *What will her market share be?* Calculations of market share are important in any business plan. For example, if the total market value for washing machine repairs in a small town was £100 000 a year and Jane expected to take 5% of this, then she would have a turnover of only £5000. However, if she expected to take 50%, she would have a turnover of £50 000.

■ *When will her customers buy?* Jane needs to identify the peak periods of the year, i.e when customers would be using washing machines most. She also needs to find out on what days of the week people are most likely to require washing machine repairs. She can then tailor her business activities to meet customer requirements.

■ *What price will consumers be prepared to pay?* Market research might indicate that £12 per hour is too high a price. It will also indicate quantities that can be sold at different prices. Jane can then work out ways of maximising revenues.

■ *Is the market growing or contracting?* Jane would need to provide hard evidence that people are keeping machines as they get older rather than simply replacing them. Perhaps newer models will be more reliable and require less servicing. She also needs to check on how long after-sales service agreements from the suppliers of new washing machines generally last. Perhaps she should look at published sources of consumer trends. If she can show that her market is growing by 10% a year, then she can start to quantify her likely sales figures in future years.

It should now be obvious that marketing provides a business with valuable evidence for a business plan. It can tell us details of:

■ market size
■ market share
■ market growth
■ acceptable prices
■ quantities (demand).

When providing quantitative information you may want to present different scenarios – an optimistic scenario (if things go really well), a likely scenario (if things do not change a lot), and a pessimistic scenario (if things go badly).

Of course, a bank will tend to err on the cautious side when weighing up figures from a marketing plan.

Task

1 Jill runs a business supplying sandwiches to business premises. In 1994 she calculated that the value of the delivered sandwich market in her home town was worth £50 000. She expected to be able to win 40% of this market. The market is expected to grow at 10% a year. Calculate Jill's expected sales revenue for 1995.

2 Kevin is a freelance graphics artist producing business stationery and posters. The market in which he operates is currently worth £400 000. Kevin estimates that the market will increase in value by £50 000 next year. However, economic forecasts suggest that the value of the market is likely to fall by between 10% and 20% next year. Kevin is likely to win 10% of the total market. He is seeking a bank loan, but because of recent experience the bank is taking a pessimistic view. What value would the bank place on Kevin's likely sales next year?

The case of Jane Brown showed the importance of basing a marketing plan on careful research. Once you have clarified a business proposal you should start to look at existing businesses that are similar to the one you propose. There may be an estate agent in your town who deals with business and commercial properties and who might be able to provide you with leads to similar businesses. You may also be able to interview people who run similar businesses, but it could make sense to do this in a neighbouring town in which businesses will not be in direct competition with your own. People will be reluctant to talk with and provide assistance to potential competitors!

Look at published statistics that refer to the relevant business sector. A library should be able to provide you with copies of government–produced Business Monitors. These examine different business sectors, so find the one that is relevant to you.

We can now say a little bit more about selling activities.

Pricing is a crucial element in the marketing mix. A low price might make you competitive but it may lead consumers to question the quality of your product. In your plan you need to explain and justify the price you have chosen, by showing how it is related to market research. You also need to bear in mind that the price needs to be pitched at an appropriate level to guarantee profits.

When you start a new business you need to tell customers of your existence through **advertising and promotion.** You then need to get people to try out your product, possibly by giving away free samples or by sending out special offers or invitations to view.

The next step will be to get people to buy, and you want customers to come back for more.

Your promotion plan should therefore show:

- why you need to promote your product
- what aspects of the product you are promoting
- what the promotions are and why they are likely to be successful
- how much the promotions will cost, and when
- how much profits the promotions will generate
- ways of evaluating the effectiveness of the promotions.

The sales plan will need to set out:

- the expected volume of sales
- the expected value of sales
- how, where and when goods will be sold
- the cost of making sales
- the likely profits generated from sales
- ways of evaluating the effectiveness of the selling operation.

In looking at **distribution** you will need to show how your goods will reach the consumers. Market research will have revealed important information about consumers' preferences for distribution. The distribution plan additionally needs to indicate plans for getting goods to consumers in the right place, and the costs stemming from such operations.

Once a sale has been made, it is necessary to maintain customer support for the product. Your marketing plan therefore needs to indicate that you have researched consumer preferences for **after-sales service**, and how and when you will provide the required service.

Effective marketing costs money, but in return it should generate substantial revenues. The costs of marketing should be far smaller than the rewards.

Interested consumers will buy goods and services, and satisfied consumers will return to make repeat purchases and pass on the message about the product. Budgeting includes deciding what marketing activities to spend money on, when to spend, and how much.

You need to have a clear idea of when you are going to carry out particular marketing and sales activities. You also need to understand why you are carrying out a specific activity at a particular time.

 Evidence collection point

You should now be able to produce Part Two of your five-part business plan:

- Part Two: Marketing – stating how, where and to whom the plan's products or services will be marketed and sold to achieve planned objectives.

The marketing plan should include details of:

- demand for the product or service
- names which you have chosen for products (and for the business)
- pricing
- packaging
- promoting
- distributing
- merchandising
- selling
- timing
- marketing communications
- after-sales support.

Work you produce for Part Two of the business plan will enable you to show evidence of the Core Skills of Communication, Application of Number and Information Technology.

Outlining a production plan for a business enterprise

The next part of the planning outline that you will need to produce is the production plan. A production plan is a statement of how a business intends to create the goods and/or services to satisfy the expected demand.

It will be important to outline how the goods or services will be acquired (as raw materials or finished goods), designed and processed (how and by whom) and tested for quality.

Design

Design of your product may include a number of areas. If you are producing a manufactured product such as biscuits you will need to create a design which takes account of factors such as size, shape, texture, colour, flavour, etc.

The design of your product will need primarily to focus on consumer requirements for good design. There is no point in designing what you think consumers *should* like. At all stages in the design process you will need to keep in touch with your customers through market research by asking questions such as: 'What design features would you most like to see in a .....?' You should then take your

initial designs to customers, ask them what they think and how the design could be improved.

Evidence collection point

Set out some notes outlining who will be responsible for the design of your product, how you will involve consumers in the design process, what the key stages will be in designing your product, and a time schedule of design steps.

Product development

In the section on marketing planning we outlined a number of important stages in product development (Figure 27.2).

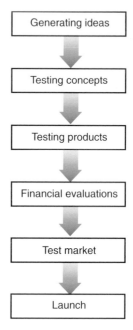

Figure 27.2 Stages in product development

Let us assume that you have already generated an idea for your business. How effective will it be? You need to test the concept by working with others, including potential buyers, to find out what their perception is of the product. Does it appeal to them? Does it meet their needs? What improvements could be made?

Once you have thrashed these ideas around you will want to produce some prototypes of the product to get a clearer idea of what it will look like, how it will work, and whether there will be any unforeseen problems.

Financial evaluation involves working out the cost of producing different quantities of the product. You may find that the costs of producing the product in quantity are excessive.

Test marketing involves actually trialling the product in a smaller version of your intended marketplace. You will need to choose a test market which is representative of the 'real' market that you will be selling in. For example, if your product is aimed at females who are over 60 then you should test your product on a sample of females in this age bracket.

Once you have successfully negotiated all these stages you will be in a position to launch your product.

Evidence collection point

Explain how you intend to go through the various stages of product development outlined above.

Production process

The production processes which you use will depend on the type of product you are producing. For example, you may be engaged in producing personalised stationery, involving the computerised generation of such materials. You will need to set out clearly each of the processes involved. It is helpful if you can set out a step-by-step description of the process, outlining the time taken at each stage and how activities interrelate.

Evidence collection point

Set out a step-by-step description of the production processes involved in your chosen enterprise activity. (This is as relevant for services as it is for manufacturing.)

Production levels

Production levels are the quantities of outputs you anticipate achieving in a particular period of time. You will best be able to set out feasible production levels when you have produced final versions of your product, or have outlined (and practised) steps involved in service activities. It may be helpful to set out a few different production levels which are contingent on different conditions – an optimistic, a likely, and a pessimistic production level.

Evidence collection point

Set out in your production plan the production levels that you expect to achieve, and what the major factors are which will determine whether these levels can be achieved.

Premises

In business planning, once a business has decided on the approximate location it desires, it is possible to look for specific premises. It is necessary to assess the amount of space required to store materials and to make goods or provide a service. It is necessary to consider the services that are required – water, telephone, electricity, etc. If deliveries need to be made to your business then it may be necessary to be near a road.

It will be important to find out whether you would be given planning permission to carry out a particular business activity, particularly if you have chosen a site which will need alteration. You would be wise to consult a planning officer about such changes.

If you want to produce food or to carry out dangerous activities then you will need to comply with special requirements.

You will need to decide whether you are going to rent, lease or purchase the property.

Evidence collection point

Outline the premises which you hope to use and show what research you have done to

This looks ideal for our new hairdressing business.

Let's see if we can borrow the keys from the estate agent to measure up the premises, and see what services are available.

find out about the regulations and requirements with which you will need to comply. Show how you will set out and use the premises that you have chosen for your business.

Machinery

If you are creating a business plan for a manufacturing operation then you will have to consider the types of machinery that you will use. You will need to do some research to identify appropriate models, and obtain prices of different types of machinery. You will need to decide whether you will buy outright or hire the machinery. If you are producing a service, then the acquisition of machinery will be equally relevant – computers, company vehicles, etc.

Evidence collection point

Make some notes setting out the types of machinery you will need for your business, the strengths and weaknesses of different models, prices, etc.

Raw materials

All business activities involve the processing of raw materials, whether they be cocoa and milk in chocolate production, hair dye and shampoo in hairdressing, or paper in office work. You will need to identify the main raw materials required in your chosen type of business activity. Set out a time schedule showing what these raw materials are, when they will be required and how much they will cost.

Evidence collection point

Produce a chart showing a time schedule for raw material requirements for your business proposition.

Labour

If you are going to obtain support for your business proposal from outside backers you will need to bear in mind that they will look closely at your business and the people who run it and ask whether you have employed the right people. By setting out a table like the one below for each of your employees, you can identify any strengths and weaknesses and have replies ready when asked.

Evidence collection point

Use a desktop publishing package to set out an employee analysis report for each of your employees, perhaps using the outline shown below:

Name:

Job title:

Age:

Professional qualifications:

Identified training needs:

Career history:

Personal strengths and weaknesses:

'People' skills:

Commitment to the business:

Potential future contribution:

Quality assurance

In Chapter 15 we emphasised the importance of quality assurance in business. In recent years, many organisations have adopted a broad approach to quality under the umbrella of quality assurance. With this approach, goods provided in the marketplace are expected to be of an appropriate quality and the operations of the organisation providing the good or service are designed in such a way as to assure that this quality is achieved. The idea is that this approach makes sure that an organisation gets the quality right first time and thus avoids problems arising from failure.

We can illustrate the process of quality assurance by taking the example of photography booths of the kind that you find in post offices, railway stations, large shops, etc. In the past, consumers wanting a passport photograph would sit in the booth, adjust the curtains, press the button, and sit uncomfortably as the camera flashed four times. They then went and stood outside for two or three minutes wondering what the photo would look like. Frequently they were disappointed with the end results, which showed them with their eyes closed, looking as if they had just staggered out of bed or the pub.

Today, the process is radically different. You go into the photography booth, which will then record your image on a short video film. You can run through the film and choose the images you want.

Quality assurance involves assuring 'fitness for purpose' and providing the quality standards that consumers require. You need to set out ways of ensuring quality standards. What procedures will you employ?

 Evidence collection point

Set out some brief notes setting out how you will assure quality in the production of your good or service. For example, how will you:

- set the quality required by the customer
- plan to achieve the right quality
- monitor the production process
- correct any problems?

Timing

Like any other aspect of planning, you will need to explain how your production plan will be phased in terms of what will be achieved and when.

 Evidence collection point

Set out a flow-chart showing how the various aspects of your production plan will be phased.

 Evidence collection point

You should now be able to produce Part Three of your five-part business plan:

- Part Three: Production – stating production intentions and schedules.

Outlining the resource requirements for marketing and production

Business planning and organisation is all about resource management. The four main resources that will be used are:

- human
- physical
- financial
- time.

We have been examining the requirements for producing marketing and production plans. Each aspect of these plans demands resources. For example, in the design process you will need to decide:

- who will be responsible for the design, how many hours will be required from each person, and what skills they will need to contribute – i.e. the human resource
- what physical resources will be required for the design process, e.g. computers and other equipment, a site to do the designing – i.e. the physical resource
- how much money will need to be ploughed into the design function, what percentage of the overall company budget this will involve, how the design will be financed, e.g. from cash reserves, borrowing – i.e. the financial resource
- how much time will need to be allocated to design, and how much to specific aspects of design, e.g. designing the logo, designing the product – i.e. the time resource.

You therefore need to identify all of the activities involved in marketing and production, and work out how many resources will be needed for each activity.

It is almost inevitable that you will find you require far more resources than you actually have available. This will force you to prioritise activities, and to decide which are critical. However, it is better to do this at the planning stage rather than finding that you run out of money or time halfway through a project.

Evidence collection point

Produce a list of all the activities that will be involved in marketing and production. Set out your resource requirements for each activity. Place activities in rank order so that you can decide what is most important, and what is feasible.

When coming up with a business proposal we tend to concentrate on opportunities. However, it is vital that we also list all the constraints. These are barriers that may prevent our business from being a success. Here are some of the constraints we should think about:

- *Personal constraints*
  - Have I enough time to put into the business?
  - Have I the skill or experience?
  - Is my health good enough?
  - Am I well organised? Can I manage time, stress, paperwork and people effectively?
- *Financial constraints*
  - Do I have enough cash, or will the business generate enough cash to meet the day-to-day needs of the business?
  - Can I raise enough medium-term and long-term finance to meet the capital requirements of the business?
  - Do I have an effective financial record-keeping system?
- *Marketing constraints*
  - Do I have enough resources to put into the marketing of the product?
  - What is the competition like?
  - What price are customers prepared to pay?
  - Can I supply at this price?
  - Where do customers want the product? Can I get it there?
  - Can I supply the product that customers want?
  - Can I put enough resources into promotion to make customers aware of the product?
- *Selling constraints*
  - Have I enough resources to put into selling?
  - Have I the experience to deal with customers and get them to buy the product?
- *Legal constraints*
  - How is the business proposal affected by employment law?
  - How is the proposal affected by health and safety regulations?

    For example, producers of gingerbread would need to look at food safety; setting up a market stall would involve considerations of public liability.
  - How is the proposal affected by consumer protection laws (e.g. the Trades Descriptions Act)?
- *Economic constraints*
  - Are we in a boom or recession?
  - Are interest rates high or low?
  - Does the product belong to a growing or declining sector of the market?
  - Can the product compete in international markets?

Evidence collection point

You should now be able to produce Part Four of your five-part business plan:

- Part Four: Resource requirements – stating the resources required for marketing and production.

The production of financial data and forecasts to support the business plan

The financial part of any business plan is crucial to its success. In the financial plan you should indicate how the plan will be financed in each part and in total, and where the finance will come from (e.g. loan from a bank, profit generated from sales).

Time period

The time period is a very important concept in business. In the long term the business needs to have enough assets to cover its long-term liabilities, and to generate profits over a period of time.

In the short term it needs to have enough cash flow to more than cover its short-term debts and other outflows. All too often a business fails because of inability to match inflows and outflows. It concentrates on long-term profits and fails to notice its short-term vulnerability because of a pressing debt that needs to be paid to a creditor.

When we looked at the constraints on business activity above we stressed that:

1 The business needs to have enough cash to meet its day-to-day needs.
2 The business needs to be able to raise enough medium-term and long-term finance.

You will need to provide evidence of both short-term and long-term financial viability in your financial data and forecasts.

Cash flow

It is imperative that you set out a cash-flow forecast for your business. We show a possible cash-flow form here. Bear in mind that it needs to cover a twelve-month period.

In each column you should list your target figure for cash received in the month. These will need to be related to your estimated billings in the profitability

Cash Targets		Month		Month		Month		Month	
		Budget	Actual	Budget	Actual	Budget	Actual	Budget	Actual
Orders									
Sales									
Purchases									
Receipts									
Sales – cash									
– debtors									
Loans/grants received									
Capital injected									
Asset disposals									
Other income									
Total receipts (CR)									
Payments									
Purchases – cash									
– creditors									
Wages, salaries, PAYE									
Rent, property taxes									
Light, heat, power									
Insurance									
Transport, packaging									
Maintenance									
Advertising									
Telephone									
Postage									
Professional fees									
VAT (net)									
HP payments, leasing charges									
Bank, finance charges and interest									
Drawings, fees									
Loan repayments									
Tax									
Dividends									
Capital expenditure									
Sundry expenses									
Total payments (DR)									
Net cash flow	CR								
	DR								
Opening bank balance	CR								
Balance brought forward	DR								
Closing bank balance	CR								
	DR								
Agreed overdraft facility									

forecast, which we look at below. For example, sales created in January may be paid for in March. As you are talking about actual cash sums, VAT should be included.

Remember that the items you include in your cash flow forecast will depend on the business you are in. The items we have included here are typical of the sorts of payments most businesses would make.

- *Capital* includes any finance raised from financial sources, partners or shareholders and used as working capital.
- *Finance repayments* includes hire purchase and other finance agreements.
- *Rent/property taxes* Items paid quarterly, etc., should be shown in the month of payment.
- *Fixed asset purchases* lists target figures for the purchase of assets such as plant and machinery.
- *Net cash flow* shows the difference between your targets for total receipts and total payments of cash.
- *Cumulative cash flow* adds all receipts and payments for the period under consideration, and includes the opening bank balance. If you do this for each month, then you obtain a forecast of the closing credit balance (or overdraft) for each month.

Evidence collection point

Set out a cash-flow forecast for the first twelve months of trading of your business.

Start-up balance sheet

Before proceeding to produce a balance sheet for your business you should review the notes on balance sheets in Chapter 24.

A balance sheet is a list of all the assets (what the firm owns) and liabilities (what the firm owes). These assets may be:

- *fixed assets* – e.g. land, buildings, plant and machinery, furniture, fixtures and fittings
- *current (short-term) assets* – stocks, debtors, cash, petty cash
- *intangible assets* – relationships with customers, business and technical know-how, which have a value but no physical existence.

On the liabilities side we have the investors' capital, because the firm owes it to the investor! Similarly,

the business is, in effect, being funded by money owed by the firm to Her Majesty's Inspector of Taxes and other creditors, as well as money owed to the bank (loan or overdraft). Set out a balance sheet for your business like the one shown here.

Balance sheet of Student Enterprises as at 1st January, 1999		
	(£)	(£)
Fixed assets		
Buildings		
Furniture		
Plant		
Vehicles		
Current assets		
Stocks		
Debtors		
Bank		
Cash		
Less current liabilities		
Bank overdraft		
WORKING CAPITAL		
Less long-term liabilities		
Bank loan		
Mortgage		
Financed by		
Capital		

Evidence collection point

Set out a starting balance sheet for your business.

Projected profit and loss

You should now set out a projected profit and loss account using the outline shown here. In each column, show your target figures for income and expenditure each month. Do this activity for a twelve-month period (exclude VAT).

The following notes may be helpful in putting together your anticipated profit and loss account:

- *Sales* Remember to allow for seasonal

fluctuations, and break sales down by product groups. Choose the groups according to the markets you have targeted and the sales patterns which characterise each. (For example, if you were selling ice-creams and hot dogs, you might expect the sales of ice-creams to rise in summer and fall in winter, and the reverse situation to apply to hot dogs!)

■ *Expenditure* This is the reverse side of income, so be accurate! Even if some overheads, e.g. rent, are paid quarterly, spread the amounts over the whole period.

■ *Depreciation* This figure is the part of your profits set aside to pay for replacement assets when the ones you have wear out or become unsuitable.

■ *Net profit or loss* The difference between monthly income and expenditure. Where the expenditure is more than the income (a loss), put the figures in brackets.

Profitability Targets	Month		Month		Month	
	Target	Actual	Target	Actual	Target	Actual
Income						
Sales						
Other income						
Total income						
Expenditure						
Materials						
Administration						
Accountancy/legal						
Bank charges						
Depreciation						
Equipment						
General expenditure						
Insurance						
Maintenance						
Marketing						
Power/heat/light						
Postage/carriage						
Printing/stationery						
Rent/property taxes						
Telephone						
Training						
Transport						
Wages/salaries						
Total expenditure						
Net profit (loss)						
Cumulative P/(L)						

Evidence collection point

Set out a projected profit and loss account for the first year of trading of your business.

Projected balance sheets

You should have set out a balance sheet showing the anticipated opening balance of your business. You can now set out a projected balance sheet showing the balance at the end of the first few months of trading.

Evidence collection point

You should now be in a position to complete Part Five of your five-part business plan:

■ Part Five: Financial data – providing for a given time period cash-flow forecast, start-up balance sheet, projected profit and loss and balance sheet, and monthly profit and loss and balance sheet for monitoring and review.

Work that you produce will enable you to provide evidence of your capability in the Core Skills of Communication, Application of Number and Information Technology.

Identification of monthly profit and loss and balance sheet monitoring and review procedures for the business plan

The plan that you create should explain how financial data and forecasts will be reviewed. It should state who will carry out the review, its frequency (time intervals), what authority exists to make changes, which records will be kept (cash-flow forecast, projected profit and loss forecasts), and the distribution of information (its circulation and frequency).

Evidence collection point

Set out in a series of action points how you intend to monitor and review financial procedures for the business plan.

Evidence indicators

You should now put together the five sections of your business plan into a neat and attractive file that you would be proud to show to an outside provider of finance. Try to be clear and concise.

Success in communication will depend on the quality of your presentation. If people can easily understand your plan then you will be successful.

You must prepare and deliver an oral and visual presentation of your plan to an invited audience. You will need to prepare a series of overhead transparencies and other illustrations to highlight the key points of your talk. Refer to the notes on presentation skills on page xliv.

In order to meet the performance criteria associated with the GNVQ element 'Produce and present a business plan' you should be able to tick the following boxes:

I have prepared a five-part business plan for a small business enterprise, presented on paper or electronically, which includes:

■ Part One   Introduction and objectives – explaining the key objectives of the plan. ☐

■ Part Two   Marketing – stating how, where and to whom the plan's products or services will be marketed and sold to achieve planned objectives. ☐

■ Part Three   Production – stating production intentions and schedules. ☐

■ Part Four   Resource requirements – stating the resources required for marketing and production. ☐

■ Part Five   Financial data – providing for a given time period cash-flow forecast, start-up balance sheet, projected profit and loss and balance sheet, and monthly profit and loss and balance sheet for monitoring and review. ☐

Planning for employment or self-employment

It is fitting that the last chapter in this book should be concerned with looking forward to the world of employment and self-employment and encouraging you to prepare a personal plan for this time. A major feature of the GNVQ in Business is that it is a vocationally focused course.

In this chapter we therefore set out to help you to:

1 identify and give examples of types of employment or self-employment
2 identify statutory requirements for employment or self-employment
3 identify sources of information and collect information for employment or self-employment
4 identify opportunities for employment or self-employment
5 analyse and discuss skills to support employment or self-employment
6 propose a personal plan for employment or self-employment.

Types of employment or self-employment

There are a number of opportunities facing you in the world of work. You could take paid employment in the private or public sectors, do voluntary work, set up your own business, go into partnership with someone else, or take out a franchise to produce or sell a product.

Paid employment

Most people when they finish their education take paid employment in either the public or the private sector of the economy.

You need to have a fairly clear idea about the sort of work that you are looking for. It may be helpful to list what you need and are looking for. You can consider the following.

Job content

What sorts of things are you good at? What portfolio of existing skills do you have and how would you like to use them? What sorts of jobs have the sort of work content that you are looking for? Remember that employment is not just about pay, it is concerned with all those other things such as job satisfaction, variety, responsibility, etc.

Working is important for the feelings of self-worth it gives as well as for being a way of earning a living. As the American writer Studs Terkel suggests in his book *Working*:

> It is about a search too, for daily meaning as well as daily bread, for recognition as well as for cash, for astonishment rather than torpor; in short, for a sort of life rather than a Monday-through-Friday sort of dying.

Job status

What level of responsibility are you aiming for? Are you more interested in personal performance or in administration, management and leadership? Do you want to practise a specialism, perhaps to act as an IT specialist, or do you want to have a more general management or supervisory role in an organisation?

Salary

a What is the minimum you need to keep up your lifestyle?
b What are you realistically hoping for?

Location

Where do you want to work? To what extent is this dependent on family commitments?

Prospects

How ambitious are you? How hard are you prepared to work at furthering your career? (For example, does this mean that you will need to move depending on where a company wants you to work? To what extent will you have to fit in with the company's hours rather than your preferred working hours?)

In looking for employment in the private and public sectors you will need to bear in mind what we have been saying about organisations shedding labour in recent times. Organisations like BP, British Telecom and British Gas have been shedding large numbers of full-time employees in recent times in the private sector. At the same time we read about cutbacks in the numbers of teachers, civil servants, the armed forces and many other public sector employees.

You therefore need to make sure that you build up a portfolio of skills that make you employable.

Evidence collection point

Interview a personnel officer in (a) a private sector, and (b) a public sector organisation to find out what sorts of skills and qualifications they are looking for in people similar to yourself that they are currently recruiting. Discuss your findings with other members of your class. This will help you to provide evidence of capability in the Core Skill of Communication.

Voluntary employment

Voluntary work can involve you in anything from being a good neighbour, to working with charities or your local social services department (perhaps visiting old people). There are hundreds of organisations which need people to help them out.

By doing voluntary work you can gain valuable experience as well as serving the community. For instance, it may help you to:

- show employers that you are a responsible person and that you care about the community. (Evidence of work can be set out in your Records of Achievement folder.)
- give you experience of working with others
- help you to keep fit and active
- help you use and improve your skills (particularly communication and teamworking skills)
- enable you to learn new skills
- put you in touch with people who may be able to help you find a job.

To get involved in voluntary work you could:

1 Directly contact a national organisation that you would like to work with so that you can obtain information about helping as a volunteer in your area. You may be able to find this information in your local library or office of a voluntary organisation.
2 Contact your local Volunteer Bureau. There are over 300 Bureaux nationwide. Every Bureau has a database of the hundreds of opportunities available. Details of local Volunteer Bureaux in England, Wales and Northern Ireland can be obtained from:

National Association of Volunteer Bureaux
St Peter's College
College Road
Saltley
Birmingham
B8 3TE

For Bureaux in Scotland:

Volunteer Development Scotland
80 Murray Place
Stirling
FK8 2BX

Alternatively you could contact the Volunteer Centre UK to ask them to do a search of 'Signpost', their computerised database. Tell them what sort of work you want to do and they will provide you with a list of agencies in your local area which may involve volunteers. Their address is:

29 Lower King's Road
Berkhamsted
Hertfordshire
HP4 2AB

Evidence collection point

Investigate local opportunities for doing voluntary work. Find out how you can become involved in such work.

Running your own business

More and more young people today are becoming involved in running or helping to run businesses. One way into this field is to help in a family business, or one belonging to people who are close to you. You will find that the knowledge and skills that you have developed during your Business course will be invaluable for this work. At the same time you will find that the insights from working in the family business are invaluable in helping you to meet the performance criteria for the GNVQ in Business.

Many other young people are taking the opportunity to start up a business of their own from scratch.

People start up their own business for a variety of reasons. Some have a bright idea that they think will make them rich; others find themselves unemployed and start their own business to survive. Some can only be themselves when they are their own bosses; others want to make a particular contribution and can see no other way of doing it except by setting up on their own.

We have already looked at the importance of business planning, which is the key to a successful start-up. Key aspects of setting up will be making sure that you have the finance required, and that you have assessed the market in depth.

However, you will also need to assess yourself by examining:

- your skills
- your interests
- your knowledge
- your experience.

Are you able to use any of these in self-employment? Do you need to update existing skills or learn new ones? Have you got enough push to go out and sell yourself and your products? Can you keep to time deadlines and cope with pressure? Are you healthy?

A useful way of starting up in business for a young person with limited capital is to join the Enterprise Allowance Scheme. Note that this scheme goes by different names in different areas, e.g. New Business Schemes, Business Start-up.

If you have been unemployed for at least six weeks, and would like to set up your own business, the Training and Enterprise Council (TEC) may be able to offer financial help through their programme. The length of the programme and the level of financial assistance will be agreed by yourself and your local TEC. You can also get free advice on setting up and running your own business – this applies whether you are setting up alone, in partnership, as a limited company or as a cooperative.

Evidence collection point

Set out a list of the advantages and pitfalls that might result from you setting up a business of your own in an area in which you think you could be successful.

Partnership

If you do not think that you could cope with the responsibility or raise the necessary money to set up on your own, but still feel that you could create an effective business, then you might consider joining an existing partnership or setting up a new partnership.

A partnership is a group of people who join together to run a business. You and your partners would share the management of the business and also the profits, usually in proportion to the amount of money you have put in (you also share the debts).

You need to choose partners that you can work well with, and who are prepared to take on responsibilities.

Another way would be to set up a cooperative. As a member of a cooperative you would jointly own, control and work for the business, and share responsibility and decison-making. In many cooperatives members receive equal pay.

Franchises

A franchise is a 'business marriage' between an existing proven business and a newcomer. The newcomer (known as the 'franchisee') buys permission to copy the business idea of the existing company. The franchisee commits his or her capital and effort, while the franchisor commits experience and existing management infrastructure, the trading name, and often supplies equipment. In 1995 there were more than 700 franchise opportunities available in the UK.

As a franchisee you would buy a licence to reproduce the franchisor's whole business system and then pay them ongoing royalties or management fees depending on how successful you are (i.e. size of turnover).

As a franchisee you must be prepared to work hard, put in long hours and use your initiative in getting your business off the ground and then developing it. It is important to choose the right franchise for you.

You will need to consult a solicitor or accountant who has had previous experience of dealing with franchising. You do not want to sink your savings into a franchise that is a non-starter – you may be better off working for someone else. A franchise should not be a millstone around your neck.

The *United Kingdom Franchise Directory* lists all established franchise opportunities in the UK and gives a description of them. The *Franchise Magazine* provides up-to-date information about franchising.

Both of these publications are available for reference at all Job Centres. Copies can be obtained from:

Franchise Development Service Ltd
Castle House
Castle Meadow
Norwich
NR2 1PJ

Statutory requirements for employment or self-employment

There are a number of statutory requirements covering employment and self-employment. These include: making arrangements to pay taxes at agreed intervals with the Inland Revenue; advising the Benefits Agency local offices of imminent self-employed status; registering your company with Companies House; paying National Insurance Contributions (NIC) at the self-employed rate; keeping business records for annual audit and presentation to the Inland Revenue and VAT offices; applying for passports and work visas when travelling abroad.

Income tax

For taxation purposes earnings subject to income tax may include:

- all wages and salaries, including tips, bonuses, benefits in kind such as company car, cheap loans etc.
- interest from banks and building societies
- dividends/profits from investments such as stocks and shares
- state benefits
- pensions by the state or by a former employer.

Employers have a responsibility to see that everybody pays their tax. They do this through the PAYE system. PAYE stands for Pay As You Earn. Employers deduct tax from wages and then hand it over to the Inland Revenue. This saves each individual from having to pay the tax themselves at once at the end of the tax year.

(Note: the tax year runs from 6 April of one year to 5 April of the following year.)

Employees do *not* have to pay tax on all of their earnings. Everybody can earn or receive certain amounts of income during the tax year without having to pay tax. **Tax allowances** represent the amount of income an individual can receive before starting to pay tax.

The main tax allowances are:

- the personal allowance – every UK resident is entitled to a personal allowance
- the married couple's allowance – a married man who is living with his wife for any part of the tax year is entitled to a married couple's allowance as well as his personal allowance (husbands/wives

can elect for the married couple's allowance to be given to the wife instead, or be split equally between them)

- the additional personal allowance – mainly for single parents
- the widow's bereavement allowance
- the blind person's allowance.

As well as tax allowances there are tax reliefs. Tax reliefs are not allowances but they affect tax in the same way. This is because the amount of income an individual receives before paying tax can also depend upon outgoings (payments they make out of income). Tax reliefs may be obtained on the following:

- interest on loans to buy property. Most people get basic tax relief through the MIRAS system which automatically involves individuals making lower interest payments to their bank or building society. Tax relief is available on the first £30 000 of a mortgage
- interest on other loans such as improving property to rent out or to buy a car or machinery necessary to carry out work
- donations to charity
- where expenses at work are incurred – this may include subscriptions to professional bodies
- against pension scheme contributions.

Task

Identify your main tax allowances and tax reliefs.

Taxable income is calculated by deducting personal allowances and tax reliefs from gross income. These are reflected by the tax code. Everybody's tax code will normally comprise a number and a letter. The number is the total amount of allowances, but with the last figure left off. For example, allowances of £3695 would give a code of 369. Most people who start their first job would have the letter L after the code number, which reflects the basic personal allowance. There are other letters for married men, single parents and people over 65 years of age.

Case study – calculating a tax code

EXAMPLE 1

Sally Nicholls works for a local plumber. She has a tool allowance of £90 a year.

For the tax year 1995–96

	£
Personal allowance	3445
Tool allowance	90
Total allowances	3535

Allowances to set against income £3535.

To turn these allowances into a tax code, the last figure is taken off and the letter L is added because Sally is single. So her tax code is 353L.

EXAMPLE 2

Ramesh Patel is 36 and married.

For the tax year 1995–96

	£
Personal allowance	3445
Married couple's allowance	1720
Total allowances	5165

Allowances to set against income £5165.

To turn these allowances into a tax code, the last figure is taken off and the letter H is added because Ramesh is married. So his tax code is 516H.

1 How much can Sally earn per year before having to pay tax?
2 Explain the difference between the code for a single person and the code for a married person with a married couple's allowance.
3 If Ramesh earns £12 000 per annum, calculate his taxable income.
4 If Ramesh is taxed at 25 per cent on his taxable income, how much tax will he pay over the year?

Everybody receives a notification of income tax coding on a form P2(T). Under PAYE the total of the allowances is spread equally among the number of pay days in the tax year. This would be 52 for weekly paid workers and 12 for employees paid monthly.

Case study – Why do we have to pay tax?

It is very easy either to say or think 'we are being taxed too heavily' or 'why should we have to pay for this?', but the effectiveness of our government in providing goods and services is really dependent upon the ability of the taxpayer to supply adequate revenues for it to do so.

Imagine what it might be like if no-one paid a fair share towards the expenses of our country. We might immediately find ourselves threatened by other nations because we would not have a defence budget. Many parents would not be able to afford to send their children to school. The protection of the essential services such as the police or the fire brigade would not exist. If people could not afford health care their lives could be cut short. Each of these areas and many more, such as consumer protection, housing, social services, a legal system, road and sanitation are involved in ensuring that we all enjoy a good 'quality of life'. Many of us take this quality of life for granted because we have always had it.

It is generally agreed by people of all political persuasions that everyone should pay a fair share towards the expenses of our country. For example, we all pay taxes when we purchase many of the articles which we buy in the shops, in the form of VAT. There are also more than 26 million income tax payers in the UK. Total tax receipts in the UK exceed £140 billion. Each year the Chancellor of the Exchequer prepares a budget which includes an estimate of what the government will spend in the coming year as well as an explanation of how the money will be raised.

1 Make a list of the services provided by the government and then number them in order of importance to you.
2 Express your views upon the amount of tax you are asked to pay. To what extent are these views dependent upon your political persuasion?
3 Identify areas where you feel that government spending should be (i) expanded or (ii) cut.

Other than the P2T mentioned earlier, two other tax forms are of particular importance.

a The **P45** helps an employer to work out the tax of a new employee. The form records the tax code, the total pay and the total pax paid to date. Part 1 of the P45 is sent to the Tax Office to inform them that an employee has left their job. Part II shows the starting point for tax deductions and Part III informs the Tax Office of the new employer.
b The **P60** is received by all employees at the end of the year and provides them with a certificate of the tax paid in that year.

Case study – The Taxpayer's Charter

In 1992 Inland Revenue issued the following Taxpayer's Charter:

> *You are entitled to expect the Inland Revenue*
> *To be fair*
> * *By settling your tax affairs impartially*
> * *By expecting you to pay only what is due under the law*
> * *By treating everyone with equal fairness*
> *To help you*
> * *To get your tax affairs right*
> * *To understand your rights and obligations*
> * *By providing clear leaflets and forms*
> * *By giving information and assistance at enquiry offices*
> * *By being courteous at all times*
> *To provide an efficient service*
> * *By settling your tax affairs promptly and accurately*
> * *By keeping private affairs strictly confidential*
> * *By using the information provided only as allowed by the law*
> * *By keeping to a minimum your cost of complying with the law*
> * *By keeping our costs down*
> *To be accountable for what we do*
> * *By publishing standards for ourselves and publishing how well we live up to them*

In response to the Taxpayer's Charter the Inland Revenue has worked hard to improve their levels of customer service. In doing this they have set up Mobile Enquiry Centres, produced a range of leaflets, reviewed their forms, initiated a system of Customer Service Managers in various parts of the country and set up a Minicom System to help the hearing impaired.

1 Explain briefly what the Taxpayer's Charter is designed to do
2 Who benefits from the Charter?
3 Suggest two further ways in which the Inland Revenue could improve their levels of customer service.

Employees also have to make **National Insurance contributions** from their earnings. The payment of National Insurance enables an employee to claim a variety of benefits from the State such as a retirement pension and sickness benefits.

Owners of small businesses will also be expected to pay income tax.

In setting up as a small business it is important to keep records of everything you spend right from the start so that you can claim these as expenses, if appropriate, against your eventual income tax payments. Ask about this at your local Inland Revenue Office.

You should keep all bank and building society records, sales invoices, receipted bills, etc, and records of your personal bank or building society accounts, especially if there have been transfers between your personal accounts and the business.

Your turnover is all the money earned by your business. You can deduct from your turnover the costs you incur for the sole purpose of earning business profits, such as:

■ everyday costs of the business and maintaining its equipment
■ goods or materials sold or used in your business
■ loose tools and other small articles used in your business
■ business travel
■ interest on business loans.

Business expenses are deducted from turnover to give a figure for profit.

You can then deduct any capital expenses such as vehicles bought, new computers or machinery. Deduct these from profits to work out your taxable income.

You only need to provide accounts to the Inland Revenue if your turnover is more than £15 000.

Any Enterprise Allowance that you receive should not be included in your tax return.

The amount of National Insurance you pay is usually worked out on your profits plus any Enterprise Allowance you receive.

See Figure 28.1 for a summary of this advice on filling in your income tax form.

Figure 28.1 Advice for filling in your income tax form for self-employment

Evidence collection point

1 Set out figures showing the income tax which would be paid by a single person earning £15 000 a year using current income tax tables. Explain your figures.
2 Set out figures showing the income tax that would be paid by a self-employed person who earned £20 000 this year. Make up figures to show turnover, business expenses, business profits, capital expenses, and taxable income.

This will help you to provide evidence of capability in the Core Skill of Application of Number.

Value Added Tax

You may not have to register for VAT payments at once if you set up in business. It will, however, be useful to register in advance so that you can reclaim

VAT paid on equipment and materials. You will find out about paying VAT at your local Customs and Excise Office.

We can illustrate the process of VAT by taking a simple example. For the sake of making the mathematics easy we assume that VAT is 10% in this country. (In fact the standard rate at present is 17½%).

A retailer buys from a wholesaler at a VAT-exclusive (not including VAT) price of £100. She will actually pay £110 (cost price plus 10% VAT). Now let us assume that she sells all these goods at a mark-up of 100% (profit margin of 50%). She will receive £200 plus 10% VAT on selling prices, a total of £220. The VAT she paid is known as her input tax and is reclaimable. The VAT she charged on the sales, which is known as her output tax, is payable to the Customs and Excise. The VAT actually due is the difference between her output tax of £20 (VAT on sales) and her input tax of £10 (VAT on cost of goods), a total of £10, which is exactly 10% of £100, the value added to the goods.

Evidence collection point

Interview the owner of a business to find out how he or she pays Value Added Tax.

National Insurance

Most working people between 16 and state pension age must pay contributions into the National Insurance (NI) scheme. These help you gain entitlement to get benefits including:

- Sickness benefit
- Invalidity benefit
- Maternity allowance
- Retirement pension
- Widow's benefits
- Unemployment benefit.

You can only get these benefits if you (or, for some benefits, your husband) have already paid or been credited with enough of the right class of contributions at the right time.

Your National Insurance (NI) number is personal to you. You keep it all your working life. It looks something like this:

AB123456C

If you work for an employer, tell him or her your NI number as soon as you start work. Then all NI

contributions and credits for you can be put on your personal contributions record.

There are four classes of NI contributions:

- *Class 1*
  These are contributions for employed persons. The more you earn, the more you pay, up to an upper limit. Your employer takes your contributions out of your pay and also has to pay employer's contributions for all employees who earn at least the lower earnings limit.

- *Class 2*
  These are contributions for self-employed persons. You must pay Class 2 NI contributions at a flat rate every week, including holiday periods.

  You can pay Class 2 by direct debit once a month or by quarterly bill, every thirteen weeks.

- *Class 3*
  These are voluntary contributions. If you are not working or you are not earning enough to pay Class 1 contributions or not have to pay Class 2 contributions you can pay Class 3 voluntary contributions. These are paid at a flat rate and can help protect your retirement pension.

- *Class 4*
  These are further contributions that may have to be made by a self-employed person. They are calculated on your profits and you have to pay them as well as Class 2 payments if your profits are more than a certain level.

Evidence collection point

Produce a short leaflet for school leavers explaining what National Insurance is and why it is important for people to pay into this pool.

This will enable you to show capability in the Core Skills of Communication and Information Technology.

Pension arrangements

You can get a basic Retirement Pension when you reach pension age (currently 60 for a woman, 65 for a man) if you have paid enough full-rate Class 1, Class 2 or Class 3 National Insurance contributions. The pension is not affected by any work you do or by any earnings that you have.

In 1994 a full basic Retirement Pension was £57.60 a week, and £34.50 for a married woman claiming on her husband's contributions.

People are sent a claim form BR1 a few months before they reach pension age. Pension payments can be made directly into a bank or building society, or a book of orders can be cashed at a post office.

One problem that you need to be aware of is that this country is faced with an increasingly ageing population. Working people are having to support a larger and larger number of retired people on pensions. By the time you come to retire, the state may no longer be in a position to provide pension support in the way it does today.

You are strongly advised to make some form of extra provision for your own retirement, e.g. by joining a private pension scheme or saving in some other way. Many jobs have occupational pension schemes – for example, a teacher would pay sums of money each month into such a scheme, to draw on when he or she retires.

Evidence collection point

Investigate a private pension scheme to find out how much you would be expected to contribute each month and what the eventual return would be. You could also investigate an occupational pension scheme in the same way.

Company registration

To set up a company it is necessary to go through a number of legal procedures in order to be recognised. This mainly involves the presentation of various records and documents to the Registrar of Companies. These documents are open to scrutiny by the general public. Companies must present a Memorandum and Articles of Association (see Chapter 4). Once it has lodged these documents and had them accepted it will be given a Certificate of Trading and can start to trade.

All companies must file each year a set of audited accounts with the Registrar of Companies. These accounts will include a directors' report, auditors' report, profit and loss account, balance sheet, source and application of funds, and an explanation of these accounts.

Benefits

If your profits or earnings are low there are a number of benefits that you can claim:

■ *Income Support*
Income Support is a Social Security benefit to help people aged 18 or over whose income is below a certain level and who are not working 16 hours a week or more. It can be paid on top of other benefits and does not depend on having paid National Insurance contributions.

To get Income Support you must be available for work and show that you are taking reasonable steps to get a job.

Income Support is paid to people who sign on at the Employment Service or Job Centre and is paid two weeks in arrears.

■ *Housing Benefit*
Housing Benefit is paid by local councils to people who need support to pay their rent. It is not paid to help with the costs of:
– mortgage interest payments
– fuel costs
– meals.

■ *Council Tax benefit*
Most owner-occupiers or tenants, including council tenants, have to pay the Council Tax. There is one bill for each dwelling. If you are on a low income and find it hard to pay your full Council Tax you may be able to get help from your local council, whether you are working or not.

If you are under 18, you will not have to pay the Council Tax so the benefit scheme does not apply to you.

■ *Family Credit*
Family Credit is a tax-free benefit for working families with children. It is not a loan and does not have to be paid back.

To get Family Credit, you must be responsible for at least one child under 16 (or under 19 if in full-time education up to GNVQ Advanced standard). You or your partner must be working at least 16 hours a week.

■ *Social Fund*
The Social Fund helps people with expenses which are difficult to pay for out of regular income. Social Fund payments include:

- *Maternity Payments* – For example, £100 to help buy things for a new baby.
- *Funeral Payment* – If you have only a small amount of savings you can get help to pay for a funeral.
- *Cold Weather Payment* – This payment is available to help with heating bills if temperatures fall below 0°C (freezing point) for seven consecutive days.
- *Community Care Grants* – These are available to help people with special priorities, e.g. elderly or disabled people. It is there to help them to lead independent lives in the community.
- *Crisis Loans* – These are to help people who cannot meet their immediate short-term expenses in an emergency.

Benefits available for those who have paid National Insurance Contributions include:

■ *Sickness Benefits* – If you are employed and incapable of work and you cannot get Statutory Sick Pay from your employer, or you are self-employed or non-employed, you may be able to get Sickness Benefit for up to 28 weeks.

■ *Invalidity Benefit* – This is made up of Invalidity Pension, Invalidity Allowance and Additional Pension.

Invalidity Benefit is tax free.

Invalidity Pension is usually paid automatically if you are still incapable of work after 28 weeks, when your Sickness Benefit ends.

Invalidity Allowance may be paid on top of Invalidity Pension depending on your age when your illness began.

■ *Maternity Benefit* – If you are pregnant and cannot get Statutory Maternity Pay because you are self-employed, you may be able to get Maternity Allowance. To get Maternity Allowance you must have paid standard rate employed and/or self-employed National Insurance Contributions at a certain time.

■ *Widow's benefits* – There are three main benefits:
- Widow's Payment
- Widowed Mother's Allowance
- Widow's Pension.

■ *Unemployment Benefit* – To get Unemployment Benefit you must have paid a set amount of full-time Class 1 National Insurance contributions.

Evidence collection point

Look at the details of the benefits described above. Identify specific benefits which are of most relevance to you, or which may be of most relevance to you in the next few years. Carry out some research to find out more details of these benefits by visiting your local Social Security Office and asking for details. Pamphlets describing benefits are available from:

Benefits Agency Distribution and Storage Centre
Manchester Road
Heywood
Lancashire
OL10 2PZ

Sources of information for employment or self-employment

Where, then, will you be able to get all the information that you require about employment and self-employment?

Obvious sources are:

■ Job Centres
■ Employment/recruitment agencies
■ The media
■ The Federation of Small Businesses
■ Chambers of Commerce
■ Banks
■ Training and Enterprise Councils (TECs)
■ Department of Trade and Industry
■ Charitable organisations

Job Centres

Job Centres are very good places to start your job search – whether you are looking for your first job or want to get back into the job market after being made redundant.

The first thing you notice is how job vacancies are clearly displayed on cards. You just write down the ones that interest you and, if you want to know more, ask at the reception desk. The receptionist will have more ideas about where you can look for work in your area – for example, local papers, local employers and private employment agencies.

When you are looking for work it will pay to go to your Job Centre at regular intervals because jobs become available frequently.

If you have been unemployed for a while, there are plenty of other ways Job Centres can help your job search, such as through seminars and Jobclubs to boost your confidence, help brush up your interview technique, prepare your CV and plenty more. You will be given a Client Adviser to talk to about the kind of work you want and advise you about what benefits you can claim while looking.

Job Centres are run by the Employment Service, which is part of the Employment Department, to offer you what you need to find a job – it's all there under one roof.

All Job Centres are listed in your local phonebook under Employment Service or Job Centre.

Evidence collection point

Visit your local Job Centre in order to look at the facilities on offer. Make a few notes about these facilities.

Employment/recruitment agencies

There is a wide variety of private employment agencies that help businesses to recruit staff. Fields in which these agencies are particularly common are professional staff agencies, secretarial work, high-technology areas, nursing and casual work.

A business looking for staff will approach an agency, which will either undertake to interview applicants itself or will send suitable applicants to the firm to be interviewed.

The agency will take a commission based on the salary of the worker. The employment agency does not therefore charge the jobseeker a fee, although it may charge for helping you with your CV and for giving careers guidance.

Recruitment consultancies and agencies are in business to supply people to companies who have slots to fill. You can therefore expect them to be interested in you if there is a good chance that they can place you.

To find appropriate agencies/consultancies you should look at the Yellow Pages, or *The Yearbook of Recruitment and Employment Services,* which is produced by the Federation of Recruitment and Employment Services.

Evidence collection point

Carry out some research to find out what recruitment/employment agencies are working in your immediate area, and what they do.

The media

The media are frequently used to advertise job vacancies so be on the lookout in newspapers and television and listen to the radio to find appropriate job opportunities.

Newspaper advertisements are an obvious source of information about jobs. A good newspaper advert gives a substantial amount of information. Jobs demanding limited skills can often be advertised locally, whereas jobs requiring specialist skills may be advertised in national, specialist papers and journals.

Evidence collection point

Study the table in Figure 28.2 to find out which papers specialise in advertising the sorts of job vacancies that you are most interested in, and on which days these vacancies are advertised. Then buy or read the newspapers on the days identified. Pick out particular jobs that appeal to you. Explain how newspaper advertising helps people to find work and/or self-employment opportunities such as franchises.

The Federation of Small Businesses

The Federation of Small Businesses is an organisation which has been specifically set up to provide advice, guidance and support for those wishing to set up in business on their own. It gives advice on such matters as business planning, tax matters, and where to get further help.

Area of employment	Widest choice	Also recommended							
		Daily Telegraph	Guardian	Independent	Financial Times	Daily Mail	Daily Express	Times	Today
Arts & communication	Guardian	Mon	M/Th	F/W	–	–	Tues	Wed	T/Th
Academics & teachers	Guardian	Th	Tues	Th	–	–	T/Th	Mon	–
Accounts & finance	Financial Times	Mon	Th	Tues	W/Th	Wed	Tues	Th	Tues
Civil service & local government	Guardian	Mon	W/Fri	Th	–	Wed	Tues	Th	Th
Computing	Daily Telegraph	Mon	Th	Mon	–	Th	Th	Tues	Tues
Economics & statisticians	Financial Times	Th	Wed	Tues	Wed	–	Tues	Th	–
Engineers: civil electrical mechanical/ production	Daily Telegraph	T/Th	Th	Mon	–	Th	Mon/T	Th	Th
Draughtsmen/women	Daily Express	Tues	Fri	M/Th	–	Th	Th	Th	Th
Management services	Daily Telegraph	Th	M/Th	Th	Wed	Th	–	Th	T/Th
Production, operation& works management	Daily Telegraph	Th	Mon	M/Th	–	Th	Th	Th	T/Th
Professional	Times	Th	Th	Th	Wed	Th	Wed	Th	T/Th
Sales representatives	Daily Telegraph	W/Th	M/Th	Wed	Wed	Tues	Wed	Th	T/Th
Sales & marketing management	Daily Telegraph	M/Th	Mon	Wed	Wed	Th	Wed	Th	Tues
Scientists & technologists	Daily Telegraph	M/Th	Th	Mon	–	Th	Th	Th	Th
Top management	Sunday Times	T/Sat	M/W/Th	Sun	Wed	Th	M/W/Th	Th	Tues
Secretarial/clerical	Daily Telegraph	–	–	–	–	Tues	Tues	M/T/W	–

Figure 28.2 Recruitment advertising in the national press

Chambers of Commerce

Most towns of a reasonable size have a Chamber of Commerce which is made up of business people in the town. The Chamber will serve both as a pressure group looking after the interests of local business and as an organisation servicing the needs of its members. In particular, people setting up a new business enterprise of their own will benefit from those with greater experience who will be able to provide advice and support.

Banks

A major part of the business of banks is to provide finance to business, coupled with advice and support. Not only do the banks provide an extensive literature on employment and self-employment, but they also run an advisory service to support people seeking self-employment. Most High Street banks today have a Small Firms Advisory Service.

Of course, banks have a vested interest. If they look after businesses that are starting out, they may go on to handle much larger accounts if these businesses grow to be multi-million pound enterprises.

Training and Enterprise Councils (TECs)

Your local Training and Enterprise Council (TEC) can provide information and advice about:

- training for a new job
- adding to your existing skills
- starting or expanding you own business.

TECs contract with other organisations to offer these and other services.

Training and Enterprise Councils are directed by top business and community leaders. They aim to make sure that training and enterprise opportunities exist so that everyone can develop their skills and make the best use of their potential.

In Scotland, local enterprise companies (LECs) have similar training and enterprise functions.

Your local Job Centre will give you details of TECs/LECs in your area.

Department of Trade and Industry

The Department of Trade and Industry also plays a part in encouraging enterprise initiatives in this country by providing advice and some financial support for businesses which are just starting up.

Charitable organisations

Prince Charles is the patron of the Prince's Youth Business Trust (PYBT), an example of a charitable organisation which seeks to encourage people to be enterprising and to set up their own businesses. The Trust gives grants and awards to young people, particularly in inner city and deprived areas, who have a good idea supported by an effective business plan.

Other charitable organisations, e.g. Voluntary Service Overseas (VSO), provide opportunities for voluntary work, whereby young people (and not so young people) can give of their skills and services to work in other countries.

Evidence collection point

Construct a database containing information about organisations in your area that provide information about employment and self-employment. You will need to create records which show what services each organisation offers to those seeking employment or self-employment.

Producing this database will help you to provide evidence of capability in Core Skills of Communication, Application of Number and Information Technology. It should also provide an invaluable resource for other students at your school or college.

Identifying opportunities for employment or self-employment

You should now set out to identify some opportunities for employment and self-employment for yourself. Clearly, you are the person with the greatest insight into this, because you know best about your own skills, likes and preferences.

However, you may well benefit from going to see a careers adviser. A careers specialist will ask you to fill in a questionnaire relating to your personality, interests, likes and dislikes. The results of the questionnaire can then be fed into a computer which will use a program designed to match your interests and aptitudes with jobs which are available (a bit like computer dating). The printout will inform you of the sorts of qualifications and training you will need to pursue to get into a particular occupation.

645

Produce a summary of at least three types of employment in which you are interested. For at least one of these types of employment you should produce a list of opportunities with relevant sources of information and statutory requirements.

The skills required to support employment or self-employment

A number of important skills are required to support employment or self-employment. These skills are often referred to as being transferable, in that they can be used in a wide variety of employment rather than being job-specific.

We will identify some of these skills below before asking you to carry out an evaluation of your own current skills.

Evaluating own strengths and weaknesses

Self-evaluation is very important. You need to be able to recognise what you are good at and what you are not so good at. Identifying your strengths should help to give you a positive self-image, and pinpointing your weaknesses should provide you with areas to work at.

By thinking about your past and recent experiences, it is possible to build a picture of the sort of person that you are. However, character assessment is not easy – it often takes us a long time to find out about our real qualities.

Instead of trying to write a detailed appraisal of your character, try to use a series of key words about yourself, such as friendly, generous, nervous, timid, hard-working. Do not be afraid to use words which are not complimentary.

Copy out the following table in order to evaluate your own strengths and weaknesses:

Personal evaluation of character	
My main strengths are	My main weaknesses are

Working with others

It requires a lot of ability to work well with other people. Working with other people is not just about working with friends, it also involves working with people who may not have quite the same outlook on life as yourself.

Working with others therefore requires a lot of maturity and strength of character. In the world of work, people frequently work in teams, and they are expected to share joint responsibility for the functioning of that team.

Whenever a group works together there will be three strands involved in moving from the start of the decision-making process to the finish. These strands are illustrated in Figure 28.3.

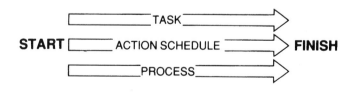

Figure 28.3 The three strands of decision-making

Task

The task is the content of the work. For example, the task of a student meeting may be to choose a student representative. The task of a piece of groupwork may be to produce an effective assignment. The task is the conversion of the information and opinions from members into recommendations, reports or other outcomes. In general terms, this covers what has to be done and why. Most groups give a lot of attention to the task.

Action schedule

The action schedule is concerned with how a group will be organised to do a given task. The schedule will cover such questions as who will fill the necessary roles, how progress will be checked and monitored, and how it will be ensured that the group finishes the task on time. It will also deal with the procedures of decision-making: how to ensure that everyone has a say, how conflict will be dealt with, etc.

In general, the action schedule will cover the 'where' and 'how' of decision-making.

An action schedule for a meeting might set down when the meeting will take place, who will attend, who will run the meeting, how decisions will be voted on and other procedural matters.

Process

The process is the interaction which takes place between members of a group. It is about how people work together, their relationships and the feelings created by their behaviour within the group. It involves interpersonal skills such as listening to others and helping others to join in a discussion. It involves expressions of feelings and the giving and receiving of feedback. In general, it covers 'who does what' and 'when'. Many groups, unfortunately, pay little attention to process.

The three threads of group working are all important in group decision-making.

It is obvious that a group that concentrates on its action schedule and its process entirely may have a wonderful time, but it may not achieve the task. It will not be long before morale will suffer and the group disintegrates.

In contrast, concentration purely on the task is likely to lead to arguments about how things should be

organised, and inattention to group members' thoughts and feelings will lead to mishandled resources and to misunderstandings.

Because teamwork is an important personal skill you will need to be aware of the three elements outlined above. Do not forget the importance of process. When you carry out tasks involving small groups, some students can act as process observers. The process observer will need to watch how the group works together, and report the results back to the group at the end of the work session.

The process observer should look at aspects of groupwork including:

- Who initiated activities?
- Who supported others in the group by helping them when appropriate?
- Who harmonised the group by seeking consensus and common purposes?
- Who listened to others and respected their contributions?
- Who collected and organised information for the group?
- Who made it easier for the group to make progress by involving others?
- Who in the group was reliable?
- Who blocked progress?
- Who interrupted others?
- Did anyone carry out actions which damaged the confidence of others?

The information provided by the process observers can be used to reflect on group dynamics and group interaction. Steps can then be taken to improve the quality of group working.

 Evidence collection point

Working in a group of three or four, make a list of important process skills. Here are four to start your list:

- starting a discussion
- helping others to join in
- building bridges between team members
- knowing when to stop talking

Produce the list on one sheet of paper. The sheet should be easy to understand, and provide a simple checklist so that you can monitor your progress in developing process skills.

During the course you should review your process skills profile to see what progress you are making. You could discuss your profile with other students (peer group assessment).

647

Skill	Good at:	Quite good at:	Poor at:
Starting a discussion			
Helping others to join in			

Self-assessment of group skills

When managing changes, it is essential to know how successful we have been. We can more effectively develop these skills by looking at ourselves more critically.

The profile form in Figure 28.4 gives the opportunity for self-assessment in terms of the personal and social skills required to operate as a member of a group. The form can be adapted for self-assessment in other areas. The tick boxes are intended to be filled in according to the following pointers:

1 = I am highly experienced at this
2 = I have some experience of this
3 = I have no experience of this

and

1 = I was very successful at this
2 = I was reasonably successful at this
3 = I was rarely successful at this

Working independently

Working life is not just about working in teams. There are many occasions when individuals have to graft for themselves and produce work using their own independent efforts. Organisations will value individuals who can be trusted to 'get on with things', who can work independently.

Evidence collection point

Evaluate your own performance in working independently. Explain how important this particular ability is. Use examples from situations that you are familiar with.

Planning

Planning means having a method or a scheme which helps to create an organised way of going about a task. Later on in this chapter we invite you to set out a personal plan for employment or self-employment. Some of the important things that planning will enable you to do are the following:

- organise your life in a more structured way
- save time
- reduce stress
- establish goals and objectives
- reflect on your own personal strengths and weaknesses
- take more responsibility for your own learning and career development.

Evidence collection point

What things have you been involved in planning in detail in recent times? How effective was your planning? What do you consider to be your main strengths and weaknesses in planning?

Time management

Using time effectively is a very important skill. It is very important that you learn to prioritise activities and tasks. Avoid 'butterflying', where you flit from one task to another without getting anything done well. For example in carrying out a task you should decide:

- What are the most important elements of the task?
- Which tasks take longer?
- What sequence do the activities need to follow?

It is important that you put most time and effort into those activities which are the key to meeting your objectives. Many people waste a lot of time on minor problems, rather than concentrating upon essential activities.

Pareto showed during the nineteenth century that 20% of the population owned 80% of the national wealth. Lothar Seiwart uses this rule to show that 20% of time and effort used well will produce 80% of the results (Figure 28.5).

Seiwart claims that the 80:20 rule applies in the following situations:

As a member of any group have you experience of:	Experience			Success		
	1	2	3	1	2	3
*Contributing ideas						
*Listening to other people's ideas and making use of them						
*Compromising when your opinion was not shared by others						
*Taking notes of what went on in the group						
*Carrying out an agreed task in co-operation with others						
*Carrying out part of a task assigned to you as an individual						
*Showing flexibility						
*Asking for things to be explained even though you could have looked silly						
*Getting the task finished						
*Choosing a person to do a particular task						
*Keeping a check on how far the group had got in carrying out a task						
*Chairing a meeting						
*Giving instructions to others						
*Trying to influence others in a group						
*Contributing ideas to a group discussion						
*Making a formal presentation to a group						
*Producing visual material as part of a presentation						
*Helping to organise a major event						
*Deciding on the best solution and planning a way forward						
*Encouraging people to carry on even when they were uninterested						
*Getting the group to finish on time						
*Sharing any praise						

Figure 28.4 A self-assessment questionnaire

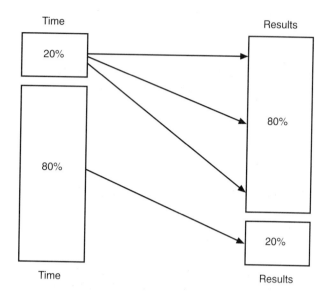

Figure 28.5 Pareto's law

- 20% of customers or goods account for 80% of a firm's sales.
- 20% of production errors cause 80% of rejects.
- 20% of a newspaper contains 80% of the news.
- 20% of meeting time produces 80% of the decisions.
- 20% of desk work makes possible 80% of the success in one's tasks.

By planning our time well we can be more effective. Eight minutes of planning our time can make sure that we can carry out one hour of effective work. When you have an assignment to complete, think of the 80:20 rule.

One way of making sure that time is well spent is to undertake a value analysis of the use of time. This is called ABC analysis (Figure 28.6)

A TASKS Very important	B TASKS Important	C TASKS Trivial/routine

Figure 28.6 ABC analysis

Time is frequently wasted on trivial problems (C) while the few essential tasks (A) are left undone. Good time management involves ranking activities as A, B and C and then listing them in order of priority:

- A tasks are most important and need the most time and resources to be done properly.
- B tasks are of less importance and can be delegated.
- C tasks are often routine but can command a large share of the work.

The important thing is to make sure that each day a few A tasks are done, rather than pushing them down the list.

Evidence collection point

How effective are you in using your time? Make a list of your strengths and weaknesses in time management.

Setting targets

In planning any activity, you need to think about your aims and objectives. In other words, what exactly are you trying to achieve? In military terms your aim is the main focus of your concern – for example, to win a war. Your objectives are the main means you establish to pursue your aim – for example, to be successful in a number of battles.

You will need to set a number of targets. These might include gaining promotion at work by a certain date, or saving £x to buy a new car.

Evidence collection point

What targets have you recently set yourself? How effective have you been in setting and meeting targets?

Reviewing progress

When you establish targets for yourself and objectives to be achieved, you will periodically need to review progress towards their achievement.

The problem that many people have is that they fail to monitor progress so that they have no clear idea of how they are performing against the standards which they have set.

In setting out a plan or a target, you should also construct a review process. This will involve deciding *when* you will review progress, *who* will be involved in the review, and *what* they will be reviewing.

Evidence collection point

How effective are you in reviewing progress? Do you set dates, and processes for reviewing performance and achievement?

Decision-making

Decision-making involves weighing up alternatives in order to make an appropriate decision. It requires a considerable amount of skill. You should not simply choose the first solution that comes to mind. You need to have the ability to visualise alternatives and choose the most appropriate way of doing something. We use the word 'decisive' to define the act of making a decision in a positive way.

Decision-making therefore involves outlining a range of alternatives and then selecting the best solution.

Evidence collection point

How effective are you at making decisions? Are you able to set out a range of alternatives and choose a 'best' course of action? Are you decisive in your approach?

Problem-solving

One way of looking at problem-solving is to define a problem as something that needs to be understood and solved, e.g. how to tackle a difficult assignment.

Another view of problem-solving is that a problem is seen as existing when there is a discrepancy between the desired state of affairs and the actual state of affairs. The problem-solving is, therefore, concerned with finding out what went wrong and then putting it right.

Evidence collection point

What problems have you been involved in solving lately? What are your main strengths and weaknesses in problem-solving situations?

Information seeking and handling

Pages xv–xxx are concerned with ways of seeking information and then handling that information. How effective are you at seeking and handling information?

Communicating

Pages xiv–xv set out the main areas of the skill of communication. What are your main strengths and weaknesses in using communication skills?

Applying number

Pages xxxviii–xxxix set out the main areas of skill of applying number. What are your main strengths and weaknesses in the application of number?

Information technology

Pages xlviii–xlix set out the main areas of the skill of information technology. What are your main strengths and weaknesses in information technology?

Occupational skills

Occupational skills refer to professional, career, vocational and job-specific skills. People in employment have to have a variety of occupational skills which vary according to each job, career or profession.

Evidence collection point

What types of occupational skills do you currently possess? What skills do you currently lack which would enable you to gain employment or self-employment in a chosen field?

Evidence collection point

You should now be in a position to carry out a detailed skills evaluation using the grid shown below. Clearly, you may need to put extra effort into those activities which you record as being poor.

Skills	Ranking				
	Very good 1	2	3	4	Poor 5
Evaluating own strengths and weaknesses					
Working with others					
Working independently					
Planning					
Time management					
Setting targets					
Reviewing progress					
Decision-making					
Problem-solving					
Information seeking and handling					
Communicating					
Applying number					
Using IT					
Occupational skills					

You should then outline a short action plan for each of the skills which feature as being poor. The action plan should identify the objectives you have related to improving specific skills, how you will review progress, and the time period involved in making the improvement.

A personal plan for employment or self-employment

You should set out a personal plan in four sections which proposes:

- The time needed for you to realise employment or self-employment opportunities.

  This should cover both the short term, i.e. 1–12 months, and the long term, i.e. 1–5 years.

- Information needed, including sources.
- Actions to be taken for you to become employed or self-employed.
- Statutory requirements for identified employment or self-employment opportunities.

Evidence indicators

In order to provide evidence that you can meet the performance criteria for this element you could produce a variety of pieces of evidence.

The evidence that you provide in carrying out this work will enable you to show capability in the Core Skills of Application of Number, Communication and Information Technology.

The following list should serve as a checklist. Please tick off each of the following when you have successfully covered them. You need to be able to confirm that:

- I have produced a summary of at least three types of employment which I have selected on the basis of potential interest. ☐
- For one type of employment I have produced a list of opportunities with relevant sources of information and statutory requirements. ☐
- I have produced a record of a discussion which analyses my personal strengths and weaknesses in relation to skills for identified employment or self-employment opportunities. ☐

- I have produced a personal plan in four sections which proposes:
  - The time needed to realise employment or self-employment ☐
  - Information needed, including sources ☐
  - Actions to take to become employed or self-employed ☐
  - Statutory requirements for the identified employment or self-employment opportunity. ☐

Answers

Business in the Economy: Unit Test 1

1	b	11	b	21	d	31	c	41	b
2	b	12	c	22	a	32	a	42	d
3	d	13	c	23	b	33	c	43	a
4	a	14	d	24	b	34	c	44	b
5	b	15	a	25	c	35	d	45	a
6	c	16	c	26	d	36	c	46	b
7	b	17	b	27	c	37	c	47	b
8	b	18	c	28	b	38	c	48	d
9	c	19	c	29	d	39	c	49	b
10	a	20	b	30	a	40	b	50	c

Business in the Economy: Unit Test 2

1	c	11	b	21	b	31	c	41	b
2	a	12	b	22	c	32	a	42	a
3	b	13	a	23	c	33	d	43	b
4	b	14	c	24	a	34	a	44	c
5	c	15	d	25	b	35	a	45	c
6	a	16	b	26	b	36	c	46	d
7	c	17	c	27	d	37	b	47	c
8	c	18	d	28	c	38	a	48	b
9	a	19	a	29	d	39	a	49	c
10	c	20	c	30	d	40	c	50	b

Business Organisations and Systems: Unit Test 1

1	c	11	a	21	d	31	b	41	b
2	d	12	b	22	a	32	a	42	c
3	a	13	b	23	c	33	b	43	a
4	b	14	b	24	c	34	a	44	c
5	d	15	c	25	b	35	b	45	d
6	c	16	c	26	b	36	c	46	b
7	c	17	b	27	a	37	b	47	c
8	a	18	c	28	d	38	d	48	c
9	b	19	d	29	c	39	a	49	d
10	d	20	b	30	a	40	b	50	c

Business Organisations and Systems: Unit Test 2

1	a	11	c	21	d	31	d	41	a
2	c	12	a	22	b	32	c	42	b
3	b	13	d	23	d	33	d	43	d
4	a	14	a	24	b	34	c	44	b
5	b	15	b	25	c	35	b	45	c
6	c	16	b	26	c	36	b	46	d
7	b	17	c	27	c	37	b	47	c
8	d	18	a	28	b	38	c	48	c
9	a	19	b	29	d	39	a	49	d
10	b	20	b	30	a	40	c	50	d

Marketing: Unit Test 1

1	c	11	d	21	d	31	b	41	b
2	d	12	a	22	d	32	c	42	c
3	b	13	d	23	a	33	b	43	a
4	a	14	c	24	c	34	c	44	c
5	d	15	b	25	d	35	a	45	b
6	c	16	b	26	b	36	d	46	b
7	c	17	b	27	d	37	a	47	b
8	a	18	b	28	b	38	c	48	d
9	c	19	c	29	c	39	b	49	c
10	c	20	a	30	d	40	d	50	c

Marketing: Unit Test 2

1	a	11	b	21	c	31	c	41	d
2	a	12	b	22	b	32	b	42	b
3	c	13	c	23	d	33	b	43	a
4	b	14	c	24	d	34	a	44	d
5	b	15	d	25	a	35	d	45	b
6	c	16	d	26	b	36	d	46	d
7	c	17	d	27	c	37	c	47	a
8	b	18	d	28	b	38	d	48	b
9	b	19	c	29	d	39	b	49	b
10	c	20	b	30	c	40	b	50	c

Human Resources: Unit Test 1

1	c	11	d	21	c	31	b	41	b
2	a	12	d	22	b	32	c	42	b
3	b	13	c	23	d	33	c	43	d
4	c	14	d	24	c	34	b	44	a
5	b	15	c	25	c	35	d	45	c
6	d	16	c	26	d	36	b	46	c
7	b	17	d	27	d	37	c	47	b
8	c	18	a	28	d	38	d	48	c
9	b	19	b	29	c	39	a	49	c
10	c	20	c	30	c	40	c	50	c

Human Resources: Unit Test 2

1	c	11	a	21	c	31	b	41	c
2	d	12	d	22	c	32	a	42	b
3	a	13	b	23	b	33	b	43	d
4	a	14	a	24	d	34	b	44	b
5	d	15	d	25	b	35	c	45	c
6	c	16	c	26	a	36	c	46	a
7	a	17	c	27	c	37	d	47	d
8	b	18	b	28	c	38	b	48	b
9	b	19	b	29	b	39	b	49	b
10	c	20	d	30	a	40	a	50	b

Production and Employment in the Economy: Unit Test 1

1	c	11	a	21	b	31	c	41	b
2	b	12	a	22	c	32	b	42	c
3	b	13	b	23	b	33	c	43	b
4	c	14	b	24	a	34	b	44	d
5	c	15	a	25	c	35	c	45	a
6	d	16	b	26	d	36	c	46	d
7	b	17	d	27	b	37	b	47	b
8	a	18	d	28	c	38	a	48	d
9	c	19	c	29	c	39	c	49	d
10	d	20	b	30	d	40	a	50	c

Production and Employment in the Economy: Unit Test 2

1	a	11	b	21	d	31	c	41	c
2	b	12	b	22	c	32	a	42	d
3	d	13	d	23	b	33	c	43	b
4	c	14	d	24	d	34	b	44	a
5	c	15	a	25	a	35	b	45	a
6	d	16	b	26	b	36	b	46	b
7	c	17	b	27	b	37	d	47	b
8	a	18	d	28	c	38	b	48	a
9	c	19	d	29	b	39	c	49	c
10	d	20	d	30	d	40	c	50	c

Financial Transactions, Costing and Pricing: Unit Test 1

1	c	11	b	21	b	31	c	41	b
2	a	12	c	22	c	32	c	42	b
3	c	13	d	23	b	33	b	43	d
4	d	14	d	24	b	34	d	44	c
5	a	15	b	25	a	35	c	45	c
6	b	16	b	26	d	36	b	46	d
7	b	17	b	27	c	37	a	47	b
8	b	18	a	28	c	38	b	48	d
9	c	19	d	29	a	39	d	49	b
10	d	20	d	30	b	40	b	50	a

Financial Transactions, Costing and Pricing: Unit Test 2

1	c	11	b	21	b	31	c	41	b
2	b	12	d	22	b	32	a	42	d
3	d	13	a	23	c	33	a	43	c
4	b	14	c	24	b	34	d	44	d
5	c	15	b	25	b	35	d	45	b
6	d	16	b	26	c	36	a	46	b
7	c	17	d	27	c	37	c	47	d
8	d	18	d	28	d	38	b	48	d
9	a	19	c	29	b	39	a	49	a
10	c	20	c	30	d	40	c	50	a

Financial Forecasting and Monitoring: Unit Test 1

1	c	11	b	21	b	31	a	41	d
2	d	12	c	22	c	32	a	42	b
3	b	13	d	23	d	33	b	43	b
4	d	14	c	24	b	34	d	44	b
5	c	15	d	25	b	35	c	45	b
6	b	16	b	26	d	36	d	46	c
7	c	17	a	27	d	37	b	47	b
8	d	18	b	28	a	38	d	48	d
9	d	19	d	29	b	39	b	49	b
10	c	20	a	30	c	40	c	50	c

Financial Forecasting and Monitoring: Unit Test 2

1	b	11	c	21	d	31	a	41	a
2	d	12	d	22	a	32	b	42	d
3	a	13	d	23	c	33	c	43	b
4	c	14	b	24	c	34	b	44	a
5	c	15	a	25	d	35	c	45	c
6	c	16	b	26	c	36	c	46	c
7	b	17	a	27	b	37	c	47	c
8	c	18	b	28	c	38	d	48	c
9	d	19	b	29	b	39	d	49	d
10	d	20	c	30	b	40	a	50	b

Index

BUSINESS

for
HIGHER AWARDS

BUSINESS *for* HIGHER AWARDS

Dave Needham • Rob Dransfield
Rod Harris • Martin Coles

Heinemann

You can order Business for Higher Awards by filling in the form below and returning it to:

Orders Department, Heinemann Educational, FREEPOST PO Box 381, Oxford OX2 8BR

Or place your order now by phoning (01865) 314333

Once you have successfully completed your GNVQ Business Advanced award, you are ready for further study or the world of work. **Business for Higher Awards** has been written by the same authors to enable you to achieve a BTEC Higher National Certificate or Higher National Diploma as well as other higher level awards in business.

Business for Higher Awards offers you a broad-based approach to business and management. It draws on recent research and up-to-date case studies to give you the very latest in business thinking. Above all, it is a book designed to be read, that will give you a firm foundation in business skills and from which you can go on to develop specialist knowledge and skills.

Business for Higher Awards also offers you

▶ coverage of all the core modules of the Higher National programmes and the most common option modules

▶ extensive case studies and discussion points to develop underpinning skills and knowledge

▶ text which relates your learning to work experience and the business environment

▶ practical advice on research, reference sources and further reading

Contents

▶ Market Relations

▶ Operating Environment

▶ Managing Finance and Information

▶ Managing People and Activities

▶ Organisational Structures and Processes

▶ Financial Accounting Framework

▶ Marketing

▶ Personnel Management in the Organisation

▶ Planning and Decision Making

Business for Higher Awards Order Form

Title (Mr/Mrs/Miss/Ms)

First Name(s) and Surname

Address*

Post code

Signed

Date

Tel. no.

* If paying by credit card, use address shown on your statement

For the purpose of the Data Protection Act 1984, Heinemann Educational is collecting this information on behalf of Reed International Books Limited

Please accept this as my official order for

☐ **Business for Higher Awards**
435 28534 3 £24.99

Quantity
Value

☐ I enclose payment by cheque/postal order made payable to Heinemann Educational

☐ **Credit card:** ☐ Visa ☐ Access
☐ American Express ☐ Diners

Credit Card Number

Exp. Date

Name of cardholder